Grammar codes

[C] countable: a noun that can be counted and has a plural form: *This is a **dictionary.*** | *There are many **dictionaries** in the library.*

[U] uncountable: a noun that cannot be counted, and that has no plural form: *We drink **milk** with our dinner.* | *There isn't much **milk** left.* | *The book contained some interesting **information** about the town.*

[P] plural: a noun that is used only with a plural verb or pronoun, and that has no singular form: *These **trousers** are too tight.*

[S] singular: a noun that is used only in the singular, and that has no plural form: *There was a **babble** of voices.* | *Let me have a **think** about it.*

[the] a noun that is the name of an actual place, organization, etc., and that is always used with the definite article: *the **White House*** | *This land belongs to the **Crown**.*

vt a transitive verb: a verb that is followed by a direct object, which can be either a noun phrase or a clause: *She **rides** a bicycle to school.* | *He **made up** a good excuse.* | *We **decided** to leave.* | *I've **given up** eating meat.*

vi an intransitive verb: a verb that has no direct object: *They all **came** yesterday.* | *We **set off** at 7 o'clock.*

LONGMAN

HANDY LEARNER'S DICTIONARY

LONGMAN

HANDY LEARNER'S DICTIONARY

Longman

Longman Group UK Limited,
Longman House, Burnt Mill, Harlow,
Essex CM20 2JE, England
and Associated Companies throughout the world

First published 1988
Fifth impression 1991

British Library Cataloguing in Publication Data

Longman handy learner's dictionary.
  1. English language – Dictionaries
  423   PE1628

  ISBN 0-582-96413-X

Set in 6/7pt Times Roman.

Printed in Great Britain
by Wm. Collins Sons & Co. Ltd., Glasgow

Publisher
Susan Maingay

Lexicographers
John Ayto
Janet Whitcut

Editors
Margaret Costa
Stephen Crowdy
Fiona McIntosh

Pronunciation Editor
Dinah Jackson

Design
Douglas Williamson
Giles Davies

Cover
Geoff Sida
Margaret Camp

Production
Clive McKeough

Contents

Guide to the dictionary

Spelling

different spelling

age·is·m, agism /'eɪdʒɪzəm/ n [U] the making of unfair differences between people because of their age, exp. treating young people more favourably than old people **ageist** adj, n

British spelling
American spelling

an·aes·thet·ic ‖ also **anes-** AmE /ˌænɪs'θetɪk/ n [C;U] substance that stops one from feeling pain, either in a part of the body (a **local anaesthetic**) or in the whole body, making one unconscious (a **general anaesthetic**)

irregular plurals

a·pex /'eɪpeks/ n **-es** or **apices** /'eɪpɪˌsiːz/ highest point: the apex of a triangle

irregular verbs

a·rise /ə'raɪz/ vi **arose** /ə'rəʊz/, **arisen** /ə'rɪzən/ happen; appear

Pronunciation/Stress

pronunciations are shown using symbols from the International Phonetic Alphabet – see inside front cover

ba·by /'beɪbi/ n **1** very young child: (fig.) the baby of the class (= the youngest) **2** very young animal or bird: a baby monkey **3** AmE infml person, esp. a girl or woman **4** infml one's special responsibility

stressed syllables are clearly marked

bal·loon /bə'luːn/ n **1** bag filled with gas or air so that it can float **2** small rubber bag that can be blown up and used as a toy

British pronunciations
American pronunciations

bath /bɑːθ‖bæθ/ n **baths** /bɑːðz, bɑːθs‖bæðz, bæθs/ **1** container in which one sits to wash the whole body **2** act of washing one's whole body at one time

Meaning

clear and simple explanations using a defining vocabulary of 2000 words

beam[1] /biːm/ n long heavy piece of wood, esp. used to support a building

words with the same spelling but different use or meaning

an·tique /æn'tiːk/ adj old and therefore valuable ♦ n valuable old object

more than one meaning

be·come /bɪ'kʌm/ v **became**, **become** **1** begin to be: become king|become warmer **2** vt be suitable for: Such behaviour hardly becomes someone in your position.

Words that you may not know are written like THIS. You can find all these words in the dictionary.

be·drag·gled /bɪˈdrægəld/ *adj* wet, LIMP, and muddy

common idioms and phrases are shown in heavy type

bee /biː/ *n* **1** stinging insect that makes honey **2 a bee in one's bonnet** fixed idea; OBSESSION **3 the bee's knees** *infml* the best person or thing

phrasal verbs (= verbs which have a special meaning when they are used with a particular adverb or preposition)

examples showing how to use the word or phrase

boil¹ /bɔɪl/ *vi/t* **1** bring or come to the temperature at which a liquid changes to gas: *100°C is the boiling point of water.* **2** cook at this temperature: *to boil eggs* **3** boil dry boil till no water remains ♦ *n* [S]: *bring the soup to the boil.*

boil away *phr vi* disappear by boiling

boil down to *phr vt* be no more than: *It all boils down to a question of money.*

boil over *phr vi* **1** (of a boiling liquid) flow over the sides of the container **2** get out of control (and develop into): *The conflict boiled over into war.*

labels showing style, region, etc.

bol·shy /ˈbɒlʃi‖ˈboʊl-/ *adj infml* (of a person or their behaviour) showing an unwillingness to help in a common aim

Grammar

parts of speech

bone-dry /ˌ ˈ ◂/ *adj* perfectly dry

bon·fire /ˈbɒnfaɪə‖ˈbɑːn-/ *n* large outdoor fire

words which are part of the same word family and which have different parts of speech are shown like this

boy /bɔɪ/ *n* young male person **~hood** *n* time of being a boy **~ish** *adj* like a boy

countable and uncountable nouns

choco·late /ˈtʃɒklɪt‖ˈtʃɑːkəlɪt, ˈtʃɔːk-/ *n* **1** [U] solid brown substance eaten as a sweet **2** [C] small sweet covered with this **3** [U] hot drink made from this ♦ *adj* dark brown

intransitive and transitive verbs

co·in·cide /ˌkəʊɪnˈsaɪd/ *vi* **1** happen at the same time **2** (of opinions, etc.) agree

com·pli·ment² /ˈkɒmplɪment‖ˈkɑːm-/ *vt* express admiration of

A

A, a /eɪ/ the 1st letter of the English alphabet

a /ə; strong eɪ/ also (before a vowel sound) **an** — indefinite article, determiner **1** one: a pencil | a doctor | a thousand pounds **2** (before some words of quantity): a few weeks | a little water **3** for each: 6 times a day | £2 a dozen

a·back /əˈbæk/ adv **be taken aback** be suddenly shocked

ab·a·cus /ˈæbəkəs/ n frame with sliding balls on wires, used for counting

a·ban·don /əˈbændən/ vt **1** leave completely **2** give up: to abandon our search **3** give (oneself) up completely to a feeling: He abandoned himself to grief. **~ment** n [U]

a·base /əˈbeɪs/ vt fml make (esp. oneself) lose self-respect

a·bashed /əˈbæʃt/ adj uncomfortable and ashamed

a·bate /əˈbeɪt/ vi fml (of wind, pain, etc.) become less fierce **~ment** n [U]

ab·at·toir /ˈæbətwɑːʳ/ n BrE for SLAUGHTERHOUSE

ab·bess /ˈæbɛs, ˈæbes/ n woman who is the head of a CONVENT

ab·bey /ˈæbi/ n house of religious men or women; MONASTERY or CONVENT

ab·bot /ˈæbət/ n man who is the head of a MONASTERY

ab·bre·vi·ate /əˈbriːvieɪt/ vt make shorter **–ation** /əˌbriːviˈeɪʃ ən/ n short form of a word

ab·di·cate /ˈæbdɪkeɪt/ vi/t give up (a position or right) officially **–cation** /ˌæbdɪˈkeɪʃ ən/ n [U]

ab·do·men /ˈæbdəmən, æbˈdəʊ-/ n part of the body containing the stomach **abdominal** /æbˈdɒmənəl‖-ˈdɑː-/ adj

ab·duct /əbˈdʌkt, æb-/ vt take (a person) away illegally; KIDNAP **~ion** /-ˈdʌkʃ ən/ n [U]

ab·er·ra·tion /ˌæbəˈreɪʃ ən/ n [C;U] change away from one's usual behaviour

a·bet /əˈbet/ vt -tt- aid and abet law give help to (a crime or criminal) **~tor** n

a·bey·ance /əˈbeɪəns/ n [U] fml **fall into abeyance** stop being done or used

ab·hor /əbˈhɔːʳ, æb-/ vt fml hate very much **~rent** /əbˈhɒrənt‖-ˈhɔːr-/ adj deeply disliked **~rence** n [U]

a·bide /əˈbaɪd/ vt **abided** or **abode**, **abode** bear; TOLERATE: I can't abide rudeness.

abide by phr vt obey (laws, etc.)

a·bid·ing /əˈbaɪdɪŋ/ adj without end: an abiding love

a·bil·i·ty /əˈbɪləti/ n [C;U] power; skill

ab·ject /ˈæbdʒekt/ adj fml **1** deserving great pity: abject poverty **2** without self-respect; HUMBLE: an abject apology **~ly** adv

a·blaze /əˈbleɪz/ adj **1** on fire; burning **2** shining brightly

a·ble /ˈeɪbəl/ adj **1** having the power, time, etc., to do something: Will you be able to come? **2** clever; skilled

a·blu·tions /əˈbluːʃənz/ n [P] fml washing oneself

a·bly /ˈeɪbli/ adv skilfully

ab·norm·al /æbˈnɔːməl‖-ˈnɔːr-/ adj not ordinary; unusual **~ly** adv **~ity** /ˌæbnɔːˈmæləti‖-nɔːr-/ n [C;U]

a·board /əˈbɔːd‖əˈbɔːrd/ adv, prep on or onto (a ship, plane, etc.)

a·bode[1] /əˈbəʊd/ n law **of/with no fixed abode** having no place as a regular home

abode[2] v past t. and p. of ABIDE

a·bol·ish /əˈbɒlɪʃ‖əˈbɑː-/ vt bring to an end by law **–ition** /ˌæbəˈlɪʃ ən/ n [U]

a·bom·in·a·ble /əˈbɒmənəbəl, -mənə-‖əˈbɑː-/ adj hateful; very bad **–bly** adv

ab·o·rig·in·al /ˌæbəˈrɪdʒənəl/ adj (of people and living things) having lived in a place from the earliest times **aboriginal** n

ab·o·rig·ine /ˌæbəˈrɪdʒəni/ n an aboriginal, esp. in Australia

a·bort /əˈbɔːt‖əˈbɔːrt/ v **1** vt cause (a child) to be born too soon for it to live **2** vi/t end before the expected time: abort the space flight **~ive** adj unsuccessful; coming to nothing **~ion** /əˈbɔːʃ ən‖əˈbɔːr-/ n [C;U] medical operation to abort a child

a·bound /əˈbaʊnd/ vi [(in, with)] exist or have in large numbers or great quantity

a·bout[1] /əˈbaʊt/ prep **1** on the subject of: a book about cats **2** in; through: walking about the streets **3** concerning: She told us all about the stars. **4** busy or concerned with: While you're about it, make me a cup of tea too. **5** **what/how about**: a(making a suggestion): How about a drink? b what news or plans have you got concerning: What about Jack?

about[2] adv **1** in all directions or places; around: papers lying about on the floor **2** somewhere near: Is there anyone about? **3** a little more or less than: about 5 miles **4** so as to face the other way **5** be going to: We're about to leave.

about-turn /·ˈ·, ·ˈ·, ·ˈ·‖·ˈ·/ n esp. BrE change to the opposite position or opinion

a·bove[1] /ə'bʌv/ prep **1** higher than; over: *fly above the clouds* **2** more than **3** too good, honest, etc. for: *He's not above stealing.* **4 above all** most important of all

above[2] adv **1** higher: *the clouds above* **2** more: *aged 20 and above* **3** earlier in a book: *the facts mentioned above* | *the above-mentioned facts*

a·bove-board /ə,bʌv'bɔːd◀, ə'bʌv-bɔːd ‖ə'bʌvbɔːrd/ adj without any trick or attempt to deceive

a·bra·sive /ə'breɪsɪv/ adj **1** causing the rubbing away of a surface **2** rough and annoying: *an abrasive personality*

a·breast /ə'brest/ adv **1** side by side **2 keep/be abreast of** know the most recent facts about

a·bridge /ə'brɪdʒ/ vt make (a book, etc.) shorter

a·bridg·ment /ə'brɪdʒmənt/ n something abridged: *an abridgment of the play for radio*

a·broad /ə'brɔːd/ adv to or in another country

ab·ro·gate /'æbrəgeɪt/ vt fml put an end to (a law, etc.)

a·brupt /ə'brʌpt/ adj **1** sudden and unexpected: *an abrupt stop* **2** (of behaviour, etc.) rough and impolite ~**ly** adv ~**ness** n [U]

ab·scess /'æbses/ n swelling on or in the body, containing PUS

ab·scond /əb'skɒnd, æb-‖æb-'skɑːnd/ vi fml go away suddenly because one has done something wrong

ab·sence /'æbsəns/ n **1** [C;U] (period of) being away: *absence from work* **2** [U] non-existence: *the absence of information about the crime*

ab·sent[1] /'æbsənt/ adj **1** not present **2** showing lack of attention: *an absent look on his face*

ab·sent[2] /əb'sent, æb-‖æb-/ vt absent (oneself) away

ab·sen·tee /,æbsən'tiː/ n person who is absent from a place

absent-mind·ed /,··'··◀/ adj so concerned with one's thoughts as not to notice what is happening, what one is doing, etc.

ab·so·lute /'æbsəluːt/ adj **1** complete; undoubted: *absolute nonsense* **2** having unlimited power: *an absolute ruler* **3** not measured by comparison with other things; not RELATIVE ~**ly** /,æbsə'luːtli◀/ adv **1** completely **2** certainly: '*Do you think so?*' '*Absolutely*'

ab·solve /əb'zɒlv‖-ɑːlv/ vt free (someone) from fulfilling a promise, or from punishment

ab·sorb /əb'sɔːb, əb'zɔːb‖-ɔːrb/ vt **1** take in (liquids, heat, etc.) **2** fill the attention of: *I was absorbed in a book.* | *an absorbing task* ~**ent** able to ABSORB (1) **absorption** /-ɔːpʃən‖

-ɔːrp-/ n [U]

ab·stain /əb'steɪn/ vi keep oneself from drinking, voting, etc. ~**er** n

ab·ste·mi·ous /əb'stiːmiəs/ adj not allowing oneself much food, etc.

ab·sten·tion /əb'stenʃən/ n [C;U] act of abstaining, esp. from voting

ab·sti·nence /'æbstɪnəns/ n [U] abstaining, esp. from alcoholic drink

ab·stract /'æbstrækt/ adj **1** existing as a quality or CONCEPT rather than as something real or solid: *Beauty is abstract but a house is not.* | *The word 'hunger' is an abstract noun.* **2** general rather than particular: *an abstract discussion of crime, without reference to actual cases* **3** (in art) not showing things as a camera would see them ♦ n **1** abstract work of art **2** short form of a statement, speech, etc.

ab·struse /əb'struːs, æb-/ adj fml difficult to understand

ab·surd /əb'sɜːd‖-ɜːrd/ adj unreasonable; (funny because) false or foolish ~**ly** adv ~**ity** /əb'sɜːdəti, -'zɜː-‖ -ɜːr-/ n [C;U]

a·bun·dant /ə'bʌndənt/ adj more than enough ~**ly** adv ~**dance** n [S;U]

a·buse[1] /ə'bjuːz/ vt **1** say bad things to or about **2** use badly: *abuse one's power*

a·buse[2] /ə'bjuːs/ n **1** [U] cruel or rude words **2** [C;U] wrong use: *the abuse of drugs* **abusive** adj using cruel or rude words

a·bys·mal /ə'bɪzməl/ adj very bad

a·byss /ə'bɪs/ n great hole that seems bottomless

ac·a·dem·ic /,ækə'demɪk◀/ adj **1** about schools and education **2** not related to practical situations; THEORETICAL: *a purely academic question* ♦ n **1** university teacher **2** someone who values skills of the mind more than practical ones ~**ally** adv

a·cad·e·my /ə'kædəmi/ n **1** society of people interested in the advancement of art, science, or literature **2** school for training in a special skill: *a military academy*

ac·cede /ək'siːd, æk-/ vi fml **1** agree to a demand, etc. **2** come to a high position

ac·cel·e·rate /ək'seləreɪt/ vi/t (cause to) move faster –**ration** /ək,selə-'reɪʃən/ n [U]

ac·cel·e·ra·tor /ək'seləreɪtə/ n instrument in a car, etc., that is used to increase its speed

ac·cent[1] /'æksənt‖'æksent/ n **1** particular way of speaking, usu. connected with a place or a social class **2** mark written over or under a letter, such as that on the 'e' of 'café' **3** importance given to a word or part of a word by saying it with more force

ac·cent² /ək'sent‖'æksent/ vt pronounce with added force

ac·cen·tu·ate /ək'sentʃuelt/ vt direct attention to; give importance to

ac·cept /ək'sept/ v 1 vi/t receive (something offered), esp. willingly 2 vt believe or agree to: *Did she accept your reasons for being late?* ~**able** adj good enough; worth accepting: *an acceptable gift* ~**ance** n [C.U]

ac·cess¹ /'ækses/ n [U] 1 way in; entrance 2 means of using or getting something: *Students need access to books.* ~**ible** /ək'sesəbəl/ adj easy to get or get to ~**ibility** /ək,sesə'bɪlɪti/ n [U]

access² vt obtain (stored information) from a computer's memory

ac·ces·sion /ək'seʃən/ n [U] coming to a high position: *the Queen's accession to the throne*

ac·ces·so·ry /ək'sesəri/ n 1 thing that is added but is not a necessary part: *car accessories such as a radio | a black dress with matching accessories* (= handbag, shoes, etc.) 2 also **accessary** — *law* person who is not present at a crime but who helps in doing it

access time /'··· ,·/ n [U] time taken by a computer to find and use a piece of information in its memory

ac·ci·dent /'æksɪdənt/ n something, usu. unpleasant, that happens unexpectedly: *serious accidents on the motorway | I met her* **by accident.** ~**al** /,æksɪ'dentl/ adj ~**ally** adv

ac·claim /ə'kleɪm/ vt greet with public approval **acclaim** n [U]

ac·cli·ma·tize /ə'klaɪmətaɪz/ vi/t make or get used to the weather in a new place **-tization** /ə,klaɪmətaɪ-'zeɪʃən‖-tə-/ n [U]

ac·co·lade /'ækəleɪd/ n strong praise

ac·com·mo·date /ə'kɒmədeɪt‖ ə'kɑ:-/ vt fml 1 provide with a place to live in 2 help by making changes: *to accommodate your wishes* **-dating** adj helpful **-dation** /ə,kɒmə'deɪʃən‖ ə,kɑ:-/ n [U] place to live; room, house, etc.

ac·com·pa·ni·ment /ə'kʌmpəni-mənt/ n 1 something which is used or provided with something else 2 music played at the same time as singing or another instrument

ac·com·pa·nist /ə'kʌmpənəst/ n player of a musical accompaniment

ac·com·pa·ny /ə'kʌmpəni/ vt 1 go with, as on a journey 2 happen at the same time as: *Lightning usually accompanies thunder.* 3 play a musical accompaniment to

ac·com·plice /ə'kʌmplɪs‖ə'kɑ:m-, ə'kʌm-/ n person who helps someone to do wrong

ac·com·plish /ə'kʌmplɪʃ‖ə'kɑ:m-, ə'kʌm-/ vt succeed in doing ~**ed** adj

skilled ~**ment** n 1 [C] something one is skilled at 2 [U] act of accomplishing something

ac·cord /ə'kɔːd‖ə'kɔːrd/ vi agree: *That does not accord with your previous statement.* ♦ n [U] 1 **in accord (with)** in agreement (with) 2 **of one's own accord** without being asked; willingly

ac·cord·ance /ə'kɔːdəns‖-ɔːr-/ n **in accordance with** in a way that agrees with

ac·cord·ing·ly /ə'kɔːdɪŋli‖-ɔːr-/ adv because of what has happened; therefore

according to /·'·· ·/ prep 1 from what is said or written: *According to my watch, it's 4 o'clock.* 2 in a way that agrees with: *paid according to the amount of work done*

ac·cor·di·on /ə'kɔːdiən‖-ɔːr-/ n musical instrument played by pressing the middle part together to force air through holes controlled by KEYS¹ (3) worked by the fingers

ac·cost /ə'kɒst‖ə'kɔːst, ə'kɑːst/ vt go up and speak to (esp. a stranger), often threateningly

ac·count¹ /ə'kaunt/ n 1 report; description: *give an account of what happened* | **By all accounts,** (= according to what everyone says) *she's a good account.* 2 record of money received and paid out 3 money kept in a bank or BUILDING SOCIETY 4 arrangement that lets one buy goods and pay for them later 5 advantage; profit: *He turned his knowledge to good account.* 6 **bring/call someone to account** cause (someone) to give an explanation 7 **of great/no account** of great/no importance 8 **on account of** because of 9 **on no account/not on any account** not for any reason 10 **take into account/take account of** give thought to; consider

account² v **account for** phr vt 1 give or be an explanation for 2 give a statement showing how money has been spent

ac·coun·ta·ble /ə'kauntəbəl/ adj responsible **-bility** /ə,kauntə'bɪlɪti/ n [U]

ac·coun·tan·cy /ə'kauntənsi/n work of an accountant

ac·coun·tant /ə'kauntənt/ n person who controls and examines money accounts

ac·cred·it·ed /ə'kredɪtəd/ adj 1 officially representing one's government in a foreign country 2 having the power to act for an organization 3 officially recognized as reaching a certain standard or quality

ac·crue /ə'kru:/ vi fml come as an increase or advantage

ac-cu-mu-late /ə'kjuːmjʊleɪt/ vi/t make or become greater; collect into a mass —**lation** /ə,kjuːmjʊ'leɪʃən/ n [C;U]

ac-cu-ra-cy /'ækjʊrəsi/ n [U] being accurate; exactness

ac-cu-rate /'ækjʊrət/ adj exactly correct ~**ly** adv

ac-cu-sa-tion /,ækjʊ'zeɪʃən/ n [C;U] (statement) accusing someone of something

ac-cuse /ə'kjuːz/ vt charge (someone) with doing wrong: He was accused of murder. | The accused (men) were found guilty. **accuser** n **accusingly** adv

ac-cus-tom /ə'kʌstəm/ vt **be accustomed to** be in the habit of; be used to

AC/DC /,·· '·· / adj sl for BISEXUAL

ace /eɪs/ n **1** playing card with one mark or spot on it **2** person of the highest skill **3** (in tennis) very fast and strong SERVE that the opponent cannot hit back ♦ adj infml very good or very skilled

a-cer-bic /ə'sɜːbɪk‖-ɜːr-/ adj (of a person or manner) clever in a rather cruel way

ache /eɪk/ vi have a continuous dull pain: My head aches. | (fig.) I'm **aching to** go to the party. **ache** n: a headache

a-chieve /ə'tʃiːv/ vt **1** finish successfully **2** get by effort: achieve results ~**ment** n **1** [U] successful finishing of something **2** [C] something achieved

A-chil-les' heel /ə,kɪliːz 'hiːl/ n small but important weakness

ac-id /'æsɪd/ adj sour; bitter **acid** n **1** [C;U] chemical substance containing HYDROGEN **2** [U] sl the drug LSD

acid rain /,·· '·/ n [U] rain containing harmful quantities of acid as a result of industrial POLLUTION

acid test /,·· '·/ n test of the value of something

ac-knowl-edge /ək'nɒlɪdʒ‖-'nɑː-/ vt **1** admit; recognize as a fact: to acknowledge defeat | an acknowledged expert **2** show one is grateful for **3** state that one has received: acknowledge a letter **4** show that one recognizes (someone) as by smiling, etc. —**edgment, -edgement** n [C;U]

ac-ne /'ækni/ n [U] skin disorder common among young people, in which spots appear on the face and neck

a-corn /'eɪkɔːn‖-ɔːrn, -ərn/ n nut of the OAK tree

a-cous-tics /ə'kuːstɪks/ n **1** [U] scientific study of sound **2** [P] qualities that make a place good or bad for hearing in **acoustic** adj

ac-quaint /ə'kweɪnt/ vt fml **1** **acquaint someone with** tell; make known to **2** **be acquainted (with)** have met socially; know ~**ance** n **1** [C] person whom one knows slightly **2** [S;U (with)] knowledge gained through experience

ac-qui-esce /,ækwi'es/ vi agree, often unwillingly —**escent** adj

ac-quire /ə'kwaɪər/ vt gain; come to possess

ac-qui-si-tion /,ækwə'zɪʃən/ n **1** [U] act of acquiring **2** [C] something acquired —**tive** /ə'kwɪzətɪv/ adj in the habit of acquiring things

ac-quit /ə'kwɪt/ vt -tt- **1** decide that (someone) is not guilty: The jury acquitted him (of murder). **2** cause (oneself) to act in the stated way: He acquitted himself rather badly. ~**tal** n [C;U]

a-cre /'eɪkər/ n a measure of land equal to 4,840 square yards

a-cre-age /'eɪkərɪdʒ/ n [S;U] area measured in acres

ac-rid /'ækrɪd/ adj (of taste or smell) bitter; stinging

ac-ri-mo-ny /'ækrəməni‖-məuni/ n [U] bitterness of manner or language —**nious** /,ækrə'məuniəs/ adj

ac-ro-bat /'ækrəbæt/ n person skilled in walking on ropes, etc., esp. at a CIRCUS —**ic** /,ækrə'bætɪk/ adj ~**ics** n [P;U]

ac-ro-nym /'ækrənɪm/ n word made from the first letters of a name, such as NATO

a-cross /ə'krɒs‖ə'krɔːs/ adv, prep from one side to the other; on or to the other side (of): a bridge across the river | Can you swim across?

a-cross-the-board /·,· · '·/ adj influencing or having effects on people or things of all types or at every level **across-the-board** adv

act[1] /ækt/ v **1** vi do something: She acted on my suggestion. | The doctor acted correctly. **2** vi/t perform in a play or film **3** vi produce an effect: Does the drug take long to act?

act up phr vi behave badly

act[2] n **1** something that one has done; an action of a particular kind: an act of terrorism | a brave act **2** law made by parliament, etc. **3** main division of a stage play **4** short event in a stage or CIRCUS performance **5** example of insincere behaviour used for effect: She was just putting on an act.

act-ing /'æktɪŋ/ adj appointed to do the duties of a position for a short time

ac-tion /'ækʃən/ n **1** [U] process of doing something: We must take **action** quickly. **2** [C] something done; ACT: Her prompt action saved his life. **3** [C;U] way something works **4** [U] effect: the action of light on photographic film **5** [C;U] military fighting or a fight [U] main events in a book, play, etc.: *The action takes place in Italy.* **7** [C;U] *law* legal charge of guilt: *bring an action against him* **8 in/into action** in/into operation **9 out of action** not working **10 take action** begin to act — see also INDUSTRIAL ACTION

ac-ti-vate /'æktɪveɪt/ vt make active **-ation** /ˌæktə'veɪʃən/ n [U]

ac-tive /'æktɪv/ adj doing things; able to take action **-ly** adv

ac-tiv-ist /'æktɪvɪst/ n person taking an active part in politics

ac-tiv-i-ty /æk'tɪvɪti/ n **1** [U] movement or action: *political activity* **2** [C] something done, esp. for interest or pleasure: *leisure activities*

ac-tor /'æktər/ **actress** /'æktrɪs/ fem. — n person who acts in a play, film, etc.

ac-tu-al /'æktʃuəl/ adj existing as a fact; real **-ly** /'æktʃuəli, -tʃəli/ adv **1** in fact; really **2** (showing surprise): *He actually offered me a drink!*

ac-u-men /'ækjʊmən, ə'kjuːmən/ n [U] fml ability to judge quickly

ac-u-punc-ture /'ækjʊˌpʌŋktʃər/ n [U] method of curing diseases by putting special needles into certain parts of the body

a-cute /ə'kjuːt/ adj **1** severe; very great: *acute shortage of water* **2** (of the mind or senses) working very well **3** (of an angle) less than 90° **4** (of a mark) put above a letter, e.g. é, to show pronunciation **-ly** adv **-ness** n [U]

ad /æd/ n *infml* advertisement

AD /ˌeɪ 'diː/ (in the year) since the birth of Christ: *in 1066 AD*

ad-age /'ædɪdʒ/ n old wise phrase; PROVERB

ad-a-mant /'ædəmənt/ adj fml refusing to change one's mind

Ad-am's ap-ple /ˌ·· '··‖'·· ˌ·/ n lump at the front of the throat that moves when one talks or swallows

a-dapt /ə'dæpt/ vt make suitable for new conditions **-able** adj able to change **-ability** /əˌdæptə'bɪlɪti/ n [U] **-ation** /ˌædæp'teɪʃən/ n [C;U] act of adapting: *an adaptation of the play for radio*

a-dap-ter, **-or** /ə'dæptər/ n **1** person who adapts **2** electrical PLUG allowing more than one piece of equipment to run from the same SOCKET

add /æd/ v **1** vt put with something else: *add a name to the list* **2** vi/t join (numbers) together **3** vt say also

add to phr vt increase: *His absence added to our difficulties.*

add up phr vi make sense; seem likely: *The facts just don't add up.*

ad-der /'ædər/ n small poisonous snake

ad-dict /'ædɪkt/ n person who cannot stop a harmful habit **~ion** /ə'dɪkʃən/ n [C;U] **~ive** /ə'dɪktɪv/ adj habit forming

ad-dic-ted /ə'dɪktɪd/ adj dependent on something, esp. a drug

ad-di-tion /ə'dɪʃən/ n **1** [U] act of adding **2** [C] something added **3 in addition (to)** as well (as) **~al** adj as well; added **~ally** adv also

ad-di-tive /'ædɪtɪv/ n substance, esp. a chemical one, added to something else

ad-dled /'ædld/ adj *infml* (of someone's brain) having become confused

add-on /'··/n piece of equipment that can be connected to a computer that increases its usefulness

ad-dress /ə'dres‖ə'dres, 'ædres/ n **1** number, town, etc., where someone lives **2** speech made to a group of people ♦ vt **1** write a name and ADDRESS (1) on **2** direct a speech to: *She addressed the crowd.*

ad-ept /'ædept, ə'dept‖ə'dept/ adj highly skilled **adept** /'ædept/ n person who is adept at something

ad-e-quate /'ædɪkwət/ adj enough; good enough **-ly** adv **-quacy** n [U]

ad-here /əd'hɪər/ vi stick firmly, as with glue **adherence** n [U] **adherent** n loyal supporter of something

adhere to phr vt remain loyal to (an idea, plan, etc.)

ad-he-sive /əd'hiːsɪv/ n, adj (a substance such as glue) that can stick **-sion** /əd'hiːʒən/ n [U]

ad hoc /ˌæd 'hɒk‖-'hɑːk, -'hoʊk/ adj made for a particular purpose

ad-ja-cent /ə'dʒeɪsənt/ adj fml very close; (almost) touching

ad-jec-tive /'ædʒɪktɪv/ n word which describes a noun, such as *black* in *a black hat* **-tival** /ˌædʒɪk'taɪvəl/ adj

ad-join /ə'dʒɔɪn/ vi/t fml be next to (one another)

ad-journ /ə'dʒɜːn‖-ɜːrn/ vi/t stop (a meeting, etc.) for a while **-ment** n [C;U]

ad-ju-di-cate /ə'dʒuːdɪkeɪt/ vi/t fml act as a judge; decide about **-cator** n **-cation** /əˌdʒuːdɪ'keɪʃən/ n [U]

ad-junct /'ædʒʌŋkt/ n something added without being a necessary part

ad-just /ə'dʒʌst/ vi/t change slightly so as to make right **~able** adj **~ment** n [C;U]

ad lib /ˌæd 'lɪb/ adv spoken, played, performed, etc., without preparation **ad-lib** vi **-bb-** invent and say without preparation

ad-min-is-ter /əd'mɪnɪstər/ vt fml **1** manage (business affairs, etc. **2** (to) give: *administer medicine/punishment*

ad-min-is-tra-tion /əd,mɪnɪ'streɪʃən/ n 1 [U] management or direction of the affairs of a business, government, etc. 2 [C] *esp. AmE* national government: *the Reagan Administration* 3 [U] act of administering **–tra-tive** /əd'mɪnɪstrətɪv‖-streɪtɪv/ *adj* **–trator** /-streɪtər/ n

ad-mi-ra-ble /'ædmərəbəl/ *adj* very good **–bly** *adv*

ad-mi-ral /'ædmərəl/ n naval officer of high rank

ad-mire /əd'maɪər/ *vt* regard with pleasure; have a good opinion of **admiring** *adj* **admirer** n **admiration** /,ædmə'reɪʃən/ n [U] feeling of pleasure and respect

ad-mis-si-ble /əd'mɪsɪbəl/ *adj* that can be accepted or considered

ad-mis-sion /əd'mɪʃən/ n 1 [U] being allowed to enter a building, join a club, etc. 2 [U] cost of entrance: *Admission £1* 3 [C] statement admitting something; CONFESSION

ad-mit /əd'mɪt/ *vt* -tt- 1 allow to enter; let in 2 agree to the truth of (something bad) **~tance** n [U] right to enter **~tedly** *adv* it must be agreed that

ad-mon-ish /əd'mɒnɪʃ‖-'mɑː-/ *vt fml* scold gently; warn **-ition** /,ædmə'nɪʃən/ n [C;U]

ad nau-se-am /,æd 'nɔːziəm/ *adv* repeatedly and to an annoying degree

a-do /ə'duː/ n **without more ado** with no further delay

ad-o-les-cent /,ædə'lesənt/ *adj, n* (of) a boy or girl who is growing up **-cence** n [S;U]

a-dopt /ə'dɒpt‖ə'dɑːpt/ *vt* 1 take (someone else's child) into one's family for ever 2 take and use (a method, suggestion, etc.) **~ive** *adj* having adopted a child **~ion** /ə'dɒpʃən‖ə'dɑːp-/ n [C;U]

a-dore /ə'dɔːr/ *vt* 1 love and respect deeply; worship 2 like very much **adorable** very lovable **adoring** loving **adoration** /,ædə'reɪʃən/ n [U]

a-dorn /ə'dɔːn‖ə'dɔːrn/ *vt* add beauty to; decorate **~ment** n [U]

a-dren-a-lin /ə'drenələn/ n [U] chemical made by the body during anger, etc., causing quick or violent action

a-drift /ə'drɪft/ *adv, adj* (of boats) floating loose; not fastened

a-droit /ə'drɔɪt/ *adj* quick and skilful **~ly** *adv*

ad-u-la-tion /,ædʒʊ'leɪʃən/ n [U] *fml* praise or admiration that is more than is necessary or deserved

ad-ult /'ædʌlt, ə'dʌlt/ *adj, n* (of) a fully grown person or animal

a-dul-ter-ate /ə'dʌltəreɪt/ *vt* make impure by adding something of lower quality

a-dul-ter-y /ə'dʌltəri/ n [U] sexual relations between a married person

and someone outside the marriage **adulterer, adulteress** /-trəs/ *fem.* — n **-terous** *adj*

ad-vance¹ /əd'vɑːns‖əd'væns/ *vi/t* go or bring forward in position, development, etc. **advanced** *adj* 1 far on in development 2 modern

advance² n 1 forward movement or development 2 money provided before the proper time 3 **in advance** before in time ♦ *adj* coming before the usual time

ad-vanc-es /əd'vɑːnsɪz‖əd'væn-/ n [P] efforts to become friends with someone

ad-van-tage /əd'vɑːntɪdʒ‖əd'væn-/ n 1 [C] something that may help one to be successful 2 [U] profit; gain 3 **take advantage of: a** make use of somebody, as by deceiving them **b** make use of; profit from **~ous** /,ædvən'teɪdʒəs, ,ædvæn-/ *adj*

ad-vent /'ædvent/ n **the advent of** the coming of (an important event, etc.)

ad-ven-ture /əd'ventʃər/ n 1 [C] exciting and perhaps dangerous experience 2 [U] excitement; risk **-turer** n 1 person who has or looks for adventures 2 person who hopes to make a profit by taking risks with his/her money **-turous** *adj* 1 also **adventuresome** /əd'ventʃəsəm‖-tʃər-/ *AmE* — fond of adventure 2 exciting

ad-verb /'ædvɜːb‖-ɜːrb/ n word which adds to the meaning of a verb, an adjective, another adverb, or a sentence, for example *slowly, tomorrow,* and *here* **~ial** /əd'vɜːbiəl‖-ɜːr-/ n, *adj*

ad-ver-sa-ry /'ædvəsəri‖'ædvərseri/ n *fml* opponent; enemy **-sarial** /,ædvə'seəriəl‖-vər-/ *adj*

ad-verse /'ædvɜːs‖-ɜːrs/ *adj fml* unfavourable: *adverse comments* **~ly** *adv* **adversity** /əd'vɜːsəti‖-ɜːr-/ n [C;U] bad luck; trouble

ad-ver-tise /'ædvətaɪz‖-ər-/ *vi/t* make (something for sale) known to people, e.g. in a newspaper **-tiser** n **-tising** n [U] business of doing this **~ment** /əd'vɜːtɪsmənt‖,ædvər'taɪz-/ also **ad, advert** /'ædvɜːt‖-ɜːrt/ *infml* — n notice of something for sale

ad-vice /əd'vaɪs/ n [U] opinion given to someone about what to do

ad-vise /əd'vaɪz/ *vt* 1 give advice to 2 ((of)) *fml* inform: *Please advise me of the cost.* 3 **well-advised/ill-advised** wise/unwise **advisory** giving advice **adviser** also **advisor** *AmE* n **advisable** *adj* sensible; wise

ad-vo-cate /'ædvəkeɪt, -kət/ n person who speaks in defence of another person or of an idea; supporter **advocate** /-keɪt/ *vt*

ae-gis /'iːdʒəs/ n **under the aegis of** with the protection or support of

aer·i·al[1] /'eəriəl/ n wire, rod, etc., that receives radio or television signals

aerial[2] adj in or from the air: aerial photography

aer·o·bat·ics /ˌeərə'bætɪks, ˌeərəʊ-/ n [U] ACROBATIC tricks done in an aircraft **aerobatic** adj

aer·o·bics /eə'rəʊbɪks/ n [U] active physical exercise done to strengthen the heart and lungs

aer·o·drome /'eərədrəʊm/ n esp. BrE small airport

aer·o·dy·nam·ics /ˌeərəʊdaɪ'næmɪks/ n [U] science of movement through the air **aerodynamic** adj 1 concerning aerodynamics 2 using the principles of aerodynamics

aer·o·nau·tics /ˌeərə'nɔːtɪks/ n [U] science of the flight of aircraft

aer·o·plane /'eərəpleɪn/ n BrE ‖ **airplane** AmE — n flying vehicle with wings and one or more engines

aer·o·sol /'eərəsɒl‖-sɔːl/ n container from which liquid is forced out in a fine mist

aer·o·space /'eərəspeɪs, 'eərəʊ-/ n [U] the air around the Earth and space beyond it

aes·thet·ics ‖ also **es-** AmE /iːs'θetɪks, es-‖es-/ n [U] science of beauty, esp. in art **aesthetic** adj **-ically** /-kli/ adv

af·fa·ble /'æfəbəl/ adj friendly and pleasant **-bly** adv

af·fair /ə'feə[r]/ n 1 event; set of events 2 something to be done; business 3 sexual relationship outside marriage — see also FOREIGN AFFAIRS

af·fect /ə'fekt/ vt cause a change in; influence: Smoking affects your health. ~**ed** adj not natural; pretended ~**ation** /ˌæfek'teɪʃən/ n [U] unnatural behaviour

af·fec·tion /ə'fekʃən/ n [U] gentle, lasting fondness ~**ate** adj ~**ately** adv

af·fi·da·vit /ˌæfə'deɪvɪt/ n law written statement for use as proof

af·fil·i·ate /ə'fɪliert/ vi/t (esp. of a group) join to a larger group **-ation** /əˌfɪli'eɪʃən/ n [C;U]

af·fin·i·ty /ə'fɪnəti/ n [C;U] close connection or liking

af·firm /ə'fɜːm‖ə'fɜːrm/ vt fml declare; state ~**ative** n, adj (statement) meaning 'yes' ~**ation** /ˌæfə'meɪʃən‖ˌæfər-/ n [C;U]

affirmative action /əˌfɜːmətɪv 'ækʃən‖-ɜːr-/ n [U] POSITIVE DISCRIMINATION

af·fix[1] /ə'fɪks/ vt fml fix; fasten

af·fix[2] /'æfɪks/ n group of letters added to the beginning or end of a word to change its meaning or use (as in 'un**tie**', 'kind**ness**')

af·flict /ə'flɪkt/ vt cause to suffer; trouble ~**ion** /ə'flɪkʃən/ n [C;U] fml

af·flu·ent /'æfluənt/ adj wealthy; rich ~**ence** n [U]

af·ford /ə'fɔːd‖ə'fɔːrd/ vt 1 be able to pay for 2 be able to risk: I can't afford to neglect my health.

af·front /ə'frʌnt/ vt be rude to; offend **affront** n

a·fi·cio·na·do /əˌfɪʃə'nɑːdəʊ/ n **-dos** someone who is keenly interested in a particular activity or subject

a·field /ə'fiːld/ adv **far afield** far away

AFL-CIO /ˌeɪ ef ˌel ˌsiː aɪ 'əʊ/ n [the] American Federation of Labor and Congress of Industrial Organizations; an association of American trade unions

a·float /ə'fləʊt/ adv, adj 1 floating 2 on a ship 3 out of debt

a·foot /ə'fʊt/ adv, adj being prepared; happening

a·fore·said /ə'fɔːsed‖ə'fɔːr-/ adj said or named before

a·fraid /ə'freɪd/ adj 1 frightened: afraid of the dark 2 sorry for something that has happened or is likely to happen: 'Are we late?' 'I'm afraid so.'

a·fresh /ə'freʃ/ adv fml again

af·ter /'ɑːftə[r]‖'æf-/ prep, conj 1 later than: after breakfast | after you leave 2 following: Your name comes after mine in the list. | It rained day after day. 3 because of: After what he did I don't want to see him. 4 in spite of: After I packed it so carefully, the clock arrived broken. 5 looking for: The police are after him. 6 fml in the style of: a painting after Rembrandt 7 **after all** in spite of everything ♦ adv later; afterwards

af·ter·ef·fect /'ɑːftərɪfekt‖'æf-/ n effect (usu. unpleasant) that follows some time after the cause

af·ter·math /'ɑːftəmæθ‖'æftər-/ n period following a bad event: the aftermath of the war

af·ter·noon /ˌɑːftə'nuːn◂‖ˌæftər-/ n [C;U] time between midday and sunset

af·ter·thought /'ɑːftəθɔːt‖'æftər-/ n idea that comes later; something added later

af·ter·wards /'ɑːftəwədz‖'æftər-wərdz/ adv later; after that

a·gain /ə'gen, ə'geɪn‖ə'gen/ adv 1 once more; another time: Say it again. 2 back to the original place or condition: He's home again now. 3 besides; further: I could eat as much (= the same amount) again. 4 **again and again** very often

a·gainst /ə'genst, ə'geɪnst‖ə'genst/ prep 1 in the direction of and meeting or touching: The rain beat against the windows. 2 in opposition to: Stealing is **against the law**. 3 as a protection from: *They were vaccinated against cholera.* **4** having as a background: *The picture looks good against that red wall.*

age /eɪdʒ/ *n* **1** [C;U] length of time someone has lived or something has existed: *What are the children's ages?* **2** [U] one of the periods of human life: *to look after her in her old age* **3** [C] period of history: *This is the nuclear age.* **4** [C] long time: *We haven't met for ages.* **5 of age** old enough (usu. at 18 or 21) to be responsible in law for one's own actions **6 under/over age** too young/too old to be legally allowed to do something ♦ *vi/t* make or become old **aged** *adj* **1** /eɪdʒd/ of the stated number of years: *a boy aged 10* **2** /'eɪdʒid/ very old: *an aged man*

age·is·m, agism /'eɪdʒɪzəm/ *n* [U] the making of unfair differences between people because of their age, esp. treating young people more favourably than old people **ageist** *adj*, *n*

a·gen·cy /'eɪdʒənsi/ *n* work or business of an agent: *an employment agency*

a·gen·da /ə'dʒendə/ *n* **-das** list of things to be talked about at a meeting

a·gent /'eɪdʒənt/ *n* **1** person who does business for other people: *An estate agent sells houses.* **2** person or thing that produces a result: *Soap is a cleansing agent.*

ag·gran·dize·ment, -disement /ə'grændʒɪzmənt/ *n* [U] increase in size, power, or rank

ag·gra·vate /'ægrəveɪt/ *vt* **1** make worse **2** annoy: *an aggravating delay* **-vation** /,ægrə'veɪʃən/ *n* [C;U]

ag·gre·gate /'ægrɪgət/ *n* [C;U] total

ag·gres·sion /ə'greʃən/ *n* [U] starting a quarrel or war without just cause **-sor** /ə'gresəʳ/ *n* person or country that does this

ag·gres·sive /ə'gresɪv/ *adj* **1** always ready to attack **2** brave and determined

ag·grieved /ə'griːvd/ *adj fml* showing hurt feelings

a·ghast /ə'gɑːst‖ə'gæst/ *adj* surprised and shocked

a·gile /'ædʒaɪl‖'ædʒəl/ *adj* able to move quickly **agility** /ə'dʒɪlɪti/ *n* [U]

ag·i·tate /'ædʒɪteɪt/ *v* **1** *vt* shake (a liquid) **2** *vt* make anxious; worry **3** *vi* **(for)** argue strongly in public **-tator** *n* person who agitates for political or social change **-tation** /,ædʒɪ'teɪʃən/ *n* [U]

a·glow /ə'gləʊ/ *adj* bright with colour or excitement

AGM /,eɪ dʒiː 'em/ *n* annual general meeting of a club, organization, etc., held once a year to elect officials, report on the year's business, etc.

ag·nos·tic /æg'nɒstɪk, əg-‖-‖-'nɑː-/ *n, adj* (person) believing that nothing can be known about God **~ism** /-tɪsɪzəm/ *n* [U]

a·go /ə'gəʊ/ *adj, adv* back in time from now: *a week ago*

a·gog /ə'gɒg‖ə'gɑːg/ *adj* excited and eager

ag·o·nize ‖ also **-ise** *BrE* /'ægənaɪz/ *vi infml* make a long and anxious effort when trying to make a decision, etc. **-nized** *adj* expressing great pain **-nizing** *adj* causing great pain

ag·o·ny /'ægəni/ *n* [C;U] great suffering

agony aunt /'·· ,·/ *n BrE* woman who gives advice in a part of a newspaper or magazine that contains letters from readers about their personal problems (an **agony column**)

ag·o·ra·pho·bi·a /,ægərə'fəʊbiə/ *n* [U] fear of open spaces

a·grar·i·an /ə'greəriən/ *adj* of land, esp. farmland

a·gree /ə'griː/ *v* **1** *vi/t* share the same opinion; say 'yes': *I agree with you.* | *We agreed to go home.* | *They met at the agreed place.* **2** *vi* (of statements, etc.) be the same; match **~able** *adj* pleasant **~ably** *adv* **~ment** *n* **1** [U] state of agreeing: *The 2 sides cannot reach agreement.* **2** [C] arrangement between people or groups; CONTRACT: *to break an agreement*

agree with *phr vt* **1** suit the health of **2** be in accordance with

ag·ri·cul·ture /'ægrɪ,kʌltʃəʳ/ *n* [U] growing crops; farming **-tural** /,ægrɪ'kʌltʃərəl◂/ *adj*

ag·ron·o·my /ə'grɒnəmi‖ə'grɑː-/ *n* [U] science of managing soil and growing crops

a·ground /ə'graʊnd/ *adv, adj* (of a ship) on or onto the shore or bottom of a sea, lake, etc.

a·head /ə'hed/ *adv, adj* **1** in front **2** into the future: *to plan ahead* **3** [(of)] in advance; succeeding better: *to get ahead of our rivals*

AI /,eɪ 'aɪ/ *n* [U] ARTIFICIAL INTELLIGENCE

aid /eɪd/ *n* **1** [U] help: *She came to my aid at once.* | *to collect £1,000 in aid of medical research* **2** [C] person or thing that helps: *an aid in learning a language* **3 What is something in aid of?** *BrE infml* What is something for?: *What's that handle in aid of?* — see also FIRST AID ♦ *vt fml* help

aide /eɪd/ *n* person who helps

AIDS, Aids /eɪdz/ *n* [U] Acquired Immune Deficiency Syndrome; very serious disease caused by a VIRUS which breaks down the body's natural defences against infection

ail /eɪl/ vi be ill: *an ailing child* ~**ment** n illness

aim /eɪm/ v 1 vi/t point (a weapon, etc.) towards 2 vi direct one's efforts; intend: *I aim to be a writer.* ♦ n 1 act of directing a shot 2 desired result; purpose: *What is your aim in life?* ~**less** adj without purpose

ain't /eɪnt/ *short for:* am not, is not, are not, has not, or have not

air[1] /eər/ n 1 [U] mixture of gases that we breathe 2 [U] space above the ground: *travel by air* 3 [C] general character of a person or place: *an air of excitement at the meeting.* 4 **clear the air** get rid of misunderstanding, etc., by stating the facts clearly 5 **in the air**: **a** (of stories, talk, etc.) being passed on from one person to another **b** uncertain 6 **on/off the air** broadcasting/not broadcasting — see also HOT AIR, THIN AIR **airs** n [P] unnatural behaviour to make one seem important

air[2] v 1 vi/t dry (clothes, etc.) in a warm place 2 vi/t make or become fresh by letting in air: *to air the room* 3 vt let people know: *He's always airing his opinions.* 4 vt broadcast **airing** n [C;U]

air-borne /'eəbɔːn‖'eərbɔːrn/ adj 1 carried by the air 2 (of aircraft) flying

air-bus /'eəbʌs‖'eər-/ n aircraft carrying many passengers on short flights

air-con-di-tion-ing /'·· ·,···/ n [U] system using machines (**air-conditioners**) to control the indoor air temperature –**tioned** adj

air-craft /'eəkrɑːft‖'eərkræft/ n -**craft** flying machine

aircraft car-ri-er /'·· ,···/ n warship that carries aircraft

air-field /'eəfiːld‖'eər-/ n place where aircraft can land

air-force /'eəfɔːs‖'eərfɔːrs/ n branch of a country's military forces that fights in the air

air-host-ess /'eə,həʊstəs‖'eər-/ n woman who looks after passengers in an aircraft

air-i-ly /'eərəli/ adv in a light AIRY (2,3) manner

air-lift /'eə,lɪft‖'eər-/ n carrying of large numbers of people or amounts of supplies by aircraft, esp. to or from a place that is difficult to get to **airlift** vt

air-line /'eəlaɪn‖'eər-/ n business that carries passengers and goods by air

air-lin-er /'eə,laɪnər‖'eər-/ n large passenger aircraft

air-lock /'eəlɒk‖'eərlɑːk/ n 1 BUBBLE in a tube, etc., that prevents the flow of liquid 2 enclosed space or room into which or from which air cannot accidentally pass

air-mail /'eəmeɪl‖'eər-/ n [U] system of sending letters, etc., by air

air-plane /'eəpleɪn‖'eər-/ n AmE for AEROPLANE

air-port /'eəpɔːt‖'eərpɔːrt/ n place where aircraft regularly land, with buildings for waiting passengers, etc.

air raid /'· ·/ n attack by military aircraft

air-ship /'eə,ʃɪp‖'eər-/ n lighter-than-air aircraft with an engine but no wings

air-space /'eəspeɪs‖'eər-/ n [U] sky above a country, regarded as that country's property

air-strip /'eə,strɪp‖'eər-/ n piece of ground where aircraft can land if necessary

air-tight /'eətaɪt‖'eər-/ adj not letting air in or out

air-to-air /,· · '·◄/ adj to be fired from one aircraft to another

air-way /'eəweɪ‖'eər-/ n AIRLINE

air-wor-thy /'eə,wɜːði‖'eər,wɜːrði/ adj (of an aircraft) in safe working condition –**thiness** n [U]

air-y /'eəri/ adj 1 open to the fresh air 2 not practical: *airy notions* 3 cheerful and careless

aisle /aɪl/ n passage between seats in a church, theatre, etc.

a-jar /ə'dʒɑːr/ adv, adj (of a door) slightly open

aka abbrev. for: also known as

a-kim-bo /ə'kɪmbəʊ/ adj, adv (of the arms) bent at the elbows and with the hand on the HIPs

a-kin /ə'kɪn/ adj [(to)] like; similar

a-lac-ri-ty /ə'lækrəti/ n [U] fml quick and willing readiness

a-larm /ə'lɑːm‖ə'lɑːrm/ n 1 [C] warning of danger 2 [U] sudden fear 3 [C] apparatus that gives a warning: *a burglar alarm* 4 [C] clock that can be set to make a noise at any time to wake people: *set the alarm (clock) for 6.30* ♦ vt frighten: *alarming news* ~**ist** n person who always expects danger, often without good reason, and says so to others ~**ist** adj

a-las /ə'læs/ interj (cry expressing sorrow)

al-be-it /ɔːl'biːɪt/ conj fml even though: *an important, albeit small, mistake*

al-bi-no /æl'biːnəʊ‖æl'baɪ-/ n person or animal with white skin, very light hair, and pink eyes

al-bum /'ælbəm/ n 1 book for sticking photographs, etc., into 2 long-playing record

al-che-my /'ælkəmi/ n [U] former science concerned with turning metals into gold –**mist** n

al-co-hol /'ælkəhɒl‖-hɔːl/ n [U] (drinks containing) the liquid that makes one drunk ~**ism** n [U] diseased condition caused by the continued drinking of too much alcohol ~**ic** /ˌælkəˈhɒlɪk◂‖-ˈhɔː-/ adj n person unable to stop drinking alcohol

al-cove /ˈælkəʊv/ n small partly enclosed space in a room for a bed, etc.

ale /eɪl/ n [U] kind of beer

al-eck /ˈælɪk/ n see SMART ALECK

a-lert /əˈlɜːt‖əˈlɜːrt/ adj quick to see and ask; watchful ♦ n 1 warning of danger 2 **on the alert** ready to deal with danger ♦ vt warn

al-fres-co /ælˈfreskəʊ/ adj, adv in the open air

al-gae /ˈældʒiː/ n [P] very small plants that live in or near water

al-ge-bra /ˈældʒəbrə/ n [U] branch of MATHEMATICS using letters to represent values

a-li-as /ˈeɪliəs/ n -**ases** false name used esp. by a criminal ♦ adv also called: Edward Ball, alias John Smith

al-i-bi /ˈæləbaɪ/ n proof that a person charged with a crime was somewhere else when it happened

a-li-en /ˈeɪliən/ n 1 foreigner who has not become a citizen of the country where he lives 2 (in films and stories) a creature from another world ♦ adj 1 foreign 2 different and strange

a-li-en-ate /ˈeɪliəneɪt/ vt make unfriendly –**ation** /ˌeɪliəˈneɪʃən/ n [U]

a-light¹ /əˈlaɪt/ vi **alighted** or **alit** /əˈlɪt/ fml get down; come down: to alight from a train

alight² adj on fire; burning

a-lign /əˈlaɪn/ vi/t 1 come or put into a line 2 **align oneself with** come into agreement with: They aligned themselves with the army. ~**ment** n [C;U]

a-like /əˈlaɪk/ adj, adv like one another; the same

al-i-men-ta-ry /ˌæləˈmentəri◂/ adj concerning food and the way it is treated: the alimentary canal (= tubelike passage leading from the mouth to the stomach)

al-i-mo-ny /ˈæləməni‖-məʊni/ n [U] money that one must pay regularly to a former wife or husband

a-live /əˈlaɪv/ adj 1 living; in existence: (fig.) The argument was kept alive by the politicians. 2 full of life; active 3 **alive to** AWARE OF 4 **alive with** covered with (insects, etc.)

al-ka-li /ˈælkəlaɪ/ n -**lis** or -**lies** [C;U] substance that forms a chemical salt when combined with an acid –**line** adj

all¹ /ɔːl/ determiner the whole of; every one of: all the bread | all these questions | He ate it all.

all² adv 1 completely: It's all dirty. | He's all alone. 2 for each side: The score was 3 all. 3 **all along** from the beginning 4 **all at once** suddenly 5

all in: a very tired b with everything included: It cost £2000 all in. 6 **all out** using all possible strength and effort 7 **all over** everywhere 8 **all right:** a safe or satisfactory b I agree; yes 9 **all the** by so much: If you help, we'll finish all the sooner 10 **all there** having a good quick mind 11 **all the same** even so; in any case 12 **all the same to** making no difference to: It's all the same to me what you do. 13 **all told** all together 14 **all up** at an end; ruined 15 **not all that** infml not very

all³ pron 1 everyone or everything: This is all I have. | I brought all of them. 2 **all in all** considering everything 3 **(not) at all** (not) in any way: I don't agree at all. 4 **in all** counting everyone or everything 5 **once and for all** for the last time

Al-lah /ˈælə/ n (the Muslim name for) God

al-lay /əˈleɪ/ vt fml make (fear, etc.) less

all clear /ˌ·ˈ·/ n [the + S] 1 signal that danger is past 2 GO-AHEAD

al-lege /əˈledʒ/ vt fml declare without proof: an alleged thief **allegedly** /əˈledʒədli/ adv **allegation** /ˌæləˈgeɪʃən/ n fml unproved statement

al-le-giance /əˈliːdʒəns/ n [U] loyalty to a leader, country, etc.

al-le-go-ry /ˈæləgəri‖-gɔːri/ n [C;U] (style of) story, poem, etc., in which the characters represent ideas and qualities

al-ler-gy /ˈælədʒi‖-ər-/ n condition of being made ill by a particular food, drug, etc. –**gic** /əˈlɜːdʒɪk‖-ɜːr-/ adj

al-le-vi-ate /əˈliːvieɪt/ vt make (pain, etc.) less –**ation** /əˌliːviˈeɪʃən/ n [U]

al-ley /ˈæli/ n 1 narrow street or path 2 track along which balls are rolled in BOWLING or SKITTLES

al-li-ance /əˈlaɪəns/ n 1 [C] close agreement or connection made between countries, etc., for a shared purpose 2 [U] act of forming an alliance or state of being in an alliance

al-li-ga-tor /ˈæləgeɪtər/ n animal like a CROCODILE

al-lo-cate /ˈæləkeɪt/ vt give as a share –**cation** /ˌæləˈkeɪʃən/ n [C;U]

al-lot /əˈlɒt‖əˈlɑːt/ vt -**tt**- allocate

al-lot-ment /əˈlɒtmənt‖əˈlɑːt-/ n 1 [C;U] allocation 2 [C] (in Britain) small piece of land rented to grow vegetables on

al-low /əˈlaʊ/ vt 1 let (someone) do something without opposing them; let (something) be done; permit: They allowed him to come. 2 provide (esp. money or time) ~**able** adj ~**ance** n 1 money provided regularly 2 **make allowances** take something into consideration

allow for *phr vt* take into consideration: *We must allow for the train being late.*

al·loy /ˈælɔɪˌˈælɒɪ, əˈlɔɪ/ *n* mixture of metals

all right /ˌ ˈ/*adj, adv* 1 safe, unharmed, or healthy 2 acceptable 3 I/we agree 4 *infml* beyond doubt 5 **That's/It's all right** (used as a reply when someone thanks you or says they are sorry for something they are doing)

all-round /ˈ · ˈ/*adj* having ability in many things, esp. in various sports **~er** /ˌ ˈ ʳ/ *n*

all-singing all-dancing /ˌ·ˈ·· ·ˈ··/*adj infml* using every possible means to attract attention

al·lude /əˈluːd/ *v* **allude to** *phr vt fml* speak about indirectly **allusion** /əˈluːʒən/ *n* [C;U]

al·lure /əˈljʊəʳˌəˈlʊəʳ/ *vt* attract or charm by the offer of something pleasant: *an alluring smile*

al·ly /ˈælaɪˌˈælaɪ, əˈlaɪ/ *n* person, country, etc., that helps one or agrees to help ◆ /əˈlaɪˌˈælaɪ, əˈlaɪ/ *vt* 1 unite by agreement, marriage, etc. 2 **allied (to)** related or connected (to)

al·ma ma·ter /ˌælmə ˈmeɪtəʳ, -ˈmɑː-ˌ -ˈmɑː-/ *n* school, college, etc., which one attended

al·ma·nac /ˈɔːlmənækˌˈɒl-, ˈæl-/ *n* book giving information about the sun, moon, sea, etc.

al·might·y /ɔːlˈmaɪti/ *adj* very great

al·mond /ˈɑːməndˌˈɑː-, ˈæ-, ˈæl-/ *n* kind of nut

al·most /ˈɔːlməʊstˌˈɔːlməʊst, ɔːlˈməʊst/ *adv* very nearly: *almost everyone|almost finished*

alms /ɑːmzˌɒmz, ɑːlmz/ *n* [P] money, food, clothes, etc., given to poor people

a·loft /əˈlɒftˌəˈlɔːft/ *adv fml* high up

a·lone /əˈləʊn/ *adv, adj* 1 without others: *He lives alone.* 2 only: *You alone can do it.* 3 **leave/let alone: a** leave untouched or unchanged **b** allow to be by oneself

a·long /əˈlɒŋˌəˈlɔːŋ/ *adv* 1 forward; on: *Come along!* 2 with others: *Bring your sister along (with you).* ◆ *prep* 1 from end to end of: *walk along the road* 2 somewhere on the length of

a·long·side /əˌlɒŋˈsaɪdˌəˌlɔːŋ-/ *adv, prep* close to the side (of)

a·loof /əˈluːf/ *adj, adv* distant in feeling; not friendly **~ness** *n* [U]

a·loud /əˈlaʊd/ *adv* in a voice that can be heard: *to read aloud*

al·pha·bet /ˈælfəbet/ letters used in writing **~ical** /ˌælfəˈbetɪkəl/ *adj* in the order of the alphabet

al·read·y /ɔːlˈredi/ *adv* 1 by or before an expected time: *Are you leaving already?* 2 before now: *I've seen the film twice already.*

al·right /ˈɔːlˈraɪt/ *adj, adv* ALL RIGHT

Al·sa·tian /ælˈseɪʃən/*n* large WOLF-like dog

al·so /ˈɔːlsəʊ/ *adv* 1 as well; besides 2 **not only ... but also ...** both ... and ...

also-ran /ˈ·· ·/*n* person who has failed to win at a sport or in an election

al·tar /ˈɔːltəʳ/ *n* table used in a religious ceremony

al·ter /ˈɔːltəʳ/ *vi/t* make or become different **~ation** /ˌɔːltəˈreɪʃən/ *n* [C;U]

al·ter·ca·tion /ˌɔːltəˈkeɪʃənˌ-tər-/ *n* [C;U] noisy argument or quarrel

alter ego /ˌæltər ˈiːɡəʊ, ˌɔːl-/ *n* **alter egos** very close and trusted friend

al·ter·nate[1] /ɔːlˈtɜːnɪtˌˈɔːltər-, ˈæl-/ *adj* (of two things) happening by turns; first one and then the other: *He works on alternate days.* **~ly** *adv*

al·ter·nate[2] /ˈɔːltəneɪtˌ-ər-/ *vi/t* happen or follow by turns **~nation** /ˌɔːltəˈneɪʃənˌ-ər-/ *n* [C;U]

al·ter·na·tive /ɔːlˈtɜːnətɪvˌɔːlˈtɜːr-, æl-/ *adj* 1 to be done or used instead; other 2 different from what is usual or TRADITIONAL: *alternative medicine* 3 not based on or not accepting the established standards of ordinary society: *alternative theatre* ◆ *n* [(to)] something that can be done or used instead **~ly** *adv*

al·though /ɔːlˈðəʊ/ *conj* though

al·ti·tude /ˈæltɪtjuːdˌ-tuːd/ *n* height above sea level

al·to /ˈæltəʊ/ *n* **-tos** (person with) a singing voice between SOPRANO and TENOR

al·to·geth·er[1] /ˌɔːltəˈɡeðəʳ/ *adv* 1 completely: *altogether different* 2 considering everything together: *Altogether, it was a good trip.*

altogether[2] *n* **in the altogether** NUDE

al·tru·is·m /ˈæltruːɪzəm/*n* [U] unselfishness **~ist** *n* **~istic** /ˌæltruːˈɪstɪk/ *adj*

a·lu·min·i·um /ˌæljuˈmɪniəm, ˌælə-/ *BrE* ‖ **aluminum** /əˈluːmɪnəm/ *AmE* *n* [U] light silver-white metal

al·ways /ˈɔːlwəz, -weɪz/ *adv* 1 at all times: *The sun always rises in the east.* 2 for ever: *I'll always love you.* 3 very often and annoyingly: *He's always complaining.*

am /m, əm; *strong* æm/ *v* 1st person sing. present tense of BE

am, AM /ˌeɪ ˈem/ *abbrev. for:* ante meridiem = *(Latin)* before midday (used after numbers expressing time)

a·mal·gam /əˈmælɡəm/ *n* mixture or combination

a·mal·gam·ate /əˈmælgəmeɪt/ vi/t (of businesses, etc.) unite; combine **–ation** /ə,mælgəˈmeɪʃən/ n [C;U]

a·mass /əˈmæs/ vt gather or collect in great amounts

am·a·teur /ˈæmətəʳ, -tʃʊəʳ, -tʃəʳ, ,æməˈtɜːʳ/ n person who does something for enjoyment and without being paid: *amateur actors | amateur sport* **–ish** adj lacking skill

a·maze /əˈmeɪz/ vt fill with great surprise: *I was amazed to hear the news. | an amazing film* **~ment** n [U] **amazingly** adv

am·a·zon /ˈæməzən‖-zɑːn, -zən/ n tall, strong woman

am·bas·sa·dor /æmˈbæsədəʳ/ n minister of high rank representing his/her own country in another country

am·bas·sa·dress /æmˈbæsədrɪs/ n 1 female ambassador 2 wife of an ambassador

am·ber /ˈæmbəʳ/ n [U] (yellow colour of) a hard substance used for jewels

am·bi·dex·trous /,æmbɪˈdekstrəs/ adj able to use both hands equally well

am·bi·ence /ˈæmbiəns/ n feeling of a place; ATMOSPHERE (3)

am·big·u·ous /æmˈbɪgjʊəs/ adj having more than one meaning; not clear **–uity** /,æmbɪˈgjuːəti/ n [C;U]

am·bi·tion /æmˈbɪʃən/ n 1 [C] strong desire for success 2 [C] whatever is desired in this way: *to achieve one's ambitions* **–tious** adj **–tiously** adv

am·biv·a·lent /æmˈbɪvələnt/ adj having opposing feelings about something **–lence** n [U]

am·ble /ˈæmbəl/ vi walk at an easy gentle rate

am·bu·lance /ˈæmbjʊləns/ n motor vehicle for carrying sick people

am·bush /ˈæmbʊʃ/ n [C;U] surprise attack from a place of hiding **ambush** vt

a·me·ba /əˈmiːbə/ n AmE for AMOEBA

a·me·li·o·rate /əˈmiːliəreɪt/ vt fml improve **–ration** /ə,miːliəˈreɪʃən/ n [U]

a·men /ɑːˈmen, eɪ-/ interj (at the end of a prayer) may this be true

a·me·na·ble /əˈmiːnəbəl/ adj willing to be influenced

a·mend /əˈmend/ vt change and improve **~ment** n [C;U]

a·mends /əˈmendz/ n [P] **make amends** pay for harm or damage done

a·me·ni·ty /əˈmiːnɪti‖əˈme-/ n something (e.g. a park or swimming pool) that makes life pleasant

A·mer·i·can foot·ball /ə,merɪkən ˈfʊtbɔːl/ n [U] BrE game played between 2 teams of 11 players using

an OVAL ball that can be handled or kicked

am·e·thyst /ˈæmɪθɪst/ n [C;U] (purple colour of) a stone used in jewellery

a·mi·a·ble /ˈeɪmiəbəl/ adj good tempered; friendly **–bly** adv

am·i·ca·ble /ˈæmɪkəbəl/ adj done in a friendly way: *reach an amicable agreement* **–bly** adv

a·mid /əˈmɪd/ also **amidst** /əˈmɪdst/ prep fml among

a·miss /əˈmɪs/ adj, adv fml 1 wrong(ly) or imperfect(ly) 2 **take something amiss** be offended

am·i·ty /ˈæmɪti/ n [U] fml friendship

am·mo·ni·a /əˈməʊniə/ n [U] gas with a strong smell, used in explosives and chemicals

am·mu·ni·tion /,æmjʊˈnɪʃən/ n [U] bullets, bombs, etc.

am·ne·si·a /æmˈniːziə‖-ʒə/ n [U] loss of memory

am·nes·ty /ˈæmnəsti/ n general act of forgiveness, esp. by a state to people guilty of political offences

a·moe·ba ‖ also **ameba** AmE /əˈmiːbə/ n **-bas** or **-bae** /-biː/ living creature that consists of only one cell **-bic** adj

a·mok /əˈmɒk‖əˈmɑːk/ also **amuck** — adv **run amok** run wildly about trying to kill people

a·mong /əˈmʌŋ/ also **amongst** /əˈmʌŋst/ — prep 1 in the middle of: *a house among the trees* 2 in the group of; one of: *He's among the best of our students. | They talked about it among themselves.* (= together) 3 to each of (more than 2): *Divide it among the 5 of you.*

a·mor·al /eɪˈmɒrəl, æ-‖eɪˈmɔː-, -ˈmɑː-/ adj having no understanding of right or wrong

am·o·rous /ˈæmərəs/ adj feeling or expressing love, esp. sexual love **~ly** adv

a·mor·phous /əˈmɔːfəs‖-ɔːr-/ adj having no fixed form or shape

a·mount¹ /əˈmaʊnt/ n quantity; total: *large amounts of money*

amount² v **amount to** phr vt be equal to

amp /æmp/ also **ampere** /ˈæmpeəʳ‖ˈæmpɪər/ — n standard measure of the quantity of electricity

am·phet·a·mine /æmˈfetəmiːn, -mɪn/ n [C;U] drug used esp. illegally, by people wanting excitement

am·phib·i·an /æmˈfɪbiən/ n animal, such as a FROG, that can live both on land and in water **–ious** adj

am·phi·thea·tre BrE ‖ **-ter** AmE /ˈæmfɪθɪətəʳ/ n open building with rows of seats round a central space

am·ple /ˈæmpəl/ adj enough; plenty **amply** adv

am·pli·fy /ˈæmpləfaɪ/ vi/t fml 1 explain in more detail 2 make (esp. sound) stronger **–fier** n instrument for making sound louder **–fication** /ˌæmpləfəˈkeɪʃən/ n [C;U]

am·pu·tate /ˈæmpjʊteɪt/ vi/t cut off (part of the body) for medical reasons **–tation** /ˌæmpjʊˈteɪʃən/ n [C;U]

a·muck /əˈmʌk/ adv AMOK

am·u·let /ˈæmjʊlət, -lət‖ˈæmjʊlət/ n object worn to protect one against evil, bad luck, etc.

a·muse /əˈmjuːz/ vt 1 cause to laugh: an amusing story 2 cause to spend time pleasantly ~**ment** n 1 [U] state of being amused 2 [C] something that passes the time pleasantly

an /ən; strong æn/ indefinite article, determiner (used before a vowel sound) a: an elephant

a·nach·ro·nism /əˈnækrənɪzəm/ n person, thing, or idea placed in the wrong period of time: To say 'Julius Caesar looked at his watch' is an anachronism. **-nistic** /əˌnækrəˈnɪstɪk/ adj

an·a·con·da /ˌænəˈkɒndə‖-ˈkɑːn-/ n large S American snake

a·nae·mi·a ‖ also **anemia** AmE /əˈniːmiə/ n [U] lack of enough red blood cells **–mic** adj

an·aes·the·si·a ‖ also **anes-** AmE /ˌænəsˈθiːziə‖-ʒə/ n [U] state of being unable to feel pain, etc.

an·aes·thet·ic ‖ also **anes-** AmE /ˌænəsˈθetɪk/ n [C;U] substance that stops one from feeling pain, either in a part of the body (a **local anaesthetic**) or in the whole body, making one unconscious (a **general anaesthetic**) **–thetist** /əˈniːsθətɪst‖əˈnes-/ n **–thetize** vt

an·a·gram /ˈænəɡræm/ n word made by changing the order of the letters in another word: 'Silent' is an anagram of 'listen'

a·nal /ˈeɪnəl/ adj of, concerning the ANUS

an·al·ge·sic /ˌænəlˈdʒiːzɪk/ n, adj (substance) which makes one unable to feel pain

a·nal·o·gy /əˈnælədʒi/ n 1 [C] degree of likeness 2 [U] explaining one thing by comparing it to something else **–gous** /-ɡəs/ adj like or alike in some ways

an·a·lyse ‖ also **-lyze** AmE/ˈænəlaɪz/ vt examine carefully, often by dividing something into parts

a·nal·y·sis /əˈnæləsəs/ n 1 [C;U] examination of something; analysing 2 [U] PSYCHOANALYSIS **analyst** /ˈænəlɪst/ n **analytic** /ˌænəˈlɪtɪk/ adj

an·ar·chy /ˈænəki‖-ər-/ n [U] 1 absence of government 2 social disorder **–chism** n [U] **–chist** n person who wishes for this **–chic**

anathema /əˈnæθəmə/ n something hated

a·nat·o·my /əˈnætəmi/ n 1 [U] scientific study of living bodies 2 [C] way a living thing works: (fig.) the anatomy of modern society **–mical** /ˌænəˈtɒmɪkəl ‖-/ adj

an·ces·tor /ˈænsəstəʳ, -səstɔː‖-ər/ n person from whom one is descended **–tral** /ænˈsestrəl/ adj

an·ces·try /ˈænsəstri, -səstri‖-ses-/ n [C;U] all one's ancestors

an·chor /ˈæŋkəʳ/ n 1 piece of heavy metal for lowering into the water to stop a ship from moving 2 something that makes one feel safe ♦ v 1 vi lower the anchor 2 vt fix firmly in position ~**age** n place where ships may anchor

an·chor·per·son /ˈæŋkəˌpɜːsən‖ˈæŋkər,pɜːrsən/ also **-man** /-ˌmæn/ masc., **-woman** /-ˌwʊmən/ fem. — n esp. AmE broadcaster usu. on television, in charge of a news broadcast, to connect one part of the broadcast with the next

an·cho·vy /ˈæntʃəvi‖ˈæntʃoʊvi/ n **-vies** or **-vy** small strong-tasting fish

an·cient /ˈeɪnʃənt/ adj 1 of times long ago: ancient Rome 2 very old

an·cil·la·ry /ænˈsɪləri‖ˈænsɪleri/ adj providing additional help

and /ənd, ən, strong ænd/ conj 1 (joining 2 things) as well as: John and Sally ‖ We're cold and hungry. 2 then; therefore: Water the seeds and they will grow. 3 (showing that something continues without stopping): We ran and ran. 4 (used instead of **to** after **come, go, try**): Try and open it.

an·droid /ˈændrɔɪd/ n (in stories) ROBOT in human form

an·ec·dote /ˈænɪkdəʊt/ n short interesting story that is true **–dotal** /ˌænɪkˈdəʊtl/ adj containing or telling anecdotes

a·ne·mi·a /əˈniːmiə/ n [U] AmE for ANAEMIA

an·es·the·si·a /ˌænəsˈθiːziə‖-ʒə/ n [U] AmE for ANAESTHESIA

a·new /əˈnjuː‖əˈnuː/ adv again

an·gel /ˈeɪndʒəl/ n 1 messenger of God 2 very kind and beautiful person ~**ic** /ænˈdʒelɪk/ adj

an·ger /ˈæŋɡəʳ/ n [U] fierce displeasure and annoyance ♦ vt make angry

an·gle[1] /ˈæŋɡəl/ n 1 space between 2 lines that meet, measured in degrees 2 corner 3 point of view 4 **at an angle** not upright or straight ♦ vt 1 turn or move at an angle 2 represent (something) from a particular point of view

angle[2] vi catch fish with a hook and line **angler** n

angle for phr vt try to get, by tricks or indirect questions: to angle for an invitation

An-gli-can /'æŋglɪkən/ n, adj (member) of the Church of England

an-gli-cize /'æŋglɪsaɪz/ vt make English

an-gry /'æŋgri/ adj 1 full of anger 2 (of the sky or clouds) stormy **angrily** adv

angst /æŋst/ n [U] anxiety and anguish caused esp. by considering the sad state of the world

an-guish /'æŋgwɪʃ/ n [U] great suffering, esp. of the mind **~ed** adj

an-gu-lar /'æŋgjʊlər/ adj 1 having sharp corners 2 (of a person) thin

an-i-mal /'ænəməl/ n 1 living creature that is not a plant 2 all these except human beings 3 MAMMAL 4 person considered as lacking a mind and behaving like a wild non-human creature ♦ adj 1 of animals 2 of the body

an-i-mate¹ /'ænəmət/ adj alive

an-i-mate² /'ænəmeɪt/ vt give life or excitement to **-mated** adj cheerful and excited: an animated discussion **-mation** /,ænə'meɪʃən/ n [U] 1 cheerful excitement 2 process of making CARTOONS

an-i-mis-m /'ænəmɪzəm/ n [U] religion according to which animals, plants, etc., are believed to have souls

an-i-mos-i-ty /,ænə'mɒsɪti‖-'maː-/ n [C;U] powerful hatred

an-kle /'æŋkəl/ n thin part of the leg, above the foot

an-nals /'ænlz/ n [P] history or record of events, etc., produced every year: It will go down in the annals (= history) of modern science.

an-nex /ə'neks‖ə'neks, 'æneks/ /,ænek'seɪʃən/ vt take control of (land, etc.) **~ation** /,ænek'seɪʃən/ n [C;U]

an-nexe /'æneks/ n building added to a larger one

an-ni-hi-late /ə'naɪəleɪt/ vt destroy completely **-lation** /ə,naɪə'leɪʃən/ n [U]

an-ni-ver-sa-ry /,ænə'vɜːsəri‖-ər-/ n day that is an exact number of years after something happened

an-no-tate /'ænəteɪt/ vt fml add notes to (a book) **-tation** /,ænə-'teɪʃən/ n

an-nounce /ə'naʊns/ vt state loudly or publicly: He announced the winner of the competition. **~ment** n public statement

an-nounc-er /ə'naʊnsər/ n person who reads the news, etc., on radio or television

an-noy /ə'nɔɪ/ vt make a little angry; cause trouble to: an annoying delay **~ance** n [C;U]

an-nu-al¹ /'ænjuəl/ adj 1 happening once every year 2 for one year; my annual salary **~ly** adv

annual² n 1 plant that lives for one year 2 book produced each year with the same name but new contents

an-nu-i-ty /ə'njuːɪti‖ə'nuː-/ n fixed sum of money paid each year to someone

an-nul /ə'nʌl/ vt **-ll-** cause (a marriage, etc.) to stop existing **~ment** n [C;U]

an-ode /'ænəʊd/ n part of an electrical instrument which collects ELECTRONs

an-o-dyne /'ænədaɪn/ adj unlikely to offend or annoy anyone

a-noint /ə'nɔɪnt/ vt put oil on, esp. in a ceremony

a-nom-a-ly /ə'nɒməli‖ə'naː-/ n fml something different from the usual type: A cat with no tail is an anomaly. **-lous** adj

a-non¹ /ə'nɒn‖ə'naːn/ adv lit soon

anon² abbrev. for ANONYMOUS

a-non-y-mous /ə'nɒnəməs‖ə'naː-/ adj without a name; not giving the name: an anonymous letter **-mity** /,ænə'nɪməti/ n [U]

an-o-rak /'ænəræk/ n short coat with a HOOD

an-o-rex-i-a /,ænə'reksiə/ n [U] dangerous condition in which there is a loss of desire to eat **-ic** adj

an-oth-er /ə'nʌðər/ determiner, pron 1 one more: Have another drink. 2 a different one: I'll do it another time. 3 more; in addition: It'll cost you another $20. 4 **one another** each other

an-swer¹ /'aːnsər‖'æn-/ n 1 what is said or written when someone asks a question or sends a letter; reply 2 something discovered by thinking: I'm getting fat — the answer is to eat less.

answer² v 1 vi/t give an answer (to): She answered with a smile. 2 vi/t attend or act in reply to (the telephone ringing, a knock at the door, etc.): Answer the phone, will you!| The dog answers to the name of Fred. 3 vi/t be as described in: He answers to the description you gave. 4 vt be satisfactory for **~able** adj 1 able to be answered 2 responsible: The school is answerable to your parents for your safety.

answer back phr vi/t reply rudely (to)

answer for phr vt 1 be responsible for 2 pay or suffer for

ant /ænt/ n insect living on the ground and famous for hard work

an-tag-o-nize ‖ also **-nise** BrE /æn'tægənaɪz/ vt make into an enemy **-nism** n [U] hatred; opposition **-nist** n opponent

Ant-arc-tic /æn'tɑːktɪk‖-ɑːr-/ adj, n (of or concerning) the very cold most southern part of the world

an·te·ce·dents /ˌæntə'siːdənts/ n [P] *fml* family or past history

an·te·cham·ber /ˈænti,tʃeɪmbər/ also **anteroom** — n small room leading to a larger one

an·te·di·lu·vian /ˌæntidɪˈluːvian/ adj very old-fashioned

an·te·lope /ˈæntəloʊp‖ˈæntəl-/ n -**lopes** or **lope** graceful animal like a deer

an·te·na·tal /ˌæntɪˈneɪtl/ adj existing or happening before birth: *an antenatal clinic*

an·ten·na /ænˈtenə/ n 1 (*pl.* -**nae** /-niː/) insect's FEELER 2 AERIAL¹

an·them /ˈænθəm/ n religious song of praise

an·thol·o·gy /ænˈθɒlədʒi‖ænˈθɑː-/ n collection of poems or other writings

an·thro·poid /ˈænθrəpɔɪd/ adj like a person

an·thro·pol·o·gy /ˌænθrəˈpɒlədʒi‖-ˈpɑː-/ n scientific study of the human race -**gist** n

an·thro·po·mor·phic /ˌænθrəpəˈmɔːfɪk‖-ɔːr-/ adj regarding a god, animal, etc, as having human qualities

an·ti·bi·ot·ic /ˌæntɪbaɪˈɒtɪk‖-ˈɑː-/ n medical substance, such as PENICILLIN, that can kill harmful bacteria in the body

an·ti·bod·y /ˈæntɪ,bɒdi‖-,bɑː-/ n substance produced in the body which fights disease

an·tic·i·pate /ænˈtɪsəpeɪt/ vt 1 expect: *We anticipate trouble.* 2 do something before (someone else) 3 guess (what will happen) and act as necessary -**pation** /æn,tɪsəˈpeɪʃən/ n [U]

an·ti·cli·max /ˌæntiˈklaɪmæks/ n unexciting end to something exciting

an·ti·clock·wise /ˌæntiˈklɒkwaɪz‖-ˈklɑːk-/ adv in the opposite direction to the movement of a clock

an·tics /ˈæntɪks/ n [P] strange, amusing movements or behaviour

an·ti·cy·clone /ˌæntiˈsaɪkloʊn/ n area of high air pressure, causing settled weather

an·ti·dote /ˈæntɪdoʊt/ n something that prevents the effects of a poison or disease

an·ti·freeze /ˈæntɪfriːz/ n [U] chemical put in water to stop it freezing. esp. in car engines

an·tip·a·thy /ænˈtɪpəθi/ n [C;U] fixed strong dislike; hatred

an·ti·quat·ed /ˈæntəkweɪtəd/ adj old-fashioned

an·tique /ænˈtiːk/ adj old and therefore valuable ♦ n valuable old object

an·tiq·ui·ty /ænˈtɪkwəti/ n 1 [U] great age 2 [U] ancient times 3 [C] something remaining from ancient times

an·ti·Sem·i·tis·m /ˌænti 'semə'tɪzəm/ n hatred of Jews -**Semitic** /-sə'mɪtɪk/ adj

an·ti·sep·tic /ˌæntəˈseptɪk/ n, adj (chemical substance) preventing disease by killing bacteria

an·ti·so·cial /ˌæntiˈsoʊʃəl/ adj 1 harmful to society 2 not liking to mix with people

an·tith·e·sis /ænˈtɪθəsəs/ n -**ses** /-siːz/ fml direct opposite

ant·ler /ˈæntlər/ n horn of a deer

an·to·nym /ˈæntənɪm/ n word opposite in meaning to another word

a·nus /ˈeɪnəs/ n hole through which solid waste leaves the bowels

an·vil /ˈænvəl/ n iron block on which metals are hammered to the shape wanted

anx·i·e·ty /æŋˈzaɪəti/ n 1 [C;U] fear and worry 2 [U] strong wish: *anxiety to please him*

anx·ious /ˈæŋkʃəs/ adj 1 worried and frightened 2 causing worry 3 wishing strongly: *anxious to please them* ~**ly** adv

an·y /ˈeni/ determiner, pron 1 no matter which: *Take any you like.* 2 some; even the smallest number or amount: *Are there any letters for me?* 3 **in any case** also **at any rate** — a whatever may happen **b** besides ♦ adv at all: *I can't stay any longer.*

an·y·bod·y /ˈeni,bɒdi, 'enibədi‖-,bɑːdi/ pron anyone

an·y·how /ˈenihaʊ/ adv 1 carelessly 2 in spite of everything

an·y·one /ˈeniwʌn/ pron 1 all people; no matter who: *Anyone can cook.* 2 even one person: *Is anyone listening?*

an·y·place /ˈenipleɪs/ adv AmE for ANYWHERE

an·y·thing /ˈeniθɪŋ/ pron 1 any object, act, event, etc.; no matter what: *He'll do anything for a quiet life.* 2 even one thing: *Can you see anything?* 3 **anything but** not at all 4 **anything like** at all like 5 **as easy as anything** very easy

an·y·way /ˈeniweɪ/ adv in spite of everything; anyhow

an·y·where /ˈeniweər/ adv 1 at or to any place 2 **anywhere near** at all near or nearly

a·or·ta /eɪˈɔːtə‖-ˈɔːr-/ n largest ARTERY in the body

a·pace /əˈpeɪs/ adv quickly

a·part /əˈpɑːt‖əˈpɑːrt/ adv 1 distant; separated: *villages 3 miles apart* 2 into parts: *to take a clock apart* 3 **apart from:** a except for b as well as 4 **tell/know apart** be able to see the difference between

a·part·heid /əˈpɑːtheɪt, -teɪt, -taɪt, -taɪd‖-ɔːr-/ n [U] (in South Africa) the system established by government of keeping different races separate

a·part·ment /əˈpɑːtmənt‖-ɑːr-/ n 1 room 2 AmE for FLAT¹ (5)

ap·a·thy /ˈæpəθi/ n [U] lack of interest in things **–thetic** /ˌæpəˈθetik/ adj

ape /eɪp/ n large monkey with no tail ♦ vt copy (behaviour) stupidly

a·per·i·tif /əˌperɪˈtiːf/ n alcoholic drink before a meal

ap·er·ture /ˈæpətʃəʳ‖ˈæpərtʃuər/ n hole; opening

a·pex /ˈeɪpeks/ n **-es** or **apices** /ˈeɪpɪsiːz/ highest point: the apex of a triangle

aph·o·ris·m /ˈæfərɪzəm/ n short wise saying

aph·ro·dis·i·ac /ˌæfrəˈdɪziæk/ n, adj (drug, etc.) causing sexual excitement

a·piece /əˈpiːs/ adv each: They cost 10p apiece.

a·plomb /əˈplɒm‖əˈplɑːm/ n [U] calm self-control

a·poc·a·lypse /əˈpɒkəlɪps‖əˈpɑː-/ n [U] (writing about) the end of the world **–lyptic** /əˌpɒkəˈlɪptɪk‖ə,pɑː-/ adj telling of great future misfortunes

a·poc·ry·phal /əˈpɒkrəfəl‖əˈpɑː-/ adj (of a story) probably untrue

a·pol·o·get·ic /əˌpɒləˈdʒetɪk‖ə,pɑː-/ adj making an apology **~ally** /-kli/ adv

ap·o·lo·gi·a /ˌæpəˈləʊdʒiə, -dʒə/ n formal defence or explanation

a·pol·o·gist /əˈpɒlədʒɪst‖əˈpɑː-/ n person who strongly supports a particular belief and can give arguments in defence of it

a·pol·o·gize /əˈpɒlədʒaɪz‖əˈpɑː-/ vi say one is sorry for a fault **–gy** n 1 statement of sorrow for a fault, for causing trouble, etc. 2 **an apology for** a very poor example of (something)

ap·o·plex·y /ˈæpəpleksi/ n [U] sudden loss of ability to move, feel, think etc.; STROKE¹ (5) **–plectic** /ˌæpəˈplektɪk/ adj 1 of or concerning apoplexy 2 violently excited and angry

a·pos·tle /əˈpɒsəl‖əˈpɑː-/ n 1 one of the 12 first followers of Christ 2 leader of a new faith

a·pos·tro·phe /əˈpɒstrəfi‖əˈpɑː-/ n the sign ('), as in I'm

a·poth·e·o·sis /əˌpɒθiˈəʊsɪs‖ə,pɑː-, ˌæpəˈθiəsɪs/ n **-ses** 1 highest possible honour and glory 2 perfect example

ap·pal BrE ‖ **appall** AmE /əˈpɔːl/ vt **-ll-** shock deeply: We were appalled to hear the news. **~ling** BrE ‖ **~ing** AmE adj 1 shocking 2 of very bad quality **–lingly** adv: an appallingly bad driver

ap·pa·ra·tus /ˌæpəˈreɪtəs‖-ˈræ-/ n [C;U] set of instruments, tools, etc. needed for a purpose

ap·par·el /əˈpærəl/ n [U] fml clothes

ap·par·ent /əˈpærənt/ adj 1 easily seen: The reason became apparent. 2 not necessarily real; seeming: her apparent lack of concern **~ly** adv it seems that

ap·pa·ri·tion /ˌæpəˈrɪʃən/ n GHOST

ap·peal /əˈpiːl/ n 1 [C;U] strong request for something: an appeal for forgiveness 2 [U] attraction; interest: He hasn't much **sex appeal**. 3 [C;U] formal request (in law, sport) for a new decision ♦ vi 1 make a strong request: to appeal for money 2 please; attract: Does the job appeal to you? 3 ask for a new decision **~ing** adj attractive

a·pear /əˈpɪəʳ/ vi 1 come into sight: Spots appeared on my skin. | They finally appeared (= arrived) at 9.00. 2 come in view of the public: Her new book appears next month. | He's appearing (= performing) at the Theatre Royal. 3 seem: He appears to be angry. 4 be present officially, as in a court of law **~ance** n [C;U] 1 (an example of) the act of appearing 2 way a person or thing looks: He changed his appearance by growing a beard. 3 **put in/make an appearance (at)** attend (a meeting, party, etc.), esp. for a short time only

ap·pease /əˈpiːz/ vt satisfy, esp. by agreeing to demands **~ment** n [C;U]

ap·pel·la·tion /ˌæpəˈleɪʃən/ n fml name; title

ap·pend /əˈpend/ vt fml add (esp. something written onto the end of a letter) **~age** n something added to, or hanging from, something else

ap·pen·di·ci·tis /əˌpendɪˈsaɪtəs/ n [U] disease of the appendix

ap·pen·dix /əˈpendɪks/ n **-dixes** or **-dices** /-dɪsiːz/ 1 small organ leading off the bowel 2 something added at the end of a book

ap·per·tain /ˌæpəˈteɪn‖-ər-/ v **appertain to** phr vt fml belong to

ap·pe·tite /ˈæpətaɪt/ n [C;U] desire, esp. for food

ap·pe·tiz·er /ˈæpətaɪzəʳ/ n something eaten to increase the appetite **–tizing** adj causing appetite: appetizing smells

ap·plaud /əˈplɔːd/ vi/t 1 praise by striking one's hands together; CLAP 2 approve strongly **applause** /əˈplɔːz/ n [U] loud praise

ap·ple /ˈæpəl/ n kind of hard round juicy fruit — see also ADAM'S APPLE

ap·pli·ance /əˈplaɪəns/ n apparatus; machine

ap·plic·a·ble /əˈplɪkəbəl, ˈæplɪkəbəl/ adj having an effect; related: The rule is applicable only to UK citizens.

ap·pli·cant /ˈæplɪkənt/ n person who applies for a job, etc.

ap·pli·ca·tion /ˌæplɪˈkeɪʃən/ *n* 1 [C;U] request: *to write applications for jobs* 2 [U] act of putting something to use 3 [C] particular practical use: *the industrial applications of this discovery* 4 [C;U] putting something on a surface 5 [U] careful effort

ap·ply /əˈplaɪ/ *v* 1 *vt* request officially: *apply for a job* 2 *vt* use for a purpose: *apply the brakes* 3 *vt* put onto a surface: *apply ointment to your skin* 4 *vi/t* give or have an effect: *Does the rule apply to me?* 5 *vt* cause to work hard: *apply oneself to the task* **applied** *adj* practical: *applied physics*

ap·point /əˈpɔɪnt/ *vt* 1 choose for a job 2 *fml* fix; decide: *the appointed time* ~**ment** *n* 1 [C;U] arrangement for a meeting 2 [C] job: *a teaching appointment*

ap·por·tion /əˈpɔːʃən‖-ɔːr-/ *vt* divide and share out

ap·po·site /ˈæpəzɪt/ *adj fml* exactly suitable

ap·praise /əˈpreɪz/ *vt fml* judge the value of **appraisal** *n*

ap·pre·cia·ble /əˈpriːʃəbəl/ *adj* noticeable: *an appreciable difference* -**bly** *adv*

ap·pre·ci·ate /əˈpriːʃieɪt/ *v* 1 *vt* be thankful for 2 *vt* understand and enjoy the good qualities of: *She appreciates good wine.* 3 *vt* understand fully: *I appreciate your difficulties.* 4 *vi* (of property) increase in value ~**ciative** /-ʃətɪv/ *adj*: *an appreciative audience* -**ciation** /əˌpriːʃiˈeɪʃən/ *n* [U]

ap·pre·hend /ˌæprɪˈhend/ *vt fml* ARREST

ap·pre·hen·sion /ˌæprɪˈhenʃən/ *n* [U] anxiety; fear -**sive** /-sɪv/ *adj* worried

ap·pren·tice /əˈprentɪs/ *n* person learning a skilled trade ♦ *vt* [(to)] send as an apprentice: *apprenticed to an electrician* ~**ship** *n* [C;U]

ap·proach¹ /əˈprəʊtʃ/ *v* 1 *vi/t* come near 2 *vt* make an offer or request to: *approach him about borrowing the money* 3 *vt* begin to consider or deal with

approach² *n* 1 act of approaching: *the approach of winter* 2 way of getting in 3 method of doing something 4 speaking to someone for the first time ~**able** *adj* easy to speak to or deal with

ap·pro·pri·ate¹ /əˈprəʊpri-ɪt/ *adj* correct; suitable ~**ly** *adv*

ap·pro·pri·ate² /əˈprəʊprieɪt/ *vt* 1 set aside for a purpose 2 take for oneself -**ation** /əˌprəʊpriˈeɪʃən/ *n* [C;U]

ap·prov·al /əˈpruːvəl/ *n* [U] 1 favourable opinion 2 official permission 3 **on approval** (of goods from a shop) to be returned without payment if unsatisfactory

ap·prove /əˈpruːv/ *v* 1 *vi* [(of)] have a favourable opinion: *I don't approve of smoking.* 2 *vt* agree officially to **approvingly** *adv*

ap·prox·i·mate /əˈprɒksəmət‖əˈprɑː-/ *adj* nearly correct but not exact ~**ly** *adv*: *approximately 300* ♦ /-meɪt/ *vi* come near -**mation** /əˌprɒksəˈmeɪʃən‖əˌprɑːk-/ *n* [C;U]

a·pri·cot /ˈeɪprɪkɒt‖ˈæprɪkɑːt/ *n* 1 [C] round orange or yellow fruit with a stone 2 [U] colour of this fruit

A·pril /ˈeɪprəl/ *n* 1 the 4th month of the year 2 **April fool** /ˌ·· ˈ·/ *n* (person who has been deceived or made fun of by) a trick played on the morning of April 1st

a·pron /ˈeɪprən/ *n* garment worn to protect the front of one's clothes

apt /æpt/ *adj* 1 likely: *apt to slip* 2 exactly suitable: *an apt remark* 3 quick to learn ~**ly** *adv* ~**ness** *n* [U]

ap·ti·tude /ˈæptɪtjuːd‖-tuːd/ *n* [C;U] natural ability

aq·ua·lung /ˈækwəlʌŋ/ *n* apparatus for breathing under water

aq·ua·ma·rine /ˌækwəməˈriːn◂/ *n* 1 [C] glass-like stone used for jewellery 2 [U] its blue-green colour

a·quar·i·um /əˈkweəriəm/ *n* -**iums** or -**ia** /-ɪə/ glass container for live fish

a·quat·ic /əˈkwætɪk, əˈkwɒt-‖əˈkwæ-, əˈkwɑː-/ *adj* living or happening in water

aq·ue·duct /ˈækwədʌkt/ *n* bridge that carries water across a valley

Ar·a·bic /ˈærəbɪk/ *n* main language of North Africa and the Middle East ♦ *adj*: *The signs 1, 2, 3, etc., are* **Arabic numerals.**

ar·a·ble /ˈærəbəl/ *adj* (of land) used for growing crops

ar·bi·ter /ˈɑːbɪtəʳ‖ˈɑːr-/ *n* someone who is in a position to make influential judgments or to settle an argument

ar·bi·trage /ˈɑːbɪtrɑːʒ‖ˈɑːr-/ *n* [U] process of buying something (esp. a CURRENCY or COMMODITY) in one place and selling it at another place at the same time in order to profit from differences in price between the two places

ar·bi·tra·ry /ˈɑːbɪtrəri‖ˈɑːrbətreri/ *adj* 1 based on chance rather than reason 2 typical of uncontrolled power ~**rily** *adv* ~**riness** *n* [U]

ar·bi·trate /ˈɑːbɪtreɪt‖ˈɑːr-/ *vi/t* act as judge in an argument -**tration** /ˌɑːbɪˈtreɪʃən‖ˌɑːr-/ *n* [U] settlement of an argument by the decision of a person or group chosen by both sides: *go to arbitration*

arc /ɑːk‖ɑːrk/ *n* part of the curve of a circle

ar·cade /ɑːˈkeɪd‖ɑːr-/ *n* covered passage with shops

ar·cane /ɑːˈkeɪn‖ɑːr-/ adj mysterious and secret

arch /ɑːtʃ‖ɑːrtʃ/ n curved part over a doorway or under a bridge ♦ vi/t make an arch: *The cat arched her back.*

ar·chae·ol·o·gy /ˌɑːkiˈɒlədʒi‖ˌɑːrkiˈɑː-/ n [U] study of ancient remains **–gist** n **–gical** /ˌɑːkiəˈlɒdʒɪkəl‖ˌɑːrkiəˈlɑː-/ adj

ar·cha·ic /ɑːˈkeɪɪk‖ɑːr-/ adj no longer used; old

arch·bish·op /ˌɑːtʃˈbɪʃəp◂‖ˌɑːrtʃ-/ n chief BISHOP

ar·cher /ˈɑːtʃəʳ‖ˈɑːr-/ n person who shoots with a BOW² (1) **~y** n [U]

ar·che·type /ˈɑːkɪtaɪp‖ˈɑːr-/ n 1 original of which others are copies 2 perfect example **–typal** /-əl/, **–typical** /ɑːˈtɪpɪkəl◂‖ɑːr-/ adj

ar·chi·pel·a·go /ˌɑːkɪˈpeləɡəʊ‖ˌɑːr-/ n area with many small islands

ar·chi·tect /ˈɑːkɪtekt‖ˈɑːr-/ n person who plans buildings **–ure** /-ˌtektʃəʳ/ n [U] art of building; way of building

ar·chives /ˈɑːkaɪvz‖ˈɑːr-/ n [P] 1 historical records 2 place where these are kept

Arc·tic /ˈɑːktɪk‖ˈɑːr-/ n, adj 1 (cap.) (of or concerning) the very cold most northern part of the world 2 very cold

ar·dent /ˈɑːdənt‖ˈɑːr-/ adj very eager **~ly** adv

ar·dour BrE **ardor** AmE /ˈɑːdəʳ‖ˈɑːr-/ n [C;U] fml strong excitement

ar·du·ous /ˈɑːdjuəs‖ˈɑːrdʒuəs/ adj fml needing effort; difficult **~ly** adv

are /əʳ, strong ɑːʳ/ v present tense pl. of BE

ar·e·a /ˈeəriə/ n 1 [C;U] size of a surface 2 [C] part of the world's surface: *a parking area behind the cinema* 3 [C] subject of activity: *the area of language teaching*

a·re·na /əˈriːnə/ n 1 enclosed space used for sports 2 place of competition: *the political arena*

aren't /ɑːnt‖ɑːrənt/ v short for: 1 are not 2 (in questions) am not

ar·got /ˈɑːɡəʊ‖-ɡɑːt/ n [C;U] speech spoken and understood by only a small group of people

ar·gue /ˈɑːɡjuː‖ˈɑːr-/ v 1 vi express disagreement; quarrel 2 vi/t give reasons for or against something **arguable** adj perhaps true, but not certain **arguably** adv: *Arguably, the criminal is a necessary member of society*

ar·gu·ment /ˈɑːɡjəmənt‖ˈɑːr-/ n 1 [C] quarrel 2 [C;U] reason given for or against; use of reason **~ative** /ˌɑːɡjəˈmentətɪv/, ˌɑːr-/ adj quarrelsome

ar·id /ˈærɪd/ adj 1 (of land) very dry 2 uninteresting; dull

a·rise /əˈraɪz/ vi arose /əˈrəʊz/, arisen /əˈrɪzən/ happen; appear

ar·is·toc·ra·cy /ˌærɪˈstɒkrəsi‖-ˈstɑː-/ n highest social class **–rat** /ˈærɪstəkræt, əˈrɪ-‖əˈrɪ-/ n member of this class **–ratic** /ˌærɪstəˈkrætɪk, əˌrɪ-‖ə,rɪ-/ adj

a·rith·me·tic /əˈrɪθmətɪk/ n calculation by numbers **~al** /ˌænθˈmetɪkəl/ adj

ark /ɑːk‖ɑːrk/ n large ship, esp. the one described in the Bible

arm¹ /ɑːm‖ɑːrm/ n 1 upper limb 2 something shaped like this: *the arm of a chair* 3 part of a garment that covers the arm 4 part or division of the armed forces 5 **arm in arm** (of 2 people) with arms joined 6 **keep someone at arm's length** avoid being friendly with someone 7 **with open arms** gladly and eagerly — see also ARMS

arm² vi/t supply with weapons: *the armed forces*

ar·ma·da /ɑːˈmɑːdə‖ɑːr-/ n collection of armed ships

Ar·ma·ged·don /ˌɑːməˈɡedn‖ˌɑːr-/ n (esp. in the Bible) great battle or war causing terrible destruction and bringing the end of the world

ar·ma·ment /ˈɑːməmənt‖ˈɑːr-/ n 1 [C] weapons and other fighting equipment of an army, etc. 2 [U] act of preparing for war

arm·chair /ˈɑːmtʃeəʳ, ˌɑːmˈtʃeəʳ‖ˈɑːrm-, ˌɑːrm-/ n chair with supports for the arms ♦ adj ready to give advice or pass judgment, but not taking an active part

ar·mi·stice /ˈɑːmɪstəs‖ˈɑːrm-/ n agreement to stop fighting for a time

ar·mour BrE **armor** AmE /ˈɑːməʳ‖ˈɑːr-/ n [U] 1 protective covering for the body in battle 2 protective metal covering on military vehicles: *an armoured car* **~y** n place where weapons are stored

arm·pit /ˈɑːmˌpɪt‖ˈɑːrm-/ n hollow place under one's arm

arms /ɑːmz‖ɑːrmz/ n [P] 1 weapons 2 **lay down one's arms** stop fighting and yield 3 **take up arms** get ready to fight with weapons 4 **up in arms** very angry and ready to argue: *They're up in arms over/about the low pay.* — see also SMALL ARMS

ar·my /ˈɑːmi‖ˈɑːr-/ n 1 military forces that fight on land 2 large group: *an army of ants*

a·ro·ma /əˈrəʊmə/ n pleasant smell **~tic** /ˌærəˈmætɪk/ adj

a·rose /əˈrəʊz/ past t. of ARISE

a·round /əˈraʊnd/ adv, prep 1 a in various places; round: *I'll show you around (the house).* b somewhere near: *Is there anyone around?* 2 a little more or less than; about: *around 10 o'clock* 3 a moving in a circle; measured in a circle: *turn around and around‖3* metres around **b** on all sides: *The children gathered around.*

a·rouse /ə'rauz/ *vt* **1** *fml* cause to wake **2** make active; excite: *arouse suspicion*

ar·range /ə'reɪndʒ/ *v* **1** *vt* put in order: *arrange flowers* **2** *vi/t* plan: *arrange to meet her* **3** *vt* set out (music) for different instruments, etc. **~ment** *n* **1** [C/U] (act of making) an agreement or plan: *make arrangements for the wedding* | *I have an arrangement with the bank.* **2** [C] something that has been put in order: *a beautiful flower arrangement* **3** [C] (example of) the setting out of a piece of music in a certain way

ar·ray /ə'reɪ/ *n* fine show, collection, or ordered group

ar·rears /ə'rɪəz||-ɔrz/ *n* [P] **1** money owed from the past: *He was two weeks in arrears with the rent.* (= he owed rent for two weeks) **2** work waiting to be done

ar·rest /ə'rest/ *vt* **1** seize by the power of the law **2** stop (a process) **3** attract (attention) ♦ *n* [C/U] act of arresting

ar·riv·al /ə'raɪvəl/ *n* **1** [U] act of arriving **2** [C] person or thing that has arrived: *to welcome the new arrivals*

ar·rive /ə'raɪv/ *vi* **1** reach a place: *arrive home* **2** happen; come: *The day arrived.* **3** win success

arrive at *phr vt* reach; come to: *arrive at a decision*

ar·ro·gant /'ærəgənt/ *adj* proud in a rude way **~ly** *adv* **-gance** *n* [U]

ar·row /'ærəu/ *n* **1** pointed stick to be shot from a BOW² (1) **2** sign ➤ used to show direction

arse¹ /ɑːs||ɑːrs/ *n* BrE *taboo sl* **1** also **ass** *AmE* — BOTTOM (2) **2** also **arsehole||asshole** *AmE* /'ɑːshəʊl,|| 'ɑːrs-/ — the ANUS **b** stupid annoying person

arse² *v* **arse about/around** *phr vi* BrE *sl* waste time

ar·se·nal /'ɑːsənəl||'ɑːr-/ *n* place where weapons are stored

ar·se·nic /'ɑːsənɪk||'ɑːr-/ *n* [U] very poisonous substance

ar·son /'ɑːsən||'ɑːr-/ *n* [U] crime of setting fire to property **~ist** *n*

art /ɑːt||ɑːrt/ *n* **1** [U] the making or expression of what is beautiful, e.g. in music, literature, or esp. painting **2** [U] things produced by art, esp. paintings: *an art gallery* **3** [C/U] skill in doing anything: *the art of conversation*

arts *n* [P] subjects of study that are not part of science — see also FINE ARTS

ar·te·fact /'ɑːtəfækt||'ɑːr-/ *n* ARTIFACT

ar·te·ry /'ɑːtəri||'ɑːr-/ *n* **1** tube that carries blood from the heart **2** main road, railway, etc.

art·ful /'ɑːtfəl||'ɑːrt-/ *adj* **1** cleverly deceitful **2** skilfully put together **~ly** *adv*

ar·thri·tis /ɑː'θraɪtəs||ɑːr-/ *n* [U] painful disease of the joints **-tic** /ɑː'θrɪtɪk|| ɑːr-/ *adj*

ar·ti·choke /'ɑːtʃtʃəʊk||'ɑːr-/ *n* [C/U] **1** also **globe artichoke** — plant whose leafy flower is eaten **2** also **Jerusalem artichoke** — plant whose potato-like root is eaten

ar·ti·cle /'ɑːtɪkəl||'ɑːr-/ *n* **1** thing; object: *an article of clothing* **2** piece of writing in a newspaper **3** complete or separate part in a written law agreement **4** word used with nouns, such as *a*, *an*, and *the* in English

ar·tic·u·late¹ /ɑː'tɪkjʊlət||ɑːr-/ *adj* **1** (of people) able to express thoughts and feelings clearly in words **2** (of speech) having clear separate sounds and words **~ly** *adv*

ar·tic·u·late² /ɑː'tɪkjʊleɪt||ɑːr-/ *v* **1** *vi/t* speak or say clearly **2** *vt* unite by joints: *an articulated lorry* **-lation** /ɑː,tɪkjʊ'leɪʃən||ɑːr-/ *n* [U]

ar·ti·fact, arte- /'ɑːtɪfækt||'ɑːr-/ *n* something made by people

ar·ti·fice /'ɑːtɪfɪs||'ɑːr-/ *n* **1** [C] clever trick **2** [U] CUNNING

ar·ti·fi·cial /,ɑːtɪ'fɪʃəl◄||,ɑːr-/ *adj* **1** made by people; not natural **2** not sincere **~ly** *adv* **~ity** /-'ælɪti/ *n* [U]

artificial in·tel·li·gence /,···· ·'···/ *n* [U] branch of computer science which aims to produce machines that can understand, make judgments, etc., in the way humans do

artificial res·pi·ra·tion /,···· ··'···/ *n* [U] making someone breathe again by pressing the chest, blowing into the mouth, etc.

ar·til·le·ry /ɑː'tɪləri||ɑːr-/ *n* [U] (part of the army that uses) large guns

ar·ti·san /,ɑːtɪ'zæn||'ɑːrtɪzən/ *n* CRAFTSMAN

art·ist /'ɑːtɪst||'ɑːr-/ *n* **1** person who works in one of the arts, esp. painting **2** inventive and skilled worker **3** also **artiste** /ɑː'tiːst||ɑːr-/ — professional singer, dancer, etc., who performs in a show **~ry** *n* [U] inventive imagination and ability **~ic** /ɑː'tɪstɪk||ɑːr-/ *adj* **1** of art or artists **2** showing skill in art **~ically** /-kli/ *adv*

art·less /'ɑːtləs||'ɑːr-/ *adj* simple and natural; almost foolish **~ly** *adv*

as¹ /əz; *strong* æz/ *adv, prep* **1** (used in comparisons and examples) equally; like: *He's as old as me.* | *small animals such as cats and dogs* | *She escaped dressed as a man.* **2** when considered as being: *As a writer, she's wonderful.*

as² *conj* **1** (used in comparisons): *He's as old as I am.* **2** in the way that: *Do as I say!|Leave it as it is.* **3** because: *As I have no car, I can't go.* **4** when; while: *He saw her as she was getting off the bus.* **5** though: *Tired as I was, I tried to help.* **6** as for when we speak of; concerning **7** as if/though in a way that seems **8** as it is in reality **9** as it were as one might say **10** as of/from starting from (a time) **11** as yet up until now

asap /ˌeɪ es eɪ ˈpiː, ˈeɪsæp/ *abbrev. for.* as soon as possible

as·bes·tos /æsˈbestəs, æz-/ *n* [U] soft grey material that protects against fire or heat

as·cend /əˈsend/ *vi/t fml* **1** go up **2** ascend the throne become king or queen ~ancy, ~ency *n* [U] controlling influence; power ~ant, ~ent *n* in the ascendant having or nearly having a controlling power or influence

as·cent /əˈsent/ *n* **1** [C;U] act or process of **2** [C] ascending; way up

as·cer·tain /ˌæsəˈteɪn/, æsər-/ *vt fml* discover; make certain ~able *adj*

as·cet·ic /əˈsetɪk/ *n, adj* (a person) avoiding physical pleasures and comforts, esp. for religious reasons ~ism /əˈsetɪsɪzəm/ *n* [U]

ASCII /ˈæski/ *n* [U] American Standard Code for Information Interchange; a set of 128 letters, numbers, etc., used for easy exchange of information between a computer and other DATA PROCESSING machinery

as·cribe /əˈskraɪb/ *v* ascribe to *phr vt* believe to be the work of: *He ascribes his success to luck.*

a·sep·tic /eɪˈseptɪk, ə-/ *adj* without bacteria; clean

a·sex·u·al /eɪˈseksjuəl/ *adj* **1** without sex **2** not interested in sex

ash /æʃ/ *n* [U] also ashes *pl.* — powder left when something has been burnt ~en *adj* pale grey ashes [P] remains of a dead body after burning

a·shamed /əˈʃeɪmd/ *adj* feeling shame

a·shore /əˈʃɔːʳ/ *adv* on or to the shore

ash·tray /ˈæʃtreɪ/ *n* dish for tobacco ash

a·side /əˈsaɪd/ *adv* to the side: *She stepped aside to let them pass.* ♦ *n* remark not intended to be heard by everyone present

ask /ɑːsk‖æsk/ *v* **1** *vi/t* say a question: *'Where is it?' she asked.|Ask him where to go.* **2** *vi/t* make a request for: *She asked him to wake her at 6.00.* **3** *vt* invite: *Ask them to tea.* **4** ask for trouble/it behave so as to cause (something bad): *If you park there, you're really asking for trouble!*

ask after *phr vt* ask for news of

a·skance /əˈskæns, əˈskɑːns‖əˈskæns/ *adv* look askance without liking or pleasure

a·skew /əˈskjuː/ *adv* not properly straight

a·sleep /əˈsliːp/ *adj* **1** sleeping **2** (of an arm or leg) unable to feel

asp /æsp/ *n* small poisonous snake

as·par·a·gus /əˈspærəgəs/ *n* [U] plant whose stems are eaten as a vegetable

as·pect /ˈæspekt/ *n* **1** particular side of a plan, problem, etc. **2** direction in which a room, building, etc., faces

as·per·sion /əˈspɜːʃən, -ʒən‖-ɜːr-/ *n fml* unkind or harmful remark: *They cast aspersions on my new book.*

as·phalt /ˈæsfælt‖ˈæsfɔːlt/ *n* [U] black material used for road surfaces

as·phyx·i·ate /æsˈfɪksieɪt, ɔs-/ *vt* kill by lack of air ~ation /æs,fɪksiˈeɪʃən, əs-/ *n* [U]

as·pire /əˈspaɪəʳ/ *vi* direct one's hopes and efforts aspiration /ˌæspəˈreɪʃən/ *n* [C;U] strong desire

as·pi·rin /ˈæsprən/ *n* -rin *or* -rins [C;U] (TABLET of) medicine that lessens pain and fever

ass /æs/ *n* **1** DONKEY **2** foolish person **3** *AmE for* ARSE¹ (1)

as·sail /əˈseɪl/ *vt fml* attack ~ant *n fml* attacker

as·sas·sin /əˈsæsən/ *n* person who assassinates

as·sas·sin·ate /əˈsæsəneɪt‖-səneɪt/ *vt* murder a ruler, politician, etc. ~ation /ə,sæsəˈneɪʃən‖-sənˈeɪ-/ *n* [C;U]

as·sault /əˈsɔːlt/ *n* [C;U] sudden violent attack assault *vt*

assault course /·ˈ· ·,/ *n* area of land on which soldiers train by climbing or jumping over objects, etc., in order to develop their fitness and courage

as·sem·ble /əˈsembəl/ *vi/t* gather or put together: *to assemble radios|A crowd assembled.*

as·sem·bly /əˈsembli/ *n* **1** [C] group of people gathered together for a purpose **2** [U] assembling of machine parts

assembly line /·ˈ·· ·/ *n* arrangement of workers and machines in which each person has a particular job, the work being passed from one worker to the next until the product is complete

as·sent /əˈsent/ *vi fml* agree ♦ *n* agreement

as·sert /əˈsɜːt‖əˈsɜːrt/ *vt* **1** declare forcefully **2** make a strong claim to: *He asserted his authority.* **3** assert oneself act in a way that shows one's power ~ive *adj* forceful; showing CONFIDENCE ~ion /əˈsɜːʃən‖-ɜːr-/ *n* forceful statement or claim

as·sess /ə'ses/ vt judge the value or amount of ~**ment** n [C;U]

as·set /'æset/ n 1 property that has value and may be sold 2 valuable quality or skill

asset-strip·ping /'·· ,·'·/ n practice of buying a company cheaply, selling all its assets to make a profit, and closing it down

ass·hole /'æshəʊl/ n AmE for ARSE¹ (2)

as·sid·u·ous /ə'sɪdjuəs‖-dʒuəs/ adj with careful attention ~**ly** adv

as·sign /ə'saɪn/ vt 1 give as a share or duty 2 decide on; name: assign a day for the meeting ~**ment** n [C] duty or piece of work 2 [U] act of assigning

as·sig·na·tion /,æsɪg'neɪʃən/ n (secret) meeting

as·sim·i·late /ə'sɪməleɪt/ vi/t take in and accept (food, ideas, foreign people) –**lation** /ə,sɪmə'leɪʃən/ n [U]

as·sist /ə'sɪst/ vi/t fml help ~**ance** n fml ~**ant** n person who helps

as·so·ci·ate /ə'səʊʃieɪt,-sieɪt/ v 1 vi/t join as friends or partners 2 vt connect in the mind **associate** /ə'səʊʃiɪt, -ʃit/ n: He's a business associate.

as·so·ci·a·tion /ə,səʊsi'eɪʃən, ə,səʊʃi-/ n 1 [C] society of people joined together 2 [U] act of joining together 3 [C;U] connecting things in the mind

Association foot·ball /·,···· '··/ [U] BrE SOCCER

as·sort·ed /ə'sɔːtɪd‖-ɔːr-/ adj of various types; mixed

as·sort·ment /ə'sɔːtmənt‖-ɔːr-/ n mixture

as·suage /ə'sweɪdʒ/ vt fml reduce (suffering)

as·sume /ə'sjuːm‖ə'suːm/ vt 1 believe without proof: Let's assume he isn't coming. 2 begin to use or perform: to assume control 3 pretend to have: to adopt an assumed name

as·sump·tion /ə'sʌmpʃən/ n 1 [C] something believed without proof 2 [U] act of assuming

as·sure /ə'ʃʊəʳ/ vt 1 tell firmly; promise 2 make (oneself) sure or certain 3 BrE insure, esp. against death **assurance** n 1 [U] belief in one's own powers 2 [C] firm promise 3 [U] BrE insurance **assured** adj certain, esp. of one's own powers

as·te·risk /'æstərɪsk/ n star-like mark (*)

a·stern /ə'stɜːn‖-ɜːrn/ adv in or at the back part of a ship

as·te·roid /'æstərɔɪd/ n very small PLANET

asth·ma /'æsmə‖'æzmə/ n [U] disease that causes difficulty in breathing ~**tic** /æs'mætɪk‖æz-/ adj

as·ton·ish /ə'stɒnɪʃ‖ə'stɑː/ vt surprise greatly: astonishingly cold ~**ment** n [U]

as·tound /ə'staʊnd/ vt shock with surprise

as·tral /'æstrəl/ adj of, from, or concerning stars

a·stray /ə'streɪ/ adj, adv off the right path

a·stride /ə'straɪd/ adv, prep with a leg on each side (of)

as·trin·gent /ə'strɪndʒənt/ adj 1 able to tighten the skin and stop bleeding 2 bitter; severe

as·trol·o·gy /ə'strɒlədʒi‖ə'strɑː-/ n [U] study of the supposed influence of the stars on events and character –**ger** n –**gical** /,æstrə'lɒdʒɪkəl‖-'lɑː-/ adj

as·tro·naut /'æstrənɔːt‖-nɑːt, -nɑːt/ n traveller in a spacecraft

as·tron·o·my /ə'strɒnəmi‖ə'strɑː-/ n [U] scientific study of the sun, stars, etc. –**mer** n –**mical** /,æstrə'nɒmɪkəl‖ -'nɑː-/ adj 1 of astronomy 2 very large: astronomical sums of money

as·tro·phys·ics /,æstrəʊ'fɪzɪks, ,æstrə-/ n [U] science of the nature of the stars and the forces that influence them –**ical** adj

as·tute /ə'stjuːt‖ə'stuːt/ adj able to see quickly something that is to one's advantage ~**ly** adv ~**ness** n [U]

a·sy·lum /ə'saɪləm/ n 1 [U] protection and shelter 2 [C] becoming rare MENTAL HOSPITAL

a·sym·met·ric /,eɪsɪ'metrɪk, ,æ-/ also –**rical** /-kəl/ adj having sides that are not alike

at /ət; strong æt/ prep 1 (showing where): at the airport 2 (showing when): at Christmas 3 towards: Look at me. 4 by: surprised at the news 5 (showing how someone does something): good at games 6 (showing a state or continued activity): at school‖at war 7 (showing price, level, age, etc.): sold at 10 cents each‖to stop work at 60 **8 at a/an** only one: He went upstairs 2 at a time.

ate /et, eɪt‖eɪt/ past t. of EAT

a·the·is·m /'eɪθi-ɪzəm/ n [U] belief that there is no God –**ist** n

ath·lete /'æθliːt/ n person who practises athletics

ath·let·ics /æθ'letɪks, əθ-/ n [U] physical exercises such as running and jumping **athletic** adj 1 of athletics 2 physically strong and active

at·las /'ætləs/ n book of maps

at·mo·sphere /'ætməsfɪəʳ/ n 1 gases surrounding a heavenly body, esp. the Earth 2 air 3 general feeling of a place –**spheric** /,ætməs'ferɪk/ adj 1 of or concerning the Earth's atmosphere 2 mysteriously beautiful and strange: atmospheric music

at·oll /ˈætɒl‖ˈætɔːl, ˈætɔːl, ˈætəʊl/ n ring-shaped CORAL island

at·om /ˈætəm/ n smallest unit of an ELEMENT ~**ic** /əˈtɒmɪk‖əˈtɑː-/ adj 1 of atoms 2 using the power that comes from splitting atoms

atom bomb /ˈ·· ·/ also **atomic bomb** /·,·· ˈ·/ — n bomb that uses the explosive power of NUCLEAR energy

a·tone /əˈtəʊn/ vi make repayment (for a crime, etc.) ~**ment** n [U]

a·tro·cious /əˈtrəʊʃəs/ adj very cruel or bad ~**ly** adv

a·troc·i·ty /əˈtrɒsəti‖əˈtrɑː-/ n 1 very cruel act 2 something very ugly

at·ro·phy /ˈætrəfi/ vi/t (cause) to lose flesh and muscle; weaken **atrophy** n [U]

at·tach /əˈtætʃ/ vt 1 fasten 2 cause to join: He attached himself to another group of tourists. 3 regard as having (special meaning or importance) 4 **be attached to** be fond of ~**ment** n [C;U]

at·tach·é/əˈtæʃeɪ‖ˌætəˈʃeɪ/ n person who helps an AMBASSADOR

attaché case/·ˈ·· ·‖,··ˈ· ·/n thin hard case with a handle, for carrying papers

at·tack /əˈtæk/ n 1 [C;U] (act of) violence 2 [C] words intended to hurt 3 [C] sudden illness ♦ vt 1 make an attack begin (something) with eagerness and interest ~**er** n

at·tain /əˈteɪn/ vt fml succeed in; reach ~**able** adj ~**ment** n 1 [U] act of attaining 2 [C] a skill

at·tempt /əˈtempt/ vt try: I attempted to leave. ♦ n 1 effort made to do something 2 **attempt on someone's life** effort to murder someone

at·tend /əˈtend/ v 1 vt be present at: attend the meeting 2 vt give attention 3 vi look after ~**ance** n 1 [C;U] act of being present 2 [C] number of people present: a large attendance ~**ant** n person who looks after a place or people

at·ten·tion /əˈtenʃən/ n [U] 1 careful thought: pay attention to the teacher 2 particular care or consideration: Old cars need lots of attention. 3 **at/to attention** (of a soldier) standing straight and still

at·ten·tive /əˈtentɪv/ adj 1 listening carefully 2 politely helpful ~**ly** adv ~**ness** n [U]

at·ten·u·ate /əˈtenjueɪt/ vi/t (cause to) become thin, weak, less valuable, etc.

at·test /əˈtest/ vt fml 1 declare to be true 2 be proof of: His success attests (to) his ability.

at·tic /ˈætɪk/ n room below the roof of a house

at·tire /əˈtaɪər/ n fml clothes ♦ vt put on clothes

at·ti·tude /ˈætɪtjuːd‖-tuːd/ n 1 way of feeling and behaving 2 fml position of the body

at·tor·ney /əˈtɜːni‖-ɜːr-/ n AmE for LAWYER

at·tract /əˈtrækt/ vt 1 excite the admiration or interest of: He was attracted by her smile. 2 draw towards: Flowers attract bees. ~**ive** adj interesting, pleasing ~**ively** adv ~**iveness** n [U] state of being attractive ~**ion** /əˈtrækʃən/ n 1 [U] power of attracting 2 [C] something attractive

at·tri·bute[1] /ˈætrɪbjuːt/ n 1 quality that belongs to a person or thing 2 something regarded as a sign of a person or position

at·tri·bute[2] /əˈtrɪbjuːt‖-bjət/ v **attribute to** phr vt I believe to be the result of: He attributes his success to hard work. 2 ASCRIBE to.

at·tri·tion /əˈtrɪʃən/ n [U] process of tiring, weakening, or destroying by continual worry, hardship, or repeated attacks: a war of attrition

at·tune /əˈtjuːn‖əˈtuːn/ v **attune to** phr vt make used to or ready for

a·typ·i·cal /eɪˈtɪpɪkəl/ adj not typical ~**ly** /-kli/ adv

au·ber·gine /ˈəʊbəʒiːn‖-bər-/ n [C;U] esp. BrE EGGPLANT

au·burn /ˈɔːbən‖-ərn/ adj, n [U] (esp. of hair) reddish brown

auc·tion /ˈɔːkʃən/ n public meeting to sell goods to whoever offers the most money ♦ vt sell by auction

auc·tio·neer /ˌɔːkʃəˈnɪər/ n person in charge of an auction, who calls out the prices

au·da·cious /ɔːˈdeɪʃəs/ adj 1 (foolishly) daring 2 disrespectful ~**ly** adv ~**city** /ɔːˈdæsɪti/ n [U]

au·di·ble /ˈɔːdəbəl/ adj able to be heard ~**bly** adv

au·di·ence /ˈɔːdiəns‖ˈɔː-, ˈɑː-/ n 1 people listening to or watching a performance 2 formal meeting with someone important: have an audience with the Pope

au·di·o /ˈɔːdi-əʊ/ adj of sound radio signals

audio-vis·u·al /ˌ··· ˈ···◀/ adj of both sight and hearing

au·dit /ˈɔːdɪt/ vt examine (business accounts) officially **audit** n ~**or** n

au·di·tion /ɔːˈdɪʃən/ n test performance given by a singer, actor, etc. **audition** vi

au·di·to·ri·um /ˌɔːdɪˈtɔːriəm/ n space where an AUDIENCE (1) sits

aug·ment /ɔːgˈment/ vi/t fml increase

au·gur /ˈɔːgər/ vi **augur well/ill (for)** be a sign of good/bad things in the future (for): This rain augurs well for farmers.

au·gust /ɔːˈgʌst/ adj noble and grand

Au·gust /'ɔːgəst/ the 8th month of the year

aunt /ɑːnt‖ænt/ n sister of one's father or mother, or wife of one's uncle

au pair /ˌəʊ 'peəʳ/ n young foreigner who lives with a family and helps with housework

au·ra /'ɔːrə/ n effect or feeling produced by a person or place

au·ral /'ɔːrəl/ adj of or related to the sense of hearing

aus·pic·es /'ɔːspǝsǝz/ n [P] fml **under the auspices of** helped by

aus·pi·cious /ɔː'spɪʃəs/ adj fml showing signs of future success ~**ly** adv

aus·tere /ɔː'stɪǝʳ, ɒ-‖ɔː-/ adj 1 without comfort; hard: an austere life 2 without decoration; plain ~**ly** adv —**terity** /ɔː'sterǝti, ɒ-‖ɔː-/ n [C;U]

au·then·tic /ɔː'θentɪk/ adj known to be real; GENUINE ~**ally** /-kli/ adv —**ate** vt prove to be authentic ~**ation** /ɔːˌθentɪ'keɪʃən/ n [U] —**ity** /ˌɔːθen'tɪsǝti/ n [U] quality of being authentic

au·thor /'ɔːθǝʳ/ **authoress** /'ɔːθǝrǝs/ fem. — n 1 writer 2 person who thinks of an idea or plan ~**ship** n [U]

au·thor·i·tar·i·an /ɔːˌθɒrɪ'teǝrɪǝn‖ ɔːˌθɑː-, ǝˌθɒː-/ n, adj (person) demanding total obedience to rules ~**ism** n [U]

au·thor·i·ta·tive /ɔː'θɒrǝtǝtɪv, ǝ-‖ ǝ'θɑːrǝteɪtɪv, ǝ'θɒː-/ adj deserving respect; able to be trusted ~**ly** adv

au·thor·i·ty /ɔː'θɒrǝti, ǝ-‖ǝ'θɑː-, ǝ'θɒː-/ n 1 [U] power to command: Who is in authority here? 2 [C] person or group with this power 3 [C] authoritative person, book, etc.: He's an authority on plants.

au·thor·ize ‖also **-ise** BrE /'ɔːθǝraɪz/ vt give formal permission for —**ization** /ˌɔːθǝraɪ'zeɪʃǝn‖ˌɔːθǝrǝ-/ n

au·to·bi·og·ra·phy /ˌɔːtǝbaɪ'ɒgrǝfi/ -baɪ'ɑː-/ n written account of one's own life —**phical** /ˌɔːtǝbaɪǝ'græfɪkǝl/ adj

au·to·crat /'ɔːtǝkræt/ n 1 ruler with unlimited power 2 person who behaves like that ~**ic** /ˌɔːtǝ'krætɪk/ adj

au·to·graph /'ɔːtǝgrɑːf‖-græf/ n SIGNATURE of someone famous ♦ vt sign one's name on

au·to·mate /'ɔːtǝmeɪt/ vt change (a process, etc) to automation

auto·mat·ic /ˌɔːtǝ'mætɪk◀/ adj 1 (esp. of a machine) able to work by itself 2 done without thought 3 certain to happen ♦ n (automatic) gun ~**ally** /-kli/ adv

au·to·ma·tion /ˌɔːtǝ'meɪʃǝn/ n [U] use of machines that need no human control

au·tom·a·ton /ɔː'tɒmǝtǝn‖ɔː'tɑː-/ n -**ta** /-tǝ/ or -**tons** 1 thing or machine that works by itself 2 person who acts without thought or feeling

au·to·mo·bile /'ɔːtǝmǝbiːl‖-mǝʊ-/ n AmE fml for car

au·ton·o·mous /ɔː'tɒnǝmǝs‖ɔː'tɑː-/ adj governing itself

au·ton·o·my /ɔː'tɒnǝmi‖ɔː'tɑː-/ n [U] self-government

au·top·sy /'ɔːtɒpsi‖-tɑːp-/ n POST-MORTEM

au·tumn /'ɔːtǝm/ n [C;U] season between summer and winter ~**al** /ɔː'tʌmnǝl/ adj

aux·il·i·a·ry /ɔːg'zɪljǝri, ɔːk-‖ɔːg-'zɪljǝri, -'zɪlǝri/ adj helping; adding support **auxiliary** n 1 helper 2 foreign soldier in the service of a country at war 3 an auxiliary verb

a·vail /ǝ'veɪl/ v **avail oneself of** fml make use of ♦ n [U] **of/to no avail** of no use; without success

a·vai·la·ble /ǝ'veɪlǝbǝl/ adj able to be got, used, etc.: Those shoes are not available in your size. —**bility** /ǝˌveɪlǝ'bɪlǝti/ n [U]

av·a·lanche /'ævǝlɑːnʃ‖-læntʃ/ n mass of snow crashing down a mountain: (fig.) an avalanche of letters

av·ant-garde /ˌævɒŋ 'gɑːd◀‖ˌævɑːŋ 'gɑːrd◀/ adj, n 1(of) people who produce the newest ideas, esp. in the arts

av·a·rice /'ævǝrǝs/ n GREED for wealth **avaricious** /ˌævǝ'rɪʃǝs/ adj

a·venge /ǝ'vendʒ/ vt punish for harm done; REVENGE: to avenge his death

av·e·nue /'ævǝnjuː‖-nuː/ n 1 road between 2 rows of trees 2 way to a result

a·ver /ǝ'vɜːʳ/ vt -**rr**- state forcefully

av·e·rage /'ævǝrɪdʒ/ n 1 [C] amount found by adding quantities together and then dividing by the number of quantities 2 [C;U] level regarded as usual ♦ adj: the average rainfall | girls of average intelligence ♦ vt 1 calculate the average of 2 be or do as an average: I average 8 hours work a day.

a·verse /ǝ'vɜːs‖ǝ'vɜːrs/ adj not liking

a·ver·sion /ǝ'vɜːʃǝn‖ǝ'vɜːrʒǝn/ n 1 [S;U] strong dislike 2 [C] hated person or thing

a·vert /ǝ'vɜːt‖ǝ'vɜːrt/ vt 1 prevent from happening: avert accidents 2 fml turn away (one's eyes)

a·vi·a·ry /'eɪviǝri‖'eɪvieri/ n cage for keeping birds in

a·vi·a·tion /ˌeɪvi'eɪʃǝn‖ˌeɪ-, ˌæ-/ n [U] flying in aircraft —**tor** n

av·id /'ævǝd/ adj extremely keen ~**ly** adv

a·vo·ca·do /ˌævǝ'kɑːdǝʊ◀/ n -**dos** or -**does** green tropical fruit

a·void /ə'vɔɪd/ vt keep away from, esp. on purpose **~able** adj **~ance** n [U]

av·oir·du·pois /ˌævədə'pɔɪz, ˌævwɑːdjuː'pwɑː‖ˌævərdə'pɔɪz/ n, adj [U] system of weights in which the standard measures are the OUNCE, POUND, and TON

a·vowed /ə'vaud/ adj openly admitted: his avowed supporters

a·vun·cu·lar /ə'vʌŋkjʊləʳ/adj of or like an uncle

a·wait /ə'weɪt/ vt fml wait for

a·wake[1] /ə'weɪk/ adj not asleep

a·wake[2] also **awaken** /ə'weɪkən/ vi/t **awoke** /ə'wəʊk/ or **awakened**, **awoken** /ə'wəʊkən/ or **awaked** wake: (fig.) People must be awakened to the dangers of nuclear weapons.

a·wak·en·ing /ə'weɪkən/ n 1 act of waking from sleep: (fig.) her awakening to social injustice 2 **rude awakening** sudden consciousness of an unpleasant state of affairs

a·ward /ə'wɔːd‖ə'wɔːrd/ vt give officially: award prizes ♦ n something awarded

a·ware /ə'weəʳ/ adj having knowledge or understanding: politically aware **~ness** n [U]

a·way[1] /ə'weɪ/ adv 1 to or at another place: Go away!|She lives 3 miles away. 2 so as to be gone: The sounds died away. 3 continuously: He's hammering away.

away[2] adj (of a sports match) played at the place, sports field, etc., of one's opponent

awe /ɔː/ n [U] respect mixed with fear

awe·in·spir·ing /'··ˌ·· /adj causing feelings of awe

awe·some /'ɔːsəm/ adj causing feelings of awe

aw·ful /'ɔːfəl/ adj 1 very bad: awful weather 2 very great: an awful lot of work **~ly** adv very

awk·ward /'ɔːkwəd‖-ərd/ adj 1 not moving skilfully: CLUMSY 2 difficult to handle 3 inconvenient: They came at an awkward time. 4 EMBARRASSING: an awkward silence **~ly** adv **~ness** n [U]

awn·ing /'ɔːnɪŋ/ n movable cloth roof put up as a protection against sun or rain

a·woke /ə'wəʊk/ past t. of AWAKE

a·wok·en /ə'wəʊkən/ past p. of AWAKE

a·wry /ə'raɪ/ adj, adv 1 not in the planned way 2 twisted or bent

axe /æks/ n 1 tool for cutting down trees 2 **have an axe to grind** have a selfish reason for one's actions ♦ vt put a sudden end to (jobs, plans, etc.)

ax·i·om /'æksɪəm/ n principle accepted as true **~atic** /ˌæksɪə'mætɪk/ adj not needing proof

ax·is /'æksɪs/ n **axes** /'æksiːz/ 1 line round which something spins: the Earth's axis 2 fixed line against which positions are measured on a GRAPH

ax·le /'æksəl/ n bar on which a wheel turns

a·ya·tol·lah /ˌaɪə'tɒlə‖-'tɑː-/ n Shiite Muslim religious leader

aye /aɪ/ n, adv (person who votes) yes

az·ure /'æʒəʳ, 'æʒjʊəʳ, 'æzjʊəʳ‖'æʒər/ adj, n [U] bright blue

B

B, b /biː/ the 2nd letter of the English alphabet

b abbrev. for: born

baa /bɑː/ vi, n (make) the sound a sheep makes

bab·ble /'bæbəl/ vi/t talk quickly and foolishly **babble** n [S]

babe /beɪb/ n lit baby

ba·boon /bə'buːn‖bæ-/ n kind of large monkey

ba·by /'beɪbi/ n 1 very young child: (fig.) the baby of the class (= the youngest) 2 very young animal or bird: a baby monkey 3 AmE infml person, esp. a girl or woman 4 infml one's special responsibility **~ish** adj like a baby

ba·by·sit·ter /'··ˌ··ʳ/ n person who looks after children while their parents are out **baby-sit** vi **-sat**; pres. p. **-sitting**

bach·e·lor /'bætʃələʳ/ n 1 unmarried man 2 person with a first university degree

back[1] /bæk/ n 1 the part of one's body opposite the chest, from the neck to the bottom of the SPINE (1) 2 the part furthest from the direction that something moves in or faces: the back of the aircraft/of the house|the back wheel of a bicycle 3 the less important side of something 4 the part of a chair that one leans against 5 the end of a book or newspaper 6 **back to back** with the backs facing each other 7 **back to front** with the back part in front 8 **be glad to see the back of** someone be glad when someone goes away 9 **behind someone's back** without their knowledge 10 **break the back of** do most or the worst part of (something) 11 **get off someone's**

back stop annoying someone 12 **have/with one's back to the wall** (be) in the greatest difficulties 13 **put one's back into** work very hard at 14 **put someone's back up** annoy someone 15 **turn one's back on someone** leave someone (esp. when one should stay) ~**less** adj: a backless dress

back² adv 1 in or into an earlier place: Put the book back on the shelf. 2 towards the back: Lean well back. 3 away from the speaker: Stand back! 4 in reply: Phone me back. 5 in an earlier time: back in 1983

back³ v 1 vi/t more backwards: back the car down the road 2 vt support and encourage 3 vt bet money on (a horse, etc.) 4 vt be or make the back of: curtains backed with satin ~**er** n 1 someone who supports a plan with money 2 someone who bets on a horse

back down phr vi give up an argument

back onto phr vt (of a place) have at the back: a house backing onto the river

back out phr vi not fulfil a promise

back up phr vt support in an argument, etc.

back·ache /'bækeik/ n [C;U] pain in the back

back·bench /,bæk'bentʃ◀/ n any of the seats in the British parliament on which members who do not hold an official position in the government or opposition may sit **backbencher** n

back·bit·ing /'bækbaitiŋ/ n [U] unkind talk about someone who is absent

back·bone /'bækbəun/ n 1 [C] SPINE (1): (fig.) She's the backbone (= main support) of the local party. 2 [U] strength of character

back·break·ing /'bækbreikiŋ/ adj (of work) very hard

back·date /,bæk'deit/ vt make effective from an earlier date

back·drop /'bækdrɒp‖-drɑːp/ n background

back·fire /,bæk'faiəʳ‖'bækfaiəʳ/ vi 1 (of a car, etc.) make a noise because the gas explodes too soon 2 have the opposite effect to that intended

back·ground /'bækɡraund/ n 1 scenery behind the main object 2 (information about) conditions existing when something happens or happened 3 person's family, experience, education, etc.

back·hand /'bækhænd/ n stroke (in tennis, etc.) with the back of the hand turned in the direction of movement ~**ed** /,bæk'hændɪd◀'bækhændɪd/ adj 1 using or made with a backhand 2 (of a remark) indirect, esp. SARCASTIC ~**er** /'bækhændəʳ/ n 1 backhand 2 BRIBE

back·ing /'bækiŋ/ n 1 help; support 2 something that makes the back of an object

back·lash /'bæklæʃ/ n sudden violent movement, esp. against a political or social movement

back·log /'bæklɒɡ‖-lɔːɡ, -lɑːɡ/ n things (esp. work) remaining to be done

back num·ber /,· '··/n newspaper, etc., earlier than the most recent one

back of be·yond /,··· ·'··/n [the + S] infml a very distant place, difficult to get to

back·pack /'bækpæk/ n esp. AmE RUCKSACK ~**er** n ~**ing** n [U]: to go backpacking in the mountains

back·ped·al /,bæk'pedl‖'bæk,pedl/ vi -ll- BrE ‖ -l- AmE 1 PEDAL backwards 2 take back a statement; change an earlier opinion

back·room boy /'bækrum ,bɔɪ, -ruːm-/ n person doing important but secret work

back seat /,· '·/n 1 [C] seat at the back of a car 2 [S] less important position

back·side /'bæksaid/ n one's BOTTOM¹ (2)

back·slap·ping /'bækslæpiŋ/ adj (of behaviour) too friendly and noisy

back·slide /,bæk'slaid‖'bækslaid/ vi go back to a worse condition −**slider** n

back·stage /,bæk'steidʒ/ adv, adj 1 behind a theatre stage 2 in private

back·street /'· ·/n street away from the main streets, esp. in a poor area of town

back·stroke /'bækstrəuk/ n way of swimming on one's back

back·track /'bæktræk/ vi 1 go back over the same path 2 BACKPEDAL (2)

back·up /'bækʌp/ n [C;U] thing or person ready to be used in place of or to help another

back·ward /'bækwəd‖-ərd/ adj 1 towards the back 2 late in development: a backward child ~**ness** n [U]

back·wards /'bækwədz‖-ərdz/ adv 1 towards the back, the beginning, or the past: say the alphabet backwards 2 with the back part in front: put one's hat on backwards 3 **know something backwards** know something perfectly

back·wa·ter /'bækwɔːtəʳ‖-wɔː-, -wɑː-/ n 1 part of a river outside the current 2 place not influenced by outside events

back·yard /,bæk'jɑːd◀‖-'jɑːrd/ n 1 yard behind a house 2 area under one's personal control

ba·con /'beikən/ n [U] salted or smoked pig meat

bac·te·ri·a /bæk'tiəriə/ n sing. -**rium** /-riəm/ [P] very small living creatures that may cause disease

bad[1] /bæd/ adj **worse** /wɜːs‖wɜːrs/, **worst** /wɜːst‖wɜːrst/ 1 unpleasant: *bad news* 2 morally wrong 3 unhealthy: *Smoking is bad for you.* 4 not of acceptable quality 5 severe: *a bad cold* 6 ROTTEN: *The apples went bad.* 7 disobedient: *a bad boy* 8 **feel bad about** be sorry or ashamed about 9 **have/get a bad name** lose or have lost people's respect 10 **in a bad way** very ill or in trouble 11 **not bad/not so bad** really rather good ~**ly** adv 1 in a bad way: *We played badly.* 2 seriously: *We were badly beaten.* 3 a great deal: *He needs help badly.*

bad blood /ˌ· '·/ n [U] angry or bitter feeling

bad debt /ˌ· '·/ n debt that is unlikely to be paid

bad-dy /'bædi/ n infml bad person

bade /bæd, beɪd/ past t. and p. of BID[2]

badge /bædʒ/ n something worn to show one's rank, membership, etc.

bad-ger[1] /'bædʒəʳ/ n black and white night animal that lives in holes in the ground

badger[2] vt ask again and again

bad-i-nage /'bædɪnɑːʒ/ n [U] playful joking talk

badly-off /ˌ·· '·/ adj 1 poor 2 lacking

bad-min-ton /'bædmɪntən/ n [U] game similar to tennis, played with a SHUTTLECOCK over a high net

bad-mouth /'· ·/ vt sl esp. AmE speak badly of

baf-fle /'bæfəl/ vt be too difficult for (someone): *a baffling question*

bag[1] /bæg/ n 1 soft container that opens at the top: *a shopping bag* 2 **bags of** esp. BrE plenty of 3 **in the bag** certain to be won, gained, etc.

bag[2] v -gg- 1 vt put into a bag 2 vt kill (animals or birds) 3 vt take possession of 4 vi be baggy

bag-gage /'bægɪdʒ/ n [U] LUGGAGE

bag-gy /'bægi/ adj hanging in loose folds: *baggy jeans*

bag-pipes /'bægpaɪps/ n [P] musical instrument with pipes and a bag of air

bail[1] /beɪl/ n [U] 1 money paid so that a prisoner may be set free until tried (TRY[1] (3)) 2 **go/stand bail** pay this money

bail[2] v bail out phr v 1 vt pay bail for someone 2 vt help someone with money 3 vi/t remove water from a boat 4 AmE BALE out (1)

bail[3] n piece of wood laid on top of STUMPS[1] in cricket

bai-liff /'beɪlɪf/ n BrE 1 law official who takes possession of goods when money is owed 2 farm manager

bait /beɪt/ n [S;U] food used to attract fish, etc., to be caught ♦ vt 1 put bait on (a hook, etc.) 2 make (an animal or a person) angry intentionally

bake /beɪk/ 1 vi/t (cause to) cook in an OVEN 2 vi/t (cause to) become hard by heating 3 vi become hot: *I'm baking!* **baker** n person who bakes bread for sale **bakery** place where bread is baked (and sold)

bak-ing pow-der /'·· ,··/ n [U] powder used to make bread and cakes light

bal-ance[1] /'bæləns/ n 1 [S;U] state in which weight is evenly spread: *It was difficult to keep my balance on the icy path.* 2 [C] instrument for weighing 3 [C] amount remaining somewhere: *my bank balance* 4 **in the balance** uncertain(ly) 5 **on balance** considering everything

balance[2] v 1 vi/t keep steady 2 vi (of 2 things, esp. debts) be equal 3 vt compare (2 things): *balance the advantages against the disadvantages*

balance of pay-ments /ˌ··· '··/ n [(the) S] the difference between the amount of money coming into a country and the amount going out, including trade in insurance, banking, etc.

balance of trade /ˌ··· '·/ n [(the) S] the difference in value between a country's IMPORTS and EXPORTS

bal-co-ny /'bælkəni/ n 1 piece of floor that sticks out from an upstairs wall 2 upstairs seats in a theatre

bald /bɔːld/ adj 1 with no hair on the head 2 plain: *a bald statement* ~**ing** adj becoming bald ~**ness** n [U]

bal-der-dash /'bɔːldədæʃ‖-dər-/ n [U] infml nonsense

bale[1] /beɪl/ n large tightly tied mass of esp. soft material: *a bale of cotton*

bale[2] v bale out phr v 1 vi BrE escape from an aircraft 2 vi/t remove water from a boat

balk /bɔːk, bɔːlk/ vi be unwilling to agree: *I balked at the price.*

ball[1] /bɔːl/ n 1 round object used in games 2 round mass: *a ball of string/ clay* 3 round part of the body: *eyeballs* 4 **on the ball** showing up-to-date knowledge and readiness to act 5 **play ball** COOPERATE 6 **start/keep the ball rolling** begin/continue something **balls** [P] taboo sl 1 TESTICLES 2 nonsense

ball[2] n 1 formal occasion for dancing 2 **have a ball** have a very good time

bal-lad /'bæləd/ n 1 poem that tells a story 2 popular love song

bal-last /'bæləst/ n [U] heavy material carried to keep a ship steady, or to be thrown from a BALLOON (1) to make it rise higher ♦ vt fill or supply with ballast

ball-cock /'bɔːlkɒk‖-kɑːk/ n hollow floating ball that opens and closes a hole through which water flows

bal-le-ri-na /ˌbælə'riːnə/ n female ballet dancer

bal·let /'bæleɪ‖bæ'leɪ, 'bæleɪ/ n 1 [C] dance with music in which a story is told 2 [C] music for such a dance 3 [S;U] art of doing such a dance 4 [C] group of ballet dancers

ball game /'· ·/n infml state of affairs

bal·lis·tic mis·sile /bə,lɪstɪk 'mɪsaɪl‖-'mɪsəl/n MISSILE that is guided as it rises into the air but then falls freely

bal·lis·tics /bə'lɪstɪks/ n [U] science of the movement of objects, such as bullets fired from a gun **ballistic** adj

bal·loon /bə'luːn/ n 1 bag filled with gas or air so that it can float 2 small rubber bag that can be blown up and used as a toy 3 **when the balloon goes up** when the action starts or the moment of danger arrives ♦ vi swell up like a balloon

bal·lot /'bælət/ n 1 [S;U] (paper used in a) secret vote 2 [C] number of votes recorded ♦ 1 vi vote or decide by secret ballot 2 vt find out the views of (a group) by holding a vote

ballot box /'·· ·/n box in which voters put their BALLOTS (1)

ball park /'· ·/n [S] infml range of numbers, prices, etc., within which the correct figure is likely to be

ball-point /'bɔːlpɔɪnt/ n pen with a ball at the end that rolls thick ink onto the paper

ball-room /'bɔːlrum, -ruːm/ n large room suitable for a BALL² (1)

balls up /'bɔːlz,ʌp/ v BrE taboo sl phr vt spoil **balls-up** /'· ·/n

bal·ly·hoo /,bæli'huː‖'bælihuː/ n [U] noise, advertising, etc., done to gain public attention

balm /bɑːm‖bɑːm, bɑːlm/ n [C;U] oily liquid used to lessen pain

balm·y /'bɑːmi‖'bɑːmi, 'bɑːlmi/ adj (of air) soft and warm

bal·sa /'bɔːlsə/ n [C;U] (light wood of) a tropical tree

bal·us·trade /,bælə's-treɪd‖'bæləs-treɪd/ n upright posts with a bar along the top, guarding an edge where people might fall

bam·boo /,bæm'buː◄/ n -boos [C;U] (hollow jointed stems of) a tropical plant of the grass family

bam·boo·zle /bæm'buːzəl/ vt sl deceive

ban /bæn/ vt -nn- forbid ♦ n order forbidding something

ba·nal /bə'nɑːl, bə'næl/ adj uninter-esting because ordinary ~ity /bə'nælɪti/ n [C;U]

ba·na·na /bə'nɑːnə‖-'næ-/ n long yel-low tropical fruit

banana skin /·'·· ·/n BrE infml event or situation likely to cause diffi-culty or make one look foolish

band¹ /bænd/ n 1 narrow piece of material for fastening, or putting round something: a rubber band 2 STRIPE (1) 3 area between measurable limits: the £10,000—£30,000 income band

band² n group of people, esp. musi-cians playing popular music — see also ONE-MAN BAND; STEEL BAND

band³ v **band together** phr vi unite for a purpose

ban·dage /'bændɪdʒ/ n narrow piece of cloth for tying round a wound ♦ vt tie up with a bandage

b and b /,biː ən 'biː/ abbrev. for: (small hotel providing) bed and breakfast

ban·dit /'bændɪt/ n armed robber — see also ONE-ARMED BANDIT

band·stand /'bændstænd/ n raised open-air place for a band to play

band·wa·gon /'bænd,wægən/ n jump on a bandwagon join some-thing that is popular, for personal gain

ban·dy¹ /'bændi/ vt bandy words quarrel

bandy² adj (of legs) curved outwards at the knees

bane /beɪn/ n cause of trouble ~ful adj harmful

bang¹ /bæŋ/ vi/t hit violently and noisily: I banged my head against the ceiling. **bang** n

bang² adv exactly: bang in the middle

bang·er /'bæŋəʳ/ n BrE 1 SAUSAGE 2 old car 3 noisy FIREWORK

ban·gle /'bæŋgəl/ n band worn as decoration

ban·ish /'bænɪʃ/ vt 1 send away as a punishment 2 stop thinking about ~ment n [U]

ban·is·ter /'bænɪstəʳ/ n also **banis-ters** — upright posts with a bar along the top, beside a staircase

ban·jo /'bændʒəʊ/ n -jos or -joes stringed instrument used esp. to play popular music

bank¹ /bæŋk/ n 1 land beside a river or lake 2 raised heap of earth, etc. 3 mass of snow, clouds, etc. 4 set of things arranged in a row: a bank of oars

bank² n 1 place where money is kept and paid out on demand 2 place where something is kept for use: a blood bank ~er n person who owns, works in, or controls a BANK² (1)

bank³ vi/t keep (money) in a bank **bank on** phr vt depend on

bank⁴ vi (of an aircraft, etc.) raise one side while turning

bank hol·i·day /,· '·· ·/n BrE official public holiday on a weekday

bank·ing /'bæŋkɪŋ/ n [U] business of a BANK² (1)

bank note /'· ·/ n piece of paper money

bank rate /'· ·/ n [the + S] the rate of interest fixed by a central bank

bank-roll /'bæŋkrəul/ n AmE supply of money ♦ vt AmE infml supply money for or pay the cost of (a business, plan, etc.)

bank-rupt /'bæŋkrʌpt/ adj unable to pay one's debts: (fig.) morally bankrupt (= completely without morals) ♦ n person who is bankrupt ♦ vt make bankrupt or very poor ~cy n [C;U] state of being bankrupt

ban-ner /'bænəʳ/ n 1 lit flag 2 piece of cloth with a political message on it, carried by marchers

banns /bænz/ n [P] public declaration of an intended marriage

ban-quet /'bæŋkwət/ n formal dinner **banquet** vi

ban-ter /'bæntəʳ/ n [U] light joking talk **banter** vi

bap-tis-m /'bæptɪzəm/ n 1 [C;U] Christian religious ceremony of touching or covering a person with water 2 **baptism of fire: a** soldier's first experience of war **b** any unpleasant first experience **–tize** /bæp'taɪz/ vt perform baptism on

bar /baːʳ/ n **i** long narrow piece of solid material: a bar of chocolate (fig.) bars of sunlight 2 length of wood or metal across a window, etc. 3 group of musical notes 4 place where drinks, etc., are served 5 bank of sand or stones under water 6 BARRIER 7 (cap.) the legal profession, esp. BARRISTERS: She was called to the Bar. (= became a barrister) 8 **behind bars** in prison 9 **prisoner at the bar** person being tried in a court of law ♦ vt -rr- 1 close with a bar: They barred themselves in. (fig.) to bar the way to success 2 forbid; prevent: He was barred from playing football. ♦ prep 1 except 2 **bar none** with no exception

barb /baːb‖baːrb/ n sharp point of a fish hook, etc., with a curved shape ~ed adj 1 with short sharp points. 2 (of speech) sharply unkind

bar-bar-i-an /baː'beəriən‖baːr-/ n wild uncivilized person

bar-bar-ic /baː'bærɪk‖baːr-/ adj 1 very cruel 2 like a barbarian **–barism** /'baːbərɪzəm‖'baːr-/ n [U] condition of being a barbarian **–barous** adj **–ity** /baː'bærəti‖baːr-/ n [C;U] great cruelty

bar-be-cue /'baːbɪkjuː‖'baːr-/ n 1 metal frame for cooking meat outdoors 2 party where this is done ♦ vt cook on a barbecue

bar-ber /'baːbəʳ‖'baːr-/ n person who cuts men's hair

bar-bi-tu-rate /baː'bɪtʃʊrət‖baːr'-bɪtʃʊrət, -reɪt/ [C;U] drug that makes people sleep

bard /baːd‖baːrd/ n 1 poet 2 **the Bard** Shakespeare

bare /beəʳ/ adj 1 without clothes or covering 2 with nothing added: the bare facts 3 empty: a room bare of furniture ♦ vt bring to view; EXPOSE ~ly adv hardly

bare-back /'beəbæk‖'beər-/ adj, adv riding, esp. a horse, without a SADDLE (1)

bare bones /· '·/n [P] simplest but most important parts or facts

bare-faced /ˌbeə'feɪst◂‖'beərfeɪst/ adj shameless

bare-foot /'beəfʊt‖'beər-/ adv without shoes

bar-gain [1] /'baːgən‖'baːr-/ n 1 agreement to do something in return for something else 2 something sold cheap 3 **into the bargain** besides everything else

bargain [2] vi talk about the conditions of a sale, etc.

bargain for/on phr vt take into account; expect

barge [1] /baːdʒ‖baːrdʒ/ n flat-bottomed boat

barge [2] vi move heavily and rudely

barge in phr vi rush in rudely; interrupt

bar-i-tone /'bærətəʊn/ n (man with) a singing voice between TENOR and BASS[1]

bark [1] /baːk‖baːrk/ v 1 vi make the noise dogs make 2 vt say in a fierce voice 3 **bark up the wrong tree** infml have a mistaken idea **bark** n 1 sharp loud noise made by a dog 2 **his bark is worse than his bite** infml he is not as bad-tempered, unfriendly, etc., as he appears

bark [2] n [U] outer covering of a tree

bar-ley /'baːli‖'baːrli/ n [U] grasslike grain plant grown as a food crop

bar-man /'baːmən‖'baːr-/ ‖ **barmaid** /'baːmeɪd‖'baːr-/ fem. — n **-men** /-mən/ person who serves drinks in a BAR (4)

barm-y /'baːmi‖'baːrmi/ adj sl foolish; mad

barn /baːn‖baːrn/ n farm building for storing things in

bar-na-cle /'baːnəkəl‖'baːr-/ n small SHELLFISH that collects on rocks, ships, etc.

ba-rom-e-ter /bə'rɒmɪtəʳ‖-'raː/ n instrument for measuring air pressure so as to judge what weather is coming: (fig.) a barometer of public opinion

bar-on /'bærən/ n 1 **baroness** fem. — British noble of the lowest rank 2 powerful businessman

bar-on-et /'bærənət, -net/ n British KNIGHT, below a baron in rank

ba-roque /bə'rɒk, bə'rəʊk/ adj 1 in a decorated style fashionable in

17th-century Europe **2** (too) greatly ornamented

bar·rack /'bærək/ *vi/t BrE* interrupt by shouting

bar·racks /'bærəks/ *n* building where soldiers live

bar·rage /'bærɑːʒ‖bɑːˈrɑːʒ/ *n* **1** heavy gunfire: (fig.) *a barrage of questions* **2** bank of earth, etc., built across a river

bar·rel /'bærəl/ *n* **1** round wooden container: *a beer barrel* **2** long tube-shaped part of a gun, etc. **3 over a barrel** in a difficult position

barrel or·gan /'·· ,··/ *n* musical instrument on wheels, played by turning a handle

bar·ren /'bærən/ *adj* **1** unable to produce children, fruit, crops, etc. **2** useless; empty: *a barren discussion* ~**ness** *n* [U]

bar·ri·cade /'bærəkeɪd, ˌbærəˈkeɪd/ *n* something quickly built to block a street, etc. ♦ *vt* close or defend with a barricade

bar·ri·er /'bæriər/ *n* something placed in the way to prevent movement: (fig.) *a barrier to success | the sound barrier*

bar·ring /'bɑːrɪŋ/ *prep* except for

bar·ris·ter /'bærəstər/ *n* (esp. in England) lawyer who has the right to speak in the highest courts

bar·row /'bærəʊ/ *n* **1** small cart to be pushed **2** WHEELBARROW

bar·tend·er /'bɑːˌtendər‖'bɑːr-/ *n AmE for* BARMAN

bar·ter /'bɑːtər‖'bɑːr-/ *vi/t* exchange goods for other goods **barter** *n* [U]

base¹ /beɪs/ *n* **1** part of a thing on which a thing stands **2** origin from which something develops or grows **3** centre from which something is controlled, plans made, etc. **4** centre for military operations, stores, etc. **5** main part or substance of a mixture: *a vegetable base* **6** point which a player must touch in BASEBALL to make a run **7 not get to first base (with)** not even begin to succeed (with) ♦ *vt* provide with a centre: *a company based in Paris* ~**less** *adj* without good reason

base on/upon *phr vt* form by using something else as a starting point: *a film based on a novel*

base² *adj* **1** *esp. lit* (of people or behaviour) dishonourable **2** (of metal) not regarded as precious ~**ly** *adv* ~**ness** *n* [U]

base·ball /'beɪsbɔːl/ *n* **1** [U] American national team game **2** [C] ball used in this game

base·ment /'beɪsmənt/ *n* room in a house below street level

base rate /'· ·/ *n* standard rate of interest on which a bank bases its

charges for lending and interest on borrowing

bas·es /'beɪsiːz/ *n pl. of* BASIS

bash /bæʃ/ *vt* hit hard ♦ *n* **1** hard blow **2 have a bash** *infml* make an attempt

bash·ful /'bæʃfəl/ *adj* SHY ~**ly** *adv*

ba·sic /'beɪsɪk/ *adj* most necessary; FUNDAMENTAL: *basic principles* ~**ally** /-kli/ *adv* in spite of surface behaviour or details; in reality **basics** *n* [P] basic parts or principles

ba·sin /'beɪsən/ *n* **1** round container for liquids; bowl **2** WASHBASIN **3** hollow place where water collects **4** large valley

ba·sis /'beɪsɪs/ *n* **bases** /'beɪsiːz/ **1** the facts, principles, etc., from which something is formed, started, or developed: *the basis of an opinion* **2** the stated way of carrying out an action, process, etc.: *working on a part-time basis*

bask /bɑːsk‖bæsk/ *vi* lie in enjoyable warmth: (fig.) *She basked in* (= enjoyed) *her employer's approval.*

bas·ket /'bɑːskət‖'bæ-/ *n* light woven container: *a shopping basket*

bas·ket·ball /'bɑːskətbɔːl‖'bæs-/ *n* **1** [U] indoor game in which players try to throw a ball into a basket **2** [C] large ball used in this game

bass¹ /beɪs/ *n* **1** (man with) the lowest human singing voice **2** instrument with the same range of notes as this: *a bass guitar* **3** DOUBLE BASS

bass² /bæs/ *n* kind of fish that can be eaten

bas·soon /bəˈsuːn/ *n* large WOODWIND musical instrument

bas·tard /'bæstəd, 'bɑː-‖'bæstərd/ *n* **1** child of unmarried parents **2** *sl* unpleasant person **3** *sl* man of the stated kind: *You lucky bastard!*

baste /beɪst/ *vt* **1** pour fat over (meat) during cooking **2** fasten with TACKs (3)

bas·ti·on /'bæstiən‖-tʃən/ *n* **1** part of a castle wall that sticks out **2** place where a principle is defended: *a bastion of freedom*

bat¹ /bæt/ *n* **1** stick for hitting the ball in cricket, BASEBALL, etc. **2 off one's own bat** without being told to do something

bat² /bæt/ *vi/t* **1** strike or hit (as if) with a bat **2 vt not bat an eyelid** show no sign of shock

bat³ *n* **1** mouselike animal that flies at night **2 as blind as a bat** not able to see well

batch /bætʃ/ *n* group; set

bat·ed /'beɪtəd/ *adj* **with bated breath** too frightened or excited to breathe

bath /bɑːθ‖bæθ/ *n* **baths** /bɑːðz, bɑːθs‖bæðz, bæθs/ **1** container in which one sits to wash the whole body **2** act of washing one's whole body at one time **3** liquid in a container used for some special purpose: *an eyebath* **4** place with a swimming pool or baths for public use ♦ **v 1** *vi* have a BATH (2) **2** *vt* give a bath to (a baby, etc.)

bathe /beɪð/ *v* **1** *vi esp. BrE* swim in the sea, etc. **2** *vi AmE* have a BATH (2) **3** *vt* put in liquid: *bathe your eyes* ♦ *n* a swim **bather** *n* swimmer

ba·thos /ˈbeɪθɒs‖-θɑːs/ *n* [U] sudden change from beautiful ideas to ordinary foolish ones

bath-robe /ˈbɑːθrəʊb‖ˈbæθ-/ *n esp. AmE* DRESSING GOWN worn before or after bathing

bath-room /ˈbɑːθrʊm, -rʊm‖ˈbæθ-/ *n* **1** room with a bath **2** *AmE for* TOILET (1)

bath-tub /ˈbɑːθtʌb‖ˈbæθ-/ *n esp. AmE for* BATH (1)

bat-man /ˈbætmən/ *n* **-men** /-mən/ British officer's servant

bat-on /ˈbætɒn‖bæˈtɔːn, bə-/ *n* short stick used by the leader of an ORCHESTRA, or as a weapon by a policeman, etc.

bats-man /ˈbætsmən/ *n* **-men** /-mən/ player in cricket who tries to hit the ball with a BAT[1] (1)

bat-tal-ion /bəˈtæljən/ *n* army unit of 500-1,000 soldiers

bat-ten /ˈbætn/ *v* **batten down** *phr vt* fasten with boards

bat-ter[1] /ˈbætə[r]/ *vi/t* **1** beat hard and repeatedly **2** cause to lose shape by continual use

batter[2] *n* [U] mixture of flour, eggs, and milk for making PANCAKEs, etc.

batter[3] *n* person who BATS[2] (1)

bat-ter-ing ram /ˈ··· ·/ *n* (in former times) heavy log used for breaking down castle doors

bat-ter-y /ˈbætəri/ *n* **1** apparatus for producing electricity **2** army unit of big guns **3** line of boxes in which hens are kept **4** set of things used together: *a battery of tests*

bat-tle /ˈbætl/ *n* short fight between enemies or opposing groups ♦ *vi* fight; struggle

bat-tle-axe *BrE* ‖ **-ax** *AmE* /ˈbætl-æks/ *n* **1** heavy axe for fighting **2** fierce woman

bat-tle-field /ˈbætlfiːld/ *n* place where a battle is fought

bat-tle-ments /ˈbætlmənts/ *n* [P] wall round a castle roof, with spaces to shoot through

bat-tle-ship /ˈbætl,ʃɪp/ *n* large warship with big guns

bat-ty /ˈbæti/ *adj sl* slightly mad

bau-ble /ˈbɔːbəl/ *n* cheap jewel

baulk /bɔːk, bɔːlk/ *v BrE for* BALK

bawd /bɔːd/ *lit* woman in charge of PROSTITUTEs

bawd-y /ˈbɔːdi/ *adj* about sex in a rude, funny way **-ily** *adv* **-iness** *n* [U]

bawl /bɔːl/ *vi/t* shout loudly

bay[1] /beɪ/ *n* **1** wide opening along a coast **2** division of a large room or building, separated by shelves, etc.

bay[2] *vi* make the deep cry of a large hunting dog

bay[3] *n* **hold/keep at bay** keep (an enemy, etc.) away

bay-o-net /ˈbeɪənət, -net/ *n* knife on the end of a RIFLE ♦ *vt* drive a bayonet into

bay win-dow /,· ˈ··/ *n* 3-sided window sticking out from a wall

ba-zaar /bəˈzɑː[r]/ *n* **1** sale to get money for some good purpose **2** market in an Eastern town

ba-zoo-ka /bəˈzuːkə/ *n* long gun that rests on the shoulder and fires ROCKETs

BC *abbrev. for:* before (the birth of) Christ

be[1] /bi; *strong* biː/ *v aux pres. t. sing.* I **am**, you **are**, he/she/it **is**; *pres. t. pl.* we/you/they **are**; *past t. sing.* I **was**, you **were**, he/she/it **was**; *past t. pl.* we/you/they **were**; *past p.* **been**; *pres. p.* **being 1** (forms continual tenses with **-ing**): *I am/was reading.* **2** (forms passives with **-ed**): *We are/were invited.* **3** (used with **to**) *a* must: *You are not to smoke.* *b* (shows future plans): *They are to be married soon.*

be[2] *v* **1** (shows that something is the same as the subject): *Today is Tuesday.* **2** (shows where or when): *He's upstairs.* **3** (shows a group or quality): *She's a doctor.* | *I'm cold.* | *Be careful!* **4** (shows that something exists): *There's a hole in your sock.*

beach /biːtʃ/ *n* sandy or stony shore ♦ *vt* move (a boat) onto a beach

beach ball /ˈ··· ·/ *n* large light ball to play with on the beach

beach bug-gy /ˈ·· ,··/ *n* motor vehicle for use on sandy beaches

beach-comb-er /ˈbiːtʃ,kəʊmə[r]/ *n* person who searches a beach for useful things to sell

beach-head /ˈbiːtʃhed/ *n* area on an enemy's shore that has been captured

beach-wear /ˈbiːtʃweə[r]/ *n* [U] clothing for the BEACH

bea-con /ˈbiːkən/ *n* fire or flashing light that gives warning

bead /biːd/ *n* **1** small ball with a hole through it, for threading on string **2** drop of liquid: *beads of sweat* **~ed** *adj*

bead-y /ˈbiːdi/ *adj* (of eyes) small and bright

bea-gle /ˈbiːgəl/ *n* short-legged hunting dog

beak /biːk/ *n* bird's hard horny mouth

bea-ker /ˈbiːkə[r]/ *n* **1** drinking cup **2** glass cup used in chemistry

beam[1] /biːm/ n long heavy piece of wood, esp. used to support a building

beam[2] n 1 line of light from some bright object 2 radio waves sent out to guide aircraft, etc. 3 bright look or smile ♦ v 1 vi (of the sun, etc.) send out light (and heat) 2 vt send out (esp. radio or television signals) in a certain direction 3 vi smile brightly

bean /biːn/ n 1 seed or POD of any of various plants, esp. used as food: baked beans | coffee beans 2 **full of beans** full of life and eagerness 3 **not have a bean** have no money at all 4 **spill the beans** tell a secret

bear[1] /beər/ n large, heavy furry animal that eats meat, fruit, and insects

bear[2] v bore /bɔːr/ borne /bɔːn‖bɔːrn/ 1 vt carry 2 vt support (a weight) 3 vt have; show: The letter bore no signature. | to bear a famous name 4 vt suffer or accept (something unpleasant) without complaining 5 vt fml give birth to 6 vi/t produce (a crop or fruit) 7 vi move in the stated direction: Cross the field, bear left, and you'll see the house. 8 vt be suitable for: His words don't bear repeating. 9 vt fml keep (a feeling toward someone) in one's mind: I don't bear him a grudge. 10 **bear in mind** remember to consider 11 **bring something to bear (on)** direct something, e.g. force or persuasion (on); EXERT ~able adj TOLERABLE ~ably adv

bear down phr v 1 vt fml defeat 2 vi use all one's strength and effort

bear down on/upon phr vt come towards forcefully and threateningly, esp. at high speed

bear on/upon phr vt relate to

bear out phr vt support the truth of

bear up phr vi show courage or strength in spite of difficulties

bear with phr vt show patience towards

beard /bɪəd‖bɪərd/ n hair on the face below the mouth ~ed adj

bear-er /ˈbeərər/ n 1 person who brings or carries something, e.g. the body at a funeral 2 person to whom a cheque is to be paid

bear-ing /ˈbeərɪŋ/ n 1 [S;U] way of behaving 2 [S;U] connection; RELEVANCE: This has no bearing on the subject. 3 [C] direction shown by a compass 4 understanding of one's position: get/lose one's bearings

bear-skin /ˈbeə‚skɪn‖ˈbeər-/ n tall black fur cap worn by certain British soldiers

beast /biːst/ n 1 4-footed animal 2 person or thing one does not like ~ly adj bad; nasty

beat[1] /biːt/ v beat, beaten /ˈbiːtn/ or beat 1 vt hit again and again, esp. with a stick: beat a drum | the rain beating against the windows 2 vt mix with a fork, etc.: beat the eggs 3 vi move regularly: I could hear his heart beating. 4 vt defeat: I beat him at tennis. 5 **beat about the bush** talk indirectly about something 6 **Beat it!** infml Go away! 7 **beat time** make regular movements to measure the speed of music ~er n tool for beating things ~ing n 1 act of giving repeated blows, usu. as punishment 2 defeat

beat[2] n 1 single stroke or blow: the beat of the drum 2 regular STRESS (4) in music or poetry 3 usual path followed by someone on duty

be·a·tif·ic /‚biːəˈtɪfɪk/ adj showing joy and peace: a beatific smile

beau·ti·cian /bjuːˈtɪʃən/ n person who gives beauty treatments

beau·ti·ful /ˈbjuːtɪfəl/ adj giving pleasure to the mind or senses ~ly adv **-tify** vt make beautiful

beau·ty /ˈbjuːti/ n 1 [U] quality of being beautiful 2 [C] someone or something beautiful

bea·ver /ˈbiːvər/ n animal like a big rat that builds dams across streams ♦ vi work hard

be·calmed /bɪˈkɑːmd‖bɪˈkɑːmd, -ˈkɑːlmd/ adj (of a sailing ship) unable to move because there is no wind

be·came /bɪˈkeɪm/ past t. of BECOME

be·cause /bɪˈkɔz, bɪˈkʌz‖bɪˈkɔːz, bɪˈkʌz/ conj 1 for the reason that: I do it because I like it. 2 **because of** as a result of: I came back because of the rain.

beck /bek/ n **at one's beck and call** always ready to do what one asks

beck·on /ˈbekən/ vi/t call with a movement of the finger

be·come /bɪˈkʌm/ v became, become 1 begin to be: become king; become warmer 2 vt be suitable for: Such behaviour hardly becomes someone in your position. **becoming** adj 1 attractive 2 suitable

bed[1] /bed/ n 1 [C] piece of furniture to sleep on 2 bottom or base: bed of a river 3 [C] piece of ground for plants 4 [U] love-making; sex

bed[2] vt -dd- 1 put in or on a bed: a machine bedded in cement 2 plant 3 have sex with

bed down phr v 1 vt make (a person or animal) comfortable for the night 2 vi make oneself comfortable for the night

bed-clothes /ˈbedkləʊðz, -kləʊz/ n [P] sheets, etc., on a bed

bed-ding /ˈbedɪŋ/ n [U] materials for a person or animal to sleep on

be·dev·il /bɪˈdevəl/ vt -ll- BrE ‖ -l- AmE cause continual trouble for

bed-fel-low /'bed,feləʊ/ n 1 person who shares a bed 2 close companion; partner

bed-lam /'bedləm/ n [S;U] place of wild noisy activity

bed of roses /,· · '··/ n [S] happy comfortable state

bed-pan /'bedpæn/ n container for a sick person's body waste

be-drag-gled /bɪ'drægəld/ adj wet, LIMP, and muddy

bed-rid-den /'bed,rɪdn/ adj too ill or old to get out of bed

bed-room /'bedrum, -ru:m/ n room for sleeping in

bed-side /'bedsaɪd/ n 1 side of a bed: bedside lamp 2 **bedside manner** way in which a doctor behaves when visiting a sick person

bed-sit-ter /,· '··/ n BrE room for both living and sleeping in

bed-sore /'bedsɔːʳ/ n sore place on the skin, caused by lying too long in bed

bed-spread /'bedspred/ n decorative cover for a bed

bed-stead /'bedsted/ n main framework of a bed

bed-time /'bedtaɪm/ n time for going to bed

bee /biː/ n 1 stinging insect that makes honey 2 **a bee in one's bonnet** fixed idea; OBSESSION 3 **the bee's knees** infml the best person or thing

beech /biːtʃ/ n large forest tree with green or copper-brown leaves

beef /biːf/ n [U] meat of farm cattle ♦ vi complain ~y adj (of a person) big and strong

bee-hive /'biːhaɪv/ n HIVE

bee-line /'biːlaɪn/ n **make a beeline for** go straight towards

been /biːn, bɪn‖bɪn/ n 1 past participle of BE 2 gone and come back: Have you ever been to India?

beer /bɪəʳ/ n [U] alcoholic drink made from MALT — see also SMALL BEER ~y adj: beery breath

beet /biːt/ n 1 root from which sugar is made 2 BEETROOT

bee-tle /'biːtl/ n insect with hard wing coverings

beet-root /'biːtruːt/ n -roots or -root [C;U] BrE large red root vegetable

be-fall /bɪ'fɔːl/ vi/t befell /-'fel/, befallen /-'fɔːlən/ fml happen (to)

be-fit /bɪ'fɪt/ vt -tt- fml be suitable for: befitting behaviour

be-fore /bɪ'fɔːʳ/ prep 1 earlier than 2 ahead of; in front of ♦ adv already; formerly: I've seen you before. ♦ conj 1 before the time when 2 rather than

be-fore-hand /bɪ'fɔːhænd‖-'fɔːr-/ adv before something else happens

be-friend /bɪ'frend/ vt fml be a friend to

beg /beg/ v -gg- 1 vi/t ask for (food, money, etc) 2 vt request politely: I beg to differ. 3 **beg the question** to take as true something that is not yet proved 4 **going begging** not wanted by anyone

be-get /bɪ'get/ v begot /bɪ'gɒt‖bɪ'gɑːt/, begotten /bɪ'gɒtn‖bɪ'gɑːtn/ lit become the father of; produce

beg-gar /'begəʳ/ n person who lives by begging ~ly adj much too little

be-gin /bɪ'gɪn/ vi/t began /bɪ'gæn/, begun /bɪ'gʌn/ 1 start; take the first step 2 **to begin with** as the first reason ~ner n person starting to learn ~ning n [C;U] starting point

be-grudge /bɪ'grʌdʒ/ vt to GRUDGE

be-guile /bɪ'gaɪl/ vt fml 1 charm 2 deceive; cheat

be-half /bɪ'hɑːf‖bɪ'hæf/ n **on behalf of** for; in the interests of: I'm speaking on John's behalf.

be-have /bɪ'heɪv/ vi 1 (of people or things) act in a particular way 2 show good manners

be-hav-iour BrE ‖ -ior AmE /bɪ'heɪvjəʳ/ n [U] way of behaving

be-head /bɪ'hed/ vt cut off the head of

be-hest /bɪ'hest/ n fml **at someone's behest** by someone's command

be-hind /bɪ'haɪnd/ prep 1 at or to the back of: hide behind the door 2 less good than: He's behind the others in mathematics. 3 in support of ♦ adv 1 behind something 2 where something was before: I've left the key behind! 3 late; slow: We're behind with the rent. ♦ n infml BUTTOCKS

be-hind-hand /bɪ'haɪndhænd/ adv fml late; slow

be-hold /bɪ'həʊld/ vt beheld /bɪ'held/ lit see

be-hold-en /bɪ'həʊldn/ adj **be beholden to** have to feel grateful to

beige /beɪʒ/ adj, n pale brown

be-ing¹ /'biːɪŋ/ n 1 existence: When did the club come into being? 2 living thing, esp. a person

being² v present participle of BE

be-lat-ed /bɪ'leɪtɪd/ adj delayed; too late

belch /beltʃ/ v 1 vi pass gas up from the stomach 2 vt send out (large amounts of smoke, etc.) belch n

be-lea-guer /bɪ'liːgəʳ/ vt fml 1 surround with an army 2 worry continuously

bel-fry /'belfri/ n tower for bells

be-lie /bɪ'laɪ/ vt fml give a false idea of

be-lief /bɪ'liːf/ n 1 [S;U] feeling that something is true, or can be trusted 2 [C] idea that is believed: religious beliefs

be·lieve /bɪˈliːv/ v 1 vt consider to be true 2 vi have religious faith **believable** adj that can be believed **believer** n

believe in phr vi 1 think that (something exists): believe in fairies 2 feel sure of the value of: believe in lots of exercise

be·lit·tle /bɪˈlɪtl/ vt fml cause to seem unimportant: Don't belittle your efforts.

bell /bel/ n 1 metal object that makes a ringing sound: church bells | a bicycle bell 2 cup-shaped object: the bell of a flower 3 **ring a bell** remind one of something

bell-bot·toms /'·ˌ··/ n [P] trousers with legs that are wider at the bottom

bel·lig·er·ent /bɪˈlɪdʒərənt/ n, adj 1 (country that is) at war 2 (person who is) ready to fight

bel·low /ˈbeləʊ/ vi/t shout in a deep voice

bel·lows /ˈbeləʊz/ n [P] **-lows** instrument for blowing air into a fire, etc.

bel·ly /ˈbeli/ n 1 infml the part of the human body between the chest and legs 2 curved surface like this: the belly of a plane ~**ful** /-fʊl/ n infml too much

bel·ly·ache /ˈbeli-eɪk/ vi complain repeatedly

belly button /'·· ˌ··/ n infml NAVEL

be·long /bɪˈlɒŋ‖bɪˈlɔːŋ/ vi be in the right place: This chair belongs upstairs. ~**ings** n [P] one's property

belong to phr vt 1 be the property of 2 be a member of

be·lov·ed /bɪˈlʌvd/ n, adj (person who is) dearly loved

be·low /bɪˈləʊ/ adv, prep in a lower place (than); under: He saw the valley below. | below the knee | see page 85 below

belt[1] /belt/ n 1 band worn round the waist 2 circular piece of material that drives a machine 3 area with a particular quality, crop, etc. 4 **below the belt** infml unfair or unfairly — see also BLACK BELT, GREEN BELT

belt[2] v 1 vt fasten with a belt 2 vt infml hit hard 3 vi sl, esp. BrE travel fast

belt out phr vt infml sing loudly

belt up phr vi sl be quiet

belt·way /ˈbeltweɪ/ n AmE for RING ROAD

be·moan /bɪˈməʊn/ vt fml express sorrow for

be·mused /bɪˈmjuːzd/ adj unable to think clearly

bench /bentʃ/ n 1 [C] long seat 2 [C] long worktable: a carpenter's bench 3 **a** [the + S] place where a judge sits in court **b** judges as a group — see also FRONT BENCH

bend /bend/ vi/t bent /bent/ (cause to) move into a curve or move away

from an upright position: bend the wire | bend down to kiss the child ♦ n 1 curve: a bend in the road 2 **round the bend** infml mad **bends** [P] pain suffered by divers who come to the surface too quickly

be·neath /bɪˈniːθ/ adv, prep fml 1 below; under 2 not worthy of: beneath contempt

ben·e·dic·tion /ˌbenɪˈdɪkʃən/ n religious blessing

ben·e·fac·tor /ˈbenɪˌfæktər/ **benefactress** /-trəs/ fem. — n person who gives money, etc. **-tion** /ˌbenɪˈfækʃən/ n 1 [U] giving of money 2 [C] money given

ben·e·fi·cial /ˌbenɪˈfɪʃəl◄/ adj (of things) helpful; useful

ben·e·fi·cia·ry /ˌbenɪˈfɪʃəri‖-ˈfɪʃieri/ n receiver of a benefit

ben·e·fit /ˈbenɪfɪt/ n 1 [U] advantage; profit: She's had the benefit of a very good education. 2 [C;U] money paid by the government to people who need it because of sickness, etc: unemployment benefit 3 [C] event to raise money for some person or special purpose 4 **the benefit of the doubt** favourable consideration given because there is no proof of guilt or wrongness ♦ v 1 vt be helpful to 2 vi gain advantage

be·nev·o·lent /bɪˈnevələnt/ adj wishing to do good; kind **-lence** n [U]

be·nign /bɪˈnaɪn/ adj kind and harmless

bent[1] /bent/ v past t. and p. of BEND 2 **bent on** determined on: She's bent on winning.

bent[2] n special natural skill: a natural bent for languages

bent[3] adj BrE sl 1 dishonest 2 HOMOSEXUAL

be·queath /bɪˈkwiːð, bɪˈkwiːθ/ vt fml give to others after death

be·quest /bɪˈkwest/ n fml something bequeathed

be·rate /bɪˈreɪt/ vt fml speak angrily to

be·reaved /bɪˈriːvd/ adj fml having lost someone by death: a bereaved mother **bereavement** n [C;U]

be·reft /bɪˈreft/ adj completely without: bereft of hope

be·ret /ˈbereɪ‖bəˈreɪ/ n round soft flat cap

ber·ry /ˈberi/ n small soft fruit with seeds

ber·serk /bəˈsɜːk, bə-‖bərˈsɜːrk, ˈbɜːrsɜːrk/ adj violently angry

berth /bɜːθ‖bɜːrθ/ n 1 sleeping place in a ship or train 2 place where a ship can be tied up in harbour 3 **give someone a wide berth** avoid someone ♦ vi/t tie up (a ship)

be·seech /bɪˈsiːtʃ/ vt besought /bɪˈsɔːt/ or beseeched fml ask eagerly

be·set /bɪ'set/ vt beset, present participle besetting attack continuously: beset by doubts

be·side /bɪ'saɪd/ prep 1 at the side of 2 in comparison with 3 **beside oneself** almost mad (with joy, etc.) 4 **beside the point** having nothing to do with the main question

be·sides /bɪ'saɪdz/ adv also ♦ prep in addition to

be·siege /bɪ'siːdʒ/ vt surround (a place) with armed forces: (fig.) They besieged her with questions.

be·sot·ted /bɪ'sɒtɪd||bɪ'sɑː-/ adj made foolish or unable to behave sensibly

be·spoke /bɪ'spəʊk/ adj (of clothes) made to someone's measurements

best¹ /best/ adj (superlative of GOOD) 1 the highest in quality or skill: the best tennis player in America 2 the **best part of** most of — see also SECOND BEST

best² adv (superlative of WELL) 1 in the best way: She did best. 2 to the greatest degree; most: He thinks he knows best. 3 **as best one can** as well as one can

best³ n [S] 1 the greatest degree of good: She wants the best for her children. 2 one's best effort: I did my best. 3 **All the best!** (used when saying goodbye) I wish you success! 4 **at its/one's best** in as good a state as possible 5 **at (the) best** if the best happens 6 **make the best of** do as well as one can with (something unsatisfactory)

bes·ti·al /'bestiəl||'bestʃəl/ adj (of human behaviour) very cruel **~ity** /,besti'æləti||,bestʃi-/ n [U]

best man /,· '·/ n man attending the BRIDEGROOM at a wedding

be·stow /bɪ'stəʊ/ vt fml give

best-sel·ler /,· '··/ n book, etc., that sells in very large numbers

bet /bet/ n 1 agreement to risk money on a future event 2 sum of money risked in this way ♦ vi/t **bet** or **betted**; pres. p. **betting** 1 risk (money) on a race, etc. 2 be sure: I bet he's angry!

be·tide /bɪ'taɪd/ vt lit **woe betide you, him, etc.** you, he, etc., will be in trouble

be·tray /bɪ'treɪ/ vt 1 be unfaithful to 2 make known (a secret): (fig.) Her face betrayed (= showed) her nervousness. **~er** n **~al** n [C;U]

be·trothed /bɪ'trəʊðd/ adj lit having promised to marry

bet·ter¹ /'betəʳ/ adj 1 higher in quality; more good: a better way to do it 2 well again after illness ♦ adv 1 in a better way: It works better now. 2 **go one better (than)** do better (than) 3 **had better** ought to; should: I'd better

not tell him. 4 **know better (than)** be sensible enough not to ♦ n **get the better of** defeat ♦ vi/t 1 improve 2 **better oneself: a** earn more **b** educate oneself **~ment** improvement **betters** n [P] people better then oneself

be·tween /bɪ'twiːn/ prep 1 in the space or time that separates: Stand between Sue and Brian. | Don't eat between meals. 2 (shows connection): an air service between London and Paris 3 (shows division or sharing): The difference between spaghetti and noodles. | Between us, we collected £17. ♦ adv 1 in the space or time between things 2 **few and far between** very rare

bev·el /'bevəl/ vt -ll- BrE | -l- AmE make a sloping edge on **bevel** n

bev·er·age /'bevərɪdʒ/ n fml liquid for drinking, esp. one that is not water or medicine

bev·y /'bevi/ n large group

be·wail /bɪ'weɪl/ vt fml express sorrow for

be·ware /bɪ'weəʳ/ vi/t (used in giving orders) Be careful!: Beware of the dog.

be·wil·der /bɪ'wɪldəʳ/ vt confuse: a bewildering mass of detail

be·witch /bɪ'wɪtʃ/ vt 1 use magic on 2 charm: a bewitching smile

be·yond /bɪ'jɒnd||bɪ'jɑːnd/ prep 1 on the further side of: beyond the mountains 2 outside the limits of; more than: beyond belief 3 **beyond me** too hard for me to understand ♦ adv further: fly to Cairo and beyond — see also BACK OF BEYOND

bi·as /'baɪəs/ n [C;U] fixed unfair opinion; PREJUDICE ♦ vt -s- or -ss- cause to form fixed opinions: a biased judgment

bib /bɪb/ n 1 piece of cloth or plastic tied under a child's chin 2 top part of an APRON

Bi·ble /'baɪbəl/ n holy book of the Christians and Jews: (fig.) This dictionary is my bible. **biblical** /'bɪblɪkəl/ adj

bib·li·og·ra·phy /,bɪbli'ɒɡrəfi||-'ɑːɡ-/ n list of writings on a subject **–pher** n person who writes such a list

bi·car·bon·ate /baɪ'kɑːbənɪt, -neɪt||-'kɑːr-/ n [U] chemical used in baking and as a medicine

bi·cen·te·na·ry /,baɪsen'tiːnəri||-'tenəri, -'sentəneri/ esp. BrE || **bicentennial** /,baɪsen'teniəl/ esp. AmE n 200th ANNIVERSARY **bicentenary** adj

bi·ceps /'baɪseps/ n **biceps** muscle of the upper arm

bick·er /'bɪkəʳ/ vi quarrel about small matters

bi·cy·cle /'baɪsɪkəl/ n 2-wheeled vehicle ridden by pushing its PEDALs **bicycle** vi

bid[1] /bɪd/ *vi/t* **bid 1** offer (a price) at a sale **2** (in card games) declare what one intends to win ♦ *n* **1** amount that is bid **2** attempt: *a rescue bid* ~**der** *n*

bid[2] *vt* **bade** /bæd, beɪd/ *or* **bid**, **bidden** /'bɪdn/ *or* **bid**; *pres. p.* **bidding** *lit* order: *She bade him come.* ~**ding** *n* [U]

bide /baɪd/ *vt* **bide one's time** wait till the right moment

bi-en-ni-al /baɪ'eniəl/ *adj* happening once every 2 years

bier /bɪəʳ/ *n* movable table for a COFFIN

bi-fo-cals /baɪ'fəʊkəlz‖'baɪfəʊ-/ [P] glasses made in 2 parts, suitable both for looking at distant objects and for reading **bifocal** *adj*

big /bɪg/ *adj* **-gg- 1** of more than average size, importance, etc: *big ears* | *a big decision* **2** generous: *big hearted* **3** *infml* very popular

big-a-my /'bɪgəmi/ *n* [U] being married to 2 people at the same time **-mist** *n* **-mous** *adj*

big game /ˌ· '·/ *n* [U] lions, elephants, etc., hunted for sport

big-head /'bɪghed/ *n infml* CONCEITED person

big-ot /'bɪgət/ *n* person who will not change an unreasonable opinion ~**ry** *n* [U] behaviour typical of a bigot

big shot /ˌ· '·/ *also* **big noise** — *n* person of great importance or influence

big-wig /'bɪgwɪg/ *n infml* important person

bi-jou /'biːʒuː/ *adj* (esp. of a building) small and pretty

bike /baɪk/ *n*, *vi* BICYCLE

bi-ki-ni /bɪ'kiːni/ *n* woman's small 2-piece swimming costume

bi-lat-er-al /baɪ'lætərəl/ *adj* with 2 sides or 2 groups: *a bilateral agreement*

bile /baɪl/ *n* [U] **1** liquid formed in the LIVER **2** bad temper

bilge /bɪldʒ/ *n* **1** ship's bottom, with dirty water in it **2** *infml* foolish talk

bi-lin-gual /baɪ'lɪŋgwəl/ *adj* using 2 languages

bil-i-ous /'bɪliəs/ *adj* sick because food is not DIGESTed properly

bill[1] /bɪl/ *n* **1** list of things that must be paid for **2** plan for a future law **3** *AmE* piece of paper money **4** printed notice **5 fill the bill** be suitable **6 foot the bill** pay and take responsibility (for) ♦ *vt* **1** send a bill to **2** advertise in printed notices **3 bill and coo** (of lovers) kiss and speak softly to each other

bill[2] *n* bird's beak

bil-let /'bɪlɪt/ *n* private home where soldiers are put to live ♦ *vt* put in billets

bill-fold /'bɪlfəʊld/ *n AmE* for WALLET

bil-liards /'bɪljədz‖-ərdz/ *n* [U] game played on a table, with balls and long sticks

bil-lion /'bɪljən/ *determiner*, *n* **billion** *or* **billions 1** one thousand million **2** *BrE* one million million ~**th** *determiner*, *n*, *adv*

bil-low /'bɪləʊ/ *n* rolling mass of smoke, etc., like a large wave **billow** *vi*

billy goat /'··· '·/ *n* male goat

bin /bɪn/ *n* large container for storing things, or for waste

bi-na-ry /'baɪnəri/ *adj* **1** double **2** using only 0 and 1 as a base: *the binary scale*

bind /baɪnd/ *v* **bound** /baʊnd/ **1** *vt* tie up: *bind the prisoner's arms* | *bind up a wound* | (fig.) *bound together by friendship* **2** *vt* fasten (a book) into its cover **3** *vi/t* (cause) to stick together in a mass **4** *vt* cause to obey, esp. by a law or a promise: *a binding agreement* | *He felt bound to tell her.* ~**er** *n* **1** person or thing that binds books **2** removable cover for holding sheets of papers, etc. ~**ing** *n* book cover

binge /bɪndʒ/ *n infml* period of drinking and wild behaviour

bin-go /'bɪŋgəʊ/ *n* [U] **1** game played for money, by covering numbered squares on a card **2** *infml* (an expression of pleasure)

bi-noc-u-lars /bɪ'nɒkjʊləz, baɪ-‖-'nɑːkjʊlərz/ *n* [P] pair of glasses like short TELESCOPEs for both eyes

bio-chem-is-try /ˌbaɪəʊ'kemɪstri/ *n* [U] chemistry of living things

bio-da-ta /ˌbaɪəʊ'deɪtə/ *n AmE* for CURRICULUM VITAE

bio-de-gra-da-ble /ˌbaɪəʊdɪ'greɪdəbəl/ *adj* able to be made harmless by the chemical action of bacteria, etc.

bi-og-ra-phy /baɪ'ɒgrəfi‖-'ɑːg-/ *n* written account of someone's life **-pher** *n* person who writes this **-phical** /ˌbaɪə'græfɪkəl/ *adj*

bi-ol-o-gy /baɪ'ɒlədʒi‖-'ɑːl-/ *n* [U] scientific study of living things **-gist** *n* **-gical** /ˌbaɪə'lɒdʒɪkəl‖-'lɑː-/ *adj*

bi-on-ic /baɪ'ɒnɪk‖-'ɑːn-/ *adj* having more than human strength, speed, etc.

bi-o-pic /'baɪəʊˌpɪk/ *n* biographical film

bi-op-sy /'baɪɒpsi‖-ɑːp-/ *n* removal of material from a living body to test it for possible disease

bio-tech-nol-o-gy /ˌbaɪəʊtek'nɒlədʒi‖-'nɑː-/ *n* [U] use of living cells, bacteria, etc., in industry

bi-ped /'baɪped/ *n* 2-footed creature

bi-plane /'baɪpleɪn/ *n* aircraft with 2 pairs of wings

birch /bɜːtʃ‖bɜːrtʃ/ *n* **1** tree with smooth wood and thin branches **2** rod made from this wood, used for punishing

bird /bɜːd‖bɜrd/ n 1 [C] creature with wings and feathers that can fly 2 [C] sl woman 3 [the + S] rude noise made as sign of disapproval 4 [U] BrE sl period of time spent in prison 5 **birds of a feather** people of the same kind — see also EARLY BIRD

bird's-eye view /ˌ· '·/ n view seen from above, like a map

bi-ro /'baɪərəʊ/ n **biros** tdmk for BALLPOINT

birth /bɜːθ‖bɜrθ/ n 1 [C;U] act, time, or process of being born: She gave birth to a fine baby. 2 [U] family origin: French by birth

birth con·trol /'· ·ˌ·/ n [U] CONTRACEPTION

birth-day /'bɜːθdeɪ‖'bɜr-/ n ANNIVERSARY of the day one was born

birth-mark /'bɜːθmɑːk‖'bɜrθmɑrk/ n mark on the skin at birth

birth-rate /'bɜːθreɪt‖'bɜr-/ n number of births during a particular time

birth-right /'bɜːθraɪt‖'bɜr-/ n something that belongs to someone because of the family or nation they were born into

bis-cuit /'bɪskɪt/ n 1 flat thin dry cake 2 AmE for SCONE 3 **take the biscuit** be very surprising

bi-sect /baɪ'sekt‖'baɪsekt/ vt divide into 2

bi-sex-u-al /baɪ'sekʃuəl/ adj sexually attracted to people of both sexes

bish-op /'bɪʃəp/ n 1 Christian priest of high rank 2 piece in CHESS ~**ric** /'bɪʃəprɪk/ n DIOCESE

bi-son /'baɪsən/ n **bisons** or **bison** large wild hairy cowlike animal

bis-tro /'biːstrəʊ/ n small BAR (4) or restaurant

bit¹ /bɪt/ v past t. of BITE

bit² n 1 small piece: bits of paper/of news 2 a short time: We walked around for a bit. 3 **a bit** rather: I'm a bit tired. 4 **bit by bit** gradually 5 **do one's bit** do one's share of work 6 **every bit as** quite as; no less: She's every bit as good as you are. 7 **not a bit of it** not at all

bit³ n single unit of computer information

bit⁴ n part of a BRIDLE that goes inside the horse's mouth

bitch /bɪtʃ/ n 1 female dog 2 derog unpleasant woman ♦ vi sl 1 complain continually 2 make nasty or hurtful remarks about others ~**y** adj making nasty remarks about people

bite /baɪt/ v **bit** /bɪt/, **bitten** /'bɪtn/ 1 vi/t cut with the teeth 2 vi/t (of snakes and insects) sting 3 vi (of fish) accept food on a hook 4 vi take firm hold: The wheels won't bite on the ice. 5 have or show an effect: The new taxes

are beginning to bite. 6 **bite off more than one can chew** attempt too much 7 **bite the bullet** suffer bravely 8 **bite the dust** infml be killed or defeated ♦ n 1 [C] piece removed by biting 2 [C;U] wound made by biting 3 [S] something to eat 4 [U;S] sharpness; bitterness **biting** adj painful: biting wind/remarks

bit-ter /'bɪtəʳ/ adj 1 not sweet; tasting like beer or black coffee 2 very cold: a bitter wind 3 causing grief: bitter disappointment 4 full of hate: bitter enemies 5 **to the bitter end** to the end in spite of all unpleasant difficulties ♦ n [U] BrE bitter beer —**ly** adv —**ness** n

bit-ter-sweet /ˌbɪtə'swiːt‖-tər-/ adj pleasant, but mixed with sadness

bi-tu-men /'bɪtjʊmən‖bə'tuː-/ n [U] sticky black substance used esp. in road-making

biv-ou-ac /'bɪvu-æk/ n camp without tents ♦ vi -**ck**- spend the night in a bivouac

bi-zarre /bə'zɑːʳ/ adj very strange ~**ly** adv

blab /blæb/ vi -**bb**- sl tell a secret

black /blæk/ adj 1 of the colour of night: Your hands are black. (= very dirty) 2 of a dark-skinned race, esp. of the Negro race 3 (of coffee) without milk 4 very bad; hopeless 5 very angry: a black look 6 (of humour) funny about unpleasant or dangerous people or events: black humour ♦ n 1 [U] black colour 2 [C] black person ♦ vt 1 make black 2 (of a British trade union) refuse to work with: Black their cargo. ~**ly** adv 1 angrily 2 sadly ~**ness** n [U]

black-ball /'blækbɔːl/ vt vote against (someone who wants to join a club)

black belt /ˌ· '·/ n (person who holds) a high rank in JUDO, KARATE, etc.

black-board /'blækbɔːd‖-ɔrd/ n board used in schools for writing on

black box /ˌ· '·/ n apparatus fitted to an aircraft to record information about an accident

black-cur-rant /ˌblæk'kʌrənt‖-'kɜr-/ n garden bush with small blue-black berries

black e-con-o-my /ˌ· ·'···/ n [the + S] business activity carried on unofficially, esp. to avoid taxation

black-en /'blækən/ vi/t make or become black: (fig.) They blackened his character by spreading lies.

black eye /ˌ· '·/ n dark skin round the eye, from being hit

black-guard /'blægɑːd, -əd‖-ərd, -ɑrd/ n SCOUNDREL

black-head /'blækhed/ n spot on the skin with a black top

black hole /ˌ· ˈ·/ n area in outer space into which everything is pulled, even light itself

black ice /ˌ· ˈ·/ n [U] ice that cannot be seen, on a road

black·leg /ˈblækleg/ n BrE person who works when others are on STRIKE² (1)

black·list /ˈblæk͵lɪst/ n list of people to be avoided or punished **blacklist** vt

black mag·ic /ˌ· ˈ··/ n magic used for evil purposes

black·mail /ˈblækmeɪl/ n [U] 1 getting money by threatening to make known unpleasant facts 2 influencing of someone's actions by threats, causing anxiety, etc.: He accused his mother of using emotional blackmail to stop him leaving home. ♦ **black·mail** vt —er n

black mar·ket /ˌ· ··◁/ n [S] unlawful buying and selling of goods, etc.: We bought our dollars on the black market. ~eer n /ˌ· ···◁/

black·out /ˈblækaʊt/ n 1 darkness, ordered by the government during wartime or caused by electrical failure 2 short loss of consciousness 3 intentional prevention of reporting: a news blackout **black out** vi/t

black pow·er /ˌ· ˈ··/ n [S] movement for the political and economic power of black people

black sheep /ˌ· ˈ·/ n family member who brings shame on it

black·smith /ˈblæk͵smɪθ/ n metalworker who makes iron things

black spot /ˈ· ·/ n part of a road where many accidents have happened

blad·der /ˈblædəʳ/ n 1 skin bag inside the body, where waste liquid collects 2 any bag that can be filled with air or liquid

blade /bleɪd/ n 1 sharp cutting part of a knife, etc. 2 flat part of an OAR, PROPELLER, or BAT¹ (1) 3 long narrow leaf: blades of grass

blame /bleɪm/ vt 1 consider responsible for something bad 2 **be to blame** be guilty ♦ n [U] responsibility for something bad ~less adj free from guilt ~worthy adj guilty

blanch /blɑːntʃ‖blæntʃ/ vi/t make or become white

blanc·mange /bləˈmɒnʒ, -ˈmɒndʒ‖ -ˈmɑː-/ n [U] sweet dish made of milk, etc.

bland /blænd/ adj 1 (of food) without much taste 2 (of people or their behaviour) showing no strong feelings or opinions, esp. so as to avoid giving offence ~ly adv ~ness n [U]

blan·dish·ments /ˈblændɪʃmənts/ n [P] FLATTERY

blank¹ /blæŋk/ adj 1 without writing 2 empty or expressionless: My mind

went blank. ~ly adv: He looked at me blankly. ~ness n [U]

blank² n 1 empty space 2 CARTRIDGE with no bullet in it 3 **draw a blank** be unsuccessful

blank cheque BrE ‖ **blank check** AmE /ˌ· ˈ·/ n 1 cheque that is signed, but with the amount left blank 2 complete freedom to do what one wants

blan·ket /ˈblæŋkɪt/ n thick bed covering: (fig.) A blanket of snow covered the hills. — see also WET BLANKET ♦ vt cover as if with a blanket ♦ adj including all cases: a blanket rule

blank verse /ˌ· ˈ·/ n [U] poetry that does not rhyme

blare /bleəʳ/ vi/t make the loud noise of a horn **blare** n [S]

bla·sé /ˈblɑːzeɪ‖blɑːˈzeɪ/ adj seeming not to be concerned or excited about something, or about things in general

blas·phe·my /ˈblæsfɨmi/ n [C;U] bad language about God and holy things —mous adj **blaspheme** /blæsˈfiːm/ vi

blast¹ /blɑːst‖blæst/ n 1 strong air movement 2 rush of air from an explosion 3 sound of a brass wind instrument 4 **at full blast** as hard as possible

blast² v 1 vi/t break up (rock, etc.) with explosives 2 vt DAMN

blast off phr vi (of a spacecraft) leave the ground **blast-off** /ˈ· ·/ n [U]

blast fur·nace /ˈ· ͵·/ n FURNACE for separating iron from the rock in which it is found

bla·tant /ˈbleɪtənt/ adj too noticeable; shameless ~ly adv —tancy n [U]

blaze /bleɪz/ n 1 [S] bright flame: (fig.) a sudden blaze of anger 2 [C] big dangerous fire 3 [C] white mark ♦ vi 1 burn or shine brightly 2 spread news about: The news was blazed across the front page. 3 **blaze a trail** lead the way

blaz·er /ˈbleɪzəʳ/ n loose-fitting JACKET, sometimes with the sign of a school, etc., on it

bleach /bliːtʃ/ vi/t make or become white or pale ♦ n [U] chemical used for bleaching cloth

bleach·ers /ˈbliːtʃəz‖-ərz/ n [the + P] AmE cheap unroofed seats for watching a BASEBALL game

bleak /bliːk/ adj cold and cheerless: bleak weather | (fig.) bleak prospects ~ly adv ~ness n [U]

blear·y /ˈblɪəri/ adj (of eyes) red and tired —ily adv —iness n [U]

bleat /bliːt/ vi, n (make) the sound of a sheep or goat

bleed /bliːd/ v bled /bled/ 1 vi lose blood 2 vt draw blood from, as doctors once did 3 vt draw off liquid or air from 4 **bleed someone dry/white** take all someone's money, esp. gradually

bleep /bliːp/ n repeated high sound made by a machine (a **bleeper**) to attract attention ♦ vi/t make, or call someone with, this sound

blem·ish /ˈblemɪʃ/ n mark, etc., that spoils perfection **blemish** vt

blench /blentʃ/ vi RECOIL

blend /blend/ vi/t mix together ♦ n mixture ~**er** kitchen mixing machine **blend in** phr vi go together well

bless /bles/ vt **blessed** or **blest** /blest/ 1 ask God's favour for 2 make holy 3 **be blessed with** be lucky enough to have ~**ed** /ˈblesɪd/ adj 1 holy 2 desirable 3 infml (used to give force to expressions of annoyance)

bless·ing /ˈblesɪŋ/ n 1 [C] God's favour 2 [C] something one is glad of 3 [U] approval

blew /bluː/ past t. of BLOW[1]

blight /blaɪt/ n 1 [U] disease of plants 2 [C] something that spoils 3 [U] condition of ugliness, disorder, and decay **blight** vt: (fig.) blighted hopes

blight·er /ˈblaɪtər/ n BrE sl BASTARD (2,3): You lucky blighter!

blind /blaɪnd/ adj 1 unable to see 2 unwilling to recognize: blind to her faults 3 without reason or purpose: blind panic 4 slightest: He didn't take a blind bit of notice. 5 **turn a blind eye (to)** pretend not to see or notice (something, esp. something illegal) ♦ vt 1 make unable to see or understand 2 **blind with science** confuse or fill with admiration by a show of detailed or specialist knowledge ~**ly** adv ~**ness** n [U]

blind al·ley /ˌ· ˈ··/ n narrow street with no way out

blind drunk /ˌ· ˈ·/ adj extremely drunk

blind·ers /ˈblaɪndəz‖-ərz/ n [P] AmE for BLINKERS

blind·fold /ˈblaɪndfəʊld/ vt cover (the eyes) with a piece of cloth ♦ n piece of material to cover the eyes ♦ adv with the eyes covered: I could do it blindfold.

blind spot /ˈ· ·/ 1 part of an area that cannot easily be seen 2 something one is never able to understand

blink /blɪŋk/ vi/t shut and open (the eyes) quickly: (fig.) The lights blinked in the distance. **blink** n 1 act of blinking 2 **on the blink** not working properly

blink·ers /ˈblɪŋkəz‖-ərz/ n [P] 1 leather pieces fixed to prevent a horse from seeing sideways 2 inability to see or understand **blinkered** adj

bliss /blɪs/ n [U] complete happiness ~**ful** adj ~**fully** adv

blis·ter /ˈblɪstər/ n 1 watery swelling under the skin 2 swelling like this on a rubber tyre, painted wood, etc. ♦ vi/t form blisters ~**ing** adj 1 very hot 2 very angry and intended to hurt: a blistering attack

blithe /blaɪð/ adj free from care ~**ly** adv

blitz /blɪts/ n 1 sudden violent attack, esp. from the air 2 period of great activity for some special purpose: an advertising blitz

bliz·zard /ˈblɪzəd‖-ərd/ n severe snowstorm

bloat·ed /ˈbləʊtɪd/ adj unpleasantly swollen

blob /blɒb‖blɑːb/ n drop of liquid or small round mass

bloc /blɒk‖blɑːk/ n group of people, nations, etc., acting as a unit — see also EN BLOC

block /blɒk‖blɑːk/ n 1 solid piece of material: a block of wood/ice 2 large building divided into parts: an office block 3 distance between one street and the next: The shop is 4 blocks away. 4 group of things considered together: a block of theatre seats 5 blockage ♦ vt 1 prevent movement through 2 shut off from view 3 prevent the success of: to block legislation

block·ade /blɒˈkeɪd‖blɑː-/ n surrounding of a place, by ships or soldiers, to stop people or goods from going in or out: to raise/lift (= end) a blockade ♦ vt surround in this way

block·age /ˈblɒkɪdʒ‖ˈblɑː-/ n something that stops movement; OBSTRUCTION: a blockage in the pipe

block·bust·er /ˈblɒk,bʌstər‖ˈblɑːk-/ n something very big, effective, or successful

block vote /ˌ· ˈ·/ n single vote made by a representative of a large group, e.g. a trade union, being regarded as representing all the group members

bloke /bləʊk/ n BrE infml man

blond /blɒnd‖blɑːnd/ adj 1 (of hair) light-coloured; yellow 2 also **blonde** fem. — having blond hair **blonde** /blɒnd‖blɑːnd/ n blonde woman

blood /blʌd/ n 1 [U] red liquid that flows through the body: blood donors 2 [U] family relationship: people of noble blood 3 [C] fashionable young man 4 **in cold blood** cruelly and on purpose 5 **make someone's blood boil** make someone very angry 6 **make someone's blood run cold** frighten someone ~**less** adj without fighting ~**y** adj 1 bleeding 2 (used for giving force to a remark): You bloody fool! ~**ily** adv

blood-and-thun·der /ˌ· · ˈ··/ adj (of a film, story, etc.) full of exciting action and meaningless violence

blood·bath /ˈblʌdbɑːθ‖-bæθ/ n merciless killing; MASSACRE

blood broth·er /ˌ· ˈ··/ n one of two or more men who have promised complete loyalty to one another

blood-cur-dling /'blʌd,kɜːdlɪŋ‖-ɜːr-/ adj very frightening

blood group /'· ·/ n class of human blood

blood-hound /'blʌdhaʊnd/ n large dog that tracks people and animals

blood poi-son-ing /'· ,···/n [U] condition in which an infection spreads from a part of the body through the BLOODSTREAM

blood pres-sure /'· ,··/n [C;U] measurable force with which blood flows through the BLOODSTREAM

blood-shed /'blʌdʃed/ n [U] killing, usu. in fighting

blood-shot /'blʌdʃɒt‖-ʃɑːt/ adj (of the eyes) red

blood sport /'· ·/ n killing of birds and animals for pleasure

blood-stain /'blʌdsteɪn/ n spot of blood ~ed adj

blood-stream /'blʌdstriːm/ n flow of blood round the body

blood-suck-er /'blʌd,sʌkəʳ/ n 1 creature that bites and then sucks blood from the wound 2 person who tries to get as much money as possible from other people

blood-thirst-y /'blʌd,θɜːstiǁ-ɜːr-/ adj eager to kill; too interested in violence

bloody-mind-ed /,·· '··◂/ adj unhelpful; unreasonable ~ness n [U]

bloom /bluːm/ n 1 flower 2 **in the bloom of** at the best time of/for ♦ vi 1 produce flowers 2 show as healthy colour 3 BLOSSOM (2)

bloom-er /'bluːməʳ/n BrE infml a big mistake

bloom-ers /'bluːməz‖-ərz/ n [P] women's short loose trousers gathered at the knee

blos-som /'blɒsəm‖'blɑː-/ n 1 flower of a tree or bush 2 **in blossom** bearing flowers ♦ vi 1 produce blossoms 2 develop favourably

blot[1] /blɒt‖blɑːt/ n 1 spot, esp. of ink 2 shameful fault: a blot on her character 3 something ugly: a blot on the landscape

blot[2] vt -tt- 1 make blots on 2 dry up (ink) 3 **blot one's copybook** spoil one's good record

blot out phr vt cover; hide: Clouds blotted out the sun.

blotch /blɒtʃ‖blɑːtʃ/ n large spot or mark ~y adj

blot-ter /'blɒtəʳ‖'blɑː-/ n large piece of BLOTTING PAPER

blotting pa-per /'·· ,··/n [U] thick soft paper used to dry wet ink after writing

blouse /blaʊz‖blaʊs/ n woman's shirt

blow[1] /bləʊ/ v blew /bluː/, blown /bləʊn/ 1 vi/t send out air; move by the force of air: The wind blew the tree down. | He blew the candle out. 2 vi/t sound made by blowing: to blow a trumpet 3 vt sl clean (one's nose) by blowing through it 4 vi/t melt (an electrical FUSE) 5 vt sl lose (a favourable chance) as the result of foolishness 6 vt infml spend (money) freely 7 vi sl leave quickly 8 vt infml DAMN: Well, I'm blowed! 9 **blow hot and cold (about)** be favourable (to) at one moment and unfavourable (at) at the next 10 **blow one's own trumpet/horn** infml praise oneself 11 **blow one's top/stack** sl explode with anger 12 **blow someone a kiss** kiss one's hand, then wave or blow over it towards someone 13 **blow someone's brains out** infml kill someone by a shot through the head 14 **blow someone's mind** sl fill someone with wonder 15 **blow the whistle on** sl cause something undesirable to stop, by bringing it to the attention of esp. the public

blow over phr vi (of a storm) stop blowing; (fig.) The scandal will soon blow over.

blow up phr v 1 vi/t explode 2 vt fill with air: blow up the tyres 3 enlarge (a photograph); (fig.) The affair was blown up by the newspapers. 4 (of bad weather) start blowing: There's a storm blowing up.

blow[2] n act of blowing: Give your nose a good blow.

blow[3] n 1 hard stroke with the hand or a weapon 2 sudden misfortune 3 **come to blows** start to fight — see also BODY BLOW

blow-by-blow /,·· '··◂/ adj with full details, given in the order in which they happened

blow-er /'bləʊəʳ/ n 1 apparatus for producing a current of air or gas 2 BrE infml telephone

blow-lamp /'bləʊlæmp/ n also **blow-torch** /-tɔːtʃ‖ -tɔːrtʃ/ — lamp that blows a flame (e.g. for burning off paint)

blown /bləʊn/ past p. of BLOW[1]

blow-out /'bləʊaʊt/ n 1 very big meal 2 bursting of a container (esp. a tyre)

blub-ber[1] /'blʌbəʳ/n [U] fat of sea creatures, esp. WHALEs

blubber[2] vi weep noisily

blud-geon /'blʌdʒən/ vt 1 hit with something heavy 2 force to do something, by threats

blue /bluː/ adj 1 of the colour of the clear sky 2 sad; DEPRESSED 3 concerned with sex; improper: blue films ♦ n [U] 1 blue colour 2 **out of the blue** unexpectedly **blues** n 1 [S;U] slow sad song or music from the southern US 2 [U] sadness

blue-blooded /ˌ· '··◁/ adj of noble birth

blue-bot-tle /ˈbluːˌbɒtl‖-bɑːtl/ n large blue-green fly

blue chip /ˌ· '·/n, adj (an industrial share) that is expensive and in which people have confidence

blue-col-lar /ˌ· '··◁/ adj of or concerning workers who do hard or dirty work with their hands

blue-eyed boy /ˈ· · ·/n infml, esp. BrE someone's favourite (male) person

blue moon /ˌ· '·/n [S] **once in a blue moon** infml almost never

blue murder /ˌ· '··/n scream/shout **blue murder** infml complain very loudly

blue-print /ˈbluːˌprɪnt/ n copy of a plan for making or building something: (fig.) a blueprint for the reforms

blue-sky /ˌ· '·◁/ adj done in order to test ideas, rather than for any particular practical purpose

blue-stock-ing /ˈbluːˌstɒkɪŋ‖-ˌstɑː-/ n woman thought to be too highly educated

bluff[1] /blʌf/ vi **1** deceive someone by pretending to be stronger or cleverer than one is: They say they'll blow up the place, but they're only bluffing. **2 bluff it out** escape trouble by continuing a deception **bluff** n [S;U] **1** action of bluffing **2 call someone's bluff** tell someone to do what they threaten to do

bluff[2] adj (of a person) rough and cheerful

blun-der /ˈblʌndəʳ/ n stupid mistake ♦ vi **1** make a blunder **2** move awkwardly ~**er** n

blunt /blʌnt/ adj **1** not sharp: a blunt pencil **2** not trying to be polite ♦ vt make less sharp ~**ly** adv roughly and plainly ~**ness** n [U]

blur /blɜːʳ/ n [S] something whose shape is not clearly seen ♦ vt -**rr**- make hard to see: (fig.) to blur a distinction

blurb /blɜːb‖blɜːrb/ n short description of the contents of a book

blurt /blɜːt‖blɜːrt/ v **blurt out** phr vt say suddenly without thinking

blush /blʌʃ/ vi become red in the face, from shame **blush** n — see also **spare someone's blushes** (SPARE) ~**ingly** adv

blus-ter /ˈblʌstəʳ/ vi **1** speak roughly and noisily **2** (of wind) blow roughly **bluster** n [U] ~**y** adj windy

B-movie /ˈbiː ˌmuːvi/ n cheaply made cinema film not considered to be of very good quality

BO /ˌbiː 'əʊ/ n [U] body odour; unpleasant smell from a person's body

board /bɔːd‖bɔːrd/ n **1** [C] flat piece of wood, etc.: floorboards | a notice board | a chessboard **2** BLACKBOARD **3**

(cost of) meals: board and lodging **4** committee of people controlling something **5 above board** completely open and honest **6 across the board** including all groups or members, as in an industry: a wage increase of £10 a week across the board **7 go by the board** (of plans) come to no result **8 on board** on a ship or public vehicle **9 sweep the board** win nearly everything ♦ v **1** vt cover with boards **2** vt go on board a ship, etc. **3** vi/t get or supply meals and lodging for payment: to board with a friend ~**er** n person who pays to live and receive meals somewhere

boarding card /ˈ·· ·/ n official card to be given up when one enters an aircraft

board-ing-house /ˈbɔːdɪŋhaʊs‖ˈbɔːr-/ n private lodging house that supplies meals

boarding school /ˈ·· ·/n [C;U] school at which children live instead of going there daily from home

boast /bəʊst/ v **1** vi talk too proudly **2** vt have (a cause for pride): This computer boasts many ingenious features. ♦ n **1** act of boasting **2** cause for pride ~**ful** adj full of self-praise

boat /bəʊt/ n **1** water vehicle, esp. smaller than a ship — see also **in the same boat** (SAME[1]) ♦ vi go in a boat, esp. for pleasure

boat-er /ˈbəʊtəʳ/n stiff hat made of STRAW

boat-swain /ˈbəʊsən/ n chief seaman on a ship

boat-train /ˈ· ·/n train that takes people to or from ships in port

bob[1] /bɒb‖bɑːb/ vi -**bb**- move quickly up and down: a boat bobbing on the water

bob[2] vt cut (a woman's hair) to shoulder-length or shorter ♦ n a bobbed haircut

bob-bin /ˈbɒbɪn‖ˈbɑː-/ n small roller for thread

bob-ble /ˈbɒbəl‖ˈbɑː-/ n ball of wool, etc., used for decoration

bob-by /ˈbɒbi‖ˈbɑːbi/ n BrE infml policeman

bobby socks, bobby sox /ˈ·· ˌ·/n [P] AmE girl's socks reaching above the ankle

bob-sleigh /ˈbɒbsleɪ‖ˈbɑːb-/ also **bobsled** /-sled/ — vi, n (ride in) a small vehicle that runs on metal blades, used for sliding down snowy slopes

bode /bəʊd/ vi **bode well/ill** be a good/bad sign for the future

bod-ice /ˈbɒdɪs‖ˈbɑː-/ n top part of a woman's dress

bod-i-ly /ˈbɒdɪli‖ˈbɑː-/ adj of the human body; PHYSICAL ♦ adv taking hold of the whole body

bod·y /'bɒdi‖'bɑːdi/ n 1 person or animal's whole physical structure, alive or dead 2 this without the head or limbs 3 main part of something: *The important news comes in the body of the letter.* 4 group of people: *an elected body* 5 object; piece of matter: *The sun is a heavenly body.* 6 large amount: *a body of water such as a lake* 7 **keep body and soul together** remain alive (by getting money for food)

body blow /'·· ·/ n 1 (in boxing BOX²) blow that falls below the breast and above the waist 2 a serious SETBACK

bod·y·guard /'bɒdigɑːd‖'bɑːdigɑːrd/ n man or group of men guarding someone important

bod·y·work /'bɒdiwɜːk‖'bɑːdiwɜːrk/ n [U] outside parts of a motor vehicle

bog¹ /bɒg‖bɑːg, bɔːg/ n [C;U] 1 area of soft wet ground 2 *BrE sl* LAVATORY ~**gy** adj

bog² v **bog down** phr vi/t -**gg**- sink into a bog: (fig.) *to get bogged down in one's work*

bo·gey /'bəʊgi/ n imaginary evil spirit

bog·gle /'bɒgəl‖'bɑː-/ vi pause in shocked surprise

bo·gus /'bəʊgəs/ adj pretended; false

bo·he·mi·an /bəʊ'hiːmiən, bə-/ adj not following accepted social customs

boil¹ /bɔɪl/ vi/t 1 bring or come to the temperature at which a liquid changes to gas: *100°C is the boiling point of water.* 2 cook at this temperature: *to boil eggs* 3 **boil dry** boil till no water remains ♦ n [S]: *Bring the soup to the boil.*

boil away phr vi disappear by boiling

boil down to phr vt be no more than: *It all boils down to a question of money.*

boil over phr vi 1 (of a boiling liquid) flow over the sides of the container 2 get out of control (and develop into): *The conflict boiled over into war.*

boil up phr v 1 vt make hot and cook 2 vi reach a dangerous level

boil² n painful infected swelling under the skin

boil·er /'bɔɪlər/ n large container for boiling water, e.g. to provide heating in a house

boiler suit /'·· ·/ n OVERALLS

bois·ter·ous /'bɔɪstərəs/ adj noisily cheerful ~**ly** adv

bold /bəʊld/ adj 1 daring; courageous 2 without respect or shame 3 clearly marked: *a bold drawing* ~**ly** adv ~**ness** n [U]

bol·lard /'bɒləd‖'bɑːlərd/ n short thick post, in the street or for tying boats to

bol·shy /'bɒlʃi‖'bɔʊl-/ adj infml (of a person or their behaviour) showing an unwillingness to help in a common aim

bol·ster¹ /'bəʊlstər/ n long PILLOW

bolster² v **bolster up** phr vt encourage; support

bolt¹ /bəʊlt/ n 1 bar that fastens a door or window 2 screw used with a NUT (2) to hold things together 3 THUNDERBOLT 4 **a bolt from the blue** something unexpected and unpleasant — see also NUTS AND BOLTS

bolt² v 1 vt fasten with a BOLT¹ (1) 2 vi run away suddenly 3 vt swallow (food) hastily ♦ n [S] 1 act of running away 2 **make a bolt for it** run away ♦ adv **bolt upright** straight and stiff

bolt-hole /'bəʊlthəʊl/ n place one can escape to

bomb /bɒm‖bɑːm/ n 1 [C] container filled with explosive 2 [the + S] the NUCLEAR bomb 3 **(go) like a bomb** (go) very well 4 **spend/cost a bomb** spend/cost a lot of money ♦ 1 vt attack with bombs 2 vi infml move quickly 3 vi AmE infml fail ~**er** n 1 aircraft that drops bombs 2 person who throws bombs

bom·bard /bɒm'bɑːd‖bɑːm'bɑːrd/ vt attack heavily with gunfire: (fig.) *He was bombarded with questions.* ~**ment** n [C;U]

bom·bas·tic /bɒm'bæstɪk‖bɑːm-/ adj using high-sounding meaningless words ~**ically** /-kli/ adv

bomb·shell /'bɒmʃel‖'bɑːm-/ n great shock

bo·na fi·de /,bəʊnə 'faɪdi◂‖'bəʊnə faɪd/ adj real

bo·nan·za /bə'nænzə, bəʊ-/ n something very profitable

bond /bɒnd‖bɑːnd/ n 1 something that unites: *a bond of friendship* 2 written promise, esp. to pay back money with interest 3 state of being stuck together ♦ vt unite; stick **bonds** n [P] chains or ropes for tying someone up

bond·age /'bɒndɪdʒ‖'bɑːn-/ n [U] lit slavery

bone /bəʊn/ n [C;U] 1 any of the various hard parts of the body which are surrounded by flesh and skin 2 **cut to the bone** reduce as much as possible 3 **feel in one's bones** believe strongly though without proof 4 **have a bone to pick with someone** have something to complain about 5 **make no bones about** feel no doubt or shame about — see also BARE BONES, FUNNY BONE ♦ vt take bones out of (fish, etc.) ~**less** adj **bony** adj 1 very thin, showing the bones 2 (of food) full of bones

bone-dry /ˌ· ˈ·◂/ adj perfectly dry

bone-i-dle /ˌ· ˈ··◂/ adj very lazy

bon-fire /'bɒnfaɪəʳ‖'bɑːn-/ n large outdoor fire

bonk /bɒŋk‖bɑːŋk, bɔːŋk/ v 1 infml hit, usu. not very hard 2 vi/t sl have sex (with) ♦ n 1 infml hit 2 sl act of having sex

bon-net /'bɒnɪt‖'bɑː-/ n 1 round hat tied under the chin 2 BrE lid over the front of a car

bon-ny /'bɒni‖'bɑːni/ adj pretty and healthy

bo-nus /'bəʊnəs/ n 1 additional payment beyond what is usual 2 anything pleasant in addition to what is expected

boo /buː/ interj, n **boos** shout of disapproval ♦ vi/t shout 'boo'

boo-by /'buːbi/ n fool

booby prize /'·· ˌ·/n prize given for the worst performance in a competition

booby trap /'·· ˌ·/ n harmless-looking thing used for surprising people unpleasantly, such as a hidden bomb ♦ **booby-trap** vt **-pp-**

book¹ /bʊk/ n 1 set of sheets of paper fastened together, to be read or written in: *books on travel*|*a bookseller*|*bookshelves*|*a bookshop* 2 collection of matches, tickets, etc., fastened like a book 3 main division of the Bible or of a long poem 4 **a closed book** subject about which one knows very little 5 **by the book** according to the rules 6 **in someone's good/bad books** in favour/disfavour with someone 7 **throw the book at** (esp. of the police) make all possible charges against **books** n [P] business accounts

book² v 1 vi/t order (tickets, etc.) in advance: *to book a seat*|*a band* 2 vt write down a legal charge against: *booked for speeding* **~able** adj

book up phr vt keep (a place or time) for people who have made arrangements in advance

book-case /'bʊk-keɪs/ n piece of furniture to hold books

book club /'· ·/ club that offers books cheaply to its members

book-end /'bʊkend/ n support for a row of books

book-ing /'bʊkɪŋ/ n a case or act of BOOKing² (1): *Buy a ticket at the booking office.*

book-keep-ing /'bʊk,kiːpɪŋ/ n [U] keeping business accounts **-er** n

book-let /'bʊklɪt/ small thin book

book-mak-er /'bʊk,meɪkəʳ/ also **bookie** /'bʊki/ infml — n person who takes BETs (2) on races

book-mark /'bʊkmɑːk‖-ɑːrk/ n something put in a book to keep one's place

book-stall /'bʊkstɔːl/ n table or open hut where books and magazines are sold

book-worm /'bʊkwɜːm‖-ɜːrm/ n person who loves reading

boom¹ /buːm/ vi 1 make a deep hollow sound 2 grow rapidly: *Business is booming.* **boom** n: *a boom in exports*

boom² n 1 long pole to which a sail is attached 2 heavy chain across a river to stop logs floating down or to prevent ships sailing up 3 long pole on the end of which a camera or MICROPHONE can be moved about

boo-mer-ang /'buːməræŋ/ n curved stick which makes a circle and comes back when thrown ♦ vi have the opposite effect to that intended

boon /buːn/ n fml comfort; help

boon-docks /'buːndɒks‖-dɑːks/ n [the + P] AmE infml rough country area where few people live

boor /bʊəʳ/ n rude person **~ish** adj **~ishly** adv

boost /buːst/ vt raise; increase **boost** n **~er** 1 something that boosts 2 additional amount of a drug

boot¹ /buːt/ n 1 heavy shoe that comes up over the ankle 2 BrE space at the back of a car for boxes, etc. 3 **give/get the boot** infml dismiss/be dismissed from a job 4 **put the boot in** sl kick someone 5 **too big for one's boots** too proud

boot² vt infml kick

boot out phr vt infml send away rudely and sometimes with force

boot³ n **to boot** in addition

booth /buːð‖buːθ/ n 1 tent, hut, etc., where goods are sold 2 small enclosed space: *a telephone/voting booth*

boot-leg /'buːtleg/ vi/t **-gg-** make, carry or sell (alcoholic drink) illegally **~ger** n

booze /buːz/ vi sl drink alcohol ♦ n [U] sl alcoholic drink **boozer** sl 1 person who boozes 2 BrE for PUB **boozy** adj sl showing signs of heavy drinking

booze-up /'·· ·/n BrE sl party with a lot of drinking

bop /bɒp‖bɑːp/ vi dance as in a DISCOTHEQUE **bop** n

bor-der¹ /'bɔːdəʳ‖'bɔːr-/ n 1 edge 2 line between 2 countries

border² vt put or be a border to

border on phr vt be very much like: *Your remarks border on rudeness.*

bor-der-line /'bɔːdəlaɪn‖'bɔːrdər-/ adj that may or may not be something: *Anne will pass the exam, but Sue is a borderline case.* (= may pass or fail) ♦ n (line marking) a border

bore¹ /bɔːʳ/ v past t. of BEAR²

bore² n dull person or activity ♦ vt make (someone) tired or uninterested:

a boring job **~dom** *n* [U] state of being bored

bore /bɔː/ *vi/t* make a round hole (in) ♦ *n* **1** hole made by boring **2** measurement of the hole inside of a gun, pipe, etc.

born /bɔːn ‖bɔːrn/ *adj* **1 be born** come into existence by birth **2** being something by nature: *a born leader* **3 born and bred** having grown up from birth in the stated place **4 born of** owing existence to

born-a·gain /ˈ· ··/ *adj* having accepted a particular religion, esp. EVANGELICAL Christianity, esp. through a deep spiritual experience: *a born-again Christian* | (fig.) *a born-again jogger*

borne /bɔːn ‖bɔːrn/ *v past p. of* BEAR²

bo·rough /ˈbʌrə ‖-rəu/ *n* town, or division of a large town

bor·row /ˈbɒrəu ‖ˈbɑː-, ˈbɔː-/ *v* **1** *vi/t* receive something that is lent, and will be returned **2** *vt* copy (ideas, words, etc.) **~er** *n*

bor·stal /ˈbɔːstl ‖ˈbɔːr-/ *n BrE* prison school for young offenders

bos·om /ˈbuzəm/ *n lit* **1** the front of the human chest, esp. the female breasts **2** place where one feels love, sorrow, etc. **3 a bosom friend** a very close friend **4 in the bosom of** in a close relationship with

boss /bɒs‖bɔːs/ *n infml* person who controls others; employer, etc. ♦ *vt* give orders to **~y** *adj* too fond of giving orders

bot·a·ny /ˈbɒtəni ‖ˈbɑː-/ *n* [U] scientific study of plants **–nist** *n* **–nical** /bəˈtænɪkəl/ *adj*

botch /bɒtʃ‖bɑːtʃ/ *vt* do a repair (something) badly ♦ *n* bad piece of work

both /bəuθ/ *determiner, pron* this one and that one: *both of us* | *both New York and London*

both·er /ˈbɒðə‖ˈbɑː-/ *v* **1** *vt* cause inconvenience to; annoy in little ways: *Does the noise bother you?* **2** *vi* trouble oneself: *Don't bother to lock the door.* ♦ *n* [C;U] trouble; inconvenience **~some** *adj* causing bother

bot·tle /ˈbɒtl‖ˈbɑːtl/ *n* **1** narrow-necked container for liquids **2** container for holding a baby's milk **3** *BrE sl* courage **4 the bottle** alcoholic drink, esp. when drunk too much: *He's on/hitting the bottle again.* ♦ *vt* put into bottles

bottle out *phr vi BrE sl* lose one's courage

bottle up *phr vt* control (feelings) unhealthily

bottle green /ˌ·· ˈ·◄/ *n, adj* [U] very dark green

bot·tle·neck /ˈbɒtlnek‖ˈbɑː-/ *n* narrow part of a road which slows down traffic: (fig.) *a bottleneck in production*

bot·tom¹ /ˈbɒtəm‖ˈbɑː-/ *n* **1** [C] base; lowest part or level: *the bottom of the stairs* | *He came bottom of the class.* **2** [C] part of the body that one sits on **3** [S] ground under the sea, a lake, etc. **4** [S] far end: *the bottom of the garden* **5** [S] cause: *get to the bottom of the trouble* **6 at bottom** really **7 from the bottom of one's heart** truly **8 knock the bottom out of** take away the necessary support on which something rests **~less** *adj* very deep

bottom² *v* **bottom out** *phr vi* reach the lowest point before rising again

bottom line /ˌ·· ˈ·/ *n* [the + S] **1** the amount of money shown (as profit or loss) at the bottom of a set of accounts **2** the most important result in the end, esp. with regard to money

bot·u·lis·m /ˈbɒtʃʊlɪzəm‖ˈbɑː-/ *n* [U] form of food poisoning

bou·doir /ˈbuːdwɑːʳ/ *n lit* woman's private room

bough /bau/ *n* large branch of a tree

bought /bɔːt/ *v past t. and p. of* BUY

boul·der /ˈbəuldəʳ/ *n* large rock

bounce /bauns/ *v* **1** *vi* (of a ball) spring back again: *The ball bounced against the wall.* **2** *vi/t* move up and down quickly: *She bounced into the room.* **3** *vi* (of a cheque) be returned by the bank as worthless ♦ *n* **1** [C;U] act of bouncing **2** [U] behaviour which is full of life **bouncer** *n* strong person employed (esp. at a club) to throw out unwelcome visitors **bouncing** *adj* (esp. of babies) strong and healthy

bound¹ /baund/ *v past t. and p. of* BIND

bound² *adj* **bound to** sure to: *It's bound to rain* **2 bound up in** busy with

bound³ *vi* jump; LEAP **bound** *n* — see also BOUNDS

bound⁴ *adj* going to (a place): *bound for home*

bound·a·ry /ˈbaundəri/ *n* outer limit; border

bound·less /ˈbaundləs/ *adj* unlimited

bounds /baundz/ *n* [P] **1** furthest limits **2 out of bounds** forbidden to be visited

boun·ty /ˈbaunti/ *n* **1** [C] something given out of kindness, or offered as a reward **2** [U] *fml* generosity **-tiful** *adj fml* generous

bou·quet /bəuˈkeɪ, buː-/ *n* **1** bunch of flowers **2** smell of a wine

bour·geois /ˈbuəʒwɑː‖buərˈʒwɑː/ *n, adj* **1** (person) of the MIDDLE CLASS **2** (person) too interested in material possessions **~ie** /ˌbuəʒwɑːˈziː‖ˌbuər-/ *n* [U] the MIDDLE CLASS

bout /baut/ *n* short period of activity or illness

bou·tique /buːˈtiːk/ *n* small fashionable shop, esp. for clothes

bo-vine /'bəʊvaɪn/ adj slow and dull, like a cow

bow[1] /baʊ/ vi/t bend forward, to show respect **bow** n

bow out phr vi give up a position or stop taking part in something

bow to phr vt obey; accept: I bow to your judgment.

bow[2] /bəʊ/ n 1 piece of curved wood with a string, for shooting arrows 2 similar piece of wood for playing stringed musical instruments 3 knot formed by doubling a string into two curved pieces ♦ vi/t 1 bend; curve 2 play (music) with a bow

bow[3] /baʊ/ n front of a ship

bowd-ler-ize /'baʊdləraɪz/ vt remove unacceptable parts from (a book)

bow-els /'baʊəlz/ n [P] 1 pipe that carries waste matter from the stomach 2 inside part: the bowels of the earth

bowl[1] /bəʊl/ n 1 deep round container for liquids, etc. 2 anything in the shape of a bowl

bowl[2] v 1 vi/t throw or roll (a ball) in a sport 2 vt (in cricket) force a player out of the game by doing this 3 vi play BOWLS or BOWLING

bowl over phr vt 1 knock down 2 surprise greatly

bow-legged /'bəʊ,legd, -,legʒd/ adj having legs curving outwards at the knees

bowl-er[1] /'bəʊlə[r]/ n person who bowls

bowler[2] n BrE man's round hard hat

bowl-ing /'bəʊlɪŋ/ n [U] indoor game in which a big ball is rolled along a track (a **bowling alley**)

bowls /bəʊlz/ n [U] outdoor game in which a big ball (a **bowl**) is rolled on grass (a **bowling green**)

bow tie /ˌbəʊ 'taɪ/ n TIE[1] (1) fastened at the front with a BOW[2](3)

bow win-dow /ˌbəʊ 'wɪndəʊ/ n curved window

box[1] /bɒks‖bɑːks/ n 1 [C] stiff container for solids: a box of chocolates 2 [C] small enclosed space: a telephone box | a box at the theatre 3 [S] BrE sl television: What's on the box? — see also BLACK BOX, PANDORA'S BOX ♦ vt put in boxes

box in phr vt enclose in a small space

box[2] vi/t fight with the FISTs, for sport: a boxing match ~er n ~ing n [U]

Boxing Day /'·· ·/ n British public holiday on the first weekday after Christmas

box num-ber /'· ,··/ n number used as a mailing address, esp. in replying to newspaper advertisements

box of-fice /'· ,··/ n place where tickets are sold in a cinema, etc.: The show was a box-office success. (= made a large profit)

boy /bɔɪ/ n young male person ~**hood** time of being a boy ~**ish** adj like a boy

boy-cott /'bɔɪkɒt‖-kɑːt/ vt refuse to trade with or take part in **boycott** n

boy-friend /'bɔɪfrend/ n woman's male companion

bo-zo /'bəʊzəʊ/ n AmE sl stupid person

bra /brɑː/ n woman's undergarment supporting the breasts

brace[1] /breɪs/ n 1 something that stiffens or supports 2 wire worn to straighten the teeth **braces** n [P] bands over the shoulders to keep trousers up

brace[2] vt 1 support 2 prepare (oneself) **bracing** adj health-giving

brace-let /'breɪslɪt/ n decoration for the wrist

brack-en /'brækən/ n [U] FERN which grows in forests

brack-et /'brækɪt/ n 1 support for a shelf, etc. 2 either of various pairs of signs used for enclosing a piece of information, for example ( ) or [ ] 3 group of people: the 16-25 age bracket ♦ vt 1 put in brackets 2 put together

brack-ish /'brækɪʃ/ adj (of water) not pure; a little salty ~**ness** n [U]

brag /bræg/ vi -gg- talk too proudly; BOAST

braid /breɪd/ n 1, vt AmE for PLAIT n [U] threads of silk, gold, etc., twisted together to make edging for material: gold braid

braille /breɪl/ n [U] type of raised printing that blind people can read

brain /breɪn/ n 1 the organ in the head that controls thought 2 mind; INTELLIGENCE 3 infml clever person 4 **have something on the brain** think about something continually, or too much ♦ vt infml hit on the head ~**less** adj stupid ~**y** adj clever

brains n [U] 1 material of which the brain consists 2 ability to think

brain-child /'breɪntʃaɪld/ n [S] someone's special idea

brain drain /'· ·/ n movement of skilled people to other countries

brain-pow-er /'breɪn,paʊə[r]/ n [U] ability to reason

brain-storm /'breɪnstɔːm‖-stɔːrm/ n 1 BrE sudden short madness 2 AmE for BRAINWAVE ~**ing** n [U] rapid exchange of ideas among a group to find answers to problems

brain-wash /'breɪnwɒʃ‖-wɔːʃ,-wɑːʃ/ vt force someone to change their beliefs ~**ing** n [U]

brain-wave /'breɪnweɪv/ n BrE sudden clever idea

braise /breɪz/ vt cook (meat or vegetables) slowly in a covered dish

brake /breɪk/ n apparatus for slowing or stopping a vehicle **brake** vi/t

bram-ble /'bræmbəl/ n common wild prickly bush

bran /bræn/ n [U] crushed skin of grain

branch[1] /brɑːntʃ‖bræntʃ/ n 1 stem growing from the trunk of a tree 2 division; part: *branch of a railway/of a family*

branch[2] vi form branches

　branch out phr vi add to one's range

brand /brænd/ 1 product of a particular producer: *my favourite brand of soup*|(fig.) *his own brand* (= special kind) *of humour* 2 mark made, esp. by burning, to show ownership ♦ vt 1 give a lasting bad name to: *He was branded as a liar.* 2 mark with a BRAND (2): (fig.) *the experience branded her for life*

bran-dish /'brændɪʃ/ vt wave (e.g. a weapon) about

brand-new /ˌ·'·◂/ adj completely unused

bran-dy /'brændi/ n [C;U] strong alcoholic drink made from wine

brash /bræʃ/ adj bold and disrespectful ~**ly** adv ~**ness** n [U]

brass /brɑːs‖bræs/ n [U] 1 bright yellow metal 2 musical instruments made of this: *a brass band* 3 BrE sl money — see also TOP BRASS

bras-siere /'bræziə‖brə'zɪər/ n fml BRA

brat /bræt/ n derog child, esp. a bad-mannered one

bra-va-do /brə'vɑːdəʊ/ n [U] unnecessary show of boldness

brave /breɪv/ adj ready to meet pain or danger; fearless ♦ vt meet (danger, etc.) without showing fear ~**ly** adv ~**ry** /'breɪvəri/ n [U]

bra-vo /'brɑːvəʊ, brɑː'vəʊ/ interj, n -**vos** (shout of) well done!

brawl /brɔːl/ n noisy quarrel **brawl** vi

brawn /brɔːn/ n [U] 1 human muscle 2 meat from the head of a pig ~**y** adj strong

bray /breɪ/ vi make the sound a DONKEY makes **bray** n

bra-zen /'breɪzən/ adj without shame

bra-zi-er /'breɪziə‖-ʒər/ n container for burning coals

breach /briːtʃ/ n 1 [C;U] act of breaking a law, promise, etc.: *breach of contract* 2 [C] hole (in a wall, etc.) 3 **breach of the peace** law fighting in public ♦ vt break through

bread /bred/ n [U] 1 food made of baked flour 2 food as a means of staying alive: *earn one's daily bread* 3 sl money 4 **bread and butter** one's way of earning money to live on 5 **know which side one's bread is buttered**

know who or what will be of most gain to oneself

bread-crumb /'bredkrʌm/ n very small bit of bread

bread-line /'bredlaɪn/ n **on the breadline** very poor

breadth /bredθ, bretθ/ n [U] 1 width 2 broad range; SCOPE

bread-win-ner /'bred,wɪnər/ n person whose wages support a family

break[1] /breɪk/ v **broke** /brəʊk/, **bro-ken** /'brəʊkən/ 1 vi/t separate suddenly into parts: *to break a window*|*The rope broke.* 2 vi/t make or become by breaking: *The box broke open.* 3 vi/t make or become useless due to damage: *a broken watch* 4 vt disobey; not keep: *break a promise/an appointment* 5 vi/t interrupt; stop: *break one's journey/the silence* 6 vi/t (cause to) fail or be destroyed: *The scandal could break him politically.* 7 vi/t bring or come into notice: *The news broke.* 8 vt do better than (a record) 9 vi (of a voice) change suddenly 10 vt discover the secret of (a CODE) 11 **break new/fresh ground** do something new and different 12 **break one's back** make every possible effort 13 **break the back of** finish the main or worst part of 14 **break the ice** begin to be friendly with people one did not know before 15 **break wind** let out gases from the bowels

　break away phr vi escape: (fig.) *break away from old traditions*

　break down phr v 1 vi/t destroy; to be reduced to pieces: (fig.) *They broke down her resistance.* 2 vi (of machinery) stop working 3 vi fail: *The peace talks have broken down.* 4 vi (of a person) lose control of one's feelings 5 vi/t separate into kinds; divide: *break the figures down into several lists*

　break even phr vi make neither a loss nor a profit

　break in phr v 1 vi enter a building by force 2 vi interrupt 3 vt make (a person or animal) accustomed to something new

　break into phr vt 1 enter by force 2 begin suddenly: *to break into song* 3 interrupt 4 use part of, esp. unwillingly: *We'll have to break into our savings.*

　break of phr vt cure (someone) of (a bad habit)

　break off phr vi/t 1 stop; end 2 separate from the main part: *A branch broke off.*

　break out phr vi 1 (of something bad) start suddenly: *War broke out.* 2 show or express something suddenly: *He broke out in a rash.* 3 escape

　break through phr vi/t 1 force a way through 2 make a new advance

break up phr v 1 vi/t divide into small pieces; separate 2 vi/t bring or come to an end: Their marriage broke up. 3 vi/t (cause to) suffer greatly 4 vi (of a crowd) cease to be together 5 vi BrE begin the school holidays 6 AmE amuse greatly

break with phr vt end one's connection with

break² n 1 act of breaking or a condition produced (as if) by breaking: a break in the clouds 2 pause for rest: a coffee break 3 change from the usual pattern or custom: a break from the past | a break in the weather 4 infml chance (esp. to make things better); piece of good luck 5 break of day DAWN 6 make a break for it try to escape

break·able /'breɪkəbəl/ adj (something) easily broken

break·age /'breɪkɪdʒ/ n [C;U] 1 example of breaking 2 something broken

break·a·way /'breɪkəweɪ/ n person or thing that escapes: a breakaway group

break·down /'breɪkdaʊn/ n 1 sudden failure in operation: a breakdown in the peace talks 2 sudden weakness or loss of power in body or mind: a nervous breakdown 3 division into kinds; detailed explanation (of figures, etc.) — see also NERVOUS BREAKDOWN

break·er /'breɪkəʳ/ n 1 large wave rolling onto the shore 2 person or thing that breaks something: an ice-breaker

break·fast /'brekfəst/ n [C;U] first meal of the day — see also CONTINENTAL BREAKFAST, ENGLISH BREAKFAST
breakfast vi

break·in /'· ·/ n entering of a building illegally and by force

break·out /'breɪkaʊt/ n violent or forceful escape from an enclosed space or a difficult situation, esp. an escape from prison

break·through /'breɪkθruː/ n important advance or discovery

break·up /'breɪkʌp/ n 1 coming to an end 2 division into parts

breast /brest/ n 1 milk-producing part of a woman's body: a breast-fed baby 2 upper front part of the body: his breast pocket | a bird with a red breast 3 make a clean breast of tell the whole truth about ♦ vt push aside with one's chest: (fig.) The ship breasted the waves.

breath /breθ/ n 1 [U] air taken into and breathed out of the lungs 2 [C] single act of breathing air in and out once 3 sign or slight movement (of something): There's a breath of spring in the air. | There wasn't a breath of

wind. 4 moment: In one breath he said he loved me, in the next that he didn't. 5 get one's breath (back) also catch one's breath — return to one's usual rate of breathing 6 hold one's breath stop breathing for a time 7 out of breath breathing very fast, as after running 8 take one's breath away surprise one greatly 9 under one's breath in a whisper 10 waste one's breath talk uselessly ~less adj ~lessly adv

breath·a·lys·er /'breθəl‑aɪzəʳ/ n apparatus used by the police to measure the amount of alcohol a driver has drunk

breathe /briːð/ v 1 vi/t take (air, etc.) into the lungs and send it out again 2 vt say softly; whisper 3 vt send out (a smell, feeling, etc.) 4 breathe again feel calm after feeling anxious 4 breathe down someone's neck infml keep too close a watch on someone 5 breathe one's last fml die ~er n short rest

breath·tak·ing /'breθ,teɪkɪŋ/ adj very exciting or unusual

breech·es /'brɪtʃɪz/ n [P] short trousers fastened at or below the knee

breed /briːd/ v bred /bred/ 1 vi/t (of animals) produce young 2 vt keep (animals, etc.) for the purpose of producing young ones 3 vt produce; cause: Flies breed disease. ♦ n kind of animal or plant: a new breed of rose ~er n person who breeds animals or plants ~ing n [U] 1 business of breeding animals, etc. 2 polite manners

breeding-ground /'·· ·/ n 1 place where the young, esp. of wild creatures, are produced 2 place or point of origin: a breeding-ground for disease

breeze /briːz/ n 1 light gentle wind 2 sl, esp. AmE something easily done ♦ vi come and go quickly and unceremoniously **breezy** adj 1 rather windy 2 cheerful in manner

breth·ren /'breðrən/ n [P] (used in church, etc.) brothers

brev·i·ty /'brevəti/ n [U] shortness

brew /bruː/ vi/t prepare (beer, tea, coffee): (fig.) Trouble is brewing. ♦ n result of brewing: a strong brew ~er n person who makes beer ~ery n place where beer is made

bribe /braɪb/ vt influence unfairly by gifts ♦ n something offered in this way: judges who take bribes ~ry /'braɪbəri/ n [U] giving or taking bribes

bric-a-brac /'brɪk ə ‚bræk/ n [U] small decorations in a house

brick /brɪk/ n 1 [C;U] (piece of) baked clay for building: brick walls 2 something shaped like a brick 3 bang/beat one's head against a

brick wall waste one's efforts by trying to do something impossible **4 drop a brick** do or say something foolish and socially uncomfortable ♦ *v* **brick in/up** *phr vt* fill or enclose with bricks

brick-bat /'brɪkbæt/ *n* an attack using words

brick-lay-er /'brɪk,leɪə^r/ *n* workman who puts bricks in place —**ing** *n* [U]

brid-al /'braɪdl/ *adj* of a bride or wedding

bride /braɪd/ *n* woman about to be married, or just married

bride-groom /'braɪdgruːm, -grum/ *n* man about to be married, or just married

brides-maid /'braɪdzmeɪd/ *n* girl attending the bride at a wedding

bridge[1] /brɪdʒ/ *n* **1** structure carrying a road or railway over a river, etc. **2** raised part of a ship where the captain and officers stand **3** upper part of the nose **4** part of a musical instrument over which the strings are stretched **5** piece of metal that keeps false teeth in place ♦ *vt* build a bridge across

bridge[2] *n* [U] card game for 4 players

bridge-head /'brɪdʒhed/ *n* position far forward in enemy land

bri-dle /'braɪdl/ *n* leather bands round a horse's head to control its movements ♦ *v* **1** *vt* put a bridle on **2** *vi* show displeasure

brief[1] /briːf/ *adj* short: *a brief visit* **2 in brief** in as few words as possible —**ly** *adv*

brief[2] *n* **1** short statement of facts or instructions **2** *BrE* set of instructions setting limits to someone's powers or duties — see also BRIEFS ♦ *vt* give necessary instructions or information

brief-case /'briːfkeɪs/ *n* flat leather case for papers

briefs /briːfs/ *n* [P] short UNDERPANTS

bri-gade /brɪ'geɪd/ *n* **1** army unit of about 5000 soldiers **2** organization with certain duties: *the Fire Brigade*

brig-a-dier /,brɪgə'dɪə^r/ *n* officer commanding a brigade

bright /braɪt/ *adj* **1** giving out light; shining **2** (of a colour) strong: *bright red* **3** cheerful; happy **4** clever **5** showing hope or signs of future success: *a bright future* —**en** *vi/t* make or become bright —**ly** *adv* —**ness** *n* [U]

bright spark /,· '·/^{r}*BrE infml* a clever or cheerful person

bril-liant /'brɪljənt/ *adj* **1** very bright: *brilliant blue* **2** very clever: *a brilliant idea* **3** very hopeful; successful: *a brilliant career* —**ly** *adv* —**liance**, **-liancy** *n* [U]

brim /brɪm/ *n* **1** edge of a cup, etc. **2** bottom part of a hat ♦ *vi* -**mm**- be full of liquid

bring /brɪŋ/ *vt* **brought** /brɔːt/ **1** carry or lead towards someone: *Bring him to the party.* **2** cause to come: *His letter brought many offers of help.* **3** be sold for **4** *law* make (a charge) officially

bring about *phr vt* cause

bring around/over/round *phr vt* persuade into a change of opinion

bring back *phr vt* **1** return or cause to return: *That song brings back memories.* **2** obtain and return with

bring down *phr vt* **1** cause to fall or come down: *bring down prices* **2** reduce or lower: *to bring someone down to your own level*

bring down on *phr vt* cause (something bad) to happen: *bring trouble down on the family*

bring forward *phr vt* **1** introduce; suggest: *bring forward a plan* **2** bring something in the future nearer to the present

bring in *phr vt* **1** cause to come; introduce **2** produce as profit; earn

bring off *phr vt* succeed in doing

bring on *phr vt* **1** cause to happen: *bring on a fever* **2** help to develop; improve

bring out *phr vt* **1** produce; cause to appear: *Responsibility brings out the best in her.* **2** cause (workers) to STRIKE[1] (6) **3** encourage, esp. to talk

bring round/to *phr vt* cause to regain consciousness

bring through *phr vt* cause to come successfully through (illness, etc.)

bring together *phr vt* cause (esp. a man and a woman) to meet

bring up *phr vt* **1** educate and care for (children) **2** mention a subject **3** *esp. BrE* VOMIT food

brink /brɪŋk/ *n* edge; VERGE: *on the brink of disaster*

brink-man-ship /'brɪŋkmənʃɪp/ *n* [U] *infml* art of trying to gain an advantage by going to the limit of safety, esp. in international politics, before stopping

brisk /brɪsk/ *adj* quick and active: *a brisk walk* —**ly** *adv* —**ness** *n* [U]

bris-tle /'brɪsl/ *n* [C;U] short stiff hair on a brush, etc. ♦ *vi* (of hair) stand up stiffly: (fig.) *bristling with anger* —**tly** /'brɪsli/ *adj*

bristle with *phr vt* have plenty of: *streets bristling with armed guards*

brit-tle /'brɪtl/ *adj* **1** hard but easily broken **2** lacking WARMTH or depth of feeling

broach /brəʊtʃ/ *vt* introduce (a subject) for conversation

broad /brɔːd/ *adj* **1** large when measured from side to side; wide **2** not limited; respecting the ideas of others: *broad opinions* | *a broadminded person* **3** not detailed: *in broad outline* **4**

full; clear: *in broad daylight* **5** (of speech) showing clearly where the speaker comes from: *a broad Scots accent* **6** not acceptable in polite society: *broad humour* **~en** *vi/t* make or become broader: *Travel broadens the mind.* **~ly** *adv* more or less; mostly **~ness** *n* [U]

broad-cast /'brɔːdkɑːst‖-kæst/ *n* radio or television presentation ♦ *v* **broadcast 1** *vi/t* send out (broadcasts) **2** *vt* make widely known: *He broadcast the news to his friends.* **~er** *n* **~ing** *n* [U]

broad-side /'brɔːdsaɪd/ *n* **1** forceful spoken or written attack **2** firing of all the guns on one side of a ship

bro-cade /brə'keɪd‖brəʊ-/ *n* [U] decorative cloth with a raised pattern

broc-co-li /'brɒkəli/ *n* vegetable similar to a CAULIFLOWER

bro-chure /'brəʊʃəʳ, -ʃʊəʳ ‖ brəʊ-'ʃʊəʳ/ *n* small book of instructions, or giving details of a service offered

brogue¹ /brəʊg/ *n* strong thick shoe

brogue² *n* Irish ACCENT (1)

broil /brɔɪl/ *vi/t* AmE for GRILL: (fig.) *broiling hot weather*

broke¹ /brəʊk/ *v* past t. of BREAK¹

broke² *adj* completely without money

bro-ken¹ /'brəʊkən/ *v* past p. of BREAK¹

broken² *adj* **1** violently separated; damaged: *a broken window* | (fig.) *broken dreams* | (fig.) *a broken man* **2** not kept to; destroyed: *a broken promise* | *a broken home* (= where a child's parents do not live together) **3** imperfectly spoken or written: *broken English*

broken-heart-ed /ˌ···'···◂/ *adj* filled with grief

bro-ker /'brəʊkəʳ/ *n* person who buys and sells shares, etc., for others

bro-ker-age /'brəʊkərɪdʒ/ *n* [U] **1** (place of) business of a broker **2** fee charged by a broker

brol-ly /'brɒli‖'brɑːli/ *n* BrE infml UMBRELLA (1)

bron-chi-al /'brɒŋkiəl‖'brɑːŋ-/ *adj* of the tubes of the WINDPIPE

bron-chi-tis /brɒŋ'kaɪtɪs‖brɑːŋ-/ *n* [U] illness of the bronchial tubes

bronze /brɒnz/ *n* [U] **1** (the reddish-brown colour of) a metal that is a mixture of copper and tin **2** MEDAL made of bronze ♦ *vt* give this colour to: *bronzed by the sun*

brooch /brəʊtʃ/ *n* decoration pinned to a dress

brood /bruːd/ *n* family of birds, etc. **~y** *adj* **1** (of a hen) wanting to sit on eggs **2** sad and silent **~ily** *adv* **~iness** *n* [U] ♦ *vi* think long and sadly about something

brook¹ /brʊk/ *n* small stream

brook² *vt* infml allow or accept without complaining

broom /bruːm, brʊm/ *n* sweeping brush with a long handle — see also NEW BROOM

broth /brɒθ‖brɔːθ/ *n* [U] thin soup

broth-el /'brɒθəl‖'brɑː-, 'brɔː-/ *n* house of PROSTITUTEs

broth-er /'brʌðəʳ/ *n* **1** male relative with the same parents **2** male member of the same profession, religious group, etc. **~hood** *n* [C] **1** condition or feeling of friendliness and companionship **2** [C] all the people in a profession, etc. **~ly** *adj* **1** like a brother **2** friendly

brother-in-law /'···ˌ·/ *n* brothers-in-law brother of one's husband or wife; one's sister's husband

brought /brɔːt/ *v* past t. and p. of BRING

brow /braʊ/ *n* **1** EYEBROW **2** FOREHEAD **3** top of a hill

brow-beat /'braʊbiːt/ *vt* -beat, -beaten /-biːtn/ frighten into doing something

brown /braʊn/ *adj, n* (of) the colour of earth or coffee ♦ *vi/t* make or become brown

browned-off /ˌ· '·◂/ *adj* BrE infml annoyed and discouraged

Brown-ie point /'braʊni ˌpɔɪnt/ *n* [usu. pl.] mark of notice and approval for something good that one has done

browse /braʊz/ *vi* **1** read without clear purpose **2** feed on young plants, grass, etc. **browse** *n* [S]

bruise /bruːz/ *n* discoloured place where the skin has been hurt ♦ *v* **1** *vt* cause a bruise on **2** *vi* show a bruise

brunch /brʌntʃ/ *n* [C;U] late breakfast or early LUNCH

bru-nette also **brunet** AmE /bruː'net/ *n* woman of a fair-skinned race with dark hair

brunt /brʌnt/ *n* **bear the brunt of** suffer the heaviest part of (an attack)

brush¹ /brʌʃ/ *n* [C] **1** instrument for sweeping, painting, etc., made of hair, nylon, etc: *a toothbrush* | *a clothes brush* **2** [C] act of brushing **3** [C] short unpleasant meeting: *a brush with the police* **4** [U] (land covered by) small rough trees and bushes **5** [C] tail of a fox

brush² *v* **1** *vt* clean with a brush **2** *vi/t* touch or move lightly

brush aside/away *phr vt* refuse to pay attention to

brush off *phr vt* refuse to listen to or have a relationship with (someone)

brush-off /'· ·/ *n* [the + S] clear refusal to be friendly: *She gave me the brush-off.*

brush up *phr vt* improve one's knowledge of (something known but partly forgotten) by study: *I must brush up my French.*

brusque /bruːsk, brusk‖brʌsk/ *adj* quick and rather impolite ~**ly** *adv* ~**ness** *n* [U]

brus·sels sprout /ˌbrʌsəlz ˈspraut/ *n* vegetable like a very small CABBAGE

bru·tal /ˈbruːtl/ *adj* without tender feeling; cruel ~**ly** *adv* ~**ty** /bruːˈtælɪti/ *n* [C;U]

brute /bruːt/ *n* 1 rough cruel person 2 animal ♦ like (that of) an animal in being cruel or very strong: *brute force*

brutish *adj* like animals rather than people

bub·ble /ˈbʌbəl/ *n* hollow ball of liquid containing air or gas ♦ *vi* 1 form, produce, or rise as bubbles: *She was bubbling (over) with happiness.* 2 make the sound of bubbles rising in liquid

bubbly *adj* 1 full of bubbles 2 showing happy feelings freely

buck[1] /bʌk/ *n* 1 [C] male of certain animals, esp. the deer, cat, and rabbit 2 [C] *sl, esp. AmE* American dollar 3 [*the* + S] responsibility: *to pass the buck*

buck[2] *v* 1 *vi* (of a horse) jump up with all 4 feet off the ground 2 *vt* throw off (a rider) by doing this

buck up *phr vt* 1 try to improve 2 make happier

buck·et /ˈbʌkɪt/ *n* 1 (contents of) an open container with a handle, for liquids 2 large quantity: *The rain came down in buckets.* ♦ *v BrE infml* rain very hard ~**ful** /-ful/ *n* contents of a bucket

bucket shop /ˈ··· /n *infml, esp. BrE* business that obtains large quantities of tickets for air travel and sells them to the public at a low price

buck·le[1] /ˈbʌkl/ *n* metal fastener for a belt, etc.

buckle[2] *vi/t* 1 fasten with a buckle 2 bend; twist: *a buckled wheel* 3 begin to yield: *Her knees buckled.*

buckle down *phr vi* begin to work seriously

bud /bʌd/ *n* 1 flower or leaf before it opens **nip something in the bud** do harm to (something), esp. so as to keep from succeeding — see also TASTE BUD ♦ *vi* -**dd**- produce buds ~**ding** *adj* beginning to develop

Bud·dhis·m /ˈbudɪzəm‖ˈbuː-, ˈbu-/ *n* [U] eastern religion taught by Buddha **Buddhist** *n, adj*

bud·dy /ˈbʌdi/ *n* 1 *infml* companion; friend 2 *AmE sl* (used as a form of address to a man)

budge /bʌdʒ/ *vi/t* move a little

bud·ger·i·gar /ˈbʌdʒərɪgɑːr/ *also* **budgie** /ˈbʌdʒi/ *infml* — *n* small brightly coloured Australian bird

bud·get /ˈbʌdʒɪt/ *n* 1 plan of how to spend money, esp. public money taken in by taxation 2 amount of money stated in this ♦ *vi* plan one's spending ♦ *adj* cheap: *budget prices*

buff[1] /bʌf/ *n, adj* [U] (of) a faded yellow colour

buff[2] *vt* polish (metal) with something soft

buff[3] *n* person interested in a subject: *a film buff*

buff·er /ˈbʌfər/ *n* spring on a railway vehicle that takes the shock when it hits anything

buffer zone /ˈ·· ·/n NEUTRAL area separating opposing forces or groups

buf·fet[1] /ˈbufeɪ‖bəˈfeɪ/ *n* table, etc., where one can get food to be eaten near by

buf·fet[2] /ˈbʌfɪt/ *vt* hit sharply: *buffeted by the wind*

buf·foon /bəˈfuːn/ *n* noisy fool

bug /bʌg/ *n* 1 *AmE* any insect 2 GERM 3 apparatus for secret listening 4 eager interest in something: *the travel bug* 5 fault in a machine, esp. a computer ♦ *vt* -**gg**- 1 fit with a BUG (3) 2 trouble (someone) continually

bug·bear /ˈbʌgbeər/ *n* something feared

bug·ger /ˈbʌgər/ *n sl, esp. BrE* 1 unpleasant person or thing 2 person of the stated kind: *You lucky bugger!* ♦ *interj* (used for adding force to expressions of displeasure) ~**y** *n* [U] SODOMY

bug·gy /ˈbʌgi/ *n* 1 light carriage 2 PUSHCHAIR

bu·gle /ˈbjuːgəl/ *n* brass musical instrument **bugler** *n*

build /bɪld/ *vi/t* **built** /bɪlt/ make by putting pieces together: *build houses/ ships* | *(fig.)Hard work builds character.* ~**er** *n* ~**ing** *n* 1 thing with a roof and walls; house, etc. 2 work of a builder

build on *phr vt* base on 2 depend on

build up *phr v* 1 *vt* increase; develop: *build up a business* 2 *vi* praise (something or someone) so as to influence the opinion of others

build[2] *n* shape and size of one's body

building so·ci·e·ty /ˈ··· ·,···/*BrE n* business organization in which people pay money in order to save it and gain interest, and which lends money to people who want to buy houses

bulb /bʌlb/ *n* 1 round root of certain plants 2 glass part of an electric lamp ~**ous** *adj* fat and round

bulge /bʌldʒ/ *n* 1 swelling on a surface 2 sudden increase ♦ *vi* swell

bulk[1] /bʌlk/ *n* 1 [U] great size or quantity 2 **in bulk** in large quantities 3 **the bulk of** most of ~**y** *adj* large and fat

bulk[2] *v* **bulk large** play an important part

bulk-head /'bʌlkhed/ n wall which divides a ship, etc., into several parts

bull /bʊl/ n 1 male of cattle and some other large animals 2 **bull in a china shop** person who is rough where care is needed 3 **take the bull by the horns** face difficulties with courage

bull-doze /'bʊldəʊz/ vt move (earth, etc.) with a powerful machine (a **bull-dozer**): (fig.) *bulldoze a plan through Parliament*

bul-let /'bʊlɪt/ n piece of shot fired from a small gun: *a* **bullet-proof** *car* — see also **bite the bullet** (BITE)

bul-le-tin /'bʊlətɪn/ n short official report

bul-lion /'bʊljən/ n [U] bars of gold or silver

bul-lish /'bʊlɪʃ/ adj marked by, tending to cause, or hopeful of rising prices (as in a STOCK EXCHANGE)

bul-lock /'bʊlək/ n BULL that cannot breed

bull's-eye /'· ·/ n centre of a TARGET

bull-shit /'bʊl,ʃɪt/ n [U] sl nonsense ♦ vi/t -tt- sl talk nonsense, esp. confidently in order to deceive, persuade, or get admiration

bul-ly /'bʊli/ n person who hurts weaker people ♦ vt hurt in this way

bul-rush /'bʊlrʌʃ/ n tall grasslike waterside plant

bul-wark /'bʊlwək||-ɔrk/ n wall built for defence

bum¹ /bʌm/ n BrE sl BUTTOCKS

bum² n AmE sl TRAMP (1) or lazy person ♦ vt -mm- sl ask for; beg

bump /bʌmp/ v 1 vi/t knock violently 2 vi move along in an uneven way ♦ n 1 (sound of) a sudden blow 2 swelling ~y adj uneven
bump into phr vt meet by chance
bump off phr vt infml kill
bump up phr vt increase

bump-er /'bʌmpəʳ/ n protective bar on the front or back of a car ♦ adj very large: *a bumper harvest*

bun /bʌn/ n 1 small round sweet cake 2 hair twisted into a tight shape

bunch /bʌntʃ/ n 1 number of small things fastened together: 2 group: *a bunch of girls* ♦ vi/t form into a bunch

bun-dle /'bʌndl/ n 1 number of articles fastened together: *a bundle of sticks/laundry* 2 a mass: *a bundle of nerves/laughs* ♦ v 1 vi/t hurry roughly 2 vt make into a bundle

bung¹ /bʌŋ/ n round piece of material to close the hole in a container

bung² vt BrE infml throw roughly
bung up phr vt block up (a hole)

bun-ga-low /'bʌŋɡələʊ/ n house all on one level

bun-gle /'bʌŋɡəl/ vt do (work) badly -gler n

bunk¹ /bʌŋk/ n bed fixed to a wall, often above or below another

bunk² n **do a bunk** BrE sl run away

bun-ker /'bʌŋkəʳ/ n 1 place to store coal 2 shelter for soldiers 3 (in GOLF) sandy place from which it is difficult to hit the ball

bun-ny /'bʌni/ n (child's word for) a rabbit

buoy /bɔɪ||'buːi, bɔɪ/ n floating object fastened to the bed of the sea to show a danger, rocks, etc.

buoy² v **buoy up** phr vt 1 keep floating 2 keep high

buoy-an-cy /'bɔɪənsi||'bɔɪənsi, 'buːjənsi/ n [U] 1 tendency to float 2 cheerfulness 3 ability, e.g. of prices or business activity, to remain or return quickly to a high level after a period of difficulty -ant adj showing buoyancy

bur-den /'bɜːdn||'bɜr-/ n fml heavy load or duty ♦ vt fml load; trouble

bur-den-some /'bɜːdnsəm||'bɜr-/ adj being a burden: *a burdensome task*

bu-reau /'bjʊərəʊ/ n bureaus or bureaux /'bjʊərəʊz/ 1 BrE writing desk with a lid 2 AmE for CHEST OF DRAWERS 3 government department 4 business office

bu-reauc-ra-cy /bjʊə'rɒkrəsi, ||-'rɑː-/ n 1 [U] group of government officials who are appointed, not elected 2 [C;U] government by such a group, usually supposed to be ineffective and full of unnecessary rules -rat /'bjʊərəkræt/ n appointed official -ratic /bjʊərə'krætɪk/ adj -ratically /-kli/ adv

bur-geon /'bɜːdʒən||'bɜr-/ vi fml grow; develop

bur-glar /'bɜːɡləʳ||'bɜr-/ n thief who breaks into buildings -gle also -glarize /'bɜːɡləraɪz||'bɜr-/ AmE — break into (a building) to steal ~y n [C;U] (example of) the crime of being a burglar

bur-i-al /'beriəl/ n [C;U] (ceremony of) burying

bur-ly /'bɜːli||'bɜrli/ adj (of a person) strong and heavy

burn¹ /bɜːn||bɜrn/ v **burnt** /bɜːnt||bɜrnt/ or **burned** 1 vt be on fire: *a burning match/house* 2 vt damage or destroy by fire or acid: *burn old letters* 3 vt use for heating or lighting: *a wood-burning stove* 4 vi be very hot: *burning sands* 5 vi feel or wish very strongly: *She's burning to tell you.* 6 **burn one's boats/bridges** destroy all means of going back, so that one must go forward 7 **burn one's fingers** also **get one's fingers burnt** infml — suffer the unpleasant results of a foolish action 8 **burn the candle at both ends** infml work or be active from very early until very late; use up all one's strength by doing too many different things **~er** *n* part of a cooker, etc. that produces flames **~ing** *adj* 1 on fire 2 very strong and urgent

burn away *phr vi* disappear by burning

burn down *phr vi* destroy (a building) by fire

burn out *phr v* 1 *vt* make (a building) hollow by fire 2 *vi* stop burning because there is nothing left to burn 3 *vi/t* stop working through damage caused by heat: (fig.) *He was burned out* (= no longer active) *at 38.*

burn up *phr vt* destroy completely by fire or great heat

burn² *n* mark or hurt place made by burning

bur·nish /'bɜːnɪʃ‖'bɜːr-/ *vt* polish by rubbing

burn-out /'bɜːnaʊt‖'bɜːr-/ *n* [C;U] moment when the engine of a ROCKET or JET uses up all its fuel and stops operating

burp /bɜːp‖bɜːrp/ *v, n* BELCH

bur·row /'bʌrəʊ‖'bɜːrəʊ/ *n* hole where a rabbit, etc., lives ♦ *vi/t* make a hole; dig

bur·sar /'bɜːsəʳ‖'bɜːr-/ *n* person in a college who has charge of money, buildings, etc.

bur·sa·ry /'bɜːsəri‖'bɜːr-/ *n* SCHOLARSHIP (1)

burst¹ /bɜːst‖bɜːrst/ *vi/t* **burst** 1 break suddenly by pressure from inside: *a burst tyre* 2 (cause to) come into the stated condition suddenly, often with force: *They burst open the door.* 3 be filled to breaking point (with a substance or usu. pleasant feeling): *I'm bursting* (= very eager) *to tell someone the news.* | *The river burst its banks.*

burst in on/upon *phr vt* interrupt noisily

burst into *phr vt* 1 enter hurriedly 2 BREAK into (2)

burst out *phr v* 1 *vi* begin suddenly (to use the voice without speaking): *They burst out laughing/crying.* 2 say suddenly

burst² *n* sudden outbreak or effort: *a burst of speed*

bur·y /'beri/ *vt* 1 put into a grave 2 hide away: *buried treasure* | (fig.) *She buried her head in her hands.*

bus /bʌs/ *n* large passenger-carrying motor vehicle ♦ *vt* **-ss-, -s-** take by bus

bush /bʊʃ/ *n* 1 [C] low woody plant: *rose bush* 2 [U] wild land in Australia 3 **beat about the bush** avoid coming to the main point **~y** *adj* (of hair) growing thickly

busi·ness /'bɪznɪs/ *n* 1 [U] trade; the getting of money 2 [C] money-earning activity; shop, etc. 3 [C;U] one's employment; duty: *A teacher's business is to teach.* 4 [S] affair; matter 5 **have no business to** have no right to 6 **like nobody's business** very fast or well 7 **Mind your own business!** Don't ask about things that don't concern you. **~like** *adj* doing things calmly and effectively

busi·ness·man /'bɪznɪsmən/, **-woman** /-,wʊmən/ *fem.* — **-men** /-mən/ *person in a business firm*

busk /bʌsk/ *vi BrE* play music in the street, etc., to earn money **busker** *n*

bus stop /'· ·/ *n* place where buses stop for passengers

bust¹ /bʌst/ *vt* **busted** or **bust** *infml* 1 break, esp. with force 2 *sl* (of the police) take to a police station 3 *sl* (of the police) enter without warning to look for something illegal 4 **-buster** *infml* person who destroys or breaks up the stated thing: *a crimebuster* ♦ *adj infml* 1 broken 2 **go bust** (of a business) fail

bust² *n* 1 human head and shoulders as shown in a SCULPTURE 2 woman's breasts

bus·tle /'bʌsəl/ *vi* be busy, often noisily **bustle** *n* [S]

bust-up /'· ·/ *n sl* 1 noisy quarrel 2 a coming to an end of a relationship or partnership

bus·y /'bɪzi/ *adj* 1 working; not free 2 full of work: *a busy morning* 3 esp. *AmE* (of telephones) in use ♦ *vt* keep (oneself) busy **busily** *adv*

but /bət; *strong* bʌt/ *conj* 1 rather; instead: *not one, but two* 2 yet at the same time; however: *I want to go, but I can't.* 3 (shows disagreement or surprise): *But I don't want to!* | *But that's wonderful!* ♦ *prep* 1 except: *nobody but me* 2 **but for** except for; without ♦ *adv lit* 1 only: *You can but try.* 2 **all but** almost ♦ *n* unwanted argument: *No buts! You're going!*

butch·er /'bʊtʃəʳ/ *n* 1 person who kills animals for food, or sells meat 2 cruel killer ♦ *vt* kill and prepare for food 2 kill bloodily **~y** *n* [U] cruel needless killing

but·ler /'bʌtləʳ/ *n* chief male servant

butt¹ /bʌt/ *vi/t* push with the head or horns

butt *phr vi* interrupt

butt² *n* 1 person that people make fun of 2 end of something: *cigarette butt* 3 BOTTOM¹ (2) 4 large barrel

but·ter /'bʌtəʳ/ *n* [U] yellow fat made from cream ♦ *vt* spread butter on

butter up *phr vt sl* praise too much; FLATTER

but·ter·cup /'bʌtəkʌp‖-ər-/ *n* yellow wild flower

but·ter·fin·gers /'bʌtə,fɪŋgəz‖ 'bʌtər,fɪŋgərz/ *n* person likely to drop things

but·ter·fly /'bʌtəflaɪ‖-ər-/ *n* **1** insect with large coloured wings **2** person who spends all his/her time running after pleasure: *a social butterfly* **3** **have butterflies in one's stomach** feel very nervous before doing something

but·ter·scotch /'bʌtəskɒtʃ‖-ər-skɑːtʃ/ *n* sweet food made from sugar and butter boiled together

but·tock /'bʌtək/ *n* either of the 2 fleshy parts on which a person sits

but·ton /'bʌtn/ *n* **1** small round object passed through a hole to fasten a garment, etc. **2** button-like object pressed to start a machine ♦ *vi/t* fasten with a button

but·ton·hole /'bʌtnhəʊl/ *n* **1** hole for a button **2** *BrE* flower to wear on one's coat or dress ♦ *vt* stop and force to listen

but·tress /'bʌtrəs/ *n* support for a wall ♦ *vt* support; strengthen

bux·om /'bʌksəm/ *adj* (of a woman) fat and healthy, esp. having large breasts

buy /baɪ/ *vi/t* **bought** /bɔːt/ **1** obtain by paying money **2** accept; believe ♦ *n* something bought ~**er** person who buys, esp. professionally for a firm

buy·out /'baɪaʊt/ *n* situation in which a person or group gains control of a company by buying all or most of its shares

buzz /bʌz/ *v* **1** *vi* make the noise that bees make: (fig.) *The room buzzed with excitement.* **2** *vi/t* call someone with an electrical signalling apparatus (a **buzzer**) **3** fly slow and fast over: *Planes buzzed the crowd.* ♦ *n* **1** [C] noise of buzzing **2** *infml* telephone call: *Give me a buzz.* **3** *sl* pleasant feeling as if from a drug

buzz off *phr vi infml* go away

buzz·word /'bʌzwɜːd‖-wɜːrd/ *n* word or phrase, esp. related to a specialized subject, which is thought to express something important but is often hard to understand

by /baɪ/ *prep, adv* **1** beside; near: *Sit by me.* **2** through; using: *enter by the door | travel by car | earn money by writing* **3** past: *He walked by (me) without speaking.* **4** before: *Do it by tomorrow.* **5** (shows who or what does something): *a play by Shakespeare | struck by lightning* **6** (shows amounts and measurements): *They overcharged me by £3. | a room 5 metres by 4 | pay by the hour* **7** (shows how or with what): *hold it by the handle* **8** (in promises, etc.): *By God, he's done it!* **9** (shows the size of groups following each other): *The animals went in two by two.* **10** during: *to sleep by day* **11** **by and by** before long **12** **by and large** on the whole; usually

bye /baɪ/ also **bye-bye** /,· '·‖'·· ·/ — *interj infml* goodbye

by-e·lec·tion , **bye-election**/'··,··/ *n* election held between regular elections, in only one place

by·gone /'baɪgɒn‖-gɔːn/ *adj* past: *in bygone days* ♦ *n* [P] **let bygones be bygones** forgive past quarrels

by·law /'baɪlɔː/ *n* law made by a local council, a railway, etc.

by-pass /'baɪpɑːs‖-pæs/ *n* road that goes round a busy town, etc. ♦ *vt* avoid by going round

by·play /'baɪpleɪ/ *n* [U] action of less importance going on at the same time as the main action

by-prod·uct /'· ,··/ *n* something produced while making something else

by·stand·er /'baɪˌstændəʳ/ *n* person who watches without taking part

byte /baɪt/ *n* unit of computer information equal to eight BITs³

by·way /'baɪweɪ/ *n* smaller road or path which is not much used or known

by·word /'baɪwɜːd‖-wɜːrd/ *n* (name of a) person, place, or thing thought to represent some (usu. bad) quality: *a byword for cruelty*

by·zan·tine /baɪˈzæntaɪn, tiːn, bɪ-‖ ˈbɪzəntiːn, -taɪn/ *adj* secret, indirect, and difficult to understand

C

C, c /siː/ the 3rd letter of the English alphabet

c *written abbrev. for:* **1** cent(s) **2** CIRCA **3** CUBIC **4** centimetre(s) **5** COPYRIGHT

C *abbrev. for:* **1** CELSIUS **2** century

cab /kæb/ *n* **1** taxi **2** the part of a bus, railway engine, etc., where the driver sits

cab·a·ret /'kæbəreɪ‖ˌkæbəˈreɪ/ *n* [C;U] performance of music and dancing in a restaurant, etc.

cab·bage /'kæbɪdʒ/ *n* **1** [C;U] round vegetable with thick green leaves **2** [C] *infml* **a** inactive person who takes no interest in anything **b** someone who has lost the ability to think, move, etc., as a result of illness, etc.

cab·in /'kæbɪn/ *n* **1** small room on a ship **2** small roughly built house

cab·i·net /'kæbənɪt/ *n* **1** piece of furniture with shelves and drawers **2** chief ministers of a government

ca·ble /'keɪbl/ *n* **1** [C;U] thick heavy rope used on ships etc.: *a cable railway*

2 [C] wire carrying electricity, telephone messages, etc. **3** [C] TELEGRAM ♦ *vi/t* send or tell by TELEGRAM

cable car /'·· ·/ *n* car supported in the air by a cable, for crossing valleys, etc.

cache /kæʃ/ *n* secret store of things

cack-hand-ed /ˌkæk 'hændəd◂/ *adj* BrE unskilful; CLUMSY

cack-le /'kækəl/ *vi* **1** make the noise a hen makes **2** laugh unpleasantly **cackle** *n*

ca-coph-o-ny /kə'kɒfəni/ʃ'kɑː-/ *n* [C;U] unpleasant mixture of loud noises **–nous** *adj*

cac-tus /'kæktəs/ *n* **-tuses** or **-ti** /-taɪ/ fleshy desert plant with PRICKLES

ca-det /kə'det/ *n* young person training in the armed forces or police

cadge /kædʒ/ *vi/t derog* get or try to get by asking; borrow

ca-dre /'kɑːdəʳ, -drə, 'keɪdəʳ ‖ 'kædri, 'kɑːdrə/ *n* (member of) an inner group of trained people

cae-sar-e-an /sɪ'zeərɪən/ *n* operation to take a baby out by cutting, instead of by ordinary birth

caf-e /'kæfeɪ‖kæ'feɪ, kə-/ *n* small restaurant serving light meals and drinks

caf-e-te-ri-a /ˌkæfə'tɪərɪə/ *n* restaurant where people collect their own food, often in a factory, college, etc.

cage /keɪdʒ/ *n* container with bars, for keeping birds or animals in ♦ *vt* put in a cage

cag-ey /'keɪdʒi/ *adj* secretive

Cain see raise Cain (RAISE)

ca-jole /kə'dʒəʊl/ *vt* persuade by praise or false promises

cake /keɪk/ *n* **1** [C;U] soft sweet food baked with flour, etc.: *a birthday cake* **2** [C] flat piece of something: *a cake of soap* **3** (sell) like hot cakes very quickly **4** have one's cake and eat it too have the advantages of something without the disadvantages that go with it — see also PIECE OF CAKE ♦ *vt* cover thickly: *shoes caked with mud*

CAL, Cal /kæl/ *abbrev. for:* computer-assisted learning

ca-lam-i-ty /kə'læməti/ *n* terrible misfortune **–tous** *adj*

cal-ci-um /'kælsɪəm/ *n* [U] metal substance found in bones and chalk

cal-cu-late /'kælkjʊleɪt/ *vt* **1** find out by using numbers: *calculate the cost* **2** plan, intend: *take a calculated risk* **-lable** *adj* able to be measured **–lator** *n* small machine that calculates **–lation** /ˌkælkjʊ'leɪʃən/ *n* [C;U]

cal-cu-lat-ing /'kælkjʊleɪtɪŋ/ *adj* coldly SHREWD

cal-en-dar /'kæləndəʳ/ *n* **1** list of the days and months of the year **2** system of naming and dividing the months, etc.

calf¹ /kɑːf‖kæf/ *n* **calves** kɑːvz‖ kævz/ **1** [C] young of cattle and some other large animals **2** [U] its leather: **calfskin** *boots*

calf² *n* **calves** back of the human leg, between knee and ankle

cal-i-bre ‖ also **-ber** *AmE*/'kæləbəʳ/ *n* **1** [S;U] quality: *work of (a) high calibre* **2** inside size of a tube or gun; bullet size

call¹ /kɔːl/ *v* **1** *vi/t* speak or say loudly **2** *vt* name: *We'll call the baby Jean.* **3** *vt* tell to come: *Call a doctor!* **4** *vi* **a** make a short visit: *Let's call at Bob's.* **b** make regular visits: *The milkman calls every day.* **5** *vi/t* telephone **6** *vt* say publicly that something is to happen: *call a meeting/an election/a strike* **7** *vt* consider to be: *She called me a coward.* **8** *vt* waken: *Please call me at 7.*

call back *phr v* **1** *vt* cause (someone) to return **2** *vi/t* return a telephone call

call by *phr vi* visit when passing

call for *phr vt* **1** demand **2** need; deserve **3** collect

call in *phr vt* ask to come: *call the doctor in*

call off *phr vt* **1** decide not to have (a planned event) **2** tell to keep away

call on/upon *phr vt* **1** visit **2** *fml* ask to do something

call out *phr vt* **1** order officially to help: *Call out the army!* **2** order to STRIKE

call up *phr vt* **1** telephone **2** BrE order to join the armed forces

call² *n* **1** shout; cry **2** telephone conversation **3** short visit **4** demand; need: *There's no call for rudeness.* **5** command to meet, come, or do something **6** on call ready to work if needed

call box /'· ·/ *n* hut with a public telephone

call-er /'kɔːləʳ/ *n* person who visits or makes a telephone call

call girl /'· ·/ *n* woman PROSTITUTE who makes her arrangements by telephone

cal-lig-ra-phy /kə'lɪgrəfi/ *n* [U] (art of) beautiful handwriting

call-ing /'kɔːlɪŋ/ *n fml* profession; trade

cal-li-pers /'kæləpəz‖-əʳz/ *n* [P] **1** instrument for measuring distance between surfaces **2** leg supports to help someone to walk

cal-lous /'kæləs/ *adj* unkind; without sympathy **~ness** *n* [U]

cal-low /'kæləʊ/ *adj* young and inexperienced

call-up /'· ·/*n* order to serve in the armed forces

cal-lus /'kæləs/ *n* an area of hard skin

calm /kɑːm‖kɑːm, kɑːlm/ *adj* **1** not excited; quiet **2** (of weather) not windy **3** (of the sea) smooth **calm** n [S;U] **calm** vi/t make or become calm: We tried to calm him down. ~**ly** adv ~**ness** n [U]

cal·o·rie /'kæləri/ n unit of heat, or of ENERGY produced by a food

calve /kɑːv‖kæv/ vi give birth to a CALF

calves /kɑːvz‖kævz/ n pl. of CALF

ca·lyp·so /kə'lɪpsəʊ/ n kind of West Indian song

cam·ber /'kæmbər/ n upward curve in the middle of a road surface

came /keɪm/ v past t. of COME

cam·el /'kæməl/ n large long-necked animal with one or two large HUMPs on its back

cam·e·o /'kæmi-əʊ/ n -os **1** piece of jewellery consisting of a raised shape on a darker background **2** short piece of fine writing or acting which shows the character of a person, place or event

cam·e·ra /'kæmərə/ n **1** apparatus for taking photographs or moving pictures **2** in camera in secret

cam·ou·flage /'kæməflɑːʒ/ n [C;U] use of colour, shape, etc. to hide an object **camouflage** vt

camp[1] /kæmp/ n **1** [C;U] place where people live in tents or huts for a short time **2** [C] group of people with the same esp. political ideas **3 break/strike camp** take up and put away tents ♦ vi set up or live in a camp: We go camping every summer. ~**er** n person who camps

camp[2] adj infml **1** (of a man) behaving or looking like a woman, esp. intentionally **2** so unreal, unnatural, etc., as to be amusing

cam·paign /kæm'peɪn/ n connected set of military, political, or business actions intended to obtain a particular result ♦ vi lead, take part in or go on a campaign

cam·pus /'kæmpəs/ n [C;U] grounds of a university, college or school: campus (= university) life

can[1] /kən; strong kæn/ v aux **1** be able to: Can you swim?|I can't hear you. **2** be allowed to; may: You can go home now. **3** (shows what is possible): He can be very annoying.|It can't be true.

can[2] /kæn/ n **1** metal container for foods or liquids: a can of beans|a petrol can **2 carry the can** esp. BrE take the blame ♦ vt -nn- preserve (food) in a can

ca·nal /kə'næl/ n watercourse dug for boats to travel along or to bring water

ca·nar·y /kə'neəri/ n small yellow songbird

can·cel /'kænsəl/ vt -ll- BrE ‖ -l- AmE **1** decide not to have (a planned event): cancel a trip **2** destroy the

value of (a cheque, etc.) by drawing a line through it ~**lation** /ˌkænsə-'leɪʃən/ n [C;U]

cancel out phr vi/t balance; equal: The 2 debts cancel each other out.

can·cer /'kænsər/ n [C;U] diseased growth in the body ~**ous** adj

can·did /'kændəd/ adj honest; sincere ~**ly** adv

can·di·date /'kændədət, -deɪt, -dət/ n **1** person to be chosen or elected for a position **2** person taking an examination –**dature** n [U] being a candidate

can·died /'kændid/ adj covered with shiny sugar

can·dle /'kændl/ n wax stick with string inside, which gives light when it burns: We ate by **candlelight**.

can·dle·stick /'kændl,stɪk/ n holder for a candle

can·dour BrE ‖ -**dor** AmE/'kændər/ n [U] being CANDID

can·dy /'kændi/ n [C;U] esp. AmE sweets, chocolate, etc.

cane /keɪn/ n **1** stem of certain tall plants, used for making furniture, for punishing children, etc. **2 the cane** punishment with this ♦ vt hit with a cane

ca·nine /'keɪnaɪn, 'kæ-‖'keɪ-/ adj, n (of, for, typical of) a dog

can·is·ter /'kænəstər/ n metal box for holding a dry substance or a gas

can·ker /'kæŋkər/ n [C;U] disease of trees, and of animal and human flesh

can·na·bis /'kænəbəs/ n [U] drug produced from HEMP, smoked in cigarettes

can·ne·ry /'kænəri/ n factory where food is put in cans

can·ni·bal /'kænəbəl/ n **1** person who eats human flesh **2** animal that eats its own kind ~**ism** n [U]

can·ni·bal·ize, -ise /'kænəbəlaɪz/ vt use parts (of a broken machine) to repair another machine of the same kind –**istic** /ˌkænəbə'lɪstɪk/ adj

can·non[1] /'kænən/ n cannons or cannon big gun, fixed to a carriage or used on military aircraft

cannon[2] vi hit or knock forcefully, esp. by accident

cannon fod·der /'·· ˌ·'/ n [U] ordinary soldiers thought of as nothing but military material without regard for their lives

can·not /'kænət, -nɒt‖-nɑːt/ v fml can not: We cannot accept.

can·ny /'kæni/ adj clever; not easily deceived

ca·noe /kə'nuː/ n light boat moved by a PADDLE

can·on /'kænən/ n **1** religious law **2** accepted standard of behaviour or thought **3** kind of Christian priest ~**ize** vt declare to be a SAINT ~**ical**

/kəˈnɒnɪkəl‖kəˈnɑː-/ *adj* according to religous law

can-o-py /ˈkænəpi/ *n* **1** cloth roof over a bed, etc.: (fig.)*a canopy of leaves* **2** cover over the front of a plane

cant /kænt/ *n* [U] insincere talk

can't /kɑːnt‖kænt/ *v short for*: can not: *I can't come tonight*

can-tan-ker-ous /kænˈtæŋkərəs/ *adj* quarrelsome

can-teen /kænˈtiːn/ *n* **1** place in a factory, office, etc., where food is served **2** *BrE* set of knives, forks, and spoons

can-ter /ˈkæntər/ *n* [S] horse's movement, slower than a GALLOP **canter** *vi/t*

can-ti-le-ver /ˈkæntɨˌliːvər/ *n* armlike beam sticking out from an upright support, esp. for a bridge

can-vas /ˈkænvəs/ *n* **1** [U] strong cloth used for tents, etc. **2** [C] oil painting done on this

can-vass /ˈkænvəs/ *vi/t* go through (a place) or to (people) to ask for votes or find out opinions ~**er** *n*

can-yon /ˈkænjən/ *n* deep narrow valley

cap /kæp/ *n* **1** soft flat head-covering with no BRIM **2** protective top of a bottle, tube, etc. ♦ *vt* -**pp-** **1** cover the top of **2** do or say better than: *He capped my joke with a funnier one.* **3** give a cap to (someone) as a sign of honour, esp. for playing in a national team

ca-pa-ble /ˈkeɪpəbəl/ *adj* **1** clever: *a very capable doctor.* **2** able to do or be: *That remark is capable of being misunderstood.* –**bly** *adv* –**bility** /ˌkeɪpəˈbɪlɨti/ *n* **1** [C;U] having skills and apparatus necessary for the stated type of war: *nuclear capability* **2** [P] undeveloped qualities and abilities

ca-pac-i-ty /kəˈpæsɨti/ *n* **1** [S;U] amount that something can hold: *The seating capacity of this theatre is 500.* **2** [C;U] ability; power **3** [C] position: *speaking in my capacity as minister* **4** **filled to capacity** completely full

cape[1] /keɪp/ *n* loose outer garment without SLEEVEs

cape[2] *n* piece of land sticking out into the sea

ca-pil-la-ry /kəˈpɪləri‖ˈkæpəleri/ *n* very thin tube, esp. a BLOOD VESSEL

cap-i-tal /ˈkæpɨtl/ *n* **1** [C] town where the centre of government is **2** [S;U] wealth, esp. when used to produce more wealth or start a business **3** [C] letter in its large form; A, B, C, etc: *write in capitals/in capital letters* **4** **make capital of** use to one's advantage ♦ *adj* punishable by death: *a capital offence*

cap-i-tal-is-m /ˈkæpɨtl-ɪzəm/ *n* [U] system based on the private ownership of wealth –**ist** *n* person who owns capital

cap-i-tal-ize, ‖ also -**ise** *BrE* /ˈkæpɨtl-aɪz/ *vt* **1** write with a capital letter **2** supply money to (a firm)

  capitalize on *phr vt* use to one's advantage

capital pun-ish-ment /ˌ··· ˈ···/*n* [U] punishment by death according to law

ca-pit-u-late /kəˈpɪtʃʊleɪt/ *vi* accept defeat; stop opposing –**lation** /kəˌpɪtʃʊˈleɪʃən/ *n* [C;U]

ca-price /kəˈpriːs/ *n* [C;U] sudden foolish change of behaviour –**pricious** /kəˈprɪʃəs/ *adj* changing; untrustworthy

cap-size /kæpˈsaɪz‖ˈkæpsaɪz/ *vi/t* (cause a boat to) turn over

cap-stan /ˈkæpstən/ *n* round object turned to raise a ship's ANCHOR, etc.

cap-sule /ˈkæpsjuːl‖-səl/ *n* **1** tiny container of medicine to be swallowed whole **2** part of a spacecraft where the pilots live

cap-tain /ˈkæptɨn/ *n* **1** leader of a team **2** person in command of a ship or aircraft **3** officer of middle rank in the armed forces ♦ *vt* be the captain of

cap-tion /ˈkæpʃən/ *n* words written above or below a picture or newspaper article

cap-ti-vate /ˈkæptɨveɪt/ *vt* charm; attract: *her captivating beauty*

cap-tive /ˈkæptɪv/ *n* prisoner, esp. taken in war ♦ *adj*: (fig.) *a captive audience* (= group not able or not allowed to stop watching or listening) –**tivity** /kæpˈtɪvɨti/ *n* [U] state or condition of being a captive

cap-tor /ˈkæptər/ *n* person who captures someone

cap-ture /ˈkæptʃər/ *vt* **1** make a prisoner of; take control of by force **2** preserve on film, in words, etc. ♦ *n* **1** [U] capturing; being captured **2** [C] person or thing captured

car /kɑːr/ *n* **1** vehicle with wheels and a motor, used for carrying people **2** railway carriage: *restaurant car*

car-a-mel /ˈkærəməl, -mel/ *n* **1** [U] burnt sugar **2** [C] sweet made of boiled sugar

car-at /ˈkærət/ *n* unit expressing the purity of gold, or the weight of a jewel

car-a-van /ˈkærəvæn/ *n* **1** *BrE* small home to be pulled by a car **2** *BrE* covered cart for living in **3** group of people with vehicles or animals crossing a desert, etc.

car-a-way /ˈkærəweɪ/ *n* plant whose strong-tasting seeds are used to give a special taste in food

car-bo-hy-drate /ˌkɑːbəʊˈhaɪdreɪt, -drət/, kɑːr-/ *n* [C;U] food such as sugar which provides heat and ENERGY, and may make one fat

car·bon /'kɑːbən‖'kɑːr-/ n 1 [U] substance found in diamonds, coal, etc. 2 [C;U] a coated paper used for making copies b copy made with this

car·bun·cle /'kɑːbʌŋkəl‖'kɑːr-/ n large painful swelling

car·bu·ret·tor BrE ‖ **-retor** AmE /ˌkɑːbj‿'retər, -bə-‖'kɑːrbəreɪtər/ n apparatus that mixes the air and petrol in a car engine

car·cass /'kɑːkəs‖'kɑːr-/ n dead body, esp. of an animal

car·cin·o·gen·ic /ˌkɑːsɪnə'dʒenɪk‖ˌkɑːr-/ adj causing CANCER

card /kɑːd‖kɑːrd/ n 1 a [C] one of 52 bits of stiff paper used for various games b [P] games played with these 2 [C] bit of stiff paper with various uses: a membership card | a birthday card | a postcard 3 [U] cardboard 4 get one's cards b be dismissed from one's job 5 lay/put one's cards on the table say what one intends to do 6 on the cards probable: They say war's on the cards. 7 play one's cards right act in the most effective manner to get what one wants

card·board /'kɑːdbɔːd‖'kɑːrdbɔːrd/ n [U] thick stiff paper: a cardboard box

car·di·ac /'kɑːdi-æk‖'kɑːr-/ adj of the heart

car·di·gan /'kɑːdɪgən‖'kɑːr-/ n short knitted (KNIT) coat with SLEEVEs, usu. fastened at the front

car·di·nal /'kɑːdənəl‖'kɑːr-/ n priest of the highest rank in the Roman Catholic church ♦ adj fml most important; main

cardinal num·ber /ˌ··· '··/ n 1, 2, 3, etc.

care¹ /keər/ n 1 [C;U] worry; anxiety: free from care | her many cares 2 [U] protection; charge: under a nurse's care 3 [U] serious attention: Take care not to drop it. 4 care of also in care of AmE — (used when addressing letters to mean) at the address of 5 take care of be responsible for 6 take into care put (esp. a child) into a home controlled by the state to make sure of proper treatment **~ful** adj attentive; CAUTIOUS **~fully** adv **~less** adj 1 not taking care; inattentive 2 free from care; not worried **~lessly** adv **~lessness** n [U]

care² vi 1 be worried; mind: I don't care where we go. 2 care to like to; want: Would you care to sit down?

care for phr vt 1 look after; nurse 2 like to have: Would you care for a drink?

ca·reer /kə'rɪər/ n 1 profession 2 general course of a person's life ♦ vi rush wildly: career down the hill

care·free /'keəfriː‖'keər-/ adj free from anxiety

ca·ress /kə'res/ n light loving touch ♦ vt give a caress to

care·tak·er /'keəˌteɪkər‖'keər-/ n person employed to look after a building

car·go /'kɑːgəʊ‖'kɑːr-/ n -goes or -gos [C;U] goods carried by a ship, plane, or vehicle

car·i·ca·ture /'kærɪkətʃuər/ n funny drawing (or written description) of someone to make them seem silly ♦ vt make a caricature of

car·nage /'kɑːnɪdʒ‖'kɑːr-/ n [U] killing of many people

car·nal /'kɑːnl‖'kɑːrnl/ adj physical, of the flesh, or esp. sexual: carnal desires

car·na·tion /kɑː'neɪʃən‖kɑːr-/ n sweet-smelling white, pink or red flower

car·ni·val /'kɑːnɪvəl‖'kɑːr-/ n [C;U] period of public rejoicing

car·ni·vore /'kɑːnɪvɔːr‖'kɑːr-/ n flesh-eating animal **-vorous** /kɑː'nɪvərəs‖kɑːr-/ adj

car·ol /'kærəl/ n religious song of joy, esp. at Christmas

carp¹ /kɑːp‖kɑːrp/ n carp or carps large FRESHWATER fish

carp² vi complain unnecessarily

car park /'· ·/ n open or enclosed place where cars and other vehicles may be left

car·pen·ter /'kɑːpəntər‖'kɑːr-/ n person who makes wooden objects **-try** n [U] work of a carpenter

car·pet /'kɑːpɪt‖'kɑːr-/ n [C;U] cloth for covering floors — see also RED CARPET ♦ vt cover (as if) with a carpet

car pool /'··/ n 1 agreement made by people to take turns driving each other to work, etc. 2 BrE number of cars owned by a company for the use of its members

car·riage /'kærɪdʒ/ n 1 [C] vehicle, esp. horse-drawn 2 [C] BrE railway passenger vehicle 3 [U] (cost of) moving goods 4 [C] movable part of a machine: the carriage of a typewriter 5 [S;U] fml way of walking

car·riage·way /'kærɪdʒweɪ/ n BrE division of a road on which traffic goes: the northbound carriageway

car·ri·er /'kæriər/ n 1 person or business that carries goods 2 person or animal that passes diseases to others without catching them 3 military vehicle or ship that carries soldiers, etc.: aircraft carrier

carrier bag /'··· ·/ n esp. BrE cheap strong paper or plastic bag, esp. with handles

car·ri·on /'kæriən/ n [U] dead or decaying flesh

car·rot /'kærət/ n long orange root vegetable

car·ry /'kæri/ v 1 vt move while supporting; have with one: *carry a gun* | *carry a child on one's back* 2 vt take from one place to another: *Pipes carry oil across the desert.* | *Flies carry disease.* 3 vt bear the weight of: *This beam carries the whole roof.* 4 vt have as a usual or necessary result: *Such a crime carries a serious punishment.* 5 vt contain; have: *All the newspapers carried the story.* 6 vt win by voting: *The motion was carried.* 7 vi reach a distance: *Her voice doesn't carry very far.* 8 **be carried away** get excited

carry off phr vt perform successfully

carry on phr vi 1 continue: *carry on talking* 2 behave in a foolish excited manner **carry-on** /'·· ·/ n piece of foolish behaviour

carry with phr vt 1 have a love affair with (someone) 2 **to carry/be carrying on with** for the present time

carry out phr vt fulfil; complete

carry through phr vt 1 help to continue: *Her courage carried her through.* 2 fulfil; complete: *carry a plan through*

cart /kɑːt‖kɑːrt/ n 1 wheeled vehicle pulled by an animal, or pulled or pushed by hand 2 **put the cart before the horse** do things in the wrong order ♦ vt 1 carry in a cart 2 carry; take: *carting these books around*

carte blanche /ˌkɑːt ˈblɑːnʃ‖ˌkɑːrt-/ n [U] full freedom

car·tel /kɑːˈtel‖kɑːr-/ n combination of independent firms, to limit competition

cart·horse /'kɑːthɔːs‖'kɑːrthɔːrs/ n heavy powerful horse, used for heavy work

car·ti·lage /'kɑːtəlɪdʒ‖'kɑːr-/ n [C;U] elastic substance found round the joints in animals

car·ton /'kɑːtn‖'kɑːrtn/ n CARDBOARD or plastic box

car·toon /kɑːˈtuːn‖kɑːr-/ n 1 humorous drawing of something interesting in the news 2 film made by photographing a set of drawings ~ist n

car·tridge /'kɑːtrɪdʒ‖'kɑːr-/ n 1 tube containing explosive and a bullet for a gun 2 part of a record player that holds the needle 3 container of MAGNETIC TAPE

cart·wheel /'kɑːtwiːl‖'kɑːrt-/ n circular movement in which a person turns over by putting their hands on the ground and moving their legs sideways in the air

carve /kɑːv‖kɑːrv/ v 1 vt make by cutting wood, stone, etc.: *carve one's*

name on a tree: | (fig.) *She carved herself (out) a good position in business.* 2 vi/t cut (cooked meat) into pieces **carver** n 1 person who carves 2 knife for carving meat **carving** n something carved from wood, etc.

cas·cade /kæˈskeɪd/ n waterfall ♦ vi pour like a waterfall

case¹ /keɪs/ n 1 [C] example; situation: *I'll make an exception in your case.* | *several cases of fever* | *police investigating a case of robbery* 2 [C] legal question to be decided; arguments supporting one side of a question: *to judge this case* | *the case for the defence* 3 [C;U] gram form of word showing the part it plays in a sentence 4 [C] person having medical treatment 5 **in any case** whatever happens 6 **in case of: a** because of anxiety about: *insure the house in case of fire* **b** if (something) happens: *In case of fire, ring the bell.* 7 **(just) in case** so as to be safe (if): *Take your coat in case it rains.*

case² n large box or container: *a packing case* | *a* **suitcase**

case·ment /'keɪsmənt/ n window that opens like a door

cash /kæʃ/ n [U] 1 money in coins or notes 2 money in any form ♦ vt exchange (a cheque, etc.) for cash

cash in on phr vt take advantage from

cash card /'· ·/ n plastic card used for obtaining one's money from a machine outside a bank, at any time of day

cash crop /'· ·/ n crop grown for sale

ca·shew /'kæʃuː, kəˈʃuː/ n (tropical American tree with) a small curved nut

cash·ier¹ /kæˈʃɪər/ n person who receives and pays out money in a bank, shop, etc.

cash·ier² /kæˈʃɪər, kə-/ vt dismiss with dishonour from service in the armed forces

cash·mere /'kæʃmɪər‖'kæʒ-, 'kæʃ-/ n [U] fine soft wool

cash reg·is·ter /'· ,··/ n machine for recording the amount of sales

cas·ing /'keɪsɪŋ/ n protective covering, as on a tyre

ca·si·no /kəˈsiːnəʊ/ n -nos building where people play cards or other games for money

cask /kɑːsk‖kæsk/ n barrel for liquids

cas·ket /'kɑːskɪt‖'kæs-/ n 1 box for jewels, letters, etc. 2 AmE for COFFIN

cas·se·role /'kæsərəʊl/ n deep dish for cooking and serving meat; food cooked in this

cas·sette /kə'set/ n container of MAGNETIC TAPE, or of photographic film

cas·sock /'kæsək/ n priest's long garment

cast¹ /kɑːst‖kæst/ vt cast 1 fml throw: cast a net | a snake casting off its skin | The sun casts long shadows. 2 give (a vote) 3 make by pouring hot metal: cast a statue 4 choose as an actor; choose actors for (a play) ~ing n thing made by pouring metal

cast aside phr vt get rid of

cast away phr vt leave (someone) somewhere as the result of a shipwreck

cast down phr vt make sad; UPSET

cast off phr vi/t unloose (a boat)

cast² n 1 actors in a play, film, etc. 2 act of throwing a fishing line, etc. 3 hard covering to protect a broken bone 4 object made by casting metal 5 general shape or quality: an inquiring cast of mind 6 slight SQUINT (1)

cas·ta·nets /ˌkæstə'nets/ n [P] musical instrument made of 2 hollow shells to be knocked together

cast·a·way /'kɑːstəweɪ‖'kæst-/ n shipwrecked person

caste /kɑːst‖kæst/ n [C;U] Hindu social class

cast·er /'kɑːstəʳ‖'kæs-/ n 1 small wheel on a chair, etc. 2 container with holes for salt or sugar

cas·ti·gate /'kæstɪgeɪt/ vt fml punish severely; CRITICIZE

casting vote /ˌ·· '·/ n deciding vote when both sides have an equal number of votes

cast i·ron /ˌ· '··/ n hard but easily breakable type of iron **cast-iron** /ˌ· '··◂/ adj 1 made of cast iron 2 very strong; unbreakable: a cast-iron stomach | a cast-iron excuse

cas·tle /'kɑːsəl‖'kæ-/ n 1 large building that can be defended against attack 2 one of the powerful pieces in the game of CHESS

cast-off /'· ·/ n, adj (piece of clothing) thrown away by the original owner

castor oil /ˌ·· '·◂/ n [U] thick vegetable oil used as a LAXATIVE

cas·trate /kæ'streɪt‖'kæstreɪt/ vt remove the sex organs of (a male) —**tration** /kæ'streɪʃən/ n [C;U]

cas·u·al /'kæʒuəl/ adj 1 informal: casual clothes 2 resulting from chance: casual meeting 3 employed for a short time: casual labour 4 not serious or thorough: the casual reader ~ly adv

cas·u·al·ty /'kæʒuəlti/ n person killed or hurt in an accident or battle

cat /kæt/ n 1 small furry animal often kept as a pet 2 animal related to this; lion, tiger, etc. 3 **let the cat out of the**

bag tell a secret (usu. unintentionally) 4 **rain cats and dogs** rain very heavily

cat·a·clys·m /'kætəklɪzəm/ n fml violent event, such as an EARTHQUAKE ~**ic** /ˌkætə'klɪzmɪk/ adj

cat·a·comb /'kætəkuːm‖-kəʊm/ n underground burial place with many rooms

cat·a·logue ‖ also **-log** AmE /'kætəlɒg‖-lɔːg, -lɑːg/ n list of places, goods for sale, etc., in order ♦ vt make a list of

cat·a·lyst /'kætl-ɪst/ n something that quickens activity without itself changing

cat·a·pult /'kætəpʌlt/ n BrE Y-shaped stick with a rubber band, for shooting small stones ♦ vt fire (as if) from a catapult: (fig.) He was catapulted to fame.

cat·a·ract /'kætərækt/ n 1 large waterfall 2 eye disease causing blindness

ca·tarrh /kə'tɑːʳ/ n [S;U] disease of the nose and throat, causing a flow of liquid

ca·tas·tro·phe /kə'tæstrəfi/ n sudden terrible misfortune —**phic** /ˌkætə'strɒfɪk‖-'strɑː-/ adj

cat bur·glar /'· ˌ··/ n thief who enters buildings by climbing walls, pipes, etc.

cat·call /'kætkɔːl/ n, v, n (make) a loud whistle or cry expressing disapproval, esp. at the theatre, etc.

catch¹ /kætʃ/ v **caught** /kɔːt/ 1 vt get hold of (a moving object) and stop it: catch a ball 2 vt make a prisoner; trap: catch a fish/a thief 3 vt discover doing something: I caught him reading my diary. 4 vt be in time for: catch a train 5 vt get (an illness) 6 vi/t get hooked or stuck: My skirt caught in the door. 7 vt hear; understand 8 vt to hit (a person or animal 9 **catch fire** start to burn 10 **catch it** infml be in trouble for doing something wrong 11 **catch one's breath** a stop breathing for a moment because of surprise or shock b rest for a short while after hard work 12 **catch sight of** see for a moment 13 **catch someone's eye** attract someone's attention by looking at them ~**ing** adj infectious

catch on phr vi 1 become popular 2 understand

catch out phr vt discover doing something wrong

catch up phr vi/t 1 come up from behind; draw level 2 **caught up in** completely interested in or involved

catch² n 1 getting and holding a ball 2 (amount of) something caught: big catch of fish 3 hook, etc. for fastening something 4 hidden difficulty; SNAG

catch-22 /ˌ· ··'··/n [U] situation from which one is prevented from escaping by something that is part of the situation itself: *I can't get a job unless I belong to the union, and I can't join the union until I've got a job — it's a catch-22 situation!*

catch-ment ar-e-a /'kætʃmənt ˌeəriə/ *n* area from which a school gets its pupils, a hospital gets its patients, etc.

catch-phrase /'kætʃfreɪz/ *n* fashionable phrase that everyone uses

catch-y /'kætʃi/ *adj* (of a tune, etc.) easy to remember

cat-e-gor-i-cal /ˌkætə'gɒrɪkəl‖-'gɔː-, -'gɑː-/ *adj* (of a statement) unconditional; made without doubt **~ly** /-kli/ *adv*

cat-e-go-ry /'kætəgəri‖-gɔːri/ *n* division in a system; class **–gorize** /-gəraɪz/ *vt* put in a category

ca-ter /'keɪtəʳ/ *vi* provide catering and drinks at a party **~er** *n*

   cater for *phr vt BrE* provide what is necessary: *magazines catering for all opinions*

cat-er-pil-lar /'kætəˌpɪləʳ‖-tər-/ *n* **1** wormlike creature that eats leaves **2** endless chain of plates on the wheels of a TRACTOR, etc.

cat-gut /'kætgʌt/ *n* [U] cord used for the strings of musical instruments

ca-thar-sis /kə'θɑːsɪs, kæ-‖kə'θɑːr-/ *n* **-ses** /-siːz/ [C;U] getting rid of bad feelings by expressing them through art or by reliving them **cathartic** *adj*

ca-the-dral /kə'θiːdrəl/ *n* chief church of a DIOCESE

cath-ode /'kæθəʊd/ *n* part of an electrical instrument from which ELECTRONs leave

cath-o-lic /'kæθəlɪk/ *adj* **1** *fml* general; broad: *catholic tastes* **2** *(cap.)* ROMAN CATHOLIC ♦ *n* *(cap.)* a ROMAN CATHOLIC

Cath-o-li-cism /kə'θɒlɪsɪzəm‖ kə'θɑː-/ *n* [U] teachings of the ROMAN CATHOLIC church

cat-nap /'kætnæp/ *n* short light sleep

cat-tle /'kætl/ *n* [P] cows and BULLs

cat-ty /'kæti/ *adj* indirectly SPITEFUL

cat-walk /'kætwɔːk/ *n* narrow raised PLATFORM (2)

cau-cus /'kɔːkəs/ *n* political meeting to decide future plans

caught /kɔːt/ *v past t. and p. of* CATCH

caul-dron /'kɔːldrən/ *n lit* large pot for boiling things

cau-li-flow-er /'kɒliˌflaʊəʳ‖'kɑː-, 'kɔː-/ *n* [C;U] green vegetable with a large white head of flowers

cause /kɔːz/ *n* **1** [C;U] thing that produces a result: *the cause of the accident* **2** [U] reason: *no cause for complaint* **3** [C] purpose strongly supported: *good causes such as famine relief* ♦ *vt* be the cause of: *to cause trouble*

cause-way /'kɔːzweɪ/ *n* raised road across water, etc.

caus-tic /'kɔːstɪk/ *adj* **1** able to burn by chemical action **2** (of remarks) bitter; nasty

cau-tion /'kɔːʃən/ *n* **1** [U] great care **2** [C] spoken warning by a policeman, etc. — see also **throw caution to the wind** (THROW) ♦ *vt* warn **~ary** *adj* giving a warning

cau-tious /'kɔːʃəs/ *adj* with caution; careful **–ly** *adv*

cav-al-cade /ˌkævəl'keɪd, 'kævəlkeɪd/ *n* procession of riders, vehicles, etc.

cav-a-lier /ˌkævə'lɪəʳ/ *adj* thoughtless; OFFHAND

cav-al-ry /'kævəlri/ *n* [U] soldiers on horseback, or (now) with armoured vehicles

cave[1] /keɪv/ *n* underground hollow place

cave[2] *v* **cave in** *phr vi* (of a roof) fall down **2** give up opposition; YIELD

ca-ve-at /'keɪviæt, 'kæv-/ *n* *law* warning

cav-ern /'kævən‖-ərn/ *n* large cave **~ous** *adj* (of a hole) very large

cav-i-ar /'kæviɑːʳ/ *n* [U] salted eggs (ROE) of a large fish

cav-il /'kævəl/ *vi* **-ll-** *BrE* ‖ **-l-** *AmE* find fault unnecessarily

cav-i-ty /'kævəti/ *n fml* hole in a solid mass, such as a tooth

ca-vort /kə'vɔːt‖-ɔːrt/ *vi infml* (esp. of a person) jump or dance about noisily

CB /ˌsiː 'biː/ *n* [U] Citizens' Band; radio by which people can speak to each other privately

cc *abbrev. for:* CUBIC centimetre

CD /ˌsiː 'diː/ *n* COMPACT DISC

CD-ROM /ˌsiː diː 'rɒm‖-'rɑːm/ *n* COMPACT DISC on which very large quantities of information can be stored for use by a computer

cease /siːs/ *vi/t* stop (an activity) **~less** *adj* unending; continuous **~lessly** *adv*

cease-fire /'··/ *n* agreement to stop fighting; TRUCE

ce-dar /'siːdəʳ/ *n* [C;U] (wood of) a tall EVERGREEN tree

cede /siːd/ *vt fml* give (esp. land, after losing a war)

cei-ling /'siːlɪŋ/ *n* **1** upper surface of a room **2** official upper limit on prices, etc.

cel-e-brate /'seləbreɪt/ *v* **1** *vt/i* mark (an event) by enjoying oneself **2** *vt* praise; honour **–brated** *adj* famous **–bration** /ˌselə'breɪʃən/ *n* [C;U]

ce-leb-ri-ty /sə'lebrəti/ *n* **1** [C] famous person **2** [U] fame

cel-e-ry /'seləri/ *n* [U] plant whose greenish-white stems are eaten as a vegetable

ce·les·ti·al /sɪˈlestɪəl‖-tʃəl/ *adj fml* of the sky or heaven

cel·i·bate /ˈselɪbət/ *n, adj* (person who is) unmarried and not sexually active, esp. for religious reasons –**bacy** *n* [U]

cell /sel/ *n* 1 small room: *prison cell* 2 small unit of living matter 3 apparatus for making electricity chemically 4 single group of people in a secret organization: *Communist cells*

cel·lar /ˈselɔʳ/ *n* underground room for storing things: *wine cellar*

cel·lo /ˈtʃeləʊ/ *n* -**los** kind of large VIOLIN held between the knees **cellist** *n* person who plays a cello

cel·lu·lar /ˈseljʊlɔʳ/ *adj* 1 having many holes; POROUS 2 consisting of CELLS (2)

cel·lu·loid /ˈseljʊlɔɪd/ *n* [U] *tdmk* 1 strong plastic formerly used for making photographic film 2 **on celluloid** on cinema film

Cel·si·us /ˈselsɪəs/ *adj, n* (in) the temperature scale in which water freezes at 0° and boils at 100°

Cel·tic /ˈkeltɪk, ˈseltɪk/ *adj* of the Celts, a European people who include the Welsh and Bretons

ce·ment /sɪˈment/ *n* [U] 1 grey powder that becomes hard like stone when mixed with water, and is used in building 2 any thick sticky glue used for filling holes or joining things ♦ *vt* join with cement: (fig.) *to cement our friendship*

cem·e·tery /ˈsemɪtri‖-teri/ *n* piece of ground used for burials

cen·o·taph /ˈsenɔtɑːf‖-tæf/ *n* MONUMENT in memory of people killed in war

cen·sor /ˈsensɔʳ/ *n* official who examines books, films, etc., to remove anything offensive ♦ *vt* examine as a censor ~**ship** *n* [U] work of a censor; censoring

cen·so·ri·ous /senˈsɔːrɪəs/ *adj fml* always looking for mistakes and faults; severely CRITICAL

cen·sure /ˈsenʃɔʳ/ *n fml* blame; disapproval ♦ *vt* express disapproval of

cen·sus /ˈsensəs/ *n* official counting, esp. of a country's population

cent /sent/ *n* (coin equal to) 0.01 of any of certain units of money, e.g. the dollar

cen·taur /ˈsentɔːr/ *n* imaginary creature, half man and half horse

cen·te·na·ry /senˈtiːnəri‖-ˈte-, ˈsentɔneri/ *n* 100th ANNIVERSARY

cen·ten·ni·al /senˈtenɪəl/ *n AmE for* centenary

cen·ter /ˈsentɔʳ/ *n, v AmE for* CENTRE

cen·ti·grade /ˈsentɔɡreɪd/ *adj, n* CELSIUS

cen·ti·me·tre *BrE* ‖ **-ter** *AmE* /ˈsentɔˌmiːtɔʳ/ *n* (unit of length equal to) 1/100 of a metre

cen·ti·pede /ˈsentɔpiːd/ *n* wormlike creature with many legs

cen·tral /ˈsentrəl/ *adj* 1 at the centre 2 most important; main ~**ly** *adv* ~**ize** *vt* bring under central control ~**ization** *n* [U] /ˌsentrəlaɪˈzeɪʃən‖-trələ-/

central heat·ing /ˌ·· ˈ··/ *n* [U] heating buildings by pipes from a single point

central pro·ces·sing u·nit /ˌ·· ˈ·· ˌ··/*n* the most important controlling part of a computer system

cen·tre *BrE* ‖ **-ter** *AmE*/ˈsentɔʳ/ *n* 1 [C] middle point 2 [C] place for a particular activity: *a shopping centre* 3 [*the* + S] a middle position, in politics, not supporting EXTREME (2) ideas ♦ *vi/t* gather to a centre: *His interests are centred on/round his family.*

cen·tre·piece /ˈsentɔpiːs‖-ɔr-/ *n* thing in the central or most important position

cen·tri·fu·gal /ˌsentrɪˈfjuːɡəl‖, senˈtrɪfjʊɡəl‖senˈtrɪfjʊɡəl/ *adj* tending to move out from the centre

cen·trist /ˈsentrɪst/ *n, adj* (of) a person who supports the CENTRE (3)

cen·tu·ry /ˈsentʃəri/ *n* 1 100 years or 100-year period counted forwards or backwards from Christ's birth 3 (in cricket) 100 runs made by one player

ce·ram·ics /sɪˈræmɪks/ *n* [U;P] (making of) pots, bricks, etc. **ceramic** *adj*

ce·re·al /ˈsɪərɪəl/ *n* 1 [C] food grain 2 [C;U] breakfast food such as CORNFLAKES

ce·re·bral /ˈserɪbrəl‖səˈriː-, ˈserɔ-/ *adj* 1 of or connected with the brain 2 showing too much serious thinking

cer·e·mo·ni·al /ˌserɔˈməʊnɪəl/ *adj* for a ceremony: *ceremonial banquet* ♦ *n* [C;U] ceremony

cer·e·mo·ni·ous /ˌserɔˈməʊnɪəs/ *adj* formally polite

cer·e·mo·ny /ˈserɔməni‖-məʊni/ *n* 1 [C] set of solemn actions to mark an important event: *a wedding ceremony* 2 [U] formal behaviour

cer·tain[1] /ˈsɜːtn‖ˈsɜːrtn/ *adj* 1 sure; without doubt: *I'm certain he saw me.* | *It's certain to rain.* 2 sure to happen: *facing certain death* 3 **make certain** do something to be sure: *Make certain he knows.* ~**ly** *adv* of course

cer·tain[2] *determiner, pron* 1 some, not named: *There are certain reasons against it.* 2 some, not a lot: *a certain amount of profit*

cer·tain·ty /ˈsɜːtnti‖ˈsɜːr-/ *n* 1 [C] established fact 2 [U] freedom from doubt

cer·tif·i·cate /sə'tɪfɪkət‖sər-/ n official paper stating facts: *marriage certificate*

cer·ti·fy /'sɜːtəfaɪ‖'sɜːr-/ vt declare officially that something is true: *to certify the prisoner insane* **–fiable** adj BrE infml mad

cer·ti·tude /'sɜːtətjuːd‖'sɜːrtɪtuːd/ n [U] fml state of being or feeling certain

cer·vi·cal /'sɜːvɪkəl‖'sɜːr-/ adj of the narrow opening (**cervix**) of the WOMB

ce·sar·e·an /sɪ,zeəriən/ n CAESAREAN

ces·sa·tion /se'seɪʃən/ n [C;U] fml short pause or stop

cess·pit /'ses,pɪt/ n underground hole where a house's SEWAGE is gathered

cf written abbrev. for: compare

ch written abbrev. for: CHAPTER (1)

chafe /tʃeɪf/ v 1 vt rub; make sore by rubbing 2 vi become impatient: *chafe at the delay*

chaff /tʃɑːf‖tʃæf/ n [U] outer covers of seeds, separated from the grain

cha·grin /'ʃægrɪn‖ʃə'grɪn/ n [U] fml annoyance and disappointment

chain /tʃeɪn/ n 1 length of metal rings joined together 2 set of connected things: *chain of mountains/of events* ♦ vt fasten with a chain: *prisoners chained to the wall*

chain re·ac·tion /,· ·'··/ n set of events so related that each causes the next

chain-smoke /'··/ vi/t smoke (cigarettes) continually **–smoker** n

chain store /'· ·/ n group of shops under one ownership

chair /tʃeər/ n 1 movable seat for one person 2 position of a chairperson 3 position of a PROFESSOR ♦ vt 1 be chairperson of 2 BrE lift and carry (someone) as a sign of admiration

chair·man /'tʃeəmən‖'tʃeər-/ -woman /-,wʊmən/ fem. n — -men /-mən/ person in charge of a meeting, or directing the work of a group

chair·per·son /'tʃeə,pɜːsən‖'tʃeər-,pɜːrsən/ n chairman or chairwoman

chal·et /'ʃæleɪ‖ʃæ'leɪ/ n 1 Swiss wooden house 2 small house or hut for holidays

chalk¹ /tʃɔːk/ n 1 [U] kind of soft white rock 2 [C;U] this material used for writing or drawing 3 **not by a long chalk** not at all **~y** adj

chalk² /tʃɔːk/ vt write with chalk

chalk up phr vt succeed in getting

chalk·board /'tʃɔːkbɔːd‖-bɔːrd/ n AmE for BLACKBOARD

chal·lenge /'tʃæləndʒ/ vt 1 invite to a fight, match, etc. 2 question the loyalty or rightness of ♦ n 1 invitation to compete 2 something exciting that needs a lot of effort **–lenging** adj difficult but exciting **–lenger** n

cham·ber /'tʃeɪmbər/ n 1 lit bedroom 2 **a** law-making body **b** room where it meets 3 enclosed space: *the 4 chambers of the heart*

cham·ber·maid /'tʃeɪmbəmeɪd‖-ər-/ n woman who cleans hotel bedrooms

chamber mu·sic /'·· ,·/ n [U] music for a small group (a **chamber orchestra**)

cha·me·le·on /kə'miːliən/ n small LIZARD that changes colour to match its surroundings

champ¹ /tʃæmp/ vi 1 (of a horse) bite noisily 2 be impatient 3 **champ at the bit** be restless and difficult to control because of being impatient to do something

champ² n infml for CHAMPION (1)

cham·pagne /ʃæm'peɪn/ n [U] expensive white wine with BUBBLEs

cham·pi·on /'tʃæmpiən/ n 1 person or animal that wins a competition 2 person who defends a principle or another person ♦ vt defend; support **~ship** n 1 competition to find the champion 2 position of being the champion 3 act of championing

chance /tʃɑːns‖tʃæns/ n 1 [U] good or bad luck 2 [C;U] likelihood: *no chance of winning* | *There* chances are (= it is likely) *he already knows.* 3 [C] favourable occasion; OPPORTUNITY: *a chance to travel* 4 [C;U] risk 5 **by chance** by accident 6 **on the (off)chance** in view of the (unlikely) possibility — see also MAIN CHANCE ♦ v 1 vt take a risk 2 vi fml happen accidentally: *We chanced to meet.* ♦ adj accidental **~y** adj risky

chan·cel /'tʃɑːnsəl‖'tʃæn-/ n eastern part of a church

chan·cel·lor /'tʃɑːnsələr‖'tʃæn-/ n (often cap.) state or legal official of high rank

chan·de·lier /,ʃændə'lɪər/ n branched hanging holder for lights

change /tʃeɪndʒ/ v 1 vi/t make or become different: *change the subject* | *water changed into ice* 2 vt give and receive in return: *change a library book* | *change pounds into dollars* 3 vi/t put different clothes on 4 vi/t leave and enter (different vehicles) 5 **change one's mind** form a new opinion ♦ n 1 changing; something new: *a change of clothes* | *Let's have fish for a change.* 2 **a** money returned when something bought costs less than the amount paid **b** low-value coins or notes — see also SEA CHANGE **~able** adj often changing

change of life /,· ·'·/ n MENOPAUSE

chan·nel¹ /'tʃænl/ n 1 narrow sea passage for liquids 3 television station 4 way along which information passes: *go through the official* *channels* vt **-ll-** BrE ‖ **-l-** AmE send through channels; direct: *channel my abilities into something useful*

chant /tʃɑːnt‖tʃænt/ vi/t sing (words) on one note **chant** n

cha-os /'keɪ-ɒs‖-ɑːs/ n [S;U] complete confusion **-otic** /keɪ'ɒtɪk‖-'ɑːtɪk/ adj

chap [1] /tʃæp/ n esp. BrE man

chap [2] vi/t **-pp-** (cause to) become sore, rough and cracked: *chapped lips*

chap-el /'tʃæpəl/ n small Christian church

chap-er-on , **-one** /'ʃæpərəʊn/ n older person who goes with a younger person and is responsible for their behaviour **chaperon, -one** vt

chap-lain /'tʃæplən/ n priest in the armed forces, a hospital, etc.

chap-ter /'tʃæptəʳ/ n 1 main division of a book, usu. numbered 2 special period of history

chapter and verse /ˌ·· ·'·/n [U] the exact details of where to find a piece of information

char [1] /tʃɑːʳ/ vi/t **-rr-** blacken by burning

char [2] n BrE CHARWOMAN

char-ac-ter /'kærəktəʳ/ n 1 [C;U] qualities that make a person or thing different from others: *a man of good character* | *the character of the town* 2 [U] moral strength, honesty, etc. 3 [C] person in a book, etc. 4 [C] person, esp. an odd one 5 [C] written letter or sign: *Chinese characters* **-less** adj ordinary; dull

char-ac-ter-is-tic /ˌkærəktə'rɪstɪk/ adj typical ♦ n special quality **-ally** /-kli/ adv

char-ac-ter-ize /'kærəktəraɪz/ vt 1 be typical of 2 describe the character of

cha-rade /ʃə'rɑːd‖ʃə'reɪd/ n 1 [C] foolish unnecessary action 2 [P] game in which words are acted by players until guessed by other players

char-coal /'tʃɑːkəʊl‖'tʃɑːr-/ n burnt wood, used for drawing with, etc.

charge /tʃɑːdʒ‖tʃɑːrdʒ/ n 1 vt/i ask in payment 2 vt record (something) to someone's debt 3 vi/t rush as if to attack 4 vt ACCUSE of a crime: *charged with stealing* 5 vt fml command; give as a duty 6 vt/i (cause to) take in electricity: *charge a battery* (fig.) *a highly charged political question* (= causing strong feelings or much argument) ♦ n 1 [C] price asked or paid 2 [U] control; responsibility: *I'll take charge of the money.* 3 [C] statement blaming a person for wrongdoing: *a charge of murder* 4 [C] rushing attack by soldiers, animals, etc. 5 [C;U] electricity put into a BATTERY 6 **in charge (of)** responsible (for)

charge card /'· ·/n plastic card which allows one to obtain goods at a particular shop and pay later

char-gé d'af-faires /ˌʃɑːʒeɪ dæ-'feəʳ‖ˌʃɑːr-/ n official who represents his/her government where there is no AMBASSADOR

char-i-ot /'tʃærɪət/ n ancient 2-wheeled horse-drawn vehicle

char-i-o-teer /ˌtʃærɪə'tɪəʳ/ n driver of a chariot

cha-ris-ma /kə'rɪzmə/ n [U] fml great charm; power to win public admiration **~tic** /ˌkærɪz'mætɪk/ adj: *charismatic leader*

char-i-ty /'tʃærəti/ n 1 [U] generosity and help to the poor, etc. 2 [U] kindness shown in judging others 3 [C] organization for helping people **-table** adj **-tably** adv

char-la-dy /'tʃɑːˌleɪdi‖'tʃɑːr-/ n CHARWOMAN

char-la-tan /'ʃɑːlətən‖'ʃɑːr-/ n person who falsely claims a special skill

charm /tʃɑːm‖tʃɑːrm/ n 1 [C;U] power to delight people 2 [C] magic words; SPELL 3 [C] object worn to bring good luck 4 **work like a charm** happen or take place with complete success ♦ vt 1 please; delight: *charming manners* 2 control by magic **~er** n person who charms **~ing** adj very pleasing

chart /tʃɑːt‖tʃɑːrt/ n 1 information in the form of a picture or GRAPH: *a sales chart* 2 map, esp. of the sea ♦ vt make a chart of

char-ter /'tʃɑːtəʳ‖-ɑːr-/ n 1 [C] official statement of rights and freedoms 2 [U] hiring of buses, planes, etc.: *charter flights* ♦ vt hire (a bus, etc.) **~ed** adj officially allowed to practise a profession: *a chartered accountant*

char-wom-an /'tʃɑːˌwʊmən‖'tʃɑːr-/ also **charlady, char** — n BrE woman who works as a cleaner

chase /tʃeɪs/ vi/t follow rapidly, in order to catch or drive away ♦ n 1 chasing something or someone 2 **give chase** chase someone

chas-m /'kæzəm/ n very deep crack in the earth

chas-sis /'ʃæsi/ n **chassis** /'ʃæsiz/ frame on which a vehicle is built

chaste /tʃeɪst/ adj avoiding wrong sexual activity

chas-ten /'tʃeɪsən/ vt improve by punishment or suffering

chas-tise /tʃæ'staɪz/ vt fml punish severely

chas-ti-ty /'tʃæstəti/ n [U] being chaste

chat /tʃæt/ vt **-tt-** talk informally **chat** n **~ty** adj 1 fond of chatting 2 having the style of informal talk: *chatty letter*

chat up *phr vt BrE infml* talk to someone (esp. of the opposite sex) in a friendly way in order to begin a relationship, persuade them to do something, etc.

chât·eau /'ʃætəʊ‖ʃæ'təʊ/ *n* -teaus *or* -teaux /'ʃætəʊz‖ʃæ'təʊz/ French castle

chat·ter /'tʃætər/ *vi* 1 talk rapidly about small things 2 (of the teeth) knock together from cold or fear ♦ *n* [U] 1 chattering talk 2 rapid speech-like sounds ~**er** *n*

chat·ter·box /'tʃætəbɒks‖-tərbɑːks/ *n* person who chatters

chauf·feur /'ʃəʊfər, ʃəʊ'fɜːr/ **chauf·feuse** /ʃəʊ'fɜːz‖-ɜːrz/ *fem.* — *n* paid driver of a private car **chauffeur** *vi/t*

chau·vin·is·m /'ʃəʊvənɪzəm/ *n* proud belief that one's own country, or one's own sex, is the best –**ist** *n, adj* — see also MALE CHAUVINIST

cheap /tʃiːp/ *adj* 1 low in price 2 a of poor quality b low or offensively unpleasant 3 without serious feeling: *cheap emotions* 4 needing little effort: *a cheap victory* 5 *AmE infml* STINGY 6 **feel cheap** feel ashamed ♦ *adv* at a low price ~**en** *vi/t* make or become cheaper ~**ly** *adv* ~**ness** *n* [U]

cheat /tʃiːt/ *vi/t* 1 act dishonestly; treat someone deceitfully: *cheating at cards* | *cheat her out of her money* 2 avoid or escape as if by deception: *to cheat death* ♦ *n* person who cheats

check /tʃek/ *n* 1 [C] examination to make sure something is correct 2 [S;U] stop; control: *keep the disease in check* 3 [C;U] pattern of squares 4 [C] *AmE* restaurant bill 5 [C] *AmE for* CHEQUE 6 [C] *AmE for* TICK¹ (2) 7 [U] (in CHESS) position of the king when under direct attack ♦ *v* 1 *vi/t* examine; make sure: *check a letter for spelling mistakes* 2 *vt* hold back; control: *check the increase in crime* 3 *vt AmE* put somewhere to be looked after: *check one's coat at the theatre* 4 *vt AmE* TICK² (2)

check in *phr vi* report one's arrival at an airport, etc. **check-in** /'· ·/ *n* [C;U]

check out *phr vi* 1 leave a hotel after paying the bill 2 a find out if something is true by making inquiries b be found to be true after inquiries have been made

check up on *phr vt* inquire thoroughly about

check·ered /'tʃekəd‖-ərd/ *adj AmE* CHEQUERED

check·list /'tʃek,lɪst/ *n* complete list; INVENTORY

check·mate /'tʃekmeɪt/ *n* [C;U] 1 (in CHESS) position of a king when under direct attack so that escape is impossible 2 (a) complete defeat ♦ *vt*

1 (in CHESS) win the game with a checkmate 2 stop; completely defeat

check-out /'tʃek-aʊt/ *n* pay desk in a self-service shop

check·point /'tʃekpɔɪnt/ *n* place where a CHECK (1) is made on people, traffic, etc.

check-up /'tʃek-ʌp/ *n* general medical examination

cheek /tʃiːk/ *n* 1 [C] either side of the face below the eye 2 [U] rude behaviour ♦ *vt esp. BrE* speak rudely to ~**y** *adj* rude

cheer /tʃɪər/ *n* 1 [C] shout of praise or joy 2 [U] happiness; good spirits ♦ *vi/t* 1 make or become happy: *cheering news* | *Cheer up!* 2 shout in approval; encourage by shouting ~**ful** *adj* happy ~**fully** *adv* ~**less** *adj* saddening ~**y** *adj* merry

cheer·i·o /,tʃɪəri'əʊ/ *interj BrE* goodbye

cheese /tʃiːz/ *n* [C;U] solid food made from milk

cheesed off /,tʃiːzd 'ɒf‖-'ɔːf/ *adj BrE sl* FED UP

chee·tah /'tʃiːtə/ *n* spotted African animal of the cat family, able to run very fast

chef /ʃef/ *n* chief cook in a restaurant, etc.

chem·i·cal /'kemɪkəl/ *adj* of chemistry ♦ *n* chemical substance

chem·ist /'kemɪst/ *n* 1 scientist specializing in chemistry 2 *BrE* person who sells medicines, soap, etc.

chem·is·try /'kemɪstri/ *n* [U] science of natural substances and how they behave

chem·o·ther·a·py /,kiːməʊ'θerəpi, ,ke-/ *n* [U] use of chemical substances to treat and control diseases

cheque *BrE* ‖ **check** *AmE*/tʃek/ *n* written order to a bank to pay money — see also BLANK CHEQUE, TRAVELLER'S CHEQUE

cheque card /'· ·/ *n BrE* card given to people by a bank, promising to pay out the money written on their cheques up to a certain amount

chequ·ered /'tʃekəd‖-ərd/ *adj BrE* partly bad and partly good: *his chequered career*

cher·ish /'tʃerɪʃ/ *vt fml* 1 care for; love 2 keep (hope, etc.) in one's mind: *cherish a memory*

cher·ry /'tʃeri/ *n* small round fruit with a stone

cher·ub /'tʃerəb/ *n* 1 pretty child, esp. one with wings in a painting 2 (*pl.* -**ubim** /-əbɪm/) kind of ANGEL ~**ic** /tʃə'ruːbɪk/ *adj*

chess /tʃes/ *n* [U] board game for 2 players

chest /tʃest/ *n* 1 upper front part of the body 2 large strong box 3 get

(something) off one's chest bring (a worry) out into the open by talking

chest-nut /'tʃesnʌt/ n 1 kind of smooth reddish-brown nut 2 joke or story so old and well-known that it is no longer funny or interesting ♦ adj reddish-brown

chest of drawers /ˌ·· '·/ n piece of furniture with drawers

chew /tʃuː/ vi/t 1 crush (food, etc.) with the teeth 2 **bite off more than one can chew** attempt more than one can deal with or succeed in finishing

chew over phr vt infml think about (a question, problem, etc.)

chewing gum /'·· ·/ n sweet sticky substance to be chewed but not swallowed

chic /ʃiːk/ adj, n [U] (with) good style

chick /tʃɪk/ n baby bird

chick-en[1] /'tʃɪkən/ n 1 [C] common farmyard bird, esp. a young one 2 [U] its meat 3 **count one's chickens before they're hatched** make plans depending on something which has not yet happened ♦ adj sl cowardly

chicken[2] v **chicken out** phr vi sl decide not to do something because one is frightened

chicken pox /'·· ·/ n [U] infectious disease that causes spots

chic-o-ry /'tʃɪkəri/ n [U] 1 plant whose leaves are eaten as a vegetable 2 powder made from its roots, added to coffee

chide /tʃaɪd/ vi/t **chided** or **chid** /tʃɪd/, **chid** or **chidden** /'tʃɪdn/ fml or lit speak to (someone) angrily; REBUKE

chief /tʃiːf/ n leader; head of something: the chief of police ♦ adj 1 highest in rank 2 main 3 **-in-chief** of the highest rank: commander-in-chief ~**ly** adv mainly; specially

chief-tain /'tʃiːftən/ n leader of a tribe, etc.

child /tʃaɪld/ n **children** /'tʃɪldrən/ 1 young human being 2 son or daughter 3 someone who behaves like a child ~**hood** n [C;U] time of being a child ~**ish** adj unsuitable for a grown person ~**less** adj having no children ~**like** adj simple; lovable

child-min-der /'tʃaɪldmaɪndəʳ/ n esp. BrE someone who looks after other people's children, esp. when the parents are at work

chill /tʃɪl/ vi/t 1 make or become cold 2 (cause to) have a feeling of cold as from fear: a chilling murder story ♦ n 1 [C] illness with coldness and shaking 2 [S] unpleasant coldness ~**y** adj 1 rather cold 2 unfriendly

chil-li /'tʃɪli/ n [C;U] (powder made from) the hot-tasting red seed case of a kind of pepper

chime /tʃaɪm/ n sound of a set of bells ♦ vi/t 1 make this sound 2 infml be in agreement

chim-ney /'tʃɪmni/ n hollow passage to let out smoke from a fire

chim-ney-pot /'tʃɪmnipɒt‖-pɑːt/ n pipe fixed on top of a chimney

chim-ney-stack /'tʃɪmnistæk/ n 1 tall chimney of a building such as a factory 2 BrE group of small chimneys

chim-ney-sweep /'tʃɪmniswiːp/ n person who cleans the insides of chimneys

chim-pan-zee /ˌtʃɪmpænˈziː, -pən-/ also **chimp** /tʃɪmp/ — n kind of African APE

chin /tʃɪn/ n the part of the face below the mouth

chi-na /'tʃaɪnə/ n [U] 1 baked clay 2 plates, cups, etc., made from this

Chi-na-town /'tʃaɪnətaʊn/ n [C;U] part of a city where there are Chinese restaurants, shops, etc.

chink[1] /tʃɪŋk/ n narrow crack

chink[2] n, v CLINK

chip[1] /tʃɪp/ n 1 small piece broken off 2 place from which this was broken 3 thin piece of potato cooked in fat: fish and chips 4 small piece of material on which an INTEGRATED CIRCUIT is formed 5 flat plastic object used for representing money in certain games 6 **a chip off the old block** a person very like their father in character 7 **have a chip on one's shoulder** be quarrelsome or easily offended, as a result of feeling badly treated 8 **when the chips are down** when a very important point is reached — see also BLUE CHIP

chip[2] vi/t **-pp-** (cause to) lose a small piece from the edge

chip in phr v infml 1 vi interrupt a conversation 2 vi/t add (one's share of money)

chi-rop-o-dist /kəˈrɒpədɪst, ʃə-‖ -'rɑː-/ n person who treats the human foot **-dy** n [U]

chirp /tʃɜːp‖tʃɜrp/ vi make the short sharp sound of small birds **chirp** n ~**y** adj (of people) cheerful

chis-el /'tʃɪzəl/ n metal tool for shaping wood or stone ♦ vi/t **-ll-**BrE ‖ **-l-**AmE cut with a chisel

chit /tʃɪt/ n signed note showing sum of money owed (for drinks, etc.)

chiv-al-ry /'ʃɪvəlri/ n [U] 1 beliefs and practices of KNIGHTs in the MIDDLE AGES 2 good manners shown by a man towards women **-rous** adj

chlo-rine /'klɔːriːn/ n [U] greenish yellow, strong-smelling substance used to DISINFECT places, esp. swimming baths

chlor-o-form /'klɒrəfɔːm, 'klɔː-‖ 'klɔːrəfɔrm/ n chemical used as an ANAESTHETIC

chock-a-block /ˌtʃɒk ə ˈblɒk◂‖ˈtʃɑːk ə ˌblɑːk/ *adj infml* very crowded
chock-full /ˌ· ˈ·◂/ *adj infml* completely full
choco-late /ˈtʃɒklət‖ˈtʃɑːkələt, ˈtʃɔːk-/ *n* **1** [U] solid brown substance eaten as a sweet **2** [C] small sweet covered with this **3** [U] hot drink made from this ♦ *adj* dark brown
choice /tʃɔɪs/ *n* **1** [C] act of choosing **2** [U] power of choosing: *have no choice but to obey* **3** [C] variety to choose from: *a big choice of shops* ♦ *adj* **1** of high quality **2** well chosen
choir /ˈkwaɪəʳ/ *n* **1** group of singers **2** part of a church where they sit
choke /tʃəʊk/ *v* **1** *vt/i* stop breathing because the breathing passage is blocked **2** *vt* fill (a passage) completely: *roads choked with traffic* ♦ *n* apparatus that controls air going into a petrol engine
choke back *phr vt* control (esp. violent or sad feelings) as if by holding in the throat: *He choked back his tears.*
chol-e-ra /ˈkɒlərə‖ˈkɑː-/ *n* [U] serious tropical disease of the stomach and bowels
cho-les-te-rol /kəˈlestərɒl‖-rəʊl/ *n* [U] substance found in all cells of the body, which helps to carry fats
choose /tʃuːz/ *vi/t* **chose** /tʃəʊz/, **chosen** /ˈtʃəʊzən/ **1** pick out from many: *choose a cake* **2** decide: *choose where to go*
chop[1] /tʃɒp‖tʃɑːp/ *vt* **-pp-** cut with a heavy tool: *chop wood/onions*
chop[2] *n* **1** quick cutting blow **2** piece of lamb or PORK with a bone in it
chop-per /ˈtʃɒpəʳ‖ˈtʃɑː-/ *n* **1** heavy tool for chopping **2** *sl* HELICOPTER
chop-py /ˈtʃɒpi‖ˈtʃɑː-/ *adj* (of water) with short rough waves
chop-sticks /ˈtʃɒpstɪks‖ˈtʃɑːp-/ *n* [P] pair of thin sticks used in East Asia for lifting food to the mouth
cho-ral /ˈkɔːrəl/ *adj* of a CHOIR
chord /kɔːd‖kɔːrd/ *n* **1** 2 musical notes sounded together **2** straight line joining 2 points on a curve — see also **strike a chord** (STRIKE[1])
chore /tʃɔːʳ/ *n* bit of regular or dull work
chor-e-og-ra-phy /ˌkɒriˈɒgrəfi, ˌkɔː-‖ˌkɔːriˈɑːg-/ *n* arranging dances for the stage **-pher** *n* **choreograph** /ˈkɒriəgrɑːf, ˈkɔː-‖ˈkɔːriəgræf/ *vt*
chor-is-ter /ˈkɒrɪstəʳ‖ˈkɔːr-, ˈkɑːr-/ *n* singer in a CHOIR
chor-tle /ˈtʃɔːtl‖ˈtʃɔːrtl/ *vi* give several laughs of pleasure and satisfaction **chortle** *n*
cho-rus /ˈkɔːrəs/ *n* **1** [C] group of singers **2** [C] part of a song repeated after each VERSE **3** [S] something said by many people together: *a chorus of groans* ♦ *vt* sing or say together
chose /tʃəʊz/ *v past t. of* CHOOSE
cho-sen /ˈtʃəʊzən/ *v past p. of* CHOOSE
Christ /kraɪst/ *n* man on whose teaching Christianity is based; Jesus
chris-ten /ˈkrɪsən/ *vt* **1** make into a member of the Christian church by BAPTISM name giving of a name **2** name (esp. a ship) at an official ceremony **3** use for the first time **~ing** *n* ceremony of BAPTISM
Chris-ten-dom /ˈkrɪsəndəm/ *n* [U] *lit* all Christian people or countries
Chris-tian /ˈkrɪstʃən, -tiən/ *n* person who believes in the teachings of Christ ♦ *adj* **1** of Christianity **2** having qualities such as kindness, generosity, etc.
Chris-ti-an-i-ty /ˌkrɪstiˈænəti/ *n* [U] the religion based on the life and teachings of Christ
Christian name /ˈ·· ·/ *n* (esp. in Christian countries) a person's FIRST NAME
Christ-mas /ˈkrɪsməs/ *n* **1** also **Christmas Day** /ˌ·· ˈ·/ — holy day in honour of Christ's birth; December 25th **2** period before and after this
chrome /krəʊm/ *n* [U] hard metal used esp. as a shiny covering on car parts, etc.
chro-mo-some /ˈkrəʊməsəʊm/ *n* tiny thread in every living cell that controls the nature of a young animal or plant
chron-ic /ˈkrɒnɪk‖ˈkrɑː-/ *adj* **1** (of a disease) lasting a long time **2** *infml* very bad: *His work is really chronic.*
chron-i-cle /ˈkrɒnɪkəl‖ˈkrɑː-/ *n* record of historical events ♦ *vt* make a chronicle of
chro-nol-o-gy /krəˈnɒlədʒi‖-ˈnɑː-/ *n* **1** [U] science that gives dates to events **2** [C] list of events in order **-ogical** /ˌkrɒnəˈlɒdʒɪkəl‖ˌkrɑːnəˈlɑː-/ *adj* arranged in order of time
chro-nom-e-ter /krəˈnɒmətəʳ‖-ˈnɑː-/ *n* very exact clock
chrys-a-lis /ˈkrɪsələs/ *n* shell-like form of an insect that will become a MOTH or BUTTERFLY
chry-san-the-mum /krɪˈsænθəməm/ *n* garden plant with large brightly-coloured flowers
chub-by /ˈtʃʌbi/ *adj* pleasantly fat
chuck /tʃʌk/ *vt* **1** throw **2** *sl* give up; leave: *chuck (in) his job*
chuck-le /ˈtʃʌkəl/ *vi* laugh quietly **chuckle** *n*
chum /tʃʌm/ *n* friend **~my** *adj* friendly
chump /tʃʌmp/ *n* **1** *sl* fool **2** thick piece of meat
chunk /tʃʌŋk/ *n* thick lump **~y** *adj* thick: *chunky sweater*
church /tʃɜːtʃ‖tʃɜːrtʃ/ *n* **1** [C] building for public Christian worship: *a regular* **churchgoer** **2** [S] profession of

priests and ministers: *enter the church* **3** [C] (*usu. cap.*) branch of Christianity: *the Catholic Church*

church-yard /'tʃɜːtʃjɑːd‖'tʃɜːrtʃjɑːrd/ *n* church burial ground

churl-ish /'tʃɜːlɪʃ‖-ɜːr-/ *adj* bad-tempered; rude ~**ly** *adv*

churn[1] /tʃɜːn‖tʃɜːrn/ *n* container in which cream is shaken to make butter

churn[2] *vi/t* shake about violently

churn out *phr vt* produce a large quantity of

chute /ʃuːt/ *n* sloped passage for something to slide down

chut-ney /'tʃʌtni/ *n* [U] hot-tasting mixture of fruits

CIA /ˌsiː aɪ 'eɪ/ *n* Central Intelligence Agency; US government department that collects information, esp. secretly

CID /ˌsiː aɪ 'diː/ *n* Central Investigation Department; branch of the UK police force made up of DETECTIVEs

ci-der /'saɪdər/ *n* [U] alcoholic drink made from apples

ci-gar /sɪ'gɑːr/ *n* roll of tobacco leaves for smoking

cig-a-rette /ˌsɪgə'ret‖ˌsɪgə'ret, 'sɪgəˌret/ *n* paper tube of cut tobacco for smoking

cin-der /'sɪndər/ *n* bit of burnt coal, etc.

cin-e-ma /'sɪnəmə/ *n* **1** [C] theatre where films are shown **2** [S] films as an art or industry

cin-na-mon /'sɪnəmən/ *n* [U] yellowish-brown SPICE used in cooking

ci-pher /'saɪfər/ *n* **1** system of secret writing **2** unimportant person

cir-ca /'sɜːkə‖'sɜːr-/ *prep fml* (used with dates) about: *circa 1000 AD*

cir-cle /'sɜːkəl‖'sɜːr-/ *n* **1** curved line on which every point is equally distant from the centre **2** ring **3** group of people **4** upper floor in a theatre ♦ *vi/t* **1** move round in a circle **2** draw a circle round

cir-cuit /'sɜːkət‖'sɜːr-/ *n* **1** circular journey round an area **2** circular path of an electric current ~**ous** /sɜː'kjuːɪtəs‖sɜːr-/ *adj* going a long way round: *a circuitous route*

cir-cu-lar /'sɜːkjələr‖'sɜːr-/ *adj* **1** shaped like a circle **2** moving in a circle **3** not direct ♦ *n* printed notice given to many people

cir-cu-late /'sɜːkjəleɪt‖'sɜːr-/ *vi/t* **1** move along a closed path **2** spread widely: *circulate rumours* **3** move about freely -**lation** /ˌsɜːkjə'leɪʃən‖ˌsɜːr-/ *n* **1** [U] flow round a closed system: *the circulation of the blood* **2** [U] passing of money among people: *the number of £5 notes in circulation* **3** [S] number of copies of a newspaper sold

cir-cum-cise /'sɜːkəmsaɪz‖'sɜːr-/ *vt* cut off the skin at the end of the male sex organ or part of the sex organ (CLITORIS) of a woman **–cision** /ˌsɜːkəm'sɪʒən‖ˌsɜːr-/ *n* [C;U]

cir-cum-fer-ence /sə'kʌmfərəns‖sər-/ *n* distance round: *the Earth's circumference*

cir-cum-nav-i-gate /ˌsɜːkəm'nævɪgeɪt‖ˌsɜːr-/ *vt fml* sail right round

cir-cum-scribe /'sɜːkəmskraɪb‖'sɜːr-/ *vt fml* limit

cir-cum-spect /'sɜːkəmspekt‖'sɜːr-/ *adj fml* careful

cir-cum-stance /'sɜːkəmstæns, -stəns‖'sɜːr-/ *n* **1** (*usu. pl.*) conditions that influence a person or event **2** **in/under no circumstances** never **3** **in/under the circumstances** because of the conditions

cir-cum-stan-tial /ˌsɜːkəm'stænʃəl‖ˌsɜːr-/ *adj fml* **1** (of a description) detailed **2** **circumstantial evidence** information worth knowing but not directly important

cir-cum-vent /ˌsɜːkəm'vent‖ˌsɜːr-/ *vt* avoid by cleverness: *circumvent the tax laws*

cir-cus /'sɜːkəs‖'sɜːr-/ *n* **1** performance of skill and daring by a group of people and animals **2** *BrE* place where several streets join **3** noisy badly behaved meeting or other such activity: *the media circus travelling with the President*

cir-rho-sis /sɪ'rəʊsəs/ *n* [U] serious LIVER disease

cissy /'sɪsi/ *n, adj BrE for* SISSY

cis-tern /'sɪstən‖-ərn/ *n* container for storing water, esp. for a TOILET

cite /saɪt/ *vt* **1** *fml* mention as an example **2** *law* call to appear in court

cit-i-zen /'sɪtəzən/ *n* **1** person living in a city or town **2** person with full membership of a country ~**ship** *n* [U]: *apply for French citizenship*

Cit-i-zens' Band /ˌ··· '·/ *n* [U] CB

cit-ric ac-id /ˌsɪtrɪk 'æsɪd/ *n* [U] weak acid from fruit juice

cit-rus /'sɪtrəs/ *adj* (of fruit) of the orange family

cit-y /'sɪti/ *n* **1** [C] large important town **2** [C] its citizens **3** [S] (*cap.*) the centre for money matters in London — see also INNER CITY

civ-ic /'sɪvɪk/ *adj* of a city or its citizens

civ-il /'sɪvəl/ *adj* **1** not military or religious **2** polite ~**ly** *adv* politely ~**ity** /sə'vɪləti/ *n* [U] politeness

civil en-gi-neer-ing /ˌ·· ··'··/ *n* [U] building of public roads, bridges, etc.

ci-vil-ian /sə'vɪljən/ *n, adj* (person) not of the armed forces

civ-i-li-za-tion ‖ *also* -**sation** *BrE* /ˌsɪvəl-aɪ'zeɪʃən‖-vəl-ə'zeɪ-/ *n* **1** [U] high level of human development and social organization **2** [C] particular civilized society: *ancient civilizations*

civ·i·lize ‖ also **-ise** BrE /'sɪvəl-aɪz/ vt **1** bring to civilization: civilized nations **2** improve in manners

civil rights /ˌ·· '·/ n [P] a citizen's rights to freedom and equality

civil ser·vant /ˌ·· '··/ n person employed in the civil service

civil ser·vice /ˌ·· '··/ n [the + S] **1** government departments, except the armed forces and law courts **2** people employed in this

civil war /ˌ·· '·/ n war between people from the same country

clad /klæd/ adj lit clothed; covered

claim /kleɪm/ v vt/i demand (something) as one's right: claim on the insurance **2** vt declare to be true: He claims to be rich. ♦ n **1** demand for something as one's right; right to something **2** something claimed, esp. money under an insurance agreement **3** statement; declaration

clai·mant /'kleɪmənt/ n fml person who claims something

clair·voy·ant /kleə'vɔɪənt‖kleər-/ adj, n (of a) person who can see what will happen in the future **-ance** n [U]

clam[1] /klæm/ n large shellfish

clam[2] v clam up phr vi become silent

clam·ber /'klæmbər/ vi climb with effort

clam·my /'klæmi/ adj unpleasantly wet and sticky

clam·our BrE ‖ **-mor** AmE /'klæmər/ n [S;U] loud confused noise, esp. of complaint ♦ vi demand noisily: a baby clamouring to be fed

clamp[1] /klæmp/ n apparatus with a screw, for fastening things together

clamp[2] vt fasten with a clamp

  clamp down on phr vt limit; prevent: clamp down on drunken driving

  clampdown /'klæmpdaʊn/ n

clan /klæn/ n Scottish family group

clan·des·tine /klæn'destən/ adj secret **~ly** adv

clang /klæŋ/ vi/t make a loud ringing sound **clang** n [S]

clang·er /'klæŋər/ n infml very noticeable mistake or unfortunate remark

clank /klæŋk/ vi/t make a sound like a heavy metal chain **clank** n [S]

clap /klæp/ v **-pp- 1** vi/t strike (one's hands) together: The audience clapped loudly. **2** vt strike lightly with the open hand: clap him on the back **3** vt infml put quickly: clapped her in jail **4 clap eyes on** infml see (someone or something) ♦ n **1** [C] loud explosive noise, esp. of thunder **2** [S] clapping: Give him a clap! **3** [S] sl GONORRHEA

clapped-out /ˌ· '·◁/ adj esp. BrE **1** (of a person) tired **2** (of a thing) old and worn out

clap·trap /'klæptræp/ n [U] nonsense

clar·et /'klærət/ n [U] red wine from Bordeaux ♦ adj deep red

clar·i·fy /'klærəfaɪ/ vt make more easily understood **-fication** /ˌklærə-fə'keɪʃən/ n [C;U]

clar·i·net /ˌklærə'net/ n kind of WOODWIND musical instrument **~tist** n person who plays the clarinet

clar·i·ty /'klærəti/ n [U] clearness

clash /klæʃ/ v vi come into opposition **2** vi (of colours) look wrong together **3** vi (of events) be planned for the same time **4** vi/t make a loud metallic noise ♦ n **1** [C] disagreement **2** [S] metallic noise

clasp /klɑːsp‖klæsp/ n **1** metal fastener **2** firm hold ♦ vt **1** seize firmly **2** fasten with a clasp

class /klɑːs‖klæs/ n **1** [C] social group of a particular rank: the ruling class **2** [U] system of dividing society into such groups **3 a** [C] group of students taught together **b** [C] period of time they are taught for **4** [C] division; level: a first-class carriage **5** [U] high quality; ELEGANCE — see also FIRST CLASS ♦ vt put into a class; consider **~y** adj fashionable and of high class

class-con·scious /'· ˌ··/ adj conscious of one's social position **~ness** n [U]

clas·sic /'klæsɪk/ adj **1** of the highest rank **2** typical: classic example **3** having a long history; TRADITIONAL ♦ n piece of literature or art, a writer or artist of lasting importance **classics** n [P] ancient Greek and Roman literature

clas·si·cal /'klæsɪkəl/ adj **1** following ancient Greek or Roman models **2** (of music) with serious artistic intentions **3** TRADITIONAL

clas·si·fy /'klæsɪfaɪ/ vt arrange into classes **-fied** adj **1** divided into classes **2** officially secret **-fication** /ˌklæsɪfə'keɪʃən/ n [C;U]

class·room /'klɑːsrʊm, -ruːm‖ 'klæs-/ n room in a school, etc., in which a class meets for a lesson

clat·ter /'klætər/ n [S;U] noise of hard objects hitting each other: a clatter of dishes ♦ vi/t make a clatter

clause /klɔːz/ n **1** gram group of words containing a subject and verb **2** law separate division of a piece of legal writing

claus·tro·pho·bi·a /ˌklɔːstrə'fəʊbiə/ n [U] fear of being shut in

claw[1] /klɔː/ n **1** sharp nail on an animal's or bird's toe **2** limb of a CRAB, etc. **3** curved end of some tools

claw[2] vi/t tear or pull with claws

  claw back phr vt take back by taxation **clawback** n

clay /kleɪ/ n [U] earth from which bricks, pots, etc., are made

clean¹ /kliːn/ *adj* 1 not dirty 2 not yet used: *clean piece of paper* 3 morally pure: *clean joke* 4 smooth; regular: *clean cut* 5 **come clean** tell the unpleasant truth ♦ *n* [S] act of cleaning ♦ *adv* completely: *I clean forgot.* | *They got clean away.*

clean² *vt* make clean **~er** *n* person or thing that cleans **–er's** *n* 1 shop where clothes, etc., are cleaned with chemicals 2 **take someone to the cleaner's** cause someone to lose all their money, etc.

clean out *phr vt* 1 make (the inside of a room, drawer, etc.) clean and tidy 2 take all someone's money

clean up *phr vi/t* 1 clean thoroughly 2 *sl* gain money as profit

clean-cut /,· '·◄/ *adj* 1 well-shaped 2 neat and clean in appearance

clean-ly¹ /'kliːnli/ *adv* in a clean way

clean-ly² /'klenli/ *adj fml* always clean **–liness** *n* [U]

cleanse /klenz/ *vt* make pure

cleanser *n* chemical, etc., used for cleaning

clean-shav-en /,· '···◄/ *adj* with no beard

clean sweep /,· '·/ *n* 1 complete change 2 complete victory

clear¹ /klɪəʳ/ *adj* 1 easy to see through: *clear glass* 2 without marks, etc.: *clear skin* | (fig) *a clear conscience* 3 easy to hear or understand 4 certain: *I'm not clear where she lives.* | *a clear case of murder* 5 open; empty: *The road's clear of snow.* 6 free; no longer touching: *We're clear of danger now.* | *He swung clear of the wall.* 7 (of wages or profit) remaining after all taxes, etc. have been paid ♦ *n* [U] **in the clear** free from guilt, debt, etc. ♦ *adv* 1 in a clear way: *shout loud and clear* 2 completely: *The prisoner got clear away.* 3 out of the way: *jump clear of the train* **~ly** *adv* 1 in a clear way: *speak clearly* 2 undoubtedly: *clearly wrong*

clear² *v* 1 *vi/t* become clear; remove something unwanted: *The sky cleared.* | *clear snow from the road* 2 *vt* get past without touching: *clear a fence* 3 *vt* give official approval to 4 *vt* free from blame 5 *vt* earn as CLEAR (7) profit or wages: *She clears £10,000 a year.*

clear away *phr vt* make an area tidy by removing

clear off *phr vi* go away

clear out *phr v* 1 *vi* go away 2 *vt* empty

clear up *phr v* 1 *vt* explain: *clear up the mystery* 2 *vt/i* tidy

clear-ance /'klɪərəns/ *n* 1 [U] official approval or acceptance 2 [C;U] distance between objects 3 [U] also **security clearance** — official acceptance that one is in no

way an enemy of one's country 4 [C] also **clearance sale** /'··· ·/ — time when a shop sells goods cheaply so as to get rid of as many as possible

clear-cut /,· '·◄/ *adj* clear in meaning

clear-ing /'klɪərɪŋ/ *n* area cleared of trees

cleav-age /'kliːvɪdʒ/ *n* 1 division caused by splitting 2 space between a woman's breasts as seen when she is wearing a dress

cleave /kliːv/ *vt* **cleaved** or **cleft** /kleft/ or **clove** /kləʊv/, **cleaved** or **cleft** or **cloven** /'kləʊvən/ divide or make by a cutting blow

cleave to *phr vt lit* remain loyal to

clef /klef/ *n* sign at the beginning of a line of written music to show the PITCH¹ (of) notes

cleft /kleft/ *v past t of* CLEAVE

cleft stick /,· '·/ *n* **(caught) in a cleft stick** (caught) in a very awkward position

clem-en-cy /'klemənsi/ *n* [U] *fml* mercy **–ent** *adj* (of weather) not severe

clench /klentʃ/ *vt* close tightly: *clench one's fists*

cler-gy /'klɜːdʒi‖-ɜːr-/ *n* [P] priests

cler-gy-man /'klɜːdʒimən‖-ɜːr-/ *n* **-men** /-mən/ Christian priest

cler-ic /,klerɪk/ *n* clergyman **–al** *adj* 1 of priests 2 of clerks

clerk /klɑːk‖klɜːrk/ *n* 1 office worker 2 official in charge of court records, etc.

clev-er /'klevəʳ/ *adj* 1 quick at learning 2 showing skill: *clever idea* **~ly** *adv* **~ness** *n* [U]

cli-ché /'kliːʃeɪ‖kliːʃeɪ/ *n* expression or idea used so often it has lost much of its force

click /klɪk/ *n* slight short sound, as of a camera ♦ *v* 1 *vi/t* make a click 2 *vi* fall into place; understand 3 *vi* be a success

cli-ent /'klaɪənt/ *n* 1 person who pays for advice from a professional person 2 customer

cli-en-tele /,kliːɒn'tel‖,klaɪən'tel, ,kliː-/ *n* clients; customers

cliff /klɪf/ *n* steep rock face, esp. on a coast

cliff-hang-er /'klɪf,hæŋəʳ/ *n* 1 competition, etc., whose result is in doubt until the very end 2 story told in parts, each of which ends at a moment of exciting uncertainty

cli-mac-tic /klaɪ'mæktɪk/ *adj* forming a climax

cli-mate /'klaɪmət/ *n* 1 average weather conditions 2 condition of opinions: *political climate* **–matic** /klaɪ'mætɪk/ *adj*

cli-max /'klaɪmæks/ *n* 1 most powerful part of a story, usu. near the end 2

ORGASM ♦ *vi/t* bring or come to a climax

climb /klaɪm/ *v* **1** *vi/t* move, esp. using hands and feet: *climb a ladder | go climbing in the Alps* **2** *vi* rise: *The road climbs steeply.* **3** *vi* (of a plant) grow upwards ♦ *n* **1** journey by climbing **2** place to climb **~er** *n* person or thing that climbs

climb down *phr vi infml* admit that one has been wrong **climb-down** /'··/ *n*

clinch[1] /klɪntʃ/ *vt* settle (an agreement) firmly

clinch[2] *n* EMBRACE

cling /klɪŋ/ *vi* **clung** /klʌŋ/ hold tightly **~ing** *adj* **1** (of clothes) tight-fitting **2** (of a person) too dependent

clin·ic /'klɪnɪk/ *n* place for specialized medical treatment **~al** *adj* **1** of clinics or hospitals **2** coldly scientific

clink /klɪŋk/ *vi/t* (cause to) make a sound like pieces of glass knocking together **clink** *n* [S]

clip[1] /klɪp/ *n* small esp. metal object for holding things together: *paper clip* **clip up -pp-**

clip[2] *vt* -pp- **1** cut with scissors, etc. **2** *sl* hit ♦ *n* **1** cutting **2** *sl* quick blow: *a clip round the ear* **~pers** *n* [P] scissor-like tool **~ping** *n* **1** piece cut off **2** CUTTING (2)

clique /kliːk/ *n derog* closely united group of people

clit·o·ris /'klɪtərɪs/ *n* small front part of the female sex organ

Cllr *BrE written abbrev. for:* COUNCILLOR

cloak /kləʊk/ *n* loose outer garment without SLEEVES ♦ *vt* keep secret

cloak-and-dag·ger /,·· '··/ *adj* (of stories, etc.) dealing with adventure and mystery

cloak·room /'kləʊkrʊm, -ruːm/ *n* room where coats, etc., may be left

clob·ber[1] /'klɒbə'‖'klɑː-/ *vt sl* **1** attack severely **2** defeat completely

clobber[2] *n sl BrE* one's belongings

clock /klɒk‖klɑːk/ *n* **1** instrument for measuring time **2** **around/round the clock** all day and all night **3** **put the clock back** return to old-fashioned ideas **4** **watch the clock** think continually of how soon work will end **5** **work against the clock** work very quickly in order to finish a job before a certain time ♦ *vt* record (time, speed, distance, etc.)

clock in/out *phr vi* record the time of arriving at/leaving work

clock up *phr vt infml* **1** record (a distance travelled, a speed reached, etc.) **2** succeed in getting

clock·wise /'klɒk-waɪz‖'klɑːk-/ *adv* in the direction of the movement of a clock

clock·work /'klɒk-wɜːk‖'klɑːk-wɜːrk/ *n* [U] **1** machinery wound up with a key **2** **like clockwork** without trouble

clod /klɒd‖klɑːd/ *n* lump or mass of clay or earth

clog[1] /klɒg‖klɑːg/ *n* wooden shoe

clog[2] *vi/t* -gg- (cause to) become blocked or filled

clois·ter /'klɔɪstə'/ *n* covered passage usu. forming part of a college, MONASTERY, etc. **~ed** *adj* sheltered from the world

clone /kləʊn/ *n* non-sexually produced descendant of a single plant or animal ♦ **clone** *vt*

close[1] /kləʊz/ *v* **1** *vt/i* shut: *close one's eyes | When does the shop close?* **2** *vt* bring to an end: *close a bank account* **3** **close a deal (with)** settle a business agreement ♦ *n* [S] *fml* end of a period of time: *at the close of play*

close down *phr vi/t* (of a factory, etc.) stop operating **closedown** /'kləʊzdaʊn/ *n*

close in *phr vi* surround gradually

close[2] /kləʊs/ *adj* **1** near: *close to the shops | a close friend* **2** thorough: *close inspection* **3** without fresh air; too warm **4** decided by a small difference: *a close finish to the race* ♦ *adv* **1** near: *close behind/together* **2** **close on** almost **3** **close to home** near the (usu. unpleasant) truth **4** (*sail*) **close to the wind** (to be) near to dishonesty or improper behaviour ♦ *n* **1** courtyard **2** BLIND ALLEY **~ly** *adv* **~ness** *n* [U]

closed shop /,· '·◄/ *n* place of work where one must belong to a particular TRADE UNION

close-knit /,kləʊs 'nɪt◄/ also **closely-knit** /,·· '·◄/ — *adj* tightly bound together by social, political, etc., beliefs and activities

close-set /,kləʊs 'set◄/ *adj* set close together: *close-set eyes*

close shave /,kləʊs 'ʃeɪv/ *n infml* situation in which something dangerous or very unpleasant is only just avoided

clos·et /'klɒzɪt‖'klɑː-, 'klɔː-/ *n esp. AmE* built-in cupboard — see also WATER CLOSET ♦ *adj* not publicly admitted; secret ♦ *vt* enclose (esp. oneself) in a private room

close-up /'kləʊs ʌp/ *n* photograph taken from very near

clo·sure /'kləʊʒə'/ *n* [C;U] closing: *hospital closures*

clot /klɒt‖klɑːt/ *n* **1** lump formed from liquid: *blood clot* **2** *sl esp. BrE* fool ♦ *vi/t* -tt- form into clots

cloth /klɒθ‖klɔːθ/ *n* [C;U] (piece of) material made by weaving

clothe /kləʊð/ *vt* provide clothes for

clothes /kləʊðz, kləʊz/ *n* [P] things to cover the body; garments

clothes-horse /'kləʊðzhɔːs, 'kləʊz-‖-ɔːrs/ n 1 BrE framework on which clothes are hung to dry, usu. indoors 2 infml esp. AmE person who is very interested in clothes and fashion

cloth-ing /'kləʊðɪŋ/ n [U] clothes

cloud /klaʊd/ n 1 [C;U] white or grey mass floating in the sky which is formed from very small drops of water 2 [C] similar floating mass: clouds of smoke/mosquitoes 3 [C] something threatening: the clouds of war 4 **have one's head in the clouds** be impractical 5 **under a cloud** out of favour ♦ v 1 vt/i cover with clouds 2 vt confuse: cloud the issue ~**y** adj 1 full of clouds 2 not clear

clout /klaʊt/ n 1 [C] blow with the hand 2 [U] influence, esp. political ♦ vt strike, esp. with the hand

clove[1] /kləʊv/ v past t. of CLEAVE

clove[2] n dried flower of a tropical tree used in cooking

clove[3] n any of the smallest pieces into which the root of the GARLIC plant can be divided

clo-ven /'kləʊvən/ v past p. of CLEAVE

clo-ver /'kləʊvəʳ/ n [C;U] 1 3-leafed plant often grown as food for cattle 2 **in clover** living in comfort

clown /klaʊn/ n 1 performer in a CIRCUS who makes people laugh 2 person acting like this ♦ vi behave foolishly

cloy /klɔɪ/ vi/t (of food) become unpleasant because too sweet: (fig.) cloying sentimentality

club[1] /klʌb/ n 1 society of people who meet for amusement; building where they meet: tennis club 2 heavy stick used as a weapon 3 stick for striking the ball in GOLF 4 playing card with one or more black three-leafed figures on it — see also BOOK CLUB ♦ vt **-bb-** hit with a heavy stick

club[2] v **club together** phr vi share the cost of something with others

cluck /klʌk/ vi make the noise a hen makes **cluck** n

clue /kluː/ n 1 something that helps to find the answer to a problem 2 **not have a clue** know nothing; be unable to understand ~**less** adj stupid

clued up /ˌkluːd ˈʌp◂/ adj infml very well-informed

clump[1] /klʌmp/ n group of trees, etc.

clump[2] vi walk heavily

clum-sy /'klʌmzi/ adj 1 awkward in movement 2 TACTLESS **-sily** adv **-siness** n [U]

clung /klʌŋ/ v past t. and p. of CLING

clus-ter /'klʌstəʳ/ n group of things close together ♦ vi form a close group

clutch[1] /klʌtʃ/ v 1 vt hold tightly 2 vi try to seize: He clutched at a branch. ♦ n 1 act of clutching 2 apparatus connecting and disconnecting the working parts of a car engine **clutches** n [P] control: in the clutches of the enemy

clutch[2] n (chickens born from) a number of eggs laid by one bird: (fig.) a clutch of new trainees

clut-ter /'klʌtəʳ/ vt make untidy ♦ n [U] scattered disorderly things

cm written abbrev. for: centimetre(s)

CND /ˌsiː en 'diː/ n [the] Campaign for Nuclear Disarmament

Co. /kəʊ/ abbrev. for: COMPANY (1)

C.O. /ˌsiː ˈəʊ◂/ n Commanding Officer; person in the armed forces in charge of others

coach /kəʊtʃ/ n 1 BrE long-distance bus 2 railway carriage 3 large horse-drawn carriage 4 person who trains people for sports, or gives private lessons ♦ vt train; teach

coach-work /'kəʊtʃwɜːk‖-wɜːrk/ n outside body of a car

co-ag-u-late /kəʊˈægjʊleɪt/ vi/t change from a liquid to a solid

coal /kəʊl/ n [C;U] (piece of) black mineral that can be burnt: a **coalmine**

co-a-lesce /ˌkəʊəˈles/ vi fml grow together; unite

coal-face /'kəʊlfeɪs/ n surface where coal is cut in a mine

coal-field /'kəʊlfiːld/ n area where there is coal under the ground

co-a-li-tion /ˌkəʊəˈlɪʃən/ n union of political parties for a special purpose

coarse /kɔːs‖kɔːrs/ adj 1 not fine; lumpy 2 rough in manner; insensitive ~**ly** adv ~**ness** n [U] **coarsen** vi/t

coast /kəʊst/ n 1 seashore 2 **the coast is clear** all danger has gone ♦ vi go downhill on a bicycle, etc., without effort or power ~**al** adj

coast-guard /'kəʊstɡɑːd‖-ɑːrd/ n 1 police organization responsible for the coast and nearby sea 2 member of the coastguard

coast-line /'kəʊstlaɪn/ n shape of a coast

coat /kəʊt/ n 1 outer garment with SLEEVES, fastened at the front 2 animal's fur, etc. 3 covering on a surface: coat of paint ♦ vt cover (a surface) ~**ing** n thin covering

coat hang-er /'· ˌ··/ n a HANGER

coat of arms /ˌ· · '·/ n **coats of arms** patterns or pictures, usu. on a shield, used by a noble family, town, etc., as their special sign

coax /kəʊks/ vt 1 persuade gently 2 obtain (something) by gently persuading

cob /kɒb‖kɑːb/ n 1 long hard central part of an ear of corn 2 strong short-legged horse 3 male SWAN

cob-ble¹ /'kɒbəl‖'kɑː-/ also **cobble-stone** /'kɒbəlstəʊn‖'kɑː-/ *n* rounded stone used for road surfaces **–bled** *adj* covered with cobbles

cobble² *vt* put together quickly and roughly

cob-bler /'kɒblə'‖'kɑː-/ *n* shoe repairer

cob-blers /'kɒbləz‖'kɑːblərz/ *n* [U] *BrE sl* nonsense

co-bra /'kɒbrə, 'kəʊ-‖'kəʊ-/ *n* kind of poisonous snake

cob-web /'kɒbweb‖'kɑːb-/ *n* a SPIDER's net of spun threads

co-caine /kəʊ'keɪn/ *n* [U] drug used against pain, or for pleasure

cock /kɒk‖kɑːk/ *n* 1 fully-grown male bird, esp. a chicken 2 hammer of a gun 3 a TAP for controlling the flow of liquid in a pipe 4 *sl* PENIS ♦ 1 *vt/i* raise up: *The horse cocked its ears.* 2 *vt* set (the hammer of a gun) in the correct position for firing 3 **cock a snook (at)** *BrE infml* show open disrespect (for)

cock-a-too /ˌkɒkə'tuː‖'kɑːkətuː/ *n* -**toos** Australian bird with a large CREST (1) on its head

cock-e-rel /'kɒkərəl‖'kɑː-/ *n* young cock

cock-eyed /ˌkɒk'aɪd◁‖ˌkɑːk-/ *adj* 1 stupid 2 CROOKED (1)

cock-le /'kɒkəl‖'kɑː-/ *n* small shellfish used for food

Cock-ney /'kɒkni‖'kɑːkni/ *n* 1 [C] person from the industrial parts of London 2 [U] the way Cockneys talk

cock-pit /'kɒk‚pɪt‖'kɑːk-/ *n* part of a plane where the pilot sits

cock-roach /'kɒk-rəʊtʃ‖'kɑːk-/ *n* large black insect which lives esp. in dirty or old houses

cock-sure /ˌkɒk'ʃʊə'‖ˌkɑːk-/ *adj* too self-confident

cock-tail /'kɒkteɪl‖'kɑːk-/ *n* 1 mixed alcoholic drink 2 mixture of fruit or SEAFOOD — see also MOLOTOV COCKTAIL

cock-up /'· ·/ *n BrE sl* confused state of affairs

cock-y /'kɒki‖'kɑːki/ *adj sl* too sure of oneself

co-coa /'kəʊkəʊ/ *n* [U] 1 brown powder tasting of chocolate 2 hot drink made from this

co-co-nut /'kəʊkənʌt/ *n* [C;U] (flesh of) a very large tropical nut

co-coon /kə'kuːn/ *n* silky covering that protects some insects in their inactive stage ♦ *vt* protect from hardship

cod /kɒd‖kɑːd/ *n* **cod** or **cods** large sea fish

cod-dle /'kɒdl‖'kɑːdl/ *vt* treat (someone) too tenderly

code /kəʊd/ *n* 1 system of signs, or of secret writing: *computer code* 2 collection of laws or social customs ♦ *vt* translate into a code

co-ed /ˌkəʊ'ed◁‖'kəʊed/ *n AmE* female student in a college open to both sexes *adj* coeducational

co-ed-u-ca-tion /ˌkəʊedjʊ'keɪʃən‖ -dʒə-/ *n* [U] education of boys and girls together **~al** *adj*

co-erce /kəʊ'ɜːs‖-'ɜːrs/ *vt fml* force to do something **-ercive** *adj* **-ercion** /kəʊ'ɜːʃən‖-'ɜːrʒən/ *n* [U]

co-ex-ist /ˌkəʊɪg'zɪst/ *vi* exist at the same time **~ence** *n* [U] (esp. of countries) existing together peacefully

cof-fee /'kɒfi‖'kɔːfi, 'kɑːfi/ *n* [C;U] (drink made by pouring boiling water onto) the (crushed) berries of a tropical tree

coffee ta-ble /'·· ‚··/ *n* low table

cof-fer /'kɒfə'‖'kɔː-, 'kɑː-/ *n* large chest for money, etc.

cof-fin /'kɒfɪn‖'kɔː-/ *n* box in which a dead person is buried

cog /kɒg‖kɑːg/ *n* 1 tooth on the edge of a wheel that moves another wheel 2 **cog in the machine** unimportant person in a very large organization

co-gent /'kəʊdʒənt/ *adj fml* forceful; CONVINCING: *cogent arguments* **cogency** *n*

cog-i-tate /'kɒdʒɪteɪt‖'kɑː-/ *vi fml* think carefully

co-gnac /'kɒnjæk‖'kəʊ-, 'kɑː-/ *n* [U] kind of BRANDY

cog-nate /'kɒgneɪt‖'kɑːg-/ *adj fml* related: *cognate languages*

co-hab-it /ˌkəʊ'hæbɪt/ *vi fml* live together as though married **~ation** /kəʊ‚hæbə'teɪʃən/ *n* [U]

co-her-ent /kəʊ'hɪərənt/ *adj* (of speech, ideas, etc.) reasonably connected; clear **~ence** *n* [U] **~ly** *adv*

co-he-sive /kəʊ'hiːsɪv/ *adj* sticking together **-sion** /-'hiːʒən/ *n* [U]

coil /kɔɪl/ *vt/i* twist into a circle ♦ *n* 1 connected set of twists: *coil of rope* 2 twisted wire that carries an electric current 3 coil of metal or plastic which is fitted inside the UTERUS to prevent a woman from having children

coin /kɔɪn/ *n* piece of metal money ♦ *vt* 1 make (coins) 2 invent (new words) 3 **coin (the) money (in)** also **coin it (in)** make or earn a lot of money very quickly

co-in-cide /ˌkəʊɪn'saɪd/ *vi* 1 happen at the same time 2 (of opinions, etc.) agree

co-in-ci-dence /kəʊ'ɪnsədəns/ *n* [C;U] accidental and surprising combination of events: *By sheer coincidence, we have the same birthday.* **–dental** /kəʊ‚ɪnsə'dentl/ *adj*

coke /kəʊk/ n [U] **1** substance left after gas has been removed from coal **2** COCAINE

col·an·der /'kʌləndəʳ, 'kɒ-‖'kʌ-, 'kɑː-/ n bowl with holes, for separating liquid from food

cold[1] /kəʊld/ adj **1** low in temperature: cold wind **2** unfriendly: a cold stare **3** (of cooked food) allowed to get cool **4** unconscious: I knocked him out cold. **5** get/have cold feet lose courage **6** give/get the cold shoulder treat/be treated unsympathetically ~ly adv ~ness n [U]

cold[2] n **1** [U] low temperature **2** [C;U] illness of the nose and throat **3** (out) in the cold not noticed; unwanted

cold-blood·ed /,· '··◄/ adj **1** (of snakes, etc.) having a body temperature that varies with the surroundings **2** cruel; without feeling: cold-blooded murder

cold-heart·ed /,· '··◄/ adj unkind

cold tur·key /,· '··/ n [U] sl (the unpleasant sick feeling caused by) the sudden stopping of the use of a drug by an ADDICT

cold war /,· '·◄/ n severe political struggle without actual fighting

col·ic /'kɒlɪk‖'kɑː-/ n [U] severe pain in the stomach and bowels

col·lab·o·rate /kə'læbəreɪt/ vi **1** work together **2** work with the enemy –rator n –ration /kə,læbə'reɪʃən/ n [U]

col·lage /'kɒlɑːʒ‖kə'lɑːʒ/ n picture made by gluing various materials or objects onto a surface

col·lapse /kə'læps/ v **1** vi fall down suddenly: The bridge collapsed under the weight of the train. **2** vi fall helpless **3** vi/t fold flat ♦ n [C;U] collapsing: (fig.) the collapse of the peace talks –lapsible adj that can be folded for packing, etc.

col·lar /'kɒləʳ‖'kɑː-/ n **1** part of a garment that fits round the neck **2** band put round an animal's neck ♦ vt seize and hold

col·lar·bone /'kɒləbəʊn‖'kɑːlər-/ n bone joining the RIBs to the shoulders

col·late /kə'leɪt/ vt fml **1** compare (copies of books, etc.) to find the differences **2** arrange (the sheets) of (esp. a book) in the proper order

col·lat·e·ral /kə'lætərəl/ n [S;U] property promised as SECURITY for a debt

col·league /'kɒliːg‖'kɑː-/ n fellow worker

col·lect[1] /kə'lekt/ v **1** vt/i gather together: collect taxes|A crowd collected in the street. **2** vt save (stamps, etc.) as a HOBBY **3** vt fetch: collect one's skirt from the cleaners **4** vt regain control of (oneself, one's thoughts, etc.) ~ed adj controlled; calm ~ive

adj shared by many people: collective ownership ~ive n business owned and controlled by the people who work in it ~ively adv: collectively responsible ~or n person who collects something: ticket collector ~ion /kə'lekʃən/ n **1** [U] collecting **2** [C] set of things, sum of money, etc., collected

col·lect[2] adj, adv AmE to be paid for by the receiver: Call me collect.

collective bar·gain·ing /·,·· '···/ n [U] talks between unions and employers about working conditions, etc.

col·lege /'kɒlɪdʒ‖'kɑː-/ n **1** school for higher education; part of a university **2** group of people with a common profession or purpose: the Royal College of Nursing

col·lide /kə'laɪd/ vi **1** crash violently **2** be opposed: The government collided with the unions.

col·li·er /'kɒliəʳ‖'kɑː-/ n **1** coal MINER **2** ship for carrying coal

col·lie·ry /'kɒljəri‖'kɑː-/ n coal mine

col·li·sion /kə'lɪʒən/ n [C;U] colliding

col·lo·qui·al /kə'ləʊkwiəl/ adj (of words, style, etc.) suitable for informal conversation ~ly adv ~ism n colloquial expression

col·lude /kə'luːd/ vi fml act in collusion

col·lu·sion /kə'luːʒən/ n fml secret agreement to deceive

co·lon[1] /'kəʊlən/ n lower part of the bowels

colon[2] n the mark (:)

colo·nel /'kɜːnl‖'kɜːr-/ n army or airforce officer of middle rank

co·lo·ni·al /kə'ləʊniəl/ adj of or about colonies (COLONY (1)) ♦ n person living or having lived in a COLONY (1) ~ism n [U] principle of having colonies

co·lo·nize /'kɒlənaɪz‖'kɑː-/ vt make into a colony: colonize Australia –nist n person living in a new COLONY (1) –nization /,kɒlənaɪ'zeɪʃən‖,kɑːlənə-/ n [U]

col·on·nade /,kɒlə'neɪd‖,kɑː-/ n row of PILLARs

col·o·ny /'kɒləni‖'kɑː-/ n **1** place lived in and controlled by people from a distant country **2** group of people of the same kind, living together

col·or /'kʌləʳ/ n AmE COLOUR

co·los·sal /kə'lɒsəl‖kə'lɑː-/ adj extremely large

co·los·sus /kə'lɒsəs‖kə'lɑː-/ n -suses or -si /-saɪ/ very large person or thing

col·our BrE ‖ **color** AmE /'kʌləʳ/ n **1** [C;U] red, blue, green, etc. **2** [C;U] paint or DYE **3** [U] appearance of the skin **4** [U] interesting details of a place, thing, or person — see also OFF

COLOUR ♦ v 1 vt give colour to 2 vi BLUSH 3 vt change; influence ~ed adj 1 having colours; not just white, or black and white 2 (of people) black or brown ~ful adj 1 brightly coloured 2 exciting ~ing n [C;U] 1 substance giving colour 2 skin colour, showing health ~less adj 1 without colour 2 dull colours n [P] 1 official flag 2 something worn as the sign of a club, team, etc. 3 show one's true colours show one's real nature or character — see also FLYING COLOURS

colour bar /'·· ·/ n customs or laws that prevent people of different colours from mixing

colour-blind /'·· ·/ adj unable to see the difference between colours

colour sup·ple·ment /'·· ,···/ n magazine printed in colour and given free with a newspaper, esp. a Sunday one

colt /kəʊlt/ n young male horse

col·umn /'kɒləm‖'kɑ:-/ n 1 PILLAR 2 something having this shape: a column of figures | a marching column of soldiers 3 a division of a page 4 newspaper article — see also FIFTH COLUMN ~ist /'kɒləmɪst, -ləmnɪst‖'kɑ:-/ n writer of a newspaper column

co·ma /'kəʊmə/ n unnatural deep sleep

co·ma·tose /'kəʊmətəʊs/ adj 1 in a coma 2 inactive and sleepy

comb /kəʊm/ n 1 [C] toothed piece of plastic, etc., for tidying the hair or as an ornament 2 [S] act of combing 3 HONEYCOMB ♦ vt 1 tidy (hair) with a comb 2 search (a place) thoroughly

com·bat /'kɒmbæt‖'kɑ:m-/ n [C;U] struggle; fight combat vt/i -tt- BrE | -t- or -tt- AmE: to combat inflation ~ant /'kɒmbətənt‖kəm'bætənt/ n person who fights ~ive adj fond of fighting

com·bi·na·tion /,kɒmbɪ'neɪʃən‖ ,kɑ:m-/ n 1 [U] combining: We worked well in combination. 2 [C] people or things combined 3 [C] numbers needed to open a special lock: combination lock

com·bine¹ /kəm'baɪn/ vi/t join together; unite

com·bine² /'kɒmbaɪn‖'kɑ:m-/ n 1 group of people, businesses, etc., acting together 2 also combine harvester /,·· ·/ machine that cuts and THRESHES grain

com·bus·ti·ble /kəm'bʌstɪbəl/ adj burning easily

com·bus·tion /kəm'bʌstʃən/ n [U] process of burning

come /kʌm/ vi came /keɪm/, come 1 move towards the speaker; arrive 2 reach a particular point: The water came up to my neck. | We came to an agreement. | The bill comes to £18.50.

3 have a particular position: Monday comes after Sunday. 4 happen: How did you come to be invited? 5 begin: I came to realize the truth. 6 become: come apart | come undone | My dream came true. 7 be offered, produced, etc.: Shoes come in different sizes. | Milk comes from cows. 8 sl have an ORGASM 9 come and go pass or disappear quickly 10 how come? how did it happen (that)? 11 to come in the future comer n 1 esp. AmE person who appears likely to be successful in their job 2 all comers everyone who comes and tries coming n [S] arrival

coming adj future: the coming winter

come about phr vi happen

come across/upon phr vt find by chance

come across phr vi be effective and well received

come along phr vi 1 improve; advance 2 arrive by chance 3 Come along! Hurry up!

come apart phr vi break into pieces without the need of force

come at phr vt advance towards in a threatening manner

come away phr vi become disconnected without being forced

come back phr vi return

come between phr vt cause trouble between

come by phr vt obtain; receive

come down phr vi 1 fall 2 come down in the world fall to a lower standard of living 3 come down in favour of/on the side of decide to support

come down on phr vt punish

come down to phr vt be no more than: It all comes down to a question of money.

come down with phr vt catch (an infectious illness)

come forward phr vi offer oneself to fill a position, give help to police, etc.

come from phr vt have (a place) as one's home

come in phr vi 1 become fashionable 2 come in handy/useful be useful

come in for phr vt receive (esp. blame)

come in on phr vt take part in

come into phr vt 1 INHERIT 2 begin to be in (a state or activity)

come of phr vt result from: No good will come of it.

come off phr v 1 vi happen as planned 2 vt come off it! stop lying or pretending

come on phr vi 1 improve; advance 2 (of weather, illness, etc.) begin 3 Come on! Hurry up!

come out phr vi 1 appear 2 become known 3 (of colour, etc.) be removed

4 STRIKE **5** (of a photograph) be successful **6** declare oneself to be HOMOSEXUAL

come out against phr vt declare one's opposition to

come out in phr vt be partly covered by (marks caused by an illness)

come out with phr vt say, esp. suddenly

come over phr v **1** vt (of feelings, etc.) influence suddenly: What's come over you? **2** vi make a short informal visit

come round phr vi **1** also **come to** — regain consciousness **2** change one's opinions **3** happen as usual

come through phr v **1** vi (of news, etc.) become known **2** vi/t SURVIVE

come to phr vt **1** enter the mind of: The idea came to me suddenly. **2** concern: He's ignorant when it comes to politics. **3** COME round

come under phr vt **1** be in (a particular class): Rabbits come under the heading of pets. **2** be governed or controlled by

come up phr vi **1** happen **2** come near

come up against phr vt meet (difficulties)

come up with phr vt think of (a plan, reply, etc.); produce

come·back /'kʌmbæk/ n return to strength or fame

co·me·di·an /kə'miːdiən/ n **1** **come·di·enne** /kə,miːdi'en/ fem. — actor who makes people laugh **2** amusing person

come·down /'kʌmdaʊn/ n fall in importance

com·e·dy /'kɒmədi‖'kɑː-/ n **1** [C;U] (type of) funny play, film, etc. **2** [U] amusing quality of something — see also BLACK COMEDY

com·et /'kɒmɪt‖'kɑː-/ n bright heavenly body with a tail

come-up·pance /,kʌm 'ʌpəns/ n well-deserved punishment or misfortune

com·fort /'kʌmfət‖-ərt/ n **1** [U] lack of pain or anxiety; physical satisfaction **2** [C] something that satisfies physical needs **3** [C;U] (person or thing that brings) help for an unhappy person ♦ vt make less unhappy

com·for·ta·ble /'kʌmftəbəl, 'kʌmfət-‖'kʌmfərt-, 'kʌmft-/ adj **1** giving comfort: a comfortable chair **2** feeling comfort; not suffering or anxious —bly adv

com·for·ta·bly off /,··· '·-/adj fairly rich

com·fy /'kʌmfi/ adj infml comfortable

com·ic /'kɒmɪk‖'kɑː-/ adj **1** funny **2** of COMEDY ♦ n **1** children's magazine

with sets of funny drawings **2** COMEDIAN ~**al** adj funny **comics** n [P] AmE part of a newspaper with funny drawings

comic strip /'·· ·/n set of drawings telling a short funny story

com·ma /'kɒmə‖'kɑːmə/ n the sign (,)

com·mand /kə'mɑːnd‖kə'mænd/ v **1** vt/i order; direct: command them to attack | your commanding officer **2** vt deserve and get: command respect **3** vt control (a place) from above ♦ n **1** [C] order, instruction **2** [U] control: take command of the army **3** [C] division of an army, air force, etc. **4** [S;U] ability to use something: a good command of spoken English —**er** n **1** naval officer of middle rank **2** any officer in command

com·man·dant /,kɒmən'dænt‖'kɑːməndænt/ n officer in charge of a military organization

com·man·deer /,kɒmən'dɪər‖,kɑ-/ vt seize (private property) for public use

com·mand·ment /kə'mɑːndmənt‖kə'mænd-/ n law given by God

command mod·ule /·' · ,·–/n part of a space vehicle from which operations are controlled

com·man·do /kə'mɑːndəʊ‖kə'mæn-/ n -**dos** or -**does** (member of) a fighting force trained to make quick RAIDS

com·mem·o·rate /kə'meməreɪt/ vt honour the memory of —**rative** adj: commemorative stamps —**ration** /kə,memə'reɪʃən/ n [U]

com·mence /kə'mens/ vi/t fml begin; start ~**ment** n [U]

com·mend /kə'mend/ vt fml **1** praise **2** put into someone's care ~**able** adj worthy of praise ~**ation** /,kɒmən'deɪʃən‖,kɑ-/ n [U] praise [C] official prize

com·men·su·rate /kə'menʃərət/ adj fml equal; suitable: a job commensurate with his abilities

com·ment /'kɒment‖'kɑː-/ n [C;U] written or spoken opinion ♦ vi/t make a comment

com·men·ta·ry /'kɒməntəri‖'kɑːmənteri/ n **1** [C] collection of opinions on a book, etc. **2** [C;U] description broadcast during an event: football commentary

com·men·tate /'kɒmənteɪt‖'kɑː-/ vi broadcast a description —**tator** n

com·merce /'kɒmɜːs‖'kɑːmɜːrs/ n [U] buying and selling; trade

com·mer·cial /kə'mɜːʃəl‖kə'mɜːr-/ adj **1** of or used in commerce: commercial law/vehicles **2** producing profit **3** (of television or radio) paid for by charges made for advertisements ♦ *n* television or radio advertisement ~**ly** *adv* ~**ize** *vt* make into a matter of profit rather than religion, art, etc.

commercial trav-el-ler /·,·· '··-/ *n* person who travels from place to place trying to get orders for a firm's goods

com-mis-e-rate /kə'mɪzəreɪt/ *v* **commiserate with** *phr vt* express sympathy for –**ration** /kə,mɪzə'reɪʃən/ *n* [C;U]

com-mis-sion /kə'mɪʃən/ *n* 1 [C;U] payment for selling goods, made to the salesman 2 [C] job or duty given to someone 3 [C] group officially appointed to find out and report on facts 4 [C] paper appointing an officer in the armed forces 5 **out of commission** (of a ship) not ready for active service ♦ *vt* 1 give a COMMISSION (2, 4) to 2 place an order for: *commission a portrait* ~**er** *n* 1 member of a COMMISSION (3) 2 government representative in certain countries — see also HIGH COMMISSIONER

com-mis-sion-aire /kə,mɪʃə'neə²/ *n esp. BrE* uniformed attendant at the entrance to a cinema, hotel, etc.

com-mit /kə'mɪt/ *vt* -**tt**- 1 do (something wrong) 2 send (someone) to prison or a MENTAL hospital 3 **commit oneself: a** make oneself responsible **b** give a firm opinion ~**ment** *n* responsibility to do something ~**tal** *n* [C;U] committing someone to prison, etc.

com-mit-tee /kə'mɪti/ *n* group chosen to do special business

com-mod-i-ty /kə'mɒdɪti‖kə'mɑː-/ *n* article of trade; product

com-mo-dore /'kɒmədɔːʳ‖'kɑː-/ *n* 1 high-ranking naval officer 2 president of a sailing club

com-mon[1] /'kɒmən‖'kɑː-/ *adj* 1 ordinary; usual: *common salt*|*the common cold* 2 shared in a group: *common knowledge* 3 rough in manner; VULGAR ~**ly** *adv*

common[2] *n* 1 area of grassland with no fences which all people are free to use 2 **in common** in shared possession

common de-nom-i-na-tor /,·· ·'····/*n* quality or belief shared by all the members of a group

com-mon-er /'kɒmənəʳ‖'kɑː-/ *n* person who is not a member of a noble family

common law /,·· '·/*n* [U] unwritten law based on custom and court decisions rather than on laws made by Parliament ♦ **common-law** /'··· ·/ *adj*

Common Mar-ket /,·· '··◁/ *n* [*the*] the EEC

common-or-gar-den /, ·· ·'····◁/ *adj BrE infml* ordinary

com-mon-place /'kɒmənpleɪs‖ 'kɑː-/ *adj* ordinary; dull

Com-mons /'kɒmənz‖'kɑː-/ *n* [*the* + S] the HOUSE OF COMMONS

common sense /,·· '·◁/ *n* [U] practical good sense gained from experience

Com-mon-wealth /'kɒmənwelθ‖ 'kɑː-/ *n* 1 association of independent states that used to be parts of the British Empire 2 official title of certain countries, such as Australia

com-mo-tion /kə'məʊʃən/ *n* [S;U] noisy confusion

com-mu-nal /'kɒmjʊnəl, kə'mjuːnl/ *adj* shared by a group

com-mune[1] /'kɒmjuːn‖'kɑː-, kə-'mjuːn/ *n* 1 group who live and work together and share their possessions 2 local government division in France, etc.

com-mune[2] /kə'mjuːn/ *vi* exchange thoughts, ideas or feelings: *commune with nature*

com-mu-ni-ca-ble /kə'mjuːnɪkəbəl/ *adj fml* (esp. of ideas, thoughts, illnesses, etc.) that can be (easily) passed from one person to another

com-mu-ni-cate /kə'mjuːnɪkeɪt/ *v* 1 *vi/t* make (opinions, ideas, etc.) known 2 *vt* pass on (a disease) 3 *vi* (of rooms) be connected –**cator** *n* person who communicates –**cation** /kə,mjuːnɪ-'keɪʃən/ *n* 1 [U] communicating 2 [C] *fml* message, letter, etc. –**cations** *n* [P] ways of travelling or sending messages

com-mu-ni-ca-tive /kə'mjuːnɪ-kətɪv/ *adj* willing to give information

com-mu-ni-on /kə'mjuːnɪən/ *n* [U] 1 *fml* sharing of beliefs, feelings, etc. 2 (*cap.*) Christian ceremony of sharing bread and wine

com-mu-ni-qué /kə'mjuːnɪkeɪ‖ kə,mjuːnɪ'keɪ/ *n* official report

com-mu-nis-m /'kɒmjʊnɪzəm‖'kɑː-/ *n* [U] 1 social and political system by which the state owns the means of production 2 (*cap.*) one-party system of government on this principle –**nist** *n, adj*

com-mu-ni-ty /kə'mjuːnɪti/ *n* 1 [C] group of people with shared interests 2 [S] people in general; the public 3 [U] shared possession

com-mute /kə'mjuːt/ *v* 1 *vi* travel regularly between home and work 2 *vt* make (a punishment) less severe –**muter** *n* person who commutes to work

com-pact[1] /kəm'pækt/ *adj* neatly packed into a small space

com-pact[2] /'kɒmpækt‖'kɑːm-/ *n* 1 container for face powder 2 *AmE* small car

compact[3] *n fml* agreement between two or more parties, countries, etc.

compact disc /,·· '·. ·, ·/*n* small circular piece of plastic on which sound, information, etc., can be stored

com·pan·ion /kəm'pænjən/ n 1 person who spends time with another 2 HANDBOOK **~able** adj friendly **~ship** n [U] friendly company

com·pa·ny /'kʌmpəni/ n 1 [C] business firm; people working together: a bus/theatre company 2 [C] group of about 120 soldiers 3 [U] a presence of companions: b I was grateful for her company. b companions, esp. guests 4 **be good/bad company** be a good/bad person to be with 5 **part company (with/from)** finish a relationship

company sec·re·ta·ry /ˌ··· '···/ n high-ranking member of a business firm who deals with accounts, legal matters, etc.

com·pa·ra·ble /'kɒmpərəbəl‖'kɑːm-/ adj similar

com·par·a·tive /kəm'pærətɪv/ adj 1 gram expressing an increase in quality or quantity: 'Worse' is the comparative form of 'bad'. 2 measured or judged by a comparison that is not stated: She's a comparative newcomer to television. (= has not been on television often) 3 making a comparison: a comparative study of European languages ♦ n gram comparative form of an adjective or adverb **~ly** adv

com·pare /kəm'peəʳ/ v 1 vt judge (one thing) against another thing, to show likeness or difference 2 vt show the likeness between (2 things) 3 vi be worthy of comparison

com·pa·ri·son /kəm'pærɨsən/ n 1 [C;U] (statement of) comparing: Paris is small in comparison with London. 2 [U] likeness: There's no comparison between them.

com·part·ment /kəm'pɑːtmənt‖-ɑːr-/ n separate division of a space; small room in a railway carriage, etc.

com·pass /'kʌmpəs/ n 1 instrument for showing direction, with a needle that points to the north 2 fml range; limit: outside the compass of this department **compasses** n [P] instrument for drawing circles

com·pas·sion /kəm'pæʃən/ n [U] sympathy; pity **~ate** adj **~ately** adv

com·pat·i·ble /kəm'pætɨbəl/ adj able to exist or work together **~bly** adv **–bility** /kəm,pætɨ'bɪlɨti/ n [U]

com·pat·ri·ot /kəm'pætriət‖-'peɪt-/ n person of the same nationality as another

com·pel /kəm'pel/ vt -ll- force to do something **~ling** adj important; urgent: compelling reasons

com·pen·sate /'kɒmpənseɪt‖ 'kɑːm-/ vi/t pay, or give something, to balance a loss **–sation** /ˌkɒmpən'seɪʃən‖ˌkɑːm-/ n [S;U] something given to compensate **–satory** /ˌkɒmpən'seɪtəri‖kəm-'pensɑːtri/ adj

com·pere /'kɒmpeəʳ‖'kɑːm-/ n BrE person who introduces a radio or television show **compere** vi/t

com·pete /kəm'piːt/ vi try to win in a competition

com·pe·tence /'kɒmpɨtəns‖ 'kɑːm-/ n [U] ability to do what is needed **–tent** adj **–tently** adv

com·pe·ti·tion /ˌkɒmpɨ'tɪʃən‖ ˌkɑːm-/ n 1 [C] test of strength, skill, etc. 2 [U] trying to win: keen competition between them 3 [U] person or people against whom one competes

com·pet·i·tive /kəm'petɨtɪv/ adj 1 decided by competition 2 liking to compete

com·pet·i·tor /kəm'petɨtəʳ/ n person, firm, etc., that competes

com·pile /kəm'paɪl/ vt make (a book, etc.) from collected facts **–piler** n **–pilation** /ˌkɒmpɨ'leɪʃən‖ˌkɑːm-/ n 1 [U] act of compiling 2 [C] something compiled

com·pla·cen·cy /kəm'pleɪsənsi/ n [U] unreasonable feeling of satisfaction **–cent** adj **–cently** adv

com·plain /kəm'pleɪn/ vi/t say that one is unhappy: to complain that the room is too hot

com·plaint /kəm'pleɪnt/ n 1 [C;U] (statement of) complaining 2 [C] illness: a liver complaint

com·ple·ment /'kɒmplɨmənt‖ 'kɑːm-/ n 1 something that completes 2 full number needed 3 gram noun or adjective after a verb such as 'be' or 'become' ♦ /-ment/ vt make complete or perfect **~ary** /ˌkɒmplɨ'mentəri‖ ˌkɑːm-/ adj supplying what is needed

com·plete /kəm'pliːt/ adj 1 having all necessary parts; whole 2 finished; ended 3 total; thorough: complete silence ♦ vt 1 make whole 2 finish **~ly** adv in every way **–pletion** /-'pliːʃən/ n [U]

com·plex¹ /'kɒmpleks‖ˌkɑːm-'pleks◂/ adj 1 difficult to understand 2 made of many connected parts **~ity** /kəm'pleksɨti/ n [C;U]

com·plex² /'kɒmpleks‖'kɑːm-/ n 1 system of many connected parts: new sports complex 2 group of unconscious fears or feelings

com·plex·ion /kəm'plekʃən/ n 1 natural appearance of the skin: good/dark complexion 2 general character of a situation

com·pli·ance /kəm'plaɪəns/ n [U] fml complying (COMPLY) **–ant** adj

com·pli·cate /'kɒmplɨkeɪt‖'kɑːm-/ vt make difficult to deal with **–cated** adj COMPLEX **–cation** /ˌkɒmplɨ'keɪʃən‖ˌkɑːm-/ n added difficulty

com·plic·i·ty /kəmˈplɪsəti/ n [U] fml taking part with someone else in a crime

com·pli·ment¹ /ˈkɒmpləmənt ‖ ˈkɑːm-/ n expression of praise **compliments** n [P] good wishes

com·pli·ment² /ˈkɒmpləment ‖ ˈkɑːm-/ vt express admiration of ~**ary** /ˌkɒmpləˈmentəri ‖ ˌkɑːm-/ adj 1 expressing admiration 2 given free: complimentary tickets

com·ply /kəmˈplaɪ/ vi fml agree to do something; obey

com·po·nent /kəmˈpəʊnənt/ n any part of a whole machine or system

com·pose /kəmˈpəʊz/ v 1 vi/t write (music, poetry, etc.) 2 vt get (oneself) under control 3 **be composed of** consist of –**posed** adj calm –**poser** n writer of music

com·pos·ite /ˈkɒmpəzɪt ‖ kɑːmˈpɑː-/ adj, n (something) made up of different parts

com·po·si·tion /ˌkɒmpəˈzɪʃən ‖ ˌkɑːm-/ n 1 [U] act of writing music, poetry, etc. 2 [C] something written 3 [U] mixture or arrangement of parts

com·pos·i·tor /kəmˈpɒzətə ‖ -ˈpɑː-/ n person who arranges material for printing

com·post /ˈkɒmpɒst ‖ ˈkɑːmpəʊst/ n [U] decayed plant matter, used to improve the soil

com·po·sure /kəmˈpəʊʒə/ n [U] calmness

com·pound¹ /ˈkɒmpaʊnd ‖ ˈkɑːm-/ adj consisting of 2 or more parts ♦ n: chemical compounds

com·pound² /kəmˈpaʊnd/ vt 1 make by combining parts 2 make worse: compound an error

com·pound³ /ˈkɒmpaʊnd ‖ ˈkɑːm-/ n enclosed area containing buildings

com·pre·hend /ˌkɒmprɪˈhend ‖ ˌkɑːm-/ vt fml 1 understand 2 include

com·pre·hen·sion /ˌkɒmprɪˈhenʃən ‖ ˌkɑːm-/ n [U] fml power of understanding –**sible** /-səbəl/ adj understandable –**sibly** adv

com·pre·hen·sive /ˌkɒmprɪˈhensɪv ‖ ˌkɑːm-/ adj 1 thorough; including a lot 2 BrE teaching pupils of all abilities together ♦ n a COMPREHENSIVE (2) school

com·press /kəmˈpres/ vt 1 force into less space 2 put (ideas, etc.) into fewer words ~**ion** /-ˈpreʃən/ n [U]

com·prise /kəmˈpraɪz/ v consist of; have as parts

com·pro·mise /ˈkɒmprəmaɪz ‖ ˈkɑːm-/ n [C;U] agreement reached by each side agreeing to some of the other side's demands ♦ v 1 vi make a compromise 2 vt put into a dishonourable position

com·pul·sion /kəmˈpʌlʃən/ n 1 [U] force that makes a person do something 2 [C] strong desire –**sive** /-sɪv/ adj caused by a compulsion: compulsive drinking

com·pul·so·ry /kəmˈpʌlsəri/ adj that must be done by law, etc. –**rily** adv

com·punc·tion /kəmˈpʌŋkʃən/ n [U] feeling of guilt

com·pute /kəmˈpjuːt/ vt calculate

com·put·er /kəmˈpjuːtə/ n ELECTRONIC machine that stores, recalls, and deals with information ~**ize** vt use or begin to use a computer to control (an operation) ~**ization** /kəmˌpjuːtəraɪˈzeɪʃən ‖ -tərə-/ n [U]

com·rade /ˈkɒmrɪd, -reɪd ‖ ˈkɑːmræd/ n 1 fml close companion 2 fellow member of a union or political party ~**ship** n [U]

con /kɒn ‖ kɑːn/ vt -**nn**- trick (a trusting person) ♦ n infml for CONFIDENCE TRICK

Con written abbrev. for: CONSERVATIVE PARTY

con·cave /ˌkɒnˈkeɪv◂, kən- ‖ ˌkɑːnˈkeɪv◂, kən-/ adj curved inwards

con·ceal /kənˈsiːl/ vt hide ~**ment** n [U]

con·cede /kənˈsiːd/ vt 1 admit as true 2 give as a right 3 end a game or match by admitting defeat

con·ceit /kənˈsiːt/ n [U] too high an opinion of oneself ~**ed** adj

con·ceive /kənˈsiːv/ v 1 vt think of; imagine 2 vi/t become PREGNANT –**ceivable** adj imaginable; possible –**ceivably** adv

con·cen·trate /ˈkɒnsəntreɪt ‖ ˈkɑːn-/ v 1 vi direct all one's attention: concentrate on the problem 2 vt/i bring or come together in one place 3 vt make (a liquid) stronger ♦ n [C;U] concentrated liquid

con·cen·tra·tion /ˌkɒnsənˈtreɪʃən ‖ ˌkɑːn-/ n 1 [U] close attention 2 [C] close gathering

concentration camp /ˌ···ˈ··· ·/ n large prison for political prisoners

con·cen·tric /kənˈsentrɪk/ adj (of circles) having the same centre

con·cept /ˈkɒnsept ‖ ˈkɑːn-/ n general idea; NOTION ~**ual** /kənˈseptʃuəl/ adj of or based on (the formation of) CONCEPTS ~**ualize** vi/t form a concept (of)

con·cep·tion /kənˈsepʃən/ n 1 [C;U] understanding 2 [U] forming of an idea 3 [C;U] fml starting of a new life by the union of a male and female sex cell

con·cern /kənˈsɜːn ‖ -ɜːrn/ vt 1 be about (a subject) 2 be of importance to: problems which concern all of us 3 worry: I'm concerned about her. ♦ n 1

[C] something that matters to someone 2 [U] worry: *no cause for concern* 3 [C] business; firm: *a going concern* ~ing *prep* about

con-cert /ˈkɒnsət‖ˈkɑːnsərt/ *n* 1 musical performance 2 **in concert: a** working together **b** playing at a concert

con-cert-ed /kənˈsɜːtɪd‖-ɜːr-/ *adj* done by agreement: *a concerted effort*

con-cer-ti-na /ˌkɒnsəˈtiːnə‖ ˌkɑːnsər-/ *n* small ACCORDION ♦ *vi* (of a vehicle) become pressed together as the result of a crash

con-cer-to /kənˈtʃɜːtəʊ‖-ˈtʃertəʊ/ *n* **-tos** piece of music for one instrument supported by an orchestra

con-ces-sion /kənˈseʃən/ *n* 1 something CONCEDEd after a disagreement 2 official permission to do something: *oil concessions in the North Sea* ~**ary** *adj* given as a concession ~**aire** /kənˌseʃəˈneəʳ/ *n* holder of a CONCESSION (2)

con-cil-i-ate /kənˈsɪliːɪt/ *vt* remove the anger of **-ation** /kənˌsɪliːˈeɪʃən/ *n* [U] **-atory** /kənˈsɪliːətəri‖-tɔːri/ *adj* trying to conciliate

con-cise /kənˈsaɪs/ *adj* expressing a lot in a few words **~ly** *adv* **~ness** *n* [U]

con-clude /kənˈkluːd/ *v fml* 1 *vt/i* bring or come to an end 2 *vt* come to believe 3 *vt* settle: *conclude an agreement*

con-clu-sion /kənˈkluːʒən/ *n* 1 decision; settlement 2 end **-sive** /-sɪv/ *adj* ending all doubt: *conclusive proof*

con-coct /kənˈkɒkt‖-ˈkɑːkt/ *vt* 1 make by mixing parts 2 invent (something false) **-ion** /-ˈkɒkʃən‖-ˈkɑːk-/ *n* mixture

con-com-i-tant /kənˈkɒmɪtənt‖-ˈkɑː-/ *adj* existing or happening together

con-cord /ˈkɒŋkɔːd‖ˈkɑːŋkɔːrd/ *n* [U] friendly agreement

con-course /ˈkɒŋkɔːs‖ˈkɑːŋkɔːrs/ *n* place where crowds can gather

con-crete /ˈkɒŋkriːt‖kɑːnˈkriːt/ *adj* 1 real or solid; not ABSTRACT: *A car is a concrete object.* 2 clear; particular: *concrete proposals* *n* [U] building material made of sand, cement, etc. ♦ *vt* cover (a path, wall, etc.) with concrete

con-cu-bine /ˈkɒŋkjʊbaɪn‖ˈkɑːŋ-/ *n* woman who has sex with, but is not married to, an Eastern ruler

con-cur /kənˈkɜːʳ/ *vi* **-rr-** *fml* 1 agree 2 happen at the same time ~**rence** /kənˈkʌrəns/ *n* [C;U] ~**rent** *adj* ~**rently** *adv*

con-cuss /kənˈkʌs/ *vt* damage (the brain) by a heavy blow ~**ion** /-ˈkʌʃən/ *n* [U]

con-demn /kənˈdem/ *vt* 1 express disapproval of 2 state the punishment for: *condemn him to death* | (fig.) *She was condemned to life in a wheelchair.* 3 declare (a building, etc.) unfit for use ~**ation** /ˌkɒndəmˈneɪʃən, -dem-‖ ˌkɑːn-/ *n* [C;U]

con-dense /kənˈdens/ *vt/i* 1 make (a gas) liquid 2 make (a liquid) thicker 3 put into fewer words **-denser** *n* **-densation** /ˌkɒndenˈseɪʃən, -dən-‖ ˌkɑːn-/ *n* [U] 1 act of condensing 2 drops of water formed when steam condenses

con-de-scend /ˌkɒndɪˈsend‖ˌkɑːn-/ *vi* 1 do something unsuited to one's social or professional position 2 *derog* behave as though one is grander than others **-scension** /-ˈsenʃən/ *n* [U]

con-di-ment /ˈkɒndɪmənt‖ˈkɑːn-/ *n fml* something used for giving taste to food

con-di-tion[1] /kənˈdɪʃən/ *n* 1 [U] state; way of being: *a car in poor condition* 2 [C] something necessary for something else: *I'll come on condition that John comes too.* 3 [C] illness 4 **in/out of condition** thoroughly fit/not fit 5 **on no condition** never **conditions** *n* [P] surrounding facts: *better working conditions* **-tional** *adj* depending on conditions **-tionally** *adv*

condition[2] *vt* 1 control; DETERMINE 2 train to behave in a certain way ~**ing** /n/

con-do-lence /kənˈdəʊləns/ *n* [C;U] expression of sympathy

con-dom /ˈkɒndəm‖ˈkɑːn-, ˈkʌn-/ *n* usu. rubber covering worn over the male sex organ during SEXUAL INTERCOURSE, as a means of birth control and as a protection against disease

con-do-min-i-um /ˌkɒndəˈmɪniːəm‖ ˌkɑːn-/ *also* **condo** /ˈkɒndəʊ‖ˈkɑːn-/ *infml* — *n AmE* block of flats which are each owned by the people living in them

con-done /kənˈdəʊn/ *vt* forgive (wrong behaviour)

con-du-cive /kənˈdjuːsɪv‖-ˈduː-/ *adj fml* likely to produce: *conducive to health*

con-duct[1] /kənˈdʌkt/ *v* 1 *vt* direct; lead 2 *vt/i* direct the playing of (musicians) 3 *vt* be the path for (electricity, etc.) 4 **conduct oneself** *fml* behave **-ive** *adj* able to conduct electricity, etc. **-ion** /-ˈdʌkʃən/ *n* [U] passage of electricity, etc.

con-duct[2] /ˈkɒndʌkt, -dəkt‖ˈkɑːndʌkt, -dəkt/ *n* [U] 1 *fml* behaviour 2 management of something

con-duc-tor /kənˈdʌktəʳ/ *n* 1 person who conducts musicians 2 **conductress** /-trɪs/ *fem.* — person who collects payments on a bus 3 *AmE* guard on a train **4** substance that conducts electricity, etc.

con-duit /'kɒndɪt, 'kɒndjuɜt‖'kɑːnduɜt/ *n* pipe for water, gas, etc.

cone /kəʊn/ *n* **1** hollow or solid object with a round base and pointed top **2** fruit of a PINE or FIR tree

con-fec-tion /kən'fekʃən/ *n fml* sweet-tasting food **~ery** *n* [U] sweets, cakes, etc. **~er** *n* person who sells these

con-fed-e-ra-cy /kən'fedərəsi/ also **con'fed·e·ra·tion** /kən,fedə'reɪʃən/ — *n* union of people, parties, or states

con-fed-e-rate /kən'fedərɨt/ *n* **1** ACCOMPLICE **2** member of a confederacy

con-fer /kən'fɜːr/ *v* **-rr-** *fml* **1** *vi* talk together **2** *vt* give (a title, etc.) to

con-fe-rence /'kɒnfərəns‖'kɑːn-/ *n* meeting for the exchange of ideas

con-fess /kən'fes/ *vi/t* admit (one's faults) **~or** *n* priest who hears one's confession **~ion** /-'feʃən/ *n* [C;U] telling of one's faults

con-fet-ti /kən'feti/ *n* [U] bits of coloured paper thrown at weddings

con-fi-dant /'kɒnfɪdænt, ,kɒnfɪ'dænt‖'kɑːnfɪdænt/ **confidante** (*same pronunciation*) *fem.* — *n* person to whom one tells secrets

confide in *phr vt* talk freely to

con-fi-dence /'kɒnfɪdəns‖'kɑːn-/ *n* **1** [U] faith; trust **2** [U] belief in one's own ability **3** [C] something told secretly **4 in confidence** secretly **-dent** *adj* sure

confidence trick /'··· ·/ *n* trick played in order to cheat a trusting person of money

con-fi-den-tial /,kɒnfɪ'denʃəl‖,kɑːn-/ *adj* **1** told in secret **2** trusted with secrets: *confidential secretary* **~ly** *adv*

con-fig-u-ra-tion /kən,fɪgjʊ'reɪʃən/ *n* shape; arrangement

con-fine /kən'faɪn/ *vt* **1** keep shut in: *confined to bed* **2** keep within the limits **~ment** *n* **1** [U] being shut up **2** [C;U] giving birth to a child: *her 3rd confinement* **3** [P] limits

con-firm /kən'fɜːm‖-ɜːrm/ *vt* **1** support; give proof of: *confirm a telephone message in writing* **2** admit (a person) to membership of the Christian church **~ed** *adj* firmly settled; unlikely to change: *confirmed bachelor* **~ation** /,kɒnfə'meɪʃən‖,kɑːnfər-/ *n* **1** proof **2** religious service in which someone is confirmed

con-fis-cate /'kɒnfɪskeɪt‖'kɑːn-/ *vt* seize (private property) officially, without payment **-cation** /,kɒnfɪ'skeɪʃən‖,kɑːn-/ *n* [C;U]

con-fla-gra-tion /,kɒnflə'greɪʃən‖,kɑːn-/ *n fml* large destructive fire

con-flate /kən'fleɪt/ *vi/t* combine **-flation** /-'fleɪʃən/ *n* [C;U]

con-flict¹ /'kɒnflɪkt‖'kɑːn-/ *n* **1** disagreement; argument **2** *fml* war

con-flict² /kən'flɪkt/ *vi* be in opposition

con-flu-ence /'kɒnfluəns‖'kɑːn-/ *n* place where two or more rivers flow together

con-form /kən'fɔːm‖-ɔːrm/ *vi* obey established rules or customs **~ist** *n* person who conforms **~ity** *n* [U]

con-found /kən'faʊnd/ *vt* confuse and surprise

con-front /kən'frʌnt/ *vt* face; meet: *confront problems* **~ation** /,kɒnfrən'teɪʃən‖,kɑːn-/ *n* [C;U] angry opposition

con-fuse /kən'fjuːz/ *vt* **1** cause to be mixed up in the mind: *I'm confused.* **2** be unable to tell the difference between: *to confuse Jack and/with Paul* **3** make less clear: *confusing the issue* **-fusion** /-'fjuːʒən/ *n* [U]

con-fute /kən'fjuːt/ *vt* prove to be wrong

con-geal /kən'dʒiːl/ *vi/t* become solid: *congealed blood*

con-ge-ni-al /kən'dʒiːniəl/ *adj* pleasant; in agreement with one's tastes **~ly** *adv*

con-gen-i-tal /kən'dʒenɨtl/ *adj* (of diseases) existing from one's birth

con-ges-ted /kən'dʒestɨd/ *adj* too full; blocked **-tion** /-'dʒestʃən/ *n* [U]

con-glom-e-rate /kən'glɒmərɨt‖-'glɑː-/ *n* large business firm producing many kinds of goods **-ration** /kən,glɒmə'reɪʃən‖-,glɑː-/ *n*

con-grat-u-late /kən'grætʃʊleɪt/ *vt* express pleasure at (someone's) success or good luck: *I congratulated them on the birth of their daughter.* **-lations** /kən,grætʃʊ'leɪʃənz/ *interj, n* [P] **I congratulate you** **-latory** /kən,grætʃʊ'leɪtəri‖-'grætʃʊlətɔːri/ *adj*

con-gre-gate /'kɒŋɡrɨɡeɪt‖'kɑːŋ-/ *vi* gather together **-gation** /,kɒŋɡrɨ'ɡeɪʃən‖,kɑːŋ-/ *n* group of people gathered together in church

con-gress /'kɒŋɡres‖'kɑːŋɡrɨs/ *n* **1** formal meeting to exchange information **2** (*cap.*) highest lawmaking body of the US, consisting of the Senate and the House of Representatives: — *congressman* **~ional** /kɒn'greʃənəl/ *adj*

con-gru-ous /'kɒŋɡruəs‖'kɑːŋ-/ *adj fml* suitable; proper

con-i-cal /'kɒnɪkəl‖'kɑː-/ *adj* CONE-shaped

co-ni-fer /'kəʊnɨfər, 'kɒ-‖'kɑː-/ *n* tree that bears cones (CONE (2))

con-jec-ture /kən'dʒektʃər/ *vi/t fml* guess ♦ *n* [C;U] **-tural** *adj*

con·ju·gal /ˈkɒndʒʊɡəl‖ˈkɑːn-/ adj fml of marriage

con·ju·gate /ˈkɒndʒʊɡeɪt‖ˈkɑːn-/ vt gram give the forms of (a verb) **–gation** /ˌkɒndʒʊˈɡeɪʃən‖ˌkɑːn-/ n class of verbs conjugated in the same way

con·junc·tion /kənˈdʒʌŋkʃən/ n 1 gram word such as 'but' or 'while' 2 **in conjunction with** in combination with

con·junc·ti·vi·tis /kənˌdʒʌŋktɪˈvaɪtɪs/ n painful eye disease

con·jure /ˈkʌndʒəʳ‖ˈkɑːn-, ˈkʌn-/ v 1 vi do clever tricks that seem magical 2 vt cause to appear as if by magic: (fig.) conjure up memories of the past 3 **a name to conjure with** name of a very influential and/or important person or thing **–jurer, -juror** n person who does conjuring tricks

con·nect /kəˈnekt/ v 1 vt/i join together: connect 2 pipes 2 vt think of as related

con·nec·tion ‖ also **con·nex·ion** BrE /kəˈnekʃən/ n 1 [C;U] being connected; relationship 2 [C] plane, train, etc. planned to take passengers arriving by another one 3 [C] person connected to others by family or business 4 **in connection with** fml with regard to

con·nive /kəˈnaɪv/ v **connive at** phr vt make no attempt to stop (something wrong) **–nivance** n [U]

con·nois·seur /ˌkɒnəˈsɜːʳ‖ˌkɑː-/ n person with special knowledge of art, wine, etc.

con·note /kəˈnəʊt/ vt fml (of a word) suggest something more than its ordinary meaning **–notation** /ˌkɒnəˈteɪʃən‖ˌkɑː-/ n: 'Skinny' has bad connotations.

con·nu·bi·al /kəˈnjuːbiəl‖-ˈnuː-/ adj fml of marriage

con·quer /ˈkɒŋkəʳ‖ˈkɑːŋ-/ vt 1 defeat (enemies): (fig.) conquer one's fear 2 take (a place) by force: a conquered city **~or** n

con·quest /ˈkɒŋkwest‖ˈkɑːŋ-/ n 1 [U] conquering 2 [C] something conquered, esp. land gained in war

con·science /ˈkɒnʃəns‖ˈkɑːn-/ n 1 [C;U] knowledge of right and wrong: to have a guilty conscience 2 **on one's conscience** causing one to feel guilty

con·sci·en·tious /ˌkɒnʃiˈenʃəs‖ˌkɑːn-/ adj careful and honest: conscientious work/workers **~ly** adv **~ness** n [U]

conscientious ob·jec·tor /ˌ···· ·ˈ··-/ n person who refuses to serve in the armed forces because of moral or religious beliefs

con·scious /ˈkɒnʃəs‖ˈkɑːn-/ adj 1 awake and able to think 2 knowing;

AWARE 3 intentional: conscious effort **~ly** adv **~ness** n [S;U]

cons·cript¹ /kənˈskrɪpt/ vt make someone serve in the armed forces **~ion** /kənˈskrɪpʃən/ n [U] practice of conscripting people

con·script² /ˈkɒnskrɪpt‖ˈkɑːn-/ n conscripted person

con·se·crate /ˈkɒnsɪkreɪt‖ˈkɑːn-/ vt 1 declare as holy: consecrated wine 2 set apart solemnly for a particular purpose: consecrate one's life to helping the poor **–cration** /ˌkɒnsɪˈkreɪʃən‖ˌkɑːn-/ n [U]

con·sec·u·tive /kənˈsekjʊtɪv/ adj following in unbroken order **~ly** adv

con·sen·sus /kənˈsensəs/ n general agreement

con·sent /kənˈsent/ vi give permission ♦ n [U] permission

con·se·quence /ˈkɒnsɪkwəns‖ˈkɑːnsɪkwens/ n 1 [C] result 2 [U] fml importance: It's of no consequence to me.

con·se·quent /ˈkɒnsɪkwənt‖ˈkɑːn-/ adj fml following as a result **~ly** adv

con·se·quen·tial /ˌkɒnsɪˈkwenʃəl‖ˌkɑːn-/ adj fml 1 consequent 2 important

con·ser·va·tion /ˌkɒnsəˈveɪʃən‖ˌkɑːnsər-/ n [U] 1 protection of animals, plants, ancient buildings, etc. 2 careful use of a limited supply, to prevent waste **~ist** n **~ism** n [U]

con·ser·va·tive /kənˈsɜːvətɪv‖-ɜːr-/ adj 1 not liking change 2 kept rather low: a conservative estimate 3 (cap.) of a British political party opposed to sudden change ♦ n 1 person who dislikes change 2 (cap.) member of the Conservative Party **~ly** adv **-tism** n [U]

Conservative Party /·ˈ···· ˌ··/n [the] British political party which tends to be opposed to sudden change

con·ser·va·to·ry /kənˈsɜːvətəri‖-ˈsɜːrvətɔːri/ n 1 GREENHOUSE 2 school of music or acting

con·serve¹ /kənˈsɜːv‖-ɜːrv/ vt use carefully; preserve: conserve one's energy

con·serve² /ˈkɒnsɜːv‖ˈkɑːnsɜːrv/ n fml fruit preserved by cooking with sugar; JAM

con·sid·er /kənˈsɪdəʳ/ v 1 vi/t think about 2 vt take into account; remember: you have to consider your wife 3 vt believe to be: consider him suitable **~ed** reached after careful thought **~ing** prep if one takes into account: She did well, considering her age.

con·sid·er·a·ble /kənˈsɪdərəbəl/ adj fairly large **-bly** adv much

con·sid·er·ate /kənˈsɪdərɪt/ adj kind and thoughtful **~ly** adv

con·sid·er·a·tion /kənˌsɪdəˈreɪʃən/ n 1 [U] thoughtful attention 2 [C] fact to be remembered when deciding something **3** [C] payment; reward **4 take something into consideration** remember when making a judgment

con-sign /kənˈsaɪn/ vt **1** send (goods) for sale **2** fml give into someone's care ~**ment** n **1** [C] goods consigned **2** [U] act of consigning

con-sist /kənˈsɪst/ v

consist in phr vt fml have as a base; depend on

consist of phr vt be made up of

con-sis-ten-cy /kənˈsɪstənsi/ n **1** [U] state of always behaving in the same way **2** [C] degree of thickness of a liquid **–tent** adj **1** not changing **2** in agreement **–tently** adv

con-sole[1] /kənˈsəʊl/ vt make less unhappy **–solation** /ˌkɒnsəˈleɪʃən‖ˌkɑːn-/ n [C;U] (person or thing giving) comfort

con-sole[2] /ˈkɒnsəʊl‖ˈkɑːn-/ n surface containing the controls for a machine

con-sol-i-date /kənˈsɒlɪdənt‖-ˈsɑː-/ vi/t **1** (cause to) become stronger **2** combine into one **–dation** /kɒnˌsɒlɪˈdeɪʃən‖-ˌsɑː-/ n

con-som-mé /kɒnˈsɒmeɪ, ˈkɒnsəmeɪ‖ˌkɑːnsəˈmeɪ/ n [U] clear soup

con-so-nant[1] /ˈkɒnsənənt‖ˈkɑːn-/ n (letter representing) a speech sound such as b, m, s, made by stopping the breath

consonant[2] adj fml in agreement

con-sort[1] /ˈkɒnsɔːt‖ˈkɑːnsɔːrt/ n wife or husband of a ruler

con-sort[2] /kənˈsɔːt‖-ɔːrt/ v **consort with** phr vi spend time in company

con-sor-ti-um /kənˈsɔːtiəm‖-ɔːr-/ n **-tiums** or **-tia** /-tiə/ combination of a number of companies, banks, etc.

con-spic-u-ous /kənˈspɪkjuəs/ adj easily seen; noticeable ~**ly** adv

con-spi-ra-cy /kənˈspɪrəsi/ n [C;U] (plan made by) conspiring

con-spi-ra-tor /kənˈspɪrətər/ n person who conspires

con-spire /kənˈspaɪər/ vi **1** plan something bad together secretly **2** (of events) combine in a bad way

con-sta-ble /ˈkʌnstəbəl‖ˈkɑːn-/ n British policeman or police officer

con-stab-u-la-ry /kənˈstæbjʊləri‖-leri/ n police force of an area

con-stant /ˈkɒnstənt‖ˈkɑːn-/ adj **1** happening all the time **2** unchanging: a constant speed **3** continuous **4** loyal ♦ n fml something that never varies ~**ly** adv **–stancy** n [U] **1** freedom from change **2** fml loyalty

con-stel-la-tion /ˌkɒnstəˈleɪʃən‖ˌkɑːn-/ n named group of stars

con-ster-na-tion /ˌkɒnstəˈneɪʃən‖ˌkɑːnstər-/ n [U] great shock and fear

con-sti-pa-tion /ˌkɒnstɪˈpeɪʃən‖ˌkɑːn-/ n [U] being unable to empty the bowels properly **–ted** /ˈkɒnstəpeɪtəd‖ˈkɑːn-/ adj

con-sti-tu-en-cy /kənˈstɪtjuənsi/ n (voters in) an area that elects a representative to Parliament

con-sti-tu-ent /kənˈstɪtjuənt/ n **1** voter **2** necessary part: the constituents of cement ♦ adj helping to make a whole

con-sti-tute /ˈkɒnstɪtjuːt‖ˈkɑːnstətuːt/ vt **1** form when added together **2** establish

con-sti-tu-tion /ˌkɒnstɪˈtjuːʃən‖ˌkɑːnstəˈtuː-/ n **1** laws and principles by which a country is governed **2** person's physical condition **3** structure of something ~**al** adj **1** by or of a political constitution **2** of a person's constitution ~**ally** adv

con-strain /kənˈstreɪn/ vt fml force (someone) to do something

con-straint /kənˈstreɪnt/ n [C;U] something that limits freedom: acted under constraint

con-strict /kənˈstrɪkt/ vt make narrower or tighter ~**ion** /-ˈstrɪkʃən/ n [C;U]

con-struct /kənˈstrʌkt/ vt make out of parts; build

con-struc-tion /kənˈstrʌkʃən/ n **1** [U] building; the building industry **2** [C] something built **3** [C] meaning given to something: put the wrong construction on his behaviour **–tive** /-tɪv/ adj helpful: constructive suggestions

con-strue /kənˈstruː/ vt place a certain meaning on

con-sul /ˈkɒnsəl‖ˈkɑːn-/ n representative of a government in a foreign city ~**ar** /-sjʊlər‖-sələr/ adj ~**ate** n consul's office

con-sult /kənˈsʌlt/ vt go to (a person, book, etc.) for advice ~**ation** /ˌkɒnsəlˈteɪʃən‖ˌkɑːn-/ n [C;U]

con-sul-tant /kənˈsʌltənt/ n **1** person who gives professional advice **2** BrE high ranking hospital doctor who gives specialist advice **–tancy** n **–tative** adj giving advice

con-sume /kənˈsjuːm‖-ˈsuːm/ vt fml **1** eat or drink **2** use up; destroy **–suming** adj main: a consuming interest in trains **–sumer** n person who buys goods

consumer dur-a-ble /·, · ˈ···/ n large article that is bought only infrequently, e.g. a car

con-sum-mate[1] /kənˈsʌmət/ adj perfect; complete

con-sum-mate[2] /ˈkɒnsəmeɪt‖ˈkɑːn-/ vt fml **1** complete (a marriage) by having sex **2** make perfect **–mation** /ˌkɒnsəˈmeɪʃən‖ˌkɑːn-/ n [C;U]

con-sump-tion /kənˈsʌmpʃən/ n **1** [S;U] consuming; amount consumed **2** [U] TUBERCULOSIS **–tive** /-tɪv/ adj suffering from TUBERCULOSIS

cont written abbrev. for: continued

con·tact /'kɒntækt‖'kɑːn-/ n 1 [U] meeting; relationship: *Have you been in contact with the disease?* 2 [C] person one knows who can help one: *some useful contacts in Spain* 3 [C] electrical part that touches another to carry electric current ♦ vt reach (someone) by telephone, letter, etc.

contact lens /'·· ·/ n plastic LENS (1) shaped to fit over the eye to improve eyesight

con·ta·gion /kən'teɪdʒən/ n 1 [U] spreading of a disease by touch 2 [C] harmful influence **–gious** adj

con·tain /kən'teɪn/ vt 1 have within itself: *Beer contains alcohol.* 2 keep under control: *I can't contain myself.*

con·tain·er /kən'teɪnəʳ/ n 1 box, bottle, etc., used to contain something 2 large metal box in which goods are packed to be carried on ships, etc.

con·tam·i·nate /kən'tæmɪneɪt/ vt make impure or dirty: *contaminated water* **–nation** /kən,tæmɪ'neɪʃən/ n [U]

con·tem·plate /'kɒntəmpleɪt‖ 'kɑːn-/ vt 1 think about; consider as possible 2 look solemnly at **–plation** /,kɒntəm'pleɪʃən‖,kɑːn-/ n [U] deep thought **–plative** /kən'templətɪv, 'kɒntəmpleɪtɪv‖kən-, 'kɑːntem-/ adj

con·tem·po·ra·ry /kən'tempərəri, -pəri‖-pəreri/ adj 1 modern; of the present 2 of the same time ♦ n person of the same age, or living at the same time

con·tempt /kən'tempt/ n [U] complete lack of respect **~ible** adj deserving contempt **~uous** adj showing contempt

contempt of court /·,· · ·'·/n [U] offence of disobeying a judge in court

con·tend /kən'tend/ v 1 vi compete; struggle 2 vt fml claim; declare **~er** n competitor

con·tent¹ /kən'tent/ adj satisfied; happy ♦ vt make happy **~ed** adj quietly happy **~edly** adv **~ment** n [U] quiet happiness

con·tent² /'kɒntent‖'kɑːn-/ n 1 [U] subject matter of a book 2 [S] amount contained in something: *a high fat content* **contents** n [P] what something contains

con·ten·tion /kən'tenʃən/ n 1 [C] claim; point of view 2 [U] struggle **–tious** adj 1 causing argument 2 quarrelsome

con·test¹ /'kɒntest‖'kɑːn-/ n struggle; competition

con·test² /kən'test/ vt fml 1 compete for 2 argue about the rightness of **~ant** n competitor

con·text /'kɒntekst‖'kɑːn-/ n 1 words that surround a word or phrase 2 surrounding conditions

con·ti·nent /'kɒntɪnənt‖'kɑːn-/ n 1 [C] large land mass; Europe, Asia, etc. 2 [the] (cap.) Europe without Britain **–al** /,kɒntɪ'nentl◂‖,kɑːn-/ adj

con·ti·nen·tal break·fast /,··· '··/n light meal usu. of bread, butter, JAM and coffee

continental quilt /,···· '·/ n BrE DUVET

con·tin·gen·cy /kən'tɪndʒənsi/ n possible event that might cause problems

con·tin·gent¹ /kən'tɪndʒənt/ adj 1 dependent on something uncertain 2 happening by chance

contingent² n 1 part of a larger force of soldiers, ships, etc. 2 part of a larger gathering of people

con·tin·u·al /kən'tɪnjuəl/ adj regular; frequent **~ly** adv

con·tin·ue /kən'tɪnjuː/ vi/t 1 go on doing something 2 start again after stopping **–uation** /kən,tɪnju'eɪʃən/ n 1 [U] act of continuing 2 [C] something which continues from something else

con·ti·nu·i·ty /,kɒntɪ'njuːɪti‖ ,kɑːntɪ'nuː-/ n [U] uninterrupted connection

con·tin·u·ous /kən'tɪnjuəs/ adj continuing unbroken: *The brain needs a continuous supply of blood.* **~ly** adv

con·tin·u·um /kən'tɪnjuəm/ n **-uums** or **-ua** /-juə/ 1 something which is without parts and the same from beginning to end 2 something that changes gradually without sudden breaks

con·tort /kən'tɔːt‖-ɔːrt/ vt twist out of shape **~ion** /-'tɔːʃən‖-'tɔːr-/ n [C;U]

con·tour /'kɒntuəʳ‖'kɑːn-/ n 1 shape of the edges of something, such as a coast 2 line on a map showing the edges of areas above a certain height

con·tra·band /'kɒntrəbænd‖'kɑːn-/ n [U] goods that it is not legal to bring into a country

con·tra·cep·tion /,kɒntrə'sepʃən‖ ,kɑːn-/ n [U] (methods for) preventing sex from resulting in PREGNANCY **–tive** /-'septɪv/ n, adj (drug, etc.) used for contraception

con·tract¹ /'kɒntrækt‖'kɑːn-/ n formal agreement to do something **~ual** /kən'træktʃuəl/ adj

contract² v **contract in/out** phr vi promise, esp. officially to/not to take part

con·tract³ /kən'trækt/ v 1 vi/t arrange by formal agreement 2 vi/t (cause to) become smaller 3 vt fml get (a disease) **~ion** /-'trækʃən/ n 1 [U] process of getting smaller 2 [C] shortened form of a word 3 [C] strong tightening of a muscle

con·trac·tor /kən'træktəʳ‖'kɑːn-

træk-/ n firm that provides supplies and/or workers, esp. for building work

con-tra-dict /ˌkɒntrə'dɪkt‖ˌkɑːn-/ v 1 vt/i say the opposite of; declare to be wrong 2 vt (of a statement, fact, etc.) be opposite to (another) **~ory** adj: contradictory reports **~ion** /-'dɪkʃən/ n [C;U]

con-tra-flow /'kɒntrəfləʊ‖'kɑːn-/ n [U] arrangement by which traffic in both directions on a road can use only one side

con-tral-to /kən'træltəʊ/ n -tos female ALTO

con-trap-tion /kən'træpʃən/ n strange-looking apparatus

con-tra-ry [1] /'kɒntrəri‖'kɑːntreri/ n [S] 1 opposite 2 **on the contrary** no, not at all 3 **to the contrary** to the opposite effect ♦ adj completely different; opposed

con-tra-ry [2] /kən'treəri/ adj (of a person) unreasonable

con-trast [1] /'kɒntrɑːst‖'kɑːntræst/ v 1 vt compare so that differences are made clear 2 vi show a difference: sharply contrasting attitudes

con-trast [2] /kən'trɑːst‖-'træst/ n [C;U] noticeable difference

con-tra-vene /ˌkɒntrə'viːn‖ˌkɑːn-/ vt fml break (a law) **-vention** /-'venʃən/ n [C;U]

con-tre-temps /'kɒntrətɒŋ‖'kɑːntrətɑːn/ n -temps /-tɒŋz‖-tɑːnz/ unlucky and unexpected event

con-trib-ute /kən'trɪbjuːt/ v 1 vt/i join with others in giving something 2 vi help in causing: contribute to good health 3 vt write (an article) for a magazine **-utor** n person who contributes **-utory** adj **-ution** /ˌkɒntrɪ'bjuːʃən‖ˌkɑːn-/ n [C;U]

con-trite /'kɒntraɪt‖kən-/ adj fml sorry for having done wrong **~ly** **-trition** /kən'trɪʃən/ n [U]

con-trive /kən'traɪv/ vt succeed in doing something: contrive to escape **-trivance** n clever plan or invention **-trived** adj unnatural and forced

con-trol /kən'trəʊl/ vt -ll- 1 direct; have power over 2 hold back; RESTRAIN ♦ n 1 [U] power to control: lose control of oneself 2 [C;U] means of controlling: wage control(s) 3 [C] place where something is controlled: controls of a plane 4 [C] standard against which the results of a study are measured 5 **out of control** in(to) a state of not being controlled 6 **under control** working properly **~ler** n person who directs something

con-tro-ver-sy /'kɒntrəvɜːsi, kən'trɒvəsi‖'kɑːntrəvɜːrsi/ n [C;U] fierce argument **-sial** /ˌkɒntrə'vɜːʃəl◄‖ˌkɑːntrə'vɜːrʃəl◄/ adj causing controversy **-sially** adv

co-nun-drum /kə'nʌndrəm/ n 1 RIDDLE 2 difficult problem

con-ur-ba-tion /ˌkɒnɜː'beɪʃən, ˌkɑːnɜːr-/ n number of towns joined into one large city or network

con-va-lesce /ˌkɒnvə'les‖ˌkɑːn-/ vi spend time getting well after an illness **-lescence** n [S;U] time spent getting well **-lescent** n, adj (person) spending time getting well

con-vene /kən'viːn/ v 1 vi meet together 2 vt call (a group) to meet **-vener, -venor** n person who convenes meetings

con-ve-ni-ence /kən'viːniəns/ n 1 [U] fitness; suitableness 2 [C] useful tool or apparatus 3 [C] TOILET 4 [U] personal comfort **-ent** adj 1 suited to one's needs 2 near **-ently** adv

con-vent /'kɒnvənt‖'kɑːnvent/ n place where NUNs live

con-ven-tion /kən'venʃən/ n 1 [C;U] accepted social custom 2 [C] meeting of a group with a shared purpose 3 [C] formal political agreement **~al** adj following accepted customs **~ally** adv

con-verge /kən'vɜːdʒ‖-ɜːr-/ vi come together and meet: roads converging at the station **-vergence** n [U]

con-ver-sant /kən'vɜːsənt‖-ɜːr-/ adj fml having knowledge or experience

con-ver-sa-tion /ˌkɒnvə'seɪʃən, ˌkɑːnvər-/ n [C;U] informal talk **~al** adj (of language) used in conversation

con-verse [1] /kən'vɜːs‖-ɜːrs/ vi fml talk informally

con-verse [2] /'kɒnvɜːs‖kən'vɜːrs/ adj, n [S] fml opposite: the converse opinion **~ly** adv

con-ver-sion /kən'vɜːʃən‖-'vɜːrʒən/ n [C;U] act of converting

con-vert [1] /kən'vɜːt‖-ɜːrt/ vt/i 1 change into another form: convert dollars into pounds 2 change to a particular religious belief, etc. **-er** n apparatus that converts something, esp. information to be put into a computer **~ible** adj (esp. of money) able to be converted **~ible** n car with a roof that can be folded back

con-vert [2] /'kɒnvɜːt‖'kɑːnvɜːrt/ n person who has accepted a particular belief

con-vex /ˌkɒn'veks◄, kən-‖ˌkɑːn'veks◄, kən-/ adj curved outwards

con-vey /kən'veɪ/ vt 1 take; carry 2 make (feelings, etc.) known **~er, ~or** n

con-vey-ance /kən'veɪəns/ n 1 [C] fml vehicle 2 [U] legal paper giving the right to property **-ancing** n [U] branch of law concerned with legal conveyances

conveyer belt, conveyor belt /·'·· ·/ n endless moving belt carrying objects from one place to another

con·vict¹ /kən'vɪkt/ vt prove (someone) to be guilty of a crime

con·vict² /'kɒnvɪkt‖'kɑːn-/ n convicted person who is sent to prison

con·vic·tion /kən'vɪkʃən/ n [C;U] 1 being convicted of a crime 2 firm belief

con·vince /kən'vɪns/ vt cause to feel sure of something **–vincing** adj: a convincing argument **–vincingly** adv

con·viv·i·al /kən'vɪvɪəl/ adj merry and friendly ~**ity** /kən,vɪvɪ'ælɪti/ n [U]

con·vo·lut·ed /'kɒnvəluːtɪd‖'kɑːn-/ adj fml 1 twisted 2 difficult to understand **–lution** /,kɒnvə'luːʃən‖,kɑːn-/ n twist

con·voy /'kɒnvɔɪ‖'kɑːn-/ n 1 group of ships or vehicles travelling together, esp. for safety 2 protecting force of warships, etc. ◆ vt go with and protect

con·vulse /kən'vʌls/ vt shake violently **–vulsive** adj **–vulsion** /-'vʌlʃən/ n

coo /kuː/ vi 1 make the soft cry of a DOVE 2 speak lovingly

cook /kʊk/ v 1 vi/t prepare (food) by using heat 2 vi (of food) be cooked 3 vt change (accounts, etc.) dishonestly ◆ n person who cooks food ~**er** n STOVE for cooking on

cook·e·ry /'kʊkəri/ n [U] art of cooking

cook·ie /'kʊki/ n esp AmE 1 BISCUIT 2 person: a smart/tough cookie.

cool¹ /kuːl/ adj 1 pleasantly cold 2 calm; unexcited: a cool-headed decision 3 not very friendly 4 (used to add force to an expression): a cool £1,000 a month ◆ n 1 cool temperature: the cool of the evening 2 calmness: lose one's cool ◆ adv play it cool act calmly ~**ness** n [U] ~**ly** /-li/ adv

cool² vi/t make or become cool

cool down/off phr vi become calmer

coop¹ /kuːp/ n cage for small creatures

coop² coop up phr vt shut into a small space

co·op·e·rate /kəʊ'ɒpəreɪt‖-'ɑːp-/ vi work together for a shared purpose **–rative** /-rətɪv/ adj helpful **–rative** n firm, farm, etc., owned by its workers **–ration** /kəʊ,ɒpə'reɪʃən‖-,ɑːp-/ n

co·opt /,kəʊ 'ɒpt‖-'ɑːpt/ vt (of an elected group) choose as a fellow member

co·or·di·nate /kəʊ'ɔːdɪneɪt‖-'ɔːr-/ vt cause to work together effectively: coordinate our efforts **–nation** /kəʊ,ɔːdɪ'neɪʃən‖-,ɔːr-/ n [U]

co·or·di·nates /kəʊ'ɔːdɪnəts‖-'ɔːr-/ n [P] separate garments in matching colours that can be worn together

cop¹ /kɒp‖kɑːp/ n sl policeman

cop² vt -pp- **cop it** sl esp. BrE be in serious trouble

cop out phr vi sl avoid responsibility **cop-out** /' ⋅ -/ n

cope /kəʊp/ vi deal with something successfully

cop·i·er /'kɒpɪəʳ‖'kɑː-/ n machine for making paper copies (COPY (1))

co·pi·ous /'kəʊpɪəs/ adj plentiful ~**ly** adv

cop·per¹ /'kɒpəʳ‖'kɑː-/ n 1 [U] a soft reddish-brown metal b its colour 2 [C] copper coin

copper² n sl policeman

copse /kɒps‖kɑːps/ n small group of trees

cop·u·late /'kɒpjˈleɪt‖'kɑːp-/ vi fml have sex **-lation** /,kɒpjˈleɪʃən/ ,kɑːp-/ n [U]

cop·y /'kɒpi‖'kɑːpi/ n 1 thing made to be like another 2 single example of a book, newspaper, etc. 3 good copy interesting news — see also HARD COPY, SOFT COPY ◆ v 1 vt make a copy of 2 vt do the same as 3 vi/t cheat in an examination, etc., by copying

cop·y·cat /'kɒpikæt‖'kɑː-/ n derog infml person who copies other people's behaviour, dress, work, etc.

cop·y·right /'kɒpiraɪt‖'kɑː-/ n [C;U] legal right to be the only seller of a book, etc.

cor·al /'kɒrəl‖'kɔː-, 'kɑː-/ n [U] white, pink, or red substance formed by small sea creatures

cord /kɔːd‖kɔːrd/ n [C;U] 1 thick string or thin rope 2 electric wire

cor·di·al¹ /'kɔːdɪəl‖'kɔːrdʒəl/ adj warm and friendly ~**ly** adv 1 in a cordial manner 2 **dislike/hate each other cordially** dislike/hate each other very strongly

cordial² n [U] nonalcoholic fruit drink

cor·don /'kɔːdn‖'kɔːrdn/ n ring of police, etc., surrounding an area ◆ v **cordon off** phr vt protect with a cordon

cords /kɔːdz‖kɔːrdz/ n [P] infml trousers made from corduroy

cor·du·roy /'kɔːdʒˈrɔɪ, -dʒˈ‖ 'kɔːrdə-/ n strong cotton cloth with raised lines on it

core /kɔːʳ/ n 1 central part: core of an apple 2 **to the core** thoroughly ◆ vt remove the core of (a fruit)

cork /kɔːk‖kɔːrk/ n 1 [U] BARK of a tree (the **cork oak**) 2 [C] piece of this used for closing a bottle ◆ vt close with a cork

corn¹ /kɔːn‖kɔːrn/ n [U] 1 BrE (seed of) various grain plants, esp. wheat 2

AmE (seed of) a tall plant with long bunches of yellow seeds

corn² *n* painful lump of hard skin on the foot

cor·ne·a /'kɔːniə/'kɔːr-/ *n* protective covering on the front surface of the eye

corned beef /,· '·◄/ *n* [U] kind of pressed cooked BEEF in tins

cor·ner /'kɔːnəʳ/'kɔːr-/ *n* **1** point where 2 lines, edges, or roads meet **2** part of the world: *remote corners of England* **3** also **corner kick** (in football) kick taken from the corner of the field **4 around/round the corner** near **5 in a tight corner** in a difficult position **6 turn the corner** become better after a period of difficulties, etc. ♦ *v* **1** *vt* force into a difficult position **2** *vt* gain control of (by buying, selling, or production of goods) **3** *vi* (of a vehicle) turn a corner

cor·ner·stone /'kɔːnəstəʊn/'kɔːr-nər-/ *n* **1** stone set at one bottom corner of a building **2** something of great importance, on which everything else is based

cor·net /'kɔːnɪt/kɔːr'net/ *n* **1** musical instrument like a TRUMPET **2** *BrE* CONE-shaped eatable container for ice-cream

corn-flakes /'kɔːnfleɪks/'kɔːrn-/ *n* [P] bits of crushed CORN¹ (2) to be eaten with milk at breakfast

cor·nice /'kɔːnɪs/'kɔːr-/ *n* decorative border at top edge of the front of a building, a column, or the walls of a room

corn·y /'kɔːni/'kɔːrni/ *adj sl* too common; old-fashioned

co·rol·la·ry /kə'rɒləri/'kɒrələri, 'kɔː-/ *n fml* something that naturally follows from something else

coronary throm·bo·sis /,kɒrənəri θrɒm'bəʊsɪs/,kɔːrəneri θrɑːm-, ,kɑː-/ also **coronary** — *n* stopping of the blood supply to the heart; kind of HEART ATTACK

cor·o·na·tion /,kɒrə'neɪʃ ən/,kɔː-, ,kɑː-/ *n* ceremony of crowning a king or queen

cor·o·ner /'kɒrənəʳ/'kɔː-, 'kɑː-/ *n* official who enquires into the cause of a person's death if it is not clearly known

cor·o·net /'kɒrənɪt/,kɔːrə'net, ,kɑː-/ *n* small crown worn by nobles, etc.

cor·po·ral¹ /'kɔːpərəl/'kɔːr-/ *adj fml* of the human body: *corporal punishment*

corporal² *n* person of low rank in an army or air force

cor·po·rate /'kɔːpərət/'kɔːr-/ *adj* **1** shared by a whole group: *corporate responsibility* **2** of a CORPORATION (1)

cor·po·ra·tion /,kɔːpə'reɪʃ ən/,kɔːr-/ *n* **1** large business organization **2** town COUNCIL

corps /kɔːʳ/ *n* **1 a** trained army group **b** branch of the army equal to 2 DIVISIONs **2** group with the same activity: *the press corps*

corpse /kɔːps/kɔːrps/ *n* dead body

cor·pu·lent /'kɔːpjʊlənt/'kɔːr-/ *adj* very fat

cor·pus·cle /'kɔːpəsəl, kɔː'pʌ-/ 'kɔːrpə-/ *n* any of the red and white cells in the body

cor·ral /kə'rɑːl, kə-/kə'ræl/ *n* enclosed area (esp. in Western America) for cattle and horses ♦ *vt* -**ll**-put in a corral

cor·rect¹ /kə'rekt/ *adj* **1** without mistakes; true **2** proper: *correct behaviour* ~**ly** *adv* ~**ness** *n* [U]

correct² *vt* make right; show the mistakes in ~**ive** *adj*, *n* ~**ion** /kə'rekʃən/ *n* **1** [U] correcting **2** [C] change that improves something **3** [U] punishment

cor·re·late /'kɒrəleɪt/'kɔː-, 'kɑː-/ *vi/t* (show to) have a close connection -**ation** /,kɒrə'leɪʃ ən/,kɔː-, ,kɑː-/ *n* close connection

cor·re·spond /,kɒrə'spɒnd/,kɔːrə'spɑːnd, ,kɑː-/ *vi* **1** be equal; match **2** exchange letters ~**ing** *adj* matching; equal

cor·re·spon·dence /,kɒrə'spɒndəns/,kɔːrə'spaːn-, ,kɑː-/ *n* [S;U] **1** letter-writing; letters **2** equality between things; likeness -**dent** *n* **1** person with whom one exchanges letters **2** someone employed by a newspaper, television or radio station, etc., to report news from a distant area

cor·ri·dor /'kɒrɪdɔːʳ/'kɔːrədɔr, 'kɑː-/ *n* passage between rows of rooms

cor·rob·o·rate /kə'rɒbəreɪt/kə'rɑː-/ *vt* support (an opinion, etc.) by proof -**ration** /kə,rɒbə'reɪʃ ən/kə,rɑː-/ *n* [U]

cor·rode /kə'rəʊd/ *vt/i* destroy slowly, esp. by chemical action

cor·ro·sion /kə'rəʊʒən/ *n* [U] **1** corroding **2** RUST, etc., produced by corroding -**sive** /-sɪv/ *adj*

cor·ru·gated /'kɒrəgeɪtɪd/'kɔː-, 'kɑː-/ *adj* having wavelike folds -**gation** /,kɒrə'geɪʃ ən/,kɔː-, ,kɑː-/ *n* [U]

cor·rupt /kə'rʌpt/ *adj* **1** morally bad, esp. dishonest **2** containing mistakes ♦ *vt/i* make or become corrupt ~**ly** *adv* ~**ion** /-'rʌpʃən/ *n* [U]

cor·set /'kɔːsɪt/'kɔːr-/ also **corsets** *pl. n* — tight-fitting undergarment worn esp. by women

cor·tege /kɔː'teɪʒ/kɔːr'teʒ/ *n* funeral procession

cosh /kɒʃ/ *n, vt, n BrE* (hit with) a short heavy pipe or filled rubber tube

cos·met·ic /kɒz'metɪk/kɑːz-/ *n* cream, powder, etc., for the skin or hair ♦ *adj* 1 of, related to, or causing increased beauty 2 dealing only with the outside appearance rather than the central part of something

cos·mic /'kɒzmɪk‖'kɑːz-/ *adj* of the whole universe

cos·mo·naut /'kɒzmənɔːt‖'kɑːz-/ *n* a Soviet ASTRONAUT

cos·mo·pol·i·tan /ˌkɒzmə'pɒlətən‖ˌkɑːzmə'pɑː-/ *adj* 1 consisting of people from many parts of the world 2 not narrow-minded ♦ *n* cosmopolitan person

cos·mos /'kɒzmɒs‖'kɑːzmɒs/ *n* the whole universe

cos·set /'kɒsɪt‖'kɑː-/ *vt* -tt- treat too kindly

cost¹ /kɒst‖kɔːst/ *n* 1 [C] price of something 2 [U] what is needed to gain something 3 **at all costs** whatever it may cost 4 **to one's cost** from one's own unpleasant experience ~**ly** *adj* expensive **costs** [P] cost of taking a matter to a court of law

cost² *vt* 1 (*past t.* and *p.* cost) have as a price: *It cost me £5.* | (fig.) *The mistake cost him his job.* 2 (*past t.* and *p.* costed) calculate the price to be charged for (a job)

co-star /'kɒʊ stɑː'/ *n* famous actor or actress who appears with another famous actor or actress in a film, etc. ♦ co-star *vi*

cost-ef·fec·tive /'·· ·,··/ *adj* bringing the best possible profits or advantages for the lowest possible cost ~**ly** *adv* ~**ness** *n* [U]

cos·tume /'kɒstjʊm‖'kɑːstuːm/ *n* [C;U] clothes, esp. as worn in plays

costume jew·ell·ery /'·· ,··/ *n* [U] precious-looking jewellery made from cheap materials

co·sy¹ /'kɒʊzi/ *adj* warm and comfortable ~**sily** *adv* ~**siness** *n* [U]

cosy² *n* covering for a teapot to keep the contents warm

cot /kɒt‖kɑːt/ *n* 1 *BrE* bed for a small child 2 *AmE* light narrow bed which folds flat

cot death /'· ,·/ *n* [C;U] unexplained death of a healthy baby

cot·tage /'kɒtɪdʒ‖'kɑː-/ *n* small house, esp. in the country

cot·ton¹ /'kɒtn‖'kɑːtn/ *n* [U] 1 soft white hair of a tropical plant 2 thread or cloth made from this 3 *AmE* COTTON WOOL

cotton² *v* **cotton on** *phr vi infml* understand

cotton wool /,·· '·/ *n* [U] *BrE* soft mass of cotton for cleaning wounds, etc.

couch¹ /kaʊtʃ/ *n* long seat like a bed

couch² *vt fml* express: *His refusal was couched in unfriendly terms.*

cou·chette /kuː'ʃet/ *n* folding bed on a train

cou·gar /'kuːgə'/ *n* large American wild cat

cough /kɒf‖kɔːf/ *v* 1 *vi* push air out noisily from the lungs 2 *vt* produce by doing this: *cough up blood* ♦ *n* 1 [C] act of coughing 2 [S] illness that makes a person cough

cough up *phr vt infml* produce (money or information) unwillingly

could /kəd; *strong* kʊd/ *v aux* 1 (describes **can** in the past): *He could read when he was 4.* 2 (used to describe what someone has said): *She asked if she could smoke.* 3 (used to show what is possible): *I think the accident could have been prevented.* 4 (used to make a request): *Could you help me?*

could·n't /'kʊdnt/ *v short for.* could not

coun·cil /'kaʊnsəl/ *n* group of people appointed or elected to manage something ♦ *adj* owned by British local government: *council flats* ~**lor** *n* member of a council

coun·sel /'kaʊnsəl/ *n* counsel 1 [C] *law* BARRISTER acting for someone 2 [C] *fml* advice ♦ *v* -**ll-** *BrE* ‖ -**l-** *AmE fml* advise ~**lor** *BrE* ‖ ~**or** *AmE* adviser

count¹ /kaʊnt/ *v* 1 *vi/t* name (numbers) in order: *count (to) 20* 2 *vt* find the total of 3 *vt* include: *6 people, counting me* 4 *vt* consider to be: *count yourself lucky* 5 *vi* have value: *Every moment counts.* ♦ *n* 1 act of counting; total 2 one of a number of crimes of which a person is thought to be guilty: *guilty on all counts* 3 **be out for the count** (in BOXING) be COUNTed out; be unconscious 4 **keep/lose count** know/no longer know the exact number ~**able** *adj* that can be counted: *Egg is a countable noun.* ~**less** *adj* very many

count down *phr vt* count backwards to zero, esp. before sending a spacecraft into space **countdown** /'kaʊntdaʊn/ *n*

count in *phr vt* include

count on/upon *phr vt* depend on; expect

count out *phr vt* 1 put down in turn while counting 2 not include 3 declare (a BOXER who fails to get up after 10 seconds) to be a loser of a fight

count² *n* European nobleman

coun·te·nance /'kaʊntənəns/ *n fml* 1 [C] face 2 [U] support; approval ♦ *vt fml* give approval to

coun·ter¹ /'kaʊntə'/ *n* 1 table where people in a shop, etc., are served 2 **over the counter** (when buying drugs) without a PRESCRIPTION 3 **under the counter** secretly and often unlawfully

counter[2] *n* **1** object used in some games instead of money **2** machine that counts

counter[3] *vt/i* meet an attack; oppose: *counter her proposal*

counter[4] *adv, adj* opposed; opposite: *act counter to all advice*

coun·ter·act /ˌkaʊntər'ækt/ *vt* reduce the effect of: *counteract a poison*

coun·ter·at·tack /'kaʊntərətæk/ *vi/ t, n* (make) an attack to oppose another

coun·ter·bal·ance /'kaʊntəˌbæləns‖-tər-/ *vt, n* (act as) a force that balances another

coun·ter·feit /'kaʊntəfit‖-tər-/ *n, adj* (thing) made as a copy of something else, to deceive: *counterfeit money* ♦ *vt* make a counterfeit of

coun·ter·foil /'kaʊntəfɔil‖-tər-/ *n* part of a cheque, etc., kept as a record

coun·ter·mand /ˌkaʊntə'mɑːnd, 'kaʊntəmɑːnd‖'kaʊntərmænd/ *vt* declare (a command already given) ineffective

coun·ter·part /'kaʊntəpɑːt‖-ərpɑːrt/ *n* person or thing that matches another, but in a different system

coun·ter·pro·duc·tive /ˌkaʊntəprə'dʌktɪv◀‖-tər-/ *adj* having an opposite effect from the one intended

coun·ter·sign /'kaʊntəsaɪn‖-ər-/ *vt* add another signature to (a paper already signed)

coun·ter·vail·ing /ˌkaʊntə'veɪlɪŋ‖-ər-/ *adj* acting with equal force but opposite effect

coun·tess /'kaʊntɪs/ *n* **a** woman who holds the rank of COUNT or EARL for herself **b** wife of a COUNT or EARL

coun·try /'kʌntri/ *n* **1** [C] nation, with its land and population **2** [S;U] also **countryside** /'kʌntrisaɪd/ -- land outside towns **3 go to the country** *esp. BrE* (of a government) call a general election ♦ *adj* of, in or from the country

country and west·ern /ˌ··· ···/also **country music** /ˌ·· '··/ — *n* [U] popular music in the style of the southern and western US

coun·try·man /'kʌntrimən/ -wo·man /-ˌwʊmən/ *fem* — -men /-mən/ **1** COMPATRIOT **2** person who does not live in a town

coun·ty /'kaʊnti/ *n* area divided from others for purposes of local government

coup /kuː/ *n* **1** clever effective action **2** also **coup d'état** /ˌkuː deɪ'tɑː‖-deɪ'tɑː/ — sudden and violent seizure of state power by a small group

cou·pé /'kuːpeɪ‖kuː'peɪ/ *n* closed car with 2 doors and a sloping back

cou·ple /'kʌpəl/ *n* **1** two things of the same kind **2** two people, esp. a husband and wife **3** a few ♦ *v* **1** *vt* join (two things) together **2** *vi* (of animals) MATE **–pling** *n* something that joins two things, esp. two railway carriages

cou·pon /'kuːpɒn‖-pɑːn/ *n* ticket showing the right of the holder to receive something

cour·age /'kʌrɪdʒ/ *n* [U] ability to control fear; bravery **–ageous** /kə'reɪdʒəs/ *adj* brave **–ageously** *adv*

cour·gette /kʊəˈʒet‖kʊr-/ *n BrE* small green MARROW

cou·ri·er /'kʊrɪə/ *n* **1** person who looks after travellers on a tour **2** official messenger

course /kɔːs‖kɔːrs/ *n* **1** path along which something moves **2** area for races or certain sports: *a golf course* **3** plan of action **4** a set of lessons, treatments, etc. **b** university studies: *a 4 year course* **5** any of several parts of a meal **6 a matter of course** that which one expects to happen **7 in due course** at the right time **8 in the course of** during **9 of course** certainly **10 run/take its/their course** (of an illness, etc.) continue to its natural end **11 stay the course** continue something through to the end in spite of difficulty ♦ *vi* (of liquid) flow quickly

court[1] /kɔːt‖kɔːrt/ *n* **1** a [C] room (**courtroom**) or building where law cases are judged **b** [U] people gathered together there **2** [C] area for certain ball games such as tennis **3** [C] king or queen with the royal family, officials, etc. **4** [C] **a** short street surrounded by buildings on three sides **b** block of flats **c** also **courtyard** /'kɔːtjɑːd‖'kɔːrtjɑːrd/ — open space surrounded by buildings

court[2] *vt* **1** try to win the favour of **2** visit and pay attention to (a woman a man hopes to marry) **3** risk foolishly: *to court disaster*

cour·te·ous /'kɜːtɪəs‖'kɜːr-/ *adj fml* polite and kind **~ly** *adv*

cour·te·sy /'kɜːtɪsi‖'kɜːr-/ *n* **1** [C;U] polite behaviour **2 by courtesy of** with the permission of

cour·ti·er /'kɔːtɪə‖'kɔːr-/ *n* person in attendance at a royal court

court-mar·tial /ˌ· '···◀‖ˌ· ,·/ *n* (trial before) a court for offences against military law ♦ *vt* **-ll-** *BrE* ‖ **-l-** *AmE* try (someone) in a court-martial

court·ship /'kɔːt-ʃɪp‖'kɔːrt-/ *n* [U] (period of) trying to attract someone to oneself, esp. with the aim of marriage

cous·in /'kʌzən/ *n* **1** child of one's uncle or aunt **2** related person or thing — see also FIRST COUSIN, SECOND COUSIN

cove /kəʊv/ *n* small BAY[1]

cov·e·nant /'kʌvənənt/ n 1 formal agreement 2 written promise to pay a fixed regular sum of money to a church, CHARITY (3), etc.

Cov·en·try /'kʌvəntri, 'kɒv-‖'kʌv-, 'kɑːv-/ n **send someone to Coventry** (of a group) refuse to speak to someone as a punishment

cov·er¹ /'kʌvər/ 1 vt spread something over; hide in this way: *cover the body with a sheet* 2 vt lie on the surface of; spread over (something): *furniture covered in dust* | *The town covers five square miles.* 3 vt travel (a distance) 4 vt include: *a talk covering the whole history of medicine* 5 vt report (an event) for a newspaper 6 vt be enough money for 7 vt protect from loss; insure 8 vt keep a gun aimed at 9 vi/t act in place of (someone who is absent)

cover up phr vt prevent (something) from being noticed **cover-up** /'·· ·/ n

cover up for phr vt hide something wrong or shameful in order to save (someone else) from punishment, blame, etc.

cov·er² n 1 [C] anything that protects or hides by covering: *cushion covers* | (fig.) *The business is a cover for illegal activity.* 2 [C] outside of a book or magazine 3 [U] shelter; protection 4 [U] insurance against loss, etc. 5 **under plain/separate cover** in a plain/separate envelope **~ing** n something that covers or hides

cov·er·age /'kʌvərɪdʒ/ n [U] time and space given to reporting an event

cov·er·alls /'kʌvərɔːlz/ n [P] AmE for OVERALLS

cover charge /'·· ·/ n charge made by a restaurant in addition to the cost of the food and drinks or of the service

covering let·ter /,··· '··/ n letter or note containing an explanation or additional information, sent with a parcel or another letter

cov·ert /'kʌvət‖'kʌuvərt/ adj hidden; secret **~ly** adv

cov·et /'kʌvɪt/ vt desire (esp. someone else's possessions) eagerly **~ous** adj

cow¹ /kau/ n female of cattle and some other large animals

cow² vt frighten into obedience

cow·ard /'kauəd‖-ərd/ n person afraid of pain or danger **~ly** adv

cow·ard·ice /'kauədɪs‖-ər-/ n [U] lack of courage

cow·boy /'kaubɔɪ/ n 1 man who looks after cattle on horseback in N America 2 BrE sl someone who is careless and dishonest in business

cow·er /'kauər/ vi bend low from fear or shame

cow-pat /'kaupæt/ n lump of cow DUNG

cox /kɒks‖kɑːks/ n person who guides and controls a rowing boat, esp. in races ♦ vi/t act as cox

coy /kɔɪ/ adj pretending not to be self-confident **~ly** adv

coy·ote /'kɔɪ-əut, kɔɪ'əutɪ‖'kaɪ-əut, kaɪ'əuti/ small WOLF

CPU /,si: pi: 'ju:/ abbrev. for CENTRAL PROCESSING UNIT

crab /kræb/ n 1 10-legged shellfish that can be eaten

crab·by /'kræbi/ adj bad-tempered

crack¹ /kræk/ v 1 vi/t break without dividing into pieces: *cracked cups* 2 vi/t make a sudden explosive sound: *crack a whip* 3 vi/t cause to break open: *crack a safe* 4 vi (of a voice) change suddenly in level 5 vi/t hit suddenly 6 vi lose strength or control: *crack (up) under the strain* 7 make (a joke) 8 discover the secret of (a CODE (1)) 9 (cause) to strike with a sudden blow 10 **cracked up to be** believed to be 11 **get cracking** be or become busy doing something in a hurried way

crack down phr vi take strong action against something **~crackdown** /'krækdaun/ n

crack² n 1 thin line caused by breaking 2 explosive sound: *crack of thunder* 3 sudden sharp blow 4 sudden change in the level of the voice 5 quick joke; clever remark 6 **at the crack of dawn** very early in the morning ♦ adj very skilful: *crack troops*

crack³ n [U] sl extremely pure form of COCAINE, taken illegally for pleasure

cracked /krækt/ adj infml slightly mad

crack·er /'krækər/ n 1 unsweetened BISCUIT 2 paper tube that makes a noise when pulled apart

crack·ers /'krækəz‖-ərz/ adj BrE infml mad

crack·le /'krækəl/ vi make small sharp sounds: *The fire crackled.* **crackle** n [S;U]

crack·pot /'krækpɒt‖-pɑːt/ adj strange; mad ♦ n crackpot person

cra·dle /'kreɪdl/ n 1 small bed for a baby 2 origin of something: *the cradle of Western civilization* 3 frame to support something ♦ vt hold gently

craft¹ /krɑːft‖kræft/ n trade needing skill, esp. with one's hands

craft² n craft boat, aircraft, or spacecraft

crafts·man /'krɑːftsmən‖'kræ-/ **crafts·wo·man** /-wumən/ fem. — n **-men** /-mən/ skilled worker **~ship** n [U]

craft·y /'krɑːfti‖'kræf-/ adj cleverly deceitful **-ily** adv **-iness** n [U]

crag /kræg/ n high steep rock ~**gy** adj 1 steep and rough 2 (esp. of a man's face) rough in appearance

cram /kræm/ v -mm- 1 vt force into a small space; fill too full: box crammed with letters 2 vi study hard for a short time: cram for an examination

cramp /kræmp/ n [C;U] sudden painful tightening of a muscle ♦ vt 1 cause to have a cramp 2 prevent natural growth or development 3 **cramp someone's style** prevent someone from showing their abilities to the full ~**ed** adj limited in space

cram-pon /'kræmpɒn/ n set of SPIKES fixed to a boot for climbing ice slopes

crane /kreɪn/ n 1 machine with a movable arm for lifting heavy objects 2 tall waterbird with long legs ♦ vi/t stretch out one's neck to see better

cra-ni-um /'kreɪniəm/ n bony part of the head, covering the brain –**al** adj

crank /kræŋk/ n 1 L-shaped handle for turning 2 person with strange ideas ♦ vt 1 move by turning a crank 2 use a CRANK (1) to start a car ~**y** adj 1 (of people or ideas) peculiar 2 AmE bad-tempered

cran-ny /'kræni/ n small narrow opening in a wall, etc.

crap /kræp/ n [U] taboo sl 1 (act of passing) solid waste from the bowel 2 nonsense ♦ **crap** vi -pp-

crash /kræʃ/ v 1 vi/t fall or hit violently: The car crashed into a tree. 2 vi make a sudden loud noise 3 vi move violently and noisily: The elephant crashed through the fence. 4 vi fail suddenly in business ♦ n 1 violent vehicle accident: a car/plane crash 2 sudden loud noise 3 sudden business failure ♦ adj intended to get quick results: a crash diet/course ♦ adv with a crash

crash hel-met /'· ,··/ n protective HELMET worn by motor cyclists, etc.

crash-land /'· ·'·/ vi/t (cause a plane) to crash in a controlled way **crash landing** n

crass /kræs/ adj fml showing great stupidity and a complete lack of feeling or respect for others

crate /kreɪt/ n large wooden or plastic box for bottles, etc.

cra-ter /'kreɪtər/ n 1 mouth of a VOLCANO 2 hole made by a bomb, etc. 3 flat-bottomed round hole on the moon's surface

cra-vat /krə'væt/ n wide piece of cloth worn like a TIE

crave /kreɪv/ vi/t have a very strong desire for (something) **craving** n

crawl /krɔːl/ vi 1 move slowly, esp. with the body close to the ground: crawling babies/(fig.) traffic 2 be covered by crawling insects, etc. 3 have an unpleasant sensation, as of insects,

etc., moving slowly over one's skin: The idea makes my flesh crawl. 4 infml try to win the favour of someone by being too nice to them ♦ n [S] 1 very slow movement 2 rapid way of swimming ~**er** n 1 someone who CRAWLS (4)

cray-on /'kreɪən, -ɒn‖-ɑːn, -ən/ n pencil or coloured chalk or wax **crayon** vi/t

craze /kreɪz/ n popular fashion that lasts a short time ♦ vt make excited or mad

cra-zy /'kreɪzi/ adj 1 mad; foolish 2 wildly excited –**zily** adv –**ziness** n [U]

creak /kriːk/ vi, n make the sound of a badly-oiled door ~**y** adj

cream /kriːm/ n [U] 1 thick liquid that rises to the top of milk 2 soft mixture like this: face cream 3 best part: the cream of the students ♦ adj yellowish-white ♦ vt 1 make into a soft mixture: creamed potatoes 2 take cream from the surface of (milk) ~**y** adj 1 containing cream 2 like cream

cream off phr vt take the best part

cream-e-ry /'kriːməri/ n DAIRY

crease /kriːs/ n 1 line made by folding 2 line marked on the ground for certain games ♦ vi/t press into CREASES (1)

cre-ate /kri'eɪt/ vt 1 cause (something new) to exist; make 2 appoint to a rank: create him a knight –**ator** n 1 [C] person who creates something 2 [the] (cap.) God –**ation** /-'eɪʃən/ n 1 [U] act of creating 2 [C] something created 3 [U] the whole universe

cre-a-tive /kri'eɪtɪv/ adj able to make new things; inventive ~**ly** adv –**tivity** /ˌkriːeɪ'tɪvəti/ n [U]

crea-ture /'kriːtʃər/ n person, animal, or being

crèche /kreʃ‖kreɪʃ,kreʃ/ n BrE public NURSERY for babies

cre-dence /'kriːdəns/ n fml acceptance as true; belief

cre-den-tials /krɪ'denʃəlz/ n [P] written proof of a person's ability and trustworthiness

credibility gap /ˌ··'···· ·/ n difference between what someone, esp. a politician, says and what they really mean or do

cred-i-ble /'kredɪbəl/ adj that can be believed –**bly** adv –**bility** /ˌkredɪ'bɪləti/ n [U]

cred-it¹ /'kredɪt/ n 1 [U] system of buying things and paying later: buy on credit 2 [U] quality of being likely to repay debts 3 [U] amount of money in someone's bank account 4 [U] belief; trust 5 [C;U] (cause of) public honour: get credit for an invention‖He's a credit to his team. 6 [C] unit of a student's work 7 **to someone's credit a**

in someone's favour **b** to/in someone's name **~able** *adj* deserving approval **~ably** *adv* **credits** *n* [P] names of actors, etc., which appear at the beginning or end of a film or television show

credit² *vt* 1 believe 2 add to an account

credit card /'·· ·/ *n* plastic card allowing one to buy goods without paying cash

cred-i-tor /'kredɪtər/ *n* person to whom money is owed

cred-u-lous /'kredjʊləs‖-dʒə-/ *adj* too willing to believe **-lity** /krɪˈdjuːlɪti‖-'duː-/ *n* [U]

creed /kriːd/ *n* system of (esp. religious) beliefs

creek /kriːk/ *n* 1 *BrE* narrow piece of water reaching in from the sea 2 *AmE* small stream

creep¹ /kriːp/ *vi* creep 1 move slowly and quietly; CRAWL 2 (of a plant) grow along the ground or a surface 3 CRAWL (3) **~er** *n* creeping plant **~y** *adj* strange and frightening **creeps** *n* [P] feeling of fear and strangeness

creep² *n infml* unpleasant SERVILE person

creepy-crawl-y /,·· '··/ *n infml esp. BrE* a creeping insect

cre-mate /krɪˈmeɪt‖'kriːmeɪt/ *vt* burn (a dead person) **-mation** /krɪˈmeɪʃən/ *n* [C;U]

crem-a-to-ri-um /,kreməˈtɔːriəm‖ ,kriː-/ *n* place where bodies are cremated

crepe /kreɪp/ *n* 1 [U] cloth, paper or rubber with a lined and folded surface 2 [C] very thin PANCAKE

crept /krept/ *v past t. and p. of* CREEP

cre-scen-do /krɪˈʃendəʊ/ *n* **-dos** gradual increase of force or loudness, esp. in music

cres-cent /'kresənt/ *n* 1 curved shape of the new moon 2 something shaped like this, such as a curved street

cress /kres/ *n* [U] small green SALAD plant

crest /krest/ *n* 1 growth of feathers on a bird's head 2 decoration like this on a soldier's HELMET 3 top of a hill, wave, etc. 4 picture used as a personal mark on letters, etc.

crest-fal-len /'krest,fɔːlən/ *adj* disappointed

cret-in /'kretɪn‖'kriːtn/ *n* 1 *sl* very stupid person 2 *med* kind of IDIOT

cre-vasse /krɪˈvæs/ *n* deep crack in ice

crev-ice /'krevɪs/ *n* narrow crack in rock, etc.

crew /kruː/ *n* 1 **a** all the people working on a ship or plane **b** all of these except the officers 2 group working

together: *a camera crew* ♦ *vi* act as ship's crew

crib /krɪb/ *n* 1 *AmE for* COT 2 book supplying a translation ♦ *vt* **-bb-** copy (someone's work) dishonestly

crick /krɪk/ *n* painful stiffening of the muscles, esp. in the back or the neck **crick** *vt*

crick-et¹ /'krɪkɪt/ *n* [U] 1 outdoor ball game played by 2 teams of 11 players each 2 **not cricket** *BrE* unfair **~er** *n* cricket player

cricket² *n* jumping insect that makes a loud noise

cried /kraɪd/ *v past t. and p. of* CRY

cries /kraɪz/ *v pres. t. of* CRY ♦ *n pl. of* CRY

crime /kraɪm/ *n* 1 [C;U] offence that is punishable by law 2 [S] a shame

crim-i-nal /'krɪmɪnəl/ *adj* of crime ♦ *n* person who is guilty of crime **~ly** *adv*

crim-son /'krɪmzən/ *n, adj* [U] deep red

cringe /krɪndʒ/ *vi* 1 bend low from fear; COWER 2 behave without self-respect towards someone

crin-kle /'krɪŋkəl/ *n* fold made by crushing ♦ *vi/t* make or get crinkles

crip-ple /'krɪpəl/ *n* person who cannot use the limbs, esp. the legs, properly ♦ *vt* 1 make into a cripple 2 damage seriously: *crippling debts*

cri-sis /'kraɪsɪs/ *n* **-ses** /-siːz/ moment of great danger or difficulty – see also MID-LIFE CRISIS

crisp /krɪsp/ *adj* 1 hard, dry, and easily broken: *crisp bacon* 2 (of weather) cold and dry 3 (of style, manners, etc.) quick and clear: *crisp reply* ♦ *n BrE* thin piece of dry cooked potato ♦ *vi/t* cook until crisp **~ly** *adv* **~ness** *n* [U] **~y** *adj*

criss-cross /'krɪskrɒs‖-krɔːs/ *vi/t* (make) a network of crossed lines

cri-te-ri-on /kraɪˈtɪəriən/ *n* **-ria** /-riə/ *or* **-rions** standard on which a judgment is based

crit-ic /'krɪtɪk/ *n* 1 person who gives judgments about art, music, etc. 2 person who expresses disapproval **~al** *adj* 1 finding fault 2 of a critic's work 3 of or at a CRISIS: *critical decisions* **~ism** /'krɪtɪsɪzəm/ *n* [C;U] 1 work of a critic 2 disapproval **~ize** *vi/t* 1 make judgments 2 find fault

cri-tique /krɪˈtiːk/ *n* book or article criticizing the work of esp. a writer

croak /krəʊk/ *vi/t, n* 1 (make) the deep low noise of a FROG makes 2 speak with a rough voice as if one has a sore throat

crock-e-ry /'krɒkəri‖'krɑː-/ *n* [U] cups, plates, pots, etc.

croc-o-dile /'krɒkədaɪl‖'krɑː-/ *n* 1 [C] large tropical river REPTILE 2 [U] its skin, used as leather **3** [C] line of people, esp. children, walking in pairs

crocodile tears /'···· ,·/n [P] insincere sorrow

cro·cus /'krəʊkəs/ n small spring plant with purple, yellow and white flowers

cro·ny /'krəʊni/ n infml friend or companion

crook /krʊk/ n **1** infml thief **2** bend or curve: *the crook of her arm* ♦ vi/t bend ~**ed** /'krʊkəd/ adj **1** not straight **2** dishonest

croon /kruːn/ vi/t sing gently in a low soft voice

crop[1] /krɒp‖krɑːp/ n **1** plant grown by a farmer **2** amount gathered in a season: *fig. this year's crop of students*

crop[2] vt -**pp**- **1** (of animals) bite off the tops of (grass etc.) **2** cut (hair, etc.) short

crop up phr vi happen unexpectedly

crop·per /'krɒpə‖'krɑː-/ n infml **come a cropper** fall heavily; fail

cro·quet /'krəʊkeɪ, -ki‖krəʊ'keɪ/ n [U] garden game in which players knock wooden balls through HOOPs

cross[1] /krɒs‖krɔːs/ n **1** the mark X or + **2 a** upright post with a bar across it, esp. that on which Christ died **b** this shape as a sign of the Christian faith **3** sorrow; pain **4** mixture of 2 things

cross[2] v **1** vi/t go or put across **2** vt oppose (someone's wishes, etc.) **3** vi (of letters) pass in opposite directions **4** vt mix different breeds of (animals or plants) **5** vt draw 2 lines across (a cheque) to show that it must be paid into a bank account **6 cross oneself** make the sign of the cross with the hand **7 cross one's mind** come into one's thoughts **8 keep one's fingers crossed** hope that nothing will happen to upset one's plans ~**ing** n **1** journey across the sea **2** place where a road, etc., may be crossed

cross off/out phr vt draw a line through (writing)

cross[3] adj angry ~**ly** adv ~**ness** n [U]

cross-bench·es /'krɒs,bentʃəz‖ 'krɔːs-/ n [P] seats in Parliament on which members sit who do not belong to the official government or opposition parties

cross-bow /'krɒsbəʊ‖'krɔːs-/ n weapon combining a BOW[2] (1) and a gun

cross-breed /'krɒsbriːd‖'krɔːs-/ n animal or plant of mixed breed –**bred** /-bred/ adj

cross-check /,··'·‖,·'·/ vt test (a calculation, etc.) by using a different method

cross-coun·try /,· '··◄/ adj, adv across the fields or open country

cross-dress·ing /'· ,··/n TRANSVESTISM

cross-ex·am·ine /,· ·'··/ vt question (esp. a witness in court) closely, to test answers given before

cross-eyed /'· ·/ adj with the eyes looking in towards the nose

cross-fire /'krɒsfaɪə‖'krɔːs-/ n [U] gunfire across one's direction of movement

cross-legged /,krɒs 'legd◄‖,krɒs 'legd◄/ adj having the knees wide apart and ankles crossed

cross-pur·pos·es /,· '···/ n **be at cross-purposes** misunderstand one another

cross-ques·tion /,· '··/ vt CROSS-EXAMINE

cross-ref·er·ence /,· '··‖'· ,·/ n note directing the reader to another place in the book

cross·roads /'krɒsrəʊdz‖'krɔːs-/ n -**roads 1** place where roads cross **2** point where a decision must be taken

cross-sec·tion /'· ,··/ n **1** (drawing of) a surface made by cutting across **2** typical example of a whole

cross·word /'krɒs,wɜːd‖ 'krɔːs,wɜːrd/ n printed game in which words are fitted into numbered squares

crotch /krɒtʃ‖krɑːtʃ/ n place between the tops of a person's legs

crotch·et /'krɒtʃət‖'krɑː-/ n a musical note

crotch·et·y /'krɒtʃəti‖'krɑː-/ adj infml bad-tempered

crouch /kraʊtʃ/ vi lower the body by bending the knees

crou·pi·er /'kruːpɪə/ n person who collects and pays out money at a CASINO

crow[1] /krəʊ/ n **1** large shiny black bird **2 as the crow flies** in a straight line

crow[2] vi **1** make the loud cry of a COCK **2** speak proudly

crow-bar /'krəʊbɑː/ n iron bar for raising heavy objects

crowd /kraʊd/ n **1** large number of people together **2** particular social group: *the college crowd* ♦ v **1** vi come together in a crowd **2** vt (esp. of people) fill: *a crowded bus*

crown /kraʊn/ n **1** [C] ring-shaped head decoration, esp. for a king or queen **2** [*the* + S] royal power **3** [C] top of a head, hat, hill, etc. **4** [C] old British coin ♦ vt **1** place a crown on the head of **2** cover the top of: *mountains crowned with snow* **3** complete worthily **4 to crown it all** to complete good or bad luck ~**ing** adj above all things

crow's feet /'· ·/n [P] line at the outer corner of a person's eye; WRINKLE

crow's nest /'· ·/ n small shelter near top of a ship's MAST from which a person can watch for danger, etc.

cru-cial /'kru:ʃəl/ adj of the greatest importance ~ly adv

cru-ci-ble /'kru:sɪbəl/ n pot for melting metals in

cru-ci-fix /'kru:sɪfɪks/ n cross with a figure of Christ on it

cru-ci-fix-ion /,kru:sɪ'fɪkʃən/ n [C;U] death by nailing to a cross

cru-ci-fy /'kru:sɪfaɪ/ vt 1 kill by crucifixion 2 be very cruel to, esp. publicly

crude /kru:d/ adj 1 in a natural state; untreated 2 without sensitive feeling: crude jokes 3 badly made ♦ n [U] crude oil ~ly adv **crudity** n [C;U]

cru-el /'kru:əl/ adj -ll- 1 liking to cause suffering 2 causing suffering: cruel disappointment ~ly adv ~ty n [C;U]

cru-et /'kru:ɪt/ n set of containers for pepper, salt, etc., at meals

cruise /kru:z/ v 1 vi sail slowly for pleasure 2 vi (of a car, etc.) move at a steady speed 3 vi/t look (in public places) for a sexual partner, esp. one of the same sex. ♦ n sea voyage for pleasure **cruiser** n 1 fast warship 2 motorboat with a CABIN

cruise mis-sile /'· ' ··/ n GUIDED MISSILE that flies low and can examine the ground

crumb /krʌm/ n small piece of dry food, esp. bread: (fig.) crumbs of information

crum-ble /'krʌmbəl/ v 1 vi/t break into small pieces 2 vi come to ruin -bly adj easily crumbled

crum-ple /'krʌmpəl/ 1 vi/t crush into irregular folds 2 vi lose strength

crunch /krʌntʃ/ v 1 vt crush (food) noisily with the teeth 2 vi make a crushing noise ♦ n [S] 1 crunching sound 2 CRISIS: when it comes to the crunch

cru-sade /kru:'seɪd/ n 1 Christian war against the Muslims in the Middle Ages 2 any united struggle: a crusade for women's rights ♦ vi take part in a crusade **-sader** n

crush /krʌʃ/ v 1 vi/t break or spoil by pressure 2 vt press; push: They crushed through the gates. 3 vt destroy completely: (fig.) He felt crushed by her cruel remark ♦ n 1 [S] crowd of people pressed together 2 [C] strong foolish and short-lived love for someone

crust /krʌst/ n [C;U] hard outer surface of something, esp. bread ~y adj 1 with a hard crust 2 bad-tempered

crus-ta-cean /krʌ'steɪʃən/ n shellfish

crutch /krʌtʃ/ n 1 stick to help someone to walk 2 something that gives moral support: He uses religion as a crutch. 3 CROTCH

crux /krʌks/ n central part of a problem

cry[1] /kraɪ/ v 1 vi produce tears from the eyes 2 vi/t call out loudly: 'Help!' he cried. 3 vi (of a bird or animal) make its natural sound 4 **cry one's eyes out** cry very bitterly 5 **for crying out loud** sl (used to give strength to a demand, etc.): Oh, for crying out loud, shut that door!

cry off phr vi refuse to fulfil a promise

cry out for phr vt need very badly

cry[2] n 1 [C] shout expressing something: cries of joy | a war cry | a cry for help 2 [S] period of crying 3 bird's or animal's natural sound 4 **a far cry from** a great deal different from (something)

cry-ba-by /'kraɪ,beɪbi/ n [C] person who cries too readily with little cause

crypt /krɪpt/ n room under a church

cryp-tic /'krɪptɪk/ adj with a hidden meaning

crys-tal /'krɪstl/ n 1 [C;U] (piece of) transparent ice-like mineral 2 [U] expensive colourless glass 3 [C] regular shape formed naturally by some substances such as sugar 4 [C] AmE transparent cover of a clock or watch face ~**lize** vi/t form into crystals 2 vi/t make (ideas, etc.) fixed in form 3 vt preserve (fruit) with sugar

crystal ball /,·· '·/ n ball used by FORTUNE-TELLERs to look into the future

cub /kʌb/ n young lion, bear, etc.

cub-by-hole /'kʌbihəʊl/ n small room or cupboard

cube /kju:b/ n 1 solid object with 6 equal square sides 2 result of multiplying a number by itself twice ♦ vt multiply a number by itself twice: 3 cubed is 27.

cu-bic /'kju:bɪk/ adj multiplying length by width and height: a cubic metre

cu-bi-cle /'kju:bɪkəl/ n small division of a large room

cuck-oo /'kʊku:||'ku:ku:, 'kʊ-/ n bird that lays its eggs in other birds' nests and makes a noise like its name

cu-cum-ber /'kju:kʌmbəʳ/ n long green vegetable eaten raw

cud /kʌd/ n [U] 1 food swallowed and brought up again by cows, etc., for further eating 2 **chew the cud** think deeply before making a decision

cud-dle /'kʌdl/ v 1 vt hold lovingly in one's arms 2 vi lie close and comfortably ♦ n [S] cuddling; HUG -**dly** adj suitable for cuddling

cud-gel /'kʌdʒəl/ n 1 CLUB (2) 2 **take up the cudgels** join in a struggle

cue[1] /kjuː/ n 1 signal for the next actor to speak in a play 2 example of how to behave

cue[2] n stick for pushing the ball in BILLIARDS

cuff[1] /kʌf/ n 1 end of a SLEEVE 2 **off the cuff** (of an answer, etc.) without preparation

cuff[2] vt hit lightly; SMACK **cuff** n

cuff link /'· ·/ n button-like object used for fastening cuffs

cui·sine /kwɪˈziːn/ n [U] style of cooking

cul-de-sac /'kʌl də ˌsæk, ˈkʊl-‖ˌkʌl də 'sæk, ˌkʊl-/ n street closed at one end

cul·i·na·ry /'kʌlənəri‖'kʌlǎneri, 'kjuːl-/ adj of, related to the kitchen or cooking

cull /kʌl/ 1 vt fml gather (information, etc.) 2 vi/t take from a group and kill (a weak or unproductive animal) ♦ n 1 act of CULLing (2) 2 animal killed this way

cul·len·der /'kʌlǎndər/ n COLANDER

cul·mi·nate /'kʌlmǎneɪt/ v

culminate in phr vt fml reach the last and highest point: the battle culminated in victory **-nation** /ˌkʌlmǎˈneɪʃən/ n [S]

cul·pa·ble /'kʌlpəbəl/ adj fml deserving blame **-bly** adv **-bility** /ˌkʌlpəˈbɪlǎti/ n [U]

cul·prit /'kʌlprǎt/ n guilty person

cult /kʌlt/ n 1 system of worship 2 popular fashion: cult films

cul·ti·vate /'kʌltǎveɪt/ vt 1 a prepare (land) for crops b grow (crops) 2 improve or develop by careful attention, study, etc. 3 pay friendly attention to (people) **-vated** adj educated and well-mannered **-vation** /ˌkʌltǎˈveɪʃən/ n [U]

cul·ture /'kʌltʃər/ n 1 [C;U] art, thought, and customs of a society: tribal cultures 2 [U] high development in art and thought 3 [U] raising animals and growing plants **-tural** adj: cultural activities **-tured** adj 1 cultivated 2 produced by humans: cultured pearls

cum·ber·some /'kʌmbəsəm‖-bər-/ adj heavy and awkward to carry

cu·mu·la·tive /'kjuːmjʊlətɪv/ adj increasing by one addition after another **~ly** adv

cun·ning /'kʌnɪŋ/ adj clever in deceiving ♦ n [U] quality of being cunning **~ly** adv

cunt /kʌnt/ n taboo 1 VAGINA 2 foolish or nasty person

cup /kʌp/ n 1 container, usu. with a handle, to drink from 2 cup-shaped thing: bra cups 3 gold or silver container given as a prize in competitions 4 AmE HOLE (5) in GOLF ♦ vt

-pp- form (one's hands) into a cup shape

cup·board /'kʌbəd‖-ərd/ n piece of furniture with doors

cup fi·nal /'· ‚·‖/ n BrE (esp. in football) last match to decide the winning team in a competition

cu·ra·ble /'kjuːrəbəl/ adj that can be cured

cu·rate /'kjuːrǎt/ n priest of the lowest rank, who helps another

cu·ra·tor /kjuˈreɪtər/ n person in charge of a MUSEUM, etc.

curb /kɜːb‖kɜrb/ n 1 controlling influence; CHECK (2) 2 AmE for KERB ♦ vt hold back; control

curd /kɜːd‖kɜrd/ n [C;U] thick soft substance that separates from milk when it becomes sour

cur·dle /'kɜːdl‖'kɜrdl/ vi/t (cause to) form into CURDS; (cause to) thicken

cure /kjuər/ vt 1 a bring back to health: (fig.) a plan to cure unemployment b make (a disease) go away 2 preserve (food, skin, tobacco) by drying, etc. ♦ n 1 something that cures a person or disease 2 a return to health after illness

cur·few /'kɜːfjuː‖'kɜr-/ n [C;U] time or signal for people to stay indoors

cu·ri·o /'kjuːriəʊ/ n -os rare or beautiful small object

cu·ri·os·i·ty /ˌkjuəriˈɒsǎti‖-'ɑːs-/ n 1 [S;U] desire to know 2 [C] interesting rare object

cu·ri·ous /'kjuːriəs/ adj 1 eager to learn 2 peculiar **~ly** adv

curl[1] /kɜːl‖kɜrl/ n 1 hanging twist of hair 2 thing this shape: curls of smoke **~y** adj having curls

curl[2] vi/t twist; wind

curl up phr vi/t (cause to) lie comfortably with the limbs drawn close to the body: curl up with a good book

cur·rant /'kʌrənt‖'kɜr-/ n 1 dried GRAPE 2 kind of black, red, or white BERRY

cur·ren·cy /'kʌrənsi‖'kɜr-/ n 1 [C;U] money in use in a country 2 [U] state of being generally believed

cur·rent[1] /'kʌrənt‖'kɜr-/ adj 1 of the present time: current fashion 2 commonly accepted 3 (of money) used as currency

current[2] n 1 flow of liquid, gas, or electricity 2 general tendency or course of events

current ac·count /'·· ·‚·/ n BrE bank account from which money can be taken out at any time

cur·ric·u·lum /kəˈrɪkjʊləm/ n -la /-lə/ or -lums course of study in a school, etc.

curriculum vi·tae /kəˌrɪkjʊləm ˈviːtaɪ/ n a CV

cur·ry[1] /'kʌri‖'kɜːri/ n [C;U] hot-tasting Indian dish of meat, vegetables, etc. ♦ vt make into curry

curry[2] v **curry favour** try to win approval dishonestly

curse /kɜːs‖kɜːrs/ n 1 words calling for evil to come to someone 2 cause of misfortune: *Foxes are a curse to farmers.* 3 word or words used in swearing ♦ vi/t 1 call down evil upon 2 use violent language (against) 3 **be cursed with** suffer from **cursed** /'kɜːsəd‖'kɜːr-/ adj hateful; annoying

cur·sor /'kɜːsə^r‖'kɜːr-/ n mark which can move around a SCREEN connected to a computer to point to a particular position

cur·so·ry /'kɜːsəri‖'kɜːr-/ adj (of work, reading, etc.) not thorough **–rily** adv

curt /kɜːt‖kɜːrt/ adj (of speech) impolitely short **~ly** adv **~ness** n [U]

cur·tail /kɜː'teɪl‖kɜːr-/ vt fml shorten; reduce **~ment** n [C;U]

cur·tain /'kɜːtn‖'kɜːrtn/ n 1 cloth hung over a window, or in front of a theatre stage: (fig.) *curtain of smoke* 2 [P] sl the end, esp. of a person's life

curt·sy /'kɜːtsi‖'kɜːr-/ vi, n (make) a woman's act of bending the knees and lowering the head to show respect

cur·va·ture /'kɜːvətʃə^r‖'kɜːr-/ n [C;U] state of being curved

curve /kɜːv‖kɜːrv/ n line that is not straight and has no angles ♦ vi/t: *The road curves to the right.*

cush·ion /'kʊʃən/ n bag filled with something soft, for lying or sitting on: (fig.) *a cushion of air* ♦ vt 1 lessen the force of 2 protect from hardship

cush·y /'kʊʃi/ adj (of a job, style of life, etc.) easy

cus·tard /'kʌstəd‖-ərd/ n [U] sweet yellow mixture of eggs and milk

cus·to·di·an /kʌ'stəʊdiən/ n person in charge of a public building

cus·to·dy /'kʌstədi/ n [U] 1 right to look after someone: *give him custody of his child* 2 being guarded or imprisoned: *in police custody*

cus·tom /'kʌstəm/ n 1 [C;U] established social behaviour 2 [C] something someone does regularly 3 [U] regular support given to a shop by its customers **customs** n [P] 1 taxes on goods entering or leaving a country 2 place where these taxes are collected

cus·tom·a·ry /'kʌstəməri‖-meri/ adj established by custom; usual

custom-built /ˌ·· '·◂/ adj made especially for one person or group of people

cus·tom·er /'kʌstəmə^r/ n person who buys things from a shop

cut[1] /kʌt/ v cut, -tt- 1 vt/i use something sharp to divide, remove, shorten, make a hole, etc.: *cut your fingers/your hair/the corn* 2 vi **a** be able to be cut **b** (of a knife, etc.) be sharp 3 vt make shorter or smaller: *cut a long speech* 4 vt make (esp. a public service) less in size, amount, etc.: *They're cutting postal deliveries/bus services.* 5 vt stay away on purpose: *cut a lecture* 6 vt put (a film) into final form 7 vt hurt the feelings of (someone): *cutting remarks* 8 vt (of a line, path, etc.) cross 9 vi stop filming a scene 10 **cut both ways** have both advantages and disadvantages 11 **cut corners** do something quickly and cheaply but not perfectly 12 **cut it fine** leave oneself too little time or money 13 **cut no/not much ice** have no/little influence 14 **cut one's losses** stop doing something before one loses any more money 15 **cut someone dead** refuse to recognize them

cut across phr vt 1 go across instead of round 2 make a different division in: *cut across party lines*

cut back phr v 1 vt PRUNE (a plant) 2 vi/t reduce **cutback** /'kʌtbæk/ n planned reduction

cut down phr vt 1 vt bring down by cutting 2 vi/t reduce: *cut down (on) smoking* 3 knock down or kill (someone) 4 **cut down to size** reduce from too great importance to true or suitable importance

cut in phr vi 1 interrupt 2 drive between moving vehicles

cut off phr vt 1 separate by cutting 2 disconnect (telephone, gas, electricity, etc.) 3 separate from others: *cut off by floods* 4 lit kill: *cut off in his prime* 5 DISINHERIT

cut out phr v 1 vt remove by cutting 2 vt make by cutting: *cut out a dress* 3 vt/i stop: *cut out smoking | engine keeps cutting out* 4 **not cut out for** not suitable for

cut up phr vt 1 cut into little pieces 2 make unhappy

cut[2] n 1 opening made by cutting 2 piece of meat, etc., cut off 3 reduction: *cuts in government spending* 4 way in which clothes, hair, etc., are shaped 5 infml someone's share of a profit 6 **a** act of removing a part, to improve or shorten **b** part removed 7 **a cut above** better

cut-and-dried /ˌ· · '·◂/ adj 1 unlikely to change; fixed

cut and thrust /ˌ·· '·/ n [the + S] the strong methods of arguing or behaving typical of a very competitive activity

cute /kjuːt/ adj 1 delightfully pretty 2 (too) clever

cu·ti·cle /'kjuːtɪkəl/ n skin at the base of one's nails

cut·lass /'kʌtləs/ n short sword with a curved blade

cut·le·ry /'kʌtləri/ n [U] knives, forks, spoons, etc.

cut·let /'kʌtlɨt/ n small piece of meat

cut-price /,· '·◄/ adj (of goods) cheap

cut·ter /'kʌtə/ n 1 person or tool that cuts 2 small fast boat

cut-throat /'kʌtθrəʊt/ adj fierce; unprincipled: *cutthroat competition*

cut·ting /'kʌtɪŋ/ n 1 piece cut from a plant to form a new one 2 BrE piece cut from a newspaper 3 unroofed passage cut through a hill for a railway, etc.

CV, cv /,si: 'vi:/ n short written account of a person's education and past employment

cy·a·nide /'saɪənaɪd/ n [U] strong poison

cy·ber·net·ics /,saɪbə'netɪks‖-bər-/ n [U] science of how information is dealt with by machines and the brain

cy·cle¹ /'saɪkəl/ n (time needed for) a set of events in regularly repeated order: *a 50-minute cycle* **cyclical** /'saɪklɪkəl/ adj fml happening in cycles

cycle² v, n bicycle **cyclist** n

cy·clone /'saɪkləʊn/ n very violent wind moving rapidly in a circle

cyl·in·der /'sɪlɨndər/ n 1 object or container with a circular base and straight sides 2 tube for a PISTON in an engine

cym·bal /'sɪmbəl/ n one of a pair of metal plates struck together to make a noise in music

cyn·ic /'sɪnɪk/ n person who sees little good in anything and shows it by making unkind remarks ~**al** adj ~**ally** /-kli/ adv ~**ism** /'sɪnɨsɪzəm/ n [U]

cy·press /'saɪprɨs/ n EVERGREEN tree with dark green leaves and hard wood

cyst /sɪst/ n hollow growth in the body, containing liquid

cyst·i·tis /sɪ'staɪtɨs/ n [U] disease of the BLADDER

czar /zɑːr/ n TSAR

D

D, d /diː/ the 4th letter of the English alphabet

D written abbrev. for: 1 died 2 DIAMETER 3 PENNY (2)

DA /,diː 'eɪ/ n district attorney

dab /dæb/ vi/t -bb- touch or cover lightly ♦ n small quantity of paint, etc.

dab·ble /'dæbəl/ v 1 vi work at something not professionally: *dabble in politics* 2 vt move (one's feet, etc.) playfully about in water

dab hand /,· '·/n BrE sl person who is clever or good at something

dachs·hund /'dækshund, -sənd/ n small dog with short legs and a long body

dad /dæd/ n infml father

dad·dy /'dædi/ n (child's word for) father

daf·fo·dil /'dæfədɪl/ n bell-shaped yellow spring flower

daft /dɑːft‖dæft/ adj BrE silly ~**ly** adv ~**ness** n [U]

dag·ger /'dægər/ n 1 short knife used as a weapon 2 **look daggers at** look angrily at

dah·li·a /'deɪliə‖'dæliə/ n big bright garden flower

dai·ly /'deɪli/ adj, adv every day ♦ n 1 newspaper sold every day but Sunday 2 also **daily help** /,·· '·/ — infml esp. BrE someone, esp. a woman, who comes to clean a house daily but does not live there

dain·ty /'deɪnti/ adj small, pretty, and delicate ~**tily** adv ~**tiness** n [U]

dair·y /'deəri/ n place where milk, butter, cheese, etc., are produced or sold

dairy cat·tle /'·· ,·/ n [P] cows kept for milk, not meat

da·is /'deɪɨs, deɪs/ n raised floor at one end of a hall

dai·sy /'deɪzi/ n 1 common small white flower that grows in grass 2 **as fresh as a daisy** not tired

dale /deɪl/ n valley

dal·li·ance /'dæliəns/ n lit FLIRTATION

dal·ly /'dæli/ vi waste time

 dally with phr vt play with (an idea)

dam¹ /dæm/ n wall built to keep back water

dam² vt -mm- make a dam across

dam up phr vt control (a feeling, esp. of anger) in an unhealthy way

dam·age /'dæmɪdʒ/ n [U] harm; loss: *brain damage* ♦ vt cause damage to **damages** n [P] money paid for damage done

dame /deɪm/ n 1 AmE sl woman 2 (cap.) British rank of honour for a woman

damn /dæm/ vt 1 (of God) punish 2 declare to be bad 3 ruin: *damning evidence* 4 **Well, I'll be damned!** infml I'm very surprised ♦ n [S] even the smallest bit: *don't care a damn* ♦ interj (used in curses): *Damn it!* That's it!

damn, also ~**ed** adj, adv (used for giving force to an expression): *run damned* (= very) *fast* | *He's a damn* *fool.* ~**able** /'dæmnəbəl/ *adj* very bad ~**ation** /dæm'neɪʃən/ *n* [U] 1 act of damning 2 **in damnation** (used for giving force to an expression of anger): *What in damnation do you mean?* **damnedest** /'dæmdɪst/ *n* do **one's damnedest** do everything possible

damp[1] /dæmp/ *adj* rather wet ♦ *n* [U] slight wetness ~**ness** *n* [U]

damp[2] also **dampen** /'dæmpən/ *vt* 1 wet slightly 2 reduce (eagerness, etc.): *damp their spirits*

damp down *phr vt* make (a fire) burn more slowly

damp course /'·· ·/ *n* material built into a wall to stop wetness from coming up

damp·er /'dæmpəʳ/ *n* 1 metal plate controlling the flow of air to a fire 2 influence reducing eagerness

damp squib /ˌ· '·/ *n* something which is intended to be exciting, effective, etc., but which fails and disappoints

dam·sel /'dæmzəl/ *n old lit* young unmarried woman of noble birth; young girl

dam·son /'dæmzən/ *n* kind of small PLUM

dance /dɑːns‖dæns/ *n* 1 [C] (music for) a set of movements performed to music 2 [C] party with dances 3 [U] art of dancing — see also SONG AND DANCE ♦ *vi/t* do a dance **dancer** *n*

dan·de·li·on /'dændɪlaɪən/ *n* common bright yellow flower

dan·druff /'dændrəf, -drʌf/ *n* bits of dead skin in the hair

dan·dy /'dændi/ *n* man who is almost too well dressed

dan·ger /'deɪndʒəʳ/ *n* 1 [U] possibility of harm 2 [C] cause of danger ~**ous** *adj* not safe ~**ously** *adv*

danger mon·ey /'·· ,·'/ *n* [U] additional pay for dangerous work

dan·gle /'dæŋgəl/ *vi/t* 1 hang loosely 2 **keep someone dangling** keep someone waiting and not knowing what the result will be

dank /dæŋk/ *adj* unpleasantly wet and cold

dap·per /'dæpəʳ/ *adj* neatly dressed

dap·pled /'dæpəld/ *adj* having cloudy spots of colour or shadow

dare /deəʳ/ *v* 1 *vi* be brave enough (to): *He didn't dare (to) ask.* 2 *vt* CHALLENGE to do something: *I dared her to jump.* ♦ *n* CHALLENGE: *She jumped for a dare.*

dare-dev·il /'deədevəl‖'deər-/ *n* foolishly adventurous person

daren't /deənt‖deərnt/ *v short for:* dare not

dare·say /deə'seɪ‖'deər-/ *v* I **daresay** *esp. BrE* I suppose (that); perhaps

dar·ing /'deərɪŋ/ *n* [U] adventurous bravery ♦ *adj* 1 brave 2 shocking ~**ly** *adv*

dark /dɑːk‖dɑːrk/ *adj* 1 without (much) light: *dark room* 2 tending towards black: *dark green* 3 secret; hidden: *keep it dark* 4 evil; sad ♦ *n* [U] 1 absence of light 2 **after/before dark** after/before night 3 **in the dark** not knowing something ~**en** *vi/t* make or become darker ~**ly** *adv* ~**ness** *n* [U]

Dark Ages /'· ,·'/ *n* [*the* + P] period in Europe between about AD 476 to AD 1000

dark horse /ˌ· '·/ *n* unknown competitor who may win

dark·room /'dɑːkruːm, -rum‖ 'dɑːrk-/ *n* room where photographs are processed

dar·ling /'dɑːlɪŋ‖'dɑːr-/ *n, adj,* dearly loved (person)

darn[1] /dɑːn‖dɑːrn/ *vt/i* mend (holes in cloth) ♦ *n* darned hole

darn[2] *n, adj, adv, interj* DAMN

dart /dɑːt‖dɑːrt/ *n* 1 pointed object to throw, esp. in a game called **darts** 2 quick movement ♦ *vi/t* move or send suddenly

dart·board /'dɑːtbɔːd‖'dɑːrtbɔːrd/ *n* circular board at which darts are thrown

dash /dæʃ/ *v* 1 *vi* run quickly 2 *vi/t* strike violently: *The waves dashed the boat against the rocks.* 3 *vt* destroy (hopes, etc.) ♦ *n* 1 [C] sudden quick run or short race 2 [C] small amount added: *a dash of pepper* 3 [C] the mark (-) 4 [U] combination of bravery and style: *I admire his dash.* ~**ing** *adj* having a lot of DASH (4)

dash·board /'dæʃbɔːd‖-bɔːrd/ *n* instrument board in a car

da·ta /'deɪtə, 'dɑːtə/ *n* [P;U] facts; information, esp. as stored in a computer's **data bank** for **data processing**

da·ta·base /'deɪtəˌbeɪs/ *n* computer's collection of data

date[1] /deɪt/ *n* 1 day, month, or year of an event 2 arrangement to meet 3 person of the opposite sex whom one arranges to meet socially 4 **out of date: a** old-fashioned **b** no longer VALID 5 **to date** up till now 6 **up to date** modern

date[2] *v* 1 *vt* guess the date of 2 *vt* write the date on 3 *vi* become old-fashioned 4 *vi/t* make a social date with **dated** *adj* old fashioned

date from also **date back** to *phr vt* have lasted since

date[3] *n* small tropical fruit with a long stone

daub /dɔːb/ *vt* cover with something sticky

daugh·ter /'dɔːtəʳ/ *n* someone's female child

daughter-in-law /'···/ n **daughters-in-law** son's wife

daunt /dɔːnt/ vt discourage ~**less** adj not discouraged

daw-dle /'dɔːdl/ vi waste time; be slow

dawn[1] /dɔːn/ n 1 [C;U] first light of morning 2 [S] first appearance: *the dawn of civilization*

dawn[2] vi begin to grow light

dawn on phr vt become known to: *The truth dawned on me.*

day /deɪ/ n 1 [C] period of 24 hours 2 [C;U] time between sunrise and sunset: *the* **daylight** *hours* | *in the* **daytime** 3 [C] hours that one works 4 [C] period; time: *the present* **day** 5 [S] period of success 6 **call it a day** finish working for the day 7 **day after day** also **day in, day out** continuously 8 **make someone's day** make someone very happy 9 **one day** at some time 10 **one's days** one's life 11 **the other day** recently 12 **these days** now

day-break /'deɪbreɪk/ n [U] DAWN (1)

day-dream /'deɪdriːm/ vi, n (have) pleasant dreamlike thoughts

day-lights /'deɪlaɪts/ n [P] **beat/knock/scare the (living) daylights out of** hit/frighten (someone) very severely

day re-lease course /,· ·'· ·/ n BrE educational course attended by workers during the usual working day

day re-turn /,· ·'·/ n BrE bus or train ticket that one can use to go and come back on the same day

day-to-day /,· · ·'··/ adj 1 happening each day: *We just live day-to-day.* 2 planning for one day at a time

daze /deɪz/ vt make unable to think clearly ♦ n dazed condition

daz-zle /'dæzəl/ vt 1 make unable to see because of too strong light 2 cause wonder to: *dazzled by success*

dea-con /'diːkən/ **-ess** /-kənɪs/ fem. — Christian church officer below a priest

dead[1] /ded/ adj 1 no longer alive 2 no longer used or usable: *dead languages* | *The telephone went dead.* 3 complete: *dead silence* 4 without activity: *the place seems dead* 5 NUMB: *My fingers went dead.* 6 (of sound or colour) dull ♦ adv 1 completely: *stop dead* 2 directly: *dead ahead* ~**en** vt cause to lose (strength, feeling, brightness): *deaden pain/noise*

dead[2] n **in the dead of** in the greatest or least active period of

dead-beat /'dedbiːt/ n lazy aimless person

dead cen-tre /,· '··/ n exact centre

dead end /,· '·◁/ n end (of a street) with no way out: (fig.) *We've reached a dead end in our talks.*

dead heat /,· '·/ n race in which the competitors finish together

dead-line /'dedlaɪn/ n fixed date for finishing something

dead-lock /'dedlɒk‖-lɑːk/ n disagreement that cannot be settled

dead-ly /'dedli/ adj 1 likely to cause death 2 total: *deadly enemies* 3 infml very dull ♦ adv 1 like death: *deadly pale* 2 very: *deadly dull*

dead-pan /'dedpæn/ adj, adv with no show of feeling, esp. when telling jokes

dead ring-er /,· '··/ n someone who looks exactly like someone else

dead-weight /'ded,weɪt/ n [S] whole weight of something that does not move

dead wood /,· '·‖'·· ·/ n [U] useless people or things

deaf /def/ adj 1 unable to hear 2 **deaf to** unwilling to listen to ~**en** vt (of loud noises) make unable to hear: *The noise was deafening.* (= very loud) ~**ness** n [U]

deaf-mute /,· '·‖'·· ·/ n, adj (person) who is deaf and cannot speak

deal[1] /diːl/ vi/t **dealt** /delt/ 1 give out (esp. playing cards) as a share 2 strike: *deal someone a blow* ~**er** n 1 person who deals cards 2 trader ~**ing** n [U] methods of business or personal relations ~**ings** n [P] personal or business relations

deal in phr vt trade in; sell

deal with phr vt 1 trade with 2 take action about 3 be about: *a book dealing with Ireland*

deal[2] n 1 [C] business arrangement 2 [C] one's turn to deal cards 3 **a good/great deal** a fairly/very large amount: *work a good deal faster*

dean /diːn/ n 1 Christian priest in charge of several others 2 important university official

dear /dɪər/ adj 1 loved; precious 2 (at the beginning of letters): *Dear Sir* 3 expensive ♦ 1 n loved person 2 a (used when speaking to someone you love): *Yes, dear.* b (used informally as a friendly form of address, esp. by or to a woman): *That's 50 pence, dear.* ♦ interj (expressing surprise, sorrow, etc.): *Oh dear!* ~**ly** adv 1 with much feeling 2 at terrible cost

dearth /dɜːθ‖dɜːrθ/ n [S] fml lack

death /deθ/ n 1 [C;U] end of life: (fig.) *the death of our hopes* 2 [U] state of being dead 3 cause of death: *Drinking will be the death of him.* 4 **at death's door** in danger of dying; about to die 5 **like death warmed up** infml very ill or tired 6 **put to death** kill, esp. officially 7 **to death** beyond proper limits: *sick/bored/worried to death* ~**less** adj unforgettable ~**ly** adj, adv like death

death du-ty /ˈ· ͵··/ n BrE tax paid on property after death

death trap /ˈ· ·/ n very dangerous thing or place

dé-bâ-cle /deɪˈbɑːkəl, dɪ-/ n sudden complete failure

de-bar /dɪˈbɑːʳ/ v -rr- debar from phr vt officially prevent from

de-base /dɪˈbeɪs/ vt make lower in value ~ment n [C;U]

de-bate /dɪˈbeɪt/ n [C;U] (process of DISCUSSION ♦ vi/t 1 hold a debate about 2 think about; wonder **debatable** adj doubtful; questionable

de-bauch /dɪˈbɔːtʃ‖dɪˈbɔːtʃ, dɪˈbɔːtʃ/ vt lead away from moral conduct, esp. in relation to sex and alcohol ♦ n ORGY ~ed adj ~ery n [U]

de-bil-i-tate /dɪˈbɪlɪteɪt/ vt make weak ~ty n [U] fml weakness

deb-it /ˈdebɪt/ n record of money owed ♦ vt charge against an account

deb-o-nair /ˌdebəˈneəʳ/ adj cheerful and fashionably dressed

de-brief /ˌdiːˈbriːf/ vt find out information from (someone on one's own side) by thorough questioning after an action

deb-ris /ˈdebriː, ˈdeɪ-‖dəˈbriː, deɪ-/ n [U] broken remains; ruins

debt /det/ n [C;U] something owed; state of owing ~or n person who owes money

de-bug /ˌdiːˈbʌɡ/ vt infml 1 remove the BUGs (3) from a room or building 2 search for and remove the BUGs (5) in (a computer PROGRAM)

de-bunk /ˌdiːˈbʌŋk/ vt point out the truth about a wrong idea

de-but /ˈdeɪbjuː, ˈdebjuː‖deɪˈbjuː, dɪ-/ n first public appearance

dec-ade /ˈdekeɪd, deˈkeɪd/ n period of 10 years

dec-a-dent /ˈdekədənt/ adj falling to a lower level of morals ~dence n [U]

de-cal /ˈdiːkæl, ˈde-‖diːkæl, dekəl/n TRANSFER (3)

de-camp /dɪˈkæmp/ vi go away quickly and esp. secretly

de-cant /dɪˈkænt/ vt pour (liquid) into another container ~er n glass container for liquid, esp. wine

de-cap-i-tate /dɪˈkæpɪteɪt/ vt BEHEAD

de-cath-lon /dɪˈkæθlɒn‖-lɑːn, -lən/ n ATHLETIC competition with 10 separate events

de-cay /dɪˈkeɪ/ vi 1 go bad: decayed teeth 2 lose health, power, etc. ♦ n [U] process of decaying

de-ceased /dɪˈsiːst/ adj fml dead ♦ n fml the dead person

de-ceit /dɪˈsiːt/ n [U] dishonesty ~ful adj dishonest ~fully adv

de-ceive /dɪˈsiːv/ vt cause to believe something false **deceiver** n

de-cel-e-rate /ˌdiːˈseləreɪt/ vi/t (cause to) go slower

De-cem-ber /dɪˈsembəʳ/ n the 12th and last month of the year

de-cent /ˈdiːsənt/ adj 1 socially acceptable; proper 2 good enough: a decent meal 3 kind **decency** n [U] being DECENT (1)

de-cen-tral-ize ‖ also, -ise BrE /ˌdiːˈsentrəlaɪz/ vi/t move (a business, etc.) from a central office or place to several smaller ones

de-cep-tion /dɪˈsepʃən/ n 1 [U] deceiving 2 [C] something that misleads **-tively** adv

dec-i-bel /ˈdesɪbel/ n unit of loudness

de-cide /dɪˈsaɪd/ v 1 vi/t make a choice or judgment: She decided to go. 2 vt make (someone) decide 3 vi/t end uncertainty **decided** adj 1 easily seen: decided improvement 2 sure of oneself **decidedly** adv certainly

   decide on phr vt decide in favour of

de-cid-u-ous /dɪˈsɪdjuəs/ adj (of trees) losing their leaves in autumn

dec-i-mal /ˈdesɪməl/ adj based on the number 10 ♦ n number such as .5 or .06 ~ize vi/t change to a decimal system of money, etc.

dec-i-mate /ˈdesɪmeɪt/ vt destroy a large part of

de-ci-pher /dɪˈsaɪfəʳ/ vt read (something difficult, esp. a CODE)

de-ci-sion /dɪˈsɪʒən/ n 1 [C;U] deciding; choice: reach a decision 2 [U] firmness of judgment

de-ci-sive /dɪˈsaɪsɪv/ adj 1 firm in judgment 2 leading to a clear result ~ly adv ~ness n [U]

deck[1] /dek/ n 1 floor of a ship or bus 2 AmE for PACK of playing cards

deck[2] vt decorate

deck-chair /ˈdektʃeəʳ/ n folding chair with a cloth seat

de-claim /dɪˈkleɪm/ vt fml say loudly, like an actor

dec-la-ra-tion /ˌdekləˈreɪʃən/ n [C;U] 1 declaring 2 official statement

de-clare /dɪˈkleəʳ/ vt 1 make known officially: declare war 2 state clearly 3 tell CUSTOMs officials about (taxable goods)

de-clas-si-fy /ˌdiːˈklæsɪfaɪ/ vt declare (esp. political and military information) no longer secret

de-cline /dɪˈklaɪn/ v 1 vi become worse or less 2 vt/i refuse (an invitation, etc.) politely ♦ n period of declining (DECLINE (1)): Interest in the arts is on the decline.

de-clutch /ˌdiːˈklʌtʃ/ vi step on the CLUTCH (2) of a car before changing GEAR (1)

de-code /ˌdiːˈkəʊd/ vt read (something written in CODE)

de·col·o·nize , **-ise** /ˌdiːˈkɒlənaɪz‖-ˈkɑː-/ vt give political independence to **-nization** /ˌdiːkɒlənaɪˈzeɪʃən‖-kɑːlənə-/ n [U]

de·com·pose /ˌdiːkəmˈpəʊz/ vi go bad; DECAY **-position** /ˌdiːkɒmpə-ˈzɪʃən‖-kɑːm-/ n [U]

de·com·press /ˌdiːkəmˈpres/ vt reduce air pressure on **-ion** /-ˈpreʃən/ n [U]

de·con·tam·i·nate /ˌdiːkənˈtæmɪneɪt/ vt remove dangerous substances from **-nation** /-ˌtæmɪˈneɪʃən/ n [U]

dé·cor /ˈdeɪkɔːr‖ˈdeɪkɔːr/ n decoration and furnishings of a place

dec·o·rate /ˈdekəreɪt/ v 1 vt add something beautiful to 2 vi/t paint, put paper, etc., on rooms 3 vt give a mark of honour, such as a MEDAL, etc. to, **-rator** n person who paints houses **-rative** /ˈdekərətɪv‖ˈdekərə-, ˈdek-əreɪ-/ adj beautiful; attractive **-ration** /ˌdekəˈreɪʃən/ n 1 [U] decorating 2 [C] something that decorates 3 [C] mark of honour, MEDAL, etc.

dec·o·rous /ˈdekərəs/ adj (of appearance or behaviour) correct

de·co·rum /dɪˈkɔːrəm/ n [U] fml correct behaviour

de·coy /ˈdiːkɔɪ/ n something used for getting a person or bird into a trap **decoy** /dɪˈkɔɪ/ vt

de·crease¹ /dɪˈkriːs/ vi/t (cause to) become less

de·crease² /ˈdiːkriːs/ n 1 [U] process of decreasing 2 [C] amount by which something decreases

de·cree /dɪˈkriː/ n official command or decision ♦ vt order officially

de·crep·it /dɪˈkrepɪt/ adj weak from old age

de·cry /dɪˈkraɪ/ vt fml speak disapprovingly of

ded·i·cate /ˈdedɪkeɪt/ vt 1 give to a serious purpose: dedicate her life to medical research | a dedicated doctor 2 declare (a book, etc.) to be in honour of someone, by printing their name at the front **-cation** /ˌdedɪˈkeɪʃən/ n 1 [C;U] act of dedicating 2 [U] words used in dedicating a book

de·duce /dɪˈdjuːs‖dɪˈduːs/ vt reach (a piece of knowledge) by reasoning

de·duct /dɪˈdʌkt/ vt take away (part) from a total **~ible** adj: expenses deductible from tax

de·duc·tion /dɪˈdʌkʃən/ n [C;U] 1 example of deducing; knowledge deduced: a brilliant deduction 2 process of deducting; something deducted: a salary of $10,000 after all deductions

deed /diːd/ n 1 lit something done; action 2 law signed agreement

deed poll /ˈ· ·/ n DEED (2) signed when changing one's name

deem /diːm/ vt fml consider; judge

deep /diːp/ adj 1 going far down from the top, or in from the outside: deep river/wound | ankle-deep in mud 2 (of colour) dark 3 (of sound) low 4 strong; extreme: deep sleep | deep distrust | in deep trouble 5 difficult to understand 6 a wise: a deep thinker b mysterious: a deep secret 7 **go off the deep end** sl lose one's temper 8 **in/into deep water** infml in/into serious trouble 9 **thrown in at the deep end** suddenly and unexpectedly faced with a difficult piece of work ♦ adv far down; far in **~en** vi/t make or become deeper **~ly** adv **~ness** n [U]

deep freeze /ˌ· ˈ·‖ˈ· ·/ vt freeze food quickly in order to preserve it ♦ n FREEZER

deep fry /ˈ· ·/ vt FRY completely under the surface of oil or fat

deep-root·ed /ˌ· ˈ··◁/ also **deep-seated** — adj strongly fixed: deep-rooted habits

deer /dɪər/ n large fast animal of which the males have ANTLERs

de·face /dɪˈfeɪs/ vt spoil the surface of **~ment** n [U]

de fac·to /ˌdeɪ ˈfæktəʊ‖ˌdɪ-, ˌdeɪ/ adj, adv fml in actual fact, though not by law

de·fame /dɪˈfeɪm/ vt fml attack the good REPUTATION of **defamation** /ˌdefəˈmeɪʃən/ n [U] **defamatory** /dɪˈfæmətəri‖-tɔːri/ adj

de·fault /dɪˈfɔːlt/ n [U] failure to fulfil a contract, pay a debt, etc. **default** vi **~er** n

de·feat /dɪˈfiːt/ vt 1 win a victory over 2 cause to fail ♦ n [C;U] (example or act of) defeating **~ism** n [U] practice of thinking or behaving in expectation of defeat **~ist** n

def·e·cate /ˈdefɪkeɪt/ vi fml pass waste matter from the bowels

de·fect¹ /ˈdiːfekt, dɪˈfekt/ n imperfection; fault **~ive** /dɪˈfektɪv/ adj

de·fect² /dɪˈfekt/ vi desert one's political party, country, etc. **~or** n **~ion** /-ˈfekʃən/ n [C;U]

de·fence ‖ also **defense** AmE/dɪˈfens/ n [U] 1 act or process of defending 2 [C] something used in defending 3 [C;U] law a arguments used in defending someone in court b lawyers who defend someone **~less** adj unable to defend oneself

de·fend /dɪˈfend/ vt 1 keep safe; protect 2 act as a lawyer for (someone charged with a crime) 3 argue in favour of

de·fen·dant /dɪˈfendənt/ n person against whom a legal charge or claim is brought

de·fen·si·ble /dɪ'fensəbəl/ adj that can be defended

de·fen·sive /dɪ'fensɪv/ adj 1 used in defence 2 (of someone) who always seems to be expecting attack ♦ n **on the defensive** prepared for attack ~**ly** adv ~**ness** n [U]

de·fer /dɪ'fɜːʳ/ vt -**rr**- POSTPONE ~**ment** n [C;U]

defer to phr vt fml accept the decision of

def·er·ence /'defərəns/ n [U] fml respect for another's wishes

de·fi·ance /dɪ'faɪəns/ n [U] open disobedience -**ant** adj -**antly** adv

de·fi·cien·cy /dɪ'fɪʃənsi/ n [C;U] lack: vitamin deficiency -**cient** adj

def·i·cit /'defəsɪt/ n amount by which something, esp. money, is too little

de·file /dɪ'faɪl/ vt fml make dirty

de·fine /dɪ'faɪn/ vt 1 give the meaning of; explain exactly 2 set, mark or show the limits of: a clearly-defined shape

def·i·nite /'defənət, 'defɪnət/ adj clear; without uncertainty ~**ly** adv 1 in a clear way 2 certainly

definite ar·ti·cle /,··· '··/ n (in English) the word THE

def·i·ni·tion /,defə'nɪʃən/ n [C;U] 1 (statement) defining something 2 [U] clearness of shape: The photograph lacks definition.

de·fin·i·tive /dɪ'fɪnətɪv/ adj that cannot be questioned; not needing change

de·flate /,diː'fleɪt, dɪ-/ v 1 vt let air or gas out of (a tyre, etc.) 2 vi/t reduce the supply of money in a country **deflation** /-'fleɪʃən/ n [U] **deflationary** adj

de·flect /dɪ'flekt/ vi/t turn aside from a straight course: (fig.) to deflect someone from their purpose ~**ion** /-'flekʃən/ n [C;U]

de·form /dɪ'fɔːm/ ‖-ɔːrm/ vt spoil the shape of ~**ity** n [C;U] imperfection of the body

de·fraud /dɪ'frɔːd/ vt deceive so as to get something: They defrauded him of £50.

de·fray /dɪ'freɪ/ vt fml pay for

de·frost /,diː'frɒst‖-'frɔːst/ vt remove ice from; unfreeze

deft /deft/ adj effortlessly skilful ~**ly** adv

de·funct /dɪ'fʌŋkt/ adj dead

de·fuse /,diː'fjuːz/ vt 1 remove the FUSE from (a bomb, etc.) 2 make harmless

de·fy /dɪ'faɪ/ vt 1 refuse to obey 2 CHALLENGE to do something impossible 3 remain unreachable by all efforts at or from: It defies description.

de·gen·e·rate /dɪ'dʒenərət/ adj having become worse than before ♦ n degenerate person ♦ vi /-nəreɪt/

become worse -**rative** /-nərətɪv/ adj -**ration** /dɪ,dʒenə'reɪʃən/ n [U]

de·grade /dɪ'greɪd/ v 1 vt bring shame to 2 vi/t change to a simpler chemical form **degradation** /,degrə'deɪʃən/ n [C;U]

de·gree /dɪ'griː/ n 1 unit of measurement of angles, or of temperature 2 stage; level: getting better by degrees 3 title given to a university student — see also THIRD DEGREE

de·hy·drate /,diːhaɪ'dreɪt‖diː'haɪdreɪt/ vt remove water from

de·i·fy /'diːɪfaɪ, 'deɪ-/ vt make a god of

deign /deɪn/ vi derog CONDESCEND

de·i·ty /'diːɪti, 'deɪ-/ n god or goddess

de·jec·ted /dɪ'dʒektɪd/ adj low in spirits; sad -**tion** /-'dʒekʃən/ n [U]

de·lay /dɪ'leɪ/ v 1 vt make later 2 vi act slowly ♦ n 1 [U] delaying 2 [C] example or time of being delayed

de·lec·ta·ble /dɪ'lektəbəl/ adj delightful; DELICIOUS

del·e·gate[1] /'delɪgət/ n person chosen to act for others

del·e·gate[2] /'delɪgeɪt/ v 1 vi/t give (power, etc.) to someone else 2 vt appoint (someone) as a delegate -**gation** /,delɪ'geɪʃən/ n [U] act of delegating 2 [C] group of delegates

de·lete /dɪ'liːt/ vt take out (written words) **deletion** /-'liːʃən/ n [C;U]

del·e·te·ri·ous /,delə'tɪərɪəs/ adj fml harmful

de·lib·e·rate[1] /dɪ'lɪbərət/ adj 1 done on purpose 2 (of speech, movement, etc.) slow; unhurried ~**ly** adv

de·lib·e·rate[2] /dɪ'lɪbəreɪt/ vi/t fml consider carefully -**ration** /dɪ,lɪbə'reɪʃən/ n fml 1 [C;U] (process of) deliberating 2 [U] being slow and unhurried

del·i·ca·cy /'delɪkəsi/ n 1 [U] being delicate 2 [C] something good to eat

del·i·cate /'delɪkət/ adj 1 easily damaged, hurt, or made ill 2 soft and fine: delicate silk 3 needing careful treatment: a delicate situation 4 pleasing but not easy to recognize: a delicate flavour 5 sensitive: delicate instruments ~**ly** adv

del·i·ca·tes·sen /,delɪkə'tesən/ n shop that sells foreign foods ready cooked

de·li·cious /dɪ'lɪʃəs/ adj (esp. of taste or smell) delightful ~**ly** adv

de·light /dɪ'laɪt/ n [U] 1 great pleasure; joy 2 [C] cause of great pleasure ♦ v 1 vt give delight to 2 vi find delight: He delights in scandal. ~**ful** adj very pleasing ~**fully** adv

de·lin·e·ate /dɪ'lɪnieɪt/ vt fml show by drawing

de·lin·quent /dɪ'lɪŋkwənt/ n, adj (person) who breaks a law -**quency** n [U]

de·lir·i·ous /dɪˈlɪərɪəs/ adj excited and dreamy, esp. because of illness ~**ly** adv –**ium** /-rɪəm/ n [U] excited dreamy state

de·liv·er /dɪˈlɪvəʳ/ vt 1 take (goods, letters, etc.) to people's houses 2 help in the birth of 3 give (a blow, kick, etc.) 4 say (a speech, etc.) 5 fml rescue ~**er** n [U] fml rescuer ~**ance** n [U] fml saving; rescue ~**y** n 1 [C;U] delivering things; things delivered 2 [C] birth of a child 3 [C;U] style of public speaking

del·ta /ˈdeltə/ n land in the shape of a triangle at the mouth of a river

de·lude /dɪˈluːd/ vt mislead; deceive

del·uge /ˈdeljuːdʒ/ n heavy rain; flood **deluge** vt

de·lu·sion /dɪˈluːʒən/ n 1 [U] deluding 2 [C] false belief

de luxe /də ˈlʌks‖-ˈluks/ adj of very high quality

delve /delv/ vi search deeply

Dem /dem/ abbrev. for: DEMOCRAT

dem·a·gogue /ˈdeməgɒg‖-gɑːg/ n leader who gains power by exciting the crowds

de·mand /dɪˈmɑːnd‖dɪˈmænd/ n 1 [C] demanding; claim 2 [S;U] desire for things that people can pay for: a great demand for teachers ♦ vt 1 ask for firmly; claim 2 need: problems demanding your attention ~**ing** adj needing a lot of attention or effort

de·mar·ca·tion /ˌdiːmɑːˈkeɪʃən‖-ɑːr-/ n [U] limits; separation

demarcation dis·pute /··· ·,·/ n disagreement between trade unions about who is to do a job

de·mean /dɪˈmiːn/ vt fml bring shame to; DEGRADE

de·mea·nour BrE ‖ –**nor** AmE/dɪˈmiːnəʳ/ n [U] fml behaviour

de·ment·ed /dɪˈmentɪd/ adj mad

de·mer·it /diːˈmerɪt/ n fml fault

de·mil·i·ta·rize ‖ also –**rise** BrE /ˌdiːˈmɪlɪtəraɪz/ vt remove armed forces from (an area) –**rization** /ˌdiːmɪlɪtəraɪˈzeɪʃən‖-tərə-/ n

de·mise /dɪˈmaɪz/ n [U] law death

de·mist /ˌdiːˈmɪst/ vt remove steam from (car windows) ~**er** n

dem·o /ˈdeməʊ/ n infml **demos** DEMONSTRATION (2)

de·mo·bi·lize /diːˈməʊbɪlaɪz/ vi/t fml send home the members of (an armed force). usu. at the end of a war

de·moc·ra·cy /dɪˈmɒkrəsi‖dɪˈmɑː-/ n 1 [U] government by elected representatives of the people 2 [C] country governed in this way 3 [U] social equality

dem·o·crat /ˈdeməkræt/ n 1 person who believes in democracy 2 (cap.) member of the Democratic Party ~**ic** /ˌdeməˈkrætɪk◄/ adj 1 of or favouring

democracy 2 (cap.) of a US political party (the **Democratic Party**) ~**ically** /-kli/ adv

Democrat n member or supporter of the **Democratic Party**, one of the two largest political parties of the US ~**ic** adj

de·mog·ra·phy /dɪˈmɒgrəfi‖-ˈmɑː-/ n [U] study of the numbers and movement of human population –**phic** /ˌdeməˈgræfɪk, ˌdiːt-◄/ adj

de·mol·ish /dɪˈmɒlɪʃ‖dɪˈmɑː-/ vt 1 pull down (buildings, etc.); destroy 2 infml eat up hungrily –**molition** /ˌdeməˈlɪʃən/ n [C;U]

de·mon /ˈdiːmən/ n 1 evil spirit 2 very active skilful person ~**ic** /dɪˈmɒnɪk‖dɪˈmɑː-/ adj of, by or like a demon

de·mon·stra·ble /dɪˈmɒnstrəbəl, ˈdemən-‖dɪˈmɑːn-/ adj fml easily proved –**bly** adv

dem·on·strate /ˈdemənstreɪt/ v 1 vt show clearly 2 vi take part in a public demonstration –**strator** n –**stration** /ˌdemənˈstreɪʃən/ n 1 [C;U] showing something 2 [C;U] also **demo** — public show of opinion, by marching, etc.

de·mon·stra·tive /dɪˈmɒnstrətɪv‖ dɪˈmɑːn-/ adj showing feelings openly

de·mor·al·ize ‖ also –**ise** BrE /dɪˈmɒrəlaɪz‖dɪˈmɔː-, dɪˈmɑː-/ vt destroy the courage and confidence of –**ization** /dɪˌmɒrəlaɪˈzeɪʃən ‖ dɪˌmɔːrələ-, dɪˌmɑː-/ n [U]

de·mote /dɪˈməʊt/ vt reduce in rank **demotion** /dɪˈməʊʃən/ n [C;U]

de·mur /dɪˈmɜːʳ/ vi -**rr**- fml show opposition to a plan

de·mure /dɪˈmjʊəʳ/ adj quiet and MODEST ~**ly** adv

den /den/ n 1 home of a wild animal 2 secret or private place 3 small, quiet room in a house

de·na·tion·al·ize ‖ also –**ise** BrE /diːˈnæʃənəlaɪz/ vt remove from state ownership –**ization** /ˌdiːnæʃənəlaɪˈzeɪʃən‖-nələ-/ n [C;U]

de·ni·al /dɪˈnaɪəl/ n 1 [U] denying (DENY) 2 [C] statement that something is false

den·i·grate /ˈdenɪgreɪt/ vt declare to be worthless

den·im /ˈdenɪm/ n [U] strong cotton cloth **denims** n [P] JEANS

den·i·zen /ˈdenɪzən/ n lit person that lives in a particular place

de·nom·i·na·tion /dɪˌnɒmɪˈneɪʃən‖ dɪˌnɑː-/ n 1 religious group 2 unit of value

de·nom·i·na·tor /dɪˈnɒmɪneɪtəʳ‖ dɪˈnɑː-/ n see COMMON DENOMINATOR

de·note /dɪˈnəʊt/ vt be the name or sign of; mean

de·noue·ment /deɪˈnuːmɒŋ‖ˌdeɪ-/

nu:'mɔːŋ/ n end of a story, when everything is explained

de-nounce /dɪ'naʊns/ vt speak or write publicly against

dense /dens/ adj 1 closely packed 2 hard to see through: *dense fog* 3 stupid ~**ly** adv **density** n [C;U]

dent /dent/ n 1 small hollow in a surface, made by a blow 2 **make a dent in** make a first step towards success in ◆ vt make a dent

den-tal /'dentl/ adj of the teeth

den-tist /'dentɪst/ n person trained to treat the teeth ~**ry** n [U]

den-tures /'dentʃəz‖-ərz/ n [P] false teeth

de-nude /dɪ'njuːd‖dɪ'nuːd/ vt fml remove the covering from: *a hill denuded of trees*

de-nun-ci-a-tion /dɪ,nʌnsi'eɪʃən/ n [C;U] act or example of denouncing (DENOUNCE)

de-ny /dɪ'naɪ/ vt 1 declare untrue 2 refuse to allow

de-o-do-rant /diː'əʊdərənt/ n [C;U] chemical that hides bad smells

de-part /dɪ'pɑːt‖-ɑːrt/ vi fml 1 leave; go away 2 **depart this life** lit to die ~**ed** adj gone for ever

  depart from phr vt turn or move away from

de-part-ment /dɪ'pɑːtmənt‖-ɑːr-/ n 1 division of a government, business, college, etc. 2 infml activity or subject for which a person is responsible ~**al** /,diːpɑːt'mentl‖-ɑːr-/ adj

department store /·'·· ·/ n large shop divided into departments

de-par-ture /dɪ'pɑːtʃər‖-ɑːr-/ n 1 going away (fig.) *a new departure* (= change from a usual course of action) *in television*

de-pend /dɪ'pend/ v 1 [it + vt] vary according to; be decided by: *It depends how much you want to spend.* 2 **That (all) depends/It all depends** That/It has not yet been decided

  depend on/upon phr vt 1 trust 2 be supported by 3 vary according to

de-pen-da-ble /dɪ'pendəbəl/ adj that can be trusted

de-pen-dant , **-dent** /dɪ'pendənt/ n person supported by another

de-pen-dence /dɪ'pendəns/ n [U] 1 being dependent: *our dependence on oil* 2 trust 3 need to have certain drugs regularly

de-pen-dent /dɪ'pendənt/ adj that depends on

de-pict /dɪ'pɪkt/ vt fml show in a picture, or in words

de-pil-a-to-ry /dɪ'pɪlətəri‖-tɔːri/ n, adj (substance) that gets rid of unwanted hair

de-plete /dɪ'pliːt/ vt fml lessen (supplies, etc.) greatly **depletion** /-'pliːʃən/ n [U]

de-plore /dɪ'plɔːr/ vt be very sorry about (and consider wrong) **deplorable** adj very bad

de-ploy /dɪ'plɔɪ/ vt arrange for effective action ~**ment** n [U]

de-pop-u-late /,diː'pɒpjʊleɪt‖-'pɑːp-/ vt reduce greatly the population

de-port /dɪ'pɔːt‖-ɔːrt/ vt send (an unwanted foreigner) out of the country ~**ation** /,diːpɔː'teɪʃən‖-pɔːr-/ n [C;U]

de-port-ment /dɪ'pɔːtmənt‖-ɔːr-/ n [U] way a person stands and walks

de-pose /dɪ'pəʊz/ vt remove (a ruler) from power

de-pos-it[1] /dɪ'pɒzɪt‖dɪ'pɑː-/ vt 1 put down 2 (of a river, etc.) leave (soil, etc.) lying 3 put in a bank, etc., to be safe ~**or** n person who deposits money

deposit[2] n 1 [C;U] material deposited by a natural process 2 first part of a payment for something, to show that an agreement will be kept

deposit ac-count /·'·· ·,·/ n BrE bank account which earns interest but from which money cannot be taken out at once

dep-ot /'depəʊ‖'diːpəʊ/ n 1 storehouse for goods 2 bus garage 3 AmE railway station

de-praved /dɪ'preɪvd/ adj wicked **depravity** /dɪ'prævəti/ n [C;U]

dep-re-cate /'deprəkeɪt/ vt fml express disapproval of

de-pre-ci-ate /dɪ'priːʃieɪt/ vi (esp. of money) fall in value **-ation** /dɪ,priːʃi'eɪʃən/ n [U]

dep-re-da-tions /,deprə'deɪʃənz/ n [P] fml acts of destruction

de-press /dɪ'pres/ vt 1 sadden: *depressing news* 2 make less active 3 fml press down ~**ed** adj 1 sad 2 suffering from low levels of business activity

de-pres-sion /dɪ'preʃən/ n 1 [C;U] sad feeling 2 [C] period of reduced business activity 3 [C] hollow in a surface 4 [C] area of low air pressure

de-prive /dɪ'praɪv/ vt prevent from having something: *deprive us of our rights* **deprivation** /,deprɪ'veɪʃən/ n [C;U]

depth /depθ/ n [C;U] 1 (degree of) being deep 2 **in depth** done thoroughly 3 **out of one's depth: a** in water deeper than one's height **b** beyond one's understanding **depths** n [the + P] deepest or most central part of: *the depths of winter/despair*

dep-u-ta-tion /,depjʊ'teɪʃən/ n group sent to act on behalf of others

dep-u-ty /'depjʊti/ n person given power to act for another **-tize** vi act as a deputy

de·rail /ˌdiːˈreɪl, dɪ-/ vt cause (a train) to run off the line ~**ment** n [C;U]

de·ranged /dɪˈreɪndʒd/ adj unbalanced in the mind

de·reg·u·late /diːˈregjʊleɪt/ vt remove from control by law ~**lation** /ˌdiːregjʊˈleɪʃən/ n [U]

der·e·lict /ˈderəlɪkt/ adj fallen into ruin ♦ n person, esp. an ALCOHOLIC, who has no home and no legal means of support ~**ion** /ˌderəˈlɪkʃən/ n 1 state of being derelict 2 failure to do one's duty

de·ride /dɪˈraɪd/ vt fml laugh unkindly at

de·ri·sion /dɪˈrɪʒən/ n [U] unkind laughter –**sive** /dɪˈraɪsɪv/ adj: derisive laughter –**sory** adj deserving derision; ABSURD

de·riv·a·tive /dɪˈrɪvətɪv/ adj derog not original or new

de·rive /dɪˈraɪv/ v 1 vt obtain from somewhere: derive pleasure from one's work 2 vi have something as an origin: words that derive from Latin **derivation** /ˌderɪˈveɪʃən/ n [C;U]

der·ma·ti·tis /ˌdɜːməˈtaɪtɪs‖ˌdɜːr-/ n [U] skin disease with redness and swelling

de·rog·a·to·ry /dɪˈrogətəri‖dɪˈrɑːgətɔːri/ adj fml (of words) showing disapproval

der·rick /ˈderɪk/ n 1 large CRANE (1) 2 tower over an oil well

de·scend /dɪˈsend/ vi/t 1 go down 2 **be descended from** have as an ANCESTOR ~**ant** n person descended from another

descend on/upon phr vt 1 arrive suddenly 2 attack suddenly

de·scent /dɪˈsent/ n 1 [C;U] going down 2 [C] downward slope 3 [U] family origins: of German descent

de·scribe /dɪˈskraɪb/ vt 1 say what something is like 2 fml draw the shape of: describe a circle

de·scrip·tion /dɪˈskrɪpʃən/ n 1 [C;U] statement that describes 2 [C] sort: birds of every description –**tive** /-tɪv/ adj 1 that describes 2 saying how a language is used

des·e·crate /ˈdesɪkreɪt/ vt spoil (a holy thing or place) –**cration** /ˌdesɪˈkreɪʃən/ n [S;U]

de·seg·re·gate /diːˈsegrɪgeɪt/ vt end racial SEGREGATION in

des·ert¹ /ˈdezət‖-ərt/ n large area of dry sandy land

de·sert² /dɪˈzɜːt‖-ɜːrt/ v 1 vt leave (a place) empty 2 vt leave (people) cruelly 3 vi leave military service without permission ~**er** n person who DESERTs (3) ~**ion** /-ˈzɜːʃən‖-ɜːr-/ n [C;U]

de·serts /dɪˈzɜːts‖-ɜːrts/ n [P] what someone deserves

de·serve /dɪˈzɜːv‖-ɜːrv/ vt be worthy of: She deserved to win. **deservedly** /dɪˈzɜːvədli‖-ɜːr-/ adv rightly **deserving** adj

des·ic·cate /ˈdesɪkeɪt/ vi/t fml dry up

de·sign /dɪˈzaɪn/ vt 1 draw a plan for (something to be made) 2 plan (something) for a purpose: books designed for use in colleges ♦ n 1 [C] plan drawn for making something 2 [U] art of designing things 3 [C] decorative pattern 4 [C] plan in the mind **designs** [P] evil plans: designs on your life

des·ig·nate /ˈdezɪgneɪt/ vt 1 choose for a particular job or purpose ♦ adj /-nət, -neɪt/ chosen for an office but not yet officially placed in it

designer¹ /dɪˈzaɪnər/ n person who makes plans or designs

designer² adj 1 made by a designer: designer jeans 2 humor or derog intended to make the user appear extremely fashionable: designer stubble/socialism

de·sir·a·ble /dɪˈzaɪərəbəl/ adj worth having; attractive –**bly** adv –**bility** /dɪˌzaɪərəˈbɪləti/ n [U]

de·sire /dɪˈzaɪər/ vt wish for; want very much ♦ n 1 [C;U] strong wish 2 [C;U] strong wish for sexual relations with 3 [C] something desired **desirous** adj feeling or having a desire

de·sist /dɪˈzɪst, dɪˈsɪst/ vi cease doing

desk /desk/ n table at which one writes or does business: airport information desk

desk·top /ˈdesktop‖-tɑːp/ adj being or using a small computer: desktop publishing

des·o·late /ˈdesələt/ adj sad and lonely –**lation** /ˌdesəˈleɪʃən/ n [U]

de·spair /dɪˈspeər/ vi lose all hope ♦ n loss of hope –**ingly** adv

de·spatch /dɪˈspætʃ/ n, v DISPATCH

des·per·ate /ˈdespərət/ adj 1 ready for any wild act because of despair 2 very dangerous and without much hope of success ~**ly** adv -**ation** /ˌdespəˈreɪʃən/ n [U]

des·pic·a·ble /dɪˈspɪkəbəl, ˈdespɪ-/ adj deserving to be despised

de·spise /dɪˈspaɪz/ vt regard as worthless

de·spite /dɪˈspaɪt/ prep fml in spite of

de·spon·dent /dɪˈspondənt‖dɪˈspɑːn-/ adj without hope; discouraged –**dency** n [U]

des·pot /ˈdespot, -ət‖ˈdespət, -ɑːt/ n ruler with total power who governs cruelly ~**ic** dɪˈspotɪk, de-‖-ˈspɑː-/ adj

des·sert /dɪˈzɜːt‖-ɜːrt/ n [C;U] sweet food served at the end of a meal

des·sert·spoon /dɪˈzɜːtspuːn‖-ɜːrt-/ n middle-sized spoon

de-sta-bil-ize ‖ also **-ise** *BrE* /diːˈsteɪbəlaɪz/ *vt* make (a government, etc.) unsteady

des-ti-na-tion /ˌdestɪˈneɪʃən/ *n* place to which someone or something is going

des-tined /ˈdestɪnd/ *adj* intended, esp. by fate: *He was destined to become famous.*

des-ti-ny /ˈdestɪni/ *n* [C;U] fate; what might happen

des-ti-tute /ˈdestɪtjuːt‖-tuːt/ *adj* **1** without food, clothes, shelter, etc. **2** *fml* lacking in: *destitute of feeling* **-tution** /ˌdestɪˈtjuːʃən‖-ˈtuː-/ *n* [U]

de-stroy /dɪˈstrɔɪ/ *vt* **1** make useless; ruin **2** kill (esp. an animal) **~er** *n* **1** someone who destroys **2** small fast warship

de-struc-tion /dɪˈstrʌkʃən/ *n* [U] destroying; ruin **-tive** /-tɪv/ *adj* **1** causing destruction **2** not helpful: *destructive criticism*

des-ul-to-ry /ˈdesəltəri, ˈdez-‖-tɔːri/ *adj fml* passing from one thing to another without plan or purpose

de-tach /dɪˈtætʃ/ *vt* separate from something larger **~ed** *adj* **1** (of a house) not joined to others **2** not influenced by personal feelings **~ment** *n* **1** [U] being DETACHED (2) **2** [C] group of soldiers, etc.

de-tail /ˈdiːteɪl‖dɪˈteɪl/ *n* **1** small fact about something **2** small working party of soldiers, etc. ♦ *vt* **1** describe fully: *a detailed account* **2** appoint (soldiers, etc.) for special work

de-tain /dɪˈteɪn/ *vt* prevent (someone) from leaving

de-tain-ee /ˌdiːteɪˈniː/ *n* person detained officially in a camp or prison

de-tect /dɪˈtekt/ *vt* notice; discover **~able** *adj* **~ive** *n* person who catches criminals **~or** *n* instrument for finding something: *a metal detector* **~ion** /-ˈtekʃən/ *n* [U]

dé-tente /ˈdeɪtɒnt, deɪˈtɒnt‖-ɑːnt/ *n* [C;U] calmer political relations between unfriendly countries

de-ten-tion /dɪˈtenʃən/ *n* [U] act of preventing a person from leaving

de-ter /dɪˈtɜːʳ/ *vt* **-rr-** discourage from doing something

de-ter-gent /dɪˈtɜːdʒənt‖-ɜːr-/ *n* [C;U] (esp. soapless) product for washing things

de-te-ri-o-rate /dɪˈtɪəriəreɪt/ *vi* become worse **-ration** /dɪˌtɪəriəˈreɪʃən/ *n*

de-ter-mi-na-tion /dɪˌtɜːmɪˈneɪʃən‖-ɜːr-/ *n* [U] **1** strong will to succeed **2** firm intention **3** finding out

de-ter-mine /dɪˈtɜːmɪn‖-ɜːr-/ *vt* **1** form a firm intention **2** limit; fix **3** find out; calculate

de-ter-min-er /dɪˈtɜːmɪnəʳ‖-ɜːr-/ *n* word that describes a noun and comes

before any adjectives that describe the same noun (such as *'his'* in *'his new car'*)

de-ter-rent /dɪˈterənt‖-ˈtɜːr-/ *n, adj* (something) that DETER*s*

de-test /dɪˈtest/ *vt* hate very much **~able** *adj*

de-throne /dɪˈθrəʊn/ *vt* remove (a king or queen) from power

det-o-nate /ˈdetəneɪt/ *vi/t* explode **-nator** *n* piece of equipment used for detonating **-nation** /ˌdetəˈneɪʃən/ *n* [C;U]

de-tour /ˈdiːtʊəʳ/ *n* way round something

de-tract /dɪˈtrækt/ *v* **detract from** *phr vt* lessen the value of

de-trac-tor /dɪˈtræktəʳ/ *n* person who says bad things about another

det-ri-ment /ˈdetrɪmənt/ *n* [U] *fml* harm; damage **~al** /ˌdetrɪˈmentl/ *adj*

deuce /djuːs‖duːs/ *n* [U] (in tennis) 40 points to each player

de-val-ue /diːˈvæljuː/ *vi/t* **1** reduce the exchange value of (money) **2** make (a person or action) seem less valuable or important **-uation** /diːˌvæljuˈeɪʃən/ *n* [C;U]

dev-a-state /ˈdevəsteɪt/ *vt* destroy completely **-station** /ˌdevəˈsteɪʃən/ *n* [U]

de-vel-op /dɪˈveləp/ *v* **1** *vi/t* (cause to) grow or become more advanced **2** *vt* use (land) for building on **3** *vt* begin to have: *develop measles* **4** *vt* cause (a photograph) to appear on paper **~er** *n* person who develops land **~ment** *n* **1** [U] developing **2** [C] new event **3** developed piece of land

de-vel-op-ing coun-try /ˌ···‖···ˈ··/ *n* poor country that is trying to improve its industry and living conditions

de-vi-ant /ˈdiːviənt/ *adj* different from an accepted standard **-ance** *n* [U]

de-vi-ate /ˈdiːvieɪt/ *vi* turn away from what is usual **-ation** /ˌdiːviˈeɪʃən/ *n* [C;U] noticeable difference

de-vice /dɪˈvaɪs/ *n* **1** instrument or tool **2** plan; trick **3 leave someone to their own devices** leave (someone) alone, without help

dev-il /ˈdevəl/ *n* **1** evil spirit **2** *sl* person: *You lucky devil!* **~ish** *adj* evil; like the devil **~ishly** *adv* very: *devilishly hard work*

devil's ad-vo-cate /ˌ··ˈ···/ *n* person who opposes an idea or plan to test how good it is

de-vi-ous /ˈdiːviəs/ *adj* not direct; not very honest

de-vise /dɪˈvaɪz/ *vt* plan; invent

de-void /dɪˈvɔɪd/ *adj* **devoid of** *fml* empty of: *a house devoid of furniture* | *devoid of human feeling*

de·vo·lu·tion /ˌdiːvəˈluːʃən/ n [U] giving of power to someone else

de·volve /dɪˈvɒlv‖dɪˈvɑːlv/ v **devolve on/upon** phr vt (of power or work) be passed to

de·vote /dɪˈvəʊt/ vt give completely to something **devoted** adj loyal; loving **devotion** /-ˈvəʊʃən/ n [U] 1 great love 2 devoutness **devotions** n [P] prayers

dev·o·tee /ˌdevəˈtiː/ n person who admires someone or something

de·vour /dɪˈvaʊər/ vt 1 eat up hungrily: (fig.) I devoured the book. 2 completely take up the attention of: devoured by hate

de·vout /dɪˈvaʊt/ adj 1 seriously religious 2 deeply felt: a devout hope ~ly adv

dew /djuː‖duː/ n [U] drops of water that form on cold surfaces in the night ~y adj wet as if with dew: a dewy-eyed look

dex·ter·i·ty /dekˈsterəti/ n [U] quick cleverness, esp. with one's hands **-terous** /ˈdekstərəs/, **-trous** /-trəs/ adj

dex·trose /ˈdekstrəʊz, -strəʊs/ n [U] form of sugar found in some fruits

di·a·be·tes /ˌdaɪəˈbiːtiːz, -tɪs/ n [U] disease in which there is too much sugar in the blood **-tic** /-ˈbetɪk/ n, adj (person) suffering from this

di·a·bol·i·cal /ˌdaɪəˈbɒlɪkəl‖-ˈbɑː-/ adj 1 very cruel or bad 2 very unpleasant and annoying: The train service was diabolical. ~ly /-kli/ adv

di·a·dem /ˈdaɪədem/ n lit crown

di·ag·nose /ˈdaɪəgnəʊz‖-nəʊs/ vt discover the nature of (a disease)

di·ag·no·sis /ˌdaɪəgˈnəʊsɪs/ n -ses /-siːz/ [C;U] (judgment made by) diagnosing **-nostic** /-ˈnɒstɪk◂‖-ˈnɑː-/ adj

di·ag·o·nal /daɪˈægənəl/ adj (of a straight line) joining opposite corners of a square, etc. ~ly adv

di·a·gram /ˈdaɪəgræm/ n plan drawn to explain a machine, idea, etc. ~matic /ˌdaɪəgrəˈmætɪk/ adj

di·al /ˈdaɪəl/ n 1 marked face of a clock, etc. 2 wheel with holes on a telephone ♦ vi/t -ll- BrE ‖ -l- AmE make a telephone call

di·a·lect /ˈdaɪəlekt/ n [C;U] variety of a language, spoken in one part of a country

di·a·lec·tic /ˌdaɪəˈlektɪk/ n [U] method of arguing according to certain rules

di·a·logue BrE ‖ **-log** AmE/ˈdaɪəlɒg‖-lɔːg, -lɑːg/ n [C;U] 1 conversation in a book or play 2 exchange of opinion between leaders, etc.

di·am·e·ter /daɪˈæmɪtər/ n distance across a circle, measured through the centre

di·a·met·ri·cal·ly /ˌdaɪəˈmetrɪkli/ adv completely: diametrically opposed/ opposite

di·a·mond /ˈdaɪəmənd/ n 1 [C;U] hard valuable precious stone 2 [C] figure with 4 equal sides, standing on one of its points 3 [C] red diamond-shaped figure on a playing card — see also ROUGH DIAMOND

di·a·per /ˈdaɪəpər‖ˈdaɪpər/ n AmE for NAPPY

di·a·phragm /ˈdaɪəfræm/ n 1 muscle separating the lungs from the stomach 2 thin plate in a telephone, camera, etc.

di·ar·rhoe·a, -rhea /ˌdaɪəˈrɪər/ n [U] illness in which the bowels are emptied too often

di·a·ry /ˈdaɪəri/ n (book for) a daily record of events in one's life **-rist** n writer of a diary

di·a·tribe /ˈdaɪətraɪb/ n fml violent attack in words

dice /daɪs/ n dice small 6-sided block with spots on it, used in games ♦ v 1 cut (food) into small squares 2 **dice with death** take a great risk ~y adj risky and uncertain

di·chot·o·my /daɪˈkɒtəmi‖-ˈkɑː-/ n fml division into 2 opposite parts or groups

dick /dɪk/ n taboo sl PENIS

dick·y /ˈdɪki/ adj infml BrE weak

dic·tate¹ /dɪkˈteɪt‖ˈdɪkteɪt/ vi/t 1 say (words) for someone else to write down 2 give (orders)

dic·tate² /ˈdɪkteɪt/ n order (esp. from within ourselves): the dictates of your own conscience

dic·ta·tion /dɪkˈteɪʃən/ n 1 [U] dictating 2 [C] piece of writing dictated

dic·ta·tor /dɪkˈteɪtər‖ˈdɪkteɪtər/ n ruler with complete power ~ship n [C;U] (country with) government by a dictator **-ial** /ˌdɪktəˈtɔːriəl/ adj

dic·tion /ˈdɪkʃən/ n [U] way in which someone pronounces words

dic·tion·a·ry /ˈdɪkʃənəri‖-neri/ n book giving a list of words in A-Z order, with their meanings

dic·tum /ˈdɪktəm/ n -ta /-tə/ or -tums formal statement of opinion

did /dɪd/ v past t. of DO

di·dac·tic /daɪˈdæktɪk, dɪ-/ adj fml intending to teach

did·dle /ˈdɪdl/ vt infml cheat

didn't /ˈdɪdnt/ v short for: did not

die¹ /daɪ/ vi **died**, pres p. **dying** /ˈdaɪ-ɪŋ/ 1 stop living; become dead: (fig.) My love will never die. ‖ His secret died with him. 2 **be dying for/to** want very badly 3 **die hard** (of beliefs, customs, etc.) take a long time to disappear

　die away phr vi fade and then cease
　die down phr vi become less: The excitement soon died down.

die off *phr vi* die one by one

die out *phr vi* become EXTINCT

die[2] *n* metal block for shaping coins, etc.

die-hard /'daɪhɑːd‖-ɑːrd/ *n* person who strongly opposes change

die-sel /'diːzəl/ *n* [U] heavy oil used instead of petrol, esp. in buses and trains

di-et /'daɪət/ *n* 1 food and drink usually taken 2 limited list of food and drink that someone is allowed for medical reasons 3 **(be/go) on a diet** (be/start) living on a limited list of food usu. in order to lose weight ♦ *vi* eat according to a DIET (2)

dif-fer /'dɪfəʳ/ *vi* 1 be different 2 disagree

dif-fe-rence /'dɪfərəns/ *n* 1 [C;U] way or fact of being different 2 [C] slight disagreement 3 **split the difference** agree on an amount halfway between

dif-fe-rent /'dɪfərənt/ *adj* 1 unlike 2 separate: *They go to different schools.* 3 various: *It comes in different colours.* 4 unusual ~**ly** *adv*

dif-fe-ren-tial /ˌdɪfə'renʃəl◄/ *n* amount of difference between things: *pay differentials*

dif-fe-ren-ti-ate /ˌdɪfə'renʃieɪt/ *vi/t* see a difference (between)

dif-fi-cult /'dɪfɪkəlt/ *adj* 1 hard to do, understand, etc. 2 (of people) not easily pleased

dif-fi-cul-ty /'dɪfɪkəlti/ *n* 1 [U] being difficult; trouble 2 [C] something difficult; problem

dif-fi-dent /'dɪfɪdənt/ *adj* lacking confidence in oneself ~**ly** *adv* ~**dence** *n* [U]

dif-fuse[1] /dɪ'fjuːz/ *vi/t fml* spread freely in all directions ~**fusion** /-'fjuːʒən/ *n*

dif-fuse[2] /dɪ'fjuːs/ *adj fml* 1 diffused[2] 2 using too many words

dig /dɪɡ/ *vi/t* **dug** /dʌɡ/, *pres p.* **digging** 1 break up and move (earth) 2 make (a hole) in this way: *dig an underground tunnel* 3 *sl* like or understand 4 **dig somone in the ribs** touch someone with one's elbow, as to share a joke ♦ *n* 1 quick push 2 place being uncovered by ARCHAEOLOGISTs 3 unpleasant remark **digs** *n* [P] *BrE* lodgings

dig at *phr vt* speak to (someone) in an unpleasant way: *Stop digging at me!*

dig in *phr v* 1 *vi/t* dig a protective place for oneself; get firmly settled 2 *vi* start eating

dig out *phr vt* get out by digging

dig up *phr vt* find (something buried) by digging: (fig.) *dig up an old scandal*

di-gest[1] /daɪ'dʒest, dɪ-/ *vt* 1 change (food) so that the body can use it 2 arrange (facts) in one's mind ~**ible** *adj* ~**ive** *adj* of or helping in digesting food ~**ion** /-'dʒestʃən/ *n* ability to digest food

di-gest[2] /'daɪdʒest/ *n* short SUMMARY

di-git /'dɪdʒɪt/ *n* 1 any number from 0 to 9 2 *fml* finger or toe ~**al** *adj* using digits: *digital watch* ~**ize** *vt* use digits to express information

dig-ni-fied /'dɪɡnɪfaɪd/ *adj* having dignity

dig-ni-ta-ry /'dɪɡnɪtəri‖-teri/ *n fml* person of high rank

dig-ni-ty /'dɪɡnɪti/ *n* [U] 1 nobleness of character 2 formal grand behaviour 3 **beneath one's dignity** below one's standard of moral or social behaviour

di-gress /daɪ'ɡres/ *vi fml* (of a writer or speaker) move away from the subject ~**ion** /-'ɡreʃən/ *n* [C;U]

dike, dyke /daɪk/ *n* 1 bank to hold back water 2 ditch

di-lap-i-dat-ed /dɪ'læpədeɪtɪd/ *adj* falling to pieces

di-late /daɪ'leɪt/ *vi/t* (cause to) become wider by stretching: *eyes dilated with terror* **dilation** /-'leɪʃən/ *n* [U]

dil-a-to-ry /'dɪlətəri‖-tɔːri/ *adj* too slow in action

di-lem-ma /dɪ'lemə, daɪ-/ *n* difficult choice between 2 things

dil-et-tan-te /ˌdɪlɪ'tænti‖-'tɑːnti/ *n, adj* (person) who enjoys art or branch of study but does not take it seriously

dil-i-gence /'dɪlɪdʒəns/ *n* [U] steady effort ~**gent** *adj* ~**gently** *adv*

di-lute /daɪ'luːt/ *vt* make (liquid) weaker and thinner **dilution** /-'luːʃən/ *n* [C;U]

dim /dɪm/ *adj* -**mm**- 1 (of light) not bright 2 not easy to see 3 *sl* stupid 4 **take a dim view of** think badly of ♦ *vi/t* -**mm**- make or become dim ~**ly** *adv* ~**ness** *n* [U]

dime /daɪm/ *n* coin of US and Canada worth 10 cents

di-men-sion /daɪ'menʃən, də-/ *n* 1 measurement of breadth, length, or height 2 particular site or part of a problem, subject, etc. 3 -**dimensional** having (so many) dimensions: *2-dimensional* **dimensions** *n* [P] size

di-min-ish /də'mɪnɪʃ/ *vi/t* make or become smaller

dim-i-nu-tion /ˌdɪmə'njuːʃən‖-'nuː-/ *n* [C;U] *fml* diminishing

di-min-u-tive /də'mɪnjʊtɪv/ *adj fml* very small

dim-ple /'dɪmpəl/ *n* small hollow in the cheek, etc.

dim-wit /'dɪmwɪt/ *n* stupid person ~**ted** /ˌ· '··◄/ *adj*

din[1] /dɪn/ *n* loud unpleasant noise

din² v din into *phr vt* repeat (something) forcefully over and over again to (someone)

dine /daɪn/ *vi fml* eat dinner
  dine off *phr vt* eat for dinner
  dine out on *phr vt* gain social success with (news or a story)

din-ghy /'dɪŋgi, 'dɪŋi/ *n* small open boat

din-gy /'dɪndʒi/ *adj* dirty and faded

dining car /'··· ·/ *n* railway carriage where meals are served

dining ta-ble /'··· ,··/ *n* table for having meals on

din-ner /'dɪnəʳ/ *n* [C;U] main meal of the day, eaten either at midday or in the evening

dinner jack-et /'··· ,··/ *n* man's black (or white) coat for formal evening occasions

di-no-saur /'daɪnəsɔːʳ/ *n* 1 large REPTILE that no longer exists 2 something very large and old-fashioned that no longer works well

dint /dɪnt/ *n* **by dint of** by means of

di-o-cese /'daɪəsɪs/ *n* area controlled by a BISHOP —**cesan** /daɪ'ɒsɪsən‖-'əs-/ *adj*

dip¹ /dɪp/ *v* -**pp**- 1 *vt* put into a liquid for a moment 2 *vi/t* drop slightly: *dip your headlights*
  dip into *phr vt* 1 read (a book) for a short time 2 use up (money)

dip² *n* 1 [C] quick bathe 2 [C] downward slope 3 [U] liquid into which food is dipped at parties 4 [C] (liquid for) dipping animals: *sheep dip*

diph-ther-i-a /dɪf'θɪəriə, dɪp-/ *n* [U] serious infectious disease of the throat

diph-thong /'dɪfθɒŋ, 'dɪp-‖-θɔːŋ/ *n* compound vowel sound

di-plo-ma /dɪ'pləʊmə/ *n* official paper showing success in studying something

di-plo-ma-cy /dɪ'pləʊməsi/ *n* [U] 1 management of relations between countries 2 skill at dealing with people

dip-lo-mat /'dɪpləmæt/ *n* person whose profession is DIPLOMACY (1) ~**ic** /,dɪplə'mætɪk◂/ *adj* of or having diplomacy ~**ically** /-kli/ *adv*

diplomatic re-la-tions /,···· ·'··/ *n* [P] connection between 2 countries that each keep an EMBASSY in the other country

dire /daɪəʳ/ *adj* terrible

di-rect¹ /dɪ'rekt, daɪ-/ *vt* 1 tell (someone) the way to a place 2 control; manage 3 *fml* command; order 4 aim

direct² *adj* 1 going straight: *direct route* 2 with nothing coming between: *direct result* 3 honest; clearly expressed: *direct answer* 4 exact: *direct opposite* ♦ *adv* without turning aside ~**ly** *adv* 1 in a direct way 2 at once ~**ness** *n* [U]

di-rec-tion /dɪ'rekʃən, daɪ-/ *n* 1 [C] point towards which a person or thing moves or faces 2 [U] control; management **directions** *n* [P] instructions

di-rec-tive /dɪ'rektɪv, daɪ-/ *n* official order

direct ob-ject /·,· '··/ *n* the noun, noun phrase, or PRONOUN that is needed to complete the meaning of a TRANSITIVE verb: *In 'I saw Mary', 'Mary' is the direct object.*

di-rec-tor /dɪ'rektəʳ, daɪ-/ *n* 1 senior manager of a firm 2 person who directs a play or film ~**ship** *n* company director's position

di-rec-to-ry /daɪ'rektəri, dɪ-/ *n* book or list of names, facts, etc.: *telephone directory*

direct speech /·,· '·/ *n* [U] *gram* actual words of a speaker

dirge /dɜːdʒ‖dɜːrdʒ/ *n* slow sad song

dirt /dɜːt‖dɜːrt/ *n* [U] 1 unclean matter; mud, etc. 2 nasty talk 3 **treat someone like dirt** treat someone as worthless ~**y** *adj* 1 not clean 2 unpleasantly concerned with sex: *dirty jokes* 3 unpleasant: *dirty looks* ~**y** *vt* make dirty ~**ily** *adv*

dirt cheap /,· '·◂/ *adj* extremely cheap

dis-a-bil-i-ty /,dɪsə'bɪləti/ *n* 1 [U] being disabled 2 [C] HANDICAP (1)

dis-a-ble /dɪs'eɪbəl/ *vt* make unable to use one's body properly —**abled** *adj* ~**ment** *n* [C;U]

dis-a-buse /,dɪsə'bjuːz/ *vt fml* free (someone) from a wrong idea

dis-ad-van-tage /,dɪsəd'vɑːntɪdʒ‖-'væn-/ *n* [C;U] unfavourable condition ~**ous** /,dɪsædvən'teɪdʒəs, -væn-/ *adj*

dis-ad-van-taged /,dɪsəd'vɑːntɪdʒd‖-'væn-/ *adj* suffering from a disadvantage with regard to one's social position, family background, etc.

dis-af-fect-ed /,dɪsə'fektɪd/ *adj* lacking (esp. political) loyalty —**fection** /-'fekʃən/ *n* [U]

dis-a-gree /,dɪsə'griː/ *vi* 1 have different opinions 2 be different ~**able** *adj* unpleasant ~**ably** *adv* ~**ment** *n* [C;U] difference of opinion
  disagree with *phr vt* (of food, etc.) make ill

dis-ap-pear /,dɪsə'pɪəʳ/ *vi* 1 go out of sight 2 cease to exist ~**ance** *n* [C;U]

dis-ap-point /,dɪsə'pɔɪnt/ *vt* fail to fulfil hopes ~**ed** *adj* sad at not seeing hopes fulfilled ~**ing** *adj* ~**ingly** *adv* ~**ment** *n* 1 [U] being disappointed 2 [C] something disappointing

dis-ap-prove /,dɪsə'pruːv/ *vi* have an unfavourable opinion —**proval** *n* [U]

dis-arm /dɪs'ɑːm‖-'ɑːrm/ *v* 1 *vt* take away weapons from 2 *vi* reduce a nation's military strength 3 *vt* drive away the anger of: *a disarming smile* ~**ingly** *adv. smile disarmingly*

dis·ar·ma·ment /dɪsˈɑːməmənt‖ -ˈɑːr-/ *n* [U] act or principle of DISARMing (2)

dis·ar·ray /ˌdɪsəˈreɪ/ *n* [U] *fml* disorder

dis·as·so·ci·ate /ˌdɪsəˈsəʊʃieɪt, -sieɪt/ *vt* DISSOCIATE

di·sas·ter /dɪˈzɑːstəʳ‖dɪˈzæ-/ *n* [C;U] sudden serious misfortune **-trous** *adj* **-trously** *adv*

dis·a·vow /ˌdɪsəˈvaʊ/ *vt fml* refuse to admit (knowledge, etc.)

dis·band /dɪsˈbænd/ *vi/t* break up a (group)

dis·be·lief /ˌdɪsbəˈliːf/ *n* [U] lack of belief

dis·be·lieve /ˌdɪsbəˈliːv/ *vi/t* refuse to believe

disc *BrE* ‖ **disk** *AmE*/dɪsk/ *n* **1** anything round and flat, such as a plate or record **2** flat piece of CARTILAGE in one's back: *a slipped disc* **3** a DISK (2)

dis·card /dɪsˈkɑːd‖-ɑːrd/ *vt* get rid of; throw away

di·scern /dɪˈsɜːn‖-ɜːrn/ *vt* see or understand esp. with difficulty ~**ible** *adj* ~**ing** *adj* able to decide and judge; having good taste ~**ment** *n* [U]

dis·charge¹ /dɪsˈtʃɑːdʒ‖-ɑːr-/ *v* **1** *vt* send (a person) away **2** *vt/i* let out (gas, liquid, etc.) **3** *vt* perform (a duty or promise) **4** *vt* pay (a debt) **5** *vt* fire (a gun, etc.)

dis·charge² /dɪsˈtʃɑːdʒ, ˈdɪstʃɑːdʒ‖ -ɑːr-/ *n* **1** [U] discharging **2** [C;U] something discharged

di·sci·ple /dɪˈsaɪpəl/ *n* follower of a (religious) leader

dis·ci·pli·nar·i·an /ˌdɪsəpləˈneəriən/ *n* person who can make others obey and believes in firm discipline

dis·ci·pli·na·ry /ˈdɪsəplɪnəri, ˌdɪsəˈplɪ-‖ˈdɪsəpləneri/ *adj* connected with punishment: *take disciplinary action*

dis·ci·pline /ˈdɪsəplən/ *n* **1** [U] training to produce obedience and self-control **2** [U] control gained by this training **3** [U] punishment **4** [C] branch of learning ♦ *vt* **1** train to be obedient **2** punish

disc jock·ey /ˈ‧ ‚‧/ *n* broadcaster who introduces records of popular music

dis·claim /dɪsˈkleɪm/ *vt* say one does not own: *disclaim responsibility* ~**er** *n* written statement which disclaims

dis·close /dɪsˈkləʊz/ *vt* make (a secret) known

dis·clo·sure /dɪsˈkləʊʒəʳ/ *n* **1** [U] act of disclosing **2** [C] disclosed secret

dis·co /ˈdɪskəʊ/ *n* **-cos** club where people dance to recorded music

dis·col·our *BrE* ‖ **-or** *AmE*/dɪsˈkʌləʳ/ *vi/t* change colour for the worse **-ora·tion** /dɪsˌkʌləˈreɪʃən/ *n* [C;U]

dis·com·fort /dɪsˈkʌmfət‖ -ərt/ *n* [C;U] (cause of) being uncomfortable

dis·con·cert /ˌdɪskənˈsɜːt‖-ɜːrt/ *vt* worry; upset ~**ingly** *adv*

dis·con·nect /ˌdɪskəˈnekt/ *vt* undo the connection of ~**ed** *adj* (of thoughts and ideas) badly arranged

dis·con·so·late /dɪsˈkɒnsələt‖ -ˈkɑːn-/ *adj* hopelessly sad

dis·con·tent /ˌdɪskənˈtent/ *n* [U] restless unhappiness ~**ed** *adj*

dis·con·tin·ue /ˌdɪskənˈtɪnjuː/ *vi/t fml* stop; end

dis·cord /ˈdɪskɔːd‖-ɔːrd/ *n* **1** [U] disagreement between people **2** [C;U] lack of musical HARMONY ~**ant** /dɪsˈkɔːdənt‖-ɔːr-/ *adj*

dis·co·theque /ˈdɪskətek, ˌdɪskəˈtek/ *n fml for* DISCO

dis·count¹ /ˈdɪskaʊnt/ *n* reduction in cost

dis·count² /dɪsˈkaʊnt‖ˈdɪskaʊnt/ *vt* regard (information) as unimportant or untrue

dis·cour·age /dɪsˈkʌrɪdʒ‖-ˈkɜːr-/ *vt* **1** take away hope from **2** persuade not to do something ~**ment** *n* [C;U]

dis·course /ˈdɪskɔːs‖-ɔːrs/ *n* [C;U] *fml* serious conversation or speech

dis·cour·te·ous /dɪsˈkɜːtiəs‖-ɜːr-/ *adj* not polite ~**ly** *adv*

dis·cov·er /dɪsˈkʌvəʳ/ *vt* find; find out ~**er** *n* ~**y** *n* **1** [U] discovering **2** [C] something found

dis·cred·it /dɪsˈkredət/ *vt* stop people from believing in ~**able** *adj* bringing shame

di·screet /dɪˈskriːt/ *adj* not saying too much; showing good sense and judgment: *a discreet silence* ~**ly** *adv*

di·screp·an·cy /dɪˈskrepənsi/ *n* difference between amounts, etc.

di·screte /dɪˈskriːt/ *adj fml* separate; not continuous

di·scre·tion /dɪˈskreʃən/ *n* [U] **1** being discreet **2** ability to decide what to do: *use your own discretion* ~**ary** *adj*

di·scrim·i·nate /dɪˈskrɪməneɪt/ *v* **1** *vi/t* recognize a difference **2** **discriminate against/in favour of** treat worse/better than others **-nating** *adj* (of a person) able to choose the best by seeing small differences **-natory** /-nətəri‖-nətɔːri/ *adj* **-nation** /dɪˌskrɪməˈneɪʃən/ *n* [U] — see also POSITIVE DISCRIMINATION

dis·cus /ˈdɪskəs/ *n* heavy plate to be thrown as a sport

di·scuss /dɪˈskʌs/ *vt* talk about ~**ion** /-ˈskʌʃən/ *n* [C;U]

dis·dain /dɪsˈdeɪn/ *n* [U] *fml* CONTEMPT ♦ *vt* regard with disdain; be too proud for: *She disdained to answer.* **~ful** *adj*

dis·ease /dɪˈziːz/ *n* [C;U] illness **-eased** *adj*: ill

dis·em·bark /ˌdɪsəmˈbɑːk‖-ɑːrk/ *vi/t* (cause to) leave a ship

dis·em·bod·ied /ˌdɪsəmˈbɒdid‖-ˈbɑː-/ *adj* existing with no body: *a disembodied voice*

dis·en·chant·ed /ˌdɪsənˈtʃɑːntɪd‖-ˈtʃænt-/ *adj* having lost belief in the value of something **-ment** *n* [U]

dis·en·fran·chise /ˌdɪsɪnˈfræntʃaɪz/ *vt* DISFRANCHISE **~ment** /-tʃɪz-‖-tʃaɪz-/ *n* [U]

dis·en·gage /ˌdɪsənˈgeɪdʒ/ *vi/t* **1** come loose and separate **2** stop fighting

dis·en·tan·gle /ˌdɪsənˈtæŋgəl/ *vt* make free from knots: (fig.) *disentangle truth from lies*

dis·fa·vour /dɪsˈfeɪvəʳ/ *n* [U] *fml* dislike; disapproval

dis·fig·ure /dɪsˈfɪgəʳ‖-ˈfɪgjər/ *vt* spoil the beauty of **~ment** *n* [C;U]

dis·fran·chise /dɪsˈfræntʃaɪz/ *vt* take away the right to vote from **~ment** /-tʃɪz-‖-tʃaɪz-/ *n* [U]

dis·gorge /dɪsˈgɔːdʒ‖-ɔːr-/ *vi/t* (cause to) flow out

dis·grace /dɪsˈgreɪs/ *n* [S;U] (cause of) shame or loss of respect ♦ *vt* bring disgrace to **~ful** *adj*

dis·grun·tled /dɪsˈgrʌntld/ *adj* annoyed and disappointed

dis·guise /dɪsˈgaɪz/ *vt* change the appearance of, to hide or deceive ♦ *n* **1** [C] something worn to disguise someone **2** [U] being disguised

dis·gust /dɪsˈgʌst, dɪz-/ *n* [U] dislike caused esp. by a bad smell or taste or bad behaviour ♦ *vt* cause disgust in **~ingly** *adv*

dish¹ /dɪʃ/ *n* **1** large plate **2** cooked food of one kind **3** *infml, esp. BrE* good-looking person

dish² *v*

dish out *phr vt* **1** serve out to several people **2 dish it out** punish or express disapproval of someone else, esp. thoughtlessly or unjustly

dish up *phr vi/t* put (a meal) into dishes

dis·heart·en /dɪsˈhɑːtn‖-ɑːr-/ *vt* discourage

di·shev·elled /dɪˈʃevəld/ *adj* (esp. of someone's hair) untidy

dis·hon·est /dɪsˈɒnəst‖-ˈɑː-/ *adj* not honest **~ly** *adv* **~y** *n* [U]

dis·hon·our *BrE* ‖ **-or** *AmE*/dɪsˈɒnəʳ‖-ˈɑː-/ *n* [S;U] *fml* (person or thing bringing) loss of honour ♦ *vt* **1** bring dishonour to **2** cause (a cheque) to BOUNCE (3) **~able** *adj*

dish·wash·er /ˈdɪʃˌwɒʃəʳ‖-ˌwɔː-, -ˌwɑː-/ *n* machine that washes dishes

dis·il·lu·sion /ˌdɪsəˈluːʒən/ *vt* tell the unpleasant truth to **~ed** *adj* **~ment** *n* [U]

dis·in·cen·tive /ˌdɪsɪnˈsentɪv/ *n* something that discourages effort

dis·in·clined /ˌdɪsɪnˈklaɪnd/ *adj* unwilling

dis·in·fect /ˌdɪsɪnˈfekt/ *vt* make (things and places) free from infection **~ant** *n* chemical that disinfects

dis·in·gen·u·ous /ˌdɪsɪnˈdʒenjuəs/ *adj* not sincere; slightly dishonest

dis·in·her·it /ˌdɪsɪnˈherɪt/ *vt* take away the right to INHERIT from

dis·in·te·grate /dɪsˈɪntɪgreɪt/ *vi/t* break up into small pieces **-gration** /dɪsˌɪntɪˈgreɪʃən/ *n* [U]

dis·in·terest·ed /dɪsˈɪntrəstɪd/ *adj* not influenced by personal advantage

dis·in·vest·ment /ˌdɪsɪnˈvestmənt/ *n* [U] reduction of INVESTMENT by selling things, etc.

dis·joint·ed /dɪsˈdʒɔɪntɪd/ *adj* (of words, ideas, etc.) not well connected **~ly** *adv*

disk /dɪsk/ *n* **1** *AmE for* DISC **2** *also* **disc** — flat circular piece of plastic used for storing computer information

disk drive /ˈ· ·/ *n* piece of electrical equipment used for passing information to and from a DISK (2)

dis·like /dɪsˈlaɪk/ *vt* not like ♦ *n* [C;U]: *have a dislike of cats*

dis·lo·cate /ˈdɪsləkeɪt‖-loʊ-/ *vt* **1** put (a bone) out of place **2** put (traffic, plans, etc.) into disorder **-cation** /ˌdɪsləˈkeɪʃən‖-loʊ-/ *n* [C;U]

dis·lodge /dɪsˈlɒdʒ‖dɪsˈlɑːdʒ/ *vt* force out of a position

dis·loy·al /dɪsˈlɔɪəl/ *adj* not loyal **~ly** *adv* **~ty** *n* [C;U]

dis·mal /ˈdɪzməl/ *adj* sad; hopeless **~ly** *adv*

dis·man·tle /dɪsˈmæntl/ *vt* take to pieces

dis·may /dɪsˈmeɪ/ *vt, n* [U] (fill with) great fear and hopelessness

dis·mem·ber /dɪsˈmembəʳ/ *vt* cut or tear (a body) apart

dis·miss /dɪsˈmɪs/ *vt* **1** *fml* remove from a job **2** send away **3** refuse to think seriously about **4** (of a judge) stop (a court case) **~al** *n* [C;U] **~ive** *adj* CONTEMPTUOUS

dis·o·be·di·ent /ˌdɪsəˈbiːdiənt, ˌdɪsəʊ-/ *adj* refusing to obey **~ly** *adv* **-ence** *n* [U]

dis·o·bey /ˌdɪsəˈbeɪ, ˌdɪsəʊ-/ *vi/t* not obey

dis·or·der /dɪsˈɔːdəʳ‖-ˈɔːr-/ *n* **1** [U] confusion **2** [C;U] public violence **3** [C;U] illness of the body or mind ♦ *vt* put into disorder **~ly** *adj*

dis·or·gan·ize ‖ *also* **-ise** *BrE* /dɪsˈɔːgənaɪz‖-ˈɔːr-/ *vt* throw into confusion

dis·or·i·en·tate /dɪsˈɔːriənteɪt/ also **disorient** /-riənt/ — vt cause (someone) to lose sense of time, direction, etc.; confuse

dis·own /dɪsˈəʊn/ vt say that one has no connection with

di·spar·age /dɪˈspærɪdʒ/ vt speak without respect of **-agingly** adv

dis·pa·rate /ˈdɪspərət/ adj fml that cannot be compared; quite different **-rity** /dɪˈspærəti/ n [C;U] inequality

dis·pas·sion·ate /dɪsˈpæʃənət/ adj calm and fair; not taking sides **~ly** adv

dis·patch , **despatch**/dɪˈspætʃ/ vt 1 send: dispatch invitations 2 finish (work, etc.) quickly 3 kill officially ♦ n 1 [C] message sent 2 [U] sending 3 [U] speed and effectiveness

di·spel /dɪˈspel/ vt -ll- drive away; scatter

dis·pen·sa·tion /ˌdɪspənˈseɪʃən, -pen-/ n 1 [C;U] permission to disobey a rule 2 [U] fml dispensing

di·spense /dɪˈspens/ vt 1 give out to people 2 prepare (medicines) **dispensary** n place where medicines are dispensed

dispense with phr vt do without

di·sperse /dɪˈspɜːs‖-ɜːrs/ vi/t scatter in different directions **dispersal** n [U]

di·spir·ited /dɪˈspɪrɪtəd/ adj lit discouraged

dis·place /dɪsˈpleɪs/ vt 1 force out of the proper place 2 take the place of **~ment** n [U]

di·splay /dɪˈspleɪ/ vt show ♦ n [C;U]: a display of skill

dis·please /dɪsˈpliːz/ vt fml annoy **-pleasure** /-ˈpleʒər/ n [U] annoyance

dis·po·sa·ble /dɪˈspəʊzəbəl/ adj 1 to be used once and then thrown away: disposable plates 2 able to be used: disposable income

dis·pos·al /dɪˈspəʊzəl/ n [U] 1 removal 2 **at one's disposal** for one to use

di·spose /dɪˈspəʊz/ v **dispose of** phr vt get rid of

dis·posed /dɪˈspəʊzd/ adj 1 willing: I don't feel disposed to help. 2 having a tendency

dis·po·si·tion /ˌdɪspəˈzɪʃən/ n fml person's natural character

dis·pos·sess /ˌdɪspəˈzes/ vt fml take property away from

dis·pro·por·tion·ate /ˌdɪsprəˈpɔːʃənət‖-ɔːr-/ adj too much or too little **~ly** adv

dis·prove /dɪsˈpruːv/ vt prove to be false

di·spute /dɪˈspjuːt/ v 1 vi/t argue (about) 2 vt question the truth of 3 vt struggle over or about (esp. in defence): disputed territory ♦ n [C;U] argument; quarrel

dis·qual·i·fy /dɪsˈkwɒlɪfaɪ‖-ˈkwɑː-/ vt make unfit to do something **-fication** /dɪsˌkwɒlɪfəˈkeɪʃən‖-ˌkwɑː-/ n [C;U]

dis·qui·et /dɪsˈkwaɪət/ vt fml make anxious ♦ n [U] anxiety

dis·re·gard /ˌdɪsrɪˈɡɑːd‖-ɑːrd/ vt pay no attention to ♦ n [U] lack of proper attention

dis·re·pair /ˌdɪsrɪˈpeər/ n [U] need for repair

dis·rep·u·ta·ble /dɪsˈrepjʊtəbəl/ adj having a bad REPUTATION

dis·re·pute /ˌdɪsrɪˈpjuːt/ n [U] loss of people's good opinion

dis·re·spect /ˌdɪsrɪˈspekt/ n [U] rudeness **~ful** adj

dis·rupt /dɪsˈrʌpt/ vt throw into disorder **~ive** adj: disruptive influence **~ion** /-ˈrʌpʃən/ n [C;U]

dis·sat·is·fy /dɪˈsætəsfaɪ, dɪsˈsæ-/ vt fail to satisfy; displease: a dissatisfied customer **-faction** /ˌdɪˌsætəsˈfækʃən, dɪsˌsæ-/ n [U]

dis·sect /dɪˈsekt, daɪ-/ vt cut up (a body) so as to study it **~ion** /-ˈsekʃən/ n [C;U]

dis·sem·i·nate /dɪˈsemɪneɪt/ vt fml spread (ideas, etc.) widely **-nation** /dɪˌsemɪˈneɪʃən/ n [U]

dis·sen·sion /dɪˈsenʃən/ n [C;U] disagreement; argument

dis·sent /dɪˈsent/ vi disagree with an opinion ♦ n [U] refusal to agree **~er** n

dis·ser·ta·tion /ˌdɪsəˈteɪʃən‖ˌdɪsər-/ n long (written) account of a subject

dis·ser·vice /dɪˈsɜːvɪs, dɪsˈsɜː-‖-ɜːr-/ n [U] harm or harmful action

dis·si·dent /ˈdɪsɪdənt/ n, adj (person) who disagrees: political dissidents

dis·sim·i·lar /dɪˈsɪmələr, dɪsˈsɪ-/ adj not similar

dis·si·pat·ed /ˈdɪsɪpeɪtəd/ adj wasting one's life in foolish or dangerous pleasure

dis·so·ci·ate /dɪˈsəʊʃieɪt, -sieɪt/ also **disassociate** — n separate in one's mind **-ation** /dɪˌsəʊʃiˈeɪʃən, siˈeɪʃən/ n [U]

dis·so·lute /ˈdɪsəluːt/ n, adj (person) who leads a bad or immoral life **~ly** adv **~ness** n [U]

dis·so·lu·tion /ˌdɪsəˈluːʃən/ n [U] breaking up of a group

dis·solve /dɪˈzɒlv‖dɪˈzɑːlv/ vi/t 1 make (a solid) become liquid 2 cause (a group) to break up: dissolve Parliament 3 fade out or away gradually: his strength/the clouds dissolved 4 lose one's self-control under the influence of strong feeling: dissolve into tears/ laughter

dis·so·nance /ˈdɪsənəns/ n 1 [C;U] combination of musical notes which do not sound pleasant together 2 [S;U] lack of agreement between beliefs and actions **-nant** adj

dis-suade /dɪ'sweɪd/ vt persuade not to –**suasion** /-'sweɪʒən/ n [U]

dis-tance /'dɪstəns/ n 1 [C;U] separation in space between places 2 [S] distant place: *watch from a distance* 3 **go the distance** (in sports) keep playing, etc. till the end of the match 4 **keep one's distance** stay far enough away 5 **keep someone at a distance** treat someone without much friendliness — see also MIDDLE DISTANCE ♦ vt separate (esp. oneself) esp. in the mind or feelings

dis-tant /'dɪstənt/ adj 1 far off 2 not close: *distant relations* 3 unfriendly ~**ly** adv

dis-taste /dɪs'teɪst/ n [U] dislike ~**ful** adj unpleasant

dis-tem-per /dɪ'stempər/ n [U] water-based paint for walls 2 infectious disease of animals

dis-tend /dɪ'stend/ vt/i fml swell

dis-til ‖ also –**till** AmE /dɪ'stɪl/ vt -**ll**- 1 make (a liquid) into gas and then make the gas into liquid, as when making alcoholic drinks 2 get or take the most important part(s) of (a book, an idea, etc.) ~**lery** n place where WHISKY, etc. is distilled ~**lation** /ˌdɪstə'leɪʃən/ n [C;U]

dis-tinct /dɪ'stɪŋkt/ adj 1 different; separate 2 clearly noticed ~**ly** adv

dis-tinc-tion /dɪ'stɪŋkʃən/ n 1 [C;U] difference 2 [S;U] unusual excellence 3 [C] mark of honour –**tive** /-tɪv/ adj showing a difference –**tively** adv

dis-tin-guish /dɪ'stɪŋgwɪʃ/ v 1 vt/i recognize a difference 2 vi/t see clearly 3 vt make different 4 **distinguish oneself** perform noticeably well ~**able** adj ~**ed** adj excellent; famous

dis-tort /dɪ'stɔːt/-ɔːrt/ vt 1 twist out of the natural shape 2 give a false account of ~**ion** /-'stɔːʃən‖-ɔːr-/ n [C;U]

dis-tract /dɪ'strækt/ vt take (someone's attention) away ~**ed** adj anxious and confused ~**ion** /-'strækʃən/ n 1 [C] amusement, etc., that distracts 2 [U] anxious confusion

dis-traught /dɪ'strɔːt/ adj very anxious and troubled

dis-tress /dɪ'stres/ n [U] 1 great suffering or sorrow 2 serious danger ♦ vt cause suffering to: *distressing news*

dis-trib-ute /dɪ'strɪbjuːt/ vt 1 give out: *distribute prizes* 2 scatter –**utor** n 1 person who distributes goods 2 instrument that distributes electric current in an engine –**ution** /ˌdɪstrə'bjuːʃən/ n [C;U]

dis-trict /'dɪstrɪkt/ n area of a country or city

dis-trust /dɪs'trʌst/ vt have no trust in ♦ n [S;U] lack of trust ~**ful** adj ~**fully** adv

dis-turb /dɪ'stɜːb‖-ɜːrb/ vt 1 interrupt 2 worry: *disturbing news* ~**ance** n [C;U] 1 act of disturbing 2 noisy disorder ~**ed** adj having or showing signs of an illness of the mind

dis-u-ni-ty /dɪs'juːnəti/ n [U] disagreement; quarrelling

dis-use /dɪs'juːs/ n [U] state of no longer being used: *to fall into disuse* –**used** /ˌdɪs'juːzd◂/ adj

ditch /dɪtʃ/ n passage cut for water to flow through ♦ vt sl get rid of

dith-er /'dɪðər/ vi be unable to decide **dither** n [S]

dit-to /'dɪtəʊ/ n -tos the same

dit-ty /'dɪti/ n short simple song

di-van /dɪ'væn‖'daɪvæn/ n bed with no back

dive /daɪv/ vi **dived** or **dove** /dəʊv/ AmE, **dived** 1 jump head first into water 2 go under water 3 (of a plane or bird) go down steeply and swiftly 4 go down quickly: *dive under the table* 5 enter quickly into some matter or activity ♦ n 1 act of diving 2 not very respectable club, etc. 3 **take a dive** sl agree to lose a match dishonestly **diver** n person who dives, or works on the sea bottom

di-verge /daɪ'vɜːdʒ, də-‖-ɜːr-/ vi separate; get further apart **divergence** n [C;U]

di-verse /daɪ'vɜːs‖də'vɜːrs, daɪ-/ adj of different kinds **diversity** /daɪ'vɜːsəti, də-‖-ɜːr-/ n [S;U] variety

di-ver-si-fy /daɪ'vɜːsəfaɪ‖də'vɜːr-, daɪ-/ vt/i make diverse: *diversify our range of products* –**fication** /daɪˌvɜːsəfə'keɪʃən‖də'vɜːr-, daɪ-/ n [U]

di-ver-sion /daɪ'vɜːʃən, də-‖-ɜːrʒən/ n 1 [C;U] diverting 2 [C] something that amuses people ~**ary** adj intended to DIVERT: *diversionary tactics*

di-vert /daɪ'vɜːt, də-‖-ɜːr-/ vt turn to another direction: *divert a river/my attention*

di-vest /daɪ'vest, də-/ vt take away from someone

di-vide /də'vaɪd/ vi/t 1 separate into parts 2 find out how many times one number is contained in another 3 be an important cause of disagreement between ♦ n something that divides **dividers** n [P] instrument for measuring lines, angles, etc.

div-i-dend /'dɪvɪdənd, -dend/ n 1 part of profit that is divided among SHAREHOLDERS 2 **pay dividends** produce an advantage

di-vine[1] /də'vaɪn/ adj 1 of God or a god 2 excellent **divinity** /də'vɪnəti/ n 1 [U] quality or state of being divine 2 [C] god or goddess 3 [U] THEOLOGY

divine² *vi/t fml* find out; guess 2 find (water or minerals) underground using a Y-shaped stick **diviner** n

div·ing-board /'daɪvɪŋbɔːd‖-bɔːrd/ n high board off which people DIVE (1) into the water

di·vis·i·ble /dɪ̆'vɪzɪ̆bəl/ adj that can be divided

di·vi·sion /dɪ̆'vɪʒən/ n 1 [U] separation or sharing 2 [C] one of the parts into which a whole is divided: *the firm's export division* 3 [C] something that separates 4 [U] disagreement 5 [U] process of dividing numbers ~**al** adj

di·vi·sive /dɪ̆'vaɪsɪv/ adj causing disunity

di·vorce /dɪ̆'vɔːs‖-ɔːrs/ n 1 [C;U] legal ending of a marriage 2 [C] separation ♦ v 1 vt/i end a marriage by law 2 vt separate completely **divorcée** /dɪ̆'vɔːsiː‖dɪ̆,vɔːr'seɪ, -'siː/ **divorcé** /dɪ̆'vɔːsiː, -seɪ‖-ɔːr/ masc. — n divorced person

di·vulge /daɪ'vʌldʒ, dɪ̆-/ vt fml tell (a secret)

DIY /,diː aɪ 'waɪ/ abbrev. for: DO-IT-YOURSELF

diz·zy /'dɪzi/ adj feeling as if things are going round and round 2 causing this feeling: *dizzy heights* 3 silly ~**zily** adv ~**ziness** n [U]

DJ /,diː 'dʒeɪ/ n 1 DISC JOCKEY 2 DINNER JACKET

DNA /,diː en 'eɪ/ n [U] acid which carries GENETIC information in a cell

do¹ /duː/ v aux did /dɪd/, done /dʌn/ 1 (used with another verb): *Do you like it?*|*He doesn't know.*|*Do be careful!* 2 (used instead of another verb): *He walks faster than I do.*|*She likes it, and so do I.*|*She sings, doesn't she?*

do² v 1 vt perform (an action); work at or produce: *do a sum/one's homework/the cooking/business/one's best/one's duty*|*do* (= study) *Science at school*|*do 80 miles an hour*|*It'll do you good.* 2 vi advance: *do well/badly* b behave: *Do as you're told!* 3 vi/t be enough or suitable (for): *Will £5 do (you)?*|*That will do!* 4 vt sl cheat: *We've been done!* 5 **do well by** treat well 6 **How do you do?** (used when one is introduced to someone) 7 **make do** use (something) even though it may not be perfect or enough 8 **nothing doing** sl no 9 **That does it!** (expression showing that enough, or too much has been done) 10 **What do you do (for a living)?** What is your work?

do away with phr vt 1 cause to end 2 kill or murder (someone or oneself)

do down phr vt 1 cause to feel ashamed or less proud of oneself 2 say bad things about (someone not present)

do for phr vt 1 kill or ruin 2 BrE infml keep house or do cleaning for (someone) 3 **What will you do for (something)?** What arrangements will you make for (something)?: *What will you do for food?*

do in phr vt 1 kill 2 tire completely

do out of phr vt cause to lose, by cheating

do over phr vt sl attack and wound

do up phr vt 1 fasten or wrap 2 repair; improve

do with phr vt 1 need; want 2 cause (oneself) to spend time doing: *I don't know what to do with myself since you've gone.* 3 (in questions with 'what') to do with regard to: *'What have you done with my pen?'* (= where have you put it?) 4 **have/be to do with** be connected with

do without phr vi/t succeed without

do³ n infml 1 esp. BrE a big party 2 **dos and don'ts** rules of behaviour

do·cile /'dəʊsaɪl‖'dɑːsəl/ adj quiet and easily taught

dock¹ /dɒk‖dɑːk/ n 1 place where ships are loaded and unloaded, or repaired: *London's dockland* 2 place in a court of law where prisoner stands ♦ vi/t 1 (cause to) sail into, or remain at, a DOCK (1) 2 (cause spacecraft) to join in space ~**er** n person who works at a dock, loading and unloading ships

dock² vt cut off the end of: (fig.) *dock someone's wages*

dock·yard /'dɒkjɑːd‖'dɑːkjɑːrd/ n SHIPYARD

doc·tor /'dɒktər‖'dɑːk-/ n 1 person trained in medicine 2 person holding one of the highest university degrees ♦ vt 1 change dishonestly: *doctor the accounts* 2 make (an animal) unable to breed

doc·tor·ate /'dɒktərɪt‖'dɑːk-/ n degree of a DOCTOR (2)

doc·tri·naire /,dɒktrɪ'neər‖,dɑːk-/ adj not questioning a doctrine; not practical: *doctrinaire socialism*

doc·trine /'dɒktrɪn‖'dɑːk-/ n [C;U] belief; set of teachings ~**trinal** /dɒk'traɪnl‖'dɑːktrɪnəl/ adj

doc·u·ment /'dɒkjḁmənt‖'dɑːk-/ n paper giving information, proof, etc. ♦ /-ment/ vt prove or support with documents ~**ation** /,dɒkjḁmən'teɪʃən, -men-‖,dɑːk-/ n [U] documents used as proof

doc·u·men·ta·ry /,dɒkjḁ'mentəri‖,dɑːk-/ adj 1 of documents 2 presenting facts through art ♦ n film, broadcast, etc., presenting facts

dod·dle /'dɒdl‖'dɑːdl/ n infml BrE something that is very easy to do

dodge /dɒdʒ‖dɑːdʒ/ v 1 vi/t avoid (something) by suddenly moving aside 2 vt avoid dishonestly ♦ n clever trick **dodger** n: tax dodger **dodgy** adj risky

doe /dəʊ/ n female of esp. the deer, rat, and rabbit

does /dəz; strong dʌz/ v 3rd pers. sing. pres. of DO

does·n't /'dʌzənt/ v short for: does not

dog /dɒg‖dɔːg/ n 1 common 4-legged animal, useful to humans 2 male of this and similar animals 3 **a dog's life** a very unhappy life 4 **let sleeping dogs lie** leave something alone — see also TOP DOG ♦ vt -gg- follow closely; PURSUE: dogged by bad luck **dogs** n [P] 1 dog races 2 **go to the dogs** be ruined

dog col·lar /'· ,··/ n 1 neckband for a dog 2 infml priest's stiff collar

dog-eared /'· ·/ adj (of pages) bent down with use

dog-eat-dog /,· · '·/adj having, showing or marked by cruel self-interest

dog·ged /'dɒgəd‖'dɔː-/ adj refusing to give up; determined ~**ly** adv

dog·house /'dɒghaʊs‖'dɔːg-/ n **in the doghouse** in a state of disfavour or shame

dog·ma /'dɒgmə‖'dɔːgmə, 'dɑːgmə/ n [C;U] (religious) belief to be accepted without reasoning ~**tic** /dɒg'mætɪk‖dɔːg-, dɑːg-/ adj trying to force one's beliefs on other people ~**tically** /-klɪ/ adv

do-good·er /,· '··‖'· ,··/n person who tries to do good things for others

dogs·bod·y /'dɒgz,bɒdi‖ 'dɔːgz,bɑːdi/ n BrE person in a low position who does the dull work

dog-tired /,· '·◄/ adj very tired

do-it-yourself /,· ··'·/n [U] doing repairs, painting the house, etc., oneself, rather than paying workmen

dol·drums /'dɒldrəmz‖'doʊl-, 'dɑːl-, 'dɔːl-/ n [P] **in the doldrums** sad and dull

dole[1] /dəʊl/ n **on the dole** receiving money from the government because one is unemployed

dole[2] v **dole out** phr vt give in small shares

dole·ful /'dəʊlfəl/ adj unhappy ~**ly** adv

doll[1] /dɒl‖dɑːl, dɔːl/ n 1 small toy figure of a person 2 AmE sl person that one likes

doll[2] v **doll up** phr vt dress prettily

dol·lar /'dɒləʳ‖'dɑː-/ n 1 unit of money, as used in the US, Canada, and other countries 2 piece of paper, coin, etc., of this value

dol·lop /'dɒləp‖'dɑː-/ n shapeless mass, esp. of food

dol·phin /'dɒlfɪn‖'dɑːl-, 'dɔːl-/ n sea-animal, two to three metres long, which swims in groups

do·main /də'meɪn, dəʊ-/ n 1 area of interest or knowledge 2 land controlled by one ruler

dome /dəʊm/ n rounded roof **domed** adj like or covered with a dome

do·mes·tic /də'mestɪk/ adj 1 of the house, home, or family 2 not foreign: domestic policies 3 (of animals) not wild ♦ n house servant ~**ally** /-kli/ adv

dom·i·cile /'dɒmɪsaɪl‖'dɑː-, 'dəʊ-/ n fml place where one lives **domicile** vt

dom·i·nant /'dɒmɪnənt‖'dɑː-/ adj most noticeable or important; dominating –**nance** n [U] controlling influence; importance

dom·i·nate /'dɒmɪneɪt‖'dɑː-/ vi/t 1 have power (over); control 2 have the most important place (in) 3 rise or be higher than: The castle dominated the whole town. –**nation** /,dɒmɪ'neɪʃən‖ ,dɑː-/ n [U]

dom·i·neer /,dɒmɪ'nɪəʳ‖,dɑː-/ vi try to control others unpleasantly

do·min·ion /də'mɪnjən/ n 1 [U] lit power to rule 2 [C] land under one government

dom·i·no /'dɒmɪnəʊ‖'dɑː-/ n -noes small flat piece of wood with spots on it, used with others in a game (**dominoes**)

domino ef·fect /'··· ·,·/n [S] situation in which one event causes similar ones to happen one after another

don /dɒn‖dɑːn/ n BrE university teacher

do·nate /dəʊ'neɪt‖'doʊneɪt/ vt give (money, etc.), esp. for a good purpose **donation** /dəʊ'neɪʃən/ n [C;U]

done /dʌn/ v 1 past p. of DO 2 finished esp. BrE socially acceptable

don·key /'dɒŋki‖'dɑːŋki/ n 1 animal like a small horse, with long ears 2 fool 3 **donkey's years** a very long time

do·nor /'dəʊnəʳ/ n person who gives or donates: blood donor

don't /dəʊnt/ v short for: do not

doo·dle /'duːdl/ vi/t draw lines, figures, etc., aimlessly while thinking of something else **doodle** n

doom /duːm/ n 1 unavoidable destruction 2 **doom and gloom** hopelessness ~**ed** DESTINED to something bad

Dooms·day /'duːmzdeɪ/ n 1 end of the world 2 **till Doomsday** forever

door /dɔːʳ/ n 1 thing that closes an entrance: bedroom/cupboard/car door 2 DOORWAY 3 (in some fixed phrases) house or building: live next door/2 doors away 4 **be on the door** have some duty at the door, such as collecting tickets 5 **by the back door** secretly or by a trick 6 **shut/close the door to/on** make impossible 7 **out of doors** OUTDOORS

door·step /'dɔːstep‖'dɔːr-/ n step in front of a door

door·step·ping /'dɔː,stepɪŋ‖'dɔːr-/ n, adj (practice of) causing people inconvenience in their homes, etc., in order to find stories for newspapers

door·way /'dɔːweɪ‖'dɔːr-/ n opening for a door

dope /dəʊp/ n 1 [U] harmful drug 2 [C] fool ♦ vt give dope to ~y adj 1 sleepy and unable to think clearly, (as if) caused by drugs 2 stupid

dor·mant /'dɔːmənt‖'dɔːr-/ adj inactive: dormant volcano

dor·mi·to·ry /'dɔːmətəri‖ 'dɔːrmətɔːri/ n bedroom for several people

dor·mouse /'dɔːmaʊs‖'dɔːr-/ n -mice /-maɪs/ small mouse

dos·age /'dəʊsɪdʒ/ n fml amount of a dose

dose /dəʊs/ n measured amount of medicine to be taken at a time ♦ vt give medicine to

doss /dɒs‖dɑːs/ v doss down phr vi sl, esp. BrE sleep, esp. not in a proper bed ~er n 1 person who sleeps in dosshouses 2 infml lazy person

doss·house /'dɒshaʊs‖'dɑːs-/ n -houses /-haʊz/ esp. BrE very cheap lodging-house

dos·si·er /'dɒsieɪ‖'dɔːsjeɪ, 'dɑː-/ n set of papers containing facts about a person or subject

dot /dɒt‖dɑːt/ n 1 small spot 2 on the dot at the exact moment — see also YEAR DOT ♦ vt -tt- 1 mark with a dot 2 cover with dots 3 dotted about scattered 4 sign on the dotted line agree to something quickly and unconditionally ~ty adj slightly mad

do·tage /'dəʊtɪdʒ/ n [U] weakness of the mind caused by old age

dote /dəʊt/ v dote on phr vt be too fond of

doub·le¹ /'dʌbəl/ adj 1 with 2 parts or uses: double doors | a double meaning 2 for 2 people: a double bed ♦ adv, predeterminer twice: cloth folded double | buy double the amount **doubly** adv twice as: doubly careful

double² n 1 [C;U] twice the amount: I'll have a double (vodka) please. 2 [C] person who looks just like another 3 at the double quickly **doubles** n [P] match between 2 pairs of players

double³ v 1 vi/t make or become twice as much 2 vt fold in half

double as phr vt have as a second use or job

double back phr vi return along the same path

double up phr vi/t bend (the body) at the waist: doubled up with pain

double bass /,dʌbəl 'beɪs/ n largest stringed musical instrument of the VIOLIN family, with a very deep sound

double-breast·ed /,··'···◄/ adj (of a coat) crossing over in front, with 2 rows of buttons

double-check /,·· '·/ vi/t examine (something) twice for exactness or quality

double chin /,·· '·/n fold of loose skin between the face and neck

double-cross /,·· '·/ vt cheat; BETRAY ~er n

double-deal·er /,·· '··/n dishonest person –ing adj, n [U]

double-deck·er /,·· '···◄/ n bus with 2 levels

double-dutch /,·· '·/n [U] speech or writing that one cannot understand

double-glaz·ing /,·· '··/n [U] 2 thicknesses of glass in a window –glaze vt

double-joint·ed /,·· '··◄/ adj having joints that move backwards as well as forwards

double-quick /,·· '·◄/ adj, adv very quick(ly)

doubt /daʊt/ vt 1 feel uncertain about 2 consider unlikely: I doubt he'll come. ♦ n 1 [C;U] (feeling of) uncertainty 2 in doubt in a condition of uncertainty 3 no doubt probably ~ful adj 1 uncertain 2 not likely ~less adv 1 without doubt 2 probably

dough /dəʊ/ n [U] 1 mixture for making bread 2 sl money

dough·nut /'dəʊnʌt/ n ring-shaped cake cooked in fat

dour /dʊəʳ‖'daʊər, dʊər/ adj hard and cold in one's nature; unfriendly ~ly adv

douse /daʊs/ vt 1 throw water over 2 put out (a light)

dove¹ /dʌv/ n 1 kind of PIGEON 2 person in favour of peace

dove² /dəʊv/ v past t. (esp. AmE) of DIVE

dove·tail /'dʌvteɪl/ n close-fitting joint for two pieces esp. of wood ♦ v 1 vt join two pieces of wood with a dovetail 2 vi fit skilfully or perfectly together

dow·a·ger /'daʊədʒəʳ/ n grand old lady

dow·dy /'daʊdi/ adj 1 dully dressed 2 (of clothes) dull

down¹ /daʊn/ adv 1 to or at a lower level: The sun's going down. | Please sit down. 2 to the south: come down from Scotland 3 on paper: write/copy it down 4 from the past: jewels handed down in the family 5 (shows reduction): Profits are down. | Turn the radio down. 6 Down with ... Let's get rid of ... ♦ prep 1 to or at a lower level on: run down the hill | swim down the river 2 along: They live down the road. 3 to: I'm just going down to the shops. ♦ adj 1 at a lower level, esp.

lying on the ground: *The telephone wires are down.* | *Prices are down.* **2** directed down: *the down escalator* **3** finished: *8 down and 2 to go* **4** sad **5** not working: *The computer/phone is down.* **6 down on** having a low opinion or dislike for ♦ *vt* **1** knock down; defeat **2** drink quickly ~**er** *n sl* **1** drug that reduces activity **2** experience or state of affairs which is saddening

down² *n* [U] soft feathers or hair ~**y** *adj*

down-and-out /ˌ· · '·◄/ *adj, n* (person who is) suffering from bad fortune, lack of money, etc.

down-cast /'daʊnkɑːst‖-kæst/ *adj* **1** downhearted **2** (of eyes) looking down

down-fall /'daʊnfɔːl/ *n* sudden ruin

down-grade /'daʊngreɪd, ˌdaʊn'greɪd‖'daʊngreɪd/ *vt* reduce to a lower position

down-heart-ed /ˌdaʊn'hɑːtɪd◄‖-ɑːr-/ *adj* low in spirits; sad

down-hill /ˌdaʊn'hɪl◄/ *adj, adv* **1** down a slope **2 go downhill** become worse

Down-ing Street /'daʊnɪŋ striːt/ *n* the government of Great Britain

down pay-ment /ˌ· '··/ *n* part of the full price paid at the time of buying, with the rest to be paid later

down-pour /'daʊnpɔːr/ *n* heavy fall of rain

down-right /'daʊnraɪt/ *adj* **1** plain; honest **2** (of something bad) complete ♦ *adv*: *downright rude*

downs /daʊnz/ *n* [P] low grassy hills

down-stairs /ˌdaʊn'steəz◄‖-eərz/ *adv, adj* on or to a lower floor

down-stream /ˌdaʊn'striːm◄/ *adv, adj* moving with the current of a river

down-time /'daʊntaɪm/ *n* [U] time during which a computer is not operating

down-to-earth /ˌ· · '·◄/ *adj* practical; sensible

down-town /ˌdaʊn'taʊn◄/ *adv, adj* to or in the town centre

down-trod-den /'daʊnˌtrɒdn‖-ˌtrɑː-/ *adj* treated badly by those in power

down-ward /'daʊnwəd‖-wərd/ *adj* going down ~**wards** *adv*

dow-ry /'daʊəri/ *n* property that a woman's father gives to her husband when she marries

doze /dəʊz/ *vi* sleep lightly **doze** *n* [S]

doz-en /'dʌzən/ *determiner, n* **dozen** *or* **dozens 1** twelve **2 talk, speak, etc., nineteen/twenty/forty to the dozen** talk quickly and continuously

Dr *written abbrev. for:* Doctor

drab /dræb/ *adj* dull ~**ness** *n* [U]

draft /drɑːft‖dræft/ *n* **1** first rough plan of something **2** written order for money from a bank **3** *AmE for*

DRAUGHT **4** *AmE for* CONSCRIPTION ♦ *vt* **1** make a DRAFT (1) of **2** *AmE for* CONSCRIPT¹

drafts-man /'drɑːftsmən‖'dræfts-/ **-woman** /-wʊmən/ *fem. n* — **-men** /-mən/ **1** person who drafts new laws **2** *AmE for* DRAUGHTSMAN

drag /dræg/ *v* **1** *vt* pull (something heavy) along **2** *vi* move too slowly: *The meeting dragged on for hours.* **3** *vt* cause to come or go unwillingly: *They dragged me to a party.* **4** *vi* move along while touching the ground: *Her long dress dragged in the dust.* **5** *vt* search the bottom of (water) with a net **6 drag one's feet/heels** act intentionally in a slow or ineffective way ♦ *n* **1** [C] someone or something that makes progress hard **2** [S] dull event or person **3** [U] *sl* the clothing of one sex worn by the other **4** [C] *sl* act of breathing in cigarette smoke

drag on *phr vi* last an unnecessarily long time

drag out *phr v* **1** *vi/t* (cause to) last an unnecessarily long time **2** *vt* force (something) to be told

drag up *phr vt* raise (a subject) unnecessarily

drag-on /'drægən/ *n* **1** imaginary fire-breathing animal **2** fierce old woman

drain /dreɪn/ *vi/t* **1** (cause to) flow away **2** make or become dry by removing liquid: *drain a field* | *wet plates on the draining-board* **3** empty by drinking the contents of **4** make weak and tired ♦ *n* **1** ditch or pipe to carry water away **2** something that uses up money, etc. **3 down the drain** used wastefully or brought to nothing ~**age** *n* [U] system for draining

drain-ing board /'·· ·/ *n* sloping board on which dishes are placed to dry

drake /dreɪk/ *n* male duck

dra-ma /'drɑːmə‖'drɑːmə, 'dræmə/ *n* **1** [C] theatrical play **2** [U] plays as a group **3** [C;U] exciting situation ~**tic** /drə'mætɪk/ *adj* **1** of the theatre **2** exciting ~**tically** /-kli/ *adv* ~**tist** /'dræmətɪst/ *n* writer of plays ~**tize** *vt* **1** turn (a story, etc.) into a play **2** present (facts) in an exciting way

drank /dræŋk/ *v past t. of* DRINK

drape /dreɪp/ *vt* **1** hang (cloth) in folds **2** cause to hang or stretch out loosely or carelessly: *He draped his legs over the arm of the chair.* ~**ry** /'dreɪpəri/ *also* **drapes** *AmE* — *n* [U] cloth, curtains, etc.

dras-tic /'dræstɪk/ *adj* sudden and violent ~**ally** /-kli/ *adv*

draught /drɑːft‖dræft/ *n* **1** current of air **2** amount of liquid swallowed **3** depth of water a ship needs **4** *BrE* round object used in playing a board game (**draughts**) ♦ adj 1 (of beer, etc.) drawn from a barrel 2 (of animals) used for pulling loads ~**y** adj with cold DRAUGHTs (1)

draughts·man /'drɑːftsmən‖ 'dræfts-/ -**woman** /-wumən/ fem. — -**men** /-mən/ n 1 person who draws parts of a new machine or building 2 person who draws well

draw¹ /drɔː/ v drew /druː/, drawn /drɔːn/ 1 vi/t make (pictures) with a pen or pencil 2 vt cause to come, go, or move by pulling: get drawn into an argument | horse-drawn cart | She drew me aside. 3 vt take or pull out: draw his sword | draw £100 from the bank | draw blood (= cause to flow) 4 vt attract: The play drew big crowds. 5 vi move steadily: The car drew ahead. 6 vt make or get by reasoning: draw a comparison/lesson/conclusion 7 vi end a game without either side winning 8 vi/t take (breath) in 9 **draw the curtains/the blinds** close or open the curtains or blinds 10 **draw the line (at)** refuse to do or accept **drawn** adj stretched out of shape: face drawn with sorrow

drawing n 1 [U] art of drawing pictures 2 [C] picture

draw away phr v 1 vi/t move (something) away 2 vi get further and further ahead

draw back phr vi be unwilling to fulfil something

draw in phr vi 1 (of days) become shorter 2 arrive

draw into phr vt encourage (someone unwilling) to join in

draw on phr vt 1 make use of 2 come near in time

draw out phr v 1 vi (of days) become longer 2 vt persuade to talk

draw up phr v 1 vt DRAFT (a plan, etc.) 2 vi (of a vehicle) arrive and stop 3 **draw oneself up** stand up straight

draw² n 1 result with neither side winning 2 LOTTERY 3 person or thing that attracts the public

draw·back /'drɔːbæk/ n disadvantage

drawer /drɔːʳ/ n sliding container in a piece of furniture

drawing room /'·· ·/ n fml LIVING ROOM

drawl /drɔːl/ vi/t speak or say slowly **drawl** n

drawn /drɔːn/ v past p. of DRAW

dread /dred/ vt fear greatly ♦ n [S;U] great fear ~**ful** adj terrible —**fully** adv

dream¹ /driːm/ n 1 image experienced during sleep 2 something hopefully desired 3 something very beautiful — see also WET DREAM ~**less** adj (of sleep) peaceful

dream² vi/t **dreamed** or **dreamt** /dremt/ 1 have a dream 2 imagine (something) 3 **not dream of** refuse to consider ~**er** n 1 person who dreams 2 impractical person ~**y** adj 1 seeming half asleep 2 peaceful and beautiful

dream up phr vt invent (esp. something silly)

drear·y /'drɪəri/ adj sad and dull –**ily** adv –**iness** n [U]

dredge /dredʒ/ vi/t bring up mud, etc. from the bottom of water

dredge up phr vt 1 bring to the surface of water 2 produce or bring up (usu. something unpleasant): dredge up the past

dregs /dregz/ n [P] 1 bits of matter that sink to the bottom of liquid 2 worthless part: the dregs of society

drench /drentʃ/ vt make thoroughly wet

dress /dres/ v 1 vi/t put clothes on 2 vi put on formal evening clothes 3 vt clean and cover (a wound) 4 vt arrange; prepare: dress a salad/a shop window 5 **dressed to kill** dressed in one's best clothes ♦ n 1 [C] woman's one-piece outer garment 2 [U] clothing — see also EVENING DRESS, MORNING DRESS ~**ing** n 1 [C] covering for a wound 2 SAUCE, etc. — see also WINDOW DRESSING ~**y** showy or too ornamental

dress up phr v 1 vi/t put special clothes on 2 vt make (something or someone) seem different or more attractive

dressing gown /'·· ·/ n loose coat for wearing indoors

dressing ta·ble /'·· ,··/ n table with a mirror, in a bedroom

dress·mak·er /'dres,meikəʳ/ n person who makes clothes

drew /druː/ v past t. of DRAW

drib·ble /'drɪbəl/ v 1 vi let SALIVA flow out slowly from the mouth 2 vi/t let (liquid) flow slowly 3 vi/t move (a ball) by many short kicks or strokes **dribble** n

dried /draid/ v past t. and p. of DRY

drift /drɪft/ n 1 mass of something blown together: snowdrifts 2 aimless movement 3 general meaning: the drift of his argument ♦ vi 1 be driven by wind or water 2 move or live aimlessly ~**er** person who DRIFTs (2)

drill¹ /drɪl/ n tool for making holes ♦ vi/t use a drill (on)

drill² n [C;U] training by repeating and following orders: army drill ♦ vi/t do or give drill

dri·ly /'draili/ adv in a DRY¹ (4) manner

drink /drɪŋk/ v **drank** /dræŋk/, **drunk** /drʌŋk/ 1 vi/t swallow (liquid) 2 vi take in (too much) alcohol ♦ n [C;U] 1 liquid to drink 2 alcohol to drink ~**able** adj ~**er** n person who drinks too much alcohol

drink to phr vt wish (someone or something) good health or success

drip /drɪp/ v/i 1 fall or let fall in drops 2 overflow with or as if with liquid: (fig.) She was dripping with diamonds. ◆ n 1 (sound of) liquid falling in drops 2 dull person ~**ping** adj very wet

drip-dry /ˌ· ˈ·◂/ adj (of clothes) that will dry smooth if hung while wet

drive[1] /draɪv/ v drove /drəʊv/, driven /'drɪvən/ 1 vi/t guide (a wheeled vehicle) 2 vt take (someone) in a vehicle 3 vt force (animals, etc.) to go 4 vt be the power for 5 vt send by hitting 6 vt force (someone) into a bad state: The pain's driving me mad. 7 vi (esp. of rain) move violently 8 **be driving at** mean; HINT **driver** n person who drives vehicles or animals

drive[2] n 1 [C] journey in a vehicle 2 [C] road through a park or garden 3 [C] stroke in a ball game 4 [C] CAMPAIGN 5 [U] force of mind: He lacks drive. 6 [C] important natural need which must be fulfilled

drive-in /'· ·◂/n, adj (place) that people can use while remaining in their cars: a drive-in restaurant/cinema/bank

driv-el /'drɪvəl/n [U] nonsense

driz-zle /'drɪzəl/ n [U] fine misty rain **drizzle** v

droll /drəʊl/ adj odd and amusing: a droll person/expression

drom-e-da-ry /'drɒmədəri‖ 'drɑːmədəri/ n camel with one HUMP (1)

drone /drəʊn/ vi make a continuous low dull sound **drone** n [S]

drone on phr vi speak for a long time in an uninteresting manner

drool /druːl/ vi let liquid flow from the mouth: (fig.) Stop drooling (= show pleasure in a foolish way) over that singer.

droop /druːp/ vi hang downwards **droop** n [S]

drop[1] /drɒp‖drɑːp/ n 1 [C] small round mass of liquid 2 [C] small round sweet 3 [S] a distance or fall straight down b fall in quantity: a drop in sales 4 **at the drop of a hat** suddenly **drops** n liquid medicine taken drop by drop

drop[2] v -pp- 1 vi/t fall or let fall 2 vi/t (cause to) become less: The temperature dropped. 3 vt let (someone) get out of a vehicle 4 vt stop; give up: drop a subject 5 vt say or write informally: drop a hint/a note 6 vt leave out (from a team)

drop back/behind phr vi get further away by moving more slowly

drop in/by/round phr vi make an unexpected visit

drop off phr vi 1 get less 2 fall asleep

drop out phr vi stop taking part **dropout** /'drɒpaʊt‖'drɑːp-/ n person who leaves a college, etc., without finishing the course

drop-pings /'drɒpɪŋz‖'drɑː-/ n [P] waste matter from the bowels of animals or birds

dross /drɒs‖drɑːs, drɔːs/ n [U] waste or impure matter

drought /draʊt/ n [C;U] long period of dry weather when there is not enough water

drove[1] /drəʊv/ v past t. of DRIVE

drove[2] n group; crowd: droves of tourists

drown /draʊn/ v 1 vi/t die or kill by being under water 2 vt cover completely with water 3 vt cover up (a sound) with a louder one 4 **drown one's sorrows** drink alcohol in an attempt to forget one's troubles

drowse /draʊz/ vi fall into a light sleep **drowsy** adj sleepy **-sily** adv **-siness** n [U]

drudge /drʌdʒ/ vi do hard dull work ◆ n person who drudges ~**ry** /'drʌdʒəri/ n [U] hard uninteresting work

drug /drʌg/ n 1 medicine 2 substance taken for pleasure: a drug addict ◆ vt -gg- 1 add harmful drugs to 2 give drugs to

drug-store /'drʌgstɔːr/ n AmE PHARMACY that also sells simple meals

drum[1] /drʌm/ n 1 musical instrument made of a skin stretched over a circular frame 2 container, etc., shaped like this: oil drum

drum[2] vi -mm- 1 beat a drum 2 make drumlike noises 3 **drum something into someone** make someone remember something by saying it often ~**mer** n person who plays a drum

drum out phr vt send away formally and disapprovingly

drum up phr vt obtain by continuous effort and esp. by advertising

drunk[1] /drʌŋk/ v past p. of DRINK

drunk[2] adj under the influence of alcohol

drunk[3] n also **drunkard** /'drʌŋkəd‖-ərd/ -- person who is (habitually) drunk

drunk-en /'drʌŋkən/ adj 1 DRUNK[2] 2 resulting from or connected with too much drinking: a drunken sleep ~**ly** adv ~**ness** n [U]

dry[1] /draɪ/ adj 1 not wet: dry clothes/climate 2 (of wine) not sweet 3 not allowing the sale of alcohol 4 amusing without appearing to be so: quietly IRONIC: dry wit 5 uninteresting ~**ly**, **drily** adv ~**ness** n [U]

dry ^{2} *v* *vi/t* make or become dry **2** *vt* preserve (food) by removing liquid ~**er, drier** *n* machine that dries

dry out *phr vi/t* **1** (cause to) give up dependence on alcohol **2** (cause to) become completely dry

dry up *phr vi* **1** (of a supply) stop coming **2** *sl* SHUT UP (1)

dry-clean /ˌ· '·/ *vt* clean (clothes) with chemicals instead of water ~**er's** *n* CLEANER'S ~**ing** *n* [U] **1** action or industry of dry-cleaning clothes **2** clothes that need to be or have just been dry-cleaned

dry dock /'· ·/ *n* place where a ship is held while water is pumped out

dry rot /ˌ· '·/ *n* [U] disease that turns wood into powder

du-al /'djuːəl‖'duːəl/ *adj* having 2 parts; double: *a dual carriageway* ~**ity** /djuˈæltǐ‖duˌ-/ *n* [U]

dub /dʌb/ *vt* **-bb-** **1** give (a name) to **2** change the spoken language of (a film)

du-bi-ous /'djuːbiəs‖'duː-/ *adj* feeling or causing doubt ~**ly** *adv*

duch-ess /'dʌtʃɪs/ *n* **a** wife of a DUKE **b** woman who holds the rank of DUKE in her own right

duch-y /'dʌtʃi/ *n* lands of a DUKE or DUCHESS

duck /dʌk/ *n* **1** [C] common swimming bird **2** [U] its meat **3** [C] *infml, esp. BrE* (used for addressing) a person one likes **4** [C] (in cricket) failure to make any runs at all **5** take to something like a duck to water learn or get used to something very easily ♦ *v* **1** *vi/t* lower (one's head) quickly **2** *vt* push (someone) under water **3** *vt* try to avoid responsibility — see also lame duck, SITTING DUCK

duck-ling /'dʌklɪŋ/ *n* young duck — see also UGLY DUCKLING

duct /dʌkt/ *n* tube that carries liquids, air, etc.

dud /dʌd/ *n sl* useless thing or person: *a dud cheque*

due /djuː‖duː/ *adj* **1** owed **2** *fml* suitable; proper **3** expected: *The train is due any minute.* **4** due to caused of ♦ *adv* (before **north, south, east, west**) exactly ♦ *n* something that rightfully belongs to one: *give him his due* **dues** *n* [P] official payments

du-el /'djuːəl‖'duːəl/ *n* fight arranged between 2 people **duel** *vi* **-ll-** *BrE* ‖ **-l-** *AmE*

du-et /djuˈet‖duˈet/ *n* piece of music for 2 performers

duffel coat /'·· ·/ *n* loose heavy coat, often with a HOOD

dug /dʌɡ/ *v past t. and p.* of DIG

dug-out /'dʌɡaʊt/ *n* **1** boat made of a hollow log **2** shelter dug in the ground

duke /djuːk‖duːk/ *n* British nobleman of the highest rank ~**dom** *n* rank or lands of a duke

dull /dʌl/ *adj* **1** not bright or shining **2** slow in thinking **3** not sharp: *a dull pain* **4** uninteresting ♦ *vt* make dull ~**ness** *n* [U]

du-ly /'djuːli‖'duːli/ *adv* properly; as expected

dumb /dʌm/ *adj* **1** unable to speak **2** unwilling to speak; silent **3** *sl* stupid ~**ly** *adv* ~**ness** *n* [U]

dumb-found /dʌmˈfaʊnd/ *vt* make dumb from surprise

dum-my /'dʌmi/ *n* **1** object made to look like a real thing or person **2** *BrE* baby's rubber TEAT for sucking **3** *sl* stupid person

dummy run /ˌ·· '·/ *n* practice attempt made before the real thing

dump /dʌmp/ *vt* **1** drop carelessly **2** sell (goods) abroad more cheaply than at home ♦ *n* place for dumping waste **2** stored supply **3** *sl* dirty untidy place **4** in the dumps sad ~**er** *n* large vehicle for carrying earth and stones ~**y** *adj* short and fat

dump-ling /'dʌmplɪŋ/ *n* ball of boiled DOUGH

dunce /dʌns/ *n* slow learner

dune /djuːn‖duːn/ *n* long low sandhill piled up by the wind

dung /dʌŋ/ *n* [U] animal MANURE

dun-ga-rees /ˌdʌŋɡəˈriːz/ *n* [P] **1** *BrE* trousers with a BIB (2), usu. made of heavy cotton **2** *AmE* JEANS for working in

dun-geon /'dʌndʒən/ *n* underground prison

dunk /dʌŋk/ *vt* dip (esp. food) into liquid while eating

du-o /'djuːəʊ‖'duːəʊ/ *n* a pair, esp. of musicians

dupe /djuːp‖duːp/ *vt* trick; deceive ♦ *n fml* person who is duped

du-pli-cate ^{1} /'djuːplɪkət‖'duː-/ *n, adj* (something that is) exactly like another

du-pli-cate ^{2} /'djuːplɪkeɪt‖'duː-/ *vt* copy exactly ~**cator** *n* machine that copies ~**cation** /ˌdjuːpləˈkeɪʃən‖ˌduː-/ *n* [U]

du-plic-i-ty /djuˈplɪsɪti‖duː-/ *n* [U] *fml* dishonesty

du-ra-ble /'djʊərəbəl‖'duː-/ *adj* long-lasting **durables** *n* [P] goods expected to last for years

du-ra-tion /djʊˈreɪʃən‖duː-/ *n* [U] *fml* **1** time during which something lasts **2** for the duration as long as something lasts

du-ress /djʊˈres‖duː-/ *n* [U] *fml* threats: *promise under duress*

dur-ing /'djʊərɪŋ‖'duː-/ *prep* **1** all through (a length of time) **2** at some moment in: *die during the night*

dusk /dʌsk/ *n* [U] time when daylight fades

dusk-y /'dʌski/ *adj* rather dark in colour

dust¹ /dʌst/ n [U] powder made of earth or other matter ~**y** adj covered with dust

dust² vt **1** clean the dust from: *dust books* **2** cover with powder: *dust crops* ~**er** n cloth for removing dust

dust off phr vt begin to use or practise again, after a period of not doing so

dust·bin /'dʌstbɪn/ n BrE container for waste materials

dust·cart /'dʌstkɑːt‖-kɑːrt/ n BrE vehicle that collects the contents of dustbins

dust jack·et /'· ‚··/ n loose paper cover on a hard cover book

dust·man /'dʌstmən/ n -**men** /-mən/ BrE person employed to empty dustbins

dust·pan /'dʌstpæn/ n flat container into which house dust is swept

dust·sheet /'dʌst-ʃiːt/ n large sheet used to cover furniture, etc., to keep off dust

Dutch /dʌtʃ/ adj **1** of the Netherlands (Holland) **2 go Dutch (with someone)** share expenses

du·ty /'djuːti‖'duːti/ n [C;U] **1** something one must do **2** tax: *customs duties* **3 heavy duty** (of machines, etc.) able to do hard work **4 on/off duty** required/not required to work

dutiful adj showing respect and obedience **dutifully** adv

duty-free /‚·· '·◄/ adj, adv (of goods) allowed to enter a country without tax

du·vet /'duːveɪ/ n large bag of feathers used as a bed covering

dwarf /dwɔːf‖dwɔːrf/ n **dwarfs** or **dwarves** /dwɔːvz‖dwɔːrvz/ very small person, animal, or plant ♦ vt cause to look small

dwell /dwel/ vi **dwelled** or **dwelt** /dwelt/ lit live (in a place) ~**er** n person or animal that lives somewhere: *city-dwellers* ~**ing** n fml home

dwell on phr vt think or speak a lot about

dwin·dle /'dwɪndl/ vi become gradually fewer or smaller

dye /daɪ/ n [C;U] substance used to colour cloth, etc. ♦ vi/t **dyes, dyed, dyeing** colour with dye

dyed-in-the-wool /‚· · · '·◄/ adj impossible to change (as to the stated or known quality): *a dyed-in-the-wool Republican*

dy·ing /'daɪ-ɪŋ/ v present p. of DIE

dyke /daɪk/ n DIKE

dy·nam·ic /daɪ'næmɪk/ adj **1** powerful and active **2** of force that causes movement ~**ally** /-kli/ adv **dynamics** n [U] science that deals with matter in movement ~**ism** /'daɪnəmɪzəm/ n [U] being DYNAMIC (1)

dy·na·mite /'daɪnəmaɪt/ n [U] **1** powerful explosive **2** something or

someone that will cause great shock, admiration, etc. ♦ vt blow up with dynamite

dy·na·mo /'daɪnəməʊ/ n -**mos** machine that turns movement into electricity

dyn·a·sty /'dɪnəsti‖'daɪ-/ n line of rulers of the same family

dys·en·te·ry /'dɪsəntəri‖-teri/ n [U] painful bowel disease

dys·lex·i·a /dɪs'leksiə/ n [U] inability to read, from difficulty in recognizing letter shapes –**ic** adj

E

E, e /iː/ the 5th letter of the English alphabet

E written abbrev. for: east(ern)

each /iːtʃ/ determiner, pron every one separately: *each child* | *each of the children* ♦ adv for or to each: *They cost fifty cents each.*

each oth·er /‚· '··/ pron with each doing something to the other: *kiss each other* | *hold each other's hands*

ea·ger /'iːgə/ adj keen; wanting very much ~**ly** adv ~**ness** n [U]

ea·gle /'iːgl/ n large meat-eating bird with a hooked beak ~**eyed** /‚·· '·◄/ adj having very good eyesight

ear¹ /ɪə/ n **1** [C] either of the 2 parts of the head with which we hear **2** [S] good recognition of sounds: *an ear for music* **3 all ears** listening eagerly **4 play by ear** play music without written notes **5 up to one's ears in** deep in; very busy with

ear² n head of a grain-producing plant

ear·ache /'ɪəreɪk/ n [C;U] pain inside the ear

ear·drum /'ɪədrʌm‖'ɪər-/ n tight skin inside the ear which allows one to hear sound

earl /ɜːl‖ɜːrl/ n British nobleman of high rank ~**dom** /'ɜːldəm‖ 'ɜːr-/ n rank or lands of an earl

ear·ly /'ɜːli‖'ɜːrli/ adv, adj **1** sooner than usual or expected: *The train arrived early.* | *an early supper* **2** near the beginning: *It happened early in the morning/in the early morning.* **3 at the earliest** and not sooner

early bird /‚·· '·/ n person who gets up or arrives early

early warn·ing sys·tem /‚·· '·· ‚··/ n RADAR network that gives advance information of enemy air attack

ear·mark /'ɪəmɑːk‖'ɪərmɑːrk/ vt set aside (money, etc.) for a particular purpose

earn /ɜːn‖ɜːrn/ v 1 vi/t get (money) by working 2 vt deserve (what one has worked for) ~**er** n ~**ings** n [P] money earned

ear·nest /'ɜːnɪst‖'ɜːr-/ adj determined and serious ♦ n **in earnest**: in a determined way **b** not joking ~**ly** adv ~**ness** n [U]

ear·plug /'ɪəplʌg‖'ɪər-/ n soft thing put into the ear to keep out noise, etc.

ear·ring /'ɪə,rɪŋ/ n decoration for the ear

ear·shot /'ɪəʃɒt‖'ɪərʃɑːt/ n **within/out of earshot** within/beyond the distance at which a sound can be heard

earth /ɜːθ‖ɜːrθ/ n 1 [S;U] (often cap.) the world we live on: the planet Earth 2 [U] its surface, as opposed to the sky: The rocket fell to earth. 3 [U] soil: a bucket of earth 4 [C] wild animal's hole 5 [C] BrE safety wire carrying electricity to the ground ♦ vt BrE connect (electrical apparatus) to the ground ~**ly** adj 1 of this world, not heaven 2 possible: no earthly reason ~**y** adj 1 like soil 2 concerned with the body, not the mind

earth·en·ware /'ɜːθənweəʳ, -ðən-‖'ɜːr-/ n [U] (pots. etc., made of) baked clay

earth·quake /'ɜːθkweɪk‖'ɜːrθ-/ n sudden violent shaking of the earth's surface

earth·work /'ɜːθwɜːk‖'ɜːrθwɜːrk/ n large structure of earth used as a protection against enemies

ear·wig /'ɪə,wɪg‖'ɪər-/ n insect with 2 curved parts on its tail

ease[1] /iːz/ n [U] 1 ability to do something easily 2 state of being comfortable 3 **ill at ease** uncomfortable

ease[2] v 1 vi/t make or become less painful or difficult 2 vt make less anxious 3 vt move slowly and carefully into a different position

  ease off/up phr vi become less active or severe

ea·sel /'iːzəl/ n wooden frame to support a picture or BLACKBOARD

east /iːst/ n [the + S] (often cap.) direction from which the sun rises ♦ adj 1 in the east 2 (of wind) from the east ♦ adv to the east ~**ward** adj, adv

Eas·ter /'iːstəʳ/ n holy day in memory of Christ's death

east·er·ly /'iːstəli‖-ərli/ adj east

east·ern /'iːstən‖-ərn/ adj of the east part of the world or of a country

eas·y /'iːzi/ adj 1 not difficult 2 comfortable; without worry ♦ adv **go easy on: a** be less severe with **b** not use too much of -**ily** adv 1 without difficulty 2 without doubt: easily the best

easy chair /,·· '·/ n an ARMCHAIR

eas·y·go·ing /,iːzi'gəʊɪŋ◂/ adj pleasantly calm and unhurried

eat /iːt/ v ate /et, eɪt ‖ eɪt/, **eaten** /'iːtn/ 1 vi/t take in (food) through the mouth 2 vt [(away, into)] destroy by chemical action 3 **be eaten up with** be full of (violent feeling) 4 **eat one's words** admit that one was wrong 5 **eat your heart out** infml be very jealous ~**able** adj ~**er** n

eaves /iːvz/ n [P] edges of a roof, beyond the walls

eaves·drop /'iːvzdrɒp‖-drɑːp/ vi -**pp**- listen secretly to conversation ~**per** n

ebb /eb/ vi grow less or lower: His courage ebbed away. ♦ n [S] **at a low ebb** in a bad state

ebb tide /,· '·/ n [C;U] outward flow of the sea

eb·o·ny /'ebəni/ adj, n [U] (of the colour of) hard black wood

e·bul·li·ent /ɪ'bʌlɪənt, ɪ'bʊ-/ adj fml full of happy excitement -**ence** n [U]

ec·cen·tric /ɪk'sentrɪk/ adj 1 (of people) unusual; peculiar 2 (of circles) not having the same centre ♦ n eccentric person ~**ity** /,eksen'trɪsɪti, -sən-/ n [C;U]

ec·cle·si·as·ti·cal /ɪ,kliːzi'æstɪkəl/ adj of the Christian church

ech·e·lon /'eʃəlɒn‖-lɑːn/ n level within an organization

ech·o /'ekəʊ/ n -**oes** sound sent back from a surface ♦ v 1 vi come back as an echo 2 vt copy or repeat (words, ideas, etc.)

éclair /ɪ'kleəʳ, eɪ-/ n finger-shaped cake with cream inside

e·clec·tic /ɪ'klektɪk/ adj fml using ideas from many different systems ~**ism** /-tɪsɪzəm/ n [U]

e·clipse /ɪ'klɪps/ n disappearance of the sun's light (cut off by the moon) or of the moon's light (cut off by the Earth) ♦ vt 1 cause an eclipse of 2 make (something) less important by comparison

e·col·o·gy /ɪ'kɒlədʒi‖ɪ'kɑː-/ n [U] relations of living things to their surroundings -**gist** n -**gical** /,iːkə'lɒdʒɪkəl ‖ -'lɑː-/ adj

ec·o·nom·ic /,ekə'nɒmɪk◂, ,iː-‖-'nɑː-/ adj 1 connected with trade, industry, and wealth 2 profitable ~**al** adj not wasteful ~**ally** /-kli/ adv

ec·o·nom·ics /,ekə'nɒmɪks, ,iː-‖-'nɑː-/ n [U] study of the way in which wealth is produced and used -**nomist** /ɪ'kɒnəməst‖ɪ'kɑː-/ n

e·con·o·mize ‖ also -**mise** vi BrE avoid waste

e·con·o·my /ɪ'kɒnəmi‖ɪ'kɑː-/ n 1 [C] economic system of a country 2 [C;U] avoidance of waste — see also BLACK

ECONOMY, MIXED ECONOMY ♦ adj cheap: an economy class air ticket

e·co·sys·tem /'i:kəʊˌsɪstəm/ n all the living things in an area and the relationship between them

ec·sta·sy /'ekstəsi/ n [C;U] great joy **ecstatic** /ɪk'stætɪk, ek-/ adj **ecstatically** -kli/ adv

e·cu·men·i·cal /ˌiːkjʊ'menɪkəl‖ˌek-/ adj favouring Christian unity

ec·ze·ma /'eksəmə‖'eksəmə, 'egzəmə, ɪg'ziːmə/ n [U] red swollen condition of the skin

ed·dy /'edi/ n circular movement of water, smoke, etc. ♦ vi move in eddies

edge /edʒ/ n 1 cutting part of a knife, etc. 2 narrowest part along the outside of an object: the edge of a coin 3 place where something begins or ends: the water's edge 4 **have the edge on** be better than 5 **on edge** nervous 6 **set someone's teeth on edge** infml give an unpleasant feeling to someone 7 **take the edge off** infml make less severe ♦ v 1 vt put a border on 2 vi/t move gradually, esp. sideways **edging** n [C;U] border **edgy** adj nervous

ed·i·ble /'edəbəl/ adj that can be eaten

e·dict /'iːdɪkt/ n official public command

ed·i·fice /'edəfəs/ n fml large fine building

ed·it /'edɪt/ vt prepare (a newspaper, film, etc.) for printing or showing **~or** n person who edits

e·di·tion /ɪ'dɪʃən/ n 1 one printing, esp. of a book 2 form in which a book is printed: a paperback edition

ed·i·to·ri·al /ˌedə'tɔːriəl/ adj of an editor ♦ n newspaper article giving the paper's opinion

ed·u·cate /'edjʊkeɪt‖'edʒə-/ vt teach; train

ed·u·ca·tion /ˌedjʊ'keɪʃən‖ˌedʒə-/ n [S;U] (knowledge resulting from) teaching or training **~al** adj

EEC /ˌiː iː 'siː/ n European Economic Community; West European organization to encourage trade and friendly relations

eel /iːl/ n long snake-like fish

ee·rie /'ɪəri/ adj frightening because of being strange: an eerie silence **eerily** adv

ef·face /ɪ'feɪs/ vt fml rub out

ef·fect /ɪ'fekt/ n [C;U] 1 result; what happens because of a cause 2 **in effect: a** in operation **b** in fact 3 **take effect** come into operation — see also SIDE EFFECT ♦ vt fml produce; cause **effects** n [P] 1 sounds, etc., produced in a film or play 2 fml personal belongings

ef·fec·tive /ɪ'fektɪv/ adj 1 producing the desired result: very effective new

laws 2 fml actual: the effective strength of our army **~ly** adv **~ness** n [U]

ef·fem·i·nate /ɪ'femɪnət/ adj (of a man) too like a woman **~nacy** n [U]

ef·fer·vesce /ˌefə'ves‖ˌefər-/ vi form bubbles of gas **-vescence** n [U] **-vescent** adj

ef·fete /ɪ'fiːt‖e-/ adj weak; EFFEMINATE

ef·fi·ca·cy /'efɪkəsi/ n [U] fml effectiveness

ef·fi·cient /ɪ'fɪʃənt/ adj working well; an efficient secretary/machine **~ly** adv **-ciency** n [U]

ef·fi·gy /'efɪdʒi/ n fml wooden, stone, etc., likeness of someone

ef·flu·ent /'efluənt/ n [C;U] liquid chemical or human waste

ef·fort /'efət‖'efərt/ n 1 [U] use of strength 2 [C] attempt: a good effort **~less** adj successful without effort **~lessly** adv

ef·fron·te·ry /ɪ'frʌntəri/ n [U] rudeness without any feeling of shame

ef·fu·sive /ɪ'fjuːsɪv/ adj showing too much feeling **~ly** adv

EFL /ˌiː ef 'el/ abbrev. for: English as a foreign language

e.g. /ˌiː 'dʒiː/ abbrev. for: for example

e·gal·i·tar·i·an /ɪˌgælɪ'teəriən/ adj believing in social equality **~ism** n [U]

egg[1] /eg/ n 1 [C] round object with a shell, containing a baby bird, snake, etc. 2 [C;U] (the contents of) an egg when used as food: a boiled egg 3 [C] female cell producing young 4 **have egg on one's face** seem foolish

egg[2] v **egg on** phr vt encourage someone, esp. to do wrong

egg·cup /'eg-kʌp/ n container for a boiled egg

egg·head /'eghed/ n derog a HIGHBROW

egg·plant /'egplɔːnt‖'egplænt/ n large purple vegetable

e·go /'iːgəʊ, 'egəʊ/ n **egos** 1 one's opinion of oneself: an enormous ego 2 tech one's conscious self — see also ALTER EGO

e·go·cen·tric /ˌiːgəʊ'sentrɪk, ˌe-/ adj thinking only about oneself; selfish

e·go·is·m /'iːgəʊɪzəm, 'e-/ n [U] selfishness **-ist** n

e·go·tis·m /'iːgətɪzəm, 'e-/ n [U] believing that one is more important than other people **-tist** n **-tistic** /ˌiːgə'tɪstɪk, ˌe-/, **-tistical** adj

ego trip /'··· ·/ n act or set of acts done mainly because it makes one feel proud of oneself

e·gre·gious /ɪ'griːdʒəs/ adj fml noticeably bad

ei·der·down /'aɪdədaʊn‖-dər-/ n bed covering filled with feathers

eight /eɪt/ determiner, n, pron 8

eighth determiner, adv, n, pron 8th

eigh·teen /ˌeɪˈtiːn◂/ determiner, n, pron 18 ~th determiner, adv, n, pron 18th

eigh·ty /ˈeɪti/ determiner, n, pron 80 -tieth determiner, adv, n, pron 80th

ei·ther¹ /ˈaɪðəʳ‖ˈiː-/ determiner, pron, conj 1 one or the other: I haven't seen either John or Sam. | I haven't met either (of them). | He either drives or walks. 2 each of two: houses on either side of the road

either² adv (used with negative expressions) also: I haven't been to France, or Germany either.

e·jac·u·late /ɪˈdʒækjʊleɪt/ vi/t 1 throw out (SPERM) suddenly from the body 2 fml cry out suddenly -lation /ˌɪdʒækjʊˈleɪʃən/ n [C;U]

e·ject /ɪˈdʒekt/ vt fml throw out ~ion /ɪˈdʒekʃən/ n [U].

ejector seat /·ˈ·· ˌ·/ BrE ‖ **ejection seat** AmE—n seat that throws one out of a plane that is burning, etc.

eke /iːk/ v **eke out** phr vt make (supplies) last as long as possible

e·lab·o·rate¹ /ɪˈlæbərət/ adj full of detail ~ly adv

e·lab·o·rate² /ɪˈlæbəreɪt/ vi add more detail -ration /ɪˌlæbəˈreɪʃən/ n [C;U]

élan /ˈeɪlɒn‖eɪˈlɑːn/ n [U] liveliness; VIGOUR

e·lapse /ɪˈlæps/ vi fml (of time) pass

e·las·tic /ɪˈlæstɪk/ adj able to spring back into shape after stretching or bending ♦ n elastic material ~ity /ˌiːlæsˈtɪsəti/ n [U]

elastic band /·ˌ·· ˈ·/ BrE for RUBBER BAND

e·lat·ed /ɪˈleɪtɪd/ adj proud and happy -ion /ɪˈleɪʃən/ n [U]

el·bow /ˈelbəʊ/ n joint where the arm bends ♦ vt push with the elbows

elbow grease /ˈ·· ·/ n [U] hard work with the hands

elbow room /ˈ·· ·/ n [U] space to move freely

el·der /ˈeldəʳ/ adj (of a family member) older: my elder sister ♦ n 1 older of 2 people 2 person in a respected official position ~ly adj rather old

elder states·man /ˌ·· ˈ··/ n old and respected person who is asked for advice because of his or her experience

el·dest /ˈeldəst/ n, adj (person who is) the oldest of 3 or more

e·lect /ɪˈlekt/ vt 1 choose by voting 2 fml decide: She elected to go. ♦ adj fml chosen, but not yet at work; president elect ~or n person with the right to vote ~oral adj ~orally adv

e·lec·tion /ɪˈlekʃən/ n [C;U] (occasion of) choosing representatives by voting — see also GENERAL ELECTION

e·lec·tion·eer·ing /ɪˌlekʃəˈnɪərɪŋ/ n [U] activity of persuading people to vote for a political party

e·lec·to·rate /ɪˈlektərət/ n all the electors

e·lec·tric /ɪˈlektrɪk/ adj 1 worked by or producing electricity: an electric razor 2 infml very exciting ~al adj concerned with or using electricity: an electrical fault ~ally /-kli/ adv

electric chair /·ˌ·· ˈ·/ n [the + S] punishment of electrocuting a criminal

e·lec·tri·cian /ɪˌlekˈtrɪʃən/ n person who fits and repairs electrical apparatus

e·lec·tri·ci·ty /ɪˌlekˈtrɪsəti/ n [U] power supply, carried usu. by wires, for heating, lighting, etc.

e·lec·tri·fy /ɪˈlektrɪfaɪ/ vt 1 use electric power for 2 excite greatly

e·lec·tro·cute /ɪˈlektrəkjuːt/ vt kill by passing electric current through the body -cution /ɪˌlektrəˈkjuːʃən/ n [C;U]

e·lec·trode /ɪˈlektrəʊd/ n point at which current enters or leaves a BATTERY (1)

e·lec·trol·y·sis /ɪˌlekˈtrɒləsəs‖-ˈtrɑː-/ n [U] the use of electricity a for separation of a liquid into its chemical parts or b for destruction of hair roots

e·lec·tron /ɪˈlektrɒn‖-trɑːn/ n small piece of matter that moves round the NUCLEUS of an atom

el·ec·tron·ic /ɪˌlekˈtrɒnɪk‖-ˈtrɑː-/ adj of, using, or produced by equipment that works by means of an electric current passing through CHIPs¹ (4), TRANSISTORs, etc. (for example, televisions, computers, etc.): electronic music/mail ~ally /-kli/ adv **electronics** n [U] study or making of such equipment

el·e·gant /ˈeləgənt/ adj graceful; stylish ~ly adv -gance n [U]

el·e·ment /ˈeləmənt/ n 1 [C] simple substance consisting of only one kind of atom 2 [S] small amount: an element of truth in what you say 3 [C] part of a whole: Honesty is an important element in his character. 4 [C] heating part of a piece of electric apparatus 5 in/out of one's element doing/not doing what one is best at **elements** n [the + P] 1 (bad) weather 2 first things to study in a subject **elemental** /ˌeləˈmentl◂/ adj of the forces of nature

el·e·men·ta·ry /ˌeləˈmentəri◂/ adj 1 easy: elementary questions 2 concerned with the beginning of something: elementary arithmetic

elementary school /·ˈ··· ˌ·/ n AmE school for the first 6 to 8 years of a child's education

el·e·phant /'elɪfənt/ n very large animal with TUSKs and a long round nose (TRUNK) — see also WHITE ELEPHANT **~ine** /,elɪ'fæntaɪn ‖ -tiːn/ adj heavy and awkward

el·e·vate /'elɪveɪt/ vt fml 1 raise 2 improve (the mind)

el·e·va·tion /,elɪ'veɪʃən/ n 1 [U] fml act of elevating 2 [S] height above sea-level 3 [C] drawing of one side of a building 4 [S] angle made with the horizon, e.g. by a gun

el·e·va·tor /'elɪveɪtə^r/ n 1 AmE for LIFT[2] (2) 2 machine for raising grain, etc.

el·e·ven /ɪ'levən/ determiner, n, pron 11 **~th** determiner, adv, n, pron 11th

el·e·ven·ses /ɪ'levənzɪz/ n BrE infml coffee, tea, or a light meal at about 11 o'clock in the morning

eleventh hour /·,··· '·/n [the + S] the very last moment

elf /elf/n elves /elvz/ small usu. male fairy **~in** adj

e·li·cit /ɪ'lɪsɪt/ vt fml get (information, etc.) from someone

e·lide /ɪ'laɪd/ vt leave out (a sound) in pronunciation

el·i·gi·ble /'elɪdʒəbəl/ adj fulfilling the conditions; suitable **-bility** /,elɪdʒə'bɪlɪti/ n [U]

e·lim·i·nate /ɪ'lɪmɪneɪt/ vt remove; get rid of **-nation** /ɪ,lɪmɪ'neɪʃən/ n [U]

e·lite /eɪ'liːt, ɪ-/ n favoured powerful group in society **elitism** n [U]

elk /elk/n very large deer

el·lipse /ɪ'lɪps/ n OVAL shape

el·lip·ti·cal /ɪ'lɪptɪkəl/ adj 1 OVAL 2 (of speech) with hidden meaning

elm /elm/ n large broad-leaved tree

el·o·cu·tion /,elə'kjuːʃən/ n [U] good clear speaking

e·lon·gate /'iːlɒŋgeɪt‖ɪ'lɔːŋ-/ vt make longer

e·lope /ɪ'ləʊp/ vi run away to get married **~ment** n [C;U]

el·o·quent /'eləkwənt/ adj 1 able to influence people by using language well 2 fml showing something very strongly: an eloquent reminder of the horrors of wars **-quence** n [U]

else /els/ adv 1 more; as well: What else can I say? 2 apart from (what is mentioned): He's here. Everyone else has gone home. 3 otherwise: You must pay or else go to prison.

else·where /els'weə^r, 'elsweə^r ‖ 'elsweər/ adv at, in, from, or to another place

ELT /,iː el 'tiː/ n [U] English language teaching

e·lu·ci·date /ɪ'luːsɪdeɪt/ v fml explain **-dation** /ɪ,luːsɪ'deɪʃən/ n [U]

e·lude /ɪ'luːd/ vt escape from

e·lu·sive /ɪ'luːsɪv/ adj hard to find or remember

elves /elvz/ pl. of ELF

e·ma·ci·a·ted /ɪ'meɪsieɪtɪd/ adj extremely thin **-ation** /ɪ,meɪsi'eɪʃən/ n [U]

em·a·nate /'eməneɪt/ v emanate from phr vi fml come out (from somewhere) **-nation** /,emə'neɪʃən/ n [C;U]

e·man·ci·pate /ɪ'mænsəpeɪt/ vt make (slaves, etc.) free **-pation** /ɪ,mænsə'peɪʃən/ n [U]

e·mas·cu·late /ɪ'mæskjʊleɪt/ vt 1 weaken 2 CASTRATE **-lation** /ɪ,mæskjʊ'leɪʃən/ n [U]

em·balm /ɪm'bɑːm/ vt preserve (a dead body) with chemicals, etc. **~er** n

em·bank·ment /ɪm'bæŋkmənt/ n wall that holds back water or carries a road or railway

em·bar·go /ɪm'bɑːgəʊ‖-ɑːr-/ n **-goes** official order forbidding trade ♦ vt put an embargo on

em·bark /ɪm'bɑːk‖-ɑːrk/ vi/t go or put onto a ship **~ation** /,embɑː'keɪʃən‖-bɑːr-/ n [C;U]

embark on/upon phr vt start (something new)

em·bar·rass /ɪm'bærəs/ vt make ashamed or socially uncomfortable: an embarrassing question/silence **~ingly** adv **~ment** n [C;U]

em·bas·sy /'embəsi/ n offices of an AMBASSADOR

em·bat·tled /ɪm'bætld/ adj surrounded by enemies or difficulties

em·bed /ɪm'bed/ vt **-dd-** fix firmly in surrounding material

em·bel·lish /ɪm'belɪʃ/ vt 1 decorate 2 add (esp. untrue) details to **~ment** n [C;U]

em·ber /'embə^r/ n [usu. pl.] piece of red-hot coal, etc., in a dying fire

em·bez·zle /ɪm'bezəl/ vi/t steal (money placed in one's care) **~ment** n [U] **-zler** n

em·bit·ter /ɪm'bɪtə^r/ vt make sad and angry

em·bla·zon /ɪm'bleɪzən/ vt show (a decoration, etc.) noticeably

em·blem /'embləm/ n sign representing something: The emblem of England is a rose.

em·bod·y /ɪm'bɒdi‖ɪm'bɑːdi/ vt fml give physical expression to **-iment** n: She's the embodiment of evil.

em·boss /ɪm'bɒs‖ɪm'bɒs, -'bɔːs/ vt decorate with a raised pattern

em·brace /ɪm'breɪs/ v 1 vi/t take (someone) lovingly in one's arms 2 vt fml include 3 vt fml become a believer in: embrace the Muslim faith ♦ n: a warm embrace

em·broi·der /ɪm'brɔɪdə^r/ vi/t 1 decorate (cloth) with needlework 2 EMBELLISH **~y** n [U]

em·broiled /ɪm'brɔɪld/ *adj* mixed up in something troublesome: *to get embroiled in an argument*
em·bry·o /'embriəʊ/ *n* **-os 1** creature in its first state before birth **2 in embryo** still incomplete **~nic** /ˌembri'ɒnɪk‖-'ɑːnɪk/ *adj*
em·bry·ol·o·gy /ˌembri'ɒlədʒi‖-'ɑːl-/ *n* [U] study of embryos
e·mend /ɪ'mend/ *vt* take mistakes out of (something written) **~ation** /ˌiːmen'deɪʃən/ *n* [C;U]
em·e·rald /'emərəld/ *n* [C;U] (colour of) a bright green precious stone
e·merge /ɪ'mɜːdʒ‖-ɜːr-/ *vi* **1** come out **2** (of facts) become known **emergence** *n* [U] **emergent** *adj* beginning to develop: *emergent nations*
e·mer·gen·cy /ɪ'mɜːdʒənsi‖-ɜːr-/ *n* dangerous happening which must be dealt with at once
em·e·ry /'eməri/ *n* [U] hard powder used for polishing
em·i·grant /'emɪgrənt/ *n* person who emigrates
em·i·grate /'emɪ̈greɪt/ *vi* leave one's own country to live in another **-gration** /ˌemɪ̈'greɪʃən/ *n* [C;U]
émigré /'emɪgreɪ/ *n fml* a REFUGEE
em·i·nence /'emɪnəns/ *n* [U] great importance
éminence grise /ˌemɪnəns 'griːz/ *n* someone who secretly has great influence, but does not have an official position of power
em·i·nent /'emɪnənt/ *adj* (of a person) famous and admired **~ly** *adv fml* extremely
e·mir /e'mɪəʳ/ *n* Muslim ruler **~ate** /'emɪrɪ̈t/ *n* lands, etc., of an emir
em·is·sa·ry /'emɪ̈səri‖-seri/ *n fml* person sent with a message or to do special work
e·mis·sion /ɪ'mɪʃən/ *n fml* **1** [U] act of emitting **2** [C] something emitted
e·mit /ɪ'mɪt/ *vt* **-tt-** *fml* send out: *to emit smoke/a humming sound*
e·mol·u·ments /ɪ'mɒljʊ̈mənts‖-'mɑːl/ *n* [P] *fml or pomp* pay; wages
e·mo·tion /ɪ'məʊʃən/ *n* **1** [C] strong feeling, such as love, sorrow, etc. **2** [U] strength of feeling: *a voice shaking with emotion* **~al** *adj* **1** concerning the emotions **2** having feelings that are (too) strong **~ally** *adv*
e·mo·tive /ɪ'məʊtɪv/ *adj* causing strong feeling
em·pa·thy /'empəθi/ *n* [S;U] ability to imagine oneself in the position of another person **-thize** *vi*
em·pe·ror /'empərəʳ/ *n* ruler of an empire
em·pha·sis /'emfəsɪ̈s/ *n* **-ses** /-siːz/ special force or attention given to something important
em·pha·size ‖ also **-sise** *BrE* /'emfəsaɪz/ *vt* place emphasis on
em·phat·ic /ɪm'fætɪk/ *adj* strongly emphasized **~ally** /-kli/ *adv*
em·pire /'empaɪəʳ/ *n* group of countries under one government
em·pir·i·cis·m /ɪm'pɪrɪ̈sɪzəm/ *n* attitude to life, etc., based on practical experience, not on books **-cal** /-rɪkəl/ *adj*
em·ploy /ɪm'plɔɪ/ *vt* **1** give paid work to **2** *fml* use **~able** *adj* suitable as a worker **~er** *n* person who employs others **~ment** *n* **1** [U] paid work **2** [C] *fml* useful activity
em·ploy·ee /ɪm'plɔɪ-iː, ˌemplɔɪ'iː/ *n* employed person
em·pow·er /ɪm'paʊəʳ/ *vt fml* give a legal power to
em·press /'emprɪ̈s/ *n* female ruler of an empire
emp·ty /'empti/ *adj* **1** containing nothing **2** insincere: *empty promises* ♦ *n* [*usu. pl.*] empty container ♦ *vt/i* make or become empty **-tiness** *n* [U]
empty-hand·ed /ˌ·· '··/ *adj* having gained nothing
empty-head·ed /ˌ·· '··◂/ *adj* silly
e·mu /'iːmjuː/ *n* large Australian flightless bird
em·u·late /'emjʊ̈leɪt/ *vt* try to do as well as or better than **-lation** /ˌemjʊ̈'leɪʃən/ *n* [U]
e·mul·sion /ɪ'mʌlʃən/ *n* [U] creamy liquid mixture, esp. paint
en·a·ble /ɪ'neɪbəl/ *vt* make able: *to enable them to walk again*
en·act /ɪ'nækt/ *vt* make (a law)
e·nam·el /ɪ'næməl/ *n* [U] **1** glassy covering on metal, etc. **2** hard surface of the teeth ♦ *vt* **-ll-** *BrE* ‖ **-l-** *AmE* cover with enamel
en·am·oured *BrE* ‖ **-ored** *AmE* /ɪ'næməd‖-ərd/ *adj* very fond (of an idea, etc.)
en bloc /ɒn 'blɒk‖ɑːn 'blɑːk/ *adv* all together as a single unit
en·camp·ment /ɪn'kæmpmənt/ *n* military camp
en·cap·su·late /ɪn'kæpsjʊ̈leɪt‖-sə-/ *vt* express in a short form
en·case /ɪn'keɪs/ *vt* cover completely
en·chant /ɪn'tʃɑːnt‖ɪn'tʃænt/ *vt* **1** delight **2** use magic on **~ing** *adj* delightful **~ingly** *adv* **~ment** *n* [C;U]
en·cir·cle /ɪn'sɜːkəl‖-ɜːr-/ *vt* surround
en·clave /'enkleɪv, 'eŋ-/ *n* part of a country surrounded by another
en·close /ɪn'kləʊz/ *vt* **1** surround with a fence, etc. **2** put (something else) into an envelope
en·clo·sure /ɪn'kləʊʒəʳ/ *n* **1** enclosed place **2** something put in with a letter **3** act of enclosing
en·com·pass /ɪn'kʌmpəs/ *vt* include; be concerned with

en·core /'ɒŋkɔːʳ‖'ɑːŋ-/ interj, n (word calling for) a repeated performance

en·coun·ter /ɪn'kaʊntəʳ/ vt fml meet (something dangerous or unexpected) ♦ n sudden (esp. unpleasant) meeting

en·cour·age /ɪn'kʌrɪdʒ‖ɪn'kɜːr-/ vt give approval to; urge: He encouraged her to try. ~ment n [C;U]

en·cour·aged /ɪn'kʌrɪdʒd‖ɪn'kɜːr-/ adj feeling new hope and confidence

en·cour·ag·ing /ɪn'kʌrɪdʒɪŋ‖ɪn-'kɜːr-/ adj causing feelings of hope and confidence: encouraging trade figures

en·croach /ɪn'krəʊtʃ/ vi go beyond what is right or usual: encroach on their territory ~ment n [C;U]

en·crust·ed /ɪn'krʌstɪd/ adj thickly covered: encrusted with jewels/mud

en·cum·ber /ɪn'kʌmbəʳ/ vt load; BURDEN -brance n

en·cy·clo·pe·di·a, -paedia /ɪn,saɪklə'piːdiə/ n book of many facts in alphabetical order **-dic** adj wide and full

end¹ /end/ n 1 point where something stops or finishes: the end of the road/of August 2 little piece remaining: cigarette ends 3 fml aim; purpose 4 at a loose end having nothing to do 5 in the end at last 6 make ends meet get just enough money 7 no end of an endless amount of 8 on end a continuously: for hours on end b upright 9 put an end to stop — see also SHARP END ~less adj never finishing ~lessly adv

end² /end/ vi/t finish ~ing n end (of a story, etc.)

end up phr vi finish one's journey

en·dan·ger /ɪn'deɪndʒəʳ/ vt cause danger to

en·dear /ɪn'dɪəʳ/ vt endear oneself to make oneself loved by ~ment n expression of love

en·deav·our BrE ‖ **-or** AmE /ɪn'devəʳ/ vi fml try ♦ n [C;U] fml effort

en·dem·ic /en'demɪk, ɪn-/ adj (esp. of something bad) often happening in a place

en·dorse /ɪn'dɔːs‖-ɔːrs/ vt 1 express approval of (opinions, etc.) 2 write one's name on (a cheque) 3 record a driving offence on (a driver's LICENCE) ~ment n [C;U]

en·dow /ɪn'daʊ/ vt 1 give a continuing income to (a school, etc.) 2 be endowed with fml have (a good quality) from birth ~ment n [C;U]

en·dur·ance /ɪn'djʊərəns‖ɪn'dʊər-/ n [U] power of enduring

en·dure /ɪn'djʊəʳ‖ɪn'dʊər/ v 1 vt suffer (pain, etc.) patiently 2 vi continue to exist

en·e·ma /'enɪmə/ n putting of a liquid, esp. a medicine, into the bowels through the RECTUM

en·e·my /'enəmi/ n 1 person who hates or opposes another person 2 country with which one is at war

en·er·get·ic /,enə'dʒetɪk‖-ər-/ adj very active ~ally /-kli/ adv

en·er·gy /'enədʒi‖-ər-/ n [U] 1 ability to be active and work hard 2 power that drives machines, etc.: nuclear energy

en·fant ter·ri·ble /,ɒnfon te'riːblə‖,ɑːnfɑːn-/ n shocking but also often interesting and amusing person

en·fee·bled /ɪn'fiːbəld/adj fml made weak

en·fold /ɪn'fəʊld/ vt take into one's arms

en·force /ɪn'fɔːs‖-ɔːrs/ vt cause (a law etc.) to be obeyed ~able adj ~ment n [U]

en·fran·chise /ɪn'fræntʃaɪz/ vt give the right to vote to ~ment n [U]

en·gage /ɪn'geɪdʒ/ v fml 1 vt arrange to employ 2 vi/t lock (machine parts) together **engaged** adj 1 having agreed to marry 2 busy or in use ~ment n 1 agreement to marry 2 arrangement to meet someone 3 fml battle

engage in phr vt fml make (someone) busy in

en·gag·ing /ɪn'geɪdʒɪŋ/ adj charming ~ly adv

en·gen·der /ɪn'dʒendəʳ/ vt fml cause; produce

en·gine /'endʒɪn/ n 1 machine that turns power into movement 2 machine that pulls a train

en·gi·neer /,endʒɪ'nɪəʳ/ n 1 person who plans machines, roads, bridges, etc. 2 person who controls engines ♦ vt cause by secret planning ~ing n [U] profession of an ENGINEER (1)

English break·fast /,ɪŋglɪʃ 'brekfəst/ n a breakfast of esp. BACON and eggs, TOAST and MARMALADE

en·grave /ɪn'greɪv/ vt cut (words, etc.) on a hard surface **engraver** n **engraving** n 1 [C] picture printed from an engraved piece of metal 2 [U] work of an engraver

en·gross /ɪn'grəʊs/ vt completely fill the attention of

en·gulf /ɪn'gʌlf/ vt swallow up: a house engulfed in flames

en·hance /ɪn'hɑːns‖ɪn'hæns/ vt increase (something good) ~ment n [U]

e·nig·ma /ɪ'nɪgmə/ n mystery ~tic /,enɪg'mætɪk/ adj ~tically /-kli/ adv

en·joy /ɪn'dʒɔɪ/ vt 1 get pleasure from 2 fml possess (something good) 3 **enjoy oneself** be happy ~able adj pleasant ~ably adv ~ment n [C;U]

en·large /ɪnˈlɑːdʒ‖-ɑːr-/ vt/i (cause to) become larger ~ment n [C;U]

　enlarge on/upon phr vt say more about

en·light·en /ɪnˈlaɪtn/ vt make free from false beliefs ~ment n [U]

en·list /ɪnˈlɪst/ v 1 vi/t (cause to) join the armed forces 2 vt obtain (help, etc.) ~ment n [C;U]

en·liv·en /ɪnˈlaɪvən/vt to make more active or cheerful

en masse /ˌɒn ˈmæs‖ˌɑːn-/ adv all together

en·mesh /ɪnˈmeʃ/ vt catch as if in a net

en·mi·ty /ˈenmɪti/ n [C;U] fml hatred

e·nor·mi·ty /ɪˈnɔːmɪti‖-ɔːr-/ n 1 [U] enormous size 2 [C;U] fml great wickedness

e·nor·mous /ɪˈnɔːməs‖-ɔːr-/ adj very large ~ly adv extremely

e·nough /ɪˈnʌf/ determiner, pron, adv 1 as much or as many as is needed: *enough food/chairs | not big enough* 2 **fair enough** infml all right 3 **oddly/strangely enough . . .** and this is strange, but . . . 4 **sure enough** as expected

en·quire /ɪnˈkwaɪəʳ/ vi/t INQUIRE ~ment n [C;U]

en·rage /ɪnˈreɪdʒ/ vt make very angry

en·rich /ɪnˈrɪtʃ/ vt 1 make rich 2 improve by adding something ~ment n [U]

en·rol , enroll vi/t -ll- (cause to) join a group officially ~ment n [C;U]

en route /ˌɒn ˈruːt‖ˌɑːn-/ adv on the way; travelling

en·sconced /ɪnˈskɒnst‖ɪnˈskɑːnst/ adj comfortably seated

en·sem·ble /ɒnˈsɒmbəl‖ɑːnˈsɑːm-/ n 1 small group of musicians 2 fml set of things

en·shrine /ɪnˈʃraɪn/ vt fml preserve as if holy

en·sign /ˈensaɪn, -sən‖ˈensən/ n 1 ship's flag 2 US naval officer

en·slave /ɪnˈsleɪv/ vt make into a slave ~ment n [U]

en·sue /ɪnˈsjuː‖ɪnˈsuː/ vi fml happen afterwards or as a result

en·sure /ɪnˈʃʊəʳ/ vt make (something) certain to happen

en·tail /ɪnˈteɪl/ vt make necessary

en·tan·gle /ɪnˈtæŋgəl/vt cause to become twisted with something else ~ment n [C;U]

en·ten·dre /ɒnˈtɒndrə‖ɑːnˈtɑːn-/ see DOUBLE ENTENDRE

en·ter /ˈentəʳ/ v 1 vi/t come or go in or into 2 vt become a member of 3 vt put into a book, list, etc.

　enter into phr vt take part in

　enter on/upon phr vt fml begin

en·ter·prise /ˈentəpraɪz‖-ər-/ n 1 [C] plan that needs courage 2 [U] willingness to take risks 3 [U] way of organizing business: *private enterprise* — see also FREE ENTERPRISE **-prising** adj having ENTERPRISE (2)

en·ter·tain /ˌentəˈteɪn‖-ər-/ v 1 vi/t amuse and interest 2 vi/t provide food and drink for (guests) 3 vt fml be willing to consider (ideas) ~er person who amuses people professionally ~ment n 1 [U] act of entertaining 2 [C] public amusement

en·thral , enthrall /ɪnˈθrɔːl/ vt -ll- hold the complete attention of

en·throne /ɪnˈθrəʊn/ vt put (a ruler) on a THRONE

en·thuse /ɪnˈθjuːz‖ɪnˈθuːz/ vi speak with enthusiasm

en·thu·si·as·m /ɪnˈθjuːziæzəm‖ɪnˈθuː-/ n [C;U] great interest and admiration **-ast** n person who is keen on something **-astic** /ɪnˌθjuːziˈæstɪk‖ɪnˌθuː-/ adj full of enthusiasm **-astically** /-kli/ adv

en·tice /ɪnˈtaɪs/ vt persuade, esp. to do wrong ~ment n [C;U]

en·tire /ɪnˈtaɪəʳ/ adj complete ~ly adv ~ty n [U] fml whole

en·ti·tle /ɪnˈtaɪtl/ vt 1 give a right (to) 2 give a title to (a book, etc.) ~ment n [U]

en·ti·ty /ˈentɪti/ n thing with separate existence

en·tou·rage /ˈɒntʊrɑːʒ‖ˈɑːn-/ n people who surround someone important

en·trails /ˈentreɪlz/ n bowels

en·trance[1] /ˈentrəns/ n 1 [C] door, etc., by which one enters 2 [C] act of entering 3 [U] right to enter

en·trance[2] /ɪnˈtrɑːns‖ɪnˈtræns/ vt fill with delight

en·trant /ˈentrənt/ n person who enters a race, profession, etc.

en·treat /ɪnˈtriːt/ vt fml beg; IMPLORE ~y n [C;U] act of entreating

en·trée /ˈɒntreɪ/ n 1 freedom to enter 2 **a** esp. BrE small meat dish eaten before the main dish of a meal **b** esp. AmE main dish of a meal

en·trenched /ɪnˈtrentʃt/ adj (of beliefs, etc.) firmly established

en·tre·pre·neur /ˌɒntrəprəˈnɜːʳ‖ˌɑːn-/ n person who starts a firm, etc., and takes business risks ~ial adj

en·trust /ɪnˈtrʌst/ vt give to someone to take care of

en·try /ˈentri/ n 1 [C;U] act of coming or going in 2 [C] something written in a list

en·twine /ɪnˈtwaɪn/ vt twist together or round

E num·ber /ˈ· ·· /n number with the letter E in front of it, used to show the chemicals contained in food

e·nu·me·rate /ɪˈnjuːməreɪt‖ɪˈnuː-/ vt fml name one by one **-ration** /ɪˌnjuːməˈreɪʃən‖ɪˌnuː-/ n [C;U]

e·nun·ci·ate /ɪˈnʌnsieɪt/ vt/i pronounce (words) clearly **-ation** /ɪˌnʌnsiˈeɪʃən/ n [U]

en·vel·op /ɪnˈveləp/ vt cover completely: *enveloped in flames* ~**ment** n [U]

en·ve·lope /ˈenvələʊp/ n paper container for a letter

en·vi·a·ble /ˈenviəbəl/ adj very desirable **-bly** adv

en·vi·ous /ˈenviəs/ adj feeling envy ~**ly** adv

en·vi·ron·ment /ɪnˈvaɪərənmənt/ n conditions in which people, animals, etc., live ~**al** /ɪnˌvaɪərənˈmentl/ adj ~**ally** adv ~**alist** n person who tries to keep our natural surroundings from being spoilt

en·vis·age /ɪnˈvɪzɪdʒ/ also **envision** /ɪnˈvɪʒən/ AmE — vt see in the mind; expect

en·voy /ˈenvɔɪ/ n messenger; representative

en·vy /ˈenvi/ n [U] **1** bad feeling one has towards someone who has better luck than oneself **2 the envy of (someone)** something which other people want to have or to be ♦ vt feel envy towards or because of

en·zyme /ˈenzaɪm/ n substance produced by living cells that causes chemical change

e·on /ˈiːən/ n an AEON

ep·au·let, -lette /ˌepəˈlet/ n shoulder decoration on a uniform

e·phem·e·ral /ɪˈfemərəl/ adj lasting only a short time

ep·ic /ˈepɪk/ n **1** long poem, film, etc., about the deeds of gods or great men **2** derog event needing a lot of time and energy ♦ adj (of stories) full of bravery and excitement

ep·i·cu·re·an /ˌepɪkjʊˈriːən/ n person who believes pleasure is very important

ep·i·dem·ic /ˌepɪˈdemɪk/ n many cases of an infectious disease at the same time

ep·i·gram /ˈepɪɡræm/ n short amusing poem or saying

ep·i·lep·sy /ˈepəlepsi/ n disease of the brain causing sudden unconsciousness **-leptic** /ˌepəˈleptɪk◂/ adj, n

ep·i·logue /ˈepəlɒɡ‖-lɔːɡ, -lɑːɡ/ n last part of a play or book

e·pis·co·pal /ɪˈpɪskəpəl/ adj of or governed by BISHOPS

ep·i·sode /ˈepɪsəʊd/ n one separate event or period of time

ep·is·tle /ɪˈpɪsəl/ n fml LETTER (1)

ep·i·taph /ˈepɪtɑːf‖-tæf/ n words written above a grave

ep·i·thet /ˈepəθet/ n adjective, esp. used of a person

e·pit·o·me /ɪˈpɪtəmi/ n something that perfectly shows a particular quality: *My son is the epitome of laziness.* **-mize** vt be typical of

e·poch /ˈiːpɒk‖ˈepək/ n period of historical time, esp. one in which some remarkable event happened ~**making** adj extremely important

eq·ua·ble /ˈekwəbəl/ adj even and regular: *an equable climate* **-bly** adv

e·qual /ˈiːkwəl/ adj **1** the same in size, value, etc. **2** equal to having enough ability, etc., for ♦ n person equal to another ♦ vt **-ll-** BrE ‖ **-l-** AmE be the same as ~**ize** vt make equal ~**ly** adv: *equally fit | to share the work equally* ~**ity** /ɪˈkwɒlɪti ‖ ɪˈkwɑ-/ n [U]: *the equality of women*

eq·ua·nim·i·ty /ˌiːkwəˈnɪmɪti, ˌekwə-/ n [U] fml calmness of mind

e·quate /ɪˈkweɪt/ vt consider as equal

e·qua·tion /ɪˈkweɪʒən/ n statement that 2 quantities are equal: $2x + 1 = 7$ is an equation.

e·qua·tor /ɪˈkweɪtəʳ/ n [the + S] imaginary line round the world, halfway between the North and South POLEs ~**ial** /ˌekwəˈtɔːriəl/ adj

e·ques·tri·an /ɪˈkwestriən/ adj of horse-riding

e·qui·lib·ri·um /ˌiːkwɪˈlɪbriəm/ n [U] fml BALANCE (1)

e·qui·nox /ˈiːkwɪnɒks, ˈe-‖-nɑːks/ n time of year when day and night are of equal length

e·quip /ɪˈkwɪp/ vt **-pp-** provide with what is necessary ~**ment** n [U] things needed for an activity

eq·ui·ta·ble /ˈekwɪtəbəl/ adj fair and just: *an equitable division of the money* **-bly** adv

eq·ui·ties /ˈekwɪtiz/ n [P] tech firm's ordinary SHAREs, on which no fixed amount of interest is paid

eq·ui·ty /ˈekwɪti/ n [U] fml fairness

e·quiv·a·lent /ɪˈkwɪvələnt/ n, adj (something) the same in value

e·quiv·o·cal /ɪˈkwɪvəkəl/ adj doubtful in meaning; questionable **-cate** vi fml speak in an equivocal way on purpose

e·ra /ˈɪərə/ n period of historical time, marked esp. by particular developments

e·rad·i·cate /ɪˈrædɪkeɪt/ vt put an end to (something bad) **-cation** /ɪˌrædɪˈkeɪʃən/ n [U]

e·rase /ɪˈreɪz‖ɪˈreɪs/ vt fml rub out **eraser** n RUBBER¹ (2)

ere /eəʳ/ prep, conj old use before

e·rect /ɪˈrekt/ adj upright ♦ vt **1** put upright: *erect a tent* **2** fml build: *erect a monument* ~**ion** /ɪˈrekʃən/ n **1** [U] the act of erecting something **2** [C] fml a building **3** [C;U] (an example of) the state of the PENIS when upright ~**ly** *adv* ~**ness** *n* [U]

er·go /'ɜːgəʊ‖'ɜːr-/ *adv* therefore

er·go·nom·ics /,ɜːgə'nɒmɪks‖,ɜːrgə-'nɑː-/ *n* [U] study of how people work best with machines -**ic** *adj* -**ically** /-kli/ *adv*

er·mine /'ɜːmɪn‖'ɜːr-/ *n* [C;U] (white fur of) the STOAT

e·rode /ɪ,rəʊd/ *vt* (of acids, water, etc.) wear away; reduce **erosion** /ɪ'rəʊʒən/ *n* [U]

e·ro·ge·nous /ɪ'rɒdʒənəs‖ɪ'rɑː-/ *adj* sexually sensitive

e·rot·ic /ɪ'rɒtɪk‖ɪ'rɑː-/ *adj* of sexual love ~**ism** /-təsɪzəm/ *n* [U]

err /ɜːʳ/ *vi fml* make a mistake

er·rand /'erənd/ *n* short journey to do or esp. buy something

er·rant /'erənt/ *adj fml* wandering away and misbehaving

er·rat·ic /ɪ'rætɪk/ *adj* changeable; not regular ~**ally** /-kli/ *adv*

er·ro·ne·ous /ɪ'rəʊniəs/ *adj fml* (of a belief) incorrect ~**ly** *adv*

er·ror /'erəʳ/ *n* **1** [C] mistake **2** [U] state of being mistaken

er·satz /'eəzæts‖'eərzɑːts/ *adj derog* used instead of something else; artificial

erst·while /'ɜːstwaɪl‖'ɜːr-/ *adj lit* former

er·u·dite /'erʊdaɪt‖'erə-/ *adj fml* full of learning

e·rupt /ɪ'rʌpt/ *vi* (of a VOLCANO) explode suddenly ~**ion** /ɪ'rʌpʃən/ *n* [C;U]

es·ca·late /'eskəleɪt/ *vi/t* (cause to) grow greater or more serious -**lation** /,eskə'leɪʃən/ *n* [U]

es·ca·la·tor /'eskəleɪtəʳ/ *n* set of moving stairs

es·ca·pade /'eskəpeɪd/ *n* wild dangerous act

es·cape /ɪ'skeɪp/ *v* **1** *vi/t* get out; get free (from) **2** *vt* avoid (something dangerous): *to escape death* **3** *vt* be forgotten by: *His name escapes me.* ♦ *n* [C;U] (act of) getting free

es·cap·is·m /ɪ'skeɪpɪzəm/ *n* [U] activity providing escape from dull reality -**ist** *adj, n*

e·scarp·ment /ɪ'skɑːpmənt‖-ɑːr-/ *n* long cliff

es·chew /ɪs'tʃuː/ *vt fml* avoid

es·cort¹ /'eskɔːt‖-ɔːrt/ *n* **1** person or people who go with another as a protection or honour **2** social companion, esp. a man

es·cort² /ɪ'skɔːt‖-ɔːrt/ *vt* go with as an escort

Es·ki·mo /'eskɪməʊ/ *n* INUIT

es·o·ter·ic /,esə'terɪk, ,iːsə-/ *adj* having deep and secret meanings understood only by a few people ~**ally** /-kli/ *adv*

ESP /,iː es 'piː/ *n* [U] extrasensory perception; knowledge obtained without using one's ordinary 5 senses

es·pe·cial·ly /ɪ'speʃəli/ *adv* **1** to a particularly great degree: *not especially hot* **2** in particular: *I like fruit, especially apples.*

es·pi·o·nage /'espiənɑːʒ/ *n* [U] spying (SPY)

es·pouse /ɪ'spaʊz/ *vt fml* support (an aim, etc.) **espousal** *n* [C;U]

es·say /'eseɪ/ *n* short piece of writing on a subject ~**ist** *n* writer of essays

es·sence /'esəns/ *n* **1** [U] most important quality of something **2** [C;U] liquid, etc., with some particular strong taste or smell: *coffee essence* **3** **of the essence** extremely important

es·sen·tial /ɪ'senʃəl/ *adj* **1** necessary **2** FUNDAMENTAL: *the essential difference between us* ♦ *n* [usu. pl.] something necessary ~**ly** *adv* basically: *She's essentially kind.*

es·tab·lish /ɪ'stæblɪʃ/ *vt* **1** begin; CREATE (an organization, set of rules, etc.) **2** settle (esp. oneself) firmly in a particular state or position: *the film which established her reputation as a director* **3** make certain of (a fact, etc.) ~**ment** *n* **1** [U] act of establishing **2** [C] *fml* place run as a business **3** [*the* + *S*] (*cap.*) often derog the powerful people who control public life

es·tate /ɪ'steɪt/ *n* **1** piece of land in the country, with one owner **2** *BrE* piece of land built on in a planned way: *a housing estate* **3** *law* whole of a person's property, esp. as left after death — see also REAL ESTATE

estate a·gent /·'·· ,··ʳ/ *n BrE* person who buys and sells houses and land for people

estate car /·'·· ·/ *n BrE* car with a door at the back and folding back seats

es·teem /ɪ'stiːm/ *n* [U] *fml* respect: *I hold him in high esteem.* ♦ *vt* **1** respect greatly **2** *fml* consider to be **estimable** /'estəməbəl/ *adj* worthy of respect

es·ti·mate¹ /'estəmeɪt/ *vt/i* calculate; form an opinion about (cost, etc.) -**mation** /,estə'meɪʃən/ *n* **1** judgment; opinion

es·ti·mate² /'estəmət/ *n* calculation of cost, number, etc.

es·trange /ɪ'streɪndʒ/ *vt* make unfriendly ~**ment** *n* [C;U]

es·tu·a·ry /'estʃuəri, -tʃəri/ *n* mouth of a river, into which the sea flows

etc., also **etcetera** /,et'setərə/ *adv* and the rest; and other things

etch /etʃ/ *vi/t* draw with a needle and acid on metal ~**ing** *n* [C;U]

e·ter·nal /ɪ'tɜːnl‖-ɜːr-/ *adj* lasting for ever ~**ly** *adv*

eternal tri·an·gle /·,·· '···/ *n* [S] difficult situation resulting from the love of two people, usu. of the same sex, for another person, usu. of the other sex

e·ter·ni·ty /ɪˈtɜːnt̬ɪ/ -ɔr-/ n 1 [C] endless time after death 2 [C] an extremely long time

e·ther /ˈiːθəʳ/ n [U] 1 liquid that easily changes to a gas 2 upper levels of the air

e·the·re·al /ɪˈθɪəriəl/ adj extremely light and delicate

eth·ic /ˈeθɪk/ n system of moral behaviour: the Christian ethic ~**al** adj 1 of morals 2 morally good ~**ally** /-kli/ adv **ethics** n 1 [U] science of morals 2 [P] moral rules

eth·nic /ˈeθnɪk/ adj of or related to a racial, national, or tribal group ~**ally** /-kli/ adv

e·thos /ˈiːθɒs/ /ˈiːθɑːs/ n [S] characteristic moral beliefs of a person or group

et·i·quette /ˈetɪket/ -kət/ n [U] formal rules of manners

et·y·mol·o·gy /ˌetəˈmɒlədʒi/ -ˈmɑː-/ n [U] study of the origins of words

eu·ca·lyp·tus /ˌjuːkəˈlɪptəs/ n tree whose oil is used as medicine for colds

eu·lo·gy /ˈjuːlədʒi/ n fml speech in praise of someone -**gize** vt praise highly -**gistic** /ˌ-ˈlɔːˈdʒɪstɪk/ adj full of praise

eu·nuch /ˈjuːnək/ n man who has been castrated (CASTRATE)

eu·phe·mis·m /ˈjuːfɪmɪzəm/ n [C;U] (use of) a pleasanter, less direct word for something unpleasant -**mistic** /ˌjuːfɪˈmɪstɪk/ adj

eu·pho·ri·a /juːˈfɔːriə/ju-/ n [U] state of happiness and cheerful excitement -**ric** /juːˈfɒrɪk ‖ -ˈfɔːrɪk, -ˈfɑː-/ adj

eu·tha·na·si·a /ˌjuːθəˈneɪziə/ -ˈneɪʒə/ n [U] painless killing of very ill or very old people

e·vac·u·ate /ɪˈvækjueɪt/ vt take all the people away from (a dangerous place) -**ation** /ɪˌvækjuˈeɪʃən/ n [C;U] -**ee** /-kjuˈiː/ n person who has been evacuated

e·vade /ɪˈveɪd/ vt avoid; escape from

e·val·u·ate /ɪˈvæljueɪt/ vt calculate the value of -**ation** /ɪˌvæljuˈeɪʃən/ n [C;U]

e·van·gel·i·cal /ˌiːvænˈdʒelɪkəl/ n, adj (often cap.) 1 (member) of those Christian churches that believe in studying the Bible rather than in ceremonies 2 (person) showing very great eagerness in spreading certain beliefs

e·van·ge·list /ɪˈvændʒəlɪst/ n travelling Christian religious teacher -**lism** n [U] ~**ic** /ɪˌvændʒəˈlɪstɪk/ adj

e·vap·o·rate /ɪˈvæpəreɪt/ vi/t change into steam and disappear -**ration** /ɪˌvæpəˈreɪʃən/ n [U]

e·va·sion /ɪˈveɪʒən/ n [C;U] the act of evading (EVADE): tax evasion -**sive** /-sɪv/ adj

eve /iːv/ n [S] 1 (usu. cap.) day before a (religious) holiday 2 time just before any event: on the eve of the election

even¹ /ˈiːvən/ adv 1 (shows that something is unexpected and surprising): John's a very good swimmer, but even he doesn't swim in the river. (= so certainly nobody else does) 2 (makes comparisons stronger): It's even colder than yesterday. 3 **even if** it does not matter if 4 **even now/so/then** in spite of that: I explained, but even then he didn't understand. 5 **even though** though

even² adj 1 smooth and regular: an even surface/temperature 2 (of things that can be compared) equal: an even chance 3 (of numbers) that can be divided by two ~**ly** adv ~**ness** n [U]

even³ v even out phr vi/t (cause to) become level or equal

even-hand·ed /ˌ·· ˈ··◂/ adj giving fair and equal treatment to all sides

eve·ning /ˈiːvnɪŋ/ n time between afternoon and bedtime

evening dress /ˈ··· ˈ·/ n 1 [U] formal clothes for the evening 2 [C] woman's formal long dress

e·vent /ɪˈvent/ n 1 (important) happening 2 one race, etc., in a day's sports 3 **at all events** in spite of everything 4 **in the event** when it actually happened 5 **in the event of** . . . if (something) happens ~**ful** adj full of important events

e·ven·tu·al /ɪˈventʃuəl/ adj happening at last ~**ly** adv in the end: They eventually succeeded. ~**ity** /ɪˌventʃuˈælɪti/ n fml possible event

ev·er /ˈevəʳ/ adv 1 at any time: Does it ever snow? | Nothing ever annoys him. | colder than ever 2 always: ever since Christmas | the ever-increasing population 3 (gives force to a question): What ever is that? 4 **ever so/such** infml very

ev·er·green /ˈevəɡriːn/ -ɔr-/ n, adj (tree) that does not lose its leaves in winter

ev·er·last·ing /ˌevəˈlɑːstɪŋ◂‖ˌevər-ˈlæ-/ adj lasting for ever

ev·ery /ˈevri/ determiner 1 each: I enjoy every minute of it. 2 (of things that can be counted) once in each: I go every 3 days. 3 as much as is possible: I have every reason to trust him. 4 **every other** the 1st, 3rd, 5th, etc., or the 2nd, 4th, 6th, etc.: Take the pills every other day 5 **every now and then** also **every so often** — sometimes, but not often

ev·ery·bod·y /ˈevribɒdi/ -bɑːdi/ pron everyone

ev·ery·day /ˈevrideɪ/ adj ordinary; common

ev·ery·one /ˈevriwʌn/ pron 1 every person: Everyone was pleased. 2 all the people usually here: *Where is everyone?*

ev·ery·thing /'evriθɪŋ/ *pron* 1 each thing; *They've eaten everything.* 2 all that matters: *Money isn't everything.*

ev·ery·where /'evriweəʳ/ ‖ also **everyplace** /-pleɪs/ *AmE—adv* at or to every place

every which way /,·· '· ·/ *adv AmE* in every direction

e·vict /ɪ'vɪkt/ *vt* force to leave a house, etc., by law **~ion** /ɪ'vɪkʃən/ *n* [C;U]

ev·i·dence /'evɪdəns/ *n* [U] 1 proof 2 answers given in a court of law 3 **in evidence** present and easily seen

ev·i·dent /'evɪdənt/ *adj* plain and clear **~ly** *adv*

e·vil /'iːvəl/ *adj* harmful; wicked ♦ *n* [C;U] *fml* wickedness or misfortune **~ly** /'iːvəl-li/ *adv*

e·voc·a·tive /ɪ'vɒkətɪv‖ɪ'vɑː-/ *adj* bringing memories: *an evocative smell*

e·voke /ɪ'vəʊk/ *vt fml* produce (a memory)

ev·o·lu·tion /,iːvə'luːʃən, ,evə-‖,evə-/ *n* [U] gradual development, esp. of living things from earlier and simpler forms

e·volve /ɪ'vɒlv‖ɪ'vɑːlv/ *vi/t* develop gradually

ewe /juː/ *n* female sheep

ex·a·cer·bate /ɪg'zæsəbeɪt‖-ər-/ *vt fml* make (something bad) worse

ex·act¹ /ɪg'zækt/ *adj* correctly measured; PRECISE: *the exact time* **~ly** *adv* 1 correctly 2 (as a reply) I agree! 3 **not exactly** not really **~ness**, also **~itude** /ɪg'zæktɪtjuːd ‖ -tuːd/ *n* [U]

ex·act² *vt fml* demand and obtain by force **~ing** *adj* demanding great effort

ex·ag·ge·rate /ɪg'zædʒəreɪt/ *vi/t* make (something) seem larger, etc., than it is **-ration** /ɪg,zædʒə'reɪʃən/ *n* [C;U]

ex·al·ta·tion /,egzɔːl'teɪʃən, ,eksɔːl-/ *n* great joy because of success

ex·alt·ed /ɪg,zɔːltɪd/ *adj* of high rank

ex·am /ɪg'zæm/ *n* test of knowledge

ex·am·i·na·tion /ɪg,zæmɪ'neɪʃən/ *n* 1 [C] *fml* exam 2 [C;U] act of examining

ex·am·ine /ɪg'zæmɪn/ *vt* 1 look carefully at 2 ask questions, to find out something or to test knowledge **-iner** *n*

ex·am·ple /ɪg'zɑːmpəl‖ɪg'zæm-/ *n* 1 something that shows a general rule: *a typical example* 2 something to be copied: *Her courage is an example to us all.* 3 **for example** (abbrev. **e.g.**) here is one of the things just spoken of 4 **make an example of someone** punish someone to frighten others

ex·as·pe·rate /ɪg'zɑːspəreɪt‖ɪg'zæ-/ *vt* annoy very much **-ratedly** *adv*

-ratingly *adv* **-ration** /ɪg,zɑːspə'reɪʃən ‖ ɪg,zæ-/ *n* [U]

ex·ca·vate /'ekskəveɪt/ *vt* 1 dig (a hole) 2 uncover by digging **-vator** *n* person or machine that excavates **-vation** /,ekskə'veɪʃən/ *n* [C;U]

ex·ceed /ɪk'siːd/ *vt* 1 be greater than 2 do more than: *to exceed the speed limit* **~ingly** *adv fml* extremely

ex·cel /ɪk'sel/ *vi* -ll- *fml* be extremely good (at something)

Ex·cel·len·cy /'eksələnsi/ *n* (title of some people of high rank in the state or church)

ex·cel·lent /'eksələnt/ *adj* very good **-lence** *n* [U]

ex·cept /ɪk'sept/ *prep* not including; but not: *Everyone except John was tired.* ♦ *vt fml* leave out; not include

ex·cep·tion /ɪk'sepʃən/ *n* 1 [C;U] (a case of) leaving out or being left out: *Everyone, without exception, must attend.* | *I don't usually see people after 5.00, but I'll make an exception in your case.* 2 **take exception to** be made angry by **~al** *adj* unusual, esp. because very good **~ally** *adv*

ex·cerpt /'eksɜːpt‖-ɜːr-/ *n* piece taken from a book, etc.

ex·cess /ɪk'ses, 'ekses/ *n, adj* [S;U] (an amount that is) greater than is usual or allowed: *an excess of violence in the film* **~ive** *adj* too much **~ively** *adv* **excesses** *n* [P] extremely bad, cruel, etc., behaviour

ex·change /ɪks'tʃeɪndʒ/ *vt* give and receive in return: *I exchanged my dollars for pounds.* ♦ *n* 1 [C;U] act of exchanging 2 [C] changing of money: *the rate of exchange* 3 [C] place where **a** telephone wires meet **b** business people meet: *the Stock Exchange* 4 [C] short period of fighting or talking — see also FOREIGN EXCHANGE

ex·cise¹ /'eksaɪz/ *n* [U] tax on goods produced inside a country

ex·cise² /ɪk'saɪz/ *vt fml* remove by cutting

ex·cite /ɪk'saɪt/ *vt* 1 cause to have strong (pleasant) feelings: *an excited little boy* 2 *fml* cause (feelings): *to excite interest* **~ment** *n* [C;U] **excitable** *adj* easily excited **exciting** *adj*: *exciting films*

ex·claim /ɪk'skleɪm/ *vi/t* speak or say suddenly

ex·cla·ma·tion /,eksklə'meɪʃən/ *n* word(s) exclaimed

exclamation mark /··'·· ·/ *BrE* ‖ **exclamation point** *AmE — n* PUNCTUATION MARK (!) written after an exclamation

ex·clude /ɪk'skluːd/ *vt* 1 keep out or leave out 2 shut out from the mind: *Don't exclude that possibility.* **excluding** *prep* not including **exclusion** /ɪk'skluːʒən/ *n* [U]

ex·clu·sive /ɪk'sklu:sɪv/ adj 1 keeping out unsuitable people 2 not shared ♦ n story appearing in only one newspaper ~ly adv only: *exclusively for women*

ex·com·mu·ni·cate /ˌekskə'mju:nɪkeɪt/ vt exclude from the Christian Church -cation /ˌekskəmju:nə'keɪʃən/ n [C;U]

ex·cre·ment /'ekskrɪmənt/ n [U] fml solid waste from the bowels

ex·crete /ɪk'skri:t/ vt pass out (waste matter)

ex·cru·ci·at·ing /ɪk'skru:ʃieɪtɪŋ/ adj (of pain) very bad ~ly adv

ex·cul·pate /'ekskʌlpeɪt/ vt fml free from blame

ex·cur·sion /ɪk'skɜ:ʃən‖ɪk'skɜ:rʒən/ n short journey for pleasure

ex·cuse[1] /ɪk'skju:z/ vt 1 forgive: *Please excuse my bad handwriting.* 2 make (bad behaviour) seem less bad 3 free from a duty 4 Excuse me (said when starting to speak to a stranger, or when one wants to get past a person, or to APOLOGIZE for something) 5 excuse oneself ask permission to be absent **excusable** adj that can be forgiven

ex·cuse[2] /ɪk'skju:s/ n reason given when asking to be excused

ex·e·cra·ble /'eksɪkrəbəl/ adj fml very bad

ex·e·cute /'eksɪkju:t/ vt 1 kill as a legal punishment 2 fml carry out; perform: *execute a plan* **-cution** /ˌeksɪ'kju:ʃən/ n 1 [C;U] legal killing 2 [U] fml carrying out; performance **-cutioner** n official who executes criminals

ex·ec·u·tive /ɪg'zekjʊtɪv/ adj concerned with managing, or carrying out decisions ♦ n 1 [C] person in an executive position in business 2 [the + S] branch of government that carries out the law

ex·ec·u·tor /ɪg'zekjʊtər/ n person who carries out the orders in a WILL[2] (5)

ex·em·pla·ry /ɪg'zemplərɪ/ adj fml suitable to be copied

ex·em·pli·fy /ɪg'zemplɪfaɪ/ vt be or give an example of **-fication** /ɪgˌzemplɪfɪ'keɪʃən/ n [C;U]

ex·empt /ɪg'zempt/ adj freed from a duty, etc. ♦ vt make exempt ~ion /ɪg'zempʃən/ n [C;U]

ex·er·cise /'eksəsaɪz‖-ər-/ n 1 [U] use of the powers of the body to improve it: *go swimming for exercise* 2 [C] something done for training: *naval exercises* 3 [S;U] use (of a power or right) ♦ 1 vi/t take or give EXERCISE (1) 2 vt use (a power or right)

ex·ert /ɪg'zɜ:t‖-ɜ:rt/ vt 1 use (strength, etc.) 2 exert oneself make an effort ~ion /ɪg'zɜ:ʃən‖-ɜ:r-/ n [C;U]

ex gra·tia /ˌeks 'greɪʃə/ adj (of a payment) made as a favour, and not because one has a legal duty to make it

ex·hale /eks'heɪl/ vi/t breathe out **exhalation** /ˌekshə'leɪʃən/ n [U]

ex·haust /ɪg'zɔ:st/ vt 1 tire out 2 use up completely ♦ n pipe by which gases escape from an engine ~ive adj thorough ~ively adv ~ion /ɪg'zɔ:stʃən/ n [U]

ex·hib·it /ɪg'zɪbɪt/ vt 1 show publicly for sale, etc. 2 fml show that one has (a quality) ♦ n something shown in a MUSEUM, etc. ~or n person showing exhibits

ex·hi·bi·tion /ˌeksə'bɪʃən/ n 1 public show of objects 2 act of exhibiting ~ism n behaviour of someone who wants to be looked at ~ist n

ex·hil·a·rate /ɪg'zɪləreɪt/ vt make cheerful and excited -ration /ɪgˌzɪlə'reɪʃən/ n [U]

ex·hort /ɪg'zɔ:t‖-ɔ:rt/ vt fml urge strongly ~ation /ˌeksɔ:'teɪʃən/ n [C;U]

ex·hume /ɪg'zju:m, eks'hju:m‖ ɪg'zu:m, ɪk'sju:m/ vt dig up (a dead body) **exhumation** /ˌeksju:'meɪʃən/ n [C;U]

ex·i·gen·cy /'eksɪdʒənsɪ, ɪg'zɪ-/ n fml urgent need

ex·ile /'eksaɪl, 'egzaɪl/ n 1 [U] unwanted absence from one's country 2 [C] someone forced into this ♦ vt send into exile

ex·ist /ɪg'zɪst/ vi have life; be real: *The problems she talks about simply don't exist.* ~ence n 1 [U] state of being real 2 [S] way of living: *lead a miserable existence* ~ent adj existing; present

ex·is·ten·tial /ˌegzɪ'stenʃəl/ adj related to existence

ex·it /'egzɪt, 'eksɪt/ n 1 way out of a building 2 act of leaving ♦ vi (used as a stage direction) he/she/it goes out

ex·o·dus /'eksədəs/ n [S] going away of many people

ex·on·e·rate /ɪg'zɒnəreɪt‖ɪg'zɑ:-/ vt fml free (someone) from blame -ration /ɪgˌzɒnə'reɪʃən‖ɪgˌzɑ:-/ n [U]

ex·or·bi·tant /ɪg'zɔ:bɪtənt ‖ -ɔ:r-/ adj (of cost) too much ~ly adv

ex·or·cize also -cise BrE /'eksɔ:saɪz‖-ɔ:r-/ vt drive out (an evil spirit, etc.) by prayers -cism n act or art of exorcizing -cist n

ex·ot·ic /ɪg'zɒtɪk‖ɪg'zɑ:-/ adj pleasantly strange: *exotic flowers/food* ~ally /-kli/ adv

ex·pand /ɪk'spænd/ vi/t (cause to) grow larger or more detailed

expand on/upon phr vt make more detailed

ex·panse /ɪk'spæns/ n wide open space

ex·pan·sion /ɪkˈspænʃən/ n [C;U] act of expanding **∼ism** n intention of expanding one's land, etc. **∼ist** n, adj

ex·pan·sive /ɪkˈspænsɪv/ adj friendly and willing to talk **∼ly** adv

ex·pa·ti·ate /ɪkˈspeɪʃieɪt/ v **expatiate on/upon** phr vt fml speak a lot about

ex·pat·ri·ate /ˈekˈspætrɪət, -trɪeɪt‖ ekˈspeɪ-/ n, adj (person) living abroad

ex·pect /ɪkˈspekt/ vt think or believe that something will happen **∼ing** adj infml PREGNANT **∼ation** /ˌekspek-ˈteɪʃən/ n **1** [U] state of expecting **2** [C] something expected

ex·pec·tant /ɪkˈspektənt/ adj **1** waiting hopefully **2** PREGNANT **∼ly** adv **-tancy** n [U] hope

ex·pec·to·rate /ɪkˈspektəreɪt/ vi fml SPIT

ex·pe·di·ent /ɪkˈspiːdɪənt/ adj (of an action) useful, esp. for one's own purposes ♦ n useful plan, esp. one thought of in a hurry because of urgent need **-ency** n [U]

ex·pe·dite /ˈekspədaɪt/ vt fml make (a plan) go faster

ex·pe·di·tion /ˌekspəˈdɪʃən/ n (people making) a journey for a purpose: an expedition to the North Pole **∼ary** adj (of an army) sent abroad to fight

ex·pel /ɪkˈspel/ vt **-ll- 1** dismiss officially from a school, etc. **2** fml force out from a container

ex·pend /ɪkˈspend/ vt spend; use up **∼able** adj that can be used up without worrying

ex·pen·di·ture /ɪkˈspendɪtʃəʳ/ n [S;U] fml spending

ex·pense /ɪkˈspens/ n [U] **1** cost **2 at someone's expense: a** with someone paying **b** (of a joke) against someone **expenses** n [P] money for a purpose: We'll pay his travelling expenses.

ex·pen·sive /ɪkˈspensɪv/ adj costing a lot **∼ly** adv

ex·pe·ri·ence /ɪkˈspɪərɪəns/ n **1** [U] knowledge gained by practice **2** [C] something that happens to: a fascinating experience ♦ vt suffer or learn by experience: to experience defeat **-enced** adj having EXPERIENCE (1)

ex·per·i·ment /ɪkˈsperɪmənt/ n [C;U] test carried out to learn something ♦ vi perform experiments **∼al** /ɪkˌsperɪˈmentl/ adj used for or based on experiments **∼ation** /ɪkˌsperəmen-ˈteɪʃən/ n [U]

ex·pert /ˈekspɜːt‖-ɜːrt/ n, adj (person) with special skill or training **∼ly** adv

ex·per·tise /ˌekspɜːˈtiːz‖-ɜːr-/ n [U] skill in a particular field

expert sys·tem /ˌ·· ˈ··/ n computer system which contains information on

a particular subject, used to solve problems

ex·pi·ate /ˈekspieɪt/ vt fml pay for (a crime) by accepting punishment **-ation** /ˌekspiˈeɪʃən/ n [U]

ex·pire /ɪkˈspaɪəʳ/ vi **1** (of something that lasts for a time) come to an end **2** lit die **expiry**, also **expiration** /ˌekspəˈreɪʃən/ n [U]

ex·plain /ɪkˈspleɪn/ v **1** vi/t make (a meaning) clear **2** vt be the reason for **explanation** /ˌekspləˈneɪʃən/ n **1** [U] act of explaining **2** [C] something that explains **explanatory** /ɪkˈsplænətəri‖ -tɔːri/ adj (of a statement) explaining

explain away phr vt give an excuse for (something) in order to avoid blame

ex·ple·tive /ɪkˈspliːtɪv‖ˈekspləɪv/ n fml word used for swearing

ex·pli·ca·ble /ˈekˈsplɪkəbəl/ adj fml (of behaviour, etc.) understandable

ex·pli·cit /ɪkˈsplɪsɪt/ adj (of a statement, etc.) clearly and fully expressed **∼ly** adv **∼ness** n [U]

ex·plode /ɪkˈspləʊd/ v **1** vi/t blow up; burst **2** vi show violent feeling

ex·ploit¹ /ɪkˈsplɔɪt/ vt **1** use (people) unfairly for profit **2** use (things) fully for profit **∼er** n **∼ation** /ˌeksplɔɪ-ˈteɪʃən/ n [U] **∼ative** /ɪkˈsplɔɪtətɪv/ adj tending to exploit

ex·ploit² /ˈeksplɔɪt/ n brave successful act

ex·plore /ɪkˈsplɔːʳ/ vt **1** travel through (a place) for discovery **2** examine (a subject) carefully **explorer** n **exploration** /ˌeksplə-ˈreɪʃən/ n [C;U] **exploratory** /ɪkˈsplɔːrətəri‖ɪkˈsplɔːrətɔːri/ adj

ex·plo·sion /ɪkˈspləʊʒən/ n **1** (noise of) exploding **2** sudden increase: the population explosion

ex·plo·sive /ɪkˈspləʊsɪv/ n, adj (substance) that explodes **∼ly** adv

ex·po·nent /ɪkˈspəʊnənt/ n someone who expresses or supports a belief

ex·port¹ /ɪkˈspɔːt‖-ɔːrt/ vi/t send (goods) abroad for sale **∼er** n

ex·port² /ˈekspɔːt‖-ɔːrt/ n **1** [U] (business of) exporting **2** [C] something exported

ex·pose /ɪkˈspəʊz/ vt **1** uncover; leave without protection **2** make known (a secret crime, etc.) **3** uncover (photographic film) to the light **4 expose oneself** show one's sexual parts on purpose, in the hope of shocking people **exposure** /ɪkˈspəʊʒəʳ/ n [C;U]

ex·po·sé /ekˈspəʊzeɪ‖ˌekspəˈzeɪ/ n public statement of something shameful

ex·po·si·tion /ˌekspəˈzɪʃən/ n [C;U] fml explaining; explanation

ex·pos·tu·late /ɪkˈspɒstʃəleɪt‖

-'spɑ:-/ *vi fml* complain loudly and firmly

ex·pound /ɪkˈspaʊnd/ *vt fml* describe (a belief, etc.) in detail

ex·press[1] /ɪkˈspres/ *vt* 1 make known by words or looks: *She expressed surprise at his decision.* 2 **express oneself** speak or write one's thoughts or feelings

express[2] *adj* 1 going quickly 2 clearly stated: *her express wish* ♦ *n* express train ♦ *adv* by express post ~**ly** *adv* 1 clearly 2 on purpose

ex·pres·sion /ɪkˈspreʃən/ *n* 1 [C;U] act of expressing: *political expression* 2 [C] word or phrase: *an odd expression to use* 3 [C] look on someone's face: *a surprised expression* 4 [U] quality of showing feeling: *singing without much expression* ~**less** *adj* without EXPRESSION (4)

ex·pres·sive /ɪkˈspresɪv/ *adj* showing feelings ~**ly** *adv*

ex·press·way /ɪkˈspreʃweɪ/ *n AmE* for MOTORWAY

ex·pro·pri·ate /ɪkˈsprəʊprieɪt/ *vt fml* take away for public use **-ation** /ɪk,sprəʊpriˈeɪʃən/ *n* [C;U]

ex·pul·sion /ɪkˈspʌlʃən/ *n* [C;U] act of expelling (EXPEL)

ex·punge /ɪkˈspʌndʒ/ *vt* remove completely from a list, etc.

ex·pur·gate /ˈekspəgeɪt/ *vt fml* remove improper words, etc., from

ex·qui·site /ɪkˈskwɪzɪt, ˈekskwɪ-/ *adj* beautifully made or done ~**ly** *adv*

ex·tant /ɪkˈstænt/ *adj fml* still existing

ex·tend /ɪkˈstend/ *v* 1 *vt* make longer or larger: *extend the car park* 2 *vt* stretch out (part of one's body) to the limit 3 *vt* fml offer, give: *extend a welcome* 4 *vi* [(**to**)] (of land) reach

ex·ten·sion /ɪkˈstenʃən/ *n* 1 [U] act of extending 2 [C] part added 3 [C] telephone line inside a set of offices, etc.

ex·ten·sive /ɪkˈstensɪv/ *adj* large in amount or area ~**ly** *adv*

ex·tent /ɪkˈstent/ *n* 1 [U] amount or length: *the extent of the damage* 2 [S] degree: *to a large extent*

ex·ten·u·a·ting /ɪkˈstenjueɪtɪŋ/ *adj* giving good reasons (for bad behaviour): *extenuating circumstances*

ex·te·ri·or /ɪkˈstɪəriər/ *n* outside of something **exterior** *adj*

ex·ter·mi·nate /ɪkˈstɜːmɪneɪt||-ɜːr-/ *vt* kill all of **-nation** /ɪk,stɜːmɪˈneɪʃən||-ɜːr-/ *n* [U]

ex·ter·nal /ɪkˈstɜːnl||-ɜːr-/ *adj* outside ~**ly** *adv*

ex·tinct /ɪkˈstɪŋkt/ *adj* 1 (of a kind of animal) no longer existing 2 (of a VOLCANO) no longer active ~**ion** /ɪkˈstɪŋkʃən/ *n* [U] state of being or becoming extinct

ex·tin·guish /ɪkˈstɪŋgwɪʃ/ *vt fml* 1 put out (a fire, etc.) 2 destroy (hope, etc.) ~**er** *n* apparatus for putting out fires

ex·tir·pate /ˈekstɜːpeɪt||-ɜːr-/ *vt fml* destroy completely

ex·tol /ɪkˈstəʊl/ *vt* **-ll-** praise highly

ex·tort /ɪkˈstɔːt||-ɔːrt/ *vt* obtain by force or threats ~**ion** /ɪkˈstɔːʃən||-ɔːr-/ *n* [C;U] ~**ionist** *n*

ex·tor·tion·ate /ɪkˈstɔːʃənət||-ɔːr-/ *adj* EXORBITANT

ex·tra /ˈekstrə/ *adj, adv* beyond what is usual or necessary: *extra money|pay extra* ♦ *n* 1 extra thing 2 film actor in a crowd scene 3 special EDITION (1) of a newspaper

ex·tract[1] /ɪkˈstrækt/ *vt* 1 pull out, esp. with difficulty 2 get (a substance) from another substance ~**ion** /ɪkˈstrækʃən/ *n* 1 [C;U] act or example of extracting 2 [U] family origin: *of Russian extraction*

ex·tract[2] /ˈekstrækt/ *n* 1 piece of writing taken from a book, etc. 2 product obtained by extracting: *beef extract*

ex·tra·cur·ric·u·lar /,ekstrəkəˈrɪkjʊlər/ *adj* outside the ordinary course of work in a school or college

ex·tra·dite /ˈekstrədaɪt/ *vt* send (a foreign criminal) home for trial **-dition** /,ekstrəˈdɪʃən/ *n* [C;U]

ex·tra·mar·i·tal /,ekstrəˈmærɪtl/ *adj* (of sexual relationships) outside marriage

ex·tra·mu·ral /,ekstrəˈmjʊərəl/ *adj* connected with but outside an organization

ex·tra·ne·ous /ɪkˈstreɪniəs/ *adj* not directly connected

extra-or·di·na·ry /ɪkˈstrɔːdənəri, ɪkˈstrɔːrdn-eri, ,ekstrəˈɔːr-/ *adj* 1 very strange 2 beyond what is ordinary: *a man of extraordinary ability* **-narily** *adv*

ex·trap·o·late /ɪkˈstræpəleɪt/ *vi/t* guess from facts already known

ex·tra·sen·so·ry per·cep·tion /,ekstrə,sensəri pəˈsepʃən||-pər-/ *n* [U] see ESP

ex·tra·ter·res·tri·al /,ekstrətəˈrestriəl/ *adj* (from) outside the Earth

ex·trav·a·gant /ɪkˈstrævəgənt/ *adj* 1 wasteful of money, etc. 2 (of ideas, behaviour, etc.) beyond what is reasonable **-gance** *n* [C;U]

ex·trav·a·gan·za /ɪk,strævəˈgænzə/ *n* very grand and expensive piece of entertainment

ex·treme /ɪkˈstriːm/ *adj* 1 furthest or greatest possible: *extreme cold|the extreme south of the country* 2 often *derog* beyond the usual limits: *extreme opinions* ♦ *n* furthest possible degree: *He's gone from one extreme to the other.* ~**ly** *adv* very

ex·trem·is·m /ɪk'striːmɪzəm/ n [U] *derog* holding of (politically) extreme opinions **-ist** n. adj

ex·trem·i·ty /ɪk'streməti/ n [S;U] highest degree   **extremities** n [P] human hands and feet

ex·tri·cate /'ekstrɪkeɪt/ vt set free from something that is hard to escape from

ex·tro·vert, extravert /'ekstrəvɜːt‖ -ɜːrt/ n cheerful person who likes to be with others

ex·u·be·rant /ɪg'zjuːbərənt‖ɪg'zuː-/ adj overflowing with life and excitement   ~**ly** adv   **-rance** n [U]

ex·ude /ɪg'zjuːd‖ɪg'zuːd/ vi/t (cause to) flow out slowly in all directions

ex·ult /ɪg'zʌlt/ vi *fml* show great delight   ~**ant** adj   ~**antly** adv ~**ation** /ˌegzʌl'teɪʃən/ n [U]

eye /aɪ/ n **1** either of the 2 parts of the head with which we see **2** way of seeing: *an experienced eye* **3** hole in a needle **4** ring into which a hook fits **5 be in the public eye** be often seen by the public **6 have an eye for** be able to judge **7 in one's mind's eye** in one's imagination **8 in the eyes of** in the opinion of **9 keep an eye on** watch carefully **10 one in the eye for** *infml* a defeat for **11 see eye to eye** agree completely **12 up to one's eyes in** *infml* very busy with ♦ vt look at closely

eye·ball /'aɪbɔːl/ n the whole of the EYE (1), including the part inside the head

eye·brow /'aɪbraʊ/ n line of hairs above each eye

eye·catch·ing /'· ˌ··/ adj unusual and attractive to look at

eye·lash /'aɪlæʃ/ n hair on the edge of the eyelid

eye·lid /'aɪlɪd/ n piece of skin that moves to close the eye

eye·o·pen·er /'· ˌ···/ n something surprising that changes one's ideas about something

eye·sight /'aɪsaɪt/ n [U] power of seeing

eye·sore /'aɪsɔːʳ/ n something ugly to look at

eye·wash /'aɪwɒʃ‖-wɔːʃ, -wɑːʃ/ n [U] *sl* nonsense

ey·rie , eyry /'ɪəri, 'eəri, 'aɪəri/n high nest of an EAGLE

F

F, f /ef/ the 6th letter of the English alphabet

F *abbrev. for:* FAHRENHEIT

fa·ble /'feɪbəl/ n short story that teaches a lesson   **fabled** adj spoken of as true; famous

fab·ric /'fæbrɪk/ n [C;U] **1** woven cloth **2** structure of a building, etc.

fab·ri·cate /'fæbrɪkeɪt/ vt invent (something false)   –**cation** /ˌfæbrɪ'keɪʃən/ n [C;U]

fab·u·lous /'fæbjʊləs/ adj **1** existing in fables **2** unbelievable: *fabulous wealth* **3** excellent   ~**ly** adv very: *fabulously rich*

fa·cade /fə'sɑːd, fæ-/ n **1** front of a building **2** false appearance

face¹ /feɪs/ n **1** [C] front part of the head **2** [C] expression on the face **3** [C] front; surface: *miners at the coal face* **4** [U] position of respect: *afraid of losing face* **5 face to face** in someone's direct presence **6 in the face of** in opposition to **7 on the face of it** APPARENTLY **8 make/pull a face/faces** make an expression with the face **9 to someone's face** openly in their presence   ~**less** adj with no clear character

face² v **1** vi/t turn the face towards **2** vt meet and oppose: *face danger* **3** vt cover the front of: *a building faced with stone*

   face up to *phr vt* be brave enough to deal with

face·cloth /'feɪsklɒθ‖-klɔːθ/ n small cloth for washing the face

face·lift /'· ˌ·/ n medical operation to make the face look younger

face·sav·ing /'· ˌ··/ adj allowing self-respect to be kept

fac·et /'fæsɪt/ n **1** one of the flat sides of a cut jewel **2** ASPECT of a subject

fa·ce·tious /fə'siːʃəs/ adj using silly jokes   ~**ly** adv

face val·ue /ˌ· '··/ n **1** [C;U] value shown on a postage stamp, etc. **2** [U] value of something as it first appears

fa·cial /'feɪʃəl/ adj of the face ♦ n facial beauty treatment

fa·cile /'fæsaɪl‖'fæsəl/ adj (of words) too easy; not deep

fa·cil·i·tate /fə'sɪlɪteɪt/ vt *fml* make easy

fa·cil·i·ty /fə'sɪlɪti/ n [U] ability to do things easily   –**ties** n [P] useful things: *shopping/sporting facilities*

fac·ing /'feɪsɪŋ/ n [U] **1** outer covering of a wall, etc. **2** material sewn in to stiffen a garment

fac·si·mi·le /fæk'sıməli/ n exact copy of a picture, etc.

fact /fækt/ n 1 [C] something known to be true 2 [U] truth 3 **in fact** really

fac·tion /'fækʃən/ n group within a larger (political) one

fac·tor /'fæktər/ n influence that helps to produce a result

fac·to·ry /'fæktəri/ n place where goods are made by machinery

facts of life /,·· '·'·/ n [P] the details of sex and birth

fac·tu·al /'fæktʃuəl/ adj based on fact ~**ly** adv

fac·ul·ty /'fækəlti/ n 1 natural power of the mind or body: *the faculty of hearing* 2 **a** university department **b** teachers in such a department

fad /fæd/ n short-lived interest in something

fade /feɪd/ v 1 vi/t (cause to) lose colour or freshness 2 vi disappear gradually

fade in/out phr vi/t (in film making and broadcasting) (cause to) appear/disappear slowly

fae·ces /'fiːsiːz/ n [P] solid waste from the bowels

fag /fæg/ n BrE 1 [S] infml tiring job 2 [C] sl cigarette 3 AmE derog sl for HOMOSEXUAL **fagged** adj BrE sl very tired

fag·got ‖ also **fagot** AmE/'fægət/ n 1 ball of cut-up meat 2 bunch of sticks for burning 3 AmE FAG (3)

Fah·ren·heit /'færənhaɪt/ n scale of temperature in which water freezes at 32° and boils at 212°

fail /feɪl/ v 1 vi/t be unsuccessful or unable 2 vi not do what is wanted: *The crops/business failed.* 3 vt judge to be unsuccessful in a test 4 vt disappoint or leave (someone) at a bad time: *My courage failed me.* 5 vi lose strength: *His health is failing.* ♦ n **without fail** certainly

fail·ing /'feɪlɪŋ/ n fault; weakness ♦ prep in the absence of

fail-safe /,· '·◄/ adj made so that any failure will stop the machine

fail·ure /'feɪljər/ n 1 [U] lack of success 2 [C] person or thing that fails 3 [C;U] non-performance; inability: *heart failure*

faint /feɪnt/ adj 1 likely to lose consciousness 2 lacking strength or courage 3 not clear or bright 4 slight: *faint chance* ♦ vi lose consciousness ♦ n act of fainting ~**ly** adv ~**ness** n [U]

faint-heart·ed /,· '··◄/ adj cowardly

fair¹ /feər/ adj 1 just and honest: *fair play* 2 quite good: *a fair knowledge of French* 3 having a good, clean appearance: *a fair copy of the report* 4 (of skin or hair) not dark 5 (of weather) not stormy ♦ adv 1 honestly: *play fair* 2

fair and square: a honestly **b** directly

3 fair enough infml all right ~**ly** adv 1 honestly 2 rather: *fairly warm*

fair² n 1 BrE FUNFAIR 2 market for farm produce 3 large show of goods: *book fair*

fair game /,· '·/ n [U] **a** something that it is reasonable to attack **b** person, idea, etc., which can easily be laughed at and CRITICIZEd

fair·ground /'feəgraund‖'feər-/ n open space for a FUNFAIR

fair sex /,· '·/ n [the] see GENTLE SEX

fair·way /'feəweɪ‖'feər-/ n part of a GOLF COURSE along which one hits the ball

fair-weath·er friend /,· ·· '·/n friend who is absent in times of trouble

fair·y /'feəri/ n 1 small imaginary person with magical powers 2 derog HOMOSEXUAL man

fairy god·moth·er /,·· '··-/n person who helps, and esp. saves, someone who is in trouble

fair·y·land /'feərilænd/ n [S] 1 land where fairies live 2 place of magical beauty

fairy light /'·· ·/ n small coloured light for decorating a Christmas tree, etc.

fairy tale /'·· ·/ n 1 story about magic 2 untrue story **fairy-tale** adj magically wonderful

fait ac·com·pli /,feɪt ə'kompli‖ -,ækɑ:m'pli:/ n faits accomplis /,feɪt ə'kompliːz‖-,ækɑ:m'pliːz/ something that has happened and cannot now be changed

faith /feɪθ/ n 1 [U] confident trust 2 [C;U] religious belief 3 [U] loyalty to a promise: *keep faith with them* ~**ful** adj 1 loyal 2 true to the facts: *faithful copy* ♦ n [the + P] religious people ~**fully** adv **Yours faithfully** (used for ending letters to strangers) ~**less** adj fml disloyal

faith heal·ing /'· ,··/ n [U] method of treating diseases by prayer, etc.

fake /feɪk/ n person or thing that is not what he/she/it looks like or pretends to be ♦ vi/t make or copy (e.g. a work of art) to deceive

fa·kir /'feɪkɪə‖'fæ-, fæ'kɪər‖fə'kɪər, fæ-/ n Hindu or Muslim holy man

fal·con /'fɔːlkən‖'fæl-/ n bird that can be trained to hunt ~**er** n person who trains falcons ~**ry** n [U] hunting with falcons

fall¹ /fɔːl/ vi **fell** /fel/, **fallen** /'fɔːlən/ 1 come or go down freely: *She fell into the lake.| The house fell down.* 2 hang loosely: *Her hair falls over her shoulders.* 3 become lower: *The temperature fell.* 4 (of land) slope down 5 happen: *Christmas falls on a Friday.* 6 become: *fall asleep/in love* 7 be wounded or killed in battle 8 be defeated **9** (of the face) take on a look of sadness, etc. **10 fall flat** produce no result **11 fall short** fail to reach a standard

fall about *phr vi* lose control of oneself (with laughter)

fall back *phr vi* RETREAT

fall back on *phr vt* use when there is failure or lack of other means

fall behind *phr vi/t* not keep level (with)

fall for *phr vt* **1** be attracted by **2** accept and be cheated by

fall off *phr vi* become less

fall on *phr vt* attack eagerly

fall out *phr vi* quarrel

fall through *phr vi* (of a plan) fail

fall² *n* **1** act of falling **2** something that has fallen: *a heavy fall of snow* **3** *AmE* for AUTUMN **falls** *n* [P] WATERFALL

fal·la·cy /ˈfæləsi/ *n* [C;U] false belief or reasoning **–lacious** /fəˈleɪʃəs/ *adj fml* based on fallacy

fal·li·ble /ˈfæləbəl/ *adj* able to make mistakes **–bility** /ˌfæləˈbɪləti/ *n* [U]

falling star /ˌ·· ˈ·/ *n* SHOOTING STAR

fal·lo·pi·an tube /fəˌləʊpiən ˈtjuːb‖ fəˈləʊpiən tuːb/ *n* tube through which eggs pass to the WOMB

fall·out /ˈfɔːlaʊt/ *n* [U] dangerous dust left in the air after a NUCLEAR explosion

fal·low /ˈfæləʊ/ *adj* (of land) dug but left unplanted

false /fɔːls/ *adj* **1** not true or correct **2** disloyal: *false friend* **3** not real: *a false nose* **4** careless; unwise: *One false move and I'll shoot you!* **~ly** *adv* **~ness** *n* [U] **~hood** *n* [C;U] lying; lie

false a·larm /ˌ· ·ˈ·/ *n* warning of something bad that does not happen

false bot·tom /ˌ· ˈ·· /*n* something that looks like the bottom of a box, etc., but hides a secret space

false pre·tenc·es /ˌ· ·ˈ··‖ˌ· ˈ··· / *n* [P] behaviour intended to deceive

false start /ˌ· ˈ·/ *n* unsuccessful beginning that means one must start again

fal·set·to /fɔːlˈsetəʊ/ *n* [C;U] **-tos** (man with an) unnaturally high voice

fal·si·fy /ˈfɔːlsəfaɪ/ *vt* make false **–fication** /ˌfɔːlsəfəˈkeɪʃən/ *n* [C;U]

fal·si·ty /ˈfɔːlsəti/ *n* [U] *fml* falseness

fal·ter /ˈfɔːltəʳ/ *vi* **1** move or behave uncertainly **2** speak unsteadily **~ingly** *adv*

fame /feɪm/ *n* [U] condition of being well known **famed** *adj* famous

fa·mil·i·al /fəˈmɪliəl/ *adj fml* of a family

fa·mil·i·ar /fəˈmɪliəʳ/ *adj* **1** often seen; common **2** too friendly **3 familiar with** knowing thoroughly **~ly** *adv* **~ity** /fəˌmɪliˈærəti/ *n* [C;U]

fa·mil·i·ar·ize /fəˈmɪliəraɪz/ *vt* make well informed

fam·i·ly /ˈfæməli/ *n* **1** one's parents, children, aunts, etc. **2** one's children **3** people descended from the same ANCESTOR **4** division of living creatures or languages: *the cat family* ♦ *adj* suitable for children: *a family film*

family plan·ning /ˌ··· ˈ··/ *n* [U] controlling of the number of children in a family by CONTRACEPTION

family tree /ˌ··· ˈ·/ *n* drawing showing the relationship of family members

fam·ine /ˈfæmən/ *n* [C;U] serious lack of food

fam·ished /ˈfæmɪʃt/ *adj* very hungry

fa·mous /ˈfeɪməs/ *adj* very well known **~ly** *adv* very well

fan¹ /fæn/ *n* instrument for making a flow of air ♦ *v* **-nn-** **1** *vt* send cool air onto **2** *vi* spread in a half circle

fan² *n* keen supporter: *football fans*

fa·nat·ic /fəˈnætɪk/ *n* person who is too keen on something: *religious fanatics* **~al** *adj* **~ally** /-kli/ *adv* **~ism** /-tɪsɪzəm/ *n* [U]

fan belt /ˈ· ·/ *n* belt driving a FAN¹ to cool an engine

fan·ci·ful /ˈfænsɪfəl/ *adj* showing imagination rather than reason **~ly** *adv*

fan·cy /ˈfænsi/ *n* **1** [U] imagination **2** [C] opinion not based on fact **3 take a fancy to** become fond of ♦ *vt* **1** wish for; like **2** imagine: *Fancy that!* **3** believe: *I fancy he's Dutch.* **4 fancy oneself** have a very high opinion of oneself ♦ *adj* **1** decorative and unusual **2** higher than the usual or reasonable price

fancy dress /ˌ·· ˈ·/ *n* [U] amusing clothes worn for a party, etc.

fan·fare /ˈfænfeəʳ/ *n* short loud piece of TRUMPET music to introduce a person or event

fang /fæŋ/ *n* long sharp tooth

fan·light /ˈfænlaɪt/ *n* small window over a door

fan mail /ˈ· ·/ *n* [U] letters to a famous person from FANS²

fan·ny /ˈfæni/ *n sl* **1** *AmE* BOTTOM¹ (2) **2** *BrE taboo* women's outer sex organs

fan·tas·tic /fænˈtæstɪk/ *adj sl* **1** wonderful **2** (of ideas) not practical **3** wild and strange **~ally** /-kli/ *adv*

fan·ta·sise ‖ also **-ize** *BrE* /ˈfæntəsaɪz/ *vi/t* have fantasies (about)

fan·ta·sy /ˈfæntəsi/ *n* [C;U] (something made by) imagination: *sexual fantasies*

far /fɑːʳ/ *adv, adj* **farther** /ˈfɑːðəʳ‖ ˈfɑːr-/ *or* **further** /ˈfɜːðəʳ‖ˈfɜːr-/ , **farthest** /ˈfɑːðəst‖ˈfɑːr-/ *or* **furthest** /ˈfɜːðəst‖ˈfɜːr-/ **1** a long way: *too far to* *walk* | *the far distance* **2** very much: *far better* **3** (of a political position) very much to the LEFT or RIGHT: *the far left* **4 as/so far as** to the degree that: *So far as I know, he's coming.* **5 far and away** by a great deal or amount: *She's far and away the best actress.* **6 far be it from me** to (used esp. to show disagreement or disapproval) I certainly would not want to **7 far from: a** very much not: *I'm far from pleased.* **b** instead of: *Far from being angry, he's delighted.* **8 so far** until now **9 So far, so good** Things are satisfactory up to this point, at least

far·a·way /ˈfɑːrəweɪ/ *adj* **1** distant **2** (of a look in someone's eyes) dreamy

farce /fɑːs‖fɑːrs/ *n* **1** light funny play **2** set of silly events **farcical** *adj*

fare /feəʳ/ *n* **1** [C] money charged for a journey **2** [U] *fml* food ♦ *vi* get on; succeed: *fare badly*

Far East /ˌ· '·◄/ *n* [S] countries east of India

fare·well /feəˈwel‖feər-/ *interj, n fml* goodbye

far-fetched /ˌfɑːˈfetʃt‖ˌfɑːr-/ *adj* hard to believe

far-flung /ˌ· '·◄/ *adj* spread over a great distance

far-gone /ˌ· '·/ *adj* in an advanced state, esp. of something bad

farm /fɑːm‖fɑːrm/ *n* area of land and buildings where crops are grown and animals raised ♦ *vi/t* use (land) as a farm

farm out *phr vt* send (work) for other people to do

farm·er /ˈfɑːməʳ‖ˈfɑːr-/ *n* person who owns or manages a farm

farm·hand /ˈfɑːmhænd‖ˈfɑːrm-/ *n* worker on a farm

farm·house /ˈfɑːmhaʊs‖ˈfɑːrm-/ *n* main house on a farm

farm·yard /ˈfɑːmjɑːd‖ˈfɑːrmjɑːrd/ *n* yard surrounded by farm buildings

far-off /ˌ· '·◄/ *adj* distant

far-reach·ing /ˌ· '··◄/ *adj* having a wide influence

far-sight·ed /ˌfɑːˈsaɪtd◄‖ˌfɑːr-/ *adj* able to judge future effects

fart /fɑːt‖fɑːrt/ *vi taboo* send out air from the bowels **fart** *n taboo* **1** escape of air from the bowels **2** *sl* extremely unpleasant person

far·ther /ˈfɑːðəʳ‖ˈfɑːr-/ *adv, adj* FURTHER

far·thest /ˈfɑːðəst‖ˈfɑːr-/ *adv, adj* FURTHEST

fas·ci·nate /ˈfæsəneɪt/ *vt* attract and interest strongly **–nating** *adj* **–nation** /ˌfæsəˈneɪʃən/ *n* [S;U]

fas·cis·m /ˈfæʃɪzəm/ *n* [U] political system marked by total state control under a single leader, and support of one's own nation and race **fascist** *n, adj*

fash·ion /ˈfæʃən/ *n* [C;U] way of dressing or behaving that is popular at a certain time **2** [S] *fml* manner of doing something: *in an orderly fashion* **3 after a fashion** not very well ♦ *vt fml* make; shape **∼able** according to the latest fashion **∼ably** *adv*

fast¹ /fɑːst‖fæst/ *adj* **1** quick: *fast cars* **2** firmly fixed: *fast colours* **3** (of a clock) showing time later than the right time ♦ *adv* **1** quickly **2** firmly **3 fast asleep** sleeping deeply **4 pull a fast one (on)** *infml* deceive (someone) with a trick

fast² *vi* eat no food, esp. for religious reasons ♦ *n* period of fasting

fas·ten /ˈfɑːsən‖ˈfæ-/ *vi/t* make or become firmly fixed **∼er** *n* thing that fastens things together **∼ing** *n* something that holds things shut

fasten on *phr vt* take eagerly and use

fast food /ˌ· '·/ *n* [U] restaurant food (e.g. fried chicken) that is easily prepared

fas·tid·i·ous /fæˈstɪdiəs/ *adj* difficult to please; disliking anything dirty or nasty **∼ly** *adv* **∼ness** *n* [U]

fat /fæt/ *n* [U] **1** material under the skins of animals and human beings which helps keep them warm **2** this substance used in cooking ♦ *adj* -tt- **1** having a lot of FAT (1) on the body **2** thick and well-filled: *fat book* **∼ness** *n* [U]

fa·tal /ˈfeɪtl/ *adj* causing death or ruin **∼ly** *adv*

fa·tal·is·m /ˈfeɪtl-ɪzəm/ *n* [U] belief that events are controlled by FATE (1) **–ist** *n*

fa·tal·i·ty /fəˈtæləti/ *n* **1** [C] violent death **2** [U] being fatal

fate /feɪt/ *n* **1** [U] power beyond human control that decides events **2** [C] end, esp. death **3** [S] the future **∼ful** *adj* important (esp. in a bad way) for the future: *fateful decision* **∼fully** *adv* **fated** *adj* **1** caused by fate **2** *infml* very unlucky

fat·head /ˈfæthed/ *n BrE* fool

fa·ther /ˈfɑːðəʳ/ *n* **1** male parent **2** (*usu. cap.*) priest ♦ *vt* become the father of **∼hood** *n* [U] **∼less** *adj* **∼ly** *adj* like a good father **fathers** *n* [P] FOREFATHERS

Father Christ·mas /ˌ·· '··/ *n esp. BrE* for SANTA CLAUS

father fig·ure /ˈ·· ˌ··/ *n* older man on whom one depends for advice

father-in-law /ˈ·· · ˌ·/ *n* **fathers-in-law** father of one's wife or husband

fa·ther·land /ˈfɑːðəlænd‖-ðər-/ *n* one's native land

fath·om /ˈfæðəm/ *n* unit of measurement (6 feet) for the depth of water ♦ *vt* understand fully

fa·tigue /fə'tiːg/ n 1 [U] tiredness 2 [U] weakness in metals caused by repeated bending 3 [C] (in the army) a job of cleaning or cooking ♦ vt fml make tired

fat·ten /'fætn/ vt make fatter

fat·ty /'fæti/ adj containing fat ♦ n sl fat person

fat·u·ous /'fætʃuəs/ adj silly: fatuous remarks ~ly adv

fau·cet /'fɔːsɪt/ n AmE for TAP (1)

fault /fɔːlt/ n 1 mistake or imperfection 2 crack in the Earth's surface 3 **at fault** in the wrong 4 **find fault with** complain about 5 **one's fault** something one can be blamed for 6 **to a fault** (of good qualities) too; too much ♦ vt find mistakes in ~less adj perfect ~y adj

fau·na /'fɔːnə/ n [U] animals of a particular area or period

faux pas /,fəʊ 'pɑː, ,fəʊ pɑː/ n faux pas /,fəʊ 'pɑːz/ social mistake

fa·vour BrE || **-vor** AmE /'feɪvə/ n 1 [U] approval: gain widespread favour 2 [C] kind act: do me a favour 3 **in favour of**: a in support of b (of a cheque) payable to 4 **in one's favour** to one's advantage ♦ vt 1 approve of 2 be unfairly fond of; treat with favour ~able adj 1 showing or winning approval 2 advantageous ~ably adv

fa·vou·rite BrE || **-vorite** AmE /'feɪvərɪt/ n 1 person or thing loved above all others 2 horse expected to win a race ♦ adj most loved **-ritism** n [U] unfairly generous treatment of one person

fawn¹ /fɔːn/ n 1 [C] young deer 2 [U] light yellowish-brown colour

fawn² v fawn on phr vt try to gain the favour of, by being too attentive

fax /fæks/ vt send (copies of printed material) in ELECTRONIC form along a telephone line

faze /feɪz/ vt AmE shock into silence

FBI /,ef biː 'aɪ/ n Federal Bureau of Investigation; US police department under central control

fear /fɪə/ n 1 [C;U] feeling that danger is near 2 [U] danger 3 **No fear!** Certainly not! ♦ vi/t fml be afraid (of) ~ful adj 1 terrible; shocking 2 fml afraid ~less adj not afraid ~lessly adv ~some adj lit frightening

fea·si·ble /'fiːzəbəl/ adj able to be done; possible **-bility** /,fiːzə'bɪləti/ n [U]

feast /fiːst/ n 1 splendid meal 2 religious FESTIVAL ♦ vi 1 eat and drink very well 2 **feast one's eyes on** look at with delight

feat /fiːt/ n difficult action successfully done

fea·ther /'feðə/ n 1 one of a bird's many light skin coverings 2 **a feather in one's cap** honour to be proud of ♦

vt 1 put feathers on or in 2 **feather one's nest** make oneself dishonestly rich while in a trusted position ~y adj soft and light

fea·ther·bed /'feðəbed‖-ər-/ vt protect (an industry) too generously

fea·ther·brained /'feðəbreɪnd‖-ər-/ adj silly and thoughtless

fea·ture /'fiːtʃə/ n 1 noticeable quality 2 part of the face 3 long newspaper article 4 film being shown at a cinema ♦ v 1 vt include as a performer 2 vi play an important part ~less adj uninteresting **features** n [P] face

Feb·ru·ary /'februəri, 'februri‖ 'febjueri/ n the 2nd month of the year

fe·ces /'fiːsiːz/ n AmE for FAECES

feck·less /'fekləs/ adj worthless and irresponsible

fec·und /'fekənd, 'fiːkənd/ adj fml FERTILE

fed /fed/ v past t. and p. of FEED

fed·e·ral /'fedərəl/ adj 1 of or being a federation 2 of the central US government as opposed to the States

fed·e·ra·tion /,fedə'reɪʃən/ n 1 [C] united group of states, organizations, etc. 2 [U] action or result of uniting in this way

fed up /, · '·/ adj sl tired and discontented

fee /fiː/ n money paid for professional services, to join a club, etc.

fee·ble /'fiːbəl/ adj weak **feebly** adv

fee·ble-mind·ed /,fiːbə'maɪndɪd◂/ adj with low INTELLIGENCE

feed /fiːd/ v fed /fed/ 1 vt give food to 2 vi (esp. of animals) eat 3 vt supply; provide: feed information into a computer ♦ n 1 animal's or baby's meal 2 [U] food for animals 3 [C] pipe, etc., through which a machine is fed

feed·back /'fiːdbæk/ n information about the results of an action, passed back to the person in charge

feel¹ /fiːl/ v felt /felt/ 1 vt learn about with the fingers 2 vt experience (the touch of something): feel the wind 3 vi search with the fingers: feel for a pencil 4 be consciously: feel hungry/happy 5 vt suffer because of: feel the cold 6 give a sensation: This sheet feels wet. 7 vt believe without reasoning: I feel they won't come. 8 **feel like** wish for; want

feel for phr vt be sorry for

feel² n [S] 1 sensation caused by touching 2 act of feeling 3 **get the feel of** become used to and skilled at

feel·er /'fiːlə/ n 1 thread-like part of an insect's head, with which it touches things 2 suggestion made to test opinion

feel·ing /'fiːlɪŋ/ n 1 [S] consciousness of something felt 2 [S] belief not based on reason 3 [U] power to feel 4 [U] excitement of mind: cause ill feeling 5

[U] sympathy **feelings** *n* [P] EMOTIONs

feet /fiːt/ *n pl.* of FOOT

feign /feɪn/ *vt fml* pretend to have or be

feint /feɪnt/ *n* false attack or blow ♦ *vi* make a feint

feist·y /ˈfaɪsti/ *adj AmE* excited and quarrelsome

fe·li·ci·ty /fɪˈlɪsəti/ *n* [U] *fml* happiness

fe·line /ˈfiːlaɪn/ *adj* of or like a cat

fell¹ /fel/ *v past t.* of FALL

fell² *vt* cut or knock down: *fell a tree/ a man*

fell³ *n* high rocky country in the north of England

fel·ler /ˈfelər/ *n sl* fellow; man

fel·low /ˈfeləʊ/ *n* **1** man **2** member of a learned society or college **3** companion: *fellow prisoners/students* ♦ *adj* another of the same group: *fellow prisoners/students* **~ship** *n* **1** [C] group or society **2** [U] companionship **3** [C] position of a college fellow

fellow feel·ing /ˌ··· ˈ···/ *n* [S;U] sympathy for someone like oneself

fellow trav·el·ler /ˌ·· ˈ···/ *n* someone who is sympathetic to COMMUNISM without actually joining the party

fel·o·ny /ˈfeləni/ *n* [C;U] serious crime (e.g. murder) **felon** *n* person guilty of felony

felt¹ /felt/ *v past t. and p.* of FEEL

felt² *n* [U] thick cloth made of pressed wool

felt-tip pen /ˌ·· ˈ·/ *n* pen with felt at the end instead of a NIB

fe·male /ˈfiːmeɪl/ *adj* **1** of the sex that produces young **2** (of plants) producing fruits **3** having a hole into which something fits: *female plug* ♦ *n* woman or female animal

fem·i·nine /ˈfemənən/ *adj* **1** suitable for a woman **2** *gram* of the class of words for females **–ninity** /ˌfeməˈnɪnəti/ *n* [U] being FEMININE (1)

fem·i·nis·m /ˈfeməˌnɪzəm/ *n* [U] principle that women should have the same rights as men **–nist** *n, adj*

fen /fen/ *n* area of low wet land

fence¹ /fens/ *n* **1** wall made of wood or wire **2** someone who buys and sells stolen goods **3** **sit on the fence** avoid taking sides in an argument ♦ *vt* surround or separate with a fence

fence² *vi* **1** fight with a long thin sword as a sport **2** avoid giving an honest answer **fencer** *n*

fenc·ing /ˈfensɪŋ/ *n* [U] **1** sword-fighting as a sport **2** material for making fences

fend /fend/ *vi*
  fend for oneself look after oneself
  fend off *phr vt* push away

fend·er /ˈfendər/ *n* **1** low wall round a fireplace **2** *AmE for* WING (4)

fer·ment¹ /fəˈment/ *vi/t* **1** change chemically so that sugar becomes alcohol **2** make or become excited **~ation** /ˌfɜːmenˈteɪʃən, ˌfɜːmən-/ *n* [U]

fer·ment² /ˈfɜːment‖ˈfɜːr-/ *n* [U] trouble and excitement

fern /fɜːn‖fɜːrn/ *n* plant with feathery green leaves

fe·ro·cious /fəˈrəʊʃəs/ *adj* fierce; violent **~ly** *adv*

fe·ro·ci·ty /fəˈrɒsəti‖fəˈrɑː-/ *n* [U] ferociousness

fer·ret /ˈferət/ *n* small fierce animal that hunts rats and rabbits ♦ *vi/t* search; find by searching

fer·rous /ˈferəs/ *adj* of or containing iron

fer·ry /ˈferi/ *also* **ferryboat** /ˈferibəʊt/ *--n* boat that carries people and things across a narrow piece of water ♦ *vt* carry (as if) on a ferry

fer·tile /ˈfɜːtaɪl‖ˈfɜːrtl/ *adj* **1** producing young, crops, etc. **2** (of a person's mind) inventive **–tility** /fɜːˈtɪləti‖fɜːr-/ *n* [U]

fer·ti·lize /ˈfɜːtəlaɪz‖ˈfɜːrtl-aɪz/ *vt* make fertile **–lizer** plant food **–liza·tion** /ˌfɜːtəlaɪˈzeɪʃən‖ˌfɜːrtələ-/ *n* [U]

fer·vent /ˈfɜːvənt‖ˈfɜːr-/ *adj* feeling strongly: *fervent hope/believer* **~ly** *adv*

fer·vid /ˈfɜːvəd‖ˈfɜːr-/ *adj fml* sharing too strong feeling

fer·vour *BrE* ‖ **-vor** *AmE*/ˈfɜːvər‖ˈfɜːr-/ *n* [U] quality of being fervent: ZEAL

fes·ter /ˈfestər/ *vi* (of a wound) become infected

fes·ti·val /ˈfestəvəl/ *n* **1** time for public happiness: *Christmas is a festival of the church.* **2** group of musical, etc., performances held regularly

fes·tive /ˈfestɪv/ *adj* joyful

fes·tiv·i·ty /feˈstɪvəti/ *n* [C;U] festive activity

fes·toon /feˈstuːn/ *vt* decorate with chains of flowers, RIBBONs, etc.

fetch /fetʃ/ *vt* **1** go and get and bring back **2** be sold for: *The house fetched £30,000.* **3** **fetch and carry** do the small duties of a servant

fete /feɪt/ *n* day of public amusement held esp. to collect money ♦ *vt* honour publicly

fet·id /ˈfiːtəd‖ˈfetəd/ *adj* smelling bad

fet·ish /ˈfetɪʃ, ˈfiː-/ *n* something to which one pays too much attention

fet·ter /ˈfetər/ *n* chain for a prisoner's foot: (fig.) *the fetters of an unhappy marriage* ♦ *vt* tie; prevent from moving

fet·tle /ˈfetl/ *n* [U] condition: *He's in fine fettle.*

fe·tus /ˈfiːtəs/ n FOETUS

feud /fjuːd/ n violent continuing quarrel ♦ vi have a feud

feud·al /ˈfjuːdl/ adj of the system of holding land in return for work, as practised in Europe from the 9th to the 15th century ~**ism** n [U]

fe·ver /ˈfiːvəʳ/ n [S;U] 1 (disease causing) high body temperature — see also YELLOW FEVER 2 excited state ~**ish** adj 1 of or having fever 2 unnaturally fast ~**ishly** adv

few /fjuː/ determiner, pron, n [P] 1 (with **a**) some: Let's invite a few friends. 2 (without **a**) not many: She has few friends.

fi·an·cé /fiˈɒnseɪ, ˌfiːɑːnˈseɪ/ **fiancée** (same pronunciation) fem. — n person one is ENGAGED to

fi·as·co /fiˈæskəʊ/ n -cos complete failure

fib /fɪb/ vi, n -bb- (tell) a small lie ~**ber** n

fi·bre BrE ‖ **fiber** AmE /ˈfaɪbəʳ/ n 1 [C] thin thread-like plant or animal growth 2 [U] mass of threads 3 [U] person's inner character **fibrous** adj

fi·bre·glass BrE ‖ **fiberglass** AmE /ˈfaɪbəɡlɑːs ‖ -bərɡlæs/ n [U] material of glass fibres used for making boats, etc.

fi·bro·si·tis /ˌfaɪbrəˈsaɪtɪs/ n [U] RHEUMATIC disorder of the muscles

fick·le /ˈfɪkəl/ adj not loyal; often changing

fic·tion /ˈfɪkʃən/ n 1 [U] stories n [S;U] untrue story ~**al** adj

fic·ti·tious /fɪkˈtɪʃəs/ adj untrue: invented

fid·dle /ˈfɪdl/ n 1 dishonest practice 2 VIOLIN 3 (as) **fit as a fiddle** perfectly healthy 4 **play second fiddle (to)** play a less important part (than) ♦ v 1 vi move things aimlessly 2 vi play the VIOLIN 3 vt sl lie about: fiddle one's taxes –**dler** n

fid·dling /ˈfɪdlɪŋ/ adj small and silly

fid·dly /ˈfɪdli/ adj needing delicate use of the fingers

fi·del·i·ty /fɪˈdelɪti/ n [U] 1 faithfulness 2 closeness to an original

fid·get /ˈfɪdʒɪt/ vi move one's body around restlessly ♦ n someone who fidgets

field¹ /fiːld/ n 1 [C] piece of farming land 2 [C] open area: a football field\an oilfield\a battlefield 3 [C] branch of knowledge 4 [S] place where practical operations actually happen: study tribal languages in the field 5 [C] area where a force is felt: gravitational field

field² v 1 vi/t (in cricket, etc.) catch or stop (the ball) 2 vt produce (a team or army) ~**er** n

field day /ˈ· ·/ n have a field day enjoy oneself very much

field e·vent /ˈ· ·,·/ n competitive sports event, such as weight-throwing or jumping

field glass·es /ˈ· ,··/ n [P] BINOCULARS

field mar·shal /ˈ· ,··/ n British army officer of highest rank

field of vi·sion /ˌ· · ˈ··/ n whole space within seeing distance

field-test /ˈ· ·/ vt try (something) out in the FIELD¹ (4)

field·work /ˈfiːldwɜːk ‖ -ɜːrk/ n [U] study done in the FIELD¹ (4)

fiend /fiːnd/ n 1 devil 2 infml someone very keen on something ~**ish** adj ~**ishly** adv

fierce /fɪəs ‖ fɪərs/ adj 1 angry, violent, and cruel 2 severe: fierce heat/ competition ~**ly** adv ~**ness** n

fi·er·y /ˈfaɪəri/ adj 1 like fire 2 violent: fiery temper

fi·es·ta /fiˈestə/ n religious holiday with public dancing, etc.

fif·teen /fɪfˈtiːn◄/ determiner, n, pron 15 ~**th** determiner, adv, n, pron 15th

fifth /fɪfθ, fɪfθ/ determiner, n, pron, adv 5th

fifth col·umn /ˌ· ˈ··/ n group of people who secretly help the enemies of their country in war

fif·ty /ˈfɪfti/ determiner, n, pron 50 ~**tieth** determiner, adv, n, pron 50th

fifty-fif·ty /ˌ··ˈ··◄/ adj, adv (of shares or chances) equal(ly)

fig /fɪɡ/ n (tree that bears) a soft sweet fruit with small seeds

fig. written abbrev. for: 1 FIGURATIVE 2 FIGURE¹ (5)

fight¹ /faɪt/ vi/t fought /fɔːt/ 1 use violence (against); struggle 2 argue ~**er** n 1 person who fights professionally: (fig.) a tireless fighter against racism 2 small military aircraft

fight back phr vt 1 recover from a bad or losing position 2 defend oneself by fighting

fight off phr vt keep away with an effort

fight out phr vt settle (a quarrel) by fighting

fight² n 1 [C] battle 2 [U] power or wish to fight 3 [C] boxing (BOX²) match

fighting chance /ˌ·· ˈ·/ n small but real chance if great effort is made

fig leaf /ˈ· ·/ n something that hides something else, esp. dishonestly

fig·ment /ˈfɪɡmənt/ n something not real: a figment of his imagination

fig·u·ra·tive /ˈfɪɡjʊrətɪv, -ɡə-/ adj (of words, phrases, etc.) used in some way other than the main or usual meaning, to suggest a picture in the mind or make a comparison ~**ly** adv: She's up to her eyes in paperwork — figuratively speaking, of course!

fig·ure¹ /ˈfɪɡəʳ‖ˈfɪɡjər/ n 1 (shape of) a human body: *a good figure* 2 person: *a leading political figure* 3 (sign for) a number 4 price 5 DIAGRAM
figure² v 1 vi take a part 2 vt esp. AmE believe 3 **That figures** infml That seems reasonable
  figure on phr vt esp. AmE plan on; include in one's plans
  figure out phr vt discover by thinking
fig·ure·head /ˈfɪɡəhed‖ˈfɪɡjər-/ n someone who is the chief in name only
figure of speech /ˌ··· ·ˈ·/ n figurative expression
fil·a·ment /ˈfɪləmənt/ n thin thread, esp. in an electric light BULB (2)
filch /fɪltʃ/ vt steal secretly (something of small value)
file¹ /faɪl/ n steel tool for rubbing or cutting hard surfaces ♦ vt rub or cut with a file: *file one's nails*
file² n 1 arrangement for storing papers on one subject
file³ vt put in a file
  file for phr vt law request officially
file⁴ n line of people one behind the other ♦ vi walk in a file
fi·li·al /ˈfɪlɪəl/ adj fml suitable to a son or daughter
fil·i·bus·ter /ˈfɪləbʌstəʳ/ vi esp. AmE delay parliamentary action by making long speeches **filibuster** n
fil·i·gree /ˈfɪləɡriː/ n [U] decorative wire work
filing cab·i·net /ˈ·· ˌ··/ n piece of office furniture for storing papers in
fil·ings /ˈfaɪlɪŋz/ n [P] very small sharp bits that have been rubbed off a metal surface with a FILE¹
fill /fɪl/ v 1 vt/i make or become full 2 vt go or be put into: *fill a vacancy* 3 fulfil ♦ n full supply **~er** n substance added to increase size **~ing** n 1 material to fill a hole, esp. in a tooth 2 food mixture folded inside pastry, SANDWICHes, etc.
  fill in phr vt 1 put in (what is necessary): *fill in a form* 2 supply the most recent information 3 take someone's place
  fill out phr v 1 vi get fatter 2 vt FILL in (1)
  fill up phr vi/t make or become full
fil·let /ˈfɪlɪt‖fɪˈlet, -leɪ, fɪˈleɪ/ n piece of meat or fish without bones ♦ vt remove bones from
filling sta·tion /ˈ·· ˌ··/ also **petrol station** BrE ‖ **gas station** AmE — n place that sells petrol and oil and may also do repairs
fil·ly /ˈfɪli/ n young female horse
film /fɪlm/ n 1 [C;U] (roll of) thin material used in photography 2 [C] esp. BrE cinema picture 3 [S;U] thin covering: *film of oil* ♦ vi/t make a

FILM (2) (of) **~y** adj very thin: *filmy silk*
film star /ˈ· ·/ n famous cinema actor or actress
film-strip /ˈfɪlm.strɪp/ n [C;U] length of photographic film that shows drawings, etc., separately as still pictures
fil·ter /ˈfɪltəʳ/ n 1 apparatus through which liquids are passed to clean them 2 glass that changes the colour or amount of light ♦ vi/t go or send (as if) through a filter: *People filtered out of the cinema.*
filter tip /ˈ·· ·/ n (cigarette with) an end that filters smoke
filth /fɪlθ/ n [U] 1 very nasty dirt 2 something rude or unpleasant **~y** adj
fin /fɪn/ n 1 winglike part of a fish 2 thing shaped like this on a car, etc.
fi·nal /ˈfaɪnl/ adj 1 last 2 (of a decision, etc.) that cannot be changed ♦ also **finals** pl. n 1 last of a set of matches 2 last and most important examinations in a college course **~ly** adv 1 at last 2 allowing no further change **~ist** n player in a final match **~ize** vt give final form to
fi·na·le /fɪˈnɑːli‖fɪˈnæli/ n last division of a piece of music
fi·nance /ˈfaɪnæns, fəˈnæns‖fəˈnæns, ˈfaɪnæns/ n [U] 1 management of (public) money 2 money, esp. provided by a bank, to help run an organization or buy something ♦ vt provide money for **finances** n [P] money owned or provided **financial** /fəˈnænʃəl, faɪ-/ adj **financially** adv
financial year /·,·· ·ˈ·/ n yearly period over which accounts are calculated
fi·nan·cier /fɪˈnænsɪəʳ, faɪˈnæn-‖ˌfɪnənˈsɪər/ n someone who controls large sums of money
finch /fɪntʃ/ n small songbird
find /faɪnd/ vt found /faʊnd/ 1 get (something lost or not known) by searching 2 learn by chance or effort: *find (out) where he lives* 3 obtain by effort: *find time to study* 4 (of a thing) arrive at: *Water finds its own level.* 5 know to exist: *Elephants are found in Africa.* 6 law decide to be: *find someone guilty* ♦ n something good or valuable that is found **~er** n **~ing** n 1 what is learnt by enquiry 2 law decision made in court 3 something learnt as the result of an official enquiry
fine¹ /faɪn/ adj 1 good; beautiful 2 very thin or small: *fine thread/dust*‖(fig.) *fine distinction* 3 (of weather) bright; not wet 4 healthy ♦ adv 1 very well 2 very thin 3 **cut it fine** allow only just enough time **~ly** adv 1 into small bits 2 delicately: *finely tuned*
fine² n money paid as a punishment ♦ vt take a fine from

fine arts /ˌ·ˈ·/ n [P] painting, music, etc.

fi·ne·ry /ˈfaɪnəri/ n [U] beautiful clothes

fi·nesse /fɪˈnes/ n [U] delicate skill

fin·ger /ˈfɪŋgəʳ/ n **1** any of the 5 end parts of the hand **2** part of a glove made to fit one of these parts **3 be/feel all fingers and thumbs** (be/feel that) one is unable to control one's hands **4 (have) a finger in every pie** (have) a part in everything that is going on **5 keep one's fingers crossed** hope for the best **6 lay a finger on** harm **7 not lift a finger** make no effort to help **8 pull one's finger out** sl start working hard **9 put one's finger on** find — see also GREEN FINGERS ♦ vt feel with one's fingers ~**ing** n [U] use of the fingers when playing music

finger-nail /ˈfɪŋgəneɪl‖-əʳ-/ n one of the hard flat pieces at the ends of the fingers

fin·ger·print /ˈfɪŋgəˌprɪnt‖-əʳ-/ n mark made by a finger pressed onto a surface ♦ vt take (someone's) fingerprints

fin·ger·tip /ˈfɪŋgəˌtɪp‖-əʳ-/ n **1** end of a finger **2 have something at one's fingertips** know it well

fin·i·cky /ˈfɪnɪki/ adj disliking many things

fin·ish /ˈfɪnɪʃ/ v **1** vi/t come or bring to an end or **2** eat or drink the rest of **3** take all one's powers, hopes of success, etc. ♦ n **1** [C] last part **2** [S;U] appearance or condition of having been properly polished, painted, etc.

    finish off phr vt kill

    finish with phr vt have no more use for

finishing school /ˈ··· ·/ n private school where rich young girls learn how to behave in social life

fi·nite /ˈfaɪnaɪt/ adj **1** limited **2** gram (of a verb) changing according to tense and subject —**ly** adv

fi·ord /ˈfiːɔːd, fjɔːd‖fiːˈɔːrd, fjɔːrd/ n FJORD

fir /fɜːʳ/ n straight tree with leaves like needles

fire[1] /faɪəʳ/ n **1** [U] condition of burning: afraid of fire **2** [C] something burning, on purpose or by accident: light a fire | forest fire **3** [C] gas or electrical apparatus for warming a room **4** [U] destruction by fire **5** [U] shooting from guns **6 catch fire** start to burn **7 on fire** burning **8 open/cease fire** start/stop shooting **9 set fire to** cause to burn **10 under fire** being shot at — see also **hang fire** (HANG[1])

fire[2] v **1** vi/t shoot off (bullets or arrows) **2** vt dismiss from a job **3** vt excite: fire one's imagination **4** vt bake (clay things) in a KILN

fire a·larm /ˈ··ˌ·/ n signal that warns people of fire

fire·arm /ˈfaɪərɑːm‖-ɑːrm/ n gun

fire-bomb /ˈfaɪəbɒm‖ˈfaɪərbɑːm/ n INCENDIARY bomb

fire-brand /ˈfaɪəbrænd‖-əʳ-/ n trouble-maker; AGITATOR

fire drill /ˈ· ·/ n [C;U] practice in leaving a burning building safely

fire en·gine /ˈ· ˌ··/ n vehicle that carries a fire brigade and their equipment

fire es·cape /ˈ· ·ˌ·/ n outside stairs for leaving a burning building

fire fighting /ˈ· ˌ··/ n [U] **1** action to put out large fires **2** actions taken to discover and remove causes of sudden trouble in organizations, etc.

fire-guard /ˈfaɪəgɑːd‖ˈfaɪərgɑːrd/ n protective framework round a fireplace

fire-man /ˈfaɪəmən‖ˈfaɪər-/ n -**men** /-mən/ **1** person who puts out fires **2** person who looks after a FURNACE, etc.

fire-place /ˈfaɪəpleɪs‖-əʳ-/ n opening for a fire in a room

fire-pow·er /ˈfaɪəˌpaʊəʳ‖-əʳ-/ n [U] ability to deliver gunfire

fire-proof /ˈfaɪəpruːf‖-əʳ-/ adj unable to be damaged by fire **fireproof** vt

fire-rais·ing /ˈ· ˌ··/ n [U] crime of starting fires on purpose

fire·side /ˈfaɪəsaɪd‖-əʳ-/ n area around the fireplace

fire sta·tion /ˈ· ˌ··/ n building for a FIRE BRIGADE

fire·wood /ˈfaɪəwʊd‖-əʳ-/ n [U] wood cut to be used on fires

fire·work /ˈfaɪəwɜːk‖ˈfaɪərwɜːrk/ n container of explosive powder, burnt to make coloured lights **fireworks** n [P] **1** show of FIREWORKs **2** show of anger

firing line /ˈ·· ·/ n [S] position of being the object of attack

firing squad /ˈ·· ˌ·/ n group of soldiers ordered to shoot an offender

firm[1] /fɜːm‖fɜːrm/ adj, adv **1** solidly fixed **2** not likely to change **3** determined; RESOLUTE ~**ly** adv ~**ness** n [U]

firm[2] n business company

fir·ma·ment /ˈfɜːməmənt‖ˈfɜːr-/ n lit the sky

first /fɜːst‖fɜːrst/ determiner, adv **1** before the others **2** for the first time: my first visit **3** rather than do something else **4 first thing** at the earliest time in the morning ♦ n, pron [S] **1** person or thing before others: the first to arrive **2** BrE university examination result of highest quality **3 at first** at the beginning **4 the first** the slightest: They haven't the first idea what it means. ~**ly** adv before anything else

first aid /ˌ· ˈ·/ n [U] treatment given by an ordinary person to someone hurt in an accident, etc.

first-born /ˈfɜːstbɔːn‖ˈfɜːrstbɔːrn/ adj, n firstborn eldest (child)

first class /ˌ· ˈ·◂/ n [U] best travelling conditions on a train, etc. **first-class** adj of the best quality

first cous·in /ˌ· ˈ·/ n child of one's aunt or uncle

first floor /ˌ· ˈ·◂/ n 1 BrE floor above the GROUND FLOOR 2 AmE ground floor

first-hand /ˌfɜːst'hænd◂‖-ɜːr-/ adj, adv (of information) directly from its origin

first la·dy /ˌ· ˈ··/n [the] (in the US) wife of the President

first name /ˈ· ·/ n name that stands before one's family name

first-rate /ˌ· ˈ·◂/ adj of the best quality

first ref·us·al /ˌ· ·ˈ··/n [U] the right to decide whether to buy something before it is offered to other people

first strike /ˌ· ˈ·◂/ n attack made on your enemy before they (can) attack you

firth /fɜːθ‖fɜːrθ/ n Scottish river ESTUARY

fis·cal /ˈfɪskəl/ adj fml of public money, taxes, etc.

fish /fɪʃ/ n **fish** or **fishes 1** [C] cold-blooded creature that lives in water **2** [U] its flesh as food **3 drink like a fish** drink too much alcohol ♦ v **1** vi try to catch fish **2** vi search indirectly: fish for compliments **3** vt bring out or up: He fished a key from his pocket. ~**y** adj **1** like fish **2** seeming false: a fishy story

fish·er·man /ˈfɪʃəmən‖-fər-/ n -**men** /-mən/ man who catches fish, esp. as a job

fish·e·ry /ˈfɪʃəri/ also -**ries** pl. part of the sea where fishing is practised

fish·ing /ˈfɪʃɪŋ/ n [U] sport or job of catching fish

fish·mon·ger /ˈfɪʃmʌŋgər‖-mɑːŋ-, -mʌŋ-/ n BrE someone who sells fish in a shop

fis·sion /ˈfɪʃən/ n [U] splitting of a cell or atom

fis·sure /ˈfɪʃər/ n deep crack in rock

fist /fɪst/ n hand when closed tightly: holding a fistful of coins

fit¹ /fɪt/ v -**tt**- **1** vi/t be the right size and shape (for): The lid doesn't fit. **2** vt put in place: fit a new lock **3** vt make suitable for ♦ n [S] **1** quality of fitting well **2** way that something fits: a tight fit ~**ted** adj fixed in place: fitted carpet ~**ter** n **1** person who fits machine parts **2** person who cuts out and fits clothes — see also GAS FITTER

fit in phr v **1** vi match; HARMONIZE **2** vt make room or time for

fit out phr vt supply; FURNISH

fit² adj **1** suitable, right: fit to eat | Do as you think fit. **2** physically healthy **3** ready to: laugh fit to burst ~**ness** n [U]

fit³ n **1** short attack of illness, etc.: fit of coughing/of pique **2** sudden loss of consciousness **3 by fits and starts** not regularly **4 have a fit** be very angry

fit·ful /ˈfɪtfəl/ adj restlessly irregular ~**ly** adv

fit·ment /ˈfɪtmənt/ n piece of fitted furniture

fit·ting /ˈfɪtɪŋ/ adj fml suitable ♦ n **1** something fixed into a building **2** occasion of trying whether clothes fit

five /faɪv/ determiner, n, pron **5 fiver** n £5 note

fix¹ /fɪks/ vt **1** fasten firmly **2** arrange; decide on: fix a price **3** repair **4** tidy: I must fix my hair **5** esp. AmE prepare (food or drink) **6** arrange the result of (something) dishonestly ~**ative** n chemical for sticking things in position ~**ation** /fɪk'seɪʃən/ n OBSESSION

fix on phr vt choose

fix up phr vt **1** provide **2** repair, change or improve

fix² n **1** awkward situation **2** sl INJECTION of a drug **3** position calculated by looking at the stars, etc.

fix·er /ˈfɪksər/ n person who is good at arranging that something happens, esp. by using influence or dishonesty

fix·ture /ˈfɪkstʃər/ n **1** something fixed into a building **2** sports event on an agreed date

fizz /fɪz/ vi, n [S] (make) a sound of BUBBLES in a liquid ~**y** adj

fiz·zle /ˈfɪzəl/ v fizzle out phr vi end disappointingly

fjord /ˈfjɔːd, fjɔːd‖fiˈɔːrd, fjɔːrd/ n narrow arm of the sea between steep cliffs, esp. in Norway

flab /flæb/ n [U] infml soft loose flesh

flab·ber·gast·ed /ˈflæbəgɑːstɪd‖-ərgæs-/ adj surprised and shocked

flab·by /ˈflæbi/ adj **1** (of muscles) too soft **2** lacking force or effectiveness ~**biness** n [U]

flac·cid /ˈflæksɪd, ˈflæksəd/ adj not firm enough

flag¹ /flæg/ n piece of cloth used as the sign of a country, etc., or to make signals — see also WHITE FLAG ♦ vt -**gg**- put a flag on

flag down phr vt signal (a vehicle) to stop

flag² vi -**gg**- become weak

flag·on /ˈflægən/ n large container for liquids

flag·pole /ˈflægpəʊl/ n long pole to raise a flag on

fla·grant /ˈfleɪgrənt/ adj openly bad ~**ly** adv

flag·ship /ˈflæg.ʃɪp/ n chief naval ship in a group

flag-staff /'flægstɑːf‖-stæf/ *n* flagpole

flag-stone /'flægstəʊn/ *n* flat stone for a floor or path

flag-wav-ing /'· ,·ˑ/ *n* [U] noisy expression of national military feeling

flail /fleɪl/ *vi* wave violently but aimlessly about

flair /fleəʳ/ *n* [S] natural ability to do something

flak /flæk/ *n* 1 gunfire directed at enemy aircraft 2 severe opposition

flake[1] /fleɪk/ *n* small leaf-like bit: *soap flakes* **flaky** *adj* 1 made up of flakes or tending to flake 2 *AmE infml* ECCENTRIC **flakiness** *n* [U]

flake[2] *vi* fall off in flakes

flake out *phr vi* fall asleep or faint because of great tiredness

flam-boy-ant /flæm'bɔɪənt/ *adj* 1 brightly coloured 2 (of a person) showy and bold

flame /fleɪm/ *n* [C;U] 1 (tongue of) burning gas 2 **in flames** burning — see also OLD FLAME ♦ *vi* 1 burn brightly 2 break out with sudden violence: (fig.) *in a flaming temper*

flam-ma-ble /'flæməbəl/ *adj AmE* INFLAMMABLE (1)

flan /flæn/ *n* open pastry case filled with fruit, etc.

flange /flændʒ/ *n* edge of a wheel, etc., that sticks out

flank /flæŋk/ *n* side of an animal, person, or moving army ♦ *vt* be placed beside

flan-nel /'flænl/ *n* 1 [U] loosely woven woollen cloth 2 [C] FACECLOTH 3 *infml, esp. BrE* meaningless words used to avoid giving a direct answer **flannels** *n* [P] flannel trousers

flap /flæp/ *n* 1 [C] flat part of anything that covers an opening 2 [S] sound of flapping 3 **in a flap** excited and anxious ♦ 1 *vi/t* wave slowly up and down: *flap its wings* 2 *vi* get excited and anxious

flare[1] /fleəʳ/ *vi* burn brightly but unsteadily ♦ *n* 1 [S] flaring light 2 [C] bright light used as a signal

flare up *phr vi* become suddenly hotter, more violent, etc. **flare-up** /'· ·/ *n*

flare[2] *vi/t* widen towards the bottom: *flared skirt* **flare** *n* **flares** *n* [P] flared trousers

flash[1] /flæʃ/ *v* 1 *vi/t* shine for a moment 2 *vi* move very fast 3 *vt* send by radio, etc.: *flash news to London*

flash[2] /flæʃ/ *n* 1 sudden bright light: (fig.) *a flash of inspiration* 2 short news report 3 FLASHLIGHT (1) 4 **in a flash** at once ♦ *adj* sudden: *flash flood* 2 modern and expensive-looking **~y** *adj* unpleasantly big, bright, etc.

flash-back /'flæʃbæk/ *n* [C;U] scene in a film, etc., that goes back in time

flash-bulb /'flæʃbʌlb/ *n* bright electric lamp for photography

flash-light /'flæʃlaɪt/ *n* 1 apparatus for taking photographs in the dark 2 *esp. AmE for* TORCH (1)

flash point /'· ·/ *n* point or place at which violence may be expected

flask /flɑːsk‖flæsk/ *n* 1 narrow-necked bottle 2 flat bottle for carrying drinks in one's pocket 3 bottle with a VACUUM between its 2 walls, for keeping liquids hot or cold

flat[1] /flæt/ *n* 1 low level plain 2 flat part or side (of) 3 (in music) flat note 4 flat piece of stage scenery 5 *BrE* set of rooms on one floor of a building 6 *esp. AmE* a flat tyre

flat[2] *adj* -tt- 1 smooth and level 2 spread out fully: *lie down flat* 3 not very thick: *flat cakes* 4 (of a tyre) without enough air in it 5 (of a BATTERY) having lost electrical power 6 (of beer, etc.) having lost its gas 7 dull and lifeless 8 (in music) below the right note 9 firm; with no more argument: *a flat refusal*

flat[3] *adv* 1 into a flat or level position 2 below the right note: *sing flat* 3 and no more: *3 minutes flat* 4 **flat broke** with no money at all 5 **flat out** at full speed

flat feet /,· '·/ *n* feet that rest too flat on the ground **flat-footed** /,· '·◁/ *adj*

flat rate /,· '·◁/ *n* one charge including everything

flat-ten /'flætn/ *vi/t* make or become flat

flat-ter /'flætəʳ/ *vt/i* 1 praise too much or insincerely 2 give pleasure to 3 (of a picture) show (a person) as more beautiful **~er** *n* **~y** *n* [U] flattering remarks

flat-u-lence /'flætjʊləns‖-tʃə-/ *n* [U] *fml* WIND[1] (3)

flaunt /flɔːnt‖flɑːnt, flɔːnt/ *vt derog* show for admiration: *flaunt her wealth*

flau-tist /'flɔːtɪst/ *n* *BrE* FLUTE-player

fla-vour *BrE* ‖ **flavor** *AmE* /'fleɪvəʳ/ *n* 1 [C;U] taste: *6 popular flavours* | *not much flavour* 2 [S] particular characteristic ♦ *vt* give taste to **~ing** *n* [C;U] something added to improve the taste **~less** *adj*

flaw /flɔː/ *n* fault or weakness **~less** *adj* **~lessly** *adv* ♦ *vt* make a flaw in

flax /flæks/ *n* [U] (thread from the stem of) a plant with blue flowers used for making LINEN

flax-en /'flæksən/ *adj lit* (of hair) pale yellow

flay /fleɪ/ *vt* 1 remove the skin from 2 attack fiercely in words

flea /fliː/ *n* wingless jumping insect that feeds on blood

flea mar-ket /'· ,··/ *n* street market where used goods are sold

flea-pit /'fliː.pɪt/ n BrE cheap dirty cinema or theatre

fleck /flek/ n small spot or grain ♦ vt mark with flecks

fledg·ling /'fledʒlɪŋ/ n 1 young bird learning to fly 2 inexperienced person

flee /fliː/ vi/t fled /fled/ fml hurry away (from); escape

fleece /fliːs/ n sheep's woolly coat ♦ vt rob by a trick; charge too much **fleecy** adj woolly

fleet /fliːt/ n 1 number of ships under one command 2 group of buses, etc. under one control

fleet·ing /'fliːtɪŋ/ adj not lasting long: fleeting glimpse

flesh /fleʃ/ n 1 [U] soft part of a person or animal that covers the bones 2 [U] soft part of a fruit 3 [S] the body as opposed to the soul 4 **flesh and blood a** human beings **b** one's relatives 5 **in the flesh** in real life ~**y** adj fat

flew /fluː/ past t. of FLY

flex[1] /fleks/ n [C;U] BrE electric wire in a protective covering

flex[2] vt bend or stretch (one's muscles)

flex·i·ble /'fleksəbəl/ adj 1 easily bent 2 easily changed: flexible plans –**bility** /ˌfleksə'bɪləti/ n [U]

flex·i·time /'fleksitaɪm/ n [U] British system by which people can choose their hours of work

flick /flɪk/ n light sudden blow or movement ♦ vt touch or strike lightly

flick·er /'flɪkər/ vi 1 burn unsteadily 2 move backwards and forwards ♦ n [S] 1 flickering 2 short-lived feeling: flicker of interest

fli·er /'flaɪər/ n person (esp. a pilot) or thing that flies

flies /flaɪz/ n [P] covered front opening on trousers

flight[1] /flaɪt/ n 1 [C;U] flying: birds in flight| (fig.) His account contained some amazing flights of fancy. 2 [C] journey by air 3 [C] aircraft making a journey: Flight Number 347 to Geneva 4 [C] group of birds or aircraft 5 [C] set of stairs ~**less** adj unable to fly

flight[2] n [C;U] (an example of) the act of running away; escape

flight path /'· ·/ n course through the air of an aircraft, etc.

flight·y /'flaɪti/ adj (of a person) too influenced by sudden desires or ideas

flim·sy /'flɪmzi/ adj light and thin; easily destroyed –**sily** adv

flinch /flɪntʃ/ vi move back in pain or fear

fling /flɪŋ/ vt flung /flʌŋ/ throw violently ♦ n [S] short time of enjoyment, often with no sense of responsibility

flint /flɪnt/ n 1 [C;U] hard stone that makes SPARKs (1) 2 bit of metal in a cigarette lighter that lights the gas or petrol

flip /flɪp/ 1 vt send spinning into the air 2 vi become mad or very angry ♦ n quick light blow

flip·pant /'flɪpənt/ adj disrespectful about serious subjects ~**ly** adv –**pancy** n [U]

flip·per /'flɪpər/ n 1 flat limb of a SEAL[2], etc. 2 rubber shoe shaped like this, for swimming

flip side /'· ·/ n less interesting side of a record

flirt /flɜːt‖flɜːrt/ vi behave as if sexually attracted ♦ n person who flirts ~**ation** /flɜː'teɪʃən‖flɜːr-/ n [C;U] ~**atious** adj liking to flirt

flirt with phr vt 1 consider, but not seriously 2 risk, esp. needlessly or lightly

flit /flɪt/ vi -tt- fly or move quickly and lightly

float /fləʊt/ v 1 vi/t (cause to) stay on the surface of liquid or be held up in air 2 vt establish (a business) by selling SHAREs 3 vi/t (allow to) vary in exchange value: float the £ 4 suggest ♦ n 1 light object that floats 2 flat vehicle drawn for use in a procession 3 money kept for use if an unexpected need arises ~**ing** adj not fixed

floating vo·ter /ˌ· '··/ n person who does not always vote for the same political party

flock /flɒk‖flɑːk/ n 1 group of sheep, goats, or birds 2 crowd 3 priest's CONGREGATION ♦ vi move in large numbers

flog /flɒg‖flɑːg/ vt -gg- 1 beat severely 2 sl sell 3 **flog a dead horse** waste time with useless efforts 4 **flog to death** infml spoil (a story idea etc.) by repeating too often

flood /flʌd/ also **floods** pl. — n 1 water covering a place that is usu. dry 2 large quantity: floods of tears ♦ vi/t 1 fill or cover with water 2 overflow 3 arrive in large numbers

flood-gate /'flʌdgeɪt/ n 1 gate for controlling water 2 **open the floodgates** suddenly let loose something that was held back

flood-light /'flʌdlaɪt/ n powerful light thrown on the outside of buildings, etc. ♦ vt -lit /-lɪt/ light with floodlights

flood tide /'· ·/ n [C;U] flow of the TIDE inwards

floor /flɔːr/ n 1 [C] surface one stands on indoors: dance floor 2 [C] level of a building — see also FIRST FLOOR, GROUND FLOOR 3 [S] part of a parliament, etc. where members sit and speak 4 **go through the floor** infml (of a price) sink to a very low level 5 **take the floor: a** speak in a DEBATE **b** start dancing at a party, etc. ♦ vt 1 provide with a floor 2 knock down; defeat 3 confuse

floor-board /'flɔːbɔːd‖'flɔːrbɔːrd/ n board in a wooden floor

floor show /'·· ·/ n CABARET

flop /flɒp‖flɑːp/ vi -pp- 1 fall awkwardly 2 fail ♦ n 1 [S] awkward fall 2 [C] failure ~py adj soft and loose: *floppy hat* ~**piness** n [U]

flop-house /'flɒphaʊs‖'flɑːp-/ n AmE cheap hotel

flop-py disk /,·· '·/ n plastic circle on which computer information is stored

flo-ra /'flɔːrə/ n [U] plants of a particular area or period

flo-ral /'flɔːrəl/ adj of flowers

flor-id /'flɒrɪd‖'flɔː-, 'flɑː-/ adj 1 over-decorated 2 having a red face

flor-ist /'flɒrɪst‖'flɔː-/ n person who sells flowers

flo-ta-tion /fləʊ'teɪʃən/ n [C;U] act of FLOATing (2) a business

flo-til-la /flə'tɪlə‖fləʊ-/ n group of small ships

flot-sam and jet-sam /,flɒtsəm ən 'dʒetsəm‖,flɑːt-, ·· ··/ n 1 [U] collection of broken unwanted things lying about in an untidy way 2 [P] people without homes or work, who move helplessly through life

flounce /flaʊns/ vi move violently to express anger or attract attention

floun-der /'flaʊndəʳ/ vi 1 make wild movements, esp. in water 2 lose control when speaking, etc.

flour /flaʊəʳ/ n [U] powder of crushed grain, used for making bread, etc.

flour-ish /'flʌrɪʃ‖'flɜːrɪʃ/ v 1 vi grow healthily: (fig.) *Business is flourishing.* 2 vt BRANDISH ♦ n noticeable fancy movement

flout /flaʊt/ vt treat (rules, etc.) without respect

flow /fləʊ/ vi (of liquid) move smoothly: (fig.)*traffic flowed past* ♦ n [S;U] steady stream or supply ~**ing** adj curving or hanging gracefully

flow-chart /'fləʊtʃɑːt‖-ɑːrt/ n drawing showing how the parts of a process are connected

flow-er /'flaʊəʳ/ n 1 [C] part of a plant that produces seeds 2 [S] lit best part: *the flower of the nation's youth* ~**less** adj ~**y** adj 1 decorated with flowers 2 (of language) FLORID (1) ♦ vi produce flowers

flow-er-bed /'flaʊəbed‖-ər-/ n small piece of ground where flowers are grown

flow-er-pot /'flaʊəpɒt‖-ərpɑːt/ n pot in which a plant is grown

flown /fləʊn/ v past p. of FLY

flu /fluː/ also **influenza** fml — n [U] infectious disease like a bad cold but more serious

fluc-tu-ate /'flʌktʃueɪt/ vi fml (of levels, etc.) change continually –**ation** /,flʌktʃu'eɪʃən/ n [C;U]

flue /fluː/ n pipe through which smoke or heat passes

flu-ent /'fluːənt/ adj 1 able to speak easily 2 (of speech) coming easily ~**ly** adv –**ency** n [U]

fluff /flʌf/ n [U] 1 soft light pieces from woolly material 2 soft fur or hair on a young animal or bird ♦ vt 1 shake or brush out: *fluff out its feathers* 2 do (something) badly or unsuccessfully ~**y** adv covered with fluff: *fluffy kitten*

flu-id /'fluːɪd/ adj 1 able to flow 2 unsettled: *Our ideas on the subject are still fluid.* ♦ n [C;U] liquid

fluke /fluːk/ n [S] piece of accidental good luck

flum-mox /'flʌməks/ vt confuse completely

flung /flʌŋ/ v past t. and p. of FLING

flunk /flʌŋk/ vt esp. AmE 1 fail (an examination, etc.) 2 mark as unsatisfactory someone's examination answers

flu-o-res-cent /flʊə'resənt‖flʊə, flɔː-/ adj giving out bright light when certain waves have passed through

flu-o-ride /'flʊəraɪd/ n [U] chemical compound said to protect teeth against decay –**ridate** /'flʊərədeɪt‖ 'flʊə-, 'flɔː-/ vt add fluoride to –**rida-tion** /,flʊərə'deɪʃən‖,flʊə-, ,flɔː-/ n [U]

flur-ry /'flʌri‖'flɜːri/ n 1 [C] sudden rush of rain, snow, etc. 2 [S] nervous excitement ♦ vt make nervous

flush /flʌʃ/ n 1 [C] (cleaning with) a rush of water 2 [S] redness of the face 3 [S] feeling of eager excitement ♦ v 1 vt clean with a rush of water 2 vi BLUSH 3 vt make (someone) leave a hiding place ♦ adj 1 level 2 sl having plenty of money ~**ed** adj proud and excited

flus-ter /'flʌstəʳ/ vt make nervous ♦ n [S] nervous state

flute /fluːt/ n WOODWIND musical instrument played by blowing sideways across it

flut-ter /'flʌtəʳ/ vi/t 1 a move (wings) quickly and lightly **b** fly by doing this 2 move in a quick irregular way: *flags fluttering* ♦ n 1 [S;U] fluttering or shaking movement 2 [S] state of excitement

flux /flʌks/ n [U] fml continual change

fly[1] /flaɪ/ v **flew** /fluː/, **flown** /fləʊn/ 1 vi move through the air as a bird or aircraft does 2 vt control (an aircraft) 3 raise (a flag) 4 FLEE 5 vi go fast: *Time flies.* | *I must fly.* (= I have to leave in a hurry) 6 **fly in the face of** DEFY 7 **fly into a rage/temper** become suddenly angry 8 **fly off the handle** infml become suddenly and unexpectedly angry 9 **let fly** attack with words, bullets or blows

fly² n 1 -winged insect 2 hook that is made to look like a fly, used in fishing 3 **fly in the ointment** infml something that spoils the perfection of something 4 **like flies** infml in very large numbers 5 **there are no flies on someone** BrE infml someone is not a fool and cannot be tricked

fly³ n FLIES

fly-blown /'flaɪbləʊn/ adj 1 covered with flies' eggs 2 old and worthless

fly-er /'flaɪəʳ/ n FLIER

flying col·ours /,·· '··/ n [P] **with flying colours** very successfully; splendidly

flying pick·et /,·· '··/ n someone who travels to PICKET a place of work other than their own

flying sau·cer /,·· '··/ n spacecraft believed to come from another world

flying squad /'·· ·/ n special police kept ready for quick action

flying start /,·· '·/ n very good beginning

flying visit /,·· '··/ n very short visit

fly-leaf /'flaɪliːf/ n -leaves /-liːvz/ empty page at the beginning or end of a book

fly-o·ver /'flaɪ-əʊvəʳ/ n BrE place where 2 roads cross at different levels

fly-past /'flaɪpɑːst‖-pæst/ n BrE ceremonial low flight by aircraft over a public gathering

foal /fəʊl/ n young horse ♦ vi give birth to a foal

foam /fəʊm/ n [U] 1 mass of BUBBLES 2 infml FOAM RUBBER ♦ vi produce foam —y adj

foam rub·ber /,·· '··◄/ n [U] soft rubber full of BUBBLES

fob /fɒb‖fɑːb/ v -bb- **fob off** phr vt deceive (someone) into accepting (something)

fo·cus /'fəʊkəs/ n -cuses or -ci /-kaɪ, -saɪ/ 1 [C] point at which beams of light, etc., meet 2 [S] centre of attention 3 **in/out of focus** (not) giving a clear picture because LENS is not correctly placed ♦ vi/t -s- or -ss- 1 come or bring to a focus 2 direct (attention) focal adj

fod·der /'fɒdəʳ‖'fɑː-/ n [U] 1 food for farm animals 2 anything that supplies a continuous demand

foe /fəʊ/ n lit enemy

foe·tus /'fiːtəs/ n creature before birth, at a later stage than an EMBRYO

fog /fɒg‖fɑːg, fɔːg/ n [C,U] (period of) thick mist ♦ vi/t -gg- (cause to) become covered with fog —gy adj 1 misty 2 not clear: I haven't the foggiest idea.

fog-bound /'fɒgbaʊnd‖'fɑːg-, 'fɔːg-/ adj prevented by fog from travelling

fog-horn /'fɒghɔːn‖'fɑːghɔːrn, 'fɔːg-/ n horn used for warning ships in fog

fog lamp /'·· ·/ n bright lamp on a vehicle, for driving through fog

fo·gy /'fəʊgi/ n derog slow uninteresting old person

foi·ble /'fɔɪbəl/ n foolish little personal habit

foil¹ /fɔɪl/ vt prevent (someone) from succeeding in a plan

foil² n 1 [U] thin sheet metal 2 [C] person or thing that provides a CONTRAST to another

foil³ n thin sword for fencing (FENCE² (1))

foist /fɔɪst/ vt force someone to accept: He tried to foist his company on them.

fold¹ /fəʊld/ v 1 bend back on itself 2 vi be able to be folded: folding table 3 vt cross (one's arms) 4 vi (of a business) fail ♦ n line made by folding —er n cardboard holder for papers

fold² n enclosure for sheep

fo·li·age /'fəʊli-ɪdʒ/ n [U] fml leaves

folk /fəʊk/ n 1 [P] people 2 [U] folk music ♦ adj of music, etc. that has grown up among ordinary people: folk singer/concert/dancing **folks** [P] one's relatives

folk-lore /'fəʊklɔːʳ/ n [U] beliefs long preserved among a tribe or nation

fol·low /'fɒləʊ‖'fɑː-/ v 1 vi/t come or go after 2 vt go along: follow the river 3 vt attend or listen to carefully 4 vi/t understand: I don't quite follow (you). 5 vt act according to: follow instructions 6 vi be a necessary result 7 **as follows** as now to be told 8 **follow suit** do what someone else has done —er n someone who follows or supports —ing n 1 next: the following day 2 to be mentioned now —ing n group of supporters

follow through phr vt carry out to the end

follow up phr vt take action to continue or add to the effect of something done before **follow-up** /'·· ·/ n: The paper's doing a follow-up next week.

fol·ly /'fɒli‖'fɑːli/ n [C,U] fml foolishness

fo·ment /fəʊ'ment/ vt fml help (something bad) to develop

fond /fɒnd‖fɑːnd/ adj 1 loving 2 foolishly hopeful: fond belief 3 having a great liking or love (for): fond of —ly adv —ness n [C,U]

fon·dle /'fɒndl‖'fɑːndl/ vt touch lovingly

font /fɒnt‖fɑːnt/ n container for water for BAPTISM

food /fuːd/ n [C,U] 1 something, esp. solid, that creatures eat 2 **food for thought** something to think about carefully

food-stuff /'fuːdstʌf/ n substance used as food

fool /fuːl/ n **1** silly person **2 make a fool of oneself** behave in a silly way ♦ v **1** vt deceive **2** vi behave in a silly way **3** vi joke ~**ish** adj silly ~**ishly** adv ~**ishness** n [U]

fool-har-dy /'fuːlhɑːdi‖-ɑːr-/ adj taking unwise risks

fool-proof /'fuːlpruːf/ adj that cannot fail

fool's par-a-dise /,· '···/ n carelessly happy state in spite of a threat of change

foot¹ /fut/ n feet /fiːt/ **1** [C] end part of the leg **2** [S] bottom: foot of the stairs **3** [C] (measure of length equal to) 12 inches (INCH) **4 a foot in the door** favourable position from which to advance, gain influence, etc. **5 on foot** walking **6 put one's feet up** rest **7 put one's foot down** speak firmly **8 put one's foot in it** esp. BrE ‖ **put one's foot in one's mouth** esp. AmE — infml say the wrong thing **9 set foot in/on** enter; visit ~**age** n [U] length of cinema film ~**ing** n **1** firm placing of the feet: lose one's footing **2** position in relation to others: on an equal footing

foot² v vt **foot the bill** infml pay the bill

foot-ball /'futbɔːl/ n **1** [U] BrE field game for 2 teams of 11 players using a round ball that is kicked **2** [C] ball used in this game **3** [U] AmE AMERICAN FOOTBALL ~**er** n

foot-bridge /'fut,brɪdʒ/ n narrow bridge to be used only by people walking

foot-hill /'fut,hɪl/ n low hill at the foot of a mountain

foot-hold /'futhəʊld/ n **1** place where a foot can stand **2** position from which to advance

foot-lights /'futlaɪts/ n [P] lights along the front of a stage floor

foot-loose /'futluːs/ adj free to go wherever one wants and do what one likes: footloose and fancy-free

foot-man /'futmən/ n -**men** /-mən/ uniformed servant who opens doors, etc.

foot-note /'futnəʊt/ n note at the bottom of a page

foot-path /'futpɑːθ‖-pæθ/ n -**paths** /-pɑːðz‖-pæðz/ narrow path for walking on

foot-plate /'futpleɪt/ n place where the driver of a railway engine stands

foot-print /'fut,prɪnt/ n mark made by a foot

foot-sore /'futsɔːʳ/ adj having sore feet from too much walking

foot-step /'futstep/ n **1** sound of a person's steps **2 follow in someone's footsteps** follow an example set by someone else in the past

foot-wear /'futweəʳ/ n [U] shoes, etc.

foot-work /'futwɜːk‖-ɜːrk/ n [U] use of the feet in sports, etc.

for¹ /fəʳ; strong fɔːʳ/ prep **1** intended to be given to, used by, or used in: a present for you | cake for tea **2** to help: lift it for you | medicine for a cold **3** (shows purpose): What's this knife for? **4** in support of: play football for England **5** towards: set off for school **6** so as to get: wait for the bus | no demand for coal **7** (shows price or amount): buy it for £1 **8** meaning: Red is for danger. **9** (shows distance or time): stay for a week **10** because of: rewarded for his bravery **11** in regard to: an ear for music | good for his health **12** considering: tall for his age **13** (introducing phrases): no need for you to go

for² conj fml and the reason is that

for-age /'fɒrɪdʒ‖'fɑː-, 'fɔː-/ n [U] food for horses and cattle ♦ vi search about

for-ay /'foreɪ‖'fɔː-, 'fɑː-/ n sudden rush into enemy country: (fig.) his unsuccessful foray into politics

for-bear¹ /fɔːˈbeəʳ, fə-‖fɔːr-, fər-/ vi -**bore** /-ˈbɔːʳ/, -**borne** /-ˈbɔːn‖-ˈbɔːrn/ fml hold oneself back from doing something ~**ance** n [U] patient forgiveness

for-bear² /'fɔːbeəʳ‖'fɔːr-/ n FOREBEAR

for-bid /fəˈbɪd‖fər-/ vt -**bade** /-ˈbeɪd‖-ˈbæd/ or -**bad** /-ˈbæd/, -**bidden** /-ˈbɪdn/ **1** refuse to allow **2 God forbid (that)** I very much hope it will not happen (that) ~**ding** adj looking dangerous

force /fɔːs‖fɔːrs/ n **1** [U] strength; violence **2** [C;U] influence **3** [C] power that produces change: the force of gravity **4** [C] group of soldiers, police, etc. — see also FORCES **5 in force** in large numbers **6 in(to) force** in/into operation **7 join forces (with)** unite (with) for a purpose ♦ vt **1** use (physical) force on **2** produce with effort: forced laughter **3** hasten the growth of (plants) **4 force someone's hand** make someone act as one wishes or before they are ready ~**ful** adj (of people, words, etc.) powerful ~**fully** adv **forcible** adj done by physical force **forcibly** adv

for-ceps /'fɔːseps, -səps‖'fɔːr-/ n [P] medical instrument for holding objects

forc-es /'fɔːsɪz‖'fɔːr-/ n [(the) P] (often cap.) the army, navy, and air force of a country

ford /fɔːd‖fɔːrd/ n place where one can cross a river without a bridge ♦ vt cross at a ford

fore /fɔːʳ/ adj front ♦ n **come to the fore** become well-known; noticeable

fore·arm /'fɔːrɑːm‖-ɑːrm/ n arm between the hand and elbow

fore·bear /'fɔːbeəʳ‖'fɔːr-/ n fml ANCESTOR

fore·bod·ing /fɔː'bəʊdɪŋ‖fɔːr-/ n [C;U] feeling of coming evil

fore·cast /'fɔːkɑːst‖'fɔːrkæst/ vt -cast or -casted say in advance (what will happen in future) ♦ n statement of future events: *weather forecast*

fore·close /fɔː'kləʊz‖fɔːr-/ vi/t take back property because a MORTGAGE has not been repaid

fore·court /'fɔːkɔːt‖'fɔːrkɔːrt/ n courtyard in front of a building

fore·fa·thers /'fɔːˌfɑːðəz‖'fɔːr-ˌfɑːðərz/ n [P] ANCESTORS

fore·fin·ger /'fɔːˌfɪŋgəʳ‖'fɔːr-/ n finger next to the thumb

fore·front /'fɔːfrʌnt‖'fɔːr-/ n [S] leading position

fore·go /fɔː'geʊ‖fɔːr-/ vt FORGO

foregone con·clu·sion /ˌ···· ·'··-/ n result that is certain from the start

fore·ground /'fɔːgraʊnd‖'fɔːr-/ n nearest part of a view

fore·hand /'fɔːhænd‖'fɔːr-/ n, adj (tennis stroke) with the inner part of hand and arm turned forward

fore·head /'fɔːhed, 'fɔːhed‖'fɔːrɪd, 'fɑːrəd, 'fɔːrhed/ n face above the eyes

for·eign /'fɒrən‖'fɔː-, 'fɑː-/ adj 1 of a country that is not one's own 2 coming or brought in from outside: *a foreign body in her eye* 3 **foreign to** not natural in ~er n foreign person

foreign affairs /ˌ·· ·'··◂/ n [P] matters concerning international relations and the interests of one's own country in foreign countries

foreign ex·change /ˌ·· ·'··/ n [U] (practice of buying and selling) foreign money

fore·man /'fɔːmən‖'fɔːr-/ **forewoman** /-ˌwʊmən/ fem. — n -men /-mən/ 1 worker in charge of others 2 leader of a JURY

fore·most /'fɔːməʊst‖'fɔːr-/ adj most important

fo·ren·sic /fə'rensɪk, -zɪk/ adj used in the law and the tracking of criminals: *forensic medicine*

fore·run·ner /'fɔːˌrʌnəʳ/ n person or thing that prepares the way for another

fore·see /fɔː'siː‖fɔːr-/ vt -saw /-'sɔː/, -seen /-'siːn/ see in advance ~able adj 1 that can be foreseen 2 **in the foreseeable future** soon

fore·shad·ow /fɔː'ʃædəʊ‖fɔːr-/ vt be a sign of (what will happen)

fore·shore /'fɔːʃɔːʳ‖'fɔːr-/ n [S] shore between the sea and ordinary land

fore·sight /'fɔːsaɪt‖'fɔːr-/ n [U] ability to imagine the future; wise planning

for·est /'fɒrəst‖'fɔː-, 'fɑː-/ n [C;U] area covered with trees ~er n person who works in a forest ~ry n [U] work of planting and caring for trees

fore·stall /fɔː'stɔːl‖fɔːr-/ vt prevent (a person or thing) by acting first

fore·taste /'fɔːteɪst‖'fɔːr-/ n [S] first experience of something that will come later

fore·tell /fɔː'tel‖fɔːr-/ vt -told /-'təʊld/ PROPHESY

fore·thought /'fɔːθɔːt‖'fɔːr-/ n [U] wise planning for the future

for·ev·er /fə'revəʳ/ adv 1 for all future time 2 continually 3 **take forever** take an extremely long time

fore·warn /fɔː'wɔːn‖fɔːr'wɔːrn/ vt warn of coming danger

fore·went /fɔː'went‖fɔːr-/ past t. of FOREGO

fore·word /'fɔːwɜːd‖'fɔːrwɜːrd/ n short introduction to a book

for·feit /'fɔːfɪt‖'fɔːr-/ vt lose as a punishment ♦ n something forfeited

for·gave /fə'geɪv‖fər-/ v past t. of FORGIVE

forge¹ /fɔːdʒ‖fɔːrdʒ/ vt 1 copy in order to deceive: *a forged passport* 2 form (metal) by heating and hammering: (fig.) *forge a new political party*

forge ahead phr vi move with a sudden increase of speed and power

forge² n place where metal is forged **forger** /'fɔːdʒəʳ‖'fɔːr-/ n 1 [U] forging of papers, etc. 2 [C] forged paper, etc.

for·get /fə'get‖fər-/ vi/t -got /-'gɒt‖-'gɑːt/, -gotten /-'gɒtn‖-'gɑːtn/ 1 fail to remember: *Don't forget to lock the door.* 2 stop thinking about: *let's just forget it* ~**ful** adj in the habit of forgetting

for·give /fə'gɪv‖fər-/ vi/t -gave /-'geɪv/, -given /-'gɪvən/ stop blaming (someone for something) -**givable** adj: *forgivable mistake* -**giving** adj willing to forgive ~**ness** n [U] act of forgiving

for·go, **fore-**/fɔː'gəʊ‖fɔːr-/ vt -went /-'went/, -gone /-'gɒn‖-'gɑːn/ fml give up

fork¹ /fɔːk‖fɔːrk/ n 1 instrument with points, for lifting food to the mouth 2 farm or gardening tool like this 3 place where a road, etc., divides; one of the divisions

fork² v 1 vt lift, etc., with a fork 2 vi divide into branches 3 vi (of a person) turn (left or right) ~**ed** adj that divides into 2 or more points at the end

fork out phr vi/t pay (money) unwillingly

fork·lift truck /'fɔːkˌlɪft ·‖'fɔːrk-/ n small vehicle with a movable apparatus for lifting goods

for-lorn /fəˈlɔːn‖fərˈlɔːrn/ adj lit alone and unhappy ~ly adv

form[1] /fɔːm‖fɔːrm/ n 1 [C] shape 2 [C] plan; kind: forms of government 3 [U] way in which a work of art is put together 4 [C] offical paper with spaces for answering questions 5 [C] class in a British school: the sixth form 6 [C] long seat with no back 7 [U] degree of skill, fitness, etc.: to be on form 8 [U] correct practice: a matter of form ~less adj shapeless

form[2] v 1 vi begin to exist: A cloud formed. 2 vt make from parts: form a government 3 vt have the shape or substance of: The buildings form a square.

form-al /ˈfɔːməl‖ˈfɔːr-/ adj 1 suitable for official occasions: formal dress/language 2 regular in shape: formal garden 3 stiff in manner and behaviour ~ly adv ~ize vt make formal ~ity /fɔːˈmælɪti‖fɔːr-/ n 1 [U] attention to rules 2 [C] act in accordance with custom: legal formalities

for-mat /ˈfɔːmæt‖ˈfɔːr-/ n size, shape, or arrangement of something ♦ vt -tt- arrange (a book, computer information, etc.) in a particular format

for-ma-tion /fɔːˈmeɪʃən‖fɔːr-/ n 1 [U] shaping of something 2 [C;U] arrangement; structure

for-ma-tive /ˈfɔːmətɪv‖ˈfɔːr-/ adj giving shape: a child's formative years

for-mer /ˈfɔːmə[r]‖ˈfɔːr-/ adj of an earlier period: her former husband ♦ n fml first of 2 things mentioned ~ly adv in earlier time

for-mi-da-ble /ˈfɔːmɪdəbəl, fəˈmɪd-‖ˈfɔːr-/ adj 1 large and frightening 2 hard to defeat -bly adv

for-mu-la /ˈfɔːmjʊlə‖ˈfɔːrmjələ/ n -las or -lae /-liː/ 1 rule expressed in a short form by letters, numbers, etc.: chemical formulae 2 list of substances used in making something: (fig.) a formula for trouble 3 combination of suggestions, plans, etc.: a peace formula

for-mu-late /ˈfɔːmjʊleɪt‖ˈfɔːrm-/ vt 1 express exactly 2 invent (a plan) -lation /ˌfɔːmjʊˈleɪʃən‖ˌfɔːr-/ n [C;U]

for-ni-cate /ˈfɔːnɪkeɪt‖ˈfɔːr-/ vi esp. law have sex outside marriage -cation /ˌfɔːnɪˈkeɪʃən‖ˌfɔːr-/ n [U]

for-sake /fəˈseɪk‖fər-/ vt -sook /-ˈsʊk/, -saken /-ˈseɪkən/ lit DESERT[2] (2)

fort /fɔːt‖fɔːrt/ n 1 building for military defence 2 **hold the fort** look after everything while someone is away

for-te /ˈfɔːteɪ‖fɔːrt/ n something someone does particularly well

forth /fɔːθ‖fɔːrθ/ adv lit 1 forward 2 **and (so on and)** so forth etc.

forth-com-ing /ˌfɔːθˈkʌmɪŋ◂‖ˌfɔːrθ◂/ adj 1 happening soon 2 supplied when needed: No answer was forthcoming. 3 ready to be helpful

forth-right /ˈfɔːθraɪt‖ˈfɔːrθ-/ adj speaking plainly; direct

forth-with /fɔːθˈwɪð, -ˈwɪθ‖fɔːrθ-/ adv fml at once

for-ti-eth /ˈfɔːtiəθ‖ˈfɔːr-/ determiner, n, pron, adv 40th

for-ti-fy /ˈfɔːtɪfaɪ‖ˈfɔːr-/ vt 1 strengthen against attack 2 make stronger: fortified wine **-fication** /ˌfɔːtɪfɪˈkeɪʃən‖ˌfɔːr-/ n 1 [C] towers, etc., for defence 2 [U] act of fortifying

for-ti-tude /ˈfɔːtɪtjuːd‖ˈfɔːrtɪtuːd/ n [U] uncomplaining courage

fort-night /ˈfɔːtnaɪt‖ˈfɔːrt-/ n BrE 2 weeks ~ly adj, adv happening once a fortnight

for-tress /ˈfɔːtrɪs‖ˈfɔːr-/ n large fort

for-tu-i-tous /fɔːˈtjuːɪtəs‖fɔːr ˈtuː-/ adj fml accidental

for-tu-nate /ˈfɔːtʃənət‖ˈfɔːr-/ adj lucky ~ly adv

for-tune /ˈfɔːtʃən‖ˈfɔːr-/ n 1 [C;U] good or bad luck 2 [C] that which will happen to a person in the future: someone's fortune 3 [C] great sum of money: diamonds worth a fortune 4 **a small fortune** a lot of money

fortune-tell-er /ˈ‥ ˌ‥/ n person who claims to be able to tell people their future

for-ty /ˈfɔːti‖ˈfɔːrti/ determiner, n, pron 40

forty winks /ˌ‥ ˈ‥/ n [P] short sleep in the day time

for-um /ˈfɔːrəm/ n place for public argument

for-ward[1] /ˈfɔːwəd‖ˈfɔːrwərd/ adj 1 towards the front or future 2 advanced in development 3 too bold often in sexual matters ♦ vt 1 send (letters, etc.) to a new address 2 fml send (goods) ♦ n attacking player in football, etc. ~ness n [U] being FORWARD[1] (2, 3)

for-ward[2] adv also **forwards** — towards the front or future

for-went /fəˈwent‖fɔːr-/ past t. of FORGO

fos-sil /ˈfɒsəl‖ˈfɑː-/ n 1 part or print of an ancient animal or plant, preserved in rock, ice etc. 2 old person with unchanging ideas ~ize vi/t 1 change into a fossil 2 (cause to) become very fixed (in ideas, etc.)

fos-ter /ˈfɒstə[r]‖ˈfɒ-, ˈfɑː-/ vt 1 fml encourage to develop take (a child) into one's home for a while

foster- see WORD BEGINNINGS, p. 486.

fought /fɔːt/ v past t. and p. of FIGHT

foul[1] /faʊl/ adj 1 very unpleasant: foul smell/language/weather 2 **fall foul of** get into trouble with ~ly adv

foul[2] n act that is against the rules

foul[3] *vi/t* 1 make dirty 2 be guilty of a FOUL[2]

foul up *phr vt infml* spoil (an occasion, etc.) **foul-up** /ˈ· ·/ *n*

foul play /ˌ· ˈ·/ *n* [U] 1 (in sports) unfair play 2 criminal violence, esp. murder

found[1] /faund/ *v past t. and p. of* FIND

found[2] *vt* 1 establish; build 2 base: *stories founded on fact* **~er** *n* person who establishes something

foun·da·tion /faunˈdeɪʃən/ *n* 1 [U] founding of an organization 2 [U] BASIS: *rumours without foundation* 3 [C] organization that gives out money

foundations *n* [P] base that supports a building: (fig.) *the foundations of her success*

foundation stone /·ˈ·· ·/ *n* first stone of a new building, often laid with public ceremony

found·er /ˈfaundəʳ/ *vi lit* (of a ship) fill with water and sink

foun·dry /ˈfaundri/ *n* place where metal is melted and poured into shapes

fount /faunt/ *n lit* SOURCE

foun·tain /ˈfauntɪn/ *n* 1 decorative structure from which water springs up 2 flow of liquid

fountain pen /ˈ·· ·/ *n* pen with ink inside

four /fɔːʳ/ *determiner, n, pron* 4

four·teen /ˌfɔːˈtiːn◂/ *determiner, n, pron* 14 **~th** *determiner, adv, n, pron* 14th

fourth /fɔːθ/ *determiner, adv, n, pron* 4th

fowl /faul/ *n* **fowls** *or* **fowl** 1 farmyard bird, esp. a hen 2 any bird

fox /foks/ˈfɑːks/ *n* doglike wild animal, said to be clever ♦ *vt* confuse; deceive

fox·hole /ˈfokshəul/ˈfɑːks-/ *n* hole where soldiers hide from the enemy

fox·hunt·ing /ˈfokshʌntɪŋ/ˈfɑːks-/ *n* [U] hunting of foxes by special dogs (**foxhounds**) and people on horses **–er** *n*

foy·er /ˈfɔɪeɪ/ˈfɔɪər/ *n* entrance hall of a theatre, etc.

frac·as /ˈfrækɑː/ˈfreɪkəs/ *n fml* noisy quarrel

frac·tion /ˈfrækʃən/ *n* 1 division of a whole number (e.g. ⅓) 2 small part: *a fraction of the cost* **~al** *adj* so small as to be unimportant

frac·tious /ˈfrækʃəs/ *adj* restless and complaining

frac·ture /ˈfræktʃəʳ/ *n* [C;U] *fml* breaking of a bone, etc. ♦ *vi/t fml* break

fra·gile /ˈfrædʒaɪl/-dʒəl/ *adj* 1 easily broken 2 having a small thin body or weak in health **–gility** /frəˈdʒɪlɪti/ *n* [U]

frag·ment[1] /ˈfrægmənt/ *n* piece broken off **~ary** *adj* incomplete

frag·ment[2] /frægˈment/ˈfrægment/ *vi/t* break into pieces **~ation** /ˌfrægmənˈteɪʃən, -men-/ *n* [U]

fra·grant /ˈfreɪgrənt/ *adj* sweet-smelling **~ly** *adv* **–grance** *n* [C;U]

frail /freɪl/ *adj* weak, esp. in body **~ty** *n* 1 [U] quality of being frail 2 [C] fault of character

frame /freɪm/ *n* 1 border into which something fits: *a window frame* 2 structure on which something is built 3 human or animal body 4 single photograph in a cinema film 5 **frame of mind** state of mind at a particular time ♦ *vt* 1 put in a FRAME(1) 2 give shape to; express: *frame a question* 3 *infml* make (a guiltless person) seem guilty of a crime

frame-up /ˈ·· ·/ *n infml* carefully prepared plan to FRAME (3) someone

frame·work /ˈfreɪmwɜːk/-ɜːrk/ *n* supporting structure

fran·chise /ˈfræntʃaɪz/ *n* 1 [S] the right to vote 2 [C] the right to sell a product

frank[1] /fræŋk/ *adj* open and honest **~ly** *adv* **~ness** *n* [U]

frank[2] *vt* stamp (a letter) by machine

frank·fur·ter /ˈfræŋkfɜːtəʳ/-ɜːr-/ *n* red smoked SAUSAGE

fran·tic /ˈfræntɪk/ *adj* wildly anxious, afraid, happy, etc. **~ally** /-kli/ *adv*

fra·ter·nal /frəˈtɜːnl/-ɜːr-/ *adj* BROTHERLY

fra·ter·ni·ty /frəˈtɜːnɪti/-ɜːr-/ *n* 1 [C] people joined by common interests 2 [U] *fml* brotherly feeling

frat·er·nize , **-ise**/ˈfrætənaɪz/-ər-/ *vi* meet and be friendly (with someone) **–nization** /ˌfrætənaɪˈzeɪʃən/-tərnə-/ *n* [U]

frat·ri·cide /ˈfrætrɪsaɪd/ *n* [U] *fml* murder of one's brother or sister

fraud /frɔːd/ *n* 1 [C;U] criminal deceit to make money 2 [C] person who falsely claims to be something

fraud·u·lent /ˈfrɔːdjʊlənt/-dʒə-/ *adj* deceitful; got or done by fraud **~ly** *adv*

fraught /frɔːt/ *adj* 1 full of: *fraught with danger* 2 *infml* **a** (of a person) worried **b** (of conditions) difficult

fray[1] /freɪ/ *vi/t* develop loose threads by rubbing: *frayed collar* | (fig.) *frayed nerves*

fray[2] *n* [S] *lit* battle

freak /friːk/ *n* 1 strange unnatural creature or event 2 person who takes a special interest in the stated thing: *a film freak* **~ish** *adj* unreasonable; unusual

freck·le /ˈfrekəl/ *n* small brown spot on the skin **freckled** *adj*

free /friː/ *adj* 1 able to act as one wants; not in prison or controlled by rules: *free speech* | *You are free to go.* **2** not busy or being used: *Is this seat free?* | *free time* **3** without payment: *free tickets* **4** (of a way or passage) not blocked **5** not fixed; loose **6 free and easy** unworried **7 free from/of** untroubled by; without: *free from dirt* | *tax free* **8 free with** ready to give **9 make free with** use (something) without respect or as if it is one's own ♦ *adv* **1** without payment **2** without control **3** in a loose position ♦ *vt* **freed** /friːd/ set free ~**ly** *adv* **1** readily; openly **2** in great amounts

free-base /ˈ· ˌˈ/ *vi sl* smoke a specially prepared mixture of COCAINE

free-bie, -bee /ˈfriːbi/ *n infml* something that is given or received without payment

free-dom /ˈfriːdəm/ *n* [U] **1** state of being free **2** [*the* + S] certain rights, often given as an honour: *the freedom of the city*

free en-ter-prise /ˌ· ˈ·—/ *n* [U] social system in which private trade, business, etc., is carried on without much government control

free-for-all /ˌ· · ˈ·/ *n* quarrel, etc., in which many people join

free-hand /ˈfriːhænd/ *adj, adv* drawn without instruments

free hand /ˌ· ˈ·/ *n* [S] unlimited freedom of action

free-hold /ˈfriːhəʊld/ *adj, adv, n* [C;U] (with) ownership of land or buildings without conditions

free-lance /ˈfriːlɑːns‖-læns/ *adj, adv, n* (done by) a writer, etc., who works for many employers **freelance** *vi* **–lancer** *n*

Free-ma-son /ˈfriːˌmeɪsən, ˌfriːˈmeɪsən/*n* man belonging to an ancient society whose members help each other

free-range /ˌ· ˈ·◄/ *adj* being or produced by hens kept under natural conditions

free rein /ˌ· ˈ·/ *n* [U] complete freedom of action

free speech /ˌ· ˈ·/ *n* [U] right to express one's ideas in public

free trade /ˌ· ˈ·◄/ *n* [U] system of allowing foreign goods freely into a country

free verse /ˌ· ˈ·/ *n* [U] poetry that does not follow the usual rules

free-way /ˈfriːweɪ/ *n AmE for* MOTORWAY

free-wheel /ˌfriːˈwiːl/ *vi* travel downhill without using power ~**ing** *adj infml* not greatly worrying about rules, responsibilities, etc.

free will /ˌ· ˈ·/ *n* [U] **1** ability to decide freely what to do **2** belief that human effort can influence events, and they are not fixed in advance by God

freeze /friːz/ *v* **froze** /frəʊz/, **frozen** /ˈfrəʊzən/ **1** *vi/t* harden into ice **2** *vi* (of weather) be at the temperature at which ice forms **3** *vi/t* stop working properly because of cold **4** *vi* feel very cold **5** *vt* preserve (food) at low temperatures **6** *vi/t* stop moving **7** *vt* fix (prices, wages, etc.) ♦ *n* [U] **1** period of freezing weather **2** fixing of prices or wages ~**er** *n* machine that freezes food

freeze out *phr vt infml* prevent from being included

freeze over *phr vi/t* (cause to) turn to ice on the surface

freight /freɪt/ *n* [U] goods carried by ship, plane, etc. ~**er** *n* ship or plane that carries goods

French fries /ˌ· ˈ·/ *n* [P] *esp. AmE* CHIPs (3)

French win-dows /ˌ· ˈ·—/ *n* [P] glass doors opening onto a garden, etc.

fre-net-ic /frɪˈnetɪk/ *adj* overexcited; feverish

fren-zy /ˈfrenzi/ *n* [S;U] violent excitement

fre-quen-cy /ˈfriːkwənsi/ *n* **1** [U] the happening of something a large number of times **2** [C;U] rate at which something happens or is repeated **3** [C] particular number of radio waves per second

fre-quent[1] /ˈfriːkwənt/ *adj* happening often ~**ly** *adv*

fre-quent[2] /frɪˈkwent‖frɪˈkwent, ˈfriːkwənt/ *vt fml* go to (a place) often

fres-co /ˈfreskəʊ/ *n* **-coes** *or* **-cos** picture painted on wet PLASTER[1] (1)

fresh /freʃ/ *adj* **1** recently made, found, etc.; not STALE: *fresh flowers* **2** (of food) not frozen or tinned **3** (of water) not salt **4** new and different: *make a fresh start* **5 a** (of wind) rather strong **b** (of weather) cold and windy **6** not tired **7** too bold with someone of the opposite sex ♦ *adv* **1** just; newly **2 fresh out of** *infml, esp. AmE* having just used up one's supplies of ~**ly** *adv* ~**ness** *n* [U]

fresh-en /ˈfreʃən/ *vi/t* **1** make or become fresh **2** (of wind) become stronger

freshen up *phr vi/t* **1** (cause to) feel less tired, look more attractive, etc. **2** (of a drink) add more liquid, esp. alcohol, to it

fresh-man /ˈfreʃmən/ *also* **fresher** /ˈfreʃəʳ/ — *n* **-men** /-mən/ student in the first year at college or university

fresh-wa-ter /ˌfreʃˈwɔːtəʳ◄‖-ˈwɔ:-, -ˈwɑ:-/ *adj* of a river or lake, not the sea

fret /fret/ *vi/t* **-tt-** worry about small things ~**ful** *adj* anxious and complaining ~**fully** *adv*

fret-saw /ˈfretsɔː/ *n* tool for cutting patterns in wood

fret-work /'fretwɜːk‖-ɜːrk/ n [U] patterns cut with a fretsaw

fri-ar /'fraɪəʳ/ n man belonging to a Christian religious group

fric-tion /'frɪkʃən/ n [U] 1 rubbing of one surface against another 2 disagreement within a group

Fri-day /'fraɪdi/ n the 5th day of the week — see also GOOD FRIDAY

fridge /frɪdʒ/ n cupboard where food is kept cold

friend /frend/ n 1 person whom one likes but who is not related 2 helper; supporter 3 **make friends** form a friendship ~**less** adj without friends ~**ly** adj 1 acting as a friend 2 not causing unpleasant feelings in competitions, etc.: a friendly game ~**liness** n [U] ~**ship** n [C;U] friendly relationship

fries /fraɪz/ n see FRENCH FRIES

frieze /friːz/ n decorative border along the top of a wall

frig-ate /'frɪgət/ n small fast warship

fright /fraɪt/ n [C;U] feeling of fear

fright-en /'fraɪtn/ vt fill with fear ~**ed** adj ~**ingly** adv

fright-ful /'fraɪtfəl/ adj terrible; very bad ~**ly** adv

fri-gid /'frɪdʒəd/ adj 1 (of a woman) disliking sex 2 very cold ~**ly** adv –**gidity** /frɪ'dʒɪdəti/ n [U]

frill /frɪl/ n 1 decorative wavy edge on cloth 2 unnecessary decoration ~**y** adj

fringe /frɪndʒ/ n 1 decorative edge of hanging threads on a curtain, etc. 2 hair hanging over the forehead 3 edge: the fringe(s) of the crowd 4 not official; not CONVENTIONAL: fringe theatre ♦ vt be the border of

fringe ben-e-fit /'· ˌ···/ n something given with a job, besides wages

frisk /frɪsk/ v 1 vi jump about playfully 2 vt search (someone) with the hands, for hidden weapons ~**y** adj joyfully playful

fris-son /'friːsɒn‖friː'sɔːn/ n feeling of excitement caused by fear

frit-ter¹ /'frɪtəʳ/ n piece of cooked BATTER² with fruit, meat, etc., inside

fritter² v **fritter away** phr vt waste: He fritters away his money.

fri-vol-i-ty /frɪ'vɒləti‖-'vɑː-/ n 1 [U] quality of being frivolous 2 [C] frivolous act or remark

friv-o-lous /'frɪvələs/ adj not serious enough; silly ~**ly** adv

friz-zy /'frɪzi/ adj (of hair) very curly, like wool

fro /frəʊ/ adv see TO AND FRO

frock /frɒk‖frɑːk/ n woman's dress

frog /frɒg‖frɑːg, frɔːg/ n 1 small jumping creature that lives on land and in water 2 **a frog in the/one's throat** difficulty in speaking because of roughness in the throat

frog-man /'frɒgmən‖'frɑːg-, 'frɔːg-/ n -**men** /-mən/ skilled underwater swimmer who uses breathing apparatus

frog-march /'frɒgmɑːtʃ‖'frɑːg-mɑːrtʃ, 'frɔːg-/ vt force (a person) to move forward with the arms held together firmly from behind

frol-ic /'frɒlɪk‖'frɑː-/ vi -**ck**- jump about happily **frolic** n ~**some** adj playful

from /frəm; strong from‖frʌm; strong frʌm, frɑːm/ prep 1 starting at (a place or time): fly from London to Paris | work from Monday till Friday 2 given or sent by: a letter from John 3 away: subtract 10 from 15 4 using: Bread is made from flour. 5 because of: suffer from heart disease 6 out of: He took a knife from his pocket. 7 in a state of protection or prevention with regard to: She saved the child from drowning. 8 judging by: From what John tells me, they're very rich.

frond /frɒnd‖frɑːnd/ n leaf of a FERN or PALM¹

front /frʌnt/ n 1 [C] part in the direction that something moves or faces: the front of the aircraft | of the house | his front teeth 2 [C] line where fighting takes place in war 3 [the + S] road beside the sea in a holiday town 4 [C] line dividing cold from warmer air 5 [C] (often false) outward appearance: present a smiling front 6 [C] combined effort or movement against opposing forces: present a united front 7 [C] particular area of activity: They have made little progress on the employment front. 8 [C] infml person, group or thing used for hiding the real nature of a secret or unlawful activity 9 **in front**: a ahead **b** in the most forward position 10 **in front of**: a ahead of **b** in the presence of 11 **up front** infml as payment in advance ♦ vi/t face (towards): The hotel fronts onto the lake. ~**al** adj at, of, or from the front

front-age /'frʌntɪdʒ/ n front width of a building or piece of land

front-bench /ˌfrʌnt'bentʃ/ n either of the two rows of seats in the British parliament on which the most important politicians of the two major parties sit **frontbencher** n

fron-tier /'frʌntɪəʳ‖frʌn'tɪər/ n edge of a country **frontiers** n [P] furthest limit: the frontiers of knowledge

front line /ˌ· '·◁/ n [S] 1 military FRONT (2) 2 most advanced position **front-line** adj

front man /'· ·/n someone who explains the views or future plans of esp. a large company to the public

front-page /'··/ *adj* very interesting; worthy of being on the front page of a newspaper: *front-page news*

front-run·ner /,· '··/ *n* person who has the best chance of success in competing for something

frost /frost‖frɔːst/ *n* 1 [U] white powder that forms on things below freezing point 2 [C;U] (period of) freezing weather ♦ *v* 1 *vi/t* (cause to) become covered with frost 2 *vt* roughen the surface (of glass) ~**y** *adj* 1 very cold 2 unfriendly: *a frosty greeting*

frost-bite /'frostbaɪt‖'frɔːst-/ *n* [U] harmful swelling etc., of the limbs, caused by cold **-bitten** *adj*

froth /froθ‖frɔːθ/ *n* 1 [U] mass of small BUBBLES on beer, etc. 2 *derog* light empty show of talk or ideas ♦ *vi* produce froth ~**y** *adj* covered with froth

frown /fraʊn/ *vi* draw the EYEBROWS together in anger or effort **frown** *n*

froze /frəʊz/ *v past t. of* FREEZE

fro-zen /'frəʊzən/ *v past p. of* FREEZE

fru-gal /'fruːgəl/ *adj* 1 not wasteful 2 small and cheap: *frugal supper*

fruit /fruːt/ *n* 1 [C;U] seed-containing part of a plant, often eatable 2 [C] also **fruits** *pl.* result or reward ♦ *vi* bear fruit ~**ful** *adj* useful; successful ~**fully** *adv* ~**less** *adj* unsuccessful ~**lessly** *adv* ~**y** *adj* 1 like fruit 2 (of a voice) rich and deep

fruit-cake /'fruːtkeɪk/ *n* 1 [C;U] cake containing small dried fruits, nuts, etc. 2 [C] *infml* a mad, silly person 3 **as nutty as a fruitcake** completely mad

fruit-er-er /'fruːtərə'/ *n* someone who sells fruit in a shop

fru·i·tion /fruː'ɪʃən/ *n* [U] *fml* fulfilment of plans, etc.

fruit ma·chine /'·· ·,·/ *n BrE* ONE-ARMED BANDIT

frus-trate /frʌ'streɪt‖'frʌstreɪt/ *vt* 1 disappoint and annoy 2 prevent the fulfilment of (plans) **-tration** /frʌ'streɪʃən/ *n* [C;U]

fry /fraɪ/ *vi/t* cook in hot fat or oil **fry** *n see* FRENCH FRIES, SMALL FRY

frying pan /'·· ,·/ *n* 1 flat pan for frying 2 **out of the frying pan into the fire** out of a bad position into an even worse one

ft *written abbrev. for:* FOOT[1] (3)

fuck /fʌk/ *vi/t taboo* have sex (with) ♦ *n taboo sl* 1 act of having sex 2 **not care/give a fuck** not to care at all **fuck off** *phr vi taboo sl* go away **fuck up** *phr vt taboo sl* spoil; ruin ♦ **fuck-up** /'·· ·/ *n*

fudge[1] /fʌdʒ/ *n* [U] creamy brown sweet made of sugar, milk, butter, etc.

fudge[2] *v* 1 *vt* put together roughly or dishonestly 2 *vi/t* avoid taking firm action (on)

fu-el /fjʊəl‖fjuːəl/ *n* [C;U] material (e.g. coal) that produces heat or power ♦ *v* **-ll-** *BrE* ‖ **-l-** *AmE* 1 *vt* provide with fuel 2 *vi* take in fuel

fugitive /'fjuːdʒɪtɪv/ *n* person escaping from something

ful-crum /'fʊlkrəm, 'fʌl-/ *n* **-crums** *or* **-cra** /-krə/ point on which a LEVER turns

ful-fil ‖ also **-fill** *AmE*/fʊl'fɪl/ *vt* **-ll-** 1 perform (a promise, duty, etc.) 2 develop fully the character and abilities (of oneself) ~**ment** *n* [U]

full /fʊl/ *adj* 1 holding as much as many as possible: *full bottle/train* 2 well fed 3 complete: *your full name* 4 highest possible: *full speed* 5 (of a garment) loose: *full skirt* 6 rounded; PLUMP 7 **full of** thinking only of ♦ *n* 1 **in full** completely 2 **to the full** thoroughly ♦ *adv* 1 straight; directly: *The sun shone full on her face.* 2 very: *They knew full well he wouldn't keep his promise.* ~**ly** *adv* 1 at least: *It's fully an hour since he left.* 2 completely ~**ness, fulness** *n* [U]

full-blown /,· '·◄/ *adj* 1 (of a flower) completely open 2 fully developed: *a full-blown war*

full-grown /,· '·◄/ *adj* completely developed

full-length /,· '·◄/ *adj* 1 (of a painting, etc.) showing someone from head to foot 2 not shorter than usual

full moon /,· '·/ *n* the moon when seen as a circle

full-scale /,· '·◄/ *adj* 1 (of a model, etc.) as big as the object represented 2 (of an activity) not lessened: *full-scale war*

full stop /,· '·/ *n* 1 a mark (.) showing esp. the end of a sentence 2 **come to a full stop** stop completely

full-time /,· '·◄/ *adj* working or studying all the usual hours

fully-fledged /,·· '·◄/ *adj* 1 (of a bird) having grown all its feathers 2 completely trained

ful-some /'fʊlsəm/ *adj* praising too much

fum-ble /'fʌmbəl/ *vi* use the hands awkwardly

fume /fjuːm/ *vi* show great anger

fumes /fjuːmz/ *n* [P] strong-smelling gas or smoke

fu-mi-gate /'fjuːmɪgeɪt/ *vt* disinfect by means of smoke or gas

fun /fʌn/ *n* [U] 1 playfulness 2 (cause of) amusement; enjoyment 3 **for fun** also **for the fun of it** — for pleasure 4 **in fun** not seriously 5 **make fun of** laugh unkindly at

func-tion /'fʌŋkʃən/ *n* 1 natural purpose of something or someone 2 important social gathering ♦ *vi* be in action; work ~**al** *adj* 1 made for use, not decoration 2 functioning

fund /fʌnd/ n supply of money for a purpose ♦ vt provide money for

fun·da·men·tal /ˌfʌndəˈmentl/ adj central; very important: *fundamental difference* ♦ n basic rule ~**ly** adv ~**ism** n [U] belief in the exact truth of the Bible ~**ist** n, adj

fu·ne·ral /ˈfjuːnərəl/ n ceremony of burying or burning a dead person

fun·fair /ˈfʌnfeəʳ/ n esp BrE travelling show, with amusements and machines to ride on

fun·gi·cide /ˈfʌndʒɪsaɪd/ n [C;U] chemical for destroying fungus

fun·gus /ˈfʌŋgəs/ n -**gi** /-dʒaɪ, -gaɪ/ or -**guses** [C;U] leafless plant that grows on wood, etc.

fu·nic·u·lar /fjuˈnɪkjʊləʳ/ n mountain railway worked by a rope

funk·y /ˈfʌŋki/ adj infml, esp AmE 1 (of JAZZ or similar music) having a simple direct style and feeling 2 attractive and fashionable

fun·nel /ˈfʌnl/ n 1 wide-mouthed tube for pouring liquids through 2 chimney on a steam engine or steamship ♦ vi/t -**ll**- BrE ‖ -**l**- AmE pass (as if) through a FUNNEL (1)

fun·ny /ˈfʌni/ adj 1 amusing 2 strange –**nily** adv

funny bone /ˈ·· ·/ n tender part of the elbow

fur /fɜːʳ/ n 1 [U] soft thick hair of a cat, rabbit, etc. 2 [C] (garment made of) the fur-covered skin of an animal 3 [U] hard covering on the inside of pots, hot-water pipes, etc. ~**ry** adj

fu·ri·ous /ˈfjʊəriəs/ adj 1 very angry 2 wild; uncontrolled ~**ly** adv

furl /fɜːl‖fɜːrl/ vt roll or fold up (a sail, flag, etc.)

fur·long /ˈfɜːlɒŋ‖ˈfɜːrlɔːŋ/ n a measure of length equal to 220 yards (201 metres)

fur·nace /ˈfɜːnɪs‖ˈfɜːr-/ n 1 enclosed space where metals, etc., are heated 2 enclosed fire to make hot water

fur·nish /ˈfɜːnɪʃ‖ˈfɜːr-/ vt 1 put furniture in 2 fml supply ~**ings** n [P] furniture, etc., for a room

fur·ni·ture /ˈfɜːnɪtʃəʳ‖ˈfɜːr-/ n [U] beds, chairs, etc.

fu·ro·re /fjʊˈrɔːri, ˈfjʊərɔːʳ‖ˈfjʊərɔːr/ n [S] sudden burst of public interest

fur·ri·er /ˈfʌriəʳ‖ˈfɜːr-/ n person who makes or sells fur garments

fur·row /ˈfʌrəʊ‖ˈfɜːr-/ n 1 track cut by a PLOUGH 2 WRINKLE ♦ vt make furrows in

fur·ther /ˈfɜːðəʳ‖ˈfɜːr-/ adv, adj 1 (comparative of FAR) at or to a greater distance or more distant point: *too tired to walk any further* 2 more: *any further questions* 3 **further to** continuing the subject of 4 **go further** give, do, or say more ♦ vt help to advance ~**ance** n [U] fml advancement ~**most** adj farthest

fur·ther·more /ˌfɜːðəˈmɔːʳ‖ˈfɜːrðərmɔːr/ adv fml also

fur·thest /ˈfɜːðɪst‖ˈfɜːr-/ adv, adj (superlative of FAR) at or to the greatest distance or degree

fur·tive /ˈfɜːtɪv‖ˈfɜːr-/ adj trying to escape notice ~**ly** adv ~**ness** n [U]

fu·ry /ˈfjʊəri/ n 1 [S;U] great anger 2 [U] wild force

fuse[1] /fjuːz/ n wire that melts to break an electric connection ♦ vi/t 1 stop working because a fuse has melted 2 join by melting

fuse[2] n 1 pipe, etc., that carries fire to an explosive article 2 part of a bomb, etc., that makes it explode

fu·se·lage /ˈfjuːzəlɑːʒ‖-sə-/ n body of an aircraft

fu·sil·lade /ˌfjuːzɪˈleɪd‖-sə-/ n rapid continuous firing of shots

fu·sion /ˈfjuːʒən/ n [C;U] join together by melting: (fig.) *a fusion of different styles of music*

fuss /fʌs/ n [S;U] 1 unnecessary show of excitement or annoyance 2 **make a fuss of** pay loving attention to ♦ vi show unnecessary anxiety ~**y** adj 1 too concerned about details 2 (of dress, etc.) overdecorated

fus·ty /ˈfʌsti/ adj 1 old and smelling bad 2 old-fashioned

fu·tile /ˈfjuːtaɪl‖-tl/ adj unsuccessful; useless; *futile attempts* **futility** /fjuːˈtɪləti/ n [U]

fu·ture /ˈfjuːtʃəʳ/ n 1 [S] time after the present: *in the future* 2 [C] that which will happen to someone or something: *an uncertain future* 3 [U] likelihood of success 4 **in future** from now on **future** adj: *his future wife* | *the future tense*

fu·tur·is·tic /ˌfjuːtʃəˈrɪstɪk/ adj of strange modern design

fuzz /fʌz/ n [U] FLUFF ~**y** adj 1 (of hair) standing up in a light short mass 2 not clear in shape 3 (of cloth, etc.) having a raised soft hairy surface ~**ily** adv ~**iness** n [U]

FYI abbrev. for: (AmE) for your information

G

G , g /dʒiː/ the 7th letter of the English alphabet

g *written abbrev. for:* GRAM(s)

gab *n* see the gift of the gab (GIFT)

gab·ar·dine, -erdine/'gæbədiːn, ˌgæbə'diːn‖'gæbərdiːn/ *n* 1 [U] strong cloth 2 [C] raincoat made from this

gab·ble /'gæbəl/ *vi/t* speak or say too quickly to be heard **gabble** *n* [S]

ga·ble /'geɪbəl/ *n* 3-cornered top of a wall between sloping roofs

gad /gæd/ *v* gad about *phr vi* travel for enjoyment

gad·get /'gædʒət/ *n* small useful machine or tool ~ry *n* [U] gadgets

Gae·lic /'geɪlɪk, 'gælɪk/ *adj, n* [U] (of or being) any of the CELTIC languages, esp. those of Scotland, Ireland, or the Isle of Man

gaffe /gæf/ *n* social mistake

gaf·fer /'gæfər/ *n* man in charge, esp. of lighting for a film

gag /gæg/ *n* 1 something put over someone's mouth to stop them from talking 2 joke ♦ *vt* -gg- put a GAG(1) on

ga·ga /'gɑːgɑː/ *adj* SENILE

gage /geɪdʒ/ *n, v AmE for* GAUGE

gag·gle /'gægəl/ *n* [S] 1 group of GEESE 2 group of noisy people

gai·e·ty /'geɪəti/ *n* [U] cheerfulness

gai·ly /'geɪli/ *adv* cheerfully

gain¹ /geɪn/ *v* 1 *vi/t* obtain (something useful) 2 *vi* (of a clock) go too fast 3 *vt fml* reach (a place) with effort ~er *n*

gain on/upon *phr vt* get close to (someone ahead in a race)

gain² *n* [C;U] increase in wealth or amount ~ful *adj* paid for: *gainful employment* ~fully *adv*

gain·say /ˌgeɪn'seɪ/ *vt* -said /-'sed/ *fml* DENY

gait /geɪt/ *n* way of walking

gai·ter /'geɪtər/ *n* covering for the lower leg

gal /gæl/ *n* girl

ga·la /'gɑːlə‖'geɪlə, 'gælə/ *n* special public entertainment

gal·ax·y /'gæləksi/ *n* large group of stars –actic /gə'læktɪk/ *adj*

gale /geɪl/ *n* 1 strong wind 2 noisy burst of laughter, etc.

gall¹ /gɔːl/ *n* [U] daring rudeness

gall² *vt* cause to feel annoyed disappointment or anger

gal·lant /'gælənt/ *adj* 1 brave 2 (of a man) polite to women ~ly *adv* ~ry *n* [U]

gall blad·der /'· ˌ··/ *n* baglike organ in which BILE is stored

gal·le·on /'gæliən/ *n* (esp. Spanish) sailing ship of the 15th to 18th centuries

gal·le·ry /'gæləri/ *n* 1 place where works of art are shown 2 upper floor of a hall or church 3 passage in a mine 4 top floor in a theatre

gal·ley /'gæli/ *n* 1 ancient ship rowed by slaves 2 ship's kitchen

Gal·lic /'gælɪk/ *adj* typical of France

gal·li·vant /'gælɪvænt/ *vi* GAD about

gal·lon /'gælən/ *n* (a measure for liquids equal to) **a** (in Britain) 4 QUARTs **b** (in America) 231 CUBIC inches

gal·lop /'gæləp/ *n* [S] movement of a horse at its fastest speed **gallop** *vi/t*

gal·lows /'gæləʊz/ *n* **gallows** wooden frame on which criminals were once killed by hanging

gallows hu·mour /'·· ˌ·ˈ·/ *n* [U] *lit* jokes about the unpleasant side of life

gall·stone /'gɔːlstəʊn/ *n* hard stone or grain that forms in the GALL BLADDER

ga·lore /gə'lɔːr/ *adj* in plenty: *bargains galore*

gal·va·nize , -nise/'gælvənaɪz/ *vt* 1 cover (another metal) with ZINC 2 shock into action

gam·bit /'gæmbɪt/ *n* action done to produce a future advantage, esp. an opening move in a game, conversation, etc.

gam·ble /'gæmbəl/ *v* 1 *vi/t* BET (1) 2 *vi* take a risk ♦ *n* [S] risky matter –bler *n*

gam·bol /'gæmbəl/ *vi* -ll- *BrE* | -l- *AmE* jump about in play

game /geɪm/ *n* 1 [C] form of play or sport 2 [C] single part of a match in tennis, etc. 3 [U] wild animals and birds hunted for food and sport 4 [C] *infml* secret trick: *give the game away* (= let a secret plan be known) 5 [C] *infml* profession or activity: *the advertising game* — see also BIG GAME, FAIR GAME ♦ *adj* brave and willing ~ly *adv* **games** *n* [P] sports competitions

game·keep·er /'geɪmˌkiːpər/ *n* man who looks after GAME (3), esp. birds

games·man·ship /'geɪmzmənʃɪp/ *n* [U] art of winning by using rules to one's own advantage but without cheating

gam·mon /'gæmən/ *n* [U] smoked or salted HAM (1)

gam·ut /'gæmət/ *n* [S] whole range of a subject

gan·der /'gændər/ *n* male GOOSE

gang¹ /gæŋ/ *n* 1 group of people working together, esp. criminals 2 group of friends

gang² *v* gang up *phr vi* work together (against someone); CONSPIRE

gang·ling /'gæŋglɪŋ/ *adj* tall, thin, and awkward

gang-plank /'gæŋplæŋk/ n movable bridge for getting into or out of a ship

gan-grene /'gæŋgri:n/ n [U] decay of a body part because blood has stopped flowing there **–grenous** /-grɪnəs/ adj

gang-ster /'gæŋstəʳ/ n member of a criminal GANG (1)

gang-way /'gæŋweɪ/ n 1 large gang-plank 2 BrE passage between rows of seats

gaol /dʒeɪl/ n, v BrE for JAIL **–er** n

gaol-bird /'dʒeɪlbɜːd ‖ -ɜːrd/ n BrE for JAILBIRD

gap /gæp/ n empty space between 2 things: (fig.) gaps in my knowledge

gape /geɪp/ vi 1 look hard in surprise 2 come apart: gaping hole

gar-age /'gæra:ʒ, -ɪdʒ ‖ gə'ra:ʒ/ n 1 building in which motor vehicles are kept 2 place that repairs them, and sells petrol and oil ♦ vt put in a garage

garb /gɑːb ‖ gɑːrb/ n [U] fml clothes

gar-bage /'gɑːbɪdʒ ‖ 'gɑːr-/ n [U] esp. AmE for RUBBISH

garbage can /'·· ·/ n AmE for DUSTBIN

gar-ble /'gɑːbəl ‖ 'gɑːr-/ vt give a confused description of

gar-den /'gɑːdn ‖ 'gɑːr-/ n 1 piece of land for growing flowers and vegetables 2 also **gardens** pl. — public park 3 **lead someone up the garden path** trick someone into believing what is not true and acting on it ♦ vi work in a garden **–er** n

garden cit-y /,·· '··/ n town planned and built to have grass and open spaces

garden par-ty /'·· ,··/ n formal party held in a garden

gar-gan-tu-an /gɑː'gæntʃuən ‖ gɑːr-/ adj extremely large

gar-gle /'gɑːgəl ‖ 'gɑːr-/ vi wash the throat by blowing through liquid ♦ n 1 [S] act of gargling 2 [C;U] liquid for gargling

gar-goyle /'gɑːgɔɪl ‖ 'gɑːr-/ n hollow figure of an ugly creature on a church roof, through which rain water runs away

gar-ish /'geərɪʃ/ adj unpleasantly bright **–ly** adv

gar-land /'gɑːlənd ‖ 'gɑːr-/ n circle of flowers for decoration ♦ vt put garlands on

gar-lic /'gɑːlɪk ‖ 'gɑːr-/ n [U] plant like an onion, used in cooking

gar-ment /'gɑːmənt ‖ 'gɑːr-/ n fml article of clothing

gar-ner /'gɑːnəʳ ‖ 'gɑːr-/ vt lit collect

gar-net /'gɑːnɪt ‖ 'gɑːr-/ n red jewel

gar-nish /'gɑːnɪʃ ‖ 'gɑːr-/ vt decorate (food) ♦ n something used to garnish

gar-ret /'gærɪt/ n lit small unpleasant room at the top of a house

gar-ri-son /'gærɪsən/ n 1 soldiers living in a town or fort 2 fort or camp where such soldiers live ♦ vt (send a group of soldiers to) guard (a place)

gar-rotte /gə'rɒt ‖ gə'rɑːt/ vt STRANGLE, esp. with a metal collar or wire

gar-ru-lous /'gærələs/ adj fml talking too much **–ly** adv

gar-ter /'gɑːtəʳ ‖ 'gɑːr-/ n elastic band to keep a STOCKING up

gas /gæs/ n -s- or -ss- 1 [C;U] substance like air 2 [U] gas used for heating, cooking, poisoning, etc. 3 [U] AmE petrol ♦ v 1 vt kill with gas 2 vi infml talk a long time **~eous** /'gæsɪəs/ adj of or like gas

gas-bag /'gæsbæg/ n infml person who talks too much

gas fit-ter /'· ,·ʳ/ n workman who puts in gas pipes, repairs cookers, etc.

gash /gæʃ/ vt, n (wound with) a long deep cut

gas-hold-er /'gæs,həʊldəʳ/ n large container from which gas is carried to buildings

gas-ket /'gæskɪt/ n flat piece of material placed between surfaces to prevent oil, etc., from escaping

gas-light /'gæs-laɪt/ n [U] light from burning gas

gas-man /'gæsmæn/ n -men /-men/ official who visits houses to see how much gas has been used

gas mask /'· ·/ n breathing apparatus that protects the wearer against poisonous gas

gas-o-line , **-lene** /'gæsəli:n/ n [U] AmE for PETROL

gasp /gɑːsp ‖ gæsp/ v 1 vi breathe quickly and with effort 2 vt say while gasping gasp n

gas sta-tion /'· ,·ʳ/ n AmE for FILLING STATION

gas-sy /'gæsi/ adj full of gas **-siness** n [U]

gas-tric /'gæstrɪk/ adj of the stomach: gastric juices

gas-tri-tis /gæ'straɪtɪs/ n [U] painful swelling of the lining of the stomach

gas-tro-en-te-ri-tis /,gæstrəʊ-entə'raɪtɪs/ n [U] swelling of the stomach lining and bowels

gas-tron-o-my /gæ'strɒnəmi ‖ gæ-'strɑː-/ n [U] art of good eating

gas-works /'gæswɜːks ‖ -ɜːr-/ n **gasworks** place where gas is made from coal

gate /geɪt/ n 1 frame closing an opening in a wall, fence, etc. 2 way in or out at an airport 3 (money paid by) the number of people attending a match, etc.

gâ-teau /'gætəʊ ‖ gɑː'təʊ/ n **-teaux** /-təʊz/ large rich cake

gate-crash /'geɪtkræʃ/ vi/t go to (a party) uninvited **~er** n

gate-post /'geɪtpəʊst/ n post from which a gate is hung

gate-way /'geɪt-weɪ/ n 1 [C] opening for a gate 2 [S] way of finding: *the gateway to success*

gath-er /'gæðəʳ/ v 1 vi/t come or bring together 2 vt obtain gradually: *gather facts/speed* 3 vt collect (flowers, crops, etc.) 4 vt understand: *I gather she's ill.* 5 vt draw (cloth) into small folds: *gathered skirt* ~**ing** n meeting

gauche /ɡəʊʃ/ adj socially awkward

gau-dy /'ɡɔːdi/ adj too bright; overdecorated –**dily** adv

gauge ‖ also **gage** AmE /geɪdʒ/ n 1 instrument for measuring 2 thickness or width of e.g. a gun barrel 3 distance between the RAILS of a railway ♦ vt 1 measure 2 make a judgment about

gaunt /ɡɔːnt/ adj 1 thin, as if ill or hungry 2 (of a place) bare and unattractive ~**ness** n [U]

gaunt-let /'ɡɔːntlɪt/ n long GLOVE protecting the wrist

gauze /ɡɔːz/ n [U] thin net-like cloth

gave /geɪv/ v past t. of GIVE

gav-el /'ɡævəl/ n small hammer used by a chairman, etc., to get attention

ga-votte /ɡə'vɒt‖ɡə'vɑːt/ n fast French dance or its music

gaw-ky /'ɡɔːki/ adj awkward in movement –**kiness** n [U]

gawp /ɡɔːp/ vi look at something in a foolish way

gay /ɡeɪ/ adj 1 HOMOSEXUAL 2 bright: *gay colours* 3 cheerful ♦ n GAY (1) person

gaze /ɡeɪz/ vi look steadily ♦ n [S] steady fixed look

ga-zette /ɡə'zet/ n official government newspaper giving important notices, etc.

gaz-et-teer /ˌɡæzə'tɪəʳ/ n list of names of places

ga-zump /ɡə'zʌmp/ vt BrE cheat (someone who has agreed to buy a house) by selling it to someone else who offers more money

GB abbrev. for: GREAT BRITAIN

GDP /ˌdʒiː diː 'piː/ n [the + S] Gross Domestic Product; the total value of everything produced in a country, usu. in a single year, except for income received from abroad

gear[1] /ɡɪəʳ/ n 1 [C;U] set of toothed wheels in a machine 2 [U] equipment: *football gear* 3 [U] apparatus of wheels, etc.: *the landing gear of an aircraft*

gear[2] v

gear to phr vt allow (an activity or action) to be influenced by (a particular fact): *education geared to the needs of industry*

gear up phr vt infml put (esp. oneself) into a state of excited or anxious expectation

gear-box /'ɡɪəbɒks‖'ɡɪərbɑːks/ n case containing the gears of a vehicle

gear le-ver /'· ˌ··/ n rod that controls the gears of a vehicle

geese /ɡiːs/ n pl. of GOOSE

Gei-ger count-er /'ɡaɪɡə ˌkaʊntəʳ‖ -ɡər-/ n instrument that measures RADIOACTIVITY

gel-a-tine /'dʒelətiːn‖-tn/ ‖ also **-tin** /-tɪn‖-tn/ AmE — n [U] gluey material used in making jelly

geld /ɡeld/ vt remove the sexual organs of (certain male animals) ~**ing** n gelded animal, esp. a horse

gel-ig-nite /'dʒelɪɡnaɪt/ n [U] powerful explosive

gem /dʒem/ n 1 jewel 2 very valuable thing or person

gen-der /'dʒendəʳ/ n [C;U] 1 (in grammar) (division into) MASCULINE, FEMININE, or NEUTER 2 division into male and female; sex

gene /dʒiːn/ n material in a cell controlling HEREDITY

ge-ne-al-o-gy /ˌdʒiːni'ælədʒi/ n [C;U] (study of) the history of a family, often shown in a drawing like a tree –**gical** /ˌdʒiːniə'lɒdʒɪkəl‖-'lɑː-/ adj

gen-e-ra /'dʒenərə/ n pl. of GENUS

gen-e-ral /'dʒenərəl/ adj 1 concerning all: *the general feeling* 2 not detailed: *a general idea* 3 chief: *Postmaster-General* ♦ n 1 army or airforce officer of very high rank 2 **in general** usually ~**ly** adv 1 usually 2 by most people 3 without considering details –**rality** /ˌdʒenə'rælɪti/ n 1 [C] general statement 2 [U] being general

general e-lec-tion /ˌ··· ·'··/ n election in which the whole country takes part

gen-e-ral-ize /'dʒenərəlaɪz/ vi make a general statement –**ization** /ˌdʒenərəlaɪ'zeɪʃən‖-lə-/ n [C;U] (statement formed by) generalizing

general prac-ti-tion-er /ˌ··· ·'···/ n doctor trained in general medicine

general strike /ˌ··· '·/ n stopping of work by all trade unionists

gen-e-rate /'dʒenəreɪt/ vt produce: *generate heat* –**rator** n machine that generates esp. electricity –**rative** /'dʒenərətɪv/ adj able to produce

gen-e-ra-tion /ˌdʒenə'reɪʃən/ n 1 [C] length of time in which a child grows up and has children 2 [C] people of about the same age 3 [U] act of generating

ge-ner-ic /dʒɪ'nerɪk/ adj shared by a whole class ~**ally** /-kli/ adv

gen-e-ros-i-ty /ˌdʒenə'rɒsɪti‖-'rɑː-/ n 1 [U] quality of being generous 2 [C] generous act

gen-e-rous /'dʒenərəs/ adj 1 giving freely 2 more than enough ~**ly** adv

gen-e-sis /'dʒenəsɪs/ n [S] origin

ge·net·ics /dʒəˈnetɪks/ n [U] study of HEREDITY **genetic** adj **–ically** /-kli/ adv

ge·ni·al /ˈdʒiːniəl/ adj cheerful and kind **–ly** adv

gen·i·tals /ˈdʒenətlz/ n [P] outer sex organs **genital** adj

ge·ni·us /ˈdʒiːniəs/ n 1 [U] great and rare powers of thought, skill, or imagination 2 [C] person with this ability 3 [S] special ability or skill: *She has a genius for saying the wrong thing.*

gen·o·cide /ˈdʒenəsaɪd/ n [U] killing of a whole race of people

gen·re /ˈʒɒnrə‖ˈʒɑːnrə/ n fml class; kind

gent /dʒent/ n sl gentleman **gents** n BrE men's public TOILET

gen·teel /dʒenˈtiːl/ adj unnaturally polite

gen·tile /ˈdʒentaɪl/ n, adj (sometimes cap.) (person who is) not Jewish

gen·til·i·ty /dʒenˈtɪləti/ n [U] being genteel

gen·tle /ˈdʒentl/ adj not rough or violent **~ness** n [U] **–tly** adv

gen·tle·man /ˈdʒentlmən/ n **-men** /-mən/ 1 man who behaves well and can be trusted 2 any man 3 lit man of good but not noble family **~ly** adj like a GENTLEMAN (1)

gentleman's a·gree·ment /ˌ··· ·'··/ n unwritten agreement made between people who trust each other

gentle sex /ˌ·· '·/ n [the + S] females; women (now usu. considered offensive to women)

gen·tle·wo·man /ˈdʒentlˌwʊmən/ n **-women** /-ˌwɪmɪn/ lady

gen·try /ˈdʒentri/ n [P] people of high social class

gen·u·flect /ˈdʒenjʊflekt/ vi fml bend one's knee in worship **~ion** /ˌdʒenjʊˈflekʃən/ n [C;U]

gen·u·ine /ˈdʒenjuɪn/ adj real; true **~ly** adv **~ness** n [U]

ge·nus /ˈdʒiːnəs/ n **genera** /ˈdʒenərə/ division of plants or animals

ge·og·ra·phy /dʒiˈɒɡrəfi, ˈdʒɒɡrəfi‖ dʒiˈɑːɡ-/ n [U] study of the countries of the world and of seas, towns, etc. **–pher** n **–phical** /ˌdʒiəˈɡræfɪkəl/ adj **–phically** /-kli/ adv

ge·ol·o·gy /dʒiˈɒlədʒi‖-ˈɑːlə-/ n [U] study of the Earth's history as recorded in rocks **–gist** n **–gical** /ˌdʒiəˈlɒdʒɪkəl‖-ˈlɑː-/ adj **–gically** /-kli/ adv

ge·om·e·try /dʒiˈɒmətri‖-ˈɑːm-/ n [U] study of lines, angles, and surfaces and their relationships **geometric** /ˌdʒiəˈmetrɪk/ adj **geometrically** /-kli/ adv

Geord·ie /ˈdʒɔːdi‖ˈdʒɔːr-/ n person from northeast England

ge·ri·at·rics /ˌdʒeriˈætrɪks/ n [U] medical care of old people **geriatric** adj

germ /dʒɜːm‖dʒɜːrm/ n 1 bacterium carrying disease 2 beginning of an idea, etc.

ger·mane /dʒɜːˈmeɪn‖dʒɜːr-/ adj fml RELEVANT.

ger·mi·cide /ˈdʒɜːməsaɪd‖ˈdʒɜːr-/ n [C;U] chemical for killing germs

ger·mi·nate /ˈdʒɜːməneɪt‖ˈdʒɜːr-/ vi/t cause (a seed) to start growing **–nation** /ˌdʒɜːməˈneɪʃən‖ˌdʒɜːr-/ n [U]

ger·und /ˈdʒerənd/ n VERBAL NOUN

ges·ta·tion /dʒeˈsteɪʃən/ n [S;U] carrying of a young creature inside the mother's body

ges·tic·u·late /dʒeˈstɪkjʊleɪt/ vi wave the hands and arms about to express something **–lation** /dʒeˌstɪkjʊˈleɪʃən/ n [C;U]

ges·ture /ˈdʒestʃəʳ/ n 1 [C;U] movement of the body to express something 2 [C] action done to show one's feelings

get /get/ v **got** /gɒt‖gɑːt/, **got** esp. BrE ‖ **gotten** /ˈgɒtn‖ˈgɑːtn/ AmE; pres. p. **getting** 1 vt receive; obtain: *get a letter*‖*get permission* 2 vt collect; bring 3 vt catch (an illness) 4 vi/t (cause to) go or arrive: *get home*‖*get my boots off* 5 [+adj] become: *get wed*‖*married* 6 vi come or bring to the stated degree of success: *Now we're getting somewhere.* 7 vt succeed in or be allowed: *He's nice when you get to know him.*‖*I never get to drive the car.* 8 vt prepare (a meal) 9 vt hear or understand: *I don't get you.* 10 vt confuse; PUZZLE: *That's got you!* 11 vt annoy: *It's his attitude that gets me.* 12 vt infml a punish or harm (someone) in return for harm they have done you: *I'll get you for this!* b catch or attack: *The crocodiles will get them.* 13 **get (something) done: a** cause something to be done: *I must get these shoes mended.* **b** experience something that happens to one: *I got my hand caught in the door.* 14 **have got** have: *He's got red hair.* 15 **you get** infml there is/are

get about/around phr vi 1 be able to move again after an illness 2 travel 3 also **get round** BrE — (of news, etc., spread)

get across/over phr vi/t (cause to) be understood

get along phr vi 1 make progress; manage 2 GET **on** (2)

get around/round to phr vt find time for; do at last

get at phr vt 1 reach 2 mean; IMPLY 3 say unkind things

get away phr vi escape

get away with phr vt escape punishment for

get back *phr vi* 1 return 2 return to power after having lost it 3 speak or write to a person at a later time: *I can't tell you now, but I'll get back to you tomorrow.* 4 **get back at someone** also **get one's own back on someone** — punish someone in return for a wrong done to oneself

get by *phr vi* 1 continue to live; SURVIVE 2 be acceptable; be good enough but not very good

get down *phr vt* 1 swallow: *get the medicine down* 2 write down 3 DEPRESS: *This weather gets me down.*

get down to *phr vt* begin to work at

get in *phr v* 1 *vi* arrive: *The plane got in late.* 2 *vt* call (someone) to help 3 *vt* collect a supply of 4 *vt* enter (a vehicle) 5 *vt* say (something), esp. by interrupting a conversation

get into *phr vt* 1 develop (a bad condition): *get into trouble* 2 become accustomed to

get off *phr v* 1 leave; start 2 *vi/t* (cause to) escape punishment 3 *vt* leave (a public vehicle) 4 *vt* DISMOUNT

get off with *phr vt sl* start a (sexual) relationship with

get on *phr vi* 1 progress 2 be friendly: *They don't get on together.*

get onto *phr v* 1 CONTACT 2 begin to talk about: *How did we get onto that subject?*

get out *phr v* 1 *vi/t* (cause to) escape 2 *vi* become known 3 gain from

get over *phr vt* 1 get better from (illness, etc.) 2 manage to deal with 3 reach the end of (usu. something unpleasant) 4 make clear; cause to be understood 5 **I can't/couldn't get over** I am/was very much surprised at

get round *phr vt* 1 avoid; CIRCUMVENT 2 persuade to do something

get through *phr v* 1 *vi/t* pass (an examination, etc.) 2 *vi* reach someone by telephone 3 *vi* finish 4 *vi/t* (cause to) be understood by someone

get together *phr vi* have a meeting or party

get up *phr v* 1 *vi* rise from bed 2 *vt* ORGANIZE 3 *vt* decorate or change the appearance of in the stated way

get up to *phr vt* 1 do (something bad) 2 reach

get-a-way /'getəwei/ *n* [S] escape
get-to-geth-er /'· ·,··/ *n* friendly informal meeting for enjoyment
get-up /'getʌp/ *n* set of clothes
get-up-and-go /,· · · '·'/ *n* [U] *infml* forceful active quality of mind
gey-ser /'giːzəʳ‖'gaɪ-/ *n* 1 natural spring of hot water 2 *BrE* bathroom apparatus for heating water by gas
ghast-ly /'gɑːstli‖'gæstli/ *adj* very bad; terrible 2 pale and ill-looking
gher-kin /'gɜːkɪn‖'gɜːr-/ *n* small green CUCUMBER

ghet-to /'getəʊ/ *n* -tos *or* -toes part of city where poor people or foreigners live

ghetto-blast-er /'·· ,··/ *n* large TAPE RECORDER that can be carried around

ghost /gəʊst/ *n* 1 (spirit of) a dead person who appears again 2 also **ghost writer** /'· ,·'/ — person who writes material which another person gives out as his own 3 **give up the ghost** die 4 **the ghost of a** the slightest ~**ly** *adj* like a ghost ♦ *vt* write (something) as a GHOST (2)

ghost town /'· ·/ *n* empty town that was once busy

ghoul /guːl/ *n* person who likes thinking about dead bodies and nasty things ~**ish** *adj*

GI /,dʒiː 'aɪ/ *n* US soldier

gi-ant /'dʒaɪənt/ also **giantess** /-tes/ *fem.* — *n* big strong person or creature ♦ *adj* very large

gib-ber /'dʒɪbəʳ/ *vi* talk very fast and meaninglessly

gib-ber-ish /'dʒɪbərɪʃ/ *n* [U] meaningless talk

gib-bet /'dʒɪbɪt/ *n* GALLOWS

gib-bon /'gɪbən/ *n* animal like a monkey with no tail and long arms

gibe, jibe /dʒaɪb/ *n* remark that makes someone look foolish ♦ *v* **gibe at** *phr vt*

gib-lets /'dʒɪblɪts/ *n* [P] bird's heart, etc., taken out before cooking

gid-dy /'gɪdi/ *adj* 1 (causing) a feeling of unsteady movement 2 (of a person) not serious –**diness** *n* [U]

gift /gɪft/ *n* 1 something given freely 2 TALENT: *a gift for music* 3 **the gift of the gab** *infml* the ability to speak well continuously, and esp. to persuade people ~**ed** *adj* TALENTED

gift horse /'· ·/ *n* **look a gift horse in the mouth** complain about a gift

gig /gɪg/ *n* musician's performance

gi-gan-tic /dʒaɪˈɡæntɪk/ *adj* very large

gig-gle /'gɪgəl/ *vi* laugh in a silly way **giggle** *n* 1 [C] act of giggling 2 [S] *infml*, *esp. BrE* something that amuses: *We only did it for a giggle.*

gig-o-lo /'ʒɪgələʊ, 'dʒɪ-/ *n* woman's paid lover and companion

gild /gɪld/ *vt* 1 cover with gold or gold paint 2 **gild the lily** to try to improve something that is already good enough, so spoiling the effect

gill[1] /gɪl/ *n* organ through which a fish breathes

gill[2] /dʒɪl/ *n* measure of liquid

gilt /gɪlt/ *n* [U] material with which things are gilded

gilt-edged /,· '·⊲/ *adj* (of government SHARES (2)) having a fixed interest rate and therefore safe

gim-let /'gɪmlɪt/ *n* tool for making holes for screws

gim-mick /'gɪmɪk/ n trick, phrase, etc., used to draw attention **—y** adv

gin /dʒɪn/ n [U] colourless alcoholic drink

gin-ger[1] /'dʒɪndʒə^r/ n [U] **1** plant whose hot-tasting root is used in cooking **2** orange-brown colour: *ginger hair*

ginger[2] v **ginger up** phr vt make more exciting

ginger ale /,·· '·‖'·· ·/ n [C;U] gassy alcoholic drink

ginger beer /,·· '·‖'·· ·/ n [C;U] gassy non-alcoholic drink

gin-ger-bread /'dʒɪndʒəbred‖-dʒər-/ n [U] cake with ginger in it

gin-ger-ly /'dʒɪndʒəli‖-ər-/ adv carefully ♦ adj careful

ging-ham /'gɪŋəm/ n [U] cotton cloth with a pattern of squares

gip-sy , **gypsy**/'dʒɪpsi/ n member of a dark-haired people who often travel about in CARAVANs (1,2)

gi-raffe /dʒɪˈrɑːf‖-ˈræf/ n longnecked African animal

gird /gɜːd‖gɜːrd/ vt **girded** or **girt** /gɜːt‖gɜːrt/ fml fasten with a belt

gir-der /'gɜːdə^r‖'gɜːr-/ n metal beam supporting a roof, bridge, etc.

gir-dle /'gɜːdl‖'gɜːr-/ n **1** woman's light CORSET **2** lit something that surrounds something: *a girdle of islands* ♦ vt lit go all round

girl /gɜːl‖gɜːrl/ n young female person **~hood** n time of being a girl **~ish** adj like a girl

girl-friend /'gɜːlfrend‖'gɜːrl-/ n **1** man's female companion **2** woman's female friend

gi-ro /'dʒaɪərəʊ/ n **1** [U] banking system handled by one central computer **2** [C] BrE SOCIAL SECURITY payment (by cheque)

girt /gɜːt‖gɜːrt/ v past t. and p. of GIRD

girth /gɜːθ‖gɜːrθ/ n **1** [C] band round a horse's middle to hold the SADDLE firm **2** [U] fml thickness measured round something: *the girth of a tree*

gist /dʒɪst/ n [S] main points of something

give[1] /gɪv/ v **gave** /geɪv/, **given** /'gɪvən/ **1** vt cause or allow someone to have: *give him a present/a job/give me time.* **2** vt pay in exchange: *I'll give £3000 for the car.* **3** vi supply money: *give generously to charity* **4** vt provide: *Cows give milk.* **5** vt perform (an action): *give an order/a sign* **6** vt offer (an amusement, etc.): *give a party* **7** vt bend or stretch under pressure **8** vt fml cause to believe, esp. wrongly: *I was given to understand that he was ill.* **9** vt call on (people present) to drink a TOAST (2) to: *I give you the President!* **10** **give or take (a certain amount)** more or less (a certain amount) **11** **give way (to): a** admit defeat in an argument or fight **b** break **c** become

less useful or important than **d** allow oneself to show (esp. a feeling) **e** allow other traffic to go before **giver** n

give away phr vt **1** give freely **2** show the truth about

give back phr vt return (something) to the owner

give in phr v **1** vi SURRENDER **2** vt deliver

give off phr vt send out (a smell, etc.)

give out phr v **1** vt DISTRIBUTE **2** vi come to an end: *The petrol/My strength gave out.*

give up phr v **1** vi/t stop: *give up smoking* **2** vi stop trying to guess, etc. **3** vt regard as lost or hopeless **4** vt offer as a prisoner **5** vt deliver to someone: *give up one's seat in the train*

give[2] n [U] quality of bending or stretching under pressure

give-and-take /,·· '·'·/ n [U] willingness to COMPROMISE (= give way to another's wishes)

give-a-way /'gɪvəweɪ/ n [S] something unintentional that makes a secret known ♦ adj (of a price) very low

giv-en /'gɪvən/adj **1** fixed and stated: *a given time* **2** **be given to** have a tendency to ♦ prep if one takes into account: *Given her inexperience, she's done a good job.*

given name /'·· ·/ n AmE for FIRST NAME

gla-cial /'gleɪʃəl/ adj of ice or an ICE AGE

gla-ci-er /'glæsɪə^r‖'gleɪʃər/ n mass of ice that flows slowly down a valley

glad /glæd/ adj **-dd- 1** pleased **2** lit causing happiness **~ly** adv willingly **~ness** n [U]

glad-den /'glædn/ vt make glad

glade /gleɪd/ n lit open space in a forest

glad-i-a-tor /'glædɪeɪtə^r/ n (in ancient Rome) man who fought in public as an entertainment

glam-o-rize ‖ also **-rise** BrE /'glæməraɪz/ vt make (something) appear more attractive than it really is

glam-our BrE ‖ **-or** AmE/'glæmə^r/ n **1** the charm of something unusual **2** sexual attraction **~ous** adj

glance /glɑːns‖glæns/ vi give a rapid look ♦ n **1** rapid look **2 at a glance** at once

glance off phr vi/t (of a blow, etc.) hit and move off at an angle

gland /glænd/ n body organ that treats materials from the bloodstream to produce various liquid substances

glan-du-lar /'glændjʊlə^r‖-dʒə-/ adj of the glands

glare /gleə^r/ vi **1** look fiercely **2** shine too strongly **glare** n [S] **glaring** adj **1**

too bright **2** noticeably bad: *glaring injustice*

glass /glɑːs‖glæs/ *n* **1** [U] hard transparent material used in windows, etc. **2** [C] something made of this, esp. a container for drinking from **3** [C] amount held by such a container — see also GLASSES **~y** *adj* like glass: *a glassy stare* *vt*

glass-blow-er /'glɑːsˌbləʊəʳ‖'glæs-/ *n* person who shapes hot glass by blowing through a tube

glass-es /glɑːsɪz‖'glæ-/ *n* [P] two pieces of specially-cut glass in a frame, worn in front of the eyes for improving a person's ability to see

glass fi-bre /ˌ· '··◄/ *n* [U] FIBREGLASS

glass-house /'glɑːshaʊs‖'glæs-/ *n* BrE GREENHOUSE

glass-ware /'glɑːsweəʳ‖'glæs-/ *n* [U] glass objects generally

glass-works /'glɑːswɜːks‖'glæswɜːrks/ *n* **glassworks** factory where glass is made

glau-co-ma /glɔː'kəʊmə/ *n* [U] eye disease marked by increased pressure within the eyeball

glaze /gleɪz/ *v* **1** *vt* put a shiny surface on (pots, etc.) **2** *vt* fit (a window, etc,) with glass **3** *vi* (of the eyes) become dull ♦ *n* [U] shiny surface

gla-zi-er /'gleɪziəʳ‖-ʒər/ *n* workman who fits glass into windows

gleam /gliːm/ *n* **1** a gentle light **2** sudden sign of something: *a gleam of interest* ♦ *vi* send out a gleam

glean /gliːn/ *vt* gather (facts, etc.) in small amounts

glee /gliː/ *n* [U] joyful satisfaction **~ful** *adj* **~fully** *adv*

glen /glen/ *n* narrow valley, esp. in Scotland

glib /glɪb/ *adj* **-bb-** speaking or spoken too easily: *glib excuses* **~ly** *adv* **~ness** *n* [U]

glide /glaɪd/ *vi* **1** move smoothly and noiselessly **2** fly in a glider ♦ *n* gliding movement **glider** *n* plane with no engine

glim-mer /'glɪməʳ/ *vi* shine faintly ♦ *n* **1** faint light **2** small uncertain sign: *a glimmer of hope*

glimpse /glɪmps/ *n* quick incomplete view of something ♦ *vt* see for a moment

glint /glɪnt/ *vi, n* (give out) a small flash of light

glis-ten /'glɪsən/ *vi* shine as if wet

glitch /glɪtʃ/ *n* small fault in the operation of something

glit-ter /'glɪtəʳ/ *vi* flash brightly: *glittering diamonds* ♦ *n* [S;U] brightness

glit-te-ra-ti /ˌglɪtə'rɑːti/ *n* [(*the*) P] fashionable people whose social activities are widely reported

gloat /gləʊt/ *vi* look at something with unpleasant satisfaction **~ingly** *adv*

glo-bal /'gləʊbəl/ *adj* **1** of the whole world **2** taking account of all considerations **~ly** *adv*

globe /gləʊb/ *n* **1** [C] object in the shape of a ball; esp. one with a map of the Earth painted on it **2** [*the* + S] the Earth

globe-trot-ter /'gləʊbtrɒtəʳ‖-trɑː-/ *n* person who travels widely **-ting** *adj, n*

glob-u-lar /'glɒbjʊləʳ‖'glɑː-/ *adj* shaped like a ball

glob-ule /'glɒbjuːl‖'glɑː-/ *n* drop of liquid

gloom /gluːm/ *n* **1** [U] darkness **2** [S;U] sadness; hopelessness **~y** *adj* **~ily** *adv*

glo-ri-fy /'glɔːrɪfaɪ/ *vt* **1** praise; worship **2** cause to seem more important: *Her cottage is just a glorified hut.* **-fication** /ˌglɔːrɪfɪ'keɪʃən/ *n* [U]

glo-ri-ous /'glɔːriəs/ *adj* **1** having great honour: *glorious victory* **2** splendid **~ly** *adv*

glo-ry¹ /'glɔːri/ *n* [U] **1** great honour **2** splendid beauty

glory² *v* **glory in** *phr vt* enjoy, often selfishly

gloss /glɒs‖glɔːs, glɑːs/ *n* [S;U] **1** shiny brightness **2** pleasant but deceiving outer appearance **3** explanation of a piece of writing ♦ *vt* write an explanation of **~y** *adj* shiny

gloss over *phr vt* hide (faults)

glos-sa-ry /'glɒsəri‖'glɔː-, 'glɑː-/ *n* list of explanations of words

glossy mag-a-zine /ˌ··· '··‖ˌ··'··/ *n* magazine printed on shiny paper with lots of pictures, esp. of clothes

glove /glʌv/ *n* **1** covering for the hand **2 fit like a glove** fit perfectly — see also KID GLOVES

glow /gləʊ/ *vi* **1** give out heat or light without flames **2** be warm and red in the face ♦ *n* [S] glowing light **~ing** *adj* strongly approving: *a glowing account*

glow-er /'glaʊəʳ/ *vi* look with an angry expression **~ingly** *adv*

glow-worm /'·· ·/ *n* insect that gives out a greenish light

glu-cose /'gluːkəʊs/ *n* [U] sugar found in fruit

glue /gluː/ *n* [U] sticky substance for joining things ♦ *vt pres. p.* **gluing** or **glueing 1** join with glue **2 glued to** close to: *children glued to the television* **~y** *adj*

glue-snif-fing /'· ˌ··/ *n* [U] harmful breathing in of FUMES of glue to produce a state of excitement

glum /glʌm/ *adj* **-mm-** sad; GLOOMY **~ly** *adv*

glut /glʌt/ vt -tt- supply with too much: *shops glutted with fruit* ◆ n [S] too large a supply

glu·ti·nous /'gluːtɪnəs/ adj fml sticky

glut·ton /'glʌtn/ n 1 person who eats too much 2 person who is always ready to do more of something hard or unpleasant: *a glutton for punishment* ~**ous** adj GREEDY --**y** n [U] fml habit of eating too much

gly·ce·rine /'glɪsəriːn‖-rən/ also **glycerin** /-rən/ -- n [U] colourless liquid used in making soap, medicines, and explosives

gm written abbrev. for: GRAM

gnarled /nɑːld‖nɑːrld/ adj rough and twisted: *gnarled tree trunks*

gnash /næʃ/ n strike (one's teeth) together

gnat /næt/ n small flying insect that stings

gnaw /nɔː/ vi/t bite steadily (at): (fig.) *gnawing anxiety*

gnome /nəʊm/ n 1 (in stories) little (old) man who lives under the ground 2 (stone or plastic) figure representing this 3 *the gnomes of Zurich* certain powerful bankers, esp. Swiss ones

GNP /ˌdʒiː en 'piː/ n [the+S] Gross National Product; total value of everything produced in a country, usu. in a single year

go¹ /gəʊ/ v went /went/, gone /gɒn‖gɔːn/ 1 vi leave a place: *I must go now.* 2 vi move; travel: *go by bus| go shopping* 3 vi lead; reach: *This road goes to London.* 4 vi start an action: *Ready, steady, go!* 5 a become: *go mad* b be or remain: *Her protests went unnoticed.* 6 vi match; fit: *Blue and green don't go (together).| 4 into 3 won't go.| Your dress goes with your eyes.* 7 vi belong: *The knives go in this drawer.* 8 vi (of machines) work: *This clock doesn't go.* 9 vi be sold: *The house is going cheap.* 10 vt have (certain words or sounds): *Ducks go 'quack'.* 11 vi become weak or worn out: *My voice is going.* 12 vi lose one's usual powers of control: *let oneself go | He's pretty far gone.* 13 vi state or do up to or beyond a limit: *go too far* 14 vi be accepted or acceptable: *What she says goes.* 15 vi happen or develop in the stated way: *The party went well.* 16 **as someone/something goes** compared with the average person or thing of that type: *He's not a bad cook, as cooks go, but he's no expert.* 17 **be going** be present for use: *Is there any good going?* 18 **be going to** (shows the future): *Is it going to rain?* 19 **go a long way** also **go far:** a (of money) buy a lot b (of a person) succeed 20 **go and:** a go in order to: *go and fetch it* b (shows surprise): *She went and bought it!* 21 **go for it** infml

make every effort to succeed at something 22 **go it alone** act independently 23 **to go** left; remaining: *only 3 more days to go* 24 **-goer** person who goes somewhere regularly: *churchgoers*

go about phr v 1 vt perform; work at: *go about one's business* 2 vi GO **around** (1,3)

go after phr vt try to get; chase

go against phr vt 1 oppose 2 be unfavourable to: *The case may go against you.*

go ahead phr vi 1 begin 2 continue

go along phr vi continue

go along with phr vt agree with

go around/round phr vi 1 (of an illness) spread 2 be enough for everyone: *not enough chairs to go round* 3 be often out in public (with someone)

go at phr vt attack; TACKLE

go back phr vi 1 return 2 stretch back in time

go back on phr vt break (a promise), etc.)

go by phr v 1 vi pass (in place or time): *A year went by.* 2 vt act according to 3 vt judge by 4 **go by the name of** be called

go down phr vi 1 become lower 2 sink: *The sun/The ship went down.* 3 become less swollen 4 (of food) be swallowed 5 be accepted: *His speech went down well with the crowd.* 6 be recorded: *This day will go down in history.*

go down with phr vt catch (an illness)

go for phr vt 1 attack 2 GO **after** 3 like or be attracted by 4 **go for nothing** be wasted

go in phr vi 1 (of the sun, etc.) become covered by clouds 2 join

go in for phr vt 1 enter (a competition) 2 have a habit of: *go in for football*

go into phr vt 1 enter (a profession) 2 explain or examine thoroughly

go off phr v 1 vi a explode b ring or sound loudly 2 vi succeed or fail: *The conference went off well.* 3 vi go bad 4 vt lose interest in 5 vi stop operating

go off with phr vt take away without permission

go on phr v 1 vi happen: *What's going on?* 2 vi (of time) pass 3 vi a continue: *go on with your work* b talk, complain, or behave in a certain way continually 4 vi be put into operation 5 vt use as proof, etc.: *I'm going on what you told me.* 6 **go on (with you)!** BrE infml I don't believe you! 7 **to be going/go on with** infml, esp. BrE for the moment

go out phr vi 1 leave the house 2 spend time with someone 3 stop burning 4 become unfashionable 5 (of the sea) go back to its low level **6** (of feelings) be in sympathy (with)

go over *phr vt* **1** examine **2** repeat

go round *phr vi* GO **around**

go through *phr v* **1** *vi* be approved officially **2** *vt* suffer or experience **3** *vt* finish; spend **4** *vt* search

go through with *phr vt* complete

go to *phr vt* **1** make oneself have: *go to a lot of trouble* **2** start experiencing or causing (a state or action)

go under *phr vi* **1** (of a ship) sink **2** fail

go up *phr vi* **1** rise **2** be built **3** be destroyed in fire, etc.

go with *phr vt* **1** match **2** be often found with

go without *phr vi/t* **1** DO **without 2 it goes without saying** it is clear without needing to be stated

go² *n* **1** [U] quality of being very active **2** [C] attempt **3** [C] turn, esp. in a game **4 from the word go** from the beginning **5 have a go** *infml. esp. BrE* **a** to complain **b** attempt to catch or stop a wrongdoer by force **6 It's all go** it's very busy **7 make a go of** *infml* make a success of **8 on the go** very busy

goad /gəʊd/ *vt* urge by continuous annoyance ♦ *n* stick for driving cattle

go-a-head¹ /'··,·/*n* [(*the*)S] permission to take action

go-ahead² *adj* active in using new methods

goal /gəʊl/ *n* **1** one's aim or purpose **2 a** place where the ball must go to gain a point in football, etc. **b** point gained by sending the ball there — see also OWN GOAL

goal-keep-er /'gəʊl,kiːpəʳ/ *n* player responsible for keeping the ball out of a team's goal

goal-post /'gəʊlpəʊst/ *n* one of the 2 posts between which the ball must go to gain a goal

goat /gəʊt/ *n* **1** horned animal like a sheep **2 get one's goat** annoy one

goa-tee /gəʊ'tiː/ *n* small pointed beard

gob /gɒb‖gɑːb/ *n BrE sl* mouth

gob-ble /'gɒbəl‖'gɑː-/ *vi/t* eat quickly and often noisily

gob-ble-dy-gook /'gɒbəldiguːk‖ 'gɑːbəldiguk, -guːk/ *n* [U] meaningless official language

go-be-tween /'·· ·,·/ *n* person who takes messages, etc., from one person or side to another

gob-let /'gɒblət‖'gɑːb-/ *n* glass or metal drinking cup with a stem and no handle

gob-lin /'gɒblən‖'gɑːb-/ *n* unkind fairy that plays tricks on people

god /gɒd‖gɑːd/ **goddess** /'gɒdɪs‖ 'gɑː-/ *fem.* — *n* being who is worshipped — see also GODS ~**less** *adj*

fml wicked; not showing respect for or belief in God ~**like** *adj* like a god: *godlike beauty* ~**ly** *adj fml* religious; leading a good life

God *n* (in the Christian, Jewish, and Muslim religions) the maker and ruler of the world

god-child /'gɒdtʃaɪld‖'gɑːd-/ *n* boy (**godson**) or girl (**goddaughter**) for whom someone makes promises at BAPTISM

god-fa-ther /'gɒd,fɑːðəʳ‖'gɑːd-/ *n* male godparent

god-fear-ing /'· ,··/ *adj fml* good and well-behaved

god-for-sak-en /'gɒdfəseɪkən‖ 'gɑːdfəʳ-/ *adj* (of places) sad and empty

god-moth-er /'gɒd,mʌðəʳ‖'gɑːd-/ *n* female godparent

god-pa-rent /'gɒd,peərənt‖'gɑːd-/ *n* person who takes responsibility for a new Christian at BAPTISM

gods /gɒdz‖gɑːdz/ *n* [*the*+S] seats high up at the back of a theatre

god-send /'gɒdsend‖'gɑːd-/ *n* unexpected lucky chance or thing

go-fer /'gəʊfəʳ/*n* person whose job is to fetch or take things for other people

go-getter /'· '··, '··‖'·, ·, ·/*n* someone who is forceful and determined, and likely to succeed

gog-gle /'gɒgəl‖'gɑː-/ *vi* STARE with the eyes wide open **goggles** *n* [P] glasses to protect the eyes

go-go /'· ·/*adj* of or being a form of fast dancing with sexy movements

go-ing /'gəʊɪŋ/ *n* [U] speed or condition of travel: *fast/rough going* ♦ *adj* operating at present: *the going rate*|*a going concern*

goings-on /,·· '·/ *n* [P] undesirable activities

goi-tre *BrE* ‖ -**ter** *AmE*/'gɔɪtəʳ/ *n* swelling in the neck caused by lack of certain chemicals

go-kart /'gəʊ kɑːt‖-kɑːrt/ *n* small low racing car

gold /gəʊld/ *n* **1** [U] valuable yellow metal **2** [U] gold coins **3** [U] the colour of gold: *gold paint* **4** [C] gold MEDAL **5 as good as gold** very well behaved

gold-en /'gəʊldən/ *adj* **1** of or like gold **2** very favourable: *a golden opportunity*

golden hand-shake /,·· '··/ *n* large amount of money given to someone leaving a firm

golden rule /,·· '·/ *n* [S] very important rule of behaviour

gold-fish /'gəʊld,fɪʃ/ *n* **goldfish** small orange fish kept as a pet

gold leaf /,· '·/ *n* [U] thin sheets of gold

gold-mine /'gəʊldmaɪn/ *n* **1** mine where gold is found **2** profitable business

gold rush /'· ·/ n rush to newly discovered goldmines

gold-smith /'gəʊld,smiθ/ n person who makes things out of gold

golf /gɒlf‖gɑːlf, gɔːlf/ n game in which people hit a ball into holes with GOLF CLUBS ~er n

golf ball /'· ·/ n 1 small hard ball used in golf 2 ball used in an electric TYPEWRITER to press letters onto the paper

golf club /'· ·/ n 1 long-handled stick for hitting the ball in golf 2 club for golfers with buildings and land they can use

gone /gɒn‖gɔːn/ v past p. of GO: George has gone to Paris. (= he is there now)

gong /gɒŋ‖gɔːŋ, gɑːŋ/ n 1 round piece of metal that makes a ringing sound when struck 2 BrE sl MEDAL

gon-or-rhe-a, -rhoea /,gɒnə'rɪə‖ ,gɑː-/ n [U] disease passed on during sexual activity

goo /guː/ n [U] 1 sticky material 2 SENTIMENTALISM

good¹ /gʊd/ adj better /'betəʳ/, best /best/ 1 satisfactory: good food/brakes 2 pleasant: good news|have a good time 3 useful; suitable: Milk is good for you. 4 clever: good at maths 5 well-behaved 6 morally right: good deeds 7 fml kind: Be good enough to hold this. 8 thorough: have a good cry 9 **a good: a** at least: a good 3 hours **b** large in size, amount: a good distance 10 **a good deal** quite a lot 11 **all in good time** (it will happen) at a suitable later time; be patient 12 **as good as** almost the same as 13 **Good!** I agree, that's fine, etc. 14 **good and . . .** infml completely: I'll do it when I'm good and ready. 15 **good for: a** effective in use: The ticket is good for a month. **b** likely to produce: She's always good for a few pounds/a laugh. 16 **in good time** early 17 **make good** be successful

good² n [U] 1 something that is good 2 something that causes gain or improvement: It'll do you good.|It's no good. (= it's useless)|What's the good of|What good is it having a car if you don't drive? 3 **for good** forever 4 **good for you** (used to express approval and pleasure at someone's success, etc.) 5 **up to no good** doing or intending doing something bad — see also GOODS

good af-ter-noon /· ,··'·/ interj (used when meeting someone in the afternoon)

good-bye /gʊd'baɪ/ interj (used when leaving someone)

good eve-ning /· '··/ interj (used when meeting someone in the evening)

good-for-noth-ing /'· ·· ,··/ adj, n useless (person)

Good Fri-day /,· '··/ n the Friday before EASTER

good-hu-moured /,· '··◄/ adj cheerful and friendly

good-look-ing /,· '··◄/ adj attractive; beautiful

good-ly /'gʊdli/ adj 1 large 2 satisfying

good mor-ning /· '··/ interj (used when meeting someone in the morning)

good-na-tured /,· '··◄/ adj kind

good-ness /'gʊdnəs/ n [U] 1 quality of being good 2 the best part of food, etc. 3 (used in expressions of surprise and annoyance): Goodness me!|for goodness' sake

good-night /gʊd'naɪt/ interj (used when leaving someone at night, or going to sleep)

goods /gʊdz/ n [P] 1 things for sale 2 things carried by train, etc. 3 possessions 4 **come up with/deliver the goods** produce in full what is expected

good Sam-ar-i-tan /,· ··'···/ n person who kindly helps people in trouble

good-will /,gʊd'wɪl/ n [U] 1 kind feelings 2 popularity of a business, as part of its value

good-y /'gʊdi/ n something very pleasant, esp. to eat

goo-ey /'guːi/ adj 1 sticky and sweet 2 SENTIMENTAL

goof /guːf/ n infml 1 foolish person 2 silly mistake ♦ vi infml, esp. AmE make a silly mistake

goof off phr vi AmE infml waste time or avoid work

goose /guːs/ n geese /giːs/ 1 bird like a large duck 2 silly person

goose-ber-ry /'gʊzbəri, 'gʊz-, 'guːs-‖'guːsberi/ n 1 garden bush with hairy green berries 2 (of a third person) present with a man and woman who would rather be alone

goose-flesh /'guːsfleʃ/ n [U] condition in which the skin rises up in small points

goose-step /'guːs-step/ n [S] way of marching with stiff straight legs

GOP /,dʒiː əʊ 'piː/ n [the] the Republican Party in US politics

gore¹ /gɔːʳ/ vt wound with horns or TUSKS

gore² n [U] lit (esp. thick) blood **gory** adj

gorge¹ /gɔːdʒ‖gɔːrdʒ/ n 1 steep narrow valley 2 **make someone's gorge rise** make someone feel sickened

gorge² vi/t eat or feed eagerly

gor-geous /'gɔːdʒəs‖'gɔːr-/ adj wonderful; beautiful ~ly adv

go-ril-la /gə'rɪlə/ n the largest of the APES

gosh /gɒʃ‖gɑːʃ/ *interj* (expressing surprise)

go-slow /ˌ· ˈ-◂/ *n BrE* decision to work slowly, as a kind of STRIKE² (1)

gos·pel /'gɒspəl‖'gɑːs-/ *n* **1** [C] something completely true **2** (*cap.*) any of 4 accounts of Christ's life in the Bible

gos·sa·mer /'gɒsəmə*ʳ*‖'gɑː-/ *n* [U] thin silky thread

gos·sip /'gɒsɪp‖'gɑː-/ *n* **1** [S;U] talk about other people's private lives **2** [C] person who likes this kind of talk ♦ *vi* spend time in gossip

got /gɒt‖gɑːt/ *v past t. and p. of* GET

Goth·ic /'gɒθɪk‖'gɑː-/ *adj* **1** of a style of building common from the 12th to 16th centuries, with pointed arches and tall pillars **2** of a style of writing in the 18th century which produced NOVELS set in lonely fearful places

got·ten /'gɒtn‖'gɑːtn/ *v AmE past p. of* GET

gou·ache /gu'ɑːʃ, gwɑːʃ/ *n* [C;U] (picture painted by) a method using colours mixed with water and a sort of glue

gouge /gaʊdʒ/ *v* **gouge out** *phr vt* push or dig out violently

gourd /gʊəd‖gɔːrd, gʊərd/ *n* hard outer shell of a fruit

gour·met /'gʊəmeɪ‖'gʊər-, gʊər'meɪ/ *n* person who knows a lot about food and drink

gout /gaʊt/ *n* [U] disease that makes the toes and fingers swell painfully

gov·ern /'gʌvən‖-ərn/ *v* **1** *vi/t* rule (a country, etc.) **2** *vt* control: *The price is governed by the quantity produced.* **~ance** *n* [U] *fml* governing

gov·ern·ess /'gʌvənɪs‖-ər-/ *n* woman who teaches children in their home

gov·ern·ment /'gʌvənmənt, 'gʌvəmənt‖'gʌvərn-/ *n* **1** [C] group of people who govern: *the Swiss government* **2** [U] act or process of governing: *the art of government* **3** form or method of governing: *a return to democratic government* **~al** /ˌgʌvən'mentl‖ˌgʌvərn-/ *adj*

gov·er·nor /'gʌvənə*ʳ*/ *n* person who controls various sorts of place or organization: *the governor of the prison/of California* **~ship** *n* [U]

gown /gaʊn/ *n* **1** woman's dress **2** outer garment worn by judges, members of universities, etc. **3** loose garment worn for some special purpose: *a nightgown/dressing gown*

GP /ˌdʒiː 'piː/ *n* doctor who is trained in general medicine and treats people in a certain local area

grab /græb/ *vi/t* **-bb-** seize suddenly and roughly ♦ *n* **1** sudden attempt to seize something **2 up for grabs** ready for anyone to take or win

grace /greɪs/ *n* [U] **1** beauty of movement or shape **2** delay allowed as a favour: *give them a week's grace* **3** prayer of thanks before or after meals **4** God's favour towards people **5 a saving grace** pleasing quality for which the person's faults are forgiven him **6 with (a) good/bad grace** willingly/unwillingly ♦ *vt fml* give honour or beauty to **~ful** *adj* **1** having GRACE(1) **2** suitably expressed **~fully** *adv* **~less** *adj* awkward

gra·cious /'greɪʃəs/ *adj* **1** polite and pleasant **2** having those qualities made possible by wealth: *gracious living* **~ly** *adv* **~ness** *n* [U]

gra·da·tion /grə'deɪʃən/ *n fml* stage; degree: *gradations of colour*

grade /greɪd/ *n* **1** level of quality **2** *AmE* a FORM¹ (5) **b** mark given for schoolwork **c** gradient **3 make the grade** succeed; reach the necessary standard ♦ *vt* separate into levels of quality

grade school /'· ˌ·/ *n AmE for* ELEMENTARY SCHOOL

gra·di·ent /'greɪdiənt/ *n* degree of slope, as on a road

grad·u·al /'grædʒuəl/ *adj* happening slowly; not sudden **~ly** *adv* **~ness** *n* [U]

grad·u·ate¹ /'grædʒuət/ *n* **1** person with a university degree **2** *AmE* person who has completed any school or college course

grad·u·ate² /'grædʒueɪt/ *v* **1** *vi* become a graduate **2** *vt* GRADE **3** *vt* mark with degrees for measurement **–ation** /ˌgrædʒu'eɪʃən/ *n* **1** (ceremony) becoming a graduate **2** [C] mark of measurement

graf·fi·ti /græ'fiːti, grə-/ *n* [P;U] drawings or writings on a wall

graft /grɑːft‖græft/ *n* **1** [C] piece from one plant fixed inside another to grow there **2** [C] piece of skin or bone similarly fixed into the body **3** [U] *esp. AmE* practice of obtaining money or advantage by the dishonest use of esp. political influence **4** [U] *BrE infml* work ♦ *vt* put onto as a graft

grain /greɪn/ *n* **1** [C] single seed of rice, wheat, etc. **2** [U] crops from food plants like these **3** [C] small hard piece: *grains of sand* (fig.) *a grain of truth* **4** [U] natural arrangement of threads or FIBRES in wood, cloth, etc. **5 be/go against the grain** it is not what one wishes (to do, know, etc.)

gram , gramme /græm/ *n* (measure of weight equal to) 1/1000 of a kilogram

gram·mar /'græmə*ʳ*/ *n* [U] (book that teaches) rules for the use of words

gram·mar·i·an /grə'meəriən/ *n* person who studies and knows about grammar

grammar school /'·· ·/ n British school, esp. formerly, for children over 11 who study for higher examinations

gram·mat·i·cal /grə'mætɪkəl/ adj 1 concerning grammar 2 correct according to the rules of grammar

gram·o·phone /'græməfəʊn/ n BrE RECORD PLAYER

gran /græn/ n BrE infml grandmother

gra·na·ry /'grænəri‖'greɪ-, 'græ-/ n storehouse for grain

grand /grænd/ adj 1 splendid; IMPRESSIVE 2 (of people) important 3 pleasant; delightful ♦ n 1 GRAND PIANO 2 (pl. **grand**) sl 1,000 pounds or dollars

grand·dad /'grændæd/ n infml grandfather

grand·child /'græntʃaɪld/ n **grand-children** /-ˌtʃɪldrən/ boy (**grandson**) or girl (**granddaughter**) who is the child of the stated person's son or daughter

gran·dee /græn'diː/ n Spanish or Portuguese nobleman

gran·deur /'grændʒər/ n [U] quality of being grand; MAGNIFICENCE

grand·fa·ther /'grænd,faːðər/ n male grandparent

grandfather clock /'··· ·, ,··· '·/ n tall clock that stands on the floor

gran·dil·o·quent /græn'dɪləkwənt/ adj using (too many) long words

gran·di·ose /'grændiəʊs/ adj intended to seem splendid and important

grand·ma /'grænmaː/ n infml grandmother

grand·moth·er /'græn,mʌðər/ n female grandparent

grand·par·ent /'græn,peərənt/ n parent of someone's father or mother

grand pi·an·o /ˌ··'··/ n large piano with strings set parallel to the ground

grand slam /ˌ· '·/ n the winning of all of a set of important sports competitions

grand·stand /'grændstænd/ n seats arranged in rising rows, for people watching races, etc.

grand to·tal /ˌ· '··/n complete amount

gran·ite /'grænɪt/ n [U] hard usu. grey rock

gran·ny , -nie /'græni/ n infml grandmother ♦ adj for old people: a granny flat

grant /graːnt‖grænt/ vt 1 fml give: grant permission 2 admit the truth of 3 **take something for granted** accept it without question ♦ n money granted esp. officially

gran·u·lar /'grænjʊlər/ adj made of grains

gran·u·lat·ed /'grænjʊleɪtɪd/ adj (of sugar) in the form of not very fine powder

gran·ule /'grænjuːl/ n small grain

grape /greɪp/ n green or purple fruit from which wine is made — see also SOUR GRAPES

grape·fruit /'greɪpfruːt/ n large yellow fruit like a sour orange

grape·vine /'greɪpvaɪn/ n [S] unofficial way of spreading news: hear about it through the office grapevine

graph /græf, graːf‖græf/ n drawing showing the relationship between 2 changing values

graph·ic /'græfɪk/ adj 1 clear and detailed: a graphic description 2 of drawing, printing, etc. **~ally** /-kli/ adv 1 clearly 2 using graphs **graphics** n [P] drawings, etc.

graph·ite /'græfaɪt/ n [U] black substance used in pencils, etc.

grap·ple /'græpəl/ v **grapple with** phr vt seize and struggle with: (fig.) grapple with a problem

grasp /graːsp‖græsp/ vt 1 take firm hold of 2 succeed in understanding ♦ n [S] 1 firm hold 2 understanding **~ing** adj too eager for money

grass /graːs‖græs/ n 1 [U] common wild green plants that cows, etc., eat 2 [C] one of these plants: tall grasses 3 sl someone who GRASSes 4 **out to grass**: a feeding on this plant b no longer working **~y** adj ♦ vi BrE sl (esp. of a criminal) inform the police about the action of (other) criminals

grass·hop·per /'graːs,hɒpər‖'græs,haː-/ n insect which can jump high and makes a sharp noise by rubbing parts of its body together

grass roots /ˌ· '·/ n [P] ordinary people, not those with political power

grass wid·ow /ˌ· '··/n woman whose husband is away for a period of time

grate[1] /greɪt/ n metal frame in a fireplace

grate[2] /greɪt/ v 1 vt rub into pieces on a rough surface: grated cheese 2 vi make a sharp unpleasant sound **grater** n tool for grating food, etc.

grate·ful /'greɪtfəl/ adj feeling or showing thanks **~ly** adv **~ness** n [U]

grat·i·fy /'grætɪfaɪ/ vt please; satisfy **~ing** adj pleasing **-fication** /ˌgrætɪfɪ'keɪʃən/ n [C;U]

grat·ing /'greɪtɪŋ/ n network of bars to protect an opening

gra·tis /'grætɪs, 'greɪtɪs/ adv, adj fml without payment; free

grat·i·tude /'grætɪtjuːd‖-tuːd/ n [U] gratefulness

gra·tu·i·tous /grə'tjuːɪtəs‖-'tuː-/ adj fml not deserved or necessary: gratuitous insults **~ly** adv

gra·tu·i·ty /grə'tjuːɪtiǁ-'tuː-/ *n* **1** *fml* TIP³ for a service done **2** money given to someone leaving a job

grave¹ /greɪv/ *n* hole where a dead person is buried

grave² *adj* serious; solemn ~**ly** *adv*

grav·el /'grævəl/ *n* [U] small stones used for making paths, etc. ~**ly** *adj* **1** covered with gravel **2** having a low rough hard sound

grave·stone /'greɪvstəʊn/ *n* stone over a grave

grave·yard /'greɪvjɑːdǁ-ɑːrd/ *n* CEMETERY

grav·i·tate /'grævɪteɪt/ *vi* be attracted (as if) by gravity –**tation** /ˌgrævɪ'teɪʃən/ *n* [U]

grav·i·ty /'grævɪti/ *n* [U] **1** force by which objects are drawn towards each other **2** seriousness: *the gravity of his illness*

gra·vy /'greɪvi/ *n* [U] juice that comes out of meat in cooking

gravy train /'·· ·/ *n* [the + S] something from which many people can make money or profit without much effort

gray /greɪ/ *adj, n, v AmE for* GREY

graze¹ /greɪz/ *vi* (of animals) eat growing grass

graze² *vt* **1** rub the skin from **2** rub lightly while passing ♦ *n* surface wound

grease /griːs/ *n* [U] soft fat or oil ♦ *vt* **1** put grease on **2 grease someone's palm** BRIBE someone **3 like greased lightning** *infml* extremely fast **greasy** *adj*

grease·proof /'griːs-pruːf/ *adj BrE* (of paper) not letting grease pass through it

great /greɪt/ *adj* **1** excellent and important: *great writers* **2** large: *great pleasure*|*a great many people* **3** keen; active: *a great filmgoer* **4** *sl* splendid: *a great idea* **5 great-:** a parent of someone's GRANDPARENT: *his great-grandfather* **b** child of someone's GRANDCHILD: *his great-granddaughter* ~**ly** *adv* very much ~**ness** *n* [U]

Great Brit·ain /ˌgreɪt 'brɪtən/ *n* England, Scotland, and Wales (but not any part of Ireland)

greed /griːd/ *n* [U] desire for too much food, money, etc. ~**y** *adj* ~**ily** *adv*

green /griːn/ *adj* **1** of a colour between yellow and blue; the colour of leaves and grass **2** unhealthily pale in the face **3** (of fruit, plants, etc.) young or unripe **4** inexperienced and easily deceived **5 green with envy** ♦ *n* **1** [U] green colour **2** [C] smooth piece of grass: *village green*|*bowling green* ~**ness** *n* [U]

greens *n* [P] green vegetables

green belt /'· ·/ *n* [C;U] stretch of land round a town where building is not allowed, so that fields, etc., remain

green·e·ry /'griːnəri/ *n* [U] green leaves and plants

green-eyed monster /ˌ· '··/ *n* [the + S] jealousy

green fin·gers /ˌ· '··/ *n* [P] *esp. BrE* natural skill in making plants grow

green·gage /'griːngeɪdʒ/ *n* kind of green PLUM

green·gro·cer /'griːnˌgrəʊsəʳ/ *n esp. BrE* person who sells fruit and vegetables

green·house /'griːnhaʊs/ *n* glass building for growing plants in

greet /griːt/ *vt* **1** welcome **2** be suddenly seen or heard ~**ing** *n* **1** words used on meeting or writing to someone **2** a good wish: *Christmas greetings*

gre·gar·i·ous /grɪ'geəriəs/ *adj* fond of companionship

gre·nade /grə'neɪd/ *n* small bomb to be thrown by hand

grew /gruː/ *v past t. of* GROW

grey /greɪ/ *adj* **1** of the colour of black mixed with white **2** having grey hair ♦ *n* [U] grey colour ♦ *vi* become grey

grey·hound /'greɪhaʊnd/ *n* thin dog with long legs, which can run swiftly

grey mat·ter /'· ˌ··/ *n* [U] **1** the brain **2** *infml* power of thought

grid /grɪd/ *n* **1** GRATING **2** *BrE* network of electricity supply wires **3** system of numbered squares on a map

grid·i·ron /'grɪdaɪənǁ-ərn/ *n* **1** frame for cooking meat over a fire **2** field marked for AMERICAN FOOTBALL

grief /griːf/ *n* [U] **1** (cause of) great sorrow **2 come to grief** suffer harm; fail **3 Good grief!** (expression of surprise and some dislike)

griev·ance /'griːvəns/ *n* cause for complaint

grieve /griːv/ *v* **1** *vi* suffer grief **2** *vt* make unhappy

griev·ous /'griːvəs/ *adj fml* very harmful; severe ~**ly** *adv*

grill /grɪl/ *v* **1** *vi/t* cook under or over direct heat **2** *vt* question severely ♦ *n BrE* **1** shelf under direct heat, for grilling food **2** meat cooked this way: *a mixed grill*

grille /grɪl/ *n* bars filling a space, esp. in a bank or post office

grim /grɪm/ *adj* -**mm**- **1** serious; terrible: *grim news* **2** showing determination: *grim smile* ~**ly** *adv* ~**ness** *n* [U]

gri·mace /grɪ'meɪs, 'grɪməsǁ'grɪməs, grɪ'meɪs/ *vi* twist the face to express pain, etc. **grimace** *n*

grime /graɪm/ *n* [U] black dirt on a surface **grimy** *adj*

grim reaper /ˌ· '··/ n [the] (a name for death, considered as a person)

grin /grɪn/ vi 1 smile widely 2 **grin and bear it** suffer without complaint **grin** n

grind /graɪnd/ vt **ground** /graʊnd/ 1 crush into powder: grind coffee beans 2 rub (the teeth) together 3 make smooth or sharp by rubbing: grind knives 4 press upon with a strong twisting movement 5 **grind to a halt** stop noisily ♦ n infml 1 [S] hard dull work 2 [C] AmE for SWOT —**er** n person or machine that grinds

grind down phr vt keep in a state of suffering and hopelessness

grind out phr vt derog produce (esp. writing or music) continually, like a machine

grind·stone /ˈgraɪndstəʊn/ n 1 round stone that is turned to sharpen tools 2 **one's nose to the grindstone** in a state of continuous hard work

grip /grɪp/ vi/t -pp- 1 seize tightly 2 hold someone's attention: a gripping story ♦ n 1 tight hold 2 thing that grips: hairgrip 3 AmE traveller's small bag 4 **come/get to grips with** deal seriously with

gripe /graɪp/ vi sl complain continuously ♦ **gripe** n

gris·ly /ˈgrɪzli/ adj shocking and sickening

gris·tle /ˈgrɪsəl/ n [U] CARTILAGE in cooked meat

grit /grɪt/ n [U] 1 small stones and sand 2 lasting courage: determination ♦ vt -tt- 1 put grit on (esp. a road) 2 **grit one's teeth** show determination —**ty** adj

griz·zled /ˈgrɪzəld/ adj grey-haired

groan /grəʊn/ vi, n (make) a loud deep sound of suffering

gro·cer /ˈgrəʊsə/ n shopkeeper who sells dry foods and other things for the home

gro·cer·ies /ˈgrəʊsəriz/ n [P] goods sold by a grocer

grog·gy /ˈgrɒgi‖ˈgrɑːgi/ adj weak and unsteady from illness, etc. -**giness** n [U]

groin /grɔɪn/ n place where the legs meet the front of the body

groom /gruːm, grum/ n 1 person who looks after horses 2 BRIDEGROOM ♦ vt 1 brush and clean (horses) 2 make (oneself) neat and tidy 3 prepare (someone) for special work

groove /gruːv/ n long hollow in a surface

grope /grəʊp/ v 1 vi search about with the hands as in the dark 2 vt sl (try to) feel the body of (a person) to get sexual pleasure **grope** n

gross¹ /grəʊs/ adj 1 unpleasantly fat 2 rough; rude 3 clearly wrong: gross negligence 4 total: gross income ♦ vt

gain as total profit —**ly** adv —**ness** n [U]

gross² determiner, n **gross** or **grosses** 144

gro·tesque /grəʊˈtesk/ adj strange and ugly —**ly** adv

grot·to /ˈgrɒtəʊ‖ˈgrɑː-/ n -**toes** or -**tos** cave

ground¹ /graʊnd/ v past t. and p. of GRIND

ground² n 1 [S;U] surface of the earth 2 [U] soil 3 [C] piece of land used for a particular purpose: a playground 4 [U] **a** base for argument: You're on safe ground as long as you avoid the subject of politics. **b** area of knowledge or experience: It was absurd to try to cover so much ground in such a short course. 5 [U] position of advantage to be won or defended: The army has lost ground. | The idea is gaining ground. (= becoming more popular) 6 [C] AmE for EARTH (5) 7 **get off the ground** make a successful start 8 **to ground** into hiding to escape — see also GROUNDS —**less** adj without reason: groundless fears —**lessly** adv

ground³ v 1 vi (of a boat) strike against the bottom of the sea, a river, etc. 2 vt cause (a plane or pilot) to stay on the ground 3 vt base: arguments grounded on experience —**ing** n [S] first necessary training in something

ground floor /ˌ· '··/ n 1 BrE part of a building at ground level 2 **get/be in on the ground floor** be part of an activity, business operation, etc., from the time it starts

grounds /graʊndz/ n [P] 1 solid bits at the bottom of a liquid 2 gardens, etc., round a building 3 reason: grounds for divorce

ground·sheet /ˈgraʊndʃiːt/ n WATERPROOF sheet to spread on the ground

ground·work /ˈgraʊndwɜːk‖-ɜːrk/ n [U] work on which further study, etc., is based

group /gruːp/ n connected set of people or things ♦ vi/t form into groups

grouse¹ /graʊs/ vi, n GRUMBLE

grouse² n **grouse** small fat bird which is shot for food and sport

grove /grəʊv/ n lit small group of trees

grov·el /ˈgrɒvəl‖ˈgrɑː-, ˈgrʌ-/ vi -**ll**- BrE ‖ -**l**- AmE 1 lie flat in fear or obedience 2 be shamefully humble and eager to please —**ler** n

grow /grəʊ/ v **grew** /gruː/, **grown** /grəʊn/ 1 vi get bigger 2 vi (of plants) live and develop 3 vt cause (plants, etc.) to grow 4 fml become: grow old

grown adj ADULT: grown men

grow on phr vt become more pleasing to: This music will grow on you.

grow out of phr vt get too big or old for

grow up phr vi 1 develop from child to man or woman 2 start to exist: *customs that have grown up*

growl /graʊl/ vi, n (make) the threatening noise of an angry dog

grown-up /ˌ· ˈ‑◂/ adj, n ADULT

growth /grəʊθ/ n 1 [S;U] process of growing; increase 2 [C] something that has grown, esp. an unnatural lump in the body

grub[1] /grʌb/ n 1 [C] insect in the wormlike stage 2 [U] sl food

grub[2] vi/-t -bb- dig with the hands or PAWS

grub·by /ˈgrʌbi/ adj rather dirty -biness n [U]

grub·stake /ˈgrʌb·steɪk/ n money provided to develop a new business

grudge /grʌdʒ/ vt be unwilling to give: *He grudged paying so much.* ♦ n continuing feeling of anger against someone **grudgingly** adv

gru·el·ling BrE ‖ **grueling** AmE /ˈgruːəlɪŋ/ adj very tiring

grue·some /ˈgruːsəm/ adj very shocking and sickening ~**ly** adv

gruff /grʌf/ adj (of the voice) deep and rough ~**ly** adv ~**ness** n [U]

grum·ble /ˈgrʌmbəl/ vi complain ♦ n complaint

grump·y /ˈgrʌmpi/ adj bad-tempered -ily adv -iness n [U]

grunt /grʌnt/ vi, n (make) the short rough sound that pigs make

guar·an·tee /ˌgærənˈtiː/ n 1 written promise to replace an article if it is found to be imperfect 2 agreement to be responsible for a debt ♦ vt 1 give a guarantee about 2 promise: *I guarantee you'll enjoy it.*

guar·an·tor /ˌgærənˈtɔːr/ n law person who agrees to be responsible for a debt

guard /gɑːd‖gɑːrd/ n 1 [U] state of watching against attack: *soldiers on guard* 2 a [C] person keeping guard b [S] group of these people 3 [C] protective apparatus: *a fireguard* 4 [C] BrE railway official on a train — see also OLD GUARD ♦ vt 1 defend 2 watch (prisoners) to prevent escape ~**ed** adj not saying too much

guard against phr vt prevent by care: *guard against infection*

guard·i·an /ˈgɑːdiən‖ˈgɑːr-/ n person responsible for a child ~**ship** n [U]

gu·ber·na·to·ri·al /ˌguːbənəˈtɔːriəl‖-bər-/ adj of a governor

guer·ril·la /gəˈrɪlə/ n member of an unofficial army which attacks in small groups

guess /ges/ 1 vi/t form an opinion (on) without knowing all the facts 2 vt infml, esp. AmE suppose; consider likely ♦ n 1 opinion formed by guessing 2 attempt to guess

guess-work /ˈgeswɜːk‖-ɜːrk/ n [U] guessing

guest[1] /gest/ n 1 person invited to someone's home, or staying in a hotel 2 person, esp. an entertainer, invited to take part in a show, etc. 3 **be my guest!** please feel free to do so ♦ vi esp. AmE take part as a guest performer

guest-house /ˈgesthaʊs/ n small private hotel

guf·faw /gəˈfɔː/ vi laugh loudly and esp. rudely **guffaw** n

guid·ance /ˈgaɪdəns/ n [U] help; advice

guide /gaɪd/ n 1 person who shows the way 2 something that influences behaviour 3 also **guide book** — book describing a place 4 instruction book 5 member of an association (the **Guides**) for training girls in character and self-help ♦ vt act as a guide to

guided mis·sile /ˌ·· ˈ··/ n MISSILE whose flight is controlled by electrical means

guide-lines /ˈgaɪdlaɪnz/ n [P] main points on how to deal with something

guild /gɪld/ n association of people with the same interests

guile /gaɪl/ n [U] deceit ~**ful** adj ~**less** adj

guil·lo·tine /ˈgɪlətiːn/ n 1 machine for cutting off the heads of criminals 2 machine for cutting paper 3 time limit fixed for argument in Parliament ♦ vt use a GUILLOTINE (1) on

guilt /gɪlt/ n [U] 1 fact of having done wrong; blame 2 shame ~**y** adj having done wrong

guin·ea /ˈgɪni/ n £1.05 in British money

guinea pig /ˈ·· ·/ n 1 small tailless furry animal used in scientific tests 2 person on whom something is tested

guise /gaɪz/ n fml outer appearance

gui·tar /gɪˈtɑːr/ n stringed musical instrument played with the fingers

gulf /gʌlf/ n 1 piece of sea partly surrounded by land 2 division, esp. between opinions

gull /gʌl/ n any of several kinds of large seabirds

gul·let /ˈgʌlɪt/ n foodpipe in the throat

gul·li·ble /ˈgʌlɪbəl/ adj easily tricked ~**bility** /ˌgʌlɪˈbɪlɪti/ n [U]

gulp /gʌlp/ vi/t swallow hastily **gulp** n

gum[1] /gʌm/ n flesh in which the teeth are fixed

gum[2] n 1 [U] sticky plant substance 2 [C] hard jelly-like sweet 3 [U] CHEWING GUM ♦ vt -mm- stick with GUM (1) ~**my** adj sticky

gum-boot /'gʌmbuːt/ n esp. BrE WELLINGTON

gump-tion /'gʌmpʃən/ n [U] 1 practical good sense 2 courage

gun[1] /gʌn/ n weapon that fires bullets or SHELLs through a tube — see also **stick to one's guns** (STICK2)

gun[2] v

gun down phr vt shoot, causing to fall to the ground dead or wounded

gun for phr vt search for in order to attack

gun-boat /'gʌnbəʊt/ n small heavily armed warship

gun-fire /'gʌnfaɪəʳ/ n [U] (sound of) shooting

gung-ho /ˌgʌŋ 'həʊ/ adj showing extreme, often foolish, eagerness, esp. to attack an enemy

gun-man /'gʌnmən/ n -men /-mən/ armed criminal

gun-ner /'gʌnəʳ/ n soldier who uses heavy guns

gun-point /'gʌnpɔɪnt/ n **at gunpoint** under a threat of death by shooting

gun-pow-der /'gʌn,paʊdəʳ/ n [U] explosive powder

gun-run-ner /'gʌn,rʌnəʳ/ n person who unlawfully and secretly brings guns into a country **-ning** n [U]

gur-gle /'gɜːgəl‖'gɜːr-/ vi, n (make) the sound of water flowing unevenly

gu-ru /'guːruː/ n gurus 1 Indian religious teacher 2 greatly respected person whose ideas are followed

gush /gʌʃ/ v 1 vi flow out: oil gushing from a pipe 2 vt send out (liquid) in large quantities 3 vi express admiration foolishly ♦ n [S] sudden flow

gust /gʌst/ n sudden rush of wind **-y** adj

gus-to /'gʌstəʊ/ n [U] eager enjoyment

gut /gʌt/ n [U] thread made from animal bowels ♦ vt 1 take out the inner organs of: gut a fish 2 destroy the inside of (a building) ♦ adj coming from feelings rather than thought: gut reactions **guts** n [P] 1 bowels 2 bravery and determination **gutsy** n brave

gut-ter /'gʌtəʳ/ n 1 [C] ditch or pipe that carries away rainwater 2 [the + S] the poorest level of society

gutter press /'·· ,·/n newspapers which tend to be full of shocking stories

gut-tur-al /'gʌtərəl/ adj (of speech) coming from deep in the throat

guy /gaɪ/ n 1 sl a man b esp. AmE person, male or female: Come on, you guys! 2 figure of a man burnt in Britain on November 5th

guz-zle /'gʌzəl/ vi/t eat or drink eagerly

gym /dʒɪm/ n 1 [C] gymnasium 2 [U] gymnastics

gym-kha-na /dʒɪm'kɑːnə/ n esp. BrE local sports meeting, esp. for horse riding by children

gym-na-si-um /dʒɪm'neɪziəm/ n hall with apparatus for indoor exercise

gym-nas-tics /dʒɪm'næstɪks/ n [U] training of the body by physical exercises **-tic** adj

gy-nae-col-o-gy ‖ usu. **gynecology** AmE /ˌgaɪnɪ'kɒlədʒi‖-'kɑː-/ n [U] medical study and treatment of the female sex organs **-gist** n **-gical** /ˌgaɪnɪkə'lɒdʒɪkəl ‖ -'lɑː-/ adj **-gically** /-kli/ adv

gyp-sy /'dʒɪpsi/ n GIPSY

gy-rate /dʒaɪ'reɪt‖'dʒaɪreɪt/ vi fml swing round and round **gyration** /dʒaɪ'reɪʃən/ n [C;U]

gy-ro-scope /'dʒaɪrəskəʊp/ n wheel that spins inside a frame, used for keeping ships, etc., steady

H

H , h /eɪtʃ/ the 8th letter of the English alphabet

ha-be-as cor-pus /ˌheɪbiəs 'kɔːpəs ‖ -'kɔːr-/ n [U] written order that a person in prison must be brought before a court

hab-er-dash-er /'hæbədæʃəʳ‖-bər-/ n 1 BrE shopkeeper who sells thread, etc., used in sewing 2 AmE shopkeeper who sells men's hats, GLOVEs, etc. **~y** n [U] haberdasher's goods

hab-it /'hæbɪt/ n 1 [C;U] person's usual behaviour 2 [C] clothes worn by a MONK or NUN

hab-it-a-ble /'hæbɪtəbəl/ adj fit to be lived in

hab-i-tat /'hæbɪtæt/ n natural home of an animal or plant

hab-i-ta-tion /ˌhæbɪ'teɪʃən/ n fml [U] living in: houses fit for habitation

ha-bit-u-al /hə'bɪtʃuəl/ adj usual 2 (done) by habit **~ly** adv

ha-bit-u-é /hə'bɪtʃueɪ/ n fml regular attender

hack[1] /hæk/ vi/t cut roughly

hack[2] n writer who does a lot of poor quality work

hack-er /'hækəʳ/ n someone who is able to use or change information in a computer system without permission

hacking cough /,·· '·/n cough with a rough, unpleasant sound

hack-les /'hækəlz/n **make someone's hackles rise** make someone very angry

hack·neyed /'hæknɪd/ adj (of a saying) meaningless because used too often

hack·saw /'hæksɔː/ n tool with a fine-toothed blade used, esp. for cutting metal

had /d, əd, həd; strong hæd/ v past t and p. of HAVE

had·dock /'hædək/ n haddock common fish, used as food

had·n't /'hædnt/ v short for: had not

hag /hæg/ n derog ugly old woman

hag·gard /'hægəd‖-ərd/ adj (of the face) lined and hollow from tiredness

hag·gis /'hægɪs/ n Scottish food made of parts of a sheep and cooked in a skin made from a sheep's stomach

hag·gle /'hægəl/ vi argue over a price

hail¹ /heɪl/ n [U] frozen rain drops: (fig.) a hail of bullets ♦ vi (of hail) fall

hail² vi 1 call out to: hail a taxi 2 recognize (someone) as important: They hailed him king.

  hail as phr vt recognize as (something good)

  hail from phr vt come from.

hail·stone /'heɪlstəʊn/ n single piece of hail

hair /heəʳ/ n 1 [C] threadlike growth from the skin 2 [U] mass of these growths 3 **let one's hair down** infml behave as one likes after being formal 4 **make someone's hair curl** infml shock someone 5 **make one's hair stand on end** frighten one badly 6 **not turn a hair** show no fear or worry (when in difficulty) ~y adj 1 covered with hair 2 infml exciting in a way that causes fear; dangerous **~iness** n [U]

hair·do /'heəduː‖'heər-/ n -dos style a person's hair is shaped into

hair·dress·er /'heə,dresəʳ‖'heər-/ n person who cuts and shapes hair

hair·grip /'heəgrɪp‖'heər-/ n BrE flat pin with the ends pressed together, for the hair

hair·piece /'heəpiːs‖'heər-/ n piece of false hair used to make one's own hair seem thicker

hair·pin bend /,heəpɪn 'bend‖ ,heər-/ n U-shaped curve on a road

hair-rais·ing /'· ,··/ adj very frightening

hair's breadth /'· ·/ n very short distance

hair-split·ting /'· ,··/ n [U] derog act or habit of paying too much attention to unimportant differences and details

hal·cy·on /'hælsɪən/ adj lit peaceful and happy: halcyon days

hale /heɪl/ adj hale and hearty healthy

half¹ /hɑːf‖hæf/ n halves /hɑːvz‖ hæfs/ 1 either of 2 equal parts; ½: Half of 50 is 25. 2 either of 2 parts into which something is divided: He's in

the bottom half of the class. 3 coin, ticket, drink, etc., of ½ the value or amount: A pint of beer and two halves please. 4 **by halves** incompletely 5 **go halves** share something equally 6 **my/your/his/her better half** one's husband or wife

half² predeterminer, adj ½ in amount: She bought half a kilo of rice.

half³ adv 1 partly: half cooked‖half French 2 **half and half** ½ one and ½ the other 3 **not half** BrE infml **a** very: It isn't half windy today. **b** not at all: This food's not half bad. **c** very much: 'Did you like the show?' 'Not half.' 4 **not half as** not nearly as

half-baked /,· '·◄/ adj (esp. of ideas) not sensible

half-broth·er /'· ,··/ n brother related through only one parent

half-caste /'· ·/also **half-breed** — n, adj (person) with parents of different races

half-heart·ed /,· '··◄‖ ,··/ adj showing not much interest

half-life /'· ·/ n time it takes for half the atoms in a RADIOACTIVE substance to decay

half-mast /,· '·/ n 1 point near the middle of a flag-pole where the flag flies as a sign of sorrow 2 **(at) half-mast** too short: His trousers are always at half-mast.

half·pen·ny /'heɪpni/ n 1 (in Great Britain before 1985) small BRONZE coin, two of which made a penny 2 **not have two halfpennies to rub together** be very poor

half-sis·ter /'· ,··/ n sister related through only one parent

half·way /,hɑːf'weɪ◄‖,hæf-/ adj, adv 1 at the midpoint between 2 things 2 **meet someone halfway** make an agreement with someone which partly satisfies the demands of both sides

half-wit /'· ·/ n weak-minded, stupid person **~ted** /,· '·/ adj

hall /hɔːl/ n 1 passage inside the entrance of a house 2 large room for meetings, etc. 3 place where university students live or eat together

hal·le·lu·ja /,hælɪ'luːjə/ interj (expression of praise to God)

hall·mark /'hɔːlmɑːk‖-ɑːrk/ n mark proving that something is really silver or gold: (fig.) Clear expression is the hallmark of a good writer.

hal·lo /hə'ləʊ, he-, hæ-/ interj, n -los BrE for HELLO

hal·lowed /'hæləʊd/ adj fml holy

Hal·low·e'en /,hæləʊ'iːn/ n October 31, when children play tricks and dress in strange clothes

hal·lu·ci·nate /hə'luːsɪneɪt/ vi see things that are not there **-natory** /-nətəri ‖ -nətɔːri/ adj **-nation** /hə,luːsɪ'neɪʃən/ n [C;U] (experience of seeing) something which is not really there, because of illness or drugs

ha·lo /'heɪləʊ/ n -loes or -los 1 circle representing light round the heads of holy people in pictures 2 circle of light round the sun or moon

halt /hɔːlt/ vi/t fml stop **halt** n [S]

hal·ter /'hɔːltəʳ/ n rope for leading a horse

halt·ing /'hɔːltɪŋ/ adj stopping and starting uncertainly

halve /hɑːv/ vt 1 reduce by half: halve the time 2 divide into halves

halves /hɑːvz‖hævz/ n pl. of HALF

ham /hæm/ n 1 [C;U] (preserved meat from) the upper part of a pig's leg 2 [C] actor whose performance is unnatural 3 [C] non-professional radio operator ♦ vi/t perform like a HAM (2)

ham·burg·er /'hæmbɜːgəʳ‖-ɜːr-/ n flat round cake of small bits of meat, eaten in a bread ROLL² (3)

ham-fisted /ˌ· '···◄/ adj awkward in using the hands

ham·let /'hæmlət/ n small village

ham·mer¹ /'hæməʳ/ n 1 tool with a metal head for driving nails into wood 2 part of a piano, etc., that hits another part 3 **be/go at it hammer and tongs** fight or argue violently 4 **come under the hammer** be offered for sale at an AUCTION 5 **throwing the hammer** sport in which a heavy metal ball on a chain is thrown

hammer² v 1 vi/t hit with a hammer 2 vt defeat thoroughly 3 vi work continuously: hammer away at the problem 4 vt force: hammer the facts into their heads

hammer out phr vt talk about in detail and come to a decision about

ham·mock /'hæmək/ n cloth or net hung up to sleep in

ham·per¹ /'hæmpəʳ/ vt cause difficulty in movement

hamper² n large basket with a lid

ham·ster /'hæmstəʳ/ n small mouse-like animal often kept as a pet

ham·string /'hæm͵strɪŋ/ n cordlike TENDON at the back of the leg ♦ vt -strung /-͵strʌŋ/ make powerless

hand¹ /hænd/ n 1 [C] movable part at the end of the arm 2 [C] pointer on a clock, etc. 3 [C] set of playing cards held by one player 4 [S] handwriting 5 [C] worker; someone with a skill: factory hands — see also OLD HAND 6 [S] help: give/lend a hand 7 [C;U] control: get out of hand\have the matter in hand\in the hands of the police 8 [S] APPLAUSE: Give the singer a big hand. 9 **at first hand** by direct experience 10 **at hand** near in time or place 11 **at second/third/fourth hand** as information passed on through 1, 2, or 3

people 12 **by hand: a** not typed or printed **b** delivered directly, not by post 13 **change hands** go from the possession of one person to that of another 14 **get/keep one's hand in** get/stay used to an activity 15 **get the upper hand (of)** get control or power (over something/somebody difficult) 16 **give someone a free hand** let someone do things in their own way 17 **hand in glove (with)** closely connected (with someone), esp. in something bad 18 **hand in hand: a** holding each other's hands **b** in close connection 19 **hand over fist** very quickly and successfully 20 **have a hand in** be partly responsible for 21 **have one's hands full** be very busy 22 **in hand** ready for use 23 **live from hand to mouth** have just enough money, food, etc., to live 24 **on hand** ready for use or to take part 25 **on the one/other hand** (used for comparing 2 things) 26 **(out of/off) one's hands** (no longer) one's responsibility 27 **play into someone's hands** do something which gives (one's opponent) an advantage 28 **raise one's hand to/against** (make a movement) to hit 29 **show one's hand** make one's power or intentions clear, esp. after keeping them secret 30 **throw in one's hand** accept defeat 31 **to hand** within reach 32 **try one's hand (at)** attempt (an activity) 33 **turn one's hand to** begin to practise (a skill) 34 **wait on someone hand and foot** do every little thing for someone

hand² vt 1 give with one's hand(s) 2 **(have to) hand it to someone** (have to) admit the high quality or success of someone

hand down phr vt give advice to those who come later

hand in phr vt deliver

hand on phr vt give to someone else

hand out phr vt 1 give out to several people 2 give freely: He's always ready to hand out advice.

hand over phr vt give control of: We handed him over to the police.

hand·bag /'hændbæg/ n woman's small bag for money and personal things

hand·book /'hændbʊk/ n book of instructions

hand·brake /'hændbreɪk/ n BRAKE worked by the driver's hand, not by the foot

hand·cuffs /'hændkʌfs/ n [P] pair of metal rings for fastening a criminal's wrists **handcuff** ♦ vt put handcuffs on

hand·ful /'hændfʊl/ n 1 as much as can be held in one hand 2 small number (of people) 3 infml person or animal that is hard to control

hand·i·cap /'hændɪkæp/ n 1 disability of the body or mind 2 disadvantage given to the stronger competitors in a sport ♦ vt -pp- 1 give a disadvantage to 2 (of a disability of body or mind) prevent (someone) from acting or living as most people do

hand·i·craft /'hændɪkrɑːft‖-kræft/ n skill such as weaving, which uses the hands

hand·i·work /'hændɪwɜːk‖-ɜːrk/ n [U] 1 work demanding the skilful use of the hands 2 result of someone's action

hand·ker·chief /'hæŋkətʃɪf‖-kər-/ n cloth or paper for drying the nose, etc.

han·dle¹ /'hændl/ n part of a door, cup, etc., that one holds

handle² vt 1 touch or move with the hands 2 control; deal with: *handle the accounts* 3 (of a car, boat, etc.) obey controlling movements in the stated way **–dler** n person who controls an animal

han·dle·bars /'hændlbɑːz‖-ɑːrz/ n [P] curved bar above front wheel of a bicycle, etc., which controls the direction it goes in

hand·out /'hændaʊt/ n 1 something given free 2 printed sheet of information given out

hand-picked /ˌhænd'pɪkt◂/ adj carefully chosen

hand·shake /'hændʃeɪk/ n act of taking each other's hand as a greeting

hand·some /'hænsəm/ adj 1 of good appearance: *a handsome boy* 2 plentiful: *a handsome reward* **~ly** adv

hand·stand /'hændstænd/ n position in which the body is supported upside down on the hands

hand-to-mouth /ˌ·· '·◂/ adj (of a way of life) with just enough food, money, etc. to live

hand·writ·ing /'hændˌraɪtɪŋ/ n [U] (style of) writing done by hand **–written** /ˌhænd'rɪtn◂/ adj written by hand

hand·y /'hændi/ adj 1 useful 2 clever with one's hands 3 easily reached 4 **come in handy** be useful **–ily** adv

hand·y·man /'hændimæn/ n -men /-men/ person who does small repairs

hang¹ /hæŋ/ v **hung** /hʌŋ/ 1 vi/t fix or be fixed from above so that the lower part is free 2 vi/t (of certain kinds of meat) be kept in this position until ready to eat 3 vt stick (wallpaper) on a wall 4 vt (*past t. and p.* **hanged**) kill by dropping with a rope round the neck 5 **hang fire** be delayed 6 **hang one's head** appear ashamed

hang about/around *phr vi* 1 wait without purpose 2 delay

hang back *phr vi* be unwilling to move

hang on *phr vi* 1 keep hold of something 2 wait 3 pay close attention to 4 depend on

hang onto *phr vt* try to keep

hang out *phr vi infml* 1 live or spend a lot of time 2 **let it all hang out** *sl* behave exactly as you want to

hang up *phr vi* 1 finish a telephone conversation 2 put something on a hook 3 **be hung up on/about** *sl* be anxious or have a fixed idea about

hang² n get/have the hang of something understand how a machine, etc., works

han·gar /'hæŋəʳ/ n building where aircraft are kept

hang·er /'hæŋəʳ/ n hook and crosspiece to hang a garment from

hanger-on /ˌ·· '·/ n **hangers-on** person who tries to be friendly in the hope of advantage

hang glid·ing /'· ˌ··/ n [U] the sport of gliding (GLIDE (2)) using a large KITE (1) instead of a plane

hang·ings /'hæŋɪŋz/ n [P] curtains, etc., that hang

hang·man /'hæŋmən/ n -men /-mən/ man whose work is hanging criminals

hang·o·ver /'hæŋˌəʊvəʳ/ n 1 feeling of sickness, etc. the day after drinking too much alcohol 2 condition or effect resulting from an earlier event or state

hang-up /'hæŋʌp/ n sl something about which a person gets unusually worried

han·ker /'hæŋkəʳ/ v **hanker after/for** *phr vt* desire strongly **hankering** n [S]

han·kie, -ky /'hæŋki/ n handkerchief

hank·y-pank·y /ˌhæŋki 'pæŋki/ n [U] improper behaviour, esp. deceit, of a not very serious kind

hap·haz·ard /ˌhæp'hæzəd◂‖-ərd/ adj unplanned; disorderly

hap·less /'hæpləs/ adj lit unlucky

hap·pen /'hæpən/ vi 1 (of an event) take place: *When did the accident happen?* 2 be or do by chance: *We happened to meet.* 3 be true by or as if by chance: *As it happens, we do know each other.* **~ing** n event

happen on *phr vt* find by chance

hap·py /'hæpi/ adj 1 pleased; contented 2 causing pleasure: *a happy occasion* 3 (of thoughts, etc.) suitable: *a happy remark* 4 (used in good wishes): *Happy Birthday!* **–pily** adv **–piness** n [U]

happy-go-luck·y /ˌ·· · '··◂/ adj unworried; CAREFREE

happy hour /'·· ˌ·/ n limited period in the day when alcoholic drinks are sold at lower than usual prices in a bar, etc.

ha-rangue /həˈræŋ/ vt attack or try to persuade with a long angry speech **harangue** n

har-ass /ˈhærəs, həˈræs‖həˈræs, ˈhærəs/ vt worry repeatedly ~**ment** n [U]

har-bour BrE ‖ **-bor** AmE/ˈhɑːbəʳ‖ ˈhɑːr-/ n sheltered area where ships are safe ♦ vt **1** give protection to **2** keep (thoughts or feelings) in the mind

hard[1] /hɑːd‖hɑːrd/ adj **1** firm and stiff: hard skin **2** difficult: hard question **3** needing or using effort: hard work/worker **4** unpleasant; severe: hard winter | Don't be too hard on him. **5** containing minerals that stop soap from forming LATHER easily **6** (of drugs) dangerous and ADDICTIVE ~**ness** n [U]

hard[2] adv **1** with great effort: push hard **2** heavily: raining hard **3 hard at it** working hard **4 hard by** fml near **5 hard done by** unfairly treated **6 hard hit** suffering loss **7 hard put** (to) having great difficulty **8 hard up** infml not having enough (esp. money) **9 take (it) hard** suffer deeply

hard-and-fast /ˌ· · ˈ·◄/ adj (of rules) fixed

hard-back /ˈhɑːdbæk‖ˈhɑːrd-/ n book with a stiff cover

hard-ball /ˈhɑːdbɔːl‖ˈhɑːrd-/ n [U] AmE **1** BASEBALL **2 play hardball** use methods that are not gentle, and may be unfair

hard-bit-ten /ˌ· ˈ·◄/ adj (of a person) made firm in argument and decision by hard experience

hard-board /ˈhɑːdbɔːd‖ˈhɑːrdbɔːrd/ n [U] stiff cardboard, used like wood

hard-boiled /ˌ· ˈ·◄/ adj **1** (of eggs) boiled till the yellow part is hard **2** (of people) not showing feeling

hard cop-y /ˈ· ˌ·/n [U] readable information from a computer, esp. printed on paper

hard-core /ˌ· ˈ·◄/ n [U] small unchanging group within an organization **hard-core** adj **1** very strongly following a particular belief or activity **2** showing or describing sexual activity in a very detailed way: hard-core pornography

hard cur-ren-cy /ˌ· ˈ··/ n [C;U] money that can be freely exchanged

hard-en /ˈhɑːdn‖ˈhɑːrdn/ vi/t make or become hard or firm

harden to phr vt make (someone) less sensitive to (something or doing something)

hard-head-ed /ˌhɑːdˈhedɪd◄‖ˌhɑːrd-/ adj tough and practical

hard-heart-ed /ˌ· ˈ·◄/ adj not kind or gentle

hard la-bour /ˌ· ˈ··/n [U] (punishment which consists of) hard physical work such as digging, etc.

hard line /ˌ· ˈ·◄/ n firm unchanging opinion or policy **hard-liner** n

hard luck /ˌ· ˈ·◄/ n [U] bad luck

hard-ly /ˈhɑːdli‖ˈhɑːrdli/ adv **1** almost not: I can hardly wait. **2** not at all: You can hardly blame me.

hard of hear-ing /ˌ· ·· ˈ··/ adj rather DEAF

hard-pressed /ˌ· ˈ·◄/ adj experiencing severe or continual difficulties

hard sell /ˌ· ˈ·◄/ n [U] method of selling by putting pressure on buyers

hard-ship /ˈhɑːdʃɪp‖ˈhɑːrd-/ n [C;U] difficult conditions of life, such as lack of money, food, etc.

hard shoul-der /ˌ· ˈ··/ n esp. BrE hard surface beside a MOTORWAY where cars may stop if in difficulty

hard-ware /ˈhɑːdweəʳ‖ˈhɑːrd-/ n [U] **1** pans, tools, etc., for the home **2** machinery which makes up a COMPUTER **3** machinery used in war

hard-wear-ing /ˌhɑːdˈweərɪŋ◄ ‖ ˌhɑːrd-/ adj (of clothes, etc.) that last a long time

hard-wood /ˈhɑːdwʊd‖ˈhɑːrd-/ n [U] strong wood from trees such as the OAK

har-dy /ˈhɑːdi‖ˈhɑːrdi/ adj able to bear cold, hard work, etc. –**diness** n [U]

hare /heəʳ/ n fast-running animal like a large rabbit ♦ vi run fast

hare-brained /ˈheəbreɪnd‖ˈheər-/ adj impractical; foolish

hare-lip /ˌheəˈlɪp‖ˌheər-/ n top lip divided into 2 parts

har-em /ˈheərəm, hɑːˈriːm‖ˈhɑːrəm/ n (women living in) the women's part of a Muslim house

hark /hɑːk‖hɑːrk/ vi lit listen

hark at phr vi infml esp. BrE listen to (something or something that is disapproved of)

hark back phr vi talk about the past

harm /hɑːm‖hɑːrm/ n [U] **1** damage; INJURY **2 out of harm's way** safe ♦ vt cause harm to ~**ful** adj ~**less** adj not dangerous

har-mon-i-ca /hɑːˈmɒnɪkə ‖ hɑːrˈmɑː-/ n MOUTHORGAN

har-mo-ni-um /hɑːˈməʊniəm‖hɑːr-/ n musical instrument like a piano, worked by pumped air

har-mo-nize /ˈhɑːmənaɪz‖ˈhɑːr-/ vi/t **1** (cause to) be in agreement, esp. in style, colour, etc. **2** sing or play in musical HARMONY

har-mo-ny /ˈhɑːməni‖ˈhɑːr-/ n **1** [C;U] musical notes pleasantly combined **2** [U] peaceful agreement **3** [C;U] pleasant combination of colours, etc.

har·ness /'hɑːnɪs‖'hɑːr-/ n [C;U] 1 leather bands, etc., that fasten a horse to a cart 2 similar arrangement for tying something to something: *safety harness* ◆ vt 1 fasten with a harness 2 use (wind, water, etc.) to produce esp. electrical power

harp[1] /hɑːp‖hɑːrp/ n large stringed musical instrument played with the fingers ~**ist** n

harp[2] v **harp on** *phr vt* talk a lot about (one's misfortunes)

har·poon /hɑːˈpuːn‖hɑːr-/ vt, (strike with) a spear on a rope, for hunting WHALEs, etc.

harp·si·chord /'hɑːpsɪkɔːd‖'hɑːrp-sɪkɔːrd/ n kind of early piano

har·row·ing /'hærəʊɪŋ/ adj causing painful feelings

har·ry /'hæri/ vt fml trouble continually

harsh /hɑːʃ‖hɑːrʃ/ adj 1 painful to the senses: *harsh light* 2 cruel ~**ly** adv ~**ness** n [U]

har·vest /'hɑːvɪst‖'hɑːr-/ n 1 (time of) gathering the crops 2 amount of crops gathered ◆ vt gather (crops)

has /s, z, əz, həz; *strong* hæz/ v 3rd person sing. pres. t. of HAVE

hash /hæʃ/ n [U] 1 meal of (re-cooked) cut up meat 2 **make a hash of something** do something badly

hash·ish /'hæʃiːʃ, -ɪʃ/ n [U] strongest form of the drug CANNABIS

has·n't /'hæzənt/ v short for: has not

has·sle /'hæsəl/ n infml a lot of trouble ◆ vi/t cause trouble or difficulties for

haste /heɪst/ n [U] quick movement, or action

has·ten /'heɪsən/ vi/t 1 fml hurry 2 be quick (to say): *I hasten to add that no one was hurt.*

hast·y /'heɪsti/ adj 1 done (too) quickly 2 (of people) too quick in acting or deciding **-ily** adv

hat /hæt/ n 1 covering for the head 2 **keep (something) under one's hat** keep (something) secret 3 **take one's hat off to** show admiration for 4 **talking through one's hat** saying something stupid — see also OLD HAT ~**ter** n maker of hats

hatch[1] /hætʃ/ v 1 vi/t (cause to) be born from an egg 2 vt form (a plan)

hatch[2] n (cover over) a hole in a wall or floor

hatch·back /'hætʃbæk/ n car with a door at the back that opens upwards

hatch·et /'hætʃɪt/ n 1 small AXE 2 **bury the hatchet** become friends again after a bad quarrel

hatchet job /'·· ,·/ n cruel attack in speech or writing

hate /heɪt/ vt 1 dislike very much 2 be sorry: *I hate to tell you.* ◆ n [C;U]

strong dislike ~**ful** adj very unpleasant ~**fully** adv

ha·tred /'heɪtrɪd/ n [S;U] hate

hat trick /'· ·/ n (in sport) 3 successes of the same kind one after the other

haugh·ty /'hɔːti/ adj too proud; ARROGANT **-tily** adv **-tiness** n [U]

haul /hɔːl/ vi/t pull with effort ◆ n 1 a amount of fish caught b amount of something gained, esp. stolen goods 2 distance that something travels or is carried: *the long haul home*

haul·age /'hɔːlɪdʒ/ n [U] 1 carrying of goods by road 2 charge for this

haunch /hɔːntʃ/ n fleshy part of the body between the waist and knee

haunt /hɔːnt/ vt 1 (of a spirit) appear in 2 visit regularly 3 remain in the thoughts of: *haunted by the memory* | *haunting tune* ◆ n place often visited

have[1] /v, əv, həv; *strong* hæv/ v aux, pres. t. I/you/we/they **have**, he/she/it **has** /z, əz, həz; *strong* hæz/; *past t.* **had** /d, əd, həd; *strong* hæd/ **1 a** (forms perfect tenses): *I've/I have finished* **b Had (I, he, etc.)** if (I, he, etc.) had: *Had I known, I would have stayed.* 2 **had better (do/not do)** ought (not) to: *You'd better tell him about it.* 3 **have (got) to** be forced to; must: *I'll have to wash it.* 4 **have had it** infml have experienced, worked, etc., all one can: *I've had it! Let's go home.*

have[2] vt 1 also **have got** — possess: *She has/has got blue eyes.* 2 experience or enjoy: *have a party/a holiday* 3 receive: *I had some good news today.* 4 eat, drink, or smoke: *I had a cigarette.* 5 ask (someone) to one's home: *We're having some people round/over for drinks.* 6 allow: *I won't have all this noise.* 7 cause to be done: *You should have your hair cut.* 8 give birth to: *to have twins* 9 **have done with** finish 10 **have it in for** be as unkind as possible to 11 **have it off/away** with BrE infml have sex with 12 **have to do with** have a connection with

have on *phr vt* 1 be wearing 2 have arranged to do 3 play a trick on: *She's just having you on.* 4 have (unfavourable information) recorded against (someone) 5 **have nothing on** be not nearly as good as

have out *phr vt* 1 get (a tooth or organ) removed 2 settle by argument: *have the whole thing out with Bill*

have up *phr vt* BrE take to court: *had up for dangerous driving*

ha·ven /'heɪvən/ n calm safe place

have·n't /'hævənt/ v short for: have not

hav·er·sack /'hævəsæk‖-ər-/ n RUCKSACK

hav·oc /'hævək/ *n* [U] widespread damage

hawk¹ /hɔːk/ *n* **1** bird that catches creatures for food **2** person who believes in use of force, esp. military

hawk² *vt* sell (goods) on the street or at the doors of houses

hay /heɪ/ *n* [U] dried grass for animal food

hay fe·ver /'· ,··/ *n* [U] illness like a bad cold, caused by breathing in POLLEN from the air

hay·stack /'heɪstæk/ *n* large pile of stored hay

hay·wire /'heɪwaɪəʳ/ *adj* **go haywire** (of plans, etc.) become badly disordered

haz·ard /'hæzəd‖-ərd/ *n* danger; risk ♦ *vt* **1** offer (a guess or explanation) **2** put in danger ~**ous** *adj* dangerous

haze /heɪz/ *n* [S;U] light mist **hazy** *adj* **1** misty **2** uncertain: *I'm hazy about the details.*

ha·zel /'heɪzəl/ *n, adj* light greenish brown: *hazel eyes*

H-bomb /'eɪtʃ ˌbɒm‖-bɑːm/ *n* HYDROGEN BOMB

he /i, *strong* hiː/ *pron* (used for the male subject of a sentence)

head¹ /hed/ *n* **1** [C] part of the body containing the eyes, mouth, and brain **2** [(the) S] end where this rests: *the head of the bed* **3** [C] mind: *Don't put ideas into his head.* **4** [S] **a** ability: *no head for figures* **b** the power to be in control of oneself: *to keep/lose one's head in a crisis* **5** ruler; chief: *heads of state* **6** [(the) S] **a** top: *head of a hammer/a page/the stairs* **b** front: *head of a procession* **7** [S] pressure of steam or water **8 a/per head** for each person: *cost £5 a head* **9 above/over one's head** too hard to understand **10 bring/come to a head** reach a point where something must be done **11 eat/shout, etc., one's head off** *infml* eat/shout, etc., too much, loudly, etc. **12 go to one's head: a** make one drunk **b** over-excite someone **c** make someone too proud **13 head and shoulders above** very much better than **14 head over heels: a** turning over headfirst **b** completely: *head over heels in love* **15 make head or tail of** manage to understand **16 off one's head** *infml* mad **17 put our/your/their heads together** think out a plan with other people **18 turn someone's head: a** make someone too proud **b** make someone fall in love **heads** *n* [U] front of a coin

head² *v* **1** *vt* be at the top or front of: *head a procession* **2** *vt* strike (a ball) with the head **3** *vi* go somewhere: *head north/towards Rome/for the bar*

head off *phr vt* **1** cause to change direction **2** prevent

head·ache /'hedeɪk/ *n* **1** pain in the head **2** problem

head·dress /'hed-dres/ *n* decorative head covering

head·first /ˌhed'fɜːst◀‖-ɜːrst/ *adj, adv* with the rest of the body following the head

head·gear /'hedgɪəʳ/ *n* [U] covering for the head

head·hunt·er /'hed,hʌntəʳ/ *n* person who tries to find suitable people for important jobs

head·ing /'hedɪŋ/ *n* words written as a title at the top of a page

head·land /'hedlənd/ *n* piece of land sticking out into the sea

head·light /'hedlaɪt/ *also* **headlamp** /-læmp/ *n* strong light on the front of a vehicle

head·line /'hedlaɪn/ *n* **1** heading above a newspaper story **2** main point of the news on radio

head·long /'hedlɒŋ‖-lɔːŋ/ *adj, adv* **1** HEADFIRST **2** in foolish haste

head·mas·ter /ˌhed'mɑːstəʳ‖'hed,mæstər/ **-mistress** /-ˌmɪstrəs‖'hed,mɪstrəs/ *fem. n* head teacher in a school

head-on /ˌ· '·◀/ *adv, adj* with the front parts meeting, usu. violently: *a head-on collision*

head·phones /'hedfəʊnz/ *n* [P] listening apparatus that fits over the ears

head·quar·ters /'hed,kwɔːtəz, ˌhed'kwɔːtəz‖-ɔːrtərz/ *n* **-ters** central office of an organization

head·rest /'hed-rest/ *n* support for the head

head·room /'hed-rum, -ruːm/ *n* [U] space to stand or move under something

head start /ˌ· '·/ *n* [S] advantage in a race or competition

head·stone /'hedstəʊn/ *n* stone marking the top end of a grave

head·strong /'hedstrɒŋ‖-strɔːŋ/ *adj* uncontrollable; impatient

head·way /'hedweɪ/ *n* **make headway** advance; make PROGRESS

head·wind /'hed,wɪnd, ˌhed'wɪnd/ *n* wind blowing directly against one

head·y /'hedi/ *adj* **1** making one drunk **2** exciting

heal /hiːl/ *vi/t* make or become healthy again ~**er** *n*

health /helθ/ *n* [U] **1** state of being well, without disease **2** condition of body or mind: *in poor health* **3** TOAST (2): *to drink someone's health* ~**y** *adj* **1** physically strong **2** producing good health **3** showing good health: (fig.) *healthy profits*

heap /hiːp/ *n* untidy pile ♦ *vt* pile up: *heap food on the plate* **heaps** *n* [P] *infml* lots: *heaps of time*

hear /hɪəʳ/ *v* **heard** /hɜːd‖hɜːrd/ **1**

vi/t receive (sounds) with the ears **2** *vt* be told or informed: *I hear they're married.* **3** *vt* listen to with attention: *A priest heard my confession.* **4 Hear! Hear!** (shout of agreement) **5 won't/wouldn't hear of** refuse(s) to allow

hear from *phr vt* receive news from, esp. by letter

hear of *phr vt* know about: *I've never heard of him.*

hear out *phr vt* listen to, till the end

hear·ing /'hɪərɪŋ/ *n* **1** [U] ability to hear sound **2** [U] distance at which one can hear **3** [C;U] act or experience of hearing **4** [C] chance to explain **5** [C] *law* trial of a case

hearing aid /'·· ·/ *n* small electric machine to improve hearing

hear·say /'hɪəseɪ‖'hɪr-/ *n* [U] things heard but unproved

hearse /hɜːs‖hɜrs/ *n* car for carrying a body to a funeral

heart /hɑːt‖hɑrt/ *n* **1** [C] organ that pumps blood round the body **2** [C] centre of a person's feelings: *a kind heart | My heart bled* (= I was very sorry) *for him.* **3** [C] something shaped like a heart **4** [C] centre: *heart of a lettuce/of the city/of the matter* **5** [C] red heart-shaped figure on a playing card **6** [U] courage: *take/lose heart* **7 after one's own heart** of the kind that one likes **8 break someone's/one's heart** make/become very unhappy **9 by heart** from memory **10 eat one's heart out** be very troubled **11 from the (bottom of one's) heart** with real feeling **12 have one's heart in the right place** be a kind person **13 lose one's heart to** fall in love with **14 set one's heart on** want very much **15 take something to heart** feel it deeply

heart·ache /'hɑːteɪk‖'hɑrt-/ *n* [U] deep sorrow

heart at·tack /'·· ·,·/ *n* dangerous condition in which the heart beats irregularly and painfully

heart·beat /'hɑːtbiːt‖'hɑrt-/ *n* [C;U] pumping movement of the heart

heart·break /'hɑːtbreɪk‖'hɑrt-/ *n* terrible sorrow **~ing** *adj* causing heartbreak

heart·brok·en /'hɑːt,brəʊkən‖ 'hɑrt-/ *adj* BROKEN-HEARTED

heart·burn /'hɑːtbɜːn‖'hɑrtbɜrn/ *n* [U] unpleasant feeling of burning in the chest, caused by INDIGESTION

heart·en /'hɑːtn‖'hɑrt-/ *vt* encourage

heart·felt /'hɑːtfelt‖'hɑrt-/ *adj* sincere

hearth /hɑːθ‖hɑrθ/n area round the fire in a home

heart·land /'hɑːtlənd‖'hɑrt-/ *n* central and most important area

heart·less /'hɑːtləs‖'hɑrt-/ *adj* cruel **~ly** *adv* **~ness** *n* [U]

heart-rend·ing /'hɑːt,rendɪŋ ‖ 'hɑrt-/ *adj* causing great pity **~ly** *adv*

heart·strings /'hɑːt,strɪŋz‖'hɑrt-/ *n* [P] deepest feelings of love and pity

heart·throb /'hɑːtθrɒb‖'hɑrtθrɑːb/ *n infml* man who is very attractive and with whom girls fall in love

heart-to-heart /,· · '·◄/ *n* open talk about personal details **heart-to-heart** *adj*

heart·warm·ing /'hɑːt,wɔːmɪŋ‖ 'hɑrt,wɔrm-/ *adj* causing pleasant feelings: *heartwarming response*

heart·y /'hɑːti‖'hɑrti/ *adj* **1** friendly and cheerful **2** healthy **3** (of meals) large **4** *BrE* (too) cheerful in a loud way **–ily** *adv* in a hearty way **2** very: *I'm heartily sick of your questions.*

heat[1] /hiːt/ *n* **1** [U] (degree of) hotness **2** [U] hot weather: *I don't like the heat much.* **3** [U] great excitement **4** [C] part of a race, whose winners will then race against others **5 on heat** (of female dogs, etc.) in a state of sexual excitement — see also WHITE HEAT

heat[2] *vi/t* make or become hot **~ed** *adj* excited and angry **~er** *n* machine for heating air or water **~ing** *n* [U] system for keeping rooms warm

heath /hiːθ/ *n* piece of open wild land

hea·then /'hiːðən/ *n*, *adj* (person) not belonging to one of the large established religions

heath·er /'heðə[r]/ *n* [U] plant which grows on MOORS and has small pink or purple flowers

heat·stroke /'hiːtstrəʊk/ *n* [U] SUNSTROKE

heat wave /'·· ·/ *n* period of unusually hot weather

heave[1] /hiːv/ *v* **1** *vi/t* pull or lift with effort **2** *vt* throw (something heavy) **3** *vi* rise and fall regularly **4 heave a sigh** SIGH

heave[2] *vi* hove /həʊv/ **1** (esp. of a ship) move; come **2 heave into sight/view** come into one's view

heave to *phr vi* hove (of a ship) stop moving

heav·en /'hevən/ *n* **1** [U] home of God or the gods **2** (*usu. cap.*) God: *Heaven help you! | Good heavens!* **3** [C *usu. pl.*] the sky **4** [U] wonderful place or state **5 move heaven and earth** do everything possible (to cause or prevent something) — see also SEVENTH HEAVEN

heav·en·ly /'hevənli/ *adj* **1** of heaven: *The moon is a heavenly body.* **2** wonderful

heav·y[1] /'hevi/ *adj* **1** of great weight **2** of unusual amount: *heavy rain/traffic | a heavy smoker* (= someone who smokes a lot) **3** needing effort: *heavy work* **4** serious and dull: *heavy reading* **5** (of food) too solid **6** (of the sea) with big waves 7 **find it heavy going** find it very difficult 8 **make heavy weather of something** make a job or problem seem more difficult than it really is ♦ *adv* in a troublesome, dull way **–ily** *adv* **–iness** *n* [U]

heavy² *n* serious usu. male part in a play, etc., esp. a bad character

heavy-du-ty /,·· '··◁/ *adj* (of clothes, machines, etc.) strong enough for rough treatment

heav-y-hand-ed /,·· '··◁/ *adj* awkward; not careful

heav-y-heart-ed /hevi'hɑːtɪd◁ǁ-'hɑːr-/ *adj* sad

heavy in-dus-try /,·· '···/ *n* [U] industry that produces large goods, or materials such as coal, steel, etc., that are used in the production of other goods

heav-y-weight /'heviweɪt/ *n*, *adj* 1 (a FIGHTER) of the heaviest class in boxing (BOX²) 2 (a person or thing) a of more than average weight b having great importance or influence

He-brew /'hiːbruː/ *n* [U] language used by the Jews, in ancient times and at present

heck-le /'hekəl/ *vi/t* interrupt (a speaker) disapprovingly at a meeting **–ler** *n*

hec-tare /'hektɑːʳ, -teəʳǁ-teər/ *n* (a measure of area of land equal to) 10,000 square metres

hec-tic /'hektɪk/ *adj* full of hurry and excitement

hec-tor /'hektəʳ/ *vt* BULLY

he'd /id, hid; *strong* hiːd/ *short for:* 1 he would 2 he had

hedge /hedʒ/ *n* 1 row of bushes dividing gardens or fields 2 protection: *a hedge against inflation* ♦ *v* 1 *vt* make a hedge round 2 *vi* refuse to answer directly 3 **hedge one's bets** protect oneself against loss by favouring or supporting more than one side in a competition, etc.

hedge-hog /'hedʒhɒgǁ-hɔːg/ *n* small prickly animal

hedge-row /'hedʒrəʊ/ *n* row of bushes, esp. along roads, separating fields

he-don-is-m /'hiːdənɪzəm/ *n* [U] idea that pleasure is the only important thing in life **–ist** *n* **–istic** /,hiːdə'nɪstɪk/ *adj*

heed /hiːd/ *vt fml* give attention to ♦ *n* [U] *fml* attention **~less** *adj*

heel /hiːl/ *n* 1 back of the foot 2 part of a shoe, sock, etc., which covers this, esp. the raised part of a shoe under the foot 3 *esp. AmE* unpleasant person, who treats others badly 4 **at/on one's heels** close behind one 5 **bring to heel** bring under control 6 **come to heel: a** (of a dog) follow close to its owner b (of a person) obey without question 7

down at heel (of people) untidy and poor-looking 8 **kick one's heels** not have anything particular to do ♦ *vt* put a heel on (a shoe)

hef-ty /'hefti/ *adj* big and powerful

he-gem-o-ny /hɪ'geməni, 'hedʒɪmənɪǁhɪ'dʒemənɪ, 'hedʒɪməʊni/ *n* [U] *fml* power of one state over others

heif-er /'hefəʳ/ *n* young cow

height /haɪt/ *n* 1 [C;U] (degree of) being high 2 [C] measurement from top to bottom 3 [C] also **heights** *pl.* — high place 4 [S] a highest degree: *the height of fashion* b the main or most active point: *the height of the storm.*

height-en /'haɪtn/ *vi/t* make or become greater in degree

hei-nous /'heɪnəs/ *adj fml* (of wickedness) extreme

heir /eəʳ/, **heiress** /'eəɹǝs, 'eəres/ *fem.* *n* person with the legal right to receive property, etc., when the owner dies

heir-loom /'eəluːmǁ'eər-/ *n* valuable object given by older members of a family to younger ones over many years

held /held/ *v past t. and p. of* HOLD

hel-i-cop-ter /'helɪkɒptəʳǁ-kɑːp-/ *n* aircraft that flies by means of fast-turning blades on top

he-li-um /'hiːliəm/ *n* [U] very light gas used in AIRSHIPs, etc.

hell /hel/ *n* 1 [U] place where the wicked are said to be punished after death 2 [C] terrible place 3 [U] *sl* (used in anger or to give force): *What the hell's that?* | *That's a hell of a good car.* 4 **for the hell of it** for fun 5 **give someone hell** treat them roughly 6 **hell to pay** *sl* serious trouble or punishment 7 **like hell: a** very much: *I worked like hell all week.* b not at all: *'He paid, didn't he?' 'Like hell he did.'* 8 **play hell with** cause damage to ♦ *interj* (an expression of) anger or disappointment **~ish** *adj* terrible

he'll /il, hil; *strong* hiːl/ *short for:* he will

hel-lo /hə'ləʊ, he-/ *interj*, *n* **-los** 1 (used in greeting) 2 *esp. BrE* (an expression of surprise): *Hello! She's left something behind.*

helm /helm/ *n* 1 wheel or TILLER that guides a ship 2 **at the helm** in control

hel-met /'helmɪt/ *n* protective head covering

help¹ /help/ *v* 1 *vi/t* make it possible for (someone) to do something; be useful (to) 2 *vt* avoid; prevent: *I couldn't help laughing.* | *It can't be helped.* 3 *vt* give food, etc., to: *Help yourself to sugar.* | *He just helped himself to the money.* (= took) **~er** *n* person who helps **~ing** *n* serving of food

help out *phr vi/t* give help (to someone) at a time of need

help² *n* **1** [U] act of helping; AID **2** [C] someone or something that helps **3** [C] person employed to do housework **4** **there's no help for it** there's no way of avoiding it **5 Help!** Please bring help. **~ful** *adj* useful **~fully** *adv* **~less** *adj* unable to look after oneself **~lessly** *adv*

hem¹ /hem/ *n* edge of a skirt, etc., turned under and sewn

hem² *vt* **-mm-** put a hem on

   hem in *phr vt* surround closely

hem·i·sphere /'hemɪsfɪə'/ *n* **1** half a SPHERE **2** half of the Earth: *the southern hemisphere*

hem·line /'hemlaɪn/ *n* length of a skirt or dress

he·mo·phil·i·a /,hiːmə'fɪliə/ *n* [U] disease that makes the sufferer bleed badly after only a small cut **-iac** /iæk/ *n* person suffering from hemophilia

hem·or·rhage /'hemərɪdʒ/ *n* [C;U] flow of blood, esp. long and unexpected

hem·or·rhoid /'hemərɔɪd/ *n* swollen blood vessel at the lower end of the bowel

hemp /hemp/ *n* [U] plant used for making rope, rough cloth, and the drug CANNABIS

hen /hen/ *n* female bird, esp. the kind kept for its eggs on farms

hence /hens/ *adv fml* **1** for this reason **2** from here or now

hence·forth /,hens'fɔːθ, 'hensfɔːθ‖-ɔːrθ/ , **-forward** /-'fɔːwəd‖-'fɔːrwərd/ *adv fml* from now on

hench·man /'hentʃmən/ *n* **-men** /-mən/ faithful supporter who may use violent methods

hen·na /'henə/ *n* [U] reddish-brown DYE

hen-pecked /'henpekt/ *adj* (of a man) too obedient to his wife

hep·a·ti·tis /,hepə'taɪtɪs/ *n* [U] serious disease of the LIVER

her /ə', hɜː'; *strong* hɜː'/ *pron* (used for the female object of a sentence) ♦ *determiner* of her: *her car* **hers** *pron* of her; her one(s): *It's hers.*

her·ald /'herəld/ *n* (in former times) person who brought important news ♦ *vt fml* be a sign of (something coming)

her·ald·ry /'herəldri/ *n* [U] study of COATS OF ARMS

herb /hɜːb‖ɜːrb, hɜːrb/ *n* any plant used in medicine or to improve the taste of food **~al** *adj* of herbs **~alist** *n* person who uses herbs, esp. to treat disease

her·ba·ceous /hɜː'beɪʃəs‖ɜːr'beɪ-, hɜːr'beɪ-/ *adj* (of a plant) soft-stemmed: *a herbaceous border* (= border of such plants)

her·biv·o·rous /hɜː'bɪvərəs‖ɜːr-, hɜːr-/ *adj* (of animals) which eat grass or plants

Her·cu·le·an /,hɜːkjuː'liːən, hɜː-'kjuːliən‖-ɜːr-/ *adj* needing great strength or determination

herd /hɜːd‖hɜːrd/ *n* **1** group of animals together **2** people generally, thought of as acting all alike ♦ *vt* drive in a herd: (fig.) *to herd tourists into a bus*

here /hɪə'/ *adv* **1** at, in, or to this place: *'It's Professor Worth here.'* (= speaking on the telephone) **2** at this point: *Here we agree.* **3 here and there** scattered about **4 Here goes!** Now I'm going to have a try. **5 Here's to** (said when drinking a TOAST(2)) **6 neither here nor there** not connected with the matter being talked about

here·a·bouts /,hɪərə'baʊts, 'hɪərə-baʊts/ *adv* somewhere near here

here·af·ter /,hɪər'ɑːftə'‖-'æf-/ *adv fml* in the future ♦ *n* [S] life after death

here·by /,hɪə'baɪ, 'hɪəbaɪ‖-ər-/ *adv fml* by this means

he·red·i·ta·ry /hɪ'redɪtəri‖-teri/ *adj* passed down from parent to child

he·red·i·ty /hɪ'redɪti/ *n* [U] fact that qualities are passed on from parent to child

here·in /,hɪər'ɪn/ *adv fml* in this

her·e·sy /'herɪsi/ *n* [C;U] belief that goes against what is officially accepted

her·e·tic /'herɪtɪk/ *n* person guilty of heresy **~al** /hɪ'retɪkəl/ *adj*

here·with /,hɪə'wɪð/ , hɪər-/ *adv fml* with this

her·i·tage /'herɪtɪdʒ/ *n* something passed down within a family or nation

her·mit /'hɜːmɪt‖'hɜːr-/ *n* person who lives alone, esp. for religious reasons

her·mit·age /'hɜːmɪtɪdʒ‖'hɜːr-/ *n* hermit's home

her·ni·a /'hɜːniə‖'hɜːr-/ *n* [C;U] condition in which an organ, esp. in the bowel, pushes through its covering wall

he·ro /'hɪərəʊ/ **heroine** /'herəʊɪn/ *fem. n* **-roes 1** someone admired for bravery etc. **2** most important character in a story **~ic** /hɪ'rəʊɪk/ *adj* very brave **~ically** /-kli/ *adv* **~ics** *n* [P] grand speech or actions that mean nothing **~ism** /'herəʊɪzəm/ *n* [U] courage

her·o·in /'herəʊɪn/ *n* [U] drug made from MORPHINE

her·pes /'hɜːpiːz‖'hɜːr-/ *n* [U] very infectious skin disease

her·ring /'herɪŋ/ *n* sea fish used for food — see also RED HERRING

her·ring·bone /'herɪŋbəʊn/ *n* [U] V-shaped pattern

her·self /ə'self, hə-; *strong* hɜː-‖-ər-, hər-; *strong* hɜːr-/ *pron* **1** (*reflexive* *form of* **she**): *She hurt herself.* **2** (*strong form of* **she**): *She did it herself* **3** (**all**) **by herself: a** alone **b** without help **4 to herself** not shared

he's /iz, hiz; *strong* hi:z/ *short for:* **1** he is **2** he has

hes·i·tant /'hezətənt/ *adj* tending to hesitate **–tancy** *n* [U]

hes·i·tate /'hezɪteɪt/ *vi* **1** pause because one is uncertain **2** be unwilling **–tation** /ˌhezɪ'teɪʃən/ *n* [C;U]

het·e·ro·dox /'hetərədɒks‖-dɑːks/ *adj* (of beliefs, etc.) against accepted opinion

het·e·ro·ge·ne·ous /ˌhetərəʊ- 'dʒiːniəs/ *adj fml* of many different kinds

het·e·ro·sex·u·al /ˌhetərə'sekʃuəl/ *adj* attracted to people of the other sex **–ity** /ˌhetərəsekʃu'ælɪti/ *n* [U]

het up /ˌhet 'ʌp/ *adj sl* nervous and excited

hew /hjuː/ *vi/t* **hewed, hewed** *or* **hewn** /hjuːn/ *fml* cut with a heavy tool

hex·a·gon /'heksəgən‖-gɑːn/ *n* figure with 6 sides **–al** /hek'sægənəl/ *adj*

hey·day /'heɪdeɪ/ *n* [S] time of greatest success

hi·a·tus /haɪ'eɪtəs/ *n fml* space where something is missing

hi·ber·nate /'haɪbəneɪt ‖ -ər-/ *vi* (of some animals) sleep during the winter **–nation** /ˌhaɪbə'neɪʃən‖-ər-/ *n* [U]

hic·cup, hiccough /'hɪkʌp, -kəp/ *n* sudden stopping of the breath with a sharp sound **hiccup** *vi*

hide¹ /haɪd/ *v* **hid** /hɪd/ , **hidden** /'hɪdn/ **1** *vt* put out of sight **2** *vi* keep oneself from being seen

hide² *n* **1** animal's skin **2 hide or/nor hair of** *infml* any sign of

hide³ *n* place where one may watch animals, birds, etc., without being seen by them

hide·bound /'haɪdbaʊnd/ *adj* not willing to consider new ideas

hid·e·ous /'hɪdiəs/ *adj* very ugly; horrible **~ly** *adv*

hide·out /'haɪdaʊt/ *also* **hideaway** /'haɪdəweɪ/ -- *n* place where one can go to avoid people

hid·ing¹ /'haɪdɪŋ/ *n* beating

hiding² *n* [U] state of being hidden: *go into hiding*

hi·er·ar·chy /'haɪərɑːkiǁ-ɑːr-/ *n* [C;U] organization with higher and lower ranks

hi·e·ro·glyph·ics /ˌhaɪərə'glɪfɪks/ *n* [P] writing that uses pictures, as in ancient Egypt

hi-fi /'haɪ faɪ, ˌhaɪ 'faɪ/ *n* **hi-fis** high-quality equipment for reproducing recorded sound

high¹ /haɪ/ *adj* **1** far above the ground: *a high mountain*|*4 metres high* **2** great: *high cost* **3** good: *high*

standards **4** (of a musical note) not deep **5** (of time) as the mid-point: *high summer*|*It's high time we were going.* (= We should go at once.) **6** (of food) not fresh **7** *infml* drunk or drugged ♦ *n* **1** high point or level: *Sales are at an all-time high.* **2** state of great excitement: *on a high* **~ly** *adv* **1** very: *highly amused* **2** very well: *highly paid*

high² *adv* **1** to or at a high level: *aim high* **2 feelings ran high** people got excited and angry **3 high and dry** deserted **4 high and low** everywhere

high-and-mighty /ˌ· · '··◂/ *adj infml* too proud and certain of one's own importance

high·brow /'haɪbraʊ/ *n, adj* (person) knowing a lot about art, books, etc.

high-class /ˌ· '·◂/ *adj* **1** of good quality **2** of high social position

high com·mis·sion·er /ˌ· ·'··/ *n* person representing one COMMON-WEALTH country in another

high court /ˌ· '·◂/ *n* most important court of justice

higher ed·u·ca·tion /ˌ··· ··'··/ *n* [U] education at a university or college

higher-up /ˌ·· '·◂/ *n* more important official person

high fi·del·i·ty /ˌ· ·'··◂/ *adj* able to reproduce sound almost perfectly

high-fli·er, -flyer /ˌ· '··/ *n* clever person who has high aims

high-grade /ˌ· '·◂/ *adj* of high quality

high-hand·ed /ˌ· '··◂/ *adj* using power too forcefully

high horse /'· ·ˌ ·'·/ *n* **on one's high horse** *infml derog* behaving as if one knows best, or more than others

high jump /'· ·/ *n* [S] **1** sport of jumping over a bar **2 be for the high jump** *BrE* be about to get a bad punishment or scolding

High·lands /'haɪləndz/ *n* [*the* + P] mountainous area

high-lev·el /ˌ· '··◂/ *adj* in or at a position of high importance

high-life /'· ·/ *n* enjoyable life of the rich and fashionable

high·light /'haɪlaɪt/ *n* **1** most important detail **2** lightest area on a picture, or in the hair ♦ *vt* throw attention onto

highly-strung /ˌ· '·◂/ *adj* nervous; excitable

high-mind·ed /ˌ· '··◂/ *adj* having high principles

High·ness /'haɪnɪs/ *n* (title of some royal persons)

high-pow·ered /ˌ· '··◂/ *adj* having great force or ability

high-rise /'· ·/ *adj* (of buildings) with many floors

high school /'· ·/ *n esp. AmE* school for children over 14

high seas /ˌ· '·/ n [the + P] oceans that do not belong to any particular country

high-sea-son /ˌ· '··/n [U] time of year when business is greatest and prices are highest

high-spir-it-ed /ˌ· '····◁/ adj active and adventurous

high spot /'· ·/n most remembered part of an activity, esp. because pleasurable

high street /'· ·/ n BrE main street of a town

high tea /ˌ· '·/ n [U] BrE early-evening meal

high tech-nol-o-gy /ˌ· ·'····/ n [U] use of the most modern machines, processes, etc., in business or industry **high tech, hi-tech** adj

high-way /'haɪweɪ/ n broad main road

high-way-man /'haɪweɪmən/ n -men /-mən/ (in former times) man who used to stop people on the roads and rob them

hi-jack /'haɪdʒæk/ vt 1 take control of (esp. an aircraft) by force 2 stop and rob (a train, etc.) ~er n

hike /haɪk/ vi, n (go for) a long country walk **hiker** n

hi-lar-i-ous /hɪ'leəriəs/ adj full of or causing laughter ~ly adv

hi-lar-i-ty /hɪ'lærəti/ n [U] cheerful laughter

hill /hɪl/ n 1 raised piece of land, not as high as a mountain 2 slope in a road, etc. ~y adj

hilt /hɪlt/ n 1 handle of a sword 2 **(up) to the hilt** completely

him /ɪm; strong hɪm/ pron (used for the male object of a sentence)

him-self /ɪm'self; strong hɪm-/ pron 1 (reflexive form of he): He shot himself. 2 (strong form of he): He made it himself. 3 (all) by himself: a alone b without help 4 to himself not shared

hind[1] /haɪnd/ adj (of animals' legs) back

hind[2] n hinds or hind female deer

hin-der /'hɪndəʳ/ vt delay the progress of –drance n [C;U]

hind-most /'haɪndməʊst/ adj furthest behind

hind-quar-ters /'haɪndˌkwɔːtəz‖-ˌkwɔːrtərz/ n [P] animal's back legs

hind-sight /'haɪndsaɪt/ n [U] ability to understand the past, and esp. what went wrong

Hin-du /'hɪnduː, hɪn'duː/ n -dus person whose religion is Hinduism **Hindu** adj

Hin-du-is-m /'hɪnduː-ɪzəm/ n [U] chief religion of India, notable for its CASTE system and belief in REINCARNATION

hinge[1] /hɪndʒ/ n metal joint on which a door, etc., swings

hinge[2] vt fix on hinges

hinge on/upon phr vt depend on

hint /hɪnt/ n 1 small or indirect suggestion: (fig.) There's a hint of summer in the air. 2 useful advice ♦ vi/t suggest indirectly

hin-ter-land /'hɪntəlænd‖-ər-/ n [S] inner part of a country

hip /hɪp/ n fleshy part where the legs join the body

hip-pie , -py /'hɪpi/ n (young) person who is against the standards of ordinary society

hip-po-pot-a-mus /ˌhɪpə'pɒtəməs‖ -'pɑː-/ also **hippo** /'hɪpəʊ/ — n -muses or -mi /-maɪ/ large African river animal

hire /haɪəʳ/ vt get the use or services of something or someone for a limited time, for payment: hire a car ♦ n [U] (money for) being hired

hire pur-chase /ˌ· '··/ n [U] BrE system of paying small sums regularly for goods already received

his /ɪz; strong hɪz/ determiner of him: his shoes ♦ pron of him; his one(s): It's his.

hiss /hɪs/ vi, t make a sound like 's', esp. to show disapproval **hiss** n

his-to-ri-an /hɪ'stɔːriən/ n person who studies history

his-tor-ic /hɪ'stɒrɪk‖-'stɔː-, -'stɑː-/ adj important in history: an historic event

his-tor-i-cal /hɪ'stɒrɪkəl‖-'stɔː-, -'stɑː-/ adj about history: historical research/novels ~ly /-kli/ adv

his-to-ry /'hɪstəri/ n 1 [U] study of past events 2 [C] account of past events 3 [C] record of someone's past: her medical history 4 **make history** do something important which will be remembered — see also NATURAL HISTORY

his-tri-on-ics /ˌhɪstri'ɒnɪks‖-'ɑːn-/ n [P] insincere behaviour, like a theatrical performance **histrionic** adj

hit[1] /hɪt/ vt hit, pres. p. hitting 1 come, or bring something, hard against: He hit the ball with the bat. | The car hit the wall. 2 reach: hit the main road 3 have a bad effect on 4 **hit it off** have a good relationship 5 **hit the bottle** infml drink too much alcohol 6 **hit the nail on the head** say or do the right thing 7 **hit the road** infml start on a journey 8 **hit the roof** show or express great anger

hit back phr vi reply forcefully to an attack on oneself

hit on/upon phr vt find by chance

hit out at/against phr vt attack in words

hit[2] n 1 blow 2 successful performance

hit-and-miss /ˌ· · '·/adj depending on chance

hitch /hɪtʃ/ v 1 vt fasten by hooking a rope or metal part on something 2 vi hitchhike 3 **get hitched** get married ♦ n 1 difficulty or delay 2 kind of knot

hitch up phr vt pull up into place

hitch-hike /ˈhɪtʃhaɪk/ vi travel by getting rides in other people's cars **hitchhiker** n

hi-tech /ˌhaɪˈtek/ adj of or using HIGH TECHNOLOGY

hith-er-to /ˌhɪðəˈtuː◂‖-ər-/ adv fml until now

hit list /ˈ··/ n infml list of people or organizations against whom some (bad) action is planned

hit man /ˈ··/ n infml, esp. AmE criminal who is employed to kill someone

hit-or-miss /ˌ·ˈ·◂/ adj HIT-AND-MISS

hit pa-rade /ˈ··ˌ·/ n list of popular songs in the order of the numbers which are sold of each

HIV /ˌeɪtʃaɪˈviː/ n [(the) S] VIRUS carried in the blood that usually develops into the disease AIDS: He's HIV positive. (= He has the HIV virus.)

hive[1] /haɪv/ n 1 box, etc., where bees are kept 2 crowded busy place

hive[2] v **hive off** phr vt make separate from a larger organization

HMS /ˌeɪtʃemˈes/ abbrev. for His/Her Majesty's Ship: title for a ship in the British Navy

hoard /hɔːd‖hɔːrd/ n (secret) store of something valuable ♦ vt save; store, esp. secretly

hoard-ing /ˈhɔːdɪŋ‖ˈhɔːr-/ n BrE high fence, esp. for sticking advertisements on

hoarse /hɔːs‖hɔːrs/ adj (of a voice) sounding rough ~**ly** adv ~**ness** n [U]

hoar-y /ˈhɔːri/ adj (of hair) white with age: (fig.) hoary old jokes

hoax /həʊks/ n trick to deceive someone **hoax** vt

hob /hɒb‖hɑːb/ n flat top of a modern COOKER

hob-ble /ˈhɒbəl‖ˈhɑː-/ n 1 vi walk with difficulty 2 vt tie 2 legs of (a horse)

hob-by /ˈhɒbi‖ˈhɑː-/ n pleasant activity for one's free time

hob-by-horse /ˈhɒbihɔːs‖ˈhɑːbihɔːrs/ n 1 children's toy like a horse's head on a stick 2 fixed idea to which a person keeps returning in conversation

hob-nail /ˈhɒbneɪl‖ˈhɑːb-/ n heavy nail in the SOLE of a boot or shoe

hob-nob /ˈhɒbnɒb‖ˈhɑːbnɑːb/ vi -**bb**- have a social relationship (with)

hock[1] /hɒk‖hɑːk/ n [U] esp. BrE German white wine

hock[2] vt sl for PAWN[2]

hock-ey /ˈhɒki‖ˈhɑːki/ n [U] 1 BrE field team game played with sticks and a ball 2 esp. AmE for ICE HOCKEY

hod /hɒd‖hɑːd/ n box on a stick, for carrying bricks

hoe /həʊ/ n garden tool for breaking up the soil **hoe** vi/t

hog /hɒg‖hɑːg, hɔːg/ n 1 pig 2 person who eats too much 3 **go the whole hog** infml do something thoroughly — see also ROAD HOG ♦ vt take and keep (all of something) for oneself

Hog-ma-nay /ˈhɒgməneɪ‖ˌhɑːgməˈneɪ/ n NEW YEAR'S EVE in Scotland

hogs-head /ˈhɒgzhed ‖ ˈhɑːgz-, ˈhɔːgz-/ n large barrel for beer, etc.

hoist /hɔɪst/ vt pull up on a rope ♦ n 1 upward push 2 apparatus for lifting heavy goods

hold[1] /həʊld/ v held /held/ 1 vt keep in the hands, etc. 2 vt keep in a particular position: hold one's head up | Hold it! (= don't move) 3 vt support: The branch won't hold me. 4 vt not allow to leave: The police held 2 men. 5 vt not use: hold one's breath 6 vt defend against attack 7 vi remain unchanged: What I said still holds. 8 vt have room for: The cinema holds 500. 9 vt possess: hold the office of chairman 10 vt believe 11 vt cause to happen: hold an election 12 vt keep (the interest or attention) of (someone) 13 **hold court** receive admirers in a group 14 **hold good** be true 15 **Hold it!** infml Don't move. 16 **hold one's own** have a (strong) position 17 **hold one's tongue** not talk 18 **hold the line** keep a telephone connection 19 **hold water** seem to be true

hold against phr vt allow (something bad) to influence one's feelings about (someone)

hold back phr v 1 vt control 2 vt keep secret 3 vi be unwilling to act

hold down phr vt 1 keep in a low position 2 keep (a job)

hold forth phr vi talk at length

hold off phr v 1 vt keep at a distance 2 vi/t delay

hold on phr vi 1 wait (esp. on the telephone) 2 continue in spite of difficulties

hold onto phr vt keep possession of

hold out phr vi 1 continue to exist; last 2 offer

hold out for phr vt demand firmly and wait in order to get

hold over phr vt POSTPONE

hold to phr vt keep to: I'll hold you to your promise.

hold up phr vt 1 delay 2 rob by force

hold with phr vt approve of

hold[2] n 1 [U] holding 2 [C] something to hold, esp. in climbing 3 [C] influence

hold[3] n bottom of a ship, where goods are stored

hold-all /ˈhəʊldɔːl/ n bag for travelling

hold·er /ˈhəʊldəʳ/ n **1** person who possesses something **2** container

hold·ing /ˈhəʊldɪŋ/ n land, etc., that one possesses

hold-up /ˈhəʊld-ʌp/ n **1** delay, as in traffic **2** attempt at armed robbery

hole¹ /həʊl/ n **1** empty space in something solid **2 a** home of a small animal **b** small unpleasant living-space **3** infml difficult position **4** (in GOLF) hollow place in the ground into which the ball must be hit: an 18-hole golf course **5 make a hole in** infml use up a large part of **6 pick holes in** find faults in — see also BLACK HOLE

hole² vt **1** make a hole in **2** vi/t hit (the ball) into a hole in GOLF

hole up phr vi sl hide as a means of escape

hol·i·day /ˈhɒlɪdi‖ˈhɑːlɪdeɪ/ n **1** time of rest from work **2 on holiday** having a holiday ♦ vi have a period of holiday ~**maker** n person on holiday

hol·i·er-than-thou /,··· ' ·'/ adj derog thinking oneself to be morally better than other people

hol·i·ness /ˈhəʊlinɪs/ n [U] **1** being holy **2** (cap.) (title of the Pope)

ho·lis·tic /həʊˈlɪstɪk/ adj concerning the whole of something or someone, not just its parts: holistic medicine

hol·low /ˈhɒləʊ‖ˈhɑː-/ adj **1** having an empty space inside **2** lacking flesh: hollow cheeks **3** (of sounds) as if made by striking an empty container **4** insincere ♦ n wide hole ♦ vt make hollow

hol·ly /ˈhɒli‖ˈhɑːli/ n [C;U] tree whose red berries are used for Christmas decoration

hol·o·caust /ˈhɒləkɔːst‖ˈhɑː-/ n great destruction and the loss of many lives, esp. by burning

hol·o·gram /ˈhɒləgræm‖ˈhɑʊləgræm, ˈhɑː-/ n picture made with laser light so that it appears to be solid rather than flat

hol·o·graph·y /həˈlɒgrəfi‖həʊˈlɑː-/ n [U] science of producing holograms

hol·ster /ˈhəʊlstəʳ/ n leather holder for a PISTOL

ho·ly /ˈhəʊli/ adj **1** connected with, or serving, religion **2** leading a pure and blameless life

home¹ /həʊm/ n **1** [C] place where one lives **2** [C;U] one's house and family: She came from a poor home. **3** [S] a place where a plant or animal is found **b** place where something was originally discovered, made or developed **4** [C] place for the care of people or animals: an old people's home **5** [U] (in sports) place which a player must try to reach **6 be/feel at home** feel comfortable **7 make oneself at home** behave freely **8 nothing to write home about** nothing special ~**less** adj

home² adv **1** to or at one's home: go home **2** to the right place: strike a nail home **3 bring/come home to one** make/become clearly understood **4 home and dry** infml, esp. BrE having safely or successfully completed something

home³ adj **1** of or related to one's home or origin **2** not foreign **3** prepared or made in the home: home grown **4** (of a sports match) played at the place, sports field, etc., of one's home area

home⁴ /həʊm/ v **home in on** phr vt aim exactly towards — see also HOMING

home-com·ing /ˈhəʊm,kʌmɪŋ/ n arrival home, esp. after a long absence

home help /,· '·/ n someone sent in by the British Social Services to clean, etc.

home·land /ˈhəʊmlænd, -lənd/ n **1** country where one was born **2** area set aside for the South African black population

home·ly /ˈhəʊmli/ adj **1** simple and plain **2** AmE not good-looking

ho·me·op·a·thy /,həʊmi-ˈɒpəθi‖-ˈɑːp-/ n [U] system of treating disease with small amounts of substances that in larger amounts would produce a similar illness -**opathic** /,həʊmiəˈpæθɪk/ adj

home·sick /ˈhəʊm,sɪk/ adj unhappy because away from home ~**ness** n [U]

home truth /,· '·/ n unpleasant fact about someone

home·ward /ˈhəʊmwəd‖-wərd/ adj going towards home **homewards** ‖ also **homeward** AmE adv

home·work /ˈhəʊmwɜːk‖-ɜːrk/ n [C] **1** schoolwork done outside the classroom **2** preparations done before taking part in an important activity

hom·ey , **homy** /ˈhəʊmi/ adj AmE infml pleasant, like home

hom·i·cide /ˈhɒmɪsaɪd‖ˈhɑː-/ n [C;U] fml murder -**cidal** /,hɒmɪˈsaɪdl◄, hɑː-/ adj

hom·i·ly /ˈhɒmɪli‖ˈhɑː-/ n long speech on moral behaviour

hom·ing /ˈhəʊmɪŋ/ adj of or having the ability to **a** guide oneself home **b** (of machines) guide themselves towards the place they are aimed at

ho·mo·ge·ne·ous /,həʊməˈdʒiːniəs/ adj formed of parts of the same kind

ho·mo·ge·nize, -nise /həˈmɒdʒənaiz‖-'mɔ:-/ *vt* make (the parts of a whole, esp. a mixture) become evenly spread

ho-mo-sex-u-al /ˌhəumə'sekʃuəl, ˌhɒ-‖ˌhəu-/ *n, adj* (person) sexually attracted to people of the same sex ~**ity** /ˌhəumə,sekʃu'ælšti, ˌhɒ-‖ˌhəu-/ *n* [U]

hon-est /'ɒnšst‖'a:n-/ *adj* 1 not likely to lie or cheat 2 (of actions, etc.) showing these qualities ~**ly** *adv* 1 in an honest way 2 really

hon-es-ty /'ɒnšsti‖'a:n-/ *n* [U] quality of being honest

hon-ey /'hʌni/ *n* 1 [U] sweet substance that bees make 2 [C] *esp. AmE for* DARLING

hon-ey-comb /'hʌnikəum/ *n* wax structure that bees make to store honey

hon-ey-moon /'hʌnimu:n/ *n* 1 holiday taken by 2 people who have just got married 2 short period of good relations, etc., at the beginning of a period in office, etc. ♦ *vi* spend one's honeymoon **honeymooner** *n*

honk /hɒŋk‖haːŋk, hɔ:ŋk/ *vi, n* (make) the sound of a car horn

hon-or-ar-y /'ɒnšrəri‖'a:nšreri/ *adj* 1 (of a rank, etc.) given as an honour 2 unpaid: *honorary chairman*

hon-our *BrE* ‖ **honor** *AmE* /'ɒnšr‖'a:nšr/ *n* 1 [U] great public respect 2 [U] high standards of behaviour: *men of honour* 3 [S] person or thing that brings pride: *He's an honour to his parents.* 4 [C] (*cap.*) (used as a title for a judge) ♦ *vt* 1 bring honour to 2 keep (an agreement) **honours** *n* [P] 1 marks of respect: *full military honours* 2 specialized university degree or a level gained in it

hon-our-a-ble *BrE* ‖ **honorable** *AmE* /'ɒnšrəbəl‖'a:n-/ *adj* 1 bringing or showing honour 2 (*cap.*) (title for certain high officials, children of noblemen, etc.) **-bly** *adv*

hood /hud/ *n* 1 covering for the head and neck **a** except the face, so that it can be pushed back **b** including the face, to avoid recognition 2 folding cover over a car, etc. 3 *AmE for* BONNET (2)

hood-wink /'hud,wɪŋk/ *vt* deceive

hoof /hu:f‖huf/ *n* **hoofs** *or* **hooves** /hu:vz‖hufs/ horny foot of a horse, etc.

hook /huk/ *n* 1 curved piece of metal or plastic for catching, hanging, or fastening things 2 (in boxing (BOX²)) blow given with the elbow bent 3 **by hook or by crook** by any means possible 4 **off the hook** no longer in a difficult situation ♦ *vt* catch, hang, or fasten with a hook ~**ed** *adj* 1 hook-shaped 2 dependent (on drugs, etc.)

hoo-li-gan /'hu:lšgən/ *n* noisy violent person who breaks things, etc. ~**ism** *n* [U]

hoop /hu:p‖hup, hu:p/ *n* circular band of wood or metal

hoo-ray /hu'rei/ *interj, n* HURRAY

hoot /hu:t/ *n* 1 sound made by an OWL or a car's horn 2 shout of dislike 3 **not care/give a hoot/two hoots** not care at all ♦ *vi/t* (cause to) make a hoot ~**er** *n* horn, whistle, etc.

hoo-ver /'hu:vəʳ/ *n tdmk BrE* (type of) VACUUM CLEANER ♦ *vi/t* clean with any VACUUM CLEANER

hooves /hu:vz/ hufs/ *pl. of* HOOF

hop¹ /hɒp‖haːp/ *vi* **-pp-** 1 (of people) jump on one leg 2 (of small creatures) jump 3 get into or onto a vehicle 4 **Hop it!** Go away! ♦ *n* 1 jump 2 distance flown by a plane without landing 3 **catch someone on the hop** meet someone when they are unprepared

hop² *n* climbing plant used for giving taste to beer

hope /həup/ *n* 1 [C;U] expectation that something good will happen 2 [C] person or thing that may bring success 3 **beyond/past hope** with no chance of success 4 **hold out hope** give encouragement — see also WHITE HOPE ♦ *vi/t* wish and expect ~**ful** *adj* feeling or giving hope ~**fully** *adv* 1 in a hopeful way 2 if our hopes succeed ~**less** *adj* 1 feeling or giving no hope 2 not skilled: *hopeless at maths* ~**lessly** *adv*

hop-per /'hɒpəʳ‖'haː-/ *n* large FUNNEL for grain or coal

horde /hɔːd‖hɔːrd/ *n* large moving crowd

ho-ri-zon /hə'raizən/ *n* 1 line where the sky seems to meet the earth or sea 2 **broaden one's horizons** increase the range of one's experience

hor-i-zon-tal /ˌhɒrš'zɒntl‖ˌhɔːrš-'za:ntl/ *adj* flat; level ♦ *n* [C;U] a horizontal line, surface or position ~**ly** *adv*

hor-mone /'hɔːməun‖'hɔːr-/ *n* substance produced in the body that influences growth, etc.

horn /hɔːn‖hɔːrn/ *n* 1 [C] pointed growth on an animal's head 2 [U] material that this is made of: **horn-rimmed** *glasses* 3 [C] apparatus, e.g. in a car, that makes a warning sound 4 [C] musical instrument played by blowing ~**y** *adj* 1 hard and rough 2 *taboo sl* sexually excited

hor-net /'hɔːnšt‖'hɔːr-/ *n* large stinging insect

horn-pipe /'hɔːnpaɪp‖'hɔːrn-/ *n* dance performed esp. by sailors

hor-o-scope /'hɒrəskəup‖'hɔː-, 'hɑː-/ *n* set of ideas about someone's character, life and future gained by knowing the position of the stars or PLANETs at time of their birth

hor-ren-dous /hɒ'rendəs‖'hɑː-, hɔː-/ adj really terrible ~**ly** adv

hor-ri-ble /'hɒrɪbəl‖'hɑː-, 'hɔː-/ adj 1 causing horror 2 very unpleasant –**bly** adv

hor-rid /'hɒrɪd‖'hɑː-, 'hɔː-/ adj nasty

hor-rif-ic /hɒ'rɪfɪk‖hɔː-, hɑː-/ adj horrifying ~**ally** –kli/ adv

hor-ri-fy /'hɒrɪfaɪ‖'hɑː-, 'hɔː-/ vt fill with horror: *horrifying news*

hor-ror /'hɒrəʳ‖'hɑː-, 'hɔː-/ n 1 [C;U] (something causing) great shock and fear 2 [C] unpleasant person, usu. a child 3 **have a horror of** hate ♦ adj frightening: *horror films* **horrors** n *infml* [*the* + P] state of great fear, worry or sadness

horror-strick-en /'·· ,··/ also **horror-struck** /'·· ·/ — adj deeply shocked

hors d'oeu-vre /,ɔː 'dɜːv‖,ɔːr 'dɜːrv/ n -**hors d'oeuvres** /-dɜːv‖-dɜːrvz/ small things served at the beginning of a meal

horse[1] /hɔːs‖hɔːrs/ n 1 large 4-legged animal that people ride on, etc. 2 apparatus for jumping over 3 **eat like a horse** eat a lot 4 **(straight) from the horse's mouth** (of information) directly from the person concerned — see also DARK HORSE, HIGH HORSE, TROJAN HORSE

horse[2] v **horse around/about** phr vi *infml* play roughly or waste time in rough play

horse-back /'hɔːsbæk‖'hɔːrs-/ n **on horseback** riding a horse ♦ adj, adv esp. AmE on the back of a horse: *horseback riding*

horse-box /'hɔːsbɒks‖'hɔːrsbɑːks/ n vehicle in which a horse can travel

horse-man /'hɔːsmən‖'hɔːrs-/ **horsewoman** /-,wʊmən/ fem. — n -**men** /-mən/ person riding a horse

horse-play /'hɔːspleɪ‖'hɔːrs-/ n [U] rough noisy behaviour

horse-pow-er /'hɔːs,paʊəʳ‖'hɔːrs-/ n horsepower unit measuring the power of an engine

horse-shoe /'hɔːʃ-ʃuː, 'hɔːs-‖'hɔːr-/ n U-shaped shoe for a horse, believed to bring good luck

hors-y /'hɔːsi‖'hɔːrsi/ adj 1 interested in horses 2 looking like a horse

hor-ti-cul-ture /'hɔːtɪ,kʌltʃəʳ‖'hɔːr-/ n [U] science of growing fruit, flowers, and vegetables –**tural** /,hɔːtɪ-'kʌltʃərəl‖,hɔːr-/ adj

hose[1] /həʊz/ also **hosepipe** /'həʊzpaɪp/ — n tube used for watering gardens, etc. ♦ vt use a hose on

hose[2] n [U] socks and STOCKINGS

ho-siery /'həʊzjəri‖'həʊʒəri/ n [U] socks, stockings, etc.

hos-pice /'hɒspɪs‖'hɑː-/ n 1 hospital for people with incurable illnesses 2 house made for travellers to rest

hos-pi-ta-ble /'hɒspɪtəbəl, hɒ'spɪ-‖hɒ'spɪ-, 'hɑːspɪ-/ adj offering a friendly welcome to guests –**bly** adv

hos-pi-tal /'hɒspɪtl‖'hɑː-/ n place where people who are ill or injured are treated —**ize** vt put into hospital

hos-pi-tal-i-ty /,hɒspɪ'tælɪti‖,hɑː-/ n [U] being hospitable

host[1] /həʊst/ n 1 man who receives guests 2 person who introduces performers, e.g. on a TV show ♦ vt act as a host

host[2] n large number: *a host of difficulties*

hos-tage /'hɒstɪdʒ‖'hɑː-/ n prisoner kept by an enemy so that the other side will obey demands, etc.

hos-tel /'hɒstl‖'hɑː-/ n building where students, etc., can live and eat

host-ess /'həʊstɪs‖n 1 female host 2 AIRHOSTESS 3 young woman who acts as companion, dancing partner, etc., in a social club

hos-tile /'hɒstaɪl‖'hɑːstl, 'hɑːstaɪl/ adj 1 unfriendly 2 belonging to an enemy

hos-til-i-ty /hɒ'stɪlɪti‖hɑː-/ n [U] unfriendliness –**ties** n [P] war

hot[1] /hɒt‖hɑːt/ adj -tt- 1 having a high temperature 2 having a burning taste: *hot pepper* 3 fierce; excitable: *hot temper* 4 (of news) very recent 5 well-informed on and interested in: *She's very hot on jazz.* 6 **hot and bothered** worried by a feeling that things are going wrong 7 **hot on someone's trail** following someone closely 8 **not so hot** *infml* not very good ~**ly** adv 1 angrily 2 eagerly: *hotly pursued*

hot[2] v -tt- **hot up** phr vi become more exciting or dangerous

hot air /,· '·/ n [U] meaningless talk

hot-bed /'hɒtbed‖'hɑːt-/ n place where something bad can develop: *a hotbed of crime*

hot-blood-ed /,· '···◁/ adj PASSIONATE

hotch-potch /'hɒtʃpɒtʃ‖'hɑːtʃpɑːtʃ/ n confused mixture

hot dog /,· '·‖'·· ·/ n FRANKFURTER in a long bread ROLL[2] (3)

ho-tel /həʊ'tel/ n building where people can stay in return for payment

ho-tel-i-er /həʊ'telieɪ, -lɪəʳ/ n hotel manager

hot-foot /,hɒt'fʊt◁‖'hɑːtfʊt/ adv fast and eagerly

hot-head /'hɒthed‖'hɑːt-/ n person who acts in haste, without thinking ~**ed** /,hɒt'hedɪd◁‖,hɑːt-/ adj

hot-house /'hɒthaʊs‖'hɑːt-/ n heated GREENHOUSE

hot line /'·· ·/ n direct telephone line between heads of government

hot-plate /'hɒtpleɪt‖'hɑːt-/ n metal surface on which food is cooked

hot seat /'·· ·/ n infml position of difficulty from which one must make important decisions

hot spot /'· ·/ place where there is likely to be unrest and perhaps war

hot-tem-pered /ˌ· '···◁/ adj easily made angry

hot wa-ter /ˌ· '··/ n [U] trouble: get into hot water

hot-water bot-tle /ˌ· '·· ˌ·/ n rubber container for hot water, to warm a bed

hound /haʊnd/ n hunting dog ♦ vt chase and worry

hour /aʊəʳ/ n 1 period of 60 minutes 2 time when a new hour starts: arrive on the hour 3 distance one can travel in this period of time: It's only an hour away. 4 period of time: my lunch hour 5 **after hours** later than the usual times of work or business 6 **at all hours** (at any time) during the whole day and night — see also ELEVENTH HOUR, HAPPY HOUR, SMALL HOURS ~ly adj, adv once every hour

house¹ /haʊs/ n **houses** /'haʊzɪz/ 1 a building for people to live in, esp. on more than one level b people in such a building: You'll wake the whole house. 2 building for a stated purpose: a hen house | the Houses of Parliament | the House of Lords 3 (often cap.) noble or royal family 4 a division of a school b business firm: the house magazine 5 people voting after a DEBATE 6 theatre, or the people in it 7 **bring the house down** cause loud admiration 8 **get on like a house on fire** be very friendly 9 **keep house** run or control the cleaning, cooking, etc. 10 **on the house** (of drinks) paid for by the people in charge 11 **(as) safe as houses** BrE very safe

house² /haʊz/ vt provide a home, or space, for

house-boat /'haʊsbəʊt/ n boat for living in

house-bound /'haʊsbaʊnd/ adj unable to leave one's home

house-break-er /'haʊsˌbreɪkəʳ/ n thief who enters a house by force

house-bro-ken /'haʊsˌbrəʊkən/ adj AmE for HOUSE-TRAINED

house-coat /'haʊskəʊt/ n garment worn by women at home

house-hold /'haʊshəʊld/ n all the people living in a house ♦ adj concerned with the management of a house: household expenses ~er n person who owns or is in charge of a house

household name /ˌ·· '·/ also **household word** — n person or thing that is very well known or talked about by almost everyone

house-keep-er /'haʊsˌkiːpəʳ/ n person paid to run a house

house-keep-ing /'haʊsˌkiːpɪŋ/ n 1 work of running a house 2 money set aside for food, etc.

house-maid /'haʊsmeɪd/ n female servant who does housework

house-man /'haʊsmən/ n -men /-mən/ BrE low-ranking doctor completing hospital training

house-mas-ter /'haʊsˌmɑːstəʳ‖ -ˌmæ-/ **housemistress** /ˌmɪstrɪs/ fem. — n teacher in charge of a school HOUSE¹ (4a)

House of Com-mons /ˌ· · '··/ n [the] the lower but more powerful of the 2 parts of the British or Canadian parliament

House of Lords /ˌ· · '·/ n [the] the upper but less powerful of the 2 parts of the British parliament, the members of which are not elected

House of Rep-re-sen-ta-tives /ˌ· ··'···/ n [the] the larger and lower of the 2 parts of the central law-making body in such countries as New Zealand, Australia, and the US

house-proud /'· ·/ adj keeping one's home very clean and tidy

house-trained /'· ·/ adj BrE (of pets) trained to empty the bowels and BLADDER outside the house

house-warm-ing /'haʊsˌwɔːmɪŋ‖ -ˌwɔːr-/ n party given for friends when one has moved into a new house

house-wife /'haʊs-waɪf/ n -wives /-waɪvz/ woman who works at home for her family, cleaning, cooking, etc.

house-work /'haʊswɜːk‖-ɜːrk/ n [U] cleaning, etc., in a house

hous-ing /'haʊzɪŋ/ n 1 [U] places to live 2 [C] protective cover for a machine

hove /həʊv/ v past t. and p. of HEAVE² (2)

hov-el /'hɒvəl‖'hʌ-, 'hɑː-/ n dirty little house or hut

hov-er /'hɒvəʳ‖'hʌ-, 'hɑː-/ vi 1 (of birds, etc.) stay in the air in one place 2 (of people) wait around

hov-er-craft /'hɒvəkrɑːft‖ 'hʌvərkræft, 'hɑː-/ n -craft or -crafts boat that moves over land or water supported by a strong force of air

how /haʊ/ adv 1 (used in questions) a in what way: How do you spell it? b in what state of health: How are you? c (in questions about number, size, etc.): How big is it? 2 (showing surprise): How kind of you! 3 **How come . . . ?** infml Why is it that . . . ? 4 **How do you do?** (used when formally introduced to someone; this person replies with the same phrase) ♦ conj the way in which; the fact that: I remember how they laughed.

how-ev-er /haʊˈevər/ adv 1 in whatever degree or way: *We'll go, however cold it is.* 2 in spite of this 3 in what way (showing surprise): *However did you get here?*

howl /haʊl/ vi/t, n (make) a long loud cry ~**er** n silly laughable mistake

HP /ˌ·ˈ·/ abbrev. for: 1 HORSEPOWER 2 HIRE PURCHASE

HQ /ˌeɪtʃ ˈkjuː/ n [C;U] HEADQUARTERS

hr, hrs written abbrev. for: hour(s)

HRH abbrev. for: His/Her Royal Highness; title for certain members of the British royal family

hub /hʌb/ n 1 centre of a wheel 2 centre of activity

hub-bub /ˈhʌbʌb/ n [S] mixture of loud noises

hub-cap /ˈhʌbkæp/ n metal covering for the centre of a wheel on a car

hud-dle /ˈhʌdl/ vi/t crowd together ♦ n crowded group

hue /hjuː/ n fml colour

hue and cry /ˌ· · ˈ·/ n expression of worry, anger, etc., by noisy behaviour

huff /hʌf/ n [S] bad temper ~**y** adj

hug /hʌg/ vt -gg- 1 hold tightly in one's arms 2 travel along beside: *The boat hugged the coast.* **hug** n

huge /hjuːdʒ/ adj very big ~**ly** adv very much

huh /hʌh/ interj (used for asking a question or for expressing surprise or disapproval)

hulk /hʌlk/ n 1 old broken ship 2 heavy, awkward person or creature

hulk-ing /ˈhʌlkɪŋ/ adj big and awkward

hull /hʌl/ n body of a ship or aircraft

hul-lo /hʌˈləʊ/ interj, n -los BrE for HELLO

hum /hʌm/ v -mm- 1 vi BUZZ (1) 2 vi/t sing with closed lips 3 vi be full of activity **hum** n [U]

hu-man /ˈhjuːmən/ adj 1 of people 2 kind, etc., as people should be: *He's really very human.* ♦ n person ~**ism** n [U] system of belief based on people's needs, and not on religion ~**ize** vt make human or humane ~**ly** adv according to human powers: *not humanly possible*

hu-mane /hjuːˈmeɪn/ adj 1 showing human kindness and the qualities of a civilized person 2 trying not to cause pain: *a humane method of killing animals* ~**ly** adv

hu-man-i-tar-i-an /hjuːˌmænɪˈteəriən/ n, adj (person) trying to improve life for human beings by improving living conditions, etc. ~**ism** n [U]

hu-man-i-ty /hjuːˈmænɪti/ n [U] 1 being human or humane 2 people in general

hum-ble /ˈhʌmbəl/ adj 1 low in rank; unimportant 2 having a low opinion of oneself and a high opinion of others; not proud ♦ vt make humble **-bly** adv

hum-bug /ˈhʌmbʌg/ n 1 [U] insincere nonsense 2 [C] BrE hard boiled sweet

hum-drum /ˈhʌmdrʌm/ adj dull and ordinary

hu-mid /ˈhjuːmɪd/ adj (of air) DAMP ~**ify** /hjuːˈmɪdɪfaɪ/ vt make humid ~**ity** n [U]

hu-mil-i-ate /hjuːˈmɪlieɪt/ vt cause to feel ashamed **-ation** /hjuːˌmɪliˈeɪʃən/ n [C;U]

hu-mil-i-ty /hjuːˈmɪlɪti/ n [U] quality of being HUMBLE (2)

hu-mor-ist /ˈhjuːmərɪst‖ˈhjuː-, ˈjuː-/ n person who makes jokes in speech or writing

hu-mor-ous /ˈhjuːmərəs‖ˈhjuː-, ˈjuː-/ adj funny ~**ly** adv

hu-mour BrE ‖ **humor** AmE /ˈhjuːməʳ‖ˈhjuː-, ˈjuː-/ n [U] ability to be amused or cause amusement ♦ vt keep (someone) happy by acceptance of their foolish wishes, behaviour, etc.

hump /hʌmp/ n 1 [C] round lump, esp. on a camel's back 2 [the + S] BrE infml feeling of bad temper: *It's giving me the hump.* 3 **over the hump** infml past the worst part of the work ♦ v 1 vt infml carry (something heavy), esp. with difficulty 2 vi/t taboo sl have sex with

hunch¹ /hʌntʃ/ n idea based on feeling rather than reason

hunch² vt pull (part of the body) into a rounded shape: *hunched shoulders*

hunch-back /ˈhʌntʃbæk/ n (person with) a back mis-shaped by a round lump ~**ed** adj

hun-dred /ˈhʌndrəd/ determiner, n, pron **-dred** or **-dreds** 100 ~**th** determiner, adv, n, pron 100th

hun-dred-weight /ˈhʌndrədweɪt/ n -**weight** (a measure of weight equal to) **a** 45.36 kilograms or **b** 50.8 kilograms

hung /hʌŋ/ v past t. and p. of HANG — see also **be hung up on** (HANG up)

hun-ger /ˈhʌŋgəʳ/ n 1 [U] need for food 2 [S] strong wish ♦ vi feel hunger -**gry** adj feeling hunger

hunger strike /ˈ·· ·/ n refusal to eat as a sign of strong dissatisfaction

hunk /hʌŋk/ n 1 thick piece of food, etc. 2 infml good-looking man

hunt /hʌnt/ vi/t 1 chase (animals) for food or sport 2 search (for) ♦ n 1 chasing or searching 2 people hunting foxes ~**er** n

hunt down/out/up phr vt find by searching

hur-dle /ˈhɜːdl‖ˈhɜːr-/ n 1 frame to jump over in a race 2 difficulty to be dealt with

hurl /hɜːl‖hɜːrl/ vt throw violently: (fig.) *He hurled abuse at the other driver.*

hur·ly-bur·ly /'hɜːli ˌbɜːli‖ˌhɜːrli 'bɜːrli/ n [S;U] noisy activity

hur·ray /hʊ'reɪ/ interj, n (shout of joy or approval)

hur·ri·cane /'hʌrɪkən‖'hɜːrɪˌkeɪn/ n violent storm with a strong fast circular wind

hur·ry /'hʌri‖'hɜːri/ vi/t (cause to) go or do something (too) quickly: *Hurry up!* (= Be quick!) ♦ n [S;U] 1 quick activity 2 need to hurry −ried adj done (too) quickly −riedly adv

hurt /hɜːt‖hɜːrt/ v hurt 1 vt cause pain or damage to 2 vt cause pain (to the feelings of (a person)) 3 vi feel pain 3 vi/t matter (to): *It won't hurt (you) to wait.* ♦ n [C;U] harm; damage ~ful adj ~fully adv

hur·tle /'hɜːtl‖'hɜːrtl/ vi move or rush with great force

hus·band /'hʌzbənd/ n man to whom a woman is married

hush /hʌʃ/ vi/t (cause to) be silent ♦ n [S;U] silence
    hush up phr vt keep secret

husk /hʌsk/ n dry outer covering of some fruits and seeds

hus·ky /'hʌski/ adj 1 (of a voice) HOARSE 2 (of a person) big and strong −kily adv

hus·tings /'hʌstɪŋz/ n [P] speeches, etc., before an election

hus·tle /'hʌsl/ vt 1 push or drive hurriedly 2 persuade someone forcefully, esp. to buy something ♦ n [U] hurried activity **hustler** n 1 infml busy, active person, esp. one who tries to persuade people to buy things, etc. 2 sl. esp. AmE for PROSTITUTE

hut /hʌt/ n small simple building

hutch /hʌtʃ/ n cage for rabbits, etc.

hy·brid /'haɪbrɪd/ n animal or plant of mixed breed

hy·drant /'haɪdrənt/ n water pipe in the street

hy·drau·lic /haɪ'drɒlɪk, -'drɔː-‖-'drɔː-/ adj using water pressure

hy·dro·e·lec·tric /ˌhaɪdrəʊ-ɪ'lektrɪk/ adj producing electricity by water power

hy·dro·foil /'haɪdrəfɔɪl/ n large motor boat which raises itself out of the water as it moves

hy·dro·gen /'haɪdrədʒən/ n [U] light gas that burns easily

hydrogen bomb /'··· ·/n bomb made using hydrogen which explodes when the central parts of the atoms join together

hy·giene /'haɪdʒiːn/ n [U] cleanness, to prevent the spreading of disease **hygienic** /haɪ'dʒiːnɪk‖-'dʒe-, -'dʒiː-/

hymn /hɪm/ n song of praise to God

hype /haɪp/ vt infml try to get a lot of public attention for, esp. more than is deserved **hype** n [U] attempts to do this

hyped up /ˌ· '·/adj infml very excited and anxious

hy·per·ac·tive /ˌhaɪpər'æktɪv/ adj unable to rest or be quiet

hy·per·bo·le /haɪ'pɜːbəli‖-ɜːr-/ n EXAGGERATION

hy·per·mar·ket /'haɪpəˌmɑːkɪt‖-pərˌmɑːr-/ n BrE very large SUPERMARKET

hy·phen /'haɪfən/ n the mark (-) joining words or word parts ~ate vt join with a hyphen

hyp·no·sis /hɪp'nəʊsəs/ n [U] sleep-like state in which a person can be influenced by the person who produced the state −tic /-'nɒtɪk‖-'nɑː-/ adj −tism /'hɪpnətɪzəm/ n [U] production of hypnosis −tist n −tize vt produce hypnosis in

hy·po·chon·dri·ac /ˌhaɪpə'kɒndriæk‖-'kɑːn-/ n someone who worries unnecessarily about their health

hy·poc·ri·sy /hɪ'pɒkrəsi‖-'pɑː-/ n [U] pretending to be different from and usu. better than one is

hyp·o·crite /'hɪpəkrɪt/ n person who practises hypocrisy −**critical** /ˌhɪpə'krɪtɪkəl/ adj

hy·po·der·mic /ˌhaɪpə'dɜːmɪk‖-ɜːr-/ adj, n (of) a needle for putting drugs into the body

hy·pot·e·nuse /haɪ'pɒtənjuːz‖-'pɑːtənuːs, -nuːz/ n longest side of a right-angled TRIANGLE which is opposite the right angle

hy·poth·e·sis /haɪ'pɒθəsəs‖-'pɑː-/ n idea that may explain facts −etical /ˌhaɪpə'θetɪkəl/ adj not yet proved

hys·te·ri·a /hɪ'stɪəriə‖-'steriə/ n [U] uncontrolled nervous excitement −rical /hɪ'sterɪkəl/ adj −rics n [P] attack(s) of hysteria

I¹, i /aɪ/ n the 9th letter of the English alphabet

I² pron (used for the person speaking, as the subject of a sentence)

ice¹ /aɪs/ n 1 [U] frozen water 2 [C] frozen sweet food 3 **skating on thin ice** taking risks 4 **keep something on ice** take no immediate action about something — see also BLACK ICE

ice² *vt* **1** make cold with ice **2** cover with ICING

ice over/up *phr vi* become covered with ice

ice age /'· ·/ *n* period when ice covered many northern countries

ice-berg /'aɪsbɜːg‖-ɜːrg/ *n* **1** mass of floating ice in the sea **2** the tip of the iceberg a small sign of a much larger situation, problem, etc.

ice-box /'aɪsbɒks‖-bɑːks/ *n* **1** box where food is kept cool with ice **2** *AmE old-fash for* FRIDGE

ice-break-er /'aɪs,breɪkəʳ/ *n* **1** ship that cuts through floating ice **2** action which makes people who have just met more relaxed

ice cap /'· ·/ *n* lasting covering of ice, e.g. at the POLES² (1)

ice cream /,· '◄‖'·· ·/ *n* [C;U] frozen creamy food mixture

ice floe /'· ·/*n* large area of floating ice

ice hock-ey /'· ,··/ *n* [U] game like HOCKEY¹ played on ice

ice lol-ly /,· '··/ *n BrE* piece of ICE¹ (2) on a stick

ice pack /'· ·/ *n* bag of ice to put on the body

ice pick /'· ·/ *n* tool for breaking ice

ice-skate /'· ·/ *n* SKATE (1) **ice-skate** *vi*

i-ci-cle /'aɪsɪkəl/ *n* pointed stick of ice, formed when water freezes as it runs down

ic-ing /'aɪsɪŋ/ *n* [U] mixture of powdery sugar with liquid, used to decorate cakes

i-con-o-clast /aɪ'kɒnəklæst‖-'kɑː-/ *n* person who attacks established beliefs ~**ic** /aɪ,kɒnə'klæstɪk‖-'kɑː-/ *adj*

ic-y /'aɪsi/ *adj* **1** very cold **2** covered with ice **icily** *adv*

I'd /aɪd/ *short for:* **1** I would **2** I had

i-dea /aɪ'dɪə/ *n* **1** [C] plan, thought, or sugestion for a possible course of action **2** [C;U] picture in the mind; CONCEPTION **3** [C] opinion or belief: *strange ideas* **4** understanding: *They've got no idea how to run a house.* **5** [C] guess; feeling of probability: *I've an idea she doesn't like him.*

i-deal /aɪ'dɪəl/ *adj* **1** perfect **2** too good to exist ♦ *n* **1** *[often pl.]* (belief in) high principles or perfect standards **2** perfect example ~**ist** *n* ~**ize** *vt* imagine as perfect ~**ly** *adv* **1** in an ideal way: *ideally suited* **2** if things were perfect

i-deal-ism /aɪ'dɪəlɪzəm/ *n* [U] quality or habit of living according to one's ideals, or the belief that such a way of life is possible ~**ist** *n* ~**istic** *adj* /,aɪdɪə'lɪstɪk/ ~**istically** /-kli/

i-den-ti-cal /aɪ'dentɪkəl/ *adj* **1** exactly alike **2** the same ~**ly** /-kli/ *adv*

i-den-ti-fy /aɪ'dentɪfaɪ/ *vt* show the identity of ~**fication** /aɪ,dentɪfɪ-'keɪʃən/ *n* [U] **1** identifying **2** paper, etc., that proves who one is

identify with *phr vt* **1** consider (someone) to be connected with **2** feel sympathy for

i-den-ti-ty /aɪ'dentɪti/ *n* **1** [C;U] who or what a person or thing is **2** [U] sameness

i-de-ol-o-gy /,aɪdi'ɒlədʒi‖-'ɑːlə-/ *n* [C;U] set of (political or social) ideas ~**ogical** /,aɪdiə'lɒdʒɪkəl‖-'lɑː-/ *adj*

id-i-o-cy /'ɪdiəsi/ *n* **1** [U] stupidity **2** [C] stupid act

id-i-om /'ɪdiəm/ *n* phrase that means something different from the meanings of its separate words: *'Kick the bucket' is an idiom meaning 'die'.*

id-i-o-mat-ic /,ɪdiə'mætɪk/ *adj* typical of natural speech ~**ally** /-kli/ *adv*

id-i-o-syn-cra-sy /,ɪdiə'sɪŋkrəsi/ *n* personal peculiarity ~**tic** /,ɪdiəsɪn-'krætɪk/ *adj* ~**tically** /-kli/ *adv*

id-i-ot /'ɪdiət/ *n* **1** fool **2** weak-minded person ~**ic** /,ɪdi'ɒtɪk‖-'ɑːt-/ *adj*

i-dle /'aɪdl/ *adj* **1** not working **2** lazy **3** useless: *idle threats* ~**ness** *n* **idly** *adv*

idle² *vi* **1** waste time **2** (of an engine) run slowly because it is disconnected **idler** *n*

idle away *phr vt* waste (time)

i-dol /'aɪdl/ *n* **1** image worshipped as a god **2** someone greatly admired ~**ize** *vt* worship as an idol

i-dol-a-try /aɪ'dɒlətri‖-'dɑː-/ *n* [U] worshipping of idols ~**trous** *adj* **idolater** *r*

id-yll-ic /ɪ'dɪlɪk‖aɪ-/ *adj* simple and happy

i.e. /,aɪ 'iː/ that is; by which is meant: *open to adults, i.e. people over 18*

if /ɪf/ *conj* **1** on condition that: *I'll come if I can.* **2** even though: *It was nice, if expensive.* **3** whether: *I don't know if he'll come.* **4** (after words expressing feeling): *I'm sorry if she's annoyed.* **5 if I were you** (used when giving advice): *If I were you, I'd burn it.* **6 it isn't/it's not as if** it's not true that ♦ *n* **ifs and buts** reasons given for delay

ig-nite /ɪg'naɪt/ *vi/t fml* start to burn **ig-ni-tion** /ɪg'nɪʃən/ *n* **1** [C] electrical apparatus that starts an engine **2** [U] *fml* action of igniting

ig-no-ble /ɪg'nəʊbəl/ *adj fml* not honourable ~**bly** *adv*

ig-no-mi-ny /'ɪgnəmini/ *n* [C;U] (act of) shame ~**nious** /,ɪgnə'mɪniəs/ *adj*

ig-no-ra-mus /,ɪgnə'reɪməs/ *n* ignorant person

ig-no-rant /'ɪgnərənt/ *adj* **1** without knowledge **2** rude, esp. because of lack of social training ~**rance** *n* [U]

ig-nore /ɪg'nɔːʳ/ *vt* refuse to notice

ill adj **worse** /wɜːs‖wɜːrs/, **worst** /wɜːst‖wɜːrst/ **1** sick **2** bad: *ill luck* ♦ adv **1** badly: *The child was ill-treated.* **2** not enough: *ill fed* ♦ n bad thing: *the social ills of poverty and unemployment*

I'll /aɪl/ short for: I will or I shall

ill-ad·vised /ˌ·····◁/ adj unwise

ill-bred /ˌ· '·◁/ adj badly behaved

il·le·gal /ɪˈliːɡəl/ adj against the law ~**ly** adv ~**ity** /ɪˈɡælɪti/ n [C;U]

il·le·gi·ble /ɪˈledʒəbəl/ adj impossible to read

il·le·git·i·mate /ˌɪlɪˈdʒɪtəmət/ adj **1** born to unmarried parents **2** against the rules ~**ly** adv

ill-got·ten /ˌ· '··◁/ adj dishonestly obtained

il·li·cit /ɪˈlɪsɪt/ adj against the law or the rules ~**ly** adv

il·lit·e·rate /ɪˈlɪtərət/ adj unable to read or write ~**racy** n [U]

ill-na·tured /ˌ· '···◁/ adj bad-tempered

ill·ness /ˈɪlnəs/ n [C;U] disease

il·lo·gi·cal /ɪˈlɒdʒɪkəl‖ɪˈlɑː-/ adj against LOGIC; not sensible ~**ly** /-kli/ adv

il·lu·mi·nate /ɪˈluːməneɪt, ɪˈljuː-‖ɪˈluː-/ vt **1** give light to **2** decorate with lights **3** (esp. in former times) decorate with gold and bright colours ~**nating** adj helping to explain: *illuminating remark* ~**nation** /ɪˌluːməˈneɪʃən, ɪˌljuː-‖ɪˌluː-/ n [U] act of illuminating or state of being illuminated ~**nations** n [P] coloured lights to decorate a town

il·lu·sion /ɪˈluːʒən/ n something seen wrongly; false idea ~**sory** /ɪˈluːsəri/ adj fml unreal

il·lus·trate /ˈɪləstreɪt/ vt **1** add pictures to **2** explain by giving examples ~**trator** n person who draws pictures for a book, etc. ~**tration** /ˌɪləˈstreɪʃən/ n **1** [C] picture **2** [C] example **3** [U] act of illustrating ~**trative** /ˈɪləstreɪtɪv, -strət-‖ɪˈlʌstrətɪv/ adj used as an example

il·lus·tri·ous /ɪˈlʌstriəs/ adj famous

I'm /aɪm/ short for: I am

im·age /ˈɪmɪdʒ/ n **1** picture in the mind, or seen in a mirror **2** general opinion about a person, etc.. that has been formed or intentionally created in people's minds **3** copy; likeness: *He's the image of his father.* **4** IDOL (1) ~**ry** n [U] METAPHORs, etc., in literature

i·ma·gi·na·ry /ɪˈmædʒənəri‖-dʒəneri/ adj unreal

i·ma·gine /ɪˈmædʒən/ vt **1** form (an idea) in the mind: *imagine a world without cars* **2** believe; suppose: *I imagine they've forgotten.* ~**ginable** adj that can be imagined ~**ginative** adj good at imagining ~**gination**

/ɪˌmædʒəˈneɪʃən/ n **1** [C;U] ability to imagine **2** [U] something only imagined

im·bal·ance /ɪmˈbæləns/ n lack of balance or equality

im·be·cile /ˈɪmbəsiːl‖-səl/ n IDIOT ~**cility** /ˌɪmbəˈsɪlɪti/ n **1** [U] being an imbecile **2** [C] foolish act

im·bibe /ɪmˈbaɪb/ vi/t fml drink or take in

im·bro·gli·o /ɪmˈbrəʊliəʊ/ n -os confused situation

im·bue /ɪmˈbjuː/ v imbue with phr vt fill with (a feeling, etc.)

im·i·tate /ˈɪmɪteɪt/ vt **1** copy **2** take as an example ~**tator** n ~**tative** /-tətɪv‖-teɪtɪv/ adj following an example; not inventive ~**tation** /ˌɪmɪˈteɪʃən/ n **1** [C;U] act or act of imitating **2** [C] copy of the real thing

im·mac·u·late /ɪˈmækj ᵿ lət/ adj clean; pure ~**ly** adv

im·ma·te·ri·al /ˌɪməˈtɪəriəl/ adj **1** unimportant **2** without physical substance

im·ma·ture /ˌɪməˈtʃʊə‖-ˈtjʊər/ adj not fully formed or developed ~**turity** n [U]

im·mea·su·ra·ble /ɪˈmeʒərəbəl/ adj too big to be measured ~**bly** adv

im·me·di·ate /ɪˈmiːdiət/ adj **1** done or needed at once: *an immediate reply* **2** nearest: *the immediate future* ~**ly** adv **1** at once **2** with nothing between: *immediately in front* ~**ly** conj as soon as: *Immediately your application is accepted, you will be informed* ~**acy** n [U] nearness or urgent presence of something

im·me·mo·ri·al /ˌɪməˈmɔːriəl/ adj see TIME IMMEMORIAL

im·mense /ɪˈmens/ adj very large ~**ly** adv very much **immensity** n [U]

im·merse /ɪˈmɜːs‖-ɜːrs/ vt put deep into liquid: (fig.) *immersed in my work* **immersion** /ɪˈmɜːʃən, -ʒən‖-ɜːr-/ n [U]

immersion heat·er /·'··· ,··/ n electric water heater in a TANK

im·mi·grate /ˈɪmɪɡreɪt/ vi come to live in a country ~**grant** n person who does this ~**gration** /ˌɪmɪˈɡreɪʃən/ n [U]

im·mi·nent /ˈɪmɪnənt/ adj going to happen soon ~**ly** adv

im·mo·bile /ɪˈməʊbaɪl‖-bəl/ adj unmoving; unable to move ~**bility** /ˌɪməʊˈbɪlɪti/ n [U] ~**bilize** /ɪˈməʊbɪlaɪz/ vt make immobile

im·mor·al /ɪˈmɒrəl‖ɪˈmɔːr-/ adj **1** not good or right **2** sexually improper ~**ity** /ˌɪməˈrælɪti/ n [C;U]

im·mor·tal /ɪˈmɔːtl‖-ɔːr-/ adj living or remembered for ever ♦ n immortal being ~**ize** vt give endless life or fame to ~**ity** /ˌɪmɔːˈtælɪti‖-ɔːr-/ n endless life

im·mune /ɪˈmjuːn/ *adj* unable to be harmed; protected **immunity** *n* [U]
 immunize /ˈɪmjʊˌnaɪz/ *vt* protect from disease

immune sys·tem /·'·· ,·'·/ *n* bodily system that fights substances that cause disease

imp /ɪmp/ *n* **1** little devil **2** troublesome child ~**ish** *adj*

im·pact /ˈɪmpækt/ *n* **1** force of one object hitting another **2** influence; effect **3** on impact at the moment of hitting

im·pair /ɪmˈpeəʳ/ *vt* spoil; weaken

im·pale /ɪmˈpeɪl/ *vt* run something sharp through: *impaled on the spikes*

im·pal·pa·ble /ɪmˈpælpəbəl/ *adj fml* not easily felt or understood

im·part /ɪmˈpɑːt‖-ɑːrt/ *vt fml* give (knowledge, etc.)

im·par·tial /ɪmˈpɑːʃəl‖-ɑːr-/ *adj* fair; just ~**ly** *adv* ~**ity** /ɪm,pɑːʃiˈælɪti‖-ɑːr-/ *n* [U]

im·pass·a·ble /ɪmˈpɑːsəbəl‖ɪmˈpæ-/ *adj* (of roads, etc.) impossible to travel over

im·passe /æmˈpɑːs‖ˈɪmpæs/ *n* point where further movement is blocked

im·pas·sioned /ɪmˈpæʃənd/ *adj* full of deep feelings: *impassioned speech*

im·pas·sive /ɪmˈpæsɪv/ *adj* showing no feelings; calm ~**ly** *adv*

im·pa·tient /ɪmˈpeɪʃənt/ *adj* **1** not patient **2** eager: *impatient to go* ~**ly** *adv* ~**ience** *n* [U]

im·peach /ɪmˈpiːtʃ/ *vt* charge with a crime against the state ~**ment** *n* [C;U]

im·pec·ca·ble /ɪmˈpekəbəl/ *adj* faultless –**bly** *adv*

im·pe·cu·ni·ous /ˌɪmpɪˈkjuːniəs/ *adj fml* without money; poor

im·pede /ɪmˈpiːd/ *vt* get in the way of

im·ped·i·ment /ɪmˈpedɪmənt/ *n* something that makes action difficult or impossible: *a speech impediment*

im·pel /ɪmˈpel/ *vt* **-ll-** (of an idea, etc.) cause (someone) to act

im·pend·ing /ɪmˈpendɪŋ/ *adj* (esp. of something bad) about to happen

im·pen·e·tra·ble /ɪmˈpenɪtrəbəl/ *adj* **1** that cannot be gone through **2** impossible to understand

im·per·a·tive /ɪmˈperətɪv/ *adj* urgent; that must be done ◆ *n* gram verb form expressing a command (e.g. 'Come!') ~**ly** *adv*

im·per·fect /ɪmˈpɜːfɪkt‖-ɜːr-/ *adj* not perfect ◆ *n gram* verb form showing incomplete action in the past (e.g. *was walking*) ~**ly** *adv* ~**ion** /ˌɪmpəˈfekʃən‖-pər-/ *n* [C;U] **1** [U] imperfect state **2** [C] fault

im·pe·ri·al /ɪmˈpɪəriəl/ *adj* of an EMPIRE or its ruler ~**ly** *adv* ~**ism** *n* [U] (belief in) the making of an EMPIRE ~**ist** *n, adj*

im·per·il /ɪmˈperəl/ *vt* **-ll-** *BrE* ‖ **-l-** *AmE* put in danger

im·pe·ri·ous /ɪmˈpɪəriəs/ *adj fml* (too) commanding; expecting obedience from others

im·per·son·al /ɪmˈpɜːsənəl‖-ɜːr-/ *adj* without personal feelings: *large impersonal organizations* ~**ly** *adv*

im·per·so·nate /ɪmˈpɜːsəneɪt‖-ɜːr-/ *vt* pretend to be (another person) –**nation** /ɪm,pɜːsəˈneɪʃən‖-,pɜːr-/ *n* [C;U]

im·per·ti·nent /ɪmˈpɜːtɪnənt‖-ɜːr-/ *adj* not properly respectful ~**ly** *adv* –**nence** *n* [U]

im·per·tur·ba·ble /ˌɪmpəˈtɜːbəbəl‖-pərˈtɜːr-/ *adj* unworried; calm –**bly** *adv*

im·per·vi·ous /ɪmˈpɜːviəs‖-ɜːr-/ *adj* **1** not letting water, etc., through **2** not easily influenced: *impervious to criticism*

im·pet·u·ous /ɪmˈpetʃuəs/ *adj* acting quickly but without thought ~**ly** *adv* –**osity** /ɪm,petʃuˈɒsɪti‖-ˈɑːs-/ *n* [U]

im·pe·tus /ˈɪmpɪtəs/ *n* **1** force of something moving **2** [S;U] STIMULUS: *a fresh impetus to industry*

im·pinge /ɪmˈpɪndʒ/ *v* **impinge on/upon** *phr vt* have an effect on

im·pi·ous /ˈɪmpiəs/ *adj* without respect for religion ~**ly** *adv*

im·plac·a·ble /ɪmˈplækəbəl/ *adj* impossible to satisfy or PLACATE

im·plant /ɪmˈplɑːnt‖ɪmˈplænt/ *vt* fix deeply into

im·plau·si·ble /ɪmˈplɔːzəbəl/ *adj* seeming to be untrue or unlikely

im·ple·ment¹ /ˈɪmplɪmənt/ *n* tool or instrument

im·ple·ment² /ˈɪmplɪment/ *vt* carry out (plans, etc.)

im·pli·cate /ˈɪmplɪkeɪt/ *vt fml* show (someone) to be concerned: *a letter implicating him in the crime*

im·pli·ca·tion /ˌɪmplɪˈkeɪʃən/ *n* **1** [C;U] (example of) the act of implying **2** [C] possible later effect of something **3** [U] act of implicating

im·plic·it /ɪmˈplɪsɪt/ *adj* **1** meant though not expressed **2** unquestioning: *implicit trust* ~**ly** *adv*

im·plore /ɪmˈplɔːʳ/ *vt* beg; request strongly: *implore them to go*

im·ply /ɪmˈplaɪ/ *vt* **1** express indirectly: *He implied that he had not yet made a decision* **2** make necessary

im·pon·de·ra·ble /ɪmˈpɒndərəbəl‖-ˈpɑːn-/ *n, adj* (thing) whose effects cannot be measured exactly

im·port¹ /ɪmˈpɔːt‖-ɔːrt/ *vt* bring in (goods) from abroad ~**er** *n* ~**ation** /ˌɪmpɔːˈteɪʃən‖-pɔːr-/ *n* [C;U]

im·port² /ˈɪmpɔːt‖-ɔːrt/ *n* **1** [C] something imported **2** [U] *fml* importance

im-por-tant /ɪmˈpɔːtənt‖-ɔːr-/ adj mattering very much ~**ly** adv –**tance** n [U]

im-pose /ɪmˈpəʊz/ v 1 vt establish (a tax, etc.) 2 vt force the acceptance of 3 vi take unfair advantage **imposing** adj large and IMPRESSIVE **imposition** /ˌɪmpəˈzɪʃən/ n [C;U] act of imposing

im-pos-si-ble /ɪmˈpɒsɪbəl‖ɪmˈpɑː-/ adj 1 not possible 2 hard to bear: make life impossible –**bly** adv –**bility** /ɪmˌpɒsɪˈbɪlɪti‖ɪmˌpɑː-/ n [U]

im-pos-tor /ɪmˈpɒstər‖ɪmˈpɑːs-/ n someone who deceives by pretending to be someone else

im-po-tent /ˈɪmpətənt/ adj 1 powerless 2 (of a man) unable to perform the sex act ~**ly** adv –**tence** n [U]

im-pound /ɪmˈpaʊnd/ vt take away officially

im-pov-e-rish /ɪmˈpɒvərɪʃ‖ɪmˈpɑː-/ vt make poor

im-prac-ti-ca-ble /ɪmˈpræktɪkəbəl/ adj that cannot be used in practice

im-prac-ti-cal /ɪmˈpræktɪkəl/ adj not practical; not sensible or reasonable

im-preg-na-ble /ɪmˈpregnəbəl/ adj impossible to enter by attack

im-preg-nate /ˈɪmpregneɪt‖ɪmˈpreg-/ v 1 make wet; SATURATE: cloth impregnated with polish 2 fml make PREGNANT

im-pre-sa-ri-o /ˌɪmprɪˈsɑːriəʊ/ n -os person who arranges theatre or concert performances

im-press /ɪmˈpres/ vt 1 fill with admiration 2 tell (someone) that something matters: impress on them that they must work ~**ive** adj causing admiration ~**ively** adv ~**ion** /-ˈpreʃən/ n 1 effect produced on the mind 2 mark left by pressing 3 attempt to copy a person's appearance or behaviour, esp. in theatre, etc. ~**ionable** adj easily influenced

im-print[1] /ɪmˈprɪnt/ vt press (a mark) on

im-print[2] /ˈɪmprɪnt/ n 1 mark left on or in something 2 name of the PUBLISHER as it appears on a book

im-pris-on /ɪmˈprɪzən/ vt put in prison ~**ment** n [U]

im-prob-a-ble /ɪmˈprɒbəbəl‖-ˈprɑː-/ adj unlikely –**bly** adv –**bility** /ɪmˌprɒbəˈbɪlɪti‖-ˌprɑː-/ n [C;U]

im-promp-tu /ɪmˈprɒmptjuː‖ ɪmˈprɑːmptuː/ adj, adv without preparation

im-prop-er /ɪmˈprɒpər‖-ˈprɑː-/ adj 1 not suitable or correct 2 socially unacceptable ~**ly** adv

im-prove /ɪmˈpruːv/ vi/t make or become better ~**ment** n [C;U] (sign of) improving

im-pro-vise /ˈɪmprəvaɪz/ vi/t 1 do (something one has not prepared for) 2 invent (music) while one plays

–**visation** /ˌɪmprəvaɪˈzeɪʃən‖-prəvə-/ n [C;U]

im-pu-dent /ˈɪmpjʊdənt/ adj shamelessly disrespectful ~**ly** adv –**dence** n [U]

im-pulse /ˈɪmpʌls/ n 1 [C;U] sudden urge 2 sudden force: nerve impulse **impulsive** /ɪmˈpʌlsɪv/ adj acting on IMPULSE (1)

im-pu-ni-ty /ɪmˈpjuːnɪti/ n [U] with impunity without being punished

im-pure /ɪmˈpjʊər/ adj 1 mixed with something else 2 morally bad **impurity** n [C;U]

in[1] /ɪn/ prep 1 contained or surrounded by: in a box‖in a field‖in France 2 (of time) **a** during: in the summer **b** at the end of: finish in 5 minutes 3 included as part of: people in a story 4 wearing: the girl in red 5 using: write in pencil‖pay in dollars 6 (shows an area of employment): a job in insurance 7 (shows direction): the sun in my eyes 8 (shows the way something is done or happens): in public‖in a hurry‖in danger 9 divided or arranged: in rows 10 for each: a slope of 1 in 3 11 with regard to: weak in judgment 12 as a/an: What did you give him in return? 13 **in all** as the total

in[2] adv 1 (in order to be) contained or surrounded; away from the outside: Open the bag and put the money in. 2 towards or at home or the usual place: Let's stay in tonight. 3 into a surface: knock a nail in 4 from lots of people or places: Letters came pouring in. 5 so as to be added: Fill in your name. 6 (in sport) **a** having a turn to BAT **b** (of a ball) inside the line 7 fashionable: Long hair is in again. 8 so as to have a position of power: The Nationalist Party are sure to get in. 9 **be in for** be about to have (esp. something bad) 10 **be in on** take part in 11 **be in with** infml be friendly with

in[3] adj 1 directed inwards: a letter in my in tray 2 infml fashionable: the in place to go 3 shared by only a few favoured people: an in joke

in[4] n **the ins and outs (of something)** infml the details (of a difficult situation, etc.)

in-a-bil-i-ty /ˌɪnəˈbɪlɪti/ n [S;U] lack of power or skill

in-ac-ces-si-ble /ˌɪnəkˈsesɪbəl/ adj impossible to reach

in-ac-cu-rate /ɪnˈækjʊrɪt/ adj not correct ~**ly** adv –**racy** n [C;U]

in-ad-e-quate /ɪnˈædɪkwɪt/ adj not good enough ~**ly** adv

in-ad-ver-tent /ˌɪnədˈvɜːtənt‖-ɜːr-/ adj done by accident ~**ly** adv

in-a-li-e-na-ble /ɪnˈeɪliənəbəl/ adj fml (of rights, etc.) that cannot be taken away

i-nane /ɪˈneɪn/ adj stupid ~ly adv **inanity** /ɪˈnænəti/ n [C;U]

in-an-i-mate /ɪnˈænəmət/ adj not living: *Stones are inanimate.*

in-ap-pro-pri-ate /ˌɪnəˈprəʊpri-ət/ adj not suitable ~ly adv ~ness n [U]

in-ar-tic-u-late /ˌɪnɑːˈtɪkjʊlɪt‖-ɑːr-/ adj 1 (of speech) not clear 2 (of people) not speaking clearly ~ly adv

in-as-much as /ˌɪnəzˈmʌtʃ əz/ conj fml to the degree that; because

in-au-gu-rate /ɪˈnɔːgjʊreɪt/ vt 1 start or introduce with a special ceremony 2 be the beginning of (a period of time) ~ral adj: *his inaugural speech* ~ration /ɪˌnɔːgjʊˈreɪʃən/ n [C;U]

in-board /ˈɪnbɔːd‖-bɔːrd/ adj inside a boat

in-born /ˌɪnˈbɔːn◂‖-ɔːrn/ adj present from one's birth

in-bred /ˌɪnˈbred◂/ adj 1 inborn 2 produced by inbreeding

in-breed-ing /ˈɪnbriːdɪŋ/ n [U] breeding between closely related family members

in-built /ˌɪnˈbɪlt◂/ adj INHERENT

Inc /ɪŋk/ adj incorporated; (of a US firm) formed into a legal CORPORATION

in-cal-cu-la-ble /ɪnˈkælkjʊləbəl/ adj too great to be counted –bly adv

in-can-des-cent /ˌɪnkænˈdesənt‖-kən-/ adj shining brightly when heated –cence n [U]

in-can-ta-tion /ˌɪnkænˈteɪʃən/ n [C;U] words used in magic

in-ca-pac-i-tate /ˌɪnkəˈpæsəteɪt/ vt make unable (to do something) –ty n [S;U] lack of ability

in-car-ce-rate /ɪnˈkɑːsəreɪt‖-ɑːr-/ vt fml imprison –ration /ɪnˌkɑːsəˈreɪʃən‖-ɑːr-/ n [U]

in-car-nate /ɪnˈkɑːnət‖-ɑːr-/ adj in human form: *the devil incarnate* –nation /ˌɪnkɑːˈneɪʃən‖-ɑːr-/ n 1 [U] state of being incarnate 2 [C] any of a person's many lives 3 [the] (cap.) the coming of God to Earth in the body of Jesus Christ

in-cen-di-a-ry /ɪnˈsendiəri‖-dieri/ adj 1 causing fires: *incendiary bomb* 2 causing violence: *incendiary speech*

in-cense /ˈɪnsens/ n [U] substance burnt to make a sweet smell

in-censed /ɪnˈsenst/ adj fml extremely angry

in-cen-tive /ɪnˈsentɪv/ n [C;U] encouragement to get things done

in-cep-tion /ɪnˈsepʃən/ n fml beginning

in-ces-sant /ɪnˈsesənt/ adj (of something bad) never stopping ~ly adv

in-cest /ˈɪnsest/ n [U] sexual relationship between close relatives ~uous /ɪnˈsestʃuəs/ adj

inch /ɪntʃ/ n 1 a measure of length equal to 2.54 centimetres 2 small

amount 3 **every inch** completely 4 **within an inch of** very near ♦ vi/t move slowly

in-ci-dence /ˈɪnsədəns/ n [S] rate of happening: *a high incidence of disease*

in-ci-dent /ˈɪnsədənt/ n 1 event, esp. one that is unusual 2 event that includes or leads to violence, danger, or serious disagreement: *The spy scandal caused a diplomatic incident.*

in-ci-dent-al /ˌɪnsəˈdentl/ adj happening in connection with something else: *incidental expenses* ♦ n something (esp. a fact or detail) that is unimportant ~ally adv (used to introduce a new subject in talking)

in-cin-e-rate /ɪnˈsɪnəreɪt/ vt fml burn (unwanted things) –rator n machine for burning things

in-cip-i-ent /ɪnˈsɪpiənt/ adj fml at an early stage

in-cise /ɪnˈsaɪz/ vt cut into **incisor** n front cutting tooth **incisive** adj going directly to the point: *incisive comments* **incision** /ɪnˈsɪʒən/ n [C;U] (act of making) a cut, done with a special tool

in-cite /ɪnˈsaɪt/ vt encourage (violence, or people to be violent) ~ment n [U]

in-cline¹ /ɪnˈklaɪn/ v 1 vt encourage to feel or think 2 vi tend: *I incline to take the opposite view.* 3 vi/t slope 4 vt (cause to) move downward: *He inclined his head (in greeting).* **inclined** adj tending: *The handle is inclined to stick.* **inclination** /ˌɪnkləˈneɪʃən/ n 1 [C;U] liking 2 [C] tendency 3 [C] act of inclining

in-cline² /ˈɪnklaɪn/ n slope

in-clude /ɪnˈkluːd/ vt 1 have as a part 2 put in with something else **inclusion** /ɪnˈkluːʒən/ n [U] **inclusive** /-ˈkluːsɪv/ adj including everything

in-cog-ni-to /ˌɪnkɒgˈniːtəʊ‖ˌɪnkɑːg-/ adj, adv taking another name

in-co-her-ent /ˌɪnkəʊˈhɪərənt/ adj not clearly expressed ~ly adv –ence n [U]

in-come /ˈɪŋkʌm, ˈɪn-/ n money received regularly

income tax /ˈ·· ·/ n tax on one's income

in-com-ing /ˈɪnkʌmɪŋ/ adj coming in, starting a period in office

in-com-mu-ni-ca-do /ˌɪnkəmjuːnɪˈkɑːdəʊ/ adv (of people) prevented from giving or receiving messages

in-com-pa-ra-ble /ɪnˈkɒmpərəbəl‖-ˈkɑːm-/ adj unequalled; very great –bly adv

in-com-pat-i-ble /ˌɪnkəmˈpætəbəl/ adj not suitable to be together –bility /ˌɪnkəmpætəˈbɪləti/ n [U]

in-com-pe-tent /ɪnˈkɒmpətənt‖-ˈkɑːm-/ adj not skilful ~ly adv –tence n [U]

in·com·pre·hen·si·ble /ˌɪnˌkɒmprɪ'hensəbəl‖-, kɑːm-/ *adj* impossible to understand **-sion** /'henʃən-/ *n* [U] failure to understand **-bility** /ɪnˌkɒmprɪhensə'bɪlɪti‖-, kɑːm-/ *n* [U]

in·con·cei·va·ble /ˌɪnkən'siːvəbəl/ *adj* impossible to imagine

in·con·gru·ous /ɪn'kɒŋgruəs‖-'kɑːŋ-/ *adj* out of place **-ity** /ˌɪnkən'gruːɪti/ *n* [C;U]

in·con·se·quen·tial /ɪnˌkɒnsɪ-'kwenʃəl‖-, kɑːn-/ *adj* 1 unimportant 2 not RELEVANT **~ly** *adv*

in·con·sid·er·ate /ˌɪnkən'sɪdərɪt/ *adj* not thinking of other people **~ly** *adv*

in·con·so·la·ble /ˌɪnkən'səʊləbəl/ *adj* too sad to be comforted **-bly** *adv*

in·con·ti·nent /ɪn'kɒntɪnənt‖-'kɑːn-/ *adj* unable to control one's bowels and BLADDER **-nence** *n* [U]

in·con·tro·vert·i·ble /ɪnˌkɒntrə-'vɜːtəbəl‖ɪnˌkɑːntrə'vɜːr-/ *adj* *fml* which cannot be disproved **-bly** *adv*

in·con·ve·ni·ence /ˌɪnkən'viːniəns/ *n* (cause of) state of difficulty when things do not suit one ♦ *vt* cause inconvenience to **-ent** *adj* causing inconvenience **-ently** *adv*

in·cor·po·rate /ɪn'kɔːpəreɪt‖-ɔːr-/ *vt* include in something larger **-ration** /ɪnˌkɔːpə'reɪʃən‖-ɔːr-/ *n* [U]

in·cor·ri·gi·ble /ɪn'kɒrədʒəbəl‖-'kɔːr-/ *adj* bad, and impossible to improve **-bly** *adv*

in·crease /ɪn'kriːs/ *vi/t* (cause to) become larger **increasingly** *adv* more and more **increase** /'ɪŋkriːs/ *n* rise in amount, numbers, or degree

in·cred·i·ble /ɪn'kredəbəl/ *adj* 1 unbelievable 2 *infml* wonderful **-bly** *adv*

in·cred·u·lous /ɪn'kredjʊləs‖-dʒə-/ *adj* not believing **~ly** *adv* **-lity** /ˌɪnkrɪ'djuːlɪti‖-'duː-/ *n* [U] disbelief

in·cre·ment /'ɪŋkrɪmənt/ *n* increase in money or value

in·crim·i·nate /ɪn'krɪmɪneɪt/ *vt* cause (someone) to seem guilty of a crime or fault

in·cu·bate /'ɪŋkjʊbeɪt/ *vt* keep (eggs) warm until they HATCH **-bator** *n* apparatus for keeping eggs warm, or for keeping PREMATURE babies alive **-bation** /ˌɪŋkjʊ'beɪʃən/ *n* [U] 1 act of incubating 2 period between infection and the appearance of a disease

in·cul·cate /'ɪŋkʌlkeɪt‖ɪn'kʌl-/ *vt* fix (ideas) in someone's mind

in·cum·bent /ɪn'kʌmbənt/ *adj* be **incumbent on** *fml* be the moral duty of ♦ *n* person holding a (political) office

in·cur /ɪn'kɜːr/ *vt* **-rr-** bring (esp. something bad) on oneself: *incur expenses*

in·cur·a·ble /ɪn'kjʊərəbəl/ *adj* that cannot be cured **-bly** *adv*

in·cur·sion /ɪn'kɜːʃən, -ʒən‖ɪn'kɜːrʒən/ *n* *fml* sudden entrance; INVASION

in·debt·ed /ɪn'detɪd/ *adj* grateful **~ness** *n* [U]

in·de·cent /ɪn'diːsənt/ *adj* 1 sexually offensive 2 unsuitable **~ly** *adv* **-cency** *n* [U]

in·de·ci·sion /ˌɪndɪ'sɪʒən/ *n* [U] inability to decide

in·deed /ɪn'diːd/ *adv* 1 certainly; really: *'Did you see him?' 'Indeed I did.'* 2 (used with **very** to make the meaning stronger): *It's very cold indeed.* 3 (showing surprise): *Did he, indeed?*

in·de·fat·i·ga·ble /ˌɪndɪ'fætɪgəbəl/ *adj* tireless **-bly** *adv*

in·de·fen·si·ble /ˌɪndɪ'fensəbəl/ *adj* that cannot be defended: *indefensible behaviour*

in·de·fi·na·ble /ˌɪndɪ'faɪnəbəl/ *adj* impossible to describe **-bly** *adv*

in·def·i·nite /ɪn'defənɪt/ *adj* not clear or fixed **~ly** *adv* for an unlimited period

indefinite ar·ti·cle /·ˌ···· '···/ *n* (in English) A or AN

in·del·i·ble /ɪn'deləbəl/ *adj* that cannot be rubbed out **-bly** *adv*

in·del·i·cate /ɪn'delɪkɪt/ *adj* not polite or modest **~ly** *adv* **-cacy** *n* [U]

in·dem·ni·fy /ɪn'demnɪfaɪ/ *vt* pay (someone) in case of loss **-nity** *n* [C;U] protection against loss; payment for loss

in·dent /ɪn'dent/ *vi/t* start (a line of writing) further into the page than the others **~ation** /ˌɪnden'teɪʃən/ *n* 1 [C;U] (act of making) a space at the beginning of a line of writing 2 space pointing inwards: *the indentations of a coastline*

in·de·pen·dent /ˌɪndɪ'pendənt◂/ *adj* 1 self-governing 2 not depending on advice, money, etc., from others ♦ *n* (*often cap.*) person who does not always favour the same political party **~ly** *adv* **-dence** *n* [U]

in-depth /'·◂·/ *adj* very thorough

in·de·scri·ba·ble /ˌɪndɪs'kraɪbəbəl/ *adj* that cannot be described **-bly** *adv*

in·de·struc·ti·ble /ˌɪndɪ'strʌktəbəl/ *adj* too strong to be destroyed

in·de·ter·mi·nate /ˌɪndɪ'tɜːmɪnɪt‖-ɜːr-/ *adj* not fixed as one thing or another

in·dex /'ɪndeks/ *n* **-dexes** or **-dices** /-dɪsiːz/ 1 **a** alphabetical list of subjects mentioned in a book **b** also **card index** — similar alphabetical list, e.g. of books and writers that can be found in a library, written on separate cards 2 **a** sign by which something can be measured **b** system of comparing prices with their former level: *the cost of living index* ♦ *vt* make, include in, or provide with an INDEX (1)

index fin·ger /'·· ,··/ *n* FOREFINGER

In·di·an /'ɪndɪən/ *n, adj* **1** (person) from India **2** (member) of the original peoples of North, South, or Central America except the INUIT

in·di·cate /'ɪndɪkeɪt/ *vt* **1** point at; show **2** *vi/t* show (the direction in which one is turning in a vehicle) by hand signals, lights, etc. —**cator** *n* **1** flashing light on a car that shows which way it will turn **2** needle or pointer showing measure-ment—**cation** /,ɪndɪ'keɪʃən/ *n* [C;U] sign or suggestion indicating something —**cative** /ɪn'dɪkətɪv/ *adj* showing

in·di·ces /'ɪndɪsiːz/ *n pl.* of INDEX

in·dict /ɪn'daɪt/ *vt* charge officially with a crime ~**able** *adj* for which one can be indicted: *indictable offence* ~**ment** *n* [C;U]

in·dif·fer·ent /ɪn'dɪfərənt/ *adj* **1** not interested **2** not very good ~**ly** *adv* —**ence** *n* [U]

in·di·ge·nous /ɪn'dɪdʒənəs/ *adj* NATIVE to a place: *indigenous flowers*

in·di·ges·tion /,ɪndɪ'dʒestʃən/ *n* [U] illness from not being able to DIGEST food

in·dig·nant /ɪn'dɪgnənt/ *adj* angry, esp. at something unjust ~**ly** *adv* —**nation** /,ɪndɪg'neɪʃən/ *n* [U] indignant feeling

in·dig·ni·ty /ɪn'dɪgnɪti/ *n* [C;U] treatment that makes one feel ashamed

in·di·rect /,ɪndɪ'rekt/ *adj* **1** not straight; not directly connected to: *indirect route* | *indirect result* **2** (of taxes) paid by increasing the cost of goods or services **3** meaning something which is not directly mentioned: *an indirect answer* ~**ly** *adv*

indirect ob·ject /,··· '··/ *n* person or thing that the DIRECT OBJECT is given to, made for, done to, etc.: *In 'I asked him a question', 'him' is the indirect object.*

indirect speech /,··· '·/ *n* [U] *gram* speech reported without repeating the actual words (e.g. *She said, 'I'm coming.'* becomes *She said she was coming.*)

in·dis·creet /,ɪndɪ'skriːt/ *adj* not acting carefully or politely ~**ly** *adv* —**cre·tion** /-'skreʃən/ *n* **1** [U] state or quality of being indiscreet **2** [C] indiscreet act: *youthful indiscretions*

in·dis·crim·i·nate /,ɪndɪ'skrɪmɪnət/ *adj* not choosing or chosen carefully ~**ly** *adv*

in·di·spen·sa·ble /,ɪndɪ'spensəbl/ *adj* necessary

in·dis·posed /,ɪndɪ'spəʊzd/ *adj fml* **1** not very well **2** unwilling

in·dis·pu·ta·ble /,ɪndɪ'spjuːtəbl/ *adj* beyond doubt: *indisputable proof* —**bly** *adv*

in·dis·tin·guish·a·ble /,ɪndɪ'stɪŋgwɪʃəbl/ *adj* impossible to tell apart: *indistinguishable from silk*

in·di·vid·u·al /,ɪndɪ'vɪdʒuəl/ *adj* **1** single; separate **2** (of a manner, style, or way of doing things) particular to a person, thing, etc. ♦ *n* single person (in a group) ~**ly** *adv* separately ~**ism** *n* [U] belief in the rights of each person in society ~**ist** *n, adj* (person) independent and unlike other people ~**istic** /,ɪndɪ,vɪdʒuə'lɪstɪk/ *adj* ~**ity** /,ɪndɪ,vɪdʒu'ælɪti/ *n* [U] qualities that make a person unusual

in·doc·tri·nate /ɪn'dɒktrɪneɪt‖ɪn'dɑː-/ *vt* train to accept ideas without question —**nation** /ɪn,dɒktrɪ'neɪʃən‖-,dɑːk-/ *n* [U]

in·do·lent /'ɪndələnt/ *adj fml* lazy —**lence** *n* [U]

in·dom·i·ta·ble /ɪn'dɒmɪtəbl‖ɪn'dɑː-/ *adj* too strong to be discouraged

in·door /'ɪndɔːr/ *adj* inside a building **indoors** *adv*

in·du·bi·ta·ble /ɪn'djuːbɪtəbl‖ɪn'duː-/ *adj fml* unquestionable —**bly** *adv*

in·duce /ɪn'djuːs‖ɪn'duːs/ *vt* **1** persuade **2** cause; produce —**ment** *n* [C;U] (something, esp. money, which provides) encouragement to do something

in·duc·tion /ɪn'dʌkʃən/ *n* **1** [U] act or ceremony of introducing a person to a new job, organization, etc. **2** [C;U] (action of causing) birth of a child which has been hastened by the use of drugs **3** [U] way of reasoning using known facts to produce general laws

in·dulge /ɪn'dʌldʒ/ *v* **1** *vt* allow to do or have something nice **2** *vi* allow oneself pleasure: *indulge in a cigar* **indul·gence** *n* [U] indulging **2** [C] something in which one indulges **indulgent** *adj* (too) kind

in·dus·tri·al /ɪn'dʌstrɪəl/ *adj* of or having INDUSTRY (1) ~**ly** *adv* ~**ism** *n* [U] system in which industries are important ~**ist** *n* owner or manager of an industry ~**ize** *vi/t* (cause to) become industrially developed

industrial action /·,··· '··/ *n* [U] *esp. BrE* action by workers to try to make their employers agree to their demands

industrial es·tate /·,··· ·'·/ *n BrE* area where factories are built

in·dus·tri·ous /ɪn'dʌstrɪəs/ *adj* hard-working —**ly** *adv*

in·dus·try /'ɪndəstri/ *n* **1** [C;U] (branch of) the production of goods for sale: *the clothing industry* **2** [U] continual hard work

i·ne·bri·at·ed /ɪˈniːbrɪeɪtəd/ adj fml drunk

in·ed·i·ble /ɪnˈedəbəl/ adj unsuitable for eating

in·ef·fec·tive /ˌɪnəˈfektɪv/ adj unable to produce the right results ~**ly** adv ~**ness** n [U]

in·ef·fec·tu·al /ˌɪnəˈfektʃuəl/ adj which does not give a good enough effect, or who is not able to get things done ~**ly** adv

in·ef·fi·cient /ˌɪnəˈfɪʃənt/ adj not working well ~**ly** adv –**ciency** n [U]

in·el·i·gi·ble /ɪnˈelədʒəbəl/ adj not fulfilling the conditions –**bility** /ɪnˌelədʒəˈbɪləti/ n [U]

in·ept /ɪˈnept/ adj 1 foolishly unsuitable 2 totally unable to do things ~**ly** adv ~**itude** n [C;U]

in·e·qual·i·ty /ˌɪnɪˈkwɒləti/‖-ˈkwɑː-/ n [C;U] lack of fairness or equality

in·ert /ɪˈnɜːt/‖-ɜːrt/ adj 1 unable to move 2 not acting chemically: inert gases

in·er·tia /ɪˈnɜːʃə/‖-ɜːr-/ n [U] 1 force that keeps a thing in the same state until pushed 2 laziness

in·es·ca·pa·ble /ˌɪnɪˈskeɪpəbəl/ adj unavoidable

in·es·ti·ma·ble /ɪnˈestəməbəl/ adj fml too good to be measured –**bly** adv

in·ev·i·ta·ble /ɪˈnevətəbəl/ adj 1 unavoidable 2 infml expected and familiar: The head teacher made his inevitable joke about school food. –**bly** adv –**bility** /ɪˌnevətəˈbɪləti/ n [U]

in·ex·cu·sa·ble /ˌɪnɪkˈskjuːzəbəl/ adj unforgivable –**bly** adv

in·ex·o·ra·ble /ɪnˈeksərəbəl/ adj fml impossible to change or prevent –**bly** adv

in·ex·pli·ca·ble /ˌɪnɪkˈsplɪkəbəl/ adj too strange to be explained –**bly** adv

in·ex·pres·si·ble /ˌɪnɪkˈspresəbəl/ adj too great to be expressed –**bly** adv

in·ex·tri·ca·ble /ɪnˈekstrɪkəbəl, ˌɪnɪkˈstrɪ-/ adj fml impossible to escape from, or to untie –**bly** adv

in·fal·li·ble /ɪnˈfæləbəl/ adj 1 never making mistakes 2 always effective: infallible cure –**bility** /ɪnˌfælɪˈbɪləti/ n [U]

in·fa·mous /ˈɪnfəməs/ adj wicked –**my** n [C;U] wickedness

in·fan·cy /ˈɪnfənsi/ n [S;U] early childhood

in·fant /ˈɪnfənt/ n very young child

in·fan·tile /ˈɪnfəntaɪl/ adj childish

in·fan·try /ˈɪnfəntri/ n [U] foot soldiers

in·fat·u·at·ed /ɪnˈfætʃueɪtəd/ adj foolishly loving –**ation** /ɪnˌfætʃuˈeɪʃən/ n [C;U]

in·fect /ɪnˈfekt/ vt give disease to: (fig.) She infected the whole class with her laughter. (= everyone laughed) ~**ion** /-ˈfekʃən/ n [C;U] (disease

spread by) infecting ~**ious** adj able to infect: (fig.) infectious laughter

in·fer /ɪnˈfɜː/ vt -**rr**- draw (meaning) from facts: I inferred from his letter that he had not made a decision ~**ence** /ˈɪnfərəns/ n [C;U]

in·fe·ri·or /ɪnˈfɪəriə/ adj less good; low(er) in rank ♦ n inferior person ~**ity** /ɪnˌfɪəriˈɒrəti/‖-ˈɔːr-/ n [U]

in·fer·nal /ɪnˈfɜːnl/‖-ɜːr-/ adj terrible; like HELL

in·fer·no /ɪnˈfɜːnəʊ/‖-ɜːr-/ n -**nos** place of very great heat and large uncontrollable flames

in·fer·tile /ɪnˈfɜːtaɪl/‖-ɜːrtl/ adj not FERTILE: infertile eggs

in·fest /ɪnˈfest/ vt (of something bad) be present in large numbers

in·fi·del·i·ty /ˌɪnfəˈdeləti/ n [C;U] 1 (act of) disloyalty 2 (act of) sex with someone other than one's marriage partner

in·fight·ing /ˈɪnfaɪtɪŋ/ n [U] disagreement between members of a group

in·fil·trate /ˈɪnfɪltreɪt‖ɪnˈfɪltreɪt, ˈɪnfɪl-/ vt enter secretly, with an unfriendly purpose –**tration** /ˌɪnfɪlˈtreɪʃən/ n [U]

in·fi·nite /ˈɪnfənət/ adj without limits; endless ~**ly** adv

in·fin·i·tive /ɪnˈfɪnətɪv/ n verb form that can follow other verbs and be used with to (e.g. 'go' in I can go and I want to go)

in·fin·i·ty /ɪnˈfɪnəti/ n [U] endless space or quantity

in·firm /ɪnˈfɜːm/‖-ɜːrm/ adj fml weak in body or mind ~**ity** n [C;U]

in·fir·ma·ry /ɪnˈfɜːməri‖-ɜːr-/ n 1 hospital 2 room where sick people are given treatment

in·flame /ɪnˈfleɪm/ vt make violent **inflamed** red and swollen: inflamed eye

in·flam·ma·ble /ɪnˈflæməbəl/ adj 1 which can easily be set on fire and which burns quickly 2 easily excited or made angry

in·flam·ma·tion /ˌɪnfləˈmeɪʃən/ n [C;U] inflamed condition

in·flam·ma·to·ry /ɪnˈflæmətəri‖-tɔːri/ adj likely to inflame: inflammatory speeches

in·flate /ɪnˈfleɪt/ v 1 vt blow up (a tyre, etc.) 2 vi/t increase the supply of money in a country **inflated** adj too big: inflated prices | an inflated opinion of oneself

in·fla·tion /ɪnˈfleɪʃən/ n [U] 1 act of inflating or state of being inflated 2 rise in prices caused by increased production costs or an increase in money supply ~**ary** adj likely to cause INFLATION (2)

in·flec·tion /ɪnˈflekʃən/ n [C;U] a gram change in the form of a word to show difference in its use **b** movement up or down of the voice

in·flex·i·ble /ɪnˈfleksəbəl/ adj impossible to bend or change **–bly** adv **–bility** /ɪnˌfleksəˈbɪləti/ n [U]

in·flict /ɪnˈflɪkt/ vt force (punishment, etc.) on ~**ion** /-ˈflɪkʃən/ n [C;U]

in·flow /ˈɪnfləʊ/ n [C;U] flowing in

in·flu·ence /ˈɪnfluəns/ n [C;U] **1** (power to have) an effect **2** someone with this power: *She's a bad influence on you.* **3 under the influence** drunk ♦ vt have an influence on

in·flu·en·tial /ˌɪnfluˈenʃəl/ adj having great influence

in·flu·en·za /ˌɪnfluˈenzə/ n [U] fml FLU

in·flux /ˈɪnflʌks/ n [C;U] arrival in large numbers or quantities

in·form /ɪnˈfɔːm‖-ɔːrm/ vt fml give information to ~**ant** n person who gives information ~**ed** adj **1** knowing things: *well-informed* **2** having and using suitable knowledge: *an informed guess* ~**er** n person who tells the police about someone

inform against/on phr vt tell the police that (someone) is guilty

in·for·mal /ɪnˈfɔːməl‖-ɔːr-/ adj not formal; without ceremony: *an informal meeting*/*informal clothes* ~**ly** adv ~**ity** /ˌɪnfɔːˈmæləti‖-ɔːr-/ n [U]

in·for·ma·tion /ˌɪnfəˈmeɪʃən‖-ər-/ n [U] knowledge given; facts

information tech·nol·o·gy /··· ···ˈ···/n [U] science of collecting and using information by means of computer systems

in·for·ma·tive /ɪnˈfɔːmətɪv‖-ɔːr-/ adj telling one useful things

in·fra·red /ˌɪnfrəˈred◂/ adj of the heat-giving light RAYS of longer wave-length than those we can see

in·fra·struc·ture /ˈɪnfrəˌstrʌktʃəʳ/n underlying systems (e.g. of power, roads, laws, banks) needed to keep a country going

in·fringe /ɪnˈfrɪndʒ/ vt/i fml go against (a law, or someone's rights) ~**ment** n [C;U]

in·fu·ri·ate /ɪnˈfjʊərieɪt/ vt make very angry

in·fuse /ɪnˈfjuːz/ vt **1** fill (someone) with a quality **2** put (tea, etc.) into hot water to make a drink **infusion** /-ˈfjuːʒən/ n [C;U] (liquid made by) infusing

in·ge·ni·ous /ɪnˈdʒiːniəs/ adj clever at making or inventing: *ingenious person*/*excuse* ~**ly** adv **–nuity** /ˌɪndʒɪˈnjuːəti‖-ˈnuː-/ n [U]

in·gen·u·ous /ɪnˈdʒenjuəs/ adj simple and inexperienced ~**ly** adv

in·glo·ri·ous /ɪnˈɡlɔːriəs/ adj lit shameful ~**ly** adv

in·got /ˈɪŋɡət/ n (brick-shaped) lump of metal

in·grained /ɪnˈɡreɪnd/ adj deeply fixed: *ingrained dirt*/*habits*

in·gra·ti·ate /ɪnˈɡreɪʃieɪt/ vt make (oneself) pleasant, so as to gain favour ~**ating** adj ~**atingly** adv

in·grat·i·tude /ɪnˈɡrætətjuːd‖-tuːd/ n [U] ungratefulness

in·gre·di·ent /ɪnˈɡriːdiənt/ n one of a mixture of things, esp. in baking

in·group /ˈ· ·/n group that treats members better than non-members

in·hab·it /ɪnˈhæbət/ vt fml live in (a place) ~**ant** n person living in a place

in·hale /ɪnˈheɪl/ vi/t breathe in **inhaler** n apparatus for inhaling medicine to make breathing easier **inhalation** /ˌɪnhəˈleɪʃən/ n [C;U]

in·her·ent /ɪnˈhɪərənt/ adj necessarily present; *problems inherent in the system* ~**ly** adv

in·her·it /ɪnˈherət/ vi/t receive (property, etc.) from someone who has died: (fig.) *He's inherited his father's meanness* ~**ance** n **1** [C] something inherited **2** [U] inheriting ~**or** n person who inherits

in·hib·it /ɪnˈhɪbət/ vt prevent; HINDER ~**ion** /ˌɪnhəˈbɪʃən/ n feeling of being unable to do what one really wants to

in·hu·man /ɪnˈhjuːmən/ adj cruel ~**ity** /ˌɪnhjuːˈmænəti/ n [C;U]

in·hu·mane /ˌɪnhjuːˈmeɪn/ adj unkind; not HUMANE n [C;U] ~**ly** adv

in·im·i·ta·ble /ɪˈnɪmətəbəl/ adj too good to be copied **–bly** adv

in·iq·ui·tous /ɪˈnɪkwətəs/ adj fml very unjust or wicked ~**ly** adv **–ty** n [C;U]

i·ni·tial /ɪˈnɪʃəl/ adj at the beginning ♦ n first letter of someone's name ♦ vt **-ll-** BrE ‖ **-l-** AmE write one's initials on ~**ly** adv at first

i·ni·ti·ate[1] /ɪˈnɪʃieɪt/ vt **1** start (something) working **2** introduce (someone) into a group, etc. **–ation** /ɪˌnɪʃiˈeɪʃən/ n [C;U]

i·ni·ti·ate[2] /ɪˈnɪʃiət/ n person instructed or skilled in some special field

i·ni·tia·tive /ɪˈnɪʃətɪv/ n **1** [U] ability to act without help or advice **2** [C] first step: *take the initiative*

in·ject /ɪnˈdʒekt/ vt put (a drug, etc.) into someone with a needle: (fig.) *inject new life, interest, etc., into something* ~**ion** /-ˈdʒekʃən/ n [C;U]

in·junc·tion /ɪnˈdʒʌŋkʃən/ n fml official order

in·jure /ˈɪndʒəʳ/ vt hurt; damage **injured** adj, n hurt (people) **injury** n **1** [U] harm; damage **2** [C] wound, etc.

in·jus·tice /ɪnˈdʒʌstəs/ n [C;U] (act of) unfairness

ink /ɪŋk/ n [C;U] coloured liquid for writing, printing, etc. ~**y** adj black

ink-ling /'ɪŋklɪŋ/ n [S;U] slight idea

in-laid /ˌɪn'leɪd/ adj set ornamentally into another substance: *inlaid gold*

in-land /'ɪnlənd/ adj, adv inside a country: *inland trade*

Inland Rev-e-nue /ˌ·· '···/ n [the] (in Britain) office that collects taxes

in-laws /'·· ·/ n [P] relatives by marriage

in-let /'ɪnlet, 'ɪnlət/ n narrow piece of water reaching into the land

in-mate /'ɪnmeɪt/ n person living in a prison, hospital, etc.

in-most /'ɪnməʊst/ also **innermost** /'ɪnəməʊst‖-nər-/ -- adj furthest inside; most well-hidden

inn /ɪn/ n small pub or hotel, esp. one built many centuries ago

in-nards /'ɪnədz‖-ər-/ n [P] inside parts, esp. of the stomach

in-nate /ˌɪ'neɪt◄/ adj (of a quality) present from birth ~**ly** adv

in-ner /'ɪnər/ adj 1 on the inside; close to the middle 2 secret, esp. if of the spirit: *inner meaning/life*

in-ning /'ɪnɪŋ/ n period of play in BASEBALL **innings** n 1 period when a cricket team or player BATS 2 BrE *infml* time when one is active

inn-keep-er /'ɪn‚ki:pər/ n manager of an INN

in-no-cent /'ɪnəsənt/ adj 1 not guilty 2 harmless 3 unable to recognize evil; simple ~**ly** adv ~**cence** n [U]

in-noc-u-ous /ɪ'nɒkjuəs‖ɪ'nɑːk-/ adj harmless

in-no-va-tion /ˌɪnə'veɪʃən/ n 1 [C] new idea 2 [U] introducing new things ~**vate** /'ɪnəveɪt/ vi make changes ~**vator** n ~**vative** /'ɪnə‚veɪtɪv/, also -**vatory** /-təri/ adj

in-nu-en-do /ˌɪnju'endəʊ/ n -**does** or -**dos** [C;U] unpleasant indirect remark(s)

in-nu-me-ra-ble /ɪ'nju:mərəbəl‖ ɪ'nju:-, ɪ'nu:-/ adj too many to count

in-nu-mer-ate /ɪ'nju:mərət‖ɪ'nju:-, ɪ'nu:-/ adj BrE unable to calculate with numbers ~**acy** n [U]

i-noc-u-late /ɪ'nɒkjʊleɪt‖ɪ'nɑː-/ vt introduce a weak form of a disease into (someone) as a protection ~**lation** /ɪˌnɒkjʊ'leɪʃən‖ɪˌnɑː-/ n [C;U]

in-of-fen-sive /ˌɪnə'fensɪv/ adj not causing dislike; not rude ~**ly** adv

in-op-por-tune /ɪn'ɒpətju:n‖ˌɪnɑːpər'tu:n/ adj fml at the wrong time ~**ly** adv

in-or-di-nate /ɪ'nɔːdənət‖-ɔːr-/ adj fml beyond reasonable limits ~**ly** adv

in-put /'ɪnpʊt/ n [S;U] something put in for use, esp. information into a computer ♦ vt -**tt**-; past t.) p. **inputted** or **input** put (information) into a computer

in-quest /'ɪnkwest/ n official inquiry, esp. when someone dies unexpectedly

in-quire /ɪn'kwaɪər/ vi/t ask for information (about) **inquiring** adj that shows an interest in knowing **inquiry** n 1 [C;U] (act of) inquiring 2 [C] set of meetings, etc., to find out why something happened

    inquire after phr vt ask about the health of

    inquire into phr vt look for information about

in-qui-si-tion /ˌɪnkwə'zɪʃən/ n thorough and esp. cruel inquiry

in-quis-i-tive /ɪn'kwɪzətɪv/ adj asking too many questions ~**ly** adv

in-roads /'ɪnrəʊdz/ n 1 attack upon or advance into a new area 2 effort or activity that lessens the quantity or difficulty of what remains afterwards

ins and outs /ˌ· · '·/ n [the + P] details of a situation, problem, etc.)

in-sane /ɪn'seɪn/ adj mad ~**ly** adv **insanity** /ɪn'sænəti/ n [U]

in-san-i-ta-ry /ɪn'sænətəri‖-teri/ adj dirty enough to cause disease

in-sa-tia-ble /ɪn'seɪʃəbəl/ adj impossible to satisfy ~**bly** adv

in-scribe /ɪn'skraɪb/ vt fml write (words) on **inscription** /ɪn'skrɪpʃən/ n piece of writing inscribed, esp. on stone

in-scru-ta-ble /ɪn'skru:təbəl/ adj mysterious: *inscrutable smile* ~**bly** adv

in-sect /'ɪnsekt/ n small creature with 6 legs

in-sec-ti-cide /ɪn'sektəsaɪd/ n [C;U] chemical used to kill insects

in-se-cure /ˌɪnsɪ'kjʊər/ adj 1 not safe 2 not sure of oneself ~**ly** adv ~**curity** n [U]

in-sem-i-na-tion /ɪnˌsemə'neɪʃən/ n [U] putting of male seed into a female

in-sen-si-ble /ɪn'sensəbəl/ adj 1 unconscious 2 lacking knowledge of ~**bility** /ɪnˌsensə'bɪləti/ n [U]

in-sen-si-tive /ɪn'sensətɪv/ adj not SENSITIVE ~**ly** adv ~**tivity** /ɪnˌsensə'tɪvəti/ n [S;U]

in-sep-a-ra-ble /ɪn'sepərəbəl/ adj impossible to separate

in-sert /ɪn'sɜːt‖-ɜːrt/ vt put into something: *insert a key in a lock* ♦ /'ɪnsɜːt‖-ɜːrt/ n written or printed material put in between pages of a book ~**ion** /ɪn'sɜːʃən‖-ɜːr-/ n [C;U]

in-ser-vice /ˌ· '··◄/ adj (taking place) during one's work: *in-service training*

in-set /'ɪnset/ n picture, etc., in the corner of a larger one

in-side /ɪn'saɪd, 'ɪnsaɪd/ n 1 [the + S] **a** part nearest to the middle, or that faces away from the open air **b** infml position in which one is able to know special or secret information 2 [C] also **insides** *pl.* — *infml* one's stomach 3 **inside out: a** with the inside parts on the outside **b** thoroughly: *know it inside out* ♦ *adj* 1 facing or at the inside: *the inside pages of a newspaper* 2 from someone closely concerned: *inside information* ♦ *adv* to or in the inside, esp. indoors: *The children are playing inside.* ♦ *prep* 1 to or on the inside of: *inside the car* 2 in less time than: *inside an hour* **insider** /ɪnˈsaɪdəʳ/ *n* person accepted in a social group, esp. someone with special information or influence

insider dealing , also **insider trad·ing**/·, ·· ′·-′/ *n* [U] illegal practice of buying and selling business shares by people who use their knowledge of the business affairs of the companies they work for

in·sid·i·ous /ɪnˈsɪdiəs/ *adj* secretly harmful ~**ly** *adv*

in·sight /ˈɪnsaɪt/ *n* [C;U] understanding: *insight into their lives*

in·sig·ni·a /ɪnˈsɪgniə/ *n* [P] objects worn as signs of rank

in·sig·nif·i·cant /ˌɪnsɪgˈnɪfɪkənt/ *adj* not important ~**ly** *adv* –**cance** *n* [U]

in·sin·u·ate /ɪnˈsɪnjueɪt/ *vt* 1 suggest (something unpleasant) indirectly 2 gain acceptance for (esp. oneself) by secret means –**ation** /ɪnˌsɪnjuˈeɪʃən/ *n* [C;U]

in·sip·id /ɪnˈsɪpɪd/ *adj derog* lacking a strong character, taste, or effect

in·sist /ɪnˈsɪst/ *vi/t* 1 order: *insist that he should go* 2 declare firmly: *He insists he wasn't there.* ~**ent** *adj* repeatedly insisting ~**ence** *n* [U]

in si·tu /ˌɪn ˈsɪtjuː‖, ˌɪn ˈsaɪtuː/ *adv* in its original place

in so far as /ˌ· · ′· ·/*conj* to the degree that

in·so·lent /ˈɪnsələnt/ *adj* disrespectful; rude –**lence** *n* [U]

in·so·lu·ble /ɪnˈsɒljʊbəl‖ɪnˈsɑː-/ *adj* 1 impossible to answer 2 impossible to DISSOLVE

in·sol·vent /ɪnˈsɒlvənt‖ɪnˈsɑːl-, ɪnˈsɔːl-/ *n, adj* (someone) unable to pay their debts –**vency** *n* [U]

in·som·ni·a /ɪnˈsɒmniə‖-ˈsɑːm-/ *n* [U] inability to sleep **insomniac** /-niæk/ *n, adj* (someone) who habitually cannot sleep

in·sou·ci·ance /ɪnˈsuːsiəns/ *n* [U] not caring about anything –**ant** *adj*

in·spect /ɪnˈspekt/ *vt* examine closely ~**or** *n* 1 official who inspects something 2 police officer of middle rank ~**ion** /-ˈspekʃən/ *n* [C;U]

in·spire /ɪnˈspaɪəʳ/ *vt* 1 encourage to act 2 fill with a feeling: *inspire them with confidence* **inspiration**

/ˌɪnspəˈreɪʃən/ *n* 1 [U] act of inspiring or state of being inspired 2 [C] something that inspires 3 [C] sudden good idea **inspired** *adj* very clever

in·sta·bil·i·ty /ˌɪnstəˈbɪlɪti/ *n* [U] 1 unsteadiness 2 (of people) tendency to act in changeable ways

in·stall /ɪnˈstɔːl/ *vt* 1 put (a machine, etc.) somewhere 2 settle (someone) in a position ~**ation** /ˌɪnstəˈleɪʃən/ *n* 1 [U] installing 2 [C] apparatus, etc., installed

in·stal·ment /ɪnˈstɔːlmənt/ *n* 1 single part of a story, etc., that appears in regular parts 2 single regular payment

in·stance /ˈɪnstəns/ *n* 1 EXAMPLE (1) 2 **for instance** for example ♦ *vt* give as an example

in·stant /ˈɪnstənt/ *n* moment of time ♦ *adj* happening or produced at once ~**ly** *adv* at once

in·stan·ta·ne·ous /ˌɪnstənˈteɪniəs/ *adj* happening at once ~**ly** *adv*

in·stead /ɪnˈsted/ *adv* 1 in place of that 2 **instead of** in place of: *You go instead of me.*

in·step /ˈɪnstep/ *n* upper surface of the foot

in·sti·gate /ˈɪnstɪgeɪt/ *vt fml* cause to do or happen ~**gator** *n* –**gation** /ˌɪnstɪˈgeɪʃən/ *n*

in·stil /ɪnˈstɪl/ *vt* -**ll**- put (ideas) into someone's mind

in·stinct /ˈɪnstɪŋkt/ *n* [C;U] natural tendency to act in a certain way ~**ive** *adj*: *instinctive fear of snakes* ~**ively** *adv*

in·sti·tute /ˈɪnstɪtjuːt‖-tuːt/ *n* society formed for a special purpose ♦ *vt fml* start; establish

in·sti·tu·tion /ˌɪnstɪˈtjuːʃən‖-ˈtuː-/ *n* 1 [C] (building for) a hospital, school, etc., where people are looked after 2 [C] established custom 3 [U] act of instituting ~**al** *adj* ~**alize** 1 *vt* make into an INSTITUTION (2) 2 *vi* (of people) to become unable to live or work anywhere except in an INSTITUTION (1)

in·struct /ɪnˈstrʌkt/ *vt* 1 give orders to 2 teach 3 *law* inform officially ~**ive** *adj* teaching something useful ~**or** *n* teacher

in·struc·tion /ɪnˈstrʌkʃən/ *n* 1 [C] order 2 [U] act of instructing; teaching **instructions** *n* [P] advice on how to do something: *Follow the instructions on the packet.*

in·stru·ment /ˈɪnstrəmənt/ *n* 1 thing that helps in work 2 apparatus for playing music ~**al** /ˌɪnstrəˈmentl/ *adj* 1 for musical instruments 2 helpful; causing: *His information was instrumental in catching the thief.* ~**alist** *n* player of a musical instrument

in·sub·or·di·nate /ˌɪnsəˈbɔːdənət‖ -ɔːr-/ adj disobedient **–nation** /ˌɪnsəbɔːdəˈneɪʃən‖-ɔːr-/ n [C;U]

in·sub·stan·tial /ˌɪnsəbˈstænʃəl/ adj not firm or solid

in·suf·fer·a·ble /ɪnˈsʌfərəbəl/ adj unbearable

in·suf·fi·cient /ˌɪnsəˈfɪʃənt/ adj not enough **~ly** adv **–ciency** n [S;U]

in·su·lar /ˈɪnsjʊlərʳ‖ˈɪnsələr/ adj 1 narrow-minded 2 of an island **~ity** /ˌɪnsjʊˈlærəti‖-sə-/ n [U]

in·su·late /ˈɪnsjʊleɪt‖ˈɪnsə-, ˈɪnʃə-/ vt 1 cover, to prevent the escape of heat, electricity, etc. 2 protect from experiences **–lator** n thing that insulates**–lation** /ˌɪnsjʊˈleɪʃən‖ˌɪnsə-/ n [U] (material for) insulating

in·sult[1] /ɪnˈsʌlt/ vt be rude to

insult[2] /ˈɪnsʌlt/ n 1 rude remark or action 2 **add insult to injury** do or say something more against someone when one has already harmed them enough

in·su·pe·ra·ble /ɪnˈsjuːpərəbəl‖ɪnˈsuː-/ adj impossible to deal with

in·sup·por·ta·ble /ˌɪnsəˈpɔːtəbəl‖-ˈpɔːr-/ adj unbearable

in·sur·ance /ɪnˈʃʊərəns/ n 1 [U] agreement to pay money in case of misfortune 2 [U] money paid by or to an insurance company for this 3 [S;U] protection against anything

in·sure /ɪnˈʃʊəʳ/ vt protect by insurance: *insured against fire*

in·sur·gent /ɪnˈsɜːdʒənt‖-ɜːr-/ n, adj REBEL **–gency** n [C;U]

in·sur·moun·ta·ble /ˌɪnsəˈmaʊntəbəl‖-sər-/ adj too large, difficult, etc., to be dealt with

in·sur·rec·tion /ˌɪnsəˈrekʃən/ n [C;U] REBELLION

in·tact /ɪnˈtækt/ adj undamaged

in·take /ˈɪnteɪk/ n 1 [S] amount or number taken in 2 [C] pipe to let in gas, water, etc.

in·tan·gi·ble /ɪnˈtændʒəbəl/ adj 1 which cannot be known by the senses or described: *an intangible quality* 2 which is hidden or not material, but known to be real: *intangible assets of the business, such as the loyalty of its customers* **–bly** adv **–bility** n [U]

in·te·ger /ˈɪntɪdʒəʳ/ n a whole number

in·te·gral /ˈɪntɪɡrəl/ adj necessary to complete something: *an integral part of the argument*

in·te·grate /ˈɪntɪɡreɪt/ vi/t (cause to) mix with other races or people **–gra·tion** /ˌɪntɪˈɡreɪʃən/ n [U] **–grationist** n believer in integration

integrated cir·cuit /ˌ···· ˈ··/ n set of electrical connections printed esp. on a CHIP[1] (4)

in·teg·ri·ty /ɪnˈteɡrəti/ n [U] 1 honesty; trustworthiness 2 wholeness

in·tel·lect /ˈɪntəlekt/ n [C;U] ability to think **~ual** /ˌɪntəˈlektʃuəl/ adj 1 of the intellect 2 clever and well-educated **~ual** n intellectual person **~ually** adv

in·tel·li·gence /ɪnˈtelədʒəns/ n [U] 1 ability to learn and understand 2 (people who gather) information about enemies **–gent** adj clever **–gently** adv

in·tel·li·gent·si·a /ɪnˌtelɪˈdʒentsiə/ n [P] intellectuals as a social group

in·tel·li·gi·ble /ɪnˈtelədʒəbəl/ adj understandable **–bly** adv **–bility** /ɪnˌtelədʒəˈbɪləti/ n [U]

in·tend /ɪnˈtend/ vt have as one's purpose; mean

in·tense /ɪnˈtens/ adj strong (in quality or feeling) **~ly** adv **intensity** n [U] quality or appearance of being intense

in·ten·si·fy /ɪnˈtensəfaɪ/ vi/t make or become more intense **–fication** /ɪnˌtensəfɪˈkeɪʃən/ n [U]

in·ten·sive /ɪnˈtensɪv/ adj giving a lot of attention **~ly** adv

in·tent[1] /ɪnˈtent/ n [U] 1 purpose: *enter with intent to steal* 2 **to all intents and purposes** in almost every way

intent[2] adj 1 with fixed attention 2 determined

in·ten·tion /ɪnˈtenʃən/ n 1 [C;U] plan; purpose 2 **good intentions** wish to bring about a good result **~al** adj done on purpose **~ally** adv

in·ter /ɪnˈtɜːʳ/ vt **-rr-** fml bury

in·ter·act /ˌɪntərˈækt/ vi have an effect on each other **~ion** /-ˈækʃən/ n [C;U]

in·ter·ac·tive /ˌɪntərˈæktɪv/ adj 1 that interacts 2 allowing the exchange of information between a computer and a user while a PROGRAM is in operation

in·ter·cede /ˌɪntəˈsiːd‖-ər-/ vi speak in favour of someone

in·ter·cept /ˌɪntəˈsept‖-ər-/ vt stop (someone or something moving between 2 places) **~ion** /-ˈsepʃən/ n [C;U]

in·ter·ces·sion /ˌɪntəˈseʃən‖-tər-/ n 1 [U] act of interceding 2 [C;U] prayer which asks for other people to be helped

in·ter·change /ˌɪntəˈtʃeɪndʒ‖-ər-/ vi/t exchange **~able** adj ♦ n /ˈɪntətʃeɪndʒ‖-tər-/ 1 [C;U] (act of) interchanging 2 [C] system of smaller roads connecting main roads

in·ter·ci·ty /ˌɪntəˈsɪti◀‖-tər-/ adj travelling fast between cities

in·ter·com /ˈɪntəkɒm‖ˈɪntərkɑːm/ n system for talking through a machine to people fairly near

in·ter·con·ti·nen·tal /ˌɪntəkɒntɪˈnentl◀‖-tərkɑːn-/ adj between CONTINENTs

in·ter·course /'ɪntəkɔːs‖'ɪntɔrkɔːrs/ n [U] **1** SEXUAL INTERCOURSE **2** fml conversation, etc., between people

in·ter·de·pen·dent /ˌɪntədɪ'pendənt‖-tər-/ adj depending on each other

in·terest /'ɪntrɪst/ n **1** [S;U] willingness to give attention: *take an interest* **2** [U] quality that makes people give attention: *That's of no interest to her.* **3** [C] activity or subject that one likes to give time to **4** [C] also **interests** pl. — advantage: *It's in your interest to go.* **5** [U] money paid for the use of money: *10% interest* **6** [C] share in a business ♦ vt cause to feel INTEREST (1) —**ed** adj feeling INTEREST (1) **2** personally concerned —**ing** adj having INTEREST (2)

in·ter·face /'ɪntəfeɪs‖-ər-/ n point where 2 systems meet and act on each other ♦ vi/t connect or be connected by means of an interface

in·ter·fere /ˌɪntə'fɪə‖-tər-/ vi **1** enter into a matter that does not concern one and in which one is not wanted **2** prevent something from working properly —**ference** n [U] **1** act of interfering **2** noises, etc., that stop radio or television from working properly

interfere with phr vt **1** get in the way of **2** touch or move (something) in a way that is not allowed **3** annoy or touch sexually

in·ter·ga·lac·tic /ˌɪntəgə'læktɪk‖-tər-/ adj between the galaxies (GALAXY)

in·ter·im /'ɪntərɪm/ adj done as part of something to follow later: *interim report*

in·te·ri·or /ɪn'tɪərɪə/ n inside of something **interior** adj

in·ter·ject /ˌɪntə'dʒekt‖-ər-/ vi/t fml make (a sudden remark) between others —**ion** /-'dʒekʃən/ n **1** [C] word or phrase interjected, such as 'Good heavens!' **2** [U] act of interjecting

in·ter·lock /ˌɪntə'lɒk‖ˌɪntər'lɑːk/ vi/t fasten or be fastened together

in·ter·loc·u·tor /ˌɪntə'lɒkjʊtə‖ˌɪntər'lɑːk-/ n fml person one is talking with

in·ter·lop·er /'ɪntələʊpə‖-tər-/ n person found in a place, esp. among others, with no right to be there

in·ter·lude /'ɪntəluːd‖-ər-/ n period of time between 2 parts or activities

in·ter·mar·ry /ˌɪntə'mæri‖-ər-/ vi (of groups of people) become connected by marriage —**marriage** n [U]

in·ter·me·di·a·ry /ˌɪntə'miːdɪəri‖ˌɪntər'miːdieri/ n person who persuades opposing sides to agree

in·ter·me·di·ate /ˌɪntə'miːdiət‖-tər-/ adj between 2 others; halfway

in·ter·ment /ɪn'tɜːmənt‖-ɜːr-/ n [C;U] fml burial

in·ter·mi·na·ble /ɪn'tɜːmɪnəbəl‖-ɜːr-/ adj long and dull; (seeming) endless —**bly** adv

in·ter·mis·sion /ˌɪntə'mɪʃən‖-tər-/ n esp. AmE for INTERVAL (2)

in·ter·mit·tent /ˌɪntə'mɪtənt‖-tər-/ adj not continuous —**ly** adv

in·tern¹ /ɪn'tɜːn‖-ɜːrn/ vt put in prison, esp. in wartime —**ment** n [U]

in·tern² /'ɪntɜːn‖-ɜːrn/ n esp. AmE person who has recently completed professional training, esp. in medicine, and is gaining practical experience, esp. in a hospital

in·ter·nal /ɪn'tɜːnl‖-ɜːr-/ adj **1** inside **2** not foreign: *internal trade* —**ly** adv

Internal Rev·e·nue /ˌ··· '···‖/ n [the] (in the US) office that collects taxes

in·ter·na·tion·al /ˌɪntə'næʃənəl◁‖-tər-/ adj between nations ♦ n **1** international sports match **2** person who plays for his or her country's team in such a match —**ly** adv —**ism** n [U] principle that nations should work together

in·ter·ne·cine /ˌɪntə'niːsaɪn‖ˌɪntər'niːsɔːn, -'nesiːn/ adj fml (of fighting, etc.) inside a group

in·ter·play /'ɪntəpleɪ‖-ər-/ n [U] INTERACTION

in·ter·po·late /ɪn'tɜːpəleɪt‖-ɜːr-/ vt fml put in (words); interrupt —**lation** /ɪnˌtɜːpə'leɪʃən‖-ɜːr-/ n [C;U]

in·ter·pose /ˌɪntə'pəʊz‖-tər-/ vt fml put or say between things

in·ter·pret /ɪn'tɜːprɪt‖-ɜːr-/ v **1** understand or explain the meaning of **2** vi/t turn (spoken words) into another language —**er** n person who INTERPRETs (2) —**ation** /ɪnˌtɜːprɪ'teɪʃən‖-ɜːr-/ n [C;U] **1** explanation **2** (example of) a performance of music, theatre, etc., by someone giving their own idea of the COMPOSER's writer's, etc., intentions

in·ter·ro·gate /ɪn'terəgeɪt/ vt **1** question formally esp. for a long time and often with the use of threats or violence **2** (try to) get direct information from: *to interrogate a computer* —**gation** /ɪnˌterə'geɪʃən/ n [C;U] —**gative** /ˌɪntə'rɒgətɪv‖-'rɑː-/ adj asking a question

in·ter·rupt /ˌɪntə'rʌpt/ vi/t break the flow of (speech, etc.) —**ion** /-'rʌpʃən/ n [C;U]

in·ter·sect /ˌɪntə'sekt‖-ər-/ vi/t cut across: *intersecting paths* —**ion** /-'sekʃən/ n **1** [U] act of intersecting **2** [C] CROSSROADS

in·ter·sperse /ˌɪntə'spɜːs‖ˌɪntər'spɜːrs/ vt put here and there among other things

in·ter·stice /ɪnˈtɜːstɪs‖-ɜːr-/ n small space or crack between things placed close together

in·ter·twine /ˌɪntəˈtwaɪn‖-ər-/ vi/t twist together

in·ter·val /ˈɪntəvəl‖-tər-/ n 1 time between events 2 BrE time between the parts of a play, etc. 3 distance between things

in·ter·vene /ˌɪntəˈviːn‖-ər-/ vi 1 interrupt so as to stop something 2 (of time) happen between events **-vention** /-ˈvenʃən/ n [C;U]

in·ter·view /ˈɪntəvjuː‖-ər-/ n meeting where a person is asked questions ♦ vt ask (someone) questions in an interview **~ee** n person who is being or is to be interviewed, esp. for a job **~er** n person who interviews

in·tes·tate /ɪnˈtesteɪt, -stət/ adj law not having made a WILL[2] (5)

in·tes·tine /ɪnˈtestən/ also **-tines** pl n bowels **-tinal** adj

in·ti·ma·cy /ˈɪntəməsi/ n 1 [U] state of being intimate 2 [C] remark or action of a kind that happens only between people who know each other very well 3 [U] the act of sex

in·ti·mate[1] /ˈɪntəmət/ adj 1 having a close relationship: intimate friends 2 private: her intimate thoughts 3 resulting from close study: intimate knowledge **~ly** adv

in·ti·mate[2] /ˈɪntəmeɪt/ vt fml make known; suggest **-mation** /ˌɪntəˈmeɪʃən/ n [C;U]

in·tim·i·date /ɪnˈtɪmədeɪt/ vt frighten by threats **-dation** /ɪnˌtɪməˈdeɪʃən/ n [U]

in·to /ˈɪntə: before vowels ˈɪntʊ; strong ˈɪntuː/ prep 1 so as to be in: jump into the water | get into trouble 2 so as to be: translate it into French 3 against: bump into a tree 4 (used when dividing): 7 into 11 won't go.

in·tol·e·ra·ble /ɪnˈtɒlərəbəl‖-ˈtɑː-/ adj unbearable **-bly** adv

in·tol·e·rant /ɪnˈtɒlərənt‖-ˈtɑː-/ adj not TOLERANT **-rance** n [U]

in·to·na·tion /ˌɪntəˈneɪʃən/ n [C;U] rise and fall of the voice in speech

in·tone /ɪnˈtəʊn/ vi/t say (a prayer, etc.) in a level voice

in·tox·i·cate /ɪnˈtɒksəkeɪt‖ɪnˈtɑːk-/ vt make drunk: (fig.) intoxicated by success **-cation** /ɪnˌtɒksəˈkeɪʃən‖-ˌtɑːk-/ n [U]

in·trac·ta·ble /ɪnˈtræktəbəl/ adj difficult to control or deal with

in·tran·si·gent /ɪnˈtrænsɪdʒənt/ adj fml refusing to change; STUBBORN **-gence** n [U]

in·tran·si·tive /ɪnˈtrænsɪtɪv/ adj (of a verb) having a subject but no object: 'Break' is intransitive in the sentence 'My cup fell and broke' but transitive in 'I broke my cup'.

in·tra·ve·nous /ˌɪntrəˈviːnəs/ adj into a VEIN: intravenous injection

in·trep·id /ɪnˈtrepɪd/ adj fml fearless **~ly** adv

in·tri·ca·cy /ˈɪntrɪkəsi/ n 1 [U] being intricate 2 [C] something intricate

in·tri·cate /ˈɪntrɪkət/ adj having many details; COMPLICATED **~ly** adv

in·trigue /ɪnˈtriːg/ v 1 vt interest greatly 2 vi make PLOTs ♦ n /ˈɪntriːg, ɪnˈtriːg/ 1 [U] act or practice of secret planning 2 [C] PLOT **intriguing** adj very interesting, esp. because of some strange quality

in·trin·sic /ɪnˈtrɪnsɪk, -zɪk/ adj belonging naturally; INHERENT **~ally** /-kli/ adv

in·tro·duce /ˌɪntrəˈdjuːs‖-ˈduːs/ vt 1 make (people) known to each other 2 bring or put in **-duction** /-ˈdʌkʃən/ n 1 [U] act of introducing 2 [C] occasion of telling people each other's names 3 [C] explanation at the beginning of a book, etc. 4 [C] simple book about a subject **-ductory** /-ˈdʌktəri/ adj happening or said at the beginning

in·tro·spec·tion /ˌɪntrəˈspekʃən/ n [U] thinking about one's own thoughts and feelings **-tive** adj

in·tro·vert /ˈɪntrəvɜːt‖-ɜːrt/ n quiet introspective person **~ed** adj

in·trude /ɪnˈtruːd/ vi come in when not wanted **intruder** n person who intrudes, esp. intending to steal **intrusive** /-ˈtruːsɪv/ adj intruding **intrusion** /-ˈtruːʒən/ n [C;U]

in·tu·i·tion /ˌɪntjuˈɪʃən‖-tuː-, -tjuː-/ n 1 [U] power of knowing something without reasoning or learned skill 2 [C] something known in this way **-tive** /ɪnˈtjuːɪtɪv‖-ˈtuː-, -ˈtjuː-/ adj **-tively** adv

In·u·it /ˈɪnjuɪt/ n member of a race of people living in the icy far north of N America

in·un·date /ˈɪnəndeɪt/ vt flood: (fig.) inundated with letters **-dation** /ˌɪnənˈdeɪʃən/ n [C;U]

in·ured /ɪˈnjʊəd‖-ərd/ adj accustomed (by long experience): inured to the smell

in·vade /ɪnˈveɪd/ vt 1 attack and take control of (a country) 2 crowd into **invader** n **invasion** /-ˈveɪʒən/ n [C;U]

in·val·id[1] /ɪnˈvælɪd/ adj not VALID: invalid argument/ticket **~ate** vt make invalid **~ation** /ɪnˌvælɪˈdeɪʃən/ n [U]

in·va·lid[2] /ˈɪnvəliːd, -lɪd‖-lɪd/ n person weakened by illness

invalid[3] v **invalid out** phr vt allow to leave the armed forces because of ill-health

in·val·u·a·ble /ɪnˈvæljʊbəl/ adj too valuable for the worth to be measured

in·var·i·a·ble /ɪnˈveəriəbəl/ adj unchanging **-bly** adv always

in·vec·tive /ɪnˈvektɪv/ n [U] *fml* angry language

in·veigh /ɪnˈveɪ/ v **inveigh against** *phr vt fml* attack in words

in·vei·gle /ɪnˈveɪɡəl, -ˈviː-‖-ˈveɪ-/ v **inveigle into** *phr vt* trick (someone) into (doing something)

in·vent /ɪnˈvent/ vt **1** produce for the first time **2** think of (something untrue) **~ive** *adj* able to invent **~or** n **~ion** /-ˈvenʃən/ n **1** [U] act of inventing **2** [C] something invented

in·ven·to·ry /ˈɪnvəntri‖-tɔːri/ n list, esp. one of all the goods in a place

in·verse /ˌɪnˈvɜːs◄‖-ɜːrs◄/ n, adj opposite

in·vert /ɪnˈvɜːt‖-ɜːrt/ vt *fml* turn upside down **inversion** /-ˈvɜːʃən‖-ˈvɜːrʒən/ n [C;U]

in·ver·te·brate /ɪnˈvɜːtəbrət, -breɪt‖-ɜːrt-/ n animal without a BACKBONE

inverted com·ma /·ˌ··ˈ··/ n BrE for QUOTATION MARK

in·vest /ɪnˈvest/ vt use (money) to make more money **~ment** n **1** [U] act of investing **2** [C] (something bought with) money invested **~or** n

invest in *phr vt* buy

invest with *phr vt fml* give officially to: *power invested in him* ‖ (fig.) *Don't invest his words with too much meaning!* (= take them too seriously)

in·ves·ti·gate /ɪnˈvestɪɡeɪt/ vi/t inquire carefully (about): *investigate a crime* **-gator** n **-gative** /-ɡətɪv‖-ɡeɪtɪv/ adj **-gation** /ɪnˌvestɪˈɡeɪʃən/ n [C;U]

in·ves·ti·ture /ɪnˈvestɪtʃəʳ‖-tʃʊəʳ/ n ceremony of investing someone with rank

in·vet·e·rate /ɪnˈvetərət/ adj fixed in a bad habit: *inveterate liar*

in·vid·i·ous /ɪnˈvɪdiəs/ adj tending to cause ill-will or make people unnecessarily offended or jealous

in·vi·gi·late /ɪnˈvɪdʒəleɪt/ vi/t BrE watch over (students in an examination) **-lator** n

in·vig·o·rate /ɪnˈvɪɡəreɪt/ vt give health and strength: *an invigorating swim*

in·vin·ci·ble /ɪnˈvɪnsəbəl/ adj too strong to be defeated **-bly** adv

in·vi·o·la·ble /ɪnˈvaɪələbəl/ adj fml impossible to VIOLATE: *inviolable rights*

in·vis·i·ble /ɪnˈvɪzəbəl/ adj that cannot be seen **-bly** adv **-bility** /ɪnˌvɪzəˈbɪləti/ n [U]

in·vite /ɪnˈvaɪt/ vt **1** ask to come **2** ask politely for: *invite questions* **inviting** adj attractive **invitingly** adv **invitation** /ˌɪnvəˈteɪʃən/ n **1** [C] request to come: *invitations to a wedding* **2** [U] act of inviting: *entrance by invitation only* **3** [C] encouragement to an action

in vi·tro /ɪn ˈviːtrəʊ/ adj (done) outside a living body, in a piece of scientific equipment

in·vo·ca·tion /ˌɪnvəˈkeɪʃən/ n fml **1** [U] act of invoking **2** [C] prayer for help

in·voice /ˈɪnvɔɪs/ vt, n (send) a bill for goods received

in·voke /ɪnˈvəʊk/ vt fml **1** call to (God, the law) for help **2** beg for **3** cause to appear by magic

in·vol·un·ta·ry /ɪnˈvɒləntəri‖-ˈvɑːl-ənteri/ adj done without intention: *an involuntary smile* **-rily** adv

in·volve /ɪnˈvɒlv‖ɪnˈvɑːlv/ vt **1** have as a necessary result **2** cause to become concerned **involved** adj **1** COMPLICATED **2** (of a person) closely concerned in relationships and activities with others, esp. in a personal or sexual way **~ment** n [U]

in·vul·ne·ra·ble /ɪnˈvʌlnərəbəl/ adj that cannot be harmed

i·o·dine /ˈaɪədiːn‖-daɪn/ n [U] chemical used to prevent infection in wounds

i·on /ˈaɪən‖ˈaɪən, ˈaɪɑːn/ n atom with an electrical CHARGE **~izer** n machine that produces negative ions, believed to make the air more healthy

i·on·o·sphere /aɪˈɒnəsfɪəʳ‖aɪˈɑː-/ n [the + S] part of the atmosphere which is used in helping to send radio waves around the Earth

i·o·ta /aɪˈəʊtə/ n [S] very small amount

IOU /ˌaɪ əʊ ˈjuː/ n 'I owe you'; signed piece of paper saying one owes money

ip·so fac·to /ˌɪpsəʊ ˈfæktəʊ/ adv fml (proved) by the fact itself

IQ /ˌaɪ ˈkjuː/ n intelligence quotient; measure of INTELLIGENCE

IRA /ˌaɪ ɑːʳ ˈeɪ/ n Irish Republican Army; illegal organization whose aim is to unite Northern Ireland and the Republic of Ireland

i·ras·ci·ble /ɪˈræsəbəl/ adj fml easily made angry

i·rate /ˌaɪˈreɪt◄/ adj angry **~ly** adv

ir·i·des·cent /ˌɪrɪˈdesənt/ adj changing colour as light falls on it **-cence** n [U]

i·ris /ˈaɪərɪs/ n **1** tall yellow or purple flower **2** coloured part of the eye

irk /ɜːk‖ɜːrk/ vt annoy **~some** adj annoying

i·ron¹ /ˈaɪən‖ˈaɪərn/ n **1** [U] common hard metal used in making steel, etc. **2** [C] heavy object for making cloth smooth **3** **have several irons in the fire** have various different interests, activities, or plans at the same time ♦

adj very firm: *iron will* **irons** *n* [P] chains for a prisoner

iron² *vt* make smooth with an iron
　iron out *phr vt* remove (difficulties, etc.)

Iron Age /'· ·/ *n* [*the*] time in the history of mankind when iron was used for tools, etc.

Iron Curtain /,·· '··/ *n* border between western Europe and the COMMUNIST countries

i-ron-ic /aɪ'rɒnɪk ‖ aɪ'rɑː-/ *also* ~al /-kəl/ — *adj* expressing IRONY ~ally /-kli/ *adv*

ironing board /'··· ·/ *n* narrow table for ironing clothes on

Iron lung /,·· '·/ *n* machine fitted over the body which helps one breathe in and out

i-ron-mon-ger /'aɪən,mʌŋgəʳ ‖ 'aɪərn,mʌŋ-, -,mɑːŋ-/ *n BrE* person who sells HARDWARE (1)

i-ron-y /'aɪərəni/ *n* 1 [U] intentional use of words which are opposite to one's real meaning, in order to be amusing or to show annoyance 2 [C;U] event or situation which is the opposite of what one expected

ir-ra-di-ate /ɪ'reɪdieɪt/ *vt* 1 *fml* throw bright light on 2 treat with X-RAYS or similar beams of force 3 treat (food) with X-RAYS to kill bacteria and make it last longer

ir-ra-tion-al /ɪ'ræʃənəl/ *adj* not reasonable — **ly** *adv*

ir-rec-on-ci-la-ble /ɪ,rekən'saɪləbəl/ *adj* impossible to bring into agreement — **bly** *adv*

ir-re-fu-ta-ble /,ɪrɪ'fjuːtəbəl/ *adj fml* too strong to be disproved

ir-reg-u-lar /ɪ'regjʊləʳ/ *adj* 1 uneven 2 *fml* against the usual rules 3 not following the usual pattern — **ly** *adv* — **ity** /ɪ,regjʊ'lærɪti/ *n* [C;U]

ir-rel-e-vant /ɪ'reləvənt/ *adj* not RELEVANT — **vance** *n* [C;U]

ir-rep-a-ra-ble /ɪ'repərəbəl/ *adj* too bad to be put right — **bly** *adv*

ir-re-place-a-ble /,ɪrɪ'pleɪsəbəl/ *adj* too special for anything else to REPLACE it

ir-re-proa-cha-ble /,ɪrɪ'prəʊtʃəbəl/ *adj fml* faultless — **bly** *adv*

ir-re-sis-ti-ble /,ɪrɪ'zɪstəbəl/ *adj* so nice, powerful, etc., that one cannot RESIST it — **bly** *adv*

ir-res-o-lute /ɪ'rezəluːt/ *adj fml* unable to make decisions — **ly** *adv*

ir-re-spec-tive /,ɪrɪ'spektɪv/ *adv* irrespective of without regard to

ir-re-spon-si-ble /,ɪrɪ'spɒnsəbəl ‖ -'spɑːn-/ *adj* not trustworthy; careless — **bly** *adv* — **bility** /,ɪrɪspɒnsə'bɪlɪti ‖ -spɑːn-/ *n* [U]

ir-re-trie-va-ble /,ɪrɪ'triːvəbəl/ *adj* impossible to get back or put right — **bly** *adv*

ir-rev-e-rent /ɪ'revərənt/ *adj* not respectful, esp. of holy things — **ly** *adv* — **rence** *n* [U]

ir-rev-o-ca-ble /ɪ'revəkəbəl/ *adj* unchangeable once made or started: *irrevocable decision* — **bly** *adv*

ir-ri-gate /'ɪrɪgeɪt/ *vt* supply water to (land) — **gation** /,ɪrɪ'geɪʃən/ *n* [U]

ir-ri-ta-ble /'ɪrɪtəbəl/ *adj* easily annoyed — **bly** *adv* — **bility** /,ɪrɪtə'bɪlɪti/ *n* [U]

ir-ri-tate /'ɪrɪteɪt/ *vt* 1 annoy 2 make sore — **tation** /,ɪrɪ'teɪʃən/ *n* [C;U]

is /s, z, əz; *strong* ɪz/ *v* 3rd person sing. present tense of BE

Is-lam /'ɪslɑːm, 'ɪz-, ɪs'lɑːm/ *n* (people and countries that practise) the Muslim religion ~ic /ɪz'læmɪk, ɪs-/ *adj*

is-land /'aɪlənd/ *n* 1 piece of land surrounded by water 2 raised place where people can wait in the middle of a road for traffic to pass — **er** *n* person living on an island

isle /aɪl/ *n lit* island

isn't /'ɪzənt/ *v short for*: is not

i-so-late /'aɪsəleɪt/ *vt* keep separate from others — **lated** *adj* alone; only: *an isolated case* — **lation** /,aɪsə'leɪʃən/ *n* [U]

is-sue /'ɪʃuː, 'ɪsjuː ‖ 'ɪʃuː/ *n* 1 [C] subject to be talked about or argued about — see also SIDE ISSUE 2 [C] printing at one time of a magazine, etc. 3 [U] *law* children ♦ *vt* produce or provide officially: *issue a statement/new uniforms*

isth-mus /'ɪsməs/ *n* narrow piece of land joining 2 larger pieces

it /ɪt/ *pron* 1 that thing already mentioned: *'Where's my dinner?' 'The cat ate it'.* 2 that person: *'Who's that?' 'It's me.'* 3 (used in statements about weather, time, or distance): *It's raining.* | *It's Thursday.* | *It's not far to Paris.* 4 (used when the real subject comes later): *It's a pity you forgot.* 5 (making part of a sentence more important): *It was Jane who told me.* ♦ *n* 1 *infml* a very important person: *He thinks he's it.* **b** the important point: *This is it, I have to decide.* 2 **That's it: a** That's complete; there's nothing more to come **b** That's right

IT /,aɪ 'tiː/ *n* INFORMATION TECHNOLOGY

i-tal-ics /ɪ'tælɪks/ *n* [P] sloping printed letters — **icize** /-ɪsaɪz/ *vt* print in italics

itch /ɪtʃ/ *vi* 1 have the feeling of wanting to SCRATCH the skin 2 **be itching to/for** want very much ♦ *n* 1 itching feeling 2 strong desire — see also SEVEN-YEAR ITCH ~**y** *adj*

itchy feet /,·· '·/ *n* [P] *infml* desire to travel

itchy palm /,·· '·/ n infml great desire for money, esp. as payment for unfair favours

it'd /'ɪtəd/ short for: 1 it would 2 it had

i-tem /'aɪtəm/ n 1 single thing on a list, etc. 2 piece of news ~**ize** vt make a detailed list of

i-tin-e-rant /aɪ'tɪnərənt/ adj travelling from place to place

i-tin-e-ra-ry /aɪ'tɪnərəri‖-nəreri/ n plan for a journey

it'll /'ɪtl/ short for: it will

its /ɪts/ determiner of it: its ears

it's short for: 1 it is 2 it has

it-self /ɪt'self/ pron 1 (reflexive form of it): The cat washed itself. 2 (strong form of it): I had the copy, but the letter itself was missing. 3 (all) by itself: a alone b without help 4 in itself without considering the rest 5 to itself not shared

IUD /,aɪ juː 'diː/ n plastic or metal object fitted inside a woman's WOMB as a form of CONTRACEPTION

I've /aɪv/ short for: I have

i-vo-ry /'aɪvəri/ n [U] 1 hard white substance of which elephants' TUSKs are made 2 creamy white colour of this

ivory tow-er /,··· '··/ n place where people avoid the difficult realities of ordinary life

i-vy /'aɪvi/ n [U] climbing plant with shiny leaves **ivied** adj covered with ivy

Ivy League /,·· '·◄/ adj AmE belonging to or typical of a group of old and respected universities of the eastern US

J

J, j /dʒeɪ/ the 10th letter of the English alphabet

jab /dʒæb/ vi/t -bb- push with force (something pointed) ♦ n 1 sharp forceful push 2 infml, esp. BrE INJECTION

jab-ber /'dʒæbər/ vi/t talk or say quickly **jabber** n [S;U]

jack¹ /dʒæk/ n 1 apparatus for lifting a car, etc. 2 playing card between the 10 and the queen

jack² v

jack in phr vt BrE sl stop; be unwilling to continue

jack up phr vt lift with a jack

jack-al /'dʒækɔːl, -kəl‖-kəl/ n kind of wild dog

jack-boot /'dʒækbuːt/ n 1 [C] high military boot 2 [S] cruel military rule

jack-et /'dʒækɪt/ n 1 short coat with SLEEVEs 2 potato skin 3 cover for a machine, pipe, etc. 4 loose paper book cover

jack knife /'· ·/ n large pocket knife, the blade of which folds into the handle

jack-knife vi (of a vehicle) bend suddenly in the middle

jack-pot /'dʒækpɒt‖-pɑːt/ n biggest money prize to be won in a game

Ja-cuz-zi /dʒə'kuːzi/ n tdmk bath fitted with a system of hot water currents

jade /dʒeɪd/ n [U] (colour of) a green precious stone

ja-ded /'dʒeɪdɪd/ adj tired because of having had too much of something, esp. experience

jag-ged /'dʒægɪd/ adj with a rough uneven edge

jag-u-ar /'dʒægjuə'‖'dʒægwɑːr/ n large spotted wild cat of S America

jail /dʒeɪl/ n [C;U] prison ♦ vt put in jail ~**er** n person in charge of prisoners

jam¹ /dʒæm/ n [U] fruit boiled in sugar, for spreading on bread

jam² v -mm- 1 vt crush or press tightly: jam clothes into a bag | jam the brakes on 2 vi get stuck: The door jammed. 3 vt block (radio messages) ♦ n 1 closely jammed mass: traffic jam 2 in a jam in a difficult situation

jam-bo-ree /,dʒæmbə'riː/ n large party or gathering

jam-packed /,· '·◄/ adj with many people or things very close together

jan-gle /'dʒæŋgəl/ vi/t (cause to) make the noise of metal striking metal

jan-i-tor /'dʒænɪtər/ n CARETAKER

Jan-u-a-ry /'dʒænjuəri, -njuri‖-jueri/ n the 1st month of the year

jar¹ /dʒɑːr/ n short wide pot or bottle

jar² v -rr- 1 vi make a nasty sound 2 vt give a nasty shock to 3 vi go badly together: jarring colours

jar-gon /'dʒɑːgən‖'dʒɑːrgən, -gɑːn/ n [U] language used by a particular group: computer jargon

jaun-dice /'dʒɔːndɪs ‖ 'dʒɔːn-, 'dʒɑːn-/ n [U] disease that makes the skin yellow **jaundiced** adj mistrustful and CYNICAL: jaundiced opinions

jaunt /dʒɔːnt‖dʒɔːnt, dʒɑːnt/ n short pleasure trip ~**y** adj cheerful and confident

jav-e-lin /'dʒævəlɪn/ n light spear for throwing

jaw /dʒɔː/ n one of the 2 bony structures where the teeth are fixed ♦ vi/t infml talk (to) for a long time **jaws** n [P] 1 animal's mouth 2 two parts of a tool, etc., that hold things tightly: (fig.) *the jaws of death*

jay-walk /'dʒeɪwɔːk/ *vi* cross streets carelessly

jazz¹ /dʒæz/ *n* [U] music with a strong beat, originated by black Americans ~**y** *adj* brightly coloured

jazz² *v* **jazz up** *phr vt* make brighter or more interesting

jeal-ous /'dʒeləs/ *adj* 1 unhappy at not being liked as much as someone else: *jealous husband* 2 very ENVIOUS 3 wanting to keep what one has ~**ly** *adv*

jeal-ous-y /'dʒeləsi/ *n* [C;U] jealous feeling

jeans /dʒiːnz/ *n* [P] strong cotton trousers

jeep /dʒiːp/ *n* (military) car for travelling on rough ground

jeer /dʒɪəʳ/ *vi/t* laugh rudely (at) **jeer** *n* ~**ingly** *adv*

jel-ly /'dʒeli/ *n* 1 [C;U] soft gluey food made with GELATINE, or from fruit juice boiled with sugar 2 [S;U] any material between a liquid and a solid state

jeop-ar-dize , **-dise** /'dʒepədaɪz‖-ər-/ *vt fml* put in danger

jeop-ar-dy /'dʒepədi‖-ər-/ *n* [U] *fml* danger: *put one's future in jeopardy*

jerk¹ /dʒɜːk‖dʒɜːrk/ *n* sudden quick pull or movement ♦ *vi/t* pull or move with a jerk ~**y** *adj* not smooth in movement

jerk² *n sl* foolish and ungraceful person

jer-kin /'dʒɜːkɪn‖-ɜːr-/ *n* short coat without SLEEVES

jerry-built /'·· ·/ *adj* built cheaply and badly

jer-sey /'dʒɜːzi‖-ɜːr-/ *n* SWEATER

jest /dʒest/ *vi fml* joke **jest** *n* [C;U] ~**er** *n* man kept formerly to amuse a ruler

jet¹ /dʒet/ *n* 1 narrow stream of gas or liquid forced out of a hole 2 hole from which this comes 3 aircraft whose engine (**jet engine**) works on this principle ♦ *vi* 1 come in a JET (1) 2 travel by JET (3)

jet² /dʒet/ *n* [U] hard shiny black mineral: (fig.) *jet-black hair*

jet-foil /'dʒetfɔɪl/ *n* HYDROFOIL

jet lag /'· ·/ *n* [U] tiredness after flying to a place where the time is different

jet-sam /'dʒetsəm/ *n* [U] see FLOTSAM AND JETSAM

jet set /'· ·/ *n* [S] international social group of rich fashionable people

jet-ti-son /'dʒetɪsən, -zən/ *vt* throw away

jet-ty /'dʒeti/ *n* small PIER

Jew /dʒuː/ *n* person descended from the people of ancient Israel whose history is told in the Bible ~**ish** *adj*

jew-el /,dʒuːəl/ *n* 1 (real or artificial) precious stone 2 very valuable person or thing ~**ler** *BrE* ‖ ~**er** *AmE* person who sells jewels ~**lery** *BrE* ‖ ~**ry** *AmE* [U] jewels worn as decoration

jib¹ /dʒɪb/ *v* **jib at** *phr vt* be unwilling to do something: *jib at signing the contract*

jib² *n* long arm of a CRANE (1) from which the hook hangs down

jibe /dʒaɪb/ *n, v* GIBE

jif-fy /'dʒɪfi/ *n* [S] moment: *I'll come in a jiffy.*

jig /dʒɪg/ *n* (music for) a quick merry dance ♦ *vi* jump up and down

jig-gle /'dʒɪgəl/ *vi/t* shake from side to side

jig-saw /'dʒɪgsɔː/ also **jigsaw puzzle** /'·· ,·/ — *n* picture cut into pieces to be fitted together for fun

jilt /dʒɪlt/ *vt* unexpectedly refuse (an accepted lover)

jin-gle /'dʒɪŋgəl/ *n* 1 sound as of small bells ringing 2 simple poem used esp. for advertisement ♦ *vi/t* (cause to) sound with a jingle

jin-go-is-m /'dʒɪŋgəʊɪzəm/ *n* [U] *derog* extreme warlike NATIONALISM

jinx /dʒɪŋks/ *n* something that brings bad luck

jit-ters /'dʒɪtəz‖-ərz/ *n* [P] anxiety before an event **-tery** *adj*

jive /dʒaɪv/ *n* [U] (dance performed to) a kind of popular music with a strong beat ♦ *vi* dance to jive music

Jnr *written abbrev. for:* JUNIOR

job /dʒɒb‖dʒɑːb/ *n* 1 [C] regular paid employment: *out of a job* (= unemployed) 2 [C] piece of work 3 [C] *sl* crime, esp. a robbery — see also INSIDE JOB 4 [S] something hard to do: *You'll have a job to open it.* 5 [S] one's affair; duty: *It's not my job to interfere.* 6 [C] *infml* example of a certain type: *That new Rolls of yours is a beautiful job.* 7 [C] *infml* a PLASTIC SURGERY operation: *a nose job* 8 **a good/bad job** *infml* a good/bad thing 9 **just the job** exactly the thing wanted or needed 10 **make the best of a bad job** do as much or as well as possible in unfavourable conditions 11 **on the job** while working; at work ~**ber** *n* member of the STOCK EXCHANGE who does not deal directly with the public ~**bing** *adj* paid by the JOB (2) ~**less** *adj* unemployed

job lot /'· ·, · '·/ *n* group of things of different kinds bought or sold together

jock-ey /'dʒɒki‖'dʒɑːki/ *n* professional rider in horse races ♦ *vi/t* try by all possible means to get into a good position: *jockey for position*

joc·u·lar /'dʒɒkjʊlər‖'dʒɑː-/ adj fml joking; not serious ~**ly** adv

joc·und /'dʒɒkənd‖'dʒɑː-/ adj lit merry

jodh·purs /'dʒɒdpəz‖'dʒɑːdpərz/ n [P] trousers for horse riding

jog /dʒɒg‖dʒɑːg/ v -**gg**- **1** vt knock slightly **2** vi run slowly for exercise **3 jog someone's memory** make someone remember ♦ n ~**ger** n someone who JOGs (2)

jog along phr vi move slowly and uneventfully

join /dʒɔɪn/ v **1** vt fasten; connect: join 2 ropes **2** vi/t come together (with); meet: join me for a drink | The stream joins the river. **3** vt become a member of: join the army ♦ n place where 2 things are joined

join in phr vi take part in an activity

join up phr vi offer oneself for military service

join·er /'dʒɔɪnər/ n woodworker who makes doors, etc., inside buildings ~**y** n [U] trade of a joiner

joint¹ /dʒɔɪnt/ n **1** place where things (esp. bones) join **2** BrE large piece of meat **3** sl public place for drinking, etc. **4** sl cigarette containing CANNABIS

joint² adj shared: joint bank account ~**ly** adv

joist /dʒɔɪst/ n beam supporting a floor

joke /dʒəʊk/ n **1** something said or done to amuse people **2 play a joke on someone** do something to make other people laugh at someone ♦ vi tell jokes **joker** n **1** person who makes jokes **2** additional playing card with no fixed value

jol·ly¹ /'dʒɒli‖'dʒɑːli/ adj happy; pleasant

jolly² infml persuade; urge gently

jolly along phr vt encourage in a joking or friendly way

jolly up phr vt make (esp. a place) bright and cheerful

jolly³ adv infml very: jolly difficult

jolt /dʒəʊlt/ vi/t shake or shock **jolt** n

Jo·nah /'dʒəʊnə/ n person who seems to bring bad luck

Jones·es /'dʒəʊnzɪz/ n **keep up with the Joneses** derog compete with one's neighbours socially, esp. by buying the same expensive new things that they buy

joss stick /'dʒɒs ˌstɪk‖'dʒɑːs-/ n stick of INCENSE

jos·tle /'dʒɒsl‖'dʒɑː-/ vi/t knock or push (against)

jot /dʒɒt‖dʒɑːt/ n [S] very small bit: not a jot of truth ♦ vt -**tt**- write quickly ~**ter** n notebook ~**ting** n rough note

jour·nal /'dʒɜːnəl‖-ɜːr-/ n **1** magazine **2** DIARY ~**ism** n profession of writing for newspapers ~**ist** n person whose profession is journalism

jour·nal·ese /ˌdʒɜːnəˈliːz‖-ɜːr-/ n [U] derog language of newspapers

jour·ney /'dʒɜːni‖-ɜːr-/ n long trip, esp. by land ♦ vi lit travel

jo·vi·al /'dʒəʊviəl/ adj friendly and cheerful ~**ly** adv

jowl /dʒaʊl/ n lower part of the face

joy /dʒɔɪ/ n **1** [U] great happiness **2** [C] something that causes joy **3** [U] BrE infml success: I tried phoning her but didn't have any joy. (= I wasn't able to) ~**ful** adj fml full of or causing joy ~**fully** adv ~**ous** adj lit joyful

joy·ride /'dʒɔɪraɪd/ n ride for pleasure in a (stolen) car

JP /ˌdʒeɪ 'piː/ n Justice of the Peace; MAGISTRATE

Jr written abbrev. for: JUNIOR

jub·i·lant /'dʒuːbɪlənt/ adj joyful; delighted –**lation** /ˌdʒuːbɪˈleɪʃən/ n [U] rejoicing

ju·bi·lee /'dʒuːbɪliː, ˌdʒuːbɪˈliː/ n **1** time of rejoicing at an ANNIVERSARY **2 diamond / golden / silver jubilee** 60th/50th/25th return of an important date

Ju·da·is·m /'dʒuːdeɪ-ɪzəm, 'dʒuːdə-‖'dʒuːdə-, 'dʒuːdi-/ n [U] religion of the Jews

jud·der /'dʒʌdər/ vi BrE (of a vehicle) shake violently

judge /dʒʌdʒ/ n **1** public official who decides legal cases **2** person who decides in a competition, etc. **3** person who can give a valuable opinion: I'm no judge of music. ♦ vi/t act as a judge (in); form an opinion (about)

judg·ment, judgement /'dʒʌdʒmənt/ n **1** [U] ability to decide correctly: a man of sound judgment **2** [C] opinion **3** [C;U] decision of a judge or court of law: She passed (= gave) judgment on the accused man.

judgment day /'·· ·/ n day when God will judge everyone

ju·di·cial /dʒuːˈdɪʃəl/ adj of law courts and judges ~**ly** adv

ju·di·cia·ry /dʒuːˈdɪʃəri‖-ʃieri, -ʃəri/ n all the judges, as a group

ju·di·cious /dʒuːˈdɪʃəs/ adj fml sensible ~**ly** adv

ju·do /'dʒuːdəʊ/ n [U] type of self-defence, from Asia

jug /dʒʌg/ n esp. BrE pot for liquids, with a handle and a lip for pouring

jug·ger·naut /'dʒʌgənɔːt‖-ər-/ n BrE very large TRUCK

jug·gle /'dʒʌgəl/ vi/t **1** keep (objects) in the air by throwing and catching them **2** play tricks (with), esp. to deceive: juggling the figures **juggler** n

juice /dʒuːs/ n [C;U] liquid from fruit, vegetables, or meat **juicy** adj **1** having a lot of juice **2** infml interesting esp. because providing details about improper behaviour

juke-box /'dʒuːkbɒks‖-bɑːks/ n coin-operated music machine

Ju-ly /dʒu'laɪ/ n the 7th month of the year

jum-ble /'dʒʌmbəl/ vi/t mix in disorder ♦ n 1 [S] disorderly mixture 2 [U] BrE things for a JUMBLE SALE

jumble sale /'··· ·/ n BrE sale of used articles to get money for CHARITY, etc.

jum-bo /'dʒʌmbəʊ/ adj very large: jumbo jet

jump¹ /dʒʌmp/ v 1 vi push oneself off the ground with one's leg muscles 2 vt cross in this way: jump a stream 3 vi move suddenly: The noise made me jump. 4 vi rise sharply: Oil prices have jumped. 5 vt attack suddenly 6 vt leave, pass or escape from (something) illegally 7 **jump down someone's throat** infml attack someone in words, strongly and unexpectedly 8 **jump the gun** start something too soon 9 **jump the queue** get something before those who have waited longer 10 **jump to it!** hurry

jump at phr vt accept eagerly

jump on phr vt infml speak to sharply

jump² n 1 act of jumping 2 thing to jump over 3 **be/stay one jump ahead** do the right thing because one knows or guesses what one's competitors are going to do ~**y** adj nervously excited

jumped-up /,·· '·◄/ adj having too great an idea of one's own importance

jump-er /'dʒʌmpər/ n 1 BrE for SWEATER 2 horse or person that jumps

jump-suit /'dʒʌmpsuːt, -sjuːt‖-suːt/ n a one-piece garment combining top and trousers

junc-tion /'dʒʌŋkʃən/ n place of joining: railway junction

junc-ture /'dʒʌŋktʃər/ n fml point in time

June /dʒuːn/ n the 6th month of the year

jun-gle /'dʒʌŋgəl/ n [C;U] thick tropical forest

ju-ni-or /'dʒuːniər/ n, adj 1 (someone) younger 2 (someone) of low or lower rank

Junior adj esp. AmE the younger (of two men in the same family with the same name)

junior school /'··· ,·/ n BrE school for children between 7 and 11 years old

junk /dʒʌŋk/ n [U] 1 old useless things 2 sl dangerous drug, esp. HEROIN ♦ vt infml get rid of as worthless

jun-ket /'dʒʌŋkɪt/ n 1 [C] infml, often derog trip, esp. one made by a government official and paid for with

government money 2 [U] kind of thick sweet milk

junk food /'· ·/ n [U] infml unhealthy food

junk-ie , -y /'dʒʌŋki/ n sl person who takes HEROIN: (fig.) I'm a real sugar junkie.

junk mail /'· ·/ n [U] mail, usu. for advertising, sent to people although they have not asked for it

jun-ta /'dʒʌntə, 'huntə/ n (military) government that has seized power by armed force

Ju-pi-ter /'dʒuːpɪtər/ n the largest PLANET, 5th in order from the sun

jur-is-dic-tion /,dʒuərɪs'dɪkʃən/ n [U] legal power

ju-ror /'dʒuərər/ n member of a jury

ju-ry /'dʒuəri/ n 1 group of people chosen to decide questions of fact in a court of law 2 group of people chosen to judge a competition of any kind

just¹ /dʒəst; strong dʒʌst/ adv 1 exactly: sitting just here 2 completely: It's just perfect! 3 at this moment: I'm just coming. 4 only a short time (ago): just after breakfast | They've only just left. 5 almost not: She arrived just in time. 6 only: no dinner, just coffee 7 **just about** very nearly 8 **just as well: a** lucky or suitable: It's just as well I brought my coat — it's freezing! **b** with good reason, considering the situation: Since there's no more work to do, we might just as well go home. 9 **just now: a** at this moment: We're having dinner just now — come back later. **b** a moment ago: Paul telephoned just now to say he'll be late. 10 **just yet** quite yet

just² /dʒʌst/ adj fair; according to what is deserved ~**ly** adv

jus-tice /'dʒʌstɪs/ n 1 [U] quality of being just; fairness 2 [U] the law: court of justice 3 [C] JUDGE (1) 4 **do justice to someone** also **do someone justice** — treat someone in a fair way

Justice of the Peace /,··· ·'·/ n MAGISTRATE

jus-ti-fy /'dʒʌstɪfaɪ/ vt give or be a good reason for –**fiable** adj –**fiably** adv –**fication** /,dʒʌstɪfɪ'keɪʃən/ n [U] good reason

jut /dʒʌt/ vi -tt- stick out or up further than the things around it

ju-ve-nile /'dʒuːvənaɪl‖-nəl, -naɪl/ n 1 young person 2 actor or actress who plays such a person ♦ adj 1 of or for juveniles 2 childish or foolish

juvenile de-lin-quen-cy /,··· ·'···/n [U] crimes by JUVENILEs (1) –**quent** n

jux-ta-pose /,dʒʌkstə'pəʊz‖'dʒʌkstəpəʊz/ vt fml put side by side –**posi-tion** /,dʒʌkstəpə'zɪʃən/ n [U]

K

K , **k**/keɪ/ the 11th letter of the English alphabet

K *written abbrev. for:* **1** 1024 BYTES of computer DATA **2** *infml* one thousand: **a** £20K salary

kaf-tan /'kæftæn‖kæf'tæn/ *n* CAFTAN

ka-lei-do-scope /kə'laɪdəskəʊp/ *n* tube containing mirrors, and often bits of coloured glass, turned to produce changing patterns **–scopic** /kə,laɪdə'skɒpɪk‖-'skɑ:-/ *adj* changing quickly and often

kan-ga-roo /,kæŋgə'ru:◂/ *n* Australian animal that jumps along on its large back legs, and carries its baby in a pocket

ka-o-lin /'keɪəlɪn/ *n* [U] fine white clay used in medicine, etc.

ka-pok /'keɪpɒk‖-pɑːk/ *n* [U] cotton-like material used to fill sleeping bags, etc.

kar-at /'kærət/ *n* CARAT

ka-ra-te /kə'rɑːti/ *n* [U] Asian style of fighting using the hands and feet

kay-ak /'kaɪæk/ *n* light covered CANOE

K.C. /,keɪ 'siː/ *n* (title, while a king is ruling, for) a British lawyer of high rank

ke-bab /kə'bæb‖kə'bɑːb/ *n* small pieces of meat cooked on a stick

kedg-e-ree /'kedʒəri/ *n* [U] dish of rice, fish, and eggs

keel¹ /kiːl/ *n* **1** bar along the bottom of a boat **2 on an even keel** steady

keel² *v* **keel over** *phr vi* fall over sideways

keen /kiːn/ *adj* **1** having a strong interest: *keen students*| *keen on football* **2** (of the 5 senses) good, strong, quick, etc.: *keen eyesight* **3** (of edges) sharp; cutting: (fig.) *keen wind* **~ly** *adv* **~ness** *n* [U]

keep¹ /kiːp/ *v* **kept** /kept/ **1** *vt* continue to have; not lose or give back **2** *vi/t* (cause to) continue being: *keep them warm*| *Keep off the grass!* **3** *vi* continually do something: *He keeps complaining.* **4** *vt* fulfil (a promise) **5** *vt* prevent: *keep them from knowing* **6** *vt* not tell (a secret) **7** *vt* make records of or in: *keep accounts*| *a diary* **8** *vt* support with money, etc. **9** *vt* own or manage: *keep chickens*| *a shop* **10** *vi* remain fresh: *This fish won't keep.* **11** *vt* take suitable notice of (a holiday, etc): *keep Christmas* **12 keep (one-self) to oneself** not mix with or talk to other people very much **13 keep one's head** remain calm **14 keep one's shirt on** also **keep one's hair on** *BrE*

— *infml* to remain calm; not to become upset or angry **15 keep some-one company** remain with someone

keep at *phr vt* continue working at (something)

keep back *phr vt* not tell or give; WITHHOLD

keep down *phr vt* **1** prevent from increasing **2** OPPRESS

keep from *phr vt* **1** not to tell (someone) about something **2** prevent oneself from (doing something)

keep in with *phr vt* remain friendly with

keep on *phr v* **1** *vi* continue talking **2** *vt* continue to employ (someone) **3** *vi* continue to have (something)

keep on at *phr vt* ask repeatedly

keep out *phr vi/t* (cause to) stay away or not enter

keep to *phr vt* **1** stay in: *keep to the left* **2** limit oneself to: *keep to the point* **3** keep (something) private to (oneself)

keep up *phr v* **1** *vi* stay level **2** *vt* continue doing **3** *vt* prevent from going to bed **4** *vt* prevent from falling or dropping: *a belt to keep my trousers up*|(fig.) *Keep your spirits up!* (= remain cheerful)

keep² *n* **1** [U] (cost of) necessary food, etc: *earn one's keep* **2** [C] central tower of a castle **3 for keeps** *infml* for ever

keep-er /'kiːpə'/ *n* person who guards or looks after: *shopkeeper*

keep-ing /'kiːpɪŋ/ *n* [U] **1** care; charge: *leave her jewels in my keeping* **2 in/out of keeping with** suitable/not suitable for

keep-sake /'kiːpseɪk/ *n* thing kept to remind one of the giver

keg /keg/ *n* small barrel

ken /ken/ *n* **beyond one's ken** outside one's knowledge

ken-nel /'kenl/ *n* house for a dog **kennels** *n* place where dogs are bred (BREED (2)) or looked after

kept /kept/ *v past t. and p. of* KEEP¹

kerb /kɜːb‖kɜːrb/ *n* *BrE* stone edge of a PAVEMENT

ker-nel /'kɜːnl‖'kɜːr-/ *n* **1** centre of a nut, seed, etc. **2** important part of a subject

kes-trel /'kestrəl/ *n* red-brown European bird which eats mice, birds, and insects

ketch-up /'ketʃəp/ *n* [U] thick liquid made from TOMATO juice

ket-tle /'ketl/ *n* pot with a SPOUT, for boiling water

ket-tle-drum /'ketldrʌm/ *n* large metal drum

key¹ /kiː/ *n* **1** shaped piece of metal for locking a door, etc.: *car keys* **2** something that explains or helps one to understand **3** any of the parts of a piano, etc., to be pressed to produce the desired sound or effect: *typewriter keys* **4** musical notes starting at a particular base note: *the key of C* ♦ *adj* very important; necessary: *key industries | a key position in the firm*

key² *vt* **1** make suitable: *factories keyed to military needs* **2** keyboard (information) **3** keyed up excited and nervous

key·board /'ki:bɔːd‖-bɔːrd/ *n* row of KEYs (3) ♦ *vt* put (information) into a machine by working a keyboard

key·hole /'ki:həʊl/ *n* hole for a KEY (1)

key·note /'ki:nəʊt/ *n* central idea of a speech, etc.)

kg *written abbrev. for:* KILOGRAM(s)

kha·ki /'kɑːki‖'kæki, 'kɑːki/ *n* **1** [U] yellowish-brown colour **2** cloth of this colour, esp. as worn by soldiers

kib·butz /kɪ'bʊts/ *n* **-zim** /-sɪm/ *or* **-zes** farm or settlement in Israel where many families live and work together

kick¹ /kɪk/ *v* **1** *vt* hit with the foot **2** *vi* move the feet as if to kick **3** *vi* (of a gun) move violently when fired **4** *vt sl* stop or give up (a harmful activity) **5** kick someone in the teeth *infml* discourage or disappoint someone very much **6** kick the bucket *sl* die

  kick about/around *phr v* **1** *vt* be unnoticed in (a place) **2** *vt* beat roughly

  kick against *phr vt* oppose or dislike

  kick off *phr vi* begin

  kick out *phr vt* remove or dismiss (someone), esp. violently

  kick up *phr vt* make (trouble): *kick up a fuss*

kick² *n* **1** [C] act of kicking **2** [C] *sl* excitement: *drive fast for kicks* **3** [S;U] *infml* strength **4** [C] extremely strong new interest: *She's on a health food kick.*

kick-off /'kɪk-ɒf‖ -ɔːf/ *n* first kick in football

kid¹ /kɪd/ *n* **1** [C] child or young person **2** [C;U] (leather from) a young goat

kid² *vi/t* **-dd-** *sl* pretend; deceive

kid gloves /ˌ· '·/ *n* [P] gentle methods of dealing with people

kid·nap /'kɪdnæp/ *vt* **-pp-** take (someone) away by force, so as to demand money, etc. **~per** *n*

kid·ney /'kɪdni/ *n* organ that separates waste liquid from the blood

kidney ma·chine /'··· ,·/ *n* hospital machine that can do the work of human kidneys

kill /kɪl/ *vt* **1** cause to die: (fig.) *My feet are killing me.* (= hurting very much) | (fig.) *The boss will kill me* (= be very angry) *when she finds out.* **2** destroy; spoil **3** kill time make time

pass quickly **4** kill two birds with one stone get two good results from one action ♦ *n* [S] **1** bird or animal killed **2** act or moment of killing **~er** *n* **~ing** *n* **1** murder **2** make a killing make a lot of money suddenly

kill-joy /'kɪldʒɔɪ/ *n* person who spoils other people's pleasure

kiln /kɪln/ *n* apparatus for baking pots, bricks, etc.

ki·lo /'kiːləʊ/ *n* kilos kilogram

kil·o·byte /'kɪləbaɪt/ *n* 1000 or 1024 BYTEs of computer information

kil·o·gram , **-gramme** /'kɪləgræm/ *n* (a measure of weight equal to) 2.2 pounds

kil·o·me·tre *BrE* ‖ **-ter** *AmE* /'kɪlə-ˌmiːtə', kɪ'lɒmɪtə'‖'kɪ'lɑːmətər/ *n* (a measure of length equal to) 0.62 of a mile

kil·o·watt /'kɪləwɒt‖-wɑːt/ *n* 1000 WATTs

kilt /kɪlt/ *n* short skirt worn esp. by Scotsmen

ki·mo·no /kɪ'məʊnəʊ/ *n* **-nos** **1** long loose Japanese garment **2** loose DRESSING GOWN

kin /kɪn/ *n* [P] next of kin one's closest relative(s) — see also KITH AND KIN

kind¹ /kaɪnd/ *n* **1** type; sort: *all kinds of people* **2** a kind of an unclear or unusual sort of: *I had a kind of feeling she'd phone.* **3** in kind (of payment) in goods, not money **4** kind of *infml* in a certain way; rather **5** of a kind: **a** of the same kind: *They're two of a kind.* **b** of a not very good kind: *It was coffee of a kind, but we couldn't drink it.*

kind² *adj* helpful and friendly **~ness** *n* [U] quality of being kind **2** [C] kind act

kin·der·gar·ten /'kɪndəgɑːtn‖-dərgɑːrtn/ *n* school for young children, usu. between the ages of 4 and 6

kind-heart·ed /ˌ· '··◄‖ˌ· '··/ *adj* having a kind nature **~ly** *adv* **~ness** *n* [U]

kin·dle /'kɪndl/ *vt/i* (cause to) start burning **–dling** *n* [U] materials for starting a fire

kind·ly /'kaɪndli/ *adv* **1** in a kind way **2** (showing annoyance) please **3** take kindly to accept willingly ♦ *adj fml* kind

kin·dred /'kɪndrəd/ *adj* **1** related **2** kindred spirit person with almost the same habits, interests, etc.

ki·net·ic /kɪ'netɪk, kaɪ-/ *adj fml* of or about movement

king /kɪŋ/ *n* **1** (title of) the male ruler of a country **2** most important man or animal **3** playing card with a picture of a king

king·dom /'kɪŋdəm/ *n* **1** country governed by a king or queen **2** any of the three divisions of natural objects: *the animal/plant/mineral kingdom*

king-pin /'kɪŋ,pɪn/ *n* most important person in a group

king-size /'· ·/ *adj* above the standard size

kink /kɪŋk/ *n* **1** twist in hair, a pipe, etc. **2** strangeness of character ~**y** *adj* sexually unnatural

kins-man /'kɪnzmən/ **kinswoman** /-,wʊmən/ *fem.* — *n* **-men** /-mən/ *fml* relative

ki-osk /'ki:ɒsk‖-ɑ:sk/ *n* **1** small open hut for selling newspapers, etc. **2** *BrE fml* public telephone box

kip /kɪp/ *vi* **-pp-** *BrE sl* sleep **kip** *n* [S;U]

kip-per /'kɪpər/ *n* salted HERRING treated with smoke

kiss /kɪs/ *vi/t* touch with the lips as a sign of love or a greeting **kiss** *n* act of kissing

kiss of death /,·· '·/ *n* [*the* + S] *infml* something that makes someone fail

kiss of life /,· · '·/ *n* [*the* + S] *esp. BrE* method of preventing death of a person by breathing into his/her mouth

kit¹ /kɪt/ *n* **1** necessary clothes, tools, etc.: *a sailor's/carpenter's kit* **2** set of pieces to be put together: *model aircraft kit*

kit² *v* **-tt- kit out/up** *phr vt* supply with necessary clothes, etc.

kit bag /'· ·/ *n* bag for carrying a soldier's or sailor's kit

kitch-en /'kɪtʃɪn/ *n* room for cooking in

kitch-en-ette /,kɪtʃɪ'net/ *n* very small kitchen

kite /kaɪt/ *n* **1** frame covered with paper or cloth, for flying in the air **2** kind of HAWK¹ (1)

kith and kin /,kɪθ ən 'kɪn/ *n* one's friends and relatives

kitsch /kɪtʃ/ *n* objects, works of literature which pretend to be art but are considered silly, funny, or worthless

kit-ten /'kɪtn/ *n* **1** young cat **2 have kittens** *BrE infml* be in a very nervous anxious condition

kit-ty /'kɪti/ *n* money collected by several people for an agreed purpose

ki-wi /'ki:wi:/ *n* **1** flightless New Zealand bird **2** *infml* New Zealander

Kleen-ex /'kli:neks/ *n* [C;U] *tdmk* paper handkerchief

klep-to-ma-ni-a /,kleptə'meɪniə/ *n* [U] disease of the mind that makes one steal **-ac** /-niæk/ *n* person with kleptomania

km *written abbrev. for:* kilometre(s)

knack /næk/ *n* special skill

knack-ered /'nækəd‖-kərd/ *adj BrE sl* very tired

knave /neɪv/ *n* **1** JACK (2) **2** *old use* dishonest man

knead /ni:d/ *vt* mix (flour and water, etc.) by pressing with the hands **2** press and rub (muscles) to cure pain, stiffness, etc.

knee /ni:/ *n* **1** middle joint of the leg **2** part of a pair of trousers, etc., that covers the knee **3 bring someone to his knees** defeat someone completely ◆ *vt* hit with the knee

knee-cap¹ /'ni:kæp/ *n* bone at the front of the knee

kneecap² *vt* **-pp-** shoot the kneecaps of (someone), usu. as an unofficial punishment

knee-deep /,· '·◄/ *adj* deep enough to reach the knees: (fig.) *knee-deep in debt* (= in trouble over debt)

knee-jerk /'· ·/ *adj derog* (of opinion) held without thought

kneel /ni:l/ *vi* **knelt** /nelt/ *or* (*esp. AmE*) **kneeled** go down on one's knees

knell /nel/ *n* sound of a bell rung slowly for a death

knew /nju:‖nu:/ *v past t. of* KNOW¹

knick-er-bock-ers /'nɪkə,bɒkəz‖ 'nɪkər,bɑ:kərz/ *n* [P] short trousers fitting tightly below the knees

knick-ers /'nɪkəz‖-ərz/ *n* [P] *BrE* **1** women's UNDERPANTS **2 get one's knickers in a twist** become angry ◆ *interj BrE sl* (used as an expression of fearless disrespect)

knick-knack /'nɪk næk/ *n* small decorative object

knife /naɪf/ *n* **knives** /naɪvz/ **1** blade with a handle, for cutting **2 have/get one's knife into someone** treat someone as an enemy and try to harm them ◆ *vt* wound with a knife

knife-edge /'· ·/ *n* **1** something sharp and narrow **2 on a knife-edge** in an extremely uncertain position

knight /naɪt/ *n* **1** (in former times) noble soldier **2** man who has been given the British title SIR **3** piece in chess ~**hood** *n* [C;U] rank of a knight ◆ *vt* make (someone) a KNIGHT (2)

knit /nɪt/ *vi/t* **knitted** *or* **knit 1** make (clothes, etc.) by forming a network of threads with long needles (**knitting needles**) **2** join closely; grow together ~**ting** *n* something being knitted

knit-wear /'nɪt-weər/ *n* [U] knitted clothing

knives /naɪvz/ *n pl. of* KNIFE

knob /nɒb‖nɑ:b/ *n* **1** round handle or control button **2** round lump: *knob of butter*

knob-bly /'nɒbli‖'nɑ:bli/ *BrE* ǁ **knobby** /'nɒbi‖'nɑ:-/ *AmE adj* having KNOBs (2): *knobbly knees*

knock¹ /nɒk‖nɑ:k/ *v* **1** *vi/t* hit: *knock on the door* **2** *vt sl* say bad things about **3** (of a car engine) make a noise like hitting **4 knock someone's block off** *infml* hit someone very severely **5**

knock spots off *BrE infml* defeat easily

knock about/around *phr v* **1** *vi/t* be present or active (in) **2** *vt* treat roughly **3** *infml* travel continuously **4** *infml* be seen in public (with someone); have a relationship (with someone)

knock back *phr vt* **1** drink quickly **2** shock

knock down *phr vt* **1** destroy (a building) with blows **2** strike to the ground: *knocked down by a bus* **3** reduce (a price)

knock off *phr v* **1** *vi/t* stop (work) **2** *vt* take from a total payment: *knock £2 off the price* **3** *vt sl* steal **4** *vt* finish quickly **5** *vt sl* murder

knock out *phr vt* **1** make unconscious by hitting **2** (of a drug) make (someone) go to sleep **3** cause someone to be dismissed from a competition **4** *sl* fill with great admiration

knock up *phr v* **1** *vt BrE* make quickly **2** *vt BrE* awaken by knocking **3** *vt AmE sl* make PREGNANT **4** *vi BrE* practise before beginning a real game

knock² *n* **1** sound of knocking **2** *infml* piece of bad luck

knock-down /'nɒkdaʊn‖'nɑːk-/ *adj* (of a price) the lowest possible

knock-er /'nɒkə'‖'nɑː-/ *n* instrument fixed to a door, for knocking

knock-ers /'nɒkəz‖'nɑːkərz/ *n* [P] *sl* a woman's breasts (usu. considered offensive to women)

knock-kneed /ˌ· '·◄‖'· ·/ *adj* with knees that touch when walking

knock-on /'· ·/ *adj* marked by a set of events, actions, etc., each of which is caused by the one before: *price rises which will have a knock-on effect throughout the economy*

knock-out /'nɒk-aʊt‖'nɑːk-/ *n* **1** act of knocking a BOXER unconscious **2** competition from which losers are dismissed **3** person or thing causing admiration ♦ *adj infml* causing great admiration

knoll /nəʊl/ *n* small round hill

knot /nɒt‖nɑːt/ *n* **1** fastening made by tying rope, etc. **2** hard lump in wood, etc. **3** small group of people **4** a measure of the speed of a ship, about 1853 metres per hour **4 get tied (up) into knots (over)** become confused (about) ♦ *vt* **-tt-** **1** make a knot in; join with a knot **2 Get knotted!** *BrE sl* (expresses great annoyance at a person) **~ty** *adj* **1** (of wood) with KNOTs (2) **2** difficult: *knotty problem*

know¹ /nəʊ/ *v* **knew** /njuː‖nuː/, **known** /nəʊn/ **1** *vi/t* have (information) in the mind **2** *vt* know well: *Do you know Paris*

well? **4** *vt* be able to recognize: *You'll know him by his red hair.* **5** [*only in past and perfect tenses*] see, hear, etc.: *I've known him to run 10 miles before breakfast.* — see also **let someone know** (LET)

know apart *phr vt* be able to tell the difference between

know backwards *phr vt* know or understand perfectly

know of *phr vt* have heard of or about: *I know of him, but I've never met him.*

know² *n* **in the know** well-informed

know-all /'· ·/ *n* person who behaves as if he/she knew everything

know-how /'· ·/ *n* [U] practical ability

know-ing /'nəʊɪŋ/ *adj* having secret understanding ~**ly** *adv* **1** in a knowing way **2** intentionally

knowl-edge /'nɒlɪdʒ‖'nɑː-/ *n* [S;U] **1** understanding **2** learning **3** information about something **4 to the best of one's knowledge** so far as one knows — see also WORKING KNOWLEDGE

knowl-edge-a-ble /'nɒlɪdʒəbəl‖ 'nɑː-/ *adj* well-informed

known¹ /nəʊn/ *past p. of* KNOW

known² *adj* **1** publicly recognized: *known criminals* **2 known as: a** generally recognized as **b** also publicly called

knuck-le¹ /'nʌkəl/ *n* **1** finger joint **2 near the knuckle** *infml* almost improper

knuckle² *v*

knuckle down *phr vi* start working hard

knuckle under *phr vi* be forced to accept the orders of someone more powerful

KO /ˌkeɪ 'əʊ/ *n infml for* KNOCKOUT (1)

ko-a-la /kəʊ'ɑːlə/ *n* type of small Australian animal like a bear

kook-y /'kuːki/ *adj AmE infml* behaving in a silly unusual manner

Ko-ran /kɔː'rɑːn, kə-‖kɔː'rɑːn, -'rɑːn/ *n* [*the*] the holy book of the Muslims

ko-sher /'kəʊʃə'/ *adj* **1** (of food) prepared according to Jewish law **2** *infml* honest and trustworthy

kow-tow /ˌkaʊ'taʊ/ *vi* obey without question

Krem-lin /'kremlən/ *n* (buildings containing) the government of the Soviet Union

ku-dos /'kjuːdɒs‖'kuːdɑːs/ *n* [U] public admiration and glory (for something done)

kung fu /ˌkʌŋ 'fuː/ *n* [U] Chinese style of fighting, like KARATE

kw *written abbrev. for:* KILOWATT(s)

L

L, l /el/ the 12th letter of the English alphabet

l *written abbrev. for:* **1** litre(s) **2** line **3** (*often cap.*) lake

lab /læb/ *n* laboratory

Lab *written abbrev. for:* LABOUR PARTY

la·bel /'leɪbəl/ *n* piece of paper, etc., fixed to something to say what it is, who owns it, etc. ♦ *vt* **-ll-** *BrE* ‖ **-l-** *AmE* **1** fix a label on **2** describe as: *They labelled him a thief.*

la·bo·ra·tory /ləˈbɒrətri‖ˈlæbrətɔːri/ *n* building or room where a scientist works

la·bo·ri·ous /ləˈbɔːriəs/ *adj* needing great effort **~ly** *adv*

la·bour¹ *BrE* ‖ **labor** *AmE* /ˈleɪbəʳ/ *n* **1** [U] hard work **2** [U] workers as a group **3** [S;U] act of giving birth ♦ *adj* (*cap.*) of the LABOUR PARTY **~er** *n* man who does heavy unskilled work

labour under *phr vt* suffer from: *labour under a delusion*

labour² *BrE* ‖ **labor** *AmE* *v* **1** *vi* work hard **2** *vt* work something out in too great detail: *labour the point*

Labour Par·ty /'·· ,·'/ *n* [*the*] political party in favour of social improvement for esp. workers and less wealthy people

lab·y·rinth /ˈlæbərɪnθ/ *n* MAZE

lace /leɪs/ *n* **1** [U] netlike decorative cloth **2** [C] cord for fastening shoes, etc. ♦ *vt* **1** fasten with a lace **2** make (a drink) stronger by adding alcohol **lacy** *adj* like LACE (1)

la·ce·rate /ˈlæsəreɪt/ *vt fml* cut; wound **-ration** /ˌlæsəˈreɪʃən/ *n* [C;U]

lach·ry·mose /ˈlækrɪməʊs/ *adj fml* **1** in the habit of weeping **2** tending to cause weeping

lack /læk/ *vt* be without (enough of) ♦ *n* [S;U] absence: need **~ing** *adj* **1** missing **2 be lacking in** without the usual or needed amount of

lack·a·dai·si·cal /ˌlækəˈdeɪzɪkəl/ *adj* without enough effort; careless

lack·ey /ˈlæki/ *n derog* person who obeys without question

lack·lus·tre *BrE* ‖ **-ter** *AmE* /ˈlæk,lʌstəʳ/ *adj* lifeless; dull

la·con·ic /ləˈkɒnɪk‖-ˈkɑː-/ *adj fml* using few words **~ally** /-kli/ *adv*

lac·quer /ˈlækəʳ/ *n* [U] transparent substance that makes a hard shiny surface, or keeps hair in place ♦ *vt* cover with lacquer

la·crosse /ləˈkrɒs‖ləˈkrɔːs/ *n* [U] field game for 2 teams, using sticks with nets at the end

la·cu·na /ləˈkjuːnə‖-ˈkuː-/ *n* **-nae** /-niː/ *or* **-nas** *fml* empty space, esp. in written matter or knowledge

lad /læd/ *n* **1** boy; youth **2** *infml* playfully rude man: *a bit of a lad* **lads** *n* [*the* + P] *BrE infml* group of men one knows and likes

lad·der /ˈlædəʳ/ *n* **1** bars joined to each other by steps, for climbing: (fig.) *the promotion ladder* **2** *BrE* ladder-shaped fault in a STOCKING, etc. ♦ *vi/t* develop a LADDER (2) (in)

la·den /ˈleɪdn/ *adj* heavily loaded: (fig.) *laden with sorrow*

la·dle /ˈleɪdl/ *n* large spoon for serving liquids ♦ *vt* serve with a ladle

ladle out *phr vt* give out freely

la·dy /ˈleɪdi/ *n* **1** woman **2** woman of good manners or high social rank **3** (*cap.*) (title for) a woman of noble rank **~like** *adj* (of a woman) behaving like a LADY (1) **~ship** *n* (title for) a woman called LADY (3): *your ladyship*

lag¹ /læg/ *vi* **-gg-** move too slowly: *lag behind the others*

lag² *vt* **-gg-** cover (water pipes, etc.) to prevent loss of heat

la·ger /ˈlɑːgəʳ/ *n* [U] light kind of beer

la·goon /ləˈguːn/ *n* lake of sea water, (partly) separated from the sea

laid /leɪd/ *v past t. and p. of* LAY²

laid-back /ˌ·ˈ·◄/ *adj infml* cheerfully informal and unworried

lain /leɪn/ *v past p. of* LIE²

lair /leəʳ/ *n* home of a wild animal

la·i·ty /ˈleɪəti/ *n* [P] LAY³ people

lake /leɪk/ *n* large mass of water surrounded by land

lamb /læm/ *n* **1** [C] young sheep **2** [U] its meat **3** [C] harmless gentle person ♦ *vi* give birth to lambs

lam·baste /ˈlæmbeɪst/ *also* **lambast** /-bæst/ *vt infml* beat or attack fiercely

lame /leɪm/ *adj* **1** unable to walk properly **2** (of excuses, etc.) weak ♦ *vt* make lame **~ly** *adv* **~ness** *n* [U]

lame duck /ˌ·ˈ·/ *n* **1** helpless person or business **2** *esp. AmE* political official whose period in office will soon end

la·ment /ləˈment/ *vi/t* **1** express grief or sorrow (for) **2 the late lamented** the recently dead (person) ♦ *n* song, etc., expressing sorrow **~able** /ˈlæməntəbəl, ləˈmentəbəl/ *adj fml* **1** unsatisfactory **2** worthy of blame **~ation** /ˌlæmənˈteɪʃən/ *n* [C;U] *fml*

lam·i·na·ted /ˈlæmɪneɪtɪd/ *adj* made by joining thin sheets of a material

lamp /læmp/ *n* **1** apparatus for giving light **2** apparatus for producing health-giving sorts of heat: *an INFRARED lamp*

lam·poon /læmˈpuːn/ *n* written attack that makes someone look foolish **lampoon** *vt*

lamp-post /'læmp-pəʊst/ n post supporting a street lamp

lamp-shade /'læmpʃeɪd/ n cover for a lamp

lance /lɑːns‖læns/ n long spearlike weapon ♦ vt cut open with a lancet

lan-cet /'lɑːnsɪt‖'læn-/ n doctor's knife for cutting flesh

land¹ /lænd/ n 1 [U] solid dry part of the Earth's surface 2 [C] country; nation 3 [U] earth for farming 4 [U] also **lands** pl. — ground owned as property 5 **see how the land lies** try to discover the present state of affairs before taking action ~**ed** adj owning a lot of land

land² v 1 vi/t come or bring to land 2 vt succeed in getting: land the top job

land in phr vt bring (someone) into (an undesirable state or position): Her resignation landed us in a real mess.

land up phr vi reach the stated (often undesirable) state or position: He landed up in prison.

land with phr vt give (someone) (something unwanted): I got landed with organizing the Christmas party.

land-ing /'lændɪŋ/ n 1 level space at the top of a set of stairs 2 arrival on land: crash landing 3 place where people and goods are loaded, esp. from a ship

landing craft /'··· ·/ n flat boat for landing soldiers and their vehicles on shore

landing gear /'··· ·/ n [U] wheels and UNDERCARRIAGE of an aircraft

land-la-dy /'lænd,leɪdi/ n 1 woman a who runs a small hotel b from whom one rents a room 2 a female LANDLORD

land-locked /'lændlɒkt‖-lɑːkt/ adj surrounded by dry land

land-lord /'lændlɔːd‖-ɔːrd/ n 1 person from whom one rents land or buildings 2 man who owns or runs a pub, etc.

land-mark /'lændmɑːk‖-ɑːrk/ n 1 recognizable object from which one can tell one's position 2 important event, discovery, etc.

land-scape /'lændskeɪp/ n (picture of) country scenery ♦ vt make (land) into a garden

land-slide /'lændslaɪd/ n 1 sudden fall of earth and rocks 2 great success in an election

lane /leɪn/ n 1 narrow road 2 division of a wide road, to keep fast and slow vehicles apart 3 path used regularly by ships or aircraft 4 path marked for each competitor in a race

lan-guage /'læŋgwɪdʒ/ n [C;U] 1 system of human expression by means of words: the origins of language 2 particular system as used by a people or nation: the English language 3 system

of signs: computer languages 4 particular style or manner of expression: poetic language 5 words and phrases considered shocking: bad language

language la-bo-ra-tory /'·· ·,···‖'··
,····/ n room where foreign languages are taught using TAPE RECORDERs, etc.

lan-guid /'læŋgwɪd/ adj lacking strength, will ~**ly** adv

lan-guish /'læŋgwɪʃ/ vi fml 1 experience long suffering 2 become weak

lan-guor /'læŋgəʳ/ n 1 tiredness of mind or body 2 pleasant or heavy stillness

lank /læŋk/ adj (of hair) straight and lifeless

lank-y /'læŋki/ adj ungracefully tall and thin

lan-tern /'læntən‖-ərn/ n container round the flame of a light

lap¹ /læp/ n front of a seated person between the waist and the knees

lap² v -pp- 1 vt drink as a cat does 2 vi (of water) move with soft sounds ♦ n act or sound of lapping

lap³ n single journey round a racing track ♦ -pp- 1 vt pass (another racer) so as to be one lap ahead 2 vi race completely round the track

la-pel /lə'pel/ n part of the front of a coat that is joined to the collar and folded back

lapse /læps/ n 1 small fault or mistake 2 failure in correct behaviour, belief, etc. 3 passing away of time ♦ vi 1 sink gradually: lapse into silence 2 (of time) pass 3 (of business agreements, etc.) come to an end **lapsed** adj 1 no longer practising, esp. one's religion 2 law no longer in use

lar-ce-ny /'lɑːsəni‖'lɑːr-/ n [C;U] law (an act of) stealing

lard /lɑːd‖lɑːrd/ n [U] pig's fat used in cooking ♦ vt 1 put lard on 2 use lots of noticeable phrases in one's speech or writing

lar-der /'lɑːdəʳ‖'lɑːr-/ n storeroom or cupboard for food

large /lɑːdʒ‖lɑːrdʒ/ adj 1 big 2 **at large: a** free **b** as a whole: the country at large ~**ly** adv mostly

lar-gesse /lɑː'ʒes‖lɑːr'dʒes/ n [U] money given generously

lark¹ /lɑːk‖lɑːrk/ n 1 bit of fun; joke

lark² v **lark about/around** phr vi play rather wildly

lar-va /'lɑːvə‖'lɑːrvə/ n -vae /-viː/ wormlike young of an insect

la-ryn-gi-tis /ˌlærən'dʒaɪtəs/ n [U] painful swelling of the larynx

lar-ynx /'læɪŋks/ n hollow boxlike part in the throat, where voice is produced by the VOCAL CORDS

las-civ-i-ous /lə'sɪviəs/ adj causing, showing or feeling uncontrolled sexual desire ~**ly** adv

la·ser /'leɪzə^r/ n apparatus producing a strong narrow beam of light

lash[1] /læʃ/ v 1 vi/t whip 2 vi/t move about violently 3 vt tie firmly

lash out phr vi 1 attack violently 2 give out (esp. money) in large quantities: *We lashed out on a new car.*

lash[2] n 1 (a hit with) the thin striking part of a whip: (fig.) *the lash of the waves* 2 EYELASH

lash·ings /'læʃɪŋz/ n [P] esp. BrE plenty; lots

lass /læs/ n girl

las·si·tude /'læsɬtjuːd‖'læsɬtjuːd, -tuːd/ n [U] fml tiredness

las·so /lə'suː, 'læsəʊ/ n -s rope for catching horses and cattle ♦ vt catch with a lasso

last[1] /lɑːst‖læst/ determiner, adv 1 after the others 2 only remaining: *my last £5* 3 most recent(ly): *When did we last meet?* 4 least suitable or likely: *He's the last person I'd have expected to see here.* 5 **every last** every, not leaving out any ♦ n, pron [(the) S] 1 person or thing after all others: *the last to leave* 2 the only remaining: *the last of the wine* 3 the one or ones before the present one: *the week before last* (= 2 weeks ago) 4 **at (long) last** in the end ~**ly** adv in the end

last[2] v 1 vi continue 2 vi/t be enough (for): *The food will last (us) a week.* ~**ing** adj continuing for a long time

last-ditch /ˌ· '·◂/ adj done as one last effort before accepting defeat

last straw /ˌ· '·/ n [the + S] the difficulty, etc., that makes the total unbearable when it is added to one's present difficulties

last word /ˌ· '·/ n [the + S] 1 remark that ends an argument 2 most modern example of something

latch[1] /lætʃ/ n 1 small bar for fastening a door, gate, window, etc. 2 spring lock for a house door which can be opened from outside with a key

latch[2] vt

latch on phr vi understand

latch onto phr vt 1 LATCH on 2 refuse to leave (someone)

late /leɪt/ adj, adv 1 after the usual time: *The train was late.* 2 near the end: *in late September* 3 recently dead: *his late wife* 4 recent: *the latest fashions* | *Have you heard the latest?* (= most recent news) 5 **at the latest** not later than 6 **of late** lately ~**ly** adv not long ago

la·tent /'leɪtənt/ adj existing but not yet noticeable or developed: *latent talent* **latency** n [U]

lat·e·ral /'lætərəl/ adj of, from, or to the side ~**ly** adv

lateral thinking /ˌ··· '··/ n [U] making of unusual connections in the mind to find a new and clever answer to a problem

la·tex /'leɪteks/ n [U] liquid from which natural rubber is made

lathe /leɪð/ n machine that turns a piece of wood or metal to be shaped

la·ther /'lɑːðə^r‖'læ-/ n [S;U] 1 FROTH made with soap and water 2 **in a lather** infml worried ♦ v 1 vi make a lather 2 vt cover with lather

Lat·in /'lætɪn‖'lætn/ n, adj (of) the language of the ancient Romans

Latin A·mer·i·can /ˌ··· ·'···◂/ adj of the Spanish- or Portuguese-speaking countries of Central and S America

lat·i·tude /'lætɬtjuːd‖-tuːd/ n [S;U] 1 distance north or south of the EQUATOR, measured in degrees 2 freedom of choice **latitudes** n [P] area at a particular latitude

la·trine /lə'triːn/ n outdoor TOILET in a camp, etc.

lat·ter /'lætə^r/ adj of a later period: *his latter years* ♦ n fml second of 2 things mentioned ~**ly** adv recently

latter-day /ˌ·· '·/ adj modern

lat·tice /'lætɬs/ n wooden or metal frame used as a fence, etc.

laud /lɔːd/ vt lit praise ~**able** adj deserving praise

laugh /lɑːf‖læf/ vi 1 express amusement, happiness, etc., by breathing out forcefully so that one makes sounds with the voice, usu. while smiling 2 **no laughing matter** serious ♦ n 1 act or sound of laughing 2 something done for a joke 3 **have the last laugh** win after earlier defeats 4 **laugh up one's sleeve** infml laugh secretly and often unkindly ~**able** adj foolish

laugh·ing·stock /'···/ n someone or something regarded as foolish

laugh·ter /'lɑːftə^r‖'læf-/ n [U] laughing

launch /lɔːntʃ/ vt 1 send (a newly-built boat) into the water 2 send (a ROCKET, etc.) into the sky 3 begin (an activity): *launch an attack/a company* ♦ n 1 act of launching 2 large motorboat ~**er** n

launch into phr vt begin with eagerness, force, etc.

launch out phr vi begin something new

launch·ing pad /'··· ·/ n base from which spacecraft, etc., are launched

laun·der /'lɔːndə^r/ vt wash and iron (clothes)

laun·der·ette /ˌlɔːn'dret/ n place where the public pay to wash their clothes in machines

laun·dry /'lɔːndri/ n 1 [C] place where clothes are laundered 2 [U] clothes (needing to be) laundered

lau·re·ate /'lɔːriɬt/ adj see POET LAUREATE

laur-el /'lɒrəl‖'lɔː-, 'lɑː-/ n EVER-GREEN bush with shiny leaves **laurels** n [P] 1 honour gained for something done 2 **rest on one's laurels** be satisfied with what one has done already, and not do any more 3 **look to one's laurels** guard against competition

la-va /'lɑːvə/ n [U] melted rock that flows from a VOLCANO

lav-a-to-ry /'lævətəri‖-tɔːri/ n TOILET

lav-en-der /'lævəndəʳ/ n [U] (pale purple colour of) a plant with strongly smelling flowers

lav-ish /'lævɪʃ/ adj 1 generous 2 given or produced in (too) great quantity: lavish praise ♦ vt give freely: She lavishes money on them. ~ly adv

law /lɔː/ n 1 [C] rule made by a government 2 [U] all these rules: Stealing is against the law. 3 [C] statement of what always happens in certain conditions: the laws of physics 4 [the + S] infml police or a policeman 5 **be a law unto oneself** do exactly what one wishes 6 **law and order** respect for the law 7 **lay down the law** give an opinion in an unpleasant commanding manner ~**ful** adj allowed or recognized by law ~**fully** adv ~**less** adj not governed by laws ~**lessness** n [U]

law-a-bid-ing /'· ·,··/ adj obeying the law

lawn /lɔːn/ n area of closely cut grass

lawn ten-nis /,· '··/ n [U] tennis played on a grass court

law-suit /'lɔːsuːt, -sjuːt‖-suːt/ n non-criminal case in a law court

law-yer /'lɔːjəʳ/ n person whose profession is the LAW (2)

lax /læks/ adj careless and uncontrolled ~**ity** n [C;U]

lax-a-tive /'læksətɪv/ n, adj (medicine) helping the bowels to empty

lay¹ /leɪ/ v past t. of LIE²

lay² /leɪ/ v laid /leɪd/ 1 vt a put, esp. carefully, in a flat position: She laid his coat on the bed. b set in proper order or position: to lay bricks 2 vt arrange for use: lay the table for dinner 3 vt cause to settle or disappear: lay his fears to rest 4 vi/t (of a bird, insect, etc.) produce (eggs) 5 vt make (a statement, claim, etc.) in a serious or official way: lay charges against someone 6 vt sl have sex with: He only goes to parties to **get laid**. 7 **lay hold of** catch and hold firmly 8 **lay waste** destroy completely

lay down phr vt 1 state firmly: lay down the law 2 give up (one's life) 3 store (esp. wine) for the future

lay in phr vt get and store a supply of

lay into phr vt attack with words or blows

lay low phr vt 1 knock down 2 make ill

lay off phr vt 1 stop employing 2 give up

lay on phr vt 1 provide: lay on lunch 2 **lay it on** tell something in a way that goes beyond the truth

lay out phr vt 1 arrange or plan: lay out a garden 2 knock (someone) down 3 spend (money)

lay up phr vt 1 keep in bed with an illness: laid up with flu 2 collect and store for future use

lay³ /leɪ/ adj 1 of or by people who are not priests 2 not professional

lay-a-bout /'leɪəbaʊt/ n lazy person

lay-by /'· ·/ n BrE space next to a road where vehicles may park

lay-er /'leɪəʳ/ n 1 thickness of some substance laid over a surface: layers of rock 2 bird that lays eggs

lay-man /'leɪmən/ n -men /-mən/ LAY³ person

lay-off /'· ·/ n stopping of a worker's employment

lay-out /'leɪaʊt/ n (planned) arrangement: the layout of the room

laze /leɪz/ vi rest lazily

la-zy /'leɪzi/ adj 1 avoiding work 2 spent in inactivity **lazily** adv **laziness** n [U]

la-zy-bones /'leɪzibəʊnz/ n lazy person

lb written abbrev. for: POUND¹ (1)

LCD /,el siː 'diː/ n liquid crystal display; part of an apparatus on which numbers, etc., are shown by passing an electric current through a special liquid

L-driver /'· ,··/ n BrE person learning to drive

lead¹ /liːd/ v led /led/ 1 vi/t guide, esp. by going first 2 vi (of a road, etc.) go somewhere: (fig.) The plan led to trouble. 3 vt influence: What led you to do it? 4 vt control or govern: lead an army 5 vi/t be ahead (of) in sports 6 vt experience (a kind of life) 7 vi (of a newspaper) have as a main story ~**ing** adj most important; chief

lead on phr vt influence (someone) to do something wrong or believe something untrue

lead up to phr vt be a preparation for

lead² /liːd/ n 1 [C] guiding suggestion 2 [S] a chief or front position b distance by which one competitor is ahead 3 [C] (person playing) the chief acting part in a play or film 4 [C] main or most important article in a newspaper 5 [C] chain, etc., for leading a dog 6 [C] wire carrying electrical power

lead³ /led/ n 1 [U] heavy greyish metal used for water pipes, etc. 2 [C;U] (stick of) GRAPHITE used in pencils

lead-en /'ledn/ *adj* **1** dull grey **2** heavy and sad

lead-er /'liːdəʳ/ *n* **1** person who leads **2** *BrE* for EDITORIAL ~**ship** *n* [U] position or qualities of a leader

leading ar-ti-cle /ˌliːdɪŋ 'ɑːtɪkəl, -'ɔːr-/ *n BrE* for EDITORIAL

leading light /ˌliːdɪŋ 'laɪt/ *n* person of importance

leading ques-tion /ˌliːdɪŋ 'kwestʃən/ *n* question formed so as to suggest the answer

leaf¹ /liːf/ *n* **leaves** /liːvz/ **1** flat green part of a plant, joined to its stem **2** sheet of paper or metal **3** part of a tabletop that can be slid or folded out **4 take a leaf out of someone's book** follow someone's example **5 turn over a new leaf** begin a new course of improved behaviour, habits, etc. ~**y** *adj*

leaf² *v* **leaf through** *phr vt* turn the pages (of a book, etc.) quickly without reading much

leaf-let /'liːflət/ *n* small sheet of printed matter ♦ *vi* give out (political) leaflets

league /liːg/ *n* **1** group of people, countries, etc., joined together for a shared aim **2** group of sports clubs that play against each other **3** level of quality: *They're not in the same league.* **4 in league (with)** working together secretly

leak /liːk/ *n* **1** accidental hole through which something flows **2** spreading of secret news: *security leak* ♦ *v* **1** *vi/t* (allow to) pass through a leak **2** *vt* make (secrets) publicly known ~**y** *adj*

leak-age /'liːkɪdʒ/ *n* [C;U] process or amount of leaking

lean¹ /liːn/ *v* **leant** /lent/ or **leaned** **1** *vi* bend from an upright position **2** *vi/t* support or rest in a sloping position: *lean a ladder against a tree* **3 lean over backwards** make every possible effort (to) ~**ing** *n* tendency: *have artistic leanings*

  lean on/upon *phr vt* **1** depend on **2** *infml* influence (someone) by threats

  lean towards *phr vt* favour (a plan or opinion)

lean² *adj* **1** not fat **2** producing little profit: *a lean year for business*

leap¹ /liːp/ *v* **leapt** /lept/ or **leaped** /lept ‖ liːpt/ jump

leap² *n* **1** jump **2** sudden increase in number, quantity, etc. **3 by leaps and bounds** very quickly **4 a leap in the dark** action or risk taken without knowing what will happen

leap-frog /'liːpfrɒg‖-frɔːg, -frɑːg/ *n* [U] game in which players jump over each other ♦ *vi/t* -**gg**- go ahead of (each other) in turn

leap year /'· ·/ *n* a year, every 4th year, in which February has 29 days

learn /lɜːn‖lɜːrn/ *vi/t* **learned** or **learnt** /lɜːnt ‖ lɜːrnt/ **1** gain (knowledge or skill): *learn French | learn to swim* **2** fix in the memory: *learn a poem* **3** become informed (of): *learn of his success* ~**er** *n* —**ing** *n* [U] knowledge gained by study —**ed** /'lɜːnɪd ‖ 'lɜːr-/ *adj* having great knowledge

lease /liːs/ *n* **1** contract for the use of a place in return for rent **2 a new lease of life** (*BrE*)/**on life** (*AmE*) new strength or desire to be happy, etc. ♦ *vt* give or take (a place) on a lease

lease-hold /'liːshəʊld/ *adj, adv* (of a place) held on a lease ~**er** *n* person who has a place on a lease

leash /liːʃ/ *n* LEAD³ (5)

least¹ /liːst/ *determiner, pron* **1** smallest number, amount, etc.: *Buy the one that costs (the) least.* **2 at least:** **a** not less than: *at least £100* **b** if nothing else: *At least it's legal.* **3 in the least** *at all*

least² *adv* (*superlative* of LITTLE) **1** less than anything else or than any others **2 not least** partly, and quite importantly

leath-er /'leðəʳ/ *n* preserved animal skin used for making shoes, etc. ~**y** *adj* stiff like leather

leave¹ /liːv/ *v* **left** /left/ **1** *vi/t* go away (from) **2** *vt* allow to remain: *leave the door open | Is there any coffee left?* **3** *vt* fail to take or bring: *I've left my coat behind.* **4** *vt* give by a WILL² (5) **5** *vt* allow something to be the responsibility of (someone) *I'll leave you to buy the tickets.* **6** *vt* have remaining in a sum: *2 from 8 leaves 6.* **7 leave go/hold of** stop holding **8 leave it at that** do or say no more **9 leave someone/something alone** stop behaving annoyingly in someone's presence or touching something **10 leave someone/something standing** *infml* be much better than someone or something **leaver** *n*: *school leavers*

  leave off *phr vi/t* stop (doing something)

  leave out *phr vt* **1** not include **2 Leave it out!** *BrE sl* Stop lying/pretending, etc.

leave² *n* **1** [C;U] time spent away from work **2** [U] *fml* permission **3 take leave of** say goodbye to: *She must have taken leave of her senses.* (= gone mad)

leaves /liːvz/ *n pl.* of LEAF¹

lech-er-ous /'letʃərəs/ *adj derog* wanting continual sexual pleasure ~**ly** *adv*

lech-er-y /'letʃəri/ *n* [U] *derog* being lecherous

lec·tern /ˈlektən‖-ərn/ n sloping table to hold a book

lec·ture /ˈlektʃəʳ/ n **1** speech given as a method of teaching **2** long solemn scolding or warning ♦ vi/t give a lecture (to) **-turer** n person who gives (university) lectures

led /led/ v. past t. and p. of LEAD¹

ledge /ledʒ/ n shelf sticking out from a wall, rock, etc.

ledg·er /ˈledʒəʳ/ n account book of a business

lee /liː/ n fml shelter from the wind ♦ adj on the side away from the wind

leech /liːtʃ/ n **1** wormlike creature that sucks blood **2** person who makes profit from others

leek /liːk/ n vegetable with long fleshy stem and broad leaves that tastes slightly of onions

leer /lɪəʳ/ vi, n (look with) an unpleasant smile

lee·ward /ˈliːwəd, tech ˈluːəd‖-ərd/ adj **1** with or in the direction of the wind: a leeward engine **2** away from the wind: the leeward side of the ship

lee·way /ˈliːweɪ/ n additional time, money, etc., allowing the chance of success

left¹ /left/ past t. and p. of LEAVE¹

left² adj **1** on the side of the body that contains the heart **2** in the direction of one's left side **3** belonging to or favouring the LEFT³ (2) in politics

left³ n [U] **1** left side or direction **2** political parties that favour more change and more state control ♦ adv towards the left **-ist** n, adj (a supporter) of the left political side

left-hand /ˌ· '·◄/ adj on the left side **~ed** adj using the left hand for most actions **~er** left-handed person

left lug·gage of·fice /ˌ· '·· ˌ·/ n BrE place in a station where one can leave one's bags

left-o·vers /ˈleft͵əʊvəz‖-ərz/ n [P] food remaining uneaten after a meal

left wing /ˌ· '·◄/ n [U] LEFT³ (2)

leg /leg/ n **1** limb that includes the foot, used for walking **2** part of a garment that covers this **3** support of a table, etc. **4** single stage of a journey **5** give someone a leg up BrE help someone to climb onto something by supporting the lower part of their leg **6** not have a leg to stand on have no good reason or excuse **7** on one's/its last legs: **a** very tired **b** nearly worn out **c** nearly dead **8** pull someone's leg make fun of a person in a playful way

leg·a·cy /ˈlegəsi/ n **1** money, etc., left in someone's WILL **2** something left behind: Disease is often a legacy of war.

le·gal /ˈliːɡəl/ adj of, allowed, or demanded by the law **~ly** adv **~ize** vt make legal **~ity** /lɪˈɡælɪti/ n [U]

le·gal·ist·ic /ˌliːɡəˈlɪstɪk◄/ adj derog placing too great an importance on keeping exactly to what the law says

legal ten·der /ˌ·· '··/ n fml money that must by law be accepted in payment

le·ga·tion /lɪˈɡeɪʃən/ n offices of a minister below the rank of AMBASSADOR, representing one country in another country

le·gend /ˈledʒənd/ n **1** [C] old story which may not be true **2** [U] such stories collectively **3** [C] famous person or act **4** [C] words that explain a picture, etc., in a book **~ary** adj famous in legends

leg·gings /ˈleɡɪnz/ n [P] outer coverings to protect the legs

le·gi·ble /ˈledʒəbəl/ adj that can be read easily **-bly** adv **-bility** /ˌledʒəˈbɪlɪti/ n [U]

le·gion /ˈliːdʒən/ n **1** division of an army, esp. in ancient Rome **2** large group of people ♦ adj fml very many **~ary** n member of a legion (1)

le·gion·naire's dis·ease /ˌliːdʒə-ˈneəʳz dɪˌziːz/ n [U] serious infectious disease of the lungs

le·gis·late /ˈledʒəsleɪt/ vi make laws **-lator** n **-lation** /ˌledʒəsˈleɪʃən/ n [U] **1** law or set of laws **2** act of making laws

le·gis·la·tive /ˈledʒəslətɪv‖-leɪtɪv/ adj having the power and duty to make laws: a legislative assembly

le·gis·la·ture /ˈledʒəsleɪtʃəʳ, -lətʃəʳ/ n body of people who make the laws

le·git·i·mate /lɪˈdʒɪtəmət/ adj **1** legally correct **2** born of parents married to each other **3** reasonable: legitimate conclusion **~ly** adv **-macy** n [U]

le·git·i·mize ‖ also **-mise** BrE /lɪˈdʒɪtəmaɪz/ also **legitimatize**, **-tise** BrE /lɪˈdʒɪtəmətaɪz/ vt **1** make legal; make acceptable **2** make (a child) legitimate

leg·less /ˈleɡləs/ adj infml, esp. BrE very drunk

lei·sure /ˈleʒəʳ‖ˈliː-/ n [U] **1** free time **2** at one's leisure at a convenient time **leisured** adj **1** having leisure **2** leisurely

lei·sure·ly /ˈleʒəli‖ˈliːʒərli/ adj unhurried

lem·on /ˈlemən/ n **1** [C] sour fruit with a hard yellow skin **2** [U] light bright yellow **3** [C] BrE sl foolish person **4** [C] sl something unsatisfactory or worthless

lem·on·ade /ˌleməˈneɪd/ n [U] **1** drink made of lemons, sugar, and water **2** BrE FIZZY drink tasting of lemons

lend /lend/ *v* **lent** /lent/ **1** *vt/i* give something for a limited time: *lend him £10 till tomorrow* **2** *vt* give; add: *The flags lent colour to the streets.* **3 lend a hand** give help **4 lend itself to** be suitable for ~**er** *n*

length /leŋθ/ *n* **1** [C;U] measurement of something from one end to the other or of its longest side **2** [U] quality or condition of being long: *the length of the exam paper* **3** [C] distance from front to back of a horse or boat in a race: *win by 3 lengths* **4** [C] amount of time from beginning to end **5** [C] piece of something: *a length of string* **6 at length: a** in many words *b fml* finally **7 go to any/great lengths** be prepared to do anything ~**y** *adj* (too) long

length-en /ˈleŋθən/ *vi/t* make or become longer

length-ways /ˈleŋθweɪz/ also **lengthwise** /-waɪz/ -- *adv* in the direction of the longest side

le-ni-ent /ˈliːniənt/ *adj* not severe in judgment ~**ly** *adv* -**ence**, -**ency** *n* [U]

lens /lenz/ *n* **1** curved piece of glass in a camera, microscope, etc. **2** part of the eye that can FOCUS light **3** CONTACT LENS

lent /lent/ *v past t. and p. of* LEND

Lent *n* the 40 days before EASTER

len-til /ˈlentl/ *n* small beanlike seed used for food

leop-ard /ˈlepəd‖-ərd/ **leopardess** /ˈlepədɪs ‖ -pər-/ *fem.* —*n* large spotted catlike animal

le-o-tard /ˈliːətɑːd‖-ɑːrd/ *n* close fitting one-piece garment worn by dancers, etc.

lep-er /ˈlepər/ *n* **1** person with leprosy **2** person avoided by other people for social or moral reasons

lep-ro-sy /ˈleprəsi/ *n* [U] disease in which the skin becomes rough, flesh and nerves are destroyed and fingers, toes, etc., drop off -**rous** *adj*

les-bi-an /ˈlezbiən/ *adj, n* (of or being) a woman HOMOSEXUAL ~**ism** *n* [U]

le-sion /ˈliːʒən/ *n fml* wound

less[1] /les/ *determiner, pron, (comparative of* LITTLE) *n* **1** smaller amount: *less noise | less than a mile* **2 less and less** (an amount) that continues to become smaller **3 less than no time** a very short time **4 none the less** but in spite of everything **5 think (the) less of** have a lower opinion of

less[2] *adv* **1** not so; to a smaller degree (than): *less cold* **2** not so much: *to work less* **3** *less and less* increasingly rarely **4** *much/still less* and certainly not

less[3] *prep* but we subtract; MINUS: *I earned $100, less tax.*

les-see /leˈsiː/ *n* person who LEASES a property

less-en /ˈlesən/ *vi/t* make or become less

less-er /ˈlesər/ *adj, adv* smaller: *the lesser of 2 evils*

les-son /ˈlesən/ *n* **1** (period of) teaching something in school, etc. **2** experience from which to learn: *The accident taught him a lesson.* **3** short piece read from the Bible

lest /lest/ *conj fml* for fear that

let /let/ *vt* **let**; *pres. p.* **letting 1** allow (to do or happen): *He let his beard grow.* **2** (the named person) must, should, or can: *Let each man decide for himself.* | (when suggesting a plan) '*Let's have a party!*' **3** give the use of (a place) for rent **4 let alone** and certainly not: *He can't walk, let alone run.* **5 let/leave go** stop holding **6 let oneself go: a** behave freely **b** stop taking care of one's appearance **7 let someone go: a** set someone free **b** dismiss someone from a job **8 let someone know** tell someone, esp. at a later date **9 let someone/something alone** stop behaving annoyingly in someone's presence or touching something **10 let well (enough) alone** allow existing conditions to remain as they are, for fear of making things worse

let down *phr vt* **1** make (clothes) longer **2** disappoint

let in for *phr vt* cause (esp. oneself) to have (something unwanted)

let into/in on *phr vt* allow to share (a secret)

let off *phr vt* **1** excuse from punishment **2** explode: *let off fireworks*

let on *phr vi* tell a secret

let out *phr vt* **1** give (a shout, etc.) **2** make (clothes) wider

let up *phr vi* lessen or stop

let-down /ˈletdaʊn/ *n* disappointment

le-thal /ˈliːθəl/ *adj* causing death

leth-ar-gy /ˈleθədʒi‖-ər-/ *n* [U] tiredness and laziness -**gic** /lɪˈθɑːdʒɪk‖ -ɑːr-/ *adj*

let-ter /ˈletər/ *n* **1** [C] written message sent to someone **2** [C] sign representing a sound **3** [(*the*) S] actual words of something: *the letter of the law* ~**ing** *n* [U] style and size of written letters **letters** *n* [U] *fml* literature

letter bomb /ˈ··ˌ·/ *n* small bomb posted in an envelope

let-ter-box /ˈletəbɒks‖ˈletərbɑːks/ *n esp. BrE* **1** hole in a door for letters **2** box in a post office or street, in which letters may be posted

let-ter-head /ˈletəhed‖-ər-/ *n* name and address printed at the top of the owner's writing paper

let-ting /ˈletɪŋ/ *n esp. BrE* house or flat to be rented

let-tuce /ˈletɪs/ *n* [C;U] green leafy vegetable, eaten raw

let-up /'letʌp/ n [C;U] lessening of activity

leu-ke-mia ‖ also **-kae-** BrE /luː'kiːmiə/ n [U] serious disease in which the blood has too many white cells

lev-el¹ /'levəl/ adj 1 flat; HORIZONTAL 2 equal: *The teams finished level.* 3 **(at) level pegging** *infml* having the same score 4 **one's level best** all that one can do

level² n [C;U] 1 line or surface parallel with the ground; position of height in relation to a flat surface: *The garden is on 2 levels.* | (fig.) *The decision was taken at ministerial level.* 2 standard of quality or quantity: *increase production levels* 3 **on the level** honest(ly)

level³ vt/i -ll- BrE ‖-l- AmE make or become level

level at/against phr vt 1 aim (a weapon) at 2 bring (a charge) against (someone)

level off/out phr vi stop rising or falling

level with phr vt infml speak truthfully to

lev-el⁴ adv so as to be level: *a missile flying level with the ground*

level cross-ing /,·· '··/ n BrE place where a road and a railway cross, usu. protected by gates

level-head-ed /,·· '··◄/ adj calm and sensible

le-ver /'liːvəʳ‖'le-, 'liː-/ n 1 bar that turns on its middle point, to lift things 2 rod that works a machine 3 something which may be used for influencing ♦ vt move with a lever: *Lever it into position.*

le-ver-age /'liːvərɪdʒ‖'le-, 'liː-/ n [U] power of a lever: (fig.) *use political leverage*

lev-i-tate /'levɪteɪt/ vi rise into the air as if by magic **-tation** /,levɪ'teɪʃən/ n [U]

lev-i-ty /'levɪti/ n [U] fml lack of proper seriousness

lev-y /'levi/ vt demand and collect (esp. taxes) officially

lewd /luːd/ adj sexually dirty: *lewd songs* **~ly** adv **~ness** n [U]

lex-i-cal /'leksɪkəl/ adj of words **~ly** /-kli/ adv

lex-i-cog-ra-phy /,leksɪ'kɒgrəfi‖-'kɑː-/ n [U] writing of dictionaries **-pher** n

lex-i-con /'leksɪkən‖-kɑːn, -kən/ n dictionary or wordlist

li-a-bil-i-ty /,laɪə'bɪləti/ n 1 [U] condition of being liable 2 [C] debt that must be paid 3 [C] someone or something that limits one's activities or freedom

li-a-ble /'laɪəbl/ adj 1 responsible in law 2 **liable to** having a tendency to

li-aise /li'eɪz/ vi form a LIAISON (1)

li-ai-son /li'eɪzən‖'liːəzɑːn, li'eɪ-/ n 1 [S;U] working association between groups 2 [C] sexual relationship between an unmarried couple

li-ar /'laɪəʳ/ n person who tells lies

lib /lɪb/ n [U] LIBERATION: — see also WOMEN'S LIB

Lib written abbrev. for: LIBERAL PARTY

li-bel /'laɪbəl/ n [C;U] damaging written statement about someone ♦ vt -ll- BrE ‖ -l- AmE make a libel against **~lous** BrE ‖ **~ous** AmE adj: *a libellous remark*

lib-e-ral /'lɪbərəl/ adj 1 willing to respect the opinions of others 2 (of education) leading to wide general knowledge 3 given freely: *liberal supplies* 4 (cap.) of the LIBERAL PARTY ♦ n (cap.) member of the LIBERAL PARTY **~ism** n [U] LIBERAL (1) opinions **~ize** vt remove limits on freedom: *liberalize the divorce laws* **~ization** /,lɪbərəlaɪ'zeɪʃən‖-rələ-/ n [U]

lib-e-ral-i-ty /,lɪbə'ræləti/ n [U] fml 1 generosity 2 broadness of mind

Liberal Par-ty /'··· ,··/n [the] political party that favours liberal opinions, esp. a British party that has a position between the CONSERVATIVE PARTY and the LABOUR PARTY

lib-e-rate /'lɪbəreɪt/ vt fml set free **-rated** adj socially and sexually free **-rator** n /-rator /,lɪbə'reɪʃən/ n [U]

lib-er-tar-i-an /,lɪbə'teəriən‖-bər-/ n believer in freedom of thought **~ism** n [U]

lib-er-tine /'lɪbətiːn‖-ər-/ n man who leads a (sexually) immoral life

lib-er-ty /'lɪbəti‖-ər-/ n [U] 1 personal or political freedom 2 chance or permission to do or use something 3 **at liberty** free 4 **take liberties** behave too freely

li-bid-i-nous /lɪ'bɪdɪnəs/ adj fml LASCIVIOUS **~ly** adv

li-bi-do /lɪ'biːdəʊ/ n **-dos** tech the sexual urge

li-brar-i-an /laɪ'breəriən/ n person in charge of a library **~ship** n [U]

li-bra-ry /'laɪbrəri, -bri‖-breri/ n (room or building with) a collection of books, records, etc.

lice /laɪs/ n pl. of LOUSE

li-cence ‖ usu. **license** AmE /'laɪsəns/ n 1 [C;U] (paper showing) official permission to do something 2 [U] fml uncontrolled freedom

li-cense ‖ also **licence** AmE /'laɪsəns/ vt give a LICENCE (1) to **licensee** /,laɪsən'siː/ n person with a licence, esp. to sell alcohol

li-cen-tious /laɪ'senʃəs/ adj sexually uncontrolled **~ly** adv **~ness** n [U]

lick /lɪk/ vt **1** move the tongue across **2** (of flames or waves) pass lightly over **3** infml defeat ♦ n **1** [C] act of licking **2** [C] small amount (of paint, etc.) **3** [S] BrE infml speed

lic-o-rice /ˈlɪkərɪs, -rɪʃ/ n [U] LIQUORICE

lid /lɪd/ n **1** movable cover of a container **2** EYELID

li-do /ˈliːdəʊ, ˈlaɪ-‖ˈliːdəʊ/ n -dos place for swimming and lying in the sun

lie[1] /laɪ/ vi, n lied, pres. p. lying (make) a false statement — see also WHITE LIE

lie[2] vi lay/leɪ/, lain/leɪn/, pres. p. lying /ˈlaɪ-ɪŋ/ **1** be or remain in a flat position on a surface **2** be or remain in a particular position or state: The town lies 2 miles to the east. | The machinery was lying idle. **3** be the responsibility of: The decision lies with you. **4** lie low be in hiding or avoid being noticed ♦ n [S] **1** way something lies **2** the lie of the land BrE **a** appearance, slope, etc., of a piece of land **b** the state of affairs at a particular time

lie about phr vi be lazy; do nothing
lie behind phr vt be the reason for
lie down phr vi **1** lie down on the job do work that is not good enough in quantity or quality **2** take something lying down suffer something bad without complaining or trying to stop it

lie in phr vi stay in bed late

lie de-tec-tor /ˈ· ·,··/ n instrument that is said to show when someone is telling LIEs[1]

lie-down /ˈ· ·/ n BrE infml a short rest

lie-in /ˈ· ·/ n infml, esp. BrE a stay in bed later than usual in the morning

lieu /ljuː, luː‖luː/ n **in lieu (of)** instead of

lieu-ten-ant /lefˈtenənt‖luːˈten-/ n officer of low rank in the armed forces

life /laɪf/ n lives /laɪvz/ **1** [U] active force that makes animals and plants different from stones or machines **2** [U] living things: There is no life on the moon. **3** [U] human existence: Life is full of surprises. **4** [C] period or way of being alive: their busy lives | (fig.) during the life of this government | (fig.) The machine has a life of 10 years. **5** [C] person: No lives were lost. **6** [U] activity; movement; strength: full of life **7** [U] existence as a collection of widely different experiences: You see life in the navy. **8** [U] also **life imprisonment** — punishment of being put in prison for a long time **9** [C] BIOGRAPHY **10** [the + S] person or thing that is the cause of enjoyment in a group: the life and soul of the party **11** [U] using a

living person as the subject of a painting, etc.: painted from life **12 as large as life** unexpectedly but unmistakably the real person **13 come to life: a** regain one's senses after fainting **b** show or develop interest, excitement, etc. **14 for dear life** with the greatest effort **15 Not on your life!** Certainly not! **16 take one's life** kill oneself **17 take one's life in one's (own) hands** be in continual danger **18 take someone's life** kill them ~**less** adj **1** dead **2** not active; dull ~**lessly** adv ~**like** adj like a real person

life belt /ˈ· ·/ n belt worn to keep a person from sinking in water

life-blood /ˈlaɪfblʌd/ n [U] something that gives continuing strength

life-boat /ˈlaɪfbəʊt/ n boat for saving people in danger at sea

life buoy /ˈ· ·/ n floating ring to hold onto in the water

life cy-cle /ˈ· ,··/ n all the stages of development through which a creature passes during its life

life-guard /ˈlaɪfɡɑːd‖-ɑːrd/ n swimmer employed to help other swimmers in danger

life jack-et /ˈ· ,··/ n garment worn to support a person in water

life-line /ˈlaɪflaɪn/ n **1** rope for saving life **2** something on which one's life depends

life-long /ˈlaɪflɒŋ‖-lɔːŋ/ adj lasting all one's life

life of Ri-ley /,·· ˈ··/ n [the + S] infml a very easy untroubled life

life-size, **life-sized** /ˈ· ·/ adj (of a work of art) as big as what it represents

life-span /ˈlaɪfspæn/ n length of a creature's life

life-style /ˈlaɪfstaɪl/ n way of living

life-time /ˈlaɪftaɪm/ n time during which someone is alive

lift[1] /lɪft/ v **1** vt raise to a higher level **2** vt improve: lift my spirits **3** vi (of clouds, etc.) disappear **4** vt bring to an end: lift a ban **5** vt steal

lift off phr vi (of an aircraft or spacecraft) leave the ground **lift-off** /ˈ· ·/ n

lift[2] n **1** act of lifting **2** BrE apparatus in a building for taking people and goods from one floor to another **3** free ride in a vehicle **4** feeling of increased strength, higher spirits, etc.

lig-a-ment /ˈlɪɡəmənt/ n band that joins bones together

lig-a-ture /ˈlɪɡətʃəʳ/ n thread used for tying, esp. in medicine

light[1] /laɪt/ n **1** [U] force by which we see things: sunlight **2** [C] lamp, etc., that gives light **3** [C] (something that will make) a flame **4** [C] bright part of a painting, etc. **5** [S;U] brightness in the eyes **6** [C] way in which something is regarded: see it in a different light **7**

bring/come to light make or become known **8 in a good/bad light** in a favourable/unfavourable way **9 in the light of** taking into account **10 see the light: a** be born **b** be made public **c** understand or accept an idea or truth **11 throw/shed light on** explain

light² *v* lit /lɪt/ *or* **lighted** *1 vi/t* (cause to) start burning **2** *vt* give light to: *lighted streets* ~**ing** *n* system or quality of lights in a place

light up *phr v* **1** *vi/t* become or become bright **2** *vi* start smoking

light³ *adj* **1** not dark: *a light room* **2** pale: *light green*

light⁴ *adj* **1** not heavy **2** small in amount: *light meals/traffic* **3** easy to bear or do: *light duties* **4** gentle: *light touch* **5** quick and graceful **6** (of wine, etc.) not very strong **7** not serious: *light reading* **8** (of sleep) not deep **9 make light of** treat as of little importance ♦ *adv* with few travelling cases or possessions: *to travel light* ~**ly** *adv* **1** gently **2** slightly **3** not seriously ~**ness** *n* [U]

light⁵ *vt* lit *or* **lighted** come down from flight and settle: (fig.) *I finally lit on the idea of going to Paris.*

light bulb *n* BULB (2)

light-en /ˈlaɪtn/ *vi/t* make or become **a** brighter **b** less heavy, or **c** more cheerful

light-er /ˈlaɪtər/ *n* instrument for lighting cigarettes, etc.

light-fin-gered /ˌ· ˈ··◁/ *adj infml* having the habit of stealing small things

light-head-ed /ˌ· ˈ··◁/ *adj* **1** unable to think clearly **2** not sensible

light-heart-ed /ˌ· ˈ··◁/ *adj* cheerful

light-house /ˈlaɪthaʊs/ *n* tower with a powerful light to guide ships

light-ning /ˈlaɪtnɪŋ/ *n* [U] electric flash of light in the sky ♦*adj* very quick, short, or sudden: *a lightning visit*

lightning con-duc-tor /ˈ·· ·ˌ··/ *n* BrE wire leading from the top of a building to the ground, as a protection against lightning

light-weight /ˈlaɪt-weɪt/ *n* **1** person or thing of less than average weight **2** someone who does not think deeply or seriously **lightweight** *adj*

light year /ˈ· ·/ *n* **1** distance that light travels in a year **2** *infml* a very long time

li-ka-ble, likeable /ˈlaɪkəbəl/ *adj* (esp. of people) pleasant; attractive

like¹ /laɪk/ *vt* **1** regard with pleasure or fondness **2** be willing (to): *I don't like to ask.* **3** (with **should** *or* **would**) wish or choose (to have): *I'd like a boiled egg.* | *Would you like to read it?* **4 How do you like . . . ?** (used when asking for an opinion) **5 I'd like to . . .** I would be surprised/interested to **6 I**

like that! That's very annoying! **7 if you like** if that is what you want **lik-ing** *n* [S] **1** fondness **2 to one's liking** which suits one's ideas or expectations **likes** *n* [P] things that one likes

like² *prep* **1** in the same way as; similar to: *Do it like this.* **2** typical of: *It's not like her to be late.* **3** such as: *Houses like that are expensive.* **4 something like** about ♦ *n* **1** something of the same kind: *running, swimming, and the like* **2** the likes of people or things of the stated type ♦ *adj fml* similar ♦ *conj infml* as: *Make it like you make tea.*

like-li-hood /ˈlaɪklɪhʊd/ *n* [U] probability

like-ly /ˈlaɪkli/ *adj* **1** probable **2 (That's) a likely story!** *infml* (said to show that one disbelieves what someone has said) ♦ *adv* **1** most/very likely **2 Not likely!** *infml* Certainly not!

like-mind-ed /ˌ· ˈ···◁/ *adj* having the same ideas, interests, etc.

lik-en /ˈlaɪkən/ *v* likened to *phr vt* to compare to

like-ness /ˈlaɪknəs/ *n* [C;U] sameness in appearance: *a family likeness*

like-wise /ˈlaɪk-waɪz/ *adv* similarly; also

li-lac /ˈlaɪlək/ *n* **1** [C] bush with pinkish-purple or white flowers **2** [U] pinkish-purple

lilt /lɪlt/ *n* [S] pleasant pattern of rising and falling sound ~**ing** *adj*

lil-y /ˈlɪli/ *n* plant with large esp. white flowers: *her lily-white skin*

lily-liv-ered /ˌ·· ˈ··◁/ *adj lit* cowardly

limb /lɪm/ *n* **1** leg, arm, or wing **2** branch of a tree **3 out on a limb** alone without support **4 tear limb from limb** tear (a person) apart

lim-ber /ˈlɪmbər/ *v* limber up *phr vi* exercise the muscles before a game, etc.

lim-bo /ˈlɪmbəʊ/ *n* [U] state of uncertainty

lime¹ /laɪm/ *n* [U] white substance used in making cement

lime² *n* tree with sweet-smelling yellow flowers

lime³ *n* sour fruit like a LEMON

lime-light /ˈlaɪmlaɪt/ *n* [the + S] the centre of public attention

lim-e-rick /ˈlɪmərɪk/ *n* funny poem with 5 lines

lim-it /ˈlɪmət/ *n* **1** farthest point or edge **2** *infml* someone or something too bad to bear **3 off limits** where one is not allowed to go **4 within limits** up to a reasonable point — see also TIME LIMIT ♦ *vt* keep below a limit ~**ed** *adj* **1** small; having limits **2** (*abbrev.* Ltd) (of a British firm) having a reduced duty to pay back debts: *a limited company* ~**less** *adj* endless

lim·i·ta·tion /ˌlɪmɪˈteɪʃn/ n 1 [U] limiting 2 [C] condition that limits

lim·ou·sine /ˈlɪməziːn, ˌlɪməˈziːn/ n expensive car with the driver's seat separated from the back

limp[1] /lɪmp/ vi, n [S] (walk with) an uneven step

limp[2] adj lacking firmness; not stiff ~**ly** adv

lim·pet /ˈlɪmpɪt/ n kind of SHELL-FISH that holds tightly to the rock: (fig.) cling to him like a limpet

lim·pid /ˈlɪmpɪd/ adj lit clear and transparent

linch·pin /ˈlɪntʃˌpɪn/ n person or thing that keeps something together

linc·tus /ˈlɪŋktəs/ n [U] BrE liquid cough medicine

line[1] /laɪn/ n 1 long narrow mark on a surface: a line drawing (= done with pen or pencil) 2 limit; border: the finishing line in a race — see also BOTTOM LINE 3 a row: boys standing in (a) line b row of words on a printed page: The actor forgot his lines. 4 row of military defences 5 a direction followed: the line of fire 6 piece of string, wire, etc.: fishing line 7 telephone connection: Hold the line, please. 8 railway 9 system of travel: airline 10 method of action: new line of approach | You're on the right lines. (= following the right method) 11 an official POLICY (1): the party line 12 trade or profession 13 family following one another: line of kings 14 a short letter 15 area of interest 16 type of goods: a new line in hats 17 in line for being considered for 18 in line with in accordance with 19 (step) out of line (act) differently from others or from what is expected 20 (reach) the end of the line (reach) the last stages, esp. a point of failure 21 read between the lines find hidden meanings

line[2] vt 1 mark with lines or WRINKLES: lined paper | His face is very lined. 2 form rows along: crowds lining the streets

line up phr v 1 vi/t form into a row 2 vt arrange (an event)

line[3] vt 1 cover the inside of (something) with material: fur-lined boots 2 **line one's pocket(s)/purse** make money for oneself **lining** n [C;U]: brake linings

lin·e·age /ˈlɪni-ɪdʒ/ n [C;U] fml line of descent from one person to another in a family

lin·e·ar /ˈlɪniəʳ/ adj 1 in lines 2 of length: linear measurement

lin·en /ˈlɪnən/ n [U] 1 cloth made from FLAX 2 sheets, tablecloths, etc.

line print·er /ˈ· ˌ··ʳ/ n machine that prints computer information

lin·er /ˈlaɪnəʳ/ n 1 large passenger ship 2 something used to LINE[3] something

lines·man /ˈlaɪnzmən/ n -men /-mən/ (in sport) official who says whether a ball has gone outside the limits

line-up /ˈlaɪn-ʌp/ n 1 collection of people, esp. side by side in a line looking forward 2 competitors in a race or game 3 set of events

lin·ger /ˈlɪŋgəʳ/ vi be slow to disappear; delay going: lingering illness

lin·ge·rie /ˈlænʒəriː‖ˌlɑːnʒəˈreɪ, ˈlænʒəriː/ n [U] fml women's underclothes

lin·go /ˈlɪŋgəʊ/ n -goes sl language

lin·guist /ˈlɪŋgwɪst/ n 1 person who studies and is good at foreign languages 2 person who studies language in general ~**ic** /lɪŋˈgwɪstɪk/ adj of language ~**ics** n [U] study of language

lin·i·ment /ˈlɪnɪmənt/ n [U] liquid for rubbing on stiff muscles

link /lɪŋk/ n 1 connection 2 one ring of a chain — see also LINKS ♦ vt/i join; connect

link·age /ˈlɪŋkɪdʒ/ n [C;U] system or way of connection

links /lɪŋks/ n **links** GOLF COURSE

li·no·le·um /lɪˈnəʊliəm/ also **lino** /ˈlaɪnəʊ/ BrE — n [U] smooth hard floor-covering

lint /lɪnt/ n [U] soft material for protecting wounds

li·on /ˈlaɪən/ **lioness** /ˈlaɪənes, -nɪs/ fem. — n 1 large yellow catlike animal 2 famous and important person: a literary lion 3 the lion's share the biggest part ~**ize** vt treat (someone) as important

lip /lɪp/ n 1 edge of the mouth 2 edge of a cup, etc. 3 **lick/smack one's lips** think of or remember something (esp. food) with enjoyment — see also STIFF UPPER LIP

lip-read /ˈlɪp riːd/ vi/t understand speech by watching lip movements

lip ser·vice /ˈ· ˌ··/ n [U] **pay lip service to** support in words, but not in fact

lip·stick /ˈlɪpˌstɪk/ n [C;U] (stick of) coloured substance put on the lips

liq·ue·fy /ˈlɪkwɪfaɪ/ vi/t fml make or become liquid —**faction** /ˌlɪkwɪˈfækʃən/ n [U]

li·queur /lɪˈkjʊəʳ‖lɪˈkɜːr/ n [C;U] strong sweet alcoholic drink

liq·uid /ˈlɪkwɪd/ n [C;U] a substance which is not a solid or a gas, which flows freely and is wet ♦ adj 1 in the form of a liquid 2 clear and wet-looking 3 (of sounds) pure and flowing 4 easily exchanged for money: liquid assets ~**ize** vt crush into juice ~**izer** n BrE for BLENDER

liq·ui·date /ˈlɪkwɪˌdeɪt/ v 1 vt kill 2 vi/t arrange the end of (an unsuccessful company) **–dation** /ˌlɪkwɪˈdeɪʃən/ n [U]

liq·uid·i·ty /lɪˈkwɪdɪti/ n [U] 1 state of being liquid 2 state of having LIQUID (4) money

liq·uor /ˈlɪkəʳ/ n [U] alcoholic drink

liq·uo·rice /ˈlɪkərɪs, -rɪʃ/ n [U] black substance used in medicine and sweets

lisp /lɪsp/ vi pronounce /s/ to sound like /θ/ **lisp** n [S]

list[1] /lɪst/ n set of things written in order: shopping list — see also HIT LIST ♦ vt put into a list

list[2] vi (of a ship) lean or slope to one side **list** n

lis·ten /ˈlɪsən/ vi 1 give attention in hearing 2 **Don't listen to someone** Don't believe or do what someone says **~er** n

  listen in phr vi 1 listen to (a broadcast on) the radio 2 listen to other people's conversation when one should not

list·less /ˈlɪstləs/ adj tired and not interested **~ly** adv **~ness** n [U]

list price /ˈ·ˌ·/ n price suggested for an article by the makers

lit /lɪt/ v past t. and p. of LIGHT[2] or LIGHT[5]

lit·a·ny /ˈlɪtəni/ n form of long Christian prayer: (fig.) a long litany of complaints

li·ter /ˈliːtəʳ/ n AmE for LITRE

lit·e·ra·cy /ˈlɪtərəsi/ n [U] state or condition of being literate

lit·e·ral /ˈlɪtərəl/ adj 1 giving one word for each word: a literal translation 2 following the usual meaning of words **~ly** adv 1 really 2 word by word

lit·e·ra·ry /ˈlɪtərəri‖ˈlɪtəreri/ adj of literature or writers

lit·e·rate /ˈlɪtərɪt/ adj 1 able to read and write 2 well-educated

lit·e·ra·ture /ˈlɪtərətʃəʳ‖-tʃuər/ n [U] 1 written works of artistic value 2 printed material giving information: sales literature

lithe /laɪð/ adj (of people or animals) able to bend easily

litho·graph /ˈlɪθəɡrɑːf‖-ɡræf/ n picture printed from stone or metal

lit·i·ga·tion /ˌlɪtɪˈɡeɪʃən/ n [U] fml process of taking action in law, in non-criminal matters

li·ti·gious /lɪˈtɪdʒəs/ adj often derog fond of litigation

lit·mus /ˈlɪtməs/ n [U] substance that turns red in acid and blue in ALKALI

li·tre BrE ‖ **-ter** AmE /ˈliːtəʳ/ n (a measure of liquid equal to) 1.76 PINTS

lit·ter /ˈlɪtəʳ/ n 1 [U] paper, etc., scattered untidily: a litter bin 2 [C] family of young animals ♦ vt scatter litter on

lit·tle[1] /ˈlɪtl/ adj 1 small: little birds 2 short: a little while 3 young 4 unimportant ♦ adv 1 not much: little-known facts 2 fml not at all: They little thought that I was watching.

little[2] determiner, pron, n less, least 1 [U] (without a or only) not much: I have very little (money) left. 2 [S] (with a or the) a small amount, but at least some: a little milk | stay a little longer 3 **little by little** gradually

little fin·ger /ˌ·· ˈ··/ n smallest finger on the hand

lit·ur·gy /ˈlɪtədʒi‖-ər-/ n form of Christian worship **–gical** /lɪˈtɜːdʒɪkəl‖-ɜːr-/ adj

live[1] /lɪv/ v 1 vi be alive 2 vi remain alive: The doctor says he'll live. 3 vi have one's home: live in Paris 4 vi lead (a kind of life) 5 **live and let live** be TOLERANT 6 **live it up** infml have a lot of fun

  live down phr vt cause (a bad action) to be forgotten, by later good behaviour

  live off phr vt 1 produce one's food or income from 2 get money for one's needs from

  live on phr v 1 vt have as one's food or income 2 vi continue in life or use

  live out phr v 1 vt live till the end of 2 vt experience in reality: live out one's fantasies 3 vi (esp. of a servant) live in a place away from one's place of work

  live through phr vt remain alive during: live through 2 world wars

  live together phr vi live as if married

  live up to phr vt keep to the high standards of

  live with phr vt 1 live as if married with 2 accept (an unpleasant thing)

live[2] /laɪv/ adj 1 alive 2 able to explode or shock: live bomb/wire 3 (of broadcasting) seen or heard as it happens

live·li·hood /ˈlaɪvlihʊd/ n way one earns one's money

live·ly /ˈlaɪvli/ adj 1 full of quick movement and thought 2 bright: lively colours **–liness** n [U]

liv·en /ˈlaɪvən/ v **liven up** phr vi/t make or become lively

liv·er /ˈlɪvəʳ/ n 1 [C] organ in the body that cleans the blood 2 [U] animal's liver as food

live·ry /ˈlɪvəri/ n uniform worn by servants, etc.

lives /laɪvz/ n pl. of LIFE

live·stock /ˈlaɪvstɒk‖-stɑːk/ n [P] farm animals

live wire /ˌlaɪv ˈwaɪəʳ/ n very active person

liv·id /ˈlɪvɪd/ adj 1 bluish-grey 2 very angry

liv·ing[1] /ˈlɪvɪŋ/ adj 1 alive 2 still in use: living language

living² n 1 [S] LIVELIHOOD 2 [U] manner of life

living room /'·· ·/ n main room for general use in a house

liz·ard /'lɪzəd‖-ərd/ n 4-legged REPTILE with a long tail

ll abbrev. for: lines

load /ləʊd/ n 1 something being carried 2 a amount the stated vehicle can carry b weight borne by the frame of a building 3 amount of work to be done 4 a load off someone's mind the removing of a great worry 5 loads of infml a lot of ♦ v 1 vt/i put a load on or in 2 vt put a bullet, etc., into (a gun) or film into (a camera) ~ed adj 1 containing a hidden trap: a loaded question 2 sl very rich 3 sl drunk

loaf¹ /ləʊf/ n loaves /ləʊvz/ 1 [C] single mass of baked bread 2 [C;U] food prepared in a solid piece: meat loaf 3 [C] sl head: Use your loaf! (= think!)

loaf² vi waste time ~er n

loan /ləʊn/ n 1 something lent 2 amount of money lent 3 on loan being borrowed ♦ vt lend

loath, loth /ləʊθ/ adj unwilling

loathe /ləʊð/ vt hate very much loathing n [S;U]

loath·some /'ləʊðsəm/ adj DISGUSTING

loaves /ləʊvz/ n pl. of LOAF

lob /lɒb‖lɑːb/ vt -bb- send (a ball) in a high curve ♦ n lobbed ball

lob·by /'lɒbi‖'lɑːbi/ n 1 hall or passage in a public building 2 group of people who try to influence those in power: the clean-air lobby ♦ vi/t 1 meet (a member of Parliament) in order to persuade him/her to support one's actions, etc. 2 be publicly active in trying to bring about change ~ist n

lobe /ləʊb/ n 1 lower fleshy part of the ear 2 division of the brain or lungs

lob·ster /'lɒbstər‖'lɑːb-/ n 1 [C] 8-legged sea animal with CLAWs 2 [U] its meat as food

lo·cal /'ləʊkəl/ adj 1 of a certain place: our local doctor 2 limited to one part: local anaesthetic ♦ n 1 person living in a place 2 BrE local pub ~ly adv

local au·thor·i·ty /ˌ·· ·'···/ n BrE group of people elected or paid to the government of a particular area

lo·cal·i·ty /ləʊ'kælɪti/ n fml place; area

lo·cal·ize /'ləʊkəlaɪz/ vt keep inside a small area

lo·cate /ləʊ'keɪt‖'ləʊkeɪt/ vt fml 1 learn the position of 2 fix in a particular place: offices located in the town centre **location** /ləʊ'keɪʃən/ n 1 [C] position 2 [U] act of locating 3 on location in a town, country, etc., to make a film

loch /lɒx, lɒk‖lɑːk, lɑːx./ n ScotE lake

lock¹ /lɒk‖lɑːk/ n 1 apparatus for fastening a door, etc. 2 piece of water closed off by gates, so that the level can be raised or lowered 3 BrE amount that a STEERING WHEEL can be turned 4 lock, stock, and barrel completely

lock² v 1 vi/t fasten with a lock 2 vi become fixed or blocked

lock away phr vt keep safe or secret, as by putting in a locked place

lock in/out phr vt keep (a person or criminal) inside/outside a place by locking the door

lock onto phr vt (esp. of a MISSILE) find and follow (the object to be attacked) closely

lock up phr v 1 vi/t make a (building) safe by locking the doors 2 vt put in a safe place and lock the door: He should be locked up! (= in prison)

lock³ n small piece of hair: his curly locks

lock·er /'lɒkər‖'lɑː-/ n small cupboard for clothes, etc., esp. at school, in a sports building, etc.

lock·et /'lɒkɪt‖'lɑː-/ n case for a small picture, etc., worn on a chain round the neck

lo·co·mo·tion /ˌləʊkə'məʊʃən/ n [U] movement from place to place

lo·co·mo·tive /ˌləʊkə'məʊtɪv/ adj of movement ♦ n fml railway engine

lo·cum /'ləʊkəm/ n esp. BrE doctor or priest doing the work of another who is away

lo·cust /'ləʊkəst/ n large flying insect that destroys crops

lodge¹ /lɒdʒ‖lɑːdʒ/ v 1 vi stay somewhere and pay rent 2 vi/t (cause) to become fixed: The chicken bone lodged in his throat. 3 vt make (a report, etc.) officially: lodge a complaint 4 vt put in a safe place: papers lodged with the bank **lodger** n person who pays to live in someone's house

lodge² n 1 small house on the land of a larger one 2 house in wild country for hunters, etc.: skiing lodge

lodg·ing /'lɒdʒɪŋ‖'lɑː-/ n [S;U] place to stay **lodgings** n [P] rented furnished rooms

loft /lɒft‖lɔːft/ n ATTIC

loft·y /'lɒfti‖'lɔːfti/ adj 1 (of ideas, etc.) noble 2 proud 3 lit high ~ily adv

log¹ /lɒg‖lɔːg, lɑːg/ n 1 thick piece of wood from a tree 2 official record of a journey 3 sleep like a log sleep deeply without moving

log² vt -gg- record in a LOG¹ (2)

log in/on phr vi begin a period of using a computer system by performing a fixed set of operations

log off/out phr vi finish a period of using a computer system by performing a fixed set of operations

log-book /'lɒgbʊk‖'lɔːg-, 'lɑːg-/ n 1 LOG¹ (2) 2 BrE for REGISTRATION DOCUMENT

log-ger-heads /'lɒgəhedz‖'lɔːgər-, 'lɑːg-/ n **at loggerheads** always disagreeing

lo-gic /'lɒdʒɪk‖'lɑː-/ n [U] 1 science of formal reasoning 2 good sense ~**al** adj ~**ally** /-kli/ adv

lo-gis-tics /lə'dʒɪstɪks‖ləʊ-/ n [P] detailed planning of an operation

lo-go /'ləʊgəʊ/ n -os sign, pattern, etc., representing a business firm

loin /lɔɪn/ n [C;U] (piece of) meat from the lower part of an animal **loins** n [P] human body between the waist and legs

loin-cloth /'lɔɪnklɒθ‖-klɔːθ/ n cloth worn round the loins

loi-ter /'lɔɪtə/ vi stand somewhere for no clear reason ~**er** n

loll /lɒl‖lɑːl/ vi 1 lie lazily 2 (allow to) hang down loosely

lol-li-pop /'lɒlipɒp‖'lɑːlipɑːp/ n hard sweet made of boiled sugar or frozen fruit juice on a stick

lol-ly /'lɒli‖'lɑːli/ n BrE 1 [C] ICE LOLLY 2 [U] sl money

lone /ləʊn/ adj fml alone; single

lone-ly /'ləʊnli/ adj 1 alone and unhappy 2 (of places) without people ~**liness** n [U]

lone-some /'ləʊnsəm/ adj LONELY (1)

long¹ /lɒŋ‖lɔːŋ/ adj 1 large when measured from beginning to end: long hair | a long time | 2 metres long 2 (of a drink) cool, containing little or no alcohol, and served in a long glass 3 **long on** with a lot of

long² adv 1 (for) a long time: long ago | Will you be long? 2 **as/so long as** on condition that 3 **no longer/(not) any longer** (not) any more 4 **so long** goodbye for now ♦ n 1 a long time: It won't take long. 2 **before long** soon 3 **the long and (the) short of it** infml the general result, expressed in a few words

long³ vi wish very much: longing to go ~**ing** adj, n [C;U] (showing) a strong wish ~**ingly** adv

long for phr vt want very much

long-dis-tance /ˌ··'··◂/ adj covering a long distance ♦ adv to or from a distant point

lon-gev-i-ty /lɒn'dʒevɪti‖lɑːn-, lɔːn-/ n [U] fml long life

long-hand /'lɒŋhænd‖'lɔːŋ-/ n [U] ordinary writing by hand

lon-gi-tude /'lɒndʒɪtjuːd‖'lɑːndʒɪtuːd/ n [C;U] distance east or west of Greenwich, measured in degrees ~**tidinal** /ˌlɒndʒɪ'tjuːdɪnəl‖ˌlɑːndʒɪ'tuː-/ adj going along, not across

long jump /'··/ n [S] sport of jumping as far as possible along the ground

long-range /ˌ·'·◂/ adj covering a long distance or time

long-sight-ed /ˌlɒŋ'saɪtɪd◂‖ˌlɔːŋ-/ adj able to see things only when they are far away

long-stand-ing /ˌlɒŋ'stændɪŋ◂‖ˌlɔːŋ-/ adj having existed for a long time: long-standing rivalry

long-suf-fer-ing /ˌlɒŋ'sʌfərɪŋ◂‖ˌlɔːŋ-/ adj patient under continued difficulties

long-term /ˌ·'·◂/ adj for or in the distant future

long wave /ˌ·'·◂/ n [U] radio broadcasting on waves of more than 1000 metres

long-wind-ed /ˌlɒŋ'wɪndɪd◂‖ˌlɔːŋ-/ adj saying too much; dull

loo /luː/ n **loos** BrE infml for TOILET

look¹ /lʊk/ v 1 vi use the eyes to see something 2 seem; appear: You look tired. 3 vi face: The window looks east. 4 **look as if/like** seem probable: It looks as if he's gone. 5 **(not) look one-self** (not) appear healthy 6 **look well** fml be attractive

look after phr vt take care of

look ahead phr vi plan for the future

look around/round phr vi search

look at phr vt 1 watch 2 consider; examine 3 **not much to look at** not attractive in appearance

look back phr vi 1 remember 2 **never look back** continue to succeed

look down on phr vt DESPISE

look for phr vt try to find

look forward to phr vt expect to enjoy

look in phr vi infml make a short visit

look into phr vt examine; INVESTIGATE

look on phr v 1 vi watch 2 vt regard as

look out phr vi take care; keep watching

look over phr vt examine quickly

look round phr vi/t examine (a place)

look through phr vt examine for points to be noted

look to phr vt 1 depend on: I look to you for support. 2 pay attention to

look up phr v 1 vi improve 2 vt find (information) in a book 3 vt find and visit

look up to phr vt respect

look² n 1 act of looking 2 appearance 3 **I don't like the look of it/the looks of this.** This (state of affairs, etc.) suggests something bad to me **looks** n [P] person's (attractive) appearance

look-in /'·· ·/ n [S] chance to take part or succeed

look·ing glass /'·· ·/ n mirror

look-out /'luk-aut/ n [S] **1** state of watching **2** person who keeps watch **3** one's personal problem: *It's your own lookout if you're caught.*

loom[1] /luːm/ n machine for weaving cloth

loom[2] vi appear in a threatening way: *Fear of failure loomed large in his life.*

loon-y /'luːni/ n, adj sl LUNATIC

loop /luːp/ n (shape of) a piece of string, etc., curved back on itself ♦ vi/t make (into) a loop

loop-hole /'luːphəʊl/ n way of escape: *loopholes in the tax laws*

loose /luːs/ adj **1** not firmly fixed: *a loose tooth* **2** free from control: *loose cattle* **3** not packed together: *loose biscuits* **4** (of clothes) too wide **5** not exact: *a loose translation* **6** without sexual morals: *loose living* **7 at a loose end** having nothing to do **8 cut loose** break away from a group or situation ~**ly** adv

loose end /,· '·/ n [usu. pl.] **1** part not properly completed **2 at a loose end** BrE ∥ **at loose ends** AmE having nothing to do

loos-en /'luːsən/ vi/t make or become looser

loot /luːt/ n [U] goods taken illegally by soldiers, etc. ♦ vi/t take loot (from) ~**er** n

lop /lɒp/||lɑːp/ vt **-pp-** cut (branches) from a tree

lop-sid-ed /,· '··◁/ adj with one side lower than the other

loq-ua-cious /ləʊ'kweɪʃəs/ adj fml talking a great deal ~**ly** adv **-city** /-'kwæsɪti/ n [U]

lord /lɔːd||lɔːrd/ n **1** ruler; master **2** nobleman: *the Lords* (= members of) the HOUSE OF LORDS) **3** (cap.) God **4** (cap.) (title for certain official people): *Lord Mayor* ~**ship** n (title for) a Lord: *your lordship*

lord-ly /'lɔːdli||-ɔːr-/ adj proud; grand

lor-ry /'lɒri||'lɔːri, 'lɑːri/ n BrE heavy motor vehicle; TRUCK[1]

lose /luːz/ v lost /lɒst||lɔːst/ **1** vt be unable to find: *lose a book/one's way* **2** vt have taken away: *lose one's job* **3** vi/t fail to win: *lose a battle* **4** vt have less of: *lose weight/money* **5** vi (of a clock) go too slowly **6** vt (cause to) fail to hear, see, or understand: *You've lost me; could you explain that again?* **7 lose oneself in something** give all one's attention to something so as not to notice anything else **8 lose sight of** forget **seen** n person who loses

lose out phr vi **1** make a loss **2** be defeated

loss /lɒs||lɔːs/ n **1** [U] act of losing; failure to keep **2** [C] person, thing, or amount lost: *The army suffered heavy losses.* **3** [C] failure to make a profit **4 at a loss** uncertain what to do or say **5 be a dead loss** infml have no worth or value

lost /lɒst||lɔːst/ v past t. and p. of LOSE

lost cause /,· '·/ n something which has no chance of success

lot[1] /lɒt||lɑːt/ n **1** a great number or amount: *a lot of people* | *lots (and lots) of money* **2** group or amount: *a new lot of students* **3 a lot** much: *a lot better* **4 a fat lot** infml none at all **5 the lot** the whole; all

lot[2] n **1** [C] article sold at an AUCTION **2** [C] esp. AmE piece of land **3** [C;U] (use of) different objects to make a decision by chance: *choose the winner by lot* **4** [S] fml one's fate **5 a bad lot** a bad person

loth /ləʊθ/ adj LOATH

lo-tion /'ləʊʃən/ n [C;U] liquid mixture for the skin or hair to make it clean and healthy

lot-te-ry /'lɒtəri||'lɑː-/ n system of giving prizes to people who bought numbered tickets, chosen by chance

loud /laʊd/ adj **1** producing a lot of sound **2** unpleasantly colourful ♦ adv in a loud way ~**ly** adv ~**ness** n [U]

loud-speak-er /,laʊd'spiːkə[r], 'laʊd-,spiːkə[r]/ n part of a radio or record player from which the sound comes out

lounge /laʊndʒ/ vi stand or sit lazily ♦ n comfortable room to sit in

lounge bar /'· ·/ n BrE SALOON BAR

lounge suit /'· ·/ n man's daytime suit

louse /laʊs/ n lice **1** insect that lives on people's and animals' bodies **2** worthless person

lou-sy /'laʊzi/ adj **1** very bad: *lousy weather* **2** covered with lice

lout /laʊt/ n rough awkward man or boy ~**ish** adj

lov-a-ble /'lʌvəbəl/ adj deserving, causing or worthy of love

love /lʌv/ n **1** [U] great fondness for someone **2** [S;U] warm interest: *a love of music* **3** [C] loved person or thing **4** [U] (in tennis) NIL **5 give/send someone one's love** send friendly greetings **6 make love (to)** have sex (with) **7 not for love or/nor money** infml not by any means ♦ v **1** vi/t feel love (for) **2** vt like very much: *I'd love a drink.* **lov-ing** adj fond

love af-fair /'· ·,·/ n sexual relationship: (fig.) *a love affair with Russian literature* (= a great interest and liking)

love-ly /'lʌvli/ adj **1** beautiful: *lovely girl/view* **2** very pleasant: *lovely dinner*

lov-er /'lʌvə[r]/ n **1** person (usu. a man) who has a sexual relationship with another person outside marriage

2 person who is fond of the stated thing: *art lovers*

love·sick /'lʌv,sɪk/ *adj* sad because of unreturned love

low /ləʊ/ *adj* **1** not high: *low wall/cost/standards* **2** (of a supply) nearly finished **3** (of sounds) **a** deep **b** not loud **4** unhappy **5** not fair or honest: *a low trick* **6** for a slow speed: *a low gear* ♦ *adv* to or at a low level: *bend low* ♦ *n* low point or level

low-brow /'ləʊbraʊ/ *n, adj* (person) not interested in art, books, etc.

low-down /'ləʊdaʊn/ *n* [S] *sl* the plain facts

low-down /'· ·/ *adj* worthless; dishonourable

low·er¹ /'ləʊəʳ/ *adj* at or nearer the bottom: *the lower leg*

lower² *vt* **1** make less high **2 lower oneself** bring oneself down in people's opinion

low·er³ /'laʊəʳ/ *vi* **1** be dark and threatening **2** FROWN severely

lower class /,·· '·◄/ *n* social class of lowest rank **lower-class** *adj*

low-key /,· '·◄/ *adj* quiet and controlled

low·lands /'ləʊləndz/ *n* [P] land lower than its surroundings

low·ly /'ləʊli/ *adj* low in rank; HUMBLE **–liness** *n* [U]

low sea·son /'· ,··/ *n* [U] time of year when business is least and prices are lowest

low-spir·it·ed /,· '···◄/ *adj* unhappy

loy·al /'lɔɪəl/ *adj* faithful to one's friends, country, etc. **~ist** *n* person who remains loyal to a ruler **~ly** *adv*

loy·al·ty /'lɔɪəlti/ *n* **1** [U] being loyal **2** [C] connection that binds one to someone or something to which one is loyal

loz·enge /'lɒzɪndʒ‖'lɑː-/ *n* medical sweet: *cough lozenge*

LP /,el 'piː/ *n* record that plays for about 20 minutes each side

L-plate /'el pleɪt/ *n* letter L, fixed to a British vehicle to show that the driver is a learner

LSD /,el es 'diː/ *n* [U] illegal drug that causes HALLUCINATIONS

Ltd *written abbrev. for:* LIMITED (2)

lu·bri·cant /'luːbrɪkənt/ *n* [C;U] substance that lubricates; oil, etc.

lu·bri·cate /'luːbrɪkeɪt/ *vt* make (machine parts) work without friction

lu·cid /'luːsɪd/ *adj* **1** easy to understand **2** able to think clearly **~ly** *adv* **~ity** /luː'sɪdəti/ *n* [U]

luck /lʌk/ *n* [U] **1** what happens to someone by chance **2** success: *wish them luck* **3 be down on one's luck** have bad luck, esp. be without money **4 be in/out of luck** have/not have good fortune **~y** *adj* having or bringing good luck **~ily** *adv*

lu·cra·tive /'luːkrətɪv/ *adj* profitable

lud·dite /'lʌdaɪt/ *n* (*often cap.*) *derog* someone who is opposed to change, esp. the introduction of new work methods and machinery

lu·di·crous /'luːdɪkrəs/ *adj* causing laughter; foolish **~ly** *adv*

lug /lʌg/ *vt* **-gg-** pull or carry with difficulty

lug·gage /'lʌgɪdʒ/ *n* [U] bags, etc., of a traveller

lu·gu·bri·ous /luː'guːbrɪəs/ *adj fml* sorrowful **~ly** *adv*

luke·warm /,luːk'wɔːm◄‖-ɔːrm◄/ *adj* **1** (of liquid) neither warm nor cold **2** not eager

lull /lʌl/ *vt* cause to rest ♦ *n* [S] calm period

lul·la·by /'lʌləbaɪ/ *n* song to make a child go to sleep

lum·ba·go /lʌm'beɪgəʊ/ *n* [U] pain in the lower back

lum·ber¹ /'lʌmbəʳ/ *v* **1** *vi* move heavily and awkwardly **2** *vt* give (someone) an unwanted object or job

lumber² *n* **1** useless articles stored away **2** *AmE for* TIMBER

lu·mi·na·ry /'luːmənəri‖-neri/ *n fml* famous respected person

lu·mi·nous /'luːmənəs/ *adj* shining in the dark **–nosity** /,luːmə'nɒsəti‖ -'nɑː-/ *n* [U]

lump /lʌmp/ *n* **1** solid mass: *lump of coal/sugar* **2** hard swelling **3 lump in the throat** tight sensation in the throat caused by unexpressed pity, sorrow, etc. ♦ *v* **lump it** accept bad conditions without complaint **~y** *adj*: *lumpy sauce*

lump together *phr vt* consider (2 or more things) as a single unit

lump sum /,· '·/ *n* money given as a single payment rather than in parts

lu·na·cy /'luːnəsi/ *n* madness

lu·nar /'luːnəʳ/ *adj* of the moon

lu·na·tic /'luːnətɪk/ *adj, n* mad or foolish (person)

lunch /lʌntʃ/ *also* **luncheon** *fml* /'lʌntʃən/ *-- n* [C;U] meal eaten at about midday **lunch** *vi*

lung /lʌŋ/ *n* either of the 2 breathing organs in the chest

lunge /lʌndʒ/ *vi* (make) a sudden forward movement

lurch¹ /lɜːtʃ‖lɜːrtʃ/ *vi* move irregularly **lurch** *n*

lurch² *n* **1** lurching movement **2 leave someone in the lurch** leave them when they are in difficulty

lure /lʊəʳ, ljʊəʳ‖lʊəʳ/ *n* something that attracts: *the lure of wealth* ♦ *vt* attract into trouble

lu·rid /'lʊərɪd, 'ljʊərɪd‖'lʊərɪd/ *adj* **1** unnaturally bright: *lurid colours* **2** shocking; unpleasant

lurk /lɜːk‖lɜːrk/ *vi* wait in hiding, esp. for a bad purpose

lus·cious /'lʌʃəs/ adj 1 having a ripe sweet taste 2 sexually attractive

lush[1] /lʌʃ/ adj (of plants) growing thickly

lush[2] n sl. esp. AmE ALCOHOLIC

lust /lʌst/ n [C;U] strong (sexual) desire: lust for power **lust** vi ~**ful** adj

lus·tre BrE ‖ **-ter** AmE /'lʌstəʳ/ n [S;U] 1 brightness of a polished surface 2 glory

lust·y /'lʌsti/ adj strong and healthy

lute /luːt/ n old stringed musical instrument

lux·u·ri·ant /lʌg'zjuəriənt, ləg'ʒuəriənt‖ləg'ʒuəriənt/ adj growing well and thickly ~**ly** adv –**ance** n [U]

lux·u·ri·ate /lʌg'zjuəriət, ləg'ʒuəriət‖ləg'ʒuəri-/ **luxuriate in** phr vt enjoy oneself lazily in

lux·u·ri·ous /lʌg'zjuəriəs, ləg'ʒuəriəs‖ləg'ʒuəriəs/ adj comfortable and esp. expensive

lux·u·ry /'lʌkʃəri/ n 1 [U] great comfort, as provided by wealth 2 [C] something pleasant, but not necessary and not often had or done

ly·ing /'laɪ-ɪŋ/ v pres. p. of LIE[1] and LIE[2]

lynch /lɪntʃ/ vt (esp. of a crowd) kill without a legal trial

lyr·ic /'lɪrɪk/ n, adj (short poem) expressing strong feelings in songlike form ~**al** adj full of joyful feeling

lyrics n [P] words of a popular song

M

M,m /em/ the 13th letter of the English alphabet

m written abbrev. for: 1 metre(s) 2 mile(s) 3 million 4 married 5 male

ma /mɑː/ n sl mother

ma'am /mæm. mɑːm, məm‖mæm/ n (polite way of addressing a woman)

mac /mæk/ n BrE coat that keeps out the rain

ma·ca·bre /mə'kɑːbrə, -bəʳ/ adj causing fear, esp. because connected with death

ma·caw /mə'kɔː/ n large S American PARROT

mace /meɪs/ n ceremonial rod carried by an official

Mach /mæk‖mɑːk/ n speed of an aircraft in relation to the speed of sound: Mach 2 (= twice the speed of sound)

ma·chet·e /mə'ʃeti, mə'tʃeti/ n large heavy knife

Mach·i·a·vel·li·an /,mækiə'veliən/ adj skilful in using indirect means to get what one wants; CUNNING

mach·i·na·tions /,mækɪ'neɪʃənz, ,mæʃ-/ n [P] secret efforts or plans to do harm

ma·chine /mə'ʃiːn/ n 1 instrument or apparatus that uses power to work 2 group that controls and plans activities of a political party ♦ vt make or produce by machine

ma·chine-gun /mə'ʃiːngʌn/ n gun that fires continuously

machine-read·a·ble /·,· '···‖/ adj in a form that can be understood and used by a computer

ma·chin·e·ry /mə'ʃiːnəri/ n [U] 1 machines: farm machinery 2 working parts of a machine or engine 3 operation of a system or organization

ma·chis·mo /mə'tʃɪzməʊ, - ·'kɪz‖mɑː-, mə-/ n [U] usu. derog quality of being macho

ma·cho /'mætʃəʊ‖'mɑː-/ adj (trying to seem) strong and brave

mack·e·rel /'mækərəl/ n mackerel or mackerels sea fish, often eaten

mack·in·tosh /'mækɪntɒʃ‖-tɑːʃ/ n esp. BrE MAC

mac·ro·bi·ot·ic /,mækrəʊbaɪ'ɒtɪk◄‖-'ɑːtɪk◄/ adj of a type of food (esp. vegetable products grown without chemicals) thought to produce good health

mad /mæd/ adj -**dd**- 1 ill in the mind 2 very foolish 3 angry 4 filled with strong interest: She's mad about politics. 5 **like mad** very hard, fast, loud, etc. 6 **mad keen** BrE infml extremely keen ~**ly** adv. madly (= very much) in love ~**ness** n [U] ~**den** vt annoy extremely

mad·am /'mædəm/ n (often cap.) (polite way of addressing a woman)

made /meɪd/ v past t. and p. of MAKE

ma·don·na /mə'dɒnə‖-'dɑː-/ n (in the Christian religion) (picture or figure of) Mary, the mother of Christ

mad·ri·gal /'mædrɪgəl/ n song for several singers without instruments

mael·strom /'meɪlstrəm/ n lit 1 violent WHIRLPOOL 2 destructive force of events

maes·tro /'maɪstrəʊ/ n -tros great or famous musician

ma·fi·a /'mɑːfiə‖'mɑː-, 'mæ-/ n 1 (usu. cap.) organization of criminals, esp. in the US 2 influential group who support each other without any concern for people outside the group: the medical mafia

mag·a·zine /,mægə'ziːn‖'mægəziːn/ n 1 sort of book with a paper cover, which contains writing, photographs, and advertisements, that is printed every week or month and is of interest to a particular group of people 2 part of a gun in which bullets are stored

ma·gen·ta /mə'dʒentə/ adj dark purplish red

mag·got /'mægət/ n wormlike young of flies and other insects

mag·ic /'mædʒɪk/ n 1 use of strange unseen forces, or of tricks, to produce effects 2 special wonderful quality: the magic of the theatre — see also BLACK MAGIC ♦ adj caused by or used in magic: a magic trick/ring ~al adj strange and wonderful ~ally /-kli/ adv

ma·gi·cian /mə'dʒɪʃən/ n person who practises magic

ma·gis·te·ri·al /,mædʒə'stɪəriəl/ adj fml showing complete and undoubted control

ma·gis·trate /'mædʒəstreɪt, -strət/ n official who judges cases in the lowest law courts

mag·nan·i·mous /mæg'nænəməs/ adj fml very generous ~ly adv -mity /,mægnə'nɪməti/ n [U]

mag·nate /'mægneɪt, -nət/ n wealthy and powerful person

mag·ne·si·um /mæg'niːziəm/ n silver-white metal

mag·net /'mægnət/ n 1 piece of iron or steel that draws other metal objects towards it 2 person or thing that attracts or interests people greatly ~ism n [U] magnetic force ~ize vt ~ic /mæg'netɪk/ adj: a magnetic personality ~ically /-kli/ adv

magnetic tape /·,·· '·/ n [C;U] TAPE on which sound or other information can be recorded

mag·nif·i·cent /mæg'nɪfəsənt/ adj extremely fine or good -cence n [U] ~ly adv

mag·ni·fy /'mægnəfaɪ/ vt cause to look or seem larger -fication /,mægnəfə'keɪʃən/ n [U]

magnifying glass /'···· ·/ n curved LENS (1) for magnifying things

mag·ni·tude /'mægnətjuːd/ n [U] fml degree of size or importance

mag·pie /'mægpaɪ/ n noisy black and white bird which likes to steal bright objects

ma·ha·ra·jah /,mɑːhə'rɑːdʒə/ n (title of) an Indian prince

ma·ha·ra·ni /,mɑːhə'rɑːni/ n (title of) the wife of a maharajah

ma·hog·a·ny /mə'hogəni‖mə'hɑː-/ n [U] dark reddish wood used for furniture

maid /meɪd/ n 1 female servant 2 maiden — see also OLD MAID

maid·en /'meɪdn/ n lit young unmarried woman ♦ adj 1 first: the ship's maiden voyage 2 unmarried: my maiden aunts

maiden name /'···· ·/ n family name a woman has or had before marriage

mail¹ /meɪl/ n [U] 1 the postal system: It came by airmail. 2 letters, etc.,

that one posts or receives ♦ vt esp. AmE for POST² (1,2)

mail² n [U] soldiers' protective clothing in former times, made of small metal rings

mail·shot /'meɪlʃɒt‖-ʃɑːt/ n sending of advertisements, etc., to large numbers of people by post

maim /meɪm/ vt wound very seriously and usu. lastingly

main¹ /meɪn/ adj chief; most important: its main function ~ly adv: His money comes mainly from investments.

main² n 1 large pipe or wire supplying water, gas, or electricity 2 **in the main** mostly

main chance /,· '·/ n [the + S] possibility of making money or other personal gain

main·frame /'meɪnfreɪm/ n the largest and most powerful kind of computer

main·land /'meɪnlənd, -lænd/ n a land mass, considered without its islands **mainland** adj

main·line /'meɪnlaɪn/ vi/t INJECT an illegal drug into one of the chief veins of the body

main·spring /'meɪn,sprɪŋ/ n 1 chief spring in a watch 2 chief force or reason that makes something happen

main·stay /'meɪnsteɪ/ n someone or something which provides the chief means of support

main·stream /'meɪnstriːm/ n main or usual way of thinking or acting in relation to a subject

main·tain /meɪn'teɪn, mən-/ vt 1 keep in good condition 2 support with money 3 continue to have or do 4 continue to say, believe, or argue

main·te·nance /'meɪntənəns/ n [U] 1 keeping in good condition 2 money given to wives and/or children by a husband/father who does not live with them

mai·son·ette /,meɪzə'net/ n flat that is part of a larger house

maize /meɪz/ n [U] esp. BrE for CORN (2)

ma·jes·ty /'mædʒəsti/ n 1 (cap.) (used as a title for kings and queens) 2 [U] fml grandness -tic /mə'dʒestɪk/ adj: majestic scenery -tically /-kli/ adv

ma·jor¹ /'meɪdʒər/ adj of great importance or seriousness: a major problem/major surgery

major² n army officer, above CAPTAIN — see also SERGEANT MAJOR

major³ v **major in** phr vt esp. AmE study as the chief subject(s) for a university degree

ma·jor·i·ty /mə'dʒɒrəti‖mə'dʒɑː-, mə'dʒɔː-/ n 1 [(the) S] most 2 [C] difference in number between a large and small group: *win by a majority of 300 votes*

make¹ /meɪk/ *vt* **made** /meɪd/ **1** produce: *make a cake/a noise/a decision/a bag made of leather/wine made from local grapes* **2** cause to be: *It made me happy.* **3** force; cause: *I can't make him understand.* **4** earn (money) **5** calculate or be counted as: *What time do you make it?|That makes the fourth glass you've had!* **6** add up to: *2 and 2 make 4* **7** tidy (a bed that has been slept in) **8** have the qualities of: *That story makes good reading.* **9** reach: *We made harbour by night fall.* **10** complete: *That picture really makes the room.* **11** **make believe** pretend **12** **make do** use something for lack of any better: *We had to make do with water.* **13** **make it: a** arrive in time **b** succeed **14** **make one's way** go: *I made my way home.* **15** **make or break** which will cause success or complete failure **maker** *n* **1** person who makes something: *a watchmaker* **2** (*usu. cap.*) God **–making 1** be the making of cause to improve greatly **2** have the makings of have the possibility of developing into

make for *phr vt* **1** move in the direction of: *I made for the exit.* **2** result in: *Large print makes for easy reading.*

make into *phr vt* use in making: *He made the bottle into an interesting ornament.*

make of *phr vt* **1** understand by: *I don't know what to make of the situation.* **2** give (the usu. stated importance) to: *She makes too much of her problems.*

make off *phr vi* leave in a hurry

make off with *phr vt* steal

make out *phr v* **1** *vt* write in complete form **2** *vt* see, hear, or understand properly **3** *vt* claim; pretend **4** *vi* succeed **5** *vt* argue as proof: *make out a case* (= give good reasons)

make over *phr vt* **1** pass over to someone else, esp. legally **2** *esp. AmE* remake

make up *phr v* **1** *vt* invent (a story, etc.), esp. to deceive **2** *vi/t* use special paint and powder on the face to look beautiful or change the appearance **3** *vt* prepare for use: *A pharmacist made up the doctor's prescriptions.* **4** *vt* form as a whole: *Oil makes up half of our exports.* **5** *vi* become friends again after a quarrel

make up for *phr vt* give something good to take away disappointment: *I bought him a present to make up for my bad behaviour.*

make² *n* **1** type of product **2** **on the make** searching for personal gain

make-be·lieve /'· ·,·/ *n* [U] pretending

make·shift /'meɪk,ʃɪft/ *adj* used because there is nothing better

make-up /'· ·/ *n* [C;U] **1** paint, powder, etc., worn on the face **2** combination of members or qualities

mal·ad·just·ed /,mælə'dʒʌstɪd◄/ *adj* not fitting in well with other people or with life generally

ma·laise /mɒ'leɪz/ *n* [C;U] **1** failure to be active and successful **2** feeling of not being well

mal·a·prop·is·m /'mæləprɒpɪzəm|| -prɑː-/ *n* often amusing misuse of a word; use of a word that is similar to the intended word but means something completely different

ma·lar·i·a /mə'leəriə/ *n* [U] tropical disease passed on by MOSQUITOes

mal·con·tent /'mælkəntent||,mælkən'tent/ *n fml* dissatisfied person who is likely to make trouble

male /meɪl/ *n, adj* (person or animal) of the sex that does not give birth

male chau·vin·ist /,· '····◄/ *n derog* man who behaves unreasonably towards women because he thinks they are less able, strong, etc., than him

mal·e·fac·tor /'mælɪfæktəʳ/ *n fml or lit* person who does evil

ma·lev·o·lent /mə'levələnt/ *adj lit* wishing to do evil to others **~ly** *adv* **–lence** *n* [U]

mal·formed /,mæl'fɔːmd||-ɔːr-/ *adj* made or shaped badly: *a malformed limb* ♦ **-formation** /,mælfɔː'meɪʃən|| -ɔːr-/ *n* [C;U]

mal·func·tion /mæl'fʌŋkʃən/ *n* fault in operation ♦ **malfunction** *vi*

mal·ice /'mælɪs/ *n* [U] desire to hurt or harm **–icious** /mə'lɪʃəs/ *adj*: *a malicious attack* **-iciously** *adv*

ma·lign /mə'laɪn/ *adj fml* bad; causing harm ♦ *vt* say bad things about

ma·lig·nant /mə'lɪgnənt/ *adj* **1** (of disease) likely to kill **2** *fml* malign **~ly** *adv*

ma·lin·ger /mə'lɪŋgəʳ/ *vi* avoid work by pretending to be ill **~er** *n*

mall /mɔːl, mæl||mɔːl/ *n AmE* area of streets with no cars, where one can shop

mal·le·a·ble /'mæliəbəl/ *adj* (of metal) easy to shape; soft: (fig.) *a malleable personality*

mal·let /'mælɪt/ *n* wooden hammer

mal·nu·tri·tion /,mælnjuː'trɪʃən|| -nuː-/ *n* [U] lack of (proper) food

mal·prac·tice /,mæl'præktɪs/ *n* [C;U] failure to do one's professional duty properly or honestly

malt /mɔːlt/ *n* [U] partly grown grain used esp. for making beer and WHISKY

mal·treat /mæl'triːt/ *vt fml* treat roughly and/or cruelly **~ment** *n* [U]

233 manoeuvre

ma-ma¹ /'mɑːmə/ *n AmE infml* mother

ma-ma² /mə'mɑː/ *n BrE lit* mother

mam-mal /'mæməl/ *n* animal of the sort fed on the mother's milk when young

mam-moth /'mæməθ/ *adj* extremely large

man /mæn/ *n* **men** /men/ **1** [C] adult male person **2** [U] the human race: *Man must change in a changing world.* **3** [C] person: *All men must die.* **4** [C] male of low rank: *officers and men* **5** [C] male member of a team **6** [C] object used in board games: *chess men* **7 a man of the world** man with a lot of experience **8 man and wife** *fml* married **9 one's own man** independent in action **10 the man in the street** the average person **11 to a man** every person: *They agreed, to a man.* — see also BEST MAN, FRONT MAN ♦ *vt* **-nn-** provide with people for operation ~**hood** *n* [U] quality or time of being a (brave) man

man-a-bout-town /ˈ·· '·/*n* (rich) man who spends a great deal of time at fashionable social events, and often does not work

man-a-cle /'mænəkəl/ *n* metal ring for fastening a prisoner's hands or feet

man-age /'mænɪdʒ/ *v* **1** *vt* be in charge of; run **2** *vi/t* succeed in doing: *I only just managed to get out of the way.* **3** *vi* succeed in living, esp. on a small amount of money: *We don't earn much, but we manage.* ~**able** *adj* easy or possible to deal with ~**ment** *n* [U] **1** managing **2** the people in charge **manager** *n* person who runs a business, hotel, sports team, etc. ~**agerial** /ˌmænəˈdʒɪəriəl/ *adj*: *managerial responsibilities*

man-da-rin /'mændərɪn/ *n* **1** high-ranking government official in the former Chinese empire **2** *often derog* high-ranking official

man-date /'mændeɪt/ *n* government's right or duty to act according to the wishes of the electors

man-da-to-ry /'mændətəri‖-tɔːri/ *adj fml* which must be done

man-di-ble /'mændɪbəl/ *n* med jaw

man-do-lin /ˌmændə'lɪn/ *n* 8-stringed musical instrument

mane /meɪn/ *n* long hair on a horse's or lion's neck

ma-neu-ver /mə'nuːvəʳ/ *n, v AmE* for MANOEUVRE

man-ful-ly /'mænfəli/ *adv* bravely and determinedly

man-ger /'meɪndʒəʳ/ *n* **1** long open container for animals' food **2 a dog in the manger** someone who does not want others to use something even though they themselves do not need it

man-gle /'mæŋgəl/ *vt* crush and tear so as to ruin

man-go /'mæŋgəʊ/ *n* **-goes** or **-gos** tropical fruit with sweet yellow flesh

man-gy /'meɪndʒi/ *adj* of bad appearance, esp. because of loss of hair or fur

man-han-dle /'mænhændl/ *vt* hold or move forcefully or roughly

man-hole /'mænhəʊl/ *n* opening in the road leading to underground pipes, wires, etc.

ma-ni-a /'meɪniə/ *n* [C;U] madness **2** extreme interest or desire: *a mania for collecting matchboxes* | *soccer mania* **maniac** /-niæk/ *n* ~**cal** /mə'naɪəkəl/ *adj*: *maniacal laughter*

man-i-cure /'mænɪkjʊəʳ/ *vt, n* (give) treatment for the hands, esp. the fingernails, including cleaning, cutting, etc. **-curist** *n*

man-i-fest¹ /'mænɪfest/ *adj fml* plain to see or understand; OBVIOUS ~**ly** *adv*

manifest² *vt* show plainly ~**ation** /ˌmænɪfe'steɪʃən‖-fə-/ *n* [C;U]

man-i-fes-to /ˌmænɪ'festəʊ/ *n* **-tos** or **-toes** statement of intentions or opinions, esp. as made by a political party before an election

man-i-fold¹ /'mænɪfəʊld/ *adj* many in number or kind

manifold² *n tech* pipe with holes, to allow gases to enter or escape from an engine, such as in a car

ma-nip-u-late /mə'nɪpjɵleɪt/ *vt* **1** *fml* handle skilfully **2** control and influence for one's own purposes **-lative** /-lətɪv/ *adj* **-lation** /mə,nɪpjɵ'leɪʃən/ *n* [U]

man-kind /ˌmæn'kaɪnd/ *n* [U] human beings

man-ly /'mænli/ *adj* having qualities (believed to be) suitable to a man **-liness** *n* [U]

man-made /ˌ· '·◁/ *adj* **1** produced by people **2** (of materials) not made from natural substances

man-ner /'mænəʳ/ *n* **1** *fml* way: *a meal prepared in the Japanese manner* **2** way of behaving towards people: *a rude manner* **3 all manner of** *fml* every sort of **4 -mannered** having the stated way of behaving: *bad-mannered* **5 (as) to the manner born** as if one is used to (something, esp. social position) from birth **manners** *n* [U] (polite) social practices: *It's bad manners to make a noise while you eat.*

man-ner-ism /'mænərɪzəm/ *n* (bad or strange) way of behaving that has become a habit

ma-noeu-vre *BrE* ‖ **maneuver** *AmE* /mə'nuːvəʳ/ *n* **1** skilful movement **2** secret trick to gain a purpose **3 on manoeuvres** doing battle training ♦ *vt* move or turn, esp. skilfully or deceivingly: *The car manoeuvres well in wet weather.* **–vrable** *BrE* ‖ **-verable** *AmE adj*

man of straw /,··'/n 1 *esp. BrE* person of weak character 2 *esp. AmE* imaginary opponent whose arguments can easily be defeated

man·or /'mænər/ *n* area of land owned by the local lord in former times

man·pow·er /'mæn,pauər/ *n* [U] number of workers employed

man·qu55e/'moŋkeı‖mɑːŋ'keı/ *adj fml* that failed to become the stated thing

man·sion /'mænʃən/ *n* large grand house

man-sized /'·'·/ *adj* large

man·slaugh·ter /'mæn,slɔːtər/ *n* [U] crime of killing someone unintentionally

man·tel·piece /'mæntlpiːs/ *n* shelf above a fireplace

man·tle /'mæntl/ *n* 1 covering: *a mantle of snow* 2 (sign of) general or official recognition: *He took over the mantle of world heavyweight champion.*

man-to-man /,· · '·◀/ *adj, adv* open(ly) and honest(ly)

man·u·al¹ /'mænjuəl/ *adj* of or using the hands **–ly** *adv*

manual² *n* book giving information or instructions

man·u·fac·ture /,mænjǔ'fæktʃər/ *vt* make in large quantities using machinery ♦ *n* [U] manufacturing: *goods of foreign manufacture* **~turer** *n*

ma·nure /mə'njuər‖mə'nuər/ *n* [U] animal waste matter put on land to make crops grow ♦ *vt* put manure on

man·u·script /'mænjǔskript/ *n* 1 first copy of a book, etc., handwritten or typed 2 old book written by hand

man·y /'meni/ *determiner, pron* 1 a large number (of): *I haven't got as many as you.* | *many people* 2 **a good/great many** many 3 **one too many** *infml* too much (alcohol) to drink

map /mæp/ *n* 1 representation of (part of) the Earth's surface as if seen from above: *a map of France* 2 **(put something) on the map** (cause something to be) considered important ♦ *vt* **-pp-** make a map of

mar /mɑː/ *vt* **-rr-** *fml* spoil

mar·a·thon /'mærəθən‖-θɑːn/ *n* 1 running race of about 26 miles (42 kilometres) 2 (hard) activity that lasts a long time: *a marathon speech of 6 hours*

ma·raud·ing /mə'rɔːdıŋ/ *adj* moving around looking for things or people to attack **-er** *n*

mar·ble /'mɑːbəl‖'mɑːr-/ *n* [U] 1 hard smooth usu. white stone used for STATUEs or buildings 2 small glass ball rolled against others in a game (**marbles**)

march /mɑːtʃ‖mɑːrtʃ/ *v* 1 *vi* walk with regular forceful steps like a soldier 2 *vt* force to go: *They marched him off to prison.* ♦ *n* act of marching: (fig.) *the march* (= steady advance) *of history*

March *n* the 3rd month of the year

marching or·ders /'·· ,·'/ *n* [P] *BrE* being told officially that one must leave

mare /meər/ *n* female horse

mar·ga·rine /,mɑːdʒə'riːn, ,mɑːgə-‖'mɑːrdʒərǎn/ *n* butter-like food substance

mar·gin /'mɑːdʒǐn‖'mɑːr-/ *n* 1 space down the edge of a page, with no writing or printing in it 2 amount by which one thing is greater than another: *We won by a decisive margin.* 3 area on the outside edge of a larger area: *the margin of the stream*

mar·gin·al /'mɑːdʒǎnəl‖'mɑːr-/ *adj* 1 small in importance or amount: *a marginal difference* 2 (of a SEAT (3) in parliament) in danger of being lost to another party in an election **~ly** *adv* **~ize** *vt* push out to the edge of (a group)

mar·i·jua·na /,mærǐ'wɑːnə, -'hwɑːnə/ *n* [U] form of the drug CANNABIS

ma·ri·na /mə'riːnə/ *n* small harbour for pleasure boats

mar·i·nade /,mærǐ'neıd/ *n* [C;U] mixture of oil, wine, etc., into which food is put for a time before being cooked **–nate** /'mærǐneıt/ *vt* keep in a marinade

ma·rine /mə'riːn/ *adj* 1 of the sea 2 of ships and sailing ♦ *n* soldier who serves on a naval ship

mar·i·ner /'mærǐnər/ *n* sailor

mar·i·o·nette /,mærıə'net/ *n* PUPPET with strings

mar·i·tal /'mærǐtl/ *adj* of marriage

mar·i·time /'mærǐtaım/ *adj* 1 MARINE 2 near the sea

mark¹ /mɑːk‖mɑːrk/ *n* 1 something on or put onto a surface: *dirty marks on the wall* | *tyre marks in the snow* 2 a number that represents a judgment of quality: *The top mark in the test was 8 out of 10.* 3 something that shows a quality: *They all stood as a mark of respect.* 4 printed or written sign: *, punctuation mark* 5 particular type of machine: *the new Mark 4 gun* 6 **make one's mark (on)** gain success, fame, etc., (in) 7 **quick/slow off the mark** *infml* quick/slow in understanding or acting 8 **up to the mark: a** of an acceptable standard **b** in good health 9

wide of the mark not correct or close to the subject

mark[2] /maːk‖maːr/ vi/t spoil with marks: *Hot cups have marked the table.* | *The table marks easily.* **2** vt give MARKS[1] (2) to **3** vt stay close to (an opposing player) to spoil their play **4** vt be a sign of: *A cross marks his grave.* | *The election marks a turning point in our affairs.* **5 mark time** spend time on work, etc., without making any advance **6 (You) mark my words!** You will see later that I am right. ~**ed** adj noticeable ~**edly** /ˈmaːkɪdli‖ˈmaːr-/ adv

mark down/up phr vt lower/raise the price of

mark out phr vt **1** also **mark off** — draw lines round (an area) **2** [(for)] show or choose as likely to become (successful) or gain (success)

mark[3] n German unit of money

mark·er /ˈmaːkəʳ‖ˈmaːr-/ n **1** tool for making marks **2** object for marking a place

mar·ket[1] /ˈmaːkɪt‖ˈmaːr-/ n **1** (place for) a gathering of people to buy and sell goods **2** desire to buy; demand: *There's no market for coats at this time of year.* **3** area where goods are sold: *the foreign/domestic market* **4** trade: *the tea market* **5 in the market** wishing to buy **6 on the market** (of goods) for sale **7 play the market** buy and sell business shares to try to make a profit — see also BLACK MARKET, COMMON MARKET

market[2] vt present and offer for sale ~**ing** n [U] **1** skills of advertising, supplying, and selling goods **2** AmE shopping ~**able** adj: (fig.) *marketable skills* ~**ability** /ˌmaːkɪtəˈbɪlɪti‖ˌmaːr-/ n [U]

market gar·den /ˌ··· ˈ··/ n BrE area for growing vegetables and fruit for sale

mar·ket·place /ˈmaːkɪtpleɪs ‖ˈmaːr-/ n **1** place where a market is held **2** activities of buying and selling

market re·search /ˌ··· ·ˈ·‖ˌ·· ˈ··/ n [U] study of what people buy and why

mark·ing /ˈmaːkɪŋ‖ˈmaːr-/ n [C;U] (any of a set of) coloured marks on an animal's fur or feathers

marks·man /ˈmaːksmən‖ˈmaːrks-/ **marks·wom·an** /-ˌwomən/ fem. — -**men** /-mən/ person who can shoot well ~**ship** n [U]

mark·up /ˈmaːk-ʌp‖ˈmaːrk-/ n price increase by a seller

mar·ma·lade /ˈmaːməleɪd‖ˈmaːr-/ n [U] JAM made from oranges

ma·roon[1] /məˈruːn/ vt put or leave in a lonely or dangerous place, without help

maroon[2] adj dark red

mar·quee /maːˈkiː‖maːr-/ n very large tent

mar·riage /ˈmærɪdʒ/ n [C;U] **1** ceremony to marry people **2** state of being husband and wife ~**able** adj suitable for marriage

mar·row /ˈmærəʊ/ n **1** [C] very large long round dark green vegetable **2** [U] soft fatty substance inside bones

mar·ry /ˈmæri/ v **1** vt take (as) a husband or wife: *He never married.* | *She married a soldier.* **2** vt join in marriage: *The priest married them.* **3** vt [(off)] cause to get married: *They married their daughter (off) to a young diplomat.* **married** adj **1** having a husband or wife: *a married man* **2** of MARRIAGE (2): *married life* **3 married to** having as a husband or wife: *She's married to a doctor.*

Mars /maːz‖maːrz/ n the PLANET 4th in order from the sun

marsh /maːʃ‖maːrʃ/ n [C;U] (area of) soft wet land —**y** adj

mar·shal[1] /ˈmaːʃəl‖ˈmaːr-/ n **1** US law official, like a SHERIFF (1) **2** military officer of very high rank **3** organizer of an event, such as a ceremony or race

marshal[2] vt -ll- BrE ‖ -l- AmE **1** arrange (esp. facts) in good order **2** lead (people) carefully

marsh·mal·low /ˌmaːʃˈmæləʊ ‖ˈmaːrʃmeləʊ/ n type of soft round sweet

mar·su·pi·al /maːˈsjuːpiəl‖maːrˈsuː-/ n animal, esp. Australian, that carries its young in a pocket of skin

mar·tial /ˈmaːʃəl‖ˈmaːr-/ adj fml of war, soldiers, etc.

martial art /ˌ·· ˈ·/ n Eastern fighting sport: *Judo is a martial art.*

martial law /ˌ·· ˈ·/ n [U] government by the army under special laws

Mar·tian /ˈmaːʃən‖ˈmaːr-/ n, adj (creature) from MARS

mar·ti·net /ˌmaːtɪˈnet‖ˌmaːr-/ n very STRICT person

mar·tyr /ˈmaːtəʳ‖ˈmaːr-/ n **1** someone who dies or suffers for their (religious) beliefs **2 make a martyr of oneself** give up one's own wishes to help others, or in the hope of being praised ♦ vt kill as a martyr

mar·vel /ˈmaːvəl‖ˈmaːr-/ n wonderful thing or example: *the marvels of modern science* ♦ vi -ll- BrE ‖ -l- AmE fml be filled with surprise and admiration ~**lous** BrE ‖ ~**ous** AmE adj very pleasing or good ~**lously** adv

Marx·is·m /ˈmaːksɪzəm‖ˈmaːr-/ n [U] teaching of Karl Marx on which COMMUNISM is based —**ist** n, adj

mar·zi·pan /ˈmaːzɪpæn‖ˈmaːrtsɪ-, ˌmaːrtsɪˈ-/ n [U] sweet paste made from ALMONDs

mas·ca·ra /mæˈskaːrə‖mæˈskærə/ n [U] dark substance for colouring the EYELASHes

mas·cot /'mæskət‖'mæskɔːt/ *n* object, animal, or person thought to bring good luck

mas·cu·line /'mæskjɣlɪ̆n/ *adj* 1 (in grammar) referring to males 2 of or like a man **—linity** /,mæskjɣ'lɪn̆ti/ [U]

mash /mæʃ/ *vt* [(UP)] crush into a soft substance ♦ *n* [U] mashed potatoes

mask /mɑːsk‖mæsk/ *n* covering for the face, to hide or protect it ♦ *vt* hide **~ed** *adj* wearing a mask

mas·o·chis·m /'mæsəkɪzəm/ *n* [U] 1 gaining pleasure from being hurt 2 wish to be hurt so as to gain sexual pleasure **—chist** *n* **—chistic** /,mæsə-'kɪstɪk/ *adj*

ma·son /'meɪsən/ *n* 1 STONEMASON 2 (*usu. cap.*) FREEMASON **~ic** /mə-'sɒnɪk‖-'sɑː-/ *adj*

ma·son·ry /'meɪsənri/ *n* [U] stone building blocks

mas·que·rade /,mæskə'reɪd/ *vi* pretend: *thieves masquerading as bank employees* ♦ *n* 1 hiding of the truth 2 dance where people wear MASKs

mass /mæs/ *n* 1 [C] large lump, heap, or quantity: *a mass of clouds* 2 [C] also **masses** *pl.* — *infml* lots: *masses of work to do* 3 [U] (in science) amount of matter in a body ♦ *vi/t* gather in large numbers or quantity **masses** *n* [*the* + P] ordinary people in society

Mass *n* (in the Catholic and Orthodox churches) important religious ceremony

mas·sa·cre /'mæsəkər/ *n* killing of large numbers of people ♦ **massacre** *vt*

mas·sage /'mæsɑːʒ‖mə'sɑːʒ/ *n* [C;U] (act of) pressing and rubbing someone's body, esp. to cure pain or stiffness ♦ *vt* 1 give a massage to 2 change (facts, figures, etc.) usu. in a dishonest way

mas·seur /mæ'sɜːr, mə-/ **masseuse** /mæ'sɜːz, mə-/ *fem.* — *n* person who gives massages

mas·sive /'mæsɪv/ *adj* extremely big **~ly** *adv* **~ness** *n* [U]

mass me·di·a /,· '···/ *n* [*the*+S] the MEDIA

mass·pro·duce /,· ·'·/ *vt* produce (goods) in large numbers to the same pattern **mass production** *n* [U]

mast /mɑːst‖mæst/ *n* 1 long upright pole for carrying sails 2 tall framework for AERIALs

mas·tec·to·my /mæ'stektəmi/ *n* operation for the removal of a breast

mas·ter[1] /'mɑːstər‖'mæ-/ *n* 1 **mistress** *fem.* — person in control of people, animals, or things 2 **mistress** *fem.* — teacher 3 great artist, writer, etc. — see also OLD MASTER 4 captain

of a ship 5 something from which copies are made: *a master tape* **~ful** *adj* able or eager to control others **~fully** *adv* **~ly** *adj* showing great skill.

master[2] *vt* 1 learn or gain as a skill: *master the art of public speaking* 2 control and defeat: *He mastered his fear of heights.*

mas·ter·mind /'mɑːstəmaɪnd‖ 'mæstər-/ *vt* plan cleverly: *mastermind a crime* ♦ *n* very clever person

master of ce·re·mo·nies /,·· '····/ *n* person who introduces speakers or performers at a public event

mas·ter·piece /'mɑːstəpiːs‖ 'mæstər-/ *n* piece of work, esp. of art, done with extreme skill

mas·ter·y /'mɑːstəri‖'mæ-/ *n* [U] 1 power to control 2 great skill or knowledge

mas·tur·bate /'mæstəbeɪt‖-ər-/ *vi/t* excite the sex organs (of) by handling, rubbing, etc. **—bation** /,mæstə'beɪʃən‖ -tər-/ *n* [U]

mat /mæt/ *n* 1 piece of strong material for covering part of a floor 2 small piece of material for putting under objects on a table

mat·a·dor /'mætədɔːr/ *n* person who kills the BULL in a BULLFIGHT

match[1] /mætʃ/ *n* 1 sports or other competition between two people or sides; game: *a football match* 2 one who is equal to or better than another: *I'm no match for her at maths.* 3 good combination: *The hat and shoes are a perfect match.* 4 marriage: *Both her daughters made good matches.* ♦ *v* 1 *vi/t* be similar (to) or combine well (with): *The curtains and carpets don't match.* 2 *vt* be equal to or find an equal for: *a restaurant that can't be matched for service*

match[2] *n* short thin stick that burns when its end is rubbed against a rough surface **~box** *n* box for holding matches

match·mak·er /'mætʃ,meɪkər/ *n* person who tries to arrange other's love affairs

mate[1] /meɪt/ *n* 1 friend, or person one works or lives with: *We're mates/ schoolmates/flatmates.* 2 either of a male-female pair 3 officer on a non-navy ship 4 *BrE sl* (used for addressing a man)

mate[2] *vi* (esp. of animals) join sexually to produce young

mate[3] *n, v* CHECKMATE

ma·te·ri·al /mə'tɪəriəl/ *n* 1 [C;U] substance of which things are or can be made 2 [U] cloth 3 [U] knowledge of facts from which a (written) work may be produced: *She's collecting material* *for a book.* ♦ *adj* **1** of matter or substance. not spirit **2** *fml* important or necessary ~**ly** *adv*

ma·te·ri·al·is·m /məˈtɪərɪəlɪzəm/ *n* [U] (too) great interest in the pleasures of the world. money. etc. **–ist** *n* **–istic** /məˌtɪərɪəˈlɪstɪk/ *adj*

ma·te·ri·al·ize, ‖ also **-ise** *BrE* /məˈtɪərɪəlaɪz/ *vi* **1** become able to be seen **2** become real or actual: *Her hopes never materialized.* **3** come; arrive **–ization** /məˌtɪərɪəlaɪˈzeɪʃən‖-lə-/ *n* [U]

ma·ter·nal /məˈtɜːnl‖-ɜːr-/ *adj* **1** of or like a mother **2** related through the mother's part of the family: *my maternal grandmother*

ma·ter·ni·ty /məˈtɜːnɪti‖-ɜːr-/ *n* [U] motherhood ♦ *adj* for women who are going to give birth: *a maternity hospital/dress*

math·e·mat·ics /ˌmæθɪˈmætɪks/ also **maths** /mæθs/ *BrE* ‖ **math** /mæθ/ *AmE* — *n* [U] science of numbers **–ical** *adj* **–ically** /-klɪ/ *adv* **–ician** /ˌmæθəməˈtɪʃən/ *n*

mat·i·née /ˈmætɪneɪ‖ˌmætˈneɪ/ *n* afternoon performance of a play, film. etc.

ma·tri·arch /ˈmeɪtrɪɑːk‖-ɑːrk/ *n* woman who controls a (family) group ~**al** /ˌmeɪtrɪˈɑːkəl◂‖-ˈɑːr-/ *adj* ruled by women

mat·ri·cide /ˈmætrɪsaɪd/ *n* [C;U] murder of one's mother

ma·tric·u·late /məˈtrɪkjʊleɪt/ *vi* become a member of a university **–lation** /məˌtrɪkjʊˈleɪʃən/ *n* [U]

mat·ri·mo·ny /ˈmætrɪmənɪ‖-məʊni/ *n* [U] being married **–nial** /ˌmætrɪˈməʊnɪəl/ *adj*

ma·tron /ˈmeɪtrən/ *n* **1** chief nurse **2** woman in charge of living arrangements in a school **3** *lit* older married woman. esp. of quiet behaviour ~**ly** *adj* (of a woman) rather fat **2** with the DIGNITY of a MATRON (3)

matt /mæt/ *adj* not shiny

mat·ted /ˈmætɪd/ *adj* twisted in a thick mass

mat·ter¹ /ˈmætə/ *n* **1** [C] subject; affair: *several important matters to discuss* **2** [*the*+S] trouble; cause of pain, illness, etc.: *Is anything the matter?* **3** [U] substance of which things are made: *all the matter in the universe* — see also GREY MATTER **4** [U] things of a particular kind or for a particular purpose: *reading matter* (= magazines, books, etc.) **5 a matter of: a** a little more or less than: *It's only a matter of hours before the doctor arrives.* **b** needing as a part: *Learning is a matter of concentration.* **6 a matter of course** a usual event **7 as a matter of fact** in fact; really **8 for that matter** (used when mentioning another possibility)

9 no matter . . . it makes no difference: *No matter how hard I tried, I couldn't move it.* **10 That's a matter of opinion.** My opinion is different from yours.

matter² *vi* be important

matter-of-fact /ˌ···'··◂/ *adj* without feelings or imagination

mat·ting /ˈmætɪŋ/ *n* [U] rough woven material. esp. for the floor

mat·tress /ˈmætrɪs/ *n* large filled cloth case for sleeping on

ma·ture /məˈtʃʊə/ *adj* **1** fully developed **2** sensible, like a mature person **3** *fml* carefully thought about ♦ *vi/t* become or make mature **–turity** *n* [U]

maud·lin /ˈmɔːdlɪn/ *adj* stupidly sad. esp. when drunk

maul /mɔːl/ *vt* hurt by handling roughly: *mauled by a lion*

mau·so·le·um /ˌmɔːsəˈlɪəm/ *n* grand building containing a grave

mauve /məʊv/ *adj* pale purple

mav·e·rick /ˈmævərɪk/ *n* person who acts differently from the rest of a group

mawk·ish /ˈmɔːkɪʃ/ *adj* expressing love and admiration in a silly way

max·im /ˈmæksəm/ *n* rule for sensible behaviour

max·i·mize ‖ also **-ise** *BrE* /ˈmæksəmaɪz/ *vt* make as big as possible

max·i·mum /ˈmæksəməm/ *n. adj* **-ma** /-mə/ *or* **-mums** largest (amount, number, etc.): *our maximum offer* | *He smokes a maximum of 10 cigarettes a day.* **–mal** *adj*

may /meɪ/ *v aux* **1** (shows a possibility): *He may come and he may not.* | *She may have missed the train.* (= perhaps she has missed it) **2** have permission to; be allowed to: *You may come in now.* | *May we go home, please?* **3** (used when expressing a wish): *May you live happily ever after!* **4 may as well** have no strong reason not to: *It's late, so I may as well go to bed.*

May *n* the 5th month of the year

may·be /ˈmeɪbɪ/ *adv* perhaps

may·hem /ˈmeɪhem/ *n* [U] violent disorder and confusion

may·on·naise /ˌmeɪəˈneɪz‖ˈmeɪəneɪz/ *n* [U] thick liquid made from eggs and oil, poured on food

may·or /meə/‖ˈmeɪər/ *n* person elected each year by a town council to be head of that city or town

may·or·ess /ˈmeərɪs‖ˈmeɪərəs/ *n* **1** woman who is a MAYOR **2** wife of a MAYOR

maze /meɪz/ *n* arrangement of twisting paths in which one becomes lost

MC /ˌem ˈsiː/ *n* **1** MASTER OF CEREMONIES **2** Member of Congress

MCP /ˌem siː ˈpiː/ *abbrev. for:* MALE CHAUVINIST pig

MD /ˌem ˈdiː/ *abbrev. for:* **1** Doctor of Medicine **2** Managing Director

me /miː *strong* miː/ *pron* (object form of I)

mead·ow /ˈmedəʊ/ *n* field of grass

mea·gre *BrE* ‖ **-ger** *AmE*/ˈmiːgəʳ/ *adj* not big enough **~ly** *adv* **~ness** *n* [U]

meal[1] /miːl/ *n* (food eaten at) an occasion for eating

meal[2] *n* [U] crushed grain

mealy-mouthed /ˌ·· ˈ·◄/ *adj* expressing (unpleasant) things too indirectly

mean[1] /miːn/ *vt* **meant** /ment/ **1** (of words, signs, etc.) represent an idea: 'Melancholy' means 'sad'. | The red light means 'stop'. **2** intend: He said Tuesday, but meant Thursday. | I said I'd help and I meant it. (= I am determined to do so) **3** be a sign of: This could mean war. **4** be of importance to the stated degree: Her work means a lot/everything to her. **5 be meant to** *esp. BrE* ought to: be supposed to **6 mean business** act with serious intentions **7 mean well** act with good intentions **~ing** *n* [C;U] **1** idea intended to be understood, esp. from words: 'Measure' has several meanings. **2** importance or value: His life lost its meaning when his wife died. **~ing** *adj* suggesting a hidden thought: a meaning look **~ingful** *adj: a meaningful look* **~ingless** *adj*

mean[2] *adj* **1** ungenerous **2** unkind; nasty **3** *esp. AmE* bad-tempered **4 no mean** very good: He's no mean cook.

mean[3] *n. adj* average

me·an·der /miˈændəʳ/ *vi* **1** wander **2** (of a stream) flow slowly and twistingly

means /miːnz/ *n* **means 1** [C] method; way **2** [P] money, esp. enough to live on **3 by all means** (a polite way of giving permission) **4 by means of** using; with **5 by no means** *fml* not at all **5 live beyond/within one's means** spend more than/not more than one can afford

means test /ˈ· ·/ *n* inquiry into the amount of money someone has, esp. to find out if they need money from the state

meant /ment/*v past t. and p. of* MEAN[1]

mean·time /ˈmiːntaɪm/ *n* **in the meantime** MEANWHILE (1)

mean·while /ˈmiːnwaɪl/ *adv* **1** in the time between 2 events **2** during the same period of time

mea·sles /ˈmiːzəlz/ *n* [U] infectious disease in which the sufferer has small red spots on the skin

meas·ly /ˈmiːzli/ *adj sl* too small

mea·sure[1] /ˈmeʒəʳ/ *vt* **1** find or show the size, amount, degree, etc., of: Measure the (height of the) cupboard first. | A clock measures time. **2** be of the stated size: The river measured 200 metres from side to side. **-surable** *adj* **-surably** *adv*

measure off/out *phr vt* take from a longer length or larger quantity

measure up *phr vi* show good enough qualities (for)

measure[2] *n* **1** [U] measuring system **2** [C] unit in such a system **3** [S;U] *fml* amount: She's had a certain measure of success. **4** [C] act to bring about an effect: The government was forced to take strong measures. **5 for good measure** in addition **6 take someone's measure/get the measure of someone** judge what someone is like **-sured** *adj* careful and steady **~ment** *n* **1** [U] act of measuring **2** [C] length, height, etc., measured

meat /miːt/ *n* [U] **1** flesh of animals (not fish) for eating **2** valuable matter, ideas, etc.: It was a clever speech, but there was no real meat in it. **~y** *adj*

mec·ca /ˈmekə/ *n* place that many people wish to reach

me·chan·ic /mɪˈkænɪk/ *n* person skilled in using or repairing machinery

me·chan·i·cal /mɪˈkænɪkəl/ *adj* **1** of or worked or produced by machinery **2** without new thought or strong feeling **~ly** /-kli/ *adv*

me·chan·ics /mɪˈkænɪks/ *n* **1** [U] science of the action of forces on objects **2** [U] science of machinery **3** [P] way in which something works

mech·a·nis·m /ˈmekənɪzəm/ *n* machine or the way it works: (fig.) the mechanism of the brain

mech·a·nize ‖ also **-ise** *BrE* /ˈmekənaɪz/ *vt* (start to) use machines for or in **-ization** /ˌmekənaɪˈzeɪʃən|-nə-/ *n* [U]

med·al /ˈmedl/ *n usu.* coinlike object given as a mark of honour, esp. for bravery **~list** *BrE* ‖ **~ist** *AmE n* person who has won a medal, esp. in sport

me·dal·li·on /mɪˈdæliən/ *n* large medal, or piece of jewellery like a medal

med·dle /ˈmedl/ *vi* take action in a matter which does not concern one **~dler** *n*

me·di·a /ˈmiːdiə/ *n* [U;P] television, radio, newspapers, etc. — see also MEDIUM[2]

me·di·ate /ˈmiːdieɪt/ *vi* act so as to bring agreement after a quarrel **-ator** *n* **-ation** /ˌmiːdiˈeɪʃən/ *n* [U]

med·ic /ˈmedɪk/ *n infml* doctor or medical student

med·ic·aid /ˈmedɪkeɪd/ *n* [U] (*often cap.*) (in the US) system by which the government helps to pay the medical costs of people on low incomes

med·i·cal /ˈmedɪkəl/ adj of or for the treatment of illness, esp. with medicine rather than operations ♦ n medical examination of the body ~**ly** /-kli/ adv

me·dic·a·ment /mɪˈdɪkəmənt, ˈmedɪ-/ n medicine

med·i·care /ˈmedɪkeəʳ/ n [U] (often cap.) (in the US) system of medical care provided by the government, esp. for old people

med·i·ca·tion /ˌmedɪˈkeɪʃən/ n [C;U] medicine, esp. a drug

me·di·ci·nal /məˈdɪsɪnəl/ adj as medicine; curing ~**ly** adv

med·i·cine /ˈmedsən‖ˈmedəsən/ n 1 [C;U] substance for treating illness 2 [U] science of treating illness 3 a **taste/dose of one's own medicine** deserved punishment

medicine man /ˈ··· ·‖ˈ··· ·/ n (in certain tribes) man with magical powers, esp. for curing people

med·i·e·val /ˌmedɪˈiːvəl‖ˌmiː-/ adj of the MIDDLE AGES

me·di·o·cre /ˌmiːdɪˈəʊkəʳ/ adj rather bad **–crity** /ˌmiːdɪˈɒkrɪti‖-ˈɑːk-/ n [U]

med·i·tate /ˈmedɪteɪt/ v 1 vi think deeply, esp. to gain calmness or before making a decision 2 vt plan or consider carefully **–tation** /ˌmedɪˈteɪʃən/ n [C;U]

me·di·um¹ /ˈmiːdɪəm/ adj of middle size, amount, quality, etc.

medium² n **-dia** /-dɪə/ or **-diums** 1 method of artistic expression or of giving information 2 condition or surroundings in which things exist 3 middle position: a happy medium between eating all the time and not eating at all

medium³ n **-diums** person who claims to receive messages from the spirits of the dead

med·ley /ˈmedli/ n mass of different types mixed together

meek /miːk/ adj gentle and uncomplaining ~**ly** adv ~**ness** n [U]

meet¹ /miːt/ v met /met/ 1 vi/t come together (with): I met an old friend in the street. | Our lips met (in a kiss). 2 vi/t be introduced (to) 3 vt find or experience: She met her death in a plane crash. 4 vt follow (as if) in answer: His speech was met with boos. 5 vt satisfy: Their offer meets all our needs. 6 vt pay: Have you enough money to meet your debts? 7 **meet someone halfway** make an agreement which partly satisfies both sides 8 **more (in/to something) than meets the eye** hidden facts or reasons (in or for something) ~**ing** n occasion of coming together, esp. to talk

meet up phr vi infml meet, esp. by informal arrangements

meet with phr vt 1 experience: I met with an accident. 2 esp. AmE have a meeting with

meet² n gathering of people for (BrE) FOXHUNTING or (AmE) sports events

meg·a·lo·ma·ni·a /ˌmegələʊˈmeɪnɪə/ n [U] belief that one is more important, powerful, etc., than one really is **-niac** /-nɪæk/ n

meg·a·phone /ˈmegəfəʊn/ n horn-shaped instrument to make the voice louder

mel·an·chol·y /ˈmelənkəli‖-kɑːli/ adj, n [U] sad(ness) **-ic** /ˌmelənˈkɒlɪk‖-ˈkɑːlɪk/ n

mé·lange /meɪˈlɑːnʒ/ n mixture

me·lee /ˈmeleɪ‖ˈmeɪleɪ, meɪˈleɪ/ n struggling or disorderly crowd

mel·low /ˈmeləʊ/ adj 1 suggesting gentle ripeness 2 (of colour) soft and warm ♦ vi/t become or make mellow ~**ness** n [U]

mel·o·dra·mat·ic /ˌmelədrəˈmætɪk/ adj too full of excited feeling ~**ally** /-kli/ adv

mel·o·dy /ˈmelədi/ n 1 tune 2 song **–dic** /məˈlɒdɪk‖-ˈlɑː-/ adj of or having melody **–dious** /məˈləʊdɪəs/ adj tuneful

mel·on /ˈmelən/ n large round juicy fruit

melt /melt/ v 1 vi/t become or make liquid: The sun melted the ice. 2 vi go away: disappear 3 vi become more sympathetic

melt down phr vt make (a metal object) liquid by heating

melt·down /ˈmeltdaʊn/ n dangerous situation in which material burns through the bottom of an atomic REACTOR

melting pot /ˈ·· ·/ n 1 place where many different things are mixed together 2 **in the melting pot** not fixed or decided

mem·ber /ˈmembəʳ/ n 1 someone who belongs to a club, group, etc. 2 part of the body, such as an organ or limb ~**ship** n 1 [U] state of being a MEMBER (1) 2 [C] all the members of a club, society, etc.

mem·brane /ˈmembreɪn/ n [C;U] soft thin skin

me·men·to /məˈmentəʊ/ n **-tos** object that brings back pleasant memories

mem·o /ˈmeməʊ/ n **-os** also **memorandum** — note from one person or office to another within an organization

mem·oirs /ˈmemwɑːz‖-ɑːrz/ n [P] AUTOBIOGRAPHY

mem·o·ra·bil·i·a /ˌmemərəˈbɪlɪə/ n [P] interesting things connected with a famous person or event

mem·o·ra·ble /'memərəbəl/ adj worth remembering, esp. because good **–bly** adv

mem·o·ran·dum /ˌmemə'rændəm/ n **–da** /-də/ fml MEMO

me·mo·ri·al /mə'mɔːriəl/ n something, esp. a stone MONUMENT, in memory of a person, event, etc.

mem·o·rize ‖ also **-rise** BrE /'meməraiz/ vt learn and remember (words, etc.), on purpose

mem·o·ry /'meməri/ n **1** [C;U] ability to remember: *She's got a good memory.* **2** [C] example of remembering: *one of my earliest memories* **3** [U] time during which things happened which can be remembered: *within living memory* **4** [U] opinion held of someone after their death: *to praise his memory* **5** [C] part of a computer in which information is stored **6 in memory of** as a way of remembering or being reminded of

men /men/ n pl. of MAN

men·ace /'menɪs/ n **1** [C;U] threat; danger **2** [C] troublesome person or thing ♦ vt threaten

mé·nage à trois /ˌmeɪnɑːʒ ɑː 'trwɑː‖məˌnɑːʒ-/ n [S] relationship in which two people and the lover of one of them live together

me·nag·e·rie /mə'nædʒəri/ n collection of wild animals kept privately or for the public to see

mend /mend/ v **1** vt repair **2** vi regain one's health **3 mend one's ways** improve one's behaviour ♦ n **1** repaired place **2 on the mend** regaining one's health **~er** n

me·ni·al /'miːniəl/ adj (of a job) humble and not interesting or important ♦ n someone who does menial work

men·in·gi·tis /ˌmenɪn'dʒaɪtɪs/ n [U] serious brain illness

men·o·pause /'menəpɔːz/ n [the + S] time of life when a woman's PERIODs[1] (3) stop

men·stru·al /'menstruəl/ adj of a woman's PERIOD(s)

men·stru·ate /'menstrueɪt/ vi have a PERIOD **–ation** /ˌmenstru'eɪʃən/ n [U]

men·tal /'mentl/ adj **1** of or in the mind: *mental stress‖a mental picture* **2** of or for illness of the mind: *a mental hospital* **3** infml mad **~ly** adv

men·tal·i·ty /men'tæləti/ n **1** [U] abilities and powers of the mind **2** [C] person's character and way of thought

men·thol /'menθɒl‖-θɔːl, -θɑːl/ n [U] substance which smells and tastes of MINT[1] **~ated** /ˌθəleɪtɪd/ adj

men·tion /'menʃən/ vt **1** tell of or about, esp. in a few words **2 Don't mention it** (polite reply to thanks) **3 not to mention** and in addition

there's … ♦ n **1** short remark about **2** naming of someone, esp. to honour them

men·tor /'mentɔːʳ/ n person who habitually advises another

men·u /'menjuː/ n list of food one can order in a restaurant

MEP /ˌem 'iː piː/ abbrev. for: Member of the European Parliament

mer·can·tile /'mɜːkəntaɪl‖'mɜːkəntiːl, -taɪl/ adj fml of trade and business

mer·ce·na·ry /'mɜːsənəri‖'mɜːsəneri/ adj influenced by the wish for money ♦ n soldier who fights for whoever will pay him

mer·chan·dise /'mɜːtʃəndaɪz, -daɪs‖'mɜːr-/ n [U] things for sale

mer·chant /'mɜːtʃənt‖'mɜːr-/ n person who buys and sells goods in large amounts ♦ adj used in trade, not war: *the merchant navy*

merchant bank /ˌ·· '·/ n bank that provides banking services for businesses rather than for ordinary people

mer·cu·ry /'mɜːkjʊri‖'mɜːr-/ n [U] **1** silvery liquid metal **2** (cap.) the PLANET nearest the sun **–rial** /mɜː'kjʊəriəl‖mɜːr-/ adj quick, active, and often changing

mer·cy /'mɜːsi‖'mɜːrsi/ n [U] **1** willingness to forgive, not to punish; kindness and pity **2** fortunate event **3 at the mercy of** defenceless against **merciful** adj **merciless** adj

mere /mɪəʳ/ adj only; nothing more than: *a mere child* **~ly** adv only

mer·e·tri·cious /ˌmerə'trɪʃəs/ adj fml (seeming) attractive but of no real value **~ly** adv **~ness** n [U]

merge /mɜːdʒ‖mɜːrdʒ/ v **1** vi combine, esp. gradually, so as to become a single thing **2** vi/t join together: *The two companies merged.* **merger** n joining together of 2 or more companies

me·rid·i·an /mə'rɪdiən/ n **1** imaginary line over the Earth's surface from the top to the bottom, used on maps **2** highest point, esp. of a star

me·ringue /mə'ræŋ/ n [C;U] (light cake made from) a mixture of sugar and the white part of eggs

mer·it /'merɪt/ n [C;U] good quality ♦ vt fml deserve

mer·i·toc·ra·cy /ˌmerə'tɒkrəsi‖-'tɑː-/ n social system which gives the highest positions to those with the most ability

mer·maid /'mɜːmeɪd‖'mɜːr-/ n (in stories) woman with a fish's tail

mer·ry /'meri/ adj **1** full of or causing laughter and fun **2** BrE infml rather drunk **–rily** adv **–riment** n [U]

merry-go-round /'···,·/ n machine with large model animals on which children ride round and round

mesh¹ /meʃ/ n [C;U] 1 net, esp. with small holes 2 threads in such a net

mesh² vi (of the teeth of GEARS) to connect: (fig.) *Their characters just don't mesh.* (= fit together suitably)

mes·mer·ize ‖ also **-ise** *BrE* /'mezmǝraɪz/ vt hold the complete attention of, as if by a strong force

mess¹ /mes/ n 1 [S;U] (state of) untidiness or dirt 2 [S] bad situation; trouble 3 [C] room where soldiers, etc., eat 4 **make a mess of** ruin; spoil ~y adj

mess² v

mess about/around phr v 1 vi act or speak stupidly 2 vi spend time with no particular plan or purpose 3 vt treat badly

mess up phr vt ruin; spoil

mes·sage /'mesɪdʒ/ n 1 piece of information passed from one person to another 2 main moral idea of a story, picture, etc. 3 **get the message** understand what is meant

mes·sen·ger /'mesǝndʒǝʳ/ n person who brings a message

mes·si·ah /mǝ'saɪǝ/ n 1 new leader in a religion 2 (cap.) Jesus Christ

met /met/ v past t. and p. of MEET¹

me·tab·o·lis·m /mǝ'tæbǝlɪzǝm/ n process by which a body lives, esp. by changing food into ENERGY **–lic** /,metǝ'bɒlɪk‖-'baː-/ adj

met·al /'metl/ n [C;U] usu. solid shiny material, such as iron, copper, or silver ~lic /mǝ'tælɪk/ adj

met·al·lur·gy /'metǝlɜːdʒi‖-ɜːr-/ n [U] scientific study of metals adj **–gist** n –gical /,metǝ'lɜːdʒɪkǝl‖-'lɜːr-/

met·al·work /'metlwɜːk‖-ɜːrk/ n [U] making of metal objects

met·a·mor·pho·sis /,metǝ'mɔːfǝsǝs‖-ɔːr-/ n -ses /-siːz/ complete change from one form to another

met·a·phor /'metǝfǝʳ, -fɔːʳ‖-fɔːr/ n [C;U] (use of) a phrase which describes one thing by stating another thing with which it can be compared (as in *the roses in her cheeks*) — see also MIXED METAPHOR ~ical /,metǝ'fɔːrɪkǝl‖-'fɔː-,-'faː-/ adj **–ically** /kli/ adv

met·a·phys·i·cal /,metǝ'fɪzɪkǝl/ adj 1 concerned with the science of being and knowing 2 (of ideas) at a high level and difficult to understand

mete /miːt/ v

mete out phr vt fml or lit give (esp. punishment)

me·te·or /'miːtiǝʳ/ n small piece of matter that flies through space and can be seen burning if it comes near the Earth ~ic /,miːti'ɒrɪk‖-'ɔːrɪk, -'aːrɪk/ adj very fast: *a meteoric rise to fame* ~ically /kli/ adv

me·te·o·rite /'miːtiǝraɪt/ n meteor that lands on the Earth

me·te·o·rol·o·gy /,miːtiǝ'rɒlǝdʒi‖ -'raː-/ n [U] scientific study of weather **–gist** n **–gical** /,miːtiǝrǝ'lɒdʒɪkǝl‖ -'laː-/ adj

me·ter¹ /'miːtǝʳ/ n machine that measures something: *a gas meter*

meter² n AmE for METRE

me·thane /'miːθeɪn‖'me-/ n [U] gas that burns easily

meth·od /'meθǝd/ n 1 [C] way of doing something 2 [U] proper planning and arrangement ~ical /mǝ'θɒdɪkǝl‖mǝ'θaː-/ adj careful; using an ordered system ~ically /-kli/ adv

meth·o·dol·o·gy /,meθǝ'dɒlǝdʒi‖ -'daː-/ n set of methods

meth·yl·at·ed spir·its /,meθǝleɪtǝd 'spɪrǝts/ also **meths** /meθ/ *BrE infml* — n alcohol for burning in lamps, heaters, etc.

me·tic·u·lous /mǝ'tɪkjʊlǝs/ adj very careful, with great attention to detail ~ly adv

mé·ti·er /'metieɪ, 'meɪ-‖me'tjeɪ, 'metjeɪ/ n fml one's type of work

me·tre¹ *BrE* ‖ **meter** *AmE* /'miːtǝʳ/ n a measure of length equal to 39.37 inches

metre² *BrE* ‖ **meter** *AmE* n [C;U] arrangement of beats in poetry

met·ric /'metrɪk/ adj using a measured system (**metric system**) based on the metre and kilogram ~ation /,metrɪ'keɪʃǝn/ n [U] changing to a metric system

met·ro /'metrǝʊ/ n -ros underground railway in France and certain other countries

me·trop·o·lis /mǝ'trɒpǝlǝs‖ mǝ'traː-/ n main or capital city **–litan** /,metrǝ'pɒlǝtǝn‖-'paː-/ adj

met·tle /'metl/ n 1 fml will to continue bravely in spite of difficulties 2 **be on one's mettle/put someone on their mettle** have to make/force someone to make the best possible effort

mew /mjuː/ vi, n (make) the crying sound a cat makes

mews /mjuːz/ n mews small city street with houses and flats, at the back of larger houses

mez·za·nine /'mezǝniːn, 'metsǝ-‖ 'mezǝ-/ n floor that comes between 2 other floors of a building

mg written abbrev. for MILLIGRAM(s)

MHR abbrev. for: Member of the House of Representatives

mi·aow /mi'aʊ/ vi, n (make) the crying sound a cat makes

mice /maɪs/ pl. of MOUSE

mick·ey /'mɪki/ n **take the mickey (out of)** sl for TEASE

Mickey Mouse /'·· ,·/ adj infml small and unimportant, not to be taken seriously

mi·crobe /'maɪkrǝʊb/ n bacterium

mi·cro·bi·ol·o·gy /ˌmaɪkrəʊ-baɪ'ɒlədʒi‖-'ɑːl-/ n [U] scientific study of very small living creatures –**gist** n

mi·cro·chip /ˈmaɪkrəʊˌtʃɪp/ n CHIP[1] (4)

mi·cro·com·put·er /ˌmaɪkrəʊkəm'pjuːtər/also **micro** infml — n the smallest type of computer, used esp. in the home, in schools, or by small businesses

mi·cro·cos·m /ˈmaɪkrəʊkɒzəm‖-kɑː-/ n something small that represents all the qualities, activities, etc., of something larger

mi·cro·film /ˈmaɪkrəʊˌfɪlm/ n [C;U] film for photographing something in a very small size ♦ vt photograph on microfilm

mi·cro·or·gan·is·m /ˌmaɪkrəʊ-'ɔːgənɪzəm‖-'ɔːr-/ n bacterium

mi·cro·phone /ˈmaɪkrəfəʊn/ n electrical instrument for collecting sound, so as to make it louder or broadcast it

mi·cro·pro·ces·sor /ˌmaɪkrəʊ-'prəʊsesər/ n central controlling CHIP[1] (4) in a small computer

mi·cro·scope /ˈmaɪkrəskəʊp/ n scientific instrument that makes things look larger, used for studying extremely small things –**scopic** /ˌmaɪkrə'skɒpɪk‖-'skɑː-/ adj 1 very small 2 using a microscope –**scopically** /-kli/ adv

mi·cro·wave ov·en /ˌmaɪkrəweɪv 'ʌvən/also **microwave** — n box that cooks food using very short electric waves

mid·air /ˌmɪd'eər◀/ n [U] point up in the sky

mid·day /ˌmɪd'deɪ◀‖'mɪd-deɪ/ n [U] 12 o'clock in the morning

mid·dle /ˈmɪdl/ adj, n [S:U] (in or at) the centre or a point halfway between 2 ends

middle age /ˌ·· '·◀/ n [U] period between youth and old age **middle-aged** adj

middle aged spread /ˌ·· '·/n [U] increase of flesh round the waist which tends to happen as people grow older

Middle Ag·es /ˌ·· '·◀/ n [the + P] period between about AD 1100 and 1500 in Europe

mid·dle·brow /ˈmɪdlbraʊ/ n person who likes books, paintings, etc., that are of average quality but not too difficult ♦ **middlebrow** adj

middle class /ˌ·· '·◀/ n social class of business and professional people, office workers, etc. **middle-class** adj

middle dis·tance /ˌ·· '·◀/ n [U] part of a view between what is close and what is far away

Middle East /ˌ·· '·◀/ n [the + S] countries in Asia west of India ~**ern** adj

mid·dle·man /ˈmɪdlmæn/ n -**men** /-men/ someone who buys from a producer and sells to a customer

middle name /ˌ·· '·/ n 1 name coming between the FIRST NAME and the SURNAME 2 infml something for which a person is well known: 'Generosity's my middle name.

middle-of-the-road /ˌ· · · · '·◀/ adj favouring a course of action that most people would agree with

mid·dling /ˈmɪdlɪŋ/ adj average

midge /mɪdʒ/ n small winged insect that bites

midg·et /ˈmɪdʒət/ adj, n very small (person)

Mid·lands /ˈmɪdləndz/ n [the + P] central parts of England, between the North and the South

mid-life cri·sis /ˌ· '··/n continuing feeling of unhappiness, lack of confidence, etc., suffered by someone in the middle years of life

mid·night /ˈmɪdnaɪt/ n [U] 12 o'clock at night

mid·riff /ˈmɪdrɪf/ n front of the body below the chest

midst /mɪdst/ n **in the midst of** in the middle of; among

mid·way /ˌmɪd'weɪ◀‖'mɪdweɪ/ adj, adv halfway

mid·wife /ˈmɪdwaɪf/ n -**wives** /-waɪvz/ nurse who helps women giving birth –**wifery** /ˈmɪd,wɪfəri‖-,waɪfəri/ n [U]

miffed /mɪft/ adj infml slightly angry

might[1] /maɪt/ v aux 1 (used for expressing slight possibility): He might come, but it's unlikely. 2 past t. of MAY: I thought it might rain. 3 ought; should: You might have offered to help! 4 **might well** be likely to 5 **might as well** have no strong reason not to

might[2] n [U] power; strength ~**y** adj very great: a mighty blow

mi·graine /ˈmiːgreɪn, ˈmaɪ-‖ˈmaɪ-/ n [C;U] very severe headache

mi·grant /ˈmaɪgrənt/ n migrating person or bird: migrant workers

mi·grate /maɪ'greɪt‖'maɪgreɪt/ vi 1 (of birds or fish) travel regularly from one part of the world to another, according to the season 2 move from one place to another, esp. for a limited period –**gration** /maɪ'greɪʃən/ n [C;U] –**gratory** /maɪ'greɪtəri‖'maɪgrə,tɔːri/ adj

mike /maɪk/ n sl for MICROPHONE

mild /maɪld/ adj not strong, forceful, or severe; gentle ~**ly** adv ~**ness** n [U]

mil·dew /ˈmɪldjuː‖-duː/ n [U] whitish growth on plants and on things kept a long time in slightly wet conditions ~**ed** adj

mile /maɪl/ n **1** a measure of length equal to 1.609 kilometres **2** also **miles** pl. — infml a lot: I feel miles better now.

mile·age /'maɪlɪdʒ/ n [C;U] **1** distance travelled, measured in miles **2** fixed amount of money paid for each mile travelled **3** amount of use: The newspapers are getting a lot of mileage out of the royal wedding.

mile-om-e-ter /maɪ'lɒmətəʳ‖-'lɑː-/ n BrE instrument that tells how far a car, etc., has travelled

mile·stone /'maɪlstəʊn/ n **1** stone beside the road, saying how far to the next town **2** important event

mi·lieu /'miːljɜː‖miː'ljɜː, -'ljuː/ n -s or -x /-ljɜːz, -ljɜː‖-'ljɜːz, -'ljuːz, -'ljuː/ person's social surroundings

mil·i·tant /'mɪlɪtənt/ n, adj (person) taking a strong active part in a struggle ~**ly** adv **–tancy** n [U]

mil·i·ta·rism /'mɪlɪtərɪzəm/ n [U] derog belief in the use of armed force **–rist** n **–ristic** /ˌmɪlɪtə'rɪstɪk/ adj

mil·i·ta·ry /'mɪlɪtəri‖-teri/ adj of, for, or by soldiers, armies, or war ◆ n [the+P] the army

mil·i·tate /'mɪlɪteɪt/ v **militate against** phr vt act, serve, or have importance as a reason against

mi·li·tia /mə'lɪʃə/ n force trained to be soldiers in time of special need

milk /mɪlk/ n [U] **1** white liquid produced by human or animal females to feed their young **2** white liquid produced by certain plants: coconut milk ◆ v **1** vt take milk from (a cow, etc.) **2** vi (of a cow, etc.) give milk **3** vt get money, knowledge of a secret, etc., from (someone or something) by clever or dishonest means **4** vt get poison from (a snake) ~**y** adj

milk·maid /'mɪlkmeɪd/ n (esp. in former times) woman who milks cows

milk·man /'mɪlkmən/ n **-men** /-mən/ person who delivers milk to houses

milk run /'· ·/ n infml familiar and frequently travelled journey

milk shake /ˌ· '·‖'· ·/ n drink of milk with an added taste of fruit, chocolate, etc.

mill¹ /mɪl/ n **1** (building containing) a machine for crushing grain to flour **2** factory: a cotton mill **3** small machine for crushing: a coffee mill **4** put someone through/go through the mill (cause someone to) pass through (a time of) hard training, hard experience, etc. ◆ vt crush or produce in a mill ~**er** n person who owns or works a flourmill

mill² v **mill about/around** phr vi move purposelessly in large numbers

mil·len·ni·um /mɪ'leniəm/ n **-nia** /-niə/ **1** [C] 1,000 years **2** the millennium future age in which everyone will be happy

mil·let /'mɪlɪt/ n [U] small seeds of a grasslike plant, used as food

mil·li·gram, **-gramme** /'mɪlɪgræm/ n a measure of weight equal to 0.001 GRAMS

mil·li·me·tre BrE ‖ **-ter** AmE /'mɪlɪˌmiːtəʳ/ n a measure of length equal to 0.001 METRES

mil·li·ner /'mɪlɪnəʳ/ n maker of women's hats ~**y** n [U] articles made and sold by a milliner

mil·lion /'mɪljən/ determiner, n, pron **million** or **millions** **1** 1,000,000 **2** also **millions of** — very large number ~**th** determiner, n, pron, adv

mil·lion·aire /ˌmɪljə'neəʳ/ **million·airess** /-'ris/ fem. — n person who has a million or more pounds or dollars; very wealthy person

mil·li·pede /'mɪlɪpiːd/ n small wormlike creature with many legs

mill·stone /'mɪlstəʊn/ n **1** circular crushing stone in a flourmill **2** cause of great trouble and anxiety

mime /maɪm/ n [C;U] use of actions without language to show meaning, esp. as a performance ◆ n actor who does this ◆ vi/t act in mime

mim·ic /'mɪmɪk/ vt **-ck- 1** copy (someone or something) amusingly **2** appear very like (something else) ◆ n person who mimics others ◆ adj not real

min·a·ret /ˌmɪnə'ret, 'mɪnəret/ n tall thin tower in a MOSQUE

mince /mɪns/ v **1** vt cut (esp. meat) into very small pieces **2** vi walk in a silly unnatural way **3** not to mince one's words speak of something sad or unpleasant using plain direct language ◆ n [U] **1** BrE meat that has been cut into very small pieces **2** AmE MINCEMEAT

mince·meat /'mɪns-miːt/ n [U] **1** mixture of dried fruit used as a filling for pastry **2** make mincemeat of defeat or destroy (a person, belief, etc.) completely

mince pie /ˌ· '·/ n small pastry case filled with mincemeat

mind¹ /maɪnd/ n **1** [C;U] person's (way of) thinking or feeling; thoughts: She has a very quick mind. **2** [U] memory: I'll bear/keep it in mind. (= not forget it) | I can't call it to mind. (= remember it) | You put me in mind of (= remind me of) my brother. **3** [C] attention: Keep your mind on your work. | You need something to take your mind off the problem. **4** [C;U] intention: Nothing was further from my mind. | I've got a good mind to (= I think I may) *report you.* **5** [C;U] opinion: *We are of one/of the same mind on this matter.* | **To my mind** (= in my opinion) *you're quite wrong.* **6** [C] person considered for his/her ability to think well: *She's one of the finest minds in the country.* **7 be in two minds (about something)** be unable to reach a decision **8 change one's mind** change one's intentions or opinions **9 have half a mind** have a desire or intention that is not firmly formed **10 in one's right mind** not mad **11 know one's own mind** know what one wants **12 make up one's mind** reach a decision **13 mind over matter** control over events or material objects by the power of the mind **14 on one's mind** causing anxiety **15 out of one's mind** mad **16 speak one's mind** express plainly one's thoughts and opinions ~ful *adj* giving attention −less *adj* not needing or using thought; stupid ~lessly *adv* −lessness *n* [U]

mind [2] *v* **1** *vi/t* be opposed to (a particular thing): *'Coffee or tea?' 'I don't mind.'* (= I'd like either) | *Would you mind opening* (= please open) *the window?* **2** *vi/t* be careful (of): *Mind the step!* **3** *vt* take care of; look after **4 Do you mind!** I am offended and annoyed **5 mind one's own business** not INTERFERE **6 mind you** also **mind** — take this into account also **7 never mind:** **a** don't worry **b** it doesn't matter **8 never you mind** it is not your business ~er *n* person who looks after: *a childminder*

mind-bog-gling /'·· ,··/ *adj sl* very surprising

mind's eye /,·'·/ *n* [U] imagination; memory

mine [1] /main/ *pron* of me; my one(s): *This pen's mine, not yours.*

mine [2] *n* **1** place where coal or metal are dug from the ground: *a goldmine.* (fig.) *He's a mine of information.* (= can tell you a lot) **2** sort of bomb placed just under the ground or in the sea ♦ *v* **1** *vi/t* dig or get from a MINE[2] (1) **2** *vt* put MINES[2] (2) in or under **3** *vt* destroy by MINES[2] (2) **miner** *n* worker in a MINE[2] (1)

mine-field /'mainfi:ld/ *n* **1** place where MINES[2] (2) have been put **2** something full of hidden dangers

min-e-ral /'mɪnərəl/ *n* substance formed naturally in the earth, such as stone, metal, coal, salt, or oil

min-e-ral-o-gy /,mɪnə'rælədʒi‖-'rɑ:-, -'ræ-/ *n* [U] scientific study of minerals −gist *n*

mineral wa-ter /'··· ,··/ *n* [U] **1** water from a spring, containing minerals **2** *BrE* FIZZY bottled drink

mine-sweep-er /'maɪn,swi:pəʳ/ *n* ship for finding and destroying MINES[2] (2)

min-gle /'mɪŋgəl/ **1** *vi/t* mix so as to form an undivided whole **2** *vi infml* talk to different people at a party

min-i /'mɪni/ *n* anything that is smaller than other things of the same kind: *a mini (skirt)*

min-i-a-ture /'mɪniətʃəʳ, 'mɪnətʃəʳ‖ 'mɪniətʃuəʳ/ *adj, n* very small (thing, esp. a copy of a bigger one) −turize *vt*

min-i-bus /'mɪnibʌs/ *n* small bus for between 6 and 12 people

min-i-mal /'mɪnəməl/ *adj* as little as possible −ly *adv*

min-i-mize ‖ also −ise *BrE* /'mɪnəmaɪz/ *vt* **1** reduce as much as possible **2** treat as if not serious

min-i-mum /'mɪnəməm/ *n, adj* −ma /-mə/ *or* −mums smallest (amount, number, etc.)

min-ing /'maɪnɪŋ/ *n* [U] digging minerals out of the earth

min-ion /'mɪnjən/ *n* slavelike helper

min-is-cule /'mɪnəskju:l/ *adj* extremely small

min-is-ter [1] /'mɪnəstəʳ/ *n* **1** politician in charge of a government department: *the Minister of Defence* **2** Christian priest −ial /,mɪnə'stɪəriəl/ *adj*

minister [2] *v* **minister to** *phr vt fml* help: *ministering to the sick*

min-is-tra-tion /,mɪnə'streɪʃən/ *n* [C;U] giving of help and service

min-is-try /'mɪnəstri/ *n* **1** [C] government department **2** [the + S] job of being a priest: *to enter the ministry* (= become a priest)

mink /mɪŋk/ *n* mink [C;U] (valuable brown fur of) a small fierce animal

mi-nor [1] /'maɪnəʳ/ *adj* of small importance or seriousness: *a minor problem | minor surgery*

minor [2] *n law* person too young to be held responsible

mi-nor-i-ty /maɪ'nɒrəti‖maɪ'nɔ:-, mə'nɑ:-/ *n* **1** [C] less than half: *A minority of people favour it.* **2** [C] small part of a population different from the rest: *minority rights | minority interest* (= supported by a small number of people) **3** [U] *law* state or time of being a minor

min-ster /'mɪnstəʳ/ *n* great or important church: *Westminster*

min-strel /'mɪnstrəl/ *n* travelling singer in former times

mint [1] /mɪnt/ *n* **1** [C] PEPPERMINT **2** [U] plant with fresh-smelling leaves used in food ~y *adj*

mint [2] *n* **1** place where coins are made **2 make a mint** earn a lot of money ♦ *vt* make (a coin) ♦ *adj* (of a stamp, coin, etc.) unused and in perfect condition

min·u·et /ˌmɪnjuˈet/ n (music for) a slow graceful dance

mi·nus /ˈmaɪnəs/ prep **1** made less by: 10 minus 4 is 6. **2** below freezing point: It was minus 10 today. (= −10°) **3** infml without ♦ n also **minus sign** a sign (−) showing a number less than zero, or that one number is to be taken away from another ♦ adj less than zero

min·us·cule, miniscule /ˈmɪnəs-kjuːl/ adj extremely small

min·ute[1] /ˈmɪnɪt/ n **1** 60th part of an hour **2** short time: Wait a minute! **3** 60th part of a degree of angle **4** short note of an official nature, such as on a report — see also MINUTES **5** the **min·ute (that)** as soon as ♦ vt record in the MINUTES

mi·nute[2] /maɪˈnjuːt‖-ˈnuːt/ adj very small ~**ness** n [U]

min·utes /ˈmɪnɪts/ n [(the) P] written record of a meeting

mi·nu·ti·ae /maɪˈnjuːʃiaɪ, mə-‖ mɑˈnuː-/ n [P] small exact details

mir·a·cle /ˈmɪrəkəl/ n **1** unexplainable but wonderful act or event, esp. as done by a holy person: (fig.) It's a miracle the explosion didn't kill her. **2** wonderful example (of a quality, ability, etc.): a miracle of modern science −**culous** /mɪˈrækjŝləs/ adj

mi·rage /ˈmɪrɑːʒ‖mŝˈrɑːʒ/ n something seen that is not really there, esp. as caused by the hot desert air

mire /maɪəʳ/ n [U] esp. lit deep mud

mir·ror /ˈmɪrəʳ/ n piece of glass in which one can see oneself ♦ vt show truly (as if) in a mirror

mirror im·age /ˈ·· ˌ··/ n image in which the right side appears on the left, and the left side on the right

mirth /mɜːθ‖mɜːrθ/ n [U] laughter

mis·ad·ven·ture /ˌmɪsədˈventʃəʳ/ n [C;U] esp. lit accident or piece of bad luck

mis·an·throp·ic /ˌmɪsənˈθrɒpɪk‖ -ˈθrɑː-/ adj disliking everyone ~**ally** /-kli/ adv −**ist** /ˈmɪsˈænθrəpŝst/ n

mis·ap·pre·hen·sion /ˌmɪsæprɪ-ˈhenʃən/ n fml mistaken belief; misunderstanding

mis·ap·pro·pri·ate /ˌmɪsəˈprəʊ-priett/ vt take dishonestly (and use)

mis·be·have /ˌmɪsbɪˈheɪv/ vi/t behave (oneself) badly

misc. written abbrev. for: MISCELLANEOUS

mis·cal·cu·late /ˌmɪsˈkælkjŝleɪt/ vi/t calculate wrongly; form a wrong judgment of something −**lation** /ˌmɪsˌkælkjŝˈleɪʃən/ n

mis·car·riage /ˌmɪsˈkærɪdʒ, ˈmɪskærɪdʒ/ n giving birth to a child too early for it to live

miscarriage of justice /·ˌ··ˈ··/ n unjust legal decision

mis·car·ry /mɪsˈkæri/ vi **1** have a miscarriage **2** fml (of a plan) go wrong

mis·cel·la·ne·ous /ˌmɪsəˈleɪniəs/ adj of many different kinds

mis·cel·la·ny /mɪˈseləni‖ˈmɪsŝleɪni/ n mixture of various kinds

mis·chance /ˌmɪsˈtʃɑːns‖-ˈtʃæns/ n [C;U] (piece of) bad luck

mis·chief /ˈmɪstʃŝf/ n **1** slightly bad behaviour, esp. by children **2** damage; harm

mis·chie·vous /ˈmɪstʃŝvəs/ adj **1** playfully troublesome **2** causing harm, esp. intentionally ~**ly** adv

mis·con·ceive /ˌmɪskənˈsiːv/ vt **1** make (a plan) badly **2** understand

mis·con·cep·tion /ˌmɪskənˈsepʃən/ n case of wrong understanding

mis·con·duct /ˌmɪsˈkɒndʌkt‖ -ˈkɑːn-/ n [U] fml bad behaviour, esp. sexual

mis·con·struc·tion /ˌmɪskən-ˈstrʌkʃən/ n [C;U] wrong understanding

mis·deed /ˌmɪsˈdiːd/ n fml wrong act

mis·de·mea·nour BrE ‖ −**nor** AmE /ˌmɪsdɪˈmiːnəʳ/ n crime or wrong act which is not very serious

mi·ser /ˈmaɪzəʳ/ n person who loves money and hates spending it ~**liness** n [U] ~**ly** adj

mis·e·ra·ble /ˈmɪzərəbəl/ adj **1** very unhappy **2** causing lack of cheerfulness: miserable weather **3** very low in quality or very small in amount: a few miserable pounds −**bly** adv

mis·e·ry /ˈmɪzəri/ n **1** [C;U] great unhappiness or suffering **2** [C] esp. BrE complaining person

mis·fire /ˌmɪsˈfaɪəʳ/ vi **1** (of a gun) not fire properly **2** (of a plan or joke) not have the intended effect

mis·fit /ˈmɪs,fɪt/ n someone who cannot live or work happily in their surroundings

mis·for·tune /mɪsˈfɔːtʃən‖-ɔːr-/ n [C;U] **1** bad luck, esp. of a serious nature **2** very unfortunate event, condition, etc.

mis·giv·ing /ˌmɪsˈgɪvɪŋ/ n [C;U] feeling that it might be better not to do a thing

mis·guid·ed /mɪsˈgaɪdŝd/ adj showing bad judgment; foolish ~**ly** adv

mis·hap /ˈmɪshæp/ n slight unfortunate happening

mis·judge /ˌmɪsˈdʒʌdʒ/ vt judge wrongly, esp. form a wrong or unfairly bad opinion −**judgment** n [C;U]

mis·lay /mɪsˈleɪ/ vt −**laid** /-ˈleɪd/ lose for a short time

mis·lead /mɪsˈliːd/ vt −**led** /-ˈled/ cause to think or act mistakenly

mis·man·age /ˌmɪsˈmænɪdʒ/ vt control or deal with (private, public or business affairs) badly ~**ment** n [U]

mis·no·mer /ˌmɪsˈnəʊməʳ/ n unsuitable name

mi·so·gy·nist /məˈsɒdʒənɪst‖ məˈsɑː-/ n woman-hater

mis·place /ˌmɪsˈpleɪs/ vt **1** put in the wrong place: (fig.) misplaced trust **2** mislay

mis·print /ˈmɪs-prɪnt/ n mistake in printing

mis·rep·re·sent /ˌmɪsreprɪˈzent/ vt give an intentionally untrue account or explanation of ~ation /ˌmɪsreprɪzenˈteɪʃən/ n [C;U]

miss[1] /mɪs/ v **1** vi/t fail to hit, catch, meet, see, hear, etc.: He shot at me, but missed. | I missed the train. | She narrowly missed being killed. **2** vt feel unhappy at the absence or loss of ♦ n **1** failure to hit, etc. **2** give something a miss esp. BrE not do, take, etc., something — see also NEAR MISS ~ing adj not in the proper place; lost **miss out** phr v **1** vt fail to include or **2** vi lose a chance to gain advantage or enjoyment

miss[2] n (usu. cap.) (title of a girl or unmarried woman): Miss Browne

mis·sile /ˈmɪsaɪl‖ˈmɪsəl/ n **1** explosive flying weapon **2** object or weapon thrown: They threw bottles and other missiles at the police.

mis·sion /ˈmɪʃən/ n **1** special job, duty, or purpose: He felt his mission in life was to help others. | They were sent on a secret mission. **2** group of people sent abroad: a trade mission **3** place where missionaries work

mis·sion·a·ry /ˈmɪʃənəri‖-neri/ n person sent abroad to teach and spread religion

mis·sive /ˈmɪsɪv/ n fml or lit letter

mis·spent /ˌmɪsˈspent◂/ adj wasted

mist /mɪst/ n [C;U] thin FOG: (fig.) lost in the mists of time ♦ vi/t cover with mist: The windscreen had misted up. ~y: (fig.) misty memories

mis·take /məˈsteɪk/ v -**took** /məˈstʊk/, -**taken** /məˈsteɪkən/ **1** have a wrong idea about: He mistook my meaning. **2** fail to recognize ♦ n [C;U] something done through carelessness, lack of knowledge or skill, etc.: I made a terrible mistake. | I did it by mistake.
mistake for phr vt think wrongly that (a person or thing) is (someone or something else): I mistook him for his brother.

mis·tak·en /məˈsteɪkən/ adj wrong; incorrect ~**ly** adv

mis·tle·toe /ˈmɪsltəʊ/ n [U] plant with white berries, used for Christmas decorations

mis·took /məˈstʊk/ past t. of MISTAKE

mis·tress /ˈmɪstrəs/ n **1** woman in control **2** man's unmarried female

sexual partner **3** esp. BrE female teacher

mis·trust /mɪsˈtrʌst/ vt not trust ♦ n [U] lack of trust ~**ful** adj

mis·un·der·stand /ˌmɪsʌndəˈstænd‖-ər-/ vi/t -**stood** /stʊd/ understand wrongly ~**ing** n [C;U] lack of correct understanding, esp. with slight disagreement

mit·i·gate /ˈmɪtɪgeɪt/ vt fml lessen the severity of -**gation** /ˈmɪtɪˈgeɪʃən/ n [U]

mi·tre BrE ‖ **miter** AmE /ˈmaɪtəʳ/ n BISHOP's tall pointed hat

mitt /mɪt/ n type of protective mitten

mit·ten /ˈmɪtn/ n GLOVE without separate finger parts

mix /mɪks/ v **1** vi/t combine so that the parts no longer have a separate shape, appearance, etc.: Oil and water don't mix. | Mix blue and yellow to make green. | She mixed herself a cocktail. **2** vi be or enjoy being in the company of others ~**ed** adj **1** of different kinds **2** for both sexes **3** mixed up in connected with (something bad) ~**er** n ♦ n [C;U] MIXTURE (1): cake mix

mixed bag /ˌ· ˈ·/ n [S] collection of things of many different kinds (and qualities)

mixed bles·sing /ˌ· ˈ··/ n [S] something that is bad as well as good

mixed economy /ˌ· ·ˈ···/ n operation of a country's money supply, industry, and trade by a mixture of CAPITALIST and SOCIALIST principles

mixed met·a·phor /ˌ· ˈ···/ n use of 2 METAPHORs together with a foolish or funny effect

mix·ture /ˈmɪkstʃəʳ/ n **1** [C;U] set of substances (to be) mixed together **2** [S] combination: a mixture of amusement and disbelief **3** [U] act of mixing

mix-up /ˈ· ·/ n state of disorder and confusion

mm written abbrev. for MILLIMETRES

mne·mon·ic /nɪˈmɒnɪk‖nɪˈmɑː-/ adj, n (something) used for helping one to remember

MO /ˌem ˈəʊ/ **1** medical officer **2** MODUS OPERANDI

moan /məʊn/ vi, n (make a) **a** low sound of pain **b** discontented complaint

moat /məʊt/ n long deep usu. water-filled hole round esp. a castle

mob /mɒb‖mɑːb/ n **1** noisy (violent) crowd **2** group of criminals ♦ vt -**bb**- gather round **a** to attack **b** because of interest or admiration

mo·bile /ˈməʊbaɪl‖-bəl, -biːl/ adj (easily) movable; not fixed -**bility** /məʊˈbɪləti/ n [U]

mo·bil·ize ‖ also -**ise** BrE /ˈməʊbəlaɪz/ vt bring into action, esp. ready for war -**ization** /məʊbəlaɪˈzeɪʃən‖-lə-/ n [U]

moc·ca·sin /'mɒkəsɪn‖'mɑː-/ n simple soft leather shoe

mock[1] /mɒk‖mɑːk/ vt laugh at unkindly or unfairly

mock[2] adj not real; pretended: a mock battle

mock·e·ry /'mɒkəri‖'mɑː-/ n 1 [U] mocking 2 [S] something unworthy of respect 3 **make a mockery of** show to be foolish or untrue

mock-up /'· ·/ n full-size model of something to be built

modal aux·il·i·a·ry /,·· '····/ n verb that goes in front of another, such as can, may, or would

mod con /,· '·/ n **all mod cons** (esp. in newspaper advertisements for houses) with all modern conveniences (such as hot water, central heating, etc.)

mode /məʊd/ n way of doing something

mod·el /'mɒdl‖'mɑːdl/ n 1 small copy: a model aeroplane 2 person who models clothes 3 person to be painted or photographed 4 person or thing of the highest quality: a model student 5 type of vehicle, machine, weapon, etc.: His car is the latest model. ♦ v -ll- BrE | -l- AmE 1 vt make a small copy 2 vi/t wear (clothes) to show them to possible buyers

model on phr vt form as a copy of: She modelled herself on her mother.

mo·dem /'məʊdəm‖'məʊ,dem/ n ELECTRONIC apparatus for changing information from a form which a computer understands into a form which can be sent along a telephone line, etc., to another computer

mod·e·rate[1] /'mɒdərət‖'mɑː-/ adj 1 neither too much nor too little; middle 2 not politically extreme —**ly** adv not very —**ration** /,mɒdə'reɪʃən‖,mɑː-/ n [U] 1 self-control 2 reduction in force or degree 3 **in moderation** within sensible limits

mod·e·rate[2] /'mɒdəreɪt‖'mɑː-/ vi/t lessen in force, degree, etc.

mod·e·rate[3] /'mɒdərət‖'mɑː-/ n person whose opinions are MODERATE[1] (2)

mod·ern /'mɒdn‖'mɑːdərn/ adj 1 of the present time 2 new and different from the past —**ize** v 1 vt make suitable for modern use 2 vi start using more modern methods —**ization** /,mɒdənaɪ'zeɪʃən‖,mɑːdərnə-/ n [C;U]

mod·est /'mɒdɪst‖'mɑː-/ adj 1 not too proud 2 not large 3 not sexually improper —**ly** adv —**y** n [U]

mod·i·cum /'mɒdɪkəm‖'mɑː-/ n small amount

mod·i·fy /'mɒdɪfaɪ‖'mɑː-/ vt 1 change, esp. slightly 2 make (a claim, condition, etc) less hard to accept or bear 3 (esp. of an adjective or adverb)

go with and describe (another word) —**fication** /,mɒdɪfɪ'keɪʃən‖,mɑː-/ n [C;U]

mod·u·late /'mɒdjʊleɪt‖'mɑːdʒə-/ vt vary the strength, nature, etc., of (a sound) —**lation** /,mɒdjʊ'leɪʃən‖,mɑːdʒə-/ n [C;U]

mod·ule /'mɒdjuːl‖'mɑːdʒuːl/ n 1 standard part used in building, making furniture, etc. 2 part of a spacecraft for independent use —**ular** /'mɒdjʊləʳ‖'mɑːdʒə-/ adj

mo·dus op·e·ran·di /,məʊdəs ,opə'rændiː‖,ɑːpə-/ n [S] method of doing something

modus vi·ven·di /,məʊdəs vɪ-'vendiː/ n [S] way of living (together)

mo·gul /'məʊgəl/ n person of very great power and wealth

mo·hair /'məʊheəʳ/ n [U] (cloth from) the long silky hair of a sort of goat

Mo·ham·me·dan /məʊ'hæmədən, mə-/ n, adj Muslim

moist /mɔɪst/ adj slightly wet ~**en** /'mɔɪsən/ vi/t make or become moist ~**ure** /'mɔɪstʃəʳ/ n [U] liquid in or on something ~**urize** /'mɔɪstʃəraɪz/ vt remove the dryness from

mo·lar /'məʊləʳ/ n large back tooth

mold /məʊld/ n, v AmE for MOULD

mol·der /'məʊldəʳ/ v AmE for MOULDER

mole[1] /məʊl/ n 1 small furry animal that lives underground 2 BrE SPY who works inside an organization

mole[2] n small, dark brown mark on the skin

mol·e·cule /'mɒlɪkjuːl‖'mɑː-/ n very small piece of matter, made of 2 or more atoms —**cular** /mə'lekjʊləʳ/ adj

mole·hill /'məʊl,hɪl/ n small pile of earth thrown up by a mole — see also **make a mountain out of a molehill** (MOUNTAIN)

mo·lest /mə'lest/ vt 1 attack; harm 2 attack (esp. a woman or child) sexually

mol·li·fy /'mɒlɪfaɪ‖'mɑː-/ vt make less angry

mol·lusc | also **mollusk** AmE /'mɒləsk‖'mɑː-/ n any of a class of soft-bodied limbless animals, usu. with a shell

mol·ly·cod·dle /'mɒli,kɒdl‖'mɑːli,kɑːdl/ vt take too much care of (a person or animal)

Mol·o·tov cock·tail /,mɒlətɒf 'kɒkteɪl‖,mɑːlətɔːf 'kɑːk-, ,məʊl-/ n petrol-filled bottle used as a bomb

molt /məʊlt/ v AmE for MOULT

mol·ten /'məʊltən/ adj (of metal or rock) melted

mo·ment /'məʊmənt/ n 1 very short period of time 2 particular point in time 3 importance: a matter of great moment 4 **the moment (that)** as soon

as ~**ary** adj lasting a moment
~**arily** /ˈməʊməntərəli‖ˌməʊmən-ˈterəli/ adv 1 for just a very short time 2 esp. AmE very soon; in a moment
moment of truth /ˌ‥‥ˈ‥/ n moment when something important will happen

mo·men·tous /məʊˈmentəs, mə-/ adj extremely important ~**ness** n [U]

mo·men·tum /məʊˈmentəm, mə-/ n [U] measurable quantity of movement in a body: (fig.) The campaign had lost its momentum.

mon·arch /ˈmɒnək‖ˈmɑːnərk, -ɑːrk/ n non-elected ruler; king, queen, etc.
~**y** n 1 [U] rule by a monarch 2 [C] country ruled by a monarch

mon·as·tery /ˈmɒnəstri‖ˈmɑːnəsteri/ n building in which MONKs live

mo·nas·tic /məˈnæstɪk/ adj of MONKs or monasteries

Mon·day /ˈmʌndi/ n the 1st day of the week, between Sunday and Tuesday

mon·e·ta·ris·m /ˈmʌnɪtərɪzəm‖ˈmɑː-/ n [U] (in ECONOMICS) belief that the best way of controlling the ECONOMY of a country is to control its money supply – **rist** n, adj

mon·e·ta·ry /ˈmʌnɪtəri‖ˈmɑːnɪteri/ adj of or about money

mon·ey /ˈmʌni/ n [U] 1 something used for paying, esp. coins or paper notes 2 wealth: We're in the money. (= rich) 3 **for my money** in my opinion 4 **one's money's worth** full value for the money one has spent

money-grub·ber /ˈmʌniˌɡrʌbər/ n person unpleasantly determined to gain money

money-spin·ner /ˈ‥ ˌ‥/ n something that brings in a lot of money

money sup·ply /ˈ‥‥ˌ‥/ n [the + S] all the money that exists and is being paid and spent in a country in the form of coins, notes, and CREDIT

mon·grel /ˈmʌŋɡrəl‖ˈmɒŋ-, ˈmʌŋ-/ n 1 dog of mixed breed 2 person or thing of mixed race or origin

mon·i·tor /ˈmɒnɪtər‖ˈmɑː-/ vt watch or listen to carefully for a special purpose ♦ n 1 television used to show the view seen by a television camera 2 instrument for monitoring a bodily condition: a heart monitor 3 a screen for use with a computer b parts of a computer operation that make sure that the computer system is working properly 4 person who listens to foreign radio news, etc., and reports on its content 5 pupil chosen to help the teacher: dinner money monitor

monk /mʌŋk/ n member of an all-male religious group that lives together

mon·key¹ /ˈmʌŋki/ n 1 small tree-climbing long-tailed animal 2 infml child full of playful tricks 3 **make a monkey (out) of someone** infml make someone appear foolish

monkey² v **monkey about/around** phr vi play foolishly

monkey busi·ness /ˈ‥ ˌ‥/ n [U] infml secret behaviour which causes trouble

mon·o /ˈmɒnəʊ‖ˈmɑː-/ adj (of sound) coming from only one place: a mono record

mon·o·chrome /ˈmɒnəkrəʊm‖ˈmɑː-/ adj 1 in only one colour 2 in black and white only

mon·o·cle /ˈmɒnəkəl‖ˈmɑː-/ n LENS for one eye only, to help the sight

mo·nog·a·my /məˈnɒɡəmi‖məˈnɑː-/ n [U] having only one husband or wife at a time –**mous** adj

mon·o·gram /ˈmɒnəɡræm‖ˈmɑː-/ n combined letters, esp. someone's INITIALs ~**med** adj

mon·o·lith·ic /ˌmɒnəˈlɪθɪk◀‖ˌmɑː-/ adj 1 like a large stone pillar 2 often derog forming an unchangeable whole

mon·o·logue /ˈmɒnəlɒɡ‖ˈmɑːnəlɔːɡ, -lɑːɡ/ n long speech by one person

mo·nop·o·ly /məˈnɒpəli‖məˈnɑː-/ n 1 unshared control or right to do or produce something: (fig.) He thinks he's got a monopoly on brains. (= that he alone is clever) –**lize** vt keep unshared control of

mon·o·rail /ˈmɒnəʊreɪl, -nə-‖ˈmɑː-/ n railway with one rail

mon·o·sod·i·um glu·tam·ate /ˌmɒnəʊˌsəʊdiəm ˈɡluːtəmeɪt ˌmɑːnə-/ n [U] chemical compound added to certain foods, to make their taste stronger

mon·o·syl·la·ble /ˈmɒnəˌsɪləbəl‖ˈmɑː-/ n word of one SYLLABLE –**bic** /ˌmɒnəsɪˈlæbɪk‖ˌmɑː-/ adj

mon·o·tone /ˈmɒnətəʊn‖ˈmɑː-/ n [S] way of speaking or singing in which the voice continues on the same note: to speak in a monotone

mo·not·o·ny /məˈnɒtəni‖məˈnɑː-/ n [U] dull sameness –**onous** adj dull; boring (BORE²) –**onously** adv

mon·soon /mɒnˈsuːn‖mɑːn-/ n (time of) very heavy rains in and near India

mon·ster /ˈmɒnstər‖ˈmɑːn-/ n 1 strange usu. large and frightening creature 2 very evil person ♦ adj unusually large: a monster potato — see also GREEN-EYED MONSTER

mon·stros·i·ty /mɒnˈstrɒsəti‖mɑːnˈstrɑː-/ n something very ugly and usu. large

mon·strous /ˈmɒnstrəs‖ˈmɑːn-/ adj 1 extremely bad; shocking 2 unnaturally large, strange, etc. ~**ly** adv

mon·tage /'mɒntɑːʒ‖mɑːn'tɑːʒ/ n [C;U] picture made from separate parts combined

month /mʌnθ/ n 12th part of a year; 4 weeks ~**ly** adj

mon·u·ment /'mɒnjʊmənt‖'mɑː-/ n 1 something built in honour of a person or event 2 historical old building or place 3 work, esp. a book, worthy of lasting fame ~**al** /ˌmɒnjʊ'mentl◂‖ˌmɑː-/ adj 1 intended as a monument 2 very large 3 (esp. of something bad) very great in degree ~**ally** adv extremely

moo /muː/ vi,n (make) the sound of a cow

mooch /muːtʃ/ vt AmE sl get by asking for it

mooch about/around phr vi wander about rather unhappily with no purpose

mood¹ /muːd/ n 1 state of feeling: in a cheerful mood 2 state of feeling in which one is bad-tempered or angry ~**y** adj often having bad moods ~**ily** adv

mood² n any of the three sets of verb forms that express **a** a fact or action (INDICATIVE), **b** a command (IMPERATIVE), or **c** a doubt, wish, etc. (SUBJUNCTIVE)

moon¹ /muːn/ n 1 large body that moves round the Earth and shines at night 2 body that moves round a PLANET other than the Earth 3 infml **over the moon** very happy — see also BLUE MOON

moon² v **moon about/around** phr vi wander about in an aimless unhappy way

moon·beam /'muːnbiːm/ n beam of light from the moon

moon·light¹ /'muːnlaɪt/ n [U] light of the moon

moonlight² vi -**ed** have a second job in addition to a regular one, esp. without the knowledge of a government department

moor¹ /mʊəʳ/ also **moors** pl., **moorland** /'mʊələnd‖'mʊər-/ n [C;U] esp. BrE (area of) high hilly usu. treeless land

moor² vi/t fasten (a boat) to land, etc., by means of ropes, etc. ~**ings** n [P] 1 ropes, ANCHORs, etc., for mooring 2 also **mooring** — place where a boat is moored

moose /muːs/ n **moose** large North American deer

moot /muːt/ vt state (a question, matter, etc.) for consideration

moot point /ˌ· '·/ n undecided matter, on which people have different opinions

mop¹ /mɒp‖mɑːp/ n 1 long stick with thick string or a SPONGE at one end, for washing floors 2 thick untidy mass of hair

mop² vt -**pp**- wash or dry (as if) with a mop: She mopped her brow.

mop up phr vt 1 remove liquid, dirt, etc., with a mop 2 finish dealing with: mop up small enemy groups

mope /məʊp/ vi be continuously sad

mo·ped /'məʊped/ n small motorcycle

mor·al /'mɒrəl‖'mɔː-/ adj 1 of or based on the difference between good and evil or right and wrong: She has high moral principles. 2 pure and honest in character and behaviour ♦ n lesson that can be learnt from a story or event ~**ize** vi give one's opinions on right and wrong, esp. when unwelcome **morals** n [P] standards of (sexual) behaviour ~**ity** /mə'rælɪti/ n [U] rightness or pureness of behaviour or of an action

mo·rale /mə'rɑːl‖mə'ræl/ n [U] pride and confidence, esp. in relation to a job to be done

moral ma·jor·i·ty /ˌ··'····/n [the+S] a movement, esp. in the US, that favours very severe Christian religious principles and is against political change

moral sup·port /ˌ·· '·/n [U] encouragement

mo·rass /mə'ræs/ [C] esp. lit MARSH: (fig.) bogged down in a morass of detail

mor·a·to·ri·um /ˌmɒrə'tɔːriəm‖ˌmɔː-/ n -**ria** /-riə/ official period during which a particular thing is not done

mor·bid /'mɔːbɪd‖'mɔːr-/ adj unhealthily interested in death ~**ly** adv ~**ity** /mɔː'bɪdɪti‖mɔːr-/ n [U]

mor·dant /'mɔːdənt‖'mɔːr-/ adj fml cruel and cutting in speech

more¹ /mɔːʳ/ adv 1 (forms COMPARATIVES): more difficult 2 to a greater degree: He likes this one more than that one. 3 again: Do it just once more.

more² determiner, pron (comparative of **many**, **much**) 1 a greater or additional number or quantity (of): He wants more food. | I can't eat any more. 2 **more and more** increasingly 3 **more or less: a** nearly **b** about

more·o·ver /mɔːˈrəʊvəʳ/ adv fml in addition; besides

mo·res /'mɔːreɪz/ n [P] fml fixed moral customs in a social group

morgue /mɔːg‖mɔːrg/ n MORTUARY

mor·i·bund /'mɒrɪbʌnd‖'mɔː-, 'mɑː-/ adj completely inactive and near to the end of existence

morn·ing /'mɔːnɪŋ‖'mɔːr-/ n 1 time between sunrise and midday 2 **in the morning** tomorrow morning

morn·ing-af·ter pill /ˌ·· ˈ·· ˌ·/ n drug taken by mouth by a woman within 72 hours of having sex, to prevent her from having a baby

morning dress /ˈ·· ·/ n [U] formal dress worn by a man at official or social ceremonies in the morning or afternoon

mo·ron /ˈmɔːrɒn‖ˈmɔːrɑːn/ n very stupid person ~ic /məˈrɒnɪk‖ məˈrɑː-/ adj

mo·rose /məˈrəʊs/ adj angry and silent ~ly adv

mor·phine /ˈmɔːfiːn‖ˈmɔːr-/ n [U] powerful drug for stopping pain

Morse code /ˌmɔːs ˈkəʊd‖ˌmɔːrs-/ n [U] system of sending messages with letters represented by combinations of long and short signals

mor·sel /ˈmɔːsəl‖ˈmɔːr-/ n small piece, esp. of food

mor·tal /ˈmɔːtl‖ˈmɔːrtl/ adj 1 that will die 2 of human beings 3 causing death: a mortal wound ♦ n human being ~ly adv 1 so as to cause death 2 very much: mortally offended ~ity /mɔːˈtælɪti‖mɔːr-/ n [U] 1 rate or number of deaths 2 state of being mortal

mor·tar[1] /ˈmɔːtər‖ˈmɔːrtl/ n [U] mixture of lime, sand, and water, used in building

mortar[2] n 1 apparatus for firing small bombs 2 thick bowl in which things are crushed

mort·gage /ˈmɔːɡɪdʒ‖ˈmɔːr-/ n 1 agreement to borrow money to buy esp. a house, which belongs to the lender until the money is repaid 2 the amount borrowed ♦ vt give up the ownership of (a house, etc.) for a time in return for money lent

mor·ti·cian /mɔːˈtɪʃən‖mɔːr-/ AmE for UNDERTAKER

mor·ti·fy /ˈmɔːtɪfaɪ‖ˈmɔːr-/ vt make ashamed −fication /ˌmɔːtɪfɪˈkeɪʃən‖ ˌmɔːr-/ n [U]

mor·tu·a·ry /ˈmɔːtʃuəri‖ˈmɔːrtʃueri/ n place where dead bodies are kept until a funeral

mo·sa·ic /məʊˈzeɪ-ɪk/ n pattern or picture formed by small pieces of coloured stone or glass

Mos·lem /ˈmɒzləm‖ˈmɑːz-/ n, adj Muslim

mosque /mɒsk‖mɑːsk/ n building in which Muslims worship

mos·qui·to /məˈskiːtəʊ/ n -tos or -toes small blood-sucking flying insect

moss /mɒs‖mɔːs/ n [U] (thick flat mass of) a small usu. green plant of wet places

most[1] /məʊst/ adv 1 (forms SUPERLATIVES): the most difficult question 2 more than anything else: He likes bananas most of all. 3 fml very: I was most upset.

most[2] determiner, pron (superlative of many, much) 1 nearly all: Most people dislike him. 2 at (the) most not more than 3 for the most part mainly 4 make the most of get the best advantage from ~ly adv mainly

MOT /ˌem əʊ ˈtiː/ n (in Britain) regular official examination of cars to make sure they are in good enough condition to be driven

mo·tel /məʊˈtel/ n hotel specially built for MOTORISTs

moth /mɒθ‖mɔːθ/ n large-winged insect that flies mainly at night

moth·ball /ˈmɒθbɔːl‖ˈmɔːθ-/ n 1 ball of strong-smelling chemical for keeping moths away from clothes 2 in mothballs stored and not used

moth-eat·en /ˈ· ˌ··/ adj 1 (of clothes) eaten by the young of moths 2 very worn out

moth·er /ˈmʌðər/ n 1 female parent 2 (usu. cap.) female head of a CONVENT: mother superior ♦ vt care for or protect (too) lovingly ~hood n [U] ~ly adj like a good mother

mother coun·try /ˈ·· ˌ·/ n country one was born in or came from originally

mother-in-law /ˈ·· · ·/ n mothers-in-law or mother-in-laws wife's or husband's mother

mother-of-pearl /ˌ·· · ˈ◂/ n [U] shiny substance from inside certain shells, used decoratively

mother tongue /ˌ·· ˈ·/ n first language one spoke

mo·tif /məʊˈtiːf/ n (repeated) artistic or musical pattern

mo·tion /ˈməʊʃən/ n 1 [U] act, way, or process of moving: the ship's rolling motion 2 [C] single movement 3 [C] suggestion formally made at a meeting 4 go through the motions do something without care or interest 5 put/set in motion start (a machine or process) ♦ vi/t signal or direct by a movement of esp. the hand −less adj unmoving

motion pic·ture /ˌ·· ˈ··◂/ n AmE for FILM (2)

mo·ti·vate /ˈməʊtɪveɪt/ vt 1 give (someone) a (strong) reason for doing something; encourage 2 be the reason why (something) was done −vation /ˌməʊtɪˈveɪʃən/ n [U]

mo·tive /ˈməʊtɪv/ n reason for action

mot·ley /ˈmɒtli‖ˈmɑːtli/ adj usu. derog of many different kinds and qualities

mo·to·cross /ˈməʊtəʊkrɒs‖-krɑːs/ n [U] motorcycle racing across rough country

mo·tor /ˈməʊtər/ n 1 machine that changes power into movement: an electric motor 2 BrE infml a car ♦ adj 1 driven by an engine: a motor mower

2 of cars, etc.: *the motor trade* ♦ *vi* go by car **~ist** *n* car driver

mo·tor·car /'məʊtəkɑːʳ‖-tər-/ *n BrE fml* car

mo·tor·cy·cle /'məʊtə،saɪkəl‖-tər-/ *n* also **motorbike** /-،baɪk/ *BrE infml* — large heavy bicycle driven by an engine

motor scoot·er /'·· ،··/ *n* SCOOTER (2)

mo·tor·way /'məʊtəweɪ‖-tər-/ *n BrE* wide road for fast long-distance travel

mot·tled /'mɒtld‖'mɑː-/ *adj* irregularly marked with colours and/or shapes

mot·to /'mɒtəʊ‖'mɑː-/ *n* **-toes** *or* **-tos** phrase or short sentence used as a guiding principle

mould[1] *BrE* ‖ **mold** *AmE*/məʊld/ *n* container into which a soft substance is poured, to take on the shape of the container when it sets ♦ *vt* shape or form (something solid): (fig.) *influences that moulded her character* **~ing** *n* [C;U] decorative stone, plastic, or wood band(s)

mould[2] *BrE* ‖ **mold** *AmE* *n* [U] soft often greenish growth on old food, etc. **~y** *adj*: *mouldy cheese*

moul·der *BrE* ‖ **molder** *AmE* /'məʊldəʳ/ *vi* decay gradually

moult *BrE* ‖ **molt** *AmE*/məʊlt/ *vi* (of a bird or animal) lose most of its feathers, fur, etc.

mound /maʊnd/ *n* **1** pile **2** small hill

mount[1] /maʊnt/ *v* **1** *vi* rise: *Costs mounted.* **2** *vt* get on (a horse, bicycle, etc.) **3** *vt* provide with a horse, etc.: *the mounted police* **4** *vt* prepare and produce: *mount an exhibition/an attack* **5** *vt* fix on a support or in a frame **6** *vt* go up; climb ♦ *n* animal for riding

mount[2] *n* (*usu. cap.*) (used before names of mountains): *Mount Everest*

moun·tain /'maʊntɪn/ *n* **1** very high rocky hill **2** very large amount **3 make a mountain out of a molehill** make a problem seem more difficult than it is **~ous** *adj* **1** full of mountains **2** extremely large

moun·tain·eer /،maʊntɪ'nɪəʳ/ *n* mountain climber **~ing** *n* [U]

mourn /mɔːn‖mɔːrn/ *vi/t* feel or express grief (for), esp. when someone dies **~er** *n* **~ful** *adj* (too) sad **~ing** *n* [U] **1** grief **2** funeral clothes, usu. black

mouse /maʊs/ *n* **mice** /maɪs/ **1** long-tailed furry animal, like a rat but smaller **2** quiet nervous person **3** small box connected to a computer by a wire which, when moved by hand, causes a CURSOR to move around on a VDU so that choices can be made within the PROGRAM in use **mousy** *adj* **1** (of hair) dull pale brown **2** (of a person) unattractively plain and quiet

mousse /muːs/ *n* [C;U] dish made from flavoured cream and eggs

mous·tache /mə'stɑːʃ‖'mʌstæʃ/ *n* hair on the upper lip

mouth[1] /maʊθ/ *n* **mouths** /maʊðz/ **1** opening in the face for eating and speaking **2** opening; entrance: *the mouth of the cave* **3 down in the mouth** not cheerful **4 keep one's mouth shut** keep silent

mouth[2] /maʊð/ *vt* **1** say by moving the lips soundlessly **2** repeat without understanding or sincerity

mouth·ful /'maʊθful/ *n* **1** amount put into the mouth **2** long word or phrase, difficult to say

mouth·or·gan /'maʊθ،ɔːgən‖-،ɔːr-/ *n* musical instrument played by moving the mouth up and down it and blowing

mouth·piece /'maʊθpiːs/ *n* **1** part of a musical instrument, telephone, etc., held in or near the mouth **2** person, newspaper, etc., that only expresses the opinions of others

mouth·wa·ter·ing /'·· ،···/ *adj* (of food) very attractive

move[1] /muːv/ *v* **1** *vi/t* (cause to) change place or position: *Sit still and don't move!* **2** *vi* act: *I had to move fast to clinch the deal.* **3** *vi* also **move house** — change one's home **4** *vt* cause to have strong feelings, esp. of pity: *a very moving story* **5** *vi/t* make (a formal suggestion) at a meeting **~ment** *n* **1** [C;U] (act of) moving: *Police are watching his movements.* (= activities) **2** [C] group of people in a united effort: *the trade-union movement* — see also WOMEN'S MOVEMENT **3** [C] separate part of a large piece of music

move in *phr vi* **1** take possession of a new home **2** (prepare to) take control, attack, etc.

move off *phr vi* leave

move on *phr v* **1** *vi* change (to something new) **2** *vi/t* go away to another place or position

move out *phr vi* leave one's former home

move over *phr vi* change position in order to make room for someone or something else

move[2] *n* **1** change of position or place, esp. in games like CHESS **2** set of actions to bring about a result: *new moves to settle the dispute* **3 get a move on** *infml* hurry up **4 make a move: a** (start to) leave **b** begin to take action **5 on the move: a** travelling about **b** having started to move or happen

mov·ie /'muːvi/ *n esp. AmE for* FILM (2) **movies** *n* [*the* + P] *esp. AmE for* CINEMA

mow /məʊ/ *vt* **mowed, mowed** *or* **mown** /məʊn/ cut (grass, corn. etc.) ~**er** *n*

mow down *phr vt* knock down or kill, esp. in large numbers

MP /ˌem 'piː/ *n* **1** Member of Parliament **2** (member of) the MILITARY police

mpg *written abbrev. for:* miles per GALLON

mph *written abbrev. for:* miles per hour

Mr /'mɪstə^r/ *n* (ordinary man's title): *Mr Smith*

Mrs /'mɪsɪz/ *n* (married woman's title)

Ms /mɪz, məz/ *n* (unmarried or married woman's title)

Mt *written abbrev. for:* MOUNT²

much¹ /mʌtʃ/ *adv* **1** a lot: *much better* | *much too small* **2** to the stated degree: *I liked it very much.* | *She would so much like to go.* **3** in most ways: *much the same as usual* **4** much as although

much² *determiner, pron* **more, most 1** large amount or part (of): *He gave me too much cake.* | *How much is it?* (= What does it cost?) | *I didn't get much.* | (fig.) *I don't think much of that.* (= I have a low opinion of it) **2** I thought as much I had expected that. **3** make much of: a treat as important b understand **4** much as although **5** not much of a not a very good **6** not up to much not very good **7** so much for that is the end of **8** too much for too difficult for

muck¹ /mʌk/ *n* [U] **1** dirt **2** worthless or improper material **3** MANURE ~**y** *adj*

muck² *v*

muck about/around *phr vi esp. BrE* **1** behave in a silly way **2** treat without consideration

muck in *phr vi* join in work or activity (with others)

muck up *phr vt* **1** spoil or do wrong **2** make dirty

muck-rak-ing /'mʌk-reɪkɪŋ/ *n* [U] *derog* finding and telling unpleasant stories about well-known people **–ing** *adj* –**er** *n*

mu-cous mem-brane /ˌ·· '··/ *n* [U] smooth wet skin, as inside the mouth

mu-cus /'mjuːkəs/ *n* [U] slippery body liquid, as produced in the nose

mud /mʌd/ *n* [U] **1** very wet earth **2** one's name is mud one is spoken badly of after causing trouble ~**dy** *adj*

mud-dle¹ /'mʌdl/ *n* state of confusion and disorder

muddle² *vt* **1** put into disorder **2** confuse the mind of

muddle along *phr vi* continue confusedly, with no plan

muddle through *phr vi* succeed in spite of having no plan or good method

mud-guard /'mʌdɡɑːd‖-ɑːrd/ *n* protective cover over a cycle wheel

mud-pack /'mʌdpæk/ *n* health treatment in which mud is put on the face

mues-li /'mjuːzli/ *n* [U] breakfast dish of grain, nuts, fruit, etc.. with milk

muff¹ /mʌf/ *n* fur or cloth cover to keep the hands or ears warm

muff² *vt* spoil a chance to do (something) well

muf-fle /'mʌfəl/ *vt* make (sound) less easily heard

muf-fler /'mʌflə^r/ *n* **1** scarf worn to keep one's neck warm **2** *AmE for* SILENCER

mug¹ /mʌɡ/ *n* **1 a** large straight-sided drinking cup with a handle **b** the contents of this: *a mug of tea* **2** *BrE sl* foolish person **3** *sl* face

mug² *vt* -**gg**- rob violently ~**ger** *n*

mug-gy /'mʌɡi/ *adj* (of weather) unpleasantly warm with heavy wet air

mug-wump /'mʌɡ-wʌmp/ *n AmE derog* person who tries to be independent of the leaders in politics

Mu-ham-ma-dan /mʊ'hæmɪdən, mə-/ *adj, n* Muslim

mu-lat-to /mjuː'lætəʊ‖mʊ-/ *n* -**tos** *or* -**toes** *lit* person with one black parent and one white one

mule /mjuːl/ *n* animal that is the young of a donkey and a horse **mul-ish** *adj* unwilling to change or agree; STUBBORN

mull /mʌl/ *vt* heat (wine) with sugar, SPICEs, etc.

mull over *phr vt* consider carefully

mul-ti-far-i-ous /ˌmʌltɪ'feəriəs/ *adj fml* of many different types

mul-ti-lat-er-al /ˌmʌltɪ'lætərəl/ *adj* including more than 2 groups, countries, etc. ~**ly** *adv*

mul-ti-na-tion-al /ˌmʌltɪ'næʃənəl◂/ *adj* having factories, offices, etc., in many different countries **multinational** *n*

mul-ti-ple /'mʌltɪpəl/ *adj* of many different types or parts ◆ *n* number which contains a smaller number an exact number of times

multiple scle-ro-sis /ˌ···· ·'··/ *n* [U] serious nerve disease in which one can no longer control one's bodily movements and actions

mul-ti-pli-ci-ty /ˌmʌltɪ'plɪsɪti/ *n* [S;U] large number or great variety

mul-ti-ply /'mʌltɪplaɪ/ *v* **1** *vt* add (a number) to itself the stated number of times: *2 multiplied by 3 is 6.* **2** *vi/t* increase in number or amount **3** *vi* breed –**plication** /,mʌltɪpləˈkeɪʃən/ n [C;U]

mul-ti-tude /'mʌltɪtjuːd‖-tuːd/ n **1** large number **2** large crowd

mum [1] /mʌm/ n mother

mum [2] adj infml not saying or telling anything: *Mum's the word.* (= silence must/will be kept about this)

mum-ble /'mʌmbəl/ vi/t speak or say unclearly

mum-bo jum-bo /,mʌmbəʊ 'dʒʌmbəʊ/ n [U] derog meaningless talk or actions, esp. in religion

mum-mi-fy /'mʌmɪfaɪ/ vt preserve as in MUMMY[2]

mum-my [1] /'mʌmi/ n BrE (child's word for) mother

mummy [2] n dead body preserved from decay, esp. in ancient Egypt

mumps /mʌmps/ n [U] infectious illness with swelling in the throat

munch /mʌntʃ/ vi/t eat (something hard) with a strong jaw movement

mun-dane /mʌnˈdeɪn/ adj ordinary; with nothing exciting or interesting in it

mu-ni-ci-pal /mjuːˈnɪsəpəl‖mjuː-/ adj of a town or its local government

mu-ni-ci-pal-i-ty /mjuː,nɪsəˈpælɪti‖ mjuː-/ n town, city, etc., with its own local government

mu-nif-i-cent /mjuːˈnɪfɪsənt‖mjuː-/ adj fml very generous –**cence** n [U]

mu-ni-tions /mjuːˈnɪʃənz‖mjuː-/ n [P] bombs, guns, etc.; war supplies

mu-ral /'mjʊərəl/ n painting done directly on a wall

mur-der /'mɜːdə‖'mɜːr-/ n [C;U] **1** crime of killing someone intentionally **2** very difficult or tiring experience — see also BLUE MURDER ♦ vt kill illegally and intentionally —**er** n —**ous** adj **1** intending or likely to cause murder **2** violent (in appearance)

murk-y /'mɜːki‖'mɜːr-/ adj unpleasantly dark

mur-mur /'mɜːmə‖'mɜːr-/ n **1** [C] soft low continuous sound **2** [S] complaint ♦ vi/t make or express in a murmur: *She murmured her approval.*

mus-cle [1] /'mʌsəl/ n **1** [C;U] (one of) the pieces of elastic material in the body which can tighten to produce movement **2** [U] strength **3 not move a muscle** stay quite still

muscle [2] v **muscle in** phr vi force one's way into (esp.) a group activity, so as to gain a share in what is produced

muscle-bound /'··· ·/ adj having large stiff muscles

mus-cu-lar /'mʌskjʊlə‖-lər/ adj **1** of muscles **2** with large muscles; strong

muse [1] /mjuːz/ vi think deeply

muse [2] n **1** (often cap.) any of 9 ancient Greek goddesses representing an art or science **2** force or person that

seems to help someone write, paint, etc.

mu-se-um /mjuːˈzɪəm‖mjuː-/ n building where objects of historic, scientific, or artistic interest are kept and shown

mush /mʌʃ/ n [U] soft mass of half-liquid, half-solid material —**y** adj

mush-room /'mʌʃrʊm, -rʊm/ n type of FUNGUS that is often eaten ♦ vi grow and develop fast

mu-sic /'mjuːzɪk/ n [U] **1** sounds arranged in patterns, usu. with tunes **2** art of making music **3** printed representation of music **4 face the music** admit to blame, responsibility, etc., and accept the results, esp. punishment or difficulty —**ian** /mjuːˈzɪʃən‖ mjuː-/ n

mu-si-cal /'mjuːzɪkəl/ adj **1** of music **2** skilled at music ♦ n play or film with songs and usu. dances —**ly** /-kli/ adv

musical chairs /,··· '·/ n [U] party game in which people have to find seats when the music stops

music hall /'·· ·/ n [C;U] (in Britain in former times) (theatre for) performances of songs, jokes, acts of skill, etc.

musk /mʌsk/ n [U] strong-smelling substance used in PERFUMEs —**y** adj

mus-ket /'mʌskɪt/ n early type of long-barrelled gun

Mus-lim /'mʌzlɪm, 'mʊz-, 'mʌs-/ n, adj (follower) of the religion started by Mohammed

mus-lin /'mʌzlɪn/ n [U] very fine thin cotton

mus-sel /'mʌsəl/ n sea animal with a black shell, often eaten

must /məst; strong mʌst/ vi 3rd person sing. **must 1** (shows what is necessary): *It's an order; you must obey.* **2** (shows what is likely): *You must be cold.* ♦ n something that should be done, seen, etc.

mus-tache /məˈstɑːʃ‖'mʌstæʃ/ n AmE for MOUSTACHE

mus-tard /'mʌstəd‖-ərd/ n [U] hot-tasting yellow substance made from a plant and usu. eaten with meat

mus-ter /'mʌstə‖/ vt gather; collect

must-n't /'mʌsənt/ short for: must not

must-y /'mʌsti/ adj with an unpleasant smell as if old –**iness** n [U]

mu-tant /'mjuːtənt/ n strangely-shaped creature

mu-ta-tion /mjuːˈteɪʃən/ n [C;U] (example or result of) a process of change in living cells, causing a new part or type

mute /mjuːt/ adj not speaking or spoken; silent ♦ n **1** person who cannot speak **2** object put on or in a musical instrument to make it sound softer ~**ly** *adv* **muted** *adj* (of sound or colour) softer than usual

mu·ti·late /'mjuːtḁleɪt/ *vt* wound and make ugly or useless **–lation** /ˌmjuːtḁ'leɪʃən/ *n* [C;U]

mu·ti·neer /ˌmjuːtḁ'nɪər, -tən-/ *n* person who mutinies

mu·ti·ny /'mjuːtḁni, -təni/ *n* [C;U] (an example of) the act of taking power from the person in charge, esp. on a ship **–nous** *adj* 1 taking part in a mutiny 2 angrily disobedient **–nously** *adv* ♦ *vi* take part in a mutiny

mutt /mʌt/ *n* dog of no particular breed

mut·ter /'mʌtər/ *vi/t* speak or say quietly and unclearly

mut·ton /'mʌtn/ *n* [U] meat from a sheep

mu·tu·al /'mjuːtʃuəl/ *adj* 1 equal for both sides: *their mutual dislike* (= they dislike each other) 2 shared by both: *mutual interests/friends* ~**ly** *adv*

mu·zak /'mjuːzæk/ *n* [U] *tdmk* recorded music played continuously though usu. not loudly in restaurants, etc.

muz·zle /'mʌzəl/ *n* 1 animal's nose and mouth 2 covering for an animal's muzzle, to stop it biting 3 front end of a gun barrel ♦ *vt* 1 put a muzzle on (an animal) 2 force to keep silent

my /maɪ/ *determiner* of me: *my parents* ♦ *interj* (expresses surprise)

my·o·pi·a /maɪ'əʊpiə/ *n* [U] inability to see distant objects clearly **–pic** /maɪ'ɒpɪk‖-'ɑːpɪk/ *adj*

myr·i·ad /'mɪriəd/ *n, adj* large and varied number (of)

my·self /maɪ'self/ *pron* 1 (*reflexive form of* I): *I hurt myself.* 2 (*strong form of* I): *I'll do it myself.* 3 (in) my usual state of mind or body: *I'm not myself today.* (= I feel ill) 4 (**all**) **by myself a** alone **b** without help 5 **to myself** not shared

mys·te·ry /'mɪstəri/ *n* 1 [C] something which cannot be explained or understood 2 [U] strange secret quality **–rious** /mɪ'stɪəriəs/ *adj* 1 unexplainable: *his mysterious disappearance* 2 hiding one's intentions **–riously** *adv* **–riousness** *n* [U]

mys·tic /'mɪstɪk/ *n* person who practises mysticism

mys·ti·cis·m /'mɪstḁsɪzəm/ *n* gaining of secret religious knowledge **mystical**, **mystic** *adj* **mystically** /-kli/ *adv*

mys·ti·fy /'mɪstḁfaɪ/ *vt* cause (someone) to wonder or be unsure: *her mystifying disappearance*

mys·tique /mɪ'stiːk/ *n* special quality that makes a person or thing seem mysterious and different, esp. causing admiration

myth /mɪθ/ *n* 1 story from ancient times 2 widely believed false story or idea ~**ical** *adj* 1 of myths 2 not real

my·thol·o·gy /mɪ'θɒlədʒi‖-'θɑː-/ *n* [U] myths: *heroes of Greek mythology* **–gical** /ˌmɪθə'lɒdʒɪkəl‖-'lɑː-/ *adj*

N

N, n /en/ the 14th letter of the English alphabet

N *written abbrev. for:* north(ern)

nab /næb/ *vt* **-bb-** *sl* 1 ARREST 2 get; take

na·dir /'neɪdɪər‖-dər/ *n* lowest point of misfortune, failure, etc.

naff /næf/ *adj* BrE *sl* (of things, ideas, behaviour, etc.) foolish or worthless, esp. in a way that shows a lack of good TASTE (3)

nag[1] /næg/ *vi/t* **-gg-** continuously complain (at) ~**ging** *adj* continuously hurting or worrying: *a nagging headache*

nag[2] *n* old horse

nail[1] /neɪl/ *n* 1 thin pointed piece of metal for hammering into a piece of wood 2 hard flat piece at the end of each finger and toe 3 **hard as nails** without any tender feelings 4 **hit the nail on the head** do or say exactly the right thing

nail[2] *vt* 1 fasten with a nail 2 *sl* catch; trap

nail down *phr vt* force to tell plans or wishes clearly

nail-bit·ing /'· ˌ··/ *adj* causing excitement and anxiety

nail var·nish /'· ˌ··/ *n* [U] liquid for giving a hard shiny surface on finger and toenails

na·ive /naɪ'iːv‖nɑː'iːv/ *adj* 1 without experience of life 2 too willing to believe without proof ~**ly** *adv* ~**ty** /naɪ'iːvti‖nɑː,iːvə'teɪ/ *n* [U] quality of being naive

na·ked /'neɪkḁd/ *adj* 1 with no clothes on 2 uncovered: *a naked light* | (fig.) *the naked truth* 3 **with the naked eye** without a microscope, TELESCOPE, etc. ~**ness** *n* [U]

nam·by-pam·by /ˌnæmbi 'pæmbi◂/ *adj* too weak, childish, or easily frightened

name /neɪm/ *n* 1 [C] what someone (or something) is called: *Her name is Mary.* 2 [C] usu. offensive title for someone: *to call someone names* 3

[S;C] opinion others have of one; REPUTATION: *The restaurant has a good name.* | *He made a name for himself* (= became famous) *in show business.* **4** [C] well-known person: *There were several big names* (= famous people) *at the party.* **5 in name only** in appearance or by title but not in fact **6 in the name of** by the right or power of: *Open up, in the name of the law!* **7 the name of the game** quality or object which is most necessary or important **8 to one's name** (esp. of money) as one's property: *He hasn't a penny to his name.* ◆ *vt* **1** give a name to: *They named their daughter Mary.* **2** say what the name of (someone or something) is: *Can you name this plant?* **3** appoint; choose ~**less** *adj* **1** whose name is not known or told **2** too terrible to mention —**ly** *adv* and that is/they are: *There are two factors, namely cost and availability.*

name-drop /'neɪmdrɒp‖-drɑːp/ *vi* -**pp**- mention famous people as if one knew them well ~**per** *n*

name-sake /'neɪmseɪk/ *n* person with the same name

nan-ny /'næni/ *n* woman employed to take care of children

nanny goat /'·· ·/ *n* female goat

nap[1] /næp/ *n* short sleep ◆ *vi* **1** have a nap **2 catch someone napping** find or take advantage of someone unprepared

nap[2] *n* soft furry surface of cloth

na-palm /'neɪpɑːm‖-pɑːm, -pɑːlm/ *n* [U] fiercely burning petrol jelly, used in bombs

nape /neɪp/ *n* back (of the neck)

nap-kin /'næpkɪn/ *n* piece of cloth or paper used at meals for protecting clothes and cleaning the lips and fingers

nap-py /'næpi/ *n BrE* cloth worn by a baby to take up waste matter from its body

nar-cis-sis-m /'nɑːsɪsɪzəm‖'nɑːr-/ *n* [U] too great love for one's own appearance or abilities —**sist** *n* –**sistic** /ˌnɑːsɪˈsɪstɪk‖ˌnɑːr-/ *adj*

nar-cot-ic /nɑːˈkɒtɪk‖nɑːrˈkɑː-/ *n* sleep-producing drug, harmful in large amounts

nar-rate /nəˈreɪt‖ˈnæreɪt, næˈreɪt, nə-/ *vt* tell (a story) or describe (events) —**rator** *n* –**ration** /nəˈreɪʃən‖ næ-, nə-/ *n* [C;U]

nar-ra-tive /'nærətɪv/ *n* **1** [C;U] *fml* story **2** [U] art of narrating

nar-row[1] /'nærəʊ/ *adj* **1** small from one side to the other **2** limited **3** only just successful: *a narrow escape* **4** not open to new ideas: *a narrow mind* — see also STRAIGHT AND NARROW ~**ly** *adv* only just ~**ness** *n* [U]

narrow[2] *vi/t* become or make narrower

narrow down *phr vt* reduce, limit

narrow-mind-ed /ˌ··ˈ··◁‖ˈ··ˌ·/ *adj* unwilling to respect the opinions of others when different from one's own ~**ness** *n* [U]

narrow squeak /ˌ·· ˈ·/ *n infml* CLOSE SHAVE

na-sal /'neɪzəl/ *adj* of the nose

nas-cent /'næsənt/ *adj* starting to develop

nas-ty /'nɑːsti‖'næsti/ *adj* **1** not nice; unpleasant **2** dangerous or painful: *a nasty cut* — see also VIDEO NASTY –**tily** *adv* –**tiness** *n* [U]

na-tion /'neɪʃən/ *n* (all the people belonging to) a country

na-tion-al /'næʃənəl/ *adj* **1** of or being a nation, esp. as opposed to **a** any of its parts: *a national newspaper* (= one read everywhere in the country) **b** another nation or other nations: *The national news comes after the international news.* **2** owned or controlled by the central government of a country: *a national bank* | *the National Health Service* ◆ *n* person from a usu. stated country —**ly** *adv* ~**ism** *n* [U] **1** love of and pride in one's country **2** desire to become a separate independent country —**ist** *adj, n* –**istic** /ˌnæʃənəˈlɪstɪk/ *adj* showing too great nationalism —**ity** /ˌnæʃəˈnælɪti/ *n* [C;U] membership of a nation by a person, esp. when abroad: *people of the same nationality*

na-tion-al-ize ‖ also -**ise** *BrE* /'næʃənəlaɪz/ *vt* take (a business or industry) into government control –**ization** /ˌnæʃənəlaɪˈzeɪʃən‖-nələ-/ *n* [U]

na-tion-wide /ˌneɪʃənˈwaɪd◁/ *adj, adv* happening over the whole country

na-tive /'neɪtɪv/ *adj* **1** of or being one's place of birth **2** found naturally in a place: *native species* **3** not learned: *native ability* ◆ *n* **1** person born in a place **2** local person, esp. non-European **3** native animal or plant

Na-tiv-i-ty /nəˈtɪvɪti/ *n* the birth of Christ

NATO /'neɪtəʊ/ *n* the North Atlantic Treaty Organisation; a group of countries which give military help to each other

nat-ter /'nætə/ *vi, n* [S] *BrE* (have) a long unimportant talk

nat-ty /'næti/ *adj sl* neat in appearance –**tily** *adv*: *nattily dressed*

nat-u-ral /'nætʃərəl/ *adj* **1** existing or happening ordinarily in the world, esp. not made by people: *death from natural causes* **2** usual; to be expected: *It's natural to feel nervous.* **3** existing from birth; not learned: *a natural talent* **4** having natural skill: *a natural musician* **5** ordinary; not AFFECTED ◆ *n* person with natural skill ~**ly** *adv* **1** as a natural skill: *Swimming comes naturally to her.* **2** in an ordinary way **3** of course ~**ist** *n* person who studies animals and plants ~**istic** /,nætʃərə'lıstık/ *adj* showing things exactly as they are: *a naturalistic painting* ~**istically** /-kli/ *adv*

natural his·to·ry /,··· '···/ *n* [U] study of animals and plants

nat·u·ral·ize ∥ also **-ise** *BrE* /'nætʃərəlaız/ *vt* make (someone born elsewhere) a citizen of a country **-iza·tion** /,nætʃərəlaı'zeıʃən/ *n* [C;U] share

natural se·lec·tion /,··· ·'··/ *n* [U] process by which creatures well suited to their conditions live and those less well suited die

na·ture /'neıtʃə'/ *n* **1** [U] everything that exists in the world independently of people, such as animals and plants, the land, and the weather **2** [C;U] character: *She has a very kind nature.* — see also SECOND NATURE **3** [S] *fml* kind; sort

naugh·ty /'nɔːti∥'nɔːti, 'nɑːti/ *adj* **1** (esp. of a child) behaving badly **2** sexually improper **-tily** *adv* **-tiness** *n* [U]

nau·se·a /'nɔːzıə, -sıə∥-zıə, -sə, -ʃə/ *n* feeling of sickness and desire to VOMIT **-ous** *adj* **-ate** /'nɔːzıeıt, -sı-∥-zı-, -ʃı-/ *vt* cause to feel nausea: (fig.) *nauseating hypocrisy*

nau·ti·cal /'nɔːtıkəl/ *adj* of ships or sailing

na·val /'neıvəl/ *adj* of a navy or warships

nave /neıv/ *n* long central part of a church

na·vel /'neıvəl/ *n* small sunken place in the middle of the stomach

nav·i·ga·ble /'nævɪgəbəl/ *adj* (of a river, etc.) deep and wide enough to let ships pass

nav·i·gate /'nævɪgeıt/ *vi/t* direct the course of (a ship, aircraft, etc., or a car) **-gator** *n* **-gation** /,nævɪ'geıʃən/ *n* [U]

na·vy /'neıvi/ *n* ships and sailors for fighting

navy blue /,·· '·◄/ *n* [U] dark blue

NB (used in writing) take notice of (this)

near /nıə'/ *adj* **1** at a short distance; close: *Christmas/My office is near.* **2 nearest and dearest** one's family ◆ *adv, prep* not far (from): *Don't go near the edge.* ◆ *vi/t* come closer (to) ~**ly** *adv* **1** almost **2 not nearly** not at all ~**ness** *n* [U]

near·by /,nıə'baı◄∥,nıər-/ *adj, adv* near

Near East /,· '·/ *n* [*the* + S] countries round the Eastern Mediterranean Sea, including Turkey and North Africa

near miss /,· '·/ *n* something that comes close to succeeding or (of a bomb) hitting

near·side /'nıəsaıd∥'nıər-/ *adj.* (on) the left-hand side, esp. of a vehicle

near·sight·ed /,nıə'saıtɪd◄∥ 'nıərsaıtɪd/ *adj esp. AmE* for SHORTSIGHTED

near thing /,· '·/ *n* something bad that nearly happened but didn't

neat /niːt/ *adj* **1** tidy **2** simple and effective: *a neat trick* **3** (of an alcoholic drink) with no water, etc., added ~**ly** *adv* ~**ness** *n* [U]

neb·u·lous /'nebjʊləs/ *adj* not clear, esp. in meaning or expression ~**ly** *adv*

ne·ces·sa·ry /'nesəsəri∥-seri/ *adj* that is needed or must be done **-rily** *adv* in a way that must be so: *Food that looks good doesn't necessarily taste good.*

ne·ces·si·tate /nɪ'sesɪteıt/ *vt fml* make necessary

ne·ces·si·ty /nɪ'sesɪti/ *n* **1** [S;U] condition of being necessary; need: *There's no necessity to stay.* **2** [C] something necessary, esp. for life

neck¹ /nek/ *n* **1** part of the body joining the head to the shoulders **2** part of a garment that goes round this **3** narrow part sticking out from a broader part: *the neck of a bottle* **4 get it in the neck** *infml* be severely scolded and punished **5 neck and neck** doing equally well in a competition **6 neck of the woods** *infml* area or part of the country **7 up to one's neck (in)** deeply concerned (with or by): *He's up to his neck in debt.* (= he owes a lot of money)

neck² *vi infml* kiss and CUDDLE

neck·lace /'nek-lɪs/ *n* decorative chain or string of jewels, worn round the neck

neck·tie /'nektaı/ *n esp. AmE* TIE (1)

nec·tar /'nektə'/ *n* [U] **1** sweet liquid collected by bees from flowers **2** sweet and good-tasting drink

née /neı/ *adj* (used to show a woman's name before she married): *Sheila Smith, née Brown*

need¹ /niːd/ *n* **1** [S;U] condition in which something necessary or desirable is missing: *a need for better medical services* **2** [S;U] necessary duty: *There's no need for you to come.* **3** [C] something one must have **4** [U] state of lacking food, money, etc.: *children in need* **5 if need be** if necessary ~**less** *adj* **1** unnecessary **2 needless**

to say of course ~**lessly** adv ~**y** adj poor

need² vt have a need for: REQUIRE To survive, plants need water.

need³ v, negative short form **needn't** have to; must: 'Was he late?' 'Need you ask!' (= of course he was)| Do you think I need go to the meeting?

nee-dle /'niːdl/ n 1 thin pointed pin or rod used in sewing or knitting (KNIT) 2 something long, thin, and sharp, such as a leaf, a pointer on a compass, or the part of a HYPODERMIC which is pushed into someone's skin 3 STYLUS ♦ vt annoy

nee-dle-work /'niːdlwɜːk‖-wɜːrk/ n [U] sewing

ne'er-do-well /'neə duː ˌwel‖ 'neər-/ n lit useless lazy person

ne-far-i-ous /nɪ'feəriəs/ adj fml wicked ~**ly** adv

ne-gate /nɪ'geɪt/ vt cause to have no effect **negation** /nɪ'geɪʃən/ n [U]

neg-a-tive /'negətɪv/ adj 1 saying or meaning 'no': a negative reply 2 not useful or encouraging: negative advice 3 less than zero 4 (of electricity) of the type carried by ELECTRONS ♦ n 1 word, expression, or statement saying or meaning 'no': The answer was in the negative. 2 film showing dark areas as light and light as dark

ne-glect /nɪ'glekt/ vt 1 give too little attention or care to 2 fail (to do something) esp. because of carelessness ♦ n [U] neglecting or being neglected ~**ful** adj tending to neglect things ~**fully** adv ~**fulness** n [U]

neg-li-gee /'neglɪʒeɪ‖ˌneglə'ʒeɪ/ n light thin NIGHTDRESS

neg-li-gent /'neglɪdʒənt/ adj not taking enough care ~**ly** adv —**gence** n [U]

neg-li-gi-ble /'neglɪdʒəbəl/ adj too slight or unimportant to worry about

ne-go-ti-a-ble /nɪ'gəʊʃiəbəl, -ʃə-/ adj 1 that can be settled or changed by being negotiated: 2 infml that can be travelled through, along, etc.

ne-go-ti-ate /nɪ'gəʊʃieɪt/ v 1 vi/t talk to someone in order to try to get (an agreement) 2 vt travel safely along or through —**ator** n —**ation** /nɪˌgəʊʃi'eɪʃən/ n [C;U]

Ne-gro /'niːgrəʊ/ **Negress** /'niːgrɪs/ fem. — n. -**es** tech or not polite black person

neigh /neɪ/ vi, n (make) the sound of a horse

neigh-bour BrE ‖ -**bor** AmE /'neɪbə˞/ n someone who lives near another ~**hood** n 1 area in a town 2 the area around a point or place: (fig.) a price in the neighbourhood of (= about) £500 ~**ing** adj (of a place) near ~**ly** adj friendly

nei-ther /'naɪðə˞‖'niː-/ determiner, pron, conj not one and not the other:

Neither book/Neither of the books is very good. ♦ adv also not: I can't swim and neither can my brother.

nem-e-sis /'neməsɪs/ n [U] lit (force bringing) just and unavoidable punishment

ne-o-clas-sic-al /ˌniːəʊ'klæsɪkəl/ adj done recently, but in the style of ancient Greece and Rome

ne-o-co-lo-ni-al-is-m /ˌniːəʊkə-'ləʊniəlɪzəm/ n [U] derog indirect control of smaller countries by more powerful ones

ne-o-lith-ic /ˌniːə'lɪθɪk/ adj of a period about 10,000 years ago

ne-ol-o-gis-m /niː'ɒlədʒɪzəm‖-'ɑːl-/ n new word or expression

ne-on /'niːɒn‖-ɑːn/ n [U] gas used in making bright electric lights

neph-ew /'nefjuː, 'nev-‖'nef-/ n son of one's brother or sister

nep-o-tis-m /'nepətɪzəm/ n [U] giving unfair favour and advantages to one's relations

Nep-tune /'neptjuːn‖-tuːn/ n the PLANET 8th in order from the sun

nerve /nɜːv‖nɜːrv/ n 1 [C] threadlike part in the body that carries feelings and messages to and from the brain 2 [U] courage: I meant to do it, but I lost my nerve. 3 [S;U] disrespectful rudeness: He had the nerve to say I was a fool! ♦ vt give courage to (someone, esp. oneself) **nerves** n [P] 1 great nervousness 2 **get on someone's nerves** make someone annoyed or bad-tempered **nervous** adj 1 a rather frightened b easily excited and worried 2 of the nerves: The brain is at the centre of the **nervous system**. **nervously** adv **nervousness** n [U]

nerve cen-tre /'· ˌ··/ n place from which a system, organization, etc., is controlled

nerve-rack-ing /'· ˌ··/ adj that causes great worry or fear

nervous break-down /ˌ·· '··/ n serious medical condition of deep worrying, anxiety, and tiredness which stops one working

nest /nest/ n 1 hollow place built or used by a bird as a home and a place to keep its eggs 2 group of similar objects which fit closely into or inside one another: a nest of tables ♦ vi build or use a nest

nest egg /'· ·/ n amount of money saved for special future use

nes-tle /'nesəl/ vi/t settle, lie, or put in a close comfortable position: She nestled down (into the big chair) and began to read.

nest-ling /'nestlɪŋ, 'neslɪŋ/ n very young bird

net¹ /net/ n [C;U] (piece of) material made of strings, wires, etc., tied together with regular spaces between

them: *the fisherman's nets* ♦ *vt* -tt-
catch in a net ~**ting** *n* string, wire,
etc., made into a net

net² also **nett** *adj* left after nothing
further is to be taken away: *a net profit*
♦ *vt* -tt- gain as a profit

net-ball /'netbɔːl/ *n* [U] women's
team game in which points are gained
by throwing a ball into a net

neth-er /'neðəʳ/ *adj lit* lower; under

net-tle /'netl/ *n* wild plant with stinging leaves

net-work¹ /'netwɜːk‖-wɜːrk/ *n* 1
large system of lines, wires, etc., that
cross or meet each other 2 group of
radio or television stations — see also
OLD-BOY NETWORK

network² *vi/t* connect (computers)
to form a NETWORK¹ (1), to share
information

neu-rol-o-gy /njʊˈrɒlədʒi‖nʊˈrɑː-/ *n*
[U] scientific study of nerves and their
diseases **-gist** *n*

neu-ro-sis /njʊˈrəʊsɪs‖nʊ-/ *n* **-ses** *a*
disorder of the mind in which one suffers from strong unreasonable fears
and has troubled relations with other
people **-rotic** /njʊˈrɒtɪk‖nʊˈrɑː-/ *adj*
of or suffering from a neurosis

neu-ter /'njuːtəʳ‖'nuː-/ *adj* (in grammar) belonging to the class of words
that mainly includes things rather
than males or females ♦ *vt* remove
part of the sex organs of (an animal)

neu-tral¹ /'njuːtrəl‖'nuː-/ *adj* 1 not
supporting either side in a war, argument, etc. 2 having no strong or
noticeable qualities: *a neutral colour*
~**ize** *vt* cause to have no effect ~**ity**
/njuːˈtrælɪti‖nuː-/ *n* [U]

neutral² *n* 1 [U] the position of a
car's GEARs in which the engine is not
connected with the wheels 2 [C] a neutral person or country

neu-tron /'njuːtrɒn‖'nuːtrɑːn/ *n* a
very small piece of matter that is part
of an atom and carries no electricity

nev-er /'nevəʳ/ *adv* not ever: *It never
snows in the desert.*

never-never /ˌ·· '··/ *n* **on the never-
never** *BrE sl* for on HIRE PURCHASE

nev-er-the-less /ˌnevəðəˈles‖-vər-/
adv in spite of that; yet: *It was a cold
day but nevertheless very pleasant.*

new /njuː‖nuː/ *adj* 1 only recently
made or begun: *a new film* 2 different
from the one before: *She's looking for
a new job.* 3 having only recently
arrived or started: *I'm new here.* 4 **new**
newly; recently: *a new-laid egg* 5 **new
to** just beginning to know about or do;
unfamiliar with ~**ly** *adv* that has just
happened or been done; recently: *a
newly-built house* ~**ness** *n* [U]

new blood /ˌ· '·/ *n* [U] new members
of a group, bringing new ideas,
ENERGY, etc.

new broom /ˌ· '·/ *n esp. BrE* newly
appointed person who is eager to
make changes

new-com-er /'njuːkʌməʳ‖'nuː-/ *n*
someone who has just arrived

new-fan-gled /ˌnjuːˈfæŋgəld◄‖
ˌnuː-/ *adj* new but neither necessary
nor better

new-ly-wed /'njuːliwed‖'nuː-/ *n*
recently married person

news /njuːz‖nuːz/ *n* 1 [U] facts that
are reported about a recent event: *a
piece of news* 2 [the+S] regular report
of recent events on radio or television

news-a-gent /'njuːzˌeɪdʒənt‖'nuːz-/
BrE ‖ **news dealer** /'· ˌ·ʳ/ *AmE* — *n*
someone who sells newspapers in a
shop

news-cast-er /'njuːzˌkɑːstəʳ‖'nuːz-
ˌkæ-/ also **newsreader** /-ˌriːdəʳ/ *BrE*
— *n* person who reads the news on
television

news-hound /'njuːzhaʊnd‖'nuːz-/ *n*
very eager newspaper reporter

news-pa-per /'njuːsˌpeɪpəʳ‖'nuːz-/
n paper printed with news, notices,
advertisements, etc., that comes out
every day or every week

new-speak /'njuːspiːk‖'nuː-/ *n* [U]
language whose meanings are slightly
changed to make people believe things
that are not quite true

news-print /'njuːzˌprɪnt‖'nuːz-/ *n*
[U] paper on which newspapers are
printed

news-wor-thy /'njuːz ˌwɜːði‖'nuːz
ˌwɜːrði/ *adj* important or interesting
enough to be reported as news

newt /njuːt‖nuːt/ *n* 4-legged animal
living both on land and water

new year /ˌ· '·/ *n (often caps.)* a year
which has just begun or will soon
begin

next /nekst/ *adj* 1 with nothing
before or between; nearest: *the house
next to mine* 2 the one following or
after: *I'm coming next week.* ♦ *adv* 1
just afterwards: *First, heat the oil;
next, add the onions.* 2 the next time:
when next we meet 3 **next to** almost:
next to impossible

next door /ˌ· '·/ *adv* 1 in the next
building: *She lives next door.* 2 **next
door to** almost the same as

NHS /ˌen entʃ 'es/ *n* [the] National
Health Service; the British system of
medical treatment for everyone, paid
for by taxes

nib /nɪb/ *n* pointed piece on the end
of a pen, out of which ink flows

nib-ble /'nɪbəl/ *vi/t* eat with small
bites ♦ *n* small bite

nice /naɪs/ *adj* 1 good; pleasant: *a
nice holiday* 2 showing or needing
careful understanding; SUBTLE: *a nice
distinction* 3 *infml* bad: *He got us into
a nice mess.* 4 **nice and** pleasantly; as

was wanted: *The soup was nice and hot.* ~**ly** *adv* ~**ness** *n* [U]

ni-ce-ty /'naɪsɪti/ *n* fine or delicate point; detail

niche /nɪtʃ, niːʃ‖nɪtʃ/ *n* 1 hollow place in a wall, where something is put 2 suitable place, job, etc.

nick[1] /nɪk/ *n* 1 small cut 2 *BrE infml* prison 3 **in the nick of time** only just in time; almost too late ♦ *vt* 1 make a small cut in 2 *BrE sl* ARREST 3 *BrE infml* steal

nick[2] *n* [U] *BrE sl* a stated condition: *The car's in good nick.*

nick-el /'nɪkəl/ *n* 1 [U] hard silver-white metal 2 [C] US 5-cent coin

nick-name /'nɪkneɪm/ *n* informal name used instead of someone's real name ♦ *vt*: *They nicknamed him 'Baldy'.*

nic-o-tine /'nɪkətiːn/ *n* [U] poisonous chemical found in tobacco

niece /niːs/ *n* daughter of one's brother or sister

nif-ty /'nɪfti/ *adj infml* very good, attractive, or effective

nig-gard-ly /'nɪgədli‖-ər-/ *adj* very ungenerous

nig-gle /'nɪgəl/ *vi* be continually annoying or troubling

night /naɪt/ *n* 1 [C;U] dark part of the day, between sunrise and sunset: *Did you have a good night?* (= sleep well) 2 **at night:** **a** during the night **b** at the end of the day 3 **by night** during the night 4 **make a night of it** spend all or most of the night in enjoyment 5 **night after night** every night 6 **night and day** also **day and night** — all the time

night-cap /'naɪtkæp/ *n* drink before going to bed

night-club /'naɪtklʌb/ *n* restaurant open late at night where people may drink, dance, and see a show

night-dress /'naɪtdres/ also **nightie** /'naɪti/ -- *n* woman's garment worn in bed

night-fall /'naɪtfɔːl/ *n* [U] beginning of night

nigh-tin-gale /'naɪtɪŋgeɪl/ *n* bird with a beautiful song

night-life /'naɪtlaɪf/ *n* [U] evening entertainment or social activity

night-ly /'naɪtli/ *adj, adv* (happening, done, etc.) every night

night-mare /'naɪtmeər/ *n* 1 frightening dream 2 terrible experience or event

night-shirt /'naɪt-ʃɜːt‖-ʃɜːrt/ *n* man's long loose shirt worn in bed

night watch-man /ˌ· '··/ *n* man who guards a building at night

ni-hi-lis-m /'naɪɪlɪzəm/ *n* [U] belief that nothing has meaning or value -**ist** *n*

nil /nɪl/ *n* nothing; zero

nim-ble /'nɪmbəl/ *adj* 1 quick, light, and neat in movement 2 quick in thought or understanding -**bly** *adv* ~**ness** *n* [U]

nine /naɪn/ *determiner, n, pron* 9

ninth *determiner, adv, n, pron* 9th

nine days' won-der /ˌ· '··/ *n* event or event that causes excitement for a short time and is then forgotten

nine-pins /'naɪn.pɪnz/ *n* like ninepins (falling or being destroyed) quickly and in large numbers

nine-teen /ˌnaɪn'tiːn◂/ *determiner, n, pron* 19 ~**th** *determiner, adv, n, pron* 19th

nine-ty /'naɪnti/ *determiner, n, pron* 90 -**tieth** *determiner, adv, n, pron* 90th

nip /nɪp/ *v* -**pp-** 1 *vt* catch in a sharp tight usu. painful hold 2 *vi BrE* go quickly; hurry 3 **nip something in the bud** stop something before it has properly started ♦ *n* [S] 1 sharp tight hold or bite 2 coldness: *a nip in the air*

nip-per /'nɪpər/ *n infml* child

nip-ple /'nɪpəl/ *n* round pointed dark-skinned area on a breast

nip-py /'nɪpi/ *adj* 1 cold 2 quick in movement

nir-va-na /nɪə'vɑːnə, nɜː-‖nɪər-, nɜːr-/ *n* [U] (*usu. cap.*) (in Buddhism and Hinduism) calm state of union with the spirit of the universe

nit /nɪt/ *n BrE* silly person

nit-pick-ing /'nɪt.pɪkɪŋ/ *n* [U] habit of paying too much attention to small unimportant details **nitpicking** *adj*

ni-trate /'naɪtreɪt, -trət/ *n* chemical used esp. to improve the soil for growing crops

ni-tric ac-id /ˌ· '··/ *n* [U] powerful acid which destroys other materials

ni-tro-gen /'naɪtrədʒən/ *n* [U] gas that forms most of the Earth's air

ni-tro-gly-ce-rine /ˌnaɪtrəʊˈglɪsəriːn, -trə-, -rɪn‖-rən/ *n* [U] powerful liquid explosive

nit-ty-grit-ty /ˌnɪti 'grɪti/ *n* **get down to the nitty-gritty** *sl* deal with the difficult, practical, and important part of a matter

nit-wit /'nɪt.wɪt/ *n* silly person

no /nəʊ/ *adv* 1 (used for refusing or disagreeing): *'Do you like it?' 'No!'* 2 not any: *He felt no better.* ♦ *determiner* 1 not a; not any: *She felt no fear.* | *I'm no fool!* 2 (shows what is not allowed): *No smoking* (on a sign) ♦ *n* answer or decision of no: *a clear no*

no. *written abbrev. for:* number

No. 10 NUMBER TEN

nob-ble /'nɒbəl‖'nɑː-/ *vt BrE sl* 1 prevent (a racehorse) from winning by using drugs 2 get or persuade dishonestly

no·bil·i·ty /nəʊˈbɪləti, nə-/ n [U] **1** people of high social rank with titles **2** state of being noble

no·ble /ˈnəʊbəl/ adj **1** of high moral quality; fine and unselfish **2** grand **3** of high social rank ♦ n lord in former times **–bly** adv

no·ble·man /ˈnəʊbəlmən/ , . **–woman** /-, wʊmən/ fem. — n **–men** /-mən/ member of the nobility

no·bod·y /ˈnəʊbədi‖-, bɑːdi, -bədi/ pron no one ♦ n unimportant person

no-claim bo·nus /ˌ· · ˈ· ·/ n reduction in the regular payments made to an insurance company (esp. for motor vehicles) given to someone who has not made any claims within a particular period

noc·tur·nal /nɒkˈtɜːnl‖nɑːkˈtɜːr-/ adj happening or active at night

nod /nɒd‖nɑːd/ vi/t **-dd-** bend (one's head) forward and down, esp. to show agreement or give a sign ♦ n act of nodding

nod off phr vi fall asleep unintentionally

nod·ding ac·quaint·ance /ˌ· · ·ˈ· ·/ n [S] slight familiarity

nod·ule /ˈnɒdjuːl‖ˈnɑːdʒuːl/ n small round lump or swelling

noise /nɔɪz/ n [C;U] sound, esp. loud and unpleasant — see also BIG NOISE

noisy adj making a lot of noise **nois·ily** adv **noisiness** n [U]

no·mad /ˈnəʊmæd/ n member of a tribe that does not settle long in one place **~ic** /nəʊˈmædɪk/ adj

no-man's-land /ˈ· · ·, ·/ n [S;U] land no one owns or controls, esp. between two armies or borders

no·men·cla·ture /nəʊˈmeŋklətʃə‖ˈnəʊmənkleɪ-/ n [C;U] system of naming things

nom·i·nal /ˈnɒmənəl‖ˈnɑː-/ adj **1** not really what the name suggests: He's only the nominal head of the business; his son really runs it. **2** (of an amount of money) very small **3** of or being a noun **~ly** adv

nom·i·nate /ˈnɒməneɪt‖ˈnɑː-/ vt to suggest officially that (someone) should be chosen or elected **–nation** /ˌnɒməˈneɪʃən‖ˌnɑː-/ n [C;U]

nom·i·nee /ˌnɒməˈniː‖ˌnɑː-/ n person who has been nominated

non·a·ligned /ˌnɒn-əˈlaɪnd‖ˌnɑːn-/ adj (of a country) not supporting any particular powerful nation

non·cha·lant /ˈnɒnʃələnt‖ˌnɑːnʃəˈlɑːnt/ adj calm and usu. uninterested **~ly** adv **–lance** n [U]

non-com·mis·sion·ed of·fi·cer /ˌnɒnkəˌmɪʃənd ˈɒfɪsə‖ˌnɑːn-; -ˈɔːf-, -ˈɑːf-/ n person in the army, navy, etc., below the rank of officer but with some power to command others

non-com·mit·tal /ˌnɒnkəˈmɪtl‖ˌnɑːn-/ adj not showing what you really think or intend **~ly** adv

non-con·form·ist /ˌnɒnkənˈfɔːmɪst◂‖ˌnɑːnkənˈfɔːr-/ n, adj **1** (person) not following customary ways of living, thinking, etc. **2** (cap.) (member) of a Christian group separated from the Church of England

non-de·script /ˈnɒndə̩skrɪpt‖ˌnɑːndəˈskrɪpt/ adj very ordinary-looking and dull

none /nʌn/ pron not any: She has several, but I have none. | None of the wine was drinkable. ♦ adv **1** none the not at all: My car is none the worse for (= not damaged by) its accident. **2** none too not very

non-en·ti·ty /nɒˈnentəti‖nɑː-/ n person without much ability, character, or importance

none-the-less /ˌnʌnðəˈles◂/ adv in spite of that; NEVERTHELESS

non-e·vent /ˌ· ·ˈ·/ n something much less important, interesting, etc., than expected

non-fic·tion /ˌnɒnˈfɪkʃən‖ˌnɑːn-/ n [U] writing about facts, not stories

no-non·sense /ˌ· ˈ· ·/ adj practical and direct

non·plus /ˌnɒnˈplʌs‖ˌnɑːn-/ vt **-ss-** to surprise (someone) so much that they do not know what to think or do

non·sense /ˈnɒnsəns‖ˈnɑːnsens/ n [U] **1** meaningless words **2** foolish words, ideas, or actions **–sensical** /nɒnˈsensɪkəl‖nɑːn-/ adj foolish

non se·qui·tur /nɒn ˈsekwɪtə‖ˌnɑːn-/ n statement that does not follow by correct reasoning from what has been said before

non-start·er /ˌnɒnˈstɑːtə‖ˌnɑːnˈstɑːr-/ n BrE person or idea with no chance of success

non-stick /ˌnɒnˈstɪk◂‖ˌnɑːn-/ adj with a special surface that food will not stick to when cooked

non-stop /ˌnɒnˈstɒp◂‖ˌnɑːnˈstɑːp◂/ adj, adv without a pause or interruption

noo·dle /ˈnuːdl/ n long thin piece of pasta made from flour, cooked in soup or boiling water

nook /nʊk/ n **1** sheltered private place **2** nooks and crannies hidden or little-known places

noon /nuːn/ n [U] 12 o'clock in the daytime

no one /ˈ· ·/ pron not anyone; no person

noose /nuːs/ n ring formed by the end of a rope, which closes tighter as it is pulled

nor /nɔːr/ conj **1** (used after neither or not) also not; or: neither hot nor cold — just warm **2** and also not: 'I don't like it.' 'Nor do I.'

norm /nɔːm‖nɔːrm/ n usual or average way of happening or behaving

nor-mal /'nɔːməl‖'nɔːr-/ adj according to what is usual, expected, or average ~**ly** adv: *Normally I go to bed at 11 o'clock.* ~**ity** || also ~**cy** AmE — n [U]

nor-mal-ize || also **-ise** BrE /'nɔːməlaɪz‖'nɔːr-/ vi/t (cause to) become normal, esp. to bring or come back to a good or friendly state **-ization** n [U]

north /nɔːθ‖nɔːrθ/ n (often cap.) direction which is on the left of a person facing the rising sun ♦ adj 1 in the north 2 (of wind) from the north ♦ adv 1 towards the north 2 **up north** to or in the north ~**ward** adj, adv

north-east /ˌnɔːθ'iːst◂‖ˌnɔːrθ-/ n, adj, adv (direction) halfway between north and east ~**ern** adj

nor-ther-ly /'nɔːðəli‖'nɔːrðərli/ adj towards or in the north

nor-thern /'nɔːðən‖'nɔːrðərn/ adj of the north part of the world or of a country ~**er** n person who lives in or comes from the northern part of a country

northwest /ˌnɔːθ'west◂‖ˌnɔːrθ-/ n, adj, adv (direction) halfway between north and west ~**ern** adj

nos. written abbrev. for: numbers

nose /nəʊz/ n 1 [C] the part of the face above the mouth that is used for breathing and smelling 2 [C] (pointed) front end: *the nose of the rocket* 3 [S] ability to find out: *I have a nose for trouble. | Just follow your nose.* (= use this ability) 4 [C] too great an interest in things which do not concern one: *Stop* **poking your nose** *into my affairs!* 5 **get up someone's nose** BrE infml annoy someone very much 6 **keep one's nose clean** keep out of trouble 7 **pay through the nose (for)** pay a great deal too much money (for) 8 **put someone's nose out of joint** make someone jealous by taking their place as the centre of attention 9 **turn one's nose up at** consider (something) not good enough to enjoy 10 **under someone's (very) nose** quite openly in front of someone ♦ vi 1 move ahead slowly and carefully 2 try to find out about things that do not concern you

nose-bleed /'nəʊzbliːd/ n case of bleeding from the nose

nose-cone /'nəʊzkəʊn/ n pointed front part of a spacecraft or MISSILE

nose-dive /'nəʊzdaɪv/ vi 1 (of a plane) drop suddenly, front end first 2 fall suddenly and greatly: *Prices nosedived.* **nosedive** n

nose-gay /'nəʊzgeɪ/ n lit small bunch of flowers

nosh /nɒʃ‖nɑːʃ/ n [S;U] BrE sl meal, food

nos-tal-gia /nɒ'stældʒə‖nɑː-/ n [U] fondness for past times **-gic** adj

nos-tril /'nɒstrəl‖'nɑː-/ n either of the 2 openings in the nose

nos-y, nosey /'nəʊzi/ adj interested in things that do not concern one

nosy park-er /ˌ·· '··/ n BrE infml nosy person

not /nɒt‖nɑːt/ adv 1 (used for showing the opposite meaning): *He's happy, but I'm not. | It's a cat, not a dog! | Will he come, or not?| Not one* (= none) *remained.* 2 **not at all** (a polite answer to thanks) 3 **not that** I don't mean that: *Not that it matters, but where were you last night?*

no-ta-ble /'nəʊtəbəl/ adj unusual or good enough to be especially noticed **-bly** adv particularly

no-ta-ry /'nəʊtəri/ n public official who watches the signing of written statements and makes them official

no-ta-tion /nəʊ'teɪʃən/ n [C;U] system of signs for writing something down: *musical notation*

notch /nɒtʃ‖nɑːtʃ/ n V-shaped cut ♦ vt 1 make a notch in 2 win: *We notched up our third victory.*

note /nəʊt/ n 1 [C] short written record to remind one of something 2 [C] short piece of additional information in a book 3 [C] short informal letter 4 [C] piece of paper money 5 [C] (sign representing) a musical sound 6 [S] stated quality or feeling: *a note of anger in his voice* 7 [U] fml fame; importance: *a composer of some note* 8 **compare notes** tell one's experiences and opinions of something to 9 **take note of** pay attention to ♦ vt 1 record in writing: *The policeman noted down his address.* 2 notice and remember **noted** adj famous

note-book /'nəʊtbʊk/ n book of plain paper in which one writes NOTES¹ (1)

note-pa-per /'nəʊtˌpeɪpər/ n [U] paper for writing letters on

note-wor-thy /'nəʊtˌwɜːði‖-ɜːr-/ adj NOTABLE

noth-ing /'nʌθɪŋ/ pron 1 not anything: *There's nothing in this box — it's empty.* 2 something of no importance: *My debts are nothing to* (= much less than) *his.* 3 **for nothing**: a free **b** with no good result 4 **nothing but** nothing other than: *He's nothing but a criminal.* 5 **nothing doing**: a I won't! **b** no result, interest, etc. 6 **nothing for it** no other way 7 **nothing like** not nearly: *It's nothing like as cold as yesterday.* 8 **think nothing of** treat as easy or unimportant

no-tice /'nəʊtɪs/ n 1 [C] written or printed sign giving information 2 [U] information that something is going to happen; warning: *The rules may be* *changed without notice.* **3** [U] attention: *Don't* **take any notice** *of* (= pay no attention to) *him.* ♦ *vi/t* see, hear, etc., so as to be conscious and remember: *She was wearing a new dress, but he didn't even notice (it).* **~able** *adj* big enough to be noticed **~ably** *adv*

no·ti·fy /'nəʊtɪfaɪ/ *vt* tell (someone), esp. formally **–fication** /ˌnəʊtɪfɪˈkeɪʃən/ *n* [U]

no·tion /'nəʊʃən/ *n* idea; opinion

no·to·ri·e·ty /ˌnəʊtəˈraɪəti/ *n* [U] state of being notorious

no·to·ri·ous /nəʊˈtɔːriəs, nə-/ *adj* famous for something bad: *a notorious liar* **~ly** *adv*

not·with·stand·ing /ˌnɒtwɪθˈstændɪŋ, -wɪð-‖ˌnɑːt-/ *adv fml* in spite of that

nou·gat /'nuːgɑː‖-gət/ *n* [U] sweet made of sugar, nuts, fruit, etc.

nought /nɔːt/ *n BrE* zero

noun /naʊn/ *n* word that is the name of a thing, quality, action, etc., and can be used as the subject or object of a verb

nour·ish /'nʌrɪʃ‖'nɜːrɪʃ, 'nʌ-/ *vt* 1 keep alive and healthy by giving food 2 keep (a feeling, plan, etc.) alive **~ment** *n* [U] food

nous /naʊs‖nuːs/ *n* [U] *BrE* good practical judgment

nou·velle cuis·ine /ˌnuːvel kwiːˈziːn/ *n* [U] style of cooking that tries to bring out the true taste of food and to present it attractively, often thought of as being served in amounts which are (too) small

nov·el¹ /'nɒvəl‖'nɑː-/ *n* long written story **~ist** *n* novel writer

novel² *adj* new and rather clever

nov·el·ty /'nɒvəlti‖'nɑː-/ *n* 1 [U] interesting newness 2 [C] something new and unusual 3 [C] small cheap object, usu. not very useful

No·vem·ber /nəʊˈvembəʳ, nə-/ *n* the 11th month of the year

nov·ice /'nɒvɪs‖'nɑː-/ *n* person who has just begun and has no experience

now /naʊ/ *adv* 1 at this present time: *He used to be fat, but now he's slim.* 2 next; at once: *Now for* (= now we will have) *the next question.* 3 (used for attracting attention or giving a warning): *Now then, what's all this?* 4 **(every) now and again/then** at times; sometimes ♦ *conj* because: *Now (that) you've arrived, we can begin.*

now·a·days /'naʊədeɪz/ *adv* in these modern times

no way /ˌ·'·/ *adv, interj sl* no; certainly not

no·where /'nəʊweəʳ/ *adv* 1 not anywhere 2 **nowhere near** not at all near or nearly

nox·ious /'nɒkʃəs‖'nɑːk-/ *adj* harmful; poisonous

noz·zle /'nɒzəl‖'nɑː-/ *n* short tube at the end of a pipe for controlling the flow of a liquid

nth /enθ/ *adj* **to the nth degree** to the highest, greatest, furthest, etc., degree or form: *dull to the nth degree*

nu·ance /'njuːɑːns‖'nuː-/ *n* slight delicate difference in meaning, colour, etc.

nub /nʌb/ *n* most important point

nu·bile /'njuːbaɪl‖'nuːbəl/ *adj* (of a young woman) sexually attractive

nu·cle·ar /'njuːkliəʳ‖'nuː-/ *adj* being, using, or producing the great power you get by breaking up atoms: *nuclear energy|nuclear warfare* (= with nuclear bombs)

nuclear fam·i·ly /ˌ···ˈ···/ *n* family unit that consists only of husband, wife, and children, without grandmothers, uncles, etc.

nuclear win·ter /ˌ···ˈ···/ *n* period which, according to scientists, would follow a nuclear explosion, when there would be no light, warmth, or growth because the sun would be hidden by dust

nu·cle·us /'njuːkliəs‖'nuː-/ *n* **-clei** /-klaɪ/ 1 central part of a an atom b a CELL (2) 2 original part round which the rest is built

nude /njuːd/ *adj* with no clothes on ♦ *n* 1 (piece of art showing) a nude person 2 **in the nude** with no clothes on

nudge /nʌdʒ/ *vt* push gently, esp. with the elbow **nudge** *n*

nud·ism /'njuːdɪzəm‖'nuː-/ *n* [U] practice of going around with no clothes on, usu. in a special place (**nudist camp**) **nudist** *n*

nu·di·ty /'njuːdɪti‖'nuː-/ *n* [U] state of being nude

nug·get /'nʌgɪt/ *n* small rough lump: *gold nuggets|(fig.) a nugget of information*

nui·sance /'njuːsəns‖'nuː-/ *n* annoying person, animal, thing, or situation

nuke /njuːk/ *vt infml* attack with NUCLEAR weapons

null and void /ˌ· · '·/ *adj* having no legal effect

nul·li·fy /'nʌlɪfaɪ/ *vt* cause to have no effect

numb /nʌm/ *adj* unable to feel: *fingers numb with cold* **numb** *vt* **~ness** *n* [U]

num·ber /'nʌmbəʳ/ *n* 1 [C] (written sign for) a member of the system used in counting and measuring: *1, 2 and 3 are numbers.* 2 [C;U] quantity; amount: *A large number of people came.* 3 [C] (copy of) a magazine printed at a particular time — see also BACK NUMBER 4 [C] piece of music 5 **have someone's number** have knowledge useful in annoying or defeating someone — see also E NUMBER, OPPO-SITE NUMBER ♦ *vt* 1 give a number to: *numbered pages* 2 reach as a total: *The audience numbered over 5000.* 3 *fml* include: *I number him among my friends.* 4 **someone's days are numbered** someone cannot continue or live much longer ~**less** *adj* too many to count

number one /,·· '·/ *n* 1 chief person or thing 2 oneself and no one else: *Look after number one.*

Number Ten /,·· '·/ *n* home of the British PRIME MINISTER, in London

nu·me·ral /'njuːmərəl‖'nuː-/ *n* sign that represents a number — see also ROMAN NUMERAL

nu·me·rate /'njuːmərət‖'nuː-/ *adj* able to calculate with numbers

nu·mer·i·cal /njuː'merɪkəl‖nuː-/ *adj* of or using numbers ~**ly** *adv*

nu·me·rous /'njuːmərəs‖'nuː-/ *adj* many

nun /nʌn/ *n* member of an all-female religious group that lives together ~**nery** *n* building where they live

nurse /nɜːs‖nɜrs/ *n* person who takes care of sick, hurt, or old people, esp. in hospital ♦ *vt* 1 take care of as or like a nurse 2 hold in the mind: *nurse a grudge* 3 handle carefully or lovingly: *He nursed the battered plane home.* 4 feed (a baby) with breast milk **nursing** *n* [U] job of being a nurse

nurse-maid /'nɜːsmeɪd‖'nɜrs-/ *n* woman employed to take care of a young child

nur·se·ry /'nɜːsəri‖'nɜrs-/ *n* 1 place where young children are taken care of 2 area where garden plants are grown to be sold

nursery rhyme /'··· ·/ *n* song or poem for young children

nursery school /'··· ·/ *n* school for young children of 2 to 5 years of age

nursing home /'·· ·/ *n* place where old or sick people can live and be looked after

nur·ture /'nɜːtʃəʳ‖'nɜr-/ *vt lit* give care and food to, so as to help development

nut /nʌt/ *n* 1 fruit with a hard shell and a softer dry seed inside which is eaten 2 small piece of metal with a hole through it for screwing onto a BOLT (2) 3 *sl* mad person 4 **a hard/tough nut to crack** a difficult question, person, etc., to deal with 5 **do one's nut** *infml* be very worried and/or angry 6 **off one's nut** *sl* mad **nuts** *adj sl* mad ~**ty** *adj* 1 like or full of nuts 2 *sl* mad

nut·case /'nʌtkeɪs/ *n sl* mad person

nut-crack·er /'nʌt,krækəʳ/ *n* tool for cracking the shell of a nut

nu·tri·ent /'njuːtriənt‖'nuː-/ *n, adj* (a chemical or food) providing life or growth

nu·tri·tion /nju:'trɪʃən‖nuː-/ *n* [U] process of giving or getting food –**tious** *adj* valuable to the body as food

nuts and bolts /,·· '·/ *n* [(*the*) P] the simple facts or skills of a subject or job

nut·shell /'nʌt-ʃel/ *n* **in a nutshell** described in as few words as possible

nuz·zle /'nʌzəl/ *vi/t* press closely, esp. with the nose

ny·lon /'naɪlɒn‖-lɑːn/ *n* [U] strong man-made material made into cloth, plastic, etc.

nymph /nɪmf/ *n* (in Greek and Roman literature) goddess of nature living in trees, streams, mountains, etc.

nym·pho·ma·ni·a /,nɪmfə'meɪniə/ *n* [U] strong sexual desire in a woman to a degree considered as unhealthy or socially unacceptable –**niac** *n* woman with nymphomania

O, o /əʊ/ 1 the 15th letter of the English alphabet 2 (in speech) zero

oaf /əʊf/ *n* rough stupid awkward person

oak /əʊk/ *n* large broad tree with hard wood and curly leaves

OAP /,əʊ eɪ 'piː/ *n BrE* old age pensioner; person old enough to receive an OLD AGE PENSION

oar /ɔːʳ/ *n* 1 long pole with a flat blade, used for rowing a boat 2 **put/shove/stick one's oar in** *sl for* INTERFERE

o·a·sis /əʊ'eɪsɪs/ *n* -**ses** /-siːz/ place with water and trees in a desert

oath /əʊθ/ *n* **oaths** /əʊðz/ 1 solemn promise 2 use of bad angry words; curse 3 **be on/under oath** have promised to tell the truth

oat·meal /'əʊtmiːl/ *n* [U] crushed oats

oats /əʊts/ *n* [P] sort of grain used as food — see also WILD OATS

ob·du·rate /'ɒbdʒʊrət‖'ɑːbdə-/ *adj fml* unwilling to think or act differently ~**ly** *adv* –**racy** *n* [U]

o·be·di·ent /ə'biːdiənt/ *adj* doing what one is told to do ~**ly** *adv* –**ence** *n* [U]

o·bei·sance /əʊˈbeɪsəns/ n [C;U] fml show of respect and obedience, esp. by bowing (BOW[1])

ob·e·lisk /ˈɒbəlɪsk∥ˈɑː-, ˈəʊ-/ n tall pointed stone pillar

o·bese /əʊˈbiːs/ adj fml unhealthily fat **obesity** n [U]

o·bey /əʊˈbeɪ, ə-/ vi/t do what one is told to do (by someone in a position of power)

o·bit·u·a·ry /əˈbɪtʃʊəri∥-tʃueri/ n report in a newspaper, etc., of someone's death

ob·ject¹ /ˈɒbdʒɪkt∥ˈɑːb-/ n 1 thing that can be seen or felt 2 purpose 3 gram word or words that represent a the person or thing (the **direct object**) that something is done to (such as door in She closed the door) or b the person (the **indirect object**) who is concerned in the result of an action (such as her in I gave her the book) 4 person or thing that produces the stated feeling: She has become an object of pity. 5 **be no object** not be a difficulty

ob·ject² /əbˈdʒekt/ vi be against something or someone: I object to paying so much.

ob·jec·tion /əbˈdʒekʃən/ n 1 statement or feeling of dislike or opposition 2 reason or argument against

ob·jec·tio·na·ble /əbˈdʒekʃənəbəl/ adj unpleasant –**bly** adv

ob·jec·tive¹ /əbˈdʒektɪv/ adj 1 not influenced by personal feelings; fair 2 existing outside the mind; real –**tivity** /ˌɒbdʒekˈtɪvɪti∥ˌɑːb-/ n [U]

objective² n purpose of a plan

object les·son /ˈ·· ˌ··/ n event or story from which one can learn how or how not to behave

ob·jet d'art /ˌɒbʒeɪ ˈdɑːʳ∥ˌɑːb-/ n **objets d'art** small object of some value as art

ob·li·ga·tion /ˌɒblɪˈgeɪʃən∥ˌɑːb-/ n [C;U] duty: You're under **no obligation** (to do sth.) (= you don't have to) –**tory** /əˈblɪgətəri∥-tɔːri/ adj

o·blige /əˈblaɪdʒ/ vt fml 1 make it necessary for (someone) to do something: We were obliged to (= had to) leave. 2 do a favour for 3 **(I'm) much obliged (to you)** (used for thanking someone politely)

o·blig·ing /əˈblaɪdʒɪŋ/ adj kind and eager to help ~**ly** adv

o·blique /əˈbliːk/ adj 1 indirect: an oblique hint 2 sloping

o·blit·er·ate /əˈblɪtəreɪt/ vt remove all signs of; destroy –**ation** /əˌblɪtəˈreɪʃən/ n [U]

o·bliv·i·on /əˈblɪviən/ n [U] 1 state of being completely forgotten 2 state of being unconscious or not noticing one's surroundings

o·bliv·i·ous /əˈblɪviəs/ adj not noticing: He was oblivious to the danger.

ob·long /ˈɒblɒŋ∥ˈɑːblɔːŋ/ n right-angled figure with 4 sides, 2 long and 2 shorter ones **oblong** adj

ob·nox·ious /əbˈnɒkʃəs∥-ˈnɑːk-/ adj extremely unpleasant ~**ly** adv

o·boe /ˈəʊbəʊ/ n musical instrument made of a black wooden tube, played by blowing **oboist** n player of an oboe

ob·scene /əbˈsiːn/ adj very offensive or shocking, esp. sexually **obscenity** /əbˈsenɪti/ n [C;U] obscene word or behaviour

ob·scure /əbˈskjʊəʳ/ adj 1 hard to understand; not clear 2 not well known ♦ vt hide **obscurity** n [U] state of being obscure

ob·se·qui·ous /əbˈsiːkwiəs/ adj too eager to obey or serve ~**ly** adv ~**ness** n [U]

ob·ser·vance /əbˈzɜːvəns∥-ɜːr-/ n fml 1 [U] doing something in accordance with a law, custom, etc. 2 [C] part of a religious ceremony

ob·ser·vant /əbˈzɜːvənt∥-ɜːr-/ adj quick at noticing things

ob·ser·va·tion /ˌɒbzəˈveɪʃən∥ˌɑːbzər-/ n 1 [C;U] action of noticing 2 [U] ability to notice things 3 [C] fml remark, esp. about something noticed 4 **under observation** being carefully watched during a period of time

ob·ser·va·to·ry /əbˈzɜːvətəri∥əbˈzɜːrvətɔːri/ n place where scientists look at and study the stars, moon, etc.

ob·serve /əbˈzɜːv∥-ɜːrv/ vt 1 watch carefully 2 fml act in accordance with (a law, custom, etc.) 3 fml say **observer** n 1 someone who observes 2 someone who attends meetings, etc., only to listen, not take part

ob·sess /əbˈses/ vt completely fill (someone's) mind, so they cannot think about anything else: She was obsessed by the fear of failure. ~**ive** adj that is an obsession ~**ion** /-ˈseʃən/ n fixed and often unreasonable idea or pattern of behaviour

ob·so·les·cent /ˌɒbsəˈlesənt∥ˌɑːb-/ adj becoming obsolete –**cence** n [U]

ob·so·lete /ˈɒbsəliːt∥ˌɑːbsəˈliːt/ adj no longer used; out of date

ob·sta·cle /ˈɒbstəkəl∥ˈɑːb-/ n something that prevents action, movement, or success

ob·ste·tri·cian /ˌɒbstəˈtrɪʃən∥ˌɑːb-/ n doctor concerned with obstetrics

ob·stet·rics /əbˈstetrɪks/ n [U] branch of medicine concerned with the birth of children

ob·sti·nate /ˈɒbstɪnɪt∥ˈɑːb-/ adj 1 not willing to obey or change one's opinion 2 difficult to control or defeat: obstinate resistance ~**ly** adv –**nacy** n [U]

ob-strep-er-ous /əb'strepərəs/ adj noisy and uncontrollable ~ly adv ~ness n [U]

ob-struct /əb'strʌkt/ vt 1 block 2 put difficulties in the way of ~ive adj intentionally obstructing ~ion /əb'strʌkʃən/ n 1 [C] act of obstructing 2 [U] something that obstructs

ob-tain /əb'teɪn/ vt fml get: How did you obtain this information? ~able adj

ob-tru-sive /əb'truːsɪv/ adj fml unpleasantly noticeable ~ly adv

ob-tuse /əb'tjuːs‖-'tuːs/ adj 1 fml annoyingly slow to understand 2 (of an angle) more than 90° ~ly adv ~ness n [U]

ob-verse /'ɒbvɜːs‖'ɑːbvɜːrs/ n 1 front side of a coin, etc. 2 opposite

ob-vi-ate /'ɒbvieɪt‖'ɑːb-/ vt fml make unnecessary

ob-vi-ous /'ɒbviəs‖'ɑːb-/ adj easy to see and understand; clear: an obvious lie ~ly adv

oc-ca-sion /ə'keɪʒən/ n 1 [C] time when something happens: May I take this occasion (= this chance) to thank you for your help. 2 [U] fml reason: He had no occasion to be so rude. 3 [C] special event or ceremony 4 **on occasion** fml occasionally — see also SENSE OF OCCASION ♦ vt fml cause

oc-ca-sion-al /ə'keɪʒənəl/ adj happening sometimes; not regular ~ly adv

oc-ci-den-tal /ˌɒksɪ'dentəl‖ˌɑːk-/ n,adj (person) of the western part of the world

oc-cult /'ɒkʌlt, ə'kʌlt‖ə'kʌlt, 'ɑː-/ adj magical and mysterious ♦ n [the + S]

oc-cu-pant /'ɒkjʊpənt‖'ɑːk-/ n person who is living in a house, room, etc. -pancy n [U] (period of) being an occupant

oc-cu-pa-tion /ˌɒkjʊ'peɪʃən‖ˌɑːk-/ n 1 [C] job 2 [C] something done to pass time 3 [U] taking possession of ~al adj of one's job

oc-cu-py /'ɒkjʊpaɪ‖'ɑːk-/ vt 1 be in: The seat was occupied. (= someone was sitting in it) 2 fill (space or time): Writing occupies most of my spare time. 3 take possession of: an occupied country 4 keep busy -pier n

oc-cur /ə'kɜː/ vi -rr- 1 happen 2 be found; exist: a disease that occurs in children ~rence /ə'kʌrəns‖ə'kɜː-/ n 1 [C] event 2 [U] process of occurring **occur to** phr vt (of an idea) come to (someone's) mind

o-cean /'əʊʃən/ n 1 [U] great mass of salt water that covers most of the Earth 2 [C] any of the great seas into which this is divided: the Atlantic Ocean ~ic /ˌəʊʃi'ænɪk/ adj

o'clock /ə'klɒk‖ə'klɑːk/ adv (used in telling the time when it is exactly a numbered hour): at 5 o'clock

oc-ta-gon /'ɒktəgən‖'ɑːktəgɑːn/ n flat figure with 8 sides and 8 angles

oc-tane /'ɒkteɪn‖'ɑːk-/ n number showing the power and quality of petrol: high-octane fuel

oc-tave /'ɒktɪv, -teɪv‖'ɑːk-/ n space of 8 degrees between musical notes

Oc-to-ber /ɒk'təʊbər‖ɑːk-/ n the 10th month of the year

oc-to-ge-nar-ian /ˌɒktəʊdʒə-'neəriən, -tə-‖ˌɑːk-/ n a person who is between 80 and 90 years old

oc-to-pus /'ɒktəpəs‖'ɑːk-/ n deep-sea creature with 8 limbs

odd /ɒd‖ɑːd/ adj 1 strange; unusual 2 (of a number) that cannot be exactly divided by two 3 separated from its pair or set: an odd shoe 4 not regular: doing odd jobs 5 rather more than the stated number: 20-odd years ago ~ly adv strangely ~ity n 1 [C] strange thing, person, etc. 2 [U] strangeness

odd man out /ˌ· · '·/ n person or thing different from or left out of a group

odd-ment /'ɒdmənt‖'ɑːd-/ n something left over: a few oddments of cloth

odds /ɒdz‖ɑːdz/ n [P] 1 probability of something happening: The odds are (= it is likely) that she will fail. 2 **at odds** in disagreement 3 **it/that makes no odds** BrE it/that makes no difference; has no importance

odds and ends /ˌ· · '·/ n [P] small articles of various kinds

ode /əʊd/ n long poem

o-di-ous /'əʊdiəs/ adj fml very unpleasant

o-di-um /'əʊdiəm/ n [U] fml widespread hatred

o-dour BrE ‖ **-dor** AmE /'əʊdər/ n fml smell

oe-soph-a-gus /ɪ'sɒfəgəs‖ɪ'sɑː-/ n med food tube from the mouth to the stomach

oes-tro-gen /'iːstrədʒən‖'es-/ n [U] substance in females that changes the body ready for the production of young

of /əv, ə; strong ɒv‖əv, ə; strong ɑːv/ prep 1 belonging to: the wheels of the car 2 made from: a crown of gold 3 containing: a bag of potatoes 4 (shows a part or amount): 2 pounds of sugar 5 **a** that is/are: a friend of mine / some fool of a boy (= some foolish boy) **b** happening in or on: the Battle of Waterloo 6 in relation to; in connection with: a teacher of English / fond of swimming 7 **a** done by: the plays of Shakespeare **b** done about: a picture of Shakespeare 8 with; having: a matter of no importance 9 (shows what someone or something is or does): the *laughter of the children* | *How kind of you!* **10** (used in dates): *the 27th of February* **11** during: *We often go there of an evening.*

off¹ /ɒf||ɔːf/ *adv, adj* **1** disconnected; removed: *The handle fell off.* **2** (esp. of electrical apparatus) not lit or working: *The TV is off.* **3** away: *She drove off.* | *2 miles off* **4** away or free from work: *She's taken this week off.* **5** so as to be finished or destroyed: *They were all killed off.* **6** not going to happen after all: *The party's off!* **7** no longer good to eat or drink **8** provided with what you need: *They're not well off.* (= have not got much money) | *You'd be better off with a bike than that old car!* **9 a** *infml* not quite right; not as good as usual: *It was a bit off, not answering my letter.* | *having an off day* **b** quiet and dull: *the off season* **10 off and on** sometimes **11 on the off chance** just in case **12 right/straight off** at once

off² *prep* **1** away from: *I jumped off the bus.* | *I cut a piece off the loaf.* | *The ship was blown off course.* **2** (of a road) turning away from (a larger one) **3** in the sea near: *an island off the coast* **4** not wanting: *She's off her food.*

of·fal /ˈɒfəl||ˈɔː-, ˈɑː-/ *n* [U] the inside organs of an animal used as food

off·beat /ˌɒfˈbiːt◄, ˌɔːf-/ *adj* not CONVENTIONAL

off col·our /ˌ···◄/ *adj* **1** slightly ill **2** sexually improper

of·fence *BrE* || **offense** *AmE*/əˈfens/ *n* **1** [C] wrong act, esp. a crime **2** [U] cause for hurt feelings: *Don't take offence.* (= feel offended)

of·fend /əˈfend/ *v* **1** *vt* hurt the feelings of; upset **2** *vt* displease greatly **3** *vi* do wrong: *to offend against good manners* ~**er** *n* person who offends, esp. a criminal: *a first offender* (= someone found guilty of a crime for the first time) ~**ing** *adj* causing displeasure, discomfort, or inconvenience

of·fen·sive /əˈfensɪv/ *adj* **1** extremely unpleasant **2** for attacking ♦ *n* **1** continued military attack **2 on the offensive** attacking ~**ly** *adv* ~**ness** *n* [U]

of·fer /ˈɒfəʳ||ˈɔː-, ˈɑː-/ *v* **1** *vt/i* say one will give or do: *The police are offering a big reward.* | *She offered to drive me there.* **2** *vt* provide; give: *The situation doesn't offer much hope.* | *He offered no resistance.* **3** give (to God): *She offered (up) a prayer.* ♦ *n* **1** statement offering something **2** what is offered ~**ing** *n* something offered

off·hand /ˌɒfˈhænd◄, ˌɔːf-/ *adv, adj* **1** careless; disrespectful **2** without time to think or prepare

of·fice /ˈɒfɪs||ˈɔː-, ˈɑː-/ *n* **1** [C] room or building where written work is done **2** [C] place where a particular

service is provided: *a ticket office* **3** [C] government department: *the Foreign Office* **4** [C;U] important job or position of power: *the office of president*

of·fi·cer /ˈɒfɪsəʳ||ˈɔː-, ˈɑː-/ *n* **1** person in command in the army, navy, etc. **2** person in a government job: *a local government officer* **3** policeman

of·fi·cial /əˈfɪʃəl/ *adj* of, from, or decided by someone in a position of power and responsibility: *official permission* ♦ *n* person who holds an OFFICE (4) ~**ly** *adv* **1** formally by an official **2** as stated publicly (but perhaps not really) ~**dom** *n* [U] officials as a group ~**ese** /əˌfɪʃəˈliːz/ *n* [U] *infml* language of government officials, considered unnecessarily hard to understand

of·fi·ci·ate /əˈfɪʃieɪt/ *vi* perform official duties

of·fi·cious /əˈfɪʃəs/ *adj* too eager to give orders ~**ly** *adv* ~**ness** *n* [U]

off·ing /ˈɒfɪŋ||ˈɔː-, ˈɑː-/ *n* **in the offing** coming soon

off-li·cence /ˈ··/ *n* *BrE* shop where alcoholic drink is sold to be taken away

off-load /ˌ·ˈ·/ *vt* *BrE* get rid of (something unwanted)

off-peak /ˌ·ˈ·◄/ *adj* **1** less busy **2** existing during less busy periods

off-put·ting /ˈ·ˌ··/ *adj esp. BrE* unpleasant and making one not want to continue

off·set /ˈɒfset, ˌɒfˈset||ˈɔːfset, ˌɔːfˈset/ *vt* -**set**; *present p.* -**setting** make up for; balance: *They offset the cost by charging higher prices.*

off·shoot /ˈɒfʃuːt||ˈɔːf-/ *n* new stem or branch; (fig.) *an offshoot of a large company*

off·shore /ˌɒfˈʃɔːʳ◄||ˌɔːf-/ *adj, adv* **1** in the sea near the coast: *offshore islands* **2** away from the coast: *offshore winds*

off·side /ˌɒfˈsaɪd◄||ˌɔːf-/ *adj, adv* **1** (in certain sports) ahead of the ball, which is against the rules **2** (on) the right-hand side, esp. of a vehicle

off·spring /ˈɒfˌsprɪŋ||ˈɔːf-/ *n* offspring *fml* someone's child or children

off-the-rec·ord /ˌ· · ˈ··◄/ *adj, adv* unofficial and not to be formally recorded

off-the-wall /ˌ· · ˈ·◄/ *adj esp. AmE* amusingly foolish

off-white /ˌ· ˈ·◄/ *adj* greyish or yellowish white

of·ten /ˈɒfən, ˈɒftən||ˈɔː-/ *adv* **1** many times: *He was often ill.* **2** in many cases: *Very fat people are often unhealthy.* **3 as often as not** at least 50% of the time **4 every so often** sometimes **5 more often than not** more than 50% of the time

o·gle /'əʊgəl/ *vi/t* look (at) with great sexual interest

o·gre /'əʊgər/ **ogress** /'əʊgrəs/ *fem.* — *n* **1** fierce creature in fairy stories, like a very large person **2** frightening person

oh /əʊ/ *interj* (expresses surprise, fear, etc.)

oil /ɔɪl/ *n* [U] thick fatty liquid that burns easily, esp. PETROLEUM ♦ *vt* put oil on or into ~**y** *adj* **1** like or covered with oil **2** too polite **oils** *n* [P] paints containing oil

oil·field /'ɔɪlfiːld/ *n* area with oil underneath it

oil paint·ing /'· ˌ··/ *n* [C;U] painting done using paint made with oil: *She's/ he's no oil painting.* (= is not beautiful)

oil-rig /'ɔɪl,rɪg/ *n* large apparatus for getting oil up from under the sea

oil-skin /'ɔɪl,skɪn/ *n* [C;U] (garment made of) cloth treated with oil so as not to let water through

oil well /'· ·/ *n* hole made in the ground to get oil

oint·ment /'ɔɪntmənt/ *n* **1** [C;U] oily usu. medicinal substance rubbed on the skin **2 a/the fly in the ointment** one small unwanted thing that spoils the happiness of an occasion

o·kay /əʊ'keɪ/ *adj, adv* **1** all right; satisfactory **2** (expresses agreement or permission) ♦ *n* approval; permission ♦ *vt* give permission for

old /əʊld/ *adj* **1** having lived or existed a long time **2** of a particular age: *The baby is 2 years old.* **3** having been so a long time: *an old friend* **4** former: *He got his old job back.* | *an old boy/girl* (= former pupil of a school) **5 of old: a** in the past **b** for a long time ♦ *n* [*the* + S] old people

old age /ˌ· '·◁/ *n* [U] part of one's life when one is old

old age pen·sion /ˌ· · '··/ *n* money paid regularly by the state to old people ~**er** *n*

old-boy net·work /'·· ·ˌ··/*n BrE* tendency of former pupils of the same school (esp. PUBLIC SCHOOLs) to favour each other, esp. in gaining positions of importance

old·en /'əʊldən/ *adj lit* past; long ago: *in olden times*

olde worl·de /ˌəʊldi 'wɜːldi‖-ɜːr-/ *adj BrE* of a perhaps too consciously old-fashioned style

old-fash·ioned /ˌ· '··◁/ *adj* **1** once usual or fashionable but now less common **2 an old-fashioned look** *BrE* a look that suggests disapproval

old flame /ˌ· '·/ *n* someone with whom one used to be in love

old guard /ˌ· ˌ·/ *n* [*the* + S] group of people with old-fashioned ideas who are against change

old hand /ˌ· '·/ *n* very experienced person

old hat /ˌ· '·/ *adj* old-fashioned

old maid /ˌ· '·/ *n* old unmarried woman

old mas·ter /ˌ· '··/ *n* (picture by) an important painter of esp. the 15th to 18th centuries

old tim·er /ˌ· '··/*n* **1** person who has been somewhere or done something for a long time **2** *AmE* old man

old wives' tale /ˌ· '· ·/ *n* ancient and not necessarily true belief

ol·fac·to·ry /ɒl'fæktəri‖ɑːl-, əʊl-/ *adj med* of the sense of smell

ol·i·gar·chy /'ɒləgɑːki‖'ɑːləgɑːrki, 'əʊ-/ *n* **1** [U] government by a small usu. unrepresentative group **2** [C] state governed in this way

ol·ive /'ɒləv‖'ɑː-/ *n* **1** [C] small fruit of the **olive tree**, grown in Mediterranean countries and eaten raw or made into **olive oil** for cooking **2** [U] dull pale green

olive branch /'··· ·/ *n* sign of a wish for peace

om·buds·man /'ɒmbʊdzmən‖ 'ɑːm-/ *n* -**men** /-mən/ person who deals with complaints about an organization

om·e·lette /'ɒmlət‖'ɑːm-/ *n* flat round mass of eggs beaten together and cooked

o·men /'əʊmən/ *n* sign of something that will happen

om·i·nous /'ɒmənəs‖'ɑː-/ *adj* seeming to show that something bad will happen ~**ly** *adv*

o·mis·sion /əʊ'mɪʃən, ə-/ *n* **1** [U] act of omitting **2** [C] something left out

o·mit /əʊ'mɪt, ə-/ *vt* **1** not include: *An important detail was omitted.* **2** *fml* not do; fail: *They omitted to tell me.*

om·ni·bus /'ɒmnɪbəs, -,bʌs‖'ɑːm-/ *n* **1** book containing several works, esp. by one writer **2** *old use for* BUS

om·nip·o·tent /ɒm'nɪpətənt‖ɑːm-/ *adj fml* having unlimited power —**tence** *n* [U]

om·nis·ci·ent /ɒm'nɪʃənt, -'nɪsiənt‖ ɑːm'nɪʃənt/ *adj* knowing everything —**ence** *n* [U]

om·niv·o·rous /ɒm'nɪvərəs‖ɑːm-/ *adj* (esp. of an animal) eating anything

on¹ /ɒn‖ɔːn, ɑːn/ *prep* **1** touching, supported by, hanging from, or connected with: *a lamp on the table* **2** towards; in the direction of **3** directed towards: *a tax on beer* **4** in (a large vehicle): *on a train* **5** (shows when something happens): *She's coming on Tuesday.* **6** about: *a book on golf* **7** by means of: *A car runs on petrol.* **8** in a state of: *on fire* | *on holiday* **9** working for; belonging to: *She's on the committee.* **10** directly after and because of: *I* *acted on your advice.* **11** paid for by: *The drinks are on me!*

on² *adv, adj* **1** continuously, instead of stopping: *He kept on talking.* **2** further; forward: *We walked on to the next one.* **3** (so as to be) wearing: *He put his coat on.* | *He had nothing on.* **4** with the stated part in front: *They crashed head on.* **5** in(to) a vehicle: *The bus stopped and we got on.* **6** (esp. of electrical apparatus) lit or working: *The TV was on.* **7** (of something arranged) happening or going to happen: *What's on at the cinema?* | *I've got nothing on on Tuesday.* (= I'm not doing anything) **8** with the stated part forward: *Look at it sideways on.* **9 and so on** etc. **10 be on about/at** keep talking (about something/to someone) in a dull, complaining way: *What's he on about now?* | *She's always on at me to* (= trying to persuade me to) *have my hair cut.* **11 not on** impossible; not acceptable **12 on and off** from time to time **13 on and on** without stopping

once /wʌns/ *adv* **1** one time: *We've only met once.* **2** formerly: *He was once a famous singer.* **3 all at once** suddenly **4 at once: a** now; without delay: *Come at once!* **b** together: *Don't all speak at once!* **5 for once** for this one time only: *Just for once he was telling the truth.* **6 once and for all** now, so as to be settled, with no further change **7 once in a while** sometimes, but not often **8 once more** again ◆ *conj* from the moment that: *Once he's arrived, we can start.*

once-o·ver /'· ,··/ *n infml* a quick look or examination

on·com·ing /'ɒn,kʌmɪŋ‖'ɔːn-, 'ɑːn-/ *adj* coming towards you: *oncoming traffic*

one¹ /wʌn/ *determiner, n* **1** (the number) 1 **2** a certain: *They'll come back one day.* | *The victim was one Roy Malkin.* **3** the same: *They all ran in one direction.* **4** particular type or example (of): *He can't tell one tree from another.* **5 at one** *fml* in agreement **6 be one up (on)** have the advantage (over) **7 for one** as one (person, thing, reason, etc.) out of several **8 in one** combined: *It's a table and desk all in one.* **9 one and all** every one **10 one and the same** exactly the same **11 one of** a member of: *Our dog's like one of the family.* **12 one or two** a few

one² *pron* **1** single thing or person of the sort mentioned: *Have you any books on gardening?* | *I'd like to borrow one.* **2** *fml* any person; you: *One should do one's duty.*

one an·oth·er /,· ·'··/ *pron* EACH OTHER: *They hit one another*

one-armed ban·dit /,· · '··/ *n* machine with a long handle, into which people put money to try to win more money

one-man band /,· · '··/ *n* **1** a street musician who plays different instruments all at one time **2** activity which someone does all on their own

one-night stand /,· · '··/ *n* **1** performance of music or a play given only once in each of a number of places **2** sexual relationship which lasts only one night

one-off /,· '··/ *adj esp. BrE* **1** happening or done only once **2** made as a single example **one-off** *n*

one-piece /'· ·/ *adj* made in one piece only

o·ner·ous /'ɒnərəs, 'əʊ-‖'ɑː-, 'əʊ-/ *adj fml* difficult; hard to bear: *an onerous duty*

one·self /wʌn'self/ *pron* **1** (*reflexive form of* ONE² (2)): *to wash oneself* **2** (*strong form of* ONE² (2)): *One shouldn't try and do everything oneself.* **3 (all) by oneself a** alone **b** without help **4 to oneself** not shared

one-sid·ed /,· '··◄/ *adj* with one side stronger or more favoured than the other: *a one-sided football match*

one-time /'wʌntaɪm/ *adj* former

one-to-one /,· · '··◄/ *adj, adv* **1** matching one another exactly **2** between only two people

one-up-man·ship /wʌn'ʌpmənʃɪp/ *n* [U] art of getting an advantage without actually cheating

one-way /,· '··◄/ *adj* moving or allowing movement in one direction only: *a one-way street*

on·go·ing /'ɒn,gəʊɪŋ‖'ɑːn-/ *adj* continuing: *an ongoing problem*

on·ion /'ʌnjən/ *n* strong-smelling round white vegetable

on·line /'ɒnlaɪn‖'ɔːn-, 'ɑːn-/ *adj* directly connected to and/or controlled by a computer **online** *adv*

on·look·er /'ɒn,lʊkə‖'ɔːn-, 'ɑːn-/ *n* person watching something happen

on·ly¹ /'əʊnli/ *adj* **1** with no others in the same group: *my only friend* **2** best: *She's the only person for this job.*

on·ly² *adv* **1** and no one or nothing else: *There were only 5 left.* **2 if only** (expresses a strong wish): *If only she were here!* **3 only just: a** a moment before **b** almost not **4 only too** very; completely: *I'm afraid it's only too true.*

on·ly³ *conj* except that; but: *She wants to go, only she hasn't got enough money.*

on·rush /'ɒnrʌʃ‖'ɔːn-, 'ɑːn-/ *n* strong movement forward

on·set /'ɒnset‖'ɔːn-, 'ɑːn-/ *n* start, esp. of something bad

on-shore /ˌɒnˈʃɔːʳ◀/, ˌɔːnˈʃɔːr, ˌɑːn-/ adv, adj towards the coast: *onshore winds*

on-slaught /ˈɒnslɔːt‖ˈɑːn-, ˈɑːn-/ n fierce attack

on-to /ˈɒntʊ, -tə‖ˈɑːn-, ˈɑːn-/ prep 1 to a position or point on: *He jumped onto the train.* 2 **be onto** have found out about (someone or something wrong or illegal)

o-nus /ˈəʊnəs/ n [S] duty; responsibility: *The onus is on you to do it.*

on-ward /ˈɒnwəd‖ˈɑːnward, ˈɑːn-/ adj, adv forward in space or time

oo-dles /ˈuːdlz/ n [P] infml lots

ooze /uːz/ v 1 vi (of thick liquid) pass or flow slowly 2 vt have (liquid) oozing out: (fig.) *He oozes charm.* ♦ n [U] mud or thick liquid

o-pac-i-ty /əʊˈpæsɪti/ n [U] opaqueness

o-pal /ˈəʊpəl/ n white precious stone with colours in it

o-paque /əʊˈpeɪk/ adj which you cannot see through ~ness n [U]

OPEC /ˈəʊpek/ n Organization of Petroleum Exporting Countries

o-pen[1] /ˈəʊpən/ adj 1 not shut: *an open window/book* | (fig.) *an open mind* (= not closed to new ideas) 2 not surrounded by anything: *open country* 3 without a roof: *an open boat* 4 not fastened or folded: *with his shirt open* 5 not completely decided or answered: *an open question* 6 that one can go into as a visitor or customer: *Is the bank open yet?* 7 (of a job) not filled 8 not hiding or secret; honest 9 that anyone can enter: *an open competition* 10 spread out: *The flowers are open.* 11 (of a cheque) payable to the person whose name is written on it 12 **keep open house** encourage visitors to come at any time 13 **open to:** a not safe from: *open to criticism* b willing to receive: *open to suggestions* 14 **with open arms** in a very friendly way ~**ly** adv not secretly ~**ness** n [U]

o-pen[2] vi/t 1 make or become open: *Open your mouth!* 2 spread; unfold: *open a map* 3 (cause to) start: *The story opens in a country village.* 4 (cause to) begin business: *The shops open at 9 o'clock.* 5 **open fire** start shooting 6 **open someone's eyes (to something)** make someone know or understand something ~**er** n

  open into/onto phr vt provide a means of entering or reaching

  open out phr vi speak more freely

  open up phr v 1 vt make possible the development of 2 vi open the door 3 vi speak more freely

o-pen[3] n [the + S] 1 the outdoors 2 **in(to) the open** (of opinions, secrets, etc.) in(to) the consciousness of the

people around one **open-air** /ˌ·· ˈ·◀/ adj of or in the outdoors: *an open-air theatre*

open-and-shut /ˌ··· ˈ·◀/ adj easy to prove

open-cast /ˈ·· ·/ adj where coal is dug from an open hole in the ground and not from a passage deep underground

open-door pol-i-cy /ˌ·· · ˈ···/ n idea of allowing traders from all countries to trade freely in a certain country

open-end-ed /ˌ·· ˈ·◀/ adj with no limit set in advance

open-hand-ed /ˌ·· ˈ·◀/ adj generous

o-pen-ing /ˈəʊpənɪŋ/ n 1 hole or clear space 2 favourable set of conditions 3 unfilled job ♦ adj first; beginning

open-plan /ˌ·· ˈ·◀/ adj (of a large room) not divided into a lot of little rooms

op-e-ra /ˈɒpərə‖ˈɑː-/ n musical play in which (most of) the words are sung ~**tic** /ˌɒpəˈrætɪk◀‖ˌɑː-/ adj

op-e-ra-ble /ˈɒpərəbl‖ˈɑː-/ adj (of a disease, etc.) that can be cured by an operation

op-e-rate /ˈɒpəreɪt‖ˈɑː-/ v 1 vi/t (cause to) work: *learning to operate the controls* 2 vi carry on trade or business: *We operate throughout Europe.* 3 vi cut the body to cure or remove diseased parts, usu. in a special room (**operating theatre**) 4 vi produce effects: *The new law operates in our favour.*

operating sys-tem /ˈ···· ˌ··/ n set of PROGRAMS inside a computer that controls the way it works and helps it to handle other programs

op-e-ra-tion /ˌɒpəˈreɪʃən‖ˌɑː-/ n 1 [U] condition or process of working 2 [C] thing (to be) done; activity 3 [C] cutting of the body to cure or remove a diseased part 4 [C] planned military movement ~**al** adj 1 of operations: *operational costs* 2 ready for use

op-e-ra-tive /ˈɒpərətɪv‖ˈɑːpərə-, ˈɑːpəreɪ-/ adj 1 (of a plan, law, etc.) working; producing effects 2 most important: *'Fast' is the operative word.* ♦ n worker

op-e-ra-tor /ˈɒpəreɪtəʳ‖ˈɑː-/ n person who works a machine, apparatus, or esp. telephone SWITCHBOARD

o-pin-ion /əˈpɪnjən/ n 1 [C] what someone thinks about something, based on personal judgment rather than facts: *In my opinion, it's crazy.* 2 [U] what people in general think about something 3 [C] professional judgment or advice ~**ated** adj too sure that what one thinks is right

o-pi-um /ˈəʊpɪəm/ n [U] sleep-producing drug

op·po·nent /ə'pəʊnənt/ n **1** person who takes the opposite side in a competition or fight **2** person who opposes someone or something

op·por·tune /'ɒpətjuːn‖,ɑːpər'tuːn/ adj fml **1** (of time) right for a purpose **2** coming at the right time ~**ly** adv

op·por·tun·is·m /'ɒpətjuːnɪzəm‖,ɑːpər'tuː-/ n [U] taking advantage of every chance for success, sometimes to other people's disadvantage —**ist** n

op·por·tu·ni·ty /,ɒpə'tjuːnəti‖,ɑːpər'tuː-/ n [C;U] favourable moment; chance

op·pose /ə'pəʊz/ vt be or act against

op·posed /ə'pəʊzd/ adj **1** against: I'm opposed to abortion. **2** as opposed to and not

op·po·site /'ɒpəzɪt‖'ɑː-/ adj **1** as different as possible from: at opposite ends of the room **2** facing: the houses opposite ♦ n opposite thing or person: Black and white are opposites. ♦ prep facing: She sat opposite me.

opposite num·ber /,··· '··/ n one that is the same or does the same things, but in a different group

op·po·si·tion /,ɒpə'zɪʃən‖,ɑː-/ n **1** [U] act or state of opposing **2** [U] people who are against one **3** [C] (often cap.) political parties opposed to the government

op·press /ə'pres/ vt **1** rule in a hard cruel way **2** cause to feel ill or sad ~**ive** adj **1** cruel; unjust **2** causing feelings of illness and unhappiness: oppressive heat ~**or** n ~**ion** /ə'preʃən/ n [U]

opt /ɒpt‖ɑːpt/ vi make a choice: I opted for the smaller one.

opt out phr vi decide not to take part

op·tic /'ɒptɪk‖'ɑːp-/ adj of the eyes: the optic nerve

op·ti·cal /'ɒptɪkəl‖'ɑːp-/ adj **1** of or about the sense of sight: She thought she saw it, but it was an **optical illusion**. (= something that deceives the sense of sight) **2** of or using light: optical character recognition

op·ti·cian /ɒp'tɪʃən‖ɑːp-/ n person who makes and sells glasses, etc., for people's eyes

op·ti·mist /'ɒptɪmɪst‖'ɑːp-/ n person who expects good things to happen —**mism** n [U] ~**ic** /,ɒptɪ'mɪstɪk‖,ɑːp-/ adj

op·ti·mize ‖ also **-mise** BrE /'ɒptɪmaɪz‖'ɑːp-/ vt make as perfect or effective as possible

op·ti·mum /'ɒptɪməm‖'ɑːp-/ also **optimal** /'ɒptɪməl‖'ɑːp-/ adj most favourable: optimum conditions for growing rice

op·tion /'ɒpʃən‖'ɑːp-/ n **1** [U] freedom to choose: I had to do it; I had no option. **2** [C] possible course of action that can be chosen **3** [C] right to buy or sell something at a stated time in the future — see also SOFT OPTION ~**al** adj which you can choose to have or not to have

op·u·lent /'ɒpjʊlənt‖'ɑːp-/ adj **1** showing great wealth **2** in good supply —**lence** n [U]

o·pus /'əʊpəs/ n piece of work done, esp. a piece of music written

or /ə/; strong /ɔː/ conj **1** (shows different possibilities): Will you have tea or coffee? **2** if not: Wear your coat or you'll be cold. **3** (describes the same thing in a different way): a kilometre, or one thousand metres **4** or else infml (used as a threat) or something bad will happen **5** or so about: We waited for 5 minutes or so.

or·a·cle /'ɒrəkəl‖'ɔːr-, 'ɑː-/ n **1** (in ancient Greece) person through whom a god answered human questions **2** person thought to be, or who believes himself to be, wise and able to give good advice

o·ral /'ɔːrəl/ adj **1** spoken, not written: an oral exam **2** med of the mouth ~**ly** adv

or·ange /'ɒrɪndʒ‖'ɑː-, 'ɔː-/ n common round reddish-yellow fruit ♦ adj of the colour of an orange

o·rang·u·tang /ɔː,ræŋuː'tæŋ‖ə'ræŋətæŋ/ n large monkey with reddish hair and no tail

o·ra·tion /ə'reɪʃən, ɔː-/ n solemn formal public speech

or·a·tor /'ɒrətəʳ‖'ɔːr-, 'ɑː-/ n public speaker

or·a·to·ry /'ɒrətri‖'ɔːrətɔːri, 'ɑː-/ n [U] language highly decorated with long or formal words

or·bit /'ɔːbɪt‖'ɔːr-/ n **1** path of something going round something else, esp. in space **2** area of power or influence ♦ vi/t go round in an orbit: The satellite orbits the Earth. ~**al** adj

or·chard /'ɔːtʃəd‖'ɔːrtʃərd/ n place where fruit trees are grown

or·ches·tra /'ɔːkɪstrə‖'ɔːr-/ n large group of musicians playing different instruments **orchestral** /ɔː'kestrəl‖ɔːr-/ adj

or·ches·trate /'ɔːkəstreɪt‖'ɔːr-/ vt **1** arrange (music) to be played by an orchestra **2** plan (something with many parts) for best effect —**tration** /,ɔːkə'streɪʃən‖,ɔːr-/ n [C;U]

or·chid /'ɔːkɪd‖'ɔːr-/ n plant with bright strange-shaped flowers

or·dain /ɔː'deɪn‖ɔːr-/ vt **1** make (someone) a priest **2** fml (of God, the law, etc.) order

or·deal /ɔː'diːl, 'ɔːdiːl‖ɔːr'diːl, 'ɔːrdiːl/ n difficult or painful experience

or·der[1] /ˈɔːdər‖ˈɔːr-/ n 1 [U] way in which things are arranged: *in alphabetical order | in order of importance | Leave everything in good order.* (= tidily) 2 [U] fitness for use: *The phone's out of order.* (= doesn't work) 3 [U] condition in which laws and rules are obeyed: *That new teacher can't keep order in his class. | Your papers are in order.* (= acceptable according to the rules) 4 [C] command: *An officer gives orders.* 5 [C] request to supply goods: *The waiter took our order.* 6 [C] (MEDAL, etc., given to someone in) a group of specially honoured people: *the Order of Merit* 7 [C] *fml* kind; sort: *courage of the highest order* 8 [P] state of being a priest, etc.: *to take (holy) orders* 9 **in order that** *fml* so that 10 **in order to** with the purpose of 11 **in the order of** about 12 **on order** asked for but not yet supplied — see also TALL ORDER

or·der[2] v 1 vt command: *He ordered them to attack.* 2 vt/i ask for (something) to be supplied: *I ordered chicken soup.* 3 vt arrange

  order about *phr vt* give many commands to, unpleasantly

or·der·ly /ˈɔːdəli‖ˈɔːrdərli-/ adj 1 well-arranged 2 liking tidy arrangement 3 peaceful and well-behaved: *an orderly crowd* ♦ n helper in a hospital **–liness** n [U]

or·di·nal num·ber /ˌɔːdɪnl ˈnʌmbə‖ˌɔːr-/ n one of the numbers (1st, 2nd, 3rd, etc.) that show order rather than quantity

or·di·nary /ˈɔːdənri‖ˈɔːrdəneri-/ adj 1 not unusual; common 2 **out of the ordinary** unusual **–narily** /ˈɔːdənrəli‖ˌɔːrdənˈerəli/ adv usually

or·di·na·tion /ˌɔːdɪˈneɪʃən‖ˌɔːr-/ n [U;C] act of ORDAINing a priest

ore /ɔːr/ n [U] rock from which metal is obtained

or·gan /ˈɔːgən‖ˈɔːr-/ n 1 part of an animal or plant that has a special purpose, such as the heart 2 organization with a special purpose within a larger one: *Parliament is an organ of government.* 3 large musical instrument played by blowing air through pipes **–ist** n ORGAN (2) player

or·gan·ic /ɔːˈgænɪk‖ɔːr-/ adj 1 of living things or bodily organs 2 made of parts with related purposes 3 (of food) grown without chemicals **~ally** /-kli/ adv

or·gan·is·m /ˈɔːgənɪzəm‖ˈɔːr-/ n 1 living creature 2 whole made of related parts

or·gan·i·za·tion, ‖ also **-sation** BrE /ˌɔːgənaɪˈzeɪʃən‖ˌɔːrgənə-/ n 1 [C] group of people with a special purpose, such as a business or club 2 organizing; arrangement

or·gan·ize ‖ also **-ise** BrE /ˈɔːgənaɪz‖ˈɔːr-/ vt 1 arrange into a good system: *a well-organized office* 2 make necessary arrangements for: *to organize a party* **-izer** n

or·gas·m /ˈɔːgæzəm‖ˈɔːr-/ n [C;U] highest point of sexual pleasure

or·gy /ˈɔːdʒi‖ˈɔːr-/ n 1 wild party where people get drunk and have sex 2 *infml* a set of (usu. pleasant activities) close together in time

O·ri·ent /ˈɔːriənt, ˈɒri-‖ˈɔːr-/ n esp. *lit* [*the*] the eastern part of the world; Asia

orient[2] vt esp. AmE ORIENTATE

o·ri·en·tal /ˌɔːriˈentl, ˌɒ-‖ˌɔːr-/ adj (person) of or from the Orient

o·ri·en·tate /ˈɔːriənteɪt, ˈɒ-‖ˈɔːr-/ vt 1 arrange or direct with a particular purpose: *an export-orientated company* 2 find out where you are **–tation** /ˌɔːriənˈteɪʃən, ˌɒ-‖ˌɔːr-/ n [C;U]

or·i·fice /ˈɒrɪfɪs‖ˈɔːr-, ˈɑː-/ n *fml* opening, esp. in the body

or·i·gin /ˈɒrɪdʒɪn‖ˈɔː-, ˈɑː-/ n 1 [C;U] starting point 2 [U] also **origins** pl. — parents and conditions of early life: *a woman of humble origin*

o·rig·i·nal /əˈrɪdʒənəl, -dʒənl/ adj 1 first; earliest 2 new and different 3 not copied ♦ n the one from which copies have been made **~ly** adv 1 in the beginning, before changing 2 in a new and different way **~ity** /ə, rɪdʒəˈnælɪti/ n [U] quality of being ORIGINAL (2)

o·rig·i·nate /əˈrɪdʒəneɪt/ vi/t (cause to) begin **–nator** n

or·na·ment /ˈɔːnəmənt‖ˈɔːr-/ n [C;U] decorative object(s) ♦ vt /-ment/ decorate **~al** /ˌɔːnəˈmentl◂‖ˌɔːr-/ adj **~ation** /ˌɔːnəmenˈteɪʃən‖ˌɔːr-/ n [U]

or·nate /ɔːˈneɪt‖ɔːr-/ adj having (too) much ornament

or·ne·ry /ˈɔːnəri‖ˈɔːr-/ adj esp. AmE bad-tempered

or·ni·thol·o·gy /ˌɔːnɪˈθɒlədʒi‖ˌɔːrnəˈθɑː-/ n [U] scientific study of birds **–gist** n

or·phan /ˈɔːfən‖ˈɔːr-/ n child with no parents ♦ vt cause to be an orphan **~age** n place where orphans live

or·tho·dox /ˈɔːθədɒks‖ˈɔːrθədɑːks/ adj 1 generally or officially accepted or used: *orthodox methods* 2 holding orthodox opinions **~y** n [U]

or·tho·pae·dic, **-pedic** /ˌɔːθəˈpiːdɪk◂‖ˌɔːr-/ adj of the branch of medicine (**orthopaedics**) that puts bones straight

os·cil·late /ˈɒsəleɪt‖ˈɑː-/ vi 1 move regularly from side to side 2 vary between opposing choices **–lation** /ˌɒsəˈleɪʃən‖ˌɑː-/ n [C]

os·mo·sis /ɒzˈməʊsəs‖ɑːz-/ n [U] gradual passing of liquid through a

skinlike wall **–tic** /ɒz'mɒtɪk‖aːz'mɑː-/
adj

os·ten·si·ble /ɒ'stensɪbəl‖aː-/ adj
(of a reason) seeming or pretended,
but perhaps not really true **–bly** adv

os·ten·ta·tion /ˌɒstən'teɪʃən, -ten-‖
ˌaː-/ n [U] unnecessary show of
wealth, knowledge, etc. **–tious** adj

os·te·o·path /'ɒstɪəpæθ‖'aː-/ n person who treats diseases by moving and
pressing bones and muscles

os·tler /'ɒslər‖'aː-/ n (in former
times) man who took care of guests'
horses at a small hotel

os·tra·cize , -cise/'ɒstrəsaɪz‖'aː-/ vt
stop accepting (someone) into one's
group **–cism** n [U]

os·trich /'ɒstrɪtʃ‖'ɔː-, 'aː-/ n
extremely large long-legged African
bird that cannot fly

oth·er /'ʌðər/ determiner, pron **1** the
remaining one of a set; what is left as
well as that mentioned: She held on
with one hand and waved with the
other. **2** additional: Have you any
other questions? **3** not this, not oneself,
not one's own, etc.: He likes spending
other people's money. **4 one after the
other** first one, then the next, etc. **5
other than: a** except: no one other
than me **b** anything but: I can't be
other than grateful. **6 the other
day/night/afternoon/evening** on a
recent day/night/afternoon/evening

oth·er·wise /'ʌðəwaɪz‖'ʌðər-/ adv **1**
differently **2** apart from that: The soup
was cold, but otherwise the meal was
excellent. **3** if not: Go faster, otherwise
we'll be late.

ouch /aʊtʃ/ interj (expresses sudden
pain)

ought /ɔːt/ v aux **1** have a (moral)
duty: You ought to look after them better. **2** (shows what is right or sensible):
You ought to see a doctor. **3** will probably: Prices ought to come down soon.

ounce /aʊns/ n **1** [C] a measure of
weight equal to 28.35 grams **2** [S] a
small amount

our /aʊər/ determiner of us: our house

ours /aʊəz‖aʊərz/ pron of us; our
one's

our·selves /aʊə'selvz‖aʊər-/ pron **1**
(reflexive form of **we**): We saw ourselves on TV. **2** (strong form of **we**):
We built the house ourselves. **3 (all) by
ourselves a** alone **b** without help **4 to
ourselves** not shared

oust /aʊst/ vt force (someone) out

out[1] /aʊt/ adv **1** away from the
inside: Open the bag and take the
money out. **2** away from home or the
usual place: Let's go out tonight. **3**
away from a surface: The nail stuck
out. **4** to lots of people or places: Hand
out the drinks. **5** (of a fire or light) no
longer burning **6** completely: I'm tired

out. **7** aloud: Call the names out. **8** so
as to be clearly seen, understood, etc.:
Their secret is out. | Are the daffodils
out (= flowering) yet? **9** wrong in
guessing, etc.: I was 2 years out in my
estimation. **10** (of the ball in a game,
e.g. tennis) outside the line **11** no
longer fashionable **12** (of the TIDE)
away from the coast **13 out of: a** from
inside; away from: I jumped out of
bed. | (fig.) We're out of danger (= safe)
now. | (fig.) It's out of sight. (= can't be
seen) **b** from among: 4 out of 5 people
preferred it. **c** not having; without:
We're out of petrol. **d** because of: I
came out of interest. **e** (shows what
something is made from): made out of
wood **14 out of it (all): a** lonely and
unhappy because one is not included
in something **b** infml not thinking
clearly **15 out** to trying to

out[2] adj **1** directed outward **2 out-
and-out** complete; total

out·board mo·tor /ˌaʊtbɔːd
'məʊtər‖-bɔːrd-/ n motor fixed to the
back end of a small boat

out·break /'aʊtbreɪk/ n sudden
appearance or start of something bad

out·burst /'aʊtbɜːst‖-ɜːr-/ n sudden
powerful expression of feeling

out·cast /'aʊtkɑːst‖-kæst/ n someone forced from their home or
friendless

out·class /aʊt'klɑːs‖-'klæs/ vt be
very much better than

out·come /'aʊtkʌm/ n effect; result

out·crop /'aʊtkrɒp‖-krɑːp/ n rock or
rocks on the surface of the ground

out·cry /'aʊtkraɪ/ n public show of
anger

out·dat·ed /ˌaʊt'deɪtɪd◂/ adj no
longer in general use

out·do /aʊt'duː/ vt **-did** /-'dɪd/,
-done /-'dʌn/, 3rd person sing. pres. t.
-does /-'dʌz/ do or be better than

out·door /ˌaʊt'dɔːr◂/ adj existing,
happening, or used outside **outdoors**
adv

out·er /'aʊtər/ adj on the outside; furthest from the middle

outer space /ˌ·· '·/ n [U] area where
the stars and other heavenly bodies
are

out·fit /'aʊt.fɪt/ n **1** set of things esp.
clothes for a particular purpose **2**
group of people working together ♦ vt
-tt- provide with a set of esp. clothes
~er n

out·flank /aʊt'flæŋk/ vt go round the
side of (an enemy) to attack

out·go·ing /ˌaʊt'ɡəʊɪŋ◂/ adj **1** finishing a period in office **2** friendly **out-
goings** n [P] money spent

out·grow /aʊt'ɡrəʊ/ vt **-grew**
/-'ɡruː/, **-grown** /-'ɡrəʊn/ grow too
big, too old, or too fat for

out·house /'aʊthaʊs/ n small building near a larger main building

out·ing /'aʊtɪŋ/ n short journey for pleasure, esp. by a group

out·land·ish /aʊt'lændɪʃ/ adj strange and unpleasing **~ly** adv **~ness** n [U]

out·last /aʊt'lɑːst‖-'læst/ vt last longer than

out·law /'aʊtlɔː/ n (in former times) criminal being hunted ♦ vt declare (something) illegal

out·lay /'aʊtleɪ/ n money spent on something

out·let /'aʊtlet, -lət/ n way out for liquid or gas: (fig.) *an outlet for his energy*

out·line /'aʊtlaɪn/ n 1 line showing the shape of something 2 main ideas or facts, without details ♦ vt: *She outlined her plans*

out·live /aʊt'lɪv/ vt live longer than

out·look /'aʊtlʊk/ n 1 view from a place 2 future probabilities 3 one's general point of view

out·ly·ing /'aʊt,laɪ-ɪŋ/ adj distant; far from a city, etc.

out·mod·ed /aʊt'məʊdəd/ adj no longer in fashion or use

out·num·ber /aʊt'nʌmbəʳ/ vt be more in numbers than: *outnumbered by the enemy*

out-of-date /,·· '·◂/ adj no longer in use or in fashion

out-of-the-way /,··· '·◂/ adj 1 distant 2 unusual

out·pa·tient /'aʊt,peɪʃənt/ n person treated at a hospital but not staying there

out·post /'aʊtpəʊst/ n group of people or settlement far from the main group or settlement

out·put /'aʊtpʊt/ n [C;U] production: *The factory's output is 200 cars a day.*

out·rage /'aʊtreɪdʒ/ n 1 [C] very wrong or cruel act 2 [U] anger caused by such an act ♦ vt offend greatly **~ous** /aʊt'reɪdʒəs/ adj 1 very offensive 2 wildly unexpected and unusual

out·right /,aʊt'raɪt◂/ adv 1 completely: *She won outright.* 2 without delay: *He was killed outright.* 3 openly: *Tell him outright what you think.* ♦ adj complete and clear: *an outright lie*

out·set /'aʊtset/ n beginning: *There was trouble from/at the outset.*

out·shine /aʊt'ʃaɪn/ vt **-shone** /-'ʃɒn‖-'ʃəʊn/ 1 shine more brightly than 2 be much better than

out·side /aʊt'saɪd, 'aʊtsaɪd/ n 1 [(the) S] the part furthest from the middle, or that faces away from one or towards the open air: *to paint the outside of a house* 2 **at the outside** at the most ♦ adj 1 facing or at the outside: *the outside wall* 2 from elsewhere: *an outside broadcast* 3 (of a chance or possibility) slight ♦ adv to or on the outside, esp. in the open air: *go outside* ♦ prep 1 to or on the outside of: *Wait just outside the door.* 2 beyond the limits of: *outside my experience*

out·sid·er /aʊt'saɪdəʳ/ n 1 person not accepted in a social group 2 person or animal not expected to win

out·size /'aʊtsaɪz/ adj larger than the standard sizes

out·skirts /'aʊtskɜːts‖-ɜːr-/ n [P] outer areas or limits of a town

out·smart /aʊt'smɑːt‖-ɑːr-/ vt defeat by being cleverer

out·spo·ken /aʊt'spəʊkən/ adj expressing thoughts or feelings openly **~ly** adv **~ness** n [U]

out·stand·ing /aʊt'stændɪŋ/ adj 1 much better than others 2 not yet done or paid **~ly** adv

out·stay /aʊt'steɪ/ vt stay longer than: *to outstay one's welcome* (= stay too long as a guest so as to be no longer welcome)

out·strip /aʊt'strɪp/ vt **-pp-** do better than: *to outstrip one's competitors*

out·ward /'aʊtwəd‖-ərd/ adj, adv 1 away: *the outward journey* 2 on the outside but perhaps not really: *outward cheerfulness* **~ly** adv **outwards** adv

out·weigh /aʊt'weɪ/ vt be more important than

out·wit /aʊt'wɪt/ vt **-tt-** defeat by being cleverer

out·worn /aʊt'wɔːn‖-'wɔːrn/ adj (of an idea, custom, etc.) no longer used or useful

o·val /'əʊvəl/ n, adj (something) egg-shaped

o·va·ry /'əʊvəri/ n part of a female that produces eggs

o·va·tion /əʊ'veɪʃən/ n joyful expression of public approval

ov·en /'ʌvən/ n closed box for cooking, baking clay, etc.: (fig.) *It's like an oven in here.* (= uncomfortably hot)

over¹ /'əʊvəʳ/ prep 1 higher than but not touching: *the clock over the fireplace* 2 so as to cover: *Put a cloth over the jug.* 3 from side to side, esp. by going up and down: *to climb over a wall* | *a bridge over the river* 4 down across the edge of: *It fell over the cliff.* 5 in; through: *There's snow over most of Europe.* 6 in control of: *I don't want anyone over me, telling me what to do.* 7 more than: *over 10 years ago* 8 while doing, eating, etc.: *We held a meeting over lunch.* 9 by means of: *I heard it over the radio.* 10 about: *an argument over money* 11 **over and above** as well as

over² *adv* **1** downwards from an upright position: *I fell over.* **2** across an edge or distance: *The milk boiled over.* | *We flew over to America.* **3** so that another side is seen: *Turn the page over* **4** beyond: *children of 7 and over* (= older) **5** so as to be covered: *The windows are boarded over.* **6** remaining: *Was there any money over?* **7** (shows something is repeated): *I had to do it (all) over again.* **8** in all details: *Think it over carefully.* ♦ *adj* ended: *The party's over.*

o·ver·all¹ /ˌəʊvərˈɔːl◂/ *adj, adv* including everything: *overall costs*

o·ver·all² /ˈəʊvərɔːl/ *n* **1** *BrE* loose coat worn to protect clothes **2** *AmE* for OVERALLS (1)

o·ver·alls /ˈəʊvərɔːlz/ *n* [P] **1** *BrE* garment for the whole body, to protect one's clothes **2** *AmE* for DUNGAREES

o·ver·awe /ˌəʊvərˈɔː/ *vt* make quiet because of respect and fear

o·ver·bal·ance /ˌəʊvəˈbæləns‖-vər-/ *vi* become unbalanced and fall over

o·ver·bear·ing /ˌəʊvəˈbeərɪŋ‖-vər-/ *adj* forcefully trying to tell others what to do

o·ver·board /ˈəʊvəbɔːd‖ˈəʊvərbɔːrd/ *adv* **1** over the side of a boat into the water **2** **go overboard** become very or too keen

o·ver·cast /ˌəʊvəˈkɑːst◂‖ˌəʊvərˈkæst◂/ *adj* dark with clouds

o·ver·coat /ˈəʊvəkəʊt‖-vər-/ *n* long warm coat

o·ver·come /ˌəʊvəˈkʌm‖-vər-/ *vt* **-came** /-ˈkeɪm/. **-come** **1** defeat **2** make helpless: *overcome with grief*

o·ver·crowd /ˌəʊvəˈkraʊd‖-vər-/ *vt* put or allow too many people or things in (one place)

o·ver·do /ˌəʊvəˈduː‖-vər-/ *vt* **-did** /-ˈdɪd/, **-done** /-ˈdʌn/, *3rd person sing. pres. t.* **-does** /-ˈdʌz/ do, decorate, perform, etc., too much: *I've been overdoing it* (= working too hard) *lately.*

o·ver·dose /ˈəʊvədəʊs‖-vər-/ *n* too much of a drug

o·ver·draft /ˈəʊvədrɑːft‖ˈəʊvərdræft/ *n* money lent by a bank to an overdrawn person

o·ver·drawn /ˌəʊvəˈdrɔːn◂‖-vər-/ *adj* having taken more money from your bank account than it contains

o·ver·drive /ˈəʊvədraɪv‖-vər-/ *n* [U] GEAR that allows a car to go fast on less than full power

o·ver·due /ˌəʊvəˈdjuː◂‖ˌəʊvərˈduː◂/ *adj* late

o·ver·flow /ˌəʊvəˈfləʊ‖-vər-/ *vi/t* **1** flow over the edge (of): *The water's/ The bath's overflowing.* **2** go beyond the limits (of): *The crowd overflowed into the street.* ♦ /ˈəʊvəfləʊ‖-vər-/ *n* (pipe for carrying away) something that overflows

o·ver·grown /ˌəʊvəˈɡrəʊn◂‖-vər-/ *adj* **1** covered with plants growing uncontrolled **2** grown too large

o·ver·hang /ˌəʊvəˈhæŋ‖-vər-/ *vi/t* **-hung** /-ˈhʌŋ/ hang or stick out over (something) ♦ /ˈəʊvəhæŋ‖-vər-/ *n* overhanging rock, roof, etc.

o·ver·haul /ˌəʊvəˈhɔːl‖-vər-/ *vt* **1** examine thoroughly (and repair) **2** OVERTAKE ♦ /ˈəʊvəhɔːl‖-vər-/ *n* thorough examination: *The car needs an overhaul.*

o·ver·head /ˌəʊvəˈhed◂‖-vər-/ *adj, adv* above one's head: *overhead cables*

o·ver·heads /ˈəʊvəhedz‖-vər-/ *n* [P] money spent regularly to keep a business running

o·ver·hear /ˌəʊvəˈhɪəʳ‖-vər-/ *vi/t* **-heard** /-ˈhɜːd‖-ˈhɜːrd/ hear (what others are saying) without them knowing

o·ver·joyed /ˌəʊvəˈdʒɔɪd‖-vər-/ *adj* extremely pleased

o·ver·kill /ˈəʊvəkɪl‖-vər-/ *n* [U] something that goes beyond the desirable or safe limits

o·ver·la·den /ˌəʊvəˈleɪdn‖-vər-/ *past p. of* OVERLOAD

o·ver·land /ˌəʊvəˈlænd◂‖-vər-/ *adj, adv* across land and not by sea or air

o·ver·lap /ˌəʊvəˈlæp‖-vər-/ *vi/t* **-pp-** cover (something) partly and go beyond it: (fig.) *Our interests overlap.* (= are partly the same) ♦ /ˈəʊvəlæp‖-vər-/ *n* part that overlaps

o·ver·leaf /ˌəʊvəˈliːf‖ˈəʊvərliːf/ *adv* on the other side of the page

o·ver·load /ˌəʊvəˈləʊd‖-vər-/ *vt* **-loaded** *or* **-laden** /-ˈleɪdn/ **1** load too heavily **2** put too much electricity through **overload** /ˈəʊvələʊd‖-vər-/ *n*

o·ver·look /ˌəʊvəˈlʊk‖-vər-/ *vt* **1** give a view of from above **2** not notice; miss **3** forgive

o·ver·manned /ˌəʊvəˈmænd‖-vər-/ *adj* having more workers than are needed for a job **-manning** *n* [U]

o·ver·much /ˌəʊvəˈmʌtʃ◂‖-vər-/ *adv, determiner, pron* **1** *fml* too much **2** very much: *I don't like him overmuch.*

o·ver·night /ˌəʊvəˈnaɪt◂‖-vər-/ *adj, adv* **1** for or during the night **2** suddenly): *an overnight success*

o·ver·play /ˌəʊvəˈpleɪ‖-vər-/ *vt* make (something) appear more important than it really is

o·ver·pow·er /ˌəʊvəˈpaʊəʳ‖-vər-/ *vt* defeat by greater power **~ing** *adj* very strong: *an overpowering desire*

o·ver·ran /ˌəʊvəˈræn‖-vər-/ *past tense of* OVERRUN

o·ver·rate /ˌəʊvəˈreɪt‖-vər-/ *vt* give too high an opinion of

o·ver·re·act /ˌəʊvəriˈækt‖-vər-/ *vi* act too strongly as a result of (something)

o·ver·ride /ˌəʊvəˈraɪd/ vt **-rode** /-ˈrəʊd/, **-ridden** /-ˈrɪdn/ forbid obedience to or acceptance of (and take the place of): *My orders were overridden.* **–riding** adj greater than anything else: *of overriding importance*

o·ver·rule /ˌəʊvəˈruːl/ vt decide against (something already decided) by official power

o·ver·run /ˌəʊvəˈrʌn/ v **-ran** /-ˈræn/, **-run 1** vt spread over and cause harm **2** vi/t continue beyond (a time limit)

o·ver·seas /ˌəʊvəˈsiːz◂/-vər-/ adv, adj in, to, or from a foreign country across the sea

o·ver·see /ˌəʊvəˈsiː/-vər-/ vt **-saw** /-ˈsɔː/, **-seen** /-ˈsiːn/ watch to see that work is properly done **-seer** /ˈəʊvəsɪə/-vər-/ n

o·ver·shad·ow /ˌəʊvəˈʃædəʊ/-vər-/ vt **1** make worried and sadder **2** make appear less important

o·ver·shoot /ˌəʊvəˈʃuːt/-vər-/ vi/t **-shot** /-ˈʃɒt/-ˈʃɑːt/ go too far or beyond, and miss

o·ver·sight /ˈəʊvəsaɪt/-vər-/ n unintended failure to notice or do something

o·ver·sleep /ˌəʊvəˈsliːp/-vər-/ vi **-slept** /-ˈslept/ wake up too late

o·ver·spill /ˈəʊvəˌspɪl/-vər-/ n esp. BrE people who leave a crowded city and settle elsewhere

o·ver·step /ˌəʊvəˈstep/-vər-/ vt **-pp-** go beyond (the limits of what is proper or allowed)

o·vert /ˈəʊvɜːt, əʊˈvɜːt/-ɜːrt/ adj not hidden; open: *overt resistance* **~ly** adv

o·ver·take /ˌəʊvəˈteɪk/-vər-/ v **-took** /-ˈtʊk/, **-taken** /-ˈteɪkən/ **1** vi/t pass (a vehicle in front) **2** vt (of something unpleasant) reach suddenly and unexpectedly

o·ver·throw /ˌəʊvəˈθrəʊ/-vər-/ vt **-threw** /-ˈθruː/, **-thrown** /-ˈθrəʊn/ remove from power ♦ /ˈəʊvəθrəʊ/-vər-/ n: *the violent overthrow of the government*

o·ver·time /ˈəʊvətaɪm/-vər-/ n, adj [U] (money paid for or time spent working) beyond the usual working time: *to work overtime to do something* (= use much effort)

o·ver·tones /ˈəʊvətəʊnz/-vər-/ n [P] things suggested but not stated clearly

o·ver·took /ˌəʊvəˈtʊk/ past tense of OVERTAKE

o·ver·ture /ˈəʊvətjʊə, -tʃʊə, -tʃər/-vər-/ n **1** a musical introduction, esp. to an OPERA **overtures** n [P] offer to begin talks

o·ver·turn /ˌəʊvəˈtɜːn/ˌəʊvərˈtɜːrn/ v **1** vi/t turn over **2** vt bring (esp. a government) to an end suddenly

o·ver·view /ˈəʊvəvjuː/-vər-/ n usu. short account (of something) which gives a general picture but no details

o·ver·weight /ˌəʊvəˈweɪt◂/-vər-/ adj weighing too much

o·ver·whelm /ˌəʊvəˈwelm/-vər-/ vt **1** defeat or make powerless by much greater numbers **2** (of feelings) make completely helpless

o·ver·wrought /ˌəʊvəˈrɔːt◂/ adj too nervous and excited

ov·u·late /ˈɒvjʊleɪt/ˈɑːv-/ vi produce eggs from the OVARY **–lation** /ˌɒvjʊˈleɪʃən/ˌɑːv-/ n [U]

ow /aʊ/ interj (expresses sudden slight pain)

owe /əʊ/ vt **1** have to pay: *I owed her £5.* **2** feel grateful for: *We owe a lot to our parents.*

ow·ing /ˈəʊɪŋ/ adj **1** still to be paid **2** **owing to** /ˈ··· ·/ because of

owl /aʊl/ n night bird with large eyes

own¹ /əʊn/ determiner, pron **1** belonging to the stated person and no one else: *At last I had my own room/a room of my own.* **2** **come into one's own** begin to be properly respected for one's qualities **3** **have/get one's own back (on someone)** succeed in doing harm (to someone) in return for harm done to oneself **4** **hold one's own (against)** avoid defeat (by) **5** **on one's own: a** alone **b** without help

own² vt possess, esp. by legal right **~er** n **~ership** n [U]

own to phr vt admit

own up phr vi admit a fault or crime

own goal /ˌ· ˈ·/ n esp. BrE **1** (in football) a GOAL against one's own team SCOREd by mistake by one of one's own players **2** infml mistake that makes one look foolish, esp. a remark or action that is against one's own interests

ox /ɒks/ɑːks/ n **oxen** large animal of the cattle type, esp. male

ox·y·gen /ˈɒksɪdʒən/ˈɑːk-/ n [U] gas present in the air, necessary for life

oy·ster /ˈɔɪstər/ n **1** flat shellfish, often eaten **2** **the world is one's/someone's oyster** there are no limits on where one/someone can go, etc.

oz written abbrev. for: OUNCE(s)

o·zone /ˈəʊzəʊn/ n [U] **1** sea air that is pleasant to breathe **2** type of oxygen

P, p /piː/ *n* 1 the 16th letter of the English alphabet 2 **mind one's p's and q's** be careful what one says so as to avoid displeasing others

p *abbrev. for:* 1 page 2 *BrE* penny/pence

pace /peɪs/ *n* 1 speed, esp. of walking or running: *She works so fast I can't keep pace with* (= go as fast as) *her.* 2 (distance moved in) a single step 3 **put someone through his/her paces** make someone do something in order to show his/her abilities, qualities, etc. 4 **set the pace** fix the speed for others to copy 5 **show one's paces** show one's abilities/qualities ♦ *v* 1 *vi/t* walk (across) with slow regular steps 2 *vt* set the speed of movement for

pace out/off *phr vt* measure by taking steps

pace-maker /ˈpeɪsˌmeɪkər/ *n* 1 person who sets a speed or example for others to follow 2 machine used to make weak or irregular heartbeats regular

pac-i-fist /ˈpæsɨfɨst/ *n* person who believes war is wrong and refuses to fight **–fism** *n* [U]

pac-i-fy /ˈpæsɨfaɪ/ *vt* make calm and quiet, esp. less angry **–fication** /ˌpæsɨfɨˈkeɪʃən/ *n* [U]

pack¹ /pæk/ *n* 1 number of things wrapped or tied together or put in a case 2 *esp. AmE* packet 3 group of hunting animals 4 collection, group: *a pack of lies/thieves* 5 complete set of playing cards

pack² *v* 1 *vi/t* put (things) into cases, boxes, etc., for taking somewhere or storing 2 *vi/t* fit or push into a space: *Crowds of people packed into the hall.* 3 *vt* cover, fill, or surround closely with protective material 4 **pack a (hard) punch** *infml* **a** (of a fighter) able to give a strong hard blow **b** use very forceful language in an argument 5 **send someone packing** *infml* cause someone undesirable to leave quickly **~ed** *adj* full of people

pack in *phr vt infml* 1 stop doing 2 attract in large numbers: *That film is really packing them in.*

pack off *phr vt infml* BUNDLE off

pack up *phr v infml* 1 finish work 2 *vi esp. BrE* (of a machine) stop working 3 *vt* stop

pack-age /ˈpækɪdʒ/ *n* 1 number of things packed together; parcel 2 set of related things offered as a unit ♦ *vt* 1 make into a package 2 put in a special container for selling

package deal /ˈ·· ·/ *n* offer or agreement where a number of things must all be accepted together

package tour /ˈ·· ·/ *n* holiday where all travel, hotels, food, etc., are paid for together

pack-et /ˈpækɨt/ *n* 1 small container or parcel: *a packet of cigarettes* 2 *sl* large amount of money

pack-ing /ˈpækɪŋ/ *n* [U] 1 putting things in cases or boxes 2 protective material for packing things

pact /pækt/ *n* solemn agreement

pad¹ /pæd/ *n* 1 something made or filled with soft material, for protection or to give shape 2 many sheets of paper fastened together: *a writing pad* 3 LAUNCHING PAD 4 *sl* one's house or home 5 *sl* thick-skinned underpart of foot of some 4-footed animals ♦ *vt* **-dd-** 1 protect, shape, or make more comfortable with a pad or pads 2 make longer by adding unnecessary words **~ding** /ˈpædɪŋ/ *n* [U] 1 material used to pad something 2 unnecessary words or sentences

pad² *vi* **-dd-** walk steadily and usu. softly

pad-dle¹ /ˈpædl/ *n* short pole with a wide blade at one end or both ends, for rowing a small boat ♦ *vi/t* 1 row with a paddle 2 **paddle one's own canoe** *infml* depend on oneself and no one else

paddle² *vi* walk about in water a few inches deep ♦ *n* [S] act of paddling

pad-dock /ˈpædək/ *n* small field where horses are kept

pad-dy /ˈpædi/ *n* field where rice is grown in water

pad-lock /ˈpædlɒk‖-lɑːk/ *n* removable lock fastened with a U-shaped bar, for locking gates, bicycles, etc. ♦ *vt* fasten or lock with a padlock

pae-di-at-rics /ˌpiːdiˈætrɪks/ *n* [U] PEDIATRICS

pa-gan /ˈpeɪgən/ *n* person who does not believe in one's religion, or in any of the main religions ♦ *adj:* pagan tribes **~ism** *n* [U]

page¹ /peɪdʒ/ *n* one or both sides of a sheet of paper in a book, newspaper, etc.

page² *n* 1 boy servant at a hotel, club, etc. 2 boy attendant at a wedding

pag-eant /ˈpædʒənt/ *n* splendid public show or ceremony **~ry** *n* [U] splendid show of ceremonial grandness

pa-go-da /pəˈgəʊdə/ *n* temple (esp. Buddhist or Hindu) built on several floors

paid /peɪd/ *past t. and p. of* PAY — see also **put paid to** (PUT)

paid-up /ˌ· ˈ·◁/ *adj* having paid in full (esp. so as to continue being a member)

pail /peɪl/ n bucket

pain /peɪn/ n 1 [U] suffering in body or mind; hurting: Are you in pain? 2 [C] case of such suffering in a particular part: a pain in my stomach 3 [S] also **pain in the neck** /ˌ· ·ˈ·ˈ·/ —sl person, thing, or happening that makes one angry or tired 4 **on/under pain of** fml at the risk of suffering (a punishment) if something is not done ♦ vt fml cause pain to ~**ed** adj displeased or hurt in one's feelings ~**ful** adj: a painful cut ~**less** adj **pains** n [P] effort; trouble: I went to great pains to get the one you wanted. **painstaking** adj very careful and thorough

paint /peɪnt/ n [U] liquid colouring matter for decorating surfaces or making pictures ♦ vi/t 1 put paint on (a surface) 2 make a picture (of) with paint 3 describe in clear, well-chosen words 4 **paint the town red** go out and have a good time ~**ing** n 1 [U] act or art of painting 2 [C] painted picture — see also OIL PAINTING **paints** n [P] set of small containers of different-coloured paint, for painting pictures

paint-er[1] /ˈpeɪntər/ n person who paints pictures, or houses, rooms, etc.

painter[2] n rope for tying up a small boat

paint-work /ˈpeɪntwɜːk‖-wɜːrk/ n [U] painted surface

pair /peər/ n 1 two of the same kind: a pair of gloves 2 something made of two similar parts: a pair of scissors 3 two people closely connected ♦ vi/t form into one or more pairs: Jane and David paired off at the party.

pair up phr vi/t (cause to) join in pairs, esp. for work or sport

pa-ja-mas /pəˈdʒɑːməz ‖ -ˈdʒɑː-, -ˈdʒæ-/ n [P] esp. AmE PYJAMAS

pal /pæl/ n infml friend

pal-ace /ˈpælɪs/ n large grand house, esp. where a king or president lives

palace rev-o-lu-tion /ˌ·· ··ˈ··/ n removal of a president, king, etc., from power by people who worked closely with him/her

pal-a-ta-ble /ˈpælətəbəl/ adj fml 1 good to taste 2 acceptable; pleasant: not a palatable suggestion

pal-ate /ˈpælɪt/ n 1 the top inside part of the mouth 2 ability to judge good food or wine

pa-la-tial /pəˈleɪʃəl/ adj (of a building) large and splendid

pa-la-ver /pəˈlɑːvər‖-ˈlæ-/ n [U] trouble over unimportant matters; FUSS

pale[1] /peɪl/ adj 1 not bright or dark: pale blue 2 (of a face) rather white ♦ vi 1 become pale 2 seem less important, clever, etc., when compared with

pale[2] n limit of proper behaviour: beyond the pale

pal-e-on-tol-o-gy /ˌpæliɒnˈtɒlədʒi‖ ˌpeɪliɑːnˈtɑː-/ n [U] study of FOSSILS —**gist** n

pal-ette /ˈpælɪt/ n board on which a painter mixes colours

pal-ings /ˈpeɪlɪŋz/ n [P] (fence made of) pointed pieces of wood

pall[1] /pɔːl/ vi become uninteresting or dull

pall[2] n 1 [S] heavy or dark covering: a pall of smoke 2 [C] cloth spread over a COFFIN

pall-bear-er /ˈpɔːlˌbeərər/ n person who walks beside or helps carry a COFFIN

pal-let /ˈpælɪt/ n large flat frame used with a FORKLIFT for lifting heavy goods

pal-li-ate /ˈpælieɪt/ vt fml cause to be or seem less unpleasant or wrong —**ative** /ˈpæliətɪv/ n, adj: only a palliative, not a cure

pal-lid /ˈpælɪd/ adj (of skin) unhealthily pale ~**ness** n [U]

pal-lor /ˈpælər/ n [S] pallidness

palm[1] /pɑːm‖pɑːm, pɑːlm/ n tall tropical tree with no branches and a mass of large leaves at the top

palm[2] n lower surface of the hand

palm[3] v **palm off** phr vt 1 get rid of by deception 2 deceive into accepting

palm-ist /ˈpɑːmɪst‖ˈpɑːm-, ˈpɑːlm-/ n person who tells someone's future by looking at their PALM[2] ~**ry** n [U] palmist's art

palm-y /ˈpɑːmi‖ˈpɑːmi, ˈpɑːlmi/ adj (of past periods) most pleasant and successful

pal-pa-ble /ˈpælpəbəl/ adj fml easily and clearly known: a palpable lie —**bly** adv

pal-pi-tate /ˈpælpɪteɪt/ vi (of the heart) beat fast and irregularly —**tations** /ˌpælpɪˈteɪʃənz/ n [P]

pal-try /ˈpɔːltri/ adj worthlessly small or unimportant

pam-pas /ˈpæmpəz, -pəs/ n [U] wide treeless plains in South America

pam-per /ˈpæmpər/ vt treat too kindly

pam-phlet /ˈpæmflɪt/ n small book with paper covers

pan[1] /pæn/ n 1 round metal container for cooking, usu. with a long handle 2 esp. BrE bowl of a LAVATORY 3 container with holes in the bottom used for separating precious metals from other material

pan[2] v -nn- 1 vt CRITICIZE very severely 2 vi/t move (a camera) to follow the action being recorded on film or television

pan out phr vi happen in a particular way

pan-a-ce-a /ˌpænə'sɪə/ n something that will put right all troubles

pa-nache /pə'næʃ, pæ-/ n [U] showy splendid way of doing things

pan-cake /'pænkeɪk/ n thin flat cake cooked in a pan

pan-cre-as /'pæŋkrɪəs/ n bodily organ that helps in changing food chemically for use by the body

pan-da /'pændə/ n black-and-white bearlike animal from China

Panda car /'·· ·/ n BrE police car

pan-de-mo-ni-um /ˌpændɪ-'məʊnɪəm/ n [U] wild and noisy disorder

pan-der /'pændəʳ/ v pander to phr vt satisfy unworthily: The newspapers pander to people's interest in sex scandals.

Pan-do-ra's box /pæn,dɔːrəz 'bɒks‖-'bɑːks/ n open Pandora's box unintentionally cause, by taking some action, a large number of problems that did not exist or were not known about before

pane /peɪn/ n sheet of glass in a window

pan-e-gyr-ic /ˌpænɪ'dʒɪrɪk/ n fml speech or writing full of great praise

pan-el /'pænl/ n 1 flat piece of wood in a door or on a wall 2 board with instruments fixed in it: an aircraft's control panel 3 small group of people who answer questions on esp. a radio or television show 4 piece of cloth of a different colour or material, set in a dress — see also SOLAR PANEL ♦ vt -ll- BrE ‖ -l- AmE decorate with PANELS (1): oak-panelled walls ~ling BrE ‖ ~ing AmE n [U] PANELs (1)

pang /pæŋ/ n sudden sharp feeling of pain

pan-ic /'pænɪk/ n [C;U] sudden uncontrollable quickly-spreading fear or terror ♦ vi/t -ck- (cause to) feel panic ~ky adj suddenly afraid

panic sta-tions /'·· ,··/ n [U] state of confused anxiety because something needs to be done in a hurry

panic-strick-en /'·· ,··/ adj filled with panic

pan-ni-er /'pænɪəʳ/ n basket, esp. either of a pair on a bicycle

pan-o-ply /'pænəpli/ n [U] splendid ceremonial show or dress

pan-o-ra-ma /ˌpænə'rɑːmə‖-'ræmə/ n 1 complete view of a wide stretch of land 2 general representation in words or pictures **-ramic** /-'ræmɪk/ adj

pan-sy /'pænzi/ n 1 small flowering garden plant 2 infml derog a EFFEMINATE young man b male HOMOSEXUAL

pant /pænt/ vi breathe quickly, with short breaths ♦ n quick short breath

pan-the-is-m /'pænθi-ɪzəm/ n [U] religious idea that God and the universe are the same thing **-ist** n

pan-ther /'pænθəʳ/ n LEOPARD, esp. a black one

pan-ties /'pæntiz/ n [P] women's or children's short undergarment worn below the waist

pan-to-mime /'pæntəmaɪm/ also **panto** /'pæntəʊ/ infml — n [C;U] play for children based on a fairy story, produced at Christmas

pan-try /'pæntri/ n small room with shelves where food is kept

pants /pænts/ n [P] 1 BrE for panties or UNDERPANTS 2 esp. AmE trousers 3 **with one's pants down** sl awkwardly unprepared 4 **by the seat of one's pants** infml guided by one's experience rather than by a formal plan

pap /pæp/ n [U] 1 soft liquid food for babies or sick people 2 esp. AmE reading matter or entertainment intended only for amusement, which does not instruct or contain ideas of any value

pa-pa[1] /'pɑːpə/ n AmE father

pa-pa[2] /pə'pɑː/ n BrE lit father

pa-pa-cy /'peɪpəsi/ n power and office of the POPE

pa-pal /'peɪpl/ adj of the POPE

pap-a-raz-zo /ˌpæpə'rætsəʊ/ n -zi /-tsi/ newspaper writer or photographer who follows famous people about hoping to find out interesting or shocking stories about them

pa-per /'peɪpəʳ/ n 1 [U] material in thin sheets for writing or printing on, wrapping things in, etc. 2 [C] newspaper 3 [C] set of questions to be answered in an examination 4 [C] piece of writing for specialists, often read aloud 5 **on paper** as written down, but not yet tried out in reality — see also WHITE PAPER ♦ vt cover with WALLPAPER **papers** n [P] pieces of paper written on or printed, esp. used for official purposes

pa-per-back /'peɪpəbæk‖-ər-/ n book with a thin cardboard cover

pa-per-boy /'peɪpəbɔɪ‖-ər-/ n boy who delivers newspapers

paper clip /'·· ·/ n piece of curved wire for holding papers together

paper ti-ger /,·· '··/ n enemy that seems or wishes to seem powerful or threatening but is really not so

pa-per-weight /'peɪpəweɪt‖-ər-/ n heavy object put on papers to stop them being scattered

pa-per-work /'peɪpəwɜːk‖-pərwɜːrk/ n [U] writing reports and letters, keeping records, etc.

pap-ri-ka /'pæprɪkə‖pə'priːkə/ n [U] hot-tasting red powder from a plant, used in cooking

par /pɑːʳ/ n 1 [S] (nearly) equal level: Her skill is on a par with mine. 2 [U] average number of hits in GOLF **3 under par** *infml* not in the usual or average condition of health

par·a·ble /'pærəbəl/ *n* short simple story which teaches a moral lesson

pa·rab·o·la /pə'ræbələ/ *n* curved line, like a thrown ball rising and falling **–bolic** /ˌpærə'bɒlɪk‖-'bɑː-/ *adj*

par·a·chute /'pærəʃuːt/ *n* piece of cloth on long ropes, fastened to someone to allow them to fall slowly and safely from an aircraft ◆ *vi/t* drop by means of a parachute

pa·rade /pə'reɪd/ *n* **1** informal procession **2** ceremonial gathering of soldiers to be officially looked at — see also HIT PARADE ◆ *vi* **1** walk or gather in a parade **2** *vi* walk showily **3** *vt* show in order to be admired: *parading her knowledge*

par·a·dise /'pærədaɪs/ *n* **1** [U](*usu. cap.*) Heaven **2** [S;U] place or state of perfect happiness — see also FOOL'S PARADISE

par·a·dox /'pærədɒks‖-dɑːks/ *n* **1** statement that says 2 opposite things but has some truth in it **2** strange combination of opposing qualities, ideas, etc. **~ical** /ˌpærə'dɒksɪkəl‖-'dɑːk-/ *adj* **~ically** /-kli/ *adv* **1** in a paradoxical way **2** it is a paradox that

par·af·fin /'pærəfɪn/ *n* [U] *BrE* sort of oil burned for heating and lighting

par·a·gon /'pærəgən‖-gɑːn/ *n* person who is or seems to be a perfect model to copy

par·a·graph /'pærəgrɑːf‖-græf/ *n* division of a piece of writing that begins a new line

par·a·keet /'pærəkiːt/ *n* small PARROT

par·al·lel /'pærəlel/ *adj* **1** (of lines) always the same distance apart **2** comparable ◆ *n* **1** [C;U] comparable person or thing **2** [C] similarity (point of) **3** [C] line of LATITUDE ◆ *vt* **-ll-** *BrE* ‖ **-l-** *AmE* be similar to

par·al·lel·o·gram /ˌpærə'leləgræm/ *n* 4-sided figure with opposite sides equal and parallel

par·a·lyse *BrE* ‖ **-lyze** *AmE* /'pærəlaɪz/ *vt* **1** cause paralysis in **2** cause to stop working: *The strike paralysed the industry.*

pa·ral·y·sis /pə'ræləsɪs/ *n* [U] loss of movement in (some of) the body muscles **paralytic** /ˌpærə'lɪtɪk/ *adj* **1** suffering from paralysis **2** *esp. BrE infml*, very drunk

par·a·med·ic /ˌpærə'medɪk/ *n esp. AmE* someone, such as an AMBULANCE driver, who helps in the care of sick people but is not a doctor or nurse

pa·ram·e·ter /pə'ræmətər/ *n* (*usu. pl.*) any of the established limits within which something must operate

par·a·mil·i·tary /ˌpærə'mɪlətri‖-teri/ *adj* acting like an army, esp. illegally

par·a·mount /'pærəmaunt/ *adj fml* greater than all others in importance

par·a·noi·a /ˌpærə'nɔɪə/ *n* [U] disease of the mind in which you think esp. that other people are trying to harm you **–noid** /'pærənɔɪd/ *adj* (as if) suffering from paranoia

par·a·pet /'pærəpət, -pet/ *n* low protective wall at the edge of a roof, bridge, etc.

par·a·pher·na·li·a /ˌpærəfə'neɪlɪə‖-far-/ *n* [U] small articles of various kinds

par·a·phrase /'pærəfreɪz/ *vt*, *n* (make) a re-expression of (something written or said) in different words

par·a·site /'pærəsaɪt/ *n* **1** animal or plant that lives and feeds on another **2** useless person supported by others' efforts **–sitic** /ˌpærə'sɪtɪk/ *adj*

par·a·sol /'pærəsɒl‖-sɔːl, -sɑːl/ *n* SUNSHADE

par·a·troops /'pærətruːps/ *n* [P] soldiers who drop from aircraft using PARACHUTES

par·cel[1] /'pɑːsəl‖'pɑːr-/ *n* **1** something wrapped up in paper and fastened **2** **part and parcel of** a most important part that cannot be separated from the whole of

parcel[2] *v* **-ll-** *BrE* ‖ **-l-** *AmE* **parcel out** *phr vt* divide into parts or shares **parcel up** *phr vt* wrap and tie

parch /pɑːtʃ‖pɑːrtʃ/ *vt* make hot and dry

parch·ment /'pɑːtʃmənt‖'pɑːr-/ *n* [C;U] treated animal skin, used formerly for writing on

par·don /'pɑːdn‖'pɑːrdn/ *n* **1** [C;U] (act of) forgiving, esp. of a guilty person, so they will no longer be punished **2 I beg your pardon**, also **pardon me** — **a** 'Please excuse me for having accidentally touched/pushed you.' **b** 'Please repeat what you said.' ◆ *vt* give pardon to ◆ *interj* (ask for something not fully heard to be repeated) **~able** *adj* that can be forgiven

pare /peər/ *vt* cut off the edge or thin covering of: (fig.) *We must pare down* (= reduce) *costs.*

par·ent /'peərənt/ *n* father or mother **~tal** /pə'rentl/ *adj*

pa·ren·the·sis /pə'renθəsɪs/ *n* **-ses** /-siz/ *fml* **1** (*usu. pl.*) *BrE fml* or *AmE* for BRACKET (2) **2** words introduced as an added explanation or thought

pa·ri·ah /pə'raɪə, 'pærɪə‖pə'raɪə/ *n fml* person not accepted by society

par·ish /'pærɪʃ/ *n* area for which a priest has responsibility: *the parish church*

pa·rish·io·ner /pə'rɪʃənər/ *n* person who lives in a parish

par·i·ty /ˈpærəti/ n [U] fml being equal

park¹ /pɑːk‖pɑːrk/ n large usu. grassy enclosed piece of land in a town, used by the public for pleasure and rest — see also SCIENCE PARK

park² vi/t put (a vehicle) for a time: (fig.) He just came in and parked himself on the sofa.

parking me·ter /ˈ·· ˌ·ˈ/ n apparatus into which one put some money, allowing one to park near it for a time

park·land /ˈpɑːk-lænd‖ˈpɑːrk-/ n large grassy area surrounding a large country house

par·lance /ˈpɑːləns‖ˈpɑːr-/ n [U] fml particular way of speaking or use of words

par·ley /ˈpɑːli‖ˈpɑːrli/ vi, n (hold) a talk, esp. with an enemy to make peace

par·lia·ment /ˈpɑːləmənt‖ˈpɑːr-/ n body of people elected or appointed to make laws **~ary** /ˌpɑːləˈmentəri‖ ˌpɑːr-/ adj

par·lour BrE ‖ **-lor** AmE /ˈpɑːləʳ‖ ˈpɑːr-/ n 1 esp. AmE shop: an ice-cream parlour 2 LIVING ROOM

parlour game /ˈ·· ·ˈ/ n game played sitting down indoors

par·lous /ˈpɑːləs‖ˈpɑːr-/ adj fml in danger of failing

pa·ro·chi·al /pəˈrəʊkiəl/ adj 1 only interested in one's own affairs 2 of a PARISH

par·o·dy /ˈpærədi/ n [C;U] copy of a writer's or composer's style, made to amuse ♦ vt make a parody of

pa·role /pəˈrəʊl/ n [U] letting someone out of prison before their official period of imprisonment has ended ♦ vt let out of prison on parole

par·ox·ys·m /ˈpærəksɪzəm/ n sudden sharp expression of feeling or attack of pain

par·quet /ˈpɑːkeɪ, ˈpɑːkeɪ‖pɑːrˈkeɪ/ n [U] small wooden blocks making a floor

par·rot /ˈpærət/ n tropical bird with a curved beak and usu. brightly coloured feathers ♦ vt repeat (someone else's words or actions) without thought or understanding

par·ry /ˈpæri/ vt turn aside (a blow or weapon): (fig.) parrying awkward questions

par·si·mo·ni·ous /ˌpɑːsɪˈməʊniəs‖ ˌpɑːr-/ adj unwilling to spend money; STINGY **~ly** adv **~ness** n [U]

par·si·mo·ny /ˈpɑːsɪməni‖ˈpɑːrsɪ-məʊni/ n [U] fml ungenerousness; state of being parsimonious

pars·ley /ˈpɑːsli‖ˈpɑːr-/ n small plant used in cooking

pars·nip /ˈpɑːsnɪp‖ˈpɑːr-/ n plant with a long white root used as a vegetable

par·son /ˈpɑːsən‖ˈpɑːr-/ n priest in charge of a PARISH

par·son·age /ˈpɑːsənɪdʒ‖ˈpɑːr-/ n parson's house

parson's nose /ˌ·· ·ˈ/ n fleshy piece at the tail end of a cooked chicken, etc.

part¹ /pɑːt‖pɑːrt/ n 1 [C] any of the pieces into which something is divided: an engine with 100 moving parts | The travel is the best part of my job. 2 [S;U] share in an activity: Did you take part in the fighting? 3 [U] side; position: He took my part (= supported me) in the quarrel. 4 [C] (words of) a character acted in a play or film 5 **for my part** as far as I am concerned 6 **for the most part**: a mostly b in most cases 7 **in part** partly 8 **on the part of** of or by (someone) 9 **play a part in** have an influence on 10 **in good part** without being offended ♦ adv partly: The exams are part written, part practical. **~ly** adv 1 not completely 2 in some degree **parts** n [P] 1 area of a country: We don't have much rain in these parts. 2 fml **a man/woman of parts** with many different abilities

part² v 1 vi/t separate: They parted as friends. | She parted the curtains. 2 vt separate (hair on the head) along a line 3 **part company** (with): a end a relationship (with) b no longer be together (with) c disagree (with) **~ing** n 1 [U] leaving 2 [C] line on the head where the hair is parted

part with phr vt give away; stop having

par·take /pɑːˈteɪk‖pɑːr-/ vi **-took** /-ˈtʊk/, **-taken** /-ˈteɪkən/ fml eat or drink something offered

par·tial /ˈpɑːʃəl‖ˈpɑːr-/ adj 1 not complete 2 (unfairly) favouring one more than another 3 **partial to** very fond of **~ly** adv **~ity** /ˌpɑːʃiˈælɪti‖ ˌpɑːr-/ n 1 [U] being PARTIAL (2) 2 [S] fondness: a partiality for cream cakes

par·tic·i·pant /pɑːˈtɪsɪpənt‖pɑːr-/ n person who participates

par·tic·i·pate /pɑːˈtɪsɪpeɪt‖pɑːr-/ vi take part or have a share in an activity **-pation** /pɑːˌtɪsɪˈpeɪʃən‖pɑːr-/ n [U]

par·ti·ci·ple /ˈpɑːtɪsɪpəl‖ˈpɑːr-/ n PAST PARTICIPLE or PRESENT PARTICIPLE

par·ti·cle /ˈpɑːtɪkəl‖ˈpɑːr-/ n very small piece

par·tic·u·lar /pəˈtɪkjʊləʳ‖pər-/ adj 1 special; unusual: of no particular importance 2 single and different from others: this particular case 3 showing (too) much care over small matters 4 **in particular** especially ♦ n small single part of a whole; detail **~ly** adv especially

parting shot /ˌ·· ˈ·/ n remark or action made when leaving

par·ti·san /ˌpɑːtɪˈzæn‖ˈpɑːrtəzən, -sən/ n, adj 1 (person) giving strong unreasoning support to one side 2 member of an armed group that fights in secret against an enemy that has conquered its country

par·ti·tion /pɑːˈtɪʃən‖pər-, pɑːr-/ n 1 [C] thin wall indoors 2 [U] division, esp. of a country ♦ vt divide up

partition off phr vt separate with a partition

part·ner /ˈpɑːtnər‖ˈpɑːrt-/ n person you are with, doing something together: a dancing/business/marriage partner ♦ vt act as a partner to ~**ship** n 1 [U] being a partner 2 [C] business owned by 2 or more partners

part of speech /ˌ· · ˈ·/ n class of word, such as 'noun' or 'verb'

par·took v past t. of PARTAKE

part-time /ˌ· ·◄/ adj, adv (working) during only part of the regular working time

par·ty /ˈpɑːti‖ˈpɑːrti/ n 1 gathering of people for food and amusement: a birthday party 2 association of people with the same political aims: the Democratic party 3 group of people doing something together: a search party — see also WORKING PARTY 4 esp. law person or group concerned in a matter 5 be (a) party to take part in or know about (some action or activity) 6 (follow) the party line act according to the official opinion of a political party — see also THIRD PARTY ♦ vi infml, esp. AmE enjoy oneself, esp. at a party or parties

party piece /ˈ·· ˌ·/ n song, poem, etc., that is someone's usual choice when asked to give a performance, e.g. at a party

pass¹ /pɑːs‖pæs/ v 1 vi/t reach and move beyond: Several cars passed (us). 2 vi/t go through or across: A cloud passed across the sun. 3 vi/t (cause to) go: I passed a rope around the tree. 4 vi come to an end: Summer is passing. 5 vt give: Please pass me the salt. 6 vt (in sport) kick, throw, etc., (esp. a ball) to a member of one's own side 7 a vi (of time) go by b vt spend (time) 8 vt accept officially: Parliament passed a new law. 9 vi/t succeed in (an examination) 10 vt give (a judgment, opinion, etc.): The judge passed a heavy sentence on him. 11 let something pass leave (a wrong statement, mistake, etc.) without putting it right 12 pass the time of day (with) give a greeting (to), and/or have a short conversation (with)

pass away phr vi die

pass by phr vt disregard

pass for phr vt be (mistakenly) accepted or considered as

pass off phr v 1 vt present falsely: passing herself off as a doctor 2 vi take place and be completed

pass on phr vi 1 PASS AWAY 2 move on

pass out phr vi faint

pass over phr vt fail to choose

pass up phr vt fail to take advantage of; miss

pass² n 1 successful result in an examination 2 official paper showing that one is allowed to do something: a travel pass 3 act of giving the ball to someone else in sport 4 way by which one can travel through or over a place, esp. a range of mountains 5 act of trying to interest someone sexually: He made a pass at me.

pass·a·ble /ˈpɑːsəbəl‖ˈpæ-/ adj 1 (just) good enough 2 a (of a road) fit to be used b (of a river) fit to be crossed –**bly** adv

pas·sage /ˈpæsɪdʒ/ n 1 [C] long narrow connecting way, esp. a CORRIDOR 2 [C] way through: We forced a passage through the crowd. 3 [U] fml going across, through, etc.: the bill's passage through Parliament 4 [U] onward flow (of time) 5 [S] (cost of) a journey by sea or air 6 [C] short part of a speech, piece of music, etc.

pas·sé /ˈpɑːseɪ, ˈpæseɪ‖pæˈseɪ/ adj old-fashioned

pas·sen·ger /ˈpæsəndʒər, -sən-/ n person being taken in a vehicle

pass·er·by /ˌpɑːsəˈbaɪ‖ˌpæsər-/ n passersby person who is going past a place

pass·ing /ˈpɑːsɪŋ‖ˈpæ-/ n [U] 1 going by 2 ending: disappearance 3 death 4 in passing while talking about something else ♦ adj 1 moving or going by: passing traffic 2 not lasting long: I didn't give it a passing thought.

pas·sion /ˈpæʃən/ n 1 [C;U] strong deep feeling, esp. of love or anger 2 [S] a strong liking: a passion for tennis 3 the Passion the suffering and death of Christ

pas·sion·ate /ˈpæʃənɪt/ adj filled with passion ~**ly** adv

pas·sive¹ /ˈpæsɪv/ adj 1 suffering something bad without (enough) opposition 2 (of verbs or sentences) expressing an action which is done to the subject of a sentence ~**ly** adv ~**ness**, also n [U] –**sivity** /pæˈsɪvɪti/

passive² n [the + S] passive form of a verb

pass·key /ˈpɑːskiː‖ˈpæs-/ n 1 key given to only a few people 2 key that will open many different locks

pass·port /ˈpɑːspɔːt‖ˈpæspɔːrt/ n 1 small official book allowing you to enter foreign countries 2 something that lets you get something else easily: *Is money a passport to happiness?*

pass·word /'pɑːswɜːd‖'pæswɜrd/ n secret word which you have to know to be allowed into a building, etc.

past¹ /pɑːst‖pæst/ adj 1 (of time) earlier than the present: *the past few days* 2 ended: *Winter is past.* 3 gram expressing past time: *the past tense* 4 former: *a past president of our club* ♦ n [S] 1 (what happened in) the time before the present: *It happened in the past.* | *our country's glorious past* 2 derog secret former life containing wrong-doing of some kind: *a woman with a past*

past² prep 1 up to and beyond: *They rushed past us.* 2 beyond in time or age: *It's 10 minutes past four.* 3 beyond the possibility of: *I'm past caring.* (= no longer care) 4 **past it** infml no longer able to do the things one could formerly do ♦ adv by: *The children ran past.*

pas·ta /'pæstə‖'pɑː-/ n [U] food made in different shapes from flour paste

paste /peɪst/ n [U] 1 soft mixture of powder and liquid 2 liquid mixture. usu. with flour, for sticking paper together ♦ vt fasten with paste

pas·tel /'pæstl‖pæ'stel/ adj soft and light in colour

pas·teur·ize ‖ also **-ise** BrE /'pæstʃəraɪz, -stə-/ vt heat (a liquid) to destroy bacteria **-ization** /ˌpæstʃəraɪ'zeɪʃən, -stə-‖-rə-/ n [U]

pas·tiche /pæˈstiːʃ/ n work of art made of, or in the style of, other works of art

pas·tille /pæˈstiːl/ n small hard sweet, esp. containing throat medicine

pas·time /'pɑːstaɪm‖'pæs-/ n something done to pass one's time pleasantly

past mas·ter /ˌ '··/ n very skilled person

pas·tor /'pɑːstər‖'pæ-/ n Christian priest in charge of a church

pas·tor·al /'pɑːstərəl‖'pæ-/ adj 1 of a priest's duties amongst his religious group 2 of simple country life

past par·ti·ci·ple /ˌ '····/ n form of a verb used in compounds to show the passive or the PERFECT¹ (5) tenses (such as *broken* in *The cup was broken.*)

pas·try /'peɪstri/ n 1 [U] a mixture of flour, fat, and liquid, eaten when baked 2 [C] article of food made from this

pas·ture /'pɑːstʃər‖'pæs-/ n [C,U] (piece of) grassy land where farm animals feed ♦ vt put in a pasture to feed

pas·ty¹ /'pæsti/ n small pastry case filled usu. with meat

past·y² /'peɪsti/ adj (of the face) unhealthily white

pat¹ /pæt/ vt **-tt-** strike gently and repeatedly with a flat hand ♦ n 1 light friendly stroke with the hand 2 small shaped mass of butter 3 **a pat on the back** expression of praise or satisfaction for something done

pat² adj, adv (too) easily or quickly answered or known

patch /pætʃ/ n 1 irregularly shaped part of a surface different from the rest: *damp patches on the wall* 2 small piece of material to cover a hole 3 small piece of ground: *a cabbage patch* 4 piece of material worn to protect a damaged eye 5 period: *He's going through* **a bad patch.** (= a time of trouble or misfortune) 6 **not a patch on** BrE infml not nearly as good as ♦ vt put a PATCH (2) on

patch up phr vt 1 repair 2 become friends again after (a quarrel)

patch·work /'pætʃwɜːk‖-ɜrk/ n [C,U] (piece of) sewn work made by joining small bits of different materials: (fig.) *the patchwork of fields seen from an aircraft*

patch·y /'pætʃi/ adj 1 in or having patches (PATCH (1)): *patchy fog* 2 incomplete or only good in parts **-ily** adv **-iness** n [U]

pâ·té /'pæteɪ‖pɑː'teɪ, pæ-/ n [U] food made by crushing meat, esp. LIVER, into a soft mass

pa·tent /'peɪtnt, 'pæ-‖'pæ-/ n (official paper giving someone) the unshared right to make or sell a new invention ♦ adj 1 protected by a patent 2 fml clear to see: *his patent annoyance* ♦ vt obtain a patent for **~ly** adv fml clearly

patent leath·er /ˌpeɪtnt 'leθər‖ ˌpæ-/ n [U] very shiny leather. usu. black

pa·ter·nal /pəˈtɜːnl‖-ɜrr-/ adj 1 of or like a father 2 protecting people like a father but allowing them no freedom 3 related to a person through the father's side of the family **~ly** adv

pa·ter·nal·ism /pəˈtɜːnəl-ɪzəm‖-ɜrr-/ n [U] a PATERNAL (2) way of controlling people **-istic** /pəˌtɜːnəl'ɪstɪk‖ -ɜrr-/ adj **-istically** /-kli/ adv

pa·ter·ni·ty /pəˈtɜːnəti‖-ɜrr-/ n [U] esp. law origin from the male parent: *paternity leave*

path /pɑːθ‖pæθ/ n **paths** /pɑːðz‖ pæðz/ 1 track or way where you can walk 2 line along which something moves: *the path of an arrow*

pa·thet·ic /pəˈθetɪk/ adj 1 causing pity or sorrow 2 derog hopelessly unsuccessful **~ally** /-kli/ adv

pa·thol·o·gy /pəˈθɒlədʒi‖-ˈθɑː-/ n [U] study of disease **-gist** n specialist in pathology, esp. one who examines a dead body to find out how the person died **-gical** /ˌpæθəˈlɒdʒɪkəl‖-ˈlɑː-/ adj **1** of pathology **2** caused by disease, esp. of the mind **3** great and unreasonable: *pathological jealousy* **–gically** /-kli/ adv

pa·thos /ˈpeɪθɒs‖-θɑːs/ n [U] quality that causes pity and sorrow

path·way /ˈpɑːθweɪ‖ˈpæθ-/ n PATH (1)

pa·tience /ˈpeɪʃəns/ n [U] **1** ability to wait calmly, to control oneself when angered, or to accept unpleasant things without complaining **2** card game for one player

pa·tient[1] /ˈpeɪʃənt/ adj showing patience **~ly** adv

patient[2] n person being treated medically

pat·i·na /ˈpætənə/ n pleasingly smooth shiny surface

pat·i·o /ˈpætiəʊ/ n **-os** stone-floored space next to a house, for sitting out on in fine weather

pa·tois /ˈpætwɑː/ n **-tois** /-twɑːz/ [C;U] local form of speech

pa·tri·arch /ˈpeɪtriɑːk‖-ɑːrk/ n **1** old and much-respected man **2** chief BISHOP of the Eastern Churches **~al** /ˌpeɪtriˈɑːkəl‖-ˈɑːr-/ adj **1** ruled only by men **2** of a patriarch

pat·ri·cide /ˈpætrəsaɪd/ n [U] **1** murder of one's father **2** person guilty of this

pat·ri·mo·ny /ˈpætrəməni‖-məʊni/ n [S;U] property one gets from one's dead father, grandfather, etc.

pat·ri·ot /ˈpætriət, -triɒt, ˈpeɪ-‖ˈpeɪtriət, -triɒt/ n someone who loves their country **~ism** n [U] **~ic** /ˌpætriˈɒtɪk, ˌpeɪ-‖ˌpeɪtriˈɑːtɪk/ adj **~ically** /-kli/ adv

pa·trol /pəˈtrəʊl/ n **1** [U] (period of) patrolling: *warships on patrol in the Channel* **2** [C] small group on patrol ♦ vi/t go round (an area, building, etc.) repeatedly to see that there is no trouble

pa·tron /ˈpeɪtrən/ n **1** person who gives money for support: *a patron of the arts* **2** fml customer in a shop, pub, etc., esp. regularly **~age** /ˈpætrənɪdʒ/ n [U] **1** support given by a PATRON (1) **2** right to appoint people to important positions

pat·ron·ize ‖ also **-ise** BrE /ˈpætrənaɪz‖ˈpeɪ-, ˈpæ-/ vt **1** act towards (someone) as if you were better or more important than them **2** fml be a PATRON (2) of

patron saint /ˌ··ˈ·/ n SAINT giving special protection to a particular place, activity, etc.

pat·ter[1] /ˈpætər/ vi, n (run with or make) the sound of something striking lightly, quickly, and repeatedly

patter[2] n [U] fast continuous amusing talk

pat·tern /ˈpætn‖ˈpætərn/ n **1** regularly repeated arrangement, esp. with a decorative effect: *cloth with a pattern of red and white squares* **2** way in which something develops: *the usual pattern of the illness* **3** shape used as a guide for making something: *a dress pattern* ♦ vt **1** make a decorative pattern on **2** make according to a PATTERN (3)

pau·ci·ty /ˈpɔːsəti/ n [S] fml less than is needed; lack

paunch /pɔːntʃ/ n fat stomach **~y** adj

pau·per /ˈpɔːpər/ n very poor person

pause /pɔːz/ n short but noticeable break in activity, speech, etc. ♦ vi make a pause

pave /peɪv/ vt **1** cover with a hard level surface, esp. of PAVING STONES **2** **pave the way (for/to)** prepare for or make possible

pave·ment /ˈpeɪvmənt/ n BrE paved path at the side of a road

pa·vil·ion /pəˈvɪljən/ n **1** esp. BrE building beside a sports field, for the players and watchers **2** large public building usu. put up for some short time, used for EXHIBITIONs, etc.

pav·ing /ˈpeɪvɪŋ/ n **1** [U] (material for making) a paved surface **2** [C] paving stone

paving stone /ˈ·· ·/ n flat stone for making pavements, etc.

paw /pɔː/ n **1** animal's foot with CLAWs **2** infml human hand: *Keep your paws off me!* ♦ vi/t **1** (of an animal) touch or strike with the foot **2** handle roughly or roughly

pawn[1] /pɔːn/ n **1** least valuable piece in CHESS **2** unimportant person used for someone else's advantage

pawn[2] vt leave with a pawnbroker in return for money lent ♦ n [U]: *My watch is in pawn.*

pawn·bro·ker /ˈpɔːnˌbrəʊkər/ n person who lends money in return for things one brings, which he keeps if one does not repay the money

pay /peɪ/ v paid **1** vi/t give (money) to (someone) in return for goods bought, work done, etc. **2** vt settle (a bill, debt, etc.) **3** vi/t be profitable (to); be worth the trouble (to): *It doesn't pay (you) to argue with him.* **4** vt give, offer, or make: *Pay attention to what I say.* | *We paid them a visit.* **5** **pay one's way** pay money for things as one buys them so as not to get into debt **6** **pay through the nose (for)** infml pay far too much (for) ♦ n [U] **1** money received for work **2** **in the pay of** employed by **~er** n

pay back phr vt **1** return (what is owing) to (someone) **2** return bad treatment, rudeness, etc., to

pay for *phr vt* receive suffering or punishment for

pay off *phr v* **1** *vt* pay all of (a debt) **2** *vt* pay and dismiss **3** *vt* pay (someone) to keep silent about a wrong act **4** *vi* be successful

pay out *phr v* **1** *vi/t* make (a large payment) **2** *vt* allow (a rope) to be pulled out gradually

pay up *phr vi* pay a debt in full, esp. unwillingly or late

pay·a·ble /'peɪəbəl/ *adj* that must or can be paid

pay dirt /'· ·/ *n* [U] *AmE* valuable discovery

pay·ee /peɪ'iː/ *n tech* person to whom money is or should be paid

pay·load /'peɪləʊd/ *n* amount carried in a vehicle, esp. a spacecraft

pay·mas·ter /'peɪˌmɑːstəʳ‖-ˌmæ-/ *n* person who pays someone, and can therefore control their actions

pay·ment /'peɪmənt/ *n* **1** [U] act of paying **2** [C] amount of money (to be) paid — see also BALANCE OF PAYMENTS, DOWN PAYMENT

pay·off /'peɪɒf‖-ɔːf/ *n* **1** payment made to settle matters **2** ending to something, when everything is explained

pay pack·et /'· ·/ *n* (envelope containing) wages

pay·roll /'peɪrəʊl/ *n* **1** list of workers employed **2** total amount of wages paid in a particular company

PE /ˌpiː 'iː/ *n* [U] physical education; development of the body by games, exercises, etc.

pea /piː/ *n* large round green seed used as food

peace /piːs/ *n* [U] **1** period free of war **2** calmness; quietness **3** good order in a country: *The job of the police is to keep the peace.* **4** lack of anxiety: *peace of mind* **5** hold one's peace remain silent **6** make one's peace with settle a quarrel with ~**ful** *adj* **1** quiet; untroubled **2** without war ~**fully** *adv* ~**fulness** *n* [U]

peace·time /'piːstaɪm/ *n* [S] time when a nation is not at war

peach /piːtʃ/ *n* round soft juicy yellowish-red fruit

pea·cock /'piːkɒk‖-kɑːk/ *n* large bird with long beautifully coloured tail feathers

peak /piːk/ *n* **1** highest point, level, etc. **2** sharply pointed mountain top **3** part of a cap which sticks out in front ♦ *adj* highest; greatest: *at peak fitness* ♦ *vi* reach a PEAK (1)

peal /piːl/ *n* **1** loud long sound: *peals of laughter* **2** sound of bells ringing ♦ *vi* (of a bell) ring loudly

pea·nut /'piːnʌt/ *n* nut that grows in a shell underground **peanuts** *n* [P] *sl* very little money

pear /peəʳ/ *n* sweet, juicy fruit, narrow at the stem end and wide at the other

pearl /pɜːl‖pɜːrl/ *n* round silvery-white jewel formed in the shell of OYSTERs

pearl·y gates /ˌ·· '·/*n* [*the* + P] gates of Heaven

peas·ant /'pezənt/ *n* **1** person who works on the land in a poor country or in former times **2** *infml derog* uneducated or bad-mannered person

peas·ant·ry /'pezəntri/ *n* all the PEASANTs (1) in a place

peat /piːt/ *n* [U] partly decayed plant material in the earth, used for growing things or burning ~**y** *adj*

peb·ble /'pebəl/ *n* small stone –**bly** *adj*

pec·ca·dil·lo /ˌpekə'dɪləʊ/ *n* -**loes** or -**los** unimportant wrongdoing

peck /pek/ *v* **1** *vi/t* (of a bird) strike with the beak **2** *vt* kiss hurriedly ♦ *n* **1** stroke or mark made by pecking **2** hurried kiss

pecking or·der /'·· ˌ·/ *n* social order, showing who is more and less important

peck·ish /'pekɪʃ/ *adj* slightly hungry

pe·cu·li·ar /pɪ'kjuːliəʳ/ *adj* **1** strange, esp. in a displeasing way **2** belonging only to a particular place, time, etc.: *a plant peculiar to these islands* **3** rather mad **4** rather ill ~**ly** *adv* **1** especially **2** strangely ~**ity** /pɪˌkjuːli'ærɪti/ *n* **1** [U] being peculiar **2** [C] something PECULIAR (2) **3** [C] strange or unusual habit, etc.

ped·a·gog·i·cal /ˌpedə'gɒdʒɪkəl‖ -'gɑː-, -'gɑʊ-/ *adj* of teaching or the study of teaching methods ~**ly** /-kli/ *adv*

ped·a·gogue /'pedəgɒg‖-gɑːg/ *n* teacher who is too much concerned with rules

ped·al /'pedl/ *n* part pushed with the foot to drive or control a machine: *a bicycle pedal* ♦ *v* -**ll**- *BrE* ‖ -**l**- *AmE* **1** *vi* work pedals **2** *vi/t* ride (a bicycle)

ped·ant /'pednt/ *n* person who overvalues small details and formal rules ~**ic** /pɪ'dæntɪk/ *adj* ~**ically** /-kli/ *adv*

ped·dle /'pedl/ *vt* try to sell by going from place to place

ped·dler /'pedləʳ/ *n* **1** person who peddles illegal drugs **2** *AmE* for PEDLAR

ped·es·tal /'pedɪstl/ *n* **1** base on which a pillar or STATUE stands **2** put someone on a pedestal treat someone as better or nobler than anyone else

pe·des·tri·an¹ /pɪ'destriən/ *n* walker

pedestrian² *adj* **1** dull and ordinary **2** for pedestrians: *a pedestrian crossing*

pe·di·at·rics, **paediatrics** /ˌpiːdiˈætrɪks/ n [U] branch of medicine concerned with children **–rician** /ˌpiːdiəˈtrɪʃən/ n children's doctor

ped·i·gree /ˈpedəɡriː/ n [C;U] (an official description of) the set of people or animals from whom a person or animal is descended ◆ adj (of an animal) specially bred from a high-quality family of animals

ped·lar /ˈpedləʳ/ n person who PEDDLEs small articles

pee /piː/ vi infml for URINATE ◆ n infml 1 [S] act of peeing 2 [U] URINE

peek /piːk/ vi, n (take) a quick look

peel /piːl/ v 1 vt remove (the outer covering) from (esp. a fruit or vegetable): (fig.) *They peeled off their clothes and jumped in the water.* 2 vi come off in small pieces: *My skin is peeling.* 3 **keep one's eyes peeled** keep careful watch ◆ n [U] outer covering of fruits and vegetables

peep¹ /piːp/ vi, n (take) a quick often secret look

peep² n 1 [C] short weak high sound 2 [S] sound, esp. something spoken

peer¹ /pɪəʳ/ n 1 lord or lady 2 fml one's equal in rank, quality, etc.

peer² vi look very carefully or hard: *peering through the mist*

peer·age /ˈpɪərɪdʒ/ n 1 rank of a PEER¹ (1) 2 all the PEERs¹ (1)

peer·ess /ˈpɪərɪs/ n 1 female PEER¹ (1) 2 wife of a PEER¹ (1)

peer·less /ˈpɪələs‖ˈpɪər-/ adj fml better than any other

peeve /piːv/ vt annoy

peev·ish /ˈpiːvɪʃ/ adj bad-tempered ~**ly** adv ~**ness** n [U]

peg¹ /peɡ/ n short piece of wood, metal, etc., for fastening things, hanging things on, etc.

peg² vt -**gg**- fasten with a peg: (fig.) *Prices have been pegged at this year's levels.* – see also **level pegging** (LEVEL¹)

peg out phr vi infml, esp. BrE die

pe·jo·ra·tive /pɪˈdʒɒrətɪv‖-ˈdʒɔːr-, -ˈdʒɑː-/ adj (of a word or expression) saying that something is bad or worthless

pe·kin·ese /ˌpiːkəˈniːz/ n small dog with long silky hair

pel·i·can /ˈpelɪkən/ n pelicans or pelican large water bird with a large beak in which it stores fish to eat

pelican cross·ing /ˌ··· ˈ··/ n (in Britain) place where PEDESTRIANs² wishing to cross the road can stop the traffic by working special TRAFFIC LIGHTS

pel·let /ˈpelɪt/ n 1 small ball of soft material 2 small metal ball fired from a gun

pel·met /ˈpelmət/ n esp. BrE strip above a window to hide curtain tops

pelt¹ /pelt/ v 1 vt attack by throwing things 2 vi (of rain) fall very heavily 3 vi run very fast ◆ n (at) **full pelt** very fast

pelt² n animal's skin with its fur

pel·vis /ˈpelvɪs/ n bowl-shaped frame of bones at the base of the SPINE **–vic** adj

pen¹ /pen/ n instrument for writing with ink

pen² n enclosed piece of land for keeping animals in ◆ vt -**nn**- shut in a pen or small space

pe·nal /ˈpiːnl/ adj of or being legal punishment, esp. in prison

pe·nal·ize ‖ also -**ise** BrE /ˈpiːnəl-aɪz‖ˈpiː-, ˈpe-/ vt put in an unfavourable or unfair situation

pen·al·ty /ˈpenlti/ n 1 punishment or disadvantage suffered, esp. for doing wrong 2 (in sports) disadvantage suffered by a player or team for breaking a rule

pen·ance /ˈpenəns/ n [U] willing self-punishment, to show one is sorry for doing wrong

pence /pens/ n pl. of PENNY

pen·chant /ˈpɒnʃɒn, ˈpentʃənt‖ˈpentʃənt/ n liking for something

pen·cil¹ /ˈpensəl/ n narrow pointed writing instrument containing a thin stick of black material

pencil² v -**ll**- BrE ‖ -**l**- AmE **pencil in** phr vt include for now, with the possibility of being changed later

pen·dant /ˈpendənt/ n hanging piece of jewellery, esp. round the neck

pend·ing /ˈpendɪŋ/ adj waiting to be decided ◆ prep until

pen·du·lous /ˈpendjʊləs‖-dʒə-/ adj fml hanging down loosely

pen·du·lum /ˈpendjʊləm‖-dʒə-/ n weight hanging so as to swing freely, esp. as used to control a clock

pen·e·trate /ˈpenətreɪt/ v 1 vi/t go (into or through): *The knife didn't penetrate his skin.* 2 vt see into or through **–trating** adj 1 (of sight, a question, etc.) sharp and searching 2 able to understand clearly and deeply **–tration** /ˌpenəˈtreɪʃən/ n [U] 1 act of penetrating 2 ability to understand clearly and deeply

pen friend /ˈ· ·/ n usu. foreign friend that you write to but have usu. never met

pen·guin /ˈpenɡwɪn/ n black-and-white seabird of the ANTARCTIC that cannot fly

pen·i·cil·lin /ˌpenəˈsɪlən/ n [U] medicine that kills bacteria

pe·nin·su·la /pəˈnɪnsjʊlə‖-sələ/ n piece of land almost surrounded by water

pe·nis /ˈpiːnɪs/ n male sex organ

pen·i·tent /'penət̬ənt/ adj feeling sorry and intending not to do wrong again ~**tence** n [U]

pen·i·ten·tia·ry /ˌpenə'tenʃəri/ n prison, esp. in the US

pen·knife /'pen-naıf/ n -**knives** /-naıvz/ small knife with a folding blade

pen name /'· ·/ n false name used by a writer instead of his/her real name

pen·nant /'penənt/ n long narrow pointed flag

pen·ni·less /'penıləs/ adj having no money

pen·ny /'peni/ n **pennies** or **pence** 1 (in Britain since 1971) unit of money equal to 1/100th of a pound 2 (in Britain before 1971) unit of money equal to one twelfth of a SHILLING 3 **a pretty penny** a rather large amount of money 4 **in for a penny, in for a pound** if something has been begun it should be finished whatever the cost may be 5 **spend a penny** infml URINATE 6 **the penny (has) dropped** BrE infml the meaning (of something said) has at last been understood

penny-far·thing /ˌ·· '··/ n bicycle with a very large front wheel and very small back wheel

pen·sion¹ /'penʃən/ n money paid regularly to someone who can no longer earn (enough) money by working esp. because of old age or illness ~**er** person receiving a pension

pension² v **pension off** phr vt dismiss from work and pay a pension to

pen·si·on³ /'ponson‖ˌpaːnsi'əun/ n house in a non-English speaking country where one can get a room and meals

pen·sive /'pensıv/ adj deeply or sadly thoughtful ~**ly** adv ~**ness** n [U]

pen·tath·lon /pen'tæθlən/ n sports event in which the competitors take part in 5 different sports

pent·house /'penthaus/ n set of rooms built on top of a tall building

pent up /ˌ· '·◂/ adj not allowed to be free or freely expressed: pent-up emotions

pe·nul·ti·mate /pɪ'nʌltəmət̬/ adj next to the last

pe·num·bra /pə'nʌmbrə/ n fml slightly dark area between full darkness and full light

pen·u·ry /'penjʊ̈ri/ n fml being very poor ~**rious** /pə'njuːˈrıəs/ adj

peo·ple /'piːpəl/ n 1 [P] persons other than oneself; persons in general: How many people were at the meeting?‖ That sort of thing annoys people. 2 [(the) P] all the ordinary members of a nation 3 [C] race; nation: the peoples of Africa 4 [P] persons from whom one

is descended ♦ vt 1 live in (a place) 2 fill with PEOPLE (1)

pep¹ /pep/ n [U] infml keen activity and forcefulness

pep² v -**pp- pep up** sl make more active or interesting

pep·per¹ /'pepə²/ n 1 [U] hot-tasting powder made from the fruit of a tropical plant 2 [C] hollow slightly hot-tasting vegetable: green peppers

pepper² vt hit repeatedly with shots

pep·per·corn rent /ˌpepəkɔːn 'rent‖ˌpepəkɔːrn-/ n BrE very small amount of money (much less than one would expect) paid as rent

pep·per·mint /'pepəˌmınt‖-ər-/ n 1 [U] MINT¹ (2) plant with a special strong taste 2 [C] sweet with this taste

pep pill /'· ·/ n PILL (1) taken to make one quicker or happier for a short time

pep talk /'· ·/ n talk intended to make people work harder, more quickly, etc.

per /pə²; strong pɜː²/ prep 1 for each: apples at 90 pence per kilo 2 infml according to: as per your instructions

per an·num /pər 'ænəm/ adv each year

per·ceive /pə'siːv‖pər-/ vt fml (come to) have knowledge of, esp. by seeing or understanding

per cent /pə'sent‖pər-/ n, adv, adj (one part) in or for each 100: a 10 per cent pay increase

per·cen·tage /pə'sentıdʒ‖pər-/ n 1 [C] number stated as if it is part of a whole which is 100: a high percentage of babies [U] infml advantage; profit

per·cep·ti·ble /pə'septəbəl‖pər-/ adj fml noticeable -**bly** adv

per·cep·tion /pə'sepʃən‖pər-/ n [U] fml 1 action of perceiving 2 keen natural understanding

per·cep·tive /pə'septıv‖pər-/ adj having or showing PERCEPTION (2) ~**ly** adv

perch /pɜːtʃ‖pɜːrtʃ/ n 1 branch, rod, etc., where a bird sits 2 high position or place ♦ v 1 vi (of a bird) sit 2 vi/t put or be in a high or unsafe place: a house perched on top of the cliff

per·cip·i·ent /pə'sıpiənt‖pər-/ adj fml perceptive -**ence** n [U]

per·co·late /'pɜːkəlert‖'pɜːr-/ vi pass slowly through a material with small holes: (fig.) The news gradually percolated through to us. -**lator** n pot in which coffee is made by hot water percolating through the crushed beans

per·cus·sion /pə'kʌʃən‖pər-/ n [U] musical instruments played by being struck: The drum is a percussion instrument.

per·di·tion /pə'dıʃən‖pər-/ n [U] fml everlasting punishment after death

pe·remp·to·ry /pə'remptəri/ adj fml 1 impolitely quick and unfriendly 2 (of a command) that must be obeyed **–rily** adv

pe·ren·ni·al /pə'reniəl/ adj 1 lasting forever or for a long time 2 (of a plant) living for more than 2 years ♦ n perennial plant **~ly** adv

per·fect¹ /'pɜːfɪkt‖'pɜːr-/ adj 1 of the very best possible kind, standard, etc. 2 as good or suitable as possible: *Your English is almost perfect.* 3 with nothing missing; full: *a perfect set of teeth* 4 complete : *a perfect fool* 5 gram expressing an action that has happened and finished: *The perfect tense is formed with 'have' in English.* **~ly** adv

per·fect² /pə'fekt‖pər-/ vt make perfect **~ible** adj

per·fec·tion /pə'fekʃən‖pər-/ n [U] 1 being perfect 2 making perfect 3 perfect example: *His performance was sheer perfection.*

per·fec·tion·ist /pə'fekʃənɪst‖pər-/ n someone not satisfied with anything not perfect

per·fid·i·ous /pə'fɪdiəs‖pər-/ adj fml disloyal **~ly** adv **~ness** n [U]

per·fo·rate /'pɜːfəreɪt‖'pɜːr-/ v 1 make a hole through 2 make a line of holes in (paper) to make it easier to tear **–ration** /ˌpɜːfə'reɪʃən‖ˌpɜːr-/ n [C;U]

per·form /pə'fɔːm‖pər'fɔːrm/ v 1 vt do (a piece of work, ceremony, etc.): *to perform an operation* 2 vi/t act or show (a play, piece of music, etc.), esp. in public 3 vi work or carry out an activity (in the stated way): *a car that performs well on hills* **~ance** n 1 [U] action or manner of performing 2 [C] (public) show of music, a play, etc. **~er** n actor, musician, etc.

per·fume /'pɜːfjuːm‖'pɜːr-/ n [C;U] (liquid having) a sweet smell ♦ /pə'fjuːm‖pər'fjuːm/ vt cause to smell sweet

per·func·to·ry /pə'fʌŋktəri‖pər-/ adj fml done hastily and without interest or care

per·haps /pə'hæps, præps‖pər-, præps/ adv it may be; possibly

per·il /'perəl/ n [C;U] (something that causes) great danger **~ous** adj

pe·rim·e·ter /pə'rɪmɪtər/ n (length of) the border round an enclosed area, esp. a camp or airfield

pe·ri·od¹ /'pɪəriəd/ n 1 stretch of time 2 division of a school day 3 monthly flow of blood from a woman's body **~ic** /ˌpɪəri'ɒdɪk‖-'ɑː-/ adj repeated and regular **~ical** n magazine that comes out regularly **~ically** /-kli/ adv

period² adv infml (used at end of a sentence) and that is all I'm going to

say on the matter: *I'm not going, period.*

per·i·pa·tet·ic /ˌperɪpə'tetɪk/ adj fml travelling about, esp. to work

pe·riph·e·ry /pə'rɪfəri/ n outside edge **–ral** adj 1 on the periphery 2 slight: *of peripheral interest*

per·i·scope /'perɪskəʊp/ n long tube with mirrors so that people lower down can see what is above them, esp. in SUBMARINES

per·ish /'perɪʃ/ vi fml 1 die 2 (cause to) decay or lose natural qualities **~able** adj (of food) that will decay quickly **~ing**, **~ed** adj very cold

per·jure /'pɜːdʒə‖'pɜːr-/ vt **perjure oneself** tell lies in a court of law **–jury** n [U] lying in court

perk¹ /pɜːk‖pɜːrk/ n money, goods, etc., that one gets from an employer in addition to one's pay: *Having Tuesdays free is one of the perks of the job.*

perk² v **perk up** phr vi/t make or become more cheerful

perk·y /'pɜːki‖'pɜːrki/ adj confidently cheerful **–iness** n [U]

perm¹ /pɜːm‖pɜːrm/ n BrE act of putting artificial curls into hair ♦ vt give a perm to

perm² v infml for PERMUTE

per·ma·nent /'pɜːmənənt‖'pɜːr-/ adj lasting a long time or for ever **~ly** adv **–nence** n [U]

per·me·a·ble /'pɜːmiəbəl‖'pɜːr-/ adj that can be permeated

per·me·ate /'pɜːmieɪt‖'pɜːr-/ vt spread or pass through or into every part of

per·mis·si·ble /pə'mɪsəbəl‖pər-/ adj fml allowed **-bly** adv

per·mis·sion /pə'mɪʃən‖pər-/ n [U] act of allowing

per·mis·sive /pə'mɪsɪv‖pər-/ adj allowing (too) much freedom, esp. in sexual matters **~ly** adv **~ness** n [U]

per·mit¹ /pə'mɪt‖pər-/ vi/t -tt- allow

per·mit² /'pɜːmɪt‖'pɜːr-/ n offical paper allowing something

per·mute /pə'mjuːt‖pər-/ vt rearrange in a different order **–mutation** /ˌpɜːmjuː'teɪʃən‖ˌpɜːr-/ n [C;U]

per·ni·cious /pə'nɪʃəs‖pər-/ adj fml very harmful **~ly** adv **~ness** n [U]

per·nick·e·ty /pə'nɪkəti‖pər-/ adj worrying too much about small things

per·o·ra·tion /ˌperə'reɪʃən/ n fml 1 last part of a speech 2 grand, long, but meaningless speech

per·pen·dic·u·lar /ˌpɜːpən'dɪkjʊlə‖ˌpɜːr-/ adj 1 exactly upright 2 at an angle of 90° to another line or surface ♦ n [C;U] perpendicular line or position

per·pe·trate /'pɜːpətreɪt‖'pɜːr-/ vt fml be guilty of **–trator** n

per·pet·u·al /pə'petʃuəl‖pər-/ adj lasting (as if) for ever **~ly** adv

per·pet·u·ate /pə'petʃueɪt‖pər-/ vt fml make (something) continue to exist for a long time **–ation** /pə,petʃu'eɪʃən‖pər-/ n [U]

per·pe·tu·i·ty /,pɜːpɪ'tjuːɪti‖,pɜːpə'tuː-/ n **in perpetuity** fml for ever

per·plex /pə'pleks‖pər-/ vt make (someone) feel confused by being difficult to understand: a perplexing problem ~**ity** n [U]

per se /,pɜː 'seɪ‖,pɜːr 'siː, ,pɜːr 'seɪ, ,peər 'seɪ/ adv considered alone and not in connection with other things

per·se·cute /'pɜːsɪkjuːt‖'pɜːr-/ vt 1 cause to suffer, esp. for religious beliefs 2 trouble or harm continually **–cutor** n **–cution** /,pɜːsɪ'kjuːʃən‖,pɜːr-/ n [C;U]

per·se·vere /,pɜːsɪ'vɪər‖,pɜːr-/ vi continue firmly in spite of difficulties **–verance** n [U]

per·sist /pə'sɪst‖pər-/ vi 1 continue firmly in spite of opposition or warning: Do not persist in this unwise action. 2 continue to exist ~**ent** adj persisting: persistent rudeness/coughing ~**ently** adv ~**ence** n [U]

per·son /'pɜːsən‖'pɜːr-/ n 1 single human being 2 gram form of verb or PRONOUN, showing the speaker (**first person**), the one spoken to (**second person**), or the one spoken about (**third person**) 3 **in person** personally; oneself 4 **on/about one's person** carried around with one

per·so·na /pə'səunə‖pər-/ n outward character a person takes on

per·son·a·ble /'pɜːsənəbəl‖'pɜːr-/ adj fml attractive

per·son·age /'pɜːsənɪdʒ‖'pɜːr-/ n character in a play or book, or in history

per·son·al /'pɜːsənəl‖'pɜːr-/ adj 1 of, for, or by a particular person: It's a personal (= private) matter. 2 rude 3 fml of the body: personal cleanliness ~**ly** adv 1 directly and not through a representative 2 giving one's own opinion 3 privately

personal col·umn /'··· ,·/ n part of a newspaper that gives or asks for messages, news, etc., about particular people

per·son·al·i·ty /,pɜːsə'nælɪti‖,pɜːr-/ n 1 [C;U] whole nature or character of a person 2 [C;U] (person with) forceful, lively, and usu. attractive qualities of character: She's got lots of personality. 3 [C] well-known person

personality cult /·'··· ,·/ n practice of giving too great admiration to a particular person, esp. a political leader

personal pro·noun /,··· '··/ n PRONOUN showing the PERSON (2), such as I or you

personal ster·e·o /,··· '··/ n small machine for playing CASSETTEs, which has EARPHONES and is carried around with the user

per·son·i·fy /pə'sɒnɪfaɪ‖pər'sɑː-/ vt 1 be a good example of (a quality) 2 represent as being human **–fication** /pə,sɒnɪfɪ'keɪʃən‖pər,sɑː-/ n [C;U]

per·son·nel /,pɜːsə'nel‖,pɜːr-/ n 1 [P] all employed people in a company, army, etc. 2 [U] department that deals with these people and their problems

per·spec·tive /pə'spektɪv‖pər-/ n 1 [U] effect of depth, distance, and solidity in drawing and painting 2 [C;U] proper relationship of each part of a matter: We must get the problem in perspective; it's not really that serious.

per·spex /'pɜːspeks‖'pɜːr-/ n [U] strong glasslike plastic

per·spi·ca·cious /,pɜːspɪ'keɪʃəs‖,pɜːr-/ adj fml showing good judgment and understanding ~**ly** adv ~**ness** n

per·spire /pə'spaɪər‖pər-/ vi fml for SWEAT **–spiration** /,pɜːspə'reɪʃən‖,pɜːr-/ n [U] fml 1 SWEAT 2 act of sweating

per·suade /pə'sweɪd‖pər-/ vt make (someone) do something by reasoning, arguing, begging, etc.

per·sua·sion /pə'sweɪʒən‖pər-/ n 1 [U] (skill in) persuading 2 [C] particular belief: her political persuasions

per·sua·sive /pə'sweɪsɪv‖pər-/ adj able to persuade others ~**ly** adv ~**ness** n [U]

pert /pɜːt‖pɜːrt/ adj amusingly disrespectful ~**ly** adv ~**ness** n [U]

per·tain /pə'teɪn‖pər-/ v **pertain to** phr vt fml be about or connected with

per·ti·na·cious /,pɜːtɪ'neɪʃəs‖,pɜːr-/ adj fml holding firmly to an opinion or action

per·ti·nent /'pɜːtɪnənt‖'pɜːr-/ adj fml directly connected: RELEVANT ~**ly** adv **–nence** n [U]

per·turb /pə'tɜːb‖pər'tɜːrb/ vt fml worry **–ation** /,pɜːtə'beɪʃən‖,pɜːrtər-/ n [U]

pe·ruse /pə'ruːz/ vt fml read carefully **perusal** n [C;U]

per·vade /pə'veɪd‖pər-/ vt fml spread all through

per·va·sive /pə'veɪsɪv‖pər-/ adj pervading; widespread ~**ly** adv ~**ness** n [U]

per·verse /pə'vɜːs‖pər'vɜːrs/ adj 1 purposely doing wrong or unreasonable things 2 awkward and annoying ~**ly** adv

per·ver·sion /pə'vɜːʃən, -ʒən‖pər'vɜːrʒən/ n 1 [C] perverted form of what is true, reasonable, etc. 2 [C] unnatural sexual act 3 [U] act of perverting

per·ver·si·ty /pə'vɜːsɪti‖pər'vɜːr-/ n **1** [U] being Perverse **2** [C] perverse act

per·vert¹ /pə'vɜːt‖pər'vɜːrt/ vt **1** lead into wrong or unnatural (sexual) behaviour **2** use for a bad purpose

per·vert² /'pɜːvɜːt‖'pɜːrvɜːrt/ n person who does unnatural sexual acts

pes·si·mist /'pesɪmɪst/ n person who expects bad things to happen **–mism** n [U] **-mistic** /,pesɪ'mɪstɪk/ adj

pest /pest/ n **1** animal or insect that harms food products **2** annoying person

pes·ter /'pestər/ vt annoy continually, esp. with demands

pes·ti·cide /'pestɪsaɪd/ n [C:U] chemical to kill PESTs (1)

pes·ti·lence /'pestɪləns/ n fml terrible disease killing many people

pes·ti·lent /'pestɪlənt/ adj **1** fml causing a pestilence **2** unpleasantly annoying

pes·tle /'pesəl, 'pestl/ n instrument for crushing things in a thick bowl

pet /pet/ n **1** animal kept as a companion: my pet cat **2** person specially favoured ♦ v -tt- **1** vi kiss and touch sexually **2** vt touch lovingly

pet·al /'petl/ n coloured leaflike part of a flower

pet·er /'piːtər/ v peter out phr vi gradually end

pe·tite /pə'tiːt/ adj (esp. of a woman) having a small and neat figure

pe·ti·tion /pə'tɪʃən/ n request or demand to a government, etc., signed by many people ♦ vi/t make or send a petition **~er** n

pet name /,· '·/ n name for someone you like, instead of their real name

pet·ri·fy /'petrɪfaɪ/ vt **1** frighten extremely **2** turn into stone

pet·ro·dol·lar /'petrəʊ,dɒlər‖-,dɑː-/ n US dollar earned by the sale of oil, esp. by oil-producing countries in the Middle East

pet·rol /'petrəl/ n [U] BrE liquid obtained from petroleum and used for producing power in engines

pe·tro·le·um /pə'trəʊliəm/ n [U] mineral oil obtained from below the ground

petrol sta·tion /'·· ,··/n BrE FILLING STATION

pet·ti·coat /'petɪkəʊt/ n skirtlike undergarment

pet·ty /'peti/ adj **1** unimportant (by comparison) **2** showing a narrow and ungenerous mind **–tiness** n [U]

petty cash /,·· '·/ n [U] money kept for small payments

petty of·fi·cer /,·· '···◄/ n person of middle rank in the navy

pet·u·lant /'petʃʊlənt/ adj showing childish bad temper **~ly** adv **-lance** n [U]

pew /pjuː/ n seat in a church: (fig.) Take a pew. (= Sit down.)

pew·ter /'pjuːtər/ n [U] greyish metal made from lead and tin

PG /,piː 'dʒiː/ abbrev. for: parental guidance; (of a film) which may in parts be unsuitable for children under 15

pha·lanx /'fælæŋks‖'feɪ-/ n group packed closely together, esp. for attack or defence

phal·lus /'fæləs/ n image of the male sex organ **–lic** adj

phan·tom /'fæntəm/ n **1** GHOST **2** something that is not really there

pha·raoh /'feərəʊ/ n ruler of ancient Egypt

phar·ma·ceu·ti·cal /,fɑːmə'sjuːtɪkəl‖,fɑːrmə'suː-/ adj of (the making of) medicine

phar·ma·cist /'fɑːməsɪst‖'fɑːr-/ n **1** person who makes medicines **2** BrE for CHEMIST (2)

phar·ma·col·o·gy /,fɑːmə'kɒlədʒi‖,fɑːrmə'kɑː-/ n [U] study of medicine and drugs **–gist** n

phar·ma·cy /'fɑːməsi‖'fɑːr-/ n **1** [C] shop where medicines are sold **2** [U] making or giving out of medicines

phar·ynx /'færɪŋks/ n med throat

phase /feɪz/ n **1** stage of development **2** way the moon looks at a particular time ♦ vt arrange in separate phases

phase in/out phr vt introduce/remove gradually

pheas·ant /'fezənt/ n large bird often shot for food

phe·nom·e·nal /fɪ'nɒmənəl‖-'nɑː-/ adj very unusual **~ly** adv: phenomenally strong

phe·nom·e·non /fɪ'nɒmənən‖fɪ'nɑːmənɑːn, -nɒn/ n **-na** /-nə/ **1** fact or event in the world as it appears or is experienced by the senses, esp. an unusual one **2** very unusual person, thing, etc.

phi·lan·der·er /fɪ'lændərər/ n old-fash man who has too many love affairs

phi·lan·thro·pist /fɪ'lænθrəpɪst/ n kind person who gives money to those who are poor or in trouble **–py** n [U] **-pic** /,filən'θrɒpɪk‖-'θrɑː-/ adj

phi·lat·e·ly /fɪ'lætəli/ n [U] stamp collecting **–list** n

phil·is·tine /'fɪlɪstaɪn‖-stiːn/ n person who does not understand and actively dislikes art, music, beautiful things, etc.

phi·los·o·pher /fɪ'lɒsəfər‖-'lɑː-/ n **1** person who studies philosophy **2** PHILOSOPHICAL (2) person

philosopher's stone /·,··· '·/n imaginary substance thought in former times to change any metal into gold

phi·los·o·phize ‖ also **-phise** BrE /fɪˈlɒsəfaɪz‖-ˈlɑ:-/ vi talk or write like a philosopher

phi·los·o·phy /fɪˈlɒsəfi‖-ˈlɑ:-/ n 1 [U] study of the nature and meaning of existence, reality, morals, etc. 2 [C] system of thought **-ophical** /ˌfɪlə-ˈsɒfɪkəl‖-ˈsɑ:-/ adj 1 of philosophy 2 accepting things with calm courage **-ophically** /-kli/ adv

phlegm /flem/ n [U] 1 thick liquid produced in the nose and throat 2 fml calmness

phleg·mat·ic /fleɡˈmætɪk/ adj calm and unexcitable **~ally** /-kli/ adv

pho·bi·a /ˈfəʊbiə/ n strong (unreasonable) fear and dislike

phoe·nix /ˈfi:nɪks/ n imaginary bird that burnt itself up and was born again from its ashes

phone /fəʊn/ n, vi/t telephone

phone book /ˈ· ·/ n book with a list of all telephone numbers in an area

phone box /ˈ· ·/ n hut containing a public telephone

phone-in /ˈ· ·/ n show in which telephoned questions, etc., from the public are broadcast

phone-tap·ping /ˈ· ˌ·/n [U] listening secretly to other people's telephone conversations by means of special ELECTRONIC equipment

pho·net·ic /fəˈnetɪk/ adj 1 of the sounds of human speech 2 (of a language) with all the sounds spelled very much as they sound **~ally** /-kli/ adv

pho·net·ics /fəˈnetɪks/ n [U] study and science of speech sounds **-ician** /ˌfəʊnɪˈtɪʃən/ n

pho·ney /ˈfəʊni/ n, adj sl (someone or something) pretended or false

phoney war /ˌ· ·ˈ·/n infml period during which a state of war officially exists but there is no actual fighting

pho·no·graph /ˈfəʊnəɡrɑ:f‖-ɡræf/ n AmE for RECORD PLAYER

pho·nol·o·gy /fəˈnɒlədʒi‖-ˈnɑ:-/ n [U] study of the system of speech sounds in a language **-ogical** /ˌfəʊnəˈlɒdʒɪkəl‖ˌfənəˈlɑ:-/ adj

phos·phate /ˈfɒsfeɪt/ n [C;U] chemical made from phosphoric acid, esp. as used for making plants grow better

phos·pho·res·cent /ˌfɒsfəˈresənt‖ˌfɑ:s-/ adj shining faintly in the dark by a natural process **-cence** n [U]

phos·pho·rus /ˈfɒsfərəs‖ˈfɑ:s-/ n [U] yellowish waxlike chemical that burns when brought into the air **-phoric** /fɒsˈfɒrɪk‖fɑ:sˈfɔ:-, fɑ:sˈfɑ:, ˈfɑ:sfərɪk/ adj

pho·to /ˈfəʊtəʊ/ n **-tos** photograph

pho·to·cop·y /ˈfəʊtəʊˌkɒpi‖-tə,kɑ:pi/ vi/t, n (make) a photographic copy

photo fin·ish /ˌ·· ˈ·/ n very close finish to a race, etc., where a photograph is needed to show the winner

pho·to·gen·ic /ˌfəʊtəʊˈdʒenɪk, ˌfəʊtə-/ adj that looks good when photographed

pho·to·graph /ˈfəʊtəɡrɑ:f‖-ɡræf/ n picture taken with a camera and film ♦ vt take a photograph of **~er** /fəˈtɒɡrəfər‖-ˈtɑ:-/ n **~y** n [U] art or business of producing photographs or films **~ic** /ˌfəʊtəˈɡræfɪk/ adj

pho·to·sen·si·tive /ˌfəʊtəʊ-ˈsensɪtɪv‖-tə'sen-/ adj changing under the action of light

pho·to·syn·the·sis /ˌfəʊtəʊ-ˈsɪnθəsɪs‖-təˈsɪn-/ n [U] process by which plants make food using sunlight

phras·al /ˈfreɪzəl/ adj of or being a phrase: 'Blow up' is a phrasal verb.

phrasal verb /ˌ·· ˈ·/n group of words that acts like a verb and consists usu. of a verb with an adverb and/or a PREPOSITION: 'Set off' and 'put up with' are phrasal verbs.

phrase /freɪz/ n 1 group of words without a FINITE verb 2 short (suitable) expression ♦ vt express in the stated way

phrase-book /ˈfreɪzbʊk/ n book explaining foreign phrases, for use abroad

phra·se·ol·o·gy /ˌfreɪziˈɒlədʒi‖-ˈɑ:-/ n [U] choice and use of words

phys·i·cal /ˈfɪzɪkəl/ adj 1 of or being matter or material things (not the mind, etc.) 2 of the body: physical strength **~ly** /-kli/ adv 1 with regard to the body 2 according to the laws of nature: physically impossible

phy·si·cian /fɪˈzɪʃən/ n fml doctor

phys·i·cist /ˈfɪzɪsɪst/ n person who studies or works in physics

phys·ics /ˈfɪzɪks/ n [U] science dealing with matter and natural forces

phys·i·ol·o·gy /ˌfɪziˈɒlədʒi‖-ˈɑ:-/ n [U] science of how living bodies work **-gist** n **-gical** /ˌfɪziəˈlɒdʒɪkəl‖-ˈlɑ:-/ adj

phys·i·o·ther·a·py /ˌfɪziəʊˈθerəpi/ n [U] exercises, rubbing, etc., to treat sick people **-pist** n

phy·sique /fɪˈzi:k/ n shape and quality of a person's body

pi·an·o /piˈænəʊ/ n **-os** large musical instrument with wire strings, played by pressing black and white bars

pi·az·za /piˈætsə/ n public square, esp. in Italy

pic·a·resque /ˌpɪkəˈresk/ adj (of a story) dealing with a character of whom one disapproves but who is not usu. wicked

pic·co·lo /ˈpɪkələʊ/ n **-los** small FLUTE

pick¹ /pɪk/ vt 1 choose 2 pull off from a plant: picking fruit 3 take up with the fingers, a beak, or a pointed instrument **4** remove unwanted pieces from: *picking her teeth* **5** steal from: *I had my pocket picked.* **6** open (a lock) without a key **7** cause (a fight, etc.) intentionally **8** **pick and choose** choose very carefully **9** **pick holes in** find the weak points in **10** **pick one's way** walk carefully **11** **pick someone's brains** make use of someone's knowledge ~**er** *n* ~**ings** *n* [P] additional money or profits

pick at *phr vt* eat (a meal) with little interest

pick off *phr vt* shoot one by one

pick on *phr vt* choose unfairly for punishment or blame

pick out *phr vt* **1** choose specially **2** see among others, esp. with difficulty

pick up *phr v* **1** *vt* take hold of and lift up **2** *vt* gather together: *Pick up your toys.* **3** *vi/t* (cause to) start again **4** *vt* get: *I picked up a cold last week.* **5** *vt* go and meet or collect: *I'll pick you up at the station.* **6** *vi* improve, esp. in health **7** *vt* become friendly with for sexual purposes **8** *vt* catch: *The police picked up the criminals at the airport.* **9** *vt* be able to hear or receive (on a radio)

pick² *n* [U] **1** choice: *Take your pick!* **2** best: *It's the pick of the new films.*

pick³ *n* **1** PICKAXE **2** sharp, pointed, usu. small instrument

pick-axe ‖ also **-ax** *AmE/*'pɪk-æks/ *n* large tool with 2 sharp points, for digging up roads, etc.

pick-et /'pɪkɪt/ *n* **1** person or group outside a place of work trying to persuade others not to work there during a quarrel with employers **2** soldier guarding a camp **3** strong pointed stick fixed in the ground — see also FLYING PICKET ♦ *vt* surround with or as PICKETS (1)

pick-le /'pɪkəl/ *n* **1** [U] VINEGAR or salt water for preserving foods **2** [C;U] vegetable preserved in this **3** [S] dirty, difficult or confused condition: *in a pickle* ♦ *vt* preserve in pickle **-led** *adj infml* drunk

pick-me-up /'· · ˌ·/ *n infml* something, esp. a drink or medicine, that makes one feel stronger, happier, etc.

pick-pock-et /'pɪk,pɒkɪt‖-,pɑk-/ *n* person who steals from people's pockets

pick-up /'··/ *n* **1** needle and arm of a record player **2** light VAN having an open body with low sides

pic-nic /'pɪknɪk/ *n* informal outdoor meal ♦ *vi* **-ck-** have a picnic

pic-to-ri-al /pɪk'tɔːrɪəl/ *adj* having or expressed in pictures ~**ly** *adv*

pic-ture /'pɪktʃəʳ/ *n* **1** [C] representation made by painting, drawing, or photography **2** [C] what is seen on the television screen: *We don't get a very good picture.* **3** [C] cinema film **4** [C] image in the mind **5** [S] person or thing that is beautiful **6** [S] perfect example: *He's the picture of health.* (= very healthy) **7** **in the picture:** **a** knowing all the facts **b** receiving much attention ♦ *vt* **1** imagine: *Just picture the frightful scene.* **2** paint or draw **pictures** *n* [P] **1** the cinema **2** the film industry

pic-tur-esque /ˌpɪktʃə'resk/ *adj* **1** charming to look at **2** (of language) unusually forceful and descriptive

pid-dling /'pɪdlɪŋ/ *adj infml* small and unimportant

pid-gin /'pɪdʒɪn/ *n* language which is a mixture of other languages

pie /paɪ/ *n* baked dish of pastry filled with meat or fruit

pie-bald /'paɪbɔːld/ *n, adj* (horse) coloured black and white

piece¹ /piːs/ *n* **1** separate part or bit: *pieces of broken glass* **2** single object that is an example of its kind or class: *a piece of paper/music/*(fig.) *advice* **3** small object used in board games: *a chess piece* **4** *BrE* coin: *a 50p piece* **5** **give someone a piece of one's mind** *infml* tell someone angrily what you think of them **6** **go to pieces** *infml* lose the ability to think or act clearly **7** **in one piece** unharmed **8** **of a piece** similar; in agreement **9** **say one's piece** say what one wants to or has planned to, esp. in a way that is annoying or unwelcome to others — see also PARTY PIECE

piece² *v* **piece together** *phr vt* complete by finding all the bits and putting them together

pi-èce de ré-sis-tance/piː,es də rezi'stɑːns/ *n* **pièces de résistance** the best or most important thing or event

piece-meal /'piːsmiːl/ *adj, adv* (done) only one part at a time

piece of cake /ˌ· · '· ·/ *n* [S] *infml* something very easy to do

piece-work /'piːswɜːk‖-wɜrk/ *n* [U] work paid for by the amount done rather than by the hours worked

pie chart /'· ·ˌ·/ *n* circle divided into several parts showing the way in which something, e.g. money or population, is divided up

pied /paɪd/ *adj* marked with different colours

pi-ed-à-terre/ˌpjeɪd æ 'teəʳ‖pi,ed ə 'teəʳ/ *n* **pieds-à-terre** (*same pronunciation*) small additional home

pier /pɪəʳ/ *n* **1** long structure built out into the sea, esp. with entertainments on it **2** supporting pillar

pierce /pɪəs‖pɪrs/ *vt* make a hole in or through with a point: (fig.) *A cry of fear pierced the silence.* **piercing** *adj* **1**

(of wind) very strong and cold **2** (of sound) unpleasantly sharp and clear **3** searching: *a piercing look*

pi·e·ty /'paɪətɪ/ *n* [U] *fml* deep respect for God and religion

pif·fling /'pɪflɪŋ/ *adj infml* useless; worthless

pig /pɪg/ *n* **1** fat short-legged animal with no fur, kept on farms for food **2** *infml* person who is dirty or rude or eats too much **3 make a pig of oneself** *infml* eat (or drink) too much

pi·geon /'pɪdʒən/ *n* **1** quite large light-grey bird **2** responsibility: *It's not my pigeon.*

pi·geon·hole /'pɪdʒənhəʊl/ *n* **1** box-like division for putting papers in **2** neat division which separates things too simply ♦ *vt* **1** put aside and do nothing about **2** put in a PIGEONHOLE (2)

pigeon-toed /'·· ·/ *adj* having feet that point inwards

pig-gy·bank /'pɪgɪbæŋk/ *n* small usu. pig-shaped container used by children for saving coins

pig·head·ed /ˌpɪg'hedɪd◄/ *adj* very unwilling to agree or obey

pig·let /'pɪglət/ *n* young pig

pig·ment /'pɪgmənt/ *n* **1** [C;U] dry coloured powder for making paint **2** [U] natural colouring matter in plants and animals ~**ation** /ˌpɪgmən-'teɪʃən/ *n* [U]

pig·my /'pɪgmɪ/ *n* PYGMY

pig·sty /'pɪgstaɪ/ *n* **1** small building for pigs **2** very dirty room or house

pig·swill /'pɪgˌswɪl/ *n* [U] waste food given to pigs

pig·tail /'pɪgteɪl/ *n* length of twisted hair hanging down the back

pike¹ /paɪk/ *n* **pikes** or **pike** large fish-eating river fish

pike² *n* long-handled spear

pil·chard /'pɪltʃəd‖-ərd/ *n* small sea fish, often eaten

pile¹ /paɪl/ *n* **1** tidy heap: *a pile of books* **2** also **piles** *pl.* — *infml* lots: *I've got piles of work to do.* **3** *infml* very large amount of money **4** large tall building — see also PILES ♦ *v* **1** *vt* make a pile of **2** *vi* come or go in a (disorderly) crowd: *The children piled into the car.*

pile up *phr vi* form into a mass or large quantity

pile² *n* [C;U] soft surface of short threads on CARPETS or cloth

pile³ *n* heavy supporting post hammered into the ground

piles /paɪlz/ *n* [P] HEMORRHOIDS

pile-up /'paɪlʌp/ *n* traffic accident with many vehicles

pil·fer /'pɪlfər/ *vi/t* steal (small things)

pil·grim /'pɪlgrɪm/ *n* person on a journey to a holy place ~**age** *n* [C;U] pilgrim's journey

pill /pɪl/ *n* **1** [C] small ball of medicine **2** [*the* + S] (*often cap.*) pill taken as birth control

pil·lage /'pɪlɪdʒ/ *vi/t fml* steal things violently from (a place taken in war)

pil·lar /'pɪlər/ *n* **1** tall upright round post, usu. of stone, used esp. as a support for a roof **2** important member and active supporter: *a pillar of the church*

pillar-box /'·· ·/ *n BrE* large round box in the street for posting letters

pill-box /'pɪlbɒks‖-baːks/ *n* **1** small round box for PILLs (1) **2** CONCRETE shelter with a gun inside it

pil·lion /'pɪljən/ *n* passenger seat on a motorcycle

pil·lo·ry /'pɪlərɪ/ *vt* attack with words, esp. in public

pil·low /'pɪləʊ/ *n* filled cloth bag for supporting the head in bed ♦ *vt* rest (esp. one's head) on something

pil·low·case /'pɪləʊkeɪs/ *n* cloth cover for a pillow

pi·lot /'paɪlət/ *n* **1** person who flies a plane **2** person who guides ships into a harbour, etc. ♦ *adj* intended to try something out: *a pilot survey* ♦ *vt* act as the pilot of

pilot light /'·· ·/ *n* **1** small gas flame to light a main flame **2** small electric light to show an apparatus is turned on

pimp /pɪmp/ *n* man who controls and gets money from PROSTITUTES

pim·ple /'pɪmpəl/ *n* small raised diseased spot on the skin

pin /pɪn/ *n* **1** short thin pointed piece of metal for fastening things **2** *AmE* BROOCH **3** *infml* leg ♦ *vt* **-nn-** **1** fasten with a pin **2** keep in one position, esp. by weight from above **3 pin one's hopes on someone** depend on someone for help, etc.

pin down *phr vt* **1** force to give clear details, make a firm decision, etc. **2** prevent from moving

pin·a·fore /'pɪnəfɔːr/ *n* loose garment worn over (the front of) a dress to keep it clean

pin·cer /'pɪnsər/ *n* footlike part of a CRAB, LOBSTER, etc., for seizing things **pincers** *n* [P] tool for holding things tightly

pinch /pɪntʃ/ *v* **1** *vt* press tightly between 2 surfaces or between finger and thumb **2** *vi* hurt by being too tight **3** *vt infml* steal **4** *vt infml* for ARREST ♦ *n* **1** [C] act of pinching **2** [C] amount picked up with finger and thumb: *a pinch of salt* **3** [*the* + S] suffering through not having enough esp. of money: *We're beginning to feel the pinch.* **4 at a pinch** if necessary

pin-cush-ion /'pɪnˌkuʃən/ n small filled bag for sticking pins into until needed

pine[1] /paɪn/ n tall tree with thin sharp leaves that do not drop off in winter

pine[2] vi 1 lose strength and health through grief 2 have a strong desire, esp. that is impossible to fulfil

pine-ap-ple /'paɪnæpəl/ n [C;U] large tropical fruit with sweet juicy yellow flesh

ping /pɪŋ/ vi, n (make) a short sharp ringing sound

ping-pong /'··/ n [U] TABLE TENNIS

pin-ion[1] /'pɪnjən/ vt prevent from moving by tying or holding the limbs

pinion[2] n small wheel fitting against a larger one for turning

pink /pɪŋk/ adj pale red ♦ n **in the pink** in perfect health

pin mon-ey /'· ˌ··/ n [U] money earned by doing small jobs

pin-na-cle /'pɪnəkəl/ n highest point or degree: *the pinnacle of success*

pin-point /'pɪnpɔɪnt/ vt find or describe exactly

pins and nee-dles /ˌ· · '··/ n [P] slight pricking pains in a limb

pin-stripe /'pɪnstraɪp/ n 1 [C] any of a pattern of parallel pale lines on dark cloth 2 [P] also **pinstripe suit** — suit made of cloth with a pattern of pinstripes

pint /paɪnt/ n 1 a measure of liquids equal to 20 fluid ounces 2 pint of beer

pin-up /'pɪnʌp/ n picture of an attractive or admired person such as a popular singer, esp. as stuck up on a wall

pi-o-neer /ˌpaɪə'nɪər/ n person who does something first, preparing the way for others ♦ vt act as a pioneer

pi-ous /'paɪəs/ adj 1 having deep respect for God and religion 2 unlikely to be fulfilled: *a pious hope* ~**ly** adv

pip[1] /pɪp/ n small seed of an apple, orange, etc.

pip[2] n short high-sounding note, esp. as given on the radio to show the exact time

pip[3] vt BrE **pipped at the post** just beaten at the end of some struggle

pipe[1] /paɪp/ n 1 tube carrying liquid or gas 2 small tube with a bowl-like container, for smoking tobacco 3 simple tubelike musical instrument **pipes** n [P] BAGPIPES

pipe[2] vt 1 carry in pipes 2 play music on a PIPE (3) or PIPES **piper** n player of BAGPIPES

pipe down phr vi infml stop talking or being noisy

pipe up phr vi suddenly start to speak

piped mu-sic /ˌ· '··/ n [U] quiet recorded music played continuously in public places

pipe dream /'· ·/ n impossible hope, plan, or idea

pipe-line /'paɪp-laɪn/ n 1 line of joined pipes, esp. for carrying oil or gas 2 **in the pipeline** about to arrive or appear; being prepared

pip-ing[1] /'paɪpɪŋ/ n [U] PIPES[1] (1)

piping[2] adv **piping hot** very hot

pi-quant /'piːkənt/ adj 1 having a pleasant sharp taste 2 interesting and exciting to the mind –**quancy** n [U]

pique /piːk/ n [U] annoyance and displeasure because of hurt pride ♦ vt offend

pi-ra-cy /'paɪrəsi/ n [U] robbery by pirates

pi-ra-nha /pə'rɑːnjə,-nə/ n fierce S. American flesh-eating river fish

pi-rate /'paɪrət/ n 1 person who sails around robbing ships 2 person who pirates things ♦ vt make and sell (a book, record, etc., by someone else) without permission or payment

pir-ou-ette /ˌpɪru'et/ n very fast turn on one foot by a dancer **pirouette** vi

piss[1] /pɪs/ vi taboo sl URINATE ~**ed** adj taboo sl drunk

piss about/around phr vi taboo sl waste time; act in a foolish way

piss off phr v taboo sl 1 vi go away 2 vt a annoy b cause to lose interest

piss[2] n [U] taboo sl 1 URINE 2 **take the piss out of** make fun of

pis-tol /'pɪstl/ n small gun held in one hand

pis-ton /'pɪstn/ n short pipe-shaped part of an engine that goes up and down inside a tube and sends power to the engine

pit[1] /pɪt/ n 1 hole in the ground 2 coal mine 3 small hollow mark on a surface 4 space in front of a stage where musicians sit 5 esp. AmE hard central part of certain fruit 6 **pit of the stomach** place where fear is thought to be felt **pits** n [P] 1 place beside the track where cars are repaired during a race 2 infml the worst possible example of something

pit[2] vt -tt- mark with PITs[1] (3)

pit against phr vt set against in competition or fight

pitch[1] /pɪtʃ/ v 1 vt set up (a camp or tent) 2 vi (of a ship or aircraft) move along with the front and back going up and down 3 vt set the PITCH[2] (2) of (a sound, music, etc.) 4 vt throw 5 vi/t (cause to) fall suddenly forwards

pitch in phr vi infml 1 start eagerly 2 add one's help or support

pitch² n 1 BrE marked-out area for playing sport 2 degree of highness and lowness of a (musical) sound 3 level; degree: *a high pitch of excitement* 4 place in a market, etc., where somebody regularly performs, sells, etc. 5 *infml* salesman's special way of talking about goods he/she is trying to sell: *a good sales pitch*

pitch³ n [U] black substance used for keeping out water: (fig.) *a* **pitch-black** (= very dark) *night*

pitched bat·tle /ˌ· '··/n *infml* fierce and long quarrel or argument

pitch·er¹ /'pɪtʃə/ n 1 BrE large old-fashioned container for holding and pouring liquids 2 AmE JUG

pitcher² n (in BASEBALL) player who throws the ball towards the BATTER²

pitch·fork /'pɪtʃfɔːk‖-fɔːrk/ n long-handled fork for lifting dried grass on a farm ♦ vt put without warning or against someone's will

pit·e·ous /'pɪtɪəs/ adj fml causing pity ~ly adv

pit·fall /'pɪtfɔːl/ n unexpected difficulty or danger

pith /pɪθ/ n [U] soft white substance in the stems of some plants and under the skin of oranges, etc. ~y adj 1 full of pith 2 strongly and cleverly stated in few words

pit·i·a·ble /'pɪtɪəbəl/ adj 1 deserving pity 2 PITIFUL –bly adv

pit·i·ful /'pɪtɪfəl/ adj 1 causing or deserving pity 2 worthless; weak ~ly adv

pit·i·less /'pɪtɪləs/ adj merciless; cruel ~ly adv

pit·tance /'pɪtəns/ n very small amount of pay or money

pi·tu·i·ta·ry /pəˈtjuːɪtəri‖pəˈtuːɪsteri/ n small organ near the brain which helps to control growth

pit·y /'pɪti/ n 1 [U] sympathy and sorrow for others' suffering or unhappiness: *We took pity on* (= felt pity for and helped) *the homeless family.* 2 [S] unfortunate state of affairs: *It's a pity you have to go now.* 3 **for pity's sake** (used to add force to a request) please 4 **more's the pity** unfortunately ♦ vt feel pity for

piv·ot /'pɪvət/ n central point on which something turns ♦ vi/t turn on or provide with a pivot ~al adj

pix·ie, pixy /'pɪksi/ n small fairy that plays tricks

piz·za /'piːtsə/ n [C;U] flat round pastry baked with cheese, TOMATOes, etc., on top

pizz·azz /pəˈzæz/ n [U] sl exciting, forceful quality

plac·ard /'plækɑːd‖-ərd/ n board put up or carried around publicly, with information on it

pla·cate /pləˈkeɪt‖'pleɪkeɪt/ vt cause to stop feeling angry

place¹ /pleɪs/ n 1 [C] particular position in space: *the place where the accident happened*‖(fig.) *Sport never had a place in his life.* 2 [C] particular town, building, etc.: *Is London a nice place to live in?* 3 [C] usual or proper position: *Put it back in its place.* 4 position in the result of a competition, race, etc.: *I took first place in the exam.* 5 [C] position of employment, in a team, etc.: *She got a place at university.* 6 [S] numbered point in an argument, etc.: *In the first place, I can't afford it.* 7 [S] duty: *It's not my place to tell them what to do.* 8 [S] *infml* home: *Come back to my place.* 9 **go places** *infml* be increasingly successful 10 **in/out of place: a** in/not in the usual or proper position **b** suitable/unsuitable 11 **in place of** instead of 12 **know one's place** consider oneself of low rank and behave respectfully 13 **lay/set a place** put knives, forks, spoons, etc., in position on the meal table (for one person) 14 **put someone in his/her place** show someone that he/she is not as important as he/she would like to be 15 **take place** happen 16 **take the place of** act or be used instead of; REPLACE

place² vt 1 put in the stated place 2 make (an order for goods one wants to buy) 3 remember fully who (someone) is ~ment n [U] act or example of placing someone or something in position

pla·ce·bo /pləˈsiːbəʊ/ n -bos or -boes substance given instead of real medicine, without the person who takes it knowing that it is not real

pla·cen·ta /pləˈsentə/ n -tas or -tae /-tiː/ thick mass inside the WOMB joining the unborn child to its mother

plac·id /'plæsɪd/ adj not easily angered or excited ~ly adv

pla·gia·rize ‖ also -ise BrE /'pleɪdʒəraɪz/ vt take (words, ideas, etc.) from (someone else's work) and use them in one's own writings without admitting that one has done so ~rism n [C;U]

plague /pleɪg/ n 1 [C;U] quickly spreading disease that kills many people 2 [C] widespread uncontrollable mass or number: *a plague of locusts* ♦ vt trouble or annoy continually

plaice /pleɪs/ n plaice flat fish, often eaten

plaid /plæd/ n (piece of) thick cloth with a pattern of coloured squares

plain¹ /pleɪn/ adj 1 without decoration or pattern; simple 2 easy to see, hear, or understand 3 expressing thoughts clearly, honestly, and exactly

4 rather ugly ♦ *adv* completely: *plain daft* ~**ly** *adv* ~**ness** *n* [U]

plain² *n* large stretch of flat land

plain sail·ing /ˌ· ˈ··/ *n* [U] something easy to do

plain·spo·ken /ˌpleɪnˈspəʊkən◂/ *adj* (too) direct and honest in speech

plain·tiff /ˈpleɪntɨf/ *n* person who brings a legal charge or claim

plain·tive /ˈpleɪntɪv/ *adj* sad-sounding ~**ly** *adv*

plait /plæt‖pleɪt/ *vt esp. BrE* twist together into a ropelike length ♦ *n esp. BrE* plaited length of esp. hair

plan /plæn/ *n* **1** arrangement for carrying out a (future) activity **2** (maplike drawing showing) an arrangement of parts in a system ♦ *vi/t* **-nn-** make a plan (for) ~**ner** *n*

plane¹ /pleɪn/ *n* **1** aircraft **2** level; standard: *Let's keep the conversation on a friendly plane.* **3** *maths* flat surface ♦ *adj maths* completely flat

plane² *n* tool with a sharp blade for making wood smooth ♦ *vt* use a plane on

plane³ *n* broad-leaved tree common in towns

plan·et /ˈplænɨt/ *n* large body in space that moves round a star, esp. the sun ~**ary** *adj*

plan·gent /ˈplændʒənt/ *adj fml* (of a sound) expressing sorrow

plank /plæŋk/ *n* **1** long narrow wooden board **2** main principle of a political party's stated aims ~**ing** *n* [U] (floor) planks

plank·ton /ˈplæŋktən/ *n* [U] extremely small sea animals and plants

plant¹ /plɑːnt‖plænt/ *n* **1** [C] living thing with leaves and roots **2** [C] factory or other industrial building **3** [U] industrial machinery **4** [C] *infml* **a** person placed secretly in a group in order to discover facts about them **b** thing hidden on a person to make him seem guilty

plant² *vt* **1** put (plants or seeds) in the ground **2** *infml* hide (illegal goods) on someone to make them seem guilty **3** *infml* put (a person) secretly in a group **4** place firmly or forcefully ~**er** *n*

plan·ta·tion /plænˈteɪʃən, plɑːn- ‖ plæn-/ *n* area where large plants are grown as a business: *a rubber plantation*

plaque /plæk/ *n* flat metal or stone plate with writing on it, usu. fixed to a wall

plas·ma /ˈplæzmə/ *n* [U] liquid part of blood, containing the cells

plas·ter¹ /ˈplɑːstəʳ‖ˈplæ-/ *n* **1** [U] mixture of lime, water, sand, etc., which hardens when dry **2** [C;U] (a thin band of) material that can be stuck to the skin to protect small wounds **3 in plaster** in a PLASTER CAST (2)

plaster² *vt* **1** put plaster on (a wall, etc.) **2** cover too thickly ~**ed** *adj infml* drunk ~**er** *n*

plaster cast /ˌ·· ˈ·, ˈ·· ·/ *n* **1** copy of a STATUE in plaster of paris **2** case of plaster of paris supporting a broken bone

plas·tic /ˈplæstɪk/ *n* [C;U] light artificial material used for making various things ♦ *adj fml* **1** easily formed into various shapes **2** connected with the art of shaping forms in clay, wood, etc., ~**ity** /plæsˈtɪsɨti/ *n* [U]

plas·ti·cine /ˈplæstɨsiːn/ *n* [U] *tdmk* coloured claylike substance played with by children

plastic sur·ge·ry /ˌ·· ˈ···/ *n* [U] repair of body parts with pieces of skin or bone taken from other parts

plate /pleɪt/ *n* **1** [C] **a** flat dish from which food is eaten or served **b** also **plateful** /-fʊl/ -- amount of food this will hold **2** [C] flat, thin, usu. large piece of something hard **3** [U] metal covered with gold or silver **4** [C] picture in a book, usu. coloured **5 on a plate** with too little effort **6 on one's plate** to deal with ♦ *vt* cover (a metal article) thinly with gold, silver, or tin

plat·eau /ˈplætəʊ‖plæˈtəʊ/ *n* **-eaus** *or* **-eaux** /-təʊ/ **1** large area of level high land **2** steady unchanging level, period, or condition

plate glass /ˌ· ˈ·◂/ *n* [U] clear glass in large thick sheets

plat·form /ˈplætfɔːm‖-fɔːrm/ *n* **1** raised area beside the track at a railway station **2** raised floor for speakers or performers **3** main ideas and aims of a political party, esp. as stated before an election

plat·i·num /ˈplætɨnəm/ *n* [U] very valuable greyish-white metal

plat·i·tude /ˈplætɨtjuːd‖-tuːd/ *n* statement that is true but not new or interesting

pla·ton·ic /pləˈtɒnɪk‖-ˈtɑː-/ *adj* (of friendship, esp. between a man and woman) not sexual

pla·toon /pləˈtuːn/ *n* small group of soldiers

plat·ter /ˈplætəʳ/ *n* **1** *AmE for* DISH¹(1) **2** large flat esp. wooden dish

plat·y·pus /ˈplætɨpəs/ *n* small Australian animal that has a beak and lays eggs

plau·dits /ˈplɔːdɨts/ *n* [P] show of pleased approval

plau·si·ble /ˈplɔːzɨbəl/ *adj* seeming true; believable **-bly** *adv*

play¹ /pleɪ/ *n* **1** [U] activity for fun, esp. by children **2** [C] story written to be acted **3** [U] action in a sport: *Rain stopped play.* **4** [U] action; effect: *He* *had to* **bring** *all his experience* **into play.** (= use it)

play² /'·/ v 1 *vi* amuse oneself with a game, toys, etc. 2 *vi/t* produce sounds or music (from) 3 *vi/t* take part in (a sport or game) 4 *vi/t* perform (in): *Who played the part of Hamlet?* 5 *vt* plan and carry out: *They played a trick on me.* 6 pretend to be: *Stop playing the fool!* (= being foolish) 7 *vt* strike and send (a ball) 8 *vt* place (a playing card) face upwards on the table 9 *vt* aim; direct: *The firemen played their hoses on the blaze.* 10 *vi* move lightly and irregularly: *A smile played across her lips.* 11 **play ball** *infml* COOPERATE 12 **play for time** delay in order to gain time 13 **play into someone's hands** behave in a way that gives someone an advantage over one 14 **play it by ear** act according to changing conditions, rather than making fixed plans in advance 15 **play (it) safe** act so as to avoid trouble ~**er** *n* person playing a sport or a musical instrument

play along *phr vi* pretend to agree, esp. to avoid trouble

play at *phr vt* 1 PLAY² (6) 2 do in a way that is not serious

play back *phr vt* listen to or look at (something just recorded) **playback** /'pleɪbæk/ *n* playing of something just recorded, esp. on television

play down *phr vt* cause to seem less important

play off *phr v* 1 *vt* set (people or things) in opposition, esp. for one's own advantage 2 *vi* play another match in order to decide who wins **play-off** /'··/ *n* second match played to decide who wins

play on *phr vt* try to use or encourage (others' feelings) for one's own advantage

play up *phr v* 1 *vi/t* cause trouble or suffering (to) 2 *vt* give special importance to

play up to *phr vt* act so as to win the favour of

play with *phr vt* 1 consider (an idea) not very seriously 2 **play with oneself** MASTURBATE 3 **to play with** that one can use; AVAILABLE

play-act /'··/ *vi* behave with an unreal show of feeling

play-boy /'pleɪbɔɪ/ *n* wealthy (young) man who lives for pleasure

play-ful /'pleɪfəl/ *adj* 1 full of fun 2 not intended seriously ~**ly** *adv* ~**ness** *n* [U]

play-ground /'pleɪgraʊnd/ *n* piece of ground for children to play on

play-group /'pleɪgruːp/ *n* informal school for very young children

playing card /'·· ·/ *n fml for* CARD (1a)

play-mate /'pleɪmeɪt/ *n* child's friend who shares in games

play-pen /'pleɪpen/ *n* enclosed frame for a baby to play in

play-thing /'pleɪˌθɪŋ/ *n* 1 toy 2 person treated without consideration

play-wright /'pleɪraɪt/ *n* writer of plays

pla-za /'plɑːzə‖'plæzə/ *n* public square or marketplace

plc /ˌpiː el 'siː/ *abbrev. for* public LIMITED company

plea /pliː/ *n* 1 *fml* urgent or serious request 2 *law* statement by someone in a court saying whether they are guilty or not

plea bar-gain-ing /'· ˌ···/ *n* [U] practice of agreeing to say in a court of law that one is guilty of a small crime in exchange for not being charged with a greater one

plead /pliːd/ *v* 1 *vi* make continual and deeply felt requests 2 *vi law* say officially in court that one is (guilty or not guilty) 3 *vt* offer as an excuse: *He pleaded ignorance.*

pleas-ant /'plezənt/ *adj* pleasing; nice ~**ly** *adv*

pleas-ant-ry /'plezəntri/ *n fml* politely amusing remark

please /pliːz/ *v* 1 *vi/t* make (someone) happy or satisfied 2 *vi* want; like: *They can appoint whoever they please.* ♦ *interj* (used when asking politely for something) **pleased** *adj* happy; satisfied: *Are you pleased with your new car?*

plea-sur-a-ble /'pleʒərəbəl/ *adj fml* enjoyable –**bly** *adv*

plea-sure /'pleʒəʳ/ *n* 1 [U] happy feeling; enjoyment 2 [C] something that gives one pleasure 3 [S] something that is not inconvenient and that one is pleased to do: *'Thank you for helping me.' 'My pleasure.'*

pleat /pliːt/ *n* flattened narrow fold in cloth ♦ *vt* make pleats in

ple-be-ian /plɪ'biːən/ *n, adj* (member) of the lower social classes

pleb-is-cite /'plebɪsɪt‖-saɪt/ *n* vote by the people of a country to decide a matter

plec-trum /'plektrəm/ *n* small piece of plastic, metal, etc., for picking the strings of a GUITAR

pledge /pledʒ/ *n* 1 solemn promise 2 something valuable left with someone as a sign that one will fulfil an agreement 3 something given as a sign of love ♦ *vt* make a solemn promise of

ple-na-ry /'pliːnəri/ *adj fml* (of powers or rights) full; limitless

plen-i-po-ten-tia-ry /ˌplenɪpə-'tenʃəri‖-ʃieri/ *n fml* official or representative with full powers

plen-ti-ful /'plentɪfəl/ adj in large enough quantities: *plentiful supplies* **~ly** adv

plen-ty /'plenti/ pron as much as or more than is needed: *There's plenty (of food) for everyone.*

pleth-o-ra /'pleθərə/ n [S] fml too much

pli-a-ble /'plaɪəbəl/ adj 1 easily bent 2 able and willing to change; ADAPTABLE 3 PLIANT (1) **–bility** /ˌplaɪə'bɪləti/ n [U]

pli-ant /'plaɪənt/ adj 1 (too) easily influenced 2 PLIABLE (1) **–ancy** n [U]

pli-ers /'plaɪəz|-ərz/ n [P] small tool for holding small things or cutting wire

plight¹ /plaɪt/ n bad or serious condition or situation

plight² v **plight one's troth** old use make a promise of marriage

plim-soll /'plɪmsəl, -səʊl/ n BrE light shoe with a cloth top

Plimsoll line /'·· ·/ n line on a ship showing the depth to which it can go down in the water when loaded

plinth /plɪnθ/ n square block which a STATUE stands on

plod /plɒd‖plɑːd/ vi **-dd-** 1 walk slowly and with effort 2 work steadily, esp. at something dull **~der** n slow, steady, not very clever worker

plonk¹ /plɒŋk‖plɑːŋk, plɔːŋk/ vt infml put, esp. heavily or with force

plonk² n [U] infml BrE cheap wine

plop /plɒp‖plɑːp/ vi, n **-pp-** [S] (make or fall with) a sound like something falling smoothly into liquid

plot¹ /plɒt‖plɑːt/ n 1 set of connected events on which a story is based 2 secret plan to do something bad 3 small piece of ground for building or growing things

plot² v **-tt-** 1 vi/t plan together secretly (something bad) 2 vt mark (the course of a ship or aircraft) on a map 3 vt mark (a line showing facts) on special paper with squares **~ter** n

plough ‖ also **plow** AmE /plaʊ/ n farming tool for breaking up earth and turning it over ♦ v 1 vi/t break up and turn over (earth) with a plough 2 vi go forcefully or roughly

plough back phr vt put (money earned) back into a business

ploy /plɔɪ/ n something done to gain an advantage, sometimes deceivingly

pluck¹ /plʌk/ vt 1 pull the feathers off (a bird to be cooked) 2 pull out or pick up sharply 3 play an instrument by pulling (its strings) 4 esp. lit. pick (a flower)

pluck up phr vt show (courage) in spite of fear

pluck² n [U] courage **~y** adj brave

plug /plʌg/ n 1 small usu. round thing for blocking a hole, esp. in a bath, etc. 2 small object for connecting an apparatus with a supply of electricity 3 publicly stated favourable opinion about a product on radio, television, etc., intended to make people want to buy it ♦ vt **-gg-** 1 block or fill with a PLUG (1) 2 give a PLUG (3) to

plug in phr vt connect to a supply of electricity

plug-hole /'plʌghəʊl/ n BrE hole in a bath, etc., where a PLUG (1) fits

plum /plʌm/ n roundish usu. dark red fruit with a hard seed in the middle ♦ adj very desirable: *a plum job*

plum-age /'pluːmɪdʒ/ n [U] feathers on a bird

plumb¹ /plʌm/ vt 1 (try to) find the meaning of 2 **plumb the depths** reach the lowest point

plumb² adv exactly: *plumb in the centre*

plumb-er /'plʌmər/ n person who fits and repairs water pipes

plumb-ing /'plʌmɪŋ/ n [U] 1 all the water pipes and containers in a building 2 work of a plumber

plumb line /'· ·/ n string with a weight on it, for finding the depth of water or whether something is upright

plume /pluːm/ n 1 (large or showy) feather 2 rising feathery shape: *a plume of smoke* **plumed** adj

plummet /'plʌmɪt/ vi fall steeply or suddenly

plump¹ /plʌmp/ adj pleasantly fat **~ness** n [U]

plump² v **plump for** phr vt BrE infml choose

plump up phr vt make rounded and soft by shaking

plun-der /'plʌndər/ vi/t steal or rob in time of war ♦ n [U] (goods seized by) plundering **~er** n

plunge /plʌndʒ/ vi/t 1 move suddenly forwards and/or downwards 2 (of the neck of a woman's garment) have a low front or v-neck showing quite a large area of chest: *a plunging neckline* ♦ n 1 act of plunging 2 **take the plunge** at last do something one had delayed **plunger** n part of a machine that moves up and down

plu-per-fect /ˌpluːˈpɜːfɪkt‖-ɜːr-/ n verb tense that expresses action completed before a particular time, formed in English with *had*

plu-ral /'plʊərəl/ n, adj (word or form) that expresses more than one

plus /plʌs/ prep with the addition of: *3 plus 2 is 5.* ♦ adj 1 greater than zero 2 additional and desirable ♦ n 1 sign (+) for adding 2 infml welcome or favourable addition

plush /plʌʃ/ adj looking very splendid and expensive

Plu-to /'pluːtəʊ/ n the PLANET 9th in order from the sun

plu-to-crat /'pluːtəkræt/ n powerful wealthy person ~**ic** /ˌpluːtə'krætɪk/ adj

plu-to-ni-um /pluː'təʊniəm/ n [U] substance used in producing atomic power

ply¹ /plaɪ/ n [U] measure of the number of threads in wool, rope, etc., or the number of sheets in plywood

ply² v **1** vi travel regularly for hire or other business **2** vt work at (a trade)

ply with phr vt keep giving (esp. food) to

ply-wood /'plaɪwʊd/ n [U] material made of thin sheets of wood stuck together

pm, PM /ˌpiː 'em/ abbrev. for: post meridiem = (Latin) after midday (used after numbers expressing time)

P M /ˌpiː 'em/ n infml for PRIME MINISTER

pneu-mat-ic /njuː'mætɪk‖nuː-/ adj **1** worked by air pressure **2** filled with air: a pneumatic tyre

pneu-mo-ni-a /njuː'məʊniə‖nuː-/ n [U] serious lung disease

P.O. /ˌpiː 'əʊ/ abbrev. for: **1** POST OFFICE **2** POSTAL ORDER

poach¹ /pəʊtʃ/ vi/t catch or kill (animals) illegally on someone else's land: (fig.) poaching (= stealing) my ideas ~**er** n

poach² vt cook in gently boiling water

pock-et /'pɒkɪt‖'pɑːkɪt/ n **1** small baglike part in or on a garment **2** container for thin things in a case, inside a car door, etc. **3** small separate area or group: pockets of mist **4** (supply of) money: beyond my pocket (= too expensive) **5** be/live in each other's pockets infml (of 2 people) to be always together (= be) **6** out of pocket BrE having spent money without any good result ♦ adj small enough to put into one's pocket: a pocket camera ♦ vt **1** put into one's pocket **2** take (money) dishonestly

pock-et-book /'pɒkɪtbʊk‖'pɑː-/ n small notebook

pocket mon-ey /'·· ˌ··/ n [U] money given regularly to a child by its parents

pock-mark /'pɒkmɑːk‖'pɑːkmɑːrk/ n hollow mark on the skin where a diseased spot has been ~**ed** adj

pod /pɒd‖pɑːd/ n long narrow seed container of PEAs and beans

podg-y /'pɒdʒi‖'pɑː-/ adj short and fat

po-di-um /'pəʊdiəm/ n -**ums** or -**dia** /-diə/ raised part for a speaker or performer to stand on

po-em /'pəʊɪm/ n piece of writing in patterns of lines and sounds

po-et /'pəʊɪt/ n writer of poetry ~**ic** /pəʊ'etɪk/ adj **1** of poetry **2** graceful ~**ical** adj **1** written as poetry **2** poetic ~**ically** /-kli/ adv

poetic jus-tice /ˌ·· '··/ n [U] something suitably bad happening to a wrong-doer

poetic li-cence /ˌ·· '··/ n [U] poet's freedom to change facts, not to obey the usual rules of grammar, etc.

poet lau-re-ate /ˌ·· '···/ n (often caps.) poet appointed to the British royal court, who writes poems on important occasions

po-et-ry /'pəʊɪtri/ n [U] **1** art of a poet **2** poems **3** graceful quality

po-faced /ˌpəʊ 'feɪst◄/ adj BrE infml looking solemn

pog-rom /'pɒgrəm‖pə'grɑːm/ n planned killing of large numbers of people

poi-gnant /'pɔɪnjənt/ adj sharply sad ~**ly** adv **poignancy** n [U]

point¹ /pɔɪnt/ n **1** [C] sharp end: the point of a needle **2** [C] particular place or moment: a weak point in the plan | At that point I left. **3** [C] unit for recording the SCORE in a game **4** [C] single particular idea or part of an argument or statement: You've made (= expressed) an important point. **5** [C] main idea, which gives meaning to the whole: That's beside the point. (= is unimportant) **6** [U] purpose; advantage: There's no point in waiting any longer. **7** [C] place on a measuring system: the boiling point of water | the 32 points of the compass **8** [C] particular quality or ability: Spelling isn't her strong point. **9** [C] sign (.) to the left of decimals: 4.2 is read as '4 point 2'. **10** [C] SOCKET: a power point **11** case in point something that proves or is an example of the subject under consideration **12** in point of fact actually **13** make a point of take particular care to **14** on the point of just about to **15** to the point of so as to be almost **16** when it comes/came to the point when the moment for action or decision comes/came **points** n [P] BrE short rails for moving a train from one track to another

point² v **1** vi show or draw attention to something by holding out a finger, stick, etc., in its direction **2** vi/t aim or be aimed: The gun was pointed/pointing at his head. **3** vt fill in and make smooth the spaces between bricks (of a wall, etc.) with CEMENT ~**ed** adj **1** having a sharp end **2** directed against a particular person: a pointed remark ~**ly** adv

point out phr vt draw attention to

point-blank /ˌ· '·◄/ adj, adv **1** fired from a very close position **2** forceful and direct: a point-blank refusal

point-er /'pɔɪntə'/ n 1 stick for pointing at things 2 thin piece that points to numbers on a measuring apparatus 3 piece of helpful advice 4 type of hunting dog

point-less /'pɔɪntləs/ adj meaningless; useless ~**ly** adv ~**ness** n [U]

point of view /ˌ · · '·/ n particular way of considering something

poise /pɔɪz/ n [U] 1 quiet confidence and self-control 2 well-balanced way of moving ♦ vt put lightly in a place where it is hard to be steady **poised** adj ready: poised to attack showing poise

poi-son /'pɔɪzən/ n [C;U] substance that can kill or cause illness ♦ vt 1 give poison to or put poison in 2 have a damaging or evil effect on ~**ous** adj

poke /pəʊk/ vi/t 1 push out sharply: She poked her head round the corner. 2 push a pointed thing (into) 3 **poke fun at** cause (unkind) laughter at 4 **poke one's nose into something** enquire into something which does not concern one ♦ n act of poking

pok-er[1] /'pəʊkə'/ n thin metal rod for poking a fire to make it burn better

po-ker[2] n [U] card game

poker face /'·· ·/ n face that hides someone's thoughts or feelings

pok-y /'pəʊki/ adj uncomfortably small and unattractive

po-lar /'pəʊlə'/ adj of or near the North or South Poles

polar bear /ˌ·· '·/ n large white bear that lives near the North Pole

po-lar-i-ty /pə'lærəti/ n [C;U] fml having or developing 2 opposite qualities

po-lar-ize, ‖ also **-ise** BrE /'pəʊləraɪz/ vi/t form into groups based on 2 directly opposite principles **-ization** /ˌpəʊləraɪ'zeɪʃən‖-rə-/ n [U]

Po-lar-oid /'pəʊlərɔɪd/ n tdmk 1 [U] substance that makes sunshine less bright, used in SUNGLASSES 2 [C] camera that produces finished photographs in seconds

pole[1] /pəʊl/ n long straight thin stick or post

pole[2] n 1 (often cap.) point furthest north and south on the Earth 2 either end of a MAGNET 3 either of the points on a BATTERY where wires are fixed 4 either of 2 positions that are as far apart as they can be 5 **poles apart** widely separated in opinions, etc.

pole-axe /'pəʊlæks/ vt cause to fall (as if) by a heavy blow

pole-cat /'pəʊlkæt/ n small fierce animal with an unpleasant smell

po-lem-ic /pə'lemɪk/ n [C;U] fml fierce argument defending or attacking ideas or opinions ~**al** adj

pole vault /'· ·/ n jump over a high bar using a long pole

po-lice /pə'liːs/ n [P] official body for making people obey the law, catching criminals, etc. ♦ vt control or keep a watch on with policemen: (fig.) a new committee to police the nuclear industry

police of-fi-cer /·'·· ˌ···/ **po-lice-man** masc /pə'liːsmən/ **po-lice-wom-an** fem /pə'liːsˌwʊmən/ n member of the police

police state /·'· ·/ n country where people are controlled by (secret) political police

pol-i-cy /'pɒləsi‖'pɑː-/ n 1 what a government, company, political party, etc., intends to do about a particular matter 2 insurance contract

po-li-o /'pəʊliəʊ/ n [U] serious infectious nerve disease, esp. of the SPINE, which often prevents movement

pol-ish[1] /'pɒlɪʃ‖'pɑː-/ vt 1 make smooth and shiny by rubbing 2 make as perfect as possible: a polished performance ♦ n 1 [U] liquid, paste, etc., for polishing 2 [S] act of polishing 3 [U] fine quality ~**ed** adj 1 (of a piece of artistic work, a performance, etc.) done with great skill and control 2 polite and graceful ~**er** n

polish off phr vt finish (food, work, etc.) quickly or easily

polish up phr vt improve by practising

po-lit-bu-ro /pə'lɪtbjʊərəʊ, 'pɒlət-‖ 'pɑːlət-, pə'lɪt-/ n **-ros** chief Communist decision-making committee

po-lite /pə'laɪt/ adj having good manners ~**ly** adv ~**ness** n [U]

pol-i-tic /'pɒlɪtɪk‖'pɑː-/ adj fml sensible; advantageous

po-lit-i-cal /pə'lɪtɪkəl/ adj 1 of or concerning government and public affairs 2 of (party) politics 3 very interested or active in politics ~**ly** /-kli/ adv

political a-sy-lum /·,··· ·'··/ n [U] official protection given to someone who has left their country because they oppose its government

pol-i-ti-cian /ˌpɒlə'tɪʃən‖ˌpɑː-/ n person whose business is politics

pol-i-tics /'pɒlətɪks‖'pɑː-/ n 1 [U] the activity of winning and using government power, in competition with other parties: active in local politics 2 [U] art and science of government: studying politics at university 3 [P] political opinions 4 [U] activity within a group by which some members try to gain an advantage: office politics

pol-ka /'pɒlkə, 'pəʊlkə/ n quick simple dance for people dancing in pairs

poll /pəʊl/ n 1 [C] also **opinion poll** — attempt to find out the general opinion about something by questioning a number of people chosen by chance 2 [C;U] election 3 [S] number of votes given ♦ vt 1 receive (a stated

pol·len /'pɒlən‖'pɑ:-/ n [U] yellow dust that makes plants produce seeds

pol·li·nate /'pɒləneɪt‖'pɑ:-/ vt bring pollen to (a flower) **–nation** /ˌpɒlə'neɪʃən‖ˌpɑ:-/ n [U]

poll·ster /'pəʊlstər/ n person who carries out POLLs (1)

pol·lute /pə'luːt/ vt make dangerously impure or unfit for use: polluted rivers **–lution** /pə'luːʃən/ n [U] 1 act of polluting 2 polluting substance

po·lo /'pəʊləʊ/ n [U] game played on horses by hitting a ball with a long-handled hammer — see also WATER POLO

polo neck /'·· ·/ n round rolled collar

pol·ter·geist /'pɒltəgaɪst‖'pəʊltər-/ n spirit that makes noises and throws things around

pol·y·es·ter /ˌpɒli'estər, ˌpɒli'estər‖ 'pɑːliestər/ n [U] artificial material used for cloth

po·lyg·a·my /pə'lɪgəmi/ n [U] having 2 or more wives at one time **–mist** /-mɪst/ n **–mous** adj

pol·y·glot /'pɒliglɒt‖'pɑːliglɑːt/ adj fml speaking or including many languages

pol·y·gon /'pɒligən‖'pɑːligɑːn/ n figure with 5 or more straight sides

pol·y·graph /'pɒligrɑːf‖'pɑːligræf/ n LIE DETECTOR

pol·y·math /'pɒlimæθ‖'pɑː-/ n fml person who knows a lot about many subjects

pol·y·mer /'pɒlɪmər‖'pɑː-/ n simple chemical compound with large MOLECULEs

pol·yp /'pɒləp‖'pɑː-/ n 1 very simple small water animal 2 small diseased bodily growth

pol·y·sty·rene /ˌpɒli'staɪəriːn‖ˌpɑː-/ n [U] light plastic that keeps in heat

pol·y·tech·nic /ˌpɒli'teknɪk‖ˌpɑː-/ n place of higher education giving training in science, industry, etc.

pol·y·the·is·m /'pɒliθiːɪzəm‖'pɑː-/ n [U] belief in many gods

pol·y·thene /'pɒliθiːn‖'pɑː-/ n [U] strong plastic used for making many common articles

pol·y·un·sat·u·ra·ted /ˌpɒliʌn-'sætʃəreɪtɪd‖ˌpɑː-/ adj (of fat or oil) having chemicals combined in a way that is thought to be good for the health when eaten

pom·e·gran·ate /'pɒmɪgrænɪt‖ 'pʌmgrænɪt, 'pɑːm-/ n fruit with small red seeds inside

pom·mel /'pʌməl/ n rounded part at the front of a SADDLE

pomp /pɒmp‖pɑːmp/ n [U] grand solemn ceremonial show

pom-pom /'pɒmpɒm‖'pɑːmpɑːm/ n small decorative woollen ball

pom·pous /'pɒmpəs‖'pɑːm-/ adj foolishly solemn and thinking oneself important **~ly** adv **~ness, -posity** /pɒm'pɒsɪti‖pɑːm'pɑː-/

ponce /pɒns‖pɑːns/ n BrE 1 PIMP 2 sl man who behaves foolishly, showily, or womanishly ♦ v

  ponce about/around phr vi BrE sl behave like a PONCE (2)

pon·cho /'pɒntʃəʊ‖'pɑːn-/ n **-chos** cloth worn over the shoulders, with a hole for the head

pond /pɒnd‖pɑːnd/ n small area of still water

pon·der /'pɒndər‖'pɑːn-/ vi/t spend time considering

pon·der·ous /'pɒndərəs‖'pɑːn-/ adj 1 heavy, slow, and awkward 2 dull and solemn

pong /pɒŋ‖pɑːŋ/ vi, n BrE sl (make) a bad smell **~y** adj

pon·tiff /'pɒntɪf‖'pɑːn-/ n POPE

pon·tif·i·cate /pɒn'tɪfɪkeɪt‖pɑːn-/ vi give one's opinion as if it were the only right one

pon·toon¹ /pɒn'tuːn‖pɑːn-/ n floating hollow container connected with others to support a floating bridge

pontoon² n [U] BrE card game

po·ny /'pəʊni/ n small horse

po·ny·tail /'pəʊniteɪl/ n hair tied in a bunch at the back of the head

pooch /puːtʃ/ n infml dog

poo·dle /'puːdl/ n dog with curling hair, often cut in shapes

poof /puːf, puf/ n BrE derog sl male HOMOSEXUAL

pooh /puː/ interj (used when something smells bad)

pooh-pooh /ˌ· '·/ vt treat as not worth considering

pool¹ /puːl/ n 1 small area of water in a hollow place 2 small amount of liquid on a surface 3 SWIMMING POOL

pool² n 1 [C] shared supply of money, goods, workers, etc. — see also CAR POOL 2 [U] American game like SNOOKER ♦ vt combine; share

pools n [the + P] arrangement (esp. in Britain) for risking money on the results of football matches

poor /pʊər/ adj 1 having very little money 2 less or worse than usual or than expected: a poor harvest/ essay| poor weather/health 3 unlucky; deserving pity: Poor David has failed his exams. **~ness** n [U] low quality

poor·ly /'pʊəli‖'pʊərli/ adv not well; badly: poorly paid ♦ adj infml ill

poor re·la·tion /ˌ· ·'··/ n one regarded as the least important among a group of similar ones

pop[1] /pɒp‖pɑːp/ *vi/t* **-pp-** **1** (cause to) make a small explosive sound **2** come, go, or put quickly: *A button popped off his shirt.* **3 pop the question** *infml* make an offer of marriage

pop up *phr vi* happen or appear suddenly

pop[2] *n* **1** [C] small explosive sound **2** [U] sweet FIZZY drink

pop[3] *n* [U] modern popular music with a strong beat: *a pop group/concert*

pop[4] *n esp. AmE* **1** father **2** (used as a form of address to an old man)

pop[5] *abbrev. for:* population

pop-a-dum /ˈpɒpədəm‖ˈpɑː-/ *n* thin Indian bread

pop art /ˌ· ˈ◁/ *n* [U] modern art showing objects from everyday life

pop-corn /ˈpɒpkɔːn‖ˈpɑːpkɔːrn/ *n* [U] MAIZE seeds heated so that they swell

pope /pəʊp/ *n* (*often cap.*) the head of the Roman Catholic Church

pop-eyed /ˌ· ˈ◁/ *adj* with wide-open eyes

pop-ish /ˈpəʊpɪʃ/ *adj derog* Roman Catholic

pop-lar /ˈpɒplər‖ˈpɑːp-/ *n* tall straight thin tree

pop-lin /ˈpɒplɪn‖ˈpɑːp-/ *n* [U] strong cotton cloth

pop-py /ˈpɒpi‖ˈpɑːpi/ *n* plant with bright flowers, usu. red

pop-py-cock /ˈpɒpikɒk‖ˈpɑːpikɑːk/ *n* [U] nonsense

pop-si-cle /ˈpɒpsɪkəl‖ˈpɑː-/ *n AmE tdmk for* ICE LOLLY

pop-u-lace /ˈpɒpjʊləs‖ˈpɑː-/ *n* [U] all the (ordinary) people of a country

pop-u-lar /ˈpɒpjʊlər‖ˈpɑː-/ *adj* **1** liked by many people: *a popular restaurant* **2** common; widespread: *a popular name* **3** of the general public: *popular opinion* ~**ly** *adv* by most people ~**ize** *vt* ~**ity** /ˌpɒpjʊˈlærɪti‖ˌpɑː-/ *n* [U]

pop-u-late /ˈpɒpjʊleɪt‖ˈpɑː-/ *vt* live in as a population

pop-u-la-tion /ˌpɒpjʊˈleɪʃən‖ˌpɑː-/ *n* (number of) people (or animals) living in a particular area or country

pop-u-list /ˈpɒpjʊlɪst‖ˈpɑː-/ *n* person who claims to support the aims of ordinary people in politics

pop-u-lous /ˈpɒpjʊləs‖ˈpɑː-/ *adj fml* having a large population

porce-lain /ˈpɔːslɪn‖ˈpɔːrsɪlɪn/ *n* [U] (cups, plates, etc., made from) fine hard thin claylike substance

porch /pɔːtʃ‖pɔːrtʃ/ *n* roofed entrance built out from a house or church

por-cu-pine /ˈpɔːkjʊpaɪn‖ˈpɔːr-/ *n* animal with long needle-like hairs on its back

pore[1] /pɔːr/ *n* small hole in the skin, through which SWEAT passes

pore[2] *v* **pore over** *phr vt* read with close attention

pork /pɔːk‖pɔːrk/ *n* [U] meat from pigs

porn /pɔːn‖pɔːrn/ *n* [U] *infml, esp. BrE* pornography

por-nog-ra-phy /pɔːˈnɒgrəfi‖pɔːrˈnɑːg-/ *n* [U] *derog* (books, films, etc.) showing or describing sexually exciting scenes –**graphic** /ˌpɔːnəˈgræfik‖ˌpɔːr-/ *adj*

po-rous /ˈpɔːrəs/ *adj* allowing liquid to pass slowly through

por-poise /ˈpɔːpəs‖ˈpɔːr-/ *n* large fishlike sea animal

por-ridge /ˈpɒrɪdʒ‖ˈpɔː-, ˈpɑː-/ *n* [U] soft breakfast food of OATMEAL

port[1] /pɔːt‖pɔːrt/ *n* harbour

port[2] *n* [U] left side of a ship or aircraft

port[3] *n* [U] strong sweet red wine from Portugal

por-ta-ble /ˈpɔːtəbəl‖ˈpɔːr-/ *adj* that can be carried

por-tals /ˈpɔːtlz‖ˈpɔːrtlz/ *n* [P] grand entrance to a building

port-cul-lis /pɔːtˈkʌlɪs‖pɔːrt-/ *n* castle gate that can be raised and lowered

por-tend /pɔːˈtend‖pɔːr-/ *vt fml* be a sign of (a future undesirable event)

por-tent /ˈpɔːtent‖ˈpɔːr-/ *n fml* sign of a future strange or undesirable event

por-ten-tous /pɔːˈtentəs‖pɔːr-/ *adj fml* **1** threatening **2** solemnly self-important

por-ter /ˈpɔːtər‖ˈpɔːr-/ *n esp. BrE* **1** person who carries loads, esp. travellers' bags, or goods in a market **2** person in charge of the entrance to a hotel, hospital, etc.

port-fo-li-o /pɔːtˈfəʊliəʊ‖pɔːrt-/ *n* **1 a** flat case for carrying drawings, etc. **b** drawings, etc., carried in this **2** collection of business shares owned **3** office and duties of a government minister

port-hole /ˈpɔːthəʊl‖ˈpɔːrt-/ *n* window in a ship or aircraft

por-ti-co /ˈpɔːtɪkəʊ‖ˈpɔːr-/ *n* **-coes** or **-cos** grand pillared entrance to a building

por-tion[1] /ˈpɔːʃən‖ˈpɔːr-/ *n* **1** part: *the front portion of the train* **2** share **3** quantity of food for one person

portion[2] *v* **portion out** *phr vt* share

port-ly /ˈpɔːtli‖ˈpɔːr-/ *adj* (of a person) fat

port-man-teau /pɔːtˈmæntəʊ‖pɔːrt-/ *n* **-teaus** or **-teaux** /təʊz/ large case for carrying clothes

port of call /ˌ· · ˈ·/ *n* **1** port where a ship stops **2** place one visits

por-trait /ˈpɔːtrɪt‖ˈpɔːr-/ *n* **1** picture of a person **2** lifelike description in words

por·tray /pɔː'treɪ‖pɔːr-/ vt **1** represent, describe **2** act the part of ~al n [C;U]

pose /pəʊz/ v **1** vi stand or sit in a particular position to be drawn, photographed, etc. **2** vt cause (a problem) **3** vt ask (a question) ♦ n **1** position when posing (POSE (1)) **2** pretended way of behaving

pose as phr vt pretend to be

pos·er /'pəʊzəʳ/ n **1** hard question **2** poseur

po·seur /pəʊ'zɜːʳ/ n person who behaves unnaturally to produce an effect

posh /pɒʃ‖pɑːʃ/ adj **1** fashionable and splendid **2** of the upper social classes

pos·it /'pɒzɪt‖'pɑː-/ vt fml suggest as being possible

po·si·tion /pə'zɪʃən/ n **1** [C;U] place where something is **2** proper place: Is everyone in position? **3** [C] way in which something is placed or stands, sits, acts. **4** [C] situation; state: the company's current financial position **5** [C] place in a rank or group: He finished in second position. **6** [C] fml job **7** [C] fml opinion ♦ vt place

pos·i·tive /'pɒzɪtɪv‖'pɑː-/ adj **1** leaving no possibility of doubt: positive proof **2** having no doubt; sure **3** effective; actually helpful **4** more than zero **5** (of electricity) of the type carried by PROTONs **6** complete; real: a positive delight ~ly adv **1** in a POSITIVE (1,2) way **2** really; indeed

positive di·scrim·i·na·tion /ˌ··· ···'··/ n [U] practice or principle of favouring people who are often treated unfairly, esp. because of their sex or race

pos·se /'pɒsi‖'pɑːsi/ n group of people gathered together to help find a criminal

pos·sess /pə'zes/ vt **1** fml have; own **2** (of a feeling or idea) seem to control all (someone's) actions ~ed adj wildly mad ~or n

pos·ses·sion /pə'zeʃən/ n **1** [U] state of possessing; ownership **2** [C] something one owns **3** [U] control by an evil spirit

pos·ses·sive /pə'zesɪv/ adj **1** unwilling to share one's own things **2** gram showing ownership: 'My' is a possessive adjective. ~ly adv ~ness n [U]

pos·si·bil·i·ty /ˌpɒsə'bɪlɪti‖ˌpɑː-/ n **1** [S;U] (degree of) likelihood **2** [U] fact of being possible **3** [C] something possible: The house is in bad condition but it has possibilities. (= can be improved)

pos·si·ble /'pɒsəbəl‖'pɑː-/ adj **1** that can exist, happen, or be done **2** acceptable; suitable ♦ n **1** [the + S] that

which can exist, happen, or be done **2** [C] person or thing that might be suitable –**bly** adv **1** in accordance with what is possible: I'll do all I possibly can. **2** perhaps

pos·sum /'pɒsəm‖'pɑː-/ n small tree-climbing animal from America and Australia

post¹ /pəʊst/ n **1** strong thick upright pole fixed in position **2** finishing place in a race ♦ vt **1** put up a notice about **2** report as being: The ship was reported missing.

post² n [U] esp. BrE **1** official system for carrying letters, parcels, etc. **2** (a single official collection or delivery of) letters, parcels, etc, sent by this means ♦ vt **1** send by post **2** **keep someone posted** continue to give someone all the latest news about something

post³ n **1** job **2** special place of duty, esp. of a soldier **3** military base ♦ vt **1** place (soldiers, policemen, etc.) on duty **2** send to a job, esp. abroad

post·age /'pəʊstɪdʒ/ n [U] charge for carrying a letter, parcel, etc., by post

postage stamp /'·· ·/ n fml for STAMP

post·al /'pəʊstl/ adj **1** of the POST² (1,2) **2** sent by post

postal or·der /'·· ˌ··/ n official paper sent by post, to be exchanged for money by the receiver

post·bag /'pəʊstbæg/ n **1** postman's bag **2** number of letters received

post·box /'pəʊstbɒks‖-bɑːks/ n box into which people put letters for posting

post·card /'pəʊstkɑːd‖-kɑːrd/ n card for sending messages by post without an envelope

post·code /'pəʊstkəʊd/ n BrE letters and numbers added to an address to make it more exact for delivering letters

post·date /ˌpəʊst'deɪt/ vt write a date later than the actual date of writing on (esp. a cheque)

post·er /'pəʊstəʳ/ n large printed notice or picture

pos·te·ri·or /pɒ'stɪəriəʳ‖pɑː-/ adj fml nearer the back ♦ n BOTTOM¹(2)

pos·ter·i·ty /pɒ'sterɪti‖pɑː-/ n [U] people or times after one's death

poster paint /'·· ·/ n [C;U] bright-coloured artist's paints

post·grad·u·ate /ˌpəʊst'grædjuət‖ -'grædʒuət/ n, adj (person doing university studies) after getting a first degree

post·haste /ˌpəʊst'heɪst/ adv fml very quickly

post·hu·mous /'pɒstjʊməs‖ 'pɑːstʃə-/ adj after death ~ly adv

post·man /'pəʊstmən/ n -men /-mən/ person who delivers letters, etc.

post·mark /'pəʊstmɑːk‖-mɑːrk/ n official mark on a letter, showing where and when it was posted **postmark** vt

post·mor·tem /ˌpəʊst'mɔːtəm‖-'mɔːr-/ n 1 tests to find out why someone died 2 finding out why something failed

post of·fice /'· ‚··/ n place where stamps are sold, letters can be posted, and various sorts of government business are done

post·pone /pəʊs'pəʊn/ vt move to a later time **~ment** n [C;U]

post·script /'pəʊst‚skrɪpt/ n remark(s) added at the end of a letter

pos·tu·late /'pɒstjⁱleɪt‖'pɑːstʃə-/ vt fml accept as true, as a base for reasoning

pos·ture /'pɒstʃəʳ‖'pɑːs-/ n 1 bodily position 2 manner of behaving or thinking on some occasion vi 1 place oneself in fixed bodily positions, esp. in order to make other people admire one 2 pretend to be something one is not

po·sy /'pəʊzi/ n small bunch of flowers

pot¹ /pɒt‖pɑːt/ n 1 [C] round container: *a paint pot* | *a cooking pot* 2 [U] sl for MARIJUANA **3 go to pot** infml become ruined or worthless **pots** n [P] infml large amount (of money)

pot² v -tt- 1 vi/t shoot, esp. for food or sport 2 vt plant in a pot **~ted** adj 1 (of meat, fish, etc.) made into a paste 2 (of a book) in a short simple form

pot·ash /'pɒtæʃ‖'pɑː-/ n [U] sort of potassium used in farming and industry

po·tas·si·um /pə'tæsiəm/ n [U] soft silver-white metal common in nature and necessary for life

po·ta·to /pə'teɪtəʊ/ n -toes common roundish brown or yellowish vegetable that grows underground

pot·bel·ly /'pɒt‚beli‖'pɑːt-/ n infml fat stomach

pot·boil·er /'pɒt‚bɔɪləʳ‖'pɑːt-/ n book, etc., produced quickly just to earn money

po·tent /'pəʊtənt/ adj powerful: *a potent drug* **~ly** adv **potency** n [U]

po·ten·tial /pə'tenʃəl/ adj that may become so; not (yet) actual: *potential danger* ♦ n [U] possibility for developing **~ly** adv **~ity** /pə‚tenʃi'æləti/ n [C;U]

pot·hole /'pɒthəʊl‖'pɑːt-/ n 1 deep hole going far underground 2 unwanted hole in the road **-holing** n [U] sport of climbing down POTHOLEs (1)

po·tion /'pəʊʃən/ n liquid mixture intended as a medicine, poison, or magic charm

pot·luck /ˌpɒt'lʌk‖ˌpɑːt-/ n **take potluck** choose without enough information; take a chance

pot plant /'· ·/ n plant grown (indoors) in a pot

pot·shot /'pɒt-ʃɒt‖'pɑːt-ʃɑːt/ n carelessly aimed shot

pot·ter¹ /'pɒtəʳ‖'pɑː-/ n person who makes pottery

pot·ter² vi move or act slowly or purposelessly

potter about/around phr vi spend time in activities that demand little effort

pot·ter·y /'pɒtəri‖'pɑː-/ n [U] (pots, dishes, etc., made of) baked clay

pot·ty¹ /'pɒti‖'pɑːti/ adj BrE infml 1 slightly mad 2 having a strong uncontrolled interest in or admiration for: *He's potty about her.*

potty² n pot for children to URINATE into

pouch /paʊtʃ/ n 1 small leather bag 2 baglike part of an animal

poul·tice /'pəʊltɪs/ n soft wet heated mass placed on the skin to lessen pain

poul·try /'pəʊltri/ n [U] (meat from) farmyard birds such as hens, ducks, etc.

pounce /paʊns/ vi fly down or jump suddenly to seize

pounce on phr vt seize or attack eagerly

pound¹ /paʊnd/ n 1 a standard unit of money, in Britain containing 100 pence 2 a measure of weight equal to 0.4536 kilograms

pound² v 1 vt crush 2 vi/t strike repeatedly and heavily 3 vi move with quick heavy steps

pound³ n place where lost animals and cats are kept until their owners take them back

pour /pɔːr/ v 1 vi/t (cause to) flow fast and steadily 2 vi rush together in large numbers 3 vi (of rain) fall hard

pour out phr vt tell freely and with feeling

pout /paʊt/ vi push the lips forwards, esp. to show displeasure **pout** n

pov·er·ty /'pɒvəti‖'pɑːvərti/ n [U] 1 being poor 2 fml lack

poverty-strick·en /'··· ‚··/ adj extremely poor

poverty trap /'··· ‚·/ n earning slightly too much to be able to receive special government payments for poor people but not enough to live comfortably on

pow·der /'paʊdəʳ/ n 1 [C;U] very fine dry grains 2 [U] pleasant-smelling substance like this, used on the skin 3 [U] gunpowder ♦ vt put POWDER (2) on ~**ed** *adj* produced in the form of powder ~**y** *adj*

powder puff /'·· ·/ *n* soft ball for putting on POWDER (2)

powder room /'·· ·/ *n* women's public TOILET

pow·er /'pauəʳ/ *n* 1 [U] strength 2 [U] force used for driving machines, producing electricity, etc.: *nuclear power* 3 [S;U] control over others; influence 4 [U] what one can do; (natural) ability: *the power of speech* 5 [C;U] right to act: *The police now have the power to search people in the street.* 6 [C] person, nation, etc., that has influence or control 7 [S + of] a large amount: *A holiday will do you a power of good.* 8 **the powers that be** *infml* the unknown people in important positions who make decisions that have an effect on one's life — see also BLACK POWER ♦ *vt* supply power to (a machine)

pow·er·boat /'pauəbəut‖'pauər-/ *n* fast boat for racing

pow·er·ful /'pauəfəl‖'pauər-/ *adj* 1 full of force: *a powerful engine* 2 great in degree: *a powerful smell* 3 having much control or influence 4 having a strong effect: *powerful drugs* ~**ly** *adv*

pow·er·less /'pauələs‖'pauər-/ *adj* lacking strength or ability: *powerless to help*

power of at·tor·ney /,·· ·'··/ *n* [U] right to act for someone else in business or law

power plant /'·· ·/ *n* engine supplying power to a factory, aircraft, etc.

power sta·tion /'·· ,·ʳ/ *n* building where electricity is made

pow·wow /'pau,wau/ *n* meeting or council of North American Indians

pox /pɒks‖pɑːks/ *n* [U] *infml for* SYPHILIS

pp *abbrev. for:* pages

PR /,piː 'ɑːʳ/ *n* [U] 1 PUBLIC RELATIONS 2 *infml for* PROPORTIONAL REPRESENTATION

prac·ti·ca·ble /'præktɪkəbəl/ *adj* that can be done —**bility** /,præktɪkə'bɪlɪti/ *n* [U]

prac·ti·cal /'præktɪkəl/ *adj* 1 concerned with action or actual conditions, rather than ideas 2 effective or convenient in actual use: *a practical uniform* 3 clever at doing things and dealing with difficulties; sensible ~**ly** /-kli/ *adv* 1 usefully; suitably 2 almost —**ity** /,præktɪ'kælɪti/ *n* [C;U]

practical joke /,··· '·/ *n* trick played on someone to amuse others

prac·tice ‖ also -**tise** *AmE*/'præktɪs/ *n* 1 [C;U] regular or repeated doing of something, to gain skill 2 [U] experience gained by this 3 [U] actual doing

of something: *to put a plan into practice* 4 [C] business of a doctor or lawyer 5 [C;U] something regularly done 6 **in/out of practice** having/not having practised enough — see also SHARP PRACTICE

prac·tise ‖ also -**tice** *AmE*/'præktɪs/ *v* 1 *vi/t* do (an action) or perform on (esp. a musical instrument) repeatedly to gain skill 2 *vi/t* do (the work of a doctor, lawyer, etc.) 3 *vt* act in accordance with (a religion): *a practising Jew* 4 *vt fml* do (habitually) 5 **practise what one preaches** do what you advise others to do —**tised** *adj* skilled through practice

prac·ti·tion·er /præk'tɪʃənəʳ/ *n* person who works in a profession, esp. a doctor — see also GENERAL PRACTITIONER

prae·sid·i·um /prɪ'sɪdiəm, -'zɪ-/ *n* -**iums** *or* -**ia** /-diə/ PRESIDIUM

prag·mat·ic /præg'mætɪk/ *adj* concerned with actual effects rather than general principles ~**ally** /-kli/ *adv*

prai·rie /'preəri/ *n* wide grassy plain, esp. in North America

praise /preɪz/ *vt* 1 speak of with admiration 2 worship ♦ *n* [U] expression of admiration

praise·wor·thy /'preɪzwɜːði‖-ɜːr-/ *adj* deserving praise

pram /præm/ *n* small 4-wheeled hand-pushed carriage for a baby

prance /prɑːns‖præns/ *vi* 1 (of an animal) jump on the back legs 2 move happily or showily

prank /præŋk/ *n* playful but foolish trick

prat·tle /'prætl/ *vi* talk continually about unimportant things ♦ *n* [U] foolish or unimportant talk

prawn /prɔːn/ *n* small 10-legged sea creature, often eaten

pray /preɪ/ *vi* 1 speak to God or a god, often silently, often asking for something 2 wish or hope strongly: *We're praying for fine weather.*

prayer /preəʳ/ *n* 1 [C] (form of words used in) a solemn request to God or a god 2 [U] praying

preach /priːtʃ/ *v* 1 *vi/t* make (a religious speech) in public 2 *vt* urge others to accept: *preaching revolution* 3 *vi* offer unwanted advice on matters of right and wrong —**er** *n*

pre·am·ble /priː'æmbəl‖'priːæmbəl/ *n* something said or written before getting to the main part

pre·car·i·ous /prɪ'keəriəs/ *adj* not firm or steady; full of danger ~**ly** *adv*

pre·cau·tion /prɪ'kɔːʃən/ *n* action done to avoid possible trouble ~**ary** *adj*

pre·cede /prɪ'siːd/ *vt* come (just) before —**ceding** *adj: the preceding day*

pre·ce·dence /'presɪdəns/ n [U] (right to) a particular place before others, esp. because of importance

pre·ce·dent /'presɪdənt/ n 1 [U] what has usu. been done before 2 [C] earlier act which shows what may be done now

pre·cept /'priːsept/ n fml guiding rule of behaviour

pre·cinct /'priːsɪŋkt/ n 1 part of a town limited to the stated use: a shopping precinct 2 AmE division of a town for election or police purposes **precincts** n [P] space around a large (old) building, usu. inside walls

pre·cious /'preʃəs/ adj 1 of great value 2 fml (of words, manners, etc.) unnaturally fine or perfect ♦ adv very: precious few ~ness n [U]

pre·ci·pice /'presɪpɪs/ n very steep side of a mountain or cliff

pre·cip·i·tate¹ /prɪ'sɪpɪteɪt/ vt 1 fml make (an unwanted event) happen sooner 2 fml throw down suddenly 3 separate (solid matter) from liquid chemically ♦ n [C;U] precipitated matter –tation /prɪ,sɪpɪ'teɪʃən/ n [U] fml 1 precipitating 2 rain, snow, etc. 3 unwise speed

pre·cip·i·tate² /prɪ'sɪpɪtət/ adj fml too hasty ~ly adv

pre·cip·i·tous /prɪ'sɪpɪtəs/ adj fml 1 dangerously steep 2 precipitate ~ly adv ~ness n [U]

pré·cis /'preɪsiː‖preɪ'siː/ n précis shortened form of something written or said

pre·cise /prɪ'saɪs/ adj 1 exact 2 (too) careful and correct about small details ~ly adv 1 exactly 2 yes, that is correct

pre·ci·sion /prɪ'sɪʒən/ n [U] exactness ♦ adj 1 done with exactness: precision bombing 2 giving exact results: precision instruments

pre·clude /prɪ'kluːd/ vt fml prevent

pre·co·cious /prɪ'kəʊʃəs/ adj developing unusually early ~ly adv ~ness n [U]

pre·cog·ni·tion /,priːkɒg'nɪʃən‖-kɑːg-/ n [U] fml knowing about things before they happen

pre·con·cep·tion /,priːkən'sepʃən/ n opinion formed in advance without (enough) knowledge –ceived /-kən'siːvd/ adj: preconceived notions

pre·con·di·tion /,priːkən'dɪʃən/ n thing that must be agreed to if something is to be done

pre·cur·sor /prɪ'kɜːsər‖-'kɜːr-/ n one that came before and led to a later thing

pred·a·to·ry /'predətəri‖-tɔːri/ adj 1 killing and eating other animals 2 living by attacking and robbing **predator** n predatory animal

pre·de·ces·sor /'priːdɪsesər‖'pre-/ n one that came before: my predecessor as headmaster

pre·des·ti·na·tion /prɪ,destɪ'neɪʃən, ,priːdes-/ n [U] belief that everything in the world has been decided by God, and that no human effort can change it

pre·des·tine /prɪ'destɪn/ vt settle in advance, esp. as if by fate or the will of God

pre·de·ter·mine /,priːdɪ'tɜːmɪn‖-ɜːr-/ vt 1 fix unchangeably from the beginning 2 arrange in advance

pre·de·ter·min·er /,priːdɪ'tɜːmɪnər‖-ɜːr-/ n word that can be used before a DETERMINER: In the phrase 'all the boys', 'all' is a predeterminer.

pre·dic·a·ment /prɪ'dɪkəmənt/ n difficult situation

pred·i·cate /'predɪkət/ n part of a sentence which makes a statement about the subject

pre·dic·a·tive /prɪ'dɪkətɪv‖'predɪkeɪt-/ adj coming after a verb

pre·dict /prɪ'dɪkt/ vt say in advance (what will happen) ~able adj 1 that can be predicted 2 not doing anything unexpected ~ably adv ~ion /prɪ'dɪdʃən/ n [C;U] predicting or something predicted

pre·di·lec·tion /,priːdɪ'lekʃən‖,predl'ek-/ n special liking for something

pre·dis·pose /,priːdɪs'pəʊz/ vt fml make (someone) likely to do or have –position /,priːdɪspə'zɪʃən/ n

pre·dom·i·nant /prɪ'dɒmɪnənt‖-'dɑː-/ adj most powerful, noticeable, important, etc. ~ly adv –nance n [U]

pre·dom·i·nate /prɪ'dɒmɪneɪt‖-'dɑː-/ vi 1 have the main power or influence 2 be greatest in numbers

pre·em·i·nent /priː'emɪnənt/ adj better than any others ~ly adv –nence n [U]

pre·empt /priː'empt/ vt prevent by taking action in advance ~ive adj

preen /priːn/ vi/t (of a bird) clean (itself or its feathers) with its beak

pre·fab·ri·cate /priː'fæbrɪkeɪt/ vt make (the parts of a building, ship, etc.) in advance in a factory and put them together later

pref·ace /'prefɪs/ n introduction to a book ♦ vt introduce (speech or writing) in the stated way

pref·a·to·ry /'prefətəri‖-tɔːri/ adj fml acting as a preface

pre·fect /'priːfekt/ n 1 older pupil who keeps order among younger ones 2 (esp. in France) public official with government or police duties

pre·fer /prɪ'fɜːr/ vt -rr- 1 like better; choose rather: I prefer wine to beer. 2

law make (a charge) officially ~**er-able** /'prefərəbəl/ *adj* better, esp. because more suitable ~**ably** *adv*

pref·e·rence /'prefərəns/ *n* [C;U] **1** liking for one thing rather than another **2** special favour shown to one person, group, etc.

pref·e·ren·tial /ˌprefə'renʃəl/ *adj* giving or showing PREFERENCE (2) ~**ly** *adv*

pre·fix /'priːfiks/ *n* wordlike part added at the beginning of a word to change its meaning (as in *untie*) ♦ *vt* **1** add a prefix to **2** add (something) to the beginning (of)

preg·nant /'pregnənt/ *adj* **1** having an unborn child or young in the body **2** full of hidden meaning –**nancy** *n* [C;U]

pre·hen·sile /prɪ'hensaɪl‖-səl/ *adj* able to hold things: *a monkey's prehensile tail*

pre·his·tor·ic /ˌpriːhɪ'stɒrɪk‖-'stɔː-, -'stɑː-/ *adj* of times before recorded history ~**ally** /-kli/ *adv*

pre·judge /ˌpriː'dʒʌdʒ/ *vt* form an opinion about before knowing all the facts

prej·u·dice /'predʒədɪs/ *n* **1** [C;U] unfair feeling against something **2** [U] *fml* damage; harm ♦ *vt* **1** cause to have a prejudice **2** weaken; harm: *It may prejudice your chances of success.*

prej·u·di·cial /ˌpredʒʊ'dɪʃəl/ *adj fml* harmful

prel·ate /'prelət/ *n* priest of high rank

pre·lim·i·na·ry /prɪ'lɪmɪnəri‖-neri/ *adj* coming before (and preparing for) esp. the main one ♦ *n* preliminary act or arrangement

prel·ude /'preljuːd/ *n* **1** something that is followed by something larger or more important **2** short piece of music introducing a large musical work

pre·mar·i·tal /ˌpriː'mærɪtəl/ *adj* happening before marriage

pre·ma·ture /'premətʃər, -tʃʊər, ˌpremə'tʃʊər‖ ˌpriːmə'tʊər/ *adj* happening before the proper time ~**ly** *adv*

pre·med·i·tat·ed /ˌpriː'medɪteɪtɪd‖ prɪ-/ *adj* planned in advance –**tation** /prɪˌmedɪ'teɪʃən‖prɪ-/ *n* [U]

prem·i·er /'premiə‖prɪ'mɪər/ *n* PRIME MINISTER ♦ *adj fml* first in importance

prem·i·ere, -**ère**/'premieər‖ prɪ'mɪər/ *n* first public performance of a film or play ♦ *vt* give a premiere of (a play or film)

prem·ise /'premɪs/ *n fml* statement or idea on which reasoning is based

prem·is·es /'premɪsəz/ *n* [P] building and its land, considered as a piece of property

pre·mi·um /'priːmiəm/ *n* **1** money paid for insurance **2** additional charge **3 at a premium** rare or difficult to obtain **4 put a premium on** cause to be an advantage

pre·mo·ni·tion /ˌpreməˈnɪʃən, ˌpriː-/ *n* feeling that something is going to happen

pre·oc·cu·pa·tion /priːˌɒkjʊ-'peɪʃən‖-ˌɑːk-/ *n* **1** [U] being preoccupied **2** [C] something that takes up all one's attention

pre·oc·cu·py /priː'ɒkjʊpaɪ‖-'ɑːk-/ *vt* fill (someone's) thoughts, taking attention away from other things

prep·a·ra·tion /ˌprepə'reɪʃən/ *n* **1** [U] act or process of preparing **2** [C] arrangement for a future event **3** [C] *fml* (chemical) mixture for a certain purpose

pre·par·a·to·ry /prɪ'pærətəri‖-tori/ *adj* done to get ready

pre·par·a·to·ry school /·'····· ·/*n* **1** (esp. in Britain) private school for pupils up to the age of 13 **2** (in the US) private school that makes pupils ready for college

pre·pare /prɪ'peər/ *vi/t* **1** get or make ready **2** put (oneself) into a suitable state of mind –**pared** *adj* willing: *not prepared to help*

pre·pon·de·rance /prɪ'pɒndərəns‖ -'pɑːn-/ *n* [S] *fml* larger number; state of being more

prep·o·si·tion /ˌprepə'zɪʃən/ *n* word (such as *in* or *by*) used with a noun or PRONOUN to show its connection with another word ~**al** *adj*

pre·pos·sess·ing /ˌpriːpə'zesɪŋ/ *adj fml* very pleasing; charming

pre·pos·ter·ous /prɪ'pɒstərəs‖ -'pɑːs-/ *adj* foolishly unreasonable or improbable ~**ly** *adv*

prep·py /'prepi/ *adj AmE infml* typical of (former) students of expensive private schools in the US, esp. in being neat and well-dressed

pre·req·ui·site /ˌpriː'rekwɪzət/ *n fml* something needed before something else can happen

pre·rog·a·tive /prɪ'rɒgətɪv‖-'rɑː-/ *n* special right belonging to someone

pres·age /'presɪdʒ, prə'seɪdʒ/ *vt fml* be a warning or sign of (a future event)

Pres·by·te·ri·an /ˌprezbə'tɪərɪən/ *n, adj* (member) of a Protestant church governed by a body of equal-ranking officials

pre·sci·ent /'presiənt/ *adj fml* seeming to know in advance –**ence** *n* [U]

pre·scribe /prɪ'skraɪb/ *vt* **1** order a medicine or treatment **2** *fml* state (what must be done)

pre·scrip·tion /prɪ'skrɪpʃən/ *n* **1** [C] (doctor's written order for) a particular medicine or treatment **2** [U] act of prescribing

pre·scrip·tive /prɪˈskrɪptɪv/ adj saying how a language ought to be

pres·ence /ˈprezəns/ n [U] **1** fact of being present **2** fml personal appearance and manner, as having a strong effect on others

presence of mind /,·· · ·ˈ·/ n [U] ability to act quickly, calmly, and wisely when necessary

pres·ent¹ /ˈprezənt/ n gift

pre·sent² /prɪˈzent/ vt **1** give, esp. ceremonially **2** be the cause of: *That presents no difficulties.* **3** offer for consideration: *to present a report* **4** provide for the public to see in a theatre, cinema, etc. **5** introduce and take part in (a radio or television show) **6** introduce (someone) esp. to someone of higher rank **7** present itself (of something possible) happen **~er** n

pres·ent³ /ˈprezənt/ adj **1** here/there: *I was not present at the meeting.* **2** existing or being considered now: *my present address* **3** gram expressing an existing state or action: *the present tense*

present⁴ n **1** [the + S] the PRESENT (2) time **2** at present at this time **3** for the present now, but not necessarily in the future

pre·sen·ta·ble /prɪˈzentəbəl/ adj fit to be seen publicly **–bly** adv

pre·sen·ta·tion /ˌprezənˈteɪʃən‖ ˌprɪzen-, -zən-/ n [C;U] act of presenting **2** [U] way something is shown, explained, etc., to others

pres·ent-day /ˌprezənt ˈdeɪ◂/ adj existing now; modern

pre·sen·ti·ment /prɪˈzentɪ̇mənt/ n strange feeling that something (bad) is going to happen

pres·ent·ly /ˈprezəntli/ adv **1** soon **2** esp. AmE now

present par·ti·ci·ple /,·· ˈ····/ n (in grammar) a participle that is formed in English by adding -ing to the verb and can be used in compound forms of the verb to show PROGRESSIVE tenses, or sometimes as an adjective

pres·er·va·tion /ˌprezəˈveɪʃən‖ -zər-/ n [U] act of preserving or condition after a long time

pre·ser·va·tive /prɪˈzɜːvətɪv‖ -ɜːr-/ n, adj [C;U] (substance) used to PRESERVE (2) food

pre·serve /prɪˈzɜːv‖ -ɜːrv/ vt **1** keep from decaying or being destroyed or lost: *preserving old customs/one's health* **2** treat (food) so it can be kept a long time ♦ n **1** [C;U] JAM (1) **2** [C] something limited to one person or group

pre·side /prɪˈzaɪd/ vi be in charge, esp. at a meeting

pres·i·den·cy /ˈprezədənsi/ n office of president

pres·i·dent /ˈprezədənt/ n **1** head of state (and government) in countries that do not have a king or queen **2** head of a business firm, government department, club, etc. **~ial** /ˌprezəˈdenʃəl/ adj

pre·sid·i·um /prɪˈsɪdiəm, -ˈzɪ-/ n **-iums** or **-ia** /-diə/ ruling political committee, esp. in COMMUNIST countries

press¹ /pres/ v **1** vt push firmly and steadily **2** vt hold firmly as a sign of friendship, etc.: *He pressed my hand warmly.* **3** vt direct weight onto to flatten, shape, get liquid out, etc. **4** vi move strongly, esp. in a mass **5** vt give (clothes) a smooth surface and a sharp fold by using a hot iron **6** vt urge strongly: *She pressed her guests to say a little longer.* **7** vi make quick action necessary **~ed** adj not having enough: *pressed for time* **~ing** adj urgent

press for phr vt demand urgently

press on phr vi continue with determination

press² n **1** [U] (writers for) the newspapers **2** [S] treatment given in the newspapers: *The play got a good press.* **3** [S] act of pushing steadily **4** [C] printing machine **5** [C] business for printing (and sometimes also selling) books, etc. **6** [C] apparatus for pressing something: *trouser press* **7** [C] act of smoothing a garment with a hot iron **8** go to press (of a newspaper, etc.) start being printed

press box /ˈ· ·/ n place where newspaper reporters sit at sports events

press con·fer·ence /ˈ· ,···/ n meeting where someone answers reporters' questions

press-gang /ˈpresgæn/ vt force to do something unwillingly

press-up /ˈ· ·/ n form of exercise where one lies face down and pushes with one's arms

pres·sure /ˈpreʃər/ n **1** [C;U] (force produced by) pressing: *Water pressure burst the dam.* **2** [C;U] (force) of the weight of the air **3** [U] forcible influence; strong persuasion **4** [U] conditions of anxiety in life or work ♦ vt PRESSURIZE (1)

pressure cook·er /ˈ·· ,··/ n closed metal pot in which food is cooked quickly in hot steam

pres·sur·ize ‖ also **-ise** BrE /ˈpreʃəraɪz/ vt **1** (try to) make (someone) do something by forceful demands **2** control the air pressure inside

pres·tige /preˈstiːʒ/ n [U] quality of being widely admired, esp. because of being the best or connected with high rank **–tigious** /preˈstɪdʒəs‖-ˈstiː-, ˈstɪ-/ adj having or bringing prestige

pre·su·ma·bly /prɪ'zjuːməblɪ‖-'zuː-/ *adv* it may reasonably be supposed that

pre·sume /prɪ'zjuːm‖-'zuːm/ *v* 1 *vt* take as true without proof 2 *vi fml* be disrespectful enough; dare: *I wouldn't presume to argue.*

pre·sump·tion /prɪ'zʌmpʃən/ *n* [U] 1 act of supposing 2 *fml* disrespectful behaviour

pre·sump·tive /prɪ'zʌmptɪv/ *adj law* probable

pre·sump·tu·ous /prɪ'zʌmptʃuəs/ *adj* disrespectful and with too high an opinion of oneself ~**ly** *adv*

pre·sup·pose /ˌpriːsə'pəʊz/ *vt* 1 accept as true in advance without proof 2 need according to reason: *A child presupposes a mother.* **-position** /ˌpriːsʌpə'zɪʃən/ *n* [C;U]

pre·tence ‖ also **-tense** *AmE* /prɪ'tens‖'priːtens/ *n* 1 [S;U] false appearance or reason 2 [U] claim to possess: *little pretence to fairness*

pre·tend /prɪ'tend/ *v* 1 *vi/t* give an appearance of (something untrue), to deceive or as a game 2 *vi* attempt; dare

pre·tend·er /prɪ'tendər/ *n* person who makes a (doubtful or unproved) claim to some high position

pre·ten·sion /prɪ'tenʃən/ *n fml* claim to possess a skill, quality, etc.

pre·ten·tious /prɪ'tenʃəs/ *adj* claiming importance, rank, or artistic value one does not have ~**ly** *adv* ~**ness** *n* [U]

pre·ter·nat·u·ral /ˌpriːtə'nætʃərəl‖ -tər-/ *adj fml* beyond what is usual or natural ~**ly** *adv*

pre·text /'priːtekst/ *n* false reason

pret·ty /'prɪtɪ/ *adj* pleasing to look at ♦ *adv* 1 rather; quite 2 **pretty well** almost ~**tily** *adv* — see also a **pretty penny** (PENNY)

pre·vail /prɪ'veɪl/ *vi fml* 1 win 2 exist; be widespread ~**ing** *adj* 1 (of wind) that usu. blows 2 common or general (in some place or time)

prevail upon *phr vt fml* persuade

prev·a·lent /'prevələnt/ *adj fml* common in a place or at a time ~**ly** *adv* ~**lence** *n* [U]

pre·var·i·cate /prɪ'værɪkeɪt/ *vi fml* try to hide the truth ~**cation** /prɪˌværɪ'keɪʃən/ *n* [C;U]

pre·vent /prɪ'vent/ *vt* stop (something) happening or (someone) doing something ~**ion** /prɪ'venʃən/ *n* [U]

pre·ven·tive /prɪ'ventɪv/ *adj* that prevents esp. illness

pre·view /'priːvjuː/ *n* private showing or short description of film, show, etc., before it is publicly seen ♦ *vt* give a preview of

pre·vi·ous /'priːvɪəs/ *adj* before this one: *my previous employer* ~**ly** *adv*

prey¹ /preɪ/ *n* [U] 1 animal hunted and eaten by another 2 such hunting and eating: *The eagle is a bird of prey.*

prey² *v* **prey on** *phr vt* 1 hunt and eat as prey 2 trouble greatly

price /praɪs/ *n* 1 money (to be) paid for something; (fig.) *the price of freedom* 2 **at a price** at a high price 3 **not at any price** not at all ♦ *vt* fix the price of

price·less /'praɪsləs/ *adj* 1 extremely valuable 2 *infml* very funny

price tag /'· ·/ *n* 1 small ticket showing the price of an article 2 a (fixed or stated) price: *The government has not yet put a price tag on the plan.*

pric·ey /'praɪsɪ/ *adj infml, esp. BrE* expensive

prick¹ /prɪk/ *v* 1 *vt* make a small hole in with something sharp-pointed 2 *vi/t* (cause to) feel a light sharp pain on the skin 3 **prick up one's ears** start to listen carefully

prick² *n* 1 small sharp pain 2 mark made by pricking 3 *taboo* PENIS 4 *taboo sl* foolish worthless man

prick·le /'prɪkəl/ *n* [C] small sharp point on an animal or plant 2 [S] pricking sensation on the skin ♦ *vi/t* PRICK¹ (2) ~**ly** *adj* 1 covered with prickles 2 that gives one a prickling sensation 3 difficult to deal with

pride¹ /praɪd/ *n* 1 [S;U] pleasure in what you (or someone connected with you) can do or have done well 2 [U] reasonable self-respect 3 [U] too high an opinion of yourself 4 [S] most valuable one: *the pride of my collection* 5 **pride of place** *esp. BrE* highest or best position

pride² *v* **pride oneself on** *phr vt* be proud of oneself because of

priest /priːst/ *n* 1 (in the Christian Church, esp. in the ROMAN CATHOLIC Church) specially trained person who performs religious ceremonies and other religious duties 2 **priestess** /'priːstes/ *fem.* — specially trained person in certain non-Christian religions ~**hood** *n* [U] 1 position of being a priest 2 all the priests

prig /prɪg/ *n* unpleasantly moral person ~**gish** *adj*

prim /prɪm/ *adj* -**mm**- easily shocked by rude things ~**ly** *adv*

pri·ma·cy /'praɪməsɪ/ *n* [U] *fml* being first in importance, rank, etc.

prima don·na /ˌpriːmə 'dɒnə‖ -'dɑːnə/ *n* 1 main female OPERA singer 2 someone who thinks they are very important and often gets excited and angry

pri·ma fa·cie /ˌpraɪmə 'feɪʃɪ‖-ʃə/ *adj, adv law* based on what seems true

pri·mal /'praɪməl/ *adj* belonging to the earliest times

pri·ma·ri·ly /'praɪmərəli‖praɪ'merəli/ *adv* mainly

pri·ma·ry[1] /'praɪmɛri‖-meri/ *adj* 1 chief; main: *the primary purpose of his visit* 2 earliest in time or order of development: *primary education*

primary[2] *n* (esp. in the US) election in which the members of a political party in a particular area vote for the person they would like to see as their party's CANDIDATE for a political office

primary col·our /'··· ,'··/ *n* red, yellow, or blue

primary school /'··· ,'/n 1 BrE school for children between 5 and 11 years old 2 AmE ELEMENTARY SCHOOL

pri·mate[1] /'praɪmeɪt/ *n* member of the most highly developed group of MAMMALS which includes human beings, monkeys, and related animals

pri·mate[2] /'praɪmət/ *n* priest of the highest rank in the Church of England

prime[1] /praɪm/ *n* [S] time when someone is at their best

prime[2] *adj* 1 main 2 best

prime[3] *vt* 1 put PRIMER[1] (1) on 2 instruct in advance 3 put explosive powder into (a gun)

prime min·is·ter /, ···/ *n* chief minister and government leader

prime num·ber /, '··/ *n* number that can only be divided by itself and 1

prim·er[1] /'praɪmə/ *n* 1 [U] paint put on before the main painting 2 [C] tube containing explosive, esp. to set off a bomb

primer[2] /'praɪmə‖'prɪmər/ *n* simple book for beginners

prime time /'· ,/n [U] time when most people are thought to watch television

pri·me·val /praɪ'miːvəl/ *adj* very ancient

prim·i·tive /'prɪmətɪv/ *adj* 1 of the earliest stage of development 2 roughly made or done 3 old-fashioned and inconvenient *n* member of a PRIMITIVE (1) race or tribe ~**ly** *adv*

pri·mo·gen·i·ture /,praɪməʊ-'dʒenətʃə/ *n* [U] system by which a dead man's property goes to his eldest son

pri·mor·di·al /praɪ'mɔːdiəl‖-'mɔːr-/ *adj* existing from or at the beginning of time

prim·rose /'prɪmrəʊz/ *n* pale yellow spring flower

pri·mus stove /'praɪməs ,stəʊv/ *n tdmk* small metal cooking apparatus

prince /prɪns/ *n* 1 king's son 2 royal ruler of a small country ~**ly** *adj* 1 of a prince 2 splendid; generous

Prince Charm·ing /, '··/ *n* [S] wonderful male lover

prin·cess /,prɪn'ses◂‖'prɪnsəs/ *n* 1 king's daughter 2 prince's wife

prin·ci·pal /'prɪnsəpəl/ *adj* main ♦ *n* 1 [C] head of a college, school, etc. 2 [S] money lent, on which interest is paid ~**ly** *adv*

principal boy /,··· '·/ *n* chief male character in a PANTOMIME, played by a woman

prin·ci·pal·i·ty /,prɪnsə'pælɪti/ *n* country ruled by a prince

prin·ci·ple /'prɪnsəpəl/ *n* 1 [C] general truth or belief: *the principle of free speech* 2 [C;U] moral rule which guides behaviour: *She resigned on a matter of principle.* 3 [U] high personal standard of right and wrong: *a man of principle* 4 [P] general rules on which a skill, etc., is based: *Archimedes' principle* 5 **in principle** as an idea, if not in fact 6 **on principle** because it would be morally wrong

print[1] /prɪnt/ *n* 1 [U] printed letters, words, etc. 2 [C] mark made on a surface: *a thumbprint* 3 [C] photograph printed on paper 4 [C] picture printed from a metal sheet 5 **in/out of print** (of a book) that can still/no longer be obtained — see also SMALL PRINT

print[2] *v* 1 *vi/t* press (letters or pictures) on (esp. paper) with ink- or paint-covered shapes 2 *vt* make (a book, magazine, etc.) by doing this 3 *vt* cause to be included in or produced as a newspaper, etc. 4 *vt* copy (a photograph) from film onto paper 5 *vi/t* write without joining the letters ~**able** *adj* suitable for reading by anyone ~**er** *n* 1 person who prints books, etc. 2 copying machine

print·out /'prɪnt,aʊt/ *n* [C;U] printed record produced by a computer

pri·or[1] /'praɪə/ *adj* 1 earlier 2 more important 3 **prior to** before

prior[2] *n* head of a priory

pri·o·ri·tize /praɪ'ɒrətaɪz‖-'ɔːr-/ *vt* give (something) priority

pri·or·i·ty /praɪ'ɒrɪti‖-'ɔːr-/ *n* 1 [U] (right of) being first in position or earlier in time 2 [C] something that needs attention before others

pri·o·ry /'praɪəri/n (building for) a religious group

prise /praɪz/ *vt esp. BrE for* PRIZE[2]

pris·m /'prɪzəm/ *n* transparent 3-sided block that breaks up light into different colours

pris·on /'prɪzən/ *n* [C;U] large building where criminals are kept for punishment

prison camp /'··· ·/ *n* guarded camp for prisoners of war

pris·on·er /'prɪzənə/ *n* person kept in prison

prisoner of war /,··· · '·/ *n* soldier, etc., caught by the enemy in war

pris·sy /ˈprɪsi/ adj infml annoyingly exact or proper

pris·tine /ˈprɪstiːn/ adj fml fresh and clean

priv·a·cy /ˈprɪvəsi, ˈpraɪ-‖ˈpraɪ-/ n [U] 1 the (desirable) state of being away from other people 2 secrecy

pri·vate /ˈpraɪvət/ adj 1 not (to be) shared with others; secret 2 just for one person or a small group, not everyone 3 not connected with or paid for by government 4 not connected with one's work or rank; unofficial 5 quiet; without lots of people ♦ n soldier of the lowest rank ~**ly** adv

private de·tec·tive /ˌ·· ·ˈ··/ n person, not a policeman, hired to follow people, report on their actions, etc.

private en·ter·prise /ˌ·· ˈ···/ n [U] CAPITALISM

private eye /ˌ·· ˈ·/ n infml private detective

private parts /ˌ·· ˈ·/ n [P] outer sexual organs

private sec·tor /ˌ·· ˈ··◁/ n [the + S] those industries and services that are owned and run by private companies, not by the state

pri·va·tion /praɪˈveɪʃən/ n [C;U] fml lack of things necessary for life

pri·vat·ize ‖ also **-ise** BrE /ˈpraɪvətaɪz/ vt sell a (government-owned industry or organization) into private ownership **-ization** /ˌpraɪvətaɪˈzeɪʃən‖-tə-/ n [U]: the privatization of the hospital service

priv·et /ˈprɪvət/ n [U] bush often used for HEDGES

priv·i·lege /ˈprɪvəlɪdʒ/ n 1 [C] special advantage limited to a particular person or group 2 [U] unfair possession of such advantages because of wealth, social rank, etc. **-leged** adj having (a) privilege

priv·y¹ /ˈprɪvi/ adj fml sharing secret knowledge (of)

priv·y² n old use for TOILET

Privy Coun·cil /ˌ·· ˈ··/ n body of important people who advise the British king or queen

prize¹ /praɪz/ n something you get given for winning, doing well, etc. ♦ vt value highly adj 1 that has gained or is worthy of a prize: a prize hen 2 given as a prize: prize money

prize² vt lift or force with a tool or metal bar

prize-fight /ˈpraɪzfaɪt/ n public BOXING match in former times ~**er** n

pro¹ /prəʊ/ n **pros** infml a PROFESSIONAL

pro² n argument or reason in favour (of something)

pro-am /ˌprəʊ ˈæm/ n, adj (competition) including both PROFESSIONALs and AMATEURS

prob·a·bil·i·ty /ˌprɒbəˈbɪləti‖ˌprɑː-/ n 1 [S;U] likelihood 2 [C] probable event or result

prob·a·ble /ˈprɒbəbəl‖ˈprɑː-/ adj that has a good chance of happening or being true; likely **-bly** adv

pro·bate /ˈprəʊbeɪt, -bət‖-beɪt/ n [U] legal process of declaring someone's WILL(3) properly made

pro·ba·tion /prəˈbeɪʃən‖prəʊ-/ n [U] 1 (period of) testing someone's suitability 2 system of not sending law-breakers to prison if they behave well for a time

probation of·fi·cer /·ˈ··· ˌ···/ n person who watches and advises law-breakers on probation (2)

probe /prəʊb/ vi/t search or examine carefully (as if) with a long thin instrument ♦ n 1 metal tool for probing 2 spacecraft for searching through space 3 thorough inquiry

pro·bi·ty /ˈprəʊbəti/ n [U] fml perfect honesty

prob·lem /ˈprɒbləm‖ˈprɑː-/ n difficulty that needs attention and thought

prob·lem·at·ic /ˌprɒbləˈmætɪk‖ ˌprɑː-/ adj full of problems or causing problems

pro·bos·cis /prəˈbɒsəs‖-ˈbɑː-/ n long movable nose of certain animals

pro·ce·dure /prəˈsiːdʒə/ n 1 [C] set of actions for doing something 2 [U] way a meeting, trial, etc., is (to be) run **-dural** adj

pro·ceed /prəˈsiːd/ vi fml 1 begin or continue in a course of action 2 walk or travel in a particular direction

pro·ceed·ings /prəˈsiːdɪŋz/ n [P] legal action taken against someone

pro·ceeds /ˈprəʊsiːdz/ n [P] money gained from the sale of something

pro·cess¹ /ˈprəʊses‖ˈprɑː-/ n 1 set of actions that produce continuation, change, or something new 2 method, esp. for producing goods 3 **in the process of** actually doing (the stated thing) at the time ♦ vt 1 treat and preserve (food): processed cheese 2 print a photograph from (film) 3 deal with; examine

pro·cess² /prəˈses/ vi walk in a procession

pro·ces·sion /prəˈseʃən/ n [C;U] line of people or vehicles moving along, esp. ceremonially

pro·ces·sor /ˈprəʊsesə‖ˈprɑː-/ n MICROPROCESSOR — see also WORD PROCESSOR

pro·claim /prəˈkleɪm‖prəʊ-/ vt declare publicly and officially

proc·la·ma·tion /ˌprɒkləˈmeɪʃən‖ ˌprɑː-/ n 1 [C] official public statement 2 [U] act of proclaiming

pro·cliv·i·ty /prəˈklɪvəti‖prəʊ-/ n fml strong natural liking or tendency

pro·cras·ti·nate /prəˈkræstʌneɪt/ vi fml delay (annoyingly) **-nation** /prəˌkræstʌˈneɪʃən/ n

pro·cre·ate /ˈprəʊkrɪeɪt/ vi fml produce young **-ation** /ˌprəʊkrɪˈeɪʃən/ n [U]

pro·cure /prəˈkjʊəʳ‖prəʊ-/ v 1 vt fml obtain 2 vt provide (a woman) for sexual pleasure **-curer** n

prod /prɒd‖prɑːd/ v **-dd-** 1 vi/t push with a pointed object 2 vt urge sharply **prod** n

prod·i·gal /ˈprɒdɪgəl‖ˈprɑː-/ adj fml 1 carelessly wasteful, esp. of money 2 giving or producing (something) freely and in large amounts **—ity** /ˌprɒdɪˈgælʌti‖ˌprɑː-/ n [U]

pro·di·gious /prəˈdɪdʒəs/ adj wonderfully large, powerful, etc. **~ly** adv

prod·i·gy /ˈprɒdɪdʒi‖ˈprɑː-/ n 1 person with wonderful abilities: child prodigy 2 a wonder in nature

pro·duce[1] /prəˈdjuːs‖-ˈduːs/ vt 1 bring into existence; give: These trees produce rubber. | Poverty produces illhealth. 2 make (goods for sale) 3 give birth to 4 bring out and show 5 prepare and bring before the public

pro·duce[2] /ˈprɒdjuːs‖ˈprɑːduːs/ n [U] something produced, esp. on a farm

pro·duc·er /prəˈdjuːsəʳ‖-ˈduː-/ n 1 person, company, etc., that produces goods 2 person in charge of the business of putting on a play, film, etc.

prod·uct /ˈprɒdʌkt‖ˈprɑː-/ n 1 something made or produced 2 result

pro·duc·tion /prəˈdʌkʃən/ n 1 [U] act of producing 2 [U] process of making products 3 [U] amount produced: a cut in production 4 [C] play, film, or broadcast that is produced

production line /·ˈ·· ·/ n arrangement of factory workers and machines for producing goods

pro·duc·tive /prəˈdʌktɪv/ adj 1 that produces a lot 2 causing or producing (a result) **~ly** adv

pro·duc·tiv·i·ty /ˌprɒdʌkˈtɪvʌti, -dək-‖ˌprɑː-/ n [U] rate of producing goods, crops, etc.

prof /prɒf‖prɑːf/ n infml for PROFESSOR

pro·fane /prəˈfeɪn/ adj 1 showing disrespect, esp. for holy things 2 (esp. of language) socially shocking 3 fml concerned with human life in this world; SECULAR: profane art ♦ vt treat disrespectfully **~ly** adv

pro·fan·i·ty /prəˈfænʌti/ n [C;U] profane behaviour or speech

pro·fess /prəˈfes/ vt fml 1 declare openly 2 claim, usu. falsely 3 have as one's religion **—ed** adj 1 self-declared 2 pretended

pro·fes·sion /prəˈfeʃən/ n 1 form of employment, esp. a socially respected

---

one like law or medicine 2 people in a particular profession 3 fml open declaration

pro·fes·sion·al /prəˈfeʃənəl/ adj 1 working in a profession 2 doing for payment what others do for fun 3 showing high standards of work ♦ n professional person **~ism** n [U] skill or quality of professionals

pro·fes·sor /prəˈfesəʳ/ n university teacher of highest rank **~ial** /ˌprɒfəˈsɔːriəl‖ˌprɑː-/ adj

prof·fer /ˈprɒfəʳ‖ˈprɑː-/ vt fml offer

pro·fi·cient /prəˈfɪʃənt/ adj very good at doing something **~ly** adv **–ciency** n [U]

pro·file /ˈprəʊfaɪl/ n 1 side view, esp. of someone's head 2 state of being noticed by other people around me: The management is trying to keep a low profile on this issue. | a high political profile 3 short description ♦ vt draw or write a profile of

prof·it[1] /ˈprɒfɪt‖ˈprɑː-/ n 1 [C;U] money gained 2 [U] advantage gained from some action

prof·it[2] v profit by/from phr vt gain advantage or learn from

prof·it·a·bil·i·ty /ˌprɒfɪtəˈbɪlʌti‖ˌprɑː-/ n [U] state of being profitable or the degree to which a business is profitable

prof·it·a·ble /ˈprɒfɪtəbəl‖ˈprɑː-/ adj producing profit **-bly** adv

prof·i·teer /ˌprɒfɪˈtɪəʳ‖ˌprɑː-/ n person who makes unfairly large profits **profiteer** vi

profit mar·gin /ˈ·· ˌ··/ n difference between production cost and selling price

profit shar·ing /ˈ·· ˌ··/ n [U] workers sharing the profits of a business

prof·li·gate /ˈprɒflɪgət‖ˈprɑː-/ adj fml 1 foolishly wasteful 2 shamelessly immoral

pro·found /prəˈfaʊnd/ adj 1 very strongly felt; deep 2 having thorough knowledge and understanding **~ly** adv **–fundity** /prəˈfʌndʌti/ n [C;U]

pro·fuse /prəˈfjuːs/ adj produced in great quantity **~ly** adv **–fusion** /prəˈfjuːʒən/ n [S;U] (too) great amount

pro·gen·i·tor /prəʊˈdʒenʌtəʳ/ n one in the past from which someone or something is descended

prog·e·ny /ˈprɒdʒʌni‖ˈprɑː-/ n [U] fml 1 DESCENDANTS 2 children

pro·ges·ter·one /prəʊˈdʒestərəʊn/ n [U] bodily substance that prepares the UTERUS for its work

prog·no·sis /prɒgˈnəʊsʌs‖prɑːg-/ n **-ses** /-siːz/ 1 doctor's opinion of how an illness will develop 2 description of the future

prog·nos·ti·cate /prɒgˈnɒstʌkeɪt‖ prɑːgˈnɑː-/ vt fml say (what is going to happen) **–cation** /ˌprɒgˌnɒstʌ'keɪʃən‖ prɑːgˌnɑː-/ n [C;U]

pro-gram[1] /'prəʊgræm/ n 1 set of instructions for making a computer do something 2 AmE a programme

program[2] vt **-mm-** or **-m-** 1 supply (a computer) with a PROGRAM[1] 2 AmE to programme ~**mable** adj controllable by means of a PROGRAM[1](1) ~**mer** n

pro-gramme BrE ‖ **-gram** AmE/'prəʊgræm/ n 1 list of performers or things to be performed 2 television or radio show 3 plan for future action ♦ vt plan or arrange

pro-gress[1] /'prəʊgres‖'prɑː-/ n [U] 1 continual improvement or development 2 forward movement in space 3 **in progress** happening or being done

pro-gress[2] /prə'gres/ vi make progress

pro-gres-sion /prə'greʃən/ n 1 [S;U] progressing 2 [C] set of numbers that vary in a particular way

pro-gres-sive /prə'gresɪv/ adj 1 developing continuously or by stages 2 favouring change or new ideas 3 (of a verb form) showing action that is continuing ♦ n person with progressive ideas, esp. about social change ~**ly** adv

pro-hib-it /prə'hɪbɪt‖prəʊ-/ vt fml 1 forbid by law or rule 2 prevent

pro-hi-bi-tion /ˌprəʊhɪ'bɪʃən/ n 1 [U] act of prohibiting something, esp. the sale of alcohol 2 [C] fml order forbidding something

pro-hib-i-tive /prə'hɪbʌtɪv‖prəʊ-/ adj preventing or tending to discourage: prohibitive prices (= too high) ~**ly** adv

proj-ect[1] /'prɒdʒekt‖'prɑː-/ n long piece of planned work

pro-ject[2] /prə'dʒekt/ v 1 vi/t stick out beyond a surface 2 vt fml aim and throw through the air 3 vt direct (sound or light) into space or onto a surface 4 vt make plans for: our projected visit to France 5 vt judge or calculate using the information one has: projected sales figures 6 vi/t express (oneself or one's beliefs, etc.) outwardly, esp. to have a favourable effect on others

pro-jec-tile /prə'dʒektaɪl‖-tl/ n object or weapon thrown or fired

pro-jec-tion /prə'dʒekʃən/ n 1 [C] act of projecting 2 [C] something that sticks out 3 [C] guess of future possibilities based on known facts

pro-jec-tion-ist /prə'dʒekʃənʌst/ n person who works a PROJECTOR, esp. in a cinema

pro-jec-tor /prə'dʒektər/ n apparatus for projecting films, etc.

pro-lapse /prəʊ'læps/ vi fml (of an inner body organ) slip out of its right place

prole /prəʊl/ n infml derog member of the proletariat

pro-le-tar-i-at /ˌprəʊlʌ'teəriət/ n class of unskilled wage-earning workers

pro-lif-e-rate /prə'lɪfəreɪt/ vi increase rapidly in numbers **–ration** /prəˌlɪfə'reɪʃən/ n [S;U]

pro-lif-ic /prə'lɪfɪk/ adj producing a lot ~**ally** /-kli/ adv

pro-lix /'prəʊlɪks‖prəʊ'lɪks/ adj fml using too many words

pro-logue BrE ‖ **-log** AmE/'prəʊlɒg‖ -lɔːg, -lɑːg/ n 1 introduction to a play, long poem, etc. 2 event that leads up to another, bigger one

pro-long /prə'lɒŋ‖-'lɔːŋ/ vt lengthen ~**ed** adj long

prom /prɒm‖prɑːm/ n BrE 1 PROMENADE (1) 2 PROMENADE CONCERT

prom-e-nade /ˌprɒmə'nɑːd◂, 'prɒmənɑːd‖ˌprɑːmə'neɪd/ n 1 wide path along the coast in a holiday town 2 fml unhurried walk ♦ vi walk slowly up and down

promenade con-cert /ˌ··· '··/ n (esp. in Britain) concert where some listeners stand

prom-i-nent /'prɒmɪnənt‖'prɑː-/ adj 1 sticking out 2 noticeable 3 famous ~**ly** adv **-nence** n 1 [U] fact or quality of being prominent 2 [C] fml part that sticks out

pro-mis-cu-ous /prə'mɪskjuəs/ adj 1 not limited to one sexual partner 2 fml being of many sorts mixed together **-cuity** /ˌprɒmɪ'skjuːʌti‖ˌprɑː-/ n [U]

prom-ise /'prɒmʌs‖'prɑː-/ n 1 [C] statement, which one wishes to be believed, of what one will do 2 [U] signs of future success, good results, etc. ♦ v 1 vi/t make a promise: I promise I won't tell them. 2 vt cause one to expect or hope for **-ising** adj showing PROMISE (2)

Promised Land /ˌ·· '·/ n [(the) S] hoped-for condition which will bring happiness

prom-on-to-ry /'prɒməntəri‖ 'prɑːməntɔːri/ n point of land stretching out into the sea

pro-mote /prə'məʊt/ vt 1 raise to a higher position or rank 2 help to arrange (a business, concert, etc.) 3 advertise 4 fml help to bring about **-moter** n person whose job is to promote events, activities, etc.

pro-mo-tion /prə'məʊʃən/ n [C;U] 1 raising of rank or position 2 advertising activity

prompt[1] /prɒmpt‖prɑːmpt/ vt 1 cause; urge 2 remind (an actor) of forgotten words **prompt**, ~**er** n person who prompts actors

prompt[2] adj acting or done quickly or at the right time ~**ly** adv ~**ness** n [U]

prom·ul·gate /'proməlgeɪt‖'prɑː-/ vt fml 1 bring (a law, etc.) into effect by official public declaration 2 spread (a belief, etc.) widely

prone /prəʊn/ adj 1 likely to suffer: *prone to colds | accident-prone* 2 lying face downwards

prong /prɒŋ‖prɔːŋ/ n pointed part of a fork: (fig.) *a 3-pronged attack* (= from 3 directions)

pro·nom·i·nal /prəʊ'nɒmənəl ‖ -'nɑː-/ adj of a pronoun

pro·noun /'prəʊnaʊn/ n word used instead of a noun, such as *he* or *it*

pro·nounce /prə'naʊns/ vt 1 make the sound of (a letter, word, etc.) 2 fml declare officially ~**ment** n solemn declaration **-nounced** adj very strong or noticeable

pro·nun·ci·a·tion /prə,nʌnsi'eɪʃən/ n [C;U] way in which a language or word is pronounced

proof¹ /pruːf/ n 1 [C;U] way of showing that something is true 2 [C] a test or trial 3 [C] test copy of something to be printed 4 [U] standard of strength for certain alcoholic drinks

proof² adj having or giving protection: *proof against temptation | waterproof*

proof·read /'pruːf,riːd/ vi/t read and put right mistakes in (PROOFs (3)) ~**er** n

prop¹ /prop‖prɑːp/ n support for something heavy ♦ vt -**pp-** support or keep in a leaning position

prop² n small article used on stage

prop·a·gan·da /,prɒpə'gændə‖ ,prɑː-/ n [U] information spread to influence public opinion

prop·a·gate /'prɒpəgeɪt‖'prɑː-/ v 1 vi/t (cause to) increase in number by producing young 2 vt fml spread (ideas, etc.) **-gation** /,prɒpə'geɪʃən ,prɑː-/ n [U]

pro·pel /prə'pel/ vt -**ll-** move or push forward

pro·pel·lant /prə'pelənt/ n [C;U] explosive for firing a bullet or ROCKET

pro·pel·ler /prə'pelər/ n 2 or more blades on a central bar that turns to drive an aircraft or ship

pro·pen·si·ty /prə'pensəti/ n fml natural tendency

prop·er /'prɒpər‖'prɑː-/ adj 1 right; suitable; correct 2 socially acceptable 3 complete: *a proper fool* ~**ly** adv

proper noun /,·· '·/ n name of a particular thing or person, spelt with a CAPITAL letter

prop·er·ty /'prɒpəti‖'prɑːpərti/ n 1 [U] something owned; possession(s) 2 [C;U] (area of) land and/or building(s) 3 [C] natural quality or power

proph·e·cy /'prɒfəsi‖'prɑː-/ n [C;U] (statement) telling what will happen in the future

proph·e·sy /'prɒfəsaɪ‖'prɑː-/ vi/t say (what will happen in the future)

proph·et /'prɒfət‖'prɑː-/ n 1 person who makes known and explains God's will 2 person who tells about the future ~**ic** /prə'fetɪk/ adj

pro·phy·lac·tic /,prɒfə'læktɪk‖ ,prɑː-/ adj fml for preventing disease ♦ n something prophylactic, esp. a CONDOM

pro·pin·qui·ty /prə'pɪŋkwəti/ n [U] fml nearness

pro·pi·ti·ate /prə'pɪʃieɪt/ vt fml make (an angry or unfriendly person) more friendly **-ation** /prə,pɪʃi'eɪʃən/ n [U]

pro·pi·tious /prə'pɪʃəs/ adj fml favourable; advantageous

pro·po·nent /prə'pəʊnənt/ n fml person who advises the use of something

pro·por·tion /prə'pɔːʃən‖-'pɔːr-/ n 1 [C;U] relationship between one thing or part and another in size, importance, etc. 2 [C] part of a whole 3 **in/out of proportion** according/not according to real importance ♦ vt fml make in or put into suitable proportion ~**al** adj in correct proportion **proportions** n [P] size and shape

proportional rep·re·sen·ta·tion /··,··· ···'·/ n [U] system of voting in elections by which parties are represented in parliament according to the proportion of votes they receive, rather than having to get a majority of the votes in each voting area

pro·pos·al /prə'pəʊzəl/ n 1 plan; suggestion 2 offer of marriage

pro·pose /prə'pəʊz/ v 1 vt suggest 2 vt intend 3 vi/t make an offer of (marriage)

prop·o·si·tion /,prɒpə'zɪʃən‖,prɑː-/ n 1 statement giving an unproved judgment 2 suggested offer or arrangement 3 person or situation to be dealt with 4 suggested offer to have sex with someone ♦ vt infml make a PROPOSITION (esp. 4) to (someone)

pro·pound /prə'paʊnd/ vt fml put forward (an idea)

pro·pri·e·ta·ry /prə'praɪətəri‖-teri/ adj privately owned: *a proprietary brand name* 2 of or like an owner

pro·pri·e·tor /prə'praɪətər/ n owner of a business

pro·pri·e·ty /prə'praɪəti/ n [U] fml 1 social or moral correctness 2 rightness or reasonableness

pro·pul·sion /prə'pʌlʃən/ n [U] force that PROPELs ~**sive** /-sɪv/ adj

pro ra·ta /,prəʊ 'rɑːtə‖-'reɪtə/ adv, adj according to a fair share for each

pro·rogue /prəʊ'rəʊg, prə-/ vt end the meetings of (a parliament) for a time

pro·sa·ic /prəʊ'zeɪ·ɪk, prə-/ adj dull ~**ally** /-kli/ adv

pros and cons /ˌprəʊz ən ˈkɒnz‖ -ˈkɑːnz/ n [P] reasons for and against

pro·sce·ni·um /prəˈsiːnɪəm, prəʊ-/ n front arch of a theatre stage

pro·scribe /prəʊˈskraɪb/ vt fml forbid, esp. by law

prose /prəʊz/ n [U] ordinary written language (not poetry)

pros·e·cute /ˈprɒsɪkjuːt‖ˈprɑː-/ vi/t bring a criminal charge (against) in court **–cutor** n **–cution** /ˌprɒsɪˈkjuːʃən‖ˌprɑː-/ n 1 [C;U] prosecuting 2 [the + S] group of people prosecuting someone in court 3 [U] fml the carrying out of something that needs to be done

pros·e·lyte /ˈprɒsəlaɪt‖ˈprɑː-/ n fml new member of a religion

pros·e·lyt·ize /ˈprɒsəlataɪz‖ˈprɑː-/ vi fml try to persuade people to become proselytes

pros·o·dy /ˈprɒsədi‖ˈprɑː-/ n [U] arrangement of sounds and beats in poetry

pros·pect¹ /ˈprɒspekt‖ˈprɑː-/ n 1 [C;U] reasonable hope of something happening 2 [S;U] something which is likely soon 3 [C] wide or distant view

pros·pect² /prəˈspekt‖ˈprɑːspekt/ vi try to find gold, oil, etc. **–or** n

pro·spec·tive /prəˈspektɪv/ adj likely to become

pro·spec·tus /prəˈspektəs/ n small book advertising a product, college, new business, etc.

pros·per /ˈprɒspə‖ˈprɑː-/ vi 1 become successful and esp. rich 2 grow well **–ous** adj successful and rich **–ity** /prɒˈsperəti ‖ prɑː-/ n [U] success and wealth

pros·tate /ˈprɒsteɪt‖ˈprɑː-/ n male bodily organ producing a seed-carrying liquid

pros·the·sis /prɒsˈθiːsɪs‖prɑːs-/ n artificial body part

pros·ti·tute /ˈprɒstɪtjuːt‖ˈprɑːstɪtuːt/ n someone who has sex with people for money ♦ vt fml use dishonourably for money **–tution** /ˌprɒstɪˈtjuːʃən ‖ ˌprɑːstɪˈtuːʃən/ n [U]

pros·trate /ˈprɒstreɪt‖ˈprɑː-/ adj 1 lying face downwards, esp. in worship 2 without any strength or courage ♦ vt make prostrate

pro·tag·o·nist /prəʊˈtægənɪst/ n 1 main supporter of a new idea 2 someone taking part

pro·te·an /ˈprəʊtɪən, prəʊˈtiːən/ adj fml continually changing

pro·tect /prəˈtekt/ vt keep safe **–or** n **–ion** /prəˈtekʃən/ n 1 [U] act of protecting or state of being protected 2 [C] something that protects

pro·tec·tion·is·m /prəˈtekʃənɪzəm/ n [U] helping one's own country's trade by taxing foreign goods

protection rack·et /·ˈ·· ˌ··/ n getting money from shop owners, etc., by threatening to damage their property

pro·tec·tive /prəˈtektɪv/ adj 1 that protects 2 wishing to protect **–ly** adv

pro·tec·tor·ate /prəˈtektərət/ n country controlled and protected by another country

prot·é·gé /ˈprɒtɪʒeɪ‖ˈprəʊ-/ n person guided and helped by another

pro·tein /ˈprəʊtiːn/ n [C;U] food substance that builds up the body and keeps it healthy

pro tem /ˌprəʊ ˈtem/ adv for the present time only

pro·test¹ /ˈprəʊtest/ n [C;U] 1 strong expression of disapproval, opposition, etc. 2 **under protest** unwillingly

pro·test² /prəˈtest/ v 1 vi make a protest 2 vt declare strongly against opposition **–er** n

Prot·es·tant /ˈprɒtɪstənt‖ˈprɑː-/ n, adj (member) of a branch of the Christian church that separated from the Roman Catholic Church in the 16th century

prot·es·ta·tion /ˌprɒtɪˈsteɪʃən, ˌprəʊ-‖ˌprɑː-, prəʊ-/ n fml 1 [C] solemn declaration 2 [U] protesting

pro·to·col /ˈprəʊtəkɒl‖-kɔːl/ n [U] fixed rules of behaviour

pro·ton /ˈprəʊtɒn‖-tɑːn/ n very small piece of matter that is part of an atom and carries POSITIVE (5) electricity

pro·to·plas·m /ˈprəʊtəplæzəm/ n [U] substance from which all plants and creatures are formed

pro·to·type /ˈprəʊtətaɪp/ n first form of a machine, afterwards developed

pro·tract /prəˈtrækt‖prəʊ-/ vt cause to last an (unnecessarily) long time **–ion** /prəˈtrækʃən/ n [U]

pro·trac·tor /prəˈtræktə‖prəʊ-/ n instrument for measuring and drawing angles

pro·trude /prəˈtruːd‖prəʊ-/ vi fml stick out **–trusion** /prəˈtruːʒən/ n [C;U]

pro·tu·ber·ance /prəˈtjuːbərəns‖prəʊˈtuː-/ n fml swelling; BULGE

proud /praʊd/ adj 1 showing proper and reasonable self-respect 2 having too high an opinion of oneself 3 having or expressing personal pleasure in something connected with oneself: proud of her new car 4 splendid; glorious ♦ adv: do someone proud treat someone, esp. a guest, splendidly **–ly** adv

prove /pruːv/ v 1 vt show to be true 2 be (later) found to be: These revelations could prove highly embarrassing.

prov·en /ˈpruːvən; ScotE ˈprəʊvən/ adj tested and shown to be true

prov·e·nance /ˈprɒvənəns‖ˈprɑː-/ n fml (place of) origin

prov·en·der /'prɒvəndəʳ‖'prɑː-/ n [U] food for horses or cattle

prov·erb /'prɒvɜːb‖'prɒvɜːrb/ n short well-known wise saying ~**ial** /prəˈvɜːbiəl‖-ˈvɜːr-/ adj 1 widely known and spoken of 2 of, concerning, or like a proverb

pro·vide /prəˈvaɪd/ vt arrange for someone to get; supply **-vided** conj on condition that **-viding** conj provided

provide for phr vt 1 supply with necessary things 2 (of the law) make possible

prov·i·dence /'prɒvədəns‖'prɑː-/ n [U] the kindness of fate

prov·i·dent /'prɒvədənt‖'prɑː-/ adj fml careful to save for future needs

prov·i·den·tial /ˌprɒvəˈdenʃəl‖ˌprɑː-/ adj fml lucky

prov·ince /'prɒvəns‖'prɑː-/ n 1 main division of a country 2 area of knowledge, activity, etc. **-incial** /prəˈvɪnʃəl/ adj 1 of a province narrow or old-fashioned in interest, customs, etc. **provinces** n [the +P] parts of a country far from the main city

prov·ing ground /'pruːvɪŋ graʊnd/ n 1 place for scientific testing 2 situation where something new is tried out

pro·vi·sion /prəˈvɪʒən/ n 1 [U] act of providing 2 [U] preparation against future risks or for future needs 3 [C] condition in an agreement or law **provisions** n [P] food supplies

pro·vi·sion·al /prəˈvɪʒənəl/ adj for use now, but likely to be changed ~**ly** adv

pro·vi·so /prəˈvaɪzəʊ/ n **-sos** condition made in advance

prov·o·ca·tion /ˌprɒvəˈkeɪʃən‖ˌprɑː-/ n 1 [U] act of provoking 2 [C] something annoying

pro·voc·a·tive /prəˈvɒkətɪv‖-ˈvɑː-/ adj likely to cause **a** anger **b** sexual interest ~**ly** adv

pro·voke /prəˈvəʊk/ vt 1 make angry 2 cause (a feeling or action)

prow /praʊ/ n front part of a ship

prow·ess /'praʊəs/ n [U] fml great ability or courage

prowl /praʊl/ vi/t move about quietly and threateningly **prowl** n [S]

prox·im·i·ty /prɒkˈsɪməti‖prɑːk-/ n [U] fml nearness

prox·y /'prɒksi‖'prɑːksi/ n 1 [U] right to act for another person, esp. as a voter 2 [C] person given this right

prude /pruːd/ n person easily offended by rude things, esp. connected with sex **prudish** adj

pru·dent /'pruːdənt/ adj sensible and careful ~**ly** adv **-dence** n [U]

prune[1] /pruːn/ n dried PLUM

prune[2] vt 1 cut off parts of (a tree or bush) to improve shape and growth 2 remove unwanted parts of

pru·ri·ent /'prʊəriənt/ adj fml unhealthily interested in sex **-ence** n [U]

pry[1] /praɪ/ vi try to find out about someone's private affairs

pry[2] vt esp. AmE for PRIZE[2]

P.S. /ˌpiː 'es/ n note added at the end of a letter

psalm /sɑːm‖sɑːm, sɑːlm/ n religious song or poem, esp. as in the Bible

pseud /sjuːd‖suːd/ n BrE infml person who falsely claims knowledge, social position, etc.

pseu·do·nym /'sjuːdənɪm‖'suːdənɪm/ n invented name, esp. of a writer

psst /ps/ interj (used for quietly gaining someone's attention)

psych /saɪk/ v sl, esp. AmE

psych out phr vt 1 understand by INTUITION 2 frighten

psych up phr vt make (esp. oneself) keen and ready

psy·che /'saɪki/ n fml human mind or spirit

psy·che·del·ic /ˌsaɪkəˈdelɪk/ adj 1 (of a drug) causing strange and powerful feelings 2 having strong patterns of colour, lines, moving lights, noise, etc.

psy·chi·a·try /saɪˈkaɪətri‖sə-/ n [U] study and treatment of diseases of the mind **-trist** n **-tric** /ˌsaɪkiˈætrɪk/ adj

psy·chic /'saɪkɪk/ adj 1 having strange powers, such as the ability to see into the future 2 of the mind 3 connected with the spirits of the dead ~**ally** -kli/ adv

psy·cho·a·nal·y·sis /ˌsaɪkəʊəˈnæləsəs/ n [U] way of treating disorders of the mind by finding their causes in the patient's past life **-analyse** ‖ also **-analyze** AmE /ˌsaɪkəʊˈænəlaɪz/ vt **-analyst** /-ˈænəlɪst/ n

psy·cho·log·i·cal /ˌsaɪkəˈlɒdʒɪkəl‖-ˈlɑː-/ adj 1 of or connected with the way the mind works 2 infml not real **psychological war·fare** /·‧‧‧ '‧‧/ n [U] spreading fear, different political beliefs, etc., among the enemy

psy·chol·o·gy /saɪˈkɒlədʒi‖-ˈkɑː-/ n [U] study of how the mind works **-gist** n

psy·cho·path /'saɪkəpæθ/ n mad person who may be violent ~**ic** /ˌsaɪkəˈpæθɪk/ adj

psy·cho·sis /saɪˈkəʊsəs/ n **-ses** /-siːz/ serious disorder of the mind **-chotic** /saɪˈkɒtɪk‖-ˈkɑː-/ n, adj

psy·cho·so·mat·ic /ˌsaɪkəʊsəˈmætɪk‖-kəsə-/ adj (of an illness) caused by anxiety, not a real disorder of the body

psy·cho·ther·a·py /ˌsaɪkəʊˈθerəpi/ n [U] treatment of mind disorders by psychological methods (not drugs, etc.) **-pist** n

pt *written abbrev. for:* **1** part **2** PINT(*s*)
3 point **4** port

PTO /,pi: ti: 'əʊ/ *abbrev. for:* please
turn over; look at the next page

pub /pʌb/ *n* building where alcohol
may be bought and drunk

pub-crawl /'·· ,·/ *n sl, esp. BrE* visit
to several pubs

pu·ber·ty /'pju:bəti‖-ər-/ *n* period of
change from childhood to the adult
state in which one can produce
children

pu·bic /'pju:bɪk/ *adj* of or near the
sexual organs

pub·lic /'pʌblɪk/ *adj* **1** of or for people in general or everyone; not private:
public opinion **2** of the government:
public money **3** not secret **4 go public**
(of a company) become a PUBLIC COM-
PANY **5 in the public eye** often seen in
public or on television, or mentioned
in newspapers ◆ *n* [S] **1** people in general **2** people interested in the stated
thing **3 in public** openly ~**ly** *adv*

pub·li·can /'pʌblɪkən/ *n* person who
runs a PUB

pub·li·ca·tion /,pʌblɪ'keɪʃən/ *n* **1**
[U] act of publishing (PUBLISH) **2** [C]
book, magazine, etc.

public bar /,·· '·/ *n BrE* plainly furnished room in a PUB, hotel, etc.,
where drinks are cheaper than in the
SALOON BAR

public com·pa·ny /,·· '···/ *n* business company that offers shares in
itself for sale on the STOCK EXCHANGE

public con·ve·nience /,·· '·/ *n*
BrE public TOILET

public house /,·· '·/ *n fml* PUB

pub·li·cist /'pʌblɪsɪst/ *n* person who
publicizes something, esp. products

pub·lic·i·ty /pʌ'blɪsəti/ *n* [U] **1** public
notice or attention: *unwelcome publicity* **2** business of publicizing things;
advertising

pub·li·cize ‖ also **-cise** *BrE*
/'pʌblɪsaɪz/ *vt* bring to public notice

public re·la·tions /,·· '··/ *n* **1** [U]
forming of a favourable public opinion of an organization **2** [P] good relations between an organization and the
public

public school /,·· '·/ *n* British
school for older children, not run by
the state

public sec·tor /,·· '···/ *n* [*the* + S]
those industries and services that are
owned and run by the state

public spir·it /,·· '··/ *n* [U] willingness to do what is helpful for everyone
~**ed** *adj*

pub·lish /'pʌblɪʃ/ *vt* **1** bring out (a
book, newspaper, etc.) **2** make known
generally: *publishing the exam results*
~**er** *n*

puce /pju:s/ *adj* dark brownish
purple

puck /pʌk/ *n* hard flat piece of rubber used in ICE HOCKEY

puck·er /'pʌkəʳ/ *vi/t* tighten into
folds

puck·ish /'pʌkɪʃ/ *adj* harmlessly
playful

pud·ding /'pʊdɪŋ/ *n* [C;U] **1** *BrE*
sweet dish served at the end of a meal
2 boiled dish made with a covering made
from flour, fat, etc.: *steak and kidney
pudding*

pud·dle /'pʌdl/ *n* small amount of
water, esp. rain, lying in a hollow
place in the ground

pu·er·ile /'pjʊəraɪl‖-rəl/ *adj fml*
childish; silly

puff[1] /pʌf/ *v* **1** *vi* breathe rapidly and
with effort **2** *vi/t* send out or come out
as little clouds of smoke or steam: *puf-
fing at a cigarette* ~**ed** *adj infml* out
of breath

puff out/up *phr vi/t* swell

puff[2] *n* **1** sudden light rush of air,
smoke, etc. **2** hollow piece of light
pastry filled with a soft, sweet mixture
3 *infml* piece of writing praising a person or entertainment ~**y** *adj* rather
swollen

puff·ball /'pʌfbɔːl/ *n* ball-like
FUNGUS

puf·fin /'pʌfɪn/ *n* seabird with a large
brightly coloured beak

puff pas·try /,· '··/*n* [U] light
air-filled pastry

pu·gi·list /'pju:dʒɪlɪst/ *n fml* boxer
(BOX[2])

pug·na·cious /pʌg'neɪʃəs/ *adj fml*
fond of quarrelling and fighting

puke /pju:k/ *vi infml for* VOMIT

puk·ka /'pʌkə/ *adj* real; GENUINE

pull[1] /pʊl/ *v* **1** *vi/t* bring (something)
along behind one: *The horses pulled
the plough.* **2** *vi/t* move (someone or
something) towards oneself: *She pulled the door open.* **3** *vt* take with force:
He had a tooth pulled (out). **4** *vt* stretch
and damage: *pull a muscle* **5** *vi* move
in or as a vehicle: *The train pulled out.*
(= left) **6** *vt* attract **7 pull a face** make
an expression with the face to show
rude amusement, disagreement, etc. **8
pull a fast one (on)** get the advantage
(over) by a trick **9 pull a gun** take out
a gun and aim it (at someone)

pull away *phr vi* (esp. of a road
vehicle) start to move off

pull down *phr vt* destroy (a building, etc.)

pull in *phr vi* **1** (of a train) arrive at a
station **2** (of a vehicle) move to one
side (and stop)

pull off *phr vt* succeed in doing
(something difficult)

pull out *phr vi/t* **1** (cause to) stop
taking part **2** (of a train) leave a
station

pull over *phr vi/t* PULL **in** (2)

pull through phr vi/t **1** (cause to) live in spite of illness or wounds **2** (help to) succeed in spite of difficulties

pull together phr v **1** vi work together to help a shared effort **2** vt control the feelings of (oneself)

pull up phr vi (of a vehicle) stop

pull² n **1** [C;U] (act of) pulling **2** [C] rope, handle, etc. for pulling something: a bellpull **3** [S] difficult steep climb **4** [U] special (unfair) influence

pul·let /'pʊlɪt/ n young hen

pul·ley /'pʊli/ n apparatus for lifting things with a rope

pull·o·ver /'pʊl,əʊvəʳ/ n SWEATER pulled on over the head

pul·mo·na·ry /'pʌlmənəri, pu-‖ 'pʊlmənəri, 'pʌl-/ adj of the lungs

pulp /pʌlp/ n **1** [S;U] soft almost liquid mass, esp. of plant material **2** [U] book, magazine, etc., cheaply produced and containing matter of bad quality ♦ vt make into pulp

pul·pit /'pʊlpɪt/ n raised enclosure from which a priest speaks in church

pul·sar /'pʌlsɑːʳ/ n starlike object that sends out regular radio signals

pul·sate /pʌl'seɪt‖'pʌlseɪt/ vi **1** shake very rapidly and regularly **2** pulse –**sation** /,pʌl'seɪʃən/ n [C;U]

pulse¹ /pʌls/ n **1** regular beating of blood in the body's blood tubes **2** strong regular beat **3** short sound or electrical charge ♦ vi move or flow with a strong beat

pulse² n [C;U] (seeds of) beans, PEAs, etc., used as food

pul·ver·ize /'pʌlvəraɪz/ vt **1** crush to a powder **2** defeat thoroughly

pu·ma /'pjuːmə/ n -mas or -ma large fierce American wild cat

pum·mel /'pʌməl/ vt -ll- BrE ‖ -l- AmE — hit repeatedly

pump¹ /pʌmp/ n machine for forcing liquid or gas into or out of something ♦ **1** vt empty or fill with a pump **2** vt put in or remove with a pump **3** vi **a** work a pump **b** work like a pump: My heart was pumping fast. **4** vt try to get information from with questions

pump² n light shoe for dancing, etc.

pump·kin /'pʌmpkɪn/ n [C;U] extremely large round dark yellow vegetable

pun /pʌn/ n amusing use of a word or phrase with 2 meanings

punch¹ /pʌntʃ/ vt **1** hit hard with the closed hand **2** cut a hole in with a special tool: The inspector punched my ticket. ♦ n **1** [C] hard blow with the closed hand **2** [U] forcefulness **3** pull one's punches express an unfavourable opinion of someone or something less strongly than is deserved

punch² n [U] mixed sweet fruit drink usu. made with alcohol

punch³ n [C] steel tool for cutting holes

punch-drunk /'· ·/ adj suffering brain damage from blows in boxing (BOX²)

punch line /'· ·/ n funny part at the end of a joke

punch-up /'· ·/ n BrE infml fight

punc·til·i·ous /pʌŋk'tɪliəs/ adj fml very exact about details, esp. of behaviour ~ly adv

punc·tu·al /'pʌŋktʃuəl/ adj coming, happening, etc., at exactly the right time ~ly adv -ality /,pʌŋktʃu'æləti/ n [U]

punc·tu·ate /'pʌŋktʃueɪt/ vt **1** divide into sentences, phrases, etc., with punctuation marks **2** repeatedly break the flow of -**ation** /,pʌŋktʃu'eɪʃən/ n [U] **1** act or system of punctuating **2** punctuation marks

punctuation mark /,··'·· ·/ n sign used in punctuating, e.g. a FULL STOP, or a COMMA

punc·ture /'pʌŋktʃəʳ/ n small hole, esp. in a tyre ♦ vi/t (cause to) get a puncture

pun·dit /'pʌndɪt/ n EXPERT who is often asked to give an opinion

pun·gent /'pʌndʒənt/ adj (of a taste or smell) strong and sharp

pun·ish /'pʌnɪʃ/ vt **1** cause (someone) to suffer for (a crime or fault) **2** deal roughly with ~ment n **1** [U] act of punishing **2** [C] way in which someone is punished

pun·ish·ing /'pʌnɪʃɪŋ/ adj that makes one thoroughly tired and weak

pu·ni·tive /'pjuːnətɪv/ adj **1** intended as punishment **2** very severe

punk /pʌŋk/ n (since the 1970's) young person with strange clothes and often coloured hair who likes loud violent music

pun·net /'pʌnɪt/ n esp. BrE small square basket in which fruit is sold

punt /pʌnt/ n long narrow flat-bottomed river boat moved along with a pole

punt·er /'pʌntəʳ/ n esp. BrE **1** person who BETs on horse races **2** customer

pu·ny /'pjuːni/ adj small and weak

pup /pʌp/ n PUPPY

pu·pa /'pjuːpə/ n -pas or -pae /-piː/ form of an insect in a covering preparing to become an adult pupal /‖/ adj

pu·pil¹ /'pjuːpəl/ n person being taught

pupil² n small round black opening in the middle of the eye

pup·pet /'pʌpɪt/ n **1** toylike figure of a person or animal that is made to move as if it were alive **2** person or group that is controlled by someone else: a puppet government

pup·py /ˈpʌpi/ n young dog
puppy love /ˈ·· ˌ·/ n [U] young boy's or girl's love for an older person
pur·chase /ˈpɜːtʃəs‖ˈpɜːr-/ vt fml buy ♦ n fml 1 [U] act of buying 2 [C] something bought 3 [U] firm hold on a surface
pur·dah /ˈpɜːdə, -dɑː‖ˈpɜːr-/ n [U] system of keeping women out of public view, esp. among Muslims
pure /pjʊəʳ/ adj 1 not mixed with anything else 2 clean 3 free from evil 4 complete; thorough: by pure chance ~ly adv wholly; only
pu·ree /ˈpjʊəreɪ‖pjuˈreɪ/ n [C;U] soft half-liquid mass of food ♦ vt make (fruit or vegetable) into a puree
pur·ga·tive /ˈpɜːɡətɪv‖ˈpɜːr-/ n medicine that empties the bowels
pur·ga·to·ry /ˈpɜːɡətəri‖ˈpɜːrɡətɔːri/ n [U] 1 (in the Roman Catholic Church) place where the soul of a dead person is made pure and fit to enter heaven 2 situation of great suffering
purge /pɜːdʒ‖pɜːrdʒ/ vt 1 get rid of (an unwanted person) from (a state, group, etc.) by driving out, killing, etc. 2 make clean and free from (something evil) 3 empty the bowels with medicine ♦ n act of purging (PURGE (1))
pu·ri·fy /ˈpjʊərɪfaɪ/ vt make pure –fication /ˌpjʊərɪfɪˈkeɪʃən/ n [U]
pur·ist /ˈpjʊərɪst/ n someone who tries to make sure things are always done correctly and not changed, esp. in matters of grammar
pu·ri·tan /ˈpjʊərɪtn/ n 1 person with hard fixed standards of behaviour who thinks pleasure is wrong 2 (cap.) member of a former Christian group which wanted to make religion simpler and less ceremonial ~ical /ˌpjʊərɪˈtænɪkəl/ adj
pu·ri·ty /ˈpjʊərɪti/ n [U] being pure
purl /pɜːl‖pɜːrl/ n [U] knitting (KNIT) stitch done backwards ♦ vi/t use a purl stitch (on)
pur·loin /pɜːˈlɔɪn, ˈpɜːlɔɪn‖-ɜːr-/ vt fml steal
pur·ple /ˈpɜːpəl‖ˈpɜːr-/ adj of a colour that is a mixture of red and blue
purple pas·sage /ˌ·· ˈ··/ n (too) splendid part in the middle of a dull piece of writing
pur·port /ˈpɜːpɔːt, -pət‖ˈpɜːrpɔːrt/ n [U] fml meaning ♦ /pəˈpɔːt‖pɜːrˈpɔːrt/ vt have an intended appearance of being
pur·pose /ˈpɜːpəs‖ˈpɜːr-/ n 1 [C] reason for doing something 2 [C] use; effect; result: It has served its purpose. (= done what is needed) 3 [U] determined quality; willpower 4 **on purpose** intentionally ~ful adj determined ~ly adv intentionally

purpose-built /ˌ·· ˈ·◂/ adj esp. BrE originally made to be the stated thing
purr /pɜːʳ/ vi make the low continuous sound of a pleased cat
purse¹ /pɜːs‖pɜːrs/ n 1 small flat bag for carrying coins 2 amount of money offered, esp. as a prize 3 AmE for HANDBAG
purse² vt draw (esp. the lips) together in little folds
purs·er /ˈpɜːsəʳ‖ˈpɜːr-/ n ship's officer responsible for money and traveller's arrangements
purse strings /ˈ· ˌ·/ n hold the purse strings control the spending of money
pur·su·ance /pəˈsjuːəns‖pərˈsuː-/ n **in the pursuance of** fml doing
pur·su·ant /pəˈsjuːənt‖pərˈsuː-/ adj **pursuant to** fml in accordance with
pur·sue /pəˈsjuː‖pərˈsuː/ vt 1 follow in order to catch 2 fml continue steadily with: pursuing a policy of neutrality -suer n
pur·suit /pəˈsjuːt‖pərˈsuːt/ n 1 [U] act of pursuing 2 [C] fml activity, esp. for pleasure
pur·vey /pɜːˈveɪ‖pɜːr-/ vt fml supply (food or other goods) ~or n
pur·view /ˈpɜːvjuː‖ˈpɜːr-/ n [U] fml limit of one's concern, activity, or knowledge
pus /pʌs/ n [U] thick yellowish liquid produced in an infected part of the body
push¹ /pʊʃ/ v 1 vi/t use sudden or steady pressure to move (someone or something) forward, away from oneself, or to a different position: He pushed the drawer shut. 2 vt try to force (someone) by continual urging 3 vt sell (illegal drugs) 4 **be pushing** infml be nearly a (stated age) 5 **push one's luck** take a risk ~ed adj not having enough: pushed for time ~er n seller of illegal drugs
push around phr vt treat roughly and unfairly
push for phr vt demand urgently and forcefully
push off phr vi infml go away
push² n 1 act of pushing 2 large planned attack and advance 3 **at a push** if necessary 4 **if/when it comes to the push** if there's a time of special need 5 **give/get the push** infml dismiss/be dismissed from a job
push-but·ton /ˈ· ˌ··/ n small button pressed to operate something
push·chair /ˈpʊʃtʃeəʳ/ n BrE small chair on wheels for a child
push·o·ver /ˈpʊʃˌəʊvəʳ/ n [S] infml 1 something very easy to do or win 2 someone easily influenced or deceived
push·y /ˈpʊʃi/ adj too forceful in getting things done, esp. for one's own advantage

pu·sil·lan·i·mous /ˌpjuːsɪˈlænɪməs/ *adj fml* cowardly

pus·sy [1] /ˈpʊsi/ also **puss** /pʊs/, **pus·sy·cat** /ˈpʊsi,kæt/ *n* (child's name for) a cat

pussy [2] *n taboo sl* the female sex organ

pus·sy·foot /ˈpʊsifʊt/ *vi* act too carefully

pus·tule /ˈpʌstjuːl‖-tʃuːl/ *n med* small raised diseased spot on the skin

put /pʊt/ *vt* **put**, *pres. p.* -**tt**- 1 move, place, or fix to, on, or in the stated place 2 cause to be: *She put her books in order.* | *Put your mistakes right at once.* | *Put your suggestions to the committee.* 3 express in words 4 express something officially for judgment: *I'll put your suggestions to the committee.* 5 write down 6 **put paid to** *BrE* RUIN

put about *phr vt* spread (bad or false news)

put across *phr vt* cause to be understood

put aside *phr vt* save (money)

put away *phr vt* 1 remove to its usual storing place 2 *infml* eat (usu. large quantities of food) 3 place (someone) in prison or a hospital for mad people

put back *phr vt* delay

put by *phr vt* PUT aside

put down *phr vt* 1 control; defeat: *put down a rebellion* 2 record in writing 3 allow to leave a vehicle 4 kill (an old or sick animal) 5 cause to feel unimportant 6 pay (an amount) as part of the cost of something with a promise to pay the rest over a period of time

put down to *phr vt* state that (something) is caused by

put forward *phr vt* suggest

put in *phr vt* 1 do (work) or spend (time) on work 2 interrupt by saying 3 (of a ship) enter a port

put in for *phr vt* make a formal request for

put into *phr vt* add (something) to (something): *Put more effort into your work!*

put off *phr vt* 1 delay 2 discourage 3 cause to dislike

put on *phr vt* 1 cover (part of) the body with (esp. clothing) 2 operate (a radio, light, etc.) by pressing or turning a button 3 increase: *She's put on weight.* 4 provide: *They're putting on another train.* 5 perform (a play, show, etc.) on stage 6 pretend to have (a feeling, quality, etc.) 7 deceive playfully

put onto *phr vt* give information about

put out *phr vt* 1 cause to stop burning 2 trouble or annoy 3 broadcast or print 4 **put oneself out** take trouble

put over *phr vt* PUT across

put over on *phr vt* **put one over on** deceive

put through *phr vt* 1 connect (a telephone caller) 2 cause to suffer or experience

put to *phr vt* 1 ask (a question) of or make (an offer) to 2 suggest to (someone) that 3 **be hard put to it to** find it difficult to

put up *phr vt* 1 raise 2 put in a public place: *put up a notice* 3 provide food and lodging for 4 make; offer: *He didn't put up much of a fight.* 5 offer for sale 6 supply (money needed)

put up to *phr vt* give the idea of doing (esp. something bad)

put up with *phr vt* suffer without complaining

pu·ta·tive /ˈpjuːtətɪv/ *adj fml* generally supposed to be or to become

put-down /ˈ· ·/ *n infml* words that make someone feel unimportant or hurt

put-on /ˈ· ·/ *n AmE infml* something not intended seriously or sincerely

pu·tre·fy /ˈpjuːtrɪfaɪ/ *vi fml* decay —**faction** /ˌpjuːtrɪˈfækʃən/ *n* [U]

pu·tres·cent /pjuːˈtresənt/ *adj fml* decaying

pu·trid /ˈpjuːtrɪd/ *adj* 1 very decayed and bad-smelling 2 worthless; greatly disliked

putsch /pʊtʃ/ *n* sudden attempt to remove a government by force

putt /pʌt/ *vi/t* (in GOLF) hit (the ball) along the ground towards or into the hole —**er** *n* 1 CLUB [1] (3) for putting 2 person who putts

put·ty /ˈpʌti/ *n* [U] soft oily paste, esp. for fixing glass to window frames

put-up job /ˌ· · ˈ·/ *n infml* something dishonestly arranged in advance

put-up·on /ˈ· ˌ··/ *adj* (of a person) used for someone else's advantage

puz·zle /ˈpʌzəl/ *v* 1 *vt* cause (someone) difficulty in the effort to understand 2 *vi* try hard to find the answer ♦ *n* 1 game or toy to exercise the mind 2 something that puzzles one

puzzle out *phr vt* find the answer to by thinking hard

PVC /ˌpiː viː ˈsiː/ *n* [U] type of plastic

pyg·my /ˈpɪgmi/ *n* 1 (*usu. cap.*) member of an African race of very small people 2 very small person

py·ja·mas *BrE* ‖ **pajamas** *esp. AmE* /pəˈdʒɑːməz‖-ˈdʒæ-, -ˈdʒɑː-/ *n* [P] soft loose-fitting trousers and short coat worn in bed

py·lon /ˈpaɪlən‖-lɑːn, -lən/ *n* tall structure supporting electricity-carrying wires

pyr·a·mid /ˈpɪrəmɪd/ *n* 1 solid figure with 3-angled sides that slope up to meet at a point 2 large stone building in this shape, used as the burial place of kings, etc., in ancient Egypt

pyre /paɪə^r/ n high mass of wood for burning a dead body

Py·rex /paɪə^r/ n [U] *tdmk* strong glass used in making cooking containers

py·ro·tech·nics /ˌpaɪrəʊˈtekniks‖ -rə-/ n [P] a (too) splendid show of skill in words, music, etc.

py·thon /ˈpaɪθən‖-θɑːn, -θən/ n large tropical snake that crushes the animals it eats

Q

Q, q /kjuː/ the 17th letter of the English alphabet

Q.C. /ˌkjuː ˈsiː/ n (title, while a queen is ruling, for) a British lawyer of high rank

QED /ˌkjuː iː ˈdiː/ there is the proof of my argument

qua /kweɪ, kwɑː‖kwɑː/ *prep fml* thought of only as

quack[1] /kwæk/ *vi, n* (make) the sound ducks make

quack[2] n 1 person dishonestly claiming to be a doctor 2 *BrE* a doctor

quad[1] /kwɒd‖kwɑːd/ n *BrE* square open space with buildings round it

quad[2] n QUADRUPLET

quad·ran·gle /ˈkwɒdræŋɡəl‖ˈkwɑː-/ n 1 QUADRILATERAL 2 *fml for* QUAD **-rangular** /kwɒˈdræŋɡjʊlə‖kwɑː-/ *adj*

quad·rant /ˈkwɒdrənt‖ˈkwɑː-/ n 1 quarter of a circle 2 instrument for measuring angles

quad·ra·phon·ic /ˌkwɒdrəˈfɒnik‖ -ˈfɑː-/ *adj* giving sound from 4 different places

quad·ri·lat·er·al /ˌkwɒdrɪˈlætərəl‖ ˌkwɑː-/ n, *adj* (flat figure) with 4 straight sides

quad·ru·ped /ˈkwɒdruped‖ˈkwɑːdrə-/ n 4-legged creature

quad·ru·ple /ˈkwɒdrʊpəl, kwɒˈdruː-‖kwɑːˈdruː-/ *vi/t* multiply by 4 ♦ *adj, adv* 4 times as big

quad·ru·plet /ˈkwɒdrʊplət‖kwɑːˈdruːp-/ n any of 4 children born at the same time

quaff /kwɒf, kwɑːf‖kwɑːf, kwæf/ *vt fml* drink deeply

quag·mire /ˈkwæɡmaɪə^r, ˈkwɒɡ-‖ ˈkwæɡ-/ n soft wet ground

quail[1] /kweɪl/ n quail *or* quails (meat of) a type of small bird

quail[2] *vi fml* be afraid; tremble

quaint /kweɪnt/ *adj* charmingly old-fashioned **~ly** *adv*

quake /kweɪk/ *vi* shake; tremble

Quak·er /ˈkweɪkə^r/ n member of a Christian religious group that opposes violence

qual·i·fi·ca·tion /ˌkwɒlɪfɪˈkeɪʃən‖ ˌkwɑː-/ n 1 [C] something that limits the force of a statement 2 [U] act of qualifying 3 [C *often pl.*] proof that one has passed an examination **qualifications** n [P] (proof of having) the necessary ability, experience, or knowledge

qual·i·fy /ˈkwɒlɪfaɪ‖ˈkwɑː-/ v 1 *vi/t* (cause) to reach a necessary standard 2 *vt* limit the force or meaning of (a statement) **-fied** *adj* 1 having suitable qualifications 2 limited: *qualified approval*

qual·i·ta·tive /ˈkwɒlɪtətɪv‖ˈkwɑːlɪ-tei-/ *adj* of or about quality

qual·i·ty /ˈkwɒlɪti‖ˈkwɑː-/ n 1 [C;U] (high) degree of goodness 2 [C] something typical of a person or thing

qualm /kwɑːm‖kwɑːm, kwɑːlm/ n uncomfortable feeling of uncertainty

quan·da·ry /ˈkwɒndəri‖ˈkwɑːn-/ n feeling of not knowing what to do

quan·go /ˈkwæŋɡəʊ/ n -gos (in Britain) independent body with legal powers, set up by the government

quan·ti·fi·er /ˈkwɒntɪfaɪə^r‖ˈkwɑːn-/ n (in grammar) a word or phrase that is used with a noun to show quantity, such as *much, few,* and *a lot of*

quan·ti·fy /ˈkwɒntɪfaɪ‖ˈkwɑːn-/ *vt fml* measure **-fiable** *adj*

quan·ti·ta·tive /ˈkwɒntɪtətɪv‖ ˈkwɑːntɪtei-/ *adj* of or about quantity

quan·ti·ty /ˈkwɒntɪti‖ˈkwɑːn-/ n 1 [U] the fact of being measurable, amount 2 [C] amount; number — see also UNKNOWN QUANTITY

quan·tum /ˈkwɒntəm‖ˈkwɑːn-/ n -ta /-tə/ (in PHYSICS) fixed amount

quantum leap /ˌ·· ˈ·/ n very large and important advance or improvement

quantum the·o·ry /ˈ··· ˌ···/ n [U] idea that ENERGY travels in quanta

quar·an·tine /ˈkwɒrəntiːn‖ˈkwɑː-/ n [U] period when a sick person or animal is kept away from others so the disease cannot spread ♦ *vt* put in quarantine

quark /kwɑːk, kwɔːk‖kwɑːrk, kwɔːrk/ n smallest possible piece of material forming the substances of which atoms are made

quar·rel[1] /ˈkwɒrəl‖ˈkwɔː-, ˈkwɑː-/ n 1 angry argument 2 cause for or point of disagreement

quar·rel[2] *vi* -ll- *BrE* ǁ -l- *AmE* have an ARGUMENT (1) **~some** *adj* likely to argue

quarrel with *phr vt* disagree with

quar·ry[1] /'kwɒri‖'kwɔː-, 'kwɑː-/ n place where stone, sand, etc., are dug out ♦ vt dig from a quarry

quarry[2] n person or animal being hunted

quart /kwɔːt‖kwɔːrt/ n a measure of amount equal to two pints

quar·ter /'kwɔːtər‖'kwɔːr-/ n 1 [C] a 4th part of a whole: *a quarter of a mile* 2 [C] 15 minutes: *a quarter to 10* 3 [C] 3 months of the year 4 [C] part of a town: *the student quarter* 5 [C] person or place from which something comes: *no help from that quarter* 6 [U] *fml* giving of life to a defeated enemy ♦ vt 1 divide into 4 parts 2 provide lodgings for **quarters** n [P] 1 lodgings 2 **at close quarters** near together

quar·ter·deck /'kwɔːtədek‖'kwɔːrtər-/ n top part of a ship, used only by officers

quar·ter·fi·nal /ˌkwɔːtə'faɪnl‖'kwɔːrtər-/ n any of 4 matches whose winners play in SEMIFINALs

quar·ter·ly /'kwɔːtəli‖'kwɔːrtər-/ adj, adv (happening) 4 times a year ♦ n quarterly magazine

quar·ter·mas·ter /'kwɔːtəˌmɑːstər‖'kwɔːrtərˌmæ-/ n military officer in charge of supplies

quar·tet /kwɔː'tet‖kwɔːr-/ n (music for) 4 musicians

quar·to /'kwɔːtəʊ‖'kwɔːr-/ n large size of paper for books

quartz /kwɔːts‖kwɔːrts/ n [U] hard mineral used in making very exact clocks

qua·sar /'kweɪzɑːr/ n very bright very distant starlike object

quash /kwɒʃ‖kwɑːʃ, kwɔːʃ/ vt 1 officially refuse to accept 2 put an end to: *quash a rebellion*

quat·er·cen·te·na·ry /ˌkwætəsen'tiːnəri‖ˌkwɑːtərsen'te-/ n 400 years after a particular event

quat·rain /'kwɒtreɪn‖'kwɑː-/ n 4 lines of poetry

qua·ver /'kweɪvər/ vi (of a voice or music) shake ♦ n a shaking in the voice ~y adj

quay /kiː/ n place in a harbour by which ships stop and unload

quea·sy /'kwiːzi/ adj 1 feeling one is going to be sick 2 uncertain about the rightness of doing something

queen /kwiːn/ n 1 a female ruler 2 king's wife 2 leading female: *a beauty queen* 3 leading female insect in a group: *a queen bee* 4 sl male homosexual ~ly adj like, or suitable for, a queen

queen moth·er /ˌ· '··/ n mother of a ruler

queer /kwɪər/ adj 1 strange 2 *infml* slightly ill 3 *infml derog for* HOMOSEXUAL 4 **in queer street** *BrE infml* in

trouble over money matters ♦ n *infml derog* male HOMOSEXUAL

quell /kwel/ vt defeat; crush

quench /kwentʃ/ vt 1 satisfy (thirst) 2 put out (flames)

quer·u·lous /'kwerələs/ adj complaining

que·ry /'kwɪəri/ n question or doubt ♦ vt express doubt or uncertainty about

quest /kwest/ n *fml* long search

ques·tion[1] /'kwestʃən/ n 1 [C] sentence or phrase asking for information 2 [C] matter to be settled; problem 3 [C;U] doubt: *His honesty is beyond question.* 4 **in question** being talked about 5 **out of the question** impossible 6 **there's no question of** there's no possibility of

question[2] vt 1 ask (someone) questions 2 have doubts about ~**able** adj 1 uncertain 2 perhaps not true or honest ~**er** n

question mark /'·· ·/ n mark (?) written at the end of a question

question mas·ter /'·· ˌ·/ n person who asks questions in a QUIZ game

ques·tion·naire /ˌkwestʃə'neər, ˌkes-/ n set of questions asked to obtain information

queue /kjuː/ n *BrE* line of people, vehicles, etc., waiting to do something in turn ♦ vi wait in a queue

queue-jump /'·· ·/ vi join a queue in front of others who were there before you

quib·ble /'kwɪbəl/ vi argue about small unimportant points **quibble** n

quiche /kiːʃ/ n flat pastry case filled with eggs, cheese, vegetables, etc.

quick[1] /kwɪk/ adj 1 fast 2 easily showing anger: *a quick temper* ♦ adv fast ~**ly** adv ~**en** vi/t make or become quicker ~**ness** n [U]

quick[2] n 1 [U] flesh to which fingernails and toenails are joined 2 **cut (a person) to the quick** hurt a person's feelings deeply

quick·ie /'kwɪki/ n something made or done in a hurry

quick·sand /'kwɪksænd/ n [U] wet sand which sucks things down

quick·step /'kwɪkstep/ n dance with fast steps

quick-wit·ted /ˌ· '··◄/ adj swift to understand and act

quid /kwɪd/ n quid *BrE infml* pound in money

quid pro quo /ˌkwɪd prəʊ 'kwəʊ/ n something given in fair exchange

qui·es·cent /kwi'esənt, kwaɪ-/ adj *fml* inactive (for the present)

qui·et /'kwaɪət/ adj 1 with little noise 2 calm; untroubled: *a quiet life* ♦ n [U] 1 quietness 2 **keep something quiet** keep something a secret 3 **on the quiet**

secretly ~**en** vi/t make or become
quiet ~**ly** adv ~**ness** n [U]

qui·e·tude /'kwaɪətjuːd‖-tuːd/ n [U]
fml calmness; stillness

quiff /kwɪf/ n hair standing up over
the forehead

quill /kwɪl/ n 1 long feather 2 pen
made from this 3 sharp prickle on
some animals, esp. the PORCUPINE

quilt /kwɪlt/ n cloth covering for a
bed, filled with feathers, etc. ~**ed**
made with cloth containing soft material with stitching across it

quin /kwɪn/ n QUINTUPLET

quince /kwɪns/ n hard apple-like
fruit

quin·ine /'kwɪniːn‖'kwaɪnaɪn/ n [U]
drug used for treating MALARIA

quin·tes·sence /kwɪn'tesəns/ n fml
perfect type or example ~**tessential**
/ˌkwɪntɪ'senʃəl/ adj

quin·tet /kwɪn'tet/ n (music for) 5
musicians

quin·tu·plet /'kwɪntjʊplət, kwɪn-
'tjuːp-‖kwɪn'tʌp-/ n any of 5 children
born at the same time

quip[1] /kwɪp/ n clever amusing
remark ♦ vi -**pp-** make a quip

quirk /kwɜːk‖kwɜːrk/ n 1 strange
happening or accident 2 strange habit
or way of behaving ~**y** adj

quis·ling /'kwɪzlɪŋ/ n TRAITOR

quit /kwɪt/ vi/t quitted or quit, pres.
p. -**tt-** stop (doing something) and
leave ~**ter** n person who lacks the
courage to finish things when he/she
meets difficulties

quite /kwaɪt/ predeterminer, adv 1
completely; perfectly: not quite right 2
to some degree; rather: quite cold 3
esp. BrE (used for showing agreement): Quite (so). 4 **quite a/an** an
unusual: quite a party | It's quite some-
thing to be a government minister at
30.

quits /kwɪts/ adj back on an equal
level with someone after an argument,
repaying money, etc.

quiv·er[1] /'kwɪvəʳ/ vi/t (cause to)
tremble a little **quiver** n

quiver[2] n container for ARROWS

qui vive /ˌkiː 'viːv/ n **on the qui vive**
careful to notice; watchful

quix·ot·ic /kwɪk'sɒtɪk‖-'saː-/ adj
doing foolishly brave things in order
to be helpful

quiz /kwɪz/ n -**zz-** game where questions are put ♦ vt -**zz-** ask questions of
(someone), esp. repeatedly

quiz·mas·ter /'kwɪzmɑːstəʳ‖-mæ-/ n
esp. AmE for QUESTION MASTER

quiz·zi·cal /'kwɪzɪkəl/ adj (of a smile
or look) suggesting a question or
secret knowledge ~**ly** /-klɪ/ adv

quoit /kwɔɪt, kɔɪt/ n ring to be thrown
over a small post in a game

quo·rate /'kwɔːrət/ adj (of a meeting) having a quorum present

quo·rum /'kwɔːrəm/ n number of
people who must be present for a
meeting to be held

quo·ta /'kwəʊtə/ n amount officially
to be produced, received, etc., as one's
share

quo·ta·tion /kwəʊ'teɪʃən/ n 1 [C]
words QUOTEd (1) 2 [U] act of quoting
3 [C] amount QUOTEd (2)

quotation mark /·'··· ·/ n mark ('or')
showing the start or end of a QUOTA-
TION (1)

quote /kwəʊt/ v 1 vi/t repeat the
words of (a person, book, etc.) in
speech or writing 2 vt offer as a price
for work to be done ♦ n 1 infml QUO-
TATION (1, 3) 2 **in quotes** in QUOTA-
TION MARKs

quo·tient /'kwəʊʃənt/ n number got
by dividing

q.v. (used for telling readers to look in
another place in the same book to find
something out)

qwert·y /'kwɜːtɪ‖'kwɜːrtɪ/ adj (of a
KEYBOARD with letters) having the
standard arrangement of letters

R

R, r /ɑː/ the 18th letter of the English
alphabet — see also THREE R'S

R written abbrev. for: river

rab·bi /'ræbaɪ/ n Jewish priest

rab·bit[1] /'ræbɪt/ n common small
long-eared animal, often kept as a pet

rabbit[2] vi BrE infml talk continuously and annoyingly

rab·ble /'ræbəl/ n disordered noisy
crowd

rabble-rous·ing /'··· ·ˌ··/ adj causing
hatred and violence among a crowd of
listeners

Ra·be·lai·si·an /ˌræbə'leɪziən, -ʒən/
adj full of jokes about sex and the
body that are shocking but harmless

rab·id /'ræbɪd/ adj 1 suffering from
rabies 2 (of feelings or opinions)
unreasonably violent

ra·bies /'reɪbiːz/ n [U] disease passed
on by the bite of an infected animal
and causing madness and death

rac·coon /rə'kuːn, ræ-‖ræ-/ n small
North American animal with a
black-ringed tail

race[1] /reɪs/ n competition in speed:
a horse race | (fig.) a race against time

♦ vi/t **1** compete in a race (against) **2** (cause to) go very fast

race² n **1** [C;U] (any of) the main divisions of human beings, each of a different physical type **2** [C] group of people with the same history, language, etc.: *the German race* **3** [C] breed or type of animal or plant

race-course /'reɪs-kɔːs‖-kɔːrs/ n track round which horses race

race-track /'reɪs-træk/ n track round which horses, runners, cars, etc., race

ra·cial /'reɪʃəl/ adj **1** of a RACE² **2** between RACEs²: *racial tension* **~ly** adv

ra·cis·m /'reɪsɪzəm/ n [U] **1** belief that one's own RACE² is best **2** dislike or unfair treatment of other races **racist** adj, n

rack¹ /ræk/ n **1** frame or shelf with bars, hooks, etc., for holding things **2** instrument for hurting people by stretching their bodies **3** bar with teeth, moved along by a wheel with similar teeth

rack² vt **1** cause great pain or anxiety to **2 rack one's brains** think very hard

rack³ n **rack and ruin** ruined condition, esp. of a building

rack·et¹, **racquet**/'rækɪt/ n instrument with a netlike part for hitting the ball in games like tennis

racket² n **1** [S] loud noise **2** [C] dishonest business

rack·e·teer /ˌrækɪ'tɪər/ n someone who works a RACKET² (2)

rac·on·teur /ˌrækɒn'tɜːr‖ˌrækɑːn-/ n someone good at telling stories

rac·y /'reɪsi/ adj (of a story, etc.) amusing, full of life, and perhaps dealing with sex

ra·dar /'reɪdɑːr/ n [U] apparatus or method of finding solid objects by receiving and measuring the speed of radio waves seen as a SCREEN

ra·di·al¹ /'reɪdiəl/ adj like a wheel

radial² also **radial tyre** /ˌ··· '·/ — n car tyre with cords inside the rubber that go across the edge of the wheel rather than along it, so as to give better control

ra·di·ant /'reɪdiənt/ adj **1** sending out light or heat in all directions **2** (of a person) showing love and happiness **~ly** adv **-ance** n [U]

ra·di·ate /'reɪdieɪt/ vi/t send out light, heat, etc.:(fig.) *She radiates happiness.*

ra·di·a·tion /ˌreɪdi'eɪʃən/ n [U] **1** (act of) radiating **2** RADIOACTIVITY

ra·di·a·tor /'reɪdieɪtər/ n **1** apparatus, esp. of hot-water pipes, for heating a building **2** apparatus that keeps a car's engine cool

rad·i·cal /'rædɪkəl/ adj **1** (of a change) thorough and complete **2** in favour of complete political change ♦ n RADICAL (2) person **~ly** /-kli/ adv

rad·i·i /'reɪdiaɪ/ pl. of RADIUS

ra·di·o /'reɪdiəʊ/ n **1** [U] sending or receiving sounds through the air by electrical waves **2** [C] apparatus to receive such sounds **3** [U] radio broadcasting industry **4 on the radio: a** (of a sound) broadcast **b** (of a person) broadcasting

ra·di·o·ac·tiv·i·ty /ˌreɪdiəʊæk'tɪvəti/ n [U] **1** quality, harmful in large amounts to living things, that some ELEMENTs have of giving out ENERGY by the breaking up of atoms **2** the energy given out in this way: *exposed to radioactivity* **-tive** /ˌreɪdiəʊ-'æktɪv◂/ adj

ra·di·og·ra·phy /ˌreɪdi'ɒɡrəti‖-'ɑːɡ-/ n [U] taking of photographs made with X-RAYs, usu. for medical reasons **-pher** n [C] person who practises radiography

ra·di·ol·o·gy /ˌreɪdi'ɒlədʒi‖-'ɑː-/ n [U] study and medical use of radioactivity **-gist** n [C]

radio tel·e·scope /ˌ··· '···/ n radio receiver for following the movements of stars and other objects in space

rad·ish /'rædɪʃ/ n small plant with a round red root, eaten raw

ra·di·um /'reɪdiəm/ n [U] RADIOACTIVE metal used in the treatment of certain diseases

ra·di·us /'reɪdiəs/ n **-dii** /-diaɪ/ **1** (length of) a straight line from the centre of a circle to its side **2** stated circular area measured from its centre point: *houses within a ten-mile radius of the town*

raf·fia /'ræfiə/ n [U] soft string-like substance from leaves of a PALM tree, used to make baskets, etc.

raf·fish /'ræfɪʃ/ adj (of a person) happy, wild, and not very respectable

raf·fle /'ræfəl/ n way of getting money by selling chances to win prizes ♦ vt offer as a raffle prize

raft /rɑːft‖ræft/ n flat, usu. wooden, floating structure, used esp. as a boat

raf·ter /'rɑːftər‖'ræf-/ n large sloping beam that holds up a roof

rag¹ /ræɡ/ n **1** small piece of old cloth **2** old worn-out garment **3** *infml derog* newspaper

rag² n *esp. BrE* amusing public event held by college students to collect money for CHARITY

rag³ vt *esp. BrE* make fun of

rag-bag /'ræɡbæɡ/ n confused mixture

rage /reɪdʒ/ n [C;U] **1** (sudden feeling of) extreme anger **2 all the rage** very fashionable ♦ vi **1** be in a rage **2** (of bad weather, pain, etc.) be very violent

rag·ged /'rægɪd/ adj 1 old and torn 2 dressed in old torn clothes 3 rough; uneven: a ragged beard | (fig.) a ragged performance ~ly adv

rag·lan /'ræglən/ adj (of an arm of a garment) joined at the neck rather than at the shoulder

rag·time /'rægtaɪm/ n [U] popular music of the 1920s, in which the strong notes of the tune come just before the main beats

rag trade /'· ·/ n [the + S] infml garment industry

raid /reɪd/ n 1 quick attack on an enemy position 2 unexpected visit by the police in search of crime ♦ vi/t make a raid (on): (fig.) The children raided the kitchen for food. ~er n

rail[1] /reɪl/ n 1 [C] fixed bar, esp. to hang things on or for protection 2 [C] line of metal bars which a train runs on 3 [U] railway ♦ vt enclose or separate with rails ~ing n rail in a fence

rail[2] vi fml curse or complain angrily

rail·road /'reɪlrəʊd/ vt 1 hurry (someone) unfairly 2 pass (a law) or carry out (a plan) quickly in spite of opposition ♦ n AmE for RAILWAY

rail·way /'reɪlweɪ/ n BrE 1 track for trains 2 system of such tracks

rain /reɪn/ n 1 [U] water falling from the clouds 2 [S] thick fall of anything: a rain of questions 3 as right as rain in perfect health 4 (come) rain or shine whatever happens ♦ v 1 vi (of rain) fall 2 vi/t (cause to) fall thickly, like rain 3 rain cats and dogs rain very heavily ~y adj 1 with lots of rain 2 for a rainy day for a time when money may be needed

rain·bow /'reɪnbəʊ/ n arch of different colours that appears in the sky after rain

rain check /'· ·/ n AmE request to claim later something offered now

rain·fall /'reɪnfɔːl/ n [C;U] amount of rain that falls in a certain time

rain for·est /'· ͵·/ n wet tropical forest

raise /reɪz/ vt 1 lift 2 make higher in amount, size, etc. 3 collect together: raise an army 4 produce and look after (children, animals, or crops) 5 mention or introduce (a subject) for consideration 6 a make (a noise) b cause people to make (a noise) or have feelings: raise a laugh/raise doubts 7 bring to an end (something that controls or forbids): raise a siege 8 raise Cain/hell/the roof infml become very angry ♦ n AmE for RISE[2] (3)

rai·sin /'reɪzən/ n dried GRAPE

rai·son d'et·re /͵reɪzɒn 'detrə/ n reason for existing

raj /'rɑːdʒ/ n [the + S] British rule in India

ra·jah /'rɑːdʒə/ n (title of) Indian ruler

rake[1] /reɪk/ n gardening tool with a row of points at the end of a long handle

rake[2] vt 1 gather, loosen, or level with a rake 2 examine or shoot in a continuous sweeping movement

rake in phr vt infml earn or gain a lot of (money)

rake out infml find by searching

rake up phr vt 1 produce with difficulty by searching 2 remember and talk about (something that should be forgotten)

rake[3] n man who has led a wild life with regard to drink and women

rake-off /'· ·/ n infml usu. dishonest share of profits

rak·ish /'reɪkɪʃ/ adj wild and informal ~ly adv

ral·ly[1] /'ræli/ n 1 large esp. political public meeting 2 motor race over public roads 3 long exchange of hits in tennis

rally[2] v 1 vi/t come or bring together (again) for a shared purpose 2 vi recover

rally round phr vi help in time of trouble

ram /ræm/ n 1 adult male sheep that can be the father of young 2 any machine that repeatedly drops or pushes a weight onto or into something ♦ vt -mm- 1 run into (something) very hard 2 force into place with great pressure: (fig.) My father keeps ramming his ideas down my throat.

RAM /ræm/ n [U] Random-Access Memory; computer memory holding information that is needed by the computer for a limited period, and can be searched in any order one likes

ram·ble[1] /'ræmbəl/ n (long) country walk for pleasure

ramble[2] vi 1 go on a ramble 2 talk or write in a disordered wandering way –bler n –bling adj 1 (of speech or writing) disordered and wandering 2 (of a street, house, etc.) of irregular shape; winding 3 (of a plant) growing loosely in all directions

ram·i·fi·ca·tion /͵ræməfɪ'keɪʃən/ n 1 branch of a system with many parts 2 any of the results that may follow from an action or decision

ramp /ræmp/ n artificial slope connecting 2 levels

ram·page /ræm'peɪdʒ, 'ræmpeɪdʒ/ vi rush about wildly or angrily ♦ n on the rampage rampaging

ram·pant /'ræmpənt/ adj (of crime, disease, etc.) widespread and uncontrollable

ram·part /'ræmpɑːt‖-ɑːrt/ n wide bank or wall protecting a fort or city

ram-rod /'ræmrɒd‖-rɑːd/ *n* stick for pushing explosive powder into or cleaning a gun

ram-shack-le /'ræmʃækəl/ *adj* (of a building or vehicle) falling to pieces

ran /ræn/ *past t.* of RUN

ranch /rɑːntʃ‖ræntʃ/ *n* large American farm where animals are raised

ran-cid /'rænsɪd/ *adj* (of butter, cream, etc.) unpleasant because not fresh

ran-cour *BrE* ‖ **-cor** *AmE* /'ræŋkəʳ/ *n* [U] *fml* bitter unforgiving hatred **–corous** *adj*

R and D /ˌɑːr ən 'diː/ *n* [U] research and development; part of a business concerned with studying new ideas, planning new products, etc.

ran-dom /'rændəm/ *adj* without any fixed plan ◆ *n* **at random** in a random way ~**ly** *adv* ~**ness** *n* [U]

randy /'rændi/ *adj infml, esp. BrE* full of sexual desire **–iness** *n* [U]

ra-nee /'rɑːni, rɑː'niː/ *n* (title of) **a** a female Indian ruler **b** the wife of a RAJAH

rang /ræŋ/ *past t.* of RING

range¹ /reɪndʒ/ *n* **1** [S,U] distance over which something has an effect or limits between which it varies: *He shot her at close range.* | *a wide range of temperature* **2** [C] area where shooting is practised or MISSILES are tested **3** [C] connected line of mountains or hills **4** [*the*+S] (in N America) stretch of grassy land where cattle feed **5** [C] set of different objects of the same kind, esp. for sale **6** (formerly) iron fireplace and stove set into a chimney in a kitchen

range² *v* **1** *vi* vary between limits **2** *vi* wander freely: *The conversation ranged over many topics.* **3** *vt* put in position

rang-er /'reɪndʒəʳ/ *n* forest or park guard

rank¹ /ræŋk/ *n* **1** [C;U] position in the army, navy, etc.: *the rank of colonel* **2** [C;U] (high) social position **3** [C] line of people or things **4 keep/break rank(s)** (of soldiers) stay in line/fail to stay in line **5 of the first rank** among the best **6 pull rank (on someone)** use unfairly the advantage of one's higher position — see also TAXI RANK ◆ *v* **1** *vi/t* be or put in a certain class **2** *vt* arrange in regular order **ranks** *n* [P] ordinary soldiers below the rank of SERGEANT

rank² *adj* **1** (of a plant) too thick and widespread **2** (of smell or taste) very strong and unpleasant **3** (of something bad) complete: *a rank beginner at the job*

rank and file /ˌ· · '·/ *n* [S] ordinary people in an organization, not the leaders

ran-kle /'ræŋkəl/ *vi* continue to be remembered with bitterness and anger

ran-sack /'rænsæk/ *vt* **1** search thoroughly and roughly **2** search and rob

ran-som /'rænsəm/ *n* money paid to free a prisoner ◆ *vt* free by paying a ransom

rant /rænt/ *vi* talk wildly and loudly

rap¹ /ræp/ *n* **1** quick light blow **2 take the rap (for)** *infml* receive the punishment (for someone else's crime) ◆ *v* **-pp- 1** *vi/t* strike quickly and lightly **2** *vt* say sharply and suddenly

rap² *n sl, esp. AmE* **-pp- a** talk **b** speak the words of a song to a musical ACCOMPANIMENT with a steady beat

ra-pa-cious /rə'peɪʃəs/ *adj fml* taking all one can, esp. by force ~**ness**, **-pacity** /rə'pæsɪti/ *n* [U]

rape¹ /reɪp/ *vt* have sex with (someone) against their will ◆ *n* [C;U] **1** act of raping **2** spoiling **rapist** *n*

rape² *n* [U] plant grown for the oil produced from its seeds

rap-id /'ræpɪd/ *adj* fast ~**ly** *adv* ~**ity** /rə'pɪdɪti/ *n* [U]

rapid-fire /'··· /*adj* (of a gun) able to fire shots quickly one after the other: (fig.) *rapid-fire jokes/questions*

rap-ids /'ræpɪdz/ *n* [P] fast-flowing rocky part of a river

ra-pi-er /'reɪpɪəʳ/ *n* long thin sharp sword

rap-port /ræ'pɔːʳ/ *n* [U] close agreement and understanding

rapt /ræpt/ *adj* giving one's whole mind: *rapt attention*

rap-ture /'ræptʃəʳ/ *n* [U] *fml* great joy and delight **–turous** *adj*

rare¹ /reəʳ/ *adj* uncommon ~**ly** *adv* not often ~**ness** *n* [U]

rare² *adj* (of meat) lightly cooked

rar-e-fied /'reərɪfaɪd/ *adj* (of air in high places) with less oxygen than usual **2** very high or grand

rar-ing /'reərɪŋ/ *adj* very eager: *We're raring to go.*

rar-i-ty /'reərɪti/ *n* **1** [U] being uncommon **2** [C] something uncommon

ras-cal /'rɑːskəl‖'ræs-/ *n* **1** misbehaving child **2** dishonest person

rash¹ /ræʃ/ *adj* without thinking enough of the (possibly bad) results ~**ly** *adv* ~**ness** *n* [U]

rash² *n* red spots on the skin, caused by illness: *He came out in* (= became covered in) *a rash.* | (fig.) *a rash* (= sudden large number) *of complaints*

rash-er /'ræʃəʳ/ *n* thin piece of BACON

rasp /rɑːsp‖ræsp/ *vt* **1** rub with something rough **2** say in a rough voice ◆ *n* **1** [C] tool for smoothing metal, wood, etc. **2** [S] rasping sound ~**ing** *adj* (of a sound) unpleasantly rough

rasp·ber·ry /ˈrɑːzbəri‖ˈræzberi/ n 1 red berry, often eaten 2 rude sound made by putting one's tongue out and blowing

ras·ta·fa·ri·an /ˌræstəˈfeəriən/ also **ras·ta** /ˈræstə/ – n (often cap.) follower of a religion from Jamaica ~**ism** n

rat /ræt/ n 1 animal like a large mouse 2 worthless disloyal person ♦ v -**tt**- act disloyally ~**ty** adj BrE sl bad-tempered

ratch·et /ˈrætʃət/ n toothed wheel or bar that allows a part of a machine to move past it in one direction only

rate[1] /reɪt/ n 1 amount measured in relation to another: a death rate of 500 a year 2 payment fixed according to a standard scale 3 of the (numbered) quality: a first-rate performer 4 **at any rate** in any case 5 **at this/that rate** if events continue in the same way — see also FLAT RATE **rates** n [P] local tax paid in Britain by owners of buildings

rate[2] vt 1 have the stated opinion about 2 deserve 3 infml have a good opinion of: I really rate her as a singer.

ra·tea·ble val·ue /ˌreɪtəbəl ˈvæljuː/ n amount used for calculating the RATES to be charged on a building

rate-cap /ˈ· ·/ vt -**pp**- BrE (of a central government) limit the amount of RATES to be charged by (a local council)

ra·ther /ˈrɑːðəʳ‖ˈræðər/ predeterminer, adv 1 to some degree: a rather cold day 2 more willingly: I'd rather have tea than coffee. 3 more exactly: He's done it, or rather he says he has.

rat·i·fy /ˈrætɪfaɪ/ vt approve (a formal agreement) and make it official –**fica·tion** /ˌrætɪfɪˈkeɪʃən/ n [U]

rat·ing /ˈreɪtɪŋ/ n British sailor who is not an officer **ratings** n [P] list of the positions of popularity given to television shows

ra·ti·o /ˈreɪʃiəʊ‖ˈreɪʃəʊ/ n -os way one amount relates to another: The ratio of adults to children was 4 to 1.

ra·tion /ˈræʃən‖ˈræ-, ˈreɪ-/ n amount of something allowed to one person for a period ♦ vt 1 limit (someone) to a fixed ration 2 limit and control (supplies) **rations** n [P] supplies of food

ra·tion·al /ˈræʃənəl/ adj 1 (of ideas and behaviour) sensible 2 (of a person) able to reason ~**ly** adv ~**ity** /ˌræʃəˈnælɪti/ n [U]

ra·tion·ale /ˌræʃəˈnɑːl‖-ˈnæl/ n [C;U] reasons and principles on which a practice is based

ra·tion·al·ize ‖ also -**ise** BrE /ˈræʃənəlaɪz/ vi/t 1 give or claim a rational explanation for (esp. strange behaviour) 2 esp. BrE make (a system) more modern and sensible –**iza·tion** /ˌræʃəˌnaɪˈzeɪʃən‖-lə-/ n [C;U]

rat race /ˈ· ·/ n endless competition for success in business

rat·tle /ˈrætl/ v 1 vi/t (cause to) make continuous hard quick noises 2 vi move quickly while making these noises 3 vt make anxious or afraid ♦ n 1 [C] toy or other instrument that rattles 2 [S] rattling noise

rattle off phr vt repeat quickly and easily from memory

rattle on/away phr vi talk quickly and continuously

rattle through phr vt perform quickly

rattle-snake /ˈrætlsneɪk/ n poisonous American snake that rattles its tail

rat trap /ˈ· ·/n AmE dirty old building that is in very bad condition

rau·cous /ˈrɔːkəs/ adj unpleasantly loud and rough ~**ly** adv ~**ness** n [U]

raunch·y /ˈrɔːntʃi/ adj infml sexy –**ily** adv –**iness** n [U]

rav·age /ˈrævɪdʒ/ vt 1 ruin and destroy 2 rob (an area) violently **ravages** n [P] destroying effects

rave /reɪv/ vi 1 talk wildly as if mad 2 talk with extreme admiration ♦ adj full of very eager praise: rave reviews in the papers **raving** adj, adv wildly (mad)

ra·ven /ˈreɪvən/ n large black bird of the CROW family

rav·e·nous /ˈrævənəs/ adj very hungry ~**ly** adv

rav·er /ˈreɪvəʳ/n infml a modern person who leads an exciting life with sexual and social freedom

rave-up /ˈ· ·/ n infml, esp. BrE wild party

ra·vine /rəˈviːn/ n deep narrow steep-sided valley

rav·ish /ˈrævɪʃ/ vt fml 1 lit RAPE[2] 2 fill with delight ~**ing** adj very beautiful

raw /rɔː/ adj 1 not cooked 2 not yet treated for use: raw materials 3 not trained or experienced 4 (of skin) painful; sore 5 (of weather) cold and wet ~**ness** n [U]

raw deal /ˌ· ·/ n unfair treatment

ray /reɪ/ n narrow beam of light or other force: (fig.) a ray (= small bit) of hope

ray·on /ˈreɪɒn‖-ɑːn/ n [U] silklike material made from plant substances

raze /reɪz/ vt fml flatten (buildings, cities, etc.)

ra·zor /ˈreɪzəʳ/ n sharp instrument for removing hair, esp. from a man's face

raz·zle /ˈræzəl/ n **on the razzle** infml having noisy fun

razz·ma·tazz /ˌræzməˈtæz/ n [U] infml noisy showy activity

Rd written abbrev. for: Road

re /ri:/ prep fml on the subject of; with regard to

-'re /ə^r/ short for: are: We're ready.

reach /ri:tʃ/ v 1 vt arrive at 2 vt stretch out an arm or hand for some purpose 3 vi/t touch by doing this: It's too high; I can't reach it. 4 vt get by doing this: Reach me my hat. 5 vi/t stretch (as far as): The garden reaches down to the lake. 6 vt get a message to ♦ n 1 [S;U] distance one can reach 2 [C] part of a river

re-act /ri'ækt/ vi 1 act or behave as a result 2 change when mixed with another substance

re-ac-tion /ri'ækʃən/ n 1 [C;U] (way of) reacting 2 [S;U] change back to a former condition 3 [U] quality of being reactionary

re-ac-tion-a-ry /ri'ækʃənəri‖-ʃəneri/ n, adj (person) strongly opposed to change

re-ac-tor /ri'æktə^r/ n large machine that produces ENERGY from atoms

read /ri:d/ v read /red/ vi/t look at and understand (something printed or written): read a newspaper 2 vt say (written words) to others: Read me a story. 3 vi (of something written) have (the stated form or meaning) or give (the stated idea): The letter reads as follows . . . | Her letters always read well. 4 vt (of a measuring instrument) show 5 vt study at university 6 read between the lines find hidden meanings 7 take something as read accept something as true without any need to consider it further **~able** adj interesting or easy to read

read-er /'ri:də^r/ n 1 someone who reads 2 British university teacher of high rank 3 schoolbook for beginners **~ship** n [S] number or type of READERs (1)

read-ing /'ri:dɪŋ/ n 1 [U] act or practice of reading 2 [C] opinion about the meaning of something 3 [C] figure shown by a measuring instrument 4 [U] something to be read: It makes (= is) interesting reading. 5 [U] knowledge gained through books 6 [C] (in Parliament) one of the 3 official occasions on which a suggested new law is read and considered

read-out /'ri:d-aʊt/ n [U] information produced from a computer in readable form

read-y /'redi/ adj 1 prepared and fit for use 2 willing 3 (of thoughts or their expressions) quick: a ready wit ♦ adv in advance: ready-cut bread ♦ n at the **ready** READY (1)–**ily** adv 1 willingly 2 easily –**iness** n [U]

ready mon-ey /'·· '··/ n [U] coins and notes that can be paid at once

re-a-gent /ri:'eɪdʒənt/ n chemical that shows the presence of a particular substance

real /rɪəl/ adj 1 actually existing 2 complete: a real idiot 3 for real esp. AmE serious(ly) ♦ adv AmE very **~ly** adv 1 in fact; truly 2 very 3 (shows interest, doubt, or displeasure)

real es-tate /'· ·,·/ n [U] esp. AmE houses to be bought

re-a-lis-m /'rɪəlɪzəm/ n [U] 1 accepting the way things really are in life 2 (in art and literature) showing things as they really are –**list** n –**listic** /rɪə'lɪstɪk/ adj

re-al-i-ty /ri'æləti/ n 1 [U] real existence 2 [C;U] something or everything real 3 in reality in actual fact

re-a-lize also **-ise** BrE/'rɪəlaɪz/ v 1 vi/t (come to) have full knowledge and understanding (of) 2 vt make (a purpose, fear, etc.) real 3 vt get for –**lization** /,rɪəlaɪ'zeɪʃən‖-lə-/ n [U]

realm /relm/ n 1 fml kingdom 2 area of activity; world

real-time /'· ·/ adj of or being very quick information handling by a computer

real-tor /'rɪəltə^r, -tɔː^r/ n AmE for ESTATE AGENT

ream /ri:m/ n 480 pieces of paper **reams** n [P] a lot of writing

reap /ri:p/ vi/t cut and gather (a crop of grain): (fig.) He reaped (= gained) the benefit of all his hard work. **~er** n — see also GRIM REAPER

rear¹ /rɪə^r/ n, adj [U] 1 back (part) 2 bring up the rear be last

rear² v 1 vt care for until fully grown 2 vi rise upright on the back legs 3 vt raise (the head)

rear-guard /'rɪəɡɑːd‖'rɪərɡɑːrd/ n soldiers protecting the rear of an army

rearguard action /,·· '··/ n fight by the rearguard of an army being driven back by a victorious enemy

re-ar-ma-ment /ri:'ɑːməmənt‖-'ɑːr-/ n [U] providing a nation with weapons again, or with new weapons

rea-son¹ /'ri:zən/ n 1 [C;U] why something is or was done; cause 2 [U] power to think, understand and form opinions 3 [U] healthy mind that is not mad: to lose one's reason (= go mad) 4 [U] good sense 5 stand to reason be clear to all sensible people 6 within reason not beyond sensible limits

reason² v 1 vi use one's REASON¹ (2) 2 vt give as an opinion based on REASON¹ (2) **~ing** n [U] steps in thinking about or understanding something

reason with phr vt try to persuade by fair argument

rea-so-na-ble /'ri:zənəbəl/ adj 1 showing fairness or good sense 2 quite

cheap –**bly** adv **1** sensibly **2** quite: in reasonably good health

re·as·sure /ˌriːəˈʃʊər/ vt comfort and make free from worry –**surance** n [C;U]

re·bate /ˈriːbeɪt/ n official return of part of a payment

reb·el¹ /ˈrebəl/ n person who rebels

re·bel² /rɪˈbel/ vi -ll- oppose or fight against someone in control

re·bel·lion /rɪˈbeljən/ n [C;U] (act of) rebelling –**lious** adj

re·birth /ˌriːˈbɜːθ‖-ɜːrθ/ n [S] fml renewal of life; change of spirit

re·born /ˌriːˈbɔːn‖-ɔːrn/ adj fml as if born again

re·bound /rɪˈbaʊnd/ vi fly back after hitting something ♦ /ˈriːbaʊnd/ n **on the rebound: a** while rebounding **b** while in an unsettled state of mind as a result of failure in a relationship

   rebound on phr vt (of a bad action) harm (the doer)

re·buff /rɪˈbʌf/ n rough or cruel answer or refusal **rebuff** vt

re·buke /rɪˈbjuːk/ vt fml speak to angrily and blamingly **rebuke** n

re·but /rɪˈbʌt/ vt fml prove the falseness of ~**tal** n [C;U]

re·cal·ci·trant /rɪˈkælsɪtrənt/ adj fml refusing to obey –**trance** n

re·call /rɪˈkɔːl/ vt **1** remember **2** send for or take back ♦ /rɪˈkɔːl‖ˈriːkɔːl, rɪˈkɔːl/ n **1** [U] ability to remember **2** [S;U] call to return

re·cant /rɪˈkænt/ vi/t fml say publicly that one no longer holds (a religious or political opinion) ~**ation** /ˌriːkænˈteɪʃən/ n [C;U]

re·cap /ˈriːkæp/ vi/t -pp- repeat (the chief points of something said) **recap** n

re·ca·pit·u·late /ˌriːkəˈpɪtʃʊleɪt/ vi/t fml recap –**lation** /ˌriːkəpɪtʃʊˈleɪʃən/ n [C;U]

re·cede /rɪˈsiːd/ vi move back or away

re·ceipt /rɪˈsiːt/ n **1** [C] written statement that one has received money **2** [U] fml receiving **receipts** n [P] money received from a business

re·ceive /rɪˈsiːv/ vt **1** get; be given: receive a letter/a nasty shock **2** accept as a visitor or member **3** turn (radio waves) into sound or pictures –**ceived** adj generally accepted –**ceiver** n **1** part of a telephone that is held to the ear **2** radio or television set **3** official who looks after the affairs of a BANKRUPT **4** person who buys and sells stolen property

re·cent /ˈriːsənt/ adj that happened or started only a short time ago ~**ly** adv not long ago

re·cep·ta·cle /rɪˈseptəkəl/ n fml container

re·cep·tion /rɪˈsepʃən/ n **1** [C] welcome: a friendly reception **2** [C] large formal party **3** [U] place where visitors to a hotel or other large building are welcomed **4** [U] quality of radio or television signals ~**ist** n person who welcomes and deals with visitors to a hotel, shop, etc.

re·cep·tive /rɪˈseptɪv/ adj willing to consider new ideas ~**ness**, -**tivity** /ˌriːsepˈtɪvəti/ n [U]

re·cess /rɪˈses/‖ˈriːses/ n **1** pause for rest during a working period **2** space in an inside wall for shelves, cupboards, etc. **3** secret inner place ♦ /rɪˈses/ vt make or put into a RECESS (2)

re·ces·sion /rɪˈseʃən/ n **1** period of reduced business activity **2** act of receding

re·cher·ché /rəˈʃeəʃeɪ‖rəˈʃeər-, rəˌʃeərˈʃeɪ/ adj rare and strange

re·ci·pe /ˈresəpi/ n set of cooking instructions

re·cip·i·ent /rɪˈsɪpiənt/ n fml person who receives something

re·cip·ro·cal /rɪˈsɪprəkəl/ adj fml given and received in return; MUTUAL –**ly** /-kli/ adv

re·cip·ro·cate /rɪˈsɪprəkeɪt/ vi/t fml give or do (something) in return –**cation** /rɪˌsɪprəˈkeɪʃən/ n [U]

re·cit·al /rɪˈsaɪtl/ n performance of music or poetry by one person or a small group

re·cite /rɪˈsaɪt/ v **1** vi/t say (something learned) aloud in public **2** vt fml give a detailed account or list of **recitation** /ˌresɪˈteɪʃən/ n [C;U]

reck·less /ˈrekləs/ adj not caring about danger ~**ly** adv ~**ness** n [U]

reck·on /ˈrekən/ vt **1** consider; regard **2** guess; suppose **3** calculate; add up ~**ing** n [U] **1** calculation **2** punishment: a day of reckoning

   reckon on phr vt make plans in expectation of

   reckon with phr vt **1** have to deal with **2** take account of in one's plans **3 to be reckoned with** to be taken seriously as a possible opponent, competitor, etc.

re·claim /rɪˈkleɪm/ vt **1** ask for the return of **2** make (land) fit for use **reclamation** /ˌrekləˈmeɪʃən/ n [U]

re·cline /rɪˈklaɪn/ vi fml lie back or down; rest

re·cluse /rɪˈkluːs‖ˈrekluːs/ n someone who lives alone on purpose

rec·og·nize, -**ise** /ˈrekəgnaɪz, ˈrekən-/ vt **1** know again (as someone or something one has met before) **2** accept as being legal or real **3** be prepared to admit **4** show official gratefulness for –**nizable** adj –**nition** /ˌrekəgˈnɪʃən/ n [U]

re-coil /rɪ'kɔɪl/ vi **1** move back suddenly in fear or dislike **2** (of a gun) spring back when fired **recoil** /'riːkɔɪl, rɪ'kɔɪl/ n [S;U]

rec-ol-lect /ˌrekə'lekt/ vi/t remember ~**ion** /-'lekʃən/ n [C;U] memory

rec-om-mend /ˌrekə'mend/ vt **1** praise as being good for a purpose **2** advise: *I'd recommend caution.* **3** (of a quality) to make (someone or something) attractive: *A hotel with little to recommend it.* ~**ation** /ˌrekəmen-'deɪʃən/ n [C;U]

rec-om-pense /'rekəmpens/ n [S;U] fml reward or payment for trouble or suffering ♦ vt fml give recompense to

rec-on-cile /'rekənsaɪl/ vt **1** make friendly again **2** find agreement between (2 opposing things) –**cilia-tion** /ˌrekənsɪli'eɪʃən/ n [U]

   reconcile to phr vt cause (someone) to accept (something unpleasant)

re-con-di-tion /ˌriːkən'dɪʃən/ vt repair and bring back into working order: *a reconditioned engine*

re-con-nais-sance /rɪ'kɒnɪsəns‖ rɪ'kɑː-/ n [C;U] (act of) reconnoitring

re-con-noi-tre BrE ‖ **-ter** AmE /ˌrekə'nɔɪtəʳ‖,riː-/ vi/t go near the place where an enemy is) to find out information

re-con-sid-er /ˌriːkən'sɪdəʳ/ vi/t think again and change one's mind (about)

re-cord[1] /rɪ'kɔːd‖-ɔːrd/ v **1** vt write down so that it will be known **2** vi/t preserve (sound or a television show) so that it can be heard or seen again **3** vt (of an instrument) show by measuring

rec-ord[2] /'rekɔːd‖-ərd/ n **1** written statement of facts, events, etc. **2** known facts about past behaviour: *his criminal record* **3** best yet done: *the world record for the long jump* **4** circular piece of plastic on which sound is stored for playing back **5 for the record** to be reported as official **6 off the record** unofficial(ly) **7 on the record: a** (of facts or events) (ever) recorded: *the coldest winter on record* **b** (of a person) having publicly said, as if for written records ♦ adj better, faster, etc., than ever before: *finished in record time*

re-cord-er /rɪ'kɔːdəʳ‖-ɔːr-/ n **1** simple musical instrument played by blowing **2** TAPE RECORDER

re-cord-ing /rɪ'kɔːdɪŋ‖-ɔːr-/ n recorded performance, speech, or piece of music

record play-er /'·· ,··/ n machine for producing sounds from RECORDS[2] (4)

re-count[1] /ˌriː'kaʊnt/ vt count (esp. votes) again **recount** /'riːkaʊnt/ n

re-count[2] /rɪ'kaʊnt/ vt fml tell

re-coup /rɪ'kuːp/ vt get back (something lost, esp. money)

re-course /rɪ'kɔːs‖'riːkɔːrs/ n **have recourse to** fml make use of

re-cov-er /rɪ'kʌvəʳ/ v **1** vt get back (something lost or taken away) **2** vi return to the proper state of health, strength, ability, etc. ~**able** adj ~**y** n [U]

rec-re-a-tion /ˌrekri'eɪʃən/ n [C;U] (form of) amusement; way of spending free time ~**al** adj

re-crim-i-na-tion /rɪˌkrɪmɪ'neɪʃən/ n [C;U] (act of) quarrelling and blaming one another

re-cruit /rɪ'kruːt/ n new member of an organization, esp. the army, navy, etc. ♦ vi/t get recruits or as a recruit ~**ment** n [U]

rec-tan-gle /'rektæŋɡəl/ n flat shape with four straight sides forming four 90° angles –**gular** /rek'tæŋɡjʊləʳ/ adj

rec-ti-fy /'rektɪfaɪ/ vt fml put right

rec-ti-tude /'rektɪtjuːd‖-tuːd/ n [U] fml moral pureness

rec-tor /'rektəʳ/ n priest in charge of a PARISH ~**y** n rector's home

rec-tum /'rektəm/ n med lowest end of the bowel, where food waste passes out

re-cum-bent /rɪ'kʌmbənt/ adj fml lying down on the back or side

re-cu-pe-rate /rɪ'kjuːpəreɪt, -'kuː-/ vi get well again after illness [U] –**rative** /-pərətɪv/ adj helping one to recuperate –**ration** /rɪˌkjuːpə'reɪʃən, -ˌkuː-/ n

re-cur /rɪ'kɜːʳ/ vi **-rr-** happen again –**currence** /rɪ'kʌrəns‖-'kɜːr-/ n [C;U]: *frequent recurrence of the fever* –**current** adj

re-cy-cle /ˌriː'saɪkəl/ vt treat (a used substance) so that it is fit to use again

red /red/ adj **-dd-** **1** of the colour of blood **2** (of hair) brownish orange **3** (of skin) pink **4** (cap.) infml COMMUNIST **5 see red** become angry suddenly and lose control of oneself ♦ n **1** [C;U] red colour **2** [U] red clothes **3 in the red** in debt **4** infml a COMMUNIST **5 Reds under the bed** (imaginary) danger that secret COMMUNISTS are hiding in one's country ~**den** vi/t make or become red

red car-pet /ˌ· '··/ n [S] special ceremonial welcome to a guest

Red Cross /ˌ· '·/ n [the] international organization that looks after the sick and wounded

re-deem /rɪ'diːm/ vt **1** buy back (something given for money lent) **2** fml make (something bad) slightly less bad **3** fml fulfil (a promise, etc.)

   Redeemer n [the, our + S] Christ

re-demp-tion /rɪ'dempʃən/ n [U] redeeming

re-de-ploy /ˌriːdɪˈplɔɪ/ vt rearrange (soldiers, workers in industry, etc.) in a more effective way ~ment n

red-hand-ed /ˌ· ˈ··◂/ adj in the act of doing wrong

red-head /ˈredhed/ n person with RED (2) hair

red her-ring /ˌ· ˈ··/ n something introduced to draw people's attention away from the main point

red-hot /ˌ· ˈ·◂/ adj so hot that it shines red: (fig.) red-hot enthusiasm

red-let-ter day /ˌ· ˈ·· ·/ n specially good day

red-light dis-trict /ˌ· ˈ· ˌ··/ n area where PROSTITUTEs work

red-neck /ˈrednek/ n infml, esp. AmE person who lives in the country, esp. one who is uneducated or poor and has strong unreasonable opinions

red-o-lent /ˈredələnt/ adj fml making one think (of); suggesting

re-dou-ble /riːˈdʌbəl/ vi/t increase greatly

re-doubt /rɪˈdaʊt/ n fml small fort

re-doub-ta-ble /rɪˈdaʊtəbəl/ adj greatly respected and feared

re-dound /rɪˈdaʊnd/ v **redound to** phr vt fml increase (fame, honour, etc.)

re-dress /rɪˈdres/ vt fml 1 put right (a wrong, injustice, etc.) 2 **redress the balance** make things equal again ♦ n [U] something, such as money, that puts right a wrong

red tape /ˌ· ˈ·/ n [U] silly detailed unnecessary rules

re-duce /rɪˈdjuːs‖rɪˈduːs/ vt 1 make less 2 (of a person) lose weight on purpose —**duction** /rɪˈdʌkʃən/ n [C;U]: price reductions

reduce to phr vt 1 bring to (a less favourable state): The child was reduced to tears. (= made to cry) 2 bring (something) to (a smaller number or amount)

re-dun-dant /rɪˈdʌndənt/ adj 1 esp. BrE no longer employed because there is not enough work 2 fml not needed —**dancy** n [C;U]

red-wood /ˈredwʊd/ n extremely tall American CONIFEROUS tree

reed /riːd/ n 1 grasslike plant growing in wet places 2 thin piece of wood or metal in certain musical instruments, blown across to produce sound ~**y** adj 1 full of reeds 2 (of a sound) thin and high

reef /riːf/ n line of sharp rocks at or near the surface of the sea

reef-er /ˈriːfər/ n infml cigarette containing the drug MARIJUANA

reef knot /ˈ· ·/ n double knot that will not undo easily

reek /riːk/ vi, n (have) a strong unpleasant smell

reel¹ /riːl/ n 1 round object on which cotton, cinema film, etc., can be wound 2 length of time it takes to show this amount of film ♦ vt bring, take, etc., by winding

reel off phr vt say quickly and easily from memory

reel² vi 1 walk unsteadily as if drunk 2 be shocked or confused 3 seem to go round and round

re-en-try /riːˈentri/ n [C;U] entering again, esp. into the Earth's ATMOSPHERE

ref /ref/ n infml for REFEREE (1)

re-fec-to-ry /rɪˈfektəri/ n eating room in a school, college, etc.

refer /rɪˈfɜːr/ v -rr-

refer to phr vt 1 mention; speak about 2 be about or directed towards 3 look at for information 4 send to (a person or place) for information, a decision, etc.

ref-er-ee /ˌrefəˈriː/ n 1 person in charge of a game 2 person who gives a REFERENCE (3)

ref-er-ence /ˈrefərəns/ n 1 [C;U] (act of) mentioning 2 [C;U] (act of) looking at something for information 3 [C] a information about someone's character and ability, esp. when they are looking for a job b person who gives such information 4 **in/with reference to** fml about

reference book /ˈ··· ·/ n book for finding information

ref-e-ren-dum /ˌrefəˈrendəm/ n -da /-də/ or -dums direct vote by all the people to decide something

re-fine /rɪˈfaɪn/ vt make pure **refined** adj 1 made pure 2 showing education, delicacy of feeling, and good manners —**ment** n 1 [C] clever addition or improvement 2 [U] act of refining 3 [U] quality of being refined

re-fin-e-ry /rɪˈfaɪnəri/ n place where oil, sugar, etc., is refined

re-fit /ˌriːˈfɪt/ vt -tt- repair and put new machinery into (a ship) **refit** /ˈriːfɪt/ n

re-flate /riːˈfleɪt/ vi/t increase the supply of money in (a money system) —**flation** /-ˈfleɪʃən/ n [U]

re-flect /rɪˈflekt/ v 1 vt throw back (heat, sound, or an image) 2 vt give an idea of; express 3 vi think carefully —**ive** adj thoughtful ~**or** n

reflect on phr vt 1 consider carefully 2 cause to be considered in a particular way

re-flec-tion /rɪˈflekʃən/ n 1 [C] reflected image 2 [U] reflecting of heat, sound, etc. 3 [C;U] deep and careful thought

re-flex /ˈriːfleks/ n unintentional movement made in reply to an outside influence: quick/slow reflexes

re·flex·ive /rɪˈfleksɪv/ n, adj (word) showing effect on oneself: In 'I enjoyed myself', 'enjoy' is a reflexive verb.

re·form /rɪˈfɔːm‖-ɔːrm/ vi/t make or become (morally) right; improve ♦ n [C;U] action to improve conditions, remove unfairness, etc. ~**er** n

re·form /ˌriːˈfɔːm‖-ɔːrm/ vi/t (cause to) form again, esp. into ranks

ref·or·ma·tion /ˌrefəˈmeɪʃən‖-fər-/ n [U] 1 (moral) improvement 2 (cap.) 16th-century religious movement leading to the establishment of Protestant churches

re·fract /rɪˈfrækt/ vt bend (light passing through) ~**ion** /ˈfrækʃən/ n [U]

re·frac·to·ry /rɪˈfræktəri/ adj fml disobedient and troublesome

re·frain¹ /rɪˈfreɪn/ vi fml not do something

refrain² n part of a song that is repeated

re·fresh /rɪˈfreʃ/ vt 1 cause to feel fresh or active again 2 **refresh one's memory** help oneself to remember again ~**ing** adj 1 producing comfort and new strength 2 pleasingly new and interesting ~**ment** n [U] ~**ments** n [P] food and drink

re·fri·ge·rate /rɪˈfrɪdʒəreɪt/ vt make (food, drink, etc.) cold to preserve it ~**ration** /rɪˌfrɪdʒəˈreɪʃən/ n [U]

re·fri·ge·ra·tor /rɪˈfrɪdʒəreɪtə/ n fml for FRIDGE

ref·uge /ˈrefjuːdʒ/ n [C;U] (place providing) protection or shelter

ref·u·gee /ˌrefjuˈdʒiː/ n person forced to leave their country because of (political) danger

re·fund /ˈriːfʌnd/ n repayment ♦ /rɪˈfʌnd/ vt pay (money) back

re·fur·bish /ˌriːˈfɜːbɪʃ‖-ɜːr-/ vt make fit for use again

re·fus·al /rɪˈfjuːzəl/ n [C;U] (a case of) refusing — see also FIRST REFUSAL

re·fuse¹ /rɪˈfjuːz/ vi/t not accept, do, or give: He refused my offer.

re·fuse² /ˈrefjuːs/ n [U] waste material; RUBBISH

re·fute /rɪˈfjuːt/ vt fml prove that (someone or something) is mistaken **refutation** /ˌrefjuˈteɪʃən/ n [C;U]

re·gain /rɪˈɡeɪn/ vt get or win back

re·gal /ˈriːɡəl/ adj fml like a king or queen; very splendid ~**ly** adv

re·gale /rɪˈɡeɪl/ v **regale with** phr vt entertain with

re·ga·li·a /rɪˈɡeɪliə/ n [U] ceremonial clothes and decorations

re·gard¹ /rɪˈɡɑːd‖-ɑːrd/ vt 1 look at or consider in the stated way: I regard him as the finest lawyer in the country. 2 fml pay respectful attention to ~**ing** prep fml in connection with

regard² n [U] 1 respect 2 respectful attention; concern 3 **in/with regard**

to in connection with ~**less** adv 1 whatever may happen 2 regardless of without worrying about **regards** n [P] good wishes

re·gat·ta /rɪˈɡætə/ n meeting for boat races

re·gen·cy /ˈriːdʒənsi/ n [C;U] rule by a regent, esp. (cap.) from 1811 to 1820 in Britain

re·gen·e·rate /rɪˈdʒenəreɪt/ vi/t grow again ~**ration** /rɪˌdʒenəˈreɪʃən/ n [U]

re·gent /ˈriːdʒənt/ n person who governs in place of a king or queen who is ill, still a child, etc.

reg·gae /ˈreɡeɪ/ n [U] West Indian popular dance and music

re·gi·cide /ˈredʒɪsaɪd/ n [U] 1 killing a king or queen 2 person who does this

re·gime /reɪˈʒiːm/ n 1 (system of) government 2 regimen

re·gi·men /ˈredʒɪmən/ n fml fixed plan of food, exercise, etc., to improve health

re·gi·ment /ˈredʒɪmənt/ n large military group ♦ vt control too firmly ~**al** /ˌredʒɪˈment l◁/ adj

re·gion /ˈriːdʒən/ n 1 quite large area or part 2 **in the region of** about ~**al** adj **regions** n [(the) P] parts of the country away from the capital

re·gis·ter¹ /ˈredʒɪstə/ n 1 (book containing) a record or list 2 range of the voice or a musical instrument 3 words, style, etc., used by speakers and writers in particular conditions

register² v 1 vt put into a REGISTER¹ (1) 2 vi put one's name on a list, esp. of those who will take part 3 vt (of a measuring instrument) show 4 vt (of a person or face) express 5 vt send by registered post 6 vi have an effect (on a person)

registered post /ˌ··· ˈ·/ n [U] system for posting valuable things, which protects the sender against loss

re·gis·trar /ˌredʒɪˈstrɑː◁‖ˈredʒɪstrɑːr/ n keeper of official records

re·gis·tra·tion /ˌredʒɪˈstreɪʃən/ n [U] registering (REGISTER² (2))

registration num·ber /···· ˌ··/ n BrE official number shown on a vehicle

registry of·fice /ˈredʒɪstri ˌɒfɪs‖-ˌɔːfɪs, -ɑː-/ also **register office** — n (esp. in Britain) office where marriages can legally take place and where births, marriages, and deaths are officially recorded

re·gress /rɪˈɡres/ vi fml go back to a former and usu. worse condition, way of behaving, etc. ~**ion** /-ˈɡreʃən/ n [U]

re·gret¹ /rɪˈɡret/ vt -tt- be sorry about: I've never regretted my decision to leave. ~**table** adj that one should regret ~**tably** adv

regret² n [C;U] unhappiness at the loss of something, because of something one has done or not done, etc. ~**ful** adj

re-group /,ri:'gru:p/ vi/t form into new groups

reg·u·lar /'regjələr/ adj 1 not varying: a regular pulse|a regular customer 2 happening (almost) every time: regular church attendance 3 correct or usual 4 evenly shaped 5 employed continuously: a regular soldier 6 gram following the standard pattern: regular verbs 7 infml complete; thorough 8 esp. AmE pleasant and honest: a regular guy ♦ n regular visitor, customer, etc. ~**ly** adv at regular times ~**ize** vt make lawful -**lar·ity** /,regjə'lærəti/ n [U]

reg·u·late /'regjəleɪt/ vt 1 control, esp. by rules 2 make (a machine) work in a certain way -**latory** /-lətəri‖-tɔ:ri/ adj fml having the purpose of regulating

reg·u·la·tion /,regjə'leɪʃən/ n 1 [C] (official) rule 2 [U] control

re·gur·gi·tate /ri:'gɜːdʒəteɪt‖-ɜːr-/ vt fml 1 bring back (swallowed food) through the mouth 2 repeat (something heard or read) in one's own work, without thought or change

re·ha·bil·i·tate /,ri:hə'bɪləteɪt/ vt 1 make able to live an ordinary life again 2 put back into good condition 3 put back to a former high rank, position, etc. -**tation** /,ri:həbɪlə'teɪʃən/ n [U]

re·hash /ri:'hæʃ/ vt use (old ideas) again **rehash** /'ri:hæʃ/ n

re·hearse /rɪ'hɜːs‖-ɜːrs/ vi/t practise for later performance **rehearsal** n [C;U]

reign /reɪn/ n period of reigning ♦ vi 1 be the king or queen 2 exist (noticeably): Silence reigned.

reign of ter·ror /,· · '··/ n period of widespread official killing

re·im·burse /,ri:ɪm'bɜːs‖-ɜːrs/ vt pay (money) back to ~**ment** n [C;U]

rein /reɪn/ n 1 also **reins** pl. — long narrow (leather) band for controlling a horse 2 **give (free) rein to** give freedom to (feelings or desires) 3 **keep a tight rein on** control firmly — see also **FREE REIN reins** n [P] means of control: take the reins (= become the leader)

re·in·car·nate /,ri:ɪn'kɑ:neɪt‖-ɑ:r-/ vt cause to return to life in a new form after death -**nation** /,ri:ɪnkɑ:'neɪʃən‖ -kɑ:r-/ n [C;U]

rein·deer /'reɪndɪər/ n reindeer large deer from northern parts of the world

re·in·force /,ri:ɪn'fɔːs‖-'fɔːrs/ vt strengthen with additions ~**ment** n [U] ~**ments** n [P] more soldiers sent to reinforce an army

reinforced con·crete /,··· '··/ n [U] CONCRETE strengthened by metal bars

re·in·state /,ri:ɪn'steɪt/ vt put back into a position formerly held ~**ment** n [C;U]

re·it·e·rate /ri:'ɪtəreɪt/ vt fml repeat several times -**ration** /ri:,ɪtə'reɪʃən/ n [C;U]

re·ject /rɪ'dʒekt/ vt refuse to accept ♦ /'ri:dʒekt/ n something thrown away as useless or imperfect ~**ion** /rɪ'dʒekʃən/ n [C;U]

re·jig /ri:'dʒɪg/ vt -gg- rearrange, esp. so as to perform different work or to work more effectively

re·joice /rɪ'dʒɔɪs/ vi 1 feel or show great joy 2 **rejoice in the name of** be called (used when the name sounds foolish) **rejoicing** n [C;U] (public) show of joy

re·join¹ /,ri:'dʒɔɪn/ vi/t join again

re·join² /rɪ'dʒɔɪn/ vt answer, esp. angrily

re·join·der /rɪ'dʒɔɪndər/ n (rude) answer

re·ju·ve·nate /rɪ'dʒuːvəneɪt/ vt make young again -**nation** /rɪ,dʒuːvə'neɪʃən/ n [U]

re·lapse /rɪ'læps/ vi return to a bad state of health or way of life **relapse** n

re·late /rɪ'leɪt/ vt 1 see or show a connection between 2 fml tell (a story) - **related** adj of the same family or kind; connected

relate to phr vt 1 connect (one thing) with (another) 2 infml understand and accept

re·la·tion /rɪ'leɪʃən/ n 1 [C] member of one's family 2 [C;U] connection 3 **in/with relation to** fml with regard to ~**ship** n 1 [C] friendship or connection between people 2 [C;U] connection **relations** n [P] dealings between (and feelings towards) each other

rel·a·tive /'relətɪv/ n RELATION (1) ♦ adj compared to each other or something else: now living in relative comfort ~**ly** adv quite

relative clause /,··· '·/ n CLAUSE joined on by a RELATIVE PRONOUN

relative pro·noun /,··· '··/ n PRONOUN which joins a CLAUSE to the rest of a sentence, such as who, which, or that

rel·a·tiv·i·ty /,relə'tɪvəti/ n [U] relationship between time, size, and mass, said to change with increased speed

re·lax /rɪ'læks/ vi/t make or become a less active and worried b less stiff, tight, or severe -**ation** /,ri:læk-'seɪʃən/ n 1 [C;U] (something done for) rest and amusement 2 [U] act of making or becoming less severe

re·lay /'ri:leɪ/ n [C;U] 1 group that takes the place of another to keep work going continuously: In a relay

(race), each member of each team runs part of the distance. **2** (broadcast sent out by) an electrical connection for receiving and passing on signals

re·lease /rɪ'liːs/ vt **1** set free **2** allow to be seen or read publicly **3** press (a handle) so as to let something go ♦ n **1** [S;U] setting free **2** [C] new film, record, or piece of information that has been released **3 on general release** (of a film) able to be seen at all the cinemas in an area

rel·e·gate /'relɪɡeɪt/ vt put into a lower or worse place **–gation** /ˌrelɪ'ɡeɪʃən/ n [U]

re·lent /rɪ'lent/ vi become less cruel or severe **~less** adj continuously cruel or severe

rel·e·vant /'relɪvənt/ adj directly connected with the subject **~ly** adv **–vance** n [U]

re·li·a·ble /rɪ'laɪəbəl/ adj that may be trusted **–ably** adv **–ability** /rɪˌlaɪə'bɪlɪti/ n [U]

re·li·ant /rɪ'laɪənt/ adj dependent (on) **–ance** n [U] **1** dependence **2** trust

rel·ic /'relɪk/ n **1** something old that reminds us of the past **2** part of or something that belonged to a dead holy person

re·lief /rɪ'liːf/ n **1** [S;U] comfort at the ending of anxiety, pain, or dullness **2** [U] help for people in trouble **3** [C] person who takes over another's duty **4** [C;U] decoration that stands out above the rest of the surface it is on **5** [U] BrE part of one's income on which one does not have to pay tax **6 light relief** pleasant and amusing change

relief map /·'··/ n map showing the height of land

re·lieve /rɪ'liːv/ vt **1** lessen (pain or trouble) **2** take over duties from **3** give variety or interest to **4 relieve oneself** URINATE or empty the bowels **relieved** adj no longer worried

relieve of phr vt free from

re·li·gion /rɪ'lɪdʒən/ n [C;U] (system of) belief in and worship of one or more gods

re·li·gious /rɪ'lɪdʒəs/ adj **1** of religion **2** obeying the rules of a religion **3** performing the stated duties very carefully **~ly** adv regularly

re·lin·quish /rɪ'lɪŋkwɪʃ/ vt fml for GIVE **up** (5)

rel·ish /'relɪʃ/ n [U] **1** great enjoyment **2** substance eaten with a meal, to add taste and interest ♦ vt enjoy

re·live /ˌriː'lɪv/ vt experience again in the imagination

re·luc·tant /rɪ'lʌktənt/ adj unwilling **~ly** adv **–tance** n [U]

re·ly /rɪ'laɪ/ v **rely on** phr vt **1** trust **2** depend on

re·main /rɪ'meɪn/ v **1** vi stay or be left behind after others have gone **2** vi continue to be: remain calm/a prisoner **remains** n [P] **1** parts which are left **2** fml dead body

re·main·der /rɪ'meɪndər/ n what is left over ♦ vt sell (esp. books) cheap so as to get rid of them quickly

re·mand /rɪ'mɑːnd‖rɪ'mænd/ vt send back to prison from a court of law, to be tried later ♦ n [C;U]: He's on remand. (= in prison waiting for a trial)

re·mark /rɪ'mɑːk‖-ɑːrk/ n spoken or written opinion ♦ vt say

remark on phr vt fml mention

re·mar·ka·ble /rɪ'mɑːkəbəl‖-ɑːr-/ adj unusual or noticeable **–bly** adv

re·me·di·al /rɪ'miːdiəl/ adj providing a remedy

rem·e·dy /'remɪdi/ n [C;U] way of curing something ♦ vt put (something bad) right

re·mem·ber /rɪ'membər/ v **1** vt call back into the mind **2** vi/t take care not to forget **3** vt give money or a present to

remember to phr vt send greetings from (someone) to

re·mem·brance /rɪ'membrəns/ n [U] **1** act of remembering **2** something given or kept to remind one

re·mind /rɪ'maɪnd/ vt cause to remember **~er** n something to make one remember

remind of phr vt cause to remember by seeming the same

rem·i·nisce /ˌremɪ'nɪs/ vi talk pleasantly about the past **–niscence** n [U] **–niscences** n [P] written or spoken account of one's past life **–niscent** adj that reminds one (of); like

re·miss /rɪ'mɪs/ adj fml careless about a duty

re·mis·sion /rɪ'mɪʃən/ n [C;U] **1** lessening of the time someone has to stay in prison **2** fml period when an illness is less severe

re·mit /rɪ'mɪt/ vt **-tt-** fml **1** send (money) by post **2** free someone from (a debt or punishment) **~tance** n **1** [C] money remitted **2** [U] fml act of remitting money

rem·nant /'remnənt/ n part that remains

rem·on·strate /'remənstreɪt‖rɪ'mɒn-/ vi fml express disapproval

re·morse /rɪ'mɔːs‖-ɔːrs/ n [U] sorrow for having done wrong **~ful** adj **~less** adj **1** showing no remorse **2** threateningly unstoppable

re·mote /rɪ'məʊt/ adj **1** far distant in space or time **2** quiet and lonely: a remote village **3** widely separated; not close: a remote connection **4** slight: a *remote chance of success* **5** not showing interest in others ~**ly** *adv* at all: *not remotely interested* ~**ness** *n* [U]

remote con·trol /ˌ·ˈ·, ·ˈ·/ *n* [C] controlling machinery by radio signals

re·move /rɪˈmuːv/ *vt* **1** take away; get rid of **2** *fml* dismiss **3 removed from** distant or different from ♦ *n* stage; degree: *Their action was only (at) one remove from* (= was nearly) *revolution.*

   removal *n* [C;U] **–mover** *n* [C;U]

re·mu·ne·rate /rɪˈmjuːnəreɪt/ *vt fml* pay **–rative** /-rətɪv/ *adj* well-paid **–ration** /rɪˌmjuːnəˈreɪʃən/ *n* [S;U]

re·nais·sance /rɪˈneɪsəns‖ˌrenə-ˈsɑːns/ *n* renewal of interest in art, literature, etc., esp. (*cap.*) in Europe between the 14th and 17th centuries

re·nal /ˈriːnl/ *adj* med of the KIDNEYS

rend /rend/ *vt* rent *lit* **1** split **2** pull violently

ren·der /ˈrendər/ *vt fml* **1** cause to be **2** give **3** perform ~**ing**, *also* **rendi·tion** /renˈdɪʃən/ *n* performance

ren·dez·vous /ˈrɒndeɪvuː, -deɪ-‖ˈrɑːn-/ *n* **–vous** /-vuːz/ **1** (arrangement for) a meeting **2** meeting place ♦ *vi* meet by arrangement

ren·e·gade /ˈrenɪgeɪd/ *n* person who disloyally leaves one country or belief to join another

re·nege , renegue/rɪˈniːg, rɪˈneɪg‖rɪˈnɪg, rɪˈneɪg/ *vi fml* break a promise

re·new /rɪˈnjuː‖rɪˈnuː/ *vt* **1** repeat: *They renewed their attack.* **2** give new life and freshness to **3** get something new of the same kind to take the place of ~**al** *n* [C;U]

ren·net /ˈrenət/ *n* [U] substance for thickening milk to make cheese

re·nounce /rɪˈnaʊns/ *vt* say formally that one does not own or has no more connection with

ren·o·vate /ˈrenəveɪt/ *vt* put back into good condition **–vation** /ˌrenəˈveɪʃən/ *n* [C;U]

re·nown /rɪˈnaʊn/ *n* [U] fame ~**ed** *adj* famous

rent¹ /rent/ *n* [C;U] money paid regularly for the use of a house, television set, etc. ♦ *vt* **1** pay rent for the use of **2** allow to be used in return for rent ~**al** *n* sum of money fixed to be paid as rent

rent² *n* large tear

rent³ *past t.) p. of* REND

rent boy /ˈ· ·/*n BrE infml* young male PROSTITUTE

re·nun·ci·a·tion /rɪˌnʌnsiˈeɪʃən/ *n* [C;U] (act of) renouncing (RENOUNCE) something

re·or·gan·ize, -ise /riːˈɔːɡənaɪz‖-ˈɔːr-/ *vt* **1** ORGANIZE in a new and better way **–ization** *n* /riːˌɔːɡənaɪˈzeɪʃən‖riːˌɔːrɡənə-/ [C;U]

rep¹ /rep/ *n infml for* SALES REPRESENTATIVE

rep² *n* [C;U] REPERTORY (company)

Rep *written abbrev. for:* REPUBLICAN

re·pair /rɪˈpeər/ *vt* mend ♦ *n* **1** [C;U] (act or result of) mending **2** [U] condition: *in good repair*

rep·a·ra·tion /ˌrepəˈreɪʃən/ *n* [C;U] *fml* repayment for loss or damage

rep·ar·tee /ˌrepɑːˈtiː‖repərˈtiː/ *n* [U] quick amusing talk

re·past /rɪˈpɑːst‖rɪˈpæst/ *n fml* meal

re·pat·ri·ate /riːˈpætrieɪt‖riːˈpeɪ-/ *vt* send (someone) back to their own country **–ation** /ˌriːpætriˈeɪʃən‖riːˌpeɪ-/ *n* [U]

re·pay /rɪˈpeɪ/ *vt* **repaid** /rɪˈpeɪd/ **1** pay (money) back to (someone) **2** reward ~**ment** *n* [C;U]

re·peal /rɪˈpiːl/ *vt* end (a law) **repeal** [U]

re·peat /rɪˈpiːt/ *vt* **1** say or do again **2 repeat oneself** keep saying the same thing ♦ *n* performance broadcast a second time ~**ed** *adj* done again and again ~**edly** *adv*

re·pel /rɪˈpel/ *vt* **-ll- 1** drive away (as if) by force **2** cause feelings of extreme dislike in ~**lent** *adj* extremely nasty ~**lent** *n* [C;U] substance that repels esp. insects

re·pent /rɪˈpent/ *vi/t fml* be sorry for (wrongdoing) ~**ant** *adj* ~**ance** *n* [U]

re·per·cus·sion /ˌriːpəˈkʌʃən‖ˌriːpər-/ *n* far-reaching effect

rep·er·toire /ˈrepətwɑː‖-ər-/ *n* set of things one can perform

rep·er·to·ry /ˈrepətəri‖ˈrepərtɔːri/ *n* [U] performing several plays one after the other on different days with the same actors

rep·e·ti·tion /ˌrepəˈtɪʃən/ *n* [C;U] repeating **–tious, -tive** /rɪˈpetɪtɪv/ *adj* containing parts that are repeated too much

re·phrase /riːˈfreɪz/ *vt* put into different (clearer) words

re·place /rɪˈpleɪs/ *vt* **1** put back in the right place **2** take the place of **3** get another (better) one instead of ~**ment** *n* **1** [U] act of replacing **2** [C] that replaces someone or something

re·plen·ish /rɪˈplenɪʃ/ *vt* fill up again

re·plete /rɪˈpliːt/ *adj fml* very full, esp. of food **–pletion** /-ˈpliːʃən/ *n* [U]

rep·li·ca /ˈreplɪkə/ *n* close copy

rep·li·cate /ˈreplɪkeɪt/ *vt fml* copy exactly

re·ply /rɪˈplaɪ/ *vi, n* answer

re·port¹ /rɪˈpɔːt‖-ɔːrt/ *n* **1** [C] account of events, business affairs, etc. **2** [C;U] what is said generally but unofficially **3** [C] noise of an explosion

report² *v* **1** *vi/t* provide information (about); give an account of, esp. for a newspaper or radio or television **2** *vi* go somewhere and say that one is there (and ready for work) **3** *vt* make a complaint about ~**er** *n* person who reports news

re-port-age /rɪ'pɔːtɪdʒ, ˌrepɔ:'tɑ:dʒ‖ -'pɔːr-, ˌrepɑr'tɑ:ʒ/ *n* [U] (writing, film, etc., in) the style of reporters

re-port-ed-ly /rɪ'pɔːtɪdli‖-'pɔːr-/ *adv* according to what is said

reported speech /·ˌ·· '·/ *n* [U] INDIRECT SPEECH

re-pose /rɪ'pəʊz/ *n* [U] *fml* rest ♦ *vt fml* rest; lie

repose in *phr vt fml* place (trust, hope, etc.) in

re-pos-i-to-ry /rɪ'pɒzɪtəri‖rɪ'pɑːzɪ- tɔːri/ *n* place where things are stored

re-pos-sess /ˌriːpə'zes/ *vt* take back, esp. when rent has not been paid

rep-re-hen-si-ble /ˌreprɪ'hensəbəl/ *adj fml* deserving blame; bad –**bly** *adv*

rep-re-sent /ˌreprɪ'zent/ *v* **1** *vt* act or speak officially for (someone else) **2** *vt* be a picture or STATUE of; show **3** *vt* be a sign of; stand for **4** be: *This represents a considerable improvement.* ~**ation** /ˌreprɪzen'teɪʃən/ *n* **1** [U] act of representing or state of being represented **2** [C] something which REPRE- SENTs (2,3) something else

rep-re-sen-ta-tive /ˌreprɪ'zentətɪv/ *adj* **1** typical **2** (of government) in which the people and their opinions are represented ♦ *n* person who REP- RESENTs (1) others — see also HOUSE OF REPRESENTATIVES

re-press /rɪ'pres/ *vt* control; hold back ~**ive** *adj* hard and cruel ~**ion** /-'preʃən/ *n* [U] pushing unwelcome feelings into one's unconscious mind, with odd effects on behaviour

re-prieve /rɪ'priːv/ *vt* give a reprieve to ♦ *n* official order not to carry out the punishment of death (yet)

rep-ri-mand /'reprɪmɑːnd‖-mænd/ *vt* express severe official disapproval of *reprimand n*

re-pri-sal /rɪ'praɪzəl/ *n* [C;U] (act of) punishing others for harm done to oneself

re-prise /rɪ'priːz/ *n* repeating of a piece of music

re-proach /rɪ'prəʊtʃ/ *n* [C;U] **1** (word of) blame **2** above/beyond **reproach** perfect ♦ *vt* blame, not angrily but sadly ~**ful** *adj*

rep-ro-bate /'reprəbeɪt/ *n fml* per- son of bad character

re-pro-duce /ˌriːprə'djuːs‖-'duːs/ *vi/t* **1** produce the young of (oneself or one's kind) **2** produce a copy (of) –**duction** /-'dʌkʃən/ *n* [C;U] –**ductive** /-'dʌktɪv/ *adj* concerned with produc- ing young

re-proof /rɪ'pruːf/ *n* [C;U] *fml* (expression of) blame or disapproval

re-prove /rɪ'pruːv/ *vt fml* speak blamingly or disapprovingly to

rep-tile /'reptaɪl‖'reptl/ *n* animal, such as a snake, with blood that changes temperature –**tilian** /rep'tɪliən/ *adj*

re-pub-lic /rɪ'pʌblɪk/ *n* state ruled by a president and usu. an elected parlia- ment, not by a king

re-pub-li-can[1] /rɪ'pʌblɪkən/ *adj* **1** belonging to or supporting a republic

republican[2] *n* person who favours republics ~**ism** *n* [U] beliefs or prac- tices of republicans

Republican *n* member or supporter of the **Republican Party**, one of the two largest political parties of the US

re-pu-di-ate /rɪ'pjuːdieɪt/ *vt fml* **1** state that (something) is untrue **2** refuse to accept –**ation** /rɪˌpjuːdi- 'eɪʃən/ *n* [U]

re-pug-nant /rɪ'pʌɡnənt/ *adj fml* causing extreme dislike; nasty –**nance** *n* [U]

re-pulse /rɪ'pʌls/ *vt* **1** refuse coldly **2** drive back (an attack) –**pulsive** *adj* extremely unpleasant –**pulsion** /-'pʌlʃən/ *n* [U] **1** extreme dislike **2** natural force by which one body drives another away from it

re-pu-ta-ble /'repjʊtəbəl/ *adj* having a good reputation –**bly** *adv*

re-pu-ta-tion /ˌrepjʊ'teɪʃən/ *n* [C;U] opinion which people in general have about someone or something

re-pute /rɪ'pjuːt/ *n* [U] *fml* **1** reputa- tion **2** good reputation **reputed** *adj* generally supposed, but with some doubt **reputedly** *adv*

re-quest /rɪ'kwest/ *n* **1** [C;U] polite demand for **2** [C] something asked for ♦ *vt* demand politely

request stop /·' · '·/ *n* place where you can get a bus to stop by signalling

req-ui-em /'rekwiəm, 'rekwiem/ *n* (music for) a Christian ceremony for a dead person

re-quire /rɪ'kwaɪər/ *vt* **1** need **2** *fml* order, expecting obedience: *You are required to (= must) do it.* ~**ment** *n* something needed or demanded

req-ui-site /'rekwɪzɪt/ *adj* needed for a purpose

req-ui-si-tion /ˌrekwɪ'zɪʃən/ *n* [C;U] formal demand, esp. by the army ♦ *vt* demand or take officially, esp. for the army

re-scind /rɪ'sɪnd/ *vt* end (a law) or take back (a decision, order, etc.)

res-cue /'reskjuː/ *vt* save or set free from harm or danger **rescue** *n* –**cuer** *n*

re-search /rɪ'sɜːtʃ, 'riːsɜːtʃ‖-ɜːr-/ *n* [C;U] advanced and detailed study, to find out (new) facts ♦ /rɪˌsɜːtʃ‖-ɜːr-/ *vi/t* do research (on or for) ~**er** *n*

re-sem-ble /rɪ'zembəl/ *vt* look or be like –**blance** *n* [C;U] likeness

re·sent /n'zent/ *vt* feel hurt and angry because of ~**ful** *adj* ~**ment** *n* [U]

res·er·va·tion /,rezə'veɪʃən‖-zər-/ *n* 1 [C;U] limiting condition(s): *I accepted every point, without reservation.* 2 [C] private doubt in one's mind 3 [C] arrangement to have or use something: *a hotel reservation* 4 [C] area set apart for particular people to live in

re·serve /n'zɜːv‖-ɜrv/ *vt* 1 keep apart for a special purpose 2 arrange to have or use: *reserve hotel rooms* ♦ *n* 1 [C] quantity kept for future use 2 [C] piece of land kept for the stated purpose 3 [C] player who will play if another cannot 4 [U] being reserved 5 [*the* + S] also **reserves** *pl.* — military forces kept for use if needed 6 **in reserve** for future use 7 **without reserve** *fml* completely **reserved** *adj* not liking to show one's feelings or talk about oneself

res·er·voir /'rezəvwɑːʳ‖-ɔrvwɑːr, -vɔːr/ *n* 1 artificial lake for storing water 2 large supply (still unused)

re·shuf·fle /riː'ʃʌfəl/ *vt* change around the positions of people working in **reshuffle** *n*

re·side /n'zaɪd/ *vi fml* have one's home

res·i·dence /'rezədəns/ *n fml* 1 [C] (large grand) house 2 [U] state of residing 3 **in residence** actually living in a place

res·i·dent /'rezədənt/ *n, adj* (person) who lives in a place ~**ial** /,rezə'denʃəl/ *adj* 1 consisting of private houses 2 for which one must live in a place: *a residential course*

re·sid·u·al /n'zɪdjuəl/ *adj* left over; remaining

res·i·due /'rezədjuː‖-duː/ *n* what is left over

re·sign /n'zaɪn/ *vi/t* leave (one's job or position) ~**ed** *adj* calmly suffering without complaint ~**edly** /,n'zaɪnədli/ *adv*

  resign *to phr vt* cause (oneself) to accept calmly (something which cannot be avoided)

res·ig·na·tion /,rezɪg'neɪʃən/ *n* 1 [C;U] (act or written statement of) resigning 2 [U] state of being resigned

re·sil·i·ent /n'zɪliənt/ *adj* 1 able to spring back to its former shape 2 able to recover quickly from misfortune ~**ence** *n* [U]

res·in /'rezən/ *n* 1 [U] thick sticky liquid from trees 2 [C] man-made plastic substance

re·sist /n'zɪst/ *vt* 1 oppose; fight against 2 remain unharmed by 3 force oneself not to accept

re·sist·ance /n'zɪstəns/ *n* [S;U] 1 act of resisting or ability to resist 2 [U] force opposed to movement: *wind resistance* 3 [(*the*) U] secret army fighting against an enemy in control of its country 4 **the line of least resistance** the easiest way –**ant** *adj* showing resistance

re·sis·tor /n'zɪstəʳ/ *n* piece of wire, etc., for reducing the power of an electrical current

res·o·lute /'rezəluːt/ *adj* firm; determined in purpose ~**ly** *adv*

res·o·lu·tion /,rezə'luːʃən/ *n* 1 [C] formal decision at a meeting 2 [C] firm decision: *a New Year resolution to stop smoking* 3 [U] quality of being resolute 4 [U] action of resolving (RESOLVE (1))

re·solve /n'zɒlv‖n'zɑːlv, n'zɔːlv/ *vt* 1 find a way of dealing with (a problem); settle 2 decide firmly 3 make a RESOLUTION (1, 2) ♦ *n* [C;U] *fml* for RESOLUTION (2, 3)

res·o·nant /'rezənənt/ *adj* 1 (of a sound) full, clear, and continuing 2 producing RESONANCE (2) –**nance** *n* [U] 1 quality of being RESONANT (1) 2 sound produced in a body by sound waves from another

res·o·nate /'rezəneɪt/ *vi* 1 produce RESONANCE (2) 2 be RESONANT (1)

re·sort[1] /n'zɔːt‖-ɔrt/ *n* 1 holiday place 2 **as a /in the last resort** if everything else fails

resort[2] *v* **resort to** *phr vt* make use of, esp. when there is nothing else

re·sound /n'zaʊnd/ *vi* 1 be loud and clearly heard 2 be filled (with sound) ~**ing** *adj* very great: *a resounding victory*

re·source /n'zɔːs, -'sɔːs‖-ɔrs/ *n* 1 [C] something useful that one possesses 2 [U] resourcefulness 3 **leave someone to his own resources** leave someone alone to pass the time as he wishes ~**ful** *adj* able to find a way round difficulties ~**fully** *adv*

re·spect /n'spekt/ *n* 1 [U] great admiration and honour 2 [U] attention; care 3 [C] detail; point: *In some respects* (= ways) *it is worse.* 4 **with respect to** with regard to; about ♦ *vt* feel or show respect for ~**ing** *prep* in connection with **respects** *n* [P] polite formal greetings

re·spec·ta·ble /n'spektəbəl/ *adj* 1 socially acceptable 2 quite good; a *respectable income* –**bly** *adv* –**bility** /n,spektə'bɪləti/ *n* [U]

re·spect·ful /n'spektfəl/ *adj* feeling or showing RESPECT (1) ~**ly** *adv*

re·spec·tive /n'spektɪv/ *adj* particular and separate ~**ly** *adv* each separately in the order mentioned

res·pi·ra·tion /,respə'reɪʃən/ *n* [U] *fml* breathing –**piratory** /'respə-reɪtəri, n'spaɪərə-‖'resprətɔːri, n'spaɪərə-/ *adj: the respiratory system* (= lungs, etc.)

res·pi·ra·tor /'respəreitəʳ/ n apparatus to help people breathe

res·pite /'respit, -paıt‖-pɪt/ n [C;U] 1 short rest from effort, pain, etc. 2 delay before something unwelcome happens

re·splen·dent /rɪ'splendənt/ adj gloriously bright and shining ~**ly** adv

re·spond /rɪ'spɒnd‖rɪ'spɑːnd/ vi 1 answer 2 act in answer

respond to phr vt (esp. of a disease) get better as a result of

re·sponse /rɪ'spɒns‖rɪ'spɑːns/ n 1 [C] answer 2 [C;U] action done in answer

re·spon·si·bil·i·ty /rɪˌspɒnsəˈbɪləti‖ rɪˌspɑːn-/ n 1 [U] condition or quality of being responsible: *I take full responsibility for losing it.* 2 [C] something for which one is RESPONSIBLE (2) 3 [U] trustworthiness

re·spon·si·ble /rɪ'spɒnsəbəl‖ rɪ'spɑːn-/ adj 1 having done or caused something (bad); guilty 2 having a duty to do or look after something 3 trustworthy 4 (of a job) needing a trustworthy person to do it 5 **be responsible for** be the cause of –**bly** adv

re·spon·sive /rɪ'spɒnsɪv‖rɪ'spɑːn-/ adj answer readily with words or feelings: (fig.) *a disease responsive to treatment*

rest¹ /rest/ n 1 [C;U] (period of) freedom from action or something tiring 2 [U] not moving: *It came to rest* (= stopped) *just here.* 3 [C] support, esp. for the stated thing: *a headrest* 4 **set someone's mind/fears at rest** free someone from anxiety ~**ful** adj peaceful; quiet

rest² v 1 vi/t (allow to) take a rest 2 vt lean; support 3 vi lie buried: *Let him rest in peace.* 4 **rest assured** be certain

rest on phr vt 1 (of a proof, argument, etc.) depend on 2 lean on 3 (of eyes) be directed towards

rest with phr vt be the responsibility of

rest³ n 1 **the rest** ones that still remain; what is left 2 **for the rest** apart from what has already been mentioned

res·tau·rant /'restərɒnt‖-rənt, -rɑːnt/ n place where meals are sold and eaten

res·tau·ra·teur /ˌrestərəˈtɜːʳ/ n restaurant owner

res·ti·tu·tion /ˌrestəˈtjuːʃən‖ -'tuːʃən/ n [U] fml giving something back to its owner, or paying for damage

res·tive /'restɪv/ adj unwilling to keep still or be controlled ~**ly** adv

rest·less /'restləs/ adj 1 giving no rest or sleep 2 unable to stay still, esp.

from anxiety or lack of interest ~**ly** adv

res·to·ra·tion /ˌrestəˈreɪʃən/ n [C;U] 1 restoring 2 (cap.) period after 1660 in Britain

re·sto·ra·tive /rɪ'stɔːrətɪv/ n, adj (food, medicine, etc.) that brings back health and strength

re·store /rɪ'stɔːʳ/ vt 1 give back 2 bring back into existence 3 bring back to a proper state, esp. of health 4 put back into a former position 5 repair (an old painting, building, etc.) **restorer** n

re·strain /rɪ'streɪn/ vt prevent from doing something; control ~**ed** adj calm and controlled **restraint** n 1 [U] quality of being restrained or act of restraining oneself 2 [C] something that restrains: *the restraints of life in a small town*

re·strict /rɪ'strɪkt/ vt keep within a certain limit ~**ive** adj that restricts one ~**ion** /-'strɪkʃən/ n [C;U]

re·struc·ture /ˌriːˈstrʌktʃəʳ/ vt arrange (a system or organization) in a new way

re·sult /rɪ'zʌlt/ n 1 [C;U] what happens because of an action or event 2 [C;U] (a) noticeable good effect 3 [C] situation of defeat or victory at the end of a game 4 [C] answer to a sum ♦ vi happen as an effect of or RESULT (1) ~**ant** adj resulting

result in phr vt cause

re·sume /rɪ'zjuːm‖rɪ'zuːm/ v 1 vi/t begin again after a pause 2 vt fml return to

ré·su·mé /'rezjumeɪ, 'reɪ-‖ ˌrezʊ'meɪ/ n 1 shortened form of a speech, book, etc. 2 esp. AmE CURRICULUM VITAE

re·sump·tion /rɪ'zʌmpʃən/ n [U] act of resuming

re·sur·gence /rɪ'sɜːdʒəns‖-ɜːr-/ n [U] becoming active again

res·ur·rect /ˌrezəˈrekt/ vt bring back into use or fashion ~**ion** /-'rekʃən/ n 1 [U] renewal 2 [the + S] return of dead people to life at the end of the world 3 [the] (cap.) return of Christ to life after his death

re·sus·ci·tate /rɪ'sʌsəteɪt/ vt bring a person back to life –**tation** /-rɪˌsʌsəˈteɪʃən/ n [U]

re·tail¹ /'riːteɪl/ n [U] sale of goods in shops to customers, not for reselling to anyone else ♦ adv by retail ~**er** n ♦ /rɪ'teɪl/ vi/t sell by retail

re·tain /rɪ'teɪn/ vt 1 keep; avoid losing 2 hold in place 3 employ (esp. a lawyer)

re·tain·er /rɪ'teɪnəʳ/ n 1 servant 2 money paid for advice and help

re·tal·i·ate /rɪ'tælieɪt/ vi pay back evil with evil –**atory** /-lɪətəri‖-tɔːri/ adj –**ation** /rɪˌtæliˈeɪʃən/ n [U]

re·tard /rɪ'tɑːd‖-ɑːrd/ vt make slow or late ~**ed** adj slow in development of the mind

retch /retʃ/ vi try unsuccessfully to be sick

re·ten·tion /rɪ'tenʃən/ n [U] state or action of retaining (RETAIN)

re·ten·tive /rɪ'tentɪv/ adj able to remember things well

re·think /ˌriː'θɪŋk/ vt **rethought** think again and perhaps change one's mind about **rethink** /'riːθɪŋk/ n [S]

ret·i·cent /'retɪsənt/ adj unwilling to say much ~**cence** n [U]

ret·i·na /'retɪnə/ n area at the back of the eye which receives light

ret·i·nue /'retɪnjuː‖-nuː/ n group travelling with and helping an important person

re·tire /rɪ'taɪər/ vi **1** leave one's job, usu. because of age **2** leave a place of action **3** fml go away, esp. to a quiet place **4** fml go to bed ~**ment** n [U] **retired** adj having stopped working **retiring** adj liking to avoid company

re·tort¹ /rɪ'tɔːt‖-ɔːrt/ n quick or angry reply ♦ vt make a retort

retort² n long-necked bottle for heating chemicals

re·touch /ˌriː'tʌtʃ/ vt improve (a picture) with small additions

re·trace /rɪ'treɪs, riː-/ vt go back over: *She retraced her steps.* (= went back the way she had come)

re·tract /rɪ'trækt/ vt/i **1** draw back or in: *The cat retracted its claws.* **2** take back (a statement or offer one has made) ~**able** adj ~**ion** /-'trækʃən/ n [U]

re·tread /'riːtred/ n tyre with a new covering of rubber

re·treat /rɪ'triːt/ vi **1** move backwards, esp. when forced **2** escape (from something unpleasant) ♦ n **1** [C;U] (act of) retreating **2** [the + S] military signal for this **3** [C] place one goes to for peace and safety

re·trench /rɪ'trentʃ/ vi fml arrange to lessen (one's spending) ~**ment** n [C;U]

re·tri·al /ˌriː'traɪəl/ n new trial of a law case

ret·ri·bu·tion /ˌretrɪ'bjuːʃən/ n fml deserved punishment

re·trieve /rɪ'triːv/ vt **1** find and bring back **2** fml put right **retrieval** n [U] retrieving **retriever** n dog that retrieves shot birds

ret·ro·grade /'retrəgreɪd/ adj moving back to an earlier and worse state

ret·ro·gres·sion /ˌretrə'greʃən/ n [U] fml going back to an earlier and worse state ~**sive** /-'gresɪv/ adj

ret·ro·spect n **in retrospect** looking back to the past ~**ive** /ˌretrə'spektɪv/ adj **1** thinking about the past **2** (of a law) having an effect on

the past **3** also **retrospective exhibition** /ˌ····'····'··/ — n a show of the work of a painter, SCULPTOR, etc., from his or her earliest years up to the present time

re·turn¹ /rɪ'tɜːn‖-ɜːrn/ v **1** vi come or go back **2** vt give or send back **3** vt elect to parliament **4** vt give (a VERDICT) **5 return a favour** do a kind action in return for another

return² n **1** [C;U] (act of) coming or giving back **2** [C] profit **3** [C] official statement or set of figures: *a tax return* **4 by return of post** by the next post **5 in return for** in exchange (for) **6 Many happy returns (of the day)!** (used as a birthday greeting) ♦ adj BrE (of a ticket) for a journey to a place and back again

returning of·fi·cer /·'··· ,···/ n official who arranges an area's parliamentary election and gives out the result

return match /·,· '·/ n second game between the same sides

re·u·nion /ˌriː'juːnjən/ n **1** [C] meeting of former fellow-workers or friends after a separation **2** [U] state of being brought together again

rev /rev/ vt -vv- increase the speed of (an engine) ♦ n sl for REVOLUTION (3)

re·vamp /ˌriː'væmp/ vt give a new and improved form to

re·veal /rɪ'viːl/ vt allow to be seen or known

re·veil·le /rɪ'væli‖'revəli/ n [U] signal to waken soldiers in the morning

rev·el /'revəl/ v -ll- BrE ‖ -l- AmE lit pass the time in dancing, etc. ~**ler** BrE ‖ ~**er** AmE n person taking part in revelry ~**ry** n [U] wild noisy dancing and feasting

revel in phr vt enjoy greatly

rev·e·la·tion /ˌrevə'leɪʃən/ n **1** [U] making known of something secret: *forced to resign by the revelation of his unpleasant activities* **2** [C](surprising) fact made known

re·venge /rɪ'vendʒ/ n [U] punishment given in return for harm done to oneself ♦ vt do something in revenge

rev·e·nue /'revənjuː‖-nuː/ n [U] income, esp. received by the government

re·ver·be·rate /rɪ'vɜːbəreɪt‖-ɜːr-/ vi (of sound) be continuously repeated in waves ~**ration** /rɪ,vɜːbə'reɪʃən‖ -ɜːr-/ n [C;U]

re·vere /rɪ'vɪər/ vt fml respect and admire greatly

rev·e·rence /'revərəns/ n [U] fml great respect and admiration

Rev·e·rend /'revərənd/ n (title of respect for) a Christian priest

rev·e·rent /'revərənt/ adj showing (religious) reverence ~**ly** adv

rev·e·ren·tial /ˌrevə'renʃəl/ adj showing reverence ~**ly** adv

rev·e·rie /'revəri/ n [C;U] pleasant dreamlike state while awake

re·ver·sal /rɪ'vɜːsəl‖-ɜːr-/ n [C;U] (case of) being reversed 2 [C] defeat or piece of bad luck

re·verse /rɪ'vɜːs‖-ɜːrs/ adj opposite in position: the reverse side | in reverse order ♦ n 1 [U] opposite in position of a vehicle's controls that causes backward movement 2 [C] REVERSAL(2) 4 [C] back side of a coin, etc. ♦ 1 vi/t go or cause (a vehicle) to go backwards 2 vt change round or over to the opposite: reverse the order | reverse a decision 3 **reverse the charges** make a telephone call to be paid for by the receiver

re·ver·sion /rɪ'vɜːʃən‖rɪ'vɜːrʒən/ n [U] return to a former condition or habit

re·vert /rɪ'vɜːt‖-ɜːrt/ v **revert to** phr vt go back to (a former condition, habit, or owner)

re·view /rɪ'vjuː/ vt 1 consider and judge (an event or situation) 2 hold a REVIEW (2) 3 give a REVIEW (3a) of ♦ n 1 [C;U] (act of) REVIEWing (1) 2 grand show of armed forces, in the presence of a king, queen, general, etc. 3 a [C] (written) expression of judgment on a new book, play, etc. b magazine containing such judgments **~er** n

re·vile /rɪ'vaɪl/ vt fml say bad things about

re·vise /rɪ'vaɪz/ v 1 vt improve and make corrections to (written material) 2 vt change (an opinion, intention, etc.) 3 vi/t esp. BrE restudy (something already learned), esp. before an examination

re·vi·sion /rɪ'vɪʒən/ n [C;U] (act of) revising 2 [C] revised piece of writing

re·vi·sion·is·m /rɪ'vɪʒənɪzəm/ n [U] questioning of the main beliefs of a (Marxist) political system **–ist** n

re·vi·tal·ize /riː'vaɪtəl-aɪz/ vt put new strength or power into

re·vive /rɪ'vaɪv/ v 1 vi/t become or make conscious or healthy again: (fig.) The photo revived (= brought to mind) old memories. 2 vi/t come or bring back into use or existence 3 vt perform (an old play) again after many years **revival** n 1 [C;U] renewal 2 [C] new performance of an old play

rev·o·ca·tion /,revə'keɪʃən/ n [U] revoking

re·voke /rɪ'vəuk/ vt put an end to (a law, decision, permission, etc.)

re·volt /rɪ'vəult/ v 1 vi (try to) take power violently from those in power 2 vt (cause) to feel sick and shocked ♦ n [C;U] (example of) the act of REVOLTing (1) **~ing** adj extremely nasty **~ingly** adv: revoltingly dirty

rev·o·lu·tion /,revə'luːʃən/ n 1 [C;U] (time of) great social change esp. of a political system by force 2 [C] complete change in ways of thinking or acting 3 [C] one complete circular movement **~ary** adj 1 of a REVOLUTION (1) 2 completely new and different ♦ n person who favours or joins in a REVOLUTION (1) **~ize** vt cause a REVOLUTION (2) in

re·volve /rɪ'vɒlv‖rɪ'vɑːlv/ vi/t spin round on a central point

revolve around phr vt have as a centre or main subject

re·volv·er /rɪ'vɒlvə‖rɪ'vɑːl-/ n small gun with a revolving bullet-container

re·vue /rɪ'vjuː/ n theatrical show with short acts, songs, jokes, etc.

re·vul·sion /rɪ'vʌlʃən/ n [U] feeling of being REVOLTed (2)

re·ward /rɪ'wɔːd‖-ɔːrd/ n 1 [C;U] (something gained in) return for work or service 2 [C] money given for helping the police ♦ vt give a reward to or for **~ing** adj giving personal satisfaction

re·work /,riː'wɜːk‖-'wɜːrk/ vt put (music, writing, etc.) into a new or different form (in order to use again)

rhap·so·dy /'ræpsədi/ n 1 expression of too great praise and excitement 2 piece of music of irregular form **–dic** /ræp'sɒdɪk‖-'sɑː-/ adj

rhet·o·ric /'retərɪk/ n [U] 1 art of speaking persuasively 2 fine-sounding but insincere or meaningless words **~al** /rɪ'tɒrɪkəl‖-'tɔː-, -'tɑː-/ adj 1 asked or asking only for effect, and not expecting an answer: a rhetorical question 2 of or showing rhetoric **~ally** -kli/ adv

rheu·ma·tis·m /'ruːmətɪzəm/ n [U] disease causing joint or muscle pain **-matic** /ruː'mætɪk/ adj of, suffering from, or being rheumatism

rheu·ma·toid ar·thri·tis /,ruːmətɔɪd ɑː'θraɪtɪs‖-ɑːr-/ n [U] long-lasting disease causing pain and stiffness in the joints

rhine·stone /'raɪnstəʊn/ n diamond-like jewel made from glass or a transparent rock

rhi·no /'raɪnəʊ/ n **-nos** rhinoceros

rhi·no·ce·ros /raɪ'nɒsərəs‖-'nɑː-/ n large thick-skinned African or Asian animal with either 1 or 2 horns on its nose

rho·do·den·dron /,rəʊdə'dendrən/ n large bush with large bright flowers

rhom·bus /'rɒmbəs‖'rɑːm-/ n figure with 4 equal straight sides

rhu·barb /'ruːbɑːb‖-ɑːrb/ n [U] large-leaved plant whose thick red stems are eaten

rhyme /raɪm/ v 1 vi (of words or lines in poetry) end with the same sound: 'Cat' rhymes with 'mat'. 2 vt put together (words) ending with the same sound ♦ n 1 [U] (use of) rhyming words at line-ends in poetry 2 [C] word that rhymes with another 3 [C] short simple rhyming poem 4 **rhyme or reason** (any) sense or meaning

rhyth·m /'rɪðəm/ n [C;U] regular repeated pattern of sounds or movements: (fig.) *the rhythm of the seasons* **–mic** /'rɪðmɪk/, **–mical** adj **–mically** /-kli/ adv

rhythm meth·od /'·· ,··/ n [the + S] method of CONTRACEPTION which depends on having sex only at a time when the woman is not likely to CONCEIVE

rib /rɪb/ n 1 any of the curved bones enclosing the chest 2 curved rod for strengthening a frame 3 thin raised line in a pattern ♦ vt **-bb-** laugh at (someone) **~bed** adj having a pattern of RIBS (3)

rib·ald /'rɪbəld/ adj fml (of jokes or laughter) rude and disrespectful

rib·bon /'rɪbən/ n long narrow band of cloth

ribbon de·vel·op·ment /,·· ·'··/ n [U] (building) houses along main road leading out of a city

rib cage /'· ·/ n all one's RIBS (1)

rice /raɪs/ n [U] (plant with) a seed that is widely eaten

rice pa·per /'· ,··/ n [U] sort of eatable paper

rich /rɪtʃ/ adj 1 having a lot of money or property 2 having a lot: *a city rich in ancient buildings* 3 expensive, valuable, and beautiful 4 (of food) containing a lot of cream, eggs, sugar, etc. 5 (of a sound or colour) deep, strong, and beautiful 6 *infml* amusing but often rather annoying ♦ n [(the) P] *rich people* **~ly** adv 1 splendidly 2 fully: *richly deserved* **~ness** n [U]

rich·es /'rɪtʃɪz/ n [U] *esp. lit* wealth

rick¹ /rɪk/ vt twist (part of the body) slightly

rick² n large pile of dried grass

rick·ets /'rɪkɪts/ n [U] children's disease in which bones become soft and bent

rick·et·y /'rɪkɪti/ adj weak and likely to break

rick·shaw /'rɪkʃɔː/ n small East Asian carriage pulled by a man

ric·o·chet /'rɪkəʃeɪ/ n sudden change of direction by a bullet, stone, etc., when it hits a hard surface ♦ vi **-t-** or **-tt-** change direction in a ricochet

rid /rɪd/ v (**rid** or **ridded**, pres. p. **-dd-**) **rid of** phr vt 1 make free of 2 **get rid of:** a free oneself from b drive or throw away or destroy

rid·dance /'rɪdəns/ n **good riddance** (said when one is glad that someone or something has gone)

rid·dle¹ /'rɪdl/ n 1 difficult and amusing question 2 mystery

riddle² v **riddle with** phr vt make full of holes

ride /raɪd/ v **rode** /rəʊd/, **ridden** /'rɪdn/ 1 vi/t travel along on (a horse, etc., a bicycle, or a motorcycle) 2 vi travel on a bus 3 vt remain safe (and floating) through: *a ship riding a storm* 4 **let something ride** let something continue, taking no action 5 **ride high** have great success 6 **ride roughshod over** act in a hurtful way towards

rider n 1 person riding esp. a horse 2 statement added to esp. an official declaration or judgment

ride out phr vt come safely through (bad weather, trouble)

ride up phr vi (of clothing) move upwards or out of place

ride² n 1 journey on an animal, in a vehicle, etc. 2 **take someone for a ride** deceive someone

ridge /rɪdʒ/ n long narrow raised part, where 2 slopes meet

rid·i·cule /'rɪdɪkjuːl/ n [U] unkind laughter ♦ vt laugh unkindly at

ri·dic·u·lous /rɪ'dɪkjʊləs/ adj silly **~ly** adv

rife /raɪf/ adj (of a bad thing) widespread; common

rif·fle /'rɪfl/ v **riffle through** phr vt turn over (papers, etc.) quickly, searching

riff-raff /'rɪfræf/ n [U] derog worthless badly-behaved people

ri·fle¹ /'raɪfl/ n gun with a long barrel, fired from the shoulder

rifle² vt search through and steal from

rift n crack: (fig.) *a rift in their friendship*

rig¹ /rɪg/ vt **-gg-** fit (a ship) with sails, ropes, etc.

rig out phr vt dress in special or funny clothes

rig up phr vt make quickly and roughly

rig² n 1 way a ship's sails and MASTs are arranged 2 apparatus: *a drilling rig* **~ging** n [U] all the ropes, etc., holding up a ship's sails

rig³ vt **-gg-** arrange dishonestly for one's own advantage

right¹ /raɪt/ adj 1 a on the side of the body away from the heart b in the direction of one's right side: *the right bank of the river* 2 just; proper; morally good 3 correct 4 in a proper or healthy state: *to put the trouble right | Are you all right?* 5 **right enough** as was expected

right² n 1 [U] RIGHT¹ (1) side or direction 2 [U] what is RIGHT¹ (2) 3 [C;U] morally just or legal claim: *You've no right to* (= should not) *say that.* 4 [U] political parties that favour less change and less state control **5 in one's own right** because of a personal claim that does not depend on anyone else **6 in the right** not wrong or deserving blame ~**ness** n [U] *the rightness of their claim* — see also RIGHTS

right³ adv **1** towards the RIGHT² (1,2) **2** correctly **3** exactly: *right in the middle* **4** completely: *Go right back to the beginning!* **5** yes; I will: *'See you tomorrow.' 'Right!'* — see also ALL RIGHT **6** *BrE sl or old use* very **7 right away** at once

right⁴ vt put back to a correct position or condition

right an·gle /'· ,··/ n angle of 90 degrees

right·eous /'raɪtʃəs/ adj **1** morally good **2** having just cause: *righteous indignation* ~**ly** adv ~**ness** n [U]

right·ful /'raɪtfəl/ adj according to a just or legal claim ~**ly** adv

right-hand /,· '·◄/ adj on the right side ~**ed** adj using the right hand for most actions ~**er** n right-handed person

right-hand man /,·· '·/ n most useful and valuable helper

right·ly /'raɪtli/ adv **1** correctly **2** justly

right-mind·ed /,· '··◄/ adj having the right opinions, principles, etc.

right of way /,·· '·/ n rights of way **1** [U] right of a vehicle to go first **2** [C] (right to follow) a path across private land

rights /raɪts/ n [P] **1** political, social, etc., advantages to which someone has a just claim, morally or in law **2 by rights** in justice; if things were done properly **3 set/put someone/something to rights** make someone/something just, healthy, etc. **4 the rights and wrongs of** the true facts of **5 within one's rights** not going beyond one's just claims

right wing /,· '·◄/ n [U] of a political party of the RIGHT(4)

ri·gid /'rɪdʒɪd/ adj **1** stiff **2** not easy to change ~**ly** adv ~**ity** /rɪ'dʒɪdəti/ n [U]

rig·ma·role /'rɪgmərəʊl/ n [S;U] long confused story or set of actions

rig·or mor·tis /,rɪgə 'mɔːtɪs, ,raɪgɔː-‖ ,rɪgər 'mɔːr-/ n [U] stiffening of the muscles after death

rig·or·ous /'rɪgərəs/ adj **1** careful and exact **2** severe ~**ly** adv

rig·our BrE ‖ -**or** AmE /'rɪgər/ n [U] **1** severity **2** fml exactness and clear thinking

rig-out /'· ·/n infml set of clothes

rile /raɪl/ vt infml annoy

Ri·ley /'raɪli/ n see LIFE OF RILEY

rim /rɪm/ n edge. esp. of a round object ♦ vt -**mm**- be round the edge of

rime /raɪm/ n [U] lit white FROST

rind /raɪnd/ n [C;U] thick outer covering of certain fruits, or of cheese or BACON

ring¹ /rɪŋ/ n **1** (metal) circle worn on the finger **2** circular band: *smoke rings* **3** circular mark or arrangement: *a ring of troops round the building* **4** enclosed space where things are shown, performances take place, or esp. people BOX or WRESTLE **5** group of people who work together, esp. dishonestly: *a drug ring* **6 make/run rings round** do things much better and faster than ♦ vt form or put a ring round

ring² v **rang** /ræŋ/, **rung** /rʌŋ/ **1** vi/t cause (a bell) to sound **2** vi (of a bell, telephone, etc.) sound **3** vi/t esp. BrE telephone **4** vi be filled with sound **5 ring a bell** remind one of something **6 ring the changes** introduce variety in **7 ring true/false** sound true/untrue ♦ n **1** [C] (making) a bell-like sound **2** [S] certain quality: *It had a ring of truth.* (= sounded true) **3** [S] esp. BrE telephone call

ring off phr vi BrE end a telephone conversation

ring out phr vi (of a voice, bell, etc.) sound loudly and clearly

ring up phr vt **1** record (money paid) on a CASH REGISTER **2** RING²(3)

ring·er /'rɪŋər/n see DEAD RINGER

ring·lead·er /'rɪŋ,liːdər/ n person who leads others to do wrong

ring·let /'rɪŋlɪt/ n long hanging curl of hair

ring·mas·ter /'rɪŋ,mɑːstər‖-,mæ-/ n person who directs CIRCUS performances

ring road /'· ·/ n BrE road that goes round a town

ring·side /'rɪŋsaɪd/ adj, adv, n (at) the edge of a RING¹(4)

ring·worm /'rɪŋwɜːm‖-wɜːrm/ n [U] disease causing red rings on the skin

rink /rɪŋk/ n specially prepared surface for skating (SKATE)

rinse /rɪns/ vt wash in clean water, so as to get rid of soap, dirt. etc. ♦ n **1** [C] act of rinsing **2** [C;U] liquid hair colouring

ri·ot /'raɪət/ n **1** [C] noisy violent crowd behaviour **2** [S] plentiful show: *The garden is a riot of colour.* **3** [S] infml very funny and successful occasion or person **4 run riot a** become violent and uncontrollable **b** (of a plant) grow too thick and tall ♦ vi take part in a riot ~**er** n ~**ous** adj wild and disorderly

riot act /'·· ·/ n **read the riot act** warn (esp. a child) to behave well

rip /rɪp/ vi/t -**pp**- **1** tear quickly and violently **2 let something rip** infml remove control and let things develop in their own way ♦ n long tear

rip off phr vt infml **1** charge too much **2** esp. AmE steal **rip-off** /'··/ n

RIP /ˌɑːr eɪ 'piː/ abbrev. for: rest in peace (= words written on a gravestone)

rip-cord /'rɪpkɔːd‖-kɔːrd/ n cord pulled to open a PARACHUTE

ripe /raɪp/ adj **1** (fully grown and) ready to be eaten: a ripe apple **2** ready; suitable: land ripe for industrial development **3** grown-up and experienced: (humor.) He's reached the ripe old age of 20. ~**ness** n [U]

rip-en /'raɪpən/ vi/t make or become ripe

ri-poste /rɪ'pɒst, rɪ'pəʊst‖rɪ'pəʊst/ vi, n (make) a quick clever (unfriendly) reply

rip-ple /'rɪpəl/ vi/t **1** move in small waves **2** make a sound like gently running water ♦ n [C] **1** very small wave or gentle waving movement **2** sound of or like gently running water

rip-roar-ing /ˌ·'···/ adj noisy and exciting

rise¹ /raɪz/ vi rose /rəʊz/, risen /'rɪzən/ **1** go up; get higher: (fig.)My spirits rose. (= I became happier) **2** (of the sun, etc.) come above the horizon **3** (of land) slope upward **4** stand up **5** fml get out of bed **6** (of wind) get stronger **7** REBEL¹: They rose up against their leaders. **8** come back to life after being dead **9** (esp. of a river) begin **10** move up in rank **11** rise to the occasion show that one can deal with a difficult matter **rising** n UPRISING **rising** prep nearly (the stated age)

rise² n **1** [C] increase **2** [U] act of growing greater or more powerful **3** [C] BrE wage increase **4** [C] upward slope **5** give rise to cause

ris-i-ble /'rɪzəbəl/ adj fml deserving to be laughed at

rising damp /ˌ·· '·/ n [U] water that comes up into the walls of a building

risk /rɪsk/ n [C;U] **1** chance that something bad may happen **2** (in insurance) (a person or thing that is) a danger **3** at risk in danger **4** at one's own risk agreeing to bear any loss or danger **5** run/take a risk do dangerous things ♦ vt **1** place in danger **2** take the chance of: Are you willing to risk failure? ~**y** adj dangerous

ri-sot-to /rɪ'zɒtəʊ‖-sɔː-/ n [C;U] rice dish with chicken, vegetables, etc.

ris-qué /'rɪskeɪ‖rɪ'skeɪ/ adj (of a joke, etc.) slightly rude

ris-sole /'rɪsəʊl/ n small round flat mass of cut-up meat

rite /raɪt/ n ceremonial (religious) act with a fixed pattern

rit-u-al /'rɪtʃuəl/ n [C;U] (ceremonial) act or acts always repeated in the same form ♦ adj done as a rite: ritual murder

ri-val /'raɪvəl/ n person with whom one competes ♦ adj competing ♦ vt -ll- BrE ‖ -l- AmE be as good as ~**ry** n [C;U] competition

riv-en /'rɪvən/ adj fml split violently apart

riv-er /'rɪvəʳ/ n wide natural stream of water

riv-et /'rɪvɪt/ n metal pin used for fastening heavy metal plates together ♦ vt **1** fasten with rivets **2** attract and hold (someone's attention) strongly ~**ing** adj very interesting

ri-vi-e-ra /ˌrɪvi'eərə/ n stretch of coast where people take holidays

riv-u-let /'rɪvjʊlɪt/ n lit very small stream

road /rəʊd/ n **1** smooth prepared track for wheeled vehicles: (fig.) We're on the road to (= on the way to) success. **2** on the road travelling

road-block /'rəʊdblɒk‖-blɑːk/ n something placed across a road to stop traffic

road hog /'· ·/ n fast selfish careless driver

road tax /'· ·/ n [C;U] tax vehicle owners must pay

road-way /'rəʊdweɪ/ n middle part of a road, where vehicles drive

road works /'rəʊdwɜːks‖-ɜːr-/ n [P] road repairing

road-wor-thy /'rəʊd,wɜːθi‖-ɜːr-/ adj (of a vehicle) in safe condition to drive -**thiness** n [U]

roam /rəʊm/ vi/t wander around with no clear purpose

roan /rəʊn/ n, adj (horse) of mixed colour

roar /rɔːʳ/ n deep loud continuing sound: roars of laughter ♦ v **1** vi give a roar **2** vt say forcefully **3** vi laugh loudly ~**ing** adj, adv **1** very great: We're doing a roaring trade. (= doing very good business) **2** very: roaring drunk

roast /rəʊst/ vt cook (esp. meat) in an OVEN or over a fire ♦ adj roasted ♦ n large piece of roasted meat

rob /rɒb‖rɑːb/ vt -bb- steal something from ~**ber** n ~**bery** n [C;U] (example of) the crime of robbing

robe /rəʊb/ n long flowing garment

rob-in /'rɒbən‖'rɑː-/ n small brown bird with a red front — see also ROUND ROBIN

ro-bot /'rəʊbɒt‖-bɑːt, -bət/ n machine that can do some of the work of a human being ~**ics** /rəʊ'bɒtɪks‖-'bɑː-/ n [U] study of the making and use of robots

ro-bust /rə'bʌst, 'rəʊbʌst/ adj strong (and healthy) ~**ly** adv ~**ness** n[U]

rock¹ /rɒk‖rɑːk/ n **1** [C;U] stone forming part of the Earth's surface **2** [C] large piece of stone **3** [C] AmE a stone **4** [U] (in Britain) hard sticky kind of sweet made in long round bars 5 [C] *sl. esp. AmE* a diamond 6 [U] ROCK 'N' ROLL 7 **on the rocks: a** (of a marriage) likely to fail soon **b** (of a drink) with ice but no water

rock² *v* 1 *vi/t* move regularly backwards and forwards or from side to side 2 *vt* shock greatly 3 **rock the boat** spoil the existing good situation

rock and roll /,·· '·/ *n* [U] ROCK 'N' ROLL

rock bot·tom /,· '··◄/ *n* [U] the lowest point

rock cake /'· ·/ *n* small hard cake

rock·er /'rokəʳ‖'rɑː-/ *n* 1 curved piece of wood on which something rocks 2 *esp. AmE* ROCKING CHAIR 3 **off one's rocker** *infml* mad

rock·e·ry /'rokəri‖'rɑː-/ *n* (part of) a garden laid out with rocks and small plants

rock·et /'rokət‖'rɑː-/ *n* 1 tube-shaped object driven through the air by burning gases, used for travelling into space, or as a MISSILE or FIREWORK 2 **give someone/get a rocket** *BrE infml* scold someone/be scolded severely ◆ *vi* rise quickly and suddenly

rock·ing chair /'·· ·/ *n* chair with rockers

rocking horse /'·· ·/ *n* wooden horse with rockers, for a child to ride on

rock 'n' roll /,rok ən 'rəul‖,rɑːk-/ *n* [U] popular modern music with a strong beat

rock·y /'roki‖'rɑːki/ *adj* 1 full of rocks 2 *infml* unsteady; not firm

ro·co·co /rə'kəukəu/ *adj* with much curling decoration

rod /rod‖rɑːd/ *n* long thin stiff pole or bar

rode /rəud/ *past t. of* RIDE

ro·dent /'rəudənt/ *n* small plant-eating animal with long front teeth, such as a mouse, rat, or rabbit

ro·de·o /rəu'deɪəu, 'rəudi-əu/ *n* **-os** (in America) public entertainment with horse riding, cattle catching, etc.

roe /rəu/ *n* [C;U] mass of fish eggs, often eaten

roe deer /'·· ·/ *n* small European and Asian deer

ro·ger /'rodʒəʳ‖'rɑː-/ *interj* (used in radio and signalling to say one has understood)

rogue /rəug/ *n* dishonest person ◆ *adj* 1 (of a wild animal) bad-tempered and dangerous 2 not following the usual or accepted standards **roguish** *adj* playful and fond of playing tricks

rogues' gal·ler·y /,· '···/ *n* collection of (pictures of) criminal or unpleasant people

role /rəul/ *n* 1 character played by an actor 2 part someone takes in an activity

roll¹ /rəul/ *v* 1 *vi/t* turn over and over or from side to side: *The ball rolled into the hole.* 2 *vt* form into esp. a tube by curling round and round 3 *vi* move steadily and smoothly (as if) on wheels 4 *vi* swing from side to side on the sea 5 *vt* flatten with a ROLLER (1) or ROLLING PIN 6 *vi* make a long deep sound 7 *vt* cause (esp. film cameras) to begin working 8 *vt* cause (the eyes) to move round and round 9 **roll in the aisles** (esp. of people at the theatre) laugh uncontrollably 10 **roll one's r's** pronounce the sound /r/ with the tongue beating rapidly against the roof of the mouth 11 **roll one's own** *BrE infml* make one's own cigarettes instead of buying them ~**ing** *adj* 1 (of land) with long gentle slopes 2 **rolling in it** *infml* extremely rich

roll in *phr vi* arrive in large quantities

roll on *phr vi* come soon; hurry up: *Roll on, summer!*

roll out *phr vt* UNROLL

roll up *phr vi* 1 arrive 2 (used esp. asking people to see a show at a CIRCUS, etc.) come in

roll² *n* 1 act of rolling 2 rolled tube 3 small loaf for one person: *a cheese roll* (= one cut and filled with cheese) 4 long deep sound (as if) of a lot of quick strokes: *a roll of drums* 5 official list of names — see also TOILET ROLL

roll call /'· ·/ *n* calling a list of names to see who is there

roll·er /'rəuləʳ/ *n* 1 tube-shaped part for pressing, smoothing, shaping, etc., 2 long heavy wave on the coast

roller coast·er /'·· ,··/ *n* small railway with sharp slopes and curves, found in amusement parks

roller skate /'·· ·/ *n* arrangement of 4 small wheels on a shoe, for moving along on **roller-skate** *vi*

rol·lick·ing /'rolikiŋ‖'rɑː-/ *adj* noisy and merry ◆ *n BrE infml* act of expressing angry disapproval of someone

rolling pin /'·· ·/ *n* tube-shaped piece of wood, etc., for flattening pastry

rolling stock /'·· ·/ *n* [U] carriages, engines, etc., of a railway

rolling stone /,·· '·/ *n* person with no fixed home or responsibilities

ro·ly-po·ly /,rəuli 'pəuli◄/ *adj infml* (of a person) fat and round

ROM /rom‖rɑːm/ *n* read-only memory; computer memory holding information that is continuously needed by the computer

Roman *n, adj* (citizen) of Rome, esp. ancient Rome

Ro·man Cath·o·lic /,·· '····/ n, adj (member) of the branch of the Christian religion led by the POPE ~**ism** /-lɪ̍sɪzəm/ n [U]

ro·mance /rəʊˈmæns, rə-/ n 1 [C] love affair 2 [U] ROMANTIC (2) quality 3 [C] story of love, adventure, etc.

Ro·man nu·me·ral /,·· '····/ n any of the signs (such as I, II, V, X, L) used for numbers in ancient Rome and sometimes now

ro·man·tic /rəʊˈmæntɪk, rə-/ adj 1 showing warm feelings of love 2 of or suggesting love, adventure, strange happenings, etc. 3 highly imaginative; not practical: *romantic notions* 4 showing romanticism ♦ n romantic person ~**ally** /-kli/ adv ~**ism** /-tɪsɪzəm/ n [U] admiration of feeling rather than thought in art and literature ~**ize** vt make (something) seem more interesting or ROMANTIC (2) than it really is

Ro·ma·ny /ˈrəʊməni/ˈrɑː-/ n 1 [C] GIPSY 2 [U] gipsies' language

Ro·me·o /ˈrəʊmiəʊ/ n -os romantic male lover

romp /rɒmp‖rɑːmp/ vi play noisily and roughly ♦ n 1 occasion of romping 2 infml piece of amusing entertainment with plenty of action

  romp through phr vt succeed in, quickly and easily

romp·ers /ˈrɒmpəz‖ˈrɑːmpərz/ n [P] one-piece garment for babies

roof /ruːf/ n 1 top covering of a building, vehicle, etc. 2 upper part of the inside (of the mouth) ♦ vt put or be a roof on ~**ing** n [U] roof material

roof rack /'· ·/ n metal frame on top of a car, for carrying things

roof·top /ˈruːftɒp‖-tɑːp/ vt 1 roof 2 **from the rooftops** loudly, so that everyone can hear

rook[1] /rʊk/ n large black bird, like a CROW

rook[2] vt sl cheat

rook·er·y /ˈrʊkəri/ n group of rooks' nests

rook·ie /ˈrʊki/ n esp. AmE new soldier or policeman

room /ruːm, rʊm/ n 1 [C] division of a building, with its own floor, walls, and CEILING 2 [U] (enough) space 3 [U] need or possibility for something to happen: *room for improvement* ♦ vi AmE have lodgings; have a room or rooms ~**y** adj with plenty of space inside

room ser·vice /'· ,··/ n [U] hotel service providing food, etc., in people's rooms

roost /ruːst/ n 1 place where a bird sleeps 2 **rule the roost** be the leader ♦ vi 1 (of a bird) sit and sleep 2 **come home to roost** (of a bad action) have a

bad effect on the doer, esp. after a period of time

roost·er /ˈruːstəʳ/ n esp. AmE for COCK (1)

root[1] /ruːt/ n 1 part of a plant that goes down into the soil for food 2 part of a tooth, hair, etc., that holds it to the body 3 cause; beginning; origin 4 (in grammar) base part of a word to which other parts can be added 5 a number that when multiplied by itself a stated number of times gives another stated number 6 **root and branch** (of something bad to be got rid of) thoroughly 7 **take root** (of plants or ideas) become established and begin to grow ~**less** adj without a home **roots** n [P] 1 (one's connection with) one's place of origin 2 **pull up one's roots** move to a new place from one's settled home 3 **put down (new) roots** establish a (new) place, by making friends, etc. — see also GRASS ROOTS

root[2] v 1 vi/t (cause to) form roots: (fig.) *rooted to the spot* (= unable to move) *deeply rooted* (= firmly fixed) 2 vi search by turning things over

  root for phr vt support strongly

  root out phr vt get rid of completely

rope[1] /rəʊp/ n 1 [C;U] (piece of) strong thick cord 2 [C] fat twisted string (of the stated jewels) 3 [the + S] hanging as a punishment 4 **give someone (plenty of) rope** allow someone (plenty of) freedom to act

rope[2] vt tie with a rope **ropes** n [P] rules, customs, and ways of operating

  rope in phr vt infml persuade or force to join an activity

  rope off phr vt separate or enclose with ropes

rop·y, ropey /ˈrəʊpi/ adj BrE infml of bad quality or condition

ro·sa·ry /ˈrəʊzəri/ n string of BEADs used by Roman Catholics for counting prayers

rose[1] /rəʊz/ past t. of RISE

rose[2] n 1 (brightly coloured sweet-smelling flower of) a prickly-stemmed bush 2 pale to dark pink colour 3 **be not all roses** infml (of a job, situation, etc.) include some unpleasant things — see also BED OF ROSES

ro·sé /ˈrəʊzeɪ‖rəʊˈzeɪ/ n [U] light pink wine

ro·se·ate /ˈrəʊziɪt/ adj lit pink

rose-col·oured /'· ,··/also **rose-tinted** — adj **look at/see/view the world through rose-coloured spectacles/glasses** see the world, life, etc., as better and more pleasant than they really are

ro·sette /rəʊˈzet/ n flat flower-like arrangement of cloth, worn as a sign of something

rose win·dow /'· ,··/ n circular decorative church window

ros·in /'rɒzən‖'rɑ:-/ n [U] substance rubbed on the BOWS² (2)of stringed musical instruments

ros·ter /'rɒstər‖'rɑ:-/ n list of people's names and duties

ros·trum /'rɒstrəm‖'rɑ:-/ n **-trums** or **-tra** /-trə/ raised place for a public performer

ros·y /'rəʊzi/ adj **1** (esp. of skin) pink **2** (esp. of future) giving hope

rot /rɒt‖rɑ:t/ vi/t **-tt-** decay ♦ n [U] **1** decay **2** process of getting worse or going wrong **3** infml foolish nonsense

ro·ta /'rəʊtə/ n list of things to be done by different people taking turns

ro·ta·ry /'rəʊtəri/ adj rotating (ROTATE (1))

ro·tate /rəʊ'teɪt‖'rəʊteɪt/ vi/t **1** turn round a fixed point **2** (cause to) take turns or come round regularly **rota-tion** /-'teɪʃən/ n **1** [U] action of rotating **2** [C] one complete turn **3 in rotation** taking regular turns

rote /rəʊt/ n [U] fml repeated study using memory rather than understanding

rot·gut /'rɒtɡʌt‖'rɑ:t-/ n [U] infml strong low-quality alcoholic drink

ro·tor /'rəʊtər/ n **1** rotating part of a machine **2** set of HELICOPTER blades

rot·ten /'rɒtn‖'rɑ:tn/ adj **1** decayed; gone bad **2** infml nasty or unpleasant **3 feel rotten** feel ill, tired, or unhappy

ro·tund /rəʊ'tʌnd/ adj fml (of a person) fat and round

rou·ble /'ru:bəl/ n unit of money in the USSR

rouge /ru:ʒ/ n [U] red substance for colouring the cheeks

rough¹ /rʌf/ adj **1** having an uneven surface **2** stormy and violent: rough weather **3** lacking gentleness, good manners, or consideration: rough handling at the airport **4** (of food and living conditions) not delicate; simple **5** not detailed or exact **6** unfortunate and/or unfair **7** infml unwell **8 rough and ready** simple and without comfort ♦ adv **1** in uncomfortable conditions: sleeping rough **2 cut up rough** infml become angry **~ly** adv **1** in a rough manner **2** about; not exactly **~en** vi/t make or become rough **~ness** n [U]

rough² n [U] **1** areas of long grass on a GOLF course **2 in rough** in an incomplete or undetailed form **3 take the rough with the smooth** accept bad things as well as good things uncomplainingly

rough³ v **rough it** infml live simply and rather uncomfortably

  rough up phr vt infml attack roughly, usu. as a threat

rough·age /'rʌfɪdʒ/ n [U] coarse matter in food, which helps the bowels to work

rough·cast /'rʌfkɑ:st‖-kæst/ n [U] surface of little stones on the outside of a building

rough di·a·mond /,· '···/ n very kind person with rough manners

rough-hewn /,· '·◁/ adj (of wood or stone) roughly cut

rough pa·per /,· '···/ n [U] paper for making informal notes or drawings

rough·shod /'rʌfʃɒd‖-ʃɑ:d/ adv see ride roughshod over (RIDE¹)

rough stuff /'· ·/ n BrE violent behaviour

rou·lette /ru:'let/ n [U] game of chance played with a small ball and a spinning wheel — see also RUSSIAN ROULETTE

round¹ /raʊnd/ adj **1** circular **2** ball-shaped **3** (of parts of the body) fat and curved **4** (of a number) expressed to the nearest 10, 100, 1000, etc. **~ness** n [U]

round² adv **1** with a circular movement: The wheels went round. **2** surrounding a central point: Gather round. **3** to various places: travelling round **4** so as to face the other way: Turn it round. **5** everywhere or to everyone: Pass the drinks round. **6** to a particular place: We invited some friends round (= to our house) for drinks. **7 all the year round** during the whole year **8 round about** a little bit more or less than **9 the other/opposite way round** in the opposite order

round³ prep. **1** with a circular movement about: The Earth goes round the Sun. **2** surrounding: Sit around the table. **3** into all parts of: Look round the shop. **4** not going straight but changing direction: He went round the corner. **5** near (a place or amount): Do you live round here?

round⁴ n **1** number or set (of events): a continual round of parties **2** regular delivery journey: do one's rounds (= make one's usual visits) **3** number of esp. alcoholic drinks bought for everyone present: It's my round. (= I'm paying) **4 a** (in GOLF) complete game **b** (in boxing BOX²) period of fighting in a match **c** (in tennis, football, etc.) stage in a competition **d** one single shot from a gun **5** long burst: a round of applause **6** type of song for 3 or 4 voices, in which each sings the same tune, one starting a line after another has just finished **7** esp. BrE SAND-WICH made with two whole pieces of bread

round⁵ vt **1** go round: rounding the corner **2** make round: rounding his lips

round down *phr vt* reduce to a whole number

round off *phr vt* end suitably and satisfactorily

round on *phr vt* turn and attack

round up *phr vt* **1** gather together (scattered things) **2** increase (an exact figure) to the next highest whole number

round·a·bout /'raʊndəbaʊt/ *n BrE* **1** area of circular traffic flow where several roads meet **2** MERRY-GO-ROUND ♦ *adj* indirect

roun·ders /'raʊndəz‖-ərz/ *n* [U] children's game where a player hits the ball and then runs round a square area

round·ly /'raʊndli/ *adv fml* **1** completely **2** forcefully

round robin /ˌ·· ·ˈ··/ *n* letter signed by many people

round-ta·ble /ˌ·· ·ˈ··◂/ *adj* at which everyone can meet and talk equally

round-the-clock /ˌ· · ·ˈ·◂/ *adj* happening both day and night

round trip /ˌ· ·ˈ·◂/ *n* journey to a place and back again

round-up /'raʊndʌp/ *n* gathering together of scattered things, animals, or people

rouse /raʊz/ *vt fml* waken **2** make more active, interested, or excited
rousing *adj* that makes people excited

rous·ta·bout /'raʊstəbaʊt/ *n AmE* man who does heavy unskilled work

rout /raʊt/ *n* complete defeat ♦ *vt* defeat completely

route /ruːt‖ruːt, raʊt/ *n* way from one place to another — see also EN ROUTE ♦ *vt* send by a particular route

route march /'· ·/ *n* soldiers' long training march

rou·tine /ruː'tiːn/ *n* **1** [C;U] regular fixed way of doing things **2** [C] set of dance steps, songs, etc. ♦ *adj* **1** regular; not special **2** dull **~ly** *adv*

rove /raʊv/ *vi esp. lit* wander

roving com·mis·sion /ˌ··· ·ˈ··/ *n* job that takes one to many places

roving eye /ˌ·· ·ˈ·/ *n* [S] sexual interests that pass quickly from one person to another

row¹ /raʊ/ *n* **1** neat line of people or things **2 in a row** one after the other without a break

row² /raʊ/ *vi/t* move (a boat) through the water with OARs

row³ /raʊ/ *n* **1** [C] noisy quarrel **2** [S] noise ♦ *vi* quarrel (noisily)

row·dy /'raʊdi/ *adj* noisy and rough **-dily** *adv* **-diness** *n* [U] **~ism** *n* [U] rowdy behaviour

row house /'raʊ haʊs/ *n AmE for* TERRACED HOUSE

row·lock /'rɒlək‖'raʊ-: *not tech* 'raʊlɒk‖-lɑːk/ *n* fastener for an OAR on the side of a boat

roy·al /'rɔɪəl/ *adj* of a king or queen ♦ *n* member of the royal family **~ly** *adv* splendidly

royal blue /ˌ·· ·ˈ·/ *adj* of a purplish-blue colour

roy·al·ist /'rɔɪəlɪst/ *n* supporter of rule by kings and queens

roy·al·ty /'rɔɪəlti/ *n* **1** [U] people of the royal family **2** [C] payment made to the writer of a book, piece of music, etc., out of the money from its sales

rpm /ˌɑː piː 'em‖ˌɑːr-/ *abbrev. for:* revolutions per minute

RSVP /ˌɑːr es viː 'piː/ please reply (written on invitations)

rub /rʌb/ *vi/t* **-bb-** **1** press against (something or each other) with a repeated up-and-down or round-and-round movement **2 rub it in** *infml* keep talking about something that another person wants to forget **3 rub salt in the wound** make someone's suffering even worse **4 rub shoulders with** *infml* meet socially and treat as equals **5 rub someone up the wrong way** *infml* annoy ♦ *n* **1** [C] act of rubbing **2** [*the* + S] cause of difficulty: *There's the rub.* **~bing** *n* copy made by rubbing paper laid over the top

rub down *phr vt* **1** dry by rubbing **2** make smooth by rubbing

rub in *phr vt* make (liquid) go into a surface by rubbing

rub off *phr vi* come off a surface (onto another) by rubbing: (fig.) *I hope some of her good qualities rub off on you.*

rub out *phr vt BrE* remove with a RUBBER¹ (2)

rub·ber¹ /'rʌbər/ *n* **1** [U] elastic substance used for keeping out water, making tyres, etc. **2** [C] *BrE* piece of this for removing pencil marks **~y** *adj*

rubber² *n* competition, esp. in cards, which usu. consists of an odd number of games

rubber band /ˌ·· ·ˈ·/ *n* thin circle of rubber for fastening things together

rubber plant /'·· ·/ *n* decorative large-leaved house plant

rubber-stamp /ˌ·· ·ˈ·/ *n* piece of rubber with raised letters or figures, for printing ♦ *vt* approve or support (a decision) officially, without really thinking about it

rub·bish /'rʌbɪʃ/ *n* [U] *BrE* **1** waste material to be thrown away **2** nonsense

rub·ble /'rʌbəl/ *n* [U] broken stone and bricks, esp. from a destroyed building

ru·bi·cund /'ruːbɪkənd/ *adj fml* fat, red, and healthy-looking

ru·ble /'ruːbəl/ *n* ROUBLE

ru·bric /'ru:brɪk/ n fml set of printed instructions

ru·by /'ru:bi/ n deep red precious stone

ruck·sack /'rʌksæk/ n large bag carried on the back, esp. by walkers, etc.

ruck·us /'rʌkəs/ n AmE for RUMPUS

ruc·tions /'rʌkʃənz/ n [P] infml noisy complaints and anger

rud·der /'rʌdəʳ/ n blade at the back of a boat or aircraft to control its direction

rud·dy /'rʌdi/ adj 1 (of the face) pink and healthy-looking 2 lit red 3 BrE infml (used for adding force to an expression)

rude /ru:d/ adj 1 not polite; bad-mannered 2 concerned with sex: a rude joke 3 sudden and violent: a rude shock 4 old use roughly made ~**ly** adv ~**ness** n [U]

ru·di·men·ta·ry /ˌru:dɪ'mentəri/ adj 1 (of facts, knowledge, etc.) at the simplest level 2 small and not fully usable: rudimentary wings

ru·di·ments /'ru:dɪmənts/ n [the + P] simplest parts of a subject, learnt first

rue /ru:/ vt be very sorry about ~**ful** adj feeling or showing that one is sorry about something

ruff /rʌf/ n stiff wheel-shaped white collar

ruf·fi·an /'rʌfiən/ n unpleasant violent man

ruf·fle /'rʌfəl/ vt 1 make uneven 2 trouble; upset

rug /rʌg/ n 1 thick floor mat 2 warm woollen covering to wrap round oneself

rug·by /'rʌgbi/ n [U] type of football played with an egg-shaped ball which can be handled

rug·ged /'rʌgɪd/ adj large, rough, and strong-looking ~**ly** adv ~**ness** n [U]

rug·ger /'rʌgəʳ/ n [U] infml rugby

ru·in /'ru:ɪn/ n 1 [U] destruction 2 [C] also **ruins** pl. remains of a building that has fallen down or been (partly) destroyed ♦ vt 1 spoil 2 cause total loss of money to ~**ed** adj (of a building) partly or wholly destroyed ~**ous** adj causing destruction or total loss of money

ru·in·a·tion /ˌru:ɪ'neɪʃən/ n [U] (cause of) being ruined

rule[1] /ru:l/ n 1 [C] something that tells you what you must do: the rules of the game 2 [U] period or way of ruling: under foreign rule 3 [C] RULER (2) 4 **as a rule** usually **ruling** n official decision

rule[2] v 1 vi/t be in charge of (a country, people, etc.) 2 vi give an official decision 3 vt draw (a line) with a ruler

rule out phr vt 1 remove from consideration 2 make impossible

rule of thumb /ˌ· · '·/ n [C] quick inexact way of calculating or judging

rul·er /'ru:ləʳ/ n 1 person who rules 2 narrow flat rod for measuring or drawing straight lines

rum[1] /rʌm/ n [U] strong alcoholic drink made from sugar

rum[2] adj -mm- old-fash infml strange

rum·ba /'rʌmbə/ n lively Latin American dance

rum·ble /'rʌmbəl/ vi, n [S] (make) a deep continuous rolling sound

rumble[2] vt BrE infml not be deceived by

rum·bus·tious /rʌm'bʌstʃəs/ adj noisy, cheerful, and full of life

ru·mi·nant /'ru:mɪnənt/ n, adj (animal) that RUMINATES (2)

ru·mi·nate /'ru:mɪneɪt/ vi 1 think deeply 2 (of an animal) bring food back from the stomach and CHEW it again ~**native** /-nətɪv‖-neɪ-/ adj seeming thoughtful

rum·mage /'rʌmɪdʒ/ vi turn things over untidily in searching

rum·my /'rʌmi/ n [U] simple card game

ru·mour BrE ‖ -**mor** AmE /'ru:məʳ/ n [C;U] (piece of) information, perhaps untrue, spread from person to person ~**ed** adj reported unofficially

rump /rʌmp/ n part of an animal above the back legs: rump steak

rum·ple /'rʌmpəl/ vt make untidy; disarrange

rum·pus /'rʌmpəs/ n [S] noisy angry argument or disagreement

run[1] /rʌn/ v ran /ræn/, run, pres. p. -nn- 1 vi (of people and animals) move faster than a walk 2 vi take part in (a race) by running 3 vi/t (cause to) move quickly: The car ran into a tree. 4 vi/t (cause to) work: This machine runs on/by electricity. 5 vi (of a public vehicle) travel as arranged 6 vt control (an organization or system) 7 vi go; pass: The road runs south. 8 vi continue in operation, performance, etc.: The play ran for 2 years in London. 9 vi/t (cause liquid) to flow: run a bath‖ running water 10 vi pour out liquid: The baby's nose is running. 11 vi (melt and) spread by the action of heat or water 12 become: Supplies are running low. 13 vi esp. AmE try to get elected 14 vt print in a newspaper 15 vt bring into a country illegally and secretly 16 vi esp. AmE for LADDER 17 vt take (someone or something) to somewhere in a vehicle: I'll run you home. 18 **run for it** escape by running 19 **run short: a** use almost all one has and not have enough left **b** become less than enough

run across *phr vt* meet or find by chance

run after *phr vt* **1** chase **2** try to gain the attention and company of

run along *phr vi* go away

run away *phr vi* go away (as if) to escape

run away/off with *phr vt* **1** gain control of: *Don't let your temper run away with you.* **2** go away with (a lover) **3** steal

run down *phr v* **1** *vt* knock down and hurt with a vehicle **2** *vt* chase and catch **3** *vi* (esp. of a clock or BATTERY) lose power and stop working: (fig.) *The coal industry is being run down.* **4** *vt* say unfair things about

run into *phr vt* **1** meet by chance **2** cause (a vehicle) to meet (something) with force

run off *phr vt* print (copies)

run out *phr vi* **1** come to an end, so there is none left **2** have none left: *We've run out of petrol.*

run over *phr v* **1** *vt* knock down and drive over **2** *vi* overflow

run through *phr vt* **1** repeat for practice **2** read or examine quickly **3** push one's sword right through

run to *phr vt* be or have enough to pay for

run up *phr vt* **1** raise (a flag) **2** make quickly, esp. by sewing **3** cause oneself to have (bills or debts)

run up against *phr vt* be faced with (a difficulty)

run² *n* **1** [C] act of running **2** [C] ship or train journey **3** [S] continuous set of similar events, performances, etc.: *a run of bad luck* | *The play had a run of 3 months.* **4** [S] **a** eager demand to buy: *a big run on ice cream* **b** general desire to sell money or take one's money out: *a run on the pound* **5** [S] freedom to use: *He gave me the run of his library.* **6** [C] animal enclosure: *a chicken run* **7** [C] point won in cricket **8** [C] sloping course: *a ski run* **9** [C] *AmE for* LADDER (2) **10 a (good) run for one's money: a** plenty of opposition in a competition **b** good results for money spent or effort made **11 in the long run** after a long period; in the end **12 on the run** trying to escape **13 the common/ordinary run (of)** the usual sort (of)

run-a-bout /'·· ,·/ *n* small light car

run-a-round /'· ,·/ *n* [*the* + S] *sl* delaying or deceiving treatment

run-a-way /'rʌnəwei/ *adj* **1** out of control: *runaway prices* **2** having escaped by running: *a runaway child*

run-down /'·· ·/ *n* detailed report

run-down /,·· '·◂/ *adj* **1** tired, weak, and ill **2** in bad condition

rune /ruːn/ *n* letter in an alphabet formerly used in Northern Europe
runic *adj*

rung¹ /rʌŋ/ *past p. of* RING²

rung² *n* cross-bar in a ladder or on a chair

run-in /'·· ·/ *n infml* quarrel or disagreement, esp. with the police

run-nel /'rʌnl/ *n esp. lit* small stream

run-ner /'rʌnəʳ/ *n* **1** person or animal that runs **2** SMUGGLER: *a gunrunner* **3** thin blade on which something slides on ice or snow **4** stem with which a plant spreads itself along the ground

runner bean /,·· '·/ *n* bean with long eatable seed container

runner-up /,·· '·/ *n* **runners-up** one that comes second in a race, etc.

run-ning¹ /'rʌnɪŋ/ *n* **1** act or sport of running **2 in/out of the running** with some/no hope of winning **3 make the running** set the speed at which something develops

running² *adj* **1** (of water) flowing **2** continuous: *a running battle* | *a running commentary* **3** (of money) spent or needed to keep something working: *running costs* **4 in running order** (of a machine) working properly **5 take a running jump: a** a run to a point where one starts a jump **b** *infml* Go away and don't annoy me! ♦ *adv* in a row: *I won 3 times running.*

running-mate /'·· ·/ *n* (in US politics) person with whom one is trying to get elected for a pair of political positions of greater and lesser importance

run-ny /'rʌni/ *adj* **1** in a more liquid form than usual **2** (of the nose or eyes) producing liquid

run-of-the-mill /,·· · '·◂/ *adj* ordinary; dull

runt /rʌnt/ *n* **1** small badly-developed animal **2** *derog* small unpleasant person

run-through /'·· ·/ *n* act of repeating (something) for practice

run-up /'·· ·/ *n* [S] period leading up to an event

run-way /'rʌnwei/ *n* surface on which aircraft land and take off

ru-pee /ruː'piː/ *n* unit of money in India, Pakistan, etc.

rup-ture /'rʌptʃəʳ/ *n* **1** [C;U] *fml* sudden breaking **2** [C] HERNIA ♦ *v* **1** *vi/t fml* break suddenly **2** *vt* give (oneself) a HERNIA

ru-ral /'ruərəl/ *adj* of the country (not the town)

ruse /ruːz‖ruːs, ruːz/ *n* deceiving trick

rush¹ /rʌʃ/ *v* **1** *vi/t* go or take suddenly and very quickly **2** *vi* hurry **3** *vt* deal with (too) hastily **4** *vt* force (someone) to eat hastily **5** *vt* attack suddenly and all together **6 rush**

someone off his/her feet make someone hurry too much or work too hard
♦ n 1 [C] sudden rapid movement 2 [U] (need for) (too much) hurrying 3 [S] sudden demand 4 [U] period of great and hurried activity: *the Christmas rush*

rush² n grasslike water plant

rush-es /'rʌʃɪz/ n [P] (in film making) the first print of a film

rush hour /'· ·/ n busy period when most people are travelling to or from work

rusk /rʌsk/ n hard BISCUIT for babies

russet /'rʌsɪt/ adj esp. lit brownish red

Rus·sian rou·lette /ˌ·· ·'·/ n [U] dangerous game in which one fires a gun at one's head without knowing whether it is loaded

rust /rʌst/ n [U] 1 reddish brown surface formed on iron, steel, etc., that has been wet 2 the colour of this ♦ vi/t (cause to) become covered with rust ~y adj 1 covered with rust 2 infml lacking recent practice

rus·tic /'rʌstɪk/ adj typical of the country, esp. in being simple ♦ n usu. derog person from the country

rus·tle /'rʌsəl/ v 1 vi/t (cause to) make slight sounds like dry leaves moving 2 vt esp. AmE steal (cattle or horses) −tler n

　rustle up phr vt provide quickly

rut¹ /rʌt/ n 1 [C] deep narrow track left by a wheel 2 [S] dull fixed way of life ~ted adj having ruts

rut² n (season of) sexual excitement in deer ♦ vi -tt- (of an animal) be in a rut

ru·ta·ba·ga /ˌruːtə'beɪgə/ n AmE for SWEDE

ruth·less /'ruːθləs/ adj doing cruel things without pity ~ly adv ~ness n [U]

rye /raɪ/ n [U] grass plant with grain used esp. for flour

S

S, s /es/ the 19th letter of the English alphabet

S written abbrev. for: south(ern)

Sab·bath /'sæbəθ/ n [S] religious day of rest, esp. Saturday (for Jews) or (for Christians) Sunday

sab·bat·i·cal /sə'bætɪkəl/ n, adj period with pay when one is free to

leave one's ordinary job to travel and study

sa·ble /'seɪbəl/ n [C;U] (dark fur from) a small animal

sab·o·tage /'sæbətɑːʒ/ n [U] intentional damage carried out secretly ♦ vt perform sabotage against

sab·o·teur /ˌsæbə'tɜːʳ/ n person who practises sabotage

sa·bre BrE ‖ **saber** AmE /'seɪbəʳ/ n heavy military sword, usu. curved

sabre-rat·tling /'·· ˌ·/ n [U] talking about (military) power in a threatening way

sac·cha·rin /'sækərɪn/ n [U] very sweet-tasting chemical used instead of sugar

sach·et /'sæʃeɪ‖sæ'ʃeɪ/ n small plastic bag holding an amount of liquid, etc.

sack¹ /sæk/ n 1 [C] large simple bag of strong material 2 [the + S] BrE dismissal from a job 3 [the + S] infml esp. AmE bed 4 **hit the sack** infml go to bed ♦ vt BrE dismiss from a job ~ing n [U] sackcloth (1)

sack² vt destroy and rob (a defeated city) sack n [U]: *the sack of ancient Rome*

sack·cloth /'sæk-klɒθ‖-klɔːθ/ n [U] 1 also **sacking** /'sækɪŋ/ -- rough cloth for making sacks 2 **sackcloth and ashes** lit sign of sorrow for what one has done

sac·ra·ment /'sækrəmənt/ n important Christian ceremony, such as BAPTISM or marriage ~al /ˌsækrə'mentl◂/ adj

sa·cred /'seɪkrɪd/ adj 1 connected with religion 2 holy because connected with God or gods 3 that is solemn and must be respected ~ness n [U]

sacred cow /ˌ·· '·/ n derog thing so much accepted that not even honest doubts about it are allowed

sac·ri·fice /'sækrɪfaɪs/ n 1 (an offering) to gods, esp. of an animal killed ceremonially 2 loss or giving up of something of value ♦ v 1 vi/t offer (something or someone) as a SACRIFICE (1) 2 vt give up or lose, esp. for some good purpose −ficial /ˌsækrɪ'fɪʃəl◂/ adj

sac·ri·lege /'sækrɪlɪdʒ/ n [C;U] treating a holy place or thing without respect −**legious** /ˌsækrɪ'lɪdʒəs◂/ adj

sac·ro·sanct /'sækrəʊsæŋkt/ adj often derog or humor too holy or important to be treated disrespectfully or harmed

sad /sæd/ adj -dd- 1 unhappy 2 unsatisfactory ~ly adv −den vt make or become SAD (1) ~ness n [U]

sad·dle¹ /'sædl/ n 1 rider's seat on a horse, bicycle, etc. 2 piece of meat from the back of a sheep or deer 3 in

the saddle: a sitting on a SADDLE (1) **b** in control (of a job)

saddle[2] *vt* put a saddle on (a horse)

  saddle with *phr vt* give (someone) (an unpleasant or difficult duty, responsibility, etc.)

sa·dis·m /'seɪdɪzəm/ *n* [U] unnatural fondness for cruelty to others, (sometimes to gain sexual pleasure) **–dist** *n* **–distic** /sə'dɪstɪk/ *adj*

sa·do·mas·o·chis·m /ˌseɪdəʊ-'mæsəkɪzəm/*n* [U] the gaining of (sexual) pleasure from hurting oneself (or other people)

s.a.e. /ˌes eɪ 'iː/ *abbrev. for:* stamped addressed envelope

sa·fa·ri /sə'fɑːri/ *n* [C;U] journey to hunt or photograph animals, esp. in Africa

safari park /·'··· ·/ *n* park where wild animals are kept and can be looked at

safe[1] /seɪf/ *adj* **1** out of danger **2** not likely to cause danger or harm **3** (of a seat in Parliament) certain to be won in an election by a particular party **4 as safe as houses** very safe from risk **5 safe and sound** unharmed **6 on the safe side** being more careful than may be necessary **7 play it safe** take no risks **~ly** *adv* **~ness** *n* [U]

safe[2] *n* thick metal box with a lock, for keeping valuable things in

safe-con·duct /ˌ· '··/ *n* [C;U] official protection given to someone passing through an area

safe-de·pos·it box /·' ·ˌ· ·/ *n* small box for storing valuable objects, esp. in a bank

safe·guard /'seɪfgɑːd‖-gɑːrd/ *n* means of protection against something unwanted ♦ *vt* protect

safe·keep·ing /ˌseɪf'kiːpɪŋ/ *n* [U] protection from harm or loss

safe·ty /'seɪfti/ *n* [U] condition of being safe

safety pin /'·· ·/ *n* bent pin with a cover at one end, used for fastening things

safety valve /'·· ·/ *n* **1** means of getting rid of possibly dangerous forces (in a machine) **2** something that allows strong feelings to be expressed in a non-violent way

saf·fron /'sæfrən/ *n* [U] **1** deep orange substance got from a flower, used for giving colour and taste to food **2** orange-yellow colour

sag /sæg/ *vi* **-gg- 1** sink or bend downwards out of the usual position **2** become less active, happy, etc.: *My spirits sagged when I saw all the work I had to do.* **sag** *n* [S;U]

sa·ga /'sɑːgə/ *n* **1** old story, esp. about the Vikings **2** long story

sa·ga·cious /sə'geɪʃəs/ *adj fml* wise **~ly** *adv* **–city** /sə'gæsəti/ *n* [U]

sage /seɪdʒ/ *adj lit* wise, esp. from long experience ♦ *n* wise person, esp. an old man

sa·go /'seɪgəʊ/ *n* [U] white plant substance used for making sweet dishes

sahib /sɑːb‖'sɑːɪb/ *n* (used formerly in India as a title of respect for a European man)

said /sed/ *past t. and p. of* SAY ♦ *adj law* just mentioned

sail /seɪl/ *n* **1** piece of strong cloth that allows the wind to move a ship through the water **2** trip in a boat **3** wind-catching blade of a WINDMILL **4 set sail** begin a trip at sea **5 under sail** driven by sails and wind ♦ *v* **1** *vi/t* travel (across) by boat **2** *vt* direct or command (a boat) on water **3** *vi* be able to control a sailing boat: *Can you sail?* **4** *vi* begin a voyage **5** *vi* move smoothly or easily — see also **sail close to the wind** (CLOSE[2]) **~ing** *n* [U] sport of riding in or directing a small boat with sails

sail·or /'seɪlər/ *n* person who works on a ship

saint /seɪnt/ *n* **1** person officially recognised after death as especially holy by the Christian church **2** *infml* a very good and completely unselfish person **~ly** *adj* very holy

sake /seɪk/ *n* **1 for the sake of: a** in order to help, improve, or bring advantage to **b** for the purpose of **2 for Christ's/God's/goodness/pity('s)**

sake *infml* (used to give force to urgent request or sometimes an expression of annoyance): *For goodness sake, stop arguing!* | *For God's sake, what do you want from me!*

sa·la·cious /sə'leɪʃəs/ *adj fml* showing a strong (improper) interest in sex

sal·ad /'sæləd/ *n* [C;U] a mixture of usu. raw vegetables served cold, sometimes with other (stated) food added: *a cheese/chicken salad*

salad days /'··· ·/ *n* [P] one's time of youth and inexperience

sal·a·man·der /'sæləmændər/ *n* small animal like a LIZARD

sa·la·mi /sə'lɑːmi/ *n* [U] large salty SAUSAGE with a strong taste of garlic

sal·a·ry /'sæləri/ *n* [C;U] fixed regular pay each month for a job, esp. for workers of higher rank **–ried** *adj* receiving a salary (as opposed to wages)

sale /seɪl/ *n* **1** [C;U] (act of) selling **2** [C] special offering of goods at low prices **3 for sale** offered to be sold, esp. privately **4 on sale: a** offered to be sold, esp. in a shop **b** *AmE* at or in a SALE (2) **5 (on) sale or return** obtained from seller so that what is used can be paid for and the rest sent back without payment **salable** *adj* that can be sold

sales /seɪlz/ *adj* of or for selling: *a sales forecast*

sales-clerk /ˈseɪlzklɑːk‖-klɑːrk/ *n AmE for* SHOP ASSISTANT

sales-man /ˈseɪlzmən/ *n* **-men** /-mən/ a male salesperson

sales-man-ship /ˈseɪlzmənʃɪp/ *n* [U] skill in selling

sales-per-son /ˈseɪlzpɜːsən‖-pɜːr-/ *n* **-people 1** a sales representative **2** SHOP ASSISTANT, esp. a skilled one

sales rep-re-sen-ta-tive /ˈ· ··,··/ *n* person who goes from place to place, usu. within a particular area, selling and taking orders for their firm's goods

sales talk /ˈ· ·/ *n* [U] talking intended to persuade people to buy

sales-wo-man /ˈseɪlzˌwʊmən/ *n* **-women** /-ˌwɪmɪn/ a female salesperson

sa-li-ent /ˈseɪliənt/ *adj fml* most noticeable or important

sa-line /ˈseɪlaɪn/ *adj* containing salt

sa-li-va /səˈlaɪvə/ *n* [U] natural liquid produced in the mouth — **ry** *adj*

sal-low /ˈsæləʊ/ *adj* (of the skin) yellow and unhealthy-looking ~**ness** *n* [U]

sal-ly[1] /ˈsæli/ *n* **1** quick short attack **2** sharp, clever remark

sally[2] *v* **sally forth** *phr vi often humor* go out, esp. to meet a difficulty

salm-on /ˈsæmən/ *n* **salmon** or **salmons** [C;U] large pink-fleshed fish highly valued as food

sal-mo-nel-la /ˌsælməˈnelə◂/ *n* [U] bacteria that causes food poisoning

sal-on /ˈsælɒn‖səˈlɑːn/ *n* stylish or fashionable small shop: *a hairdressing salon*

sa-loon /səˈluːn/ *n* **1** large grandly furnished room for use of ship's passengers **2** *BrE* large car with a fixed roof **3** *AmE* public drinking place

saloon bar /·ˈ· ·/ *n BrE* a comfortably furnished room in a pub, with more expensive drinks than in the PUBLIC BAR

salt[1] /sɔːlt/ *n* **1** [U] common white substance used for preserving food and improving its taste: *salt water* **2** [C] chemical compound of an acid and a metal **3** [C] *infml* an old, experienced sailor: *an old salt* **4 the salt of the earth** person or people regarded as admirable and dependable **5 take something with a pinch/grain of salt** not necessarily believe all of something — see also **worth one's salt** (WORTH)

salt[2] *vt* put salt on

salt away *phr vt* save money (esp. for the future)

salt-cel-lar /ˈsɔːltˌselər/ *n* small pot with a hole for shaking salt on to food

salt-pe-tre *BrE* ‖ **-ter** *AmE* /ˌsɔːlt-**ˈpiːtər/ *n* [U] chemical used in making GUNPOWDER and matches

salt-y /ˈsɔːlti/ *adj* containing or tasting of salt

sa-lu-bri-ous /səˈluːbriəs/ *adj* **1** socially desirable or RESPECTABLE **2** *fml* health-giving

sal-u-ta-ry /ˈsæljʊtəri‖-teri/ *adj* causing an improvement in character, future behaviour, health, etc.

sal-u-ta-tion /ˌsæljʊˈteɪʃən/ *n* **1** [C;U] *fml* expression of greeting by words or actions **2** [C] word or phrase such as 'Ladies and Gentlemen', 'Dear Sir', 'Dear Miss Jones', at the beginning of a speech or letter

sa-lute /səˈluːt/ *n* **1** military sign of recognition, esp. raising the hand to the forehead **2** ceremonial firing of guns to honour someone **3 take the salute** (of a person of high rank) to stand while being SALUTEd by soldiers marching past ♦ *v* **1** *vi/t* make a SALUTE (1) (to) **2** *vt fml* honour and praise **3** *vt fml* greet

sal-vage /ˈsælvɪdʒ/ *vt* save (goods or property) from wreck or destruction ♦ *n* [U] act or process of salvaging

sal-va-tion /sælˈveɪʃən/ *n* [U] **1** (esp. in the Christian religion) the saving or state of being saved from SIN **2** something or someone that saves one from loss or failure

Salvation Ar-my /·,·· ˈ··/ *n* Christian organization with military uniforms and ranks, that helps poor people

salve /sɑːv‖sælv/ *n* [C;U] medicinal paste for putting on a wound, sore place, etc. ♦ *vt fml* make (esp. feelings) less painful

sal-ver /ˈsælvər/ *n* fine metal plate for serving food, drink, etc., formally

sal-vo /ˈsælvəʊ/ *n* **-vos** or **-voes** firing of several guns together

Sa-mar-i-tan /səˈmærɪtən/ *n* a member of the **Samaritans**, an organization that helps people in great trouble of mind with no one to talk to — see also GOOD SAMARITAN

sam-ba /ˈsæmbə/ *n* quick dance of Brazilian origin

same[1] /seɪm/ *adj* **1** not changed or different; not another or other **2** alike in (almost) every way **3 one and the same** exactly the same **4 same here** *infml* me too **5 by the same token** in the same way **6 in the same boat** in the same unpleasant situation **7 just/all the same** in spite of this

same[2] *pron* **1** the same thing, person, condition, etc. **2 the same again, please** (an order for another drink of the same kind) **3 same to you** I wish you the same (a greeting or sometimes an angry wish) ~**ness** *n* [U] **1** very close likeness **2** lack of variety

same[3] *adv* **the same (as)** in the same way (as)

sam·o·var /'sæməva:[r]/ *n* Russian water boiler for making tea

sam·ple /'sa:mpəl‖'sæm-/ *n* small part representing the whole ♦ *vt* take and examine a sample of

sam·pler /'sa:mplə[r]‖'sæm-/ *n* piece of cloth with pictures, etc., stitched on it with thread, done to show one's skill at sewing

san·a·to·ri·um /,sænə'tɔ:riəm/ *n* **-ums** *or* **-a** /riə/ sort of hospital for sick people who are getting better but still need treatment, rest, etc.

sanc·ti·fy /'sæŋktɪfaɪ/ *vt* make holy

sanc·ti·mo·ni·ous /,sæŋktɪ-'məʊniəs◄/ *adj fml* disapproving of others because one thinks one is good, right, etc., and they are not ~**ly** *adv* ~**ness** *n* [U]

sanc·tion /'sæŋkʃən/ *n* **1** [U] *fml* formal or official permission, approval, or acceptance **2** [C] action taken against a person or country that has broken a law or rule **3** [C] something that forces people to keep a rule: *a moral sanction* ♦ *vt fml* **1** accept, approve, or permit, esp. officially **2** make acceptable: *a custom sanctioned by long usage*

sanc·ti·ty /'sæŋktɪti/ *n* [U] holiness

sanc·tu·a·ry /'sæŋktʃʊəri,-tʃəri‖-tʃʊeri/ *n* **1** [C] part of a (Christian) church considered most holy **2** [C;U] (place of) protection for someone being hunted by officers of the law **3** [C] area where animals are protected

sanc·tum /'sæŋktəm/ *n* **1** holy place inside a temple **2** *infml* private place or room where one can be quiet and alone

sand /sænd/ *n* [U] **1** loose material of very small grains, found on seacoasts and in deserts **2** **build on sand** plan or do something with no good reason to believe in its success ♦ *vt* **1** make smooth by rubbing with esp. SANDPAPER **2** put sand on, esp. to stop slipping **sands** *n* [P] **1** area of sand **2** moments in time (as if measured by sand in an HOURGLASS): *The sands of time are running out.* ~**y** *adj* **1** consisting of sand or having sand on the surface **2** (of hair) yellowish brown

san·dal /'sændl/ *n* light shoe with a flat bottom and bands to hold it to the foot

sand·bag /'sændbæg/ *n* sand-filled bag, esp. for forming a protective wall

sand·blast /'sændbla:st‖-blæst/ *vt* clean or cut with a high-speed stream of sand

sand·cas·tle /'sænd,ka:səl‖-,kæ-/ *n* small model, esp. of a castle, built of sand

sand·pa·per /'sænd,peɪpə[r]/ *n* [U] paper covered with fine grainy material, for rubbing surfaces to make them smoother ♦ *vt* rub with sandpaper

sand·stone /'sændstəʊn/ *n* [U] soft rock formed from sand

sand·storm /'sændstɔ:m‖-ɔ:rm/ *n* desert windstorm in which sand is blown about

sand·wich /'sænwɪdʒ‖'sændwɪtʃ, 'sænwɪtʃ/ *n* **2** pieces of bread with other food between them ♦ *vt* fit (with difficulty) between 2 other things

sandwich board /'·· ·/ *n* advertising signs hung at the front and back of someone who walks about in public

sandwich course /'·· ·/ *n BrE* course of study including a period of work in business or industry

sane /seɪn/ *adj* **1** healthy in mind; not mad **2** sensible ~**ly** *adv* ~**ness** *n* [U]

sang /sæŋ/ *past t. of* SING

san·guine /'sæŋgwɪn/ *adj fml* quietly hopeful

san·i·tary /'sænɪtəri‖-teri/ *adj* **1** concerned with preserving health, esp. by removing dirt **2** not dangerous to health; clean

sanitary tow·el /'···· ,··/ *n* small mass of soft paper worn to take up MENSTRUAL blood

san·i·ta·tion /,sænɪ'teɪʃən/ *n* [U] methods of protecting public health, esp. by removing and treating waste

san·i·tize ‖ *also* **-tise** *BrE*/'sænɪtaɪz/ *vt derog* make less unpleasant, dangerous, strongly expressed, etc., in order not to offend people

san·i·ty /'sænɪti/ *n* [U] quality of being SANE

sank /sæŋk/ *v past t. of* SINK[1]

San·ta Claus /'sæntə klɔ:z‖'sæntɪ klɔ:z, 'sæntə-,/ *n* imaginary old man believed by children to bring presents at Christmas

sap[1] /sæp/ *n* [U] watery food-carrying liquid in plants

sap[2] *vt* **-pp-** weaken or destroy, esp. over a long time

sap·ling /'sæplɪŋ/ *n* young tree

sap·phire /'sæfaɪə[r]/ *n* [C;U] bright blue precious stone

sar·casm /'sa:kæzəm‖'sa:r-/ *n* [U] saying the clear opposite of what is meant, in order to be (amusingly) offensive **-castic** /sa:'kæstɪk‖sa:r-/ *adj* **-tically** /-kli/ *adv*

sar·coph·a·gus /sa:'kɒfəgəs‖sa:r'ka:-/ *n* **-gi** /-gaɪ/ *or* **-guses** stone box for a dead body

sar·dine /sa:'di:n‖sa:r-/ *n* **1** small young fish often preserved in oil for eating **2** **like sardines** packed very tightly together

sar·don·ic /sɑːˈdɒnɪk‖sɑːrˈdɑːnɪk/ *adj* seeming to regard oneself as too important to consider a matter, person, etc., seriously ~**ally** /-kli/ *adv*

sarge /sɑːdʒ‖sɑːrdʒ/ *n infml for* SERGEANT

sa·ri /ˈsɑːri/ *n* dress consisting of a length of cloth, worn by Hindu women

sa·rong /səˈrɒŋ‖səˈrɔːŋ, səˈrɑːŋ/ *n* Malayan skirt consisting of a length of cloth

sar·to·ri·al /sɑːˈtɔːriəl‖sɑːr-/ *adj fml* of (the making of) men's clothes

sash[1] /sæʃ/ *n* length of cloth worn round the waist or over one shoulder

sash[2] *n* window frame, esp. in a sort of window with 2 frames that slide up and down

sat /sæt/ *past t. and p. of* SIT

Sa·tan /ˈseɪtn/ *n* the Devil

sa·tan·ic /səˈtænɪk/ *adj* 1 very evil or cruel 2 of satanism ~**ally** /-kli/ *adv*

sat·an·is·m /ˈseɪtənɪzəm/ *n* [U] worship of the devil -**ist** *n*

satch·el /ˈsætʃəl/ *n* small bag carried over the shoulders

sate /seɪt/ *vt fml* satisfy with more than enough of something

sat·el·lite /ˈsætəlaɪt/ *n* 1 heavenly body that moves round a larger one 2 man-made object moving round the Earth, moon, etc. 3 country or person that depends on another

sa·ti·ate /ˈseɪʃieɪt/ *vt fml* satisfy (too) fully

sat·in /ˈsætɪn/ *n* [U] smooth shiny cloth made mainly from silk

sat·ire /ˈsætaɪər/ *n* [C;U] (piece of writing, etc.) showing the foolishness or evil of something in an amusing way -**irical** /səˈtɪrɪkəl/ *adj* -**irize** /ˈsætɪraɪz/ *vt*

sat·is·fac·tion /ˌsætɪsˈfækʃən/ *n* 1 [C;U] (something that gives) a feeling of pleasure 2 [U] *fml* fulfilment of a need, desire, etc. 3 [U] *fml* certainty: *It has been proved to my satisfaction.* 4 [U] *fml* chance to defend one's honour

sat·is·fac·to·ry /ˌsætɪsˈfæktəri/ *adj* 1 pleasing 2 good enough -**rily** *adv*

sat·is·fy /ˈsætɪsfaɪ/ *vt* 1 please 2 fulfil (a need, desire, etc.) 3 *fml* fit (a condition, rule, standard, etc.) 4 persuade fully

sat·u·rate /ˈsætʃəreɪt/ *vt* 1 make completely wet 2 fill completely: *The house market is saturated.* -**rated** *adj* (of fat or oil) having chemicals unhealthily combined -**ration** /ˌsætʃəˈreɪʃən/ *n* [U]

Sat·ur·day /ˈsætədi‖-ər-/ *n* the 6th day of the week, between Friday and Sunday

Sat·urn /ˈsætən‖-ərn/ *n* the PLANET 6th in order from the sun, with large rings round it

sat·ur·nine /ˈsætənaɪn‖-ər-/ *adj fml* sad and solemn, often in a threatening way

sauce /sɔːs/ *n* 1 [C;U] quite thick liquid put on food 2 [S;U] rude disrespectful talk **saucy** *adj* 1 amusingly disrespectful or rude 2 producing sexual interest in an amusing way

sauce·pan /ˈsɔːspæn, -pən/ *n* metal cooking pot with a handle

sau·cer /ˈsɔːsər/ *n* small plate for putting a cup on — see also FLYING SAUCER

sau·na /ˈsɔːnə, ˈsɔːnə‖ˈsaʊnə/ *n* (a room or building for) a Finnish type of bath in steam

saun·ter /ˈsɔːntər/ *vi* walk unhurriedly

saus·age /ˈsɒsɪdʒ‖ˈsɔː-/ *n* [C;U] cut-up meat in a tube of thin skin

sausage roll /ˌ·· ˈ·/ *n* small piece of sausage in a pastry covering

sav·age /ˈsævɪdʒ/ *adj* 1 forcefully cruel or violent 2 uncivilized ♦ *n* member of an uncivilized tribe ♦ *vt* attack and bite fiercely ~**ly** *adv*

sav·ag·er·y /ˈsævɪdʒəri/ *n* [C;U] (act of) savage behaviour

sa·van·na /səˈvænə/ *n* [U] flat grassy land in a warm part of the world

save[1] /seɪv/ *v* 1 *vt* make safe from danger or destruction 2 *vi/t* keep and add to an amount of (money) for later use 3 *vt* avoid the waste of (money, time, etc.) 4 *vt* keep for future use or enjoyment later 5 *vt* make unnecessary 6 *vt* (of a GOALKEEPER) stop one's opponents from getting the ball in the net 7 **save one's skin/neck/bacon** *infml* escape from a serious danger 8 **to save one's life** *infml* even with the greatest effort: *I can't play the piano to save my life.* ♦ *n* act of saving (SAVE (6)) **saver** *n* **savings** *n* [P] money saved, esp. in a bank

save[2] *prep fml* except

saving grace /ˌ·· ˈ·/ *n* the one good thing that makes something acceptable

savings and loan as·so·ci·a·tion /ˌ··· · ˈ· ···,·/ *n AmE for* BUILDING SOCIETY

sa·viour *BrE* ‖ -**vior** *AmE*/ˈseɪvjər/ *n* 1 one who saves from danger or loss 2 (*usu. cap.*) Jesus Christ

sav·oir-faire /ˌsævwɑː ˈfeər‖-wɑːr-/ *n* [U] ability to do or say the proper thing on every social occasion

sa·vour *BrE* ‖ -**vor** *AmE*/ˈseɪvər/ *n* [S;U] 1 taste or smell 2 (power to excite) interest ♦ *vt* enjoy slowly and purposefully

sa·vour·y *BrE* ‖ -**vory** *AmE*/ˈseɪvəri/ *adj* 1 not sweet; tasting of meat, cheese, etc. 2 *fml* morally good ♦ *n* a small salty dish

saw[1] /sɔː/ *past t. of* SEE

saw[2] *n* thin-bladed tool with teeth for cutting hard materials ◆ *vi/t* **sawed, sawed** *or* **sawn** /sɔːn/ cut (as if) with a saw

saw[3] *n* short well-known saying

saw·dust /'sɔːdʌst/ *n* [U] wood dust made by a saw in cutting

sax·o·phone /'sæksəfəʊn/ *also* **sax** /sæks/ *infml* — *n* metal musical instrument of the WOODWIND family, used esp. in JAZZ

say[1] /seɪ/ **said** /sed/ **1** *vt* pronounce (a sound, word, etc) **2** *vi/t* express (a thought, opinion, etc.) in words **3** *vt* give as a general opinion; claim **4** *vt* suppose; suggest: *Let's say they accept your idea — what then?* | *Would you accept, say,* (= for example) *£500?* **5 go without saying** be clear; not need stating **6 hard to say** difficult to judge **7 I say** *BrE infml* **a** a weak expression of surprise, concern, etc. **b** (used for calling someone's attention): *I say, I've just had a wonderful idea!* **8 I wouldn't say no** *BrE infml* yes, please **9 say for oneself/something** offer as an excuse or defence: *You're late again. What have you got to say for yourself?* | *The idea has little to be said for it.* **10 say no more** *infml* your/the meaning is clear **11 say to oneself** think **12 that is to say** expressed another (more exact) way **13 they say** it is usually thought **14 to say nothing of** including **15 when all is said and done** it must be remembered that **16 you don't say!** (an expression of slight surprise)

say[2] *n* [S;U] **1** power or right of (sharing in) acting or deciding **2 have one's say** (have the chance to) express one's opinion

say·ing /'seɪ-ɪŋ/ *n* well-known wise statement

say-so /'· ·/ *n* **1** personal statement without proof **2** permission

scab /skæb/ *n* **1** hard mass of dried blood formed over a wound **2** *derog* one who works while others are on STRIKE

scab·bard /'skæbəd‖-ərd/ *n* tube for holding a sword, knife, etc.

sca·bies /'skeɪbiz/ *n* [U] skin disease

sca·brous /'skeɪbrəs/ *adj fml* improper; SALACIOUS

scaf·fold /'skæfəld, -fəʊld/ *n* raised stage for the official killing of criminals ~**ing** /-fəl-/ *n* [U] structure of poles and boards round a building for workmen to stand on

scald /skɔːld/ *vt* burn with hot liquid **scald** *n*

scale[1] /skeɪl/ *n* **1** [C] set of marks on an instrument, used for measuring **2** [C] set of figures for measuring or comparing: *a temperature scale* **3** [C;U] relationship between a map or

model and the thing it represents: *a scale of 1 inch to the mile* **4** [C;U] size or level in relation to other or usual things: *a large-scale business operation* **5** [C] set of musical notes at fixed separations **6 to scale** according to a fixed rule for reducing the size of something in a drawing, etc.

scale[2] *also* **scales** *pl.* — *n* weighing apparatus

scale[3] *n* **1** any of the small flat stiff pieces covering fish, snakes, etc. **2** greyish material formed inside hot water pipes, pots in which water is boiled, etc. ◆ *vt* remove the scales from

scale[4] *vt* **1** climb up **2** increase/reduce, esp. by a fixed rate

scal·lop /'skɒləp‖'skɑː-/ *n* small sea animal (MOLLUSC) with a shell, used for food

scal·ly·wag /'skæliwæg/ *n* trouble-making child

scalp /skælp/ *n* skin on top of the head: (fig.) *He wants the Minister's scalp.* (= wants him to admit defeat and leave his job) ◆ *vt* cut off the scalp of

scal·pel /'skælpəl/ *n* small sharp knife used by doctors in operations

scam /skæm/ *n sl* clever and dishonest plan or course of action

scamp /skæmp/ *n* playfully trouble-making child

scam·per /'skæmpə[r]/ *vi* run quickly and usu. playfully

scam·pi /'skæmpi/ *n* [U] *BrE* (dish of) large PRAWNs

scan /skæn/ *v* -**nn**- **1** *vt* examine closely, esp. making a search **2** *vt* look at quickly without careful reading **3** *vi* (of poetry) have a regular pattern of repeated beats ◆ *n* act of scanning ~**ner** *n* instrument for scanning SCAN (1): *a brain scanner*

scan·dal /'skændl/ *n* **1** [C] (something causing) a public shock **2** [U] talk which brings harm or disrespect to someone ~**ize** *vt* offend (someone's) feelings of what is right or proper ~**ous** *adj* morally shocking

Scan·di·na·vi·an /ˌskændɪ-'neɪvɪən/ *adj* of Denmark, Norway, Sweden, Finland, and/or Iceland

scan·sion /'skænʃən/ *n* [U] way a line of a poem SCANs (3)

scant /skænt/ *adj* hardly enough

scant·y /'skænti/ *adj* hardly (big) enough -**ily** *adv*

scape·goat /'skeɪpgəʊt/ *n* one who takes the blame for others' faults

scar /skɑː[r]/ *n* mark left when a wound heals ◆ *vt* -**rr**- mark with a scar

scarce /skeəs‖skeərs/ *adj* **1** less than is wanted; hard to find **2 make oneself scarce** *infml* go away or keep away, esp. in order to avoid trouble

~ly adv 1 hardly; almost not 2 (almost) certainly not **scarcity** n [C;U] being scarce; lack

scare /skeə^r/ vt frighten ♦ n 1 [S] sudden fear 2 [C] (mistaken or unreasonable) public fear: *scare stories about war in the newspapers* **scary** adj frightening

scare-crow /'skeəkrəʊ‖'skeər-/ n figure dressed in old clothes set up in a field to scare birds away from crops

scare-mon-ger /'skeə,mʌŋgə^r‖ 'skeər,mɑːŋ-, -,mʌŋ-/ n person who spreads reports causing public anxiety

scarf /skɑːf‖skɑːrf/ n **scarves** /skɑːvz‖skɑːrvz/ or **scarfs** /scarfs/ piece of cloth worn round the neck or head

scar-let /'skɑːlɪt‖-ɑːr-/ adj bright red

scarlet fe-ver /,·· ˈ··/ n [U] serious disease marked by a painful throat and red spots on the skin

scar-per /'skɑːpə^r‖-ɑːr-/ vi BrE sl run away

scat /skæt/ vi -tt- (*usu. imperative*) infml go away fast

scath-ing /'skeɪðɪŋ/ adj bitterly cruel in judgment **~ly** adv

sca-tol-o-gy /skæ'tɒlədʒi‖-'tɑː-/ n [U] (writing with) OBSCENE interest in body waste **-ogical** /,skætə'lɒdʒɪkəl‖ -'lɑː-/ adj

scat-ter /'skætə^r/ v 1 vi/t separate widely 2 vt spread widely (as if) by throwing **~ed** adj far apart; irregularly separated

scat-ter-brain /'skætəbreɪn‖-ər-/ n careless or forgetful person **~ed** adj

scat-ty /'skæti/ adj BrE slightly mad or scatterbrained

scav-enge /'skævɪndʒ/ vi/t 1 (of an animal) feed on (waste or decaying flesh) 2 search for or find (usable objects) among unwanted things **-enger** n

sce-na-ri-o /sɪ'nɑːriəʊ‖-'næ-, -'neɪ-/ n -os 1 written description of the action in a film or play 2 description of a possible course of events

scene /siːn/ n 1 (in a play) division (within an act) 2 single piece of action in one place in a play or film 3 background for action of a play: *There are few scene changes.* 4 place where something happens: *the scene of the crime* 5 event regarded as like something in a play or film: *scenes of merrymaking* 6 show of angry feelings esp. between 2 people in public 7 an area of activity: *He's new to the film/political scene.* 8 **behind the scenes** secretly 9 **on the scene** present: *a report from our man on the scene in Africa* 10 **set the scene** prepare 11 **steal the scene** get all the attention and praise expected by someone else at a show, party, etc.

sce-ne-ry /'siːnəri/ n [U] 1 natural surroundings, esp. in the country 2 painted background and other articles used on stage

sce-nic /'siːnɪk/ adj showing attractive natural scenery

scent /sent/ n 1 [C] pleasant smell 2 [C] smell followed by hunting animals 3 [U] esp. BrE for PERFUME ♦ vt 1 tell the presence of by smelling 2 get a feeling of the presence of 3 fill with pleasant smells

scep-tic BrE‖**skep-** AmE /'skeptɪk/ n sceptical person **~al** adj unwilling to believe **~ally**/-kli/ adv **-ticism** /-tɪsɪzəm/ n [U] doubt

scep-tre BrE ‖ **-ter** AmE /'septə^r/ n ceremonial rod carried by a ruler

sched-ule /'ʃedjuːl‖'skedʒul, -dʒəl/ n 1 planned list or order of things to be done 2 a list of prices b esp. AmE timetable of trains, buses, etc. 3 **ahead of/on/behind schedule** before/at/after the planned or expected time ♦ vt plan for a certain future time **-uled** adj being a regular service

sche-mat-ic /skiː'mætɪk, skɪ-/ adj showing the main parts but leaving out details **~ally**/-kli/ adv

scheme /skiːm/ n 1 plan in simple form; system 2 BrE official or business plan 3 clever dishonest plan ♦ vi make SCHEMEs (3)

scher-zo /'skeətsəʊ‖-eər-/ n -zos quick piece of music

schis-m /'sɪzəm, 'skɪzəm/ n [C;U] separation between parts originally together, esp. in the church **~atic** /sɪz'mætɪk, skɪz-/ adj

schiz-oid /'skɪtsɔɪd/ adj of schizophrenia

schiz-o-phre-ni-a /,skɪtsəʊ'friːniə, -sə-/ n [U] disorder in which the mind becomes separated from the feelings **-phrenic** /-'frenɪk/ adj, n (of) someone with schizophrenia

schlep /ʃlep/ v -pp- AmE infml 1 vt carry or drag (something heavy) 2 vi spend a lot of time and effort in getting from one place to another

schmaltz, schmalz /ʃmɔːlts, ʃmælts‖ ʃmɔːlts, ʃmɑːlts/ n [U] infml art or esp. music which brings out feelings in a too easy, not serious or delicate, way **~y** adj

schmuck /ʃmʌk/ n AmE infml fool

schol-ar /'skɒlə^r‖-ɑː-/ n 1 person with great knowledge of a (non-science) subject 2 holder of a SCHOLARSHIP (1) **~ly** adj 1 concerned with serious detailed study 2 of or like a SCHOLAR (1)

schol-ar-ship /'skɒləʃɪp‖'skɑːlər-/ n 1 [C] payment so that someone can attend a college 2 [U] exact and serious study

scho·las·tic /skəˈlæstɪk/ adj of schools and teaching

school[1] /skuːl/ n 1 [C;U] (attendance or work at) a place of education for children 2 [C] body of students (and teachers) at such a place: *She was liked by the whole school.* 3 [C;U] teaching establishment: *a driving school* 4 [C;U] (in some universities) department concerned with one subject: *the School of Law* 5 [C;U] AmE UNIVERSITY 6 [C] group of people with the same methods, style, etc: *Rembrandt and his school* ♦ vt fml teach, train, or bring under control

school[2] n large group of fish swimming together

school-marm /ˈskuːlmɑːm‖-mɑːrm/ n old-fashioned, exact, and easily shocked woman who likes giving orders

school-master /ˈskuːlˌmɑːstəʳ‖ -ˌmæ-/ **schoolmistress** /-ˌmɪstrəs/ fem. — n teacher at a school

school-mate /ˈskuːlmeɪt/ n a child at the same school

school of thought /ˌ· · ·/ n group with the same way of thinking, opinion, etc.

schoo·ner /ˈskuːnəʳ/ n 1 large fast sailing ship 2 tall drinking glass esp. for SHERRY or BEER

schwa /ʃwɑː/ n vowel sound shown in this dictionary as /ə/ or /ə/

sci·at·i·ca /saɪˈætɪkə/ n [U] pain in the lower back

sci·ence /ˈsaɪəns/ n 1 [U] (study of) knowledge which depends on testing facts and stating general natural laws 2 [C] **a** a branch of such knowledge, such as PHYSICS, chemistry, or BIOLOGY **b** anything which may be studied exactly

science fiction /ˌ·· · ·/ n [U] stories about imaginary future (scientific) developments

science park /ˈ·· ·/ n an area where there are a lot of companies concerned esp. with new TECHNOLOGY and scientific study

sci·en·tif·ic /ˌsaɪənˈtɪfɪk/ adj 1 of science 2 needing or showing exact knowledge or use of a system ~ally /-kli/ adv

sci·en·tist /ˈsaɪəntɪst/ n person who works in a science

scim·i·tar /ˈsɪmɪtəʳ/ n curved sword

scin·til·late /ˈsɪntɪleɪt/ vi 1 (esp. of conversation) quick, clever and interesting 2 throw out quick flashes of light

scis·sors /ˈsɪzəz‖-ərz/ n [P] cutting tool with 2 joined blades

scle·ro·sis /skləˈrəʊsəs/ n [U] med hardening of some usu. soft bodily organ — see also MULTIPLE SCLEROSIS

scoff[1] /skɒf‖skɑːf, skɔːf/ vi speak laughingly and disrespectfully

scoff[2] vt infml eat eagerly and fast

scold /skəʊld/ vt speak angrily and complainingly to (a wrong-doer)

scone /skɒn, skəʊn‖skəʊn, skɑːn/ n small round breadlike cake

scoop /skuːp/ n 1 sort of deep spoon for lifting and moving liquids or loose material 2 news report printed, broadcast, etc., before one's competitors can do so ♦ vt 1 take up or out (as if) with a SCOOP (1) 2 make a news report before (another newspaper)

scoot /skuːt/ vi go quickly and suddenly

scoot·er /ˈskuːtəʳ/ n 1 child's 2-wheeled vehicle pushed along by one foot 2 low vehicle with two small wheels, an enclosed engine, and usu. a wide curved part at the front to protect the legs

scope /skəʊp/ n [U] 1 area within the limits of a question, subject, etc. 2 space or chance for action or thought

scorch /skɔːtʃ‖skɔːrtʃ/ v 1 vt burn the surface (of something) without destroying completely 2 vt infml travel very fast ♦ n scorched place ~er n infml 1 very hot day 2 something very exciting, angry, fast, etc.

scorched earth pol·i·cy /ˌ· '· ·,··/n destruction by an army of all useful things, esp. crops, in an area before leaving it to an advancing army

score[1] /skɔːʳ/ n 1 number of points won in a game, examination, etc. 2 a written copy of a piece of music **b** music for a film or play 3 reason: *Don't worry on that score.* 4 old disagreement or hurt kept in the mind: *to have a score to settle with someone* 5 **know the score** understand the true and usu. unfavourable facts of a situation

score[2] v 1 vi/t make (a point) in a game 2 vi record the points made in a game 3 vt gain (a success, victory, etc.) 4 vi/t make (a clever point) esp. in an argument: *She always tries to score (points) off other people in a conversation.* 5 vt arrange (music) for a particular combination of instruments 6 vt cut one or more lines on 7 vi/t sl (usu. of a man) have sex with someone 8 sl obtain and use unlawful drugs **scorer** n person who SCORES[2] (1, 2)

score[3] determiner, n score or scores esp. lit 20 **scores** n [P] a lot

score-board /ˈskɔːbɔːd‖ˈskɔːrbɔːrd/ n board on which a SCORE[1] (1) is recorded

scorn /skɔːn‖skɔːrn/ n [U] strong (angry) disrespect ♦ vt refuse to

accept or consider because of scorn or pride **~ful** adj **~fully** adv

scor-pi-on /'skɔːpiən‖-ər-/ n small animal with a long poisonous stinging tail

scotch /skɒtʃ‖skɑːtʃ/ vt fml put an end to

Scotch adj Scottish ♦ n [U] WHISKY made in Scotland

scot-free /ˌ· '·/ adj without harm or esp. punishment

Scots /skɒts‖skɑːts/ adj Scottish

Scot-tish /'skɒtɪʃ‖'skɑːtɪʃ/ adj of Scotland

scoun-drel /'skaundrəl/ n wicked, selfish, or dishonest man

scour¹ /skauə'/ vt search (an area) thoroughly

scour² vt clean by hard rubbing with a rough material **~er** n pad of rough nylon for cleaning pots and pans

scourge /skɜːdʒ‖skɜːrdʒ/ n cause of great harm or suffering ♦ vt cause great harm or suffering

scout /skaut/ n **1** member of an association (**the scouts**) for training boys in character and self-help **2** soldier sent ahead of an army to find out about the enemy **3** person who seeks out good young sportspeople, actors, etc., for new teams, shows, etc.: *a talent scout* ♦ vi go looking for something

scowl /skaul/ n angry FROWN ♦ vi make a scowl

scrab-ble /'skræbəl/ vi SCRAMBLE (1, 2)

scrag-gy /'skrægi/ adj thin and bony

scram /skræm/ vi **-mm-** [often imperative] infml get away fast

scram-ble /'skræmbəl/ vi **1** move or climb quickly and untidily **2** vi struggle or compete eagerly or against difficulty **3** vt cook (an egg) while mixing the white and yellow parts together **4** vt mix up (a radio or telephone message) so that it cannot be understood ♦ n **1** [S] act of scrambling (SCRAMBLE (1)) **2** [C] motorcycle race over rough ground

scrap¹ /skræp/ n **1** [C] small piece **2** [U] unwanted material (to be) thrown away: *She sold the car for scrap.* (= as metal to be used again) ♦ vt **-pp-** get rid of **~py** adj not well arranged or planned

scrap² n sudden short fight or quarrel ♦ vi **-pp-** fight or quarrel

scrap-book /'skræpbuk/ n book of empty pages on which cut-out pictures, etc., are stuck

scrape /skreɪp/ v **1** vi/t (cause to) rub roughly against a surface **2** vt remove or clean by pulling or pushing an edge repeatedly across a surface **3** vi live, keep a business, etc., with no more than the necessary money **4** vi succeed by doing work of the lowest acceptable quality: *She scraped through the exam.* **5 scrape a living** get just enough food or money to stay alive **6 scrape the bottom of the barrel** take, use, suggest, etc., something of the lowest quality ♦ n **1** act or sound of scraping **2** mark or wound made by scraping **3** difficult situation

scrape up/together phr vt gather (enough money) with difficulty

scrap heap /'· ·/ n **1** pile of waste material, esp. metal **2** imaginary place where unwanted things, people, or ideas go

scrap pa-per /'· ˌ··/ esp BrE ‖ usu. **scratch paper** AmE — n [U] used paper for making notes, shopping lists, etc.

scratch /skrætʃ/ vi/t **1** rub and tear or mark with something pointed or rough (a part of the body) lightly and repeatedly **3** remove (oneself, a horse, etc.) from a race or competition **4 scratch a living** get just enough food or money to stay alive **5 scratch the surface** deal with only the beginning of a matter or only a few of many cases ♦ n **1** [C] mark or sound made by scratching **2** [S] act of SCRATCHing (2) **3 from scratch** (starting) from the beginning **4 up to scratch** at/to an acceptable standard **5 without a scratch** without even the smallest amount of hurt or damage **~y** adj **1** (of a record, etc.) spoiled by scratches **2** (of clothes) hot, rough, and uncomfortable

scrawl /skrɔːl/ vt write carelessly or awkwardly ♦ n (piece of) careless or irregular writing

scraw-ny /'skrɔːni/ adj unpleasantly thin

scream /skriːm/ vi/t **1** cry out in a loud high voice: (fig.) *The wind screamed around the house.* **2** draw attention, as if by such a cry ♦ **1** [C] sudden loud cry **2** [S] infml very funny person, thing, joke, etc.

scree /skriː/ n [U] small loose stones on a mountainside

screech /skriːtʃ/ vi **1** make an unpleasant high sharp sound, esp. in terror or pain **2** (of machines, brakes, etc.) make such a noise **3 screech to a halt/standstill** stop very suddenly (as if) making this noise ♦ n very high unpleasant noise

screed /skriːd/ n long (dull) piece of writing

screen /skriːn/ n **1** something, esp. a movable upright frame, that protects, shelters, or hides **2** surface on which a cinema film is shown **3** the cinema industry: *star of stage, screen and radio* | *screen test* (= test of one's ability to act in a film) | *She first appeared* *on the screen* (= acted in her first film) *last year.* **4** front glass surface of an electrical instrument, esp. a television, on which pictures or information appear ♦ *vt* **1** shelter, protect, or hide (as if) with a screen **2** test so as to remove those that do not reach the proper standard **3** show or broadcast (a film or television show) — see also SMALL SCREEN **~ing** *n* **1** [C;U] (a) showing of a film **2** [U] process of SCREEN (2) ing

screen-play /'skri:npleɪ/ *n* story written for a film

screw /skru:/ *n* **1** metal pin having a head with a cut across it, a point at the other end, and a raised edge winding round it so that when twisted into the material it holds firmly **2** act of turning one of these **3** PROPELLER, esp. on a ship **4** *taboo sl* **a** act of having sex **b** someone considered as a person to have sex with **5 have a screw loose** *humor* be slightly mad **6 put the screws on someone** *infml* to force someone to do as one wishes, esp. by threatening ♦ *v* **1** *vt* fasten with one or more screws **2** *vi/t* tighten or fasten by turning **3** *vi/t* *taboo sl* have sex (with) **4** *sl* cheat: *We really got screwed by that salesman.*

screw up *phr v* **1** *vt* twist (a part of the face) to express disapproval or uncertainty: *She screwed up her eyes to read the sign.* **2** *vt* carelessly twist (paper, etc.) or so as to make a ball **3** *vi/t* *sl* **a** ruin **b** deal with badly: *He really screwed up on that job.* **4** *vt* **screw up one's courage** stop oneself from being afraid **5** *vt* **screwed up** *infml* very worried and confused

screw-ball /'skru:bɔːl/ *n* AmE SCREWY person

screw-driv-er /'skru:ˌdraɪvəʳ/ *n* tool with a blade that fits into the top of a screw, for turning it

screw-y /'skru:i/ *adj infml* strange or slightly mad

scrib-ble /'skrɪbəl/ *v* **1** *vi* write (meaninglessly marks) **2** *vt* write carelessly or hastily ♦ *n* [S;U] meaningless or careless writing

scribe /skraɪb/ *n* person employed to copy things in writing

scrimp /skrɪmp/ *vi* **scrimp and save** save money slowly and with great difficulty

script /skrɪpt/ *n* **1** [C] written form of a play, film, or broadcast **2** [C;U] particular alphabet: *Arabic script* **3** [S;U] *fml* handwriting **~ed** *adj* having a SCRIPT (1) **~writer** *n* writer of SCRIPTs (1)

scrip-ture /'skrɪptʃəʳ/ also **scriptures** *pl.* — *n* [U] **1** the Bible **2** holy book(s) of the stated religion **-tural** *adj*

scroll /skrəʊl/ *n* **1** rolled-up piece of paper, esp. containing official writing **2** decoration or shape like this in stone or wood

scrooge /skru:dʒ/ *n* extremely ungenerous person

scro-tum /'skrəʊtəm/ *n* **-ta** /-tə/ or **-tums** bag of flesh holding the TESTICLEs

scrounge /skraʊndʒ/ *vi/t* get (something) without work or payment or by persuading others **scrounger** *n*

scrub /skrʌb/ *v* **-bb-** **1** *vi/t* clean or remove by hard rubbing **2** *vt* no longer do or have; CANCEL ♦ *n* [S] act of scrubbing

scrub [2] *n* [U] low-growing plants covering the ground thickly

scruff [1] /skrʌf/ *n* flesh at the back (of the neck)

scruff [2] *n* BrE *infml* dirty and untidy person

scruf-fy /'skrʌfi/ *adj* dirty and untidy

scrum /skrʌm/ *n* **1** group of players trying to get the ball in RUGBY **2** disorderly struggling crowd

scrump-tious /'skrʌmpʃəs/ *adj infml* (of food) extremely good

scru-ple /'skru:pəl/ *n* **1** [C] moral principle which keeps one from doing something **2** [U] conscience

scru-pu-lous /'skru:pjʊləs/ *adj* **1** *fml* very exact **2** exactly honest **~ly** *adv*

scru-ti-ny /'skru:tɪni/ *n* [U] careful and thorough examination **-nize** *vt* examine closely

scud /skʌd/ *vi* **-dd-** (esp. of clouds and ships) move along quickly

scuff /skʌf/ *vt* make rough marks on the smooth surface of (shoes, a floor, etc.) ♦ *n* mark made by scuffing

scuf-fle /'skʌfəl/ *n* disorderly fight among a few people **scuffle** *vi*

scull /skʌl/ *vi/t* row (a small light boat) **~er** *n*

scul-le-ry /'skʌləri/ *n* room next to a kitchen, where pots and dishes are washed

sculp-tor /'skʌlptəʳ/ *n* artist who makes sculptures

sculp-ture /'skʌlptʃəʳ/ *n* **1** [U] art of shaping solid representations **2** [C;U] (piece of) work produced by this ♦ *vt* make by shaping

scum /skʌm/ *n* **1** [S;U] (unpleasant) material formed on the surface of liquid **2** [P] *often taboo* worthless immoral people: *the scum of the earth*

scup-per /'skʌpəʳ/ *vt* BrE **1** sink (one's own ship) intentionally **2** wreck or ruin (a plan)

scurf /skɜːf‖skɜːrf/ *n* [U] small bits of dead skin, esp. in the hair

scur-ri-lous /'skʌrɪləs/ *adj fml* containing very rude, improper, and usu.

untrue statements ~**ly** adv ~**ness** n [U]

scur·ry /'skʌri/ vi hurry, esp. with short quick steps ♦ n [U] movement or sound of scurrying

scur·vy /'skɜːvi‖-ɜːr-/ n [U] disease caused by lack of VITAMIN C

scut·tle[1] /'skʌtl/ n sort of bucket for holding and carrying coal

scuttle[2] vi rush with short quick steps

scuttle[3] vt sink (a ship) by making holes in the bottom

scythe /saɪð/ n grass-cutting tool with a long curving blade fixed to a handle ♦ vt cut (as if) with a scythe

SDI /ˌes diː 'aɪ/ n Strategic Defence Initiative; a US government plan for the use of special weapons to destroy enemy MISSILES in space

sea /siː/ n 1 [U] great body of salty water that covers much of the Earth's surface 2 [C] a particular (named) part of this: *the Caribbean Sea* **b** body of water (mostly) enclosed by land: *the Mediterranean Sea* 3 [C] any of a number of broad plains on the Moon: *the Sea of Tranquillity* 4 [C] large quantity spread out in front of one: *a sea of faces* 5 **at sea: a** on a voyage **b** infml not understanding 6 **by sea** on a ship 7 **go to sea** become a sailor 8 **put to sea** start a voyage

sea a·nem·o·ne /'·· ·,··/ n simple flower-like sea animal

sea·board /'siːbɔːd‖-bɔːrd/ n the part of a country along a seacoast

sea change /'· ·/ n lit a complete but usu. gradual change

sea·far·ing /'siːˌfeərɪŋ/ adj connected with the sea and sailing

sea·food /'siːfuːd/ n [U] fish and fishlike animals from the sea which can be eaten, esp. SHELLFISH

sea·front /'siːfrʌnt/ n part of a coastal (holiday) town on the edge of the sea, often with a broad path along it

sea·gull /'siːgʌl/ n GULL

sea·horse /'siːhɔːs‖-hɔːrs/ n small fish with a head and neck like those of a horse

seal[1] /siːl/ n 1 official mark put on an official paper, often by pressing a pattern onto red wax 2 something fastened across an opening to protect it 3 tight connection to keep gas or liquid in or out 4 **set the seal on** bring to an end in a suitable way ♦ vt 1 fix a SEAL (1) onto 2 fasten or close (as if) with a SEAL (2, 3): (fig.) *My lips are sealed.* 3 make (more) certain, formal, or solemn 4 **seal someone's doom/fate** fml make someone's death or punishment certain

seal off phr vt close tightly so as not to allow entrance or escape

seal[2] n large smooth-bodied sea animal with broad flat limbs for swimming

sea legs /'· ·/ n [P] ability to walk comfortably on a moving ship

sea lev·el /'· ,··/ n the average height of the sea, used as a standard for measuring heights on land

sealing wax /'·· ·/ n hard easily-melted substance used for SEALS[1] (1)

sea li·on /'· ,··/ n large SEAL[2] of the Pacific Ocean

seam /siːm/ n 1 line of stitches joining 2 pieces of cloth, etc. 2 narrow band of coal between other rocks 3 **burst at the seams** infml be very full

sea·man /'siːmən/ n -**men** /-mən/ 1 sailor, esp. of low rank 2 man skilled in handling ships at sea ~**ship** n [U] skill in handling a ship and directing its course

seam·y /'siːmi/ adj rough and immoral -**iness** n [U]

sé·ance /'seɪɒns, -ɒns‖'seɪɑːns/ n meeting where people try to talk to the spirits of the dead

sear /sɪə/ vt burn with sudden powerful heat ~**ing** adj 1 burning 2 causing or describing very strong feelings esp. of a sexual kind

search /sɜːtʃ‖sɜːrtʃ/ vi/t 1 look through or examine (a place or person) carefully and thoroughly to try to find something 2 **search me!** infml I don't know! ♦ n 1 act of searching 2 **in search of** searching for ~**ing** adj sharp and thorough: *a searching look* ~**er** n

search·light /'sɜːtʃlaɪt‖'sɜːr-/ n large powerful light that can be turned in any direction

search par·ty /'· ,··/ n group of searchers, esp. for a lost person

search war·rant /'· ,··/ n official written order allowing the police to search a place

sea·shore /'siːʃɔː/ n [U] land along the edge of the sea

sea·sick /'siːˌsɪk/ adj sick because of a ship's movement ~**ness** n [U]

sea·side /'siːsaɪd/ n [the + S] esp. BrE coast, esp. as a holiday place

sea·son /'siːzən/ n 1 spring, summer, autumn, or winter 2 period of the year marked by a particular thing: *the rainy/holiday/cricket season* 3 **in/out of season** (of food) at/not at the best time of year for eating 4 **Season's Greetings!** (a greeting on a Christmas card) — see also SILLY SEASON ♦ vt 1 give a special taste to (a food) by adding salt, pepper, a SPICE, etc. 2 dry (wood) gradually for use ~**able** adj fml suitable or useful for the time of year ~**al** adj happening or active only at a particular season ~**ed** adj having much experience ~ing n [C;U] something that seasons food

season tick·et /'·· ,··||,·· '··/ n ticket usable for a number of journeys, performances, etc., during a fixed period of time

seat /siːt/ n 1 place for sitting 2 the part on which one sits 3 place as a member of an official body: *to lose one's seat in Parliament* 4 place where a particular activity happens 5 **in the driver's seat** *infml* in control 6 **take a back seat (to someone)** *infml* allow someone else to take control or have the more important job 7 **take/have a seat** please sit down ♦ vt 1 cause or help to sit: *be seated* (= please sit down) 2 have room for seats for ~ing n [U] seats

seat belt /'· ·/ n protective belt round a seated person in a car, plane, etc.

sea ur·chin /'· ,··/ n small ball-shaped sea animal with a prickly shell

sea·weed /'siːwiːd/ n [U] plant that grows in the sea

sea·wor·thy /'siːwɜːðɪ||-ɜːr-/ adj (of a ship) fit for a sea voyage

sec·a·teurs /'sekətɜːz|,sekə'tɜːrz/ n [P] BrE strong garden scissors

se·cede /sɪ'siːd/ vi formally leave an official group or organization **secession** /-'seʃən/ n [U]

se·clude /sɪ'kluːd/ vt fml keep (esp. oneself) away from other people **secluded** adj very quiet and private **seclusion** /sɪ'kluːʒən/ n [U]

sec·ond[1] /'sekənd/ determiner, adv, pron [2nd]

second[2] n 1 length of time equal to $\frac{1}{60}$ of a minute 2 *infml* moment

second[3] n 1 [C] helper of a fighter in a boxing match (BOX[2]) or DUEL 2 [C] imperfect article sold cheaper 3 [C] British university examination result of middle to good quality 4 **second to none** *infml* the best **seconds** [P] *infml* 2nd servings of food at a meal

second[4] vt support formally (a formal suggestion at a meeting) ~**er** n

se·cond[5] /sɪ'kɒnd||sɪ'kɑːnd/ vt BrE fml move from usual duties to a special duty ~**ment** n [C;U]

sec·ond·a·ry /'sekəndərɪ||-derɪ/ adj 1 (of education or a school) for children over 11 2 not main: *of secondary importance* 3 developing from something earlier: *a secondary infection* ~**rily** adv

second best /,·· '·◄/ adj not as good as the best

second class /,·· '·◄/ n [U] travelling conditions cheaper than FIRST CLASS on a train, etc. **second-class** adj below the highest quality

second cous·in /,·· '··/ n the child of one's parent's COUSIN

second-guess /,·· '·/ vt AmE infml 1 make a judgment about (someone or something) only after an event has taken place 2 try to say in advance what (someone) will do, how (something) will happen, etc.

second-hand /,·· '·◄/ adj, adv 1 owned or used by someone else before; not new 2 (of information) not directly from its origin

second na·ture /,·· '··/ n [U] very firmly fixed habit

second-rate /,·· '·◄/ adj of low quality

second sight /,·· '·/ n [U] supposed ability to know about future or distant things

second thought /,·· '·/ n [C;U] thought that a past decision or opinion may not be right: *On second thoughts I think I will have a beer.*

second wind /,·· '·/ n [S] return of one's strength during hard physical activity, when it seemed one had become too tired to continue

se·cre·cy /'siːkrəsɪ/ n [U] 1 keeping secrets 2 being secret

se·cret /'siːkrət/ adj 1 that no one else knows or must know about 2 undeclared ♦ n 1 matter kept hidden or known only to a few 2 special way of doing something well: *the secret of baking perfect bread* 3 mystery 4 **in secret** in a private way or place ~**ly** adv

secret a·gent /,·· '··/ n person gathering information secretly esp. for a foreign government

sec·re·tar·i·at /,sekrə'teərɪət/ n official office or department concerned with the running of a large organization

sec·re·ta·ry /'sekrətərɪ||-terɪ/ n 1 person who prepares letters, keeps records, arranges meetings, etc., for another 2 government minister or high non-elected official: *the Secretary of State for Trade* 3 officer of an organization who keeps records, writes official letters, etc. –**rial** /,sekrə'teərɪəl/ adj

se·crete[1] /sɪ'kriːt/ vt (esp. of an animal or plant organ) produce (a usu. liquid substance) **secretion** /sɪ'kriːʃən/ n [C;U] (production of) a usu. liquid substance

secrete[2] vt fml hide **secretion** n [U]

se·cre·tive /'siːkrətɪv, sɪ'kriːtɪv/ adj hiding one's thoughts or plans ~**ly** adv ~**ness** n [U]

secret ser·vice /,·· '··/ n government department dealing with special police work, esp. (in the US) protecting high government officers

sect /sekt/ n small group within or separated from a larger (esp. religious) group

sec·tar·i·an /sek'teəriən/ adj of or between sects, esp. as shown in great strength and narrowness of beliefs ~**ism** n [U]

sec·tion /'sekʃən/ n 1 [C] separate part of a larger object, place, group, etc. 2 [C;U] representation of something cut through from top to bottom ~**al** adj 1 in sections (to be) put together 2 limited to one particular group or area

sec·tor /'sektər/ n 1 part of a field of activity, esp. in business or trade — see also PRIVATE SECTOR, PUBLIC SECTOR 2 area of military control

sec·u·lar /'sekjʊlər/ adj not connected with or controlled by a church

se·cure /sɪ'kjʊər/ adj 1 protected against danger or risk 2 fastened firmly 3 certain: a secure job 4 having no anxiety ♦ vt 1 close tightly 2 make safe 3 fml get —**ly** adv

se·cu·ri·ty /sɪ'kjʊərəti/ n 1 [U] state of being secure 2 [U] (department concerned with) protection, esp. against lawbreaking, violence, enemy acts, escape from prison, etc.: strict security measures | a maximum security prison 3 [U] property of value promised to a lender in case repayment is not made 4 [C] document giving the owner the right to some property: government securities

se·dan /sɪ'dæn/ n AmE for SALOON (1)

sedan chair /·,· '·/ n seat carried through the streets on poles in former times

se·date /sɪ'deɪt/ adj calm or quiet ♦ vt make sleepy or calm, esp. with a drug **sedation** /-'deɪʃən/ n [U]

sed·a·tive /'sedətɪv/ n drug that makes one calm, esp. by causing sleep

sed·en·ta·ry /'sedəntəri ||-teri/ adj fml used to or needing long periods of sitting and only slight activity

sed·i·ment /'sedəmənt/ n [S;U] solid material that settles to the bottom of a liquid ~**ary** adj

se·di·tion /sɪ'dɪʃən/ n [U] speaking, actions, etc., encouraging people to disobey the government –**tious** adj

se·duce /sɪ'djuːs/ vt 1 persuade to have sex with 2 persuade to do esp. something bad by making it seem attractive **seducer** n **seduction** /sɪ'dʌkʃən/ n [C;U] **seductive** /sɪ'dʌktɪv/ adj very desirable or attractive

sed·u·lous /'sedjʊləs||'sedʒə-/ adj fml showing steady attention, care, and determination ~**ly** adv

see¹ /siː/ v **saw** /sɔː/, **seen** /siːn/ 1 vi have or use the power of sight 2 vt

notice, recognize, or examine by looking 3 vi/t come to know or understand: I can't see why you don't like it. 4 vt form an opinion or picture of in the mind: I see little hope of any improvement. 5 vt visit, meet, or receive as a visitor 6 vi/t (try to) find out: I'll see if he's there. 7 vt make sure; take care: See you're ready at 8 o'clock. 8 vt go with: I'll see you home. 9 vt be the occasion of (an event or course in history 10 vt (have experience of: We've seen some good times together. | That sofa has seen better days. 11 (I'll) see you/be seeing you (soon/later/next week, etc.) (used when leaving a friend) 12 let me see (used for expressing a pause for thought) 13 see fit decide to 14 seeing is believing: a I'll believe it when I see it, but not before b Now I've seen it, so I believe it 15 see one's way (clear) to feel able or willing to 16 see red become very angry 17 see the back/last of someone have no more to do with 18 see the light: a understand or accept an idea b have a religious experience which changes one's belief c come into existence 19 see things think one sees something that is not there 20 so I see what you say is already clear 21 (you) see (used in explanations)

see about phr vt 1 deal with 2 consider further 3 We'll see about that! infml I will prevent that happening or continuing!

see in phr vt find attractive in: I can't think what she sees in him.

see off phr vt 1 go to the airport, station, etc., with (someone who is starting a trip) 2 chase away 3 remain firm until (something dangerous) stops

see out phr vt 1 last until the end of 2 go to the door with (someone who is leaving)

see through phr vt 1 not be deceived by 2 provide for, support, or help until the end of (esp. a difficult time)

see to phr vt attend to; take care of

see² n area governed by a BISHOP

seed /siːd/ n [C;U] 1 usu. small hard plant part that can grow into a new plant 2 [C] something from which growth begins: seeds of future trouble 3 [U] lit SEMEN 4 [C] SEEDed (3) player 5 **go/run to seed: a** (of a plant) produce seed after flowers have been produced **b** (of a person) lose one's freshness, esp. by becoming lazy, careless, old, etc. ♦ vt 1 (of a plant) grow and produce seed 2 plant seeds in (a piece of ground) 3 place (esp. tennis players at the start of a competition) in order of likelihood to win ~**less** adj

seed·ling /'siːdlɪŋ/ n young plant grown from a seed

seed·y /'siːdi/ adj 1 looking poor, dirty, and uncared for 2 infml slightly unwell and/or in low spirits **–iness** n [U]

see·ing /'siːɪŋ/ also **seeing that —** conj as it is true that; since

seek /siːk/ v sought /sɔːt/ fml or lit 1 vi/t search (for) 2 vt ask for 3 vt try

seem /siːm/ v give the idea or effect of being; appear: She seems happy. **~ing** adj that seems to be, but perhaps is not real: his seeming calmness **~ingly** adv according to what seems to be so (but perhaps is not)

seem·ly /'siːmli/ adj fml (socially) suitable **–liness** n [U]

seen /siːn/ v past t of SEE

seep /siːp/ vi (of liquid) flow slowly through small openings in a material **~age** n [U] slow seeping flow

seer /'sɪəʳ/ n lit someone who knows about the future

see·saw /'siːsɔː/ n 1 board balanced in the middle for people to sit on at opposite ends so that when one end goes up the other goes down 2 up and down movement ♦ vi move up and down esp. between opponents or opposite sides: seesawing prices

seethe /siːð/ vi 1 be in a state of anger or unrest 2 (of a liquid) move about as if boiling

see-through /' · ·/ adj (esp. of a garment) that can be (partly) seen through

seg·ment /'segmənt/ n any of the parts into which something may be cut up or divided ♦ vt /seg'ment/ divide into segments **~ation** /ˌsegmən'teɪʃən/ n [U]

seg·re·gate /'segrɪgeɪt/ vt separate or set apart, esp. from a different social or racial group **–gation** /ˌsegrɪ'geɪʃən/ n [U]

seis·mic /'saɪzmɪk/ adj of or caused by EARTHQUAKES

seis·mo·graph /'saɪzməgrɑːf‖-græf/ n instrument for measuring the force of EARTHQUAKES

seize /siːz/ vt 1 take possession of by force or official order: (fig.) She was seized by a sudden idea. 2 take hold of eagerly, quickly, or forcefully **seizure** /'siːʒəʳ/ n 1 [U] act of seizing 2 [C] sudden attack of illness

seize up phr vt BrE (of part of a machine) become stuck and stop working

sel·dom /'seldəm/ adv not often; rarely

se·lect /sɪ'lekt/ vt choose as best, most suitable, etc., from a group ♦ adj 1 limited to members of the best social group or class 2 of high quality **~or** n

~ion /-'lekʃən/ n 1 [U] act of selecting or fact of being selected 2 [C] something or someone selected 3 [C] collection of things to choose from — see also NATURAL SELECTION

se·lec·tive /sɪ'lektɪv/ adj 1 careful in choosing 2 having an effect only on certain things **~ly** adv **–tivity** /sɪˌlek'tɪvɪti/ **~ness** /sɪ'lektɪvnɪs/ n [U]

self /self/ n selves /selvz/ [C;U] whole being of a person, including their nature, character, abilities, etc.

self-ab·sorbed /ˌ · ·'·◄/ adj paying all one's attention to oneself and one's own affairs

self-ap·point·ed /ˌ · ·'·◄/ adj chosen by oneself to do something, unasked and usu. unwanted

self-as·sured /ˌ · ·'·◄/ adj confident **–surance** n [U]

self-cen·tred /ˌ · '·◄/ adj interested only in oneself **~ness** n [U]

self-con·fi·dent /ˌ · '··◄/ adj sure of one's own power to succeed **~ly** adv **–dence** n [U]

self-con·scious /ˌ · '··◄/ adj nervous and uncomfortable about oneself as seen by others **~ly** adv **~ness** adj [U]

self-con·tained /ˌ · ·'·◄/ adj 1 complete in itself; independent 2 not showing feelings or depending on others' friendship

self-con·trol /ˌ · ·'·/ n [U] control over one's feelings **–trolled** adj

self-de·fence /ˌ · ·'·/ n [U] act or skill of defending oneself: He shot the man in self-defence. (= only to protect himself)

self-de·ter·mi·na·tion /ˌ · ·'···/ n [U] country's right to govern itself

self-em·ployed /ˌ · ·'·◄/ adj earning money from one's own business, rather than being paid by an employer

self-es·teem /ˌ · ·'·/ n [U] one's good opinion of one's own worth

self-ev·i·dent /ˌ · '···◄/ adj plainly true without need of proof **~ly** adv

self-ex·plan·a·to·ry /ˌ · ·'····/ adj easily understood

self-ful·fill·ing proph·e·cy /ˌ · ·ˌ · '···/ n statement about what may happen in the future which comes true because it has been made

self-im·port·ant /ˌ · ·'·◄/ adj having too much an opinion of one's own importance **–ance** n [U]

self-in·dul·gent /ˌ · ·'·◄/ adj too easily allowing oneself pleasure or comfort **–gence** n [U]

self-in·terest /ˌ · '··/ n [U] concern for what is best for oneself **~ed** adj

self·ish /'selfɪʃ/ adj concerned with one's own advantage without care for others **~ly** adv **~ness** n [U]

self·less /'selfləs/ adj concerned with others' advantage without care for oneself **~ly** adv **~ness** n [U]

self·made /ˌ·ˈ·◄/ adj having gained success and wealth by one's own efforts alone

self-pos·sessed /ˌ·ˈ·◄/ adj calm and confident **-session** n [U]

self-re·li·ant /ˌ·ˈ··/ adj not depending on others' help **-ance** n [U]

self-re·spect /ˌ·ˈ·/n [U] proper pride in oneself **~ing** adj

self-right·eous /ˌ·ˈ··/ adj (too) proudly sure of one's own rightness or goodness **~ly** adv **~ness** n [U]

self-sac·ri·fice /ˌ·ˈ···/n [U] the giving up of things that one cares deeply about, esp. in order to help others

self·same /'selfseɪm/ adj exactly the same

self-sat·is·fied /ˌ·ˈ···/adj too pleased with oneself

self-seek·ing /ˌ·ˈ··◄/ n, adj [U] (someone) working only for their own advantage

self-serv·ice /ˌ·ˈ··◄/ adj, n [U] (working by) the system in which buyers collect what they want and pay at a special desk

self-start·er /ˌ·ˈ··/n 1 a usu. electrical apparatus for starting a car engine 2 a person able to work alone on their own ideas

self-styled /ˈ·ˈ·/adj given the stated title by oneself, usu. without any right to it

self-suf·fi·cient /ˌ·ˈ···◄/ adj able to provide everything one needs without outside help **-ciency** n [U]

self-will /ˌ·ˈ·/ n [U] strong unreasonable determination to follow one's own wishes **~ed** adj

sell¹ /sel/ v sold /səʊld/ 1 vi/t give (property or goods) to someone in exchange for money 2 vt help or cause (something) to be bought: *Bad news sells like newspapers.* 3 vt offer (goods) for sale 4 vi be bought: *The magazine sells at $5.* 5 vt make acceptable or desirable by persuading 6 **sell oneself: a** make oneself or one's ideas seem attractive to others **b** give up one's principles for money or gain 7 **sell one's soul (to the devil)** act dishonourably in exchange for money, power, etc. 8 **sell someone down the river** put someone in great trouble by being disloyal to them 9 **sell something/someone short** value something or someone too low **~er** n

sell off phr vt get rid of by selling, usu. cheaply

sell out phr v 1 vi/t (cause to) sell all of (what was for sale): *The tickets are sold out; there are none left.* 2 vi be disloyal or unfaithful, esp. for payment **sell-out** /ˈ·ˈ·/ n 1 performance,

match, etc., for which all tickets have been sold 2 act of disloyalty or unfaithfulness

sell up phr vi sell something (esp. a business) completely

sell² n [S] deception — see also HARD SELL, SOFT SELL

sel·lo·tape /'seləteɪp, 'seləʊ-/ n [U] tdmk, BrE band of thin clear sticky material ♦ vt put together or mend with sellotape

selves /selvz/ pl. of SELF

se·man·tic /sɪˈmæntɪk/ adj of meaning in language **-ally** /-kli/ adv **-tics** n [U] study of meaning

sem·a·phore /'seməfɔːʳ/n [U] system of sending messages with flags

sem·blance /'sembləns/ n [S] appearance; outward form or seeming likeness: *a semblance of order*

se·men /'siːmən/ n [U] SPERM-carrying liquid, passed into the female during the sexual act

se·mes·ter /sɪˈmestəʳ/ n either of the 2 teaching periods in the year at US colleges

sem·i·cir·cle /'semɪˌsɜːkəl‖-ɜːr-/ n half a circle

sem·i·co·lon /ˌsemɪˈkəʊlən‖'semɪˌkəʊlən/ n mark (;) used to separate independent parts of a sentence

sem·i·con·duc·tor /ˌsemɪkənˈdʌktəʳ/ n substance which allows the passing of an electric current more easily at high temperatures

sem·i·de·tached /ˌsemɪdɪˈtætʃt/ adj, n (being) one of a pair of joined houses

sem·i·fi·nal /ˌsemɪˈfaɪnl◄‖'semɪˌfaɪnl/ n either of 2 matches whose winners play in a FINAL

sem·i·nal /'semənəl/ adj 1 fml influencing future development in a new way 2 containing or producing SEMEN

sem·i·nar /'semənɑːʳ/ n small study group

sem·i·na·ry /'semənəri‖-neri/ n college for training esp. Roman Catholic priests

Se·mit·ic /sɪˈmɪtɪk/ adj of a race of people including Jews and Arabs

sem·o·li·na /ˌseməˈliːnə/ n [U] crushed wheat used esp. for PASTA and cooked milky dishes

sen·ate /'senət/ n (usu. cap.) 1 higher of the 2 parts of the law-making body in the US, France, etc. 2 highest council of state in ancient Rome 3 governing council in some universities **-ator** n member of a senate **-atorial** /ˌsenəˈtɔːriəl/ adj

send /send/ sent /sent/ 1 vt cause to go or be taken, without going oneself: *He sent her a birthday card.* 2 vt cause to become: *It sent him mad.* 3 **send word** send a message **~er** n

send away *phr vi* **1** send to another place **2** order goods to be sent by post

send down *phr vt* **1** cause to go down **2** *BrE* (of a student) to dismiss from a university for bad behaviour **3** *BrE infml* send (someone) to prison

send for *phr vt* ask or order to come: *Send for a doctor!*

send off *phr vt* **1** post (a letter, parcel, etc.) **2** *BrE* (in sport) order (a player) to leave the field because of a serious breaking of the rules **3** SEND **away** **send-off** /'·· ·/ *n* show of good wishes at the start of a journey, new business, etc.

send on *phr vt* **1** send (a letter) to the receiver's next address **2** send (belongings) in advance to a point on a journey

send out *phr vt* **1** send from a central point **2** (of a natural object) produce: *The sun sends out light.* **3** obtain something from somewhere else: *We can send out for coffee later.*

send up *phr vt* **1** cause to go up **2** *BrE* make fun of by copying **3** *AmE infml* SEND **down** (3) **send-up** /'·· ·/ *n* *BrE* something which makes fun of someone or something

se·nile /'siːnail/ *adj* of or showing old age, esp. in weakness of mind **senility** /sɪ'nɪlɪti/ *n* [U]

se·ni·or /'siːniə[r]/ *n, adj* **1** (someone) older **2** (someone) of high or higher rank ~**ity** /ˌsiːni'ɒrɪti‖-'ɔːr-,-'ɑː-/ *n* [U] **1** being senior **2** official advantage gained by length of service in an organization

Senior *adj esp. AmE* the older, esp. of two men in the same family who have the same name

sen·sa·tion /sen'seɪʃən/ *n* **1** [C;U] feeling, such as of heat or pain, coming from the senses **2** [U] general feeling in the mind or body **3** [C] (cause of) excited interest ~**al** *adj* **1** wonderful **2** causing excited interest or shock ~**ally** *adv*

sen·sa·tion·al·ism /sen'seɪʃən-əlɪzəm/ *n* [U] the intentional producing of excitement or shock, esp. by books, magazines, etc., of low quality

sense /sens/ *n* **1** [C] intended meaning **2** [U] good and esp. practical understanding and judgment **3** [C] any of the 5 natural powers of sight, hearing, feeling, tasting, and smelling — see also SIXTH SENSE **4** [C;U] power to understand and judge a particular thing: *a poor sense of direction* **5** [S] feeling, esp. one that is hard to describe **6 in a sense** partly; in one way of speaking **7 make sense**: **a** have a clear meaning **b** be a wise course of action **8 make sense (out) of** understand **9 (there's) no sense (in)** no good reason for ♦ *vt* feel in the mind: *I*

could sense danger. **senses** *n* [P] powers of (reasonable) thinking: *He must have taken leave of his senses.* (= gone mad) ~**less** *adj* **1** showing a lack of meaning, thought, or purpose **2** unconscious

sense of oc·ca·sion /ˌ··· ·'···/ *n* [S] **1** natural feeling that tells one how one should behave at a particular social event **2** suitable feeling produced in someone by an important event

sense or·gan /'· ˌ··/ *n* eye, nose, tongue, ear, etc.

sen·si·bil·i·ty /ˌsensɪ'bɪlɪti/ also **sensibilities** *pl.* — *n* [U] delicate feeling about style or what is correct, esp. in art or behaviour

sen·si·ble /'sensɪbəl/ *adj* **1** having or showing good sense; reasonable **2 sensible of** *fml* recognizing; conscious of ~**bly** *adv*

sen·si·tive /'sensɪtɪv/ *adj* **1** quick to feel or show the effect of: *sensitive to light* **2** easily offended **3** showing delicate feelings or judgment: *a sensitive performance* **4** knowing or being conscious of the feelings and opinions of others **5** (of an apparatus) measuring exactly **6** needing to be dealt with carefully so as not to cause trouble or offence: *a sensitive issue* ~**ly** *adv* ~**tivity** /ˌsensɪ'tɪvɪti/ *n* [U]

sen·si·tize, -tise /'sensɪtaɪz/ *vt* make sensitive

sen·sor /'sensə[r]/ *n* apparatus for discovering the presence of something, such as heat or sound

sen·so·ry /'sensəri/ *adj fml* of or by the bodily senses

sen·su·al /'senʃuəl/ *adj* **1** of bodily feelings **2** interested in or suggesting physical, esp. sexual, pleasure ~**ity** /ˌsenʃu'ælɪti/ *n* [U]

sen·su·ous /'senʃuəs/ *adj* **1** giving pleasure to the senses SENSUAL (2) ~**ly** *adv* ~**ness** *n* [U]

sent /sent/ *v past t. and p. of* SEND

sen·tence /'sentəns/ *n* **1** group of words forming complete statement, command, question, etc. **2** (order given by a judge which fixes) a punishment for a criminal found guilty in court **3 give/pass/pronounce sentence** (of a judge) say the order for a punishment **4 under sentence of death** having received a death sentence ♦ *vt* (of a judge) give a punishment to

sen·ten·tious /sen'tenʃəs/ *adj fml* full of supposedly wise moral remarks ~**ly** *adv*

sen·tient /'senʃənt/ *adj fml* having feelings and consciousness

sen·ti·ment /'sentəmənt/ *n* **1** [U] tender feelings of pity, love, sadness, etc., or imaginative remembrance of the past 2 [C] *fml* thought or judgment caused by a feeling ~**al** /,senti'mentl◂/ *adj* **1** caused by sentiment **2** showing too much sentiment, esp. of a weak or unreal kind ~**ally** *adv* ~**al-ity** /,sentimn'tæləti/ *n* [U] **sentiments** *n* [P] opinion

sen-ti-nel /'sentinəl/ *n lit* guard; sentry

sen-try /'sentri/ *n* soldier guarding a building, entrance, etc.

se-pal /'sepəl/ *n* small leaf underneath a flower

sep-a-ra-ble /'sepərəbəl/ *adj fml* that can be separated –**bly** *adv*

sep-a-rate[1] /'sepəreit/ *v* **1** *vi/t* move, set, keep, or break apart **2** *vi* stop living together as husband and wife –**ration** /,sepə'reiʃən/ *n* **1** [C;U] the act of separating or the fact of being separated **2** [C;U] (a time of) being or living apart **3** [U] *law* a formal agreement by a husband and wife to live apart

sep-a-rate[2] /'sepərət/ *adj* **1** different; *a word with 3 separate meanings* **2** not shared: *We have separate rooms.* **3** apart ~**ly** *adv*

sep-a-rat-is-m /'sepərətizəm/ *n* [U] belief that a particular political or religious group should be separate, not part of a larger whole –**ist** *n*

se-pi-a /'si:piə/ *n* [U] reddish-brown colour

Sep-tem-ber /sep'tembə^r/ *n* the 9th month of the year

sep-tet /sep'tet/ *n* (music for) 7 musicians

sep-tic /'septik/ *adj* infected with bacteria

sep-ti-cae-mi-a /,septi'si:miə/ *esp. BrE* ‖ **-cemia** *AmE n* [U] dangerous infection spread through the body in the blood

septic tank /'·· ·/ *n* large container in which body waste matter is broken up and changed by bacteria

sep-ul-chre *BrE* ‖ **-cher** *AmE* /'sepəlkə^r/ *n lit* burial place –**chral** /si'pʌlkrəl/ *adj fml or lit* like or suitable for a grave

se-quel /'si:kwəl/ *n* **1** something that follows, esp. as a result **2** film etc., which continues where an earlier one ended

se-quence /'si:kwəns/ *n* **1** [C] group following each other in order **2** [U] order in which things follow each other **3** [C] scene in a film

se-ques-tered /si'kwestəd ‖ -ərd/ *adj lit* quiet and hidden

se-ques-trate /si'kwestreit, 'si:-kwə-/ *vt* seize (property) by legal order until claims on it are settled –**tration** /,si:kwə'streiʃən/ *n* [U]

se-quin /'si:kwin/ *n* small round shiny piece sewn on a garment for decoration

se-ra-gli-o /sə'rɑ:liəu/ *n* -**os** HAREM

se-raph-ic /sə'ræfik/ *adj* like an ANGEL, esp. in beauty or purity ~**ally** /-kli/ *adv*

ser-e-nade /,serə'neid/ *n* piece of music played or sung to a woman by a lover ♦ *vt* sing or play a serenade to

ser-en-dip-i-ty /,serən'dipəti/ *n* [U] ability to make useful discoveries by chance

se-rene /sə'ri:n/ *adj* completely calm and peaceful ~**ly** *adv* **serenity** /sə'renəti/ *n* [U]

serf /sɜːf ‖ sɜːrf/ *n* slave-like farm worker in former times ~**dom** /'sɜːfdəm ‖ 'sɜːr-/ *n* [U] state or fact of being a serf

serge /sɜːdʒ ‖ sɜːrdʒ/ *n* [U] strong woollen cloth

ser-geant /'sɑːdʒənt ‖ 'sɑːr-/ *n* **1** soldier in charge of others, but below the officers **2** policeman of middle rank

sergeant ma-jor /,·· '··◂/ *n* soldier just above a sergeant in rank

se-ri-al[1] /'siəriəl/ *adj* of, happening or arranged in a SERIES

serial[2] *n* written or broadcast story appearing in parts at fixed times ~**ize** *vt* print or broadcast as a serial

serial num-ber /'··· ,··/ *n* number marked on something to show which one it is in a series

se-ries /'siəri:z/ *n* series group of the same or similar things coming one after another or in order

se-ri-ous /'siəriəs/ *adj* **1** causing worry and needing attention **2** not cheerful or funny **3** needing or having great skill or thought ~**ly** *adv* ~**ness** *n* [U]

ser-mon /'sɜːmən ‖ 'sɜːr-/ *n* talk given by a priest as part of a church service

ser-pent /'sɜːpənt ‖ 'sɜːr-/ *n lit* snake

ser-rat-ed /sə'reitd, se-/ *adj* having (an edge with) a row of V-shapes like teeth

ser-ried /'serid/ *adj* **serried ranks** *lit* large numbers of people, etc., close together

se-rum /'siərəm/ *n* **serums** or **sera** /-rə/ [C;U] liquid containing disease-fighting substances, put into a sick person's blood

ser-vant /'sɜːvənt ‖ 'sɜːr-/ *n* person paid to do personal services for someone, esp. in their home

serve /sɜːv ‖ sɜːrv/ *v* **1** *vi/t* do work (for); give service (to): *to serve in the army* **2** *vt* provide with something necessary or useful: *The pipeline serves the whole town.* **3** *vt* offer (food, a meal, etc.) for eating **4** *vt* attend to (a customer in a shop) **5** *vt* spend (a period of time): *She served (2 years) in* *prison.* **6** *vi/t fml* be good enough or suitable for (a purpose) **7** *vi/t* (esp. in tennis) begin play by hitting (the ball) to one's opponent **8** *vt law* deliver (an official order to appear in court) **9 if my memory serves me (right)** if I remember correctly **10 serve someone right** be suitable punishment ♦ *n* act or manner of serving (SERVE (7))

server *n* **1** something used in serving food **2** player who serves in tennis — see also TIME SERVER

ser·vice /'sɜːvɪs‖'sɜr-/ *n* **1** [C;U] act or work done for someone **2** [U] attention to guests in a hotel, restaurant, etc., or to customers in a shop **3** [C;U] (operation of) an organization doing useful work: *a bus service | the postal service* **4** [C;U] (duty in) the army, navy, etc. **5** [C] religious ceremony **6** [C;U] examination of a machine to keep it in good condition **7** [C] SERVE **8** [C] set of dishes, etc.: *a dinner service* **9 at your service** *fml* willing to help **10 of service** *fml* useful; helpful ♦ *vt* repair or put in good condition ♦ *adj* something for the use of people working in a place, rather than the public: *service stairs*

ser·vice·a·ble /'sɜːvɪsəbəl/ *adj* fit for (long or hard) use; useful

service charge /'·· ·/ *n* amount added to a bill to pay for a particular service

ser·vice·man /'sɜːvɪsmən‖'sɜr-/ **-woman** /-ˌwʊmən/ *fem.* — *n* **-men** /-mən/ member of the army, navy, etc.

service sta·tion /'·· ˌ·/ *n* GARAGE

ser·vi·ette /ˌsɜːvɪ'et‖ˌsɜr-/ *n* NAPKIN

ser·vile /'sɜːvaɪl‖'sɜrvəl, -vaɪl/ *adj* behaving like a slave **-vility** /sɜː'vɪlɪti‖sɜr-/ *n* [U]

serv·ing /'sɜːvɪŋ‖'sɜr-/ *n* amount of food for 1 person

ser·vi·tude /'sɜːvɪtjuːd‖'sɜrvɪtuːd/ *n* [U] *lit* state of being a slave or one who is forced to obey another

ses·sion /'seʃən/ *n* **1** formal meeting or group of meetings of esp. a parliament or court **2** period of time used for a particular purpose: *a recording/drinking session*

set¹ /set/ *v* **set**, *pres. p.* **-tt-** **1** *vt* put (to stay) in the stated place: *to set a ladder against a wall* **2** *vt* fix; establish: *set a date for the wedding* **3** *vt* put into the correct condition for use: *set the clock/the table* **4** *vt* cause to be: *set a prisoner free | Her words set me thinking.* **5** *vt* put: *set a load down* **6** *vt* give (a piece of work) for someone to do **7** *vt* put the action of (a film, story, etc.) in the stated place and time **8** *vi/t* (cause to) become solid: *The jelly has set.* **9** *vi* (of the sun, moon, etc.) go

below the horizon **10** *vt* write or provide music for (a poem or other words to be sung) **11** *vt* fix (a precious stone) into (a piece of jewellery) **12** *vt* put (a broken bone) into a fixed position to mend **13** *vt* arrange (hair) when wet to be in a particular style when dry **14** *vt* arrange for printing **15 set an example** offer a standard for other people to follow **16 set eyes on** see **17 set light/fire to** cause (something) to burn **18 set one's face against** oppose **19 set one's heart/hopes on** want very much **20 set one's mind to** decide firmly on

set about *phr vt* **1** begin **2** attack

set back *phr vt* **1** place at esp. the stated distance behind something: *The house is set back 15 feet from the road.* **2** delay **3** cost (a large amount)

set in *phr vi* (of bad weather, disease, etc.) begin (and continue)

set off *phr v* **1** *vi* begin a journey **2** *vt* cause to explode **3** *vt* cause (sudden activity) **4** *vt* make (one thing) look better by putting it near something different: *A white belt set off her blue dress.*

set on *phr vt* **1** attack **2** cause to attack: *I'll set the dogs on you.*

set out *phr v* **1** *vt* arrange or spread out in order **2** *vi* begin a journey **3** *vt* begin with a purpose

set to *phr vi* begin eagerly or determinedly

set up *phr vt* **1** put into position **2** prepare (a machine, instrument, etc.) for use **3** establish or arrange (an organization, plan, etc.) **4** provide with what is necessary or useful

set² *adj* **1** given or fixed for study: *set books* **2** determined: *He's very set on going.* **3** fixed; PRESCRIBEd: *set hours* **4** unmoving: *a set smile* **5** at a fixed price: *a set dinner* **6** *infml* ready: *I'm all set, so we can go.*

set³ *n* **1** group forming a whole: *a set of gardening tools* **2** television or radio receiving apparatus **3** a scenery, etc., representing the place of action in a stage play **b** place where a film is acted **4** group of games in a tennis match **5** group of people of a particular social type: *the smart set* **6** act of setting (SET¹(13)) one's hair

set·back /'setbæk/ *n* something that delays or prevents successful progress

set piece /ˌ· '·◄/ *n* something carried out using a well-known formal pattern or plan

set·square /'setskweəʳ/ *n* 3-sided right-angled plate for drawing or testing angles

set·tee /se'tiː/ *n* long soft seat with a back, for more than one person

set·ter /'setəʳ/ *n* long-haired dog used by hunters

set·ting /'setɪŋ/ n **1** the going down (of the moon, sun, etc.) **2** way or position in which an instrument is prepared for use **3** a set of surroundings **b** time and place where the action of a book, film, etc., happens **4** set of articles (dishes, knives, forks, etc.) arranged at one place on a table for eating: *a place setting*

set·tle /'setl/ v **1** vi start to live in a place **2** vi/t (place so as to) stay or be comfortable **3** vi/t come or bring to rest, esp. from above: *Dust had settled on the furniture.* **4** vi/t make or become quiet, calm, etc.: *Settle down, children!* **5** vt decide on firmly; fix: *That settles it!* (= That has decided the matter.) **6** vt provide people to live in (a place) **7** vi/t bring (a matter) to an agreement **8** vt pay (a bill) **settled** *adj* **settler** n member of a new population

settle down *phr vi* **1** (cause to) sit comfortably **2** give one's serious attention (to a job, etc.): *I must settle down to some work today.* **3** establish a home and live a quiet life **4** become used to a way of life, job, etc.

settle for *phr vt* accept (something less than hoped for)

settle in *phr vi/t* (help to) get used to a new home, job, etc.)

settle on *phr vt* decide or agree on; choose

settle up *phr vi* pay what is owed

set·tle·ment /'setlmənt/ n **1** [U] movement of a new population into a new place to live there **2** [C] newly-built small village in an area with few people **3** [C;U] agreement or decision ending an argument **4** [C;U] payment of money claimed **5** [C] a formal gift or giving of money: *He made a settlement on his daughter when she married.*

set-to /'· ·/ n [S] short fight or quarrel

set-up /'· ·/ n arrangement; organization

sev·en /'sevən/ determiner, n, pron **7** ~**th** determiner, adv, n, pron 7th

sev·en·teen /ˌsevən'tiːn/ determiner, n, pron **17** ~**th** determiner, adv, n, pron 17th

seventh heav·en /ˌ·· '··/ n complete happiness

sev·en·ty /'sevənti/ determiner, n, pron **70** ~**tieth** determiner, adv, n, pron 70th

seventy-eight /ˌ··· '·/ n record played at 78 turns a minute

seven-year itch /ˌ·· · '·/ n dissatisfaction after 7 years of marriage

sev·er /'sevər/ vt fml divide in 2, esp. by cutting: (fig.) *sever diplomatic relations* ~**ance** n [U]

sev·er·al /'sevrəl/ determiner, pron more than a few but not very many;

some ♦ *adj fml* separate: *They went their several ways.*

severance pay /'···· ·/ n [U] money paid by a company to a worker losing his job through no fault of his own

se·vere /sə'vɪər/ adj **1** causing serious harm, pain, or worry **2** not kind or gentle **3** completely plain and without decoration ~**ly** adv **severity** /sə'verəti/ n [U]

sew /səu/ vi/t sewed, sewn /səun/ fasten (esp. cloth) with thread

sew up *phr vt* **1** close or repair by sewing **2** settle satisfactorily

sew·age /'sjuːdʒ, 'suː-‖'suː-/ n [U] waste material and water carried in sewers

sew·er /'sjuːər, 'suːər‖'suːər/ n large underground pipe for carrying away sewage and water, esp. in a city

sew·er·age /'sjuːərɪdʒ, 'suː-‖'suː-/ n [U] system of removing waste material through sewers

sex /seks/ n **1** [U] condition of being male or female **2** [C] set of all male or female people **3** [U] (activity connected with) SEXUAL INTERCOURSE: *to have sex (with someone)* ♦ vt find out whether (an animal) is male or female

sex ap·peal /'· ·ˌ·/ n [U] power of being sexually exciting to other people

sex·is·m /'seksɪzəm/ n [U] (unfair treatment coming from) the belief that one sex is better, cleverer, etc., than the other –**ist** adj, n

sex or·gan /'· ˌ··/ n part of the body used in producing children

sex·tant /'sekstənt/ n instrument for measuring angles between stars, to find out where one is

sex·tet /seks'tet/ n (music for) 6 musicians

sex·ton /'sekstən/ n someone who takes care of a church building

sex·tu·plet /sek'stjuːplət‖-'stʌ-/ n any of 6 children born together

sex·u·al /'sekʃuəl/ adj of or connected with sex ~**ly** adv; sexually active ~**ity** /ˌsekʃu'æləti/ n [U] interest in, the expression of, or the ability to take part in sexual activity

sexual in·ter·course /ˌ··· '···/ n [U] bodily act between 2 people in which the sex organs are brought together

sex·y /'seksi/ adj sexually exciting –**ily** adv –**iness** n [U]

SF written abbrev. for: SCIENCE FICTION

sh , shh /ʃ/ interj (used for demanding silence)

shab·by /'ʃæbi/ adj **1** untidy, uncared-for, and worn-out **2** unfair and ungenerous –**bily** adv –**biness** n

shack¹ /ʃæk/ n small roughly built house or hut

shack² v **shack up** phr vi infml (of a person, or persons) live together without being married

shack·le /'ʃækəl/ n metal band for fastening the arms or legs: (fig.) the shackles of slavery ♦ vt fasten (as if) with shackles

shade /ʃeɪd/ n 1 [U] slight darkness, made esp. by blocking of direct sunlight 2 [C] something which provides shade or reduces light: a lampshade 3 [C] degree or variety of colour: shades of blue 4 [C] slight difference: shades of meaning 5 [S] slightly: a shade too loud 6 [C] lit GHOST 7 **put someone/something in the shade** make someone/something seem much less important by comparison ♦ v 1 vt shelter from direct light 2 vt represent shadow on (an object in a picture) 3 vi change gradually **shady** adj 1 in or producing shade 2 probably dishonest

shades /ʃeɪdz/ n [P] 1 infml SUNGLASSES 2 **shades of** this reminds me of

shad·ow /'ʃædəʊ/ n 1 [U] SHADE (1): Most of the room was in shadow. 2 [C] dark shape made on a surface by something between it and direct light: The tree cast a long shadow across the lawn. 3 [C] dark area: shadows under her eyes 4 [S] slightest bit: not a shadow of a doubt 5 [C] a form from which the real substance has gone: After his illness he was only a shadow of his former self. 6 **be afraid of one's own shadow** be habitually afraid or nervous ♦ adj (in Britain) of the party opposing the government in parliament: the shadow cabinet ♦ vt 1 make a shadow on 2 follow and watch closely, esp. secretly ~**y** adj 1 hard to see or know about clearly 2 full of shade

shadow-box /'ʃædəʊbɒks‖-bɑːks/ vi fight with an imaginary opponent ~**ing** n [U]

shaft¹ /ʃɑːft‖ʃæft/ n 1 thin rod forming the body of a weapon or tool, such as a spear or axe 2 bar which turns to pass power through a machine: a propeller shaft 3 long passage going down: a mine shaft 4 either of 2 poles that an animal is fastened between to pull a vehicle 5 beam (of light) 6 lit something shot like an arrow: shafts of wit

shaft² vt AmE sl treat unfairly and very severely

shag¹ /ʃæg/ n [U] rough strong tobacco

shag² vt -gg- BrE taboo sl have sex with

shagged out /ˌ· '·/ adj BrE sl very tired

shag·gy /'ʃægi/ adj being or covered with long uneven untidy hair **-giness** n [U]

shaggy-dog sto·ry /ˌ·· '·ˌ ··/ n long joke with a purposely pointless ending

shake /ʃeɪk/ v shook /ʃʊk/, shaken /'ʃeɪkən/ 1 vi/t move up and down and from side to side with quick short movements 2 vi/t hold (someone's right hand) and move it up and down, to show esp. greeting or agreement 3 vt trouble; upset 4 vi (of a voice) tremble 5 **shake one's head** move head from side to side to answer 'no' ♦ n 1 [C] act of shaking 2 [C] infml moment 3 [C] AmE infml MILK SHAKE 4 [S] AmE infml treatment of the stated type — see also SHAKES **shaky** adj shaking; unsteady **shakily** adv

shake off phr vt get rid of; escape from

shake up phr vt 1 make big changes in (an organization), esp. to improve it 2 mix by shaking **shake-up** /'·ˌ·/ n rearrangement of an organization

shake-down /'ʃeɪkdaʊn/ n infml 1 last test operation of a new ship or aircraft 2 AmE act of getting money dishonestly 3 place prepared as a bed

shakes /ʃeɪks/ n infml 1 [the+P] nervous shaking of the body from disease, fear, etc. 2 **no great shakes** not very good

shale /ʃeɪl/ n [U] soft rock which splits naturally

shall /ʃəl; strong ʃæl/ v aux neg. short form **shan't** (used with I and we) 1 (expresses the future tense) 2 (used in questions or offers): Shall I (= would you like me to) go?

shal·low /'ʃæləʊ/ adj 1 not deep 2 lacking deep or serious thinking **shallows** n [P] shallow area in a river, lake, etc.

sham /ʃæm/ n 1 [C] something that is not what it appears or is said to be 2 [U] falseness; PRETENCE ♦ adj not real ♦ vi/t -mm- put on a false appearance

sha·ma·teur /'ʃæmətə', -tʃʊə', -tʃə', ˌʃæmə'tɜːr/ n derog one who officially plays sport for no money but in fact receives payment

sham·ble /'ʃæmbəl/ vi walk awkwardly, dragging the feet

sham·bles /'ʃæmbəlz/ n [P] (place or scene of) great disorder

sham·bol·ic /ʃæm'bɒlɪk‖-'bɑː-/ adj BrE infml completely disordered or confused

shame /ʃeɪm/ n 1 [U] painful feeling caused by knowledge of guilt, inability, or failure 2 [U] ability to feel this 3 [U] loss of honour 4 [S] something one is sorry about: It's a shame you can't come. 5 **put someone/something to shame** show someone/something to be less good by comparison ♦ vt 1 bring dishonour to 2 cause to feel shame ~**ful** adj which one ought to feel ashamed of ~**fully** adv ~**fulness** n [U] ~**less** adj **1** not feeling suitably ashamed: a shameless liar **2** done without shame ~**lessly** adv ~**lessness** n [U]

shame-faced /ˌʃeɪmˈfeɪst◂/ adj showing suitable shame ~**ly** /-ˈfeɪsɪdli/ adv

sham-poo /ʃæmˈpuː/ n -**poos** [C;U] liquid soap for washing the hair ♦ vt -**pooed**. present p. -**pooing** wash with shampoo

sham-rock /ˈʃæmrɒk‖-rɑːk/ n [U] plant with 3 leaves on each stem that is the national sign of Ireland

shan-dy /ˈʃændi/ n [U] beer mixed with esp. LEMONADE

shang-hai /ʃæŋˈhaɪ/ vt trick or force into doing something unwillingly

Shan-gri-La /ˌʃæŋgri ˈlɑː/ n distant beautiful imaginary place where everything is pleasant

shank /ʃæŋk/ n smooth end of a SCREW (1) or DRILL

shan't /ʃɑːnt‖ʃænt/ v short for: shall not

shan-ty[1] /ˈʃænti/ n small roughly built house

shanty[2] n song sung by working sailors

shan-ty-town /ˈʃænti,taʊn/ n (part of) a town where poor people live in shanties

shape /ʃeɪp/ n **1** [C;U] outer form of something: a cake in the shape of a heart **2** [U] general character or nature of something **3** [U] (proper) condition, health, etc. **4** get/put something into shape arrange or plan something properly **5** in any shape or form of any kind; at all **6** take shape begin to be or look like the finished form ♦ v **1** vt give a particular shape to: the influences that shape one's character **2** vi develop in the stated way ~**less** adj ~**ly** adj (of a person) having an attractive shape

shape up phr vi **1** develop well or in the stated way **2** (usu. used threateningly or angrily) begin to perform more effectively, behave better, etc.

shard /ʃɑːd‖ʃɑːrd/ n broken piece of a bowl, cup, etc.

share /ʃeər/ n **1** part belonging to, owed to, or done by a particular person **2** part of the ownership of a business company, offered for sale to the public **3** go shares BrE divide cost, ownership, etc., among 2 or more people ♦ v **1** vi/t have, use, pay, etc., with others or among a group **2** vt divide and give out in shares **3** share and share alike have an equal share in everything

share-hold-er /ˈʃeə,həʊldər‖ˈʃeər-/ n owner of SHAREs (2)

share-out /ˈ· ·/ n [S] act of giving out shares of something

shark /ʃɑːk‖ʃɑːrk/ n **1** shark or sharks large dangerous fish with sharp teeth **2** n person clever at getting money from others in dishonest ways

sharp /ʃɑːp‖ʃɑːrp/ adj **1** having or being a thin cutting edge or fine point: a sharp knife **2** not rounded: a sharp nose **3** causing a sensation like that of cutting, pricking, biting, or stinging: a sharp wind|the sharp taste of lemon juice **4** quick and strong: a sharp pain|a sharp blow to the head **5** sudden: a sharp turn **6** clear in shape or detail: a sharp photo **7** quick and sensitive in thinking, seeing, etc. **8** angry **9** (in music) above the right note **10** infml smart-looking ♦ adv **1** exactly at the stated time **2** suddenly: Turn sharp right. **3** above the right note **4** Look sharp! : a be careful b hurry up ♦ n (in music) sharp note ~**ly** adv ~**en** vi/t become or make sharp or sharper ~**ener** n: a pencil sharpener ~**ness** n [U]

sharp end /ˈ· ·/ n [the + S] infml part of a job, organization, etc., where the most severe problems are experienced

sharp prac-tice /ˌ· ˈ··/ n [U] dishonest but not quite illegal activity

sharp-shoot-er /ˈʃɑːp,ʃuːtər‖ˈʃɑːrp-/ n person skilled in shooting

shat-ter /ˈʃætər/ v **1** vi/t break suddenly into very small pieces **2** vt shock very much **3** vt infml tire very much

shave /ʃeɪv/ v **1** vi/t cut off (a beard or face hair) with a RAZOR or shaver **2** vt cut hair from (a part of the body) **3** vt cut off (very thin pieces) from (a surface) **4** vt come close to or touch in passing ♦ n act of shaving — see also CLOSE SHAVE **shaver** n electric shaving tool **shaving** n very thin piece cut off from a surface

shaving cream /ˈ·· ·/ n [U] soapy paste put on the face to make shaving easier

shawl /ʃɔːl/ n large piece of cloth worn over a woman's head or shoulders or wrapped round the body

she /ʃiː; strong ʃiː/ pron (used for the female subject of a sentence) ♦ n a female: a she-goat

sheaf /ʃiːf/ n **sheaves** /ʃiːvz/ **1** bunch of grain plants tied together **2** many things held or tied together: a sheaf of notes

shear /ʃɪər/ v **sheared**, **sheared** or **shorn** /ʃɔːn‖ʃɔːrn/ **1** vt cut off wool from (a sheep) **2** vt break under a sideways or twisting force **3** be shorn of have (something) completely removed from one **shears** n [P] large cutting tool like scissors

sheath /ʃiːθ/ n **sheaths** /ʃiːðz/ **1** closefitting case for a blade **2** CONDOM

sheathe /ʃiːð/ vt put away in a SHEATH (1)

she-bang /ʃ∂'bæŋ/ n **the whole shebang** infml everything

shed[1] /ʃed/ n lightly built single-floored (wooden) building

shed[2] vt **shed; pres. p.** -**dd**- **1** cause to flow out: *shedding tears* (= crying) **2** get rid of (outer skin, leaves, hair, etc.) naturally **3** get rid of (something not wanted or needed) **4** (of a vehicle) drop (a load of goods) by accident **5** **shed blood** cause wounding or esp. killing **6** **shed light on** help to explain

she'd /ʃid; strong ʃiːd/ short for: **1** she would **2** she had

sheen /ʃiːn/ n [S;U] shiny surface

sheep /ʃiːp/ n **sheep 1** grass-eating animal farmed for its wool and meat **2** **make/cast sheep's eyes at someone** behave fondly towards someone, esp. in an awkward or silly way **3** **the sheep and the goats** those who are good, able, successful, etc., and those who are not — see also BLACK SHEEP ~**ish** adj uncomfortable because one knows one has done something wrong or foolish ~**ishly** adv ~**ishness** n [U]

sheep-dog /'ʃiːpdɒg‖-dɔːg/ n dog trained to control sheep

sheer[1] /ʃɪ∂ʳ/ adj **1** pure; nothing but: *He won by sheer luck.* **2** very steep **3** (of cloth) very thin ♦ adv straight up or down

sheer[2] vi change direction quickly

sheet /ʃiːt/ n **1** large 4-sided piece of cloth used on a bed **2** broad regularly shaped piece of a thin or flat material: *a sheet of glass/paper* **3** a broad stretch of something: *a sheet of ice* **4** moving or powerful wide mass: *The rain came down in sheets.*

sheet mu·sic /'· ‚·· · '·/n [U] music printed on single sheets

sheikh /ʃeɪk‖ʃiːk/ n Arab chief or prince ~**dom** n

shek·els /'ʃek∂lz/ n [P] sl money

shelf /ʃelf/ n **shelves** /ʃelvz/ **1** flat (narrow) board fixed against a wall or in a frame, for putting things on **2** narrow surface of rock underwater **3** **on the shelf** (of a person) with little chance to marry, esp. because one is too old

shell[1] /ʃel/ n **1** [C;U] hard outer covering of a nut, egg, fruit, or certain types of animal: *a snail shell* **2** [C] outer surface or frame of something: (fig.) *He's only a shell of a man.* **3** [C] explosive for firing from a large gun **4** **come out of one's shell** begin to be friendly or interested in others

shell[2] vt **1** remove from a SHELL[1] (1) or POD **2** fire SHELLS[1] (3) at

shell out phr vt infml pay

she'll /ʃɪl; strong ʃiːl/ short for: **1** she will **2** she shall

shel·lack·ing /ʃ∂'lækɪŋ/ n AmE infml severe defeat

shell-fish /'ʃel‚fɪʃ/ n -**fish 1** [C] soft-bodied water animal with a shell: *Oysters and lobsters are shellfish.* **2** [U] such animals as food

shell-shock /'ʃelʃɒk‖-ʃɑːk/ n [U] illness of the mind, esp. in soldiers caused by the experience of war ~**shocked** adj

shel·ter /'ʃelt∂ʳ/ n **1** [C] building or enclosure giving protection **2** [U] protection, esp. from bad weather ♦ v **1** vt give shelter to **2** vi take shelter

shelve /ʃelv/ v **1** vt put aside until a later time **2** vi slope gradually

shelves /ʃelvz/ pl. of SHELF

she-nan-i-gans /ʃ∂'nænɪg∂nz/ n [P] infml **1** rather dishonest practices **2** MISCHIEF

shep-herd /'ʃep∂d‖-∂rd/ **shepherd-ess** /'ʃep∂des‖-∂rdɪs/ fem. — n person who takes care of sheep ♦ vt lead or guide like sheep

shepherd's pie /‚·· '·/ n [U] dish of finely cut-up meat with a topping of potato

sher-bet /'ʃɜːb∂t‖'ʃɜːr-/ n [U] sweet powder, often added to water

sher-iff /'ʃerɪf/ n **1** elected law officer in a local area in the US **2** royally appointed chief officer in an English COUNTY

sher-ry /'ʃeri/ n [U] pale or dark brown wine (originally) from Spain

she's /ʃiz; strong ʃiːz/ short for: **1** she is **2** she has

shib-bo-leth /'ʃɪbəleθ‖'ʃɪbəlɪθ/ n **1** word used to test to which party, class, etc., a person belongs **2** once-important custom or phrase which no longer has much meaning

shield /ʃiːld/ n **1** something carried as a protection from being hit **2** representation of this, used for a COAT OF ARMS, BADGE, etc. **3** protective cover ♦ vt protect

shift /ʃɪft/ v **1** vi/t move from one place to another **2** vt get rid of; remove **3** **shift for oneself** take care of oneself ♦ n **1** change in position or direction **2** (period worked by) a group of workers which takes turns with others: *the night shift* **3** loose fitting simple dress ~**less** adj lazy and lacking in purpose ~**y** adj looking dishonest; not to be trusted ~**ily** adv ~**iness** n [U]

shift key /'· ·/ n KEY on a TYPE-WRITER, etc., pressed to print a capital letter

shift stick /'··/ AmE for GEAR LEVER

shil-ling /'ʃɪlɪŋ/ n former British coin worth 12 old pence (1/20 of £1)

shil·ly-shal·ly /ˈʃili ˌʃæli/ vi waste time instead of taking action

shim·mer /ˈʃɪmər/ vi shine with a soft trembling light

shin /ʃɪn/ n the part of the leg below the knee ♦ vi -nn- climb using the hands and legs, esp. quickly and easily

shine /ʃaɪn/ v **shone** /ʃɒn‖ʃoʊn/ 1 vi/t (cause to) give off light 2 vt (past t. and p. **shined**) polish 3 vi be clearly excellent ♦ n [S] 1 brightness 2 act of polishing 3 (come) rain or shine whatever happens 4 take a shine to start to like **shiny** adj bright

shin·gle /ˈʃɪŋgəl/ n [U] stones on a seashore **-gly** adj

shin·gles /ˈʃɪŋgəlz/ n [U] disease producing painful red spots, esp. round the waist

shin·ny /ˈʃɪni/ vi AmE for SHIN

ship /ʃɪp/ n 1 large boat 2 large aircraft or space vehicle 3 when one's ship comes in/home one becomes rich ♦ vt -pp- 1 send by ship 2 send over a large distance by road, air, etc. **~per** n dealer who ships goods **~ping** n [U] ships as a group

ship·board /ˈʃɪpbɔːd‖-bɔːrd/ n on shipboard on a ship

ship·mate /ˈʃɪpmeɪt/ n fellow sailor on the same ship

ship·ment /ˈʃɪpmənt/ n 1 [C] load of goods sent by sea, road, or air 2 [C;U] sending, carrying, and delivering goods

ship·shape /ˈʃɪpʃeɪp/ adj clean and neat

ship·wreck /ˈʃɪp-rek/ n [C;U] destruction of a ship, as if by hitting rocks or by sinking ♦ vt 1 cause to suffer shipwreck 2 ruin

ship·yard /ˈʃɪp-jɑːd‖-jɑːrd/ n place where ships are built or repaired

shires /ˈʃaɪəz‖ˈʃaɪərz/ n [P] areas of England away from the cities

shirk /ʃɜːk‖ʃɜːrk/ vi/t avoid (unpleasant work) because of laziness, lack of determination, etc. **~er** n

shirt /ʃɜːt‖ʃɜːrt/ n 1 cloth garment for the upper body with SLEEVEs and usu. a collar 2 lose one's shirt to lose all one has 3 put one's shirt on risk all one's money on

shirt·sleeves /ˈʃɜːtsliːvz‖ˈʃɜːrt-/ n in (one's) shirtsleeves wearing nothing over one's shirt

shirt·y /ˈʃɜːti‖ˈʃɜːr-/ adj infml angry

shit /ʃɪt/ n [U] taboo 1 solid waste from the bowels 2 something of no value: I don't give a shit. (= I don't care) 3 worthless or unpleasant person ♦ vi -tt- taboo pass solid waste from the bowels ♦ interj taboo (expressing anger or annoyance) **~ty** adj taboo sl unpleasant

shiv·er /ˈʃɪvər/ vi shake, esp. from cold or fear ♦ n feeling of shivering **~y** adj

shoal¹ /ʃoʊl/ n dangerous bank of sand near the surface of water

shoal² n large group of fish swimming together

shock¹ /ʃɒk‖ʃɑːk/ n [C;U] 1 (state or feeling caused by) an unexpected and usu. very unpleasant event 2 violent force from a hard blow, crash, explosion, etc., or from electricity ♦ vt cause unpleasant or angry surprise to ♦ adj very surprising: shock tactics **~ing** adj 1 very offensive, wrong, or upsetting 2 very bad: I've got a shocking cold.

shock² n thick mass (of hair)

shock ab·sorb·er /ˈˈ·‖·ˌ··/ n apparatus fitted to a vehicle to lessen the effect of violent movement

shod /ʃɒd‖ʃɑːd/ past t. and p. of SHOE

shod·dy /ˈʃɒdi‖ˈʃɑːdi/ adj 1 cheaply and badly done 2 ungenerous; dishonourable **-dily** adv **-diness** n [U]

shoe /ʃuː/ n 1 covering worn on the foot 2 fill someone's shoes take the place and do the job of someone 3 in someone's shoes in someone's position: I'd hate to be in your shoes. ♦ vt shod fix a HORSESHOE on

shoe·lace /ˈʃuːleɪs/ n thin cord for fastening a shoe

shoe·string /ˈʃuːstrɪŋ/ n on a shoestring with a very small amount of money

shone /ʃɒn‖ʃoʊn/ past t. and p. of SHINE

shoo /ʃuː/ interj (used for driving away esp. birds and animals) ♦ vt drive away (as if) by saying 'shoo'

shook /ʃʊk/ v past t. of SHAKE

shoot /ʃuːt/ v **shot** /ʃɒt‖ʃɑːt/ 1 vi fire a weapon 2 vt (of a person or weapon) send out (bullets, etc.) with force: (fig.) She shot him an angry glance. 3 vt hit, wound, or kill with a bullet, etc. 4 vi move very quickly or suddenly: The car shot past us. | Pain shot up my arm. | (fig.) Prices have shot up. 5 vi/t make (a photograph or film) (of) 6 vi kick, throw, etc., a ball to make a point in a game 7 vt AmE play (a game of BILLIARDS, POOL, etc.) 8 shoot one's mouth off talk foolishly about what one does not know about or should not talk about 9 shoot the bull/the breeze AmE infml have an informal not very serious conversation ♦ n 1 new growth from a plant 2 occasion for shooting, esp. of animals

shoot down phr vt 1 bring down (a flying aircraft) by shooting 2 REJECT (an idea)

shoot up *phr v* **1** *vi* go upwards, increase, or grow quickly **2** *vt infml* damage or wound by shooting **3** *vi/t sl* take (a drug) directly into the blood using a needle

shooting star /,·· '·/ *n* METEOR

shoot-out /'· ·/ *n* battle between gunfighters, esp. in the West

shop[1] /ʃɒp‖ʃɑːp/ *n* **1** [C] *BrE* building or room where goods are sold **2** [U] subjects connected with one's work: *Let's not talk shop.*

shop[2] *v* **-pp- 1** *vi* visit shops to buy things **2** *vt BrE infml* tell the police about (a criminal) ~**per** *n* ~**ping** *n* [U] goods bought when visiting shops

shop around *phr vt* compare prices or values in different shops before buying: *(fig.) Shop around before deciding which club to join.*

shop assis·tant /'· ·,··/ *n BrE* person who serves customers in a shop

shop floor /,· '·◂/ *n* area, esp. in a factory, where the ordinary workers work

shop·keep·er /'ʃɒp,kiːpə[r]‖'ʃɑːp-/ *n esp. BrE* person in charge of a small shop

shop·lift /'ʃɒp,lɪft‖'ʃɑːp-/ *vi* steal from a shop ~**er** *n*

shop-soiled /'ʃɒpsɔɪld‖'ʃɑːp-/ *adj* slightly damaged or dirty from being kept in a shop for a long time

shop stew·ard /,· '··/ *n* trade union officer representing members in a place of work

shore[1] /ʃɔː[r]/ *n* [C;U] **1** land along the edge of a sea, lake, etc. **2 on shore** on land; away from one's ship

shore[2] *v* **shore up** *phr vt* support (something in danger of falling), esp. with wood

shorn /ʃɔːn‖ʃɔːrn/ *past p. of* SHEAR

short[1] /ʃɔːt‖ʃɔːrt/ *adj* **1** measuring a small or smaller than average amount in distance, length, or height **2** lasting only a little time, or less time than usual or expected **3** a shorter (and often more usual) way of saying: *The word 'pub' is short for 'public house'.* **4** not having or providing what is needed: *I'm short of money.* **5** rudely impatient **6 little/nothing short of** *fml* nothing less than **7 make short work of** deal with or defeat quickly **8 short and sweet** short and direct in expression **9 short of: a** not quite reaching **b** except for **10 short on** without very much or enough (of): *He's a nice fellow but short on brains.*

short[2] *adv* **1** suddenly: *He stopped short.* **2 fall short (of)** be less than (good) enough (for) **3 go short (of)** be without enough (of) **4 run short (of): a** not have enough left **b** become less than enough

short[3] *n* **1** drink of strong alcohol, such as WHISKY **2** short film shown before the main film at a cinema **3** SHORT CIRCUIT **4 for short** as a shorter way of saying it **5 in short** all I mean is; to put it into as few words as possible — see also SHORTS

short·age /'ʃɔːtɪdʒ‖'ʃɔːr-/ *n* [C;U] amount lacking; not enough

short·bread /'ʃɔːtbred‖'ʃɔːrt-/ *n* [U] sweet buttery BISCUIT

short-change /,· '·/*vt* **1** give back less than enough money to a buyer **2** fail to reward fairly

short cir·cuit /,· '··/ *n* faulty electrical connection where the current flows the wrong way and usu. puts the power supply out of operation **short-circuit** *vi/t* (cause to) have a short circuit

short·com·ing /'ʃɔːt,kʌmɪŋ‖'ʃɔːrt-/ *n* fault; failing

short cut /,· '·, '· ·‖'· ·/ *n* quicker more direct way

short·en /'ʃɔːtn‖'ʃɔːrtn/ *vi/t* make or become shorter

short·fall /'ʃɔːtfɔːl‖'ʃɔːrt-/ *n* amount by which something fails to reach the expected total

short·hand /'ʃɔːthænd‖'ʃɔːrt-/ *n* [U] system of special signs for fast writing

short·hand·ed /,ʃɔːt'hændɪd◂‖ ,ʃɔːrt-/ *adj* without enough workers or helpers

short-list /'· ·/ *n BrE* list of the best ones chosen from an original long list **short-list** *vt BrE* put on a short list

short-lived /,· '·◂/ *adj* lasting only a short time

short·ly /'ʃɔːtli‖'ʃɔːrt-/ *adv* **1** soon **2** impatiently **3** in a few words

shorts /ʃɔːts‖ʃɔːrts/ *n* [P] **1** short trousers **2** *esp. AmE* short UNDERPANTS

short shrift /,· '·/*n* [U] unfairly quick or unsympathetic treatment

short-sight·ed /,ʃɔːt'saɪtɪd◂‖ ,ʃɔːrt-/ *adj* **1** unable to see distant things clearly **2** not considering what may happen in the future ~**ly** *adv* ~**ness** *n* [U]

short-term, short term /,· '·◂/ *adj, n* (concerning) a short period of time; (in or for) the near future: *short-term planning*

short wave /,· '·◂/ *n* [U] radio broadcasting on waves of less than 60 metres

shot[1] /ʃɒt‖ʃɑːt/ *v* past t. and p. of SHOOT **2 be/get shot of** *sl* get rid of

shot[2] *n* **1** [C] (sound of) shooting a weapon **2** [C] hit, kick, etc., of a ball in sport **3** [C] person who shoots with the stated skill **4** [C] attempt: *I'll have a shot at it.* **5** [U] metal balls for shooting from shotguns or CANNONS **6** [C] **a** photograph **b** single part of a film made by one camera without interruption **7** [C] INJECTION: *a shot of penicillin* **8** [C] sending up of a spacecraft or ROCKET: *a moon shot* **9** [C] a small drink (esp. of WHISKY) all swallowed at once **10 a shot in the arm** something which acts to bring back a better, more active condition **11 a shot in the dark** a wild guess unsupported by arguments **12 like a shot** quickly and eagerly — see also BIG SHOT

shot-gun /'ʃɒtgʌn‖'ʃɑːt-/ *n* gun fired from the shoulder, usu. having two barrels, used esp. to kill birds

shotgun wed-ding /,·· '··/ *n* wedding that has to take place, esp. because the woman is going to have a baby

should /ʃəd; *strong* ʃʊd/ *v aux* **1** a ought to **b** will probably **2** (used after *that* in certain expressions of feeling): *It's odd that you should mention him.* (= The fact that you have mentioned him is odd.) **3** *fml* (used instead of **shall** in conditional sentences with **I** and **we** as the subject and a past tense verb): *I should be surprised if he came.* **4** (to express humour or surprise): *As I left the house, who should I meet but my old friend Sam.* **5 I should** (when giving advice) you ought to: *I should go (if I were you).* **6 I should have thought** *esp. BrE* (shows surprise): *I should have thought you'd know the answer.* **7 I should like** *fml* I want **8 I should think** I believe **9 I should think so!/not!** of course!/of course not!

shoul-der /'ʃəʊldər/ *n* **1** a the part of the body at each side of the neck where the arms are connected **b** part of a garment which covers this part of the body **2** part where something widens slopingly: *the shoulder of a bottle* **3 head and shoulders above** very much better than **4 put one's shoulder to the wheel** start work **5 rub shoulders with** meet socially **6 shoulder to shoulder: a** side by side **b** together; with the same intentions ♦ *vt* accept (a heavy responsibility, duty, etc.)

shoulder blade /'·· ·/ *n* either of 2 flat bones in the upper back

should-n't /'ʃʊdnt/ *v short for:* should not

shout /ʃaʊt/ *vi/t* speak or say very loudly ♦ *n* loud cry or call

shout down *phr vt* prevent a speaker being heard by shouting

shout-ing /'ʃaʊtɪŋ/ *n* **1** [U] shouts **2 all over bar the shouting** the important or interesting part (of a struggle, competition, etc.) has now been (successfully) completed and the result is no longer in doubt

shove /ʃʌv/ *vi/t* **1** push, esp. roughly or carelessly **2** *infml* move oneself: *Shove over and let me sit down.* ♦ *n* strong push

shov-el /'ʃʌvəl/ *n* long-handled tool with a broad blade for lifting loose material ♦ *vi/t* **-11-** *BrE* ‖ **-l-** *AmE* move or work (as if) with a shovel

show¹ /ʃəʊ/ *v* **showed, shown** /ʃəʊn/ **1** *vt* allow or cause to be seen: *Show me your ticket.* **2** *vi* be able to be seen: *The stain won't show.* **3** *vt* go with and guide or direct: *May I show you to your seat?* **4** *vt* explain, esp. by actions: *Show me how to do it.* **5** *vt* make clear; prove: *This piece of work shows what you can do when you try.* **6** *vt* cause to be felt in one's actions: *They showed their enemies no mercy.* **7** *vi sl for* SHOW up (2) **8 it goes to show** it proves the point **9 to show for** as a profit or reward from

show off *phr v* **1** *vi derog* behave so as to try to get attention and admiration **2** *vt* show proudly or to the best effect

show up *phr v* **1** *vt* make clear the (esp. unpleasant) truth about **2** *vi* arrive; be present

show² *n* **1** [C] performance, esp. in a theatre or on television or radio **2** [C] collection of things for the public to look at: *a flower show* **3** [S] showing of some quality: DISPLAY: *a show of temper* **4** [S] outward appearance: *a show of interest* **5** [U] splendid(-seeming) appearance or ceremony **6** [S] effort; act of trying: *They've put up a very good/poor show this year.* **7 get this show on the road** *infml* start to work **8 on show** being shown to the public — see also **steal the show** (STEAL) **~y** *adj* (too) colourful, bright, attention-getting, etc.

show busi-ness /'· ,··/ *n* [U] job of people who work in television, films, the theatre, etc.

show-case /'ʃəʊkeɪs/ *n* a set of shelves enclosed in glass on which objects are placed for looking at in a shop, etc.: (fig.) *The factory is a showcase for British industry.*

show-down /'ʃəʊdaʊn/ *n* settlement of a quarrel in an open direct way

show-er /'ʃaʊər/ *n* **1** short-lasting fall of rain (or snow) **2** fall or sudden rush of many small things: *a shower of sparks* **3** (apparatus for) washing the body by standing under running water ♦ *v* **1** *vi* fall in showers **2** *vt* scatter or cover in showers **3** *vi* take a SHOWER (3) **~y** *adj* with showers of rain

show-ing /'ʃəʊɪŋ/ *n* **1** [S] performance: *a poor showing* **2** [C] act of putting on view

show jump·ing /'· ,·'/ n [U] competition for riding horses over fences

show·man /'ʃəʊmən/ n -men /mən/ 1 person whose business is producing public entertainments, etc. 2 person who is good at gaining public attention ~**ship** n [U]

shown /ʃəʊn/ past p. of SHOW

show-off /'· ·/ n person who SHOWs off (1)

show-piece /'ʃəʊpiːs/ n fine example fit to be admired

shrank /ʃræŋk/ past t. of SHRINK

shrap·nel /'ʃræpnəl/ n [U] metal scattered from an exploding bomb

shred /ʃred/ n 1 small narrow piece torn or roughly cut off 2 slightest bit: *not a shred of evidence* ♦ vt -dd- cut or tear into shreds

shrew /ʃruː/ n 1 very small mouse-like animal 2 bad-tempered scolding woman ~**ish** adj

shrewd /ʃruːd/ adj 1 showing good practical judgment 2 likely to be right: *a shrewd estimate* ~**ly** adv

shriek /ʃriːk/ vi/t, n (cry out with) a wild high cry

shrift /ʃrɪft/ n see SHORT SHRIFT

shrill /ʃrɪl/ adj (of a sound) high and (painfully) sharp **shrilly** /'ʃrɪl-li, 'ʃrɪli/ adv ~**ness** n [U]

shrimp /ʃrɪmp/ n small 10-legged sea creature

shrine /ʃraɪn/ n 1 holy place, where one worships 2 box containing the remains of a holy person's body

shrink[1] /ʃrɪŋk/ v **shrank** /ʃræŋk/, **shrunk** /ʃrʌŋk/ 1 vi/t (cause to) become smaller 2 vi move back and away ~**age** n [U] loss in size

shrink from phr vt avoid, esp. from fear

shrink[2] n infml PSYCHOANALYST or PSYCHIATRIST

shrinking vi·o·let /,·· '··'/ n shy person

shriv·el /'ʃrɪvəl/ vi/t -ll- BrE -l- AmE (cause to) become smaller by drying and twisting into small folds

shroud /ʃraʊd/ n 1 cloth for covering a dead body 2 something that covers and hides ♦ vt cover and hide

shrub /ʃrʌb/ n low bush

shrub·be·ry /'ʃrʌbəri/ n [C;U] mass or group of shrubs

shrug /ʃrʌg/ vi/t -gg- raise (one's shoulders), esp. showing doubt or lack of interest ♦ n act of shrugging

shrug off phr vt treat as unimportant or easily dealt with

shrunk /ʃrʌŋk/ past p. of SHRINK

shrunk·en /'ʃrʌŋkən/ adj having been shrunk

shud·der /'ʃʌdər/ vi shake uncontrollably for a moment ♦ n act of shuddering

shuf·fle /'ʃʌfəl/ v 1 vi/t mix up (playing cards) so as to produce a chance order 2 vi walk by dragging one's feet slowly along ♦ n 1 [C] act of shuffling cards 2 [S] slow dragging walk

shun /ʃʌn/ vt -nn- avoid with determination

shunt /ʃʌnt/ vt 1 esp. BrE move (a train) from one track to another 2 move around or away: *Smith was shunted to a smaller office.*

shush /ʃʊʃ/ interj (used for demanding silence)

shut /ʃʌt/ v shut, pres. p. -tt- 1 vi/t close: *Shut the door.* 2 vt keep or hold by closing a door, window, etc.: *He shut himself in his room.* 3 vi/t stop operating: *The shops shut at 5.30.*

shut down phr vi/t (cause to) stop operation, esp. for a long time or forever **shutdown** /'ʃʌtdaʊn/ n

shut off phr vi/t 1 stop in flow or operation, esp. by turning a handle or pressing a button 2 keep separate or away

shut up phr v 1 vi/t (cause to) stop talking 2 vt keep enclosed 3 **shut up shop** close a business at the end of a day or forever

shut·ter /'ʃʌtər/ n 1 part of a camera which opens to let light fall on the film 2 movable cover for a window 3 **put up the shutters** infml close a business at the end of the day or forever ♦ vt close (as if) with SHUTTERs (2)

shut·tle /'ʃʌtl/ n 1 (vehicle used on) a regular short journey: *a shuttle service between the town centre and the station* | *the London to Paris air shuttle* 2 reusable spacecraft 3 thread-carrier in weaving ♦ vt move by a SHUTTLE (1)

shut·tle·cock /'ʃʌtlkɒk‖-kɑːk/ n light feathered object struck in BADMINTON

shuttle di·plo·ma·cy /'·· ·,···/ n [U] international talks carried out by someone who travels between the countries concerned taking messages and suggesting answers to problems

shy[1] /ʃaɪ/ adj 1 nervous in the company of others 2 (of animals) unwilling to come near people 3 **fight shy of** try to avoid 4 **once bitten, twice shy** a person who has been tricked will be more careful in the future ~**ly** adv ~**ness** n [U]

shy[2] vi (esp. of a horse) make a sudden (frightened) movement

shy away from phr vt avoid something unpleasant

shys·ter /'ʃaɪstər/ n AmE infml dishonest person, esp. a lawyer

Siamese twin /,saɪəmiːz 'twɪn/ n either of 2 people with their bodies joined from birth

sib·i·lant /'sɪbələnt/ *adj, n fml* (making or being) a sound like *s* or *sh*

sib·ling /'sɪblɪŋ/ *n fml* brother or sister

sick /sɪk/ *adj* 1 ill 2 throwing or about to throw food up out of the stomach: *The cat's been sick on the carpet.* | *We felt sick as soon as the ship began to move.* 3 feeling annoyance, dislike, and loss of patience: *I'm sick of your complaints.* | *His hypocrisy makes me sick!* 4 unnaturally or unhealthily cruel: *a sick joke* 5 **worried sick** very worried **~ness** *n* 1 [C;U] illness 2 [U] feeling SICK (2)

sick·bay /'sɪkbeɪ/ *n* room with beds for sick people

sick·en /'sɪkən/ *v* 1 *vt* cause to feel SICK (3) 2 *vi* become ill **~ing** *adj* extremely displeasing or unpleasant

sick·le /'sɪkəl/ *n* small tool with a curved blade for cutting long grass

sick·ly /'sɪkli/ *adj* 1 weak and unhealthy 2 unhealthily pale 3 causing a sick feeling

side[1] /saɪd/ *n* 1 surface that is not the top, bottom, front, or back 2 edge; border: *A square has 4 sides.* 3 either of the 2 surfaces of a thin flat object 4 part in relation to a central line: *I live on the other side of town.* 5 place or area next to something: *On one side of the window was a mirror, and on the other a painting.* | *He never leaves his mother's side.* 6 part or quality to be considered: *Try to look at both sides of the question.* 7 (group holding) a position in a quarrel, war, etc.: *I'm on your side.* | *I never take sides.* (= support one side against the other) 8 sports team 9 part of a line of a family that is related to a particular person 10 **get on the right/wrong side of someone** *infml* win/lose someone's favour 11 **on the right/wrong side of** younger/older than (a stated age) 12 **on the side** as a (sometimes dishonest) additional activity: *She does some teaching on the side.* 13 **on the big/small/etc. side** rather; too big/small/etc. 14 **on/to one side: a** out of consideration or use for the present **b** away from other people for a private talk 15 **side by side** next to (one) another 16 **-sided** having the stated number or kind of sides

side[2] *vi* support the stated SIDE[1] (7): *She sided with me.*

side·board /'saɪdbɔːd ‖ -bɔrd/ *n* long table-like cupboard for dishes, glasses, etc.

side·boards /'saɪdbɔːdz ‖ -bɔrdz/ *BrE* ‖ **sideburns** /'saɪdbɜːnz ‖ -bɜrnz/ *AmE* — *n* [P] hair on the sides of a man's face

side·car /'saɪdkɑːʳ/ *n* small wheeled seat fastened to the side of a motorcycle

side ef·fect /'·· ‚·/ *n* effect in addition to the intended one

side is·sue /'· ‚·/ *n* question or subject apart from the main one

side·kick /'saɪdkɪk/ *n infml* a (less important) helper or companion

side·light /'saɪdlaɪt/ *n* 1 small lamp at the side of a vehicle 2 piece of additional (not very important) information

side·long /'saɪdlɒŋ ‖ -lɔːŋ/ *adj* directed sideways: *a sidelong glance*

side·sad·dle /'saɪd‚sædl/ *adv, n* (on) a woman's SADDLE on which one puts both one's legs on the same side

side·show /'saɪdʃəʊ/ *n* separate small show at a fair or CIRCUS

side·step /'saɪdstep/ *vi/t* **-pp-** 1 step aside to avoid (esp. a blow) 2 avoid (an unwelcome question, problem, etc.)

side·track /'saɪdtræk/ *vt* cause to leave one subject or activity and follow another (less important) one

side·walk /'saɪdwɔːk/ *n AmE* for PAVEMENT

side·ways /'saɪdweɪz/ *adv* 1 with one side (not the back or front) forward or up 2 towards one side

sid·ing /'saɪdɪŋ/ *n* piece of railway track where carriages are parked

si·dle /'saɪdl/ *v* **sidle up** *phr vi* walk secretively or nervously up (to someone)

siege /siːdʒ/ *n* operation by an army surrounding a city, etc., to force the people inside to accept defeat

si·es·ta /si'estə/ *n* short sleep after the midday meal

sieve /sɪv/ *n* 1 tool with a net or holes for letting liquid or small objects through 2 **head/memory like a sieve** a mind that forgets quickly ♦ *vt* put through or separate with a sieve

sift /sɪft/ *v* 1 *vt* put (something non-liquid) through a sieve 2 *vi/t* examine (things in a mass or group) closely: *sifting the evidence*

sigh /saɪ/ *vi* let out a deep breath slowly and with a sound, usu. expressing sadness, satisfaction, or tiredness: (fig.) *The wind sighed in the trees.* (= made a sound like sighing) ♦ *n* act or sound of sighing

sight /saɪt/ *n* 1 [U] power of seeing 2 [S;U] seeing of something: *I caught sight of her* (= noticed her) *in the crowd.* 3 [C] something seen 4 [U] range of what can be seen: *The train came into sight.* 5 [C] something worth seeing: *the sights of London* **6** [C] part of an instrument or weapon which guides the eye in aiming **7** [S] something which looks very bad or laughable **8** [S] *infml* a lot: *She earns a sight more than I do.* **9 a sight for sore eyes** a person or thing that one is glad to see **10 at first sight** at the first time of seeing or considering **11 at/on sight** as soon as seen or shown **12 in sight:** a in view **b** near **13 know someone by sight** recognize someone without knowing them personally or without knowing their name **14 set one's sights on** direct one's efforts (towards) — see also SECOND SIGHT ♦ *vt* see for the first time — **ed** *adj* able to see ~**ing** *n* case of someone or something being seen or noticed: *several sightings of rare birds* ~**less** *adj* blind

sight·see·ing /'saɪtsiːɪŋ/ *n* [U] visiting places of interest —**seer** *n*

sign /saɪn/ *n* **1** mark which represents a known meaning: + *is the plus sign.* **2** movement of the body intended to express a meaning **3** notice giving information, a warning, etc. **4** something that shows the presence or coming of something else: *There are signs that the economy may be improving.* **5** also **star sign** — any of the 12 divisions of the year represented by groups of stars (Leo, Taurus, etc.) **6 a sign of the times** something that is typical of the way things are just now ♦ *vi/t* **1** write (one's name) on (a written paper), esp. officially or to show that one is the writer **2** SIGNAL (1) **3** SIGN UP —**er** *n*

sign away *phr vt* give up (ownership, etc.) formally by signing a paper

sign on *phr vi/t* **1** (cause to) join a working force by signing a paper **2** state officially that one is unemployed

sign up *phr vi/t* (cause to) sign an agreement to take part in something or take a job

sig·nal /'sɪɡnəl/ *n* **1** sound or action which warns, commands, or gives a message: *a danger signal* **2** action which causes another to happen **3** apparatus by a railway track to direct train drivers **4** message sent by radio or television waves ♦ *vi* -**ll-** *BrE* ‖ -**l-** *AmE* give a signal

signal box /'··· ·/ *n* small building near a railway from which signals and POINTS are controlled

sig·nal·man /'sɪɡnəlmən/ *n* -**men** /-mən/ someone who works railway signals

sig·na·to·ry /'sɪɡnətəri‖-tɔːri/ *n* *fml* signer of an agreement, esp. among nations

sig·na·ture /'sɪɡnətʃəʳ/ *n* person's name written by himself or herself — see also TIME SIGNATURE

signature tune /'··· ,·/ *n* short piece of music used regularly to begin and end a particular radio or TV programme

sig·nif·i·cant /sɪɡ'nɪfɪkənt/ *adj* **1** of noticeable importance or effect **2** having a special meaning, indirectly expressed ~**ly** *adv* —**cance** *n* [S;U]

sig·ni·fy /'sɪɡnɪfaɪ/ *v fml* **1** *vt* mean **2** *vi/t* make known (esp. an opinion) by an action **3** *vi* matter

sign·post /'saɪnpəʊst/ *n* sign showing directions and distances ♦ *vt* esp. *BrE* provide with signposts to guide the driver

si·lage /'saɪlɪdʒ/ *n* [U] plants preserved as winter cattle food

si·lence /'saɪləns/ *n* **1** [C;U] (period of) absence of sound **2** [U] not speaking or making a noise **3** [U] failure to mention a particular thing ♦ *vt* cause or force to be silent **silencer** *n* apparatus for reducing noise

si·lent /'saɪlənt/ *adj* **1** free from noise **2** not speaking **3** failing or refusing to express an opinion, etc. **4** (of a letter) not pronounced —**ly** *adv*

sil·hou·ette /,sɪlu'et/ *n* dark shape seen against a light background ♦ *vt* cause to appear as a silhouette

sil·i·con /'sɪlɪkən/ *n* [U] simple nonmetallic substance found commonly in natural compounds

silicon chip /,··· '/ *n* a CHIP[1] (4) in a computer or other ELECTRONIC machinery

silk /sɪlk/ *n* [U] (smooth cloth from) fine thread produced by silkworms ~**en** *adj* **1** silky **2** made of silk ~**y** *adj* soft, smooth, and/or shiny

silk·worm /'sɪlkwɜːm‖-wɜːrm/ *n* CATERPILLAR which produces silk

sill /sɪl/ *n* shelflike part at the bottom of a window

sil·ly /'sɪli/ *adj* not serious or sensible; foolish —**liness** *n* [U]

silly sea·son /'·· ,··/ *n* [*the* + S] *infml* period in the summer when there is not much news so newspapers print silly stories about unimportant things

si·lo /'saɪləʊ/ *n* **1** round tower-like enclosure for storing SILAGE **2** underground MISSILE-firing base

silt /sɪlt/ *n* [U] loose mud brought by a river or current ♦ *v* **silt up** *phr vi/t* fill or become filled with silt

sil·ver /'sɪlvəʳ/ *n* **1** [U] soft whitish precious metal **2** [U] spoons, forks, dishes, etc., made of silver **3** [U] silver (-coloured) coins **4** [C] silver MEDAL ♦ *adj* **1** made of silver **2** of the colour of silver ~**y** *adj* **1** like silver in shine and colour **2** having a pleasant metallic sound

silver·smith /'sɪlvə,smɪθ‖-əʳ-/ *n* maker of jewellery, etc., in silver

silver wed·ding /,·· '··/ *n* the date that is exactly 25 years after the date of a wedding

sim·i·lar /'sɪmələʳ, 'sɪmɪləʳ/ *adj* almost but not exactly the same; alike **~ly** *adv* **~ity** /,sɪmə'lærəti/ *n* **1** [U] quality of being similar **2** [C] way in which things are similar

sim·i·le /'sɪməli/ *n* expression which describes one thing by comparing it with another (as in *as white as snow*)

sim·mer /'sɪməʳ/ *vi/t* cook gently in (nearly) boiling liquid: (fig.) *simmering with anger/excitement*

   simmer down *phr vi* become calmer

sim·per /'sɪmpəʳ/ *vi* smile in a silly unnatural way

sim·ple /'sɪmpəl/ *adj* **1** without decoration; plain **2** easy **3** consisting of only one thing or part **4** (of something non-physical) pure: *the simple truth* **5** easily tricked; foolish **–ply** *adv* **1** in a simple way **2** just; only: *I simply don't know.* **3** really; absolutely: *a simply gorgeous day*

simple-mind·ed /,·· '··◂/ *adj* **1** foolish **2** simple and unthinking in mind

sim·ple·ton /'sɪmpəltən/ *n* weak-minded trusting person

sim·plic·i·ty /sɪm'plɪsəti/ *n* [U] **1** quality of being simple **2 simplicity itself** very easy

sim·pli·fy /'sɪmpləfaɪ/ *vt* make simpler **–fication** /,sɪmpləfə'keɪʃən/ *n* [C;U]

sim·plis·tic /sɪm'plɪstɪk/ *adj derog* treating difficult matters as if they were simple **~ally** /-kli/ *adv*

sim·u·late /'sɪmjuleɪt/ *vt* give the appearance or effect of **–lation** /,sɪmju'leɪʃən/ *n* [U]

sim·ul·ta·ne·ous /,sɪməl'teɪniəs‖ ,saɪ-/ *adj* happening or done at the same moment **~ly** *adv*

sin /sɪn/ *n* [C;U] **1** offence against God or a religious law **2** *infml* something that should not be done: *He thinks it's a sin to stay in bed after 8 o'clock.* **3 live in sin** *old-fashioned or humor* (of 2 unmarried people) live together as if married ♦ *vi* **-nn-** do wrong **~ful** *adj* wicked **~ner** *n*

since /sɪns/ *adv* **1** at a time between then and now: *She left in 1979, and I haven't seen her since.* **2** from then until now: *He came here 2 years ago and has lived here ever since.* **3** ago: *I've long since forgotten his name.* ♦ *prep* from (a point in past time) until now: *I haven't seen her since 1979.* ♦ *conj* **1 a** after the past time when: *I haven't seen her since she left.* **b** continuously from the time when: *We've been friends since we met at school.* **2** as: *Since you can't answer, I'll ask someone else.*

sin·cere /sɪn'sɪəʳ/ *adj* free from deceit or falseness; honest and true **~ly** *adv* **-cerity** /sɪn'serəti/ *n* [U]

si·ne·cure /'saɪnɪkjuəʳ, 'sɪn-/ *n* paid job with few or no duties

sin·ew /'sɪnju:/ *n* [C;U] strong cord connecting a muscle to a bone **~y** *adj*

sing /sɪŋ/ *v* **sang** /sæŋ/, **sung** /sʌŋ/ **1** *vi/t* produce (music, songs, etc.) with the voice **2** *vi* make or be filled with a ringing sound: *It made my ears sing.* **~er** *n*

singe /sɪndʒ/ *vt* burn slightly

sin·gle[1] /'sɪŋgəl/ *adj* **1** being (the) only one: *a single sheet of paper* **2** considered by itself; separate: *He understands every single word I say.* **3** unmarried **4** for the use of only one person: *a single bed* **5** *BrE* (of a ticket) for a journey to a place but not back ♦ *n* **1** *BrE* a SINGLE[1] (5) ticket **2** record with only one short song on each side — see also SINGLES **–gly** *adv* one by one; not in a group

single[2] *v* **single out** *phr vt* choose from a group for special attention

single file /,·· '·/ *adv, n* (in) a line of people, vehicles, etc., one behind another

single-hand·ed /,·· '··◂/ *adj* without help from others

single-mind·ed /,·· '··◂/ *adj* having one clear aim or purpose

sin·gles /'sɪŋgəlz/ *n* singles *n* (tennis) match between 2 players

sing·song /'sɪŋsɒŋ‖-sɔːŋ/ *n* **1** [S] repeated rising and falling of the voice in speaking **2** [C] *BrE infml* gathering for singing songs

sin·gu·lar /'sɪŋgjʊləʳ/ *adj* **1** (of a word) representing only one thing **2** *fml* unusually great ♦ *n* SINGULAR (1) word or form **~ly** *adv fml* particularly

sin·is·ter /'sɪnəstəʳ/ *adj* threatening or leading to evil

sink[1] /sɪŋk/ *v* **sank** /sæŋk/, **sunk** /sʌŋk/ **1** *vi/t* (cause to) go down below a surface, out of sight, or to the bottom (of water) **2** *vi* get smaller **3** *vi* fall from lack of strength: *He sank into a chair.* **4** *vi* lose confidence or hope: *My heart sank.* **5** *vt* make by digging: *sink a well* **6** *vt* put (money, labour, etc.) into

   sink in *phr vi* become fully and properly understood

sink[2] *n* large kitchen basin for washing pans, vegetables, etc.

sinking feel·ing /'·· ,··/ *n* [S] *infml* uncomfortable feeling in stomach raised by fear or helplessness, esp. because something bad is about to happen

sin·u·ous /'sɪnjuəs/ *adj* full of curves; winding **~ly** *adv*

si·nus /'saɪnəs/ *n* any of the air-filled spaces in the bones behind the nose

sip /sɪp/ *vi/t* **-pp-** drink with very small mouthfuls ♦ *n* very small amount drunk

si-phon /'saɪfən/ *n* 1 tube for removing liquid by natural pressure 2 bottle for holding and forcing out a gas-filled drink ♦ *vt* remove with a siphon: (fig.) *The new road will siphon off traffic from the town centre.*

sir /sɜːʳ; *strong* sɜːʳ/ *n* 1 (used respectfully when speaking to an older man or one of higher rank) 2 (used at the beginning of a formal letter): **Dear Sir, . . .** 3 (*cap.*) British rank of honour for a man

sire /'saɪəʳ/ *n* 1 horse's male parent 2 *lit* (used when speaking to a king) ♦ *vt* (esp. of a horse) be the father of

si-ren /'saɪərən/ *n* 1 apparatus for making a loud long warning sound: *a police/air-raid siren* 2 dangerous beautiful woman

sir-loin /'sɜːlɔɪn‖'sɜːr-/ *n* [U] BEEF cut from the best part of the lower back

sis-sy ‖ also **cissy** *BrE* /'sɪsi/ *n* girlish or cowardly boy ♦ *adj* like a sissy

sis-ter /'sɪstəʳ/ *n* 1 female relative with the same parents 2 *BrE* nurse in charge of a hospital WARD 3 female member of a religious group 4 female member of the same group (used esp. by supporters of the WOMEN'S MOVEMENT) ♦ *adj* belonging to the same group: *our sister organization* ~**hood** *n* 1 [U] being (like) sisters 2 [C] society of women leading a religious life ~**ly** *adj* like a sister

sister-in-law /'··· ‚·/ *n* **sisters-in-law** sister of one's husband or wife; one's brother's wife

sit /sɪt/ *v* **sat** /sæt/, *present p.* **-tt-** 1 *vi* rest on a seat or on the ground with the upper body upright 2 *vi/t* (cause to) take a seat 3 *vi* (of an official body) have one or more meetings 4 *vt BrE* take (a written examination) 5 *vi* (take up a position to) be painted or photographed 6 **be sitting pretty** be in a very good position 7 **sit tight** keep in the same position; not move

sit about/around *phr vi* do nothing, esp. while waiting or while others act

sit back *phr vi* rest and take no active part

sit down *phr vi* SIT (2)

sit in *phr vi* take another's regular place, e.g. in a meeting

sit in on *phr vi* attend without taking an active part

sit on *phr vt* 1 be a member of (a committee, etc.) 2 delay taking action on

sit up *phr v* 1 *vi/t* (cause or help to) rise to a sitting position from a lying one 2 *vi* sit properly upright in a chair 3 *vi* stay up late; not go to bed 4 *vi*

show sudden interest, surprise, or fear: *Her speech really made them sit up (and take notice).*

sit-com /'sɪtkɒm‖-kɑːm/ *n* [C;U] SITUATION COMEDY

site /saɪt/ *n* place where a particular thing happened or is done ♦ *vt* put or esp. build in a particular position

sit-in /'· ·/ *n* method of expressing dissatisfaction and anger in which a group of people enter a public place, stop its usual services, and refuse to leave

sit-ting /'sɪtɪŋ/ *n* 1 serving of a meal for a number of people at one time 2 act of having one's picture made 3 meeting of an official body

sitting duck /‚·· '·/ *n* one easy to attack or cheat

sitting room /'·· ·/ *n esp. BrE* for LIVING ROOM

sit-u-at-ed /'sɪtʃueɪtɪd/ *adj* 1 in the stated place or position 2 in the stated situation: *How are you situated for money?* (= have you got enough?)

sit-u-a-tion /‚sɪtʃu'eɪʃən/ *n* 1 set of conditions, facts, and/or events 2 *fml* position with regard to surroundings 3 *fml* job

situation com-e-dy /‚···· '···/ *n* [C;U] humorous television or radio show typically having a number of standard characters who appear in different stories every week

six /sɪks/ *determiner, n, pron* 1 6 2 **at sixes and sevens** in disorder ~**th** *determiner, adv, n, pron* 6th

six-teen /‚sɪk'stiːn◂/ *determiner, n, pron* 16 ~**th** *determiner, adv, n, pron* 16th

sixth sense /‚· '·/ *n* ability to know things without using any of the 5 ordinary senses

six-ty /'sɪksti/ *determiner, n, pron* 60 –**tieth** *determiner, adv, n, pron* 60th

size¹ /saɪz/ *n* 1 [C;U] (degree of) bigness or smallness 2 bigness: *A town of some size.* 3 [C] standard measurement: *These shoes are size 9.* 4 **-sized** of the stated size 5 **cut someone down to size** show someone to be really less good, important, etc. 6 **that's about the size of it** that's a fair statement of the matter

size² *v* **size up** *phr vt* form an opinion or judgment about

size-a-ble /'saɪzəbəl/ *adj* quite large

siz-zle /'sɪzəl/ *vi* make a sound like food cooking in hot fat

skate¹ /skeɪt/ *n* 1 blade fixed to a shoe for moving along on ice 2 ROLLER SKATE 3 **get/put one's skates on** *infml* move, act, or work quickly; hurry

skate² *vi* 1 move on skates 2 (**skate**) **on thin ice** *infml* (to be) doing something risky **skater** *n*

skate over/around *phr vt* avoid treating seriously

skate-board /'skeɪtbɔːd‖-bɔːrd/ *n* short board with 2 small wheels at each end for standing on and riding

skel-e-ton /'skelɪtən/ *n* **1** structure consisting of all the bones in the body **2** structure on which more is built or added **3 skeleton in the cupboard** *BrE* ‖ *AmE* **closet** — a secret of which a person or family is ashamed ♦ *adj* enough simply to keep an operation going: *a skeleton staff* **–tal** *adj*

skeleton key /'··· ·/ *n* key that opens many different locks

skep-tic /'skeptɪk/ *n AmE for* SCEPTIC

sketch /sketʃ/ *n* **1** simple quickly made drawing **2** short description **3** short humorous scene ♦ *vi/t* draw a sketch (of) **~y** *adj* not thorough or complete

skew /skjuː/ *vt* cause to be not straight or exact: DISTORT

skew-er /'skjuːər/ *n* long pin put through meat for cooking

ski /skiː/ *n* **skis** long thin piece of wood, plastic, etc., fixed to boots for travelling on snow ♦ *vi* **skied**, *present p.* **skiing** travel on skis **~er** *n*

skid /skɪd/ *vi* **-dd-** (of a vehicle or wheel) slip sideways out of control ♦ *n* act of skidding

skil-ful ‖ usu. **skillful** *AmE*/'skɪlfəl/ *adj* having or showing skill **~ly** *adv*

skill /skɪl/ *n* [C;U] special ability to do something well **~ed** *adj* having or needing skill: *a skilled job*

skim /skɪm/ *v* **-mm-** **1** *vt* remove from the surface of a liquid **2** *vi/t* read quickly to get the main ideas **3** *vi/t* (cause to) move quickly (nearly) touching (a surface)

skimp /skɪmp/ *vi/t* spend, provide, or use less (of) than is needed **~y** *adj* not enough

skin /skɪn/ *n* **1** [U] natural outer covering of the body **2** [C] skin of an animal for use as leather, etc. **3** [C] natural outer covering of some fruits and vegetables: *banana skins* **4** [C;U] the solid surface that forms over some liquids **5 by the skin of one's teeth** only just **6 get under someone's skin** annoy or excite someone deeply **7 no skin off someone's nose** *infml* not something that upsets or causes disadvantage to someone **8 save one's skin** save oneself, esp. in a cowardly way, from death, etc. **9 skin and bone(s)** very thin ♦ *vt* **-nn-** remove the skin from **~ny** *adj* very thin

skin-deep /ˌ· '·◂/ *adj* on the surface only

skin-dive /'·· ·/ *vi* swim underwater without heavy breathing apparatus **skin diver** *n*

skin-flint /'skɪnˌflɪnt/ *n* someone who dislikes giving or spending money

skin-head /'skɪnhed/ *n* (esp. in Britain) young person with very short hair, esp. of a group who behaves violently

skint /skɪnt/ *adj BrE infml* having no money

skin-tight /ˌ· '·◂/ *adj* (of clothes) fitting tightly against the body

skip[1] /skɪp/ *v* **-pp-** **1** *vi* move in a light dancing way **2** *vi/t* leave out (something in order); not deal with (the next thing) **3** *vi* move in no fixed order **4** *vi* jump over a rope passed repeatedly beneath one's feet **5** *vi/t* leave hastily and secretly: *They have skipped the country.* **6** *vt* fail to attend or take part in (an activity) ♦ *n* light quick stepping and jumping movement

skip[2] *n BrE* large metal container for carrying away unwanted things

skip-per /'skɪpər/ *n* captain of a ship or sports team ♦ *vt* act as captain; lead

skir-mish /'skɜːmɪʃ‖-ɜːr-/ *n* short military fight, not as big as a battle

skirt[1] /skɜːt‖skɜːrt/ *n* woman's outer garment that hangs from the waist

skirt[2] *vi/t* **1** be or go round the outside (of) **2** avoid (a difficult subject)

skirting board /'··· ·/ *n* board fixed along the base of an inside wall

skit /skɪt/ *n* short acted scene making fun of something

skit-tish /'skɪtɪʃ/ *adj* (esp. of a horse) easily excited and frightened

skit-tle /'skɪtl/ *n* bottle-shaped object used in a game (**skittles**) where a player tries to knock down a set of them with a ball

skulk /skʌlk/ *vi* hide or move about slowly and secretly, through fear or shame or for some evil purpose

skull /skʌl/ *n* head bone, enclosing the brain

skunk /skʌŋk/ *n* **1** small N American animal which gives out a bad-smelling liquid when attacked **2** *infml* person who is bad, unfair, etc.

sky /skaɪ/ *n* **1** space above the Earth, where clouds and the sun, moon, and stars appear **2 the sky's the limit** there is no upper limit, esp. to the amount of money that can be spent

sky-div-ing /'skaɪˌdaɪvɪŋ/ *n* [U] sport of falling by PARACHUTE

sky-high /ˌ· '·◂/ *adj, adv* at or to a very high level

sky-jack /'skaɪdʒæk/ *vt* HIJACK (an aircraft)

sky-light /'skaɪlaɪt/ *n* window in a roof

sky-line /'skaɪlaɪn/ *n* shape or view of esp. city buildings against the sky

sky·rock·et /'skaɪ,rɒkɪt‖-,rɑ:-/ vi increase suddenly and steeply

sky·scrap·er /'skaɪ,skreɪpər/ n very tall city building

slab /slæb/ n thick flat usu. 4-sided piece: *a stone slab*

slack /slæk/ adj 1 (of a rope, etc.) not pulled tight 2 not careful or quick 3 not firm; weak: *slack discipline* 4 not busy ♦ n **take up the slack** tighten a rope, etc. ♦ vi 1 be lazy 2 reduce in speed, effort, etc. **slacks** n [P] informal trousers ~**en** vi/t make or become slack ~**ness** n [U]

slag[1] /slæg/ n 1 [U] waste material left when metal is separated from its rock 2 [C] *BrE sl* worthless or immoral woman

slag[2] v **-gg-** **slag off** phr vt *BrE sl* make extremely unfavourable remarks about

slain /sleɪn/ past p. of SLAY

slake /sleɪk/ vt *lit* satisfy (thirst) with a drink

sla·lom /'slɑːləm/ n SKI race down a very winding course

slam /slæm/ v **-mm-** 1 vi/t shut loudly and forcefully 2 vt push or put hurriedly and forcefully: *She slammed on the brakes.* 3 vt attack with words ♦ n noise of a door being slammed — see also GRAND SLAM

slan·der /'slɑːndər‖'slæn-/ n [C;U] (act of) saying something false and damaging about someone ♦ vt harm by making a false statement ~**ous** adj

slang /slæŋ/ n [U] very informal language that includes new and sometimes not polite words and meanings and is often used among particular groups of people, and not usu. in serious speech or writing ♦ vt *BrE* attack with rude angry words

slant /slɑːnt‖slænt/ v 1 vi/t (cause to) be at an angle 2 vt usu. *derog* express in a way favourable to a particular opinion ♦ n 1 [S] slanting direction or position 2 [C] particular way of looking at or expressing facts or a situation

slap /slæp/ n 1 hit with the flat hand 2 **slap in the face** an action (seeming to be) aimed directly against someone else ♦ vt **-pp-** 1 give a slap to 2 place quickly, roughly, or carelessly ♦ adv also **slap-bang** /ˌ· '·/ — directly; right: *slap in the middle of lunch*

slap·dash /'slæpdæʃ/ adj careless

slap·stick /'slæp,stɪk/ n [U] humorous acting with fast violent action and simple jokes

slap-up /'· '·/ adj *BrE* excellent and in large quantities: *a slap-up meal*

slash /slæʃ/ v 1 vi/t cut with long sweeping violent strokes: (fig.) *a slashing attack on the government* 2 vt

reduce very greatly ♦ n 1 long sweeping cut or blow 2 straight cut making an opening in a garment

slat /slæt/ n thin narrow flat piece of wood, plastic, etc.

slate[1] /sleɪt/ n 1 [U] dark grey easily splittable rock 2 [C] piece of this used in rows for covering roofs 3 [C] small board of this, used for writing on with chalk 4 [C] imaginary record of (mistakes of) the past: *a clean slate*

slate[2] vt *BrE* attack in words

slaugh·ter /'slɔːtər/ vt 1 kill (many people) cruelly or wrongly 2 kill (an animal) for food 3 *infml* defeat severely in a game ♦ n [U] slaughtering

slaugh·ter·house /'slɔːtəhaʊs‖-ər-/ n building where animals are killed for food

slave /sleɪv/ n 1 person who is owned by (and works for) another 2 person completely in the control of: *a slave to drink* ♦ vi work hard with little rest

slave driv·er /'· ,··/ n person who makes you work very hard

slav·er[1] /'sleɪvər/ n ship or person that carries or sells slaves ~**y** n [U] 1 system of having slaves 2 condition of being a slave

slav·er[2] /'slævər/ vi 1 let SALIVA run out of the mouth 2 be unpleasantly eager or excited

slav·ish /'sleɪvɪʃ/ adj 1 showing complete obedience and willingness to work for others 2 copied too exactly, without originality ~**ly** adv

slay /sleɪ/ v *esp. lit* slew /sluː/, slain /sleɪn/ kill

slea·zy /'sliːzi/ adj dirty, poor-looking, and suggesting immorality

sled /sled/ vi, n **-dd-** sledge

sledge /sledʒ/ vi, n (travel on) a vehicle for sliding along snow on 2 metal blades

sledge-ham·mer /'sledʒ,hæmər/ n heavy long-handled hammer

sleek /sliːk/ adj 1 (of hair or fur) smooth and shining 2 stylish and without unnecessary decoration ~**ly** adv

sleep /sliːp/ n 1 [U] natural unconscious resting state 2 [S] act or period of sleeping 3 **get to sleep** succeed in sleeping 4 **go to sleep: a** begin to sleep **b** (of an arm, leg, etc.) become unable to feel, or feel PINS AND NEEDLES 5 **put to sleep** kill (a suffering animal) mercifully ♦ vi sleep /slept/ 1 rest in sleep 2 provide beds or places for sleep (for a number of people): *The house sleeps 6.* ~**er** n 1 sleeping person 2 *esp. BrE* heavy piece of wood, metal, etc., supporting a railway track 3 train with beds 4 *esp. AmE* book, play, record, etc., that has a delayed or unexpected success ~**y** *adj* **1** tired **2** inactive or slow-moving ~**ily** *adv*

sleep around *phr vi derog* have sex with a lot of different people

sleep in *phr vi* sleep late in the morning

sleep off *phr vt* get rid of (a feeling or effect) by sleeping: *Sleep it off.* (= sleep until one is no longer drunk)

sleep on *phr vt* delay deciding on (a matter) until next day

sleep through *phr vt* fail to be woken by

sleep together *phr vi* (of 2 people) have sex

sleep with *phr vt* have sex with

sleeping bag /'·· ·/ *n* large cloth bag for sleeping in

sleeping car /'·· ·/ *n* railway carriage with beds for passengers

sleeping part·ner /,·· '··/ *n* business partner who does no active work in the business

sleeping pill /'·· ·/ *n* PILL which helps a person to sleep

sleeping sick·ness /'·· ,··/ *n* [U] serious African disease which causes great tiredness

sleep·less /'sliːpləs/ *adj* **1** not providing sleep: *a sleepless night* **2** unable to sleep ~**ly** *adv* ~**ness** *n* [U]

sleep·walk·er /'sliːp,wɔːkəʳ/ *n* person who walks about while asleep ~**ing** *n* [U]

sleet /sliːt/ *n* [U] partly frozen rain ♦ *vi* (of sleet) fall

sleeve /sliːv/ *n* **1** part of a garment for covering (part of) an arm **2** *esp. BrE* stiff envelope for keeping a record in **3 have/keep something up one's sleeve** kept something secret for use at the right time in the future

sleigh /sleɪ/ *n* large (horse-drawn) SLEDGE

sleight of hand /,slaɪt əv 'hænd/ *n* [U] **1** skill and quickness of the hands in doing tricks **2** clever deception

slen·der /'slendəʳ/ *adj* **1** gracefully or pleasingly thin **2** small and hardly enough: *slender resources*

slept /slept/ *v past t. and p. of* SLEEP

sleuth /sluːθ/ *n* DETECTIVE

slew¹ /sluː/ *v past t. of* SLAY

slew² *vi/t* turn or swing violently

slice /slaɪs/ *n* **1** thin flat piece cut off: *a slice of bread* | (fig.) *a slice of the profits* **2** kitchen tool with a broad blade for serving food **3 a slice of life** a representation of life as it really is ♦ *v* **1** *vt* cut into slices **2** *vi/t* hit (a ball) so that it moves away from a straight course

slick¹ /slɪk/ *adj* **1** smooth and slippery **2** skilful and effective, so as to seem easy **3** clever and able to persuade, but perhaps not honest ~**ly** *adv*

slick² *n* area of oil floating on esp. the sea

slick·er /'slɪkəʳ/ *n* **1** *infml* a well-dressed, self-confident, but probably untrustworthy person: *a city slicker* **2** *AmE* coat made to keep out the rain

slide /slaɪd/ *v* slid /slɪd/ **1** *vi/t* go or send smoothly across a surface **2** *vi* move quietly and unnoticed **3 let something slide** let a situation or condition continue, esp. getting worse, without taking action, usu. because of laziness *n* **1** slipping movement **2** fall: *a slide in living standards* **3** apparatus for sliding down **4** piece of film through which light is passed to show a picture on a surface **5** small piece of thin glass to put an object on for seeing under a microscope

slide rule /'·· ·/ *n* ruler with a middle part that slides along, for calculating numbers

sliding scale /,·· '·/ *n* system of pay, taxes, etc., calculated by rates which may vary according to changing conditions

slight¹ /slaɪt/ *adj* **1** small in degree: *a slight improvement* **2** thin and delicate **3 in the slightest** at all ~**ly** *adv* **1** a little: *slightly better* **2** in a SLIGHT (2) way: *He's very slightly built.*

slight² *vt* treat disrespectfully or rudely ♦ *n* INSULT

slim /slɪm/ *adj* -mm- **1** attractively thin **2** (of probability, hope, etc.) very small ♦ *vi* -mm- try to make oneself thinner ~**ly** *adv* ~**mer** *n*

slime /slaɪm/ *n* unpleasant thick sticky liquid **slimy** *adj* **1** unpleasantly slippery **2** *derog* trying to please in order to gain advantage for oneself

sling /slɪŋ/ *vt* slung /slʌŋ/ **1** throw roughly or with effort **2** hang **3 sling one's hook** *BrE sl* go away **4 sling mud at** say unfair and damaging things about (esp. a political opponent) ♦ *n* piece of cloth hanging from the neck to support a damaged arm

slink /slɪŋk/ *vi* slunk /slʌŋk/ move quietly and secretly, as if in fear or shame

slip¹ /slɪp/ *v* -pp- **1** *vi* slide out of place unexpectedly or by accident **2** *vi/t* move or put smoothly or unnoticed **3** *vi/t* put on or take off (a garment) quickly **4** *vi* get worse or lower: *slipping standards* **5** *vi* make a mistake **6** *vt* fail to be remembered by: *It slipped my mind.* (= I forgot) **7** give secretly: *I slipped the waiter some money.* **8 let slip: a** fail to take (a chance) **b** make known accidentally

♦ *n* **1** small mistake **2** woman's undergarment like a skirt or loose dress **3** young, slender person: *a slip of a girl* **4** SLIPWAY **5 give someone the slip** escape from someone

slip² *n* small or narrow piece of paper

slip-page /'slɪpɪdʒ/ *n* [C;U] (amount of) slipping

slipped disc /ˌ· '·/ *n* painful displacement of one of the connecting parts between the bones of the backbone

slip-per /'slɪpə'/ *n* light soft shoe worn indoors

slip-per-y /'slɪpəri/ *adj* 1 very smooth or wet, so one cannot easily hold or move on it 2 not to be trusted 3 a/the **slippery slope** a course of action that cannot be stopped and leads to ruin

slip road /'· ·/ *n BrE* road for driving onto or off a MOTORWAY

slip-shod /'slɪpʃɒd‖-ʃɑːd/ *adj* carelessly done

slip-stream /'slɪpstriːm/ *n* 1 area of low air pressure behind a fast-moving vehicle 2 stream of air driven backwards by an aircraft engine

slip-up /'· ·/ *n* usu. slight mistake

slip-way /'slɪpweɪ/ *n* sloping track for moving ships into or out of water

slit /slɪt/ *n* long narrow cut or opening ♦ *vt* slit; *present p.* -tt- make a slit in

slith-er /'slɪðə'/ *vi* 1 move smoothly and twistingly 2 slide unsteadily

sliv-er /'slɪvə'/ *n* small thin piece cut or broken off

slob /slɒb‖slɑːb/ *n* rude, dirty, lazy, or carelessly dressed person

slog /slɒg‖slɑːg/ *vi* -gg- *BrE* move or work with much effort ♦ *n* something needing much effort

slo-gan /'sləʊgən/ *n* short phrase expressing a political or advertising message

sloop /sluːp/ *n* small sailing ship

slop¹ /slɒp‖slɑːp/ *vi/t* -pp- go or cause (a liquid) to go over the side of a container: *You're slopping paint everywhere!*

slop about/around *phr vi infml* 1 move about in a lazy purposeless way 2 play in or move about in anything wet or dirty

slop² *n* [U] 1 [*usu.* P] food waste, esp. for feeding animals 2 *derog* tasteless liquid food

slope /sləʊp/ *vi* lie neither completely upright nor completely flat ♦ *n* 1 piece of sloping ground 2 degree of sloping

slope off *phr vt BrE* go away secretly esp. to avoid work

slop-py /'slɒpi‖'slɑːpi/ *adj* 1 (of clothes) loose, informal and careless 2 not careful or thorough enough 3 silly in showing feelings –**pily** *adv* –**piness** *n* [U]

slosh /slɒʃ‖slɑːʃ/ *v* 1 *vi/t* move or cause (liquid) to move about roughly and noisily, making waves 2 *vt BrE infml* hit ~**ed** *adj infml* drunk

slot /slɒt‖slɑːt/ *n* 1 long straight narrow hole 2 place or position in a list, system, organization, etc. ♦ *vi/t* -tt- 1 (be) put into a SLOT (1) 2 fit into a SLOT (2)

sloth /sləʊθ/ *n* 1 [U] *esp. lit* laziness 2 [C] slow-moving animal of S America ~**ful** *adj* lazy

slot ma-chine /'· ·ˌ·/ *n* 1 *BrE* VENDING MACHINE 2 *AmE for* ONE-ARMED BANDIT

slouch /slaʊtʃ/ *vi* walk, stand, or sit in a tired-looking round-shouldered way ♦ *n* lazy, useless person: *She's no slouch when it comes to tennis.* (= she's very good)

slough¹ /slʌf/ *v* **slough off** *phr vt* 1 (esp. of a snake) throw off (dead outer skin) 2 *esp. lit* get rid of as something worn out or unwanted

slough² /slaʊ‖sluː, slaʊ/ *n lit* bad condition that is hard to get free from

slov-en-ly /'slʌvənli/ *adj* 1 untidy 2 very carelessly done –**liness** *n* [U]

slow /sləʊ/ *adj* 1 having less than a usual speed; not fast 2 taking a long time: *a slow job* 3 (of a clock) showing a time that is earlier than the right time 4 not quick in understanding 5 not active: *Business is slow.* ♦ *vi/t* make or become slower ♦ *adv* slowly: *slow-moving traffic* ~**ly** *adv* ~**ness** *n* [U]

slow-coach /'sləʊkəʊtʃ/ *n BrE infml* slow-acting person

slow-down /'sləʊdaʊn/ *n* 1 lessening of speed or activity 2 *AmE for* GO-SLOW

sludge /slʌdʒ/ *n* [U] thick soft mud

slug¹ /slʌg/ *n* small soft limbless creature, like a SNAIL with no shell

slug² *vt* -gg- *esp. AmE* hit hard

slug³ *n esp. AmE* 1 bullet 2 *infml* amount of strong alcoholic drink taken at one swallow

slug-gish /'slʌgɪʃ/ *adj* not very active or quick ~**ly** *adv* ~**ness** *n* [U]

sluice /sluːs/ *n* passage for controlling the flow of water ♦ *vt* wash with a large flow of water

slum /slʌm/ *n* city area of bad living conditions and old unrepaired buildings ♦ *vi* 1 amuse oneself by visiting a place on a much lower social level: *go slumming* 2 **slum it** live very cheaply ~**my** *adj*

slum-ber /'slʌmbə'/ *vi, n lit* sleep

slump /slʌmp/ *vi* 1 drop down suddenly and heavily 2 decrease suddenly ♦ *n* 1 sudden decrease, esp. in business 2 time of seriously bad business conditions and high unemployment

slung /slʌŋ/ *past t. and p. of* SLING

slunk /slʌŋk/ *past t. and p. of* SLINK

slur¹ /slɜː'/ *vt* -rr- pronounce unclearly

slur² vt **-rr-** make unfair damaging remarks about ♦ n: a slur on my reputation

slurp /slɜːp‖slɜːrp/ vt drink noisily **slurp** n

slush /slʌʃ/ n [U] **1** partly melted snow **2** books, films, etc., full of silly love stories ~**y** adj

slush fund /'· ·/ n money secretly kept for dishonest payments

slut /slʌt/ n **1** sexually immoral woman **2** untidy, lazy woman ~**tish** adj

sly /slaɪ/ adj **1** secretly deceitful or tricky **2** playfully unkind: a sly joke **3 on the sly** secretly ~**ly** adv ~**ness** n [U]

smack¹ /smæk/ vt **1** hit with the flat hand **2** open and close (one's lips) noisily in eagerness to eat ♦ n blow with the open hand ♦ adv exactly; right: smack in the middle

smack² v smack of phr vt have a taste or suggestion of

small /smɔːl/ adj **1** of less than usual size, amount, importance, etc. **2** young: small children **3** doing only a limited amount of business: small shopkeepers **4** slight: small hope of success **5 feel small** feel ashamed or humble ♦ n [the + S] narrow middle part (of the back) ~**ness** n [U]

small arms /'· ·‖,· '·/ n [P] guns made to be carried in one or both hands for firing

small beer /'· ,·/ n [U] infml person or thing of little importance

small fortune /,· '··/ n [S] very large amount of money

small fry /'· ·/ n young or unimportant person

small-holding /'smɔːl,həʊldɪŋ/ n BrE small farm run by one person

small hours /'· ·/ n [P] after midnight

small-minded /,· '··/ adj having narrow or ungenerous views

small-pox /'smɔːlpɒks‖-pɑːks/ n [U] serious infectious disease which leaves marks on the skin

small print /'· ,·/ n [the + U] something that is purposely made difficult to understand or is easy not to notice, such as part of an agreement or CONTRACT

small screen /'· ,·/ n [the + S] television

small talk /'· ·/ n [U] light conversation on non-serious subjects

small-time /,· '··/ adj limited in activity, ability, profits, etc.

smarmy /'smɑːmi‖-ɑːr-/ adj BrE unpleasantly and falsely polite

smart¹ /smɑːt‖smɑːrt/ adj **1** quick or forceful: a smart blow on the head **2** esp. BrE neat and stylish **3** esp. AmE

clever **4** fashionable ~**ly** adv ~**ness** n [U]

smart² vi, n (cause or feel) a stinging pain: (fig.) She was still smarting over his unkind words.

smart aleck /'smɑːt ,ælək‖-ɑːr-/ n annoying person who pretends to know everyting

smart-en /'smɑːtn‖-ɑːr-/ v **smarten up** phr vi/t improve in appearance

smash /smæʃ/ v **1** vi/t break into pieces violently **2** vi/t go, drive, hit forcefully: The car smashed into a lamppost. **3** vt put an end to: The police have smashed the drugs ring. **4** vt hit (the ball) with a SMASH (2) ♦ n **1** (sound of) a violent breaking **2** hard downward, attacking shot, as in tennis **3** very successful new play, film, etc.: a smash hit **4** SMASH-UP ~**ing** adj esp. BrE very fine; wonderful

smash-up /'· ·/ n serious road or railway accident

smattering /'smætərɪŋ/ n limited knowledge: a smattering of German

smear /smɪə²/ vt **1** spread (a sticky or oily substance) untidily across (a surface) **2** make unproved charges against (someone) in order to produce unfavourable public opinion ♦ n **1** mark made by smearing **2** unfair unproved charge against someone: a smear campaign

smear test /'· ·/ n medical test on material from inside the body, esp. for discovering CANCER

smell /smel/ v smelled or smelt /smelt/ **1** vi have or use the sense of the nose **2** vt notice, examine, etc., (as if) by this sense: I think I smell gas! | I could smell trouble coming. **3** vi have a particular smell: The bread smells stale. **4** vi have a bad smell **5 smell a rat** guess that something wrong or dishonest is happening ♦ n **1** [U] power of using the nose to discover the presence of gases in the air **2** [C] quality that has an effect on the nose: a flower with a sweet smell **3** [C] bad smell ~**y** adj bad-smelling

smelt /smelt/ vt melt (ORE) for removing the metal

smidgin /'smɪdʒən/ n [S] infml small amount

smile /smaɪl/ n pleased or amused expression in which the mouth is turned up at the ends ♦ vi make a smile **smilingly** adv

smirk /smɜːk‖smɜːrk/ vi, n (make) a silly self-satisfied smile

smite /smaɪt/ vt smote /sməʊt/, smitten /'smɪtn/ lit strike hard

smith /smɪθ/ n maker of metal things: a silversmith

smith-e-reens /,smɪðə'riːnz/ n (in)to smithereens into extremely small bits

smit·ten /'smɪtn/ v past p. of SMITE
♦ adj suddenly in love

smock /smɒk‖smɑːk/ n long loose shirtlike garment

smog /smɒg‖smɑːg, smɔːg/ n [U] thick dark unpleasant mist in cities

smoke /sməʊk/ n 1 [U] usu. white, grey, or black gas produced by burning 2 [S] act of smoking tobacco 3 **go up in smoke** end or fail without results, esp. suddenly ♦ v 1 vi/t suck in smoke from (a cigarette, pipe, etc.) 2 vi give off smoke: *smoking chimneys* 3 vt preserve (fish, meat, etc.) with smoke
smoker n person who smokes **smoky** adj 1 filled with smoke 2 tasting of or looking like smoke **smoking** n [U] practice or habit of smoking cigarettes, etc.

smoke out phr vt fill a place with smoke to force (a person, animal, etc.) to come out from hiding

smoke-screen /'sməʊkskriːn/ n 1 cloud of smoke produced to hide something 2 something that hides one's real intentions

smoke-stack /'sməʊkstæk/ n 1 tall chimney of a factory or ship 2 AmE for FUNNEL (2)

smokestack in·dus·try /'·· ,···/ n esp. AmE the branch of industry that produces cars, ships, steel, etc.

smol·der /'sməʊldəʳ/ v AmE for SMOULDER

smooch /smuːtʃ/ vi kiss and hold lovingly

smooth¹ /smuːð/ adj 1 having an even surface; not rough 2 (of a liquid mixture) without lumps 3 even in movement, without sudden changes: *a smooth flight* 4 (too) pleasant or polite ~ly adv ~ness n [U]

smooth² vt make smooth(er)
smooth over phr vt make (difficulties) seem small or unimportant

smote /sməʊt/ v past t. of SMITE

smoth·er /'smʌðəʳ/ vt 1 cover thickly or in large numbers: *a face smothered in/with spots* 2 die or kill from lack of air 3 keep from developing or happening: *smother a yawn*

smoul·der /'sməʊldəʳ/ vi 1 burn slowly with (almost) no flame 2 have or be violent but unexpressed feelings

smudge /smʌdʒ/ n dirty mark with unclear edges ♦ vi/t make or become dirty with a smudge

smug /smʌg/ adj -gg- too pleased with oneself ~ly adv ~ness n [U]

smug·gle /'smʌgəl/ vt take in or out secretly or illegally **-gler** n **-gling** n [U] taking goods to another country without paying the necessary tax

smut /smʌt/ n 1 [C] small piece of dirt 2 [U] morally offensive talk, stories, etc. ~ty adj rude

snack /snæk/ n amount of food smaller than a meal ♦ vi AmE eat a snack

snag /snæg/ n 1 hidden or unexpected difficulty 2 rough or sharp part of something that may catch and hold things passing it ♦ vt -gg- catch on a SNAG(2)

snail /sneɪl/ n small slow-moving soft-bodied limbless creature with a shell on its back

snake /sneɪk/ n 1 long thin limbless creature, often with a poisonous bite 2 deceitful person 3 **a snake in the grass** a false friend ♦ vi move twistingly

snake charm·er /'· ,··/ n person who controls snakes by playing music

snap /snæp/ v -pp- 1 vi/t close the jaws quickly (on): *The dog snapped at my ankles.* 2 vi/t break suddenly and sharply 3 vi/t move with a sharp sound: *The lid snapped shut.* 4 vi speak quickly and angrily 5 vt infml to photograph 6 **snap one's fingers** make a noise by moving the second finger quickly along the thumb 7 **snap out of it** free oneself quickly from a bad state of mind 8 **snap someone's head off** answer someone in a short rude way ♦ n 1 act or sound of snapping 2 informal photograph ♦ adj done without warning or long consideration: *snap judgments* **--py** adj 1 stylish; fashionable 2 hasty; quick: *Make it snappy!* (= Hurry up!)

snap up phr vt take or buy quickly and eagerly

snap-shot /'snæpʃɒt‖-ʃɑːt/ n a SNAP (2)

snare /sneəʳ/ n 1 trap for small animals 2 deceiving situation ♦ vt catch in a snare

snarl¹ /snɑːl‖snɑːrl/ vi 1 (of an animal) make a low angry sound 2 speak angrily ♦ n act or sound of snarling

snarl² v **snarl up** phr vt mix together so as to make movement difficult: *The traffic had got snarled up.* **snarl-up** /'· ·/ n confused state, esp. of traffic

snatch /snætʃ/ vi/t take (something) quickly and often violently or wrongfully ♦ n 1 act of snatching 2 short incomplete part: *overhearing snatches of conversation*

snaz·zy /'snæzi/ adj infml stylishly good-looking or attractive **-zily** adv

sneak /sniːk/ vi/t **snuck** /snʌk/ AmE go or take quietly and secretly ♦ n BrE derog sl schoolchild who gives information about the wrongdoings of others ~er n AmE for PLIMSOLL ~ing adj 1 secret: *a sneaking admiration* 2 not proved but probably right: *a sneaking suspicion* ~y adj acting or done secretly or deceitfully

sneak pre-view /ˌ· ˈ··/ n a chance to see something new, esp. a film, before anyone else has done so

sneer /snɪə^r/ vi express proud dislike and disrespect, esp. with an unpleasant curling smile ♦ n sneering look or remark

sneeze /sniːz/ vi, n (have) a sudden uncontrolled burst of air from the nose

snide /snaɪd/ adj indirectly but unpleasantly expressing a low opinion ~**ly** adv

sniff /snɪf/ v 1 vi breathe in loudly, esp. in short repeated actions 2 vi/t do this to discover a smell (in or on) 3 vt take (a harmful drug) through the nose ♦ n act or sound of sniffing ~**er** n

sniff at phr vt dislike or refuse proudly

sniff out phr vt discover or find out (as if) by smelling

snig·ger /ˈsnɪgə^r/ vi laugh quietly or secretly in a disrespectful way **snigger** n

snip /snɪp/ vt **-pp-** cut with quick short strokes, esp. with scissors ♦ n 1 act of snipping 2 BrE thing cheaply bought

snipe /snaɪp/ vi 1 shoot from a hidden position 2 make an unpleasant indirect attack in words **sniper** n

snip·pet /ˈsnɪpɪt/ n small bit: a snippet of information

sniv·el /ˈsnɪvəl/ vi **-ll-** BrE ‖ **-l-** AmE act or speak in a weak complaining crying way

snob /snɒb‖snɑːb/ n person who pays too much attention to social class, and dislikes people of a lower class ~**bery** n [U] behaviour of snobs ~**bish** adj

snog /snɒg‖snɔːg/ vi **-gg-** BrE infml hold and kiss each other **snog** n

snook /snuːk‖snuk, snuːk/ n see **cock a snook** (COCK)

snoo·ker /ˈsnuːkə^r‖ˈsnu-/ n [U] game in which a player hits balls into holes round a table ♦ vt infml defeat (someone, a plan, etc.)

snoop /snuːp/ vi search about or concern oneself with other people's affairs without permission ~**er** n

snoot·y /ˈsnuːti/ adj infml proudly rude **-ily** adv **-iness** n [U]

snooze /snuːz/ vi, n (have) a short sleep

snore /snɔː^r/ vi breathe noisily while asleep ♦ n act or sound of snoring

snor·kel /ˈsnɔːkəl‖-ɔːr-/ n breathing tube for underwater swimmers ♦ vi go snorkeling

snort /snɔːt‖snɔːrt/ 1 vi make a rough noise by forcing air down the nose, often in impatience or anger 2 vt SNIFF (3) ♦ n act or sound of snorting

snot·ty-nosed /ˌsnɒti ˈnəʊzd◂‖ ˌsnɑː-/ adj (esp. of a young person) trying to act as if one is important; rude

snout /snaʊt/ n animal's long nose: a pig's snout

snow[1] /snəʊ/ n frozen rain that falls in white pieces (FLAKEs) and often forms a soft covering on the ground ~**y** adj

snow[2] vi (of snow) fall

snow in/up phr vt prevent from travelling by a heavy fall of snow

snow under phr vt cause to have more of something than one can deal with: snowed under with work

snow·ball /ˈsnəʊbɔːl/ n ball of pressed snow, as thrown by children ♦ vi increase faster and faster

snow·drift /ˈsnəʊˌdrɪft/ n deep mass of snow piled up by the wind

snow·drop /ˈsnəʊdrɒp‖-drɑːp/ n plant of early spring with a small white flower

snow·man /ˈsnəʊmæn/ n **-men** /-men/ figure of a person made out of snow

snow·plough BrE ‖ **-plow** AmE /ˈsnəʊplaʊ/ n apparatus or vehicle for clearing away snow

snow·storm /ˈsnəʊstɔːm‖-ɔːrm/ n very heavy fall of snow

Snr BrE written abbrev. for: SENIOR

snub[1] /snʌb/ vt **-bb-** treat (someone) rudely, esp. by paying no attention to them ♦ n act of snubbing

snub[2] adj (of a nose) short and flat

snuck /snʌk/ AmE past t. and p. of SNEAK

snuff[1] /snʌf/ n [U] powdery tobacco for breathing into the nose

snuff[2] vt put out (a candle) by pressing the burning part

snuff out phr vt put a sudden end to

snug /snʌg/ adj **-gg-** 1 giving warmth, comfort, protection, etc. 2 (of clothes) fitting closely and comfortably

snug·gle /ˈsnʌgəl/ vi settle into a warm comfortable position

so[1] /səʊ/ adv 1 to such a (great) degree: It was so dark I couldn't see. 2 (used instead of repeating something): He hopes he'll win and I hope so too. 3 also: He hopes he'll win and so do I. 4 very: We're so glad you could come! 5 in this way 6 yes; it is true: 'There's a fly in your soup.' 'So there is!' 7 fml therefore 8 **and so on/forth** and other things of that kind 9 **or so** more or less: It'll only cost 15p or so. 10 **so as to: a** in order to **b** in such a way as to 11 **so long!** infml goodbye 12 **so many/much: a** a certain number/amount: a charge of so much a day **b** an amount equal to: These books are just so much waste paper!

so² conj **1** with the result that: It was dark, so I couldn't see. **2** therefore: He had a headache, so he went to bed. **3** with the purpose (that): I gave him an apple so (that) he wouldn't go hungry. **4** (used at the beginning of a sentence) **a** (with weak meaning): So here we are again. **b** (to express discovery): So that's how they did it! **5 so what?** Why is that important?; Why should I care?

so³ adj **1** true: Is that really so? **2 just so** arranged exactly and tidily

soak /səʊk/ vi/t **1** (cause to) remain in liquid, becoming completely wet **2** (of liquid) enter (a solid) through the surface ♦ n [C;U] (act of) soaking ~ed adj thoroughly wet, esp. from rain ~ing adv, adj very (wet)

soak up phr vt draw in (a liquid) through a surface: (fig.) to soak up the sun | to soak up information

so-and-so /'·· ·‚·/ n **1** one not named **2** unpleasant or annoying person

soap /səʊp/ n **1** [U] usu. solid substance used with water for cleaning esp. the body **2** [C] infml SOAP OPERA — see also SOFT SOAP —y adj

soap-box /'səʊpbɒks‖-bɑːks/ n **on one's soapbox** stating one's opinions loudly and forcefully

soap op·e·ra /'·· ‚···/ n continuing television or radio story about the daily life and troubles of the same set of characters

soar /sɔːʳ/ vi **1** (of a bird) fly high without moving the wings **2** rise steeply: Prices soared.

sob /sɒb‖sɑːb/ vi -bb- cry while making short bursts of sound breathing in ♦ n act or sound of sobbing

so·ber /'səʊbəʳ/ adj **1** not drunk **2** fml thoughtful, serious, or solemn; not silly ♦ vi/t make or become SOBER (2): a sobering thought —ly adv

sober up phr vi/t make or become SOBER (1)

so·bri·e·ty /sə'braɪəti/ n fml being sober

so·bri·quet /'səʊbrɪkeɪ/ n fml for NICKNAME

sob sto·ry /'· ‚··/ n story intended to make the hearer or reader cry, feel pity, or feel sorry

so-called /‚· '·◁/ adj (undeservedly but) commonly described in the stated way

soc·cer /'sɒkəʳ‖'sɑː-/ n [U] BrE game played with a round ball between 2 teams of 11 players

so·cia·ble /'səʊʃəbəl/ adj fond of being with others; friendly —bly adv —bility /‚səʊʃə'bɪlɪti/ n [U]

so·cial /'səʊʃəl/ adj **1** of human society or its organization **2** living together by nature **3** based on rank in society: social class **4** for or spent in time or activities with friends (rather than work): an active social life | a social club —ly adv

social climb·er /‚·· '··/ n derog person who tries to get accepted into a higher social class

so·cial·is·m /'səʊʃəlɪzəm/ n [U] political system aiming at establishing a society in which everyone is equal —ist adj, n

so·cia·lite /'səʊʃəl-aɪt/ n person who goes to many fashionable parties

so·cial·ize ‖ also **-ise** BrE /'səʊʃəl-‚aɪz/ vi spend time with others in a friendly way

social sci·ence /‚·· '··‖'·· ‚·/ n [C;U] study of people in society, including SOCIOLOGY, ECONOMICS, etc.

social se·cu·ri·ty /‚·· ·'···/ n [U] government money paid to the unemployed, old, sick, etc.

social serv·ic·es /‚·· '···/n [P] esp. BrE (local) government services to help people, such as education, health care, etc.

social work /'·· ·/ n [U] work done to help the old, sick, unemployed, etc. ~er n

so·ci·e·ty /sə'saɪəti/ n **1** [U] everyone considered as a whole: Society has a right to expect obedience to the law. **2** [C;U] group of people who share laws, organization, etc.: modern Western society **3** [C] organization of people with similar aims or interests: She joined the university film society. **4** [U] fashionable people **5** [U] fml being with other people — see also BUILDING SOCIETY —tal adj of society

so·ci·o·ec·o·nom·ic /‚səʊsiəʊekə'nɒmɪk, ‚səʊʃiəʊ-, -iːkə-‖-'nɑː-/ adj based on a combination of social and money conditions

so·ci·ol·o·gy /‚səʊsi'ɒlədʒi, ‚səʊʃi-‖ -'ɑːlə-/ n [U] study of society and group behaviour —ogical /‚səʊsiə'lɒdʒɪkəl, ‚səʊʃiə-‖-'lɑː-/ adj —ogist n

sock¹ /sɒk‖sɑːk/ n **1** cloth covering for the foot **2 pull one's socks up** BrE try to improve

sock² vt sl strike hard ♦ n forceful blow

sock·et /'sɒkɪt‖'sɑː-/ n hole into which something fits

sod¹ /sɒd‖sɑːd/ n [C;U] (piece of) earth with grass and roots growing in it

sod² n BrE sl person or thing that causes a lot of trouble and difficulty

so·da /'səʊdə/ n [U] **1** SODA WATER: a whisky and soda **2** sodium

soda foun·tain /'·· ‚··/n AmE place in a shop at which fruit drinks, ice cream, etc., are served

soda wa·ter /'·· ,·'/ n [U] gas-filled water esp. for mixing with other drinks

sod·den /'sɒdn‖'sɑːdn/ adj very wet

so·di·um /'səʊdiəm/ n [U] silver-white metal found naturally only in compounds

sod·o·my /'sɒdəmi‖'sɑː-/ n [U] fml or law any of various sexual acts, esp. ANAL sex between males

sod's law /,· '·/ n [U] sl (often cap. S) natural tendency for things to go wrong

so·fa /'səʊfə/ n comfortable seat for 2 or 3 people

soft /sɒft‖sɔːft/ adj 1 not hard or stiff 2 smooth to the touch: soft skin 3 quiet 4 restful and pleasant: soft colours 5 with little force; gentle: a soft breeze 6 easy: a soft job 7 too kind 8 not in good physical condition 9 dealing with ideas not facts: one of the soft sciences like PSYCHOLOGY 10 not of the worst or most harmful kind: Cannabis is a soft drug. 11 (of a drink) containing no alcohol and usu. sweet and served cold 12 (in English pronunciation) **a** (of the letter c) having the sound /s/ and not /k/ **b** (of the letter g) having the sound /dʒ/ and not /g/ 13 (of water) free from minerals that stop soap forming LATHER easily 14 infml foolish: He's soft in the head. ~ly adv ~ness n

soft-boiled /,· '·◂/ adj (of an egg) boiled not long enough for the YOLK to become solid

soft cop·y /'· ,··/ n [U] information stored in a computer's memory or shown on a SCREEN, rather than in printed form

soft·en /'sɒfən‖'sɔ-/ vi/t (cause to) become soft(er) or more gentle ~er n: a water softener

soften up phr vt break down opposition of (someone)

soft-heart·ed /,sɒft'hɑːtd◂‖,sɔːft-'hɑːr-/ adj easily made to act kindly or feel sorry for someone

soft op·tion /,· '··/n course of action which will give one less trouble

soft-ped·al /,· '··‖'·· ,·/ vt make (a subject, fact, etc.) seem unimportant

soft sell /,· '·◂/ n [U] selling by gentle persuading

soft soap /,· '·/ n [U] saying nice things about people, esp. as a means of persuading **soft-soap** /'· ·/ vt use soft soap on

soft spot /'· ·/ n fondness

soft touch /,· '·/ n infml someone from whom it is easy to get what one wants because they are kind, easily deceived, etc.

soft·ware /'sɒftweə‖'sɔːft-/ n [U] set of PROGRAMs that control a computer

soft·wood /'sɒftwʊd‖'sɔːft-/ n [U] cheap easily-cut wood from trees such as PINE and FIR

sog·gy /'sɒgi‖'sɑːgi/ adj completely (and unpleasantly) wet –giness n [U]

soil [1] /sɔɪl/ n [U] top covering of the earth in which plants grow; ground

soil [2] vt fml make dirty

soi·ree /'swɑːreɪ‖swɑː'reɪ/ n evening party, often including an artistic performance

so·journ /'sɒdʒɜːn‖'səʊdʒɜːrn/ vi lit live for a time in a place

sol·ace /'sɒləs‖'sɑː-/ n [C;U] (something that gives) comfort for someone full of grief or anxiety

so·lar /'səʊlə/ adj of or from the sun

solar cell /,·· '·/n apparatus for producing electric power from sunlight

so·lar·i·um /səʊ'leəriəm/ n -ia /-riə/ or -iums glass-walled room for sitting in the sunshine

solar pan·el /,·· '··/n number of SOLAR CELLs working together

solar plex·us /,·· '··/ n 1 system of nerves between the stomach and the BACKBONE 2 infml stomach

solar sys·tem /'·· ,··/ n sun and the PLANETs going round it

sold /səʊld/ past t. and p. of SELL

sol·der /'sɒldə', 'sɔ-‖'sɑːdər/ n [U] easily-meltable metal used for joining metal surfaces ◆ vt join with solder

sol·dier [1] /'səʊldʒə'/ n member of an army

soldier [2] v **soldier on** phr vi continue working steadily in spite of difficulties

sole [1] /səʊl/ n bottom surface of the foot or of a shoe

sole [2] n flat fish often used for food

sole [3] adj 1 only 2 unshared: sole responsibility ~ly adv only

so·le·cis·m /'sɒləsɪzəm‖'sɑː-/ n fml doing something wrong, esp. in grammar or social behaviour

sol·emn /'sɒləm‖'sɑː-/ adj 1 without humour or lightness; serious 2 (of a promise) made sincerely and meant to be kept 3 of the grandest most formal kind ~ly adv ~ness n [U] ~ity /sə'lemnəti/ n 1 [U] solemnness 2 [C] formal act proper for a grand event

sol-fa /,sɒl 'fɑː‖,səʊl-/ n system of names given to different musical notes

so·li·cit /sə'lɪsət/ v 1 vt fml ask for 2 vi esp. law advertise oneself as a PROSTITUTE

so·lic·i·tor /sə'lɪsətə'/ n (esp. in England) lawyer who advises people, prepares contracts, etc.

so·lic·i·tous /sə'lɪsətəs/ adj fml helpful and kind ~ly adv ~ness n [U]

so·lic·i·tude /sə'lɪsətjuːd‖-tuːd/ n [U] fml solicitousness

sol·id /'sɒləd‖'sɑː-/ adj 1 not liquid or gas 2 not hollow 3 firm and well made **4** that may be depended on **5** in or showing complete agreement: *The strike was 100 per cent solid.* **6** not mixed with any other (metal): *a watch of solid gold* **7** *infml* continuous: *waiting for 4 solid hours* **8** having length, width and height ♦ *n* solid object or substance ~**ly** *adv* -**ity** /sə'lɪdɪti/ *n* [U] quality or state of being solid

sol·i·dar·i·ty /ˌsɒlɪ'dærɪti‖ˌsɑː-/ *n* [U] loyalty within a group

so·lid·i·fy /sə'lɪdɪfaɪ/ *vi/t* (cause to) become solid or hard

solid-state /ˌ·· '·◄/ *adj* having electrical parts, esp. TRANSISTORs, that run without heating or moving parts

so·lil·o·quy /sə'lɪləkwi/ *n* speech made by an actor alone on stage

sol·i·taire /ˌsɒlɪ'teə‖ˌsɑː-/ *n* [U] **1** *AmE for* PATIENCE (2) **2** (piece of jewellery having) a single jewel, esp. a diamond

sol·i·ta·ry /'sɒlɪtəri‖'sɑːləteri/ *adj* **1** (fond of being) alone **2** in a lonely place **3** single

sol·i·tude /'sɒlɪtjuːd‖'sɑːlɪtuːd/ *n* [U] *fml* state of being alone

so·lo /'səʊləʊ/ *n* **solos** something done by one person alone, esp. a piece of music for one performer ♦ *adj, adv* **1** without a companion or esp. instructor **2** as or being a musical solo ~**ist** *n* performer of a musical solo

sol·stice /'sɒlstɪs‖'sɑːl-/ *n* time of the longest and shortest days of the year

sol·u·ble /'sɒljʊbəl‖'sɑː-/ *adj* **1** that can be dissolved (DISSOLVE) **2** *fml* solvable **–bility** /ˌsɒljʊ'bɪlɪti‖ˌsɑː-/ *n* [U]

so·lu·tion /sə'luːʃən/ *n* **1** [C] answer to a problem or question **2** [C;U] liquid with a solid mixed into it

solve /sɒlv‖sɑːlv, sɔːlv/ *vt* find an answer to or explanation of **solvable** *adj*

sol·vent[1] /'sɒlvənt‖'sɑːl-, 'sɔːl-/ *adj* not in debt –**vency** *n* [U]

solvent[2] *n* [C;U] liquid that can turn solids into liquids

solvent a·buse /'·· '·,·/ *n* [U] *fml for* GLUE-SNIFFING

som·bre *BrE* ‖ -**ber** *AmE*/'sɒmbər‖ 'sɑːm-/ *adj* sadly serious or dark ~**ly** *adv* ~**ness** *n* [U]

some /səm; *strong* sʌm/ *determiner* **1** a certain number or amount of: *I bought some bread.* | *Some people like tea, others prefer coffee.* **2** an unknown or unstated one: *She went to work for some computer firm (or other).* **3** quite a large number or amount of: *The fire lasted for some time.* **4** *infml* no kind of: *Some friend you are!* **5** a fine or important: *That was some speech you made!* **6** **some ... or (an)other** one

or several which the speaker cannot or does not care to state exactly: *He's staying with some friend or other.* ♦ *pron* **1** an amount or number of the stated thing(s) **2** certain ones but not all ♦ *adv* **1** about (the stated number): *Some 50 people came.* **2** *AmE* rather; a little: *'Are you feeling better?' 'Some, I guess.'* **some more** an additional amount (of)

some·bod·y /'sʌmbədi, -bədi‖ -bɑːdi/ *pron* someone ♦ *n* [U] a person of some importance: *He thinks he's really somebody.*

some·how /'sʌmhaʊ/ *adv* **1** in some way not yet known or stated **2** for some reason: *Somehow I don't believe her.*

some·one /'sʌmwʌn/ *pron* **1** a person (but not a particular or known one) **2** **or someone** or a person like that: *We need a builder or someone.*

some·place /'sʌmpleɪs/ *adv* *AmE for* SOMEWHERE

som·er·sault /'sʌməsɔːlt‖-ər-/ *n* rolling jump in which the feet go over the head and then land on the ground **somersault** *vi*

some·thing /'sʌmθɪŋ/ *pron* **1** some unstated or unknown thing **2** better than nothing: *At least we've got the car, that's something.* **3** **make something of oneself/one's life** be successful **4** **or something** (to show that the speaker is not sure): *He's a director or something.* **5** **something of a(n)** rather a(n); a fairly good **6** **something like: a** rather like **b** *infml* about: *There were something like 1000 people there.* **7** **something over/under** rather more/less than **8** **something to do with** (having) a connection with

some·time /'sʌmtaɪm/ *adv* at some uncertain or unstated time ♦ *adj* *fml* former

some·times /'sʌmtaɪmz/ *adv* on some occasions but not all

some·what /'sʌmwɒt‖-wɑːt/ *adv* a little; rather

some·where /'sʌmweər/ *adv* **1** (at or to) some place **2** **get somewhere** begin to succeed

son /sʌn/ *n* **1** someone's male child **2** (used by an older man to a much younger man or boy): *What's your name, son?*

so·nar /'səʊnɑːr, -nər/ *n* apparatus for finding underwater objects with sound waves

so·na·ta /sə'nɑːtə/ *n* usu. 3- or 4-part piece of music for 1 or 2 instruments

song /sɒŋ‖sɔːŋ/ *n* **1** [C] short piece of music with words for singing **2** [U] act or art of singing **3** [C;U] music-like sound of birds **4** **for a song** very cheaply

song and dance /,·· '·/ n [S;U] *infml* an unnecessary or unwelcome expression of excitement, anger, etc.

son·ic /'sɒnɪk‖'sɑː-/ adj of or concerning the speed of sound or sound

son-in-law /'··· ,·/ n **sons-in-law** or **son-in-laws** daughter's husband

son·net /'sɒnɪt‖'sɑː-/ n 14-line poem

son·ny /'sʌni/ n (used in speaking to a young boy)

son-of-a-bitch /,··· '·/ n **sons-of-bitches**, **son-of-a-bitches** *taboo* someone strongly disliked

so·nor·ous /'sɒnərəs, sə'nɔːrəs‖ sə'nɔːrəs, 'sɑːnərəs/ adj having a pleasantly full loud sound **~ly** adv **-ity** /sə'nɒrɪti‖sə'nɔː-/ n [U]

soon /suːn/ adv **1** within a short time **2** quickly; early: *How soon can you finish it?* **3** willingly: *I'd sooner stay here.* **4 as soon as** at once after; when **5 no sooner ... than** when ... at once: *No sooner had she arrived than it was time to go.* **6 sooner or later** certainly, although one cannot be sure when

soot /sʊt/ n [U] black powder produced by burning **~y** adj **~iness** n [U]

soothe /suːð/ vt **1** make less angry or excited **2** make less painful **soothingly** adv

sooth·say·er /'suːθ,seɪəʳ/ n *lit* person who tells the future

sop[1] /sɒp‖sɑːp/ n something offered to gain someone's favour or stop them complaining

sop[2] v **-pp- sop up** phr vt take up (liquid) into something solid

soph·is·m /'sɒfɪzəm‖'sɑː-/ n *fml* **1** [U] SOPHISTRY **2** [C] correct-sounding but false argument

so·phis·ti·cat·ed /sə'fɪstɪkeɪtɪd/ adj **1** experienced in and understanding the ways of society **2** highly developed and including the best or most modern systems **-ion** /sə,fɪstɪ'keɪʃən/ n [U]

soph·ist·ry /'sɒfɪstri‖'sɑː-/ n [U] *fml* use of false deceptive arguments

soph·o·more /'sɒfəmɔːʳ‖'sɑː-/ n student in the second year of a US college course

sop·o·rif·ic /,sɒpə'rɪfɪk◄‖,sɑː-/ adj causing sleep

sop·ping /'sɒpɪŋ‖'sɑː-/ adv, adj very (wet)

sop·py /'sɒpi‖'sɑːpi/ adj *BrE* **1** foolish **2** too full of expressions of tender feelings

so·pra·no /sə'prɑːnəʊ‖-'præ-/ n **-nos** **1** (someone, esp. a woman, with) the highest human singing voice **2** instrument which plays notes in the highest range

sor·bet /'sɔːbət, 'sɔːbeɪ‖'sɔːrbət/ n [C;U] dish of ice with a usu. fruit taste

sor·cer·y /'sɔːsəri‖'sɔːr-/ n [U] doing of magic with the help of evil spirits **sorcerer, sorceress** *fem.* — n

sor·did /'sɔːdɪd‖'sɔːr-/ adj **1** completely lacking fine or noble qualities; low **2** dirty and badly cared for **~ly** adv **~ness** n [U]

sore /sɔːʳ/ adj **1** painful, esp. from a wound or hard use **2** likely to cause offence: *Don't joke about his weight: it's a sore point with him.* **3** *AmE* angry ♦ n painful usu. infected place on the body ♦ adv *lit* sorely **~ly** adv *fml* very much **~ness** n [U]

sor·row /'sɒrəʊ‖'sɑː-, 'sɔː-/ n [C;U] sadness; grief ♦ vi grieve **~ful** adj **~fully** adv **~fulness** n [U]

sor·ry /'sɒri‖'sɑːri, 'sɔːri/ adj **1** feeling sadness, pity, or sympathy **2** ashamed of or unhappy about an action and wishing one had not done it **3** causing pity mixed with disapproval: *You look a sorry sight.* ♦ interj **1** (used for excusing oneself or expressing polite refusal, disagreement, etc.) **2** (used for asking someone to repeat something one has not heard)

sort[1] /sɔːt‖sɔːrt/ n **1** group of people, things, etc., all sharing certain qualities; kind **2** person: *She's not such a bad sort.* **3 of sorts** of a poor or doubtful kind **4 out of sorts** feeling unwell or annoyed **5 sort of** *infml* rather

sort[2] vi/t put (things) in order

sort out phr vt **1** separate from a mass or group **2** *BrE* deal with

sor·tie /'sɔːti‖'sɔːrti/ n **1** short trip into an unfamiliar place **2** short attack by an army

SOS /,es əʊ 'es/ n urgent message for help

so-so /'· ·/ adj, adv neither very bad(ly) nor very good/well

sot·to vo·ce /,sɒtəʊ 'vəʊtʃi‖,sɑː-/ adv *fml* quietly

souf·flé /'suːfleɪ‖suː'fleɪ/ n [C;U] light airy baked dish of eggs and flour

sought /sɔːt/ past t. and p. of SEEK

sought-af·ter /'· ,·/ adj esp. *BrE* wanted because of rarity or high quality

soul /səʊl/ n **1** part of a person that is not the body and is thought not to die **2** person: *Not a soul* (= no one) *was there.* **3** perfect example: *Your secret is safe with him; he's the soul of discretion.* **4** most active part or influence: *She's the life and soul of any party.* **5** attractive quality of sincerity: *The performance lacks soul.* **6** SOUL MUSIC **7** **heart and soul** (with) all one's power and feeling **8** **keep body and soul together** have enough money, etc., to live **~ful** adj expressing deep feeling **~fully** adv **~less** adj having no attractive or tender human qualities ~**lessly** adv

soul-des-troy-ing /'· ·,··/ adj (esp. of a job) very uninteresting

soul mu-sic /'· ,··/n [U] type of popular music usu. performed by black singers

soul-search-ing /'· ,··/ n deep examination of one's mind and conscience

sound[1] /saund/ n 1 [C;U] what is or may be heard 2 [S] idea produced by something read or heard: *From the sound of it, I'd say the matter was serious.* ♦ v 1 vi seem when heard: *His explanation sounded suspicious.* 2 vi/t (cause to) make a sound: *Sound the trumpets.* 3 vt signal by making sounds: *Sound the alarm.* 4 vt pronounce 5 vt measure the depth of (water, etc.) using a weighted line

sound off phr vi express an opinion freely and forcefully

sound out phr vt try to find out the opinion or intention of

sound[2] adj 1 not damaged or diseased 2 showing good sense or judgment: *sound advice* 3 thorough 4 (of sleep) deep and untroubled 5 **as sound as a bell** in perfect condition ~**ly** adv ~**ness** n [U]

sound[3] adv **sound asleep** deeply asleep

sound bar-ri-er /'· ,··/ n point at which an aircraft, etc., reaches the speed of sound

sound ef-fects /'· ·,·/ n [P] sounds produced to give the effect of natural sounds in a radio or TV broadcast or film

sounding board /'·· ·/n means used for testing thoughts, opinions, etc.

sound-ings /'saundıŋz/ n [P] 1 measurements made by sounding (SOUND[1] (5)) water 2 carefully quiet or secret enquiries

sound-proof /'saundpru:f/ adj that sound cannot get through or into ♦ vt make soundproof

sound-track /'saundtræk/ n recorded music from a film

soup /su:p/ n [U] 1 liquid cooked food often containing pieces of meat or vegetables 2 **in the soup** in trouble

sour /sauər/ adj 1 acid-tasting: *sour green apples* 2 tasting bad because of chemical action by bacteria: *sour milk* 3 bad-tempered; unfriendly 4 **go/turn sour** go wrong ♦ vi/t (cause to) become sour ~**ly** adv ~**ness** n [U]

source /sɔːs‖sɔːrs/ n where something comes from; cause

sour grapes /,· '·/ n [U] pretending to dislike what one really desires, because it is unobtainable

sour-puss /'sauəpus‖-ər-/ n complaining humourless person

south /sauθ/ n (often cap.) **1** the direction which is on the right of a person facing the rising sun **2** [*the* + S] **a** the part of a country which is further south than the rest **b** the southeastern states of the US ♦ adj 1 in the south **2** (of wind) from the south ♦ adv towards the south ~**ward** adj, adv

south-east /,sauθ'iːst◂/ n, adj, adv (direction) halfway between south and east ~**ern** /-'iːstən‖-ərn/ adj

south-er-ly /'sʌðəli‖-ər-/ adj south

south-ern /'sʌðən‖-ərn/ adj of the south part of the world or of a country ~**ern** n (often cap.) person who lives in or comes from the southern part of a country

south-west /,sauθ'west◂/ n, adj, adv (direction) halfway between south and west ~**ern** /-'westən‖-ərn/ adj

sou-ve-nir /,suːvə'nɪər‖, 'suːvənɪər/ n object kept as a reminder of an event, journey, place, etc.

sou'west-er /sau'westər/ n hat of shiny material to keep off the rain, worn esp. by sailors

sove-reign /'sɒvrən‖'saː-v-/ n 1 fml king, queen, etc. 2 former British gold coin worth £1 ♦ adj (of a country) independent and self-governing ~**ty** n [U] 1 complete freedom and power to act or govern 2 quality of being a sovereign state

So-vi-et /'səuviət, 'sɒ-‖'sou-, 'saː-/ adj of the USSR or its people

sow[1] /səu/ vi/t **sowed, sown** /səun/ or **sowed** plant (seeds) on (a piece of ground) ~**er** n

sow[2] /sau/ n female pig

soya bean /'·· ·/ n bean of an Asian plant which produces oil and is made into a special dark liquid used in Chinese cooking

soz-zled /'sɒzəld‖'saː-/ adj BrE infml drunk

spa /spaː/ n place with a spring of mineral water where people come to be cured

space /speɪs/ n 1 [U] something measurable in length, width, or depth; room: *There's not enough space in the cupboard for all my clothes.* 2 [C;U] quantity or bit of this: *looking for a parking space* 3 [U] what is outside the Earth's air; where the stars and PLANETs are 4 [U] what surrounds all objects and continues outwards in all directions: *staring into space* 5 [C;U] period of time: *within the space of a few years* ♦ vt place apart; arrange with spaces between

space-age /'· ·/ adj very modern

space-craft /'speɪs-kraːft‖-kræft/ n vehicle able to travel in SPACE (3)

space-ship /'speɪsˌʃɪp/ n (esp. in stories) spacecraft for carrying people

space sta·tion /'· ˌ··/ large spacecraft intended to stay above the Earth and act as a base for scientific tests, etc.

space-suit /'speɪs-suːt, -sjuːt‖-suːt/ n special garment worn in SPACE (3), covering the whole body

spa·cious /'speɪʃəs/ adj having a lot of room: a spacious office ~ness n [U]

spade[1] /speɪd/ n 1 broad-bladed tool for digging 2 **call a spade a spade** speak the plain truth without being delicate or sensitive

spade[2] n playing card with one or more figures shaped like black printed leaves on it

spake /speɪk/ old use, past tense of SPEAK

span[1] /spæn/ past t. of SPIN

span[2] n 1 length between 2 limits, esp. of time: over a span of 3 years 2 length of time over which something continues: concentration span 3 (part of) a bridge, arch, etc., between supports 4 distance from the end of the thumb to the little finger in a spread hand ♦ vt -nn- 1 form an arch or bridge over 2 include in space or time

span·gle /'spæŋɡəl/ n small shiny piece sewn on for decoration ♦ vt decorate with spangles

span·iel /'spænjəl/ n dog with long ears and long wavy hair

spank /spæŋk/ vt hit (esp. a child) with the open hand for punishment, esp. on the BUTTOCKs **spank** n

span·ner /'spænəʳ/ n BrE 1 metal tool with jaws or a hollow end, for twisting NUTs (2) 2 **a spanner in the works** a cause of confusion to a plan or operation

spar[1] /spaːʳ/ vi -rr- 1 practise boxing (BOX[2]) 2 fight with words

spar[2] n pole supporting a ship's ropes or sails

spare /speəʳ/ vt 1 give up (something that is not needed): We have no money to spare. (= we have only just enough) 2 keep from using, spending, etc.: No expense was spared. (= a lot of money was spent) 3 not give (something unpleasant): Spare me the gory details. 4 esp. lit not punish or harm 5 **spare a thought** stop and consider 6 **spare someone's blushes** infml avoid making someone feel awkward, esp. by praising them too much ♦ adj 1 kept for use if needed: a spare tyre 2 free: spare time 3 rather thin ♦ n BrE for SPARE PART

spare part /ˌ· '·/ n machine part to take the place of one that is damaged

spare part sur·ge·ry /ˌ· '··ˌ/ n [U] infml fixing of organs (such as a heart

from dead people in a body to take the place of diseased organs

spare-ribs /'speəˌrɪbz/ n [P] (dish of) pig's RIBs with their meat

spark /spaːk‖spaːrk/ n 1 small bit of burning material flying through the air: (fig.) His murder was the spark that set off the war. 2 electric flash passing across a space 3 very small but important bit: not a spark of humour — see also BRIGHT SPARK ♦ vi 1 produce a spark 2 lead to (esp. something unpleasant) 3 esp. AmE encourage

spark off phr vt cause (esp. something violent or unpleasant)

spar·kle /'spaːkəl‖-aːr-/ vi shine in small flashes: (fig.) Her conversation sparkled with wit. (= was bright and interesting) ♦ n [C;U] act or quality of sparkling **-kling** adj 1 full of life and brightness 2 (of wine) giving off gas in small BUBBLEs

spark plug /'· ·/‖ also **sparking plug** /'·· ·,·/ BrE — n part inside an engine that makes a SPARK (2) to light the petrol and start the engine

spar·row /'spærəʊ/ n very common small brownish bird

sparse /spaːs‖spaːrs/ adj scattered; not crowded ~**ly** adv ~**ness** n [U]

spar·tan /'spaːtn‖-aːr-/ adj simple, severe, and without attention to comfort

spas·m /'spæzəm/ n 1 sudden uncontrolled tightening of muscles 2 sudden short period of uncontrolled activity: spasms of coughing

spas·mod·ic /spæz'mɒdɪk‖-'maː-/ adj happening irregularly or non-continuously: spasmodic interest ~**ally** /-kli/ adv

spas·tic /'spæstɪk/ n person with a disease in which some parts of the body will not move

spat /spæt/ past t. and p. of SPIT

spate /speɪt/ n [S] esp. BrE large number or amount coming together at the same time

spa·tial /'speɪʃəl/ adj fml of or in SPACE (1) ~**ly** adv

spat·ter /'spætəʳ/ vi/t scatter (drops of liquid) or be scattered on (a surface)

spat·u·la /'spætjʊlə‖-tʃələ/ n (kitchen) tool with a wide flat blade for spreading, mixing, etc.

spawn /spɔːn/ n [U] eggs of water animals like fishes and FROGs ♦ vi 1 produce spawn 2 produce esp. in large numbers

speak /spiːk/ v spoke /spəʊk/, spoken /'spəʊkən/ 1 vi say things; talk 2 vi express thoughts, ideas, etc., in some other way than this: Actions speak louder than words. 3 vt say; express: Is he speaking the truth? 4 vt be able to talk in (a language) 5 vi make a speech **6** *vi* mean in the stated way what is said: *generally/personally speaking, I agree* **7 on speaking terms** willing to talk and be polite to another **8 so to speak** as one might say **9 speak one's mind** express one's thoughts (too) directly **10 to speak of** worth mentioning ~**er** *n* **1** person making a speech **2** person who speaks a language LOUDSPEAKER

speak for *phr vt* express the thoughts, opinions, etc., of

speak out *phr vi* speak boldly, freely and plainly

speak up *phr vi* **1** speak more loudly **2** SPEAK out

speak·eas·y /'spiːkˌiːzi/ *n* (esp. in the US in the 1920s and 1930s) place for going to buy and drink alcohol illegally

spear /spɪər/ *n* weapon consisting of a sharp-pointed pole ♦ *vt* push or throw a spear into

spear·head /'spɪəhed/'spɪər-/ *n* forceful beginner and/or leader of an attack or course of action ♦ *vt* lead forcefully

spear·mint /'spɪəˌmɪnt/'spɪər-/ *n* [U] common MINT plant with a fresh taste

spec /spek/ *n* **on spec** *BrE* as a risk

spe·cial /'speʃəl/ *adj* **1** of a particular kind; not ordinary **2** particularly great or fine: *a special occasion* ♦ *n* something not of the regular kind **2** *AmE infml* an advertised reduced price in a shop ~**ly** *adv* **1** for one particular purpose **2** unusually

spe·cial·ist /'speʃəlɪst/ *n* **1** person with skill or interest in a particular subject **2** doctor who specializes in a particular sort of disease, etc.

spe·ci·al·i·ty /ˌspeʃiˈæləti/ ‖ *usu.* **specialty** /'speʃəlti/ *AmE* — *n* **1** person's particular field of work or study **2** finest product

spe·cial·ize ‖ also **-ise** *BrE* /'speʃəlaɪz/ *vi* limit one's study, business, etc., to one particular area **-ization** /ˌspeʃəlaɪˈzeɪʃən‖-lə-/ *n* [C;U]

spe·cies /'spiːʃiːz/ *n* **-cies** group of similar types of animal or plant

spe·cif·ic /spəˈsɪfɪk/ *adj* **1** detailed and exact: *specific instructions* **2** particular; fixed or named: *a specific tool for each job* ~**ally** /-kli/ *adv*

spe·ci·fi·ca·tion /ˌspesɪfɪˈkeɪʃən/ *n* **1** [C] detailed plan or set of descriptions or directions **2** [U] act of specifying

spe·ci·fy /'spesɪfaɪ/ *vt* state exactly

spe·ci·men /'spesəmən/ *n* **1** single typical thing or example **2** piece or amount of something to be shown, tested, etc.: *The doctor needs a specimen of your blood.*

spe·cious /'spiːʃəs/ *adj fml* seeming correct but in fact false ~**ly** *adv* ~**ness** *n* [U]

speck /spek/ *n* very small piece or spot: *a speck of dust*

speck·le /'spekəl/ *n* any of a number of small irregular marks **-led** *adj*

spec·ta·cle /'spektəkəl/ *n* **1** something unusual that one sees, esp. something grand and fine **2** object of laughing, disrespect, or pity **spectacles** *n* [P] GLASSES

spec·tac·u·lar /spekˈtækjʊlər/ *adj* unusually interesting and grand ♦ *n* spectacular entertainment ~**ly** *adv*

spec·ta·tor /spekˈteɪtər‖ˈspekteɪtər/ *n* person watching an event or sport

spec·tre *BrE* ‖ **-ter** *AmE* /'spektər/ *n* *fml or lit for* GHOST **1** fml idea

spec·trum /'spektrəm/ *n* **-tra** /-trə/ **1** set of bands of different colours into which light may be separated by a PRISM **2** broad and continuous range: *both ends of the political spectrum*

spec·u·late /'spekjʊleɪt/ *vi* **1** make guesses **2** buy things to sell later in the hope of profit **-lator** *n* **-lative** /-lətɪv/ *adj* **-lation** /ˌspekjʊˈleɪʃən/ *n* [C;U]

sped /sped/ *past t. and p. of* SPEED

speech /spiːtʃ/ *n* **1** [U] act, power, or way of speaking **2** [C] set of words spoken formally to a group of listeners — see also FREE SPEECH ~**less** *adj* unable to speak because of strong feeling, shock, etc.

speed /spiːd/ *n* **1** [C] rate of movement: *a speed of 2000 kilometres an hour* **2** [U] quickness of movement or action: *travelling at speed* (= fast) **3** [U] *sl for* AMPHETAMINE ♦ *v* **speeded** or **sped** /sped/ **1** *vi/t* go or take quickly **2** *vi* drive illegally fast ~**y** *adj* fast

speed up *phr vi/t* (cause to) go faster

speed·om·e·ter /spɪˈdɒmɪtər, spiː-‖ -ˈdɑː-/ *n* instrument showing how fast a vehicle is going

speed·way /'spiːdweɪ/ *n* [U] sport of racing motorcycles on a closed track

spell¹ /spel/ *v* **spelt** /spelt/ *esp. BrE* ‖ **spelled** *esp. AmE* **1** *vi* form words (correctly) from letters **2** *vt* name in order the letters of (a word) **3** *vt* (of letters) form (a word): *B-O-O-K spells 'book'.* **4** *vt* have an effect: *His disapproval spells defeat for our plan.* ~**er** *n* ~**ing** *n* way a word is spelt

spell out *phr vt* explain in the clearest possible way

spell² *n* **1** unbroken period of time: *spells of sunshine* **2** quickly passing attack of illness: *a dizzy spell*

spell³ *n* (words producing) a condition produced by magical power: (fig.) *The first time we saw Venice, we fell under its spell.*

spell-bind /'spelbaɪnd/ vt hold the complete attention of

spend /spend/ vt **spent** /spent/ 1 pay (money) for goods or services 2 pass or use (time): *He spent 3 years in prison.* ~**er** n **spent** adj 1 already used; no longer for use 2 worn out

spend-thrift /'spend,θrɪft/ n person who wastes money

sperm /spɜːm‖spɜːrm/ n male sex cell which unites with the female egg to produce new life

spew /spjuː/ vi/t (cause to) come out in a rush or flood

sphere /sfɪəʳ/ n 1 ball-shaped mass 2 area or range of existence, meaning, action, etc.: *this country's sphere of influence* **spherical** /'sferɪkəl/ adj ball-shaped

sphinx /sfɪŋks/ n 1 ancient Egyptian image of a lion with a human head 2 person who behaves or speaks in a mysterious way

spice /spaɪs/ n 1 [C;U] vegetable product used for giving taste to food 2 [S;U] (additional) interest or excitement ♦ vt add spice to **spicy** adj 1 containing (much) spice 2 slightly improper or rude

spick-and-span /ˌspɪk ən 'spæn/ adj completely clean and tidy

spi-der /'spaɪdəʳ/ n small 8-legged creature, of which many types make WEBs to catch insects ~**y** adj long and thin like a spider's legs

spike /spaɪk/ n 1 pointed piece, esp. of metal 2 metal point fixed to the bottom of a (sports) shoe 3 group of grains or flowers on top of a stem ♦ vt 1 drive a spike into 2 add a strong alcoholic drink to (a weak or non-alcoholic one) 3 stop (esp. an article in a newspaper) from being printed or spread 4 **spike someone's guns** take away an opponent's power **spiky** adj

spill /spɪl/ vi/t **spilt** /spɪlt/ esp. BrE ‖ **spilled** esp. AmE (cause to) pour out accidentally and be lost: *I've spilt some coffee on the carpet.*|(fig.) *The crowd spilt into the streets.* 2 **spill the beans** infml tell a secret too soon or to the wrong person ♦ n fall from a horse, bicycle, etc.

spin /spɪn/ v **span** /spæn/ or **spun** /spʌn/, **spun**; pres. p. -**nn**- 1 vi/t turn round and round fast 2 vi/t make (thread) by twisting (cotton, wool, etc.): (fig.) *spin a yarn* (= tell a story) 3 vt produce in threadlike form: *a spider spinning a web* ♦ n 1 [C] act of spinning 2 [S;U] fast turning movement 3 [C] short trip for pleasure 4 [S] a steep drop: *The news sent prices into a spin.* 5 **in a (flat) spin** in a confused state of mind ~**ner** n

spin out phr vt cause to last long enough or too long

spin-ach /'spɪnɪdʒ, -ɪtʃ‖-ɪtʃ/ n [U] vegetable with large soft leaves

spin-al cord /ˌ··· '·/ n thick cord of important nerves enclosed in the SPINE (1)

spin-dle /'spɪndl/ n 1 machine part round which something turns 2 pointed rod onto which thread is twisted -**dly** adj long, thin, and weak-looking

spine /spaɪn/ n 1 row of bones down the centre of the back 2 prickly animal or plant part 3 side of a book along which the pages are fastened ~**less** adj weak and cowardly **spiny** adj prickly

spine-chil-ling /'·· ,··/ adj very frightening

spin-off /'·· ·/ n (useful) indirect product of a process

spin-ster /'spɪnstəʳ/ n unmarried woman

spi-ral /'spaɪərəl/ n, adj 1 (curve) winding round and round a central line or away from a central point 2 process of continuous upward or downward change ♦ vi -**ll**- BrE ‖ -**l**- AmE move in a spiral

spire /spaɪəʳ/ n tall thin pointed roof of a church tower

spir-it /'spɪrɪt/ n 1 [C] person's mind or soul 2 [C] a being without a body, such as a GHOST 3 [U] quality of lively determination or brave effort: *a woman with spirit* | *team spirit* 4 [C] person of the stated kind of temper: *a free spirit* 5 [C] central quality or force: *the spirit of the law* (= its real intention) 6 [S;U] feeling in the mind towards something; ATTITUDE: *Please take my remarks in the spirit in which they were intended, and don't be offended.* 7 [C] strong alcoholic drink 8 **in spirit** in one's thoughts 9 -**spir-ited** having the stated feelings or spirits: *high-spirited* ♦ vt take secretly or mysteriously **spirits** n [P] state of one's mind: *in high spirits* (= cheerful) ~**ed** adj full of SPIRIT (3) ~**edly** adv ~**less** adj without SPIRIT (3) ~**lessness** n

spir-i-tu-al /'spɪrɪtʃuəl/ adj 1 of the spirit rather than the body 2 religious ♦ n religious song originally sung by US blacks ~**ly** adv

spit[1] /spɪt/ v **spat** /spæt/; pres. p. -**tt**- 1 vi/t throw out (liquid or other contents) from the mouth with force 2 vt say with effort or anger 3 vi rain very lightly ♦ n [U] SALIVA

spit[2] n 1 thin rod on which meat is cooked over a fire 2 small usu. sandy point of land running out into a stretch of water

spit and pol·ish /ˌ·· ·'··/ n [U] great military attention to a clean and shiny appearance

spite /spaɪt/ n [U] **1** desire to annoy or harm **2 in spite of** taking no notice of: *They continued, in spite of my warning.* ♦ vt annoy or harm intentionally ~**ful** adj

spitting im·age /ˌ·· '··/ n exact likeness

spit·tle /'spɪtl/ n [U] SALIVA

splash /splæʃ/ v **1** vi/t **a** (cause to) fall or move about in drops or waves, esp. wildly or noisily: *Rain splashed against the window.* **b** throw a liquid against (something): *He splashed his face with cold water.* **2** vt report as if very important, esp. in a newspaper **3** vi/t BrE spend freely: *I splashed out and bought a new dress.* ♦ n **1** (sound or mark made by) splashing **2** forceful effect: *make a splash in society*

splash down phr vi (esp. of a spacecraft) land in the sea **splashdown** /'splæʃdaʊn/ n [C;U]

splash·y /'splæʃi/ adj esp. AmE big, bright, and very noticeable

splay /spleɪ/ vi/t spread out or become larger at one end

spleen /spliːn/ n **1** organ that controls the quality of the body's blood supply **2 vent one's spleen** express one's annoyance

splen·did /'splendɪd/ adj **1** grand in appearance or style **2** very fine; excellent ~**ly** adv

splen·dour BrE ‖ -**dor** AmE /'splendər/ n [U] excellent or grand beauty

splice /splaɪs/ vt **1** fasten end to end to make one continuous length **2** BrE infml join in marriage

splint /splɪnt/ n flat piece for keeping a broken bone in place

splin·ter /'splɪntər/ n small sharp piece, esp. of wood, broken off ♦ vi/t break into splinters

splinter group /'·· ˌ·/ n group of people that has separated from a larger body

split /splɪt/ v split; pres. p. -tt- **1** vi/t divide along a length, esp. by a blow or tear **2** vi/t divide into separate parts **3** vt share **4** vi/t separate into opposing groups or parties: *Did you know John and Mary had split up?* (= their marriage had ended) **5 split hairs** concern oneself with small unimportant differences ♦ n **1** cut, break, or division made by splitting — see also SPLITS ~**ting** adj (of a headache) very bad

split per·son·al·i·ty /ˌ· ···'···/ n set of 2 very different ways of behaving present in one person

splits /splɪts/ n [the + P] movement in which a person's legs are spread

wide and touch the floor along their whole length

split sec·ond /ˌ· '··◂/ n very short moment

splurge /splɜːdʒ‖-ɜːr-/ vi/t spend more than one can usu. afford

splut·ter /'splʌtər/ vi **1** talk quickly, as if confused **2** make a wet spitting (SPIT) noise **splutter** n

spoil /spɔɪl/ v spoiled or spoilt /spɔɪlt/ **1** vt destroy the value, worth, or pleasure of; ruin **2** vt treat very or too well: *Go on, spoil yourself, have another cake.* **3** vi decay **spoils** n [P] fml or lit things taken without payment

spoil for phr vt **1** be very eager for **2** cause to be unsatisfied with: *Fine French wine spoils you for cheaper kinds.* **3 be spoilt for choice** find it difficult to decide or choose

spoil·sport /'spɔɪlspɔːt‖-ɔːrt/ n person who ruins others' fun

spoke[1] /spəʊk/ v past t. of SPEAK

spoke[2] n any of the bars connecting the outer ring of a wheel to the centre

spok·en /'spəʊkən/ v past p. of SPEAK

spoken for /'·· ·/ adj infml closely connected with a person of the opposite sex

spokes·per·son /'spəʊks.pɜːsən‖-ɜːr-/ **spokes·man** /-mən/ masc., **spokes·wom·an** /-.wʊmən/ fem. — n person chosen to speak officially for a group

sponge /spʌndʒ/ n **1** [C] simple sea creature with a rubber-like body **2** [C;U] piece of this or plastic like it, which can suck up water and is used for washing **3 throw in the sponge** accept defeat ♦ v **1** vt clean with a sponge **2** vi derog get things from people free by taking advantage of their generosity **sponger** n person who SPONGEs (2) **spongy** adj not firm

sponge cake /'··/ n [U;C] light cake made from eggs, sugar, and flour

spon·sor /'sponsər‖'spɑːn-/ n **1** company or person giving money to help others to do something **2** person who takes responsibility for a person or thing ♦ vt act as a sponsor for: *a concert sponsored by American Express* ~**ship** n [U]

spon·ta·ne·ous /spon'teɪniəs‖ spɑːn-/ adj happening naturally, without planning or another's suggestion ~**ly** adv -**taneity** /ˌspontə'niːəti, -ˈneɪti‖ˌspɑːn-/ n [U]

spoof /spuːf/ n funny untrue copy or description

spook /spuːk/ vt esp. AmE cause (esp. an animal) to be suddenly afraid ♦ n infml for GHOST

spook·y /'spuːki/ adj causing fear in a strange way -**ily** adv

spool /spuːl/ n wheel-like object onto which things are wound

spoon /spuːn/ n kitchen tool consisting of a small bowl with a handle, used esp. for eating — see also WOODEN SPOON ♦ vt take up with a spoon

spoon-feed /'· ·/ vt 1 feed with a spoon 2 teach (people) in very easy lessons

spo-rad-ic /spəˈrædɪk/ adj happening irregularly ~**ally** /-kli/ adv

spore /spɔːʳ/ n very small cell that acts like a seed: a mushroom's spores

sport /spɔːt‖spɔːrt/ n 1 [C;U] activity needing physical effort and skill and usu. done as a competition according to rules 2 [C] friendly or kind person ♦ vt wear or show publicly: sporting a brand new coat **sports** /n [P] BrE ATHLETICS competition ~**ing** adj 1 fair and generous 2 (fond) of outdoor sports ~**y** BrE infml good at and/or fond of sport

sports car /'· ·/ n low fast car

sports-man /ˈspɔːtsmən‖ˈspɔːr-/ **sports-wom-an** /-ˌwʊmən/ fem. — n -**men** /-mən/ person who plays sport(s) ~**ship** n [U] fairness to one's opponent, esp. in sport

spot /spɒt‖spɑːt/ n 1 usu. round part different from the main surface: a blue dress with white spots | You've got ink spots on your trousers. 2 small diseased mark on the skin 3 place: a beautiful spot for a picnic 4 small or limited part of something: one of the brighter spots in the news 5 BrE small amount: a spot of bother 6 infml difficult situation 7 SPOTLIGHT 8 place in a broadcast: a guest spot on TV 9 **change one's spots** change one's qualities or way of life 10 **knock spots off** be very much better than 11 **on the spot: a** at once **b** at the place of the action **c** in a position of having to make the right action or answer: The question really put me on the spot. — see also BLACK SPOT, HIGH SPOT, SOFT SPOT ♦ vt -tt- 1 see; recognize 2 mark with spots 3 AmE allow as an advantage in a game ~**less** adj completely clean ~**ter** n person who looks for the stated thing: a train spotter ~**ty** adj 1 having spots on the face 2 AmE with some parts less good than others

spot check /ˌ· '·‖ˌ· ·/ n examination of a few chosen by chance to represent all **spot-check** vt

spot-light /ˈspɒtlaɪt‖ˈspɑːt-/ n 1 (light from) a large lamp with a directable beam 2 public attention ♦ vt direct attention to

spouse /spaʊs, spaʊz/ n fml or law husband or wife

spout /spaʊt/ n 1 opening from which liquid comes out: the spout of a teapot 2 forceful (rising) stream of liquid 3 BrE infml **up the spout a** ruined **b** PREGNANT(1) ♦ v 1 vi/t come or throw out in a forceful stream 2 vt derog pour out in a stream of words

sprain /spreɪn/ vt damage (a joint in the body) by sudden twisting **sprain** n

sprang /spræŋ/ past t. of SPRING

sprawl /sprɔːl/ vi/t spread out awkwardly or ungracefully ♦ n sprawling position or area

spray /spreɪ/ vi/t send or come out in a stream of small drops (onto) ♦ n 1 [U] water blown in very small drops 2 [C;U] liquid to be sprayed out from a container under pressure: hair spray (= to keep hair in place) 3 [C] small branch with its leaves and flowers

spread /spred/ v **spread** 1 vi/t (cause to) become longer, broader, wider, etc. 2 vi/t (cause to) have an effect or influence or become known over a wider area: The fire/news soon spread. 3 vi cover a large area or period 4 vt put over (a surface): Spread butter on the bread. ♦ n 1 [U] act or action of spreading 2 [U] soft food for spreading on bread: cheese spread 3 [C] large or grand meal — see also MIDDLE AGED SPREAD

spread-ea-gle /ˌ· '··‖'· ˌ··/ vt put into a position with arms and legs spread wide

spread-sheet /ˈspredʃiːt/ n type of computer PROGRAM that allows figures (e.g. about sales, taxes, and profits) to be shown in groups on a SCREEN (4) so that quick calculations can be made

spree /spriː/ n period of much wild fun, spending, drinking, etc.

sprig /sprɪg/ n small end of a stem with leaves

spright-ly /ˈspraɪtli/ adj cheerful and active -**liness** n [U]

spring¹ /sprɪŋ/ v **sprang** /spræŋ/, **sprung** /sprʌŋ/ 1 vi move quickly and suddenly as if by jumping: The soldiers sprang to attention. | (fig.) The engine sprang into life. 2 vi/t open or close with a SPRING (2): The box sprang open. (= opened suddenly) | to spring a trap 3 vt produce (as) (a surprise): She sprang the news on us. 4 **spring a leak** (of a ship, container, etc.) begin to let liquid through a hole, etc.

spring from phr vt have as its origin

spring up phr vi come into existence suddenly

spring² n 1 [C;U] season between winter and summer 2 [C] length of wound metal that comes up again after being pressed down 3 [C] place where water comes naturally from the ground **4** [U] elastic quality **5** [C] act of springing ~**y** adj elastic

spring-board /'sprɪŋbɔːd‖-bɔːrd/ n **1** bendable board off which people who DIVE jump **2** strong starting point

spring-clean /,· '-◄/ vi/t clean (a house, etc.) thoroughly **spring-clean** /'·-/ n

sprin-kle /'sprɪŋkəl/ vt scatter (small drops or bits) on or over (a surface) **–kler** n apparatus for sprinkling drops of water

sprint /sprɪnt/ vi run very fast **sprint** n ~**er** n

sprout /spraʊt/ vi/t send or come out as new growth ♦ n **1** new growth on a plant **2** BRUSSELS SPROUT

spruce¹ /spruːs/ adj neat and clean ♦ v **spruce up** phr vt make (esp. oneself) spruce

spruce² n tree of northern countries with short needle-shaped leaves

sprung /sprʌŋ/ past p. of SPRING

spry /spraɪ/ adj (esp. of older people) active

spud /spʌd/ n infml potato

spun /spʌn/ past t. and p. of SPIN

spur /spɜːr/ n **1** sharp object fitted to a rider's boot, used to make a horse go faster **2** event or influence leading to action **3** length of high ground coming out from a mountain range **4 on the spur of the moment** without preparation or planning ♦ vt -**rr**- urge or encourage forcefully

spu-ri-ous /'spjʊəriəs/ adj **1** based on incorrect reasoning **2** pretended; false ~**ly** adv ~**ness** n [U]

spurn /spɜːn‖spɜːrn/ vt refuse or send away with angry pride

spurt /spɜːt‖spɜːrt/ vi/t **1** make a SPURT (1) **2** (cause to) flow out suddenly or violently ♦ n **1** sudden short increase of effort or speed **2** spurting of liquid or gas

sput-ter /'spʌtər/ vi make repeated soft explosive sounds

spu-tum /'spjuːtəm/ n [U] liquid coughed up

spy /spaɪ/ n **1** person employed to find out secret information **2** person who watches secretly ♦ v **1** watch or search secretly **2** vt catch sight of

sq written abbrev. for: square

squab-ble /'skwɒbəl‖'skwɑː-/ vi, n (have) a quarrel about unimportant things

squad /skwɒd‖skwɑːd/ n group of people working as a team — see also FLYING SQUAD

squad-ron /'skwɒdrən‖'skwɑː-/ n large group of soldiers with TANKs (2), of warships, or of aircraft in the airforce

squal-id /'skwɒlɪd‖'skwɑː-/ adj **1** very dirty and unpleasant **2** of low moral standards ~**ly** adv

squall /skwɔːl/ n sudden strong wind ~**y** adj

squal-or /'skwɒlər‖'skwɑː-/ n [U] SQUALID (1) conditions

squan-der /'skwɒndər‖'skwɑːn-/ vt spend foolishly and wastefully

square¹ /skweər/ n **1** shape with 4 straight equal sides forming 4 right angles **2** broad open area with buildings round it in a town **3** result of multiplying a number by itself ♦ adj **1** being a SQUARE (1) **2** of an area equal to a square with sides of the stated length: *1 square metre* **3** forming (nearly) a right angle: *a square jaw* **4** fair; honest: *a square deal* **5** equal in points: *The teams are all square.* **6** having paid and settled what is owed

square² v **1** vt put into a square shape **2** vt divide into squares **3** vt multiply by itself: *2 squared is 4.* **4** vi/t (cause to) fit a particular explanation or standard **5** vt cause (totals of points or games won) to be equal **6** vt pay or pay for **7** vt pay or settle dishonestly: *There are government officers who will have to be squared.* ♦ adv squarely ~**ly** adv directly: *He looked her squarely in the eye.*

square up phr vi settle a bill

square meal /,· '·/ n infml good satisfying meal

square one /,· '·/ n [U] the starting point

square root /,· '·/ n number which when squared (SQUARE² (3)) equals a particular number: *2 is the square root of 4.*

squash /skwɒʃ‖skwɑːʃ, skwɔːʃ/ v **1** vt flatten; crush **2** vi/t push or fit into a small space **3** vt force into silence or inactivity ♦ n **1** [S] act or sound of squashing **2** [U] game played in a 4-walled court with RACKETs and a small ball **3** [U] *BrE* sweet fruit drink **4** [C;U] *esp. AmE* any of a group of vegetables with hard skins, including MARROWs and PUMPKINs ~**y** adj soft and easy to squash

squat /skwɒt‖skwɑːt/ vi -**tt**- **1** sit with the legs drawn up under the body **2** live in an empty building without permission ♦ adj ungracefully short or low and thick ~**ter** n person who SQUATs (2)

squaw /skwɔː/ n North American Indian woman

squawk /skwɔːk/ vi **1** (of a bird) make a loud rough cry **2** complain loudly **squawk** n

squeak /skwiːk/ vi, n (make) a short very high quiet sound — see also NARROW SQUEAK ~**y** adj: *a squeaky door*

squeal /skwiːl/ n a long very high cry ♦ vi **1** make a squeal **2** sl give secret information about one's criminal friends to the police ~**er** n

squeam·ish /'skwiːmɪʃ/ adj easily shocked or upset by unpleasant things ~**ly** adv —**ness** n [U]

squeeze /skwiːz/ v 1 vt press firmly (together), esp. from opposite sides 2 vt get or force out (as if) by pressure: squeeze the juice from an orange 3 vi/t fit or go by forcing or crowding: She squeezed through the narrow opening. 4 vt cause many difficulties to: Higher lending rates are squeezing small businesses. ♦ n 1 act of squeezing 2 difficult situation caused by high costs or not enough supplies

squelch /skweltʃ/ vi, n (make) the sound of soft mud being pressed ~**y** adj

squib /skwɪb/ n small toy explosive — see also DAMP SQUIB

squid /skwɪd/ n squid or squids sea creature with 10 arms at the end of its long body

squidg·y /'skwɪdʒi/ adj BrE infml pastelike; soft and wet

squig·gle /'skwɪgəl/ n short wavy or twisting line

squint /skwɪnt/ vi 1 look with almost closed eyes 2 have a SQUINT (1) ♦ n 1 condition in which the eyes look in different directions 2 act of SQUINT·ing (1)

squire /skwaɪəʳ/ n main landowner in an English village or country area

squirm /skwɜːm‖skwɜːrm/ vi twist the body about, esp. from discomfort, shame, or nervousness

squir·rel /'skwɪrəl‖'skwɜːrəl/ n small furry tree-climbing animal

squirt /skwɜːt‖skwɜːrt/ vi/t, n (force or be forced out in) a thin stream

Sr written abbrev. for: SENIOR

SS /'es es/abbrev. for: STEAMSHIP

ssh /ʃ/ interj (used for asking for less noise)

St written abbrev. for: 1 Street 2 SAINT

stab /stæb/ vi/t -bb- strike forcefully (into) with a pointed weapon ♦ n 1 act of stabbing 2 try: I'll have a stab at it. 3 **a stab in the back** an attack from someone supposed to be a friend ~**bing** adj (of pain) sharp and sudden ~**bing** n [C;U]: a big increase in the number of stabbings at football matches

sta·ble[1] /'steɪbəl/ adj not easily moved, upset, or changed —**bilize** vi/t —**bilizer** n —**bility** /stə'bɪləti/ n [U]

stable[2] n 1 building where horses are kept 2 group of things with one owner ♦ vt keep in a stable

stac·cat·o /stə'kɑːtəʊ/ adj, adv played with very short notes

stack /stæk/ n 1 neat pile: a stack of dishes 2 large pile of dried grass stored outdoors 3 also **stacks** pl. — large amount ♦ vt make into a neat pile (on)

sta·di·um /'steɪdiəm/ n -diums or -dia /-diə/ large building containing a sports field and seats for SPECTATORs

staff /stɑːf‖stæf/ n 1 the workers in a place 2 long thick stick or pole ♦ vt provide workers for

stag /stæg/ n 1 fully grown male deer 2 for men only: a stag night/party 3 BrE person who buys shares in a new company hoping to sell them quickly at a profit

stage /steɪdʒ/ n 1 raised floor on which plays are performed: He wants to go on the stage. (= become an actor) 2 a centre of action or attention: on the centre of the political stage 3 state reached at a particular time in a course of events: The project was cancelled at an early stage. 4 part of a journey or long race 5 any of the separate driving parts of a ROCKET ♦ vt 1 perform or arrange for public show 2 cause to happen, esp. for public effect

stage·coach /'steɪdʒkəʊtʃ/ n (in former times) horse-drawn carriage providing a regular passenger service

stage-man·age /'· ·,·/ vt arrange for public effect, so that a desired result will happen as if naturally

stage man·ag·er /'· ,··/ n person in charge of a theatre stage

stage-struck /'steɪdʒstrʌk/ adj in love with the theatre and esp. wishing to be an actor

stage whis·per /ˌ· '··/ n loud whisper intended to be heard by everyone

stag·ger /'stægəʳ/ v 1 vi/t walk unsteadily, almost falling 2 vt shock greatly 3 vt arrange so as to happen at different times ♦ n unsteady movement, as if about to fall

stag·ing post /'·· ·/ n place where regular stops are made on long journeys

stag·nant /'stægnənt/ adj 1 (esp. of water) not flowing or moving, and often bad-smelling 2 not developing or growing —**nate** /stæg'neɪt‖'stægneɪt/ vi become STAGNANT (2) —**nation** /stæg'neɪʃən/ n [U]

staid /steɪd/ adj serious and dull by habit ~**ness** n [U]

stain /steɪn/ vi/t discolour in a way that is hard to repair ♦ n 1 stained place or spot 2 mark of guilt or shame

stained glass /ˌ· '·◄/ n [U] coloured glass for making patterns in windows

stain·less steel /ˌ·· '·◄/ n [U] steel that does not RUST

stair /steəʳ/ n step in a set of stairs

stairs /steəz/ n [P] number of steps for going up or down, esp. indoors: a flight of stairs

stair·case /'steəkeɪs‖'steər-/ n set of stairs with its supports and side parts

stake /steɪk/ n 1 pointed post for driving into the ground 2 share in something so that one is interested in whether it succeeds or fails 3 money risked on the result of something 4 post to which a person was tied for being killed. esp. by burning 5 **at stake** at risk ♦ vt 1 risk the loss of (something) on a result 2 **stake a claim** state that something should belong to one

stal·ac·tite /'stæləktaɪt‖stə'læktaɪt/ n sharp point of rock hanging from a cave roof

stal·ag·mite /'stæləgmaɪt‖stə'læɡmaɪt/ n sharp point of rock standing on a cave floor

stale /steɪl/ adj 1 no longer fresh: stale bread/(fig.) news 2 no longer interesting or new ~ness n [U]

stale·mate /'steɪlmeɪt/ n 1 (in CHESS) position in which neither player can win 2 situation in which neither side in a quarrel can get an advantage

stalk¹ /stɔːk/ n thin plant part with l or more leaves, fruits, or flowers on it

stalk² v 1 vt hunt by following closely and secretly 2 vi walk stiffly or proudly

stall¹ /stɔːl/ n 1 BrE small open-fronted shop or other selling place in a market 2 indoor enclosure for an animal **stalls** n [P] BrE seats on the main level of a theatre or cinema

stall² vi/t 1 (cause to) stop because there is not enough speed or engine power 2 delay ♦ n act of stalling

stal·lion /'stæljən/ n male horse kept for breeding

stal·wart /'stɔːlwət‖-ərt/ adj, n strong and dependable (person)

sta·men /'steɪmən/ n male POLLEN-producing part of a flower

stam·i·na /'stæmənə/ n [U] strength to keep going

stam·mer /'stæmər/ vi/t speak or say with pauses and repeated sounds ♦ n habit of stammering

stamp /stæmp/ v 1 vi/t put (the feet) down hard 2 vt mark by pressing: The title was stamped in gold on the book. | (fig.) His manners stamped him as a military man. 3 vt stick a stamp onto ♦ n 1 small piece of paper for sticking onto esp. a letter, parcel, etc., to be posted 2 tool for pressing or printing onto a surface: a date-stamp 3 mark made by this: (fig.) a remark which bears the stamp of truth 4 act of stamping the foot

stamp out phr vt put an end to

stam·pede /stæm'piːd/ n 1 sudden rush of frightened animals 2 sudden mass movement ♦ vi/t (cause to) go in a stampede or unreasonable rush

stamping ground /'·· ·/ n a favourite very familiar place

stance /stɑːns‖stæns/ n 1 way of standing 2 way of thinking; ATTITUDE

stan·chion /'stɑːntʃən‖'stæn-/ n strong upright supporting bar

stand¹ /stænd/ v stood /stʊd/ 1 vi support oneself on one's feet in an upright position 2 vi rise to a position of doing this: They stood (up) when he came in. 3 vi be in height: He stands 5 feet 10 inches. 4 vi/t (cause to) rest in a position, esp. upright or on a base: The clock stood on the shelf. 5 vi be in a particular state of affairs: How do things stand at the moment? 6 vi be in a position (to gain or lose): He stands to win a fortune if he comes top. 7 vt like; bear: I can't stand (= don't like) whisky. 8 vi remain true or in force: My offer still stands. 9 vt pay the cost of (something) for (someone else): He stood them a wonderful meal. 10 vi BrE compete for an office in an election: standing for Parliament 11 **know how/where one stands (with someone)** know how someone feels about one 12 **stand a chance/hope** have a chance/hope 13 **standing on one's head** with great ease: I could do the job standing on my head. 14 **stand on one's hands/head** support oneself on the hands/head and hands, with the feet in the air 15 **stand on one's own two feet** be able to do without help from others 16 **stand something on its head** change or upset violently 17 **stand to reason** be clear to all sensible people

stand by phr v 1 vt remain loyal to 2 vt keep (a promise, agreement, etc.) 3 vi be present or near 4 vi remain inactive when action is needed 5 vi wait in readiness

stand down phr vi 1 yield one's position or chance of election 2 leave the witness box in court

stand for phr vt 1 represent; mean: The B in his name stands for Brian. 2 have as a principle 3 accept without complaining

stand in phr vi take the place of the usual person for a time

stand out phr vi 1 have an easily-seen shape, colour, etc. 2 be clearly the best

stand up phr vt 1 remain in good condition in spite of: Will it stand up to continuous use? 2 be accepted as true: The charges will never stand up in court. 3 fail to meet (someone, esp. of the oposite sex) as arranged

stand up for phr vt defend; support

stand² n 1 place for selling or showing things 2 piece of furniture for putting things on: a hatstand 3 open-fronted building for watchers at a sports ground **4** raised stage: *the judge's stand* **5** strong defensive effort **6** *AmE* for WITNESS BOX — see also ONE-NIGHT STAND

stan·dard /ˈstændəd‖-ərd/ *n* **1** level of quality that is considered proper or acceptable **2** something fixed as a rule for measuring weight, value, etc. **3** ceremonial flag ♦ *adj* of the usual kind; ordinary ~**ize** *vt* make all the same in accordance with a single STANDARD (2) –**ization** /ˌstændədaɪˈzeɪʃən‖-dərd-/ *n* [U]

standard lamp /ˈ·· ·/ *n BrE* lamp on a tall base which stands on the floor

standard of liv·ing /ˌ·· · ˈ··/ *n* degree of wealth and comfort in everyday life that a person, country, etc., has

stand-by /ˈstændbaɪ/ *n* **1** one kept ready for use **2 on standby: a** ready for action **b** able to travel, esp. in a plane, only if there is a seat no one else wants

stand-in /ˈ· ·/ *n* person who takes the place or job of someone else for a time

stand·ing /ˈstændɪŋ/ *n* [U] **1** rank, esp. based on experience or respect **2** continuance: *a friend of long standing* (= who has been a friend for a long time) ♦ *adj* continuing in use or force: *a standing invitation*

standing or·der /ˌ·· ˈ··/ *n BrE* order to a bank to pay a fixed amount to someone at fixed periods

stand-off-ish /ˌstændˈɒfɪʃ‖-ˈɔːfɪʃ/ *adj* rather unfriendly ~**ly** *adv* ~**ness** *n* [U]

stand·point /ˈstændpɔɪnt/ *n* POINT OF VIEW

stand·still /ˈstændˌstɪl/ *n* [S] condition of no movement; stop

stank /stæŋk/ *past t.* of STINK

stan·za /ˈstænzə/ *n* division of a poem

sta·ple[1] /ˈsteɪpəl/ *n* piece of wire put through sheets of paper and bent to fasten them together ♦ *vt* fasten with staples **stapler** *n*

staple[2] *adj* **1** used all the time; usual; ordinary **2** main product: *a staple among British products*

star /stɑːr/ *n* **1** very large mass of burning gas in space, seen as a small bright spot in the night sky **2** figure with 5 or more points, used as a sign of something: *a five star hotel* (= a very good hotel) **3** heavenly body regarded as determining one's fate: *born under an unlucky star* **4** famous performer: *a film star* **5 stars in one's eyes** an unthinking feeling that some wonderful thing is really possible **6 see stars** see flashes of light, esp. as a result of being hit on the head ♦ *v* -**rr**- **1** *vi/t* appear or have as a main performer: *a film starring Charlie Chaplin* **2** *vt*

mark with STARs (2) ~**ry** *adj* filled with stars

star-board /ˈstɑːbəd‖ˈstɑːrbərd/ *n* [U] right side of a ship or aircraft

starch /stɑːtʃ‖-ɑːr-/ *n* [U] **1** white tasteless substance that is an important part of foods such as grain and potatoes **2** cloth-stiffening substance *vt* stiffen with STARCH (2) ~**y** *adj* **1** full of, or like, STARCH **2** stiffly correct and formal –**ily** *adv*

star·dom /ˈstɑːdəm‖ˈstɑːr-/ *n* [U] state of being a famous performer

stare /steə'/ *vi* look for a long time with great attention ♦ *n* long steady look

star-fish /ˈstɑːˌfɪʃ‖ˈstɑːr-/ *n* flat sea animal with 5 arms forming a star shape

stark /stɑːk‖stɑːrk/ *adj* **1** hard, bare, or severe in appearance **2** complete: *stark terror* ♦ *adv* completely: *stark naked* ‖ *stark staring mad* (= completely mad)

star·let /ˈstɑːlɪt‖ˈstɑːr-/ *n* young actress hoping to become famous

star·ling /ˈstɑːlɪŋ‖ˈstɑːr-/ *n* common greenish-black European bird

starry-eyed /ˌ·· ˈ·◁/ *adj* full of unreasonable hopes

stars and stripes /ˌ· ·ˈ·/ *n* [*the* + S] the flag of the US

star-stud·ded /ˈ·· ˌ··/ *adj* filled with famous performers

start /stɑːt‖stɑːrt/ *v* **1** *vi/t* begin **2** *vi/t* (cause to) come into existence: *How did the trouble start?* **3** *vi/t* (cause to) begin operation: *The car won't start.* **4** *vi* begin a journey **5** *vi* make a sudden sharp movement, esp. from surprise ~**er** *n* **1** person, animal, etc., in a race or match at the start **2** person who gives the signal for a race to begin **3** instrument for starting a machine **4** first part of a meal **5 for starters** first of all

start[2] *n* **1** [C] beginning of activity **2** [*the* + S] first part or moments **3** [C] place of starting **4** [C;U] amount by which one is ahead of another **5** [C] sudden sharp movement — see also FLYING START

start-le /ˈstɑːtl‖ˈstɑːrtl/ *vt* give a sudden slight shock to

starve /stɑːv‖stɑːrv/ *vi/t* **1** (cause to) suffer from great hunger **2** (cause to) not have enough: *starved of affection/ funds* **starvation** /stɑːˈveɪʃən‖stɑːr-/ *n* [U]

star wars /ˈ· ˌ/ *n* [U] *infml* SDI

stash /stæʃ/ *vt infml* store secretly; hide ♦ **stash** *n*

state[1] /steɪt/ *n* **1** [C] particular way of being; condition: *the current state of our economy* **2** [C] *infml esp. BrE* a very nervous, anxious condition: *Don't get in(to) such a state.* **3** [C;U] government or political organization of a country: *industry controlled by the state* | *state secrets* 4 [C] nation; country 5 [C] self-governing area within a nation: *the states of the US* 6 [U] official grandness and ceremony ~**less** *adj* belonging to no country ~**less-ness** *n* [U] ~**ly** *adj* 1 formal; ceremonious 2 grand in style or size ~**liness** *n* [U]

state[2] *vt* say or mention, esp. formally or in advance

State De·part·ment /'·· ·,··/ *n* [*the*] the American government department which deals with foreign affairs

state·ly home /,·· '·/ *n* large country house of historical interest, esp. one which people pay to visit

state·ment /'steɪtmənt/ *n* 1 (formal) written or spoken declaration 2 list showing money paid, received, etc.

state-of-the-art /,···· '·◄/ *adj* using the most modern methods or materials

state·room /'steɪtrʊm, -ruːm/ *n* passenger's private room on a ship

States /steɪts/ [*the*] *infml* the US

states·man /'steɪtsmən/ *n* -**men** /-mən/ respected political or government leader — see also ELDER STATESMAN ~**ship** *n* [U]

stat·ic /'stætɪk/ *adj* 1 not moving or changing 2 of or being electricity that collects on the surface of objects ◆ *n* [U] electrical noise spoiling radio or television signals

sta·tion /'steɪʃən/ *n* 1 a (building at) a place where the stated public vehicles regularly stop: *a bus station* b esp. *BrE* like this where trains regularly stop 2 building for the stated service or activity: *a polling station* (= where people vote) 3 broadcasting company or apparatus 4 one's position in life; social rank: *She married beneath her station.* — see also SPACE STATION ◆ *vt* put (esp. a person) into a certain place for esp. military duty

sta·tion·a·ry /'steɪʃənəri‖-neri/ *adj* not moving

sta·tion·er /'steɪʃənər/ *n* seller of stationery

sta·tion·e·ry /'steɪʃənəri‖-neri/ *n* [U] paper, pens, pencils, envelopes, etc.

sta·tion·mas·ter /'steɪʃən,mɑːstər‖ -,mæs-/ *n* person in charge of a railway station

sta·tis·tics /stə'tɪstɪks/ *n* 1 [P] numbers which represent facts or measurements 2 [U] science that deals with and explains these –**tical** *adj* –**tically** /-kli/ *adv* **statistician** /,stætɪ'stɪʃən/ *n* person who works with statistics

stat·ue /'stætʃuː/ *n* (large) stone or metal likeness of a person, animal, etc.

stat·u·esque /,stætʃu'esk/ *adj* like a statue in formal still beauty

stat·u·ette /,stætʃu'et/ *n* small statue that goes on a table or shelf

stat·ure /'stætʃər/ *n* [C;U] *fml* 1 degree to which someone is regarded as important or admirable 2 person's height

sta·tus /'steɪtəs/ *n* 1 [C;U] rank or condition in relation to others 2 [U] high social position 3 [C] state of affairs at a particular time

status quo /,steɪtəs 'kwəʊ/ *n* existing state of affairs

stat·ute /'stætʃuːt/ *n fml* law

stat·u·to·ry /'stætʃʊtəri‖-tʃətɔːri/ *adj* fixed or controlled by law

staunch[1] /stɔːntʃ‖stɑːntʃ, stɔːntʃ/ *adj* dependably loyal; firm ~**ly** *adv* ~**ness** *n* [U]

staunch[2] *vt* stop the flow of (blood)

stave /steɪv/ *v* **stave off** *phr vt* keep away: *just enough food to stave off hunger*

stay /steɪ/ *vi* 1 remain in a place rather than leave 2 continue to be; remain: *trying to stay healthy* 3 live in a place for a while: *staying at a hotel* 4 **stay put** not move 5 **stay the course** last or continue for the whole length of ◆ *n* 1 period of living in a place 2 *law* stopping or delay: *a stay of execution* (= not carrying out a punishment)

stay on *phr vt* remain after the usual leaving time

staying pow·er /'·· ,··/ *n* [U] STAMINA

St Ber·nard /sənt 'bɜːnəd‖,seɪnt bər'nɑːrd/ *n* large strong Swiss dog used in mountain rescue

stead /sted/ *n* **in someone's stead** *fml* instead of someone

stead·fast /'stedfɑːst‖-fæst/ *adj fml or lit* 1 firmly loyal 2 not moving or movable ~**ly** *adv* ~**ness** *n* [U]

stead·y /'stedi/ *adj* 1 firm; not shaking: *a steady hand* 2 not varying wildly; regular: *a steady speed* 3 not likely to change: *a steady job* 4 dependable ◆ *vi/t* make or become steady –**ily** *adv* –**iness** *n* [U]

steak /steɪk/ *n* [C;U] flat piece of meat, esp. BEEF or fish

steal /stiːl/ *v* **stole** /stəʊl/, **stolen** /'stəʊlən/ 1 *vi/t* take (what belongs to someone else) without permission 2 *vi* move secretly or quietly 3 *vt* take secretly or improperly: *stealing a look at someone* 4 **steal the show** get all the attention and praise expected by someone else, at a show or other event ◆ *n* [S] *infml*, esp. *AmE* something for sale very cheaply

stealth /stelθ/ *n* [U] acting quietly and secretly or unseen ~**y** *adj*

steam /stiːm/ *n* [U] 1 water gas produced by boiling 2 power produced by steam under pressure: *The ship sailed full steam ahead.* (= at its fastest speed) **3 let off steam** get rid of anger or unwanted ENERGY **4 under one's/its own steam** by one's/its own power or effort ♦ v **1** vi give off steam **2** vi travel by steam power **3** vt cook with steam **4** vt use steam on: *He steamed the letter open.* **~er** n **1** ship driven by steam power **2** container for cooking food with steam **~y** adj **1** of or containing steam **2** *infml* EROTIC

steam up phr vi/t **1** cover or become covered with a mist of cooling water **2** *infml* make angry or excited

steamed-up adj *infml* excited and angry

steam-roll-er /'sti:m,rəʊlə*/ n vehicle with heavy metal wheels for flattening new road surfaces ♦ vt force in spite of all opposition: *He was steamrollered into signing the agreement.*

steam-ship /'sti:m,ʃɪp/ n a large non-naval ship driven by steam power

steed /sti:d/ n *lit* horse

steel /sti:l/ n [U] hard strong metal made from iron ♦ vt make (esp. oneself) unfeeling or determined **~y** adj like steel in colour or hardness

steel band /'· ·/ n West Indian band playing drums cut from metal oil barrels

steep[1] /sti:p/ adj **1** rising or falling at a large angle **2** (esp. of a price) too high **~ly** adv **~ness** n [U]

steep[2] vt **1** keep in liquid **2 steeped in** thoroughly filled or familiar with

stee-ple /'sti:pəl/ n high pointed church tower

stee-ple-chase /'sti:pəltʃeɪs/ n long race with fences to jump over

stee-ple-jack /'sti:pəldʒæk/ n person who repairs towers, tall chimneys, etc.

steer[1] /stɪə*/ vt **1** direct the course of (esp. a boat or road vehicle) **2 steer clear (of)** keep away (from); avoid

steer[2] n young male animal of the cattle family with its sex organs removed

steer-age /'stɪərɪdʒ/ n [U] part of a passenger ship for those with the cheapest tickets

steering wheel /'·· ·/ n wheel turned to make a vehicle go left or right

stel-lar /'stelə*/ adj *fml* of the stars

stem[1] /stem/ n **1** part of a plant on which leaves or smaller branches grow **2** narrow upright support: *the stem of a wineglass*

stem[2] vt -mm- stop (the flow of)

stem from phr vt result from

stench /stentʃ/ n very strong bad smell

sten-cil /'stensəl/ n **1** card, etc., with patterns or letters cut in it **2** mark

made by putting paint, etc., through the holes in this onto paper, etc. ♦ vt -ll- *BrE* -l- *AmE* make (a copy of) with a stencil

sten-to-ri-an /sten'tɔːriən/ adj *fml* (of the voice) very loud

step[1] /step/ n **1** act of moving by raising one foot and bringing it down somewhere else **2** the sound this makes **3** short distance: *It's just a step away from here.* **4** flat edge, esp. in a set one above the other, on which the foot is placed for going up or down **5** act, esp. in a set of actions, which should produce a certain result: *We must take steps* (= take action) *to improve matters.* **6** movement of the feet in dancing **7 in/out of step: a** moving/not moving the feet at the same time as others in marching **b** in/not in accordance or agreement with others **8 step by step** gradually **9 watch one's step** behave or act carefully

step[2] vi -pp- **1** go by putting one foot usu. in front of the other **2** bring the foot down; TREAD **3 step on it!** go faster **4 step out of line** act differently from others or from what is expected

step down/aside phr vi leave one's job, position, etc.

step in phr vi INTERVENE

step up phr vt increase

step- see WORD BEGINNINGS, p. 487.

step-lad-der /'step,lædə*/ n folding 2-part ladder joined at the top

steppes /steps/ n [P] large treeless area in Russia and parts of Asia

stepping-stone /'·· ·/ n **1** any of a row of large stones for walking across a stream on **2** way of improvement or getting ahead

ster-e-o /'steriəʊ, 'stɪər-/ adj using a system of sound recording in which the sound comes from 2 different places ♦ n **-os 1** [C] stereo record player **2** [U] stereo sound — see also PERSONAL STEREO

ster-e-o-phon-ic /,steriə'fɒnɪk, ,stɪər-‖-'fɑː-/ adj *fml* stereo

ster-e-o-type /'steriətaɪp/ n usu. *derog* fixed set of ideas about what a particular type of person or thing is like ♦ vt *derog* treat as an example of a fixed general type **-typical** /,steriəʊ-'tɪpɪkəl/ adj

ster-ile /'steraɪl‖-rəl/ adj **1** which cannot produce young **2** free from all (harmful) bacteria, etc. **3** lacking new thought, imagination, etc. **4** (of land) not producing crops **-ility** /stə'rɪlɪti/ n [U] **-ilize** /'sterəlaɪz/ vt make STERILE (1,2) **-ilization** /,sterəlaɪ'zeɪʃən‖-lə-/ n [U]

ster-ling /'stɜːlɪŋ‖-ɜːr-/ n [U] British money ◆ adj **1** (esp. of silver) of standard value **2** of the highest standard, esp. in being loyal and brave

stern[1] /stɜːn‖stɜːrn/ n severe and serious: a stern look/reprimand ~**ly** adv ~**ness** n [U]

stern[2] n back part of a ship

ste-roid /'stɪərɔɪd,'ste-/ n chemical that has a strong effect on the workings of the body

steth-o-scope /'steθəskəʊp/ n tube with which doctors can listen to people's heartbeats

stet-son /'stetsən/ n hat with a wide BRIM worn by US COWBOYs

ste-ve-dore /'stiːvədɔː/ n person who loads and unloads ships

stew /stjuː‖stuː/ vi/t cook slowly and gently in liquid ◆ n **1** [C;U] dish of stewed meat and vegetables **2** [S] confused anxious state of mind

stew-ard /'stjuːəd‖'stuːərd/ n **1** **stewardess** /-dɪs/ fem. — person who serves passengers on a ship, plane, etc. **2** person in charge of a public meeting, horse race, etc. — see also SHOP STEWARD

stick[1] /stɪk/ n **1** small thin piece of wood **2** thin wooden or metal rod used for support while walking, for hitting things, etc. **3** thin rod of any material: a stick of chalk/celery **4 get the wrong end of the stick** infml misunderstand — see also STICKS

stick[2] v stuck /stʌk/ **1** vt push: She stuck her fork into the meat. **2** vi/t fasten or be fastened with glue or a similar substance **3** vi/t (cause to) become fixed in position: He got his finger stuck in the hole. **4** vt infml put: Stick your coat down over there. **5** vt esp. BrE like; bear **6** vt BrE sl keep (something unwanted) ~**er** n **1** LABEL with a message or picture, which can be stuck to things **2** infml determined person

stick around phr vi not go away

stick at phr vt continue to work hard at

stick by phr vt continue to support

stick out phr v **1** vi/t (cause to) come out beyond a surface: Her ears stick out. **2** vt continue to the end of (something difficult) **3 stick one's neck out** infml take a risk

stick out for phr vt **1** refuse to accept less than

stick to phr vt **1** refuse to leave or change: stick to one's decision **2 stick to one's guns** infml continue to express one's beliefs or carry on a course of action in spite of attacks

stick together phr vi (of 2 or more people) stay loyal to each other

stick up for phr vt defend (someone) by words or actions

stick with phr vt **1** stay close to **2 stick with it** infml continue in spite of difficulties

stick-in-the-mud /'···,·'/ n person who will not change or accept new things

stick-ler /'stɪklər/ n person who demands the stated quality: a stickler for punctuality

sticks /stɪks/ n [the + P] infml a country area far from modern life

stick-up /'·,·/ n infml robbery carried out by threatening with a gun

sticky /'stɪki/ adj **1** like or covered with glue or a similar substance **2** difficult; awkward: a sticky situation **3 come to/meet a sticky end** (suffer) ruin, death, etc. ~**iness** n [U]

stiff /stɪf/ adj **1** not easily bent or changed in shape **2** formal; not friendly **3** strong, esp. in alcohol **4** difficult; severe: stiff competition ◆ adv extremely: I was scared stiff. ◆ n sl dead body ~**ly** adv ~**en** vi/t make or become stiff ~**ness** n [U]

stiff-necked /,·'·◁/ adj proudly OBSTINATE

stiff upper lip /,·· ··'·/ n [S] ability to accept bad luck or unpleasant events without appearing upset

sti-fle /'staɪfəl/ v **1** vi/t (cause to) be unable to breathe properly **2** vt keep from happening: stifling a yawn

stig-ma /'stɪgmə/ n feeling of shame ~**tize** vt describe very disapprovingly

stig-ma-ta /'stɪgmətə, stɪg'mɑːtə/ n [P] (marks like) the nail marks on Christ's body

stile /staɪl/ n arrangement of steps for climbing over a fence or wall

sti-let-to /stɪ'letəʊ/ n -tos small thin DAGGER

stiletto heel /·,·· ·'·/ n BrE high thin heel of a woman's shoe

still[1] /stɪl/ adv **1** (even) up to this/that moment: He's still here. **2** in spite of that: It's raining. Still, we must go out. **3** even: a still greater problem **4** yet: He gave still another reason.

still[2] adj **1** not moving **2** without wind **3** silent; calm **4** (of a drink) not containing gas ~**ness** n [U]

still[3] n photograph of a scene from a (cinema) film

still[4] n apparatus for making alcohol

still-birth /'stɪlbɜːθ,ˌstɪl'bɜːθ‖-ɜːrθ/ n child born dead

still-born /'stɪlbɔːn, ˌstɪl'bɔːn‖-ɔːrn/ adj born dead

still life /,· '·◁/ n still lifes [C;U] painting of objects, esp. flowers and fruit

stilt /stɪlt/ n either of a pair of poles for walking around on high above the ground

stilt-ed /'stɪltɪd/ adj very formal and unnatural

Stil·ton /'stɪltən/ n [U] strong-tasting cheese with grey-blue marks

stim·u·late /'stɪmjʊleɪt/ vt 1 cause to become more active, grow faster, etc. 2 fml excite (the body or mind) **–lant** n 1 drug which gives one more power to be active 2 stimulus **–lation** /ˌstɪmjʊ'leɪʃən/ n [U]

stim·u·lus /'stɪmjʊləs/ n -li /-laɪ/ something that causes activity

sting /stɪŋ/ vi/t stung /stʌŋ/ 1 have, use, or prick with a STING (1) 2 (cause to) feel sharp pain: (fig.) stinging criticism ♦ n 1 pain-producing organ used by certain insects and plants for attack or protection 2 wound caused by this 3 sharp pain

stin·gy /'stɪndʒi/ adj infml ungenerous; mean **–gily** adv

stink /stɪŋk/ vi stank /stæŋk/, stunk /stʌŋk/ 1 give off a strong bad smell 2 infml be very unpleasant or bad: Your plan stinks. ♦ n strong bad smell

stink out phr vt fill with a stink

stint /stɪnt/ n limited or fixed amount, esp. of shared work ♦ vt give too small an amount (of)

sti·pend /'staɪpend/ n priest's wages

sti·pen·di·a·ry /staɪ'pendiəri‖-dieri/ adj receiving regular payment for professional services

stip·ple /'stɪpəl/ vt draw or paint (on) with dots instead of lines **–pling** n [U]

stip·u·late /'stɪpjʊleɪt/ vt state as a necessary condition **–lation** /ˌstɪpjʊ'leɪʃən/ n [C;U] statement of conditions

stir /stɜːr/ v -rr- 1 vt move around and mix (esp. liquid) with a spoon, etc. 2 vi/t make or cause a slight movement (in): She stirred in her sleep. 3 vt excite: a stirring tale of adventure 4 vi infml cause trouble between others ♦ n 1 [C] act of stirring 2 [S] (public) excitement

stir up phr vt cause (trouble)

stir·rup /'stɪrəp‖'stɜː-/ n D-shaped metal piece for a horse-rider's foot to go in

stitch /stɪtʃ/ n 1 [C] amount of thread put with a needle through cloth or through skin to close a wound 2 [C] single turn of the wool round the needle in knitting (KNIT) 3 [S] sharp pain in the side caused by running 4 [S] infml clothes: He hadn't got a stitch on. (= was completely NAKED) 5 in stitches laughing helplessly ♦ vi/t sew

stoat /stəʊt/ n small brown furry European animal

stock /stɒk‖staːk/ n 1 [C] supply: a large stock of food 2 [U] (supply of) goods for sale: Have you any blue shirts in stock? 3 [C;U] money lent to a government or company: stocks and shares 4 [U] liquid made from meat,

bones, etc., used in cooking 5 [U] farm animals, esp. cattle 6 [C;U] a family line, of the stated sort: She comes from farming/good stock. 7 take stock (of) consider a situation carefully so as to make a decision — see also STOCKS ♦ vt keep supplies of ♦ adj commonly used, esp. without much meaning: stock excuses

stock up phr vi provide oneself with a full store of goods

stock·ade /stɒ'keɪd‖staː-/ n strong defensive fence

stock·brok·er /'stɒk,brəʊkər‖'staːk-/ n someone who buys and sells STOCKs (3) and SHAREs (2) for others

stock ex·change /'· ·ˌ·/ n place where STOCKs (3) and SHAREs (2) are bought and sold

stock·ing /'stɒkɪŋ‖'staː-/ n close-fitting garment for a woman's foot and leg

stock-in-trade /ˌ· · '·/ n [U] things habitually used: A pleasant manner is part of a politician's stock-in-trade.

stock·ist /'stɒkɪst‖'staː-/ n BrE one who keeps particular goods for sale

stock·man /'stɒkmən‖'staːk-/ n -men /-mən/ man who looks after farm animals

stock mar·ket /'· ˌ··/ n STOCK EXCHANGE

stock·pile /'stɒkpaɪl‖'staːk-/ n large store for future use ♦ vt make a stockpile of

stocks /stɒks‖staːks/ n [P] wooden frame in which criminals were fastened in former times

stock-still /ˌ· '·◄/ adv not moving at all

stock·tak·ing /'stɒk,teɪkɪŋ‖'staːk-/ n [U] making a list of goods held in a business

stock·y /'stɒki‖'staː-/ adj thick, short, and strong **–ily** adv **–iness** n [U]

stodge /stɒdʒ‖staːdʒ/ n [U] unpleasantly heavy and uninteresting food **stodgy** adj 1 like stodge 2 uninteresting and difficult

sto·ic /'stəʊɪk/ n person who remains calm and uncomplaining **~al** adj patient when suffering, like a stoic **~ally** /-kli/ adv **~ism** /-ˌsɪzəm/ n [U] stoical behaviour

stoke /stəʊk/ vt fill (an enclosed fire) with FUEL **~stoker** n

stole[1] /stəʊl/ past t. of STEAL

stole[2] n long piece of material worn over the shoulders

sto·len /'stəʊlən/ past p. of STEAL

stol·id /'stɒlɪd‖'staː-/ adj showing no excitement when strong feelings might be expected

stom·ach /'stʌmək/ n 1 [C] baglike organ in the body where food is digested (DIGEST[1]) 2 [C] front part of the body below the chest 3 [S;U] desire; liking: *He's got no stomach for a fight.* ♦ *vt* accept without displeasure; bear

stomach pump /'·· ·/ *n* apparatus for drawing the contents out of the stomach

stomp /stomp‖stɑːmp, stɔːmp/ *vi* walk heavily

stone /stəʊn/ *n* 1 [C] fairly large piece of rock 2 [U] rock 3 [C] (*pl.* stone *or* stones) a measure of weight equal to 14 pounds or 6.35 kilograms 4 [C] single hard seed of certain fruits 5 [C] piece of hard material formed in an organ of the body ♦ *vt* 1 throw stones at 2 take the STONE (4) out of **stoned** *adj infml* 1 under the influence of drugs 2 very drunk **stony** *adj* 1 containing or covered with stones 2 cruel

Stone Age /'·· ·/ *n* earliest known time in human history, when stone tools were used

stone-ma-son /'stəʊn,meɪsən/ *n* person who cuts stone for building

stone's throw /'· ·/ *n* [S] short distance

stone-work /'stəʊnwɜːk‖-ɜːrk/ *n* [U] parts of a building made of stone

stony broke /,·· '·/ *adj BrE infml* having no money at all

stood /stʊd/ *past t. and p. of* STAND

stooge /stuːdʒ/ *n* person who habitually does what another wants

stool /stuːl/ *n* seat without back or arm supports

stool-pi-geon /'stuːl,pɪdʒən/ *n infml* person who helps the police to trap another

stoop /stuːp/ *vt* 1 bend the upper body forwards and down 2 stand like this habitually ♦ *n* [S] habitual stooping position

stoop to *phr vt* fall to a low standard of behaviour by allowing oneself to do (something)

stop¹ /stop‖stɑːp/ *v* -**pp**- 1 *vi/t* (cause to) no longer be moving or operating 2 *vi/t* (cause to) end: *The rain has stopped.* 3 *vt* prevent 4 *vi* pause 5 *vi esp. BrE* remain; stay: *stopping at a fine hotel* 6 *vt* block: *The pipe's stopped up.* 7 *vt* stop from being given or paid: *stop a cheque* ~**per** *n* object for closing a bottle

stop off *phr vi* make a short visit to a place while making a journey elsewhere

stop over *phr vi* make a short stay before continuing a journey

stop² *n* 1 act of stopping or the state of being stopped 2 BUS STOP 3 **pull all the stops out** do everything possible to complete an action 4 **put a stop to** stop (esp. an undesirable activity)

stop-cock /'stopkok‖'stɑːpkɑːk/ *n* turnable apparatus for controlling the flow of water in a pipe

stop-gap /'stopgæp‖'stɑːp-/ *n* something that fills a need for a time

stop-o-ver /'stop,əʊvəʳ‖'stɑːp-/ *n* short stay between parts of a journey

stop-page /'stopɪdʒ‖'stɑː-/ *n* 1 [C] stopping, esp. of work 2 [C;U] amount taken away from one's pay 3 [C;U] blocked state

stop press /,· '·◁/ *n* [*the* + S] late news put into a paper

stop-watch /'stopwotʃ‖'stɑːpwɑːtʃ, -wɔːtʃ/ *n* watch that can be started and stopped to measure periods exactly

stor-age /'stɔːrɪdʒ/ *n* [U] (price paid for) storing

store /stɔːʳ/ *vt* 1 make and keep a supply of for future use 2 keep in a special place while not in use ♦ *n* 1 supply for future use 2 place for keeping things 3 large shop 4 *esp. AmE* SHOP (1) 5 **in store:** a being stored b about to happen: *There's trouble in store.* 6 **set ... store by** feel to be of (the stated amount of) importance **stores** *n* [S;P] (building or room containing) military or naval goods and food

sto-rey *BrE* ‖ -**ry** *AmE*/'stɔːri/ *n* floor or level in a building

stork /stɔːk‖stɔːrk/ *n* large bird with a long beak, neck, and legs

storm /stɔːm‖stɔːrm/ *n* 1 rough weather condition with rain and strong wind 2 sudden violent show of feeling: *a storm of protest* 3 **take by storm:** a conquer by a sudden violent attack b win great approval from (those who watch a performance) ♦ *v* 1 *vt* attack (a place) with sudden violence 2 *vi* go angrily ~**y** *adj*

sto-ry /'stɔːri/ *n* 1 account of events, real or imagined 2 news article 3 lie: *Have you been telling stories again?* 4 *AmE for* STOREY 5 **the same old story** the usual excuse or difficulty — see also TALL STORY

sto-ry-book /'stɔːribʊk/ *adj* as perfectly happy as in a fairy story for children

story line /'·· ·/ *n* events in a film, book, or play

stout /staʊt/ *adj* 1 rather fat 2 brave and determined 3 strong and thick ♦ *n* [U] strong dark beer ~**ly** *adv* ~**ness** *n* [U]

stout-heart-ed /,staʊt'hɑːtɪd◁‖-ɑːr-/ *adj lit* brave

stove /stəʊv/ *n* enclosed apparatus that can be heated for cooking or to provide warmth

stow /stəʊ/ *vt* put away or store, esp. on a ship

stow away *phr vi* hide on a ship or plane in order to make a free journey

stow·a·way /'stəʊəweɪ/ n person who stows away

strad·dle /'strædl/ vt 1 have one's legs on either side of 2 be, land, etc., on either side of (something), rather than in the middle

strag·gle /'strægəl/ vi move, grow, or spread untidily **–gler** n one who is behind a main group **–gly** adj growing or lying untidily

straight[1] /streɪt/ adj 1 not bent or curved 2 level or upright 3 neat; tidy 4 honest, open, and truthful 5 (of the face) with a serious expression 6 (of alcohol) without added water 7 correct: *set the record straight* 8 sl HETEROSEXUAL ♦ n straight part, esp. on a race track **~ness** n [U]

straight[2] adv 1 in a straight line 2 directly (and without delay): *Get straight to the point.* 3 clearly: *I can't think straight.* 4 **go straight** leave a life of crime

straight and nar·row /ˌ·· '··/ n [U] honest life

straight·a·way /ˌstreɪtə'weɪ/ adv at once

straight·en /'streɪtn/ vt (cause to) become straight, level, or tidy

straighten out phr vt remove the confusions or difficulties in: *straighten out one's business affairs*

straighten up phr vi get up from a bent position

straight·for·ward /ˌstreɪt'fɔːwəd◂‖ -'fɔːrwərd/ adj 1 honest and open, without hidden meanings 2 simple **~ly** adv **~ness** n [U]

strain[1] /streɪn/ v 1 vt damage (a body part) through too much effort or pressure 2 vi make (too) great efforts 3 vt separate (a liquid and solid) by pouring through esp. a strainer 4 vt force beyond acceptable or believable limits: *straining the truth* ♦ n [C;U] 1 (force causing) the condition of being tightly stretched 2 troubling influence 3 damage caused by straining a body part **~ed** adj 1 not natural in behaviour; unfriendly 2 tired or nervous **~er** n instrument with a net for STRAINing (3) things

strain[2] n 1 breed or type of plant or animal 2 [U] lit tune

strait /streɪt/ also **straits** pl. — n narrow water passage between 2 areas of land **straits** n [P] difficult situation: *in dire straits*

strait·ened /'streɪtnd/ adj fml difficult because lacking money

strait-jack·et /'streɪtˌdʒækt/ n 1 garment for a violently mad person that prevents arm movement 2 something preventing free development

strait-laced /ˌstreɪt'leɪst◂/ adj having severe, rather old-fashioned ideas about morals

strand /strænd/ n single thin thread, wire, etc.

strand·ed /'strændd/ adj in a helpless position, unable to get away

strange /streɪndʒ/ adj 1 unusual; surprising 2 unfamiliar **~ly** adv **~ness** n [U]

strang·er /'streɪndʒər/ n 1 unfamiliar person 2 person in an unfamiliar place

stran·gle /'stræŋgəl/ vt 1 kill by pressing the throat to stop breathing 2 stop the proper development of **–gler** n **–gulation** /ˌstræŋgjʊ'leɪʃən/ n [U]

stran·gle·hold /'stræŋgəlhəʊld/ n strong control which prevents action

strap /stræp/ n strong narrow band used as a fastening or support: *a leather watchstrap* ♦ vt **-pp-** fasten with straps

strap·ping /'stræpɪŋ/ adj big and strong

stra·ta /'strɑːtə‖'streɪtə/ pl. of STRATUM

strat·a·gem /'strætədʒəm/ n trick or plan for deceiving or gaining an advantage

stra·te·gic /strə'tiːdʒɪk/ adj 1 part of a plan, esp. in war 2 right for a purpose **~ally** /-kli/ adv

strat·e·gist /'strætədʒst/ n person skilled in (military) planning

strat·e·gy /'strætədʒi/ n 1 [U] skilful (military) planning 2 [C] particular plan for winning success

strat·i·fy /'strætfaɪ/ vt arrange in separate levels or strata **–fication** /ˌstrætf'keɪʃən/ n [C;U]

strat·os·phere /'strætəsfɪər/ n outer air surrounding the Earth, starting at about 10 kilometres above the Earth

stra·tum /'strɑːtəm‖'streɪ-/ n -ta /-tə/ 1 band of a particular rock 2 part of something thought of as divided into different levels

straw /strɔː/ n 1 [U] dried stems of grain plants, such as wheat 2 [C] single such stem 3 [C] thin tube for sucking up liquid — see also LAST STRAW, MAN OF STRAW

straw·ber·ry /'strɔːbəri‖-beri, -bəri/ n (plant with) a small red juicy fruit

straw poll /ˌ· '·/ n unofficial examination of opinions before an election, to see what the result is likely to be

stray /streɪ/ vi wander away ♦ n animal lost from its home ♦ adj 1 wandering; lost 2 single; not in a group

streak /striːk/ n 1 thin line or band, different from what surrounds it 2 bad quality of character: *a stubborn streak* 3 period marked by a particular quality: *a lucky streak* 4 **like a streak (of lightning)** very quickly ♦ v 1 vi move very fast 2 vt cover with streaks **~y** adj marked with streaks

stream /striːm/ n 1 small river 2 something flowing: *a stream of traffic*|(fig.) *a stream of abuse* 3 group of pupils of similar ability 4 **go with/against the stream** agree/not agree with a general way of thinking, etc., in society 5 **on stream** in(to) production ♦ v 1 vi flow strongly 2 vi move in a continuous flowing mass 3 vi float in the air 4 vt esp. BrE group in STREAMs (3) — **-er** n long narrow piece of paper for throwing

stream-line /ˈstriːmlaɪn/ vt 1 give a smooth shape which moves easily through water or air 2 make more simple and effective **-lined** adj

street /striːt/ n 1 road in a town 2 **streets ahead** much better 3 **up/down one's street** in one's area of interest — see also HIGH STREET

street-cred-i-bil-i-ty /ˌ· ···ˈ···/also **street-cred** /ˈ· ·/ infml — n [U] popular acceptance among young esp. working-class people

street-wise /ˈstriːtwaɪz/ adj infml clever enough to succeed and live well in the hard world of the city streets

strength /streŋθ, strenθ/ n 1 [U] (degree of) being strong 2 [C] way in which something is good or effective: *the strengths and weaknesses of the plan* 3 [U] force measured in numbers: *The police are at full strength.* 4 **on the strength of** persuaded or influenced by — **-en** vi/t become or make strong or stronger

stren-u-ous /ˈstrenjuəs/ adj 1 needing great effort 2 showing great activity: *a strenuous denial* — **-ly** adv **-ness** n [U]

stress /stres/ n [C;U] 1 (worry resulting from) pressure caused by difficulties 2 force of weight caused by pressure 3 sense of special importance 4 degree of force put on a part of a word when spoken, or on a note in music: *In 'under' the main stress is on 'un'.* ♦ vt 1 mention strongly 2 put STRESS (4) on

stretch /stretʃ/ v 1 vi/t (cause to) become wider or longer 2 vi spread out: *The forest stretched for miles.* 3 vi be elastic 4 vi straighten one's limbs to full length: *stretch out your arms* 5 vt allow to go beyond exact limits: *stretch a rule* 6 **stretch one's legs** have a walk esp. after sitting for a long time ♦ n 1 [C] act of stretching 2 [U] elasticity 3 [C] long area of land or water 4 [C] continuous period: *14 hours at a stretch* (= without stopping) 5 **at full stretch** using all one's powers **-y** adj elastic

stretch-er /ˈstretʃəʳ/ n covered frame for carrying a sick person

strew /struː/ vt **strewed, strewn** /struːn/ or **strewed** esp. lit 1 scatter 2 lie scattered over

strick-en /ˈstrɪkən/ adj showing the effect of trouble, illness, etc.: *grief-stricken*

strict /strɪkt/ adj 1 severe in making people behave properly 2 **a** exact: *strict instructions* **b** complete: *in strict secrecy* **-ly** adv **-ness** n [U]

stric-ture /ˈstrɪktʃəʳ/ n fml expression of blame

stride /straɪd/ vi **strode** /strəʊd/, **stridden** /ˈstrɪdn/ walk with long steps ♦ n 1 long step 2 **make strides** improve or do well 3 **take something in one's stride** deal with a difficult situation easily and without complaint

stri-dent /ˈstraɪdənt/ adj with a hard sharp sound or voice **-ly** adv **-dency** n [U]

strife /straɪf/ n [U] trouble and quarrelling between people

strike[1] /straɪk/ v **struck** /strʌk/ 1 vt hit sharply 2 vt make a (sudden) attack 3 vt harm suddenly: *They were struck down with illness.* 4 vt light (a match) 5 vi/t **a** make known (the time), esp. by the hitting of a bell **b** (of time) be made known in this way 6 vi stop working because of disagreement 7 vt find; meet: *strike oil/difficulties* 8 vt have a particular effect on: *Her behaviour struck me as odd.*|*struck down with fear* 9 vt come suddenly to mind 10 vt produce (a coin or similar object) 11 vt make (an agreement): *strike a bargain/balance* 12 **strike a chord** remind someone of something 13 **strike a note** of express (a need for): *The book strikes a warning note.* 14 **strike camp** take down tents when leaving a camping place 15 **strike it rich** find sudden wealth

strike off phr vt remove (someone or their name) from (an official list)

strike out phr vi 1 go purposefully in the stated direction 2 **strike out on one's own** take up an independent life 3 CROSS out

strike up phr vt 1 begin playing or singing 2 start to make (a friendship)

strike[2] n 1 act or time of striking (STRIKE[1] (6)): *The workers are on strike.* 2 attack, esp. by aircraft 3 success in finding esp. a mineral in the earth: *an oil strike* — see also FIRST STRIKE, GENERAL STRIKE

strik-er /ˈstraɪkəʳ/ n 1 person on STRIKE[2] (1) 2 attacking player in football

strik-ing /ˈstraɪkɪŋ/ adj very noticeable, esp. because beautiful or unusual **-ly** adv

striking dis-tance /ˈ·· ˌ·ˈ·/ n **within striking distance** very close (to)

string[1] /strɪŋ/ n 1 [C;U] thin cord 2 [C] thin cord or wire stretched across a musical instrument to give sound 3 [C] set of objects on a thread: *a string of pearls* 4 [C] set of things, events, etc., following each other closely: *a whole string of complaints* 5 **no strings attached** (esp. of an agreement) with no limiting conditions 6 **pull strings** use secret influence 7 **two strings to one's bow** an additional interest, ability, etc., which can be used as well as the main one **strings** n [P] all the (players of) VIOLINs, CELLOs, etc., in an ORCHESTRA ~**y** adj 1 (of food) full of unwanted threadlike parts 2 unpleasantly thin, so that the muscles show

string[2] vt **strung** /strʌŋ/ 1 put STRINGS[1] (2) on (a musical instrument or RACKET[1]) 2 put with others onto a thread 3 **highly strung** (of a person) very sensitive and easily excited 4 **strung up** very excited, nervous, or worried

string along phr v 1 vt encourage the hopes of deceitfully 2 vi go (with someone else) for a time, esp. for convenience

string out phr vt spread out in a line

string up phr vt 1 hang high 2 kill by hanging

strin-gent /ˈstrɪndʒənt/ adj (esp. of rules, limits, etc.) severe ~**ly** adv

strip /strɪp/ v -**pp**- 1 vt remove (the covering or parts of) 2 vi/t undress, usu. completely 3 vt remove the parts of (esp. an engine) ♦ n 1 narrow piece: *a strip of paper/land* 2 clothes of a particular colour worn by a team in SOCCER ~**per** n 1 [C] striptease performer 2 [C;U] tool or liquid for removing things: *paint stripper*

strip of phr vt take away (something of value) from

strip car-toon /ˌ· ·ˈ·/n BrE COMIC STRIP

stripe /straɪp/ n 1 different-coloured band 2 usu. V-shaped sign worn on a uniform to show rank **striped** adj **stripy** adj

strip light-ing /ˈ· ˌ··, ˌ· ˈ··/ n [U] long tube-shaped lamps

strip-ling /ˈstrɪplɪŋ/ n lit young man

strip-tease /ˈstrɪptiːz, ˌstrɪpˈtiːz/ n [U] removal of clothes by a person, performed as a show

strive /straɪv/ vi **strove** /strəʊv/ or **strived**, **striven** /ˈstrɪvən/ or **strived** fml or lit make a great effort

strode /strəʊd/ past t. of STRIDE

stroke[1] /strəʊk/ vt pass the hand over gently

stroke[2] n 1 hit, esp. with a weapon 2 act of stroking 3 line made by a single movement of a pen or brush 4 act of hitting a ball 5 (single movement or set of movements that is repeated in) a method of swimming 6 sudden bursting of a blood tube in the brain 7 unexpected piece (of luck) 8 sound of a clock striking: *on the stroke of (= exactly at) 6 o'clock* 9 **at a stroke** with one direct action

stroll /strəʊl/ vi, n (take) a slow walk for pleasure ~**er** n 1 person who strolls or is strolling 2 a BrE light foldable PUSHCHAIR b AmE for PUSHCHAIR

strong /strɒŋ/ adj 1 having great power 2 not easily becoming broken, changed, destroyed, or ill 3 having a powerful effect on the mind or senses: *a strong smell* 4 (of a drink, drug, etc.) having a lot of the substance which gives taste, produces effect, etc.: *This coffee's too strong.* 5 having the stated number of members: *a club 50 strong* 6 (still) going **strong** continuing with energy, good health, etc. 7 **strong on:** a good at doing b eager and active in dealing with ~**ly** adv

strong-box /ˈstrɒŋbɒks‖ˈstrɔːŋbɑːks/ n firm lockable box for keeping valuable things in

strong-hold /ˈstrɒŋhəʊld‖ˈstrɔːŋ-/ n 1 fort 2 place where a particular activity is common

strong lan-guage /ˌ· ˈ··/n [U] swearing; curses

strong point /ˈ· ·/ n something one is good at

strong room /ˈ· ·/ n special lockable room in a bank, etc., where valuable things are kept

stron-ti-um /ˈstrɒntiəm‖ˈstrɑːn-tʃiəm, -tiəm/ n [U] soft metal, of which a harmful form (**strontium 90**) is given off by atomic explosions

strop-py /ˈstrɒpi‖ˈstrɑːpi/ adj BrE infml tending to quarrel or disobey –**pily** adv

strove /strəʊv/ past t. of STRIVE

struck /strʌk/ past t. and p. of STRIKE

struc-ture /ˈstrʌktʃəʳ/ n 1 [C;U] way in which parts are formed into a whole 2 [C] large thing built ♦ vt arrange so that each part is properly related to others –**tural** adj –**turally** adv

strug-gle /ˈstrʌgəl/ vi 1 make violent movements, esp. in fighting 2 make a great effort ♦ n hard fight or effort

strum /strʌm/ vi/t -**mm**- play carelessly or informally on (esp. a GUITAR, BANJO, or piano)

strung /strʌŋ/ past t. and p. of STRING

strut[1] /strʌt/ n supporting rod in a structure

strut[2] vi -**tt**- walk proudly

strych-nine /ˈstrɪkniːn‖-naɪn, -niːn/ n [U] poisonous drug

stub /stʌb/ n 1 short left-over part of esp. a cigarette or pencil 2 small piece left in a book of cheques or tickets after tearing out a cheque or ticket ♦ vt block — hit (one's toe) against something ~**by** adj short and thick: *stubby fingers*

stub out phr vt put out (a cigarette) by pressing

stub-ble /'stʌbəl/ n [U] 1 short growth of beard 2 remains of cut wheat —**bly** adj

stub-born /'stʌbən‖-ərn/ adj 1 having a strong will; (unreasonably) determined 2 difficult to use, move, change, etc. —**ly** adv —**ness** n [U]

stuc-co /'stʌkəʊ/ n [U] PLASTER stuck (decoratively) onto walls

stuck[1] /stʌk/ v past t. and p. of STICK

stuck[2] adj 1 unable to go further because of difficulties 2 **stuck with** having to do or have, esp. unwillingly 3 **get stuck in** infml begin forcefully

stuck-up /ˌ· '·◄/ adj infml too proud in manner

stud[1] /stʌd/ n 1 removable button-like fastener, esp. for collars 2 large-headed nail ♦ vt **-dd-** cover (as if) with STUDs[1] (2)

stud[2] n 1 number of horses kept for breeding 2 taboo man who has sex a lot and thinks he is very good at it

stu-dent /'stjuːdənt‖'stuː-/ n 1 person studying at a college or university 2 person with a stated interest: *a student of life*

stu-di-o /'stjuːdiəʊ‖'stuː-/ n 1 place where films, recordings, or broadcasts are made 2 workroom for a painter, photographer, etc.

stu-di-ous /'stjuːdiəs‖'stuː-/ adj 1 fond of studying 2 careful ~**ly** adv ~**ness** n [U]

stud-y /'stʌdi/ n 1 [U] also **studies** pl. — act of studying 2 [C] thorough enquiry into a particular subject, esp. including a piece of writing on it 3 [C] workroom; office 4 [C] drawing or painting of a detail: *a study of a flower* 5 [C] piece of music for practice ♦ v 1 vi/t spend time in learning 2 vt examine carefully **studied** adj carefully thought about or considered, esp. before being expressed: *a studied remark*

stuff[1] /stʌf/ n [U] 1 matter; material 2 one's possessions or the things needed to do something 3 **do one's stuff** show one's ability as expected 4 **know one's stuff** be good at what one is concerned with 5 **That's the stuff!** infml That's the right thing to do/say

stuff[2] vt 1 fill 2 push so as to be inside 3 put STUFFING (2) inside 4 fill the skin of (a dead animal) to make it look real 5 cause (oneself) to eat as much as possible 6 **get stuffed!** sl (an

expression of dislike, esp. for what someone has said) ~**ing** n [U] 1 filling material 2 cut-up food put inside a chicken, etc., before cooking

stuff up phr vt block

stuffed shirt /ˌ· '·, '·◄/ n dull person who thinks himself important

stuff-y /'stʌfi/ adj 1 (having air) that is not fresh 2 derog formal and old-fashioned —**ily** adv —**iness** n [U]

stul-ti-fy /'stʌltɪfaɪ/ vt fml make (someone's) mind dull —**fication** /ˌstʌltɪfəˈkeɪʃən/ n [U]

stum-ble /'stʌmbəl/ vi 1 catch one's foot on something and start to fall 2 stop and/or make mistakes in speaking

stumble across/on/upon phr vt meet or find by chance

stumbling block /'···/ n something preventing action or development

stump[1] /stʌmp/ n 1 base of a cut-down tree 2 useless end of something long that has been worn down, cut off, etc. 3 any of the 3 sticks at which the ball is aimed in cricket ~**y** adj short and thick in body

stump[2] v 1 vt leave (someone) unable to reply 2 vi walk heavily or awkwardly

stun /stʌn/ vt **-nn-** 1 make unconscious 2 shock greatly 3 delight ~**ning** adj very attractive

stung /stʌŋ/ past t. and p. of STING

stunk /stʌŋk/ past p. of STINK

stunt[1] /stʌnt/ n 1 dangerous act of skill 2 attention-getting action: *publicity stunts* 3 **pull a stunt** do a trick, sometimes silly

stunt[2] vt prevent full growth (of)

stunt man /'··/ **stunt woman** /'· ,··/ fem. — n person who does STUNTs[1] (1) in films, etc.

stu-pe-fy /'stjuːpɪfaɪ‖'stuː-/ vt fml surprise (and annoy) extremely 2 make unable to think —**faction** /ˌstjuːpɪˈfækʃən‖ˌstuː-/ n [U]

stu-pen-dous /stjuːˈpendəs‖stuː-/ adj surprisingly great or good

stu-pid /'stjuːpɪd‖'stuː-/ adj foolish ~**ly** adv ~**ity** /stjuːˈpɪdəti‖stuː-/ n [U]

stu-por /'stjuːpə‖'stuː-/ n [C,U] nearly unconscious unthinking state

stur-dy /'stɜːdi‖-ɜːr-/ adj 1 strong and firm 2 determined —**dily** adv —**diness** n [U]

stut-ter /'stʌtə/ vi/t speak or say with difficulty in pronouncing esp. the first consonant of words ♦ n habit of stuttering

sty[1], **stye** /staɪ/ n infected place on the eyelid

sty[2] n PIGSTY

style /staɪl/ n 1 [C,U] (typical) manner of doing something: *the modern* *style of architecture* | *written in a formal style* 2 [C] fashion, esp. in clothes 3 [U] high quality of social behaviour or appearance 4 [C] type or sort 5 **in style** in a grand way ♦ *vt* 1 DESIGN 2 give (a title) to: *He styles himself 'Lord'.* **stylish** *adj* fashionable and good-looking **stylist** *n* 1 person who invents styles or fashions 2 person with a (good) style of writing **stylize** *vt* present in a simplified style rather than naturally **stylistic** /staɪ'lɪstɪk/ *adj* of STYLE (1)

sty·lus /'staɪləs/ *n* -**luses** or -**li** /-laɪ/ needle-like instrument in a RECORD PLAYER that picks up sound signals from a record

suave /swɑːv/ *adj* with smooth (but perhaps insincere) good manners —**ly** *adv* ~**ness** *n* [U]

sub /sʌb/ *n infml* 1 SUBMARINE 2 SUBSTITUTE 3 *BrE* amount of money paid to someone from their wages before the usual day of payment ♦ *vt* -**bb**- SUBEDIT

sub·con·scious /ˌsʌb'kɒnʃəs ‖ -'kɑːn-/ *adj, n* (present at) a hidden level of the mind, not consciously known about ~**ly** *adv*

sub·con·ti·nent /ˌsʌb'kɒntɪnənt ‖ -'kɑːn-/ *n* large mass of land smaller than a CONTINENT, esp. India

sub·con·tract /ˌsʌbkən'trækt ‖ -'kɑːntrækt/ *vt* hire someone else to do (work which one has agreed to do) ~**or** *n* person or firm that has had work subcontracted to it

sub·cu·ta·ne·ous /ˌsʌbkjuː'teɪniəs/ *adj med* beneath the skin

sub·di·vide /ˌsʌbdɪ'vaɪd/ *vt* divide into even smaller parts —**division** /-'vɪʒən/ *n* [C;U]

sub·due /səb'djuː ‖ -'duː/ *vt* 1 gain control of 2 make gentler —**dued** *adj* 1 of low brightness or sound 2 unusually quiet in behaviour

sub·ed·it /ˌsʌb'edɪt/ *vt* look at and put right (material to be printed in a newspaper, etc.) ~**or** *n*

sub·ject[1] /'sʌbdʒɪkt/ *n* 1 thing dealt with, represented, or considered: *the subject of the painting/of the conversation* 2 branch of knowledge being studied 3 word that comes before a main verb and represents the person or thing that performs the action of the verb or about which something is stated 4 member of a state: *British subjects* ♦ *adj* 1 tending; likely: *He's subject to ill health.* 2 not independent: *a subject race* 3 **subject to** depending on: *subject to your approval* (= if you approve)

subject[2] /səb'dʒekt/ *vt fml* defeat and control ~**ion** /-'dʒekʃən/ *n* [U] 1 act of subjecting 2 state of being severely controlled by others

subject to *phr vt* cause to experience or suffer

sub·jec·tive /səb'dʒektɪv/ *adj* 1 influenced by personal feelings (and perhaps unfair) 2 existing only inside the mind; not real ~**ly** *adv* -**tivity** /ˌsʌbdʒek'tɪvəti/ *n* [U]

sub ju·di·ce /ˌsʌb 'dʒuːdɪsi ‖ ˌsub 'juːdɪkeɪ/ *adj* now being considered in a court of law, and therefore not allowed to be publicly mentioned

sub·ju·gate /'sʌbdʒʊgeɪt/ *vt* defeat and make obedient —**gation** /ˌsʌbdʒʊ'geɪʃən/ *n* [U]

sub·junc·tive /səb'dʒʌŋktɪv/ *adj, n* (of) a verb form expressing doubt, wishes, unreality, etc.: *In 'if I were you' the verb 'were' is in the subjunctive.*

sub·let /ˌsʌb'let/ *vt* -**let**, *pres. p.* -**tt**- rent (property rented from someone) to someone else

sub·li·mate /'sʌbləmeɪt/ *vt fml* replace (natural urges, esp. sexual) with socially acceptable activities —**mation** /ˌsʌblə'meɪʃən/ *n* [U]

sub·lime /sə'blaɪm/ *adj* 1 very noble or wonderful 2 *infml* complete and usu. careless or unknowing ~**ly** *adv*

sub·lim·i·nal /sʌb'lɪmɪnəl/ *adj* at a level which the ordinary senses are not conscious of

sub·ma·chine gun /ˌsʌbmə'ʃiːn gʌn/ *n* light MACHINEGUN

sub·ma·rine /'sʌbməriːn, ˌsʌbmə'riːn/ *n* (war)ship which can stay under water ♦ *adj* under or in the sea

sub·merge /səb'mɜːdʒ ‖ -ɜːr-/ *vi/t* 1 (cause to) go under the surface of water 2 cover or competely hide —**mersion** /-'mɜːʃən ‖ -'mɜːrʒən/ *n* [U] act of submerging or state of being submerged

sub·mit /səb'mɪt/ *v* -**tt**- 1 *vi* admit defeat 2 *vt* offer for consideration 3 *vt esp. law* suggest —**mission** /-'mɪʃən/ *n* 1 [C;U] submitting 2 [U] *fml* opinion 3 [U] *fml* obedience 4 [C] *law* request; suggestion —**missive** /-'mɪsɪv/ *adj* too obedient

sub·or·di·nate[1] /sə'bɔːdənət ‖ -ɔːr-/ *adj* less important ♦ *n* someone of lower rank

sub·or·din·ate[2] /sə'bɔːdɪneɪt ‖ -ɔːr-/ *vt* put in a subordinate position —**ation** /sə,bɔːdɪ'neɪʃən ‖ -ɔːr-/ *n* [U]

sub·orn /sə'bɔːn ‖ -ɔːrn/ *vt fml* persuade to do wrong, esp. tell lies in court

sub·poe·na /sə'piːnə, səb-/ *n* written order to attend a court of law **subpoena** *vt*

sub·scribe /səb'skraɪb/ *vi* pay regularly, esp. to receive a magazine —**scriber** *n*

subscribe to *phr vt* agree with; approve of

sub·scrip·tion /səbˈskrɪpʃən/ n 1 act of subscribing (to) 2 amount paid regularly, esp. to belong to a society, receive a magazine, etc.

sub·se·quent /ˈsʌbsɪkwənt/ adj coming afterwards or next ~ly adv

sub·ser·vi·ent /səbˈsɜːviənt‖-ɜːr-/ adj too willing to obey ~ly adv ~ence n [U]

sub·side /səbˈsaɪd/ vi 1 return to its usual level; become less: The flood waters/The wind/His anger subsided. 2 (of land or a building) sink down **subsidence** /səbˈsaɪdəns, ˈsʌbsɪdəns/ n [U]

sub·sid·i·a·ry /səbˈsɪdiəri‖-dieri/ adj connected with but less important than the main one ♦ n subsidiary company

sub·si·dy /ˈsʌbsɪdi/ n paid, esp. by government, to make prices lower, etc. **–dize** vt give a subsidy to (someone) or (something): subsidized school meals

sub·sist /səbˈsɪst/ vi fml remain alive ~ence n [U] 1 ability to live, esp. on little money or food 2 state of living with little money or food

sub·stance /ˈsʌbstəns/ n 1 [C] material; type of matter: a sticky substance 2 [U] fml truth: There is no substance in these rumours. 3 [U] fml real meaning, without the unimportant details 4 [U] fml wealth 5 [U] importance, esp. in relation to real life: There was no real substance in the speech.

sub·stan·tial /səbˈstænʃəl/ adj 1 solid; strongly made 2 satisfactorily large: a substantial meal 3 noticeably large (and important): substantial changes 4 concerning the main part 5 wealthy ~ly adv 1 in all important ways: They are substantially the same. 2 quite a lot

sub·stan·ti·ate /səbˈstænʃieɪt/ vt fml prove the truth of **–ation** /səb,stænʃiˈeɪʃən/ n [U]

sub·stan·tive /ˈsʌbstəntɪv/ adj fml having reality, actuality, or importance

sub·sti·tute /ˈsʌbstɪtjuːt‖-tuːt/ n one taking the place of another ♦ v 1 vt put in place of another 2 vi act or be used instead **–tution** /,sʌbstɪˈtjuːʃən‖-ˈtuː-/ n [C;U]

sub·sume /səbˈsjuːm‖-ˈsuːm/ vt fml include

sub·ter·fuge /ˈsʌbtəfjuːdʒ‖-ər-/ n [C;U] deceiving or slightly dishonest trick(s)

sub·ter·ra·ne·an /,sʌbtəˈreɪniən◄/ adj underground

sub·ti·tles /ˈsʌb,taɪtlz/ n [P] translation printed over a foreign film

sub·tle /ˈsʌtl/ adj 1 hardly noticeable: subtle differences 2 clever in arrangement: a subtle plan 3 very clever in noticing and understanding ~tly adv **–tlety** n [C;U]

sub·tract /səbˈtrækt/ vt take (a number or amount) from a larger one ~ion /-ˈtrækʃən/ n [C;U]

sub·urb /ˈsʌbɜːb‖-ɜːrb/ n outer area of a town, where people live ~an /səˈbɜːbən‖-ɜːr-/ adj

sub·ur·bi·a /səˈbɜːbiə‖-ɜːr-/ n [U] (life and ways of people who live in) suburbs

sub·vert /səbˈvɜːt‖-ɜːrt/ vt try to destroy the power and influence of **–versive** adj trying to destroy established ideas or defeat those in power **–version** /-ˈvɜːʃən‖-ˈvɜːrʒən/ n [U]

sub·way /ˈsʌbweɪ/ n 1 path under a road or railway 2 AmE underground railway

suc·ceed /səkˈsiːd/ v 1 vi do what one has been trying to do 2 vi do well, esp. in gaining position or popularity 3 vt follow after 4 vi/t be the next to take a rank or position (after): Hammond succeeded Jones as champion.

suc·cess /səkˈses/ n 1 [U] degree of succeeding; good result 2 [C] person or thing that succeeds ~ful adj ~fully adv

suc·ces·sion /səkˈseʃən/ n 1 [U] following one after the other: in quick succession 2 [S] many following each other closely: a succession of visitors 3 [U] succeeding (4)

suc·ces·sive /səkˈsesɪv/ adj following each other closely in time ~ly adv

suc·ces·sor /səkˈsesəʳ/ n person who takes an office or position formerly held by another

suc·cinct /səkˈsɪŋkt/ adj clearly expressed in few words ~ly adv

suc·cour BrE ‖ **–cor** AmE /ˈsʌkəʳ/ vt, n [U] lit help

suc·cu·lent /ˈsʌkjʊlənt/ adj juicy and tasty **–lence** n [U]

suc·cumb /səˈkʌm/ vi fml stop opposing

such /sʌtʃ/ predeterminer, determiner 1 of that kind: I dislike such people. | some flowers, such as (= for example) roses 2 to so great a degree: He's such a kind man. 3 so great; so good, bad or unusual: He wrote to her every day, such was his love for her. ♦ pron 1 any/no/some such any/no/some (person or thing) like that: No such person exists. 2 as such properly so named

such and such /ˈ· · ,/predeterminer infml a certain (time, amount, etc.) not named

such·like /ˈsʌtʃlaɪk/ adj, pron (things) of that kind

suck /sʌk/ v 1 vi/t draw (liquid) in with the muscles of the mouth 2 vt hold (something) in one's mouth and move one's tongue against it: *sucking one's thumb* **3** *vt* draw powerfully: *The current sucked them under.* **suck** *n*

suck·er /'sʌkəʳ/ *n* **1** person or thing that sucks **2** flat piece which sticks to a surface by suction **3 a** easily cheated person **b** someone who likes the stated thing very much: *a sucker for ice cream*

suck·le /'sʌkəl/ *vi/t* feed with milk from the breast

suc·tion /'sʌkʃən/ *n* [U] drawing away air or liquid, esp. to lower the air pressure between 2 objects and make them stick to each other

sud·den /'sʌdn/ *adj* happening unexpectedly and quickly ~**ly** *adv* ~**ness** *n* [U]

suds /sʌdz/ *n* [P] mass of soapy BUBBLEs

sue /sjuː‖suː/ *vi/t* bring a legal claim (against)

suede /sweɪd/ *n* [U] soft leather with a rough surface

su·et /'suːɪt, 'sjuːɪt‖'suː-/ *n* [U] hard fat used in cooking

suf·fer /'sʌfəʳ/ *v* **1** *vi* experience pain or difficulty **2** *vt* experience (something unpleasant) **3** *vt* accept without dislike: *He doesn't suffer fools gladly.* **4** *vi* grow worse: *His work has suffered since his illness.* ~**ing** *n* [U;C]

suf·fer·ance /'sʌfərəns/ *n* **on sufferance** with permission, though not welcomed

suf·fice /sə'faɪs/ *vi/t fml* **1** be enough (for) **2 suffice to say that ...** I will say only that ...

suf·fi·cient /sə'fɪʃənt/ *adj* enough ~**ly** *adv* –**ciency** *n* [S;U] *fml*

suf·fix /'sʌfɪks/ *n* group of letters or sounds added at the end of a word (as in kindness, quickly)

suf·fo·cate /'sʌfəkeɪt/ *vi/t* (cause) to die because of lack of air –**cation** /ˌsʌfə'keɪʃən/ *n* [U]

suf·frage /'sʌfrɪdʒ/ *n* [U] right to vote in national elections

suf·fuse /sə'fjuːz/ *vt* spread all through –**fusion** /-'fjuːʒən/ *n*

sug·ar /'ʃʊgəʳ/ *n* [U] sweet white or brown plant substance used in food and drinks ◆ *vt* put sugar in ~**y** *adj* **1** containing or tasting of sugar **2** too sweet, nice, kind, etc., in an insincere way

sug·ar·cane /'ʃʊgəkeɪn‖-əʳ-/ *n* [U] tall tropical plant from whose stems sugar is obtained

sugar dad·dy /'·· ˌ··‖ˌ·'··/ *n infml* older man who provides a young woman with money and presents in return for sex and companionship

sug·gest /sə'dʒest‖səg'dʒest/ *vt* **1** state as an idea for consideration: *I suggest we do it this way.* **2** give signs

(of): *The latest figures suggest that business is improving.* ~**ive** *adj* **1** (perhaps) showing thoughts of sex **2** *fml* which leads the mind into a particular way of thinking ~**ion** /sə'dʒestʃən‖səg-/ *n* [C;U] act of suggesting or something suggested

su·i·cide /'suːɪsaɪd, 'sjuː-‖'suː-/ *n* **1** [C;U] killing oneself **2** [C] person who does this **3** [U] action that destroys one's position –**cidal** /ˌsuːɪ'saɪdl, ˌsjuː-‖ˌsuː-/ *adj* **1** likely or wishing to kill oneself **2** likely to lead to death or destruction

suit [1] /suːt, sjuːt‖suːt/ *n* **1** short coat with trousers or skirt of the same material **2** garment for a special purpose: *a bathing suit* | *a suit of armour* **3** any of the 4 sets of playing cards **4 follow suit** do the same as everyone else

suit [2] *vt* **1** be convenient for; satisfy **2** match or look good on (someone): *That hairstyle doesn't suit you.* **3** be **suited (to/for)** be suitable **4 suit oneself** do what one likes

suit·a·ble /'suːtəbəl, 'sjuː-‖'suː-/ *adj* fit or right for a purpose –**bly** *adv* –**bility** /ˌsuːtə'bɪlɪti, ˌsjuː-‖ˌsuː-/ *n* [U]

suit·case /'suːtkeɪs, 'sjuːt-‖'suːt-/ *n* case for carrying clothes and possessions when travelling

suite /swiːt/ *n* **1** set of matching furniture **2** set of hotel rooms **3** piece of music made up of several parts

sui·tor /'suːtəʳ, 'sjuː-‖'suː-/ *n lit* man wishing to marry a particular woman

sulk /sʌlk/ *vi* be silently bad-tempered ~**y** *adj* ~**ily** *adv* –**iness** *n* [U]

sul·len /'sʌlən/ *adj* showing silent dislike, bad temper, lack of interest, etc. ~**ly** *adv* ~**ness** *n* [U]

sul·ly /'sʌli/ *vt lit* spoil

sul·phur *BrE* ‖ -**fur** *AmE*/'sʌlfəʳ/ *n* [U] substance found esp. as a light yellow powder

sul·phu·ric ac·id /ˌsʌlˌfjʊərɪk 'æsɪd/ *n* [U] powerful acid

sul·tan /'sʌltən/ *n* (*often cap.*) Muslim ruler

sul·ta·na /sʌl'tɑːnə‖-'tænə/ *n* **1** small dried GRAPE used in cakes, etc. **2** (*often cap.*) wife, mother, or daughter of a sultan

sul·try /'sʌltri/ *adj* **1** (of weather) hot, airless, and uncomfortable **2** causing or showing strong sexual desire

sum [1] /sʌm/ *n* **1** total produced when numbers are added together **2** amount (of money) **3** simple calculation

sum [2] *v* -**mm**- **sum up** *phr v* **1** *vi/t* SUMMARIZE **2** *vt* consider and form a judgment of

sum·ma·ry /'sʌməri/ *n* short account giving the main points ◆ *adj*

1 short **2** done at once without attention to formalities: *summary dismissal* **–rize** *vt* make a summary of

sum·mer /'sʌmə^r/ *n* [C;U] hot season between spring and autumn **~y** *adj* like or suitable for summer

sum·mit /'sʌmɪt/ *n* **1** highest point **2** top of a mountain **3** meeting between heads of government

sum·mon /'sʌmən/ *vt* order officially to come

   summon up *phr vt* get (a quality in oneself) ready for use

sum·mons /'sʌmənz/ *n, vt* order to appear in a court of law

sump /sʌmp/ *n* part of an engine holding the oil supply

sump·tu·ous /'sʌmptʃuəs/ *adj* expensive and grand **~ly** *adv*

sum to·tal /ˌ· '··/ *n* [*the* + S] the whole, esp. when less than expected or needed

sun /sʌn/ *n* **1** [*the* + S] star round which the Earth moves **2** [*the* + S;U] sun's light and heat: *sitting in the sun* **3** [C] star round which PLANETs may turn **4** **under the sun** at all ♦ *vt* **-nn-** place (oneself) in sunlight **~ny** *adj* **1** having bright sunlight **2** cheerful

sun·bathe /'sʌnbeɪð/ *vi* sit or lie in strong sunlight **–bather** *n*

sun·beam /'sʌnbiːm/ *n* a beam of sunlight

sun·belt /'sʌnbelt/ *n* [*the* + S] southern and southwestern parts of the US

sun·burn /'sʌnbɜːn/ *-ɜːrn/ *n* [U] sore skin caused by too much strong sunlight **–burnt**, **~ed** *adj*

sun·dae /'sʌndeɪ‖-di/ *n* ice cream dish with fruit, nuts, etc.

Sun·day /'sʌndi/ *n* the 7th day of the week, between Saturday and Monday

sun·der /'sʌndə^r/ *vt lit* separate

sun·di·al /'sʌndaɪəl/ *n* apparatus producing a shadow which shows the time

sun·down /'sʌndaʊn/ *n* [U] sunset

sun·dry /'sʌndri/ *adj* **1** various **2** **all and sundry** all types of people; everybody

sung /sʌŋ/ *past p. of* SING

sun·glass·es /'sʌnˌglɑːsɪz‖-ˌglæ-/ *n* [P] glasses with dark glass for protection from sunlight

sunk /sʌŋk/ *past p. of* SINK

sunk·en /'sʌŋkən/ *adj* **1** that has (been) sunk **2** below the surrounding level: *sunken eyes | a sunken garden*

sun·lamp /'sʌnlæmp/ *n* ULTRA-VIOLET lamp for browning the skin

sun·light /'sʌnlaɪt/ *n* [U] light from the sun

sun·lit /'sʌnˌlɪt/ *adj* brightly lit by the sun

sun·rise /'sʌnraɪz/ *n* [U] time when the sun appears after the night

sunrise in·dus·try /'·· ,···/ *n* industry such as ELECTRONICS or the making of computers, that is taking the place of older industries

sun·set /'sʌnset/ *n* [C;U] time when the sun disappears as night begins

sun·shade /'sʌnʃeɪd/ *n* sort of UMBRELLA for protection from the sun

sun·shine /'sʌnʃaɪn/ *n* [U] strong sunlight

sun·spot /'sʌnspɒt‖-spɑːt/ *n* dark cooler area on the sun's surface

sun·stroke /'sʌnstrəʊk/ *n* [U] illness caused by too much strong sunlight

sun·tan /'sʌntæn/ *n* brownness of the skin caused by being in strong sunlight

su·per /ˌsuːpə^r, 'sjuː-‖'suː-/ *adj* wonderful; extremely good

su·per·an·nu·at·ed /ˌsuːpər-'ænjueɪtɪd, ˌsjuː-‖ˌsuː-/ *adj fml* **1** too old for work **2** old-fashioned **–ion** /ˌsuːpərænu'eɪʃən, ˌsjuː-‖ˌsuː-/ *n* [U] *fml for* PENSION

su·perb /suː'pɜːb, sjuː-‖suː'pɜːrb/ *adj* excellent; wonderful **~ly** *adv*

su·per·cil·i·ous /ˌsuːpə'sɪliəs, ˌsjuː-‖ˌsuːpər-/ *adj fml derog* (as if) thinking that others are of little importance **~ly** *adv* **~ness** *n* [U]

su·per·con·duc·tor /ˌsuːpəkən-'dʌktə^r, ˌsjuː-‖ˌsuːpər-/ *n* metal which at very low temperatures allows electricity to pass freely

su·per·fi·cial /ˌsuːpə'fɪʃəl, ˌsjuː-‖ˌsuːpər-/ *adj* **1** on the surface; not deep **2** not thorough or complete **~ly** *adv* **~ity** /ˌsuːpəfɪʃi'æləti, ˌsjuː-‖ˌsuːpər-/ *n* [U]

su·per·flu·ous /suː'pɜːfluəs, sjuː-‖suː'pɜːr-/ *adj* more than is necessary; not needed **~ly** *adv*

su·per·grass /'suːpəɡrɑːs, 'sjuː-‖'suːpərɡræs/ *n BrE* person, esp. a criminal, who supplies the police with a lot of information about the activities of criminals

super·human /ˌsuːp'hjuːmən, ˌsjuː-◄‖ˌsuːpər'hjuː-, -'juː/ *adj* (as if) beyond or better than human powers

su·per·im·pose /ˌsuːpərɪm'pəʊz, ˌsjuː-‖ˌsuː-/ *vt* put (something) over something else, esp. so that both can be (partly) seen

su·per·in·tend /ˌsuːpərɪn'tend, ˌsjuː-‖ˌsuː-/ *vt* be in charge of and direct **~ent** *n* **1** person in charge **2** British police officer of middle rank

su·pe·ri·or /suː'pɪəriə^r, sjuː-‖suː-/ *adj* **1** of higher rank **2** better **3** of high quality **4** *derog* (as if) thinking oneself better than others ♦ *n* person of higher rank **~ity** /suːˌpɪəri'ɒrəti, sjuː-‖suː‖ˌsuːˌpɪəri'ɔː-, -'ɑː-/ *n* [U]

su·per·la·tive /suː'pɜːlətɪv, sjuː-‖suː'pɜːr-/ *adj* **1** *gram* expressing 'most'

2 extremely good ♦ *n gram* superlative form of an adjective or adverb

su·per·mar·ket /'suːpə,maːkʌt, 'sjuː-‖'suːpər,maːr-/ *n* large food shop where one serves oneself

su·per·nat·u·ral /,suːpə'nætʃərəl◂, ,sjuː-‖,suːpər-/ *adj* of or caused by the power of spirits, gods, and magic ~**ly** *adv*

su·per·pow·er /'suːpə,pauə', 'sjuː-‖ 'suːpər-/ *n* very powerful nation

su·per·sede /,suːpə'siːd, ,sjuː-‖ ,suːpər-/ *vt* take the place of

su·per·son·ic /,suːpə'sɒnɪk◂, ,sjuː-‖ ,suːpər'saː-/ *adj* (flying) faster than the speed of sound

su·per·star /'suːpəstaːʳ, 'sjuː-‖ 'suːpər-/ *n* very famous performer

su·per·sti·tion /,suːpə'stɪʃən, ,sjuː-‖ ,suːpər-/ *n* [C;U] (unreasonable) belief based on old ideas about luck, magic, etc. **–tious** *adj*

su·per·struc·ture /'suːpə,strʌktʃəʳ, 'sjuː-‖'suːpər-/ *n* upper structure built on a base

su·per·vise /'suːpəvaɪz, 'sjuː-‖ 'suːpər-/ *vt* watch (people or work) to make sure things are done properly **–visor** *n* **–visory** *adj* **–vision** /suːpə'vɪʒən, ,sjuː-‖,suːpər-/ *n* [U]

sup·per /'sʌpəʳ/ *n* [C;U] evening meal

sup·plant /sə'plaːnt‖sə'plænt/ *vt* take the place of

sup·ple /'sʌpəl/ *adj* bending easily and gracefully ~**ness** *n* [U]

sup·ple·ment /'sʌplɪmənt/ *n* **1** additional amount to supply what is needed **2** additional separate part of a newspaper, magazine, etc. — see also COLOUR SUPPLEMENT ♦ *vt* make additions to ~**ary** /,sʌplɪ'mentəri◂/ *adj* additional

sup·ple·men·ta·ry ben·e·fit /,···· '··/ *n* [U] (in Britain) government money given to those with not enough to live on

sup·ply /sə'plaɪ/ *vt* **1** provide (something) **2** provide things to (someone) for use ♦ *n* **1** amount for use: *a supply of food* **2** (system for) supplying: *the supply of electricity* **3** **in short supply** scarce — see also MONEY SUPPLY **–plier** *n* **supplies** *n* [P] things necessary for daily life, esp. food

supply and de·mand /·,·· ·'·/ *n* [U] balance between the amount of goods for sale and the amount that people actually want to buy

sup·port /sə'pɔːt‖-ɔːrt/ *vt* **1** bear the weight of, esp. so as to prevent from falling **2** approve of and encourage **3** be loyal to: *supporting the local football team* **4** provide money for (someone) to live on **5** strengthen (an idea, opinion, etc.) ♦ *n* **1** [U] state of being

supported **2** [C] something that supports **3** [U] active approval and encouragement **4** [U] money to live on ~**er** *n* person who supports a particular activity or team, defends a particular principle, etc. **~ive** *adj* providing encouragement, help, etc.

supporting part also **supporting role** /·,·· '··/ *n* small part in a play or film

sup·pose /sə'pəuz/ *vt* **1** consider to be probable: *As she's not here, I suppose she must have gone home.* **2** **be supposed to: a** ought to; should **b** be generally considered to be ♦ *conj* **1** (used for making a suggestion): *Suppose we wait a while.* **2** what would/will happen if **dly** /-zədli/ *adv* as is believed; as it appears **–posing** *conj* suppose

sup·po·si·tion /,sʌpə'zɪʃən/ *n* **1** [U] act of supposing or guessing **2** [C] guess

sup·pos·i·to·ry /sə'pɒzɪtəri‖sə-'paːzətɔːri/ *n* piece of meltable medicine placed in the RECTUM or VAGINA

sup·press /sə'pres/ *vt* **1** bring to an end by force **2** prevent from being shown or made public: *suppressing her anger/the truth* **–ion** /-'preʃən/ *n* [U]

su·preme /suː'priːm, sjuː-, sə-‖suː-, suː-/ *adj* **1** highest in degree: *supreme happiness*|*the supreme sacrifice* (= giving one's life) **2** most powerful ~**ly** *adv* extremely **supremacy** /sə'preməsi/ *n* [U]

sur·charge /'sɜːtʃaːdʒ‖'sɜːrtʃaːrdʒ/ *n* (demand for) an additional payment ♦ *vt* make (someone) pay a surcharge

sure /ʃuəʳ/ *adj* **1** having no doubt **2** certain (to happen): *You're sure to* (= certainly will) *like it.* **3** confident (of having): *I've never felt surer of success.* **4** **be sure to** don't forget to **5** **make sure: a** find out (if something is really true) **b** take action (so that something will certainly happen) **6** **sure of oneself** certain that one's actions are right ♦ *adv* **1** certainly **2** **for sure** certainly so **3** **sure enough** as was expected ~**ly** *adv* **1** I believe, hope, or expect: *Surely you haven't forgotten?* **2** safely ~**ness** *n* [U]

sure-fire /'ʃuəfaɪəʳ‖'ʃuər-/ *adj* certain to succeed

sure-foot·ed /,ʃuː'futʌd◂‖,ʃuər-/ *adj* able to walk, climb, etc., in difficult places without falling

sure·ty /'ʃuərʌti/ *n* [C;U] **1** person who takes responsibility for the behaviour of another **2** money given to make sure that a person will appear in court

surf /sɜːf‖sɜːrf/ *n* [U] white air-filled waves breaking on a shore ♦ *vi* ride as a sport over breaking waves near the shore, on a SURFBOARD ~**ing** *n* [U] sport of surfing **~er** *n* person who goes surfing

sur·face /'sɜːfɪs‖'sɜːr-/ *n* **1** outer part of an object **2** top of liquid **3** what is easily seen, not the main (hidden) part ♦ *adj* **1** not deep; SUPERFICIAL: *surface friendliness* ♦ *vi* come up to the surface of water: (fig.) *He doesn't usually surface* (= get out of bed) *until midday.*

surface mail /'··· ·/ *n* [U] post carried by land or sea

surface-to-air /,·· · '·◄/ *adj* (of a weapon) fired from the earth towards aircraft

surf·board /'sɜːfbɔːd‖'sɜːrfbɔːrd/ *n* board for riding on surf

sur·feit /'sɜːfɪt‖'sɜːr-/ *n* [S] too large an amount

surge /sɜːdʒ‖sɜːrdʒ/ *n* **1** sudden powerful forward movement **2** sudden increase of strong feeling ♦ *vi* **1** move forwards like powerful waves **2** (of a feeling) arise powerfully

sur·geon /'sɜːdʒən‖'sɜːr-/ *n* doctor who does SURGERY (1)

sur·ge·ry /'sɜːdʒəri‖'sɜːr-/ *n* **1** [U] performing of medical operations **2** [C;U] *BrE* place where or time when a doctor or DENTIST treats patients **3** [C] *BrE* period of time when people can come and see a member of parliament, lawyer, etc., to ask advice

sur·gi·cal /'sɜːdʒɪkəl‖'sɜːr-/ *adj* **1** of or used for surgery **2** (of a garment) worn as treatment for a particular physical condition **~ly** /-kli/ *adv*

sur·ly /'sɜːli‖'sɜːrli/ *adj* bad-tempered and bad-mannered **surli·ness** *n* [U]

sur·mise /sə'maɪz‖sər-/ *vt fml* suppose; guess

sur·mount /sə'maʊnt‖sər-/ *vt* **1** succeed in dealing with (a difficulty) **2** be on top of

sur·name /'sɜːneɪm‖'sɜːr-/ *n* person's family name

sur·pass /sə'pɑːs‖sər'pæs/ *vt fml* go beyond, esp. be better than

sur·plus /'sɜːpləs‖'sɜːr-/ *n, adj* (amount) additional to what is needed or used

sur·prise /sə'praɪz‖sər-/ *n* [C;U] **1** (feeling caused by) an unexpected event **2 take by surprise** come on (someone) unprepared ♦ *vt* **1** cause surprise to **2** find, catch, or attack when unprepared

sur·pris·ing /sə'praɪzɪŋ‖sər-/ *adj* unusual; causing surprise **~ly** *adv*

sur·re·al /sə'rɪəl‖sə-/ *adj* having a strange dreamlike unreal quality **~ism** *n* [U] modern art or literature that treats subjects in a surreal way **~ist** *n* (artist or writer) concerned with surrealism

sur·ren·der /sə'rendə/ *v* **1** *vi/t* give up or give in to the power (esp. of an

enemy); admit defeat **2** *vt fml* give up possession of ♦ *n* [C;U] act of surrendering

sur·rep·ti·tious /,sʌrəp'tɪʃəs/ *adj* done secretly, esp. for dishonest reasons **~ly** *adv*

sur·ro·gate /'sʌrəgeɪt, -gɪt‖'sɜːr-/ *n, adj* (person or thing) acting or used in place of another

sur·round /sə'raʊnd/ *vt* be or go all around on every side ♦ *n* (decorative) edge or border **~ing** *adj* around and nearby **~ings** *n* [P] place and conditions of life

sur·veil·lance /sə'veɪləns‖sər-/ *n* [U] close watch kept on someone or something

sur·vey[1] /sə'veɪ‖sər-/ *vt* **1** look at or examine as a whole **2** examine the condition of (a building) **3** measure (land) **~or** *n* person whose job is to SURVEY[1] (2,3)

survey[2] /'sɜːveɪ‖'sɜːr-/ *n* **1** act of surveying: *a survey of public opinion/of a house* **2** general description

sur·vive /sə'vaɪv‖sər-/ *vi/t* continue to live or exist (after), esp. after coming close to death: *She survived the accident.* **–vival** *n* **1** [U] act of surviving **2** [C] something which has survived from an earlier time **–vivor** *n*

sus·cep·ti·ble /sə'septəbəl/ *adj* **1** easily influenced (by) **2** likely to suffer (from) **–bility** /sə,septə'bɪlɪti/ *n*

sus·pect /sə'spekt/ *vt* **1** believe to be so; think likely: *I suspected he was ill but didn't like to ask him.* **2** believe to be guilty ♦ *n* /'sʌspekt/ person suspected of guilt ♦ *adj* of uncertain truth, quality, legality, etc.

sus·pend /sə'spend/ *vt* **1** *fml* hang from above **2** hold still in liquid or air **3** make inactive for a time: *The meeting was suspended while the lights were repaired.* **4** prevent from taking part for a time, esp. for breaking rules **~er** *n* fastener for holding up a woman's stockings **~ers** *n* [P] *AmE* for BRACES for trousers

sus·pense /sə'spens/ *n* [U] state of uncertainty causing anxiety or pleasant excitement

sus·pen·sion /sə'spenʃən/ *n* **1** [U] act of suspending or fact of being suspended **2** [C] apparatus fixed to a vehicle's wheels to lessen the effect of rough roads

suspension bridge /·'·· ·/ *n* bridge hung from strong steel ropes fixed to towers

sus·pi·cion /sə'spɪʃən/ *n* **1** [U] **a** a case of suspecting or being suspected (SUSPECT (2)): *under suspicion of murder* **b** lack of trust: *treat someone with suspicion* **2 a** a feeling of SUSPECTing: *I have a suspicion you're right.* **b** belief about someone's guilt: *They have their* suspicions. **3** [S] slight amount **–cious** *adj* **1** suspecting guilt or wrongdoing **2** making one suspicious: *suspicious behaviour* **–ciously** *adv*

suss /sʌs/ *vt BrE sl* discover the fact that

suss out *phr vt BrE sl* quietly or secretly find out details about

sus·tain /səˈsteɪn/ *vt* **1** keep strong or keep in existence over a long period **3** *fml* suffer: *The car sustained severe damage.* **4** *fml* hold up (the weight of)

sus·te·nance /ˈsʌstənəns/ *n* [U] *fml* food or its ability to keep people strong and healthy

swab /swɒb‖swɑːb/ *n* piece of material that can take up liquid, esp. used medically ♦ *vt* **-bb-** clean (a wound) with a swab

swag /swæg/ *n* [U] *infml* goods obtained in a robbery

swag·ger /ˈswægəʳ/ *vi* walk or behave (too) confidently or proudly **swagger** *n* [S;U]

swal·low¹ /ˈswɒləʊ‖ˈswɑː-/ *v* **1** *vi/t* move (the contents of the mouth) down the throat **2** *vt* accept patiently or with too easy belief: *It was an obvious lie, but he swallowed it.* **3** *vt* hold back (uncomfortable feelings); not show or express: *swallow one's pride* ♦ *n* act of swallowing or amount swallowed

swallow up *phr vt* take in and cause to disappear

swal·low² *n* small bird with a double-pointed tail

swam /swæm/ *past t. of* SWIM

swamp /swɒmp‖swɑːmp, swɔːmp/ *n* [C;U] (area of) soft wet land ♦ *vt* cause to have (too) much to deal with **~y** *adj* wet like a swamp

swan¹ /swɒn‖swɑːn/ *n* large white long-necked water bird

swan² *vi* **-nn-** *infml* go or travel purposelessly or irresponsibly: *She just swanned off to Italy for the summer.*

swank /swæŋk/ *vi, n* [U] *infml* (act or speak too proudly, making) false or too great claims **~y** *adj infml* very fashionable or expensive

swan-song /ˈswɒnsɒŋ‖ˈswɑːnsɔːŋ/ *n* one's last performance or piece of artistic work

swap /swɒp‖swɑːp/ *vi/t* **-pp-** exchange (goods or positions) so that each person gets what they want ♦ *n* **1** exchange **2** something (to be) exchanged

sward /swɔːd‖swɔːrd/ *n lit* piece of grassy land

swarm /swɔːm‖swɔːrm/ *n* large moving mass of insects: (fig.) *swarms of tourists* ♦ *vi* move in a crowd or mass
swarm with *phr vt* be full of (a moving crowd)

swar·thy /ˈswɔːði‖-ɔːr-/ *adj* having fairly dark skin

swash-buck·ling /ˈswɒʃˌbʌkəlɪŋ‖ˈswɑːʃ-, ˈswɔːʃ-/ *adj* full of showy adventures, sword fighting, etc.

swat /swɒt‖swɑːt/ *vt* **-tt-** hit (an insect), esp. so as to kill it

swathe /sweɪð‖swɑːð, swʌð, sweɪð/ *v* **swathe in** *phr vt* wrap round in (cloth): (fig.) *hills swathed in mist*

sway /sweɪ/ *v* **1** *vi/t* swing from side to side **2** *vt* influence, esp. so as to change opinion ♦ *n* [U] **1** swaying movement **2** *lit* influence

swear /sweəʳ/ *v* **swore** /swɔːʳ/, **sworn** /swɔːn‖swɔːrn/ **1** *vi* curse **2** *vi/t* make a solemn promise or statement, esp. by taking an OATH (1): *She swore to tell the truth/swore that she had been there.* **3** *cause to take an* OATH

swear by *phr vt* have confidence in (something)

swear in *phr vt* **1** cause (a witness) to take the OATH (1) in court **2** cause to make a promise of responsible action, etc.: *The elected President was sworn in.*

sweat /swet/ *n* **1** [U] body liquid that comes out through the skin **2** [S] anxious state **3** [S] *infml* hard work **4 no sweat** *infml* (used for saying that something will not cause any difficulty) ♦ *vi* **1** produce sweat **2** be very anxious or nervously impatient **3** **sweat blood** *infml* work unusually hard **~y** *adj* **1** covered in or smelly with sweat **2** unpleasantly hot

sweated la·bour /ˌ·· ˈ·-/ *n* [U] long hours of work for little money

sweat·er /ˈswetəʳ/ *n* (woollen) garment for the upper body, usu. without fastenings

sweat-shirt /ˈswet-ʃɜːt‖-ɜːrt/ *n* loose cotton garment for the upper body

swede /swiːd/ *n* large round yellow root vegetable

sweep¹ /swiːp/ *v* **swept** /swept/ **1** *vt* clean or remove by brushing **2** *vi/t* move (over) or carry quickly and powerfully: *A wave of panic swept over her.* | *We were swept along by the crowd.* **3** *vi* lie in a curve across land **4** *vt* win completely and easily, as in elections **5** *vi* (of a person) move in a proud, firm manner **6** **sweep someone off their feet** fill someone with sudden love or excitement **7** **sweep something under the carpet** *BrE* ‖ **under the rug** *AmE* keep (something bad or shocking) secret **~er** *n* **~ing** *adj* **1** including many or most things: *sweeping changes* **2** too general: *a sweeping statement*

sweep aside *phr vt* refuse to pay any attention to

sweep² *n* **1** act of sweeping **2** long curved line or area of country: (fig.) *the broad sweep of her narrative* (= covering all parts of the subject) **3** person who cleans chimneys **4** sweepstake

sweep-stake /'swiːpsteɪk/ *n* form of risking money, esp. on a horserace, in which the winner gets all the losers' money

sweet /swiːt/ *adj* **1** tasting like sugar **2** pleasing to the senses: *sweet music* **3** charming; lovable: *What a sweet little boy!* — see also **short and sweet** (SHORT¹) ♦ *n* BrE **1** [C] small piece of food made of sugar, chocolate, etc. **2** [C;U] (dish of) sweet food at the end of a meal — **en** *vt* **1** make sweeter **2** *infml* give money or presents in order to persuade —**ly** *adv* —**ness** *n* [U]

sweet-bread /'swiːtbred/ *n* sheep's or cow's PANCREAS used as food

sweet-en-er /'swiːtnər/ *n* **1** substance used instead of sugar to make food or drink taste sweet **2** *infml* money, a present, etc., given in order to persuade someone

sweet-heart /'swiːthɑːt‖-hɑːrt/ *n* lit person whom one loves

sweet talk /'· ·/ *n* [U] *infml* insincere talk intended to please or persuade — **sweet-talk** /'· ·/ *vt*

sweet tooth /ˌ· '·, '· ·/ *n* [S] liking for sweet and sugary things

swell /swel/ *vi/t* **swelled, swollen** /'swəʊlən/ *or* **swelled 1** increase gradually to beyond the usual or original size **2** fill or be filled, giving a full round shape ♦ *n* [S] rolling up-and-down movement of the surface of the sea ♦ *adj* AmE excellent —**ing** *n* **1** act of swelling **2** swollen place on the body

swel-ter /'sweltər/ *vi* experience the effects of unpleasantly great heat

swept /swept/ *past t. and p. of* SWEEP

swept-back /ˌ· '·◂/ *adj* having the front edge pointing backwards at an angle from the main part

swerve /swɜːv‖swɜːrv/ *vi, n* (make) a sudden change of direction

swift¹ /swɪft/ *adj* quick —**ly** *adv* —**ness** *n* [U]

swift² *n* small brown fast-flying bird like a SWALLOW²

swig /swɪɡ/ *vt* -**gg**- *infml* drink, esp. in large mouthfuls **swig** *n*

swill /swɪl/ *vt* **1** wash with large streams of water **2** *infml* drink, esp. in large amounts ♦ *n* [U] partly liquid pig food

swim /swɪm/ *v* **swam** /swæm/, **swum** /swʌm/; *present p.* -**mm**- **1** *vi* move through water using the limbs, FINs, etc. **2** *vt* cross by doing this **3** *vi* be full of or surrounded with liquid **4** *vi* seem to spin round and round: *My head was*

swimming. **5 swim with the tide** follow the behaviour of other people around one ♦ *n* [S] act of swimming **2 in the swim** knowing about and concerned in what is going on in modern life —**mer** *n*

swimming pool /'·· ·/ *n* large usu. outdoor container filled with water and used for swimming

swin-dle /'swɪndl/ *vi/t* cheat, esp. so as to get money ♦ *n* act of swindling **swindler** *n*

swine /swaɪn/ *n* **swine 1** *fml or lit* pig **2** *sl* unpleasant person

swing /swɪŋ/ *v* **swung** /swʌŋ/ **1** *vi/t* move backwards and forwards or round and round from a fixed point: *Soldiers swing their arms as they march.* **2** *vi/t* move in a smooth curve: *The door swung shut.* **3** *vi* turn quickly **4** *vi* start smoothly and rapidly: *We're ready to swing into action.* **5** *vi infml* be hanged to death, as a punishment **6 not enough room to swing a cat** *infml* very little space ♦ *n* **1** [C] act of swinging **2** [C] children's swinging seat fixed from above by ropes or chains **3** [C] noticeable change: *a big swing in public opinion* **4** [S] JAZZ music of the 1930s and 1940s with a strong regular active beat **5 go with a swing** happen successfully **6 in full swing** having reached a very active stage **7 what you lose on the swings you gain on the roundabouts** (often shortened to **swings and roundabouts**) *infml, esp. BrE* the disadvantages of a particular situation or course of action are balanced by the advantages

swinge-ing /'swɪndʒɪŋ/ *adj esp. BrE* very severe

swipe /swaɪp/ *vt* **1** hit hard **2** *infml* steal ♦ *n* sweeping blow

swirl /swɜːl‖swɜːrl/ *vi/t* move with twisting turns ♦ *n* twisting mass

swish¹ /swɪʃ/ *vi/t* move through the air with a sharp whistling noise ♦ *n* act of swishing

swish² *adj infml* fashionable and expensive

Swiss /swɪs/ *adj* of Switzerland

switch /swɪtʃ/ *n* **1** apparatus for stopping or starting an electric current **2** sudden complete change ♦ *vi/t* change or exchange: *They switched jobs. | The lights have switched to green.*

switch off/on *phr vt* turn (an electric light or apparatus) off/on with a switch

switch over *phr vi* **1** change completely **2** change from one radio or television CHANNEL(3) to another

switch-board /'swɪtʃbɔːd‖-bɔːrd/ *n* place where telephone lines in a large building are connected

swiv-el /'swɪvəl/ *vi/t* **-ll-** *BrE* ‖ **-l-** *AmE* turn round (as if) on a central point

swiz, swizz/swɪz/ *n* [S] *BrE infml* something that makes one feel cheated or disappointed

swiz-zle stick /'swɪzəl ˌstɪk/ *n* rod for mixing drinks

swol-len /'swəʊlən/ *past. p. of* SWELL

swoon /swuːn/ *vi lit* **1** experience deep joy, desire, etc. **2** FAINT

swoop /swuːp/ *vi* come down sharply, esp. to attack **swoop** *n* **1** swooping action **2 at one fell swoop** all at once

swop /swɒp‖swɑːp/ *v, n* SWAP

sword /sɔːd‖sɔːrd/ *n* **1** weapon with a long sharp metal blade and a handle **2 cross swords (with)** be opposed to (to), esp. in argument

swords-man /'sɔːdzmən‖-ɔːr-/ *n* **-men** /-mən/ (skilled) fighter with a sword ~**ship** *n* [U]

swore /swɔːʳ/ *past t. of* SWEAR

sworn /swɔːn‖swɔːrn/ *past p. of* SWEAR

swot /swɒt‖swɑːt/ *vi* **-tt-** *BrE infml* study hard, esp. to get good examination results ♦ *n derog* person who swots

swum /swʌm/ *past p. of* SWIM

swung /swʌŋ/ *past t. and p. of* SWING

syb-a-rit-ic /ˌsɪbə'rɪtɪk/ *adj fml* being or liking great and expensive comfort, physical pleasures, etc.

syc-o-phant /'sɪkəfənt/ *n* person who praises people insincerely to gain personal advantage ~**ic** /ˌsɪkə-'fæntɪk/ *adj* ~**ically** /-kli/ *adv* –**phancy** *n* [U]

syl-la-ble /'sɪləbəl/ *n* part of a word containing a single vowel sound: *There are two syllables in 'window': 'win-' and '-dow'.* **–labic** /sɪ'læbɪk/ *adj*

syl-la-bus /'sɪləbəs/ *n* arrangement of subjects for study over a period of time

syl-lo-gis-m /'sɪlədʒɪzəm/ *n* arrangement of 2 statements which must lead to a third

sylph-like /'sɪlf-laɪk/ *adj* (of a woman) gracefully thin

syl-van /'sɪlvən/ *adj lit* of or in the woods

sym-bi-o-sis /ˌsɪmbi'əʊsəs‖-baɪ-, -bi-/ *n* [U] condition in which one living thing depends on another for existence –**otic** /-'ɒtɪk‖-'ɑːtɪk/ *adj*

sym-bol /'sɪmbəl/ *n* something that represents something else: *The dove is the symbol of peace.* ~**ism** *n* [U] use of symbols ~**ize** *vt* represent by or as a symbol –**ic** /sɪm'bɒlɪk‖-'bɑː-/ *adj* representing: *The snake is symbolic of evil.* ~**ically** /-kli/ *adv*

sym-me-try /'sɪmətri/ *n* [U] **1** exact likeness in size, shape, etc., between opposite sides **2** effect of pleasing balance **symmetrical** /sɪ'metrɪkəl/ *adj*

sym-pa-thy /'sɪmpəθi/ *n* [U] **1** sensitivity to and pity for others' suffering **2** agreement and/or understanding: *I am in sympathy with their aims.* **3 come out in sympathy** support workers who have gone on STRIKE² (1) by stopping work oneself –**thize** *vt* feel or show sympathy **sympathies** *n* [P] feelings of support or loyalty –**thetic** /ˌsɪmpə'θetɪk/ *adj* feeling or showing sympathy –**thetically** /-kli/ *adv*

sym-pho-ny /'sɪmfəni/ *n* usu. 4-part piece of music for an ORCHESTRA

sym-po-si-um /sɪm'pəʊziəm/ *n* **-ums** *or* **-a** /-ziə/ meeting to talk about a subject of study

symp-tom /'sɪmptəm/ *n* **1** outward sign of a disease **2** outward sign of inner change, new feelings; etc. ~**atic** /ˌsɪmptə'mætɪk/ *adj* being a symptom

syn-a-gogue /'sɪnəgɒg‖-gɔːg/ *n* building where Jews worship

syn-chro-nize ‖ *also* **-nise** *BrE* /'sɪŋkrənaɪz/ *vt* **1** cause to happen at the same time or speed **2** cause (watches, etc.) to show the same time –**nization** /ˌsɪŋkrənaɪ'zeɪʃən‖-krənə-/ *n* [U]

syn-co-pate /'sɪŋkəpeɪt/ *vt* change (the beat of music) by giving force to the beats that are usu. less forceful –**pation** /ˌsɪŋkə'peɪʃən/ *n* [U]

syn-di-cate¹ /'sɪndɪkət/ *n* group of people or companies combined for usu. business purposes

syn-di-cate² /'sɪndɪkeɪt/ *vt* sell (written work, pictures, etc.) to many different newspapers or magazines

syn-drome /'sɪndrəʊm/ *n* **1** set of medical SYMPTOMs which represent an illness **2** any pattern of qualities, happenings, etc., typical of a general condition

syn-o-nym /'sɪnənɪm/ *n* word with the same meaning as another ~**ous** /sɪ'nɒnɪməs‖-'nɑː-/ *adj*

sy-nop-sis /sɪ'nɒpsəs‖-'nɑːp-/ *n* short account of something longer

syn-tax /'sɪntæks/ *n* [U] way in which words are ordered and connected in sentences –**tactic** /sɪn'tæktɪk/ *adj*

syn-the-sis /'sɪnθəsəs/ *n* **-ses** /-siːz/ **1** [U] combining of separate things, ideas, etc., into a complete whole **2** [C] something made by synthesis –**size** *vt* make by synthesis, esp. make (something similar to a natural product) by combining chemicals –**sizer** *n* electrical instrument, like a piano, that can produce many sorts of different sounds, used esp. in popular music

syn-thet-ic /sɪn'θetɪk/ *adj* artificial ~**ally** /-kli/ *adv*

syph·i·lis /'sɪfəlɪs/ n [U] very serious VENEREAL DISEASE

sy·phon /'saɪfən/ n, v SIPHON

sy·ringe /sɪ'rɪndʒ/ n (medical) instrument with a hollow tube for sucking in and pushing out liquid, esp. through a needle ♦ vt clean with a syringe

syr·up /'sɪrəp‖'sɜː-, 'sɪ-/ n [U] sweet liquid, esp. sugar and water

sys·tem /'sɪstəm/ n 1 [C] group of related parts which work together forming a whole: the postal system | the digestive system 2 [C] ordered set of ideas, methods, or ways of working: the American system of government 3 [C] the body, thought of as a set of working parts: Travelling always upsets my system. 4 [U] orderly methods 5 [the + S] society seen as something which uses and limits individuals: to fight the system — see also EXPERT SYSTEM, OPERATING SYSTEM ~**atic** /,sɪstə'mætɪk/ adj based on orderly methods and careful organization; thorough ~**atically** /-kli/ adv

systems an·a·lyst /'·· ,··/ n someone who studies (esp. business) activities and uses computers to plan ways of carrying them out, etc.

T

T, t /tiː/ the 20th letter of the English alphabet

ta /tɑː/ interj BrE sl thank you

tab /tæb/ n 1 small piece of paper, cloth, metal, etc., fixed to something to hold it by, open it with, etc. 2 **keep tabs on** watch closely

tab·by /'tæbi/ n cat with dark and light bands of fur

tab·er·nac·le /'tæbənækəl‖-ər-/ n container for religious objects

ta·ble /'teɪbəl/ n 1 piece of furniture with a flat top on upright legs 2 set of figures arranged in rows across and down a page 3 **turn the tables on** gain an advantage over (someone who had an advantage over you) see also WATER TABLE ♦ vt 1 BrE put forward for consideration by a committee, etc. 2 AmE leave until a later date for consideration

tab·leau /'tæbləʊ‖'tæbləʊ, tæ'bləʊ/ n scene on stage shown by a group of people who do not move or speak

ta·ble d'hôte /,tɑːbəl 'dəʊt/ n complete meal at a fixed price

ta·ble·spoon /'teɪbəlspuːn/ n large spoon for serving food

tab·let /'tæblɪt/ n 1 small solid piece of medicine 2 small block (of soap) 3 flat piece of stone or metal with words on it

table ten·nis /'·· ,·'·/ n [U] indoor game in which a small ball is hit across a net on a table

tab·loid /'tæblɔɪd/ n newspaper with small pages and many pictures

ta·boo /tə'buː, tæ'buː/ n -**boos** [C;U] strong social or religious custom forbidding something ♦ adj strongly forbidden by social custom: taboo words

tab·u·late /'tæbjʊt/ vt arrange as a TABLE (2) -**lar** adj -**lation** /,tæbjʊ'leɪʃən/ n [U]

ta·cit /'tæsɪt/ adj accepted or understood without being openly expressed: tacit approval ~**ly** adv

ta·ci·turn /'tæsɪtɜːn‖-ɜːrn/ adj tending to speak very little

tack /tæk/ n 1 small nail 2 sailing ship's direction: (fig.) He switched the conversation onto a new tack. 3 long loose stitch ♦ v 1 vt fasten with tacks 2 vi change the course of a sailing ship

tack·le /'tækəl/ n 1 [C] act of stopping or taking the ball away from an opponent in sport 2 [U] apparatus used in certain sports: fishing tackle 3 [C;U] (system of) ropes and wheels for heavy pulling and lifting ♦ v 1 vt take action in order to deal with 2 vt speak to fearlessly so as to deal with a problem 3 vi/t stop or rob with a TACKLE (1)

tack·y /'tæki/ adj 1 sticky 2 of low quality: a tacky hotel/remark (= in bad TASTE (3)) -**iness** n [U]

tact /tækt/ n [U] skill of speaking or acting without offending people ~**ful** adj ~**fully** adv ~**less** adj ~**lessly** adv

tac·tic /'tæktɪk/ n plan or method for gaining a desired result **tactics** n [U] art of arranging and moving military forces in battle **tactical** adj 1 of tactics 2 done to get a desired result in the end: a tactical retreat **tactician** /tæk'tɪʃən/ n person skilled in tactics

tac·tile /'tæktaɪl‖'tæktl/ adj of or able to be felt by the sense of touch

tad·pole /'tædpəʊl/ n small creature that grows into a FROG or TOAD

tag /tæg/ n 1 [C] small piece of paper or material fixed to something to show who owns it, its cost, etc. 2 [U] game in which one child chases the others until he/she touches one of them ♦ vt -**gg**- 1 fasten a tag to 2 provide with a name or NICKNAME

tag along phr vi go with someone by following closely behind

tag on *phr vt* add

tail[1] /teɪl/ *n* **1** long movable growth at the back of a creature's body **2** last or back part (of something long): *the tail of an aircraft/a queue* **3** person employed to follow someone ♦ **turn tail** turn round ready to run away

tails *n* [P] **1** side of a coin without a ruler's head on it **2** tailcoat

tail[2] *vt* follow (someone) closely, esp. without their knowledge

tail away/off *phr vi* lessen gradually

tail-back /'teɪlbæk/ *n* line of traffic stretching back from where its flow has been halted

tail-coat /teɪl'kəʊt, 'teɪlkəʊt/ *n* man's coat with a long back divided into 2 below the waist

tai-lor /'teɪlər/ *n* person who makes outer garments for men ♦ *vt* fit to a particular need ~**made** *adj* exactly right for a particular need, person, etc.

tail-wind /'teɪl wɪnd/ *n* wind coming from behind

taint /teɪnt/ *vt, n* [S] (spoil with) a small amount of decay, infection, or bad influence

take[1] /teɪk/ *v* **took** /tʊk/, **taken** /'teɪkən/ **1** *vt* move from one place to another: *Take the chair into the garden.*|*Take the children with you.*|*I had a tooth taken out.* **2** *vt* remove without permission: *Someone's taken my pen.* **3** *vt* subtract: *What do you get if you take 5 from 12?* **4** *vt* get possession of; seize: *Rebels have taken the airport.* **5** *vt* get by performing an action: *Take his temperature.*|*He took notes.*|*Take a seat.* **6** *vt* start to hold: *She took my arm.* **7** *vt* use for travel: *I take the train to work.* **8** *vt* be willing to accept: *Will you take a cheque?* **9** *vt* accept as true or worthy of attention: *Take my advice.*|*I took his suggestion seriously.* **10** *vt* be able to contain: *The bus takes 55 passengers.* **11** *vt* be able to accept; bear: *I can't take his rudeness.* **12** *vt* need: *The journey takes (= lasts) 2 hours.*|*It took 10 men to pull down the wall.* **13** *vt* do; perform: *He took a walk/a bath.* **14** *vt* put into the body: *take some medicine/a deep breath* **15** *vt* make by photography **16** *vt* have (a feeling): *take offence/pity* **17** *vi* have the intended effect; work: *Did the vaccination take?* **18** *vt* attract; delight: *The little house took my fancy.* **19** *vt* understand: *I take it you know each other.* **20** **be taken ill** become (suddenly) ill **21** **take it easy** *infml* RELAX **22** **take one's time: a** use as much time as is necessary **b** use too much time **23** **take something as read** agree on something without needing to talk about it

take aback *phr vt* surprise and confuse

take after *phr vt* look or behave like (an older relative)

take apart *phr vt* **1** separate into pieces **2** *sl* harm a place or person

take back *phr vt* **1** admit that (what one said) was wrong **2** cause to remember a former period in one's life: *That takes me back!*

take in *phr vt* **1** reduce the size of (a garment) **2** provide lodgings for **3** include **4** understand fully **5** deceive

take off *phr vt* **1** *vt* remove (a garment) **2** *vi* (of a plane, etc.) rise into the air to begin a flight **3** *vi* leave without warning: *One day he just took off.* **4** *vt* copy the speech or manners of; MIMIC **5** *vt* have as a holiday from work: *I took Tuesday off.*

take on *phr vt* **1** start to employ **2** begin to have (a quality or appearance) **3** start to quarrel or fight with **4** accept (work, responsibility, etc.)

take out *phr vt* **1** go somewhere with (someone) as a social activity **2** obtain officially: *take out insurance* **3** **take someone out of himself** amuse or interest someone so that their worries are forgotten **4** **take it out of someone** use all the strength of someone

take out on *phr vt* express (one's feelings) by making (someone) suffer: *He tends to take things out on his wife.*

take over *phr vi/t* gain control of and responsibility for (something)

take to *phr vt* **1** like, esp. at once **2** begin a practice or habit: *He took to drink.* **3** go to (one's bed, etc.) for rest, escape, etc.

take up *phr vt* **1** begin to interest oneself in: *I've taken up the guitar.* **2** complain, ask, or take further action about: *I'll take the matter up with my lawyer.* **3** fill or use (space or time), esp. undesirably **4** accept (someone's) offer: *I'll take you up on that.* **5** continue (a story, etc.)

take up with *phr vt* **1** become friendly with **2** be very interested in: *She's very taken up with her work.*

take[2] *n* **1** filming of a scene **2** takings

take-a-way /'teɪkəweɪ/ *n BrE* (meal from) a restaurant that sells food to eat elsewhere

take-off /'teɪk ɒf‖-ɔːf/ *n* **1** [C;U] rising of a plane, etc., from the ground **2** amusing copy of someone's typical behaviour

take-o-ver /'teɪk ˌəʊvər/ *n* act of gaining control of esp. a business company

ta-ker /'teɪkər/ *n* [*usu. pl.*] *infml* person willing to accept an offer

tak-ings /'teɪkɪŋz/ *n* [P] money received, esp. by a shop

tal·cum pow·der /'tælkəm ˌpaudəʳ/ also **talc** /tælk/ infml—n [U] crushed mineral put on the body to dry it or make it smell nice

tale /teɪl/ n 1 story 2 false story; lie

tal·ent /'tælənt/ n [S;U] special natural ability or skill **~ed** adj

tal·is·man /'tælɪzmən/ n -s object with magic protective powers

talk /tɔːk/ v 1 vi speak: Can the baby talk yet? Is there somewhere quiet where we can talk? 2 vi give information by speaking, usu. unwillingly: We have ways of making you talk. 3 vi speak about others' affairs; GOSSIP 4 vt speak about: It's time to talk business. ♦ n 1 [S] conversation 2 [C] informal LECTURE 3 [U] way of talking: baby talk 4 [the + S] subject much talked about: Her sudden marriage is the talk of the street. 5 [U] empty or meaningless speech — see also SMALL TALK, SWEET TALK **talks** n [P] formal exchange of opinions **~er** n

talk down to phr vt speak to (someone) as if one were more important, clever, etc.

talk into/out of phr vt persuade (someone) to do/not to do (something)

talk over phr vt speak about thoroughly and seriously

talk round phr vt persuade (someone) to change their mind

talk·a·tive /'tɔːkətɪv/ adj liking to talk a lot

talking point /'··· ·/ n subject of conversation or argument

talking-to /'··· ·/ n angry talk in order to blame or CRITICIZE

tall /tɔːl/ adj 1 of greater than average height 2 of the stated height from top to bottom: He is 6 feet tall.

tall or·der /ˌ· '··/ n [S] something unreasonably difficult to do

tal·low /'tæləʊ/ n [U] hard animal fat used for candles

tall sto·ry /ˌ· '··/ n story that is difficult to believe

tal·ly /'tæli/ n recorded total of money spent, points made in a game, etc. ♦ vi be exactly equal; match

tal·on /'tælən/ n sharp powerful curved nail on a hunting bird's foot

tam·bou·rine /ˌtæmbə'riːn/ n drumlike musical instrument with small metal plates round the edge

tame /teɪm/ adj 1 not fierce or wild 2 dull; unexciting ♦ vt make (an animal) tame **~ly** adv **~ness** n [U] **tamer** n

tam·per /'tæmpəʳ/ v **tamper with** phr vt touch or change without permission, esp. causing damage

tam·pon /'tæmpɒn‖-pɑːn/ n mass of cotton put into a woman's sex organ to take up the monthly bleeding

tan /tæn/ v -nn- 1 vt change (animal skin) into leather by treating with TANNIN 2 vi/t turn brown, esp. by sunlight ♦ n 1 [C] brown skin colour from sunlight 2 [U] yellowish brown colour

tan·dem /'tændəm/ n 1 bicycle for 2 riders 2 **in tandem** with both working closely together

tan·doo·ri /tæn'dʊəri/n [C;U] (meat cooked by) an Indian method of cooking in a big clay pot

tang /tæŋ/ n strong sharp taste or smell **~y** adj

tan·gent /'tændʒənt/ n 1 straight line touching the edge of a curve 2 **go/fly off at a tangent** change suddenly to a different course of action or thought

tan·ge·rine /ˌtændʒə'riːn‖'tændʒə-riːn/ n sort of small orange

tan·gi·ble /'tændʒəbəl/ adj 1 clear and certain; real: tangible proof 2 touchable **~bly** adv

tan·gle /'tæŋgəl/ vi/t (cause to) become a confused mass of twisted threads ♦ n confused mass or state

tan·go /'tæŋgəʊ/ n -gos American dance

tank /tæŋk/ n 1 large liquid or gas container 2 enclosed armoured military vehicle

tan·kard /'tæŋkəd‖-ərd/ n large usu. metal cup for beer, etc.

tank·er /'tæŋkəʳ/ n ship, road vehicle, etc., carrying large quantities of liquid or gas

tan·nin /'tænɪn/ n [U] reddish acid found in parts of certain plants

Tan·noy /'tænɔɪ/ n tdmk, esp. BrE system of LOUDSPEAKERs for public information

tan·ta·lize, -lise /'tæntəl-aɪz/ vt cause to desire something even more strongly by keeping it just out of reach

tan·ta·mount /'tæntəmaʊnt/ adj having the same effect (as): Her answer is tantamount to a refusal.

tan·trum /'tæntrəm/ n sudden uncontrolled attack of angry bad temper

tap¹ /tæp/ 1 turnable apparatus for controlling the flow of water, etc., from a pipe, barrel, etc. 2 **on tap** ready for use when needed

tap² vt -pp- 1 use or draw from: tapping our reserves of oil 2 listen secretly by making an illegal connection to (a telephone)

tap³ vi/t, n -pp- (strike with) a light short blow: She tapped her fingers on the table/tapped me on the shoulder.

tap dance /'· ˌ·/ n dance in which one makes loud sounds on the floor with special shoes

tape /teɪp/ n [C;U] 1 (long piece of) narrow material: fastening a parcel with sticky tape **2** (long piece of) narrow plastic MAGNETIC material on which sounds or pictures are recorded ♦ *vt* **1** record on TAPE (2) **2** fasten or tie with TAPE (1) **3 have something taped** *infml* understand something thoroughly or have learnt how to deal with it

tape mea·sure /'·ˌ··/ *n* narrow band of cloth or bendable metal used for measuring

ta·per /'teɪpər/ *vi/t* make or become gradually narrower towards one end ♦ *n* thin candle

tape re·cord·er /'·ˌ·ˌ··/ *n* electrical apparatus for recording and playing sound with TAPE (2)

tap·es·try /'tæpəstri/ *n* [C;U] (piece of) cloth with pictures or patterns woven into it

tar /tɑː/ *n* [U] black meltable substance used for making roads, preserving wood, etc. ♦ *vt* **-rr- 1** cover with tar **2 tarred with the same brush** having the same faults

ta·ran·tu·la /təˈræntjʊlə/ ‖-tʃələ/ *n* large poisonous SPIDER

tar·dy /'tɑːdi‖'tɑːrdi/ *adj fml or lit* **1** slow in acting or happening **2** *AmE* late **–dily** *adv* **–diness** *n*

tar·get /'tɑːɡɪt‖'tɑːr-/ *n* **1** something aimed at in shooting practice **2** place, thing, or person at which an attack is directed **3** total or object which one tries to reach: *a production target of 500 cars a week* ♦ *vt* cause to be a target

tar·iff /'tærɪf/ *n* **1** tax on goods coming into a country **2** *fml* list of prices in a hotel, restaurant, etc.

tar·mac /'tɑːmæk‖'tɑːr-/ *n* [U] **1** tar and small stones for making road surfaces **2** area where aircraft take off and land

tar·nish /'tɑːnɪʃ‖'tɑːr-/ *vi/t* make or become discoloured and less bright: *tarnished silver*/(fig.) *reputations*

tar·ot /'tærəʊ/ *n* set of 22 special cards used for telling the future

tar·pau·lin /tɑːˈpɔːlɪn‖tɑːr-/ *n* [C;U] (sheet or cover of) heavy WATERPROOF cloth

tar·ry /'tæri/ *vi lit* stay in a place for a while

tart[1] /tɑːt‖tɑːrt/ *v* **tart up** *phr vt infml derog* decorate or dress someone or something in a cheap colourful way

tart[2] *adj* bitter ♦ **~ness** *n* [U]

tart[3] *n* sexually immoral woman

tart[4] *n BrE* pastry container holding fruit or JAM

tar·tan /'tɑːtn‖'tɑːrtn/ *n* [C;U] (woollen cloth with) a pattern of bands crossing each other, esp. representing a particular Scottish CLAN

tar·tar[1] /'tɑːtər‖'tɑːr-/ *n* [U] chalklike substance that forms on teeth

tar·tar[2] *n infml* fierce person with a violent temper

task /tɑːsk‖tæsk/ *n* **1** piece of (hard) work (to be) done **2 take someone to task** speak severely to someone for a fault or failure

task force /'· ·/ *n* military or police group set up for a special purpose

task·mas·ter /'tɑːsk,mɑːstər‖ 'tæsk,mæstər/ , **-mistress** *fem.—n* someone who makes people work very hard

tas·sel /'tæsəl/ *n* tied bunch of threads hung decoratively

taste /teɪst/ *n* **1** [C;U] quality by which a food or drink is recognized in the mouth: *Sugar has a sweet taste.* **2** [U] sense which recognizes food or drink as sweet, salty, etc. **3** [U] ability to make (good) judgments about beauty, style, fashion, etc. **4** [C;U] personal liking: *She has expensive tastes in clothes.* ♦ *v* **1** *vt* experience or test the taste of **2** *vi* have a particular taste: *These oranges taste nice.* **3** *vt lit* experience: *having tasted freedom* **~ful** *adj* showing good TASTE (3) **~less** *adj* **1** not tasting of anything **2** showing bad TASTE (3) **tasty** *adj* pleasant-tasting

taste bud /'· ·/ *n* group of cells on the tongue used in tasting

tat /tæt/ *n* [U] *BrE sl* something of very low quality

ta·ta /tæˈtɑː/ *interj esp. BrE* goodbye

tat·ters /'tætəz‖-ərz/ *n* **in tatters: a** (of clothes) old and torn **b** ruined **–tered** *adj* (dressed in clothes that are) in tatters

tat·too[1] /təˈtuː, tæˈtuː/ *n* **-toos** pattern made by tattooing ♦ *vt* make (a pattern) on the skin (of) by pricking with a needle and then pouring coloured DYEs in **~ist** *n*

tat·too[2] *n* **-toos 1** outdoor military show with music **2** fast beating of drums

tat·ty /'tæti/ *adj sl. esp. BrE* untidy or in bad condition

taught /tɔːt/ *past t. & p. of* TEACH

taunt /tɔːnt/ *vt* try to upset with unkind remarks or by laughing at faults or failures ♦ *n* taunting remark

taut /tɔːt/ *adj* stretched tight **~ly** *adv* **~ness** *n* [U]

tau·tol·o·gy /tɔːˈtɒlədʒi‖tɔːˈtɑː-/ *n* [C;U] unnecessary repeating of the same idea in different words **–gical** /ˌtɔːtəˈlɒdʒɪkəl‖-ˈlɑː-/ *adj*

tav·ern /'tævən‖-ərn/ *n lit* pub

taw·dry /'tɔːdri/ *adj* cheaply showy; showing bad TASTE (3) **–driness** *n* [U]

taw·ny /'tɔːni/ *adj* brownish yellow

tax /tæks/ *n* [C;U] money which must be paid to the government ♦ *vt* **1** make (someone) pay a tax **2** charge a tax on: *Cigarettes are heavily taxed.* **3**

push to the limits of what one can bear: *Such stupid questions tax my patience.* ~**able** *adj* that can be TAXed (2) ~**ing** /'tæksɪŋ/ *adj* needing great effort ~**ation** /tæk'seɪʃən/ *n* [U] (money raised by) taxing

tax-de-duc-ti-ble /ˌ· ·'····◂/ *adj* that may legally be subtracted from one's total income before it is taxed

tax-i[1] /'tæksi/ *n* car with a driver which can be hired

taxi[2] *vi* (of an aircraft) move along the ground before taking off or after landing

tax-i-der-my /'tæksədɜːmi‖-ɜr-/ *n* [U] filling the skins of dead animals so that they look real ~**mist** *n*

taxi rank /'··· ·/ *n* place where taxis wait to be hired

TB /ˌtiː 'biː/ *abbrev. for:* TUBERCULOSIS

tea /tiː/ *n* [C;U] **1** (drink made by pouring boiling water onto) the dried cut-up leaves of an Asian bush **2** drink made like tea from the stated leaves: *mint tea* **3** (esp. in Britain) small afternoon meal — see also HIGH TEA **4 one's cup of tea** the sort of thing one likes: *Running isn't really my cup of tea.*

tea-bag /'tiːbæg/ *n* small paper bag full of tea leaves

teach /tiːtʃ/ *v* **taught** /tɔːt/ *vi/t* give knowledge or skill of (something) to (someone): *He taught me French.* **2** *vt* show (someone) the bad results of doing something: *I'll teach you to be rude to me!* (= a threat) ~**er** *n* person who teaches, esp. as a job ~**ing** *n* [U] **1** job of a teacher **2** also **teachings** *pl.* — moral beliefs taught by someone of historical importance: *the teachings of Christ*

teach-in /'· ·/ *n* organized exchange of opinions about a subject of interest

teak /tiːk/ *n* [U] hard yellowish brown wood from Asia, used for furniture

team[1] /tiːm/ *n* **1** group of people who work or esp. play together: *a football team* **2** 2 or more animals pulling the same vehicle

team[2] *v* **team up** *phr vi* work together for a shared purpose

team-ster /'tiːmstər/ *n AmE* TRUCK driver

team-work /'tiːmwɜːk‖-wɜrk/ *n* [U] (effective) combined effort

tea-pot /'tiː-pɒt‖-pɑːt/ *n* container in which tea is made and served

tear[1] /teər/ *v* **tore**/tɔːr/, **torn** /tɔːn‖ tɔːrn/ **1** *vt* pull apart by force, esp. so as to leave irregular edges **2** *vi* become torn **3** *vt* remove with sudden force: *He tore off his clothes.* **4** *vi* rush excitedly **5 be torn between** be unable to

decide between ♦ *n* hole made by tearing

tear down *phr vt* pull down; destroy

tear up *phr vt* destroy completely by tearing

tear[2] /tɪər/ *n* **1** drop of salty liquid that flows from the eye, esp. because of sadness **2 in tears** crying ~**ful** *adj* ~**fully** *adv*

tear-a-way /'teərəweɪ/ *n BrE* noisy, sometimes violent young person

tear gas /'tɪə gæs‖'tɪər-/ *n* [U] gas that stings the eyes

tear-jerk-er /'tɪəˌdʒɜːkər‖'tɪr-ˌdʒɜr-/ *n* very sad book, film, etc.

tease /tiːz/ *v* **1** *vi/t* make jokes (about) or laugh (at) unkindly or playfully **2** *vt* annoy on purpose **3** *vt* separate the threads in (wool, etc.) ♦ *n* someone fond of teasing **teaser** *n* difficult question

tea-spoon /'tiːspuːn/ *n* small spoon

teat /tiːt/ *n* **1** rubber object through which a baby sucks milk, etc., from a bottle **2** animal's NIPPLE

tea tow-el /'· ˌ··/ *n* cloth for drying washed cups, plates, etc.

tech /tek/ *n* TECHNICAL COLLEGE — see also HIGH TECH

tech-ni-cal /'teknɪkəl/ *adj* **1** concerned with scientific or industrial subjects or skills **2** needing special knowledge in order to be understood: *His arguments are rather too technical for me.* **3** according to an (unreasonably) exact acceptance of the rules ~**ly** /-kli/ *adv*

technical col-lege /'··· ˌ··/ *n* (esp. in Britain) college teaching practical subjects

tech-ni-cal-i-ty /ˌteknɪ'kæləti/ *n* small (esp. unimportant) detail or rule

tech-ni-cian /tek'nɪʃən/ *n* highly skilled scientific or industrial worker

tech-nique /tek'niːk/ *n* method of doing an activity that needs skill

tech-no-crat /'teknəkræt/ *n often derog* scientist or technician in charge of an organization

tech-nol-o-gy /tek'nɒlədʒi‖-'nɑː-/ *n* practical science, esp. as used in industrial production ~**gist** *n* ~**gical** /ˌteknə'lɒdʒɪkəl‖-'lɑː-/ *adj*

ted-dy bear /'tedi beər/ also **teddy** *infml*—*n* toy bear

te-di-ous /'tiːdiəs/ *adj* long and uninteresting ~**ly** *adv* ~**ness** *n* [U]

te-di-um /'tiːdiəm/ *n* [U] state of being tedious

tee /tiː/ *n* small object on which a GOLF ball is placed to be hit ♦ *v*

tee off *phr vi* drive the ball from a tee

tee up *phr vi/t* place (the ball) on a tee

teem /tiːm/ *vi BrE* (of rain) fall very heavily

teem with *phr vt* have (a type of creature) present in great numbers

teen-ag-er /'ti:neɪdʒəʳ/ *n* person of between 13 and 19 years old **teenage** *adj*

teens /ti:nz/ *n* [P] period of being a teenager

tee-ny wee-ny /ˌti:ni 'wi:ni◄/ *adj infml* extremely small

tee-ter /'ti:təʳ/ *vi* stand or move unsteadily

teeter-tot-ter /'·· ˌ··/ *n AmE for* SEE-SAW (1)

teeth /ti:θ/ *pl. of* TOOTH

teethe /ti:ð/ *vi* (of a baby) grow teeth

teething troub-les /'·· ˌ··/ *n* [P] problems in the early stages of using something

tee-to-tal /ˌti:'təʊtl◄/ *adj* drinking no alcohol ~**ler** *n*

Tef-lon /'teflɒn‖-lɑ:n/ *n tdmk* [U] artificial substance to which things will not stick, used on kitchen pans, etc.

tel-e-com-mu-ni-ca-tions /ˌteli-kəmju:nɪˈkeɪʃənz/ *n* [P] sending and receiving of messages by means of radio, telephone, SATELLITE, etc.

tel-e-gram /'telɪgræm/ *n* message sent by telegraph

tel-e-graph /'telɪgrɑ:f‖-græf/ *n* [U] method of sending messages along wire by electric signals ♦ *vt* send a telegraph ~**ic** /ˌtelɪˈgræfɪk◄/ *adj*

telegraph pole /'··· ˌ·/ *n* pole for supporting telephone wires

te-lep-a-thy /tɪˈlepəθi/ *n* [U] sending of messages directly from one mind to another –**thic** /ˌteliˈpæθɪk/ *adj*

tel-e-phone /'telɪfəʊn/ *n* [C;U] (apparatus for) the sending and receiving of sounds over long distances by electric means ♦ *vi/t* (try to) speak (to) by telephone

te-leph-o-nist /tɪˈlefənɪst/ *n* person whose job is to make telephone connections

tel-e-pho-to lens /ˌtelɪˈfəʊtəʊ 'lenz/ *n* special LENS used for photographing very distant objects

tel-e-scope /'telɪskəʊp/ *n* tube with a special piece of glass in it for looking at very distant objects ♦ *vi/t* shorten, esp. **a** by one part sliding over another **b** by crushing –**scopic** /ˌtelɪˈskɒpɪk‖-ˈskɑ:-/ *adj* 1 of or related to a telescope 2 that telescopes

tel-e-text /'telitekst/ *n* [U] system of broadcasting written information (e.g. news) on television

tel-e-vise /'telɪvaɪz/ *vt* broadcast on television

tel-e-vi-sion /'telɪˌvɪʒən, ˌtelɪˈvɪʒən/ *n* [C;U] (apparatus for receiving) the broadcasting of pictures and sounds by electric waves

tel-ex /'teleks/ *n* 1 [U] method of sending written messages round the world by telephone wires, SATELLITES, etc. 2 [C] message sent by telex ♦ *vt* send by telex

tell /tel/ *v* told /təʊld/ 1 *vt* make (something) known to (someone) in words: *Are you telling me the truth?| Tell me how to do it.* 2 *vt* warn; advise: *I told you it wouldn't work.* 3 *vt* order: *I told him to do it.* 4 *vi/t* find out; know: *How can you tell which button to press?| It was so dark that I couldn't tell if it was you.* 5 **all told** when all have been counted 6 **tell the time** read the time from a watch or clock 7 **there's no telling** it is impossible to know 8 **you're telling me** (used as a strong way of saying) I know this already

tell against *phr vt* count in judgment against

tell off *phr vt* speak severely to (someone who has done something wrong)

tell on *phr vt* 1 have a bad effect on 2 *infml* (used esp. by children) inform against (someone)

tell-er /'teləʳ/ *n* 1 bank clerk 2 person who counts votes

tell-ing /'telɪŋ/ *adj* sharply effective: *a telling argument*

tell-tale /'telteɪl/ *adj* being a small sign that shows something: *a few telltale hairs on the murderer's sleeve*

tel-ly /'teli/ *n sl* television

te-me-ri-ty /tɪˈmerɪti/ *n* [U] *fml* foolish confidence; rashness

temp /temp/ *n infml* secretary employed for a short time ♦ *vi infml, esp. BrE* work as a temp

tem-per /'tempəʳ/ *n* 1 [C] state of mind; MOOD: *He's in a good/bad temper.* 2 [C;U] angry or impatient state of mind 3 **keep one's temper** stay calm 4 **lose one's temper** become angry ♦ *vt* 1 harden (esp. metal) by special treatment 2 make less severe: *justice tempered with mercy*

tem-pe-ra-ment /'tempərəmənt/ *n* person's character with regard to being calm, easily excited, etc. ~**al** /ˌtempərəˈmentl◄/ *adj* 1 having or showing frequent changes of temper 2 caused by temperament ~**ally** *adv*

tem-pe-rance /'tempərəns/ *n* [U] 1 *fml* being TEMPERATE (2) 2 complete avoiding of alcohol

tem-pe-rate /'tempərɪt/ *adj* 1 (of an area's weather) neither very hot nor very cold 2 *fml* avoiding too much of anything

tem-pe-ra-ture /'tempərətʃəʳ/ *n* 1 [C;U] degree of heat or coldness: *the average temperature* 2 [S] bodily temperature higher than the correct one; fever

tem·pest /'tempɪst/ n lit violent storm

tem·pes·tu·ous /tem'pestʃuəs/ adj full of wildness or anger

tem·plate /'templeɪt,-plət/ n shape used as a guide for cutting metal, wood, etc.

tem·ple[1] /'templ/ n building where people worship a god or gods, esp. in the Hindu and Buddhist religions

temple[2] n flattish area on each side of the forehead

tem·po /'tempəʊ/ n -pos 1 rate of movement or activity 2 speed of music

tem·po·ral /'tempərəl/ adj fml 1 of practical rather than religious affairs 2 of time

tem·po·ra·ry /'tempərəri, -pəri‖-pəreri/ adj lasting for only a limited time —**rily** adv

tempt /tempt/ vt (try to) persuade (someone) to do something wrong ~**ation** /temp'teɪʃən/ n 1 [U] act of tempting 2 [C] something that tempts, esp. by being very attractive ~**ing** adj very attractive

ten /ten/ determiner, n, pron 10

ten·a·ble /'tenəbəl/ adj 1 (of a point of view, etc.) that can be reasonably supported or held 2 (of a job) that can be held for the stated period

te·na·cious /tɪ'neɪʃəs/ adj bravely firm ~**ly** adv —**city** /tɪ'næsɪti/ n [U]

ten·ant /'tenənt/ n person who pays rent for the use of a building, land, etc. -**ancy** n 1 [C] length of time a person is a tenant 2 [U] use of land, etc., as a tenant

tend[1] /tend/ vt be likely: *She tends to lose* (= often loses) *her temper if you disagree with her.*

tend[2] vt take care of

ten·den·cy /'tendənsi/ n 1 likelihood of often happening or behaving in a particular way 2 special liking and natural skill: *She has artistic tendencies.*

ten·den·tious /ten'denʃəs/ adj fml (in discussion, article, etc.) unfairly leaving out other points of view ~**ly** adv

ten·der[1] /'tendər/ adj 1 not difficult to bite through 2 needing careful handling; delicate 3 sore 4 gentle, kind, and loving ~**ly** adv ~**ness** n [U]

tender[2] v fml 1 vt present for acceptance: *She tendered her resignation.* 2 vt offer in payment of debt 3 vi make a tender ◆ n statement of the price one would charge

tender[3] n coal- or water-carrying railway vehicle — see also LEGAL TENDER

ten·der-heart·ed /,tendə'hɑːtɪd‖-dər'hɑːr-/ adj easily made to feel love, pity, or sorrow

ten·don /'tendən/ n strong cord connecting a muscle to a bone

ten·dril /'tendrəl/ n thin curling stem by which a plant holds on to things

ten·e·ment /'tenəmənt/ n large building divided into flats, esp. in a poor city area

ten·et /'tenɪt/ n fml principle; belief

ten·ner /'tenər/ n BrE sl £10

ten·nis /'tenɪs/ n [U] game played by hitting a ball over a net with a RACKET

ten·or /'tenər/ n 1 (man with) the highest man's singing voice 2 instrument with the same range of notes as this: *a tenor saxophone* 3 fml general meaning (of something written or spoken)

ten-pin /'ten,pɪn/ n any of the 10 bottle-shaped objects to be knocked over with a ball in **tenpin bowling**

tense[1] /tens/ adj 1 stretched tight 2 nervously anxious ◆ vi/t (cause to) become tense ~**ly** adv ~**ness** n [U]

tense[2] n form of a verb showing time and continuity of action: *the future tense*

ten·sile /'tensaɪl‖'tensəl/ adj of TENSION (1)

ten·sion /'tenʃən/ n 1 [C;U] degree to which something is (able to be) stretched 2 [U] nervous anxiety caused by problems, uncertain waiting, etc. 3 [C;U] anxious, untrusting, and possibly dangerous relationship: *racial tensions in the inner city* 4 [U] tech electric power: *high-tension cables*

tent /tent/ n cloth shelter supported usu. by poles and ropes, used esp. by campers

ten·ta·cle /'tentəkəl/ n long snake-like boneless limb of certain creatures: *the tentacles of an octopus*

ten·ta·tive /'tentətɪv/ adj 1 not firmly arranged or fixed: *a tentative agreement* 2 not firm in making statements or decisions ~**ly** adv

ten·ter·hooks /'tentəhʊks‖-ər-/ n **on tenterhooks** anxiously waiting

tenth /tenθ/ determiner, adv, n, pron 10th

ten·u·ous /'tenjuəs/ adj slight: *a tenuous connection* ~**ly** adv ~**ness** n [U]

ten·ure /'tenjər, -juər/ n [U] 1 act, right, or period of holding a job or land 2 right to keep one's job, esp. as a university teacher

tep·id /'tepɪd/ adj only slightly warm: *tepid water* / (fig.) *enthusiasm*

term /tɜːm‖tɜːrm/ n 1 division of the school or university year: *the summer term* 2 fixed period: *a 4-year term as president* 3 word or expression, esp. as used in a particular activity: *'Tort' is a legal term.* 4 **in the long/short term**

over a long/short period — see also TERMS ♦ *vt* name; call; describe as

ter·mi·nal /'tɜːmɪnəl‖'tɜːr-/ *adj* of or being an illness that will cause death ♦ *n* **1** main building for passengers or goods at an airport, port, etc. **2** apparatus for giving instructions to and getting information from a computer **3** place for electrical connections: *the terminals of a battery* ~ly *adv*

ter·mi·nate /'tɜːmɪneɪt‖'tɜːr-/ *vi/t fml* (cause to) come to an end **–nation** /,tɜːmɪ'neɪʃən‖,tɜːr-/ *n* [U]: *the termination of a pregnancy*

ter·mi·nol·o·gy /,tɜːmɪ'nɒlədʒi‖,tɜːrmɪ'nɑː-/ *n* [U] (use of) particular TERMs (3): *legal terminology* **–logical** /,tɜːmɪnə'lɒdʒɪkəl‖,tɜːrmɪnə'lɑː-/ *adj*

ter·mi·nus /'tɜːmɪnəs‖'tɜːr-/ *n* **-ni** /-naɪ/ *or* **-nuses** stop or station at the end of a bus or railway line

ter·mite /'tɜːmaɪt‖'tɜːr-/ *n* antlike insect

terms /tɜːmz‖tɜːrmz/ *n* [P] **1** conditions of an agreement or contract **2** conditions of sale **3 come to terms** reach an agreement **4 come to terms with** accept (something unwelcome) **5 on good/bad/friendly terms** having a good, bad, etc., relationship

ter·race /'terəs/ *n* **1** level area cut from a slope **2** flat area next to a building **3** steps on which watchers stand in football grounds **4** row of joined houses ♦ *vt* form into TERRACES (4)

terraced house /,·· '·/*n BrE* house which is part of a TERRACE (4)

ter·ra·cot·ta /,terə'kɒtə‖-'kɑː-/ *n* [U] (articles of) reddish brown baked clay

ter·rain /te'reɪn, tə-/ *n* [C;U] (area of) land of the stated sort: *rocky terrain*

ter·res·tri·al /tə'restriəl/ *adj fml* of the Earth or land, as opposed to space or the sea

ter·ri·ble /'terəbəl/ *adj* **1** extremely severe: *a terrible accident* **2** extremely bad or unpleasant: *a terrible meal* **–bly** *adv* **1** extremely severely or badly **2** extremely: *terribly sorry*

ter·ri·er /'teriər/ *n* type of small active dog

ter·rif·ic /tə'rɪfɪk/ *adj* **1** excellent **2** very great ~**ally** /-kli/ *adv* extremely

ter·ri·fy /'terəfaɪ/ *vt* frighten extremely: *a terrified horse*

ter·ri·to·ry /'terətəri‖-tɔːri/ *n* [C;U] **1** (area of) land, esp. as ruled by one government: *This island is French territory.* **2** area belonging to (and defended by) a particular person, animal, or group **3** area for which one person or group is responsible **–rial** /,terə'tɔːriəl◄/ *adj* **1** of or being land or territory **2** (of animals, birds, etc.) showing a tendency to guard one's own TERRITORY (2)

ter·ror /'terər/ *n* [U] extreme fear

ter·ror·is·m /'terərɪzəm/ *n* [U] use of violence for political purposes **-ist** *n*

ter·ror·ize ‖ *also* **-ise** *BrE*/'terəraɪz/ *vt* fill with terror by threats or acts of violence

terse /tɜːs‖tɜːrs/ *adj* using few words, often to show anger ~**ly** *adv* ~**ness** *n* [U]

ter·tia·ry /'tɜːʃəri‖'tɜːrʃieri, -ʃəri/ *adj fml* 3rd in order

TESOL /'tesɒl‖-sɑːl/ *n* [U] teaching English to speakers of other languages

test /test/ *n* **1** set of questions or jobs to measure someone's knowledge or skill: *a history/driving test* **2** short medical examination: *an eye test* **3** use of something to see how well it works: *nuclear weapon tests* **4 put to the test** find out the qualities of (something) by use ♦ *vt* **1** study or examine with a test **2** provide difficult conditions for: *a testing time* (= a difficult period) *for the country* **3** search by means of tests: *The company is testing for oil.*

tes·ta·ment /'testəmənt/ *n* **1** *fml* for WILL² (5) **2** (*cap.*) either of the 2 main parts of the Bible: *the Old Testament*

tes·ti·cle /'testɪkəl/ *n* either of the 2 round SPERM-producing organs in male animals

tes·ti·fy /'testəfaɪ/ *vi/t* **1** make a solemn statement of truth **2** show (something) clearly; prove

tes·ti·mo·ni·al /,testə'məuniəl/ *n* **1** formal written statement of someone's character and ability **2** something given or done to show respect, thanks, etc.

tes·ti·mo·ny /'testəməni‖-məuni/ *n* formal statement of facts, esp. in a court of law

test match /'· ·/ *n* international cricket or RUGBY match

test tube /'· ·/ *n* small glass tube, closed at one end, used in scientific tests

tes·ty /'testi/ *adj fml* bad-tempered **–tily** *adv*

tet·a·nus /'tetənəs/ *n* [U] serious disease, caused by infection of a cut, which causes the muscles to stiffen

tetch·y /'tetʃi/ *adj* sensitive in a bad-tempered way **–ily** *adv* **–iness** *n* [U]

tête-à-tête /,teɪt ɑː 'teɪt, ,teɪt ə 'teɪt/ *n* private conversation between 2 people

teth·er /'teðər/ *n* **1** rope, etc., to which an animal is tied **2 the end of one's tether** the condition of being unable to bear any more difficulties, annoyances, etc. ♦ *vt* fasten with a tether

text /tekst/ *n* **1** [C;U] main body of printed words in a book **2** [C;U] exact original words of a speech, etc. **3** [C] textbook: *a set text* **4** [C] sentence from the Bible used by a priest in a SERMON ~**ual** *adj*

text-book /'tekstbʊk/ *n* standard book used for studying a particular subject, esp. in schools ♦ *adj* **1** as it ought to be; IDEAL: *textbook journalism* **2** typical

tex-tile /'tekstaɪl/ *n* woven material

tex-ture /'tekstʃəʳ/ *n* [C;U] quality of roughness or smoothness, coarseness or fineness, of a surface or substance

tha-lid-o-mide /θə'lɪdəmaɪd/ *n* [U] drug no longer used because it caused unborn babies to develop wrongly

than /ðən; strong ðæn/ *conj, prep* **1** (used in comparing things): *This is bigger than that.* **2** when; as soon as: *No sooner had we started to eat than the doorbell rang.*

thank /θæŋk/ *vt* express one's gratefulness to **thanks** *n* [P] **1** (words expressing) gratefulness **2 thanks to** because of ~**ful** *adj* **1** glad **2** grateful ~**fully** *adv* ~**less** *adj* not likely to be rewarded with thanks or success

thanks /θæŋks/ *interj* thank you

thanks-giv-ing /ˌθæŋks'gɪvɪŋ◀/ *n* [C;U] **1** (an) expression of gratefulness, esp. to God **2** (*cap.*) holiday in the US

thank you /'· ·/ *interj* **1** (used for politely expressing thanks or acceptance) **2 no, thank you** (used for politely refusing an offer)

that[1] /ðæt/ *determiner, pron* **those** /ðəʊz/ **1** (being) the person, thing, or idea which is understood or has just been mentioned or shown: *Look at that man over there.* | *Who told you that?* | *I'd like these apples, not those.* **2 that's that** that is the end of the matter

that[2] *conj* **1** (used for introducing CLAUSES): *She said that she couldn't come.* **2** (used as a RELATIVE PRONOUN) which/who(m): *This is the book that I bought.*

that[3] *adv* to such a degree; so: *It wasn't that difficult.*

thatch /θætʃ/ *vt, n* [U] (make or cover with) a roof covering of STRAW: *a thatched roof* | *cottage*

thaw /θɔː/ *v* **1** *vi/t* change from a solid frozen state to being liquid or soft **2** *vi* become friendlier, less formal, etc. ♦ *n* **1** period when ice and snow melt **2** increase in friendliness

the /ðə, ði; strong ðiː/ *definite article, determiner* **1** (used for referring to a particular thing): *the sky* | *Close the door.* **2** (used with some geographical names): *the Rhine* | *the Pacific* **3** (used before a singular noun to make it general): *The lion is a wild animal.* **4** (used for making an adjective into a noun): *I like the French.* (= French people) | *To do the impossible.* **5** (used

with measures) each: *paid by the hour* | *sold by the metre* **6** (used before names of musical instruments): *She plays the piano.* **7** (used before the plural of 20, 30, etc., to show a period of 10 years): *music of the 60s* ♦ *adv* **1** (used in comparisons, to show that 2 things happen together): *The more he eats, the fatter he gets.* **2** (in comparisons to show that someone or something is better, worse, etc., than before): *She looks (all) the better for 2 weeks holiday in Spain.* **3** (to show that someone or something is more than any other): *She's the cleverest* | *the most sensible of them all.*

the-at-re /'θɪətəʳ/ *usu.* **-er** *AmE n* **1** building where plays are performed **2** the work of people involved with plays: *He's in the theatre.* **3** large room where public talks are given **4** room where medical operations are done **5** area of activity in a war **–atrical** /θi'ætrɪkəl/ *adj* **1** of the theatre **2** too showy; not natural

the-at-re-go-er /'θɪətəˌɡəʊəʳ||-tər-/ *n* person who goes regularly to THEATRES (1)

thee /ðiː/ *pron lit* (object form of **thou**)

theft /θeft/ *n* [C;U] stealing

their /ðəʳ; strong ðeəʳ/ *determiner* of them; *their house*

theirs /ðeəz||ðeərz/ *pron* of them; their one(s): *It's theirs.*

them /ðəm; strong ðem/ *pron* (object form of **they**): *I want those books; give them to me.*

theme /θiːm/ *n* **1** subject of a talk, piece of writing, etc. **2** repeated idea, image, or tune in writing, music, etc.

theme park /'· ·/ *n* enclosed outdoor area containing amusements that are all based on a single subject (e.g. space travel)

them-selves /ðəm'selvz/ *pron* **1** (*reflexive form of* **they**): *They saw themselves on television.* **2** (*strong form of* **they**): *They built it themselves.* **3 (all) by themselves: a** alone **b** without help **4 to themselves** not shared

then /ðen/ *adv* **1** at that time: *I was happier then.* **2** next; afterwards: . . . *and then we went home.* **3** in that case; as a result: *Have you done your homework? Then you can watch television.* **4** besides; also

thence /ðens/ *adv fml* from that place

the-ol-o-gy /θi'ɒlədʒi||θi'ɑː-/ *n* [U] study of religious ideas and beliefs **–ologian** /θiə'ləʊdʒən/ *n* **–ological** /θiə'lɒdʒɪkəl||-'lɑː-/ *adj*

theo-rem /'θɪərəm/ *n* MATHEMATICAL statement that can be proved by reasoning

the·o·ry /ˈθɪəri/ n 1 [C] statement intended to explain a fact or event 2 [U] general principles and methods as opposed to practice **–rize** /ˈθɪəraɪz/ vi form a theory **–retical** /θɪəˈretɪkəl/ adj existing in or based on theory, not practice or fact

ther·a·peu·tic /ˌθerəˈpjuːtɪk/ adj 1 for the treating or curing of disease 2 having a good effect on one's health or state of mind: I find swimming/knitting very therapeutic.

ther·a·py /ˈθerəpi/ n [C;U] treatment of illnesses of the body or mind **–pist** n: a speech therapist

there¹ /ðeə/ adv 1 at or to that place: He lives over there. 2 (used for drawing attention to someone or something): There goes John. 3 **all there** healthy in mind 4 **there and then** at that exact place and time 5 **there you are: a** here is what you wanted **b** I told you so ♦ interj (used for comforting someone or expressing victory, satisfaction, etc.): There, there. Stop crying. | There, I knew I was right.

there² pron (used for showing that something or someone exists or happens, usu. as the subject of **be**, **seem**, or **appear**): There's someone at the door to see you.

there·a·bouts /ˌðeərəˈbaʊts/ adv near that place, time, number, etc.

there·af·ter /ðeərˈɑːftər‖-ˈæf-/ adv fml after that

there·by /ˌðeəˈbaɪ, ˈðeəbaɪ‖-ər-/ adv fml by doing or saying that

there·fore /ˈðeəfɔːr‖ˈðeər-/ adv for that reason; as a result

there·up·on /ˌðeərəˈpɒn, ˈðeərəpɒn‖-pɑːn, -pɔːn/ adv fml 1 about that matter 2 without delay

ther·mal /ˈθɜːməl‖ˈθɜːr-/ adj of, using, producing, or caused by heat ♦ n rising current of warm air

ther·mo·dy·nam·ics /ˌθɜːməʊdaɪˈnæmɪks‖ˌθɜːr-/ n [U] scientific study of heat and its power in driving machines

ther·mom·e·ter /θəˈmɒmɪtər‖θərˈmɑː-/ n instrument for measuring temperature

ther·mos /ˈθɜːmɒs‖ˈθɜːr-/ n tdmk for FLASK (3)

ther·mo·stat /ˈθɜːməstæt‖ˈθɜːr-/ n apparatus for keeping a machine, room, etc., at an even temperature

the·sau·rus /θɪˈsɔːrəs/ n dictionary with words grouped according to similarities in meaning

these /ðiːz/ pl. of THIS

the·sis /ˈθiːsɪs/ n **-ses** /-siːz/ 1 long piece of writing on a particular subject, done to gain a higher university degree 2 opinion or statement supported by reasoned arguments

they /ðeɪ/ pron (used as the subject of a sentence) 1 those people, animals, or things 2 people in general: They say prices are going to rise. 3 (used to avoid saying **he** or **she**): If anyone knows, they should tell me.

they'd /ðeɪd/ short for: 1 they had 2 they would

they'll /ðeɪl/ short for: they will

they're /ðeər/ short for: they are

they've /ðeɪv/ short for: they have

thick /θɪk/ adj 1 having a large or the stated distance between opposite surfaces: thick walls | walls 2 metres thick 2 (of liquid) not flowing easily 3 difficult to see through: thick mist 4 full of; covered with: furniture thick with dust 5 with many objects set close together: a thick forest 6 BrE sl stupid ♦ adv 1 thickly 2 **thick and fast** quickly and in large numbers ♦ n 1 [the + S] part, place, etc., of greatest activity 2 **through thick and thin** through both good and bad times **~ly** adv **~en** vi/t make or become thicker **~ness** n 1 [C;U] being thick 2 [C] LAYER

thick·et /ˈθɪkɪt/ n thick growth of bushes and small trees

thick·set /ˌθɪkˈset◂/ adj having a broad strong body

thick-skinned /ˌ·ˈ·◂/ adj not easily offended

thief /θiːf/ n **thieves** /θiːvz/ person who steals

thieve /θiːv/ vi steal

thigh /θaɪ/ n top part of the human leg

thim·ble /ˈθɪmbəl/ n small cap put over the end of the finger when sewing

thin /θɪn/ adj **-nn-** 1 having a small distance between opposite surfaces 2 not fat 3 (of a liquid) flowing (too) easily; weak 4 with few objects widely separated: a thin audience 5 easy to see through: thin mist 6 lacking force or strength: a thin excuse 7 **thin end of the wedge** something which seems unimportant but will open the way for more serious things of a similar kind ♦ adv thinly ♦ vi/t make or become thinner **~ly** adv **~ness** n [U]

thin air /· ·ˈ·/ n [U] infml state of not being seen or not existing

thine /ðaɪn/ determiner THY ♦ pron lit (possessive form of **thou**) yours

thing /θɪŋ/ n 1 [C] unnamed or unnameable object: What do you use this thing for? 2 [C] remark, idea, or subject: What a nasty thing to say! 3 [C] act; activity: the first thing we have to do 4 [C] event: A funny thing happened today. 5 [S] that which is necessary or desirable: Cold beer's just the thing on a hot day. 6 [S] the fashion or custom: the latest thing in shoes 7 [S] sl activity satisfying to one personally: Tennis isn't really my thing. 8 **first**

thing early in the morning **9 for one thing** (used for introducing a reason) **10 have a thing about** have a strong like or dislike for **11 a good/bad thing** it's sensible/not sensible: *It's a good thing we found you.* (= it's lucky) **12 make a thing of** give too much importance to **13 a close/near thing** a situation in which something unpleasant is only just avoided **14 the thing is** what we must consider is — see also NEAR THING **things** n [P] **1** general state of affairs; situation **2** one's personal possessions: *Pack your suitcase.*

think /θɪŋk/ v **thought** /θɔːt/ **1** vi use the mind to make judgments **2** vt have as an opinion; believe: *Do you think it will rain?* **3** vt understand; imagine: *I can't think why you did it.* **4** vt have as a plan: *I think I'll go swimming tomorrow.* **5 think aloud** to speak one's thoughts as they come ♦ n [S] act of thinking ~**er** n

think of phr vt consider seriously before making a decision

think of phr vt **1** form a possible plan for **2** have as an opinion about: *what do you think of that?* **3** take into account: *But think of the cost!* **4** remember **5 not think much of** have a low opinion of **6 think better of** decide against **7 think highly/well/little of** have a good/bad, etc., opinion of someone or something **8 think nothing of** regard as usual or easy

think out/through phr vt consider carefully and in detail

think over phr vt consider seriously

think up phr vt invent (esp. an idea)

think-ing /ˈθɪŋkɪŋ/ n [U] opinion: *What's the government's thinking on this?* ♦ adj thoughtful; able to think clearly

thin-skinned /ˌ ˈ ◂/ adj easily offended

third /θɜːd‖θɜːrd/ determiner, adv, n, pron 3rd

third de-gree /ˌ ˈ ◂/ n [the + S] hard questioning and rough treatment

third par-ty /ˌ ˈ ◂/ n **1** person other than the 2 main people concerned **2** person other than the holder protected by an insurance agreement

third-rate /ˌ ˈ ◂/ adj of very low quality

Third World /ˌ ˈ ◂/ n [the] the countries of the world which are industrially less well-developed

thirst /θɜːst‖θɜːrst/ n **1** [S;U] desire for drink **2** [U] lack of drink: *I'm dying of thirst* **3** [S] strong desire: *the thirst for knowledge* ~**y** adj feeling or causing thirst

thir-teen /ˌθɜːˈtiːn◂‖ˌθɜːr-/ determiner, n, pron 13 ~**th** determiner, adv, n, pron 13th

thir-ty /ˈθɜːti‖ˈθɜːrti/ determiner, n, pron 30 ~**tieth** determiner, adv, n, pron 30th

this /ðɪs/ determiner, pron **these** /ðiːz/ **1** (one) going to be mentioned, to happen: *I'll come this morning.* | *Do it like this.* (= in the way about to be shown) **2** (one) near or nearer in place, time, thought, etc.: *Give me these, not those.* **3** infml a certain: *There were these two men standing there . . .* ♦ adv to this degree: *It was this big.*

this-tle /ˈθɪsəl/ n plant with prickly leaves and usu. purple flowers

thong /θɒŋ‖θɔːŋ/ n narrow length of leather used esp. for fastening

tho-rax /ˈθɔːræks/ n med part of the body between the neck and the ABDOMEN

thorn /θɔːn‖θɔːrn/ n **1** sharp growth on a plant **2 thorn in one's flesh/side** continual cause of annoyance ~**y** adj **1** prickly **2** difficult to deal with

thor-ough /ˈθʌrə‖ˈθʌrəʊ, ˈθʌrə/ adj **1** complete in every way: *a thorough search* **2** careful about details ~**ly** adv ~**ness** n [U]

thor-ough-bred /ˈθʌrəbred‖ˈθʌrəʊ-, ˈθʌrə-/ n, adj (animal, esp. a horse) from parents of one very good breed

thor-ough-fare /ˈθʌrəfeə‖ˈθʌrəʊ-, ˈθʌrə-/ n fml large public road

thor-ough-go-ing /ˌθʌrəˈɡəʊɪŋ◂/ adj very thorough; complete

those /ðəʊz/ pl. of THAT

thou /ðaʊ/ pron lit (used of a single person) you

though /ðəʊ/ conj, adv **1** in spite of the fact (that): *Though it's hard work, I enjoy it.* **2** but: *I'll try, though I don't think I can.* **3 as though** as if

thought¹ /θɔːt/ past t. & p. of THINK

thought² n **1** [C] something thought; idea, etc. **2** [U] thinking **3** [U] serious consideration **4** [U] intention: *I had no thought of causing any trouble.* **5** [C;U] attention; regard: *acting with no thought to her own safety* — see also SECOND THOUGHT ~**ful** adj **1** thinking deeply **2** paying attention to the wishes, needs, etc., of others ~**fully** adv ~**less** adj showing a selfish or careless lack of thought ~**lessly** adv

thou-sand /ˈθaʊzənd/ determiner, n, pron **thousand** or **thousands** 1000 ~**th** determiner, adv, n, pron 1000th

thrall /θrɔːl/ n [U] lit slavery

thrash /θræʃ/ v **1** vt beat (as if) with a whip or stick **2** vt defeat thoroughly **3** vi move wildly or violently

thrash out phr vt find an answer (to) by much talk and consideration

thread /θred/ n **1** [C;U] very fine cord made by spinning cotton, silk etc.

2 [C] line of reasoning connecting the parts of an argument or story 3 [C] raised line that winds round the outside of a screw 4 **hang by a thread** be in a very dangerous position ♦ *vt* 1 put thread through the hole in (a needle) 2 put (a film or TAPE) in place on an apparatus 3 put (things) together on a thread 4 **thread one's way through** go carefully through (crowds, etc.)

thread·bare /'θredbeəʳ/ *adj* (of cloth) very worn: (fig.) *a threadbare* (= too often used) *excuse*

threat /θret/ *n* 1 [C;U] expression of an intention to harm or punish someone 2 [C] something or someone regarded as a possible danger

threat·en /'θretn/ *v* 1 *vt* make a threat (against): *They threatened to blow up the plane.* 2 *vt* give warning of (something bad): *The sky threatened rain.* 3 *vi* (of something bad) seem likely: *Danger threatens.*

three /θriː/ *determiner, n, pron* 3

three-D /θriː 'diː◂/ *n* [U] three-dimensional form or appearance

three-di·men·sion·al /,· ·'···◂/ *adj* having length, depth, and height

three R's /,θriː 'ɑːz‖-'ɑːrz/ *n* [*the* + P] reading, writing, and ARITHMETIC, considered as forming the base of children's education

thresh /θreʃ/ *vt* separate the grain from (corn, etc.) by beating

thresh·old /'θreʃhəʊld, -ʃəʊld/ *n* 1 point of beginning: *scientists on the threshold of* (= about to make) *a research breakthrough* 2 piece of stone or wood across the bottom of a doorway

threw /θruː/ *past t. of* THROW

thrice /θraɪs/ *adv lit* 3 times

thrift /θrɪft/ *n* [U] not spending too much money ~**y** *adj*

thrill /θrɪl/ *n* (something producing) a sudden strong feeling of excitement, fear, etc. ♦ *vi/t* (cause to) feel a thrill ~**er** *n* book, film, etc., telling a very exciting (crime) story

thrive /θraɪv/ *vi* **thrived** *or* **throve** /θrəʊv/, **thrived** develop well and be healthy, strong, or successful

throat /θrəʊt/ *n* 1 passage from the mouth down inside the body 2 front of the neck

throb /θrɒb‖θrɑːb/ *vi* -**bb**- (of a machine, the action of the heart, etc.) beat heavily and regularly ♦ *n* throbbing

throes /θrəʊz/ *n* [P] *lit* sudden violent pains, esp. caused by dying 2 **in the throes of** struggling with (some difficulty)

throm·bo·sis /θrɒm'bəʊsəs‖θrɑːm-/ *n* -**ses** /-siːz/ having a thickened mass of blood in a blood tube or the heart

throne /θrəʊn/ *n* ceremonial seat of a king, queen, etc.: (fig.) *He ascended the throne.* (= became king)

throng /θrɒŋ‖θrɔːŋ/ *n* large crowd ♦ *vi/t* go as or fill with a throng

throt·tle /'θrɒtl‖'θrɑːtl/ *vt* seize (someone) by the throat to stop them breathing ♦ *n* VALVE controlling the flow of petrol, etc., into an engine

through /θruː/ *prep, adv* 1 in at one side (of) and out at the other: *Water flows through this pipe.*|*I opened the door and went through.* 2 from beginning to end (of): *I read through the letter.* 3 so as to finish successfully: *Did you get through your exam?* 4 past: *He drove through a red light.* ♦ *prep* 1 by means of; because of: *The war was lost through bad organization.* 2 *AmE* up to and including: *Wednesday through Saturday* ♦ *adv* 1 so as to be connected by telephone 2 **through and through** completely ♦ *adj* 1 finished; done: *Are you through yet?* 2 having no further relationship: *I'm through with him!* 3 allowing a continuous journey: *a through train*

through·out /θruː'aʊt/ *prep, adv* in, to, through, or during every part (of)

through·put /'θruːpʊt/ *n* amount of work, materials, etc., dealt with in a particular time

throw /θrəʊ/ *v* **threw** /θruː/, **thrown** /θrəʊn/ 1 *vi/t* send (something) through the air with a sudden movement of the arm 2 *vt* move or put forcefully or quickly: *The two fighters threw themselves at each other.*|*I'll just throw on some clothes.* 3 *vt* cause to fall to the ground: *Her horse threw her.* 4 *vt* direct: *I think I can throw some light on the mystery.* 5 *vt* operate (a SWITCH) 6 *vt* shape from wet clay when making POTTERY 7 *vt* make one's voice appear to come from somewhere other than one's mouth 8 *vt infml* arrange (a party) 9 *vt* confuse; shock: *Her reply really threw me.* 10 **throw a fit** have a sudden uncontrolled attack of anger 11 **throw oneself into** to start to work very busily at 12 **throw oneself on/upon** put complete trust in 13 **throw one's weight about** give orders to others, because one thinks one is important 14 **throw oneself at** *phr vt* **a** rush violently towards someone **b** attempt forcefully to win someone's love ♦ *n* 1 act of throwing 2 distance thrown ~**er** *n*

throw away *phr vt* 1 get rid of 2 waste (an opportunity, chance, etc.)

throw in *phr vt* 1 supply additionally without increasing the price 2

throw in the sponge/towel admit defeat

throw off *phr vt* **1** recover from **2** escape from

throw open *phr vt* allow people to enter

throw out *phr vt* **1** get rid of **2** refuse to accept

throw over *phr vt* end a relationship with

throw together *phr vt* build or make hastily

throw up *phr v* **1** *vt* stop doing (esp. a job) **2** *vt* bring to notice: *The investigation has thrown up some interesting facts.* **3** *vi sl for* VOMIT

throw-back /'θrəʊbæk/ *n* (example of) a return to something in the past

thrush¹ /θrʌʃ/ *n* common singing bird with a spotted breast

thrush² *n* [U] infectious disease of the mouth, throat, and VAGINA

thrust /θrʌst/ *vi/t* **thrust** push forcefully and suddenly ♦ *n* **1** [C] act of thrusting **2** [U] forward-moving power of an engine **3** [U] (main) meaning — see also CUT AND THRUST

thud /θʌd/ *vi, n -dd-* (make) the dull sound of something heavy falling

thug /θʌg/ *n* violent criminal

thumb¹ /θʌm/ *n* **1** short thick finger set apart from the other **4 2 all thumbs** *infml* very awkward with the hands **3 stick out like a sore thumb** *infml* seem out of place **4 thumb one's nose at** *infml* make fun of **5 thumbs up/down** an expression of approval/disapproval **6 under someone's thumb** *infml* under the control of someone — see also RULE OF THUMB

thumb² *v* **thumb a lift** ask passing motorists for a ride by signalling with one's thumb

thumb through *phr vi/t* look through (a book) quickly

thumb-nail /'θʌmneɪl/ *n* nail of the thumb ♦ *adj* small or short: *a thumbnail description/sketch*

thumb-screw /'θʌmskruː/ *n* instrument for crushing the thumbs to cause great pain

thump /θʌmp/ *v* **1** *vt* hit hard **2** *vi* make a repeated dull sound: *My heart thumped.* ♦ *n* (sound of) a heavy blow

thun-der /'θʌndə^r/ *n* [U] **1** loud explosive noise that follows lightning: (fig.) *the thunder of distant guns* **2 steal someone's thunder** spoil effect of someone's action by doing it first ♦ *v* **1** *vi* produce thunder **2** *vi* produce or go with a loud noise **3** *vt* shout loudly ~**ous** *adj* very loud: *thunderous applause*

thun-der-bolt /'θʌndəbəʊlt‖-dər-/ *n* **1** thunder and lightning together **2** event causing great shock

thun-der-clap /'θʌndəklæp‖-ər-/ *n* a single loud crash of thunder

thun-der-struck /'θʌndəstrʌk‖-ər-/ *adj* shocked

Thurs-day /'θɜːzdi‖'θɜːr-/ *n* the 4th day of the week, between Wednesday and Friday

thus /ðʌs/ *adv fml* **1** in this way **2** with this result **3 thus far** up until now

thwack /θwæk/ *n, v* WHACK

thwart /θwɔːt‖θwɔːrt/ *vt* prevent from happening or succeeding

thy /ðaɪ/ *determiner lit* (*possessive form of* **thou**) your

thy-roid /'θaɪrɔɪd/ *n* organ in the neck that controls growth and activity

ti-a-ra /ti'ɑːrə/ *n* piece of jewellery like a small crown

tic /tɪk/ *n* sudden unconscious movement of the muscles

tick¹ /tɪk/ *n* **1** short repeated sound of a watch or clock **2** mark ✓ showing esp. correctness **3** *sl, esp. BrE* moment

tick² *v* **1** *vi* make a TICK¹ (1) **2** *vt* mark with a TICK¹ (2) **3 make someone/something tick** *infml* provide a person/thing with reasons for behaving, working, etc., in a particular way

tick off *phr vt infml* speak sharply to, expressing disapproval or annoyance

tick over *phr vi* continue working at slow steady rate

tick³ *n* very small blood-sucking insect

tick⁴ *n* **on tick** *infml* on CREDIT¹ (1)

tick-et /'tɪkɪt/ *n* **1** piece of paper or card showing that payment for a service has been made: *a bus/cinema ticket* **2** piece of card showing the price, size, etc., of goods **3** printed notice of an offence against the traffic laws **4** *infml* exactly the thing needed: *This hammer is just the ticket.*

tick-le /'tɪkəl/ *v* **1** *vt* touch (someone's body) lightly to produce laughter, a feeling of nervous excitement, etc.: *Stop tickling my toes!* **2** *vi* give or feel a prickly sensation **3** *vt* delight or amuse ♦ *n* [C;U] (act or feel of) tickling **–lish** *adj* **1** sensitive to being tickled **2** (of a problem or situation) rather difficult

tid-al wave /'··· ·/ *n* very large dangerous ocean wave: (fig.) *a tidal wave of public disapproval*

tid-dler /'tɪdlə^r/ *n BrE* very small fish

tid-dly /'tɪdli/ *adj BrE infml* slightly drunk

tide¹ /taɪd/ *n* **1** regular rise and fall of the sea: *The tide's out.* (= has fallen to its lowest point) **2** current caused by this: *strong tides* **3** feeling or tendency that moves or changes like the tide: *the tide of public opinion* **tidal** *adj*

tide² v **tide over** phr vt help (someone) through (a difficult period)

tide-mark /ˈtaɪdmɑːk‖-mɑːrk/ infml mark round the inside of an empty bath showing the level to which it was filled

tid-ings /ˈtaɪdɪŋz/ n [P] lit news

ti-dy /ˈtaɪdi/ adj 1 neat 2 infml fairly large: a tidy income ♦ vi/t make (things) tidy **tidily** adv **tidiness** n [U]

tie¹ /taɪ/ n 1 band of cloth worn round the neck 2 a card, string, etc., used for fastening something 3 something that unites: the ties of friendship 4 something that limits one's freedom 5 result in which each competitor gains an equal number of points, votes, etc.

tie² v **tied; pres. p. tying 1** vt fasten by knotting: tie a parcel/one's shoe laces 2 vt make (a knot or BOW²) (3) (3) vi/t finish (a match or competition) with a TIE¹ (5)

tie down phr vt 1 limit the freedom of 2 force to be exact

tie in phr vi have a close connection

tie up phr vt 1 limit free use of (money, property, etc.) 2 connect 3 **tied up** very busy

tie-breaker /ˈtaɪˌbreɪkəʳ/ also **tiebreak** /ˈtaɪˌbreɪk/ —n number of quickly-played points to decide the winner of a tennis SET³ (4)

tie-in /ˈ· ·/ n product that is connected in some way with a new film, TV show, etc.

tie-pin /ˈtaɪˌpɪn/ n decorative CLIP for holding a TIE¹ (1) in place

tier /tɪəʳ/ n 1 any of a number of rising rows of esp. seats 2 level of organization

tiff /tɪf/ n slight quarrel

ti-ger /ˈtaɪgəʳ/ **tigress** /ˈtaɪgrəs/ fem. — n 1 large Asian wild cat that has yellowish fur with black bands 2 fierce or brave person — see also PAPER TIGER

tight /taɪt/ adj 1 firmly fixed in place; closely fastened: The cases were packed tight in the back. | Is the roof watertight? 2 fully stretched 3 fitting (too) closely; leaving no free room or time: tight shoes | a tight schedule 4 difficult to obtain: Money is tight just now. 5 marked by close competition: a tight game/finish 6 sl ungenerous with money 7 sl drunk 8 **in a tight corner/spot** in a difficult position ♦ adv tightly **—ly** adv **—en** vi/t make or become tighter **~ness** n [U] **tights** n [P] very close fitting garment covering the legs and lower body

tight-fist·ed /ˌtaɪt ˈfɪstⅆd◄/ adj infml very ungenerous, esp. with money **~ness** n [U]

tight-lipped /ˌ· ˈ·◄/ adj 1 having the lips pressed together 2 not saying anything

tight-rope /ˈtaɪt-rəʊp/ n rope tightly stretched high above the ground, on which someone walks

tile /taɪl/ n 1 thin shaped piece of baked clay, etc., used for covering roofs, walls, floors, etc. 2 **(out) on the tiles** enjoying oneself wildly ♦ vt cover with tiles

till¹ /tɪl, tl/ prep, conj until

till² n drawer where money is kept in a shop

till³ vt lit cultivate (the ground)

til-ler /ˈtɪləʳ/ n long handle for turning a boat's RUDDER

tilt /tɪlt/ vi/t (cause to) slope (as if by raising one end ♦ n [S;U] 1 slope 2 **(at) full tilt** at full speed

tim-ber /ˈtɪmbəʳ/ n 1 [U] wood for building 2 [U] growing trees 3 [C] wooden beam, esp. in a ship

time /taɪm/ n 1 [U] continuous measurable quantity from the past, through the present, and into the future 2 [S;U] period: It happened a long time ago. | I haven't got (the) time to do it. (= I am too busy doing other things) 3 period in which an action is completed, esp. in a race: Her time was just under 4 minutes. 4 [U] particular point stated in hours, minutes, seconds, etc.: The time is 4 o'clock. 5 [C;U] particular point in the year, day, etc.: We both arrived at the same time. | in summertime | It's time we were leaving. 6 [C] occasion: I've been here several times. 7 [C] experience connected with a period or occasion: We had a great time at the party. 8 [C] period in history: in ancient times 9 [U] point when something should happen: The plane arrived on time. (= not early or late) 10 [U] rate of speed of a piece of music 11 **ahead of one's time** with ideas not accepted in period in which one lives 12 **all the time** continuously 13 **at a time** singly/in groups of 2/3, etc.: We went into her office 2 at a time. 14 **at all times** always 15 **at one time** formerly 16 **at the same time: a** however; nevertheless 17 **at times** sometimes 18 **behind the times** old-fashioned 19 **buy time** infml delay an action or decision in order to give oneself more time 20 **do time** sl go to prison 21 **for a time** for a short period 22 **for the time being** for a limited period at present 23 **from time to time** sometimes 24 **have no time for someone** dislike someone 25 **in no time** very quickly 26 **in time: a** after a certain amount of time has passed **b** early or soon enough 27 **take one's time** not hurry 28 **the time of one's life** have a very enjoyable experience **29 time and (time) again/time after time** repeatedly — see also TIMES ♦ *vt* **1** arrange the time at which (something) happens **2** measure the time taken by or for **3** (in sport) make (a shot) at exactly the right moment **~less** *adj* **1** unending **2** not changed by time **~ly** *adj fml* happening at just the right time: *a timely warning* **timer** *n* person or machine that measures or records time — see also OLD TIMER

time-and-motion /ˌ· · ·ˈ··/ *adj* concerning the measurement and study of the effectiveness of work methods

time bomb /ˈ· · / *n* **1** bomb set to explode at a particular time **2** situation likely to become very dangerous

time im·me·mo·ri·al /ˌ· ··ˈ···/ *n* [U] *lit* long ago in the past

time lim·it /ˈ· ,··/ *n* period of time in which something must be done

times /taɪmz/ *n* (used to show an amount that is calculated by multiplying something the stated number of times): *Their house is at least 3 times the size of ours.* ♦ *prep* multiplied by: *3 times 3 is 9.*

time-serv·er /ˈtaɪmˌsɜːvəʳ‖-ɜːr-/ *n derog* person who acts so as to please those in power at the time **~ing** *adj,n* [U]

time-shar·ing /ˈ· ,··/*n* [U] **1** use of one main COMPUTER by many people in different places **2** several people buying or renting a house (esp. for holidays), each using it for short periods each year

time sig·na·ture /ˈ· ,···/ *n* mark, esp. 2 numbers, to show what speed music should be played at

time·ta·ble /ˈtaɪmˌteɪbəl/ *n* **1** list of the travelling times of buses, trains, etc. **2** (list of) the times of classes in a school, etc. ♦ *vt* **1** to plan for a future time: *The meeting was timetabled for tomorrow.* **2** arrange according to a TIMETABLE (2)

tim·id /ˈtɪmɪd/ *adj* fearful; lacking courage **~ly** *adv* **~ity** /tɪˈmɪdɪti/ *n* [U]

tim·o·rous /ˈtɪmərəs/ *adj fml* fearful **~ly** *adv* **~ness** *n* [U]

tin /tɪn/ *n* **1** [U] soft whitish metal **2** [C] *BrE* small closed metal container in which food is sold ♦ *vt* **-nn-** pack (food) in tins **~ny** *adj* **1** of or like tin **2** having a thin metallic sound

tinc·ture /ˈtɪŋktʃəʳ/ *n* [C;U] medical substance mixed with alcohol

tin·der /ˈtɪndəʳ/ *n* [U] material that burns easily, used esp. for lighting fires

tin·foil /ˈtɪnfɔɪl/ *n* [U] very thin bendable sheet of shiny metal

tinge /tɪndʒ/ *vt* give a small amount of colour to: *black hair tinged with*

grey | (fig.) *admiration tinged with jealousy* ♦ *n* [S] small amount

tin·gle /ˈtɪŋgəl/ *vi, n* [S] (feel) a slight, not unpleasant, stinging sensation

tin·ker /ˈtɪŋkəʳ/ *vi* work without a definite plan or useful results, making small changes, esp. when trying to repair or improve something ♦ *n* **1** [S] act of tinkering **2** [C] travelling mender of pots and pans

tin·kle /ˈtɪŋkəl/ *vi* make light metallic sounds ♦ *n* **1** tinkling sound **2** *BrE sl* telephone call

tin o·pen·er /ˈ· ,···/ *n BrE* tool for opening tins

tin pan al·ley /ˌ· · ˈ··/ *n* [U] (*often caps.*) writers, players, and producers of popular music

tin·pot /ˈ· ·/ *adj* worthless and unimportant, but perhaps thinking oneself to be important

tin·sel /ˈtɪnsəl/ *n* [U] **1** threads of shiny material used for (Christmas) decorations **2** something showy that is really cheap and worthless

tint /tɪnt/ *n* pale or delicate shade of a colour ♦ *vt* give a tint to

ti·ny /ˈtaɪni/ *adj* extremely small

tip¹ /tɪp/ *n* **1** (pointed) end of something: *the tips of one's fingers* **2** part stuck on the end: *cigarettes with tips* **3 on the tip of one's tongue** not quite able to be remembered ♦ *vt* **-pp-** put a tip on: *tipped cigarettes*

tip² *v* **-pp- 1** *vt BrE* pour **2** *vi/t* (cause to) fall over **3** *vi/t* (cause to) lean at an angle ♦ *n esp. BrE* **1** place where unwanted waste is left **2** *infml* extremely untidy dirty place: *His room is an absolute tip.*

tip³ *n* small amount of money given to someone who does a service ♦ *vi/t* **-pp-** give a tip (to)

tip⁴ *n* helpful piece of advice ♦ *vt* **-pp-** suggest as likely to succeed

tip off *phr vt* give a warning or piece of secret information to **tip-off** /ˈ··/ *n*

tip·ple /ˈtɪpəl/ *n infml* alcoholic drink

tip·ster /ˈtɪpstəʳ/ *n* person who gives advice about the likely winner of horse and dog races

tip·sy /ˈtɪpsi/ *adj infml* slightly drunk

tip·toe /ˈtɪptəʊ/ *n* **on tiptoe** on one's toes with the rest of the foot raised ♦ *vi* walk on tiptoe

tip-top /ˌ· ˈ◁/ *adj infml* excellent

ti·rade /taɪˈreɪd, tɪ-‖ˈtaɪreɪd, tɪˈreɪd/ *n* long, angry speech

tire¹ /taɪəʳ/ *vi/t* (cause to) become tired **~less** *adj* never getting tired **~some** *adj* **1** annoying **2** uninteresting

tire² *n AmE for* TYRE

tired /taɪəd‖taɪərd/ *adj* **1** needing rest or sleep **2** no longer interested: *I'm tired of doing this; let's go for a walk.* **3**

showing lack of imagination or new thought: *tired ideas* ~**ness** n [U]

tis·sue /'tɪʃuː, -sjuː‖-ʃuː/ n 1 [C;U] the material animals and plants are made of; cells: *lung tissue* 2 [U] thin light paper, esp. for wrapping 3 [C] paper handkerchief 4 [C] *fml* something formed as if by weaving threads together: *a tissue of lies*

tit¹ /tɪt/ n small bird of various sorts

tit² n sl, not polite woman's breast

ti·tan·ic /taɪ'tænɪk/ adj very great in degree: *a titanic struggle*

ti·ta·ni·um /taɪ'teɪniəm/ n [U] light strong metal used in compounds

tit·bit /'tɪt,bɪt/ n small piece of particularly nice food: (fig.) *a few titbits of information*

tit for tat /,· · '·/ n [U] something unpleasant given in return for something unpleasant one has suffered

tithe /taɪð/ n tax paid to the church in former times

tit·il·late /'tɪtɨleɪt/ vt excite, esp. sexually –**lation** /,tɪtɨ'leɪʃən/ n [U]

ti·tle /'taɪtl/ n 1 [C] name of a book, play, painting, etc. 2 [C] word such as 'Lord', 'President', or 'Doctor' used before someone's name to show rank, office, or profession 3 [S;U] legal right to ownership 4 [C] position of unbeaten winner: *the world heavyweight boxing title* **titled** adj having a noble title, such as 'Lord'

tit·ter /'tɪtər/ vi laugh quietly in a nervous or silly way **titter** n

tit·tle-tat·tle /'tɪtl ,tætl/ n [U] GOSSIP

tit·u·lar /'tɪtʃɨlər/ adj holding a title but not having any real power: *a titular head of state*

tiz·zy /'tɪzi/ n sl infml state of excited worried confusion

T-junc·tion /'tiː ,dʒʌŋkʃən/ n place where 2 roads meet in the shape of a T

TNT /,tiː en 'tiː/ n [U] powerful explosive

to /tə, tu; strong tuː/ prep 1 in a direction towards: *the road to London* 2 a (used before a verb to show it is the INFINITIVE): *I want to go.* b used in place of infinitive: *We didn't want to come but we had to.* 3 in order to: *I came by car to save time.* 4 so as to be in: *I was sent to prison.* 5 touching: *Stick the paper to the wall.* 6 as far as: *from beginning to end* 7 for the attention or possession of: *I told/gave it to her.* 8 in connection with: *the answer to a question* 9 in relation or comparison with: *That's nothing to what it could have been.* | *We won by 6 points to 3.* 10 (of time) before: *It's 10 to 4.* 11 per: *This car does 30 miles to the gallon.* ♦ adv 1 so as to be shut: *Pull the door to.* 2 into consciousness: *She came to.* 3 **close/near to** from really

close: *He doesn't look so young when you see him close to.*

toad /təʊd/ n animal like a large FROG

toad·stool /'təʊdstuːl/ n (uneatable) FUNGUS

toad·y /'təʊdi/ vi be too nice to someone of higher rank, esp. for personal advantage ♦ n person who toadies

to and fro /,· · '·/ adv forwards and backwards or from side to side: *The door swung to and fro in the breeze.*

toast /təʊst/ n 1 [U] bread made brown by heating 2 [C] act of ceremonial drinking to show respect or express good wishes: *They drank a toast to their guest.* ♦ vt 1 make brown by heating 2 warm thoroughly 3 drink a TOAST (2) to ~**er** n electrical apparatus for making TOAST (1)

toast·mas·ter /'təʊst,mɑːstər‖-,mæ-/ n person who introduces TOASTs (2) and speakers at a formal dinner

to·bac·co /tə'bækəʊ/ n [U] dried leaves of a certain plant prepared esp. for smoking in cigarettes, pipes, etc. ~**nist** /tə'bækənɪst/ n seller of tobacco, cigarettes, etc.

to·bog·gan /tə'bɒgən‖-'bɑː-/ n long board for carrying people over snow **toboggan** vi

to·day /tə'deɪ/ adv, n [U] 1 (on) this day 2 (at) this present time

tod·dle /'tɒdl‖'tɑːdl/ vi 1 walk, esp. with short unsteady steps 2 infml walk; go –**dler** n child who has just learnt to walk

to-do /tə 'duː/ n infml state of excited confusion or annoyance

toe¹ /təʊ/ n 1 any of the 5 small movable parts at the end of the foot 2 part of a shoe or sock covering these 3 **on one's toes** fully ready for action

toe² v **toe the line** act obediently

toe cap /'· ·/ n strengthened toe of a shoe

toe·hold /'təʊhəʊld/ n place for putting the end of the foot when climbing

tof·fee /'tɒfi‖'tɑːfi/ n [C;U] (piece of) a hard brown substance made from sugar and butter

toffee-nosed /'·· ·/ adj sl for SNOBBISH

to·ga /'təʊgə/ n loose outer garment worn in ancient Rome

to·geth·er¹ /tə'geðər/ adv 1 in or into a single group, body, or place 2 with each other 3 at the same time 4 in agreement; combined 5 **together with** in addition to ~**ness** n [U] friendliness

together² adj infml 1 (of a person) very much in control of life, actions, etc. 2 **get it together** have things under control

tog-gle /ˈtɒgəl‖ˈtɑː-/ n bar-shaped wooden button

togs /tɒgz‖tɑːgz, tɔːgz/ n [P] infml clothes

toil /tɔɪl/ n [U] lit hard work ♦ vi lit work or move with great effort

toi-let /ˈtɔɪlɪt/ n 1 [C] (room containing) a seatlike apparatus for receiving and taking away the body's waste matter 2 [U] fml act of washing, dressing oneself, etc.

toilet pa-per /ˈ·· ‚·ˑ/ n [U] paper for cleaning oneself after passing waste matter from the body

toi-let-ries /ˈtɔɪlɪtriz/ n [P] things used in washing, making oneself tidy, etc.

toilet roll /ˈ·· ·/ n rolled-up length of TOILET PAPER

toilet wa-ter /ˈ·· ‚·ˑ/ n [U] weak form of PERFUME

to-ken /ˈtəʊkən/ n 1 outward sign: They wore black as a token of mourning. 2 card which can be exchanged for goods: a book token — see also **by the same token** (SAME¹) ♦ adj 1 being a small part representing something greater 2 derog done so as to seem acceptable: a token effort

told /təʊld/ past t. & p. of TELL

tol-e-rate /ˈtɒləreɪt‖ˈtɑː-/ vt 1 permit (something one disagrees with) 2 suffer (someone or something) without complaining **-rable** adj fairly good; not too bad **-rably** adv fml fairly **-rance** n 1 [C;U] ability to suffer pain, hardship, etc., without being harmed or damaged: a low tolerance to cold 2 [U] allowing people to behave in a way one disagrees with, without getting annoyed 3 [U] TOLERATION (1) **-rant** adj showing or practising TOLERANCE (2) **-ration** /ˌtɒləˈreɪʃən/ ‚tɑː-/ n [U] 1 allowing opinions, customs, etc., different from one's own to be freely held or practised 2 TOLERANCE (2)

toll¹ /təʊl/ n 1 tax paid for using a road, bridge, etc. 2 bad effect of illness, misfortune, etc.: The death toll in the accident was 9.

toll² /vt/t ring (a bell) or be rung slowly and repeatedly

tom-a-hawk /ˈtɒməhɔːk‖ˈtɑː-/ n North American Indian axe

to-ma-to /təˈmɑːtəʊ‖-ˈmeɪ-/ n -toes soft red fruit eaten raw or cooked as a vegetable

tomb /tuːm/ n (large decorative cover for) a grave

tom-boy /ˈtɒmbɔɪ‖ˈtɑː-/ n spirited young girl who enjoys rough and noisy activities

tom-cat /ˈtɒmkæt‖ˈtɑː-/ n male cat

tome /təʊm/ n lit or humor large heavy book

tom-fool-e-ry /tɒmˈfuːləri‖tɑː-/ n [U] fml foolish behaviour

to-mor-row /təˈmɒrəʊ‖-ˈmɔː-, ˈmɑː-/ adv on the day following today ♦ n 1 [U] day after today 2 [S;U] future

tom-tom /ˈtɒm tɒm‖ˈtɑːm tɑːm/ n long narrow drum played with the hands

ton /tʌn/ n 1 a measure of weight equal to 1.016 TONNES 2 also **tons** pl. — a very large amount 3 **come down on someone like a ton of bricks** infml turn the full force of one's anger against someone, usu. as a punishment **tons** adv sl very much

tone¹ /təʊn/ n 1 [C] quality of sound, esp. of a musical instrument or the voice 2 [C] variety or shade of a colour 3 [U] general quality or nature 4 [U] proper firmness of bodily organs and muscles **tonal** adj

tone² v

tone down phr vt reduce in force

tone in phr vi/t (cause to) match

tone up phr vt make stronger, brighter, more effective or healthy, etc.

tone-deaf /ˌ· ˈ·◄/ adj unable to tell the difference between musical notes

tongs /tɒŋz‖tɑːŋz, tɔːŋz/ n [P] 2 movable arms joined at one end, for holding and lifting things

tongue /tʌŋ/ n 1 movable organ in the mouth in talking, licking, etc.: (fig.) She has a sharp tongue. (= a severe or unkind way of speaking) 2 object like this in shape or purpose: tongues of flame 3 fml language 4 **hold one's tongue** remain silent 5 (**with**) **tongue in cheek** saying or doing something one does not seriously mean

tongue-tied /ˈ· ·/ adj unable to speak freely, esp. because of nervousness

tongue twist-er /ˈ· ‚·ˑ/ n word or phrase difficult to say

ton-ic /ˈtɒnɪk‖ˈtɑː-/ n 1 [C] something, esp. a medicine, that increases health or strength 2 [U] tonic water: a gin and tonic

tonic wa-ter /ˈ·· ‚·ˑ/ n [U] sort of gassy water usu. mixed with strong alcoholic drink

to-night /təˈnaɪt/ adv, n (during) the night of today

ton-nage /ˈtʌnɪdʒ/ n [C;U] 1 amount of goods a ship can carry, expressed in TONS 2 ships, esp. those that carry goods

tonne /tʌn/ n a measure of weight equal to 1000 kilograms

ton-sil /ˈtɒnsəl‖ˈtɑː-/ n either of 2 small organs at the back of the throat

ton-sil-li-tis /ˌtɒnsəˈlaɪtəs‖ˌtɑː-/ n [U] painful soreness of the tonsils

too /tuː/ *adv* **1** to a greater degree than is necessary or good: *You're driving too fast.* **2** also: *I've been to Australia, and to New Zealand too.* **3** only **too** very

took /tʊk/ *past t. of* TAKE

tool /tuːl/ *n* **1** hand-held instrument, such as an axe, hammer, etc. **2 down tools** *infml* to stop working

toot /tuːt/ *vt* make a short warning sound with (a horn) **toot** *n*

tooth /tuːθ/ *n* **teeth** /tiːθ/ **1** small bony object growing in the mouth, used for biting **2** any of the pointed parts standing out from a comb, SAW, COG, etc. **3** ability to produce an effect: *The present law has no teeth.* **4 armed to the teeth** very heavily armed **5 fight tooth and nail** fight very violently **6 get one's teeth into** do a job very actively and purposefully **7 in the teeth of** against and in spite of: *in the teeth of fierce opposition* **8 lie in/through one's teeth** lie shamelessly **9 long in the tooth** *infml* old **10 set someone's teeth on edge** give someone an unpleasant sensation caused by certain acid tastes or high sounds — see also SWEET TOOTH ~less *adj* ~y *adj*

tooth-brush /'tuːθbrʌʃ/ *n* small brush for cleaning one's teeth

tooth-paste /'tuːθpeɪst/ *n* [U] paste for cleaning one's teeth

tooth-pick /'tuːθ‚pɪk/ *n* short thin pointed stick for removing food from the teeth

top[1] /tɒp‖tɑːp/ *n* **1** the highest or upper part: *the top of a tree* **2** the best or most important part or place: *at the top of the class* **3** cover: *bottle tops* **4 at the top of (one's) voice** as loudly as possible **5 from top to bottom** all through; completely **6 from top to toe** (of a person) completely **7 get on top of** *infml* be too much for: *This work is getting on top of me.* **8 on top of:** **a** able to deal with **b** in addition to **9 on top of the world** *infml* very happy **10 over the top** *infml*, *esp. BrE* more than is reasonable, sensible, or proper — see also **blow one's top** (BLOW[1]) ~**less** *adj* leaving the breasts bare ♦ *adj* highest, best, etc.: *at top speed* (= very fast)

top[2] *vt* **-pp-** **1** be higher, better, or more than: *Our profits have topped £1 million.* **2** form a top for: *a cake topped with cream* **3 top the bill** be chief actor or actress in a play
  top off *phr vt esp. AmE* complete successfully by a last action
  top up *phr vt* fill (a partly empty container) with liquid

top[3] /tɒp‖tɑːp/ *n* **1** child's toy that spins round **2 sleep like a top** sleep deeply and well

to-paz /'təʊpæz/ *n* [C;U] (precious stone cut from) a yellowish mineral

top brass /‚· '·/ *n* [U;P] *sl* officers of high rank in the armed forces

top dog /‚· '·/ *n* person in the most advantageous or powerful position

top hat /‚· '·/ *n* man's formal tall usu. black or grey hat

top-heav-y /‚· '··◂/ *adj* too heavy at the top

top-ic /'tɒpɪk‖'tɑː-/ *n* subject for conversation, writing, etc.

top-ic-al /'tɒpɪkəl‖'tɑː-/ *adj* of or being a subject of present interest ~**ly** /-kli/ *adv*

top-notch /‚· '·◂/ *adj* being one of the best

to-pog-ra-phy /tə'pɒgrəfi‖-'pɑː-/ *n* [U] (science of describing) the shape and height of land **-phical** /‚tɒpə-'græfikəl‖‚tɑː-, ‚təʊ-/ *adj*

top-ple /'tɒpəl‖'tɑː-/ *vi/t* (cause to) become unsteady and fall down: (fig.) *The scandal toppled the government.*

top-se-cret /‚· '··◂/ *adj* that must be kept extremely secret

top-sy-tur-vy /‚tɒpsi 'tɜːvi◂‖‚tɑːpsi 'tɜːrvi◂/ *adj*, *adv* in complete disorder and confusion

torch /tɔːtʃ‖tɔːrtʃ/ *n* **1** *BrE* small electric light carried in the hand **2** mass of burning material carried by hand to give light **3** *AmE for* BLOWLAMP

tore /tɔːʳ/ *past t. of* TEAR[1]

tor-ment[1] /'tɔːment‖'tɔːr-/ *n* [C;U] very great suffering

tor-ment[2] /tɔː'ment‖tɔːr-/ *vt* cause torment to ~**or** *n*

torn /tɔːn‖tɔːrn/ *past p. of* TEAR

tor-na-do /tɔː'neɪdəʊ‖tɔːr-/ *n* **-does** *or* **-dos** very violent wind that spins at great speed

tor-pe-do /tɔː'piːdəʊ‖tɔːr-/ *n* **-does** long narrow motor-driven explosive apparatus fired through the sea to destroy ships ♦ *vt* attack or destroy (as if) with a torpedo

tor-pid /'tɔːpɪd‖'tɔːr-/ *adj fml derog* inactive; slow

tor-por /'tɔːpəʳ‖'tɔːr-/ *n* [U] *fml derog* inactivity

tor-rent /'tɒrənt‖'tɔːr-, 'tɑː-/ *n* violently rushing stream of water: (fig.) *torrents of abuse* **-rential** /tə'renʃəl‖tɑː-/ *adj*: *torrential rain*

tor-rid /'tɒrɪd‖'tɔː-, 'tɑː-/ *adj* **1** (esp. of weather) very hot **2** full of strong feelings and uncontrolled activity, esp. sexual: *a torrid love affair*

tor-so /'tɔːsəʊ‖'tɔːr-/ *n* **-sos** human body without the head and limbs

tort /tɔːt‖tɔːrt/ *n law* wrongful but not criminal act

tor-toise /'tɔːtəs‖'tɔːr-/ *n* slow-moving land animal with a hard shell

tor·toise-shell /ˈtɔːtəʃel, ˈtɔːtəʃel‖ˈtɔːr-/ n [U] material from a tortoise's or TURTLE's shell, brown with yellowish marks

tor·tu·ous /ˈtɔːtʃuəs‖ˈtɔːr-/ adj 1 twisted; winding 2 not direct in speech, thought or action ~ly adv

tor·ture /ˈtɔːtʃər‖ˈtɔːr-/ vt cause great pain or suffering to out of cruelty, as a punishment, etc. ♦ n 1 [U] act of torturing 2 [C;U] severe pain or suffering -turer n

To·ry /ˈtɔːri/ n, adj (member) of the CONSERVATIVE PARTY ~ism n [U]

toss /tɒs‖tɔːs/ v 1 vt throw 2 vi/t (cause to) move about rapidly and pointlessly: He tossed and turned all night, unable to sleep. 3 vt move or lift (part of the body) rapidly: She tossed her head. 4 vt mix rapidly: toss a salad 5 vi/t throw (a coin) to decide something according to which side lands upwards: There's only one cake left — let's toss for it. ♦ n 1 [C] act of tossing 2 [S] BrE sl the least amount: I couldn't give a toss (= I don't care at all) what he thinks.

toss-up /ˈ· ·/ n [S] even chance; uncertainty

tot[1] /tɒt‖tɑːt/ n 1 very small child 2 small amount of a strong alcoholic drink

tot[2] v -tt- **tot up** phr vt add up

to·tal /ˈtəʊtl/ adj complete; whole ♦ n 1 complete — see also GRAND TOTAL, SUM TOTAL amount 2 **in total** when all have been added up ♦ v -ll- BrE ‖ -l- AmE be when added up: His debts totalled £9000. ~ly adv: totally different ~ity /təʊˈtælɪti/ n [U] fml completeness

to·tal·i·tar·i·an /təʊˌtælɪˈteəriən/ adj of or based on a centrally controlled system of government that does not allow any political opposition ~ism n [U]

tote /təʊt/ vt infml, esp. AmE carry, esp. with difficulty

to·tem /ˈtəʊtəm/ n person or thing used as sign or SYMBOL of an organization, society, etc.

tot·ter /ˈtɒtər‖ˈtɑː-/ vi move or walk unsteadily, as if about to fall: (fig.) their tottering economy

touch[1] /tʌtʃ/ v 1 vi/t be separated (from) by no space at all: Their hands touched. 2 vi/t feel or make connection (with), esp. with the hands: The model is fragile, don't touch (it). 3 vt eat or drink: You haven't touched your food. | I never touch alcohol. 4 vt compare with: Nothing can touch a cold drink on a hot day! 5 vt cause to feel pity, sympathy, etc.: a touching story 6 **touch wood** touch something made of wood to keep away bad luck ~ed adj

1 grateful 2 slightly mad ~y adj easily offended or annoyed ~ily adv ~iness n [U]

touch down phr vi (of a plane or spacecraft) land

touch off phr vt cause (a violent event) to start

touch on/upon phr vt talk about shortly

touch up phr vt 1 improve with small additions 2 sl touch a person in a sexually improper way

touch[2] n 1 [U] sense of feeling 2 [C] way something feels: the silky touch of her skin 3 [C] act of touching 4 [U] connection, esp. so as to receive information: He's gone to Australia, but we keep in touch by letter. 5 [S] particular way of doing things: a woman's touch 6 [C] small details: putting the finishing touches to the plan 7 [S] special ability: I'm losing my touch. 8 [S] slight attack of an illness: a touch of flu 9 [S] slight amount: It needs a touch more salt. 10 [U] (in football) area outside the field of play 11 **lose touch** lose contact — see also SOFT TOUCH

touch-and-go /ˌ··ˈ··◂/ adj of uncertain result; risky

touch-down /ˈtʌtʃdaʊn/ n landing of a plane or spacecraft

touch-line /ˈtʌtʃlaɪn/ n line along each of the longer sides of a football field

touch-stone /ˈtʌtʃstəʊn/ n lit something used as a test or standard

tough /tʌf/ adj 1 not easily weakened or broken 2 difficult to cut or eat: tough meat 3 difficult: a tough job/problem 4 not kind, severe: a tough new law against drunken driving 5 unfortunate: tough luck ~ly adv ~en vi/t make or become tougher ~ness n [U]

tou·pee /ˈtuːpeɪ‖tuːˈpeɪ/ n small WIG worn by a man

tour /tʊər/ n 1 act of travelling round a country, walking round a building, etc., looking at interesting things 2 period of duty in a job, esp. abroad 3 journey to take part in performances, sports matches, etc. ♦ vi/t visit as a tourist ~ism n [U] 1 travelling for pleasure, esp. on one's holidays 2 the business of providing holidays for tourists ~ist n 1 person travelling for pleasure 2 sportsman on TOUR (3)

tour de force /ˌtuə də ˈfɔːs‖ˌtʊər də ˈfɔːrs/ n [S] show of great skill

tour·na·ment /ˈtʊənəmənt, ˈtɔː-‖ˈtɜːr-, ˈtʊər-/ n 1 competition: a chess/tennis tournament 2 (in former times) competition of fighting skill

tour·ni·quet /ˈtʊənikeɪ, ˈtɔː-‖ˈtɜːrnɪkət, ˈtʊər-/ n something twisted tightly round a limb to stop bleeding

tou·sle /'taʊzəl/ vt make (hair) untidy

tout /taʊt/ vt derog try to persuade people to buy (one's goods or services) ♦ n BrE derog person who offers tickets for the theatre, etc., at very high prices

tow /təʊ/ vt pull (esp. a vehicle) with a rope or chain ♦ n 1 act of towing 2 **in tow** following closely behind 3 **on tow** being towed

to·wards /tə'wɔːdz‖tɔːrdz/ esp. BrE ‖ **toward** /tə'wɔːd‖tɔːrd/ esp. AmE — prep 1 in the direction of: He walked towards me. | She had her back towards me. 2 just before in time: We arrived towards noon. 3 in relation to: What are their feelings towards us? 4 for the purpose of: Each week we save £5 towards our holiday.

tow·el /'taʊəl/ n piece of cloth or paper for drying things ♦ vt -ll- BrE ‖ -l- AmE rub or dry with a towel

tow·el·ling BrE ‖ **toweling** AmE /'taʊəlɪŋ/ n [U] thickish cloth, used for making esp. towels

tow·er /'taʊəʳ/ n 1 tall (part of a) building: a church tower 2 tall metal framework for signalling or broadcasting ♦ vi be very tall: (fig.) Intellectually he towers above (= is much better than) them all. ~**ing** adj very great: a towering rage

tower block /'·· ·/ n esp. BrE tall block of flats or offices

tower of strength /,·· ·'·/ n person who can be depended on for help or support

town /taʊn/ n 1 [C] large group of houses and other buildings where people live and work 2 [C] all the people who live in such a place 3 [U] the business or shopping centre of a town 4 [U] the chief city in an area 5 [S] (life in) towns and cities in general 6 **go to town** act or behave freely or wildly 7 **(out) on the town** enjoying oneself, esp. at night 8 **paint the town red** have a very enjoyable time, esp. in a wild or noisy manner

town hall /,· ·'·/ n public building for a town's local government

town·ship /'taʊnʃɪp/ n (in South Africa) a place where black citizens live

tow·path /'təʊpɑːθ‖-pæθ/ n path along the bank of a CANAL or river

tox·ic /'tɒksɪk‖'tɑːk-/ adj poisonous ~**ity** /tɒk'sɪsəti‖tɑːk-/ n [U]

tox·in /'tɒksɪn‖'tɑːk-/ n poison produced in plants and animals

toy¹ /tɔɪ/ n 1 object for children to play with 2 small breed of dog

toy² v **toy with** phr vt 1 consider (an idea) not very seriously 2 play with or handle purposelessly

trace¹ /treɪs/ vt 1 find, esp. by following a course 2 copy lines or the shape of something using transparent paper ♦ n 1 [C;U] mark or sign showing the former presence of someone or something: She had vanished without trace. (= completely) 2 [C] small amount of something: traces of poison in his blood

trace² n rope, chain, etc., fastening a cart or carriage to the animal pulling it

trac·er·y /'treɪsəri/ n patterns with decorative branching and crossing lines

track¹ /træk/ n 1 marks left by a person, animal, or vehicle that has passed before 2 narrow (rough) path or road 3 railway line 4 course for racing 5 piece of music on a record or TAPE (2) 6 **cover one's tracks** keep one's movements, activities, etc., secret 7 **in one's tracks** infml where one is; suddenly 8 **keep/lose track of** keep/fail to keep oneself informed about a person, situation, etc. 9 **make tracks** leave, esp. in a hurry 10 **off the beaten track** not well-known or often visited 11 **on the right/wrong track** thinking or working correctly/incorrectly 12 **a one-track mind** infml a tendency to think only of one thing or subject

track² vt follow the TRACK¹ (1) of ~**er** n

track down phr vt find by hunting or searching

track re·cord /'træk ˌrekɔːd‖-ərd/ n degree to which someone or something has performed well or badly up to now

track·suit /'træksuːt, -sjuːt‖ -suːt/ n loose-fitting suit worn by people when training for sport

tract¹ /trækt/ n 1 wide stretch of land 2 system of related organs in an animal: the digestive tract

tract² n fml short article on a religious or moral subject

trac·ta·ble /'træktəbəl/ adj fml easily controlled or governed

trac·tion /'trækʃən/ n [U] 1 type of pulling power: steam traction 2 force that prevents a wheel from slipping 3 medical treatment with a pulling apparatus used to cure a broken bone or similar INJURY

trac·tor /'træktəʳ/ n motor vehicle for pulling farm machinery

trade¹ /treɪd/ n 1 [U] business of buying, selling, or exchanging goods, esp. between countries 2 [C] particular business: the wine trade 3 [C] job, esp. needing skill with the hands: the printer's trade 4 [S] stated amount of business: doing a good trade — see also FREE TRADE

trade² v 1 *vi* buy and sell goods 2 *vt* exchange: *I traded my radio for a typewriter.* | (fig.) *trading insults*

trade in *phr vt* give in part payment for something new: *I traded my old car in.*

trade off *phr vt* balance (one situation or quality) against another, with the aim of producing an acceptable or desirable result

trade on *phr vt* take unfair advantage of

trade-mark /'treɪdmɑːk‖-mɑːrk/ *n* 1 sign or word put on a product to show who made it 2 thing by which a person or thing may habitually be recognised

trade name /'· ·/ *n* name given by a producer to a particular product

trade off /'· ·/ *n* balance between two (opposing) situations or qualities

trades-man /'treɪdzmən/ *n* -men /mən/ 1 shopkeeper 2 worker or seller who comes to people's homes

trade un·i·on /ˌ· '···◁/ *n* workers' organization to represent their interests and deal with employers ~ist *n*

trade wind /'· ·/ *n* wind blowing almost continually towards the EQUATOR

tra·di·tion /trə'dɪʃən/ *n* 1 [C] opinion, custom, principle, etc., passed down from the past to the present 2 [U] (passing down of) such customs, etc.: *By tradition, brides in the West wear white.* ~al *adj* ~ally *adv*

traf·fic /'træfɪk/ *n* [U] 1 (movement of) vehicles on the road, planes in the sky, etc. 2 trade, esp. in illegal things 3 business done in carrying passengers or goods ◆ v -ck- **traffic in** *phr vt* trade in (esp. illegal things) ~ker *n*: *drug traffickers*

traffic lights /'·· ·/ *n* [P] set of coloured lights for controlling road traffic

traffic war·den /'·· ˌ··/ *n* BrE official who controls the parking of vehicles on streets

tra·ge·dy /'trædʒɪdi/ *n* [C;U] 1 serious play that ends sadly 2 [U] these plays considered as a group 3 terrible, unhappy, or unfortunate event

tra·gic /'trædʒɪk/ *adj* 1 of or related to TRAGEDY (2) 2 very sad, unfortunate, etc. ~ally /-kli/ *adv*

trail /treɪl/ *n* 1 track or smell followed by a hunter: *We're on their trail.* (= following them closely) 2 path across rough country 3 stream of dust, smoke, people, etc., behind something moving ◆ v 1 *vi/t* drag or be dragged along behind 2 *vt* TRACK 3 *vi* (of a plant) grow along a surface ~er *n* 1 vehicle pulled by another 2 small pieces of a new film shown to advertise it

train¹ /treɪn/ *n* 1 line of railway carriages pulled by an engine 2 set of related things one after another: *It interrupted my train of thought.* 3 part of a long garment that spreads over the ground behind the wearer 4 long line of moving people, animals or vehicles

train² v 1 *vi/t* give or be given instruction, practice, or exercise: *training a dog to jump over a fence* 2 *vt* aim (a gun, etc.) 3 *vt* direct the growth of (a plant) ~ee *n* person being trained ~er *n* ~ing *n* [S;U] 1 practical instruction 2 **in/out of training** in/not in a healthy condition for a sport, test of skill, etc.

traipse /treɪps/ *vi* walk tiredly

trait /treɪ, treɪt‖treɪt/ *n fml* particular quality of someone or something

trai·tor /'treɪtəʳ/ *n* someone disloyal, esp. to their country

tra·jec·to·ry /trə'dʒektəri/ *n fml* curved path of an object fired or thrown through the air

tram /træm/ *n* usu. electric bus that runs on metal lines set in the road

tramp /træmp/ *vi* 1 walk heavily 2 sound of heavy walking 3 walk steadily, esp. over a long distance ◆ *n* 1 esp. BrE wandering person with no home or job who begs for food or money 2 long walk

tram·ple /'træmpəl/ *vi/t* step (on) heavily; crush under the feet

tram·po·line /'træmpəliːn‖ˌtræmpə'liːn/ *n* frame with springy material on which people jump up and down

tramp steam·er /'·· ˌ··/ *n* ship that takes goods irregularly to various ports

trance /trɑːns‖træns/ *n* sleeplike condition of the mind

tran·quil /'træŋkwəl/ *adj* pleasantly calm, quiet, or free from worry ~lize BrE ‖ ~ize AmE *vt* make calm (esp. with tranquillizers) ~lizer BrE ‖ ~izer AmE *n* drug for reducing anxiety and making people calm ~lity BrE ‖ ~ity AmE /træŋ'kwɪlǝti/ *n* [U] calmness

trans·act /træn'zækt/ *vt fml* do and complete (a piece of business) ~ion /-'zækʃən/ *n* 1 [U] act of transacting 2 [C] piece of business **transactions** *n* [P] records of meetings of a society

trans·at·lan·tic /ˌtrænzət'læntɪk◁/ *adj* connecting or concerning countries on both sides of the Atlantic ocean

tran·scend /træn'send/ *vt fml or lit* go beyond (a limit or something within limits) ~ent *adj* going far beyond ordinary limits

tran·scribe /træn'skraɪb/ *vt* 1 write an exact copy of 2 write down (something said) 3 arrange (a piece of music) for instrument or voice other than the original

tran-script /'trænskrıpt/ n exact written or printed copy ~**ion** /træn'skrıpʃən/ n 1 [U] act or process of transcribing 2 [C] transcript

trans-fer[1] /træns'fɜːʳ/ v -rr- 1 vi/t move from one place, job, etc., to another 2 vt give ownership of property to another person 3 vi move from one vehicle to another ~**able** adj

transfer[2] /'trænsfəːʳ/ n 1 [C;U] act or process of transferring 2 [C] something transferred 3 [C] esp. BrE picture for sticking or printing onto a surface ~**ence** n [U]

trans-fig-ure /træns'fıgəʳ‖-gjər/ vt fml or lit change so as to be more glorious

trans-fix /træns'fıks/ vt fml make unable to move or think because of terror, shock, etc.

trans-form /træns'fɔːm‖-fɔːrm/ vt change completely ~**ation** /ˌtrænsfə-'meıʃən‖-fər-/ n [C;U]: the transformation of heat into power ~**er** /træns'fɔːməʳ‖-ɔːr-/ n apparatus for changing electrical force, esp. to a different VOLTAGE

trans-fu-sion /træns'fjuːʒən/ n [C;U] act of putting one person's blood into another's body

trans-gress /trænz'gres‖træns-/ v fml 1 vt go beyond (a proper or legal limit) 2 vi do wrong ~**ion** /-'greʃən/ n [C;U] ~**or** /-'gresəʳ/ n

tran-si-ent /'trænziənt‖'trænʃənt/ adj fml lasting or staying for only a short time ~**ence** n [U]

tran-sis-tor /træn'zıstəʳ, -'sıstəʳ/ n 1 small apparatus for controlling the flow of electric current 2 small radio with TRANSISTORs ~**ize** vt provide with transistors (1)

tran-sit /'trænsət, -zət/ n [U] going or moving of people or goods from one place to another: The parcel was lost in transit.

tran-si-tion /træn'zıʃən, -'sı-/ n [C;U] (act of) changing from one state to another ~**al** adj

tran-si-tive /'trænsətıv, -zə-/ adj (of a verb) that must have an object or a phrase acting like an object

tran-si-to-ry /'trænzətəri‖-tɔːri/ adj TRANSIENT

trans-late /træns'leıt, trænz-/ vi/t change (speech or writing) into a different language ~**lation** /-'leıʃən/ n [C;U] ~**lator** /-'leıtəʳ/ n

trans-lit-e-rate /trænz'lıtəreıt‖træns-/ vt fml write in a different alphabet

trans-lu-cent /trænz'luːsənt‖træns-/ adj allowing light to pass through (although not transparent)

trans-mit /trænz'mıt‖træns-/ v -tt- 1 vi/t broadcast: transmit a radio distress signal 2 vt pass to another person: transmit a disease 3 vt allow to pass through itself: Water transmits sound. -**mission** n 1 [U] act of transmitting 2 [C] television or radio broadcast 3 [C] parts of a vehicle that carry power to the wheels ~**ter** n broadcasting apparatus

trans-mute /trænz'mjuːt‖træns-/ vt fml change into something completely different (and better) -**mutation** /ˌtrænzmjuː'teıʃən‖ˌtræns-/ n [C;U]

trans-par-ent /træn'spærənt, -'speər-/ adj 1 that can be seen through 2 fml easily understood 3 fml clear and certain: a transparent lie -**ency** n 1 [U] quality of being transparent 2 [C] SLIDE (4)

trans-plant /træns'plɑːnt‖-'plɔːnt/ vt 1 move (a plant) from one place and plant it in another 2 move (an organ, piece of skin, hair, etc.) from one part of the body to another, or one person to another ♦ /'trænsplɑːnt‖-plænt/ n 1 something transplanted 2 act or operation of transplanting an organ: a heart transplant

trans-port /'trænspɔːt‖-ɔːrt/ vt carry (goods, people, etc.) from one place to another ♦ n 1 [U] also **transportation** /ˌtrænspɔː'teıʃən‖-spər-/ esp. AmE — (means or system of) transporting: London's public transport includes buses and trains. 2 **in a transport/in transports of** lit filled with (joy, delight, etc.) ~**er** /træn'spɔːtəʳ‖-ɔːr-/ n long vehicle on which several cars can be carried

trans-pose /træn'spəʊz/ vt fml 1 change the order or position of (2 or more things) 2 to change the KEY of a piece of music -**position** /ˌtrænspə-'zıʃən/ n [C;U]

trans-put-er /trænz'pjuːtəʳ‖træns-/ n extremely powerful computer MICROCHIP

trans-verse /trænz'vɜːs‖træns-'vɜːrs/ adj fml lying or placed across: a transverse beam ~**ly** adv

trans-ves-tite /trænz'vestaıt‖træns-/ n person who likes to wear the clothes of the opposite sex -**tism** n [U]

trap /træp/ n 1 apparatus for catching and holding an animal: a mouse-trap 2 plan for deceiving (and catching) a person: The police set a trap to catch the thief. 3 2-wheeled horse-drawn vehicle 4 sl mouth: Keep your trap shut! 5 AmE for BUNKER (3) ♦ vt -pp- 1 place or hold firmly with no hope of escape: The miners were trapped underground. 2 trick; deceive 3 catch (an animal) in a trap ~**per** n

trap-door /'træpdɔːʳ/ n small door in a roof or floor

tra·peze /trə'piːz/ n short bar hung high above the ground used by ACROBATs to swing on

trap·pings /'træpɪŋz/ n [P] articles of dress or decoration, esp. as an outward sign of rank

trash /træʃ/ n [U] 1 something of extremely low quality or value 2 AmE for RUBBISH (1) —y adj

trash·can /'træʃkæn/ n AmE for DUSTBIN

trau·ma /'trɔːmə, 'traumə/ n damage to the mind caused by a shock or terrible experience ~**tic** /trɔː'mætɪk/ adj deeply and unforgettably shocking

trav·el /'trævəl/ v -ll- BrE ‖ -l- AmE 1 vi/t make a journey (through) 2 vt cover (the stated distance) on a journey 3 vi go, pass, move, etc.: At what speed does light travel? 4 **travel light** travel without much luggage ♦ n [U] travelling: foreign travel ~**led** BrE ‖ ~**ed** AmE adj experienced in travel: a much travelled writer ~**ler** BrE ‖ ~**er** AmE 1 person on a journey 2 travelling SALESMAN — see also FELLOW TRAVELLER **travels** n [P] journeys, esp. abroad

travel a·gent /'··· ˌ··/ n someone who makes people's travel arrangements

traveller's cheque /ˌ··· '·/ n cheque that can be exchanged abroad for foreign money

trav·el·ogue ‖ also **-og** AmE /'trævəlɒg‖-lɔːg, -lɑːg/ n film or talk describing foreign travel

tra·verse /'trævɜːs‖trə'vɜːrs/ vt fml pass across, over, or through

trav·es·ty /'trævəsti/ n something that completely misrepresents the nature of the real thing: The trial was a travesty of justice. (= was very unjust)

trawl /trɔːl/ vi/t, n (fish with) a large net drawn along the sea bottom ~**er** n boat that uses a trawl

tray /treɪ/ n flat piece of plastic, metal, etc., for carrying things, esp. food

treach·e·ry /'tretʃəri/ n 1 [U] disloyalty or deceit 2 [C] disloyal or deceitful act -**rous** adj 1 very disloyal or deceitful 2 full of hidden dangers: treacherous currents -**rously** adv

trea·cle /'triːkəl/ n [U] BrE thick dark liquid made from sugar

tread /tred/ v **trod** /trɒd‖trɑːd/, **trodden** /'trɒdn‖'trɑːdn/ 1 vi put one's foot when walking; step: Don't tread on the flowers! 2 vt fml walk along: tread a path 3 vt press firmly with the feet 4 **tread on someone's toes** offend someone 5 **tread water** keep upright in water by moving the legs ♦ n 1 [S] act, way, or sound of walking 2 [C;U] pattern of raised lines on a tyre 3 [C] part of a stair on which the foot is placed

trea·dle /'tredl/ n apparatus worked by the feet to drive a machine

tread·mill /'tred‚mɪl/ n something providing repeated uninteresting work

trea·son /'triːzən/ n [U] disloyalty to one's country, esp. by helping its enemies ~**able** adj law of or being treason

trea·sure /'treʒəʳ/ n 1 [U] wealth in gold, jewels, etc. 2 [C] very valuable object or person ♦ vt keep or regard as precious: treasured memories

trea·sur·er /'treʒərəʳ/ n person in charge of an organization's money

treasure trove /'·· ·/ n [U] something valuable found in the ground and claimed by no one

trea·su·ry /'treʒəri/ n government department that controls and spends public money

treat /triːt/ vt 1 act or behave towards: He treated his horses very cruelly. 2 deal with or handle: Treat the glass carefully.\ He treated my request as a joke. 3 try to cure medically 4 put through a chemical or industrial action: metal treated against rust 5 pay for (someone's) food, drink, amusement, etc. ♦ n 1 something that gives great pleasure, esp. when unexpected: What a treat to have real champagne! 2 act of treating (TREAT (5)) someone: The meal's my treat, so put away your money. ~**ment** n 1 [U] act or way of treating someone or something 2 [C] substance or method for treating someone or something

trea·tise /'triːtɪs, -tɪz/ n serious book on a particular subject

trea·ty /'triːti/ n formally signed agreement between countries

tre·ble[1] /'trebəl/ predeterminer 3 times as much or as many as ♦ vi/t make or become 3 times as great

treble[2] n 1 [C] boy with a high singing voice 2 [U] upper half of the whole range of musical notes

tree /triː/ n 1 tall long-living plant with a wooden trunk or stem 2 treelike bush: a rose tree ~**less** adj

trek /trek/ vi, n -**kk**- (make) a long hard journey, esp. on foot

trel·lis /'trelɪs/ n light upright wooden framework on which plants are grown

trem·ble /'trembəl/ vi 1 shake uncontrollably 2 be very worried: I tremble to think what may happen. **tremble** n [S]

tre·men·dous /trɪ'mendəs/ adj 1 very great in amount or degree 2 wonderful: What a tremendous party! ~**ly** adv

trem·or /'tremə^r/ n shaking movement: *an earth tremor* (= a small EARTHQUAKE)|*a tremor in his voice*

trem·u·lous /'tremjᵿləs/ adj slightly shaking ~**ly** adv

trench /trentʃ/ n long narrow hole cut in the ground, esp. as a protection for soldiers

tren·chant /'trentʃənt/ adj (of language) forceful and effective

trend /trend/ n **1** general direction or course of development: *a rising trend of violent crime* **2** set a/**the trend** start or popularize a fashion ~**y** adj *infml* very fashionable

trend·set·ter /'trend,setə^r/ n person who starts or popularizes the latest fashion -**ting** adj

trep·i·da·tion /,trepᵻ'deɪʃən/ n [U] *fml* anxiety

tres·pass /'trespəs, -pæs/ vi go onto privately owned land without permission ♦ n **1** [C] *lit for* SIN **2** [C;U] (act of) trespassing ~**er** n

trespass on phr vt *fml* use too much

tress·es /'tresᵻz/ n [P] *lit* woman's long hair

tres·tle /'tresəl/ n wooden beam with a pair of spreading legs, used esp. for supporting a table (**trestle table**)

tri·al /'traɪəl/ n **1** [C;U] (act of) hearing and judging a person or case in a court of law: *He's on trial for murder.* **2** [C;U] (act of) testing to find out if something is good: *We gave her the job for a trial period.* **3** [C] cause of worry or trouble **4 stand trial** be tried in court **5 trial and error** trying several methods and learning from one's mistakes

trial run /,·· '·/ n testing of something new to see if it works properly

tri·an·gle /'traɪæŋgəl/ n figure or shape with 3 straight sides and 3 angles — see also ETERNAL TRIANGLE -**gular** /traɪ'æŋgjᵿlə^r/ adj

tribe /traɪb/ n people of the same race, beliefs, language, etc., living together under the leadership of a chief: *a tribe of Amazonian Indians* **tribal** adj

trib·u·la·tion /,trɪbjᵿ'leɪʃən/ n TRIAL (3)

tri·bu·nal /traɪ'bjuːnl/ n sort of court that deals with particular matters: *an industrial relations tribunal*

trib·u·ta·ry /'trɪbjᵿtəri‖-teri/ n river that flows into a larger river

trib·ute /'trɪbjuːt/ n [C;U] something said or given to show respect or admiration: *The chairman paid tribute to* (= praised) *their hard work.*

trice /traɪs/ n **in a trice** very quickly

trick /trɪk/ n **1** clever act or plan to deceive or cheat someone **2** something done to make someone look stupid:

children playing tricks on their teacher **3** amusing or confusing skilful act: *magic/card tricks* **4** quick or clever way to do something **5** cards played or won in a single part of a card game **6 do the trick** fulfil one's purpose ♦ vt deceive ♦ adj full of hidden difficulties: *a trick question* ~**ery** n [U] use of deceiving tricks ~**y** adj **1** difficult to deal with: *a tricky problem* **2** (of a person or actions) clever and deceitful

trick·le /'trɪkəl/ vi flow in drops or a thin stream ♦ n [S] thin slow flow: (fig.) *a trickle of enquiries*

trick-or-treat /,··'·/ vi (of children) go to people's houses on HALLOWE'EN and ask for TREATs (1) under threat of playing tricks on people who refuse

trick·ster /'trɪkstə^r/ n deceiver; cheater

tri·col·our *BrE* ‖ -**or** *AmE*/'trɪkʌlə^r‖ 'traɪ,kʌlər/ n 3-coloured flag, esp. the national flag of France

tri·cy·cle /'traɪsɪkəl/ n 3-wheeled bicycle

tri·dent /'traɪdənt/ n forklike weapon with 3 points

tried /traɪd/ past t. & p. of TRY

tri·er /'traɪə^r/ n person who always tries hard

tri·fle[1] /'traɪfəl/ n **1** [C;U] (esp. in Britain) sweet dish made of cake set in fruit, jelly, cream, etc. **2** [C] *fml* something of little value or importance **3 a trifle** *fml* rather: *You were a trifle rude* -**fling** adj *fml* of little value or importance

trifle[2] v **trifle with** phr vt treat without seriousness or respect

trig·ger /'trɪgə^r/ n piece pulled with the finger to fire a gun ♦ vt start (esp. a number of things that happen one after the other)

trigger-happy /'·· ,··/ adj too eager to use violent methods

trig·o·nom·e·try /,trɪgə'nomᵻtri‖ -'nɑː-/ n [U] MATHEMATICS dealing with the relationship between the sides and angles of TRIANGLEs

tril·by /'trɪlbi/ n esp. *BrE* man's soft hat with a BRIM

trill /trɪl/ vi/t. n (sing, play, or pronounce with) a rapidly repeated sound

tril·o·gy /'trɪlədʒi/ n group of 3 related books, plays, etc.

trim /trɪm/ vt -**mm**- **1** make neat by cutting **2** decorate, esp. round the edges **3** move (sails) into the correct position for sailing well ♦ n **1** [S] act of cutting **2** in (good) trim [U] proper condition ♦ adj -**mm**- pleasingly neat ~**ming** n decoration or useful addition: *roast duck with all the trimmings* (= vegetables, potatoes, SAUCE, etc.)

Trin·i·ty /'trɪnᵻti/ n [the] (in the Christian religion) the union of the 3 forms of God (the Father, Son, and Holy Spirit) as one God

trin-ket /'trɪŋkɪt/ n small decorative object of low value

tri-o /'triːəʊ/ n -os 1 group of 3 2 piece of music for 3 performers

trip /trɪp/ v -pp- 1 vi/t (cause to) catch the foot and lose balance: *I tripped over a stone and fell down.* 2 vi/t (cause to) make a mistake: *He tried to trip me up with awkward questions.* 3 vi lit move or dance with quick light steps ♦ n 1 short journey, esp. for pleasure 2 act of tripping (TRIP (1)) 3 sl period under the influence of a mind-changing drug ~per n esp. BrE person on a pleasure TRIP (1)

tripe /traɪp/ n [U] 1 wall of a cow's stomach used as food 2 sl worthless talk or writing

trip-le /'trɪpəl/ adj having 3 parts or members ♦ vi/t increase to 3 times the amount or number

trip-let /'trɪplət/ n any of 3 children born together

trip-li-cate /'trɪplɪkət/ n **in triplicate** in 3 copies, one of which is the original

tri-pod /'traɪpɒd‖-pɑːd/ n 3-legged support, esp. for a camera

trip-tych /'trɪptɪk/ n picture with 3 folding parts

trip-wire /'trɪp‚waɪəʳ/ n stretched wire that sets off a trap, explosive, etc., if touched

trite /traɪt/ adj (of a remark) common and uninteresting

tri-umph /'traɪəmf/ n [C;U] (joy or satisfaction caused by) a complete victory or success ♦ vi be victorious ~al /traɪˈʌmfəl/ adj of or marking a triumph ~ant adj (joyful because one is) victorious ~antly adv

tri-um-vir-ate /traɪˈʌmvɪrət/ n group of 3, esp. 3 people in power

triv-i-a /'trɪviə/ n [P] trivial things

triv-i-al /'trɪviəl/ adj 1 of little worth or importance 2 ordinary ~ize vt -ality /‚trɪviˈælɪti/ n [C;U]

trod /trɒd‖trɑːd/ past t. of TREAD

trod-den /'trɒdn‖'trɑːdn/ past p. of TREAD

trog-lo-dyte /'trɒglədaɪt‖'trɑːg-/ n person who lives in a CAVE

Tro-jan horse /‚trəʊdʒən ˈhɔːs/ n something or someone that attacks or weakens something secretly from within

trol-ley /'trɒli‖'trɑːli/ n 1 small cart, esp. pushed by hand 2 esp. BrE small table on wheels, for serving food and drink 3 trolleybus

trol-ley-bus /'trɒlibʌs‖'trɑː-/ n bus driven by electricity from wires above it

trom-bone /trɒmˈbəʊn‖trɑːm-/ n brass musical instrument with a long sliding tube

troop /truːp/ n 1 (moving) group of people or animals 2 group of soldiers esp. on horses ♦ vi move in a group **troops** n [P] soldiers

tro-phy /'trəʊfi/ n 1 prize for winning a competition or test of skill 2 something kept as a reminder of success

trop-ic /'trɒpɪk‖'trɑː-/ n line round the world at 23½° north (**the tropic of Cancer**) and south (**the tropic of Capricorn**) of the EQUATOR **tropics** n [P] hot area between these lines ~al 1 adj of the tropics 2 very hot: *tropical weather*

trot[1] /trɒt‖trɑːt/ n [S] 1 horse's movement, slower than a CANTER 2 slow run 3 **on the trot: a** one after another: *She won 3 races on the trot.* **b** continuously active

trot[2] vi -tt- move at the speed of a trot **trot out** phr vt repeat in an uninteresting unchanged way: *trotting out the same old excuses*

trou-ba-dour /'truːbədɔːr, -dʊəʳ/ n travelling singer and poet of former times

troub-le /'trʌbəl/ n 1 [C;U] (cause of) difficulty, worry, annoyance, etc.: *I didn't have any trouble doing it; it was easy.* 2 [U] state of being blamed: *He's always getting into trouble with the police.* 3 [S;U] inconvenience or more than usual work or effort: *I took a lot of trouble to get it right.* 4 [C;U] political or social disorder 5 [U] failure to work properly: *engine/heart trouble* 6 **ask/look for trouble** behave so as to cause difficulty or danger for oneself 7 **get a girl into trouble** infml make pregnant ♦ v 1 vi/t worry 2 vt cause inconvenience to 3 vi make an effort, BOTHER ~some adj annoying

troub-le-shoot-er /'trʌbəl‚ʃuːtəʳ/ n person who finds and removes causes of trouble in machines, organizations, etc.

trough /trɒf‖trɔːf/ n 1 long container for animal's food 2 long hollow area between waves 3 area of low air pressure

trounce /traʊns/ vt defeat completely

troupe /truːp/ n company of entertainers

trou-sers /'traʊzəz‖-ərz/ n [P] 2-legged outer garment covering the body from the waist downwards **trouser** adj: *a trouser leg*

trous-seau /'truːsəʊ, truːˈsəʊ/ n -seaux /-səʊz/ or -seaus clothes and other personal articles of a woman getting married

trout /traʊt/ n **trout** or **trouts** river (or sea) fish used for food

trove /trəʊv/ n see TREASURE TROVE

trow·el /'traʊəl/ n **1** flat-bladed tool for spreading cement, etc. **2** garden tool like a small spade

tru·ant /'truːənt/ n **1** pupil who stays away from school without permission **2 play truant** be a truant **-ancy** n [U]

truce /truːs/ n [C;U] agreement for the stopping of fighting

truck¹ /trʌk/ n **1** large motor vehicle for carrying goods **2** BrE open railway goods vehicle ♦ vt AmE carry by truck **~er** n AmE truck driver

truck² n **have no truck with** fml avoid any connection with

truck farm /'· ·/ n AmE for MARKET GARDEN

truc·u·lent /'trʌkjʊlənt/ adj willing or eager to quarrel or fight **~ly** adv **-lence** n [U]

trudge /trʌdʒ/ vi walk slowly and with effort ♦ n long tiring walk

true /truː/ adj **1** in accordance with fact or reality **2** real: true love **3** faithful; loyal **4** exact: a true likeness **5 come true** happen as was wished, expected, or dreamt **truly** adv **1** in accordance with the truth **2** really: a truly wonderful experience **3** sincerely: truly sorry ♦ n **out of true** not having correct shape or balance

true-blue /ˌ· '·◄/ adj completely loyal

truf·fle /'trʌfəl/ n underground FUNGUS highly regarded as food

tru·ism /'truːɪzəm/ n statement that is clearly true

trump¹ /trʌmp/ n **1** card of a sort (SUIT (3)) chosen to be of higher rank than other suits in a game **2 turn/come up trumps** do the right or needed thing, esp. unexpectedly at the last moment

trump² vt beat by playing a trump **trump up** phr vt invent (a false charge or reason)

trump card /'· ·/ n something that gives a clear and unquestionable advantage

trum·pet /'trʌmpɪt/ n **1** high-sounding brass musical instrument consisting of a long usu. winding tube **2 blow one's own trumpet** praise oneself ♦ v **1** vi (of an elephant) make a loud sound **2** vt declare or shout loudly **~er** n trumpet player

trun·cate /trʌŋˈkeɪt‖ˈtrʌŋkeɪt/ vt shorten (as if) by cutting off the top or end

trun·cheon /'trʌntʃən/ n short thick stick used as a weapon by a policeman

trun·dle /'trʌndl/ vi/t move heavily or awkwardly on wheels

trunk /trʌŋk/ n **1** main stem of a tree **2** large box in which things are packed for travelling **3** elephant's long nose **4** body without the head or limbs **5** AmE for BOOT¹ (2) **trunks** n [P] men's SHORTS for swimming

trunk call /'· ·/ n BrE a telephone call made over a long distance

trunk road /'· ·/ n main road for long-distance travel

truss /trʌs/ vt **1** tie up firmly and roughly **2** tie (a bird's) wings and legs in place for cooking ♦ n **1** medical supporting belt worn by someone with a HERNIA **2** framework of beams built to support a roof, bridge, etc.

trust¹ /trʌst/ n **1** [U] firm belief in the honesty, goodness, worth, etc., of someone or something **2** [C;U] (arrangement for) the holding and controlling of money for someone else: a charitable trust **3** [U] fml responsibility: employed in a position of trust **4 take on trust** accept without proof

trust² vt **1** believe in the honesty and worth of, esp. without proof **2** allow someone to do or have something: Can he be trusted with a gun? **3** depend on **4** fml hope, esp. confidently: I trust you enjoyed yourself. **~ful**; also **~ing** adj (too) ready to trust others **~fully**, **~ingly** adv **~y** adj lit dependable

trust in phr vt fml have faith in

trust·ee /trʌˈstiː/ n **1** person in charge of a TRUST¹ (2) **2** member of a group controlling the affairs of a company, college, etc.

trust·wor·thy /'trʌst,wɜːði‖-ɜːr-/ adj dependable

truth /truːθ/ n **truths** /truːðz, truːθs/ **1** [U] that which is true: Are you telling the truth? **2** [U] quality of being true: I doubted the truth of what he said. **3** [C] true fact — see also HOME TRUTH, MOMENT OF TRUTH **~ful** adj **1** (of a statement) true **2** habitually telling the truth **~fully** adv **~fulness** n [U]

try /traɪ/ v **1** vi/t make an attempt: I tried to persuade him, but failed. **2** vt test by use and experience: Have you tried this new soap? | We need to try the idea out in practice. **3** vt examine in a court of law: He was tried for murder. **4** vt cause to suffer, esp. with small annoyances: Her constant questions try my patience. | I've had a very trying day. **5** vt attempt to open (a door, window, etc.) ♦ n **1** attempt **2** winning of points in RUGBY by pressing the ball to the ground behind the opponents' line **tried** adj known to be good from experience

try on phr vt **1** put on (a garment, etc.) to see if it fits or looks well **2** infml behave badly to see if it will be tolerated: Take no notice, he's just trying it on.

try out *phr vt* test by use or experience

tsar /zɑːʳ, tsɑːʳ/ *n* (until 1917) male ruler of Russia

tsa-ri-na /zɑːˈriːnə, tsɑː-/ *n* (until 1917) **1** female ruler of Russia **2** wife of the tsar

tset-se fly /ˈtetsi flaɪ, ˈtsetsi-, ˈsetsi-/ *n* African fly that causes SLEEPING SICKNESS

T-shirt /ˈtiː ʃɜːt‖-ʃɜːrt/ *n* light informal collarless garment for the upper body

tub /tʌb/ *n* **1** round container for washing, packing, storing, etc. **2** bath

tu-ba /ˈtjuːbə‖ˈtuːbə/ *n* large brass musical instrument that produces low notes

tub-by /ˈtʌbi/ *adj infml* rather fat

tube /tjuːb‖tuːb/ *n* **1** hollow round pipe **2** small soft metal or plastic container for paint, paste, etc., which you get out by pressing: *a tube of toothpaste* **3** pipe in the body: *the bronchial tubes* **4** *BrE* for the UNDERGROUND **tubing** *n* [U] tubes **tubular** /ˈtjuːbjʊləʳ‖ˈtuː-/ *adj* in the form of tubes

tu-ber /ˈtjuːbəʳ‖ˈtuː-/ *n* fleshy underground stem, such as a potato

tu-ber-cu-lo-sis /tjuːˌbɜːkjʊˈləʊsɪs‖tuːˌbɜːr-/ *n* [U] serious infectious disease that attacks esp. the lungs **tubercular** /tjuːˈbɜːkjʊləʳ‖tuːˈbɜːr-/ *adj*

TUC /ˌtiː juː ˈsiː/ *n* [*the*] Trades Union Congress; the association of British trade unions

tuck /tʌk/ *vt* **1** put (the edge of) into a tight place for neatness, protection, etc.: *Tuck your shirt in.* | *She tucked the newspaper under her arm.* **2** put into a private or almost hidden place: *a house tucked away among the trees* ♦ *n* **1** narrow flat fold of material sewn into a garment **2** [U] *BrE* sweets, cakes, etc., as eaten by schoolchildren: *a tuck shop*

tuck in *phr vi* eat eagerly

tuck up *phr vt* make (esp. a child) comfortable in bed by pulling the sheets tight

Tues-day /ˈtjuːzdi‖ˈtuːz-/ *n* the 2nd day of the week, between Monday and Wednesday

tuft /tʌft/ *n* small bunch (of hair, grass, etc.)

tug /tʌg/ *vi/t* **-gg-** pull hard ♦ *n* **1** sudden strong pull **2** also **tugboat** /ˈtʌgbəʊt/ — small boat used for pulling and guiding ships in narrow places

tug-of-love /ˌ· · ˈ·/ *n BrE infml* situation in which a child's parent tries to get the child back from someone else, such as the child's other parent

tug-of-war /ˌ· · ˈ·/ *n* [C;U] sport in which 2 teams pull against each other on a rope

tu-i-tion /tjuːˈɪʃən‖tuː-/ *n* [U] *fml* teaching; instruction

tu-lip /ˈtjuːlɪp‖ˈtuː-/ *n* garden plant with large colourful cup-shaped flowers

tum-ble /ˈtʌmbəl/ *vi* **1** fall suddenly and helplessly, esp. rolling over **2** *infml* understand ♦ *n* fall

tumble down *phr vi* fall to pieces; COLLAPSE

tum-ble-down /ˈtʌmbəldaʊn/ *adj* nearly in ruins

tum-my /ˈtʌmi/ *n infml* stomach

tu-mour *BrE* ‖ **-mor** *AmE*/ˈtjuːməʳ‖ˈtuː-/ *n* mass of quickly growing diseased cells in the body

tu-mult /ˈtjuːmʌlt‖ˈtuː-/ *n* [S;U] confused noise and excitement **~uous** /tjuːˈmʌltʃuəs‖tuː-/ *adj* noisy

tu-na /ˈtjuːnə‖ˈtuːnə/ *n* **tuna** *or* **tunas** [C;U] large sea fish used for food

tune /tjuːn‖tuːn/ *n* **1** (pleasing) pattern of musical notes **2** **call the tune** be in a position to give orders **3** **change one's tune** change one's opinion, behaviour, etc. **4** **in/out of tune: a** at/not at the correct musical level **b** in/not in agreement or sympathy **5** **to the tune of** to the amount of ♦ *vt* **1** set (a musical instrument) to the correct musical level **2** put (an engine) in good working order **~ful** *adj* having a pleasant tune **tuner** *n* person who tunes musical instruments

tune in *phr vi* turn on a radio, esp. so as to listen to a particular radio station

tung-sten /ˈtʌŋstən/ *n* hard metal used esp. in making steel

tu-nic /ˈtjuːnɪk‖ˈtuː-/ *n* **1** loose usu. belted garment which reaches to the knees **2** short coat forming part of a uniform

tun-nel /ˈtʌnl/ *n* usu. man-made underground passage for road, railway, etc. ♦ *vi/t* **-ll-** *BrE* ‖ **-l-** *AmE* make a tunnel (under or through)

tunnel vi-sion /ˈ·· ˌ··/ *n* [U] tendency to consider only one part of a question, without even trying to examine others

tur-ban /ˈtɜːbən‖ˈtɜːr-/ *n* **1** Asian head covering made by winding cloth round the head **2** woman's small high-fitting hat

tur-bid /ˈtɜːbɪd‖ˈtɜːr-/ *adj* **1** (of a liquid) not clear; muddy **2** confused

tur-bine /ˈtɜːbaɪn‖ˈtɜːrbən, -baɪn/ *n* motor in which liquid or gas drives a wheel to produce circular movement

tur-bo-jet /ˈtɜːbəʊdʒet‖ˈtɜːr-/ *n* (aircraft) engine that forces out a stream of gases behind itself

tur-bu-lent /ˈtɜːbjələnt‖ˈtɜːr-/ *adj* violent and disorderly or irregular **-lence** *n* [U] **1** being turbulent **2** turbulent air movements

turd /tɜːd‖tɜːrd/ n taboo **1** piece of solid waste passed from the body **2** sl offensive person

tu-reen /tjʊˈriːn‖təˈriːn/ n large deep dish for serving soup from

turf[1] /tɜːf‖tɜːrf/ n **1** [U] grass surface **2** [C] piece of this **3** [the + S] horseracing

turf[2] vt cover with turf

turf out phr vt sl, esp. BrE throw out; get rid of

tur-gid /ˈtɜːdʒɪd‖ˈtɜːr-/ adj fml (of language or style) too solemn and self-important

tur-key /ˈtɜːki‖ˈtɜːrki/ n **1** [C;U] bird rather like a large chicken, used for food **2** AmE sl play in theatre which does not succeed **3** sl, esp. AmE stupid person **4 talk turkey** infml, esp. AmE speak seriously and plainly esp. about business — see also COLD TURKEY

Tur-kish bath /ˌ·· ˈ·/ n health treatment in which one sits in a very hot steamy room

tur-moil /ˈtɜːmɔɪl‖ˈtɜːr-/ n [S;U] state of confusion and trouble

turn[1] /tɜːn‖tɜːrn/ v **1** vi/t move round a central point: The wheels turned. **2** vi/t move so that a different side faces upwards or outwards: She turned the pages. **3** vi change direction: Turn right at the end of the road.|He turned to crime. (= became a criminal) **4** vi go round: The car turned the corner. **5** vi look round: She turned to wave. **6** vt aim; point: They turned their hoses on the burning building.|I turned my thoughts to home. **7** vi/t (cause to) become: His hair has turned grey.|The witch turned the prince into a frog. **8** vi go sour: The milk's turned. **9** vt pass: It's just turned 3 o'clock.|She's turned 40. **10 turn a phrase** fml say a clever thing neatly **11 turn one's hand to** begin to practise (a skill) **12 turn one's head** make one too proud **13 turn one's stomach** make one feel sick

turn against phr vt (cause to) become opposed to

turn away phr vt **1** refuse to let in **2** refuse to help

turn down phr vt **1** refuse **2** reduce the force, speed, loudness, etc., of (something) by using controls: Can you turn that radio down?

turn in phr v **1** no longer continue **2** vi go to bed **3** vt deliver to the police **4** vt give back; return **5** esp. AmE hand in; deliver: He's turned in some very poor work lately.

turn off phr vt **1** stop the flow or operation of: turn off the tap/television **2** sl cause to lose interest, often sexually

turn on phr vt **1** cause to flow or operate: turn on the tap/television **2**

depend on **3** attack suddenly and without warning **4** vt excite or interest strongly, often sexually **5** sl (cause to) take an illegal drug, esp. for the first time

turn out phr v **1** vt stop the operation of (a light) **2** vt drive out; send away **3** vi come out or gather (as if) for a meeting or public event **4** vt produce: The factory turns out 100 cars a day. **5** vt empty (a cupboard, pocket, etc.) **6** happen to be in the end: The party turned out a success. **7** vt dress: an elegantly turned-out woman

turn over phr vt **1** think about; consider **2** deliver to the police **3** (of an engine) to run at the lowest speed **4** do business

turn over to phr vt give control of (something) to

turn to phr vt go to for sympathy, help, advice, etc.

turn up phr v **1** vi be found **2** vi arrive **3** vt find **4** vt shorten (a garment) by folding up the bottom **5** vi happen **6 turn up one's nose (at something or someone)** suggest by one's behaviour that (something or someone) is not good enough for one

turn[2] n **1** act of turning (something) **2** change of direction **3** rightful chance or duty to do something: It's my turn to speak.|We took it in turns to do it. (= did it one after the other) **4** development: She's taken a turn for the worse. (= has become more ill) **5** point of change in time: at the turn of the century **6** attack of illness: He had one of his funny turns. **7** shock: You did give me a turn, appearing like that suddenly! **8** short stage performance **9 a good turn** a useful or helpful action **10 at every turn** in every place; at every moment **11 on the turn: a** about to turn or change **b** infml (of milk) about to go sour **12 out of turn** unsuitably: I hope I haven't spoken out of turn. **13 to a turn** (of food) cooked perfectly **14 turn and turn about** one after another

~ing n place where one road branches off from another

turn-coat /ˈtɜːnkəʊt‖ˈtɜːrn-/ n disloyal person

turn-ing point /ˈ·· ·/ n point at which a very important change happens

tur-nip /ˈtɜːnɪp‖ˈtɜːr-/ n [C;U] plant with a large round yellowish root used as a vegetable

turn-off /ˈ· ·/ n **1** smaller road branching off from a main road **2** infml something that causes one to feel dislike or lose interest, esp. sexually

turn-on /ˈ· ·/n infml something that excites or interests one strongly, esp. sexually

turn-out /ˈtɜːnaut‖ˈtɜːrn-/ n 1 number of people who attend 2 occasion on which one empties all unwanted things from drawers, rooms, etc. 3 AmE wide place in a narrow road

turn-o-ver /ˈtɜːnˌəuvəʳ‖ˈtɜːrn-/ n 1 [S] rate at which a particular kind of goods is sold 2 [S] amount of business done 3 [S] number of workers hired to fill the places of those who leave 4 [C] small pie: apple turnover

turn-pike /ˈtɜːnpaɪk‖ˈtɜːrn-/ n road which drivers have to pay to use

turn-stile /ˈtɜːnstaɪl‖ˈtɜːrn-/ n small gate that turns round, set in an entrance to admit people one at a time

turn-ta-ble /ˈtɜːnˌteɪbəl‖ˈtɜːrn-/ n 1 round spinning surface on which a record is placed to be played 2 machine including such a round surface

turn-up /ˈ· ·/ n 1 [C] BrE turned-up bottom of a trouser leg 2 [S] also **turn-up for the book(s)** — unexpected and surprising event

tur-pen-tine /ˈtɜːpəntaɪn‖ˈtɜːr-/ n [U] thin oil used esp. for cleaning off unwanted paint

tur-pi-tude /ˈtɜːpɪtjuːd‖ˈtɜːrpətuːd/ n [U] fml shameful wickedness

tur-quoise /ˈtɜːkwɔɪz, -kwɑːz‖ˈtɜːrkwɔɪz/ n [C;U] (piece of) a precious greenish-blue mineral ♦ adj turquoise-coloured

tur-ret /ˈtʌrɪt/ n 1 small tower at the corner of a building 2 turning structure on a warship, plane, etc., that contains a gun

tur-tle /ˈtɜːtl‖ˈtɜːrtl/ n 1 4-legged (sea) animal with a hard horny shell 2 **turn turtle** (of a ship) turn over

tur-tle-neck /ˈtɜːtlnek‖ˈtɜːr-/ n esp. AmE (garment with) a POLO NECK

tusk /tʌsk/ n very long pointed tooth, usu. one of a pair: an elephant's tusks

tus-sle /ˈtʌsəl/ vi fml fight roughly without weapons ♦ n rough struggle or fight

tut /tʌt/ interj (shows annoyance or disapproval)

tu-tor /ˈtjuːtəʳ‖ˈtuː-/ n 1 private teacher (in British colleges) teacher who guides a student's studies ♦ vt teach —**ial** /tjuːˈtɔːrɪəl ‖ tuː-/ n short period of instruction given by a TUTOR (2)

tu-tu /ˈtuːtuː/ n short stiff skirt worn by women BALLET dancers

tux-e-do /tʌkˈsiːdəu/ also **tux** /tʌks/ infml — n -**dos** AmE for DINNER JACKET

TV /ˌtiː ˈviː◂/ n [C;U] television

twad-dle /ˈtwɒdl‖ˈtwɑːdl/ n [U] infml nonsense

twain /tweɪn/ n [U] lit (set of) 2

twang /twæŋ/ n 1 quick ringing sound 2 sound of human speech (as if) produced partly through the nose ♦ vi/t (cause) to make a TWANG (1)

tweak /twiːk/ vt seize, pull, and twist: He tweaked her ear. **tweak** n

tweed /twiːd/ n [U] coarse woollen cloth **tweeds** n [P] (suit of) tweed clothes

tweet /twiːt/ vi, n (make) the short weak high noise of a small bird

tweet-er /ˈtwiːtəʳ/ n a LOUDSPEAKER that gives out high sounds

twee-zers /ˈtwiːzəz‖-ərz/ n [P] small 2-part jointed tool for picking up and pulling out very small objects

twelfth /twelfθ/ determiner, adv, n, pron 12th

twelve /twelv/ determiner, n, pron 12

twen-ty /ˈtwenti/ determiner, n, pron 20 -**tieth** determiner, adv, n, pron 20th

twerp /twɜːp‖twɜːrp/ n BrE sl fool

twice /twaɪs/ predeterminer, adv 1 2 times 2 **think twice (about something)** consider (something) carefully

twid-dle /ˈtwɪdl/ vi/t turn (something) round with one's fingers, usu. purposelessly

twig[1] /twɪg/ n small thin stem on a tree or bush

twig[2] n -gg- BrE sl to understand

twi-light /ˈtwaɪlaɪt/ n (faint darkish light at) the time when day is about to become night -**lit** adj

twill /twɪl/ n [U] strong woven cotton cloth

twin /twɪn/ n either of 2 people born to the same mother at the same time — also SIAMESE TWIN

twin bed /ˌ· ˈ·◂/ n either of 2 beds in a room for 2 people

twine /twaɪn/ n [U] strong string ♦ vi/t twist; wind

twinge /twɪndʒ/ n sudden sharp pain: (fig.) a twinge of conscience

twin-kle /ˈtwɪŋkəl/ vi 1 shine with an unsteady light: The stars twinkled. 2 (of the eyes) be bright with cheerfulness, amusement, etc. ♦ n [S] 1 twinkling light 2 brightness in the eye

twirl /twɜːl‖twɜːrl/ vi/t 1 spin 2 curl ♦ n sudden quick spin or circular movement

twist /twɪst/ v 1 vi/t bend, turn, etc., so as to change shape: She twisted the wire into the shape of a star. 2 vt wind: Twist the wires together. 3 vi move windingly 4 vt turn: She twisted her head round. 5 vt hurt (a joint or limb) by turning it sharply 6 vt derog change the true meaning of 7 **twist someone's arm** persuade someone forcefully or threateningly 8 **twist round one's little finger** be able to get someone to do what one wants ♦ n 1 act of twisting 2 bend 3 unexpected development: a strange twist of fate

~er *n* **1** dishonest cheating person **2** *AmE infml* TORNADO

twit /twɪt/ *n BrE sl* fool

twitch /twɪtʃ/ *vi/t* move with a twitch: *His eyelid twitched.* ♦ *n* repeated short sudden unconscious muscle movement **~y** *adj* nervous; anxious

twit·ter /'twɪtə^r/ *vi, n* [U] **1** (of a bird) (make) short high rapid sounds **2** **all of a twitter** (of people) in a very excited state

two /tuː/ *determiner, n, pron* **1** (the number) 2 **2 in two** in two parts **3 one or two** a few **4 put two and two together** calculate the meaning of what one sees or hears **5 two can play at that game** (used as a threat to someone who has been unfair, unkind, etc., to oneself)

two-faced /ˌtuːˈfeɪst◀/ *adj* deceitful; insincere

two·some /'tuːsəm/ *n* group of 2 people or things

two-time /' · · /' *vt* be unfaithful to (a girlfriend or boyfriend)

two-way /ˌ· ˈ·◀/ *adj* moving or allowing movement in both directions

ty·coon /taɪˈkuːn/ *n* rich powerful businessman

ty·ing /'taɪ-ɪŋ/ *pres. p. of* TIE

type /taɪp/ *n* **1** [C] sort; kind; example of a group or class: *She's just that type of person.* **2** [U] small blocks with raised letters on them, used in printing **3** [U] printed letters: *italic type* **4 true to type** behaving or acting (esp. badly) just as one would expect ♦ *vi/t* write with a typewriter or WORD PROCESSOR

type-cast /'taɪpkɑːst‖-kæst/ *vt* **-cast** repeatedly give (an actor) the same kind of part

type-face /'taɪpfeɪs/ *n* size and style of printed letters

type-script /'taɪpˌskrɪpt/ *n* typewritten copy of something

type-writ-er /'taɪpˌraɪtə^r/ *n* machine that prints letters by means of finger-operated keys

ty·phoid /'taɪfɔɪd/ *n* [U] infectious disease causing fever and often death, produced by bacteria in food or drink

ty·phoon /taɪˈfuːn/ *n* very violent tropical storm

ty·phus /'taɪfəs/ *n* [U] infectious disease that causes fever, severe headaches, and red spots on the body

typ·i·cal /'tɪpɪkəl/ *adj* showing the usual or main qualities of a particular sort of thing: *a typical British summer, with lots of rain* **~ly** /-kli/ *adv*

typ·i·fy /'tɪpɪfaɪ/ *vt* be a typical mark, sign, or example of

typ·ist /'taɪpɪst/ *n* secretary employed mainly for typing letters

ty·pog·ra·phy /taɪˈpɒɡrəfi‖-ˈpɑː-/ *n* [U] **1** preparing matter for printing **2** arrangement and appearance of printed matter **-phic** /ˌtaɪpəˈɡræfɪk◀/ *adj*

tyr·an·nize ‖ *also* **-nise** *BrE* /'tɪrənaɪz/ *vt* use power over (a person, country, etc.) with unjust cruelty

tyr·an·ny /'tɪrəni/ *n* [U] use of cruel or unjust ruling power **-ical** /tɪˈrænɪkəl/ *adj*

ty·rant /'taɪərənt/ *n* cruel unjust ruler

tyre /taɪə^r/ *n BrE* thick band of rubber round the outside edge of a wheel

tzar /zɑː^r, tsɑː^r/ *n* TSAR

tza·ri·na /zɑːˈriːnə, tsɑː-/ *n* TSARINA

U

U, u /juː/ the 21st letter of the English alphabet

u·biq·ui·tous /juːˈbɪkwətəs/ *adj fml* happening or existing everywhere

U-boat /'juː bəʊt/ *n* German SUBMARINE of the Second World War

ud·der /'ʌdə^r/ *n* milk-producing organ of a cow, female goat, etc.

UFO /'juːfəʊ, ˌjuː ef 'əʊ/ *n* UFO's *or* UFOs strange object in the sky, thought of as a spacecraft from another world

ugh /ʊx, ʌɡ/ *interj* (expresses extreme dislike)

ug·ly /'ʌɡli/ *adj* **1** unpleasant to see **2** very unpleasant or threatening: *in an ugly mood* **ugliness** [U]

ugly duck·ling /ˌ·· ˈ··/ *n* person less attractive than others in early life but becoming attractive later

UK /ˌjuːˈkeɪ/ *n* [*the*] the UNITED KINGDOM

u·ku·le·le /ˌjuːkəˈleɪli/ *n* sort of small GUITAR

ul·cer /'ʌlsə^r/ *n* sore place where the skin is broken **~ate** *vi* turn into or become covered with ulcers **~ous** *adj*

ul·te·ri·or /ʌlˈtɪəriə^r/ *adj* kept secret, esp. because bad: *an ulterior motive*

ul·ti·mate /'ʌltəmət/ *adj* being or happening after all others: *our ultimate destination* **~ly** *adv* in the end

ul·ti·ma·tum /ˌʌltɪˈmeɪtəm/ *n* **-tums** *or* **-ta** /-tə/ statement of conditions to be met, not open to argument

ul·tra·ma·rine /ˌʌltrəməˈriːn/ *adj* very bright blue

ul·tra·son·ic /ˌʌltrəˈsɒnɪk◀‖-ˈsɑː-/ *adj* (of a sound wave) beyond the range of human hearing

ul·tra·vi·o·let /ˌʌltrə'vaɪəlɪt/ adj (of light) beyond the purple end of the range of colours that can be seen by humans

um·bil·i·cal cord /ʌmˌbɪlɪkəl 'kɔːd‖-'kɔːrd/ n tube of flesh which joins an unborn creature to its mother

um·brage /'ʌmbrɪdʒ/ n **take umbrage** be offended

um·brel·la /ʌm'brelə/ n **1** folding cloth-covered frame for keeping rain off the head **2** protecting power or influence **3** anything which covers or includes a wide range of different parts

um·laut /'ʊmlaʊt/ n sign (¨)

um·pire /'ʌmpaɪə'/ n judge in charge of certain games, such as cricket and tennis ♦ vi/t act as an umpire

ump·teen /ˌʌmp'tiːn◄/ determiner, pron infml a large number (of) ~th n, determiner

un·a·ble /ʌn'eɪbəl/ adj not able

un·ac·coun·ta·ble /ˌʌnə'kaʊntəbəl/ adj fml hard to explain; surprising **–bly** adv

un·ac·cus·tomed /ˌʌnə'kʌstəmd◄/ adj **1** not used (to) **2** unusual

un·ad·vised /ˌʌnəd'vaɪzd/ adj fml not sensible

u·nan·i·mous /juː'nænɪməs/ adj with everyone agreeing: a unanimous decision ~ly adv –nimity /ˌjuːnə'nɪmɪti/ n [U]

un·an·swe·ra·ble /ʌn'ɑːsərəbəl‖ʌn'æn-/ adj that cannot be answered or argued against

un·as·sum·ing /ˌʌnə'sjuːmɪŋ◄, -'suː-‖-'suː-/ adj quiet and unwilling to make claims about one's good qualities

un·at·tached /ˌʌnə'tætʃt◄/ adj **1** not connected **2** not married or ENGAGED (1)

un·at·tend·ed /ˌʌnə'tendɪd◄/ adj alone, with no one present or in charge

un·a·vail·ing /ˌʌnə'veɪlɪŋ◄/ adj having no effect ~ly adv

un·a·wares /ˌʌnə'weəz‖-'weərz/ adv unexpectedly or without warning: I took/caught her unawares. (= surprised her by my presence)

un·bal·ance /ˌʌn'bæləns/ vt make slightly mad: an unbalanced mind

un·be·known /ˌʌnbɪ'nəʊn/ adv without the stated person knowing: Unbeknown to me, he had left.

un·bend /ʌn'bend/ v -bent /-'bent/ **1** vi/t straighten **2** vi behave more informally

un·bos·om /ˌʌn'bʊzəm/ vt fml or lit **unbosom oneself** tell one's secret troubles and worries

un·bowed /ˌʌn'baʊd◄/ adj esp. lit not defeated

un·bri·dled /ʌn'braɪdld/ adj not controlled, and esp. too active or violent

un·bur·den /ˌʌn'bɜːdn‖-ɜːr-/ vt fml free (oneself, one's mind, etc.) by talking about a secret trouble

un·called-for /ʌn'kɔːld fɔː'/ adj not deserved, necessary, or right: uncalled-for rudeness

un·can·ny /ʌn'kæni/ adj not natural or usual; mysterious –nily adv

un·ce·re·mo·ni·ous /ˌʌnserɪ-'məʊniəs/ adj **1** informal **2** rudely quick ~ly adv: He was thrown out unceremoniously into the street.

un·cer·tain /ʌn'sɜːtn‖-ɜːr-/ adj **1** doubtful **2** undecided or unable to decide **3** likely to change: uncertain weather ~ly adv ~ty n [C;U]

un·chart·ed /ʌn'tʃɑːtɪd‖-ɑːr-/ adj esp. lit (of a place) not well known enough for maps to be made

un·cle /'ʌŋkəl/ n brother of one's father or mother, or husband of one's aunt

un·clean /ˌʌn'kliːn◄/ adj not (religiously) pure

Uncle Sam /ˌʌŋkəl 'sæm/ n infml lit the US

Uncle Tom /ˌʌŋkəl 'tɒm‖-'tɑːm/ n derog black person who is very friendly or respectful to white people

un·com·for·ta·ble /ʌn'kʌmftəbəl, -'kʌmfət-‖ʌn'kʌmfərt-,-'kʌmft-/ adj **1** not comfortable **2** EMBARRASSed **–bly** adv

un·com·mon·ly /ʌn'kɒmənli‖-'kɑː-/ adv fml very

un·com·pro·mis·ing /ʌn'kɒmprə-maɪzɪŋ‖-'kɑːm-/ adj (bravely) unchangeable in one's opinions, actions, etc.

un·con·scio·na·ble /ʌn'kɒnʃənəbəl‖-'kɑːn-/ adj fml unreasonable in degree or amount **–bly** adv

un·con·scious /ʌn'kɒnʃəs‖-'kɑːn-/ adj **1** having lost consciousness **2** not intentional

un·count·a·ble /ʌn'kaʊntəbəl/ adj that cannot be counted: 'Furniture' is an uncountable noun — you can't say 'two furnitures'.

un·couth /ʌn'kuːθ/ adj fml rough and bad-mannered

un·cov·er /ʌn'kʌvə'/ vt **1** remove a covering from **2** find out (something unknown or kept secret)

un·crowned king /ˌ·· '·/un·crowned queen fem. — n person considered the best, most famous, etc., in a particular activity

unc·tu·ous /'ʌŋktʃuəs/ adj fml full of unpleasantly insincere kindness, interest, etc.

un·daunt·ed /ʌn'dɔːntɪd/ adj not at all discouraged or frightened

un·de·ceive /ˌʌndɪ'siːv/ vt fml inform (a mistaken person) of the truth

un·de·cid·ed /ˌʌndɪˈsaɪdəd/ adj not yet having (been) decided; in doubt

un·de·ni·a·ble /ˌʌndɪˈnaɪəbəl/ adj clear and certain **–bly** adv

un·der /ˈʌndəʳ/ prep **1** below; covered by: *The ball rolled under the table.* | (fig.) *She wrote under the name of George Eliot.* **2** less than: *under £5* **3** working for; controlled by: *She has 3 secretaries under her.* | *Spain under Franco.* **4** (expresses various states or relationships): *He was under threat of* (= was threatened with) *dismissal.* | *I was under the impression* (= thought) *that you'd gone.* **5** in the state or act of: *under discussion/contract* **6** **under age** too young in law, esp. for drinking alcohol, driving a car, etc. **7** **under cover (of)** hidden (by): *They escaped under cover of darkness.* ♦ adv **1** in or to a lower place **2** less: *children of 9 or under*

un·der·arm /ˈʌndərɑːm/ adj, adv (in sport) with the hand below the shoulder

un·der·bel·ly /ˈʌndəˌbeli/ -ər-/ n esp. lit weak or undefended part of a place, plan, etc.

un·der·car·riage /ˈʌndəˌkærɪdʒ/ -ər-/ n aircraft's wheels and wheel supports

und·er·charge /ˌʌndəˈtʃɑːdʒ/ ˌʌndərˈtʃɑːrdʒ/ vi/t take too small an amount of money from (someone)

un·der·clothes /ˈʌndəkləʊðz, -kləʊz/ -dər-/ n [P] UNDERWEAR

un·der·coat /ˈʌndəkəʊt/ -dər-/ n covering of paint that goes under the main covering

un·der·cov·er /ˌʌndəˈkʌvəʳ◄/ -dər-/ adj acting or done secretly, esp. as a SPY

un·der·cur·rent /ˈʌndəˌkʌrənt/ -dər-ˌkɜːr-/ n **1** hidden current of water beneath the surface **2** hidden tendency: *an undercurrent of discontent*

un·der·cut /ˌʌndəˈkʌt/ -dər-/ vt **-cut**; pres. p. **-tt-** sell things more cheaply than (a competitor)

un·der·de·vel·oped coun·try /ˌʌndədɪˌveləpt ˈkʌntri/ -dər-/ n country that needs to develop its industries and improve living conditions

un·der·dog /ˈʌndədɒg/ ˈʌndərdɔːg/ n one always treated badly by others or expected to lose in a competition

un·der·done /ˌʌndəˈdʌn◄/ -ər-/ adj not completely cooked

un·der·es·ti·mate /ˌʌndərˈestɪment/ v **1** vi/t guess, too low a value (for) **2** vt have too low an opinion of ♦ n /-stɪmət/ ESTIMATE which is too small

un·der·fed /ˌʌndəˈfed◄/ -ər-/ adj having not enough food

un·der·foot /ˌʌndəˈfʊt/ -ər-/ adv beneath the feet: *The path was stony underfoot.*

un·der·go /ˌʌndəˈgəʊ/ -dər-/ vt **-went** /-ˈwent/, **-gone** /-ˈgɒn/ -ˈgɔːn/ experience (esp. something unpleasant or difficult)

un·der·grad·u·ate /ˌʌndəˈgrædʒuət/ -ər-/ n person doing a university course for a first degree

un·der·ground /ˈʌndəgraʊnd/ -ər-/ adj **1** below the Earth's surface **2** secret; representing a political view not acceptable to the government ♦ n **1** (often cap.) underground railway system **2** secret group fighting or opposing the rulers of a country ♦ adv /ˌʌndəˈgraʊnd/ -ər-/ **go underground** hide from political view for a time

un·der·growth /ˈʌndəgrəʊθ/ -dər-/ n [U] bushes and low plants growing around trees

un·der·hand[1] /ˌʌndəˈhænd◄/ -ər-/ also **underhanded** /-ˈhændəd◄/ — adj (secretly) dishonest

underhand[2] adj, adv UNDERARM

un·der·lie /ˌʌndəˈlaɪ/ -ər-/ vt **-lay** /-ˈleɪ/, **-lain** /-ˈleɪn/ be a hidden cause or meaning of

un·der·line /ˌʌndəˈlaɪn/ -ər-/ vt **1** draw a line under **2** give additional force to, so as to show importance

un·der·ling /ˈʌndəlɪŋ/ -ər-/ n person of low rank

un·der·manned /ˌʌndəˈmænd◄/ -ər-/ adj (of a factory, etc.) having too few workers

un·der·mine /ˌʌndəˈmaɪn/ -ər-/ vt **1** weaken or destroy gradually: *Criticism undermines his confidence.* **2** wear away the ground beneath

un·der·neath /ˌʌndəˈniːθ/ -ər-/ prep, adv under; below

un·der·pants /ˈʌndəpænts/ -ər-/ n [P] underclothes for the lower part of the body

un·der·pass /ˈʌndəpɑːs/ ˈʌndərpæs/ n path or road under another road, railway, etc.

un·der·pin /ˌʌndəˈpɪn/ -ər-/ vt **-nn-** strengthen or support (an argument)

un·der·priv·i·leged /ˌʌndəˈprɪvɪlɪdʒd◄/ -dər-/ adj poor and living in bad social conditions

un·der·rate /ˌʌndəˈreɪt/ vt give too low an opinion of

un·der·sec·re·ta·ry /ˌʌndəˈsekrətəri/ ˌʌndərˈsekrəteri/ n (in Britain) high-ranking government official who advises ministers

un·der·side /ˈʌndəsaɪd/ -ər-/ n lower side or surface

un·der·signed /ˌʌndəsaɪnd/ -ər-/ n whose signature is/are beneath the writing: *We, the undersigned*

un·der·stand /ˌʌndəˈstænd/ -ər-/ v **-stood** /-ˈstʊd/ **1** vi/t know or find the meaning (of): *She spoke in Russian, and I didn't understand.* 2 *vt* know or feel closely the nature of (a person, feelings. etc.) 3 *vt* take or judge (as the meaning) 4 *vt* find have been informed: *I understand you wish to join.* 5 *vt* add (something unexpressed) in the mind to make a meaning complete 6 **make oneself understood** make one's meaning clear to others, esp. in speech ~**able** *adj* 1 that can be understood 2 reasonable ~**ably** *adv* ~**ing** *n* 1 [U] brain power; ability to understand 2 [C] private informal agreement 3 [U] sympathy ♦ *adj* sympathetic

un·der·state /ˌʌndəˈsteɪt‖-ər-/ *vt* express less strongly than one could or should ~**ment** *n* [C;U]

un·der·stud·y /ˈʌndəˌstʌdi‖-ər-/ *n* actor able to take over from another in a particular part if necessary ♦ *vt* be an understudy for

un·der·take /ˌʌndəˈteɪk‖-ər-/ *vt* -**took** /-ˈtʊk/, -**taken** /-ˈteɪkən/ *fml* 1 take up or accept (a position, work, etc.) 2 promise -**taking** /ˌʌndəˈteɪkɪŋ‖ˈʌndərˌteɪ-/ *n* 1 piece of work; job 2 *fml* promise

un·der·tak·er /ˈʌndəteɪkəʳ‖-dər-/ *n* funeral arranger -**ing** *n* [U]

un·der·tone /ˈʌndətəʊn‖-dər-/ *n* 1 low voice 2 hidden meaning or feeling

un·der·wear /ˈʌndəweəʳ‖-dər-/ *n* [U] clothes worn next to the body under other clothes

un·der·went /ˌʌndəˈwent‖-ər-/ *past t. of* UNDERGO

un·der·world /ˈʌndəwɜːld‖ˈʌndərwɜːrld/ *n* 1 criminals considered as a social group 2 home of the dead in ancient Greek stories

un·der·write /ˌʌndəˈraɪt/ *vt* -**wrote** /-ˈrəʊt/, -**written** /-ˈrɪtn/ *fml* support, esp. with money -**writer** /ˈʌndəraɪtəʳ‖-dər-/ *n* person who makes insurance contracts

un·de·si·ra·ble /ˌʌndɪˈzaɪərəbəl/ *adj fml* not wanted; unpleasant ♦ *n* someone regarded as immoral, criminal, or socially unacceptable -**bility** *n* /ˌʌndɪzaɪərəˈbɪləti/

un·de·vel·oped /ˌʌndɪˈveləpt◂/ *adj* (usu. of a place) not having industry, mining, building, etc.

un·dies /ˈʌndiz/ *n* [P] *infml* (women's) underwear

un·di·vid·ed /ˌʌndɪˈvaɪdɪd◂/ *adj* complete

un·do /ʌnˈduː/ *vt* -**did** /-ˈdɪd/, -**done** /-ˈdʌn/ 1 unfasten (something tied or wrapped) 2 remove the effects of: *The fire undid months of hard work.* ~**ing** *n* [S] cause of one's ruin, failure, etc.

un·doubt·ed /ʌnˈdaʊtɪd/ *adj* known for certain to be (so) ~**ly** *adv*

un·dress /ʌnˈdres/ *v* 1 *vi* take one's clothes off 2 *vt* take (someone's) clothes off ♦ *n* *fml* lack of clothes ~**ed** *adj* wearing no clothes

un·due /ˌʌnˈdjuː◂‖-ˈduː◂/ *adj* too much; unsuitable **unduly** *adv*: *not unduly worried*

un·du·late /ˈʌndjʊleɪt‖-dʒə-/ *vi* rise and fall like waves -**lation** /ˌʌndjʊˈleɪʃən‖-dʒə-/ *n* [C;U]

un·dy·ing /ʌnˈdaɪ-ɪŋ/ *adj lit* which will never end

un·earth /ʌnˈɜːθ‖-ˈɜːrθ/ *vt* 1 dig up 2 discover

un·earth·ly /ʌnˈɜːθli‖-ˈɜːr-/ *adj* 1 very strange and unnatural 2 *infml* (of time) very inconvenient

un·eas·y /ʌnˈiːzi/ *adj* worried; anxious -**ily** *adv* -**iness** *n* [U]

un·ec·o·nom·ic /ˌʌniːkəˈnɒmɪk, ˌʌnekə-‖-ˈnɑː-/ *also* **uneconomical** /-mɪkəl/ — *adj* not producing profit; wasteful

un·ed·i·fy·ing /ʌnˈedɪfaɪ-ɪŋ/ *adj* unpleasant or offensive to the moral sense

un·em·ployed /ˌʌnɪmˈplɔɪd◂/ *adj* not having a job ♦ *n* [*the* + S] people without jobs

un·em·ploy·ment /ˌʌnɪmˈplɔɪmənt/ *n* [U] 1 condition of lacking a job 2 lack of jobs for numbers of people in society

un·en·vi·a·ble /ʌnˈenviəbəl/ *adj* not to be wished for, esp. because of difficulty

un·e·qualled *BrE* ‖-**qualed** *AmE* /ʌnˈiːkwəld/ *adj* the greatest possible

un·e·quiv·o·cal /ˌʌnɪˈkwɪvəkəl/ *adj* totally clear in meaning

un·er·ring /ʌnˈɜːrɪŋ/ *adj* without making a mistake

un·e·ven /ʌnˈiːvən/ *adj* 1 not smooth, straight, or regular 2 ODD (2) 3 varying in quality: *uneven work* (= often rather bad) ~**ly** *adv* ~**ness** *n* [U]

un·ex·cep·tio·na·ble /ˌʌnɪkˈsepʃənəbəl/ *adj fml* satisfactory

un·ex·pur·gat·ed /ʌnˈekspəɡeɪtɪd‖-pər-/ *adj* (of a book, play, etc.) with nothing that is considered improper taken out; complete

un·fail·ing /ʌnˈfeɪlɪŋ/ *adj* continuous ~**ly** *adv*

un·faith·ful /ʌnˈfeɪθfəl/ *adj* having sex with someone other than one's regular partner

un·fath·o·ma·ble /ʌnˈfæðəməbəl/ *adj* that one cannot understand; mysterious

un·flap·pa·ble /ʌnˈflæpəbəl/ *adj* always calm, esp. in difficult situations

un·fold /ʌnˈfəʊld/ *v* 1 *vt* open from a folded position 2 *vi/t* (cause to) become clear, more fully known, etc.: *as the story unfolded*

un·for·get·ta·ble /ˌʌnfəˈgetəbəl‖ -fər-/ *adj* too strong in effect to be forgotten —**bly** *adv*

un·for·tu·nate /ʌnˈfɔːtʃənət‖-ˈfɔːr-/ *adj* 1 that makes one sorry 2 unlucky 3 slightly rude ~**ly** *adv*

un·found·ed /ʌnˈfaʊndɪd/ *adj* not supported by facts

un·frock /ʌnˈfrɒk‖ʌnˈfrɑːk/ *vt* dismiss (a priest)

un·furl /ʌnˈfɜːl‖-ɜːrl/ *vt* unroll and open (a flag, sail, etc.)

un·gain·ly /ʌnˈgeɪnli/ *adj* not graceful; awkward

un·god·ly /ʌnˈgɒdli‖-ˈgɑːd-/ *adj* 1 not religious 2 *infml* UNEARTHLY (2)

un·grate·ful /ʌnˈgreɪtfəl/*adj* 1 not grateful 2 *lit* (of work) giving no reward or result

un·guard·ed /ʌnˈgɑːdɪd‖-ɑːr-/ *adj* unwisely careless, esp. in speech

un·hand /ʌnˈhænd/ *vt lit* stop holding or touching: *Unhand me, sir!*

un·heard-of /ʌnˈhɜːd əv, -ɒv‖-ɜːrd əv, -ɑːv/ *adj* very unusual

un·hinge /ʌnˈhɪndʒ/ *vt* make mad

un·ho·ly /ʌnˈhəʊli/ *adj* terrible; unreasonable: *an unholy row*

unholy al·li·ance /ˌ··ˈ···/*n* grouping of people or esp. organizations that are usu. separate or opposed but have come together for a bad purpose

u·ni·corn /ˈjuːnɪkɔːn‖-ɔːrn/ *n* imaginary horselike animal with a single horn

u·ni·form /ˈjuːnɪfɔːm‖-ɔːrm/ *n* sort of clothes worn by all members of a group: *school/army uniform* ♦ *adj* the same all over; regular ~**ly** *adv* ~**ed** *adj*: *uniformed soldiers* ~**ity** /ˌjuːnɪˈfɔːmɪti‖-ɔːr-/ *n* [U]

u·ni·fy /ˈjuːnɪfaɪ/ *vt* bring together so as to be a single whole or all the same —**fication** /ˌjuːnɪfɪˈkeɪʃən/ *n* [U]

u·ni·lat·er·al /ˌjuːnɪˈlætərəl/ *adj* done by only one group: *unilateral disarmament*

un·im·pea·cha·ble /ˌʌnɪmˈpiːtʃəbəl/ *adj fml* that cannot be doubted or questioned

un·i·ni·ti·at·ed /ˌʌnɪˈnɪʃieɪtɪd/ *n* [*the* + P] *fml* people who are not among those who have special knowledge or experience

un·in·terest·ed /ʌnˈɪntrəstɪd/ *adj* not interested

u·nion /ˈjuːnjən/ *n* 1 [C] club or society, esp. a TRADE UNION 2 [C] group of states: *the Soviet Union* 3 [U] *fml* joining 4 [C;U] *lit* (unity in) marriage

Union Jack /ˌ··ˈ·/*n* [*the*] British flag

u·nique /juːˈniːk/ *adj* 1 being the only one of its type 2 unusual 3 better than any other ~**ly** *adv*

u·ni·sex /ˈjuːnɪseks/ *adj* of one type for both male and female

u·ni·son /ˈjuːnɪsən, -zən/ *n* [U] 1 being together in taking action 2 everyone singing or playing the same note

u·nit /ˈjuːnɪt/ *n* 1 group within a larger organization: *the hospital's X-ray unit* 2 amount forming a standard of measurement: *The pound is a unit of currency.* 3 whole number less than 10 4 piece of furniture, etc., which can be fitted with others of the same type

u·nite /juːˈnaɪt/ *v* 1 *vt* join 2 *vi* become one 3 *vi* act together for a purpose

United King·dom /·,·· ˈ··/ *n* [*the*] England, Scotland, Wales, and Northern Ireland

unit trust /ˌ·· ˈ·/ *n* company through which one can buy SHAREs in various companies

u·ni·ty /ˈjuːnɪti/ *n* [U] being united or in agreement

u·ni·verse /ˈjuːnɪvɜːs‖-ɜːrs/ *n* [*the* + S] everything which exists in all space —**versal** /ˌjuːnɪˈvɜːsəl‖-ɜːr-/ *adj* among or for everyone or in every place: *universal agreement* —**versally** *adv*

u·ni·ver·si·ty /ˌjuːnɪˈvɜːsəti◄‖-ɜːr-/ *n* 1 place of education at the highest level, where degrees are given 2 members of this place

un·kempt /ˌʌnˈkempt◄/ *adj* (esp. of hair) untidy

un·kind /ˌʌnˈkaɪnd◄/ *adj* not kind; cruel or thoughtless

unknown quan·ti·ty /ˌ·· ˈ···/*n* 1 person or thing whose qualities and abilities are not yet known 2 (in MATHEMATICS) a number represented by the letter x

un·leash /ʌnˈliːʃ/ *vt* allow (feelings, forces, etc.) to act with full force

un·less /ʌnˈles, ən-/ *conj* except if: *Don't come unless I ask you to.*

un·like·ly /ʌnˈlaɪkli/ *adj* 1 not expected; improbable 2 not likely to happen or be true

un·load /ʌnˈləʊd/ *v* 1 *vt* remove (a load) from (something) 2 *vi/t* remove bullets from (a gun) or film from (a camera) 3 *vt* get rid of

un·loose /ʌnˈluːs/ *vt* set free

un·loos·en /ʌnˈluːsən/ *vt* loosen

un·mask /ʌnˈmɑːsk‖-mæsk/ *vt* show the hidden truth about

un·men·tio·na·ble /ʌnˈmenʃənəbəl/ *adj* too shocking to be spoken about

un·mit·i·gat·ed /ʌnˈmɪtɪgeɪtɪd/ *adj* in every way (bad): *an unmitigated disaster*

un·nat·u·ral /ʌnˈnætʃərəl/ *adj* 1 unusual 2 against ordinary good ways of behaving: *unnatural sexual practices*

un·nerve /ˌʌnˈnɜːv‖-ˈɜːrv/ *vt* take away (someone's) confidence or courage

un·ob·tru·sive /ˌʌnəbˈtruːsɪv/ *adj* not (too) noticeable **–ly** *adv*

un·pack /ʌnˈpæk/ *vi/t* remove (possessions) from (a container)

un·pal·at·a·ble /ʌnˈpælətəbəl/ *adj fml* unpleasant and difficult for the mind to accept

un·pick /ʌnˈpɪk/ *vt* take out (the stitches) from (something)

un·pleas·ant /ʌnˈplezənt/ *adj* 1 not enjoyable 2 unkind

un·pre·ce·dent·ed /ʌnˈpresɪdentɪd/ *adj* never having happened before

un·pre·ten·tious /ˌʌnprɪˈtenʃəs/ *adj* not attempting to seem wealthy, important, etc.; simple

un·prin·ta·ble /ʌnˈprɪntəbəl/ *adj* too offensive to express

un·qual·i·fied /ʌnˈkwɒlɪfaɪd ‖ -ˈkwɑː-/ *adj* 1 not limited 2 not having suitable knowledge or experience

un·ques·tio·na·ble /ʌnˈkwestʃənəbəl/ *adj* which cannot be doubted; certain **–bly** *adv*

un·rav·el /ʌnˈrævəl/ *vt* **-ll-** *BrE* ‖ **-l-** *AmE* 1 *vi/t* become or cause (threads, cloth, etc.) to become separated or unwoven 2 *vt* make clear (a mystery)

un·real /ˌʌnˈrɪəl◂/ *adj* seeming imaginary or unlike reality **~ity** /ˌʌnrɪˈælɪti/ *n* [U]

un·re·mit·ting /ˌʌnrɪˈmɪtɪŋ◂/ *adj fml* (of something difficult) never stopping

un·re·quit·ed /ˌʌnrɪˈkwaɪtɪd◂/ *adj fml* not given in return

un·rest /ʌnˈrest/ *n* [U] troubled or dissatisfied confusion, often with fighting

un·ri·valled *BrE* ‖ **-valed** *AmE* /ʌnˈraɪvəld/ *adj* better than any other

un·roll /ʌnˈrəʊl/ *vi/t* open from a rolled condition

un·ru·ly /ʌnˈruːli/ *adj* 1 behaving wildly: *unruly children* 2 hard to keep in place: *unruly hair*

un·sa·vour·y *BrE* ‖ **-vory** *AmE* /ʌnˈseɪvəri/ *adj* unpleasant or unacceptable in moral values

un·scathed /ʌnˈskeɪðd/ *adj* not harmed

un·scru·pu·lous /ʌnˈskruːpjʊləs/ *adj* not caring about honesty and fairness

un·sea·so·na·ble /ʌnˈsiːzənəbəl/ *adj* unusual for the time of year, esp. bad **-bly** *adv*

un·seat /ʌnˈsiːt/ *vt* 1 remove from a position of power 2 (of a horse) throw off (a rider)

un·seem·ly /ʌnˈsiːmli/ *adj* not proper or suitable (in behaviour)

un·set·tle /ʌnˈsetl/ *vt* make more anxious, dissatisfied, etc. **-tled** *adj* (of

weather, a political situation, etc.) likely to get worse

un·sight·ly /ʌnˈsaɪtli/ *adj* ugly

un·so·cial /ʌnˈsəʊʃəl◂/ *adj* unsuitable for combining with family and social life: *working unsocial hours*

un·spea·ka·ble /ʌnˈspiːkəbəl/ *adj* terrible **-bly** *adv*

un·stint·ing /ʌnˈstɪntɪŋ/ *adj fml* very generous

un·stuck /ʌnˈstʌk/ *adj* 1 not fastened 2 **come unstuck** go wrong; be unsuccessful

un·sung /ˌʌnˈsʌŋ◂/ *adj lit* not famous (though deserving to be)

un·swerv·ing /ʌnˈswɜːvɪŋ‖-ɜːr-/ *adj* firm: *unswerving loyalty*

un·thin·ka·ble /ʌnˈθɪŋkəbəl/ *adj* that cannot be considered or accepted; impossible

un·til /ʌnˈtɪl, ən-/ *prep, conj* 1 up to (the time that): *Don't start until he arrives.* 2 as far as: *We stayed on the train until London.*

un·to /ˈʌntu/ *prep lit* to

un·told /ʌnˈtəʊld◂/ *adj* very great: *untold damage*

un·to·ward /ˌʌntəˈwɔːd‖ʌnˈtɔːrd/ *adj fml* unexpected and undesirable

un·tram·mel·led *BrE* ‖ **-meled** *AmE* /ʌnˈtræməld/ *adj fml* allowed to act or develop with complete freedom

un·truth /ʌnˈtruːθ, ˈʌntruːθ/ *n fml* lie

un·u·su·al /ʌnˈjuːʒuəl, -ʒəl/ *adj fml* 1 not common 2 interesting because different from others **~ly** *adv* 1 very 2 in an unusual way

un·ut·te·ra·ble /ʌnˈʌtərəbəl/ *adj fml* 1 terrible 2 complete: *an unutterable fool* **~bly** *adv*

un·var·nished /ʌnˈvɑːnɪʃt‖-ɑːr-/ *adj* without additional description

un·veil /ʌnˈveɪl/ *vt* 1 remove a covering from 2 show publicly for the first time

un·war·rant·ed /ʌnˈwɒrəntɪd ‖ -ˈwɔː-, -ˈwɑː-/ *adj* (done) without good reason

un·well /ʌnˈwel/ *adj* (slightly) ill

un·wiel·dy /ʌnˈwiːldi/ *adj* awkward to move, handle, or use

un·wind /ʌnˈwaɪnd/ *v* **-wound** /-ˈwaʊnd/ 1 *vi/t* undo (something wound) or become undone: *unwinding a ball of wool* 2 *vi* become calmer and free of care

un·wit·ting /ʌnˈwɪtɪŋ/ *adj* not knowing or intended: *their unwitting accomplice*

un·writ·ten rule /ˌʌnrɪtn ˈruːl/ *n* usual custom (not officially stated)

up /ʌp/ *adv* 1 to or at a higher level: *She climbed up onto the roof.* ‖ *He turned up his collar.* 2 (shows increase): *Profits are up.* ‖ *Turn the radio up.* (= louder) 3 to the north: *driving up to Scotland* 4 out of bed:

We stayed up late. **5** so as to be completely finished: *Eat up your vegetables.* **6** into small pieces: *She tore it up.* **7** firmly; tightly: *He tied up the parcel.* **8** together: *Add up the figures.* **9** more loudly: *Sing up!* **10** on top: *right side up* **11 up against** having to face (something difficult) **12 up and down: a** higher and lower: *jumping up and down* **b** backwards and forwards: *walking up and down* **13 up to: a** towards and as far as: *He walked up to me and asked my name.* **b** until: *up to now* **c** good, well, or clever enough for: *He's not up to the job.* **d** the duty or responsibility of: *I'll leave it up to you.* (= you must decide) **e** doing (something bad): *What are you up to?* **14 Up (with)** We want or approve of: *Up the workers!* ♦ *prep* **1** to or at a higher level on: *walking up the stairs* **2** to or at the top or far end of: *They live just up the road.* ♦ *adj* **1** directed up: *the up escalator* **2** (of a road) being repaired **3 be up** be happening; be the matter **4 be well up in/on** know a lot about **5 up and about** out of bed (again) and able to walk **6 up for: a** intended or being considered for **b** on trial for ♦ *vt* **-pp-** increase

up-and-com-ing /ˌ··'··◄/ *adj* new and likely to succeed

up-and-up /ˌ··'·'/ *n* **on the up-and-up** improving; succeeding

up-braid /ˌʌp'breɪd/ *vt fml for* SCOLD

up-bring-ing /'ʌpbrɪŋɪŋ/ *n* [S] (way of) training and caring for a child

up-com-ing /'ʌp‚kʌmɪŋ/ *adj* about to happen

up-date /ˌʌp'deɪt/ *vt* **1** make more modern **2** supply with the latest information

up-end /ʌp'end/ *vt* stand on a part that does not usually stand on the floor

up-front /ˌʌp'frʌnt/ *adj* very direct and making no attempt to hide one's meaning

up-grade /ˌʌp'greɪd/ *vt* give a more important position to

up-heav-al /ʌp'hiːvəl/ *n* [C;U] great change and confusion, with much activity

up-held /ˌʌp'held/ *past t. and p. of* UPHOLD

up-hill /ˌʌp'hɪl◄/ *adj, adv* **1** up a slope **2** difficult: *an uphill task*

up-hold /ˌʌp'həʊld/ *vt* **-held** /-'held/ **1** prevent from being weakened or taken away **2** declare (a decision) to be right **~er** *n*

up-hol-ster /ʌp'həʊlstə'/ *vt* cover and fill (a seat) **~er** *n* **~y** *n* [U] material covering and filling a seat

up-keep /'ʌpkiːp/ *n* [U] (cost of) keeping something repaired and in order

up-lift /ˌʌp'lɪft/ *vt fml* encourage cheerful or holy feelings in

up-mar-ket /'·‚··/ *adj* being or using goods produced to meet the demand of the higher social groups

up-on /ə'pɒn‖ə'pɑːn/ *prep fml for* ON¹ (1,3,4,6,7)

up-per /'ʌpə'/ *adj* at or nearer the top: *the upper arm* ♦ *n* **1** top part of a shoe **2 on one's uppers** *infml* very poor

upper class /ˌ·· '·◄/ *n* highest social class, esp. with noble titles **upper-class** *adj*

upper hand /ˌ·· '·/ *n* [*the* + S] control

up-per-most /'ʌpəməʊst‖-pər-/ *adv* in the highest or strongest position

up-right /'ʌp-raɪt/ *adj* **1** exactly straight up; not bent or leaning **2** completely honest ♦ *n* upright supporting beam

up-ris-ing /'ʌpˌraɪzɪŋ/ *n* act of the ordinary people suddenly and violently opposing those in power

up-roar /'ʌp-rɔː'/ *n* [S;U] confused noisy activity, esp. shouting **~ious** /ʌp'rɔːriəs/ *adj* very noisy, esp. with laughter

up-root /ˌʌp'ruːt/ *vt* **1** tear (a plant) from the earth **2** remove from a home, settled habits, etc.

ups and downs /ˌ· · '·/ *n* [P] good and bad periods

up-set /ʌp'set/ *vt* **-set**; *pres. p.* **-tt- 1** turn over, esp. accidentally, causing confusion or scattering **2** cause to be worried, sad, angry, etc. **3** make slightly ill ♦ *n* /ʌpset/ **1** slight illness: *a stomach upset* **2** unexpected result

up-shot /'ʌpʃɒt‖'ʌpʃɑːt/ *n* result in the end

up-side down /ˌʌpsaɪd 'daʊn/ *adj* **1** with the top turned to the bottom **2** in disorder

up-stage /ˌʌp'steɪdʒ/ *vt* take attention away from (someone) for oneself

up-stairs /ˌʌp'steəz◄‖-'steərz/ *adv, adj* on or to a higher floor

up-stand-ing /ˌʌp'stændɪŋ/ *adj* **1** tall and strong **2** honest

up-start /'ʌpstɑːt‖-ɑːrt/ *n* someone who has risen too suddenly or unexpectedly to a high position

up-stream /ˌʌp'striːm◄/ *adv, adj* moving against the current of a river

up-take /'ʌpteɪk/ *n* [U] ability to understand: *He's rather slow on the uptake.*

up-tight /ˌʌp'taɪt, 'ʌp'taɪt/ *adj infml* anxious and nervous

up-to-date /ˌ·· '·◄/ *adj* **1** modern **2** including or having all the latest information

up-turn /'ʌptɜːn‖-ɜːrn/ *n* a favourable change

up·ward /'ʌpwəd‖-ərd/ adj going up **upwards** adv more than

upwardly-mo·bile /,··· '··◂/ adj able or wishing to move into a higher social class and become more wealthy

u·ra·ni·um /ju'reɪnɪəm/ n [U] RADIO-ACTIVE metal used in producing atomic power

U·ra·nus /ju'reɪnəs/ n the PLANET 7th in order from the Sun

ur·ban /'ɜːbən‖'ɜːr-/ adj of towns

ur·bane /ɜː'beɪn‖'ɜːr-/ adj smoothly polite — **ly** adv **urbanity** /-'bænətɪ/ n [U]

ur·chin /'ɜːtʃən‖'ɜːr-/ n small dirty untidy child — see also SEA URCHIN

urge /ɜːdʒ‖ɜːrdʒ/ vt 1 try strongly to persuade: *He urged me to reconsider.* 2 drive forwards: *He urged the horses onwards with a whip.* ♦ n strong desire or need

ur·gent /'ɜːdʒənt‖'ɜːr-/ adj that must be dealt with at once ~**ly** adv **urgency** n [U]

u·ri·nal /'juərənəl, ju'raɪ-‖'juərə-/ n container or building for (men) urinating

u·rine /'juərən/ n [U] liquid waste passed from the body **urinary** adj **uri·nate** vi pass urine from the body **uri·nation** /,juərə'neɪʃən/ n [U]

urn /ɜːn‖ɜːrn/ n 1 large metal container for serving tea or coffee 2 container for the ashes of a burnt dead body

us /əs, s; *strong* ʌs/ pron (*object form of* we)

US /,ju: 'es◂/ abbrev. for: 1 also USA /,ju: es 'eɪ/ — the United States (of America) 2 of the United States: *the US navy*

us·age /'juːzɪdʒ, 'juːsɪdʒ/ n 1 [C;U] way of using a language: *a book on English usage* 2 [U] *fml* (type or degree of) use

use¹ /juːs/ n 1 [U] using or being used 2 [U] ability or right to use something: *He lost the use of his legs.* 3 [C;U] purpose: *A machine with many uses.* 4 [U] advantage; usefulness: *It's no use complaining.* (= complaining will have no effect) 5 **in use** being used 6 **make use of** use 7 **of use** useful ~**ful** adj that fulfils a need well ~**fully** adv ~**fulness** n [U] ~**less** adj 1 not useful 2 unable to do anything properly ~**lessly** adv

use² /juːz/ vt 1 employ for a purpose; put to use: *Oil can be used as a fuel.* 2 finish; CONSUME (2) 3 take unfair advantage of; EXPLOIT **usable** adj **used** adj that has already had an owner: *used cars* **user** n

use up phr vt finish completely

use³ /juːs/ vi (used in the past tense for showing what always or regularly happened): *I used to go there every week, but I no longer do.*

used to /'juːst tʊ,-tə/ adj no longer finding (something) strange or annoying because it has become familiar: *I'm used to the noise.*

user-friend·ly /,·· '··◂/ adj easy to use or understand

ush·er /'ʌʃər/ n someone who shows people to their seats in a public place ♦ vt *fml* bring by showing the way: (fig.) *The bombing of Hiroshima ushered in the nuclear age.*

ush·er·ette /,ʌʃə'ret/ n female usher in a cinema

USSR /,ju: es es 'ɑːr/ abbrev. for: Union of Soviet Socialist Republics; the Soviet Union; Russia

u·su·al /'juːʒʊəl, 'juːʒəl/ adj in accordance with what happens most of the time: *He lacked his usual cheerfulness.* ~**ly** adv in most cases; generally

u·surp /ju'zɜːp‖-ɜːrp/ vt *fml* steal (someone else's power or position) ~**er** n

u·su·ry /'juːʒərɪ/ n [U] *fml* lending money to be paid back at an unfairly high rate of interest ~**rer** n

u·ten·sil /juː'tensəl/ n *fml* object with a particular use, esp. a tool or container

u·te·rus /'juːtərəs/ n *med* for WOMB

u·til·i·tar·i·an /juː,tɪlə'teərɪən/ adj *fml, sometimes derog* made to be useful rather than decorative

u·til·i·ty /juː'tɪlətɪ/ n 1 [U] degree of usefulness 2 [C] public service, such as water supplies, a bus service, etc.

u·til·ize /'juːtəlaɪz/ vt *fml* for USE² (1) —**ization** /,juːtəlaɪ'zeɪʃən‖-lə-/ n [U]

ut·most /'ʌtməʊst/ adj *fml* very great: *done with (the) utmost care* ♦ n [U] the most that can be done: *I did my utmost to prevent it.*

u·to·pi·a /juː'təʊpɪə/ n [C;U] perfect society -**pian** adj impractically trying to bring social perfection

ut·ter¹ /'ʌtər/ adj (esp. of something bad) complete: *utter nonsense* ~**ly** adv

utter² vt *fml* make (a sound) or produce (words) ~**ance** n *fml* 1 [U] speaking 2 [C] something said

U-turn /'ju: tɜːn‖-ɜːrn/ n 1 turning movement in a vehicle which takes one back in the direction one came from 2 complete change, resulting in the opposite of what has gone before

u·vu·la /'juːvjʊlə/ n small piece of flesh hanging down at the top of the throat

V

V, **v** /viː/ the 22nd letter of the English alphabet

v *abbrev. for:* 1 verb 2 VERSUS 3 very

va·can·cy /'veɪkənsi/ n unfilled place. such as a job or hotel room

va·cant /'veɪkənt/ adj 1 empty 2 (of a job) having no worker to do it 3 showing lack of interest or serious thought **~ly** adv

va·cate /vəˈkeɪt, veɪ-‖ˈveɪkeɪt/ vt fml cease to use or live in: *Kindly vacate your seats.*

va·ca·tion /vəˈkeɪʃən‖veɪˈkeɪ-/ n 1 [C] a esp. AmE holiday b esp. BrE time when universities are closed 2 [U] fml vacating ♦ vi esp. AmE have a holiday

vac·cine /'væksiːn‖vækˈsiːn/ n [C;U] substance put into the body to protect it against disease **–cinate** /'væksɜ́neɪt/ vt put vaccine into **–cination** /ˌvæk-sɜ́'neɪʃən/ n [C;U]

vac·il·late /'væsɜ́leɪt/ vi keep changing one's mind **–lation** /ˌvæsɜ́'leɪʃən/ n [C;U]

vac·u·ous /'vækjuəs/ adj fml 1 showing foolishness: *a vacuous grin* 2 with no purpose or meaning **~ly** adv **–uity** /vəˈkjuːɜ́ti, væ-‖və-/ n [U]

vac·u·um /'vækjuəm, -kjum/ n space completely without air or other gas: (fig.) *Her death left a vacuum* (= emptiness) *in our lives.* ♦ vt clean with a vacuum cleaner

vacuum clean·er /'··· ,··/ n electric apparatus for sucking up dirt from floors. etc.

vacuum flask /'··· ·/ n FLASK (3)

vacuum-packed /'··· ·‖,··· '·/ adj wrapped in plastic with all air removed

vag·a·bond /'vægəbɒnd‖-bɑːnd/ n lit person who lives a wandering life

va·ga·ry /'veɪɡəri/ n chance event that has an effect on one

va·gi·na /vəˈdʒaɪnə/ n passage from the outer female sex organs to the WOMB

va·grant /'veɪɡrənt/ n fml or law person with no home who wanders around and usu. begs **vagrancy** n [U] being a vagrant

vague /veɪɡ/ adj 1 not clearly seen, described, understood, etc. 2 unable to express oneself clearly **~ly** adv **~ness** n [U]

vain /veɪn/ adj 1 admiring oneself too much 2 unsuccessful; unimportant: *a vain attempt* 3 **in vain** unsuccessfully 4 **take someone's name in vain** talk disrespectfully about someone **~ly** adv

vale /veɪl/ n (in poetry and place-names) broad low valley

val·e·dic·tion /ˌvælɜ́'dɪkʃən/ n [C;U] fml or lit (act of) saying goodbye **–tory** /-'dɪktəri/ adj used in valediction

va·len·cy /'veɪlənsi/ n measure of the power of atoms to form compounds

val·en·tine /'væləntaɪn/ n (card sent to) a lover chosen on **Saint Valentine's Day** (February 14th)

val·et /'vælɜ́t, 'væleɪ/ n 1 man's personal male servant 2 hotel servant who cleans and presses clothes

val·i·ant /'væliənt/ adj esp. fml or lit very brave **~ly** adv 1 very bravely 2 very hard: *He tried valiantly (but without success) to pass the exam.*

val·id /'vælɜ́d/ adj 1 (of a reason, argument, etc.) firmly based and acceptable 2 that can legally be used: *a ticket valid for 3 months* **~ly** adv **~ate** vt fml make valid **~ity** /vəˈlɪdɜ́ti/ n [U]

val·ley /'væli/ n land between 2 lines of hills or mountains

val·our BrE ‖ **-or** AmE /'vælər/ n [U] esp. fml or lit great bravery **–orous** adj

val·u·a·ble /'væljuəbəl, -jɣ́bəl‖'væljɣ́bəl/ adj 1 worth a lot of money 2 very useful ♦ n something VALUABLE (1)

val·u·a·tion /ˌvæljuˈeɪʃən/ n 1 [C;U] calculating how much something is worth 2 [C] value decided on

val·ue /'væljuː/ n 1 [S;U] usefulness or importance, esp. compared with other things: *The map was of great value in finding the way.* 2 [C;U] worth in esp. money: *goods to the value of £500* 3 [U] worth compared with the amount paid: *a restaurant offering the best value in town* ♦ vt 1 calculate the value of 2 consider to be of great worth **values** n [P] standards or principles; people's ideas about the worth of certain qualities: *moral values* **~less** adj **–uer** n

value-ad·ded tax /ˌ··· '·/ n [U] VAT

value judg·ment /'·· ,··/ n judgment about the quality of something, based on opinion rather than facts

valve /vælv/ n 1 part inside a pipe which opens and shuts to control the flow of liquid or gas through it 2 closed airless glass tube for controlling a flow of electricity

vam·pire /'væmpaɪər/ n imaginary evil creature that sucks people's blood

van[1] /væn/ n covered road vehicle or railway carriage for carrying esp. goods

van[2] n **in the van** fml or lit taking a leading part

van·dal /'vændl/ n person who destroys beautiful or useful things

~ism *n* [U] needless damage to esp. public buildings **~ize** *vt* destroy or damage intentionally

vane /veɪn/ *n* bladelike turning part of a machine — see also WEATHER VANE

van·guard /ˈvænɡɑːd‖-ɑːrd/ *n* 1 leading part of some kind of advancement in human affairs: *scientists in the vanguard of medical research* 2 front of a marching army

va·nil·la /vəˈnɪlə/ *n* [U] strong-smelling plant substance used in food

van·ish /ˈvænɪʃ/ *vi* 1 disappear 2 cease to exist

van·i·ty /ˈvænəti/ *n* [U] 1 being too proud of oneself 2 quality of being without lasting value

van·quish /ˈvæŋkwɪʃ/ *vt esp. lit* defeat completely

van·tage-point /ˈvɑːntɪdʒpɔɪnt‖ ˈvæn-/ *n* 1 good position from which to see 2 point of view

vap·id /ˈvæpɪd/ *adj fml* dull

va·pour *BrE* ‖ **-por** *AmE*/ˈveɪpəʳ/ *n* [U] gaslike form of a liquid, such as mist or steam **vaporize** *vi/t* change into vapour **vaporous** *adj*

var·i·a·ble /ˈveəriəbəl/ *adj* that changes or can be changed; not fixed or steady ♦ *n* variable amount **-bly** *adv*

var·i·ance /ˈveəriəns/ *n* **at variance (with)** not in agreement (with)

var·i·ant /ˈveəriənt/ *n, adj* (form, etc.) that is different and can be used instead: *variant spellings*

var·i·a·tion /ˌveəriˈeɪʃən/ *n* 1 [C;U] (example or degree of) varying: *price variations* 2 [C] any of a set of pieces of music based on a single tune

var·i·cose veins /ˌværɪkəʊs ˈveɪnz/ *n* [P] swollen blood tubes, esp. in the legs

var·ied /ˈveərid/ *adj* 1 VARIOUS (1) 2 (always) changing: *a varied life*

var·ie·gat·ed /ˈveəriɡeɪtɪd/ *adj* marked irregularly with different colours **-gation** /ˌveənˈɡeɪʃən/ *n* [U]

va·ri·e·ty /vəˈraɪəti/ *n* 1 [U] not being always the same: *a job lacking variety* 2 [S] group containing different sorts of the same thing: *a wide variety of colours* 3 [C] sort: *a new variety of wheat* 4 [U] entertainment with many short performances of singing, dancing, telling jokes, etc.

var·i·ous /ˈveəriəs/ *adj* 1 different from each other: *There are various ways of doing it.* 2 several **-ly** *adv*

var·nish /ˈvɑːnɪʃ‖ˈvɑːr-/ *n* [C;U] liquid that gives a hard shiny surface to esp. wooden articles ♦ *vt* cover with varnish

varnish over *phr vt* cover up (something unpleasant)

var·y /ˈveəri/ *v* 1 *vi* be different (from each other): *Houses vary in size.* 2 *vi/t* change, esp. continually: *varying one's work methods*

vas·cu·lar /ˈvæskjʊləʳ/ *adj* of or containing VEINs

vase /vɑːz‖veɪs, veɪz/ *n* deep decorative pot for esp. flowers

va·sec·to·my /vəˈsektəmi/ *n* operation for cutting the SPERM-carrying tubes in a man, to prevent him from becoming a father

vas·sal /ˈvæsəl/ *n* person of low social rank in the Middle Ages

vast /vɑːst‖væst/ *adj* extremely large: *a vast desert/improvement* **~ly** *adv*

vat /væt/ *n* large liquid container for industrial use: *a whisky vat*

VAT /ˌviː eɪ ˈtiː, væt/ *n* [U] tax added to the price of an article

Vat·i·can /ˈvætɪkən/ *n* (palace in Rome which is) the centre of government of the Roman Catholic Church

vau·de·ville /ˈvɔːdəvɪl, ˈvəʊ-/ *n* *AmE for* VARIETY (4)

vault[1] /vɔːlt/ *n* 1 thick-walled room for storing valuable things 2 underground room, esp. for storage or for dead bodies 3 arched roof

vault[2] *vi* jump using the hands or a pole to gain more height ♦ *n* act of vaulting **-er** *n*

vaunt /vɔːnt/ *vt esp. lit* BOAST about

VD /ˌviː ˈdiː/ *n* [U] VENEREAL DISEASE

VDU /ˌviː diː ˈjuː/ *n* visual display unit; apparatus with a SCREEN which shows information, esp. from a computer or WORD PROCESSOR

veal /viːl/ *n* [U] meat from a young cow

veer /vɪəʳ/ *vi* change direction

veg /vedʒ/ *n* [U] *BrE infml* vegetables

vege·ta·ble /ˈvedʒtəbəl/ *n* 1 plant grown for food to be eaten with the main part of a meal, rather than with sweet things: *Potatoes and carrots are vegetables.* 2 human being who exists but has little or no power of thought

veg·e·tar·i·an /ˌvedʒəˈteəriən/ *n* person who eats no meat ♦ *adj* 1 of or related to vegetarians 2 made up only of vegetables

vege·tate /ˈvedʒəteɪt/ *vi* lead a dull inactive life

vege·ta·tion /ˌvedʒəˈteɪʃən/ *n* [U] plants

ve·he·ment /ˈviːəmənt/ *adj fml* forceful **~ly** *adv* **-mence** *n* [U]

ve·hi·cle /ˈviːɪkəl/ *n* 1 something in or on which people or goods are carried, such as a car, bicycle, etc. 2 means of expressing or showing something: *He bought the newspaper company as a vehicle for his own political views.*

veil /veɪl/ n **1** covering for a woman's face **2** something that covers and hides: *a veil of mist* **3 take the veil** (of a woman) become a NUN ♦ vt cover (as if) with a veil: *veiled in secrecy* **~ed** adj expressed indirectly: *veiled threats*

vein /veɪn/ n **1** tube carrying blood back to the heart **2** thin line running through a leaf or insect's wing **3** metal-containing crack in rock **4** small but noticeable amount: *a vein of cruelty* **5** state of mind: *in a sad vein*

veld /velt/ n high flat grassland of South Africa

ve·loc·i·ty /vəˈlɒsəti‖vəˈlɑː-/ n fml speed

vel·vet /ˈvelvət/ n [U] cloth with a soft furry surface on one side only **~y** adj soft like velvet

ve·nal /ˈviːnl/ adj fml acting or done to gain unfair reward or personal advantage rather than for proper honest reasons

ven·det·ta /venˈdetə/ n long-lasting situation in which one person repeatedly tries to harm another

vending ma·chine /ˈ·· ·,·/ n machine into which one puts money to obtain small articles

vend·or /ˈvendəʳ/ n fml seller, esp. of a house, land, etc.

ve·neer /vəˈnɪəʳ/ n **1** thin covering of wood on an article **2** false outer appearance: *a veneer of respectability* ♦ vt cover with a veneer

ven·e·ra·ble /ˈvenərəbəl/ adj fml deserving respect or honour because of great age

ven·e·rate /ˈvenəreɪt/ vt fml treat (someone or something old) with great respect or honour **–ration** /ˌvenəˈreɪʃən/ n [U]

ve·ne·re·al dis·ease /·ˌ··· ·ˈ·/ n [C;U] disease passed on by sexual activity

ve·ne·tian blind /vəˌniːʃən ˈblaɪnd/ n window covering with long flat bars that can be turned to let in or shut out light

ven·geance /ˈvendʒəns/ n **1** [U] harm done in return for harm done to oneself: *He took vengeance on his tormentors.* **2 with a vengeance** infml very greatly

venge·ful /ˈvendʒfəl/ adj esp. lit fiercely wishing to take vengeance **~ly** adv

ve·ni·al /ˈviːniəl/ adj fml (of a mistake, fault, etc.) not very serious, and therefore forgivable

ven·i·son /ˈvenɪzən, -sən/ n [U] deer meat

ven·om /ˈvenəm/ n **1** liquid poison produced by certain animals **2** great anger or hatred **~ous** adj: *a venomous snake/look*

vent[1] /vent/ n **1** opening or pipe by which gas, smoke, etc., escape **2 give vent to** express freely: *giving vent to his anger*

vent[2] v **vent on** phr vt express by making (someone or something) suffer: *venting her fury on the cat*

ven·ti·late /ˈventəleɪt‖-tl-eɪt/ vt let or bring fresh air into (a room, building, etc.) **–lator** n **1** apparatus for ventilating **2** apparatus for pumping air into and out of the lungs of someone who cannot breathe properly **–lation** /ˌventəˈleɪʃən‖-tl-eɪ-/ n [U]

ven·tri·cle /ˈventrɪkəl/ n space in the bottom of the heart that pushes blood out into the body

ven·tril·o·quist /venˈtrɪləkwəst/ n someone who can make their voice seem to come from someone or somewhere else, **–quism** n [U]

ven·ture /ˈventʃəʳ/ v **1** vi risk going: *She ventured too near the cliff edge, and fell over.* **2** vt fml dare to say ♦ n (new and risky) course of action: *her latest commercial venture*

venture cap·i·tal /ˈ·· ,··/ n [U] money lent to start up a new business company, esp. a risky one

ven·ture·some /ˈventʃəsəm‖-tʃər-/ adj lit or AmE ready to take risks

ven·ue /ˈvenjuː/ n place arranged for something to happen

ve·nus /ˈviːnəs/ n the PLANET 2nd in order from the sun

ve·rac·i·ty /vəˈræsəti/ n [U] fml truthfulness

ve·ran·da, -dah /vəˈrændə/ n open area with a floor and roof beside a house

verb /vɜːb‖vɜːrb/ n word or group of words that is used in describing an action, experience, or state, such as *wrote* in *She wrote a letter*, or *put on* in *He put on his coat*

verb·al /ˈvɜːbəl‖ˈvɜːr-/ adj **1** spoken, not written **2** of words and their use **3** of a verb **~ly** adv in spoken words

verb·al·ize also **-ise** BrE /ˈvɜːbəlaɪz‖ˈvɜːr-/ vi/t express (something) in words

verbal noun /ˌ·· ·ˈ·/ n noun describing an action, formed by adding *-ing* to the verb: *In the sentence 'The building of the bridge was slow work', 'building' is a verbal noun.*

ver·ba·tim /vɜːˈbeɪtəm‖vɜːr-/ adv, adj repeating the actual words exactly

ver·bi·age /ˈvɜːbi-ɪdʒ‖ˈvɜːr-/ n [U] fml too many unnecessary words

ver·bose /vɜːˈbəʊs‖vɜːr-/ adj fml using too many words **–bosity** /-ˈbɒsəti‖-ˈbɑː-/ n [U]

ver·dant /ˈvɜːdənt‖ˈvɜːr-/ adj lit green with growing plants

ver·dict /ˈvɜːdɪkt‖ˈvɜːr-/ n **1** decision made by a JURY at the end of a trial about whether the prisoner is guilty **2** judgment; opinion

ver-dure /'vɜːdʒəʳ‖'vɜːr-/ *n* [U] *lit* (greenness of) growing plants

verge[1] /vɜːdʒ‖vɜːrdʒ/ *n* **1** edge, esp. of a path or road **2 on the verge of** nearly; about to

verge[2] *v* **verge on** *phr vt* be near to: *dark grey, verging on black*

ver-ger /'vɜːdʒəʳ‖'vɜːr-/ *n* person who looks after the inside of a church

ver-i-fy /'verɪfaɪ/ *vt* make certain that (something) is true **-fiable** *adj* **-fication** /,verɪfɪˈkeɪʃən/ *n* [U]

ver-i-si-mil-i-tude /,verəsɪˈmɪlɪtjuːd‖-tuːd/ *n* [U] *fml* quality of seeming to be true

ver-i-ta-ble /'verɪtəbəl/ *adj fml* (used to give force to an expression) real: *a veritable feast* **-bly** *adv*

ver-mil-ion /vəˈmɪljən‖vər-/ *adj* bright reddish orange

ver-min /'vɜːmɪn‖-ɜːr-/ *n* [P] **1** insects and small animals that do damage **2** people who are a trouble to society

ver-mouth /'vɜːməθ‖vərˈmuːθ/ *n* [U] drink made from wine with strong-tasting substances added

ver-nac-u-lar /vəˈnækjʊləʳ‖vər-/ *adj, n* (in or being) the language spoken in a particular place

ver-sa-tile /'vɜːsətaɪl‖'vɜːrsɒtl/ *adj* that can do many different things or has many uses **-tility** /,vɜːsəˈtɪlɪti ,vɜːr-/ *n* [U]

verse /vɜːs‖vɜːrs/ *n* **1** [U] writing in the form of poetry, esp. with RHYMES — see also BLANK VERSE, FREE VERSE **2** [C] single division of a poem **3** [C] short numbered group of sentences in the Bible or other holy book

versed /vɜːst‖vɜːrst/ *adj fml* experienced; skilled: *thoroughly versed in the arts of diplomacy*

ver-sion /'vɜːʃən‖'vɜːrʒən/ *n* **1** form of something that is slightly different from others of the same sort: *This dress is a cheaper version of the one we saw in the other shop.* **2** one person's account of an event: *The 2 eyewitnesses gave different versions of the accident.*

ver-sus /'vɜːsəs‖'vɜːr-/ *prep* in competition with; against

ver-te-bra /'vɜːtɪbrə‖'vɜːr-/ *n* **-brae** /-briː, -breɪ/ small bone in the BACKBONE

ver-te-brate /'vɜːtɪbrət, -breɪt‖ 'vɜːr-/ *n* animal with a BACKBONE

ver-ti-cal /'vɜːtɪkəl‖'vɜːr-/ *adj* forming a 90° angle with the ground or bottom; upright **-ly** /-kli/ *adv*

ver-ti-go /'vɜːtɪgəʊ‖'vɜːr-/ *n* [U] unpleasant feeling of unsteadiness at great heights

verve /vɜːv‖vɜːrv/ *n* [U] forcefulness and eager enjoyment

ve-ry /'veri/ *adv* **1** to a great degree: *a very exciting book* **2** in the highest possible degree: *I did my very best to help.* **3 very good** (used as a respectful form of agreement) of course **4 very well** (used as a (form of agreement, often with some degree of unwillingness) ◆ *adj* **1** (used for giving force to an expression) actual: *He died in that very bed.* **2 the very idea!** (used for expressing surprise at something said by someone else)

ves-pers /'vespəz/-ərz/ *n* [P;U] church service in the evening

ves-sel /'vesəl/ *n* **1** ship or large boat **2** (round) container, esp. for liquids **3** tube that carries liquid through a body or plant

vest[1] /vest/ *n* **1** *BrE* undergarment for the upper body **2** *AmE* for WAISTCOAT

vest[2] *v* **vest in/with** *phr vt fml* give the legal right to possess or use (power, property, etc.) to (someone)

ves-tal vir-gin /,vestl 'vɜːdʒən‖-ɜːr-/ *n* unmarried female temple servant in ancient Rome

vested in-terest /,·· '··/ *n* a personal reason for doing something, because one gains advantage from it

ves-ti-bule /'vestɪbjuːl/ *n fml* **1** room or passage through which larger rooms are reached **2** *AmE* enclosed passage at each end of a railway carriage which connects it with the next carriage

ves-tige /'vestɪdʒ/ *n* **1** (small) remaining part: *the last vestiges of royal power* **2** slightest bit: *not a vestige of truth*

vest-ment /'vestmənt/ *n* (priest's) ceremonial garment

ves-try /'vestri/ *n* room in a church for esp. changing into vestments

vet /vet/ *n* animal doctor ◆ *vt* **-tt-** examine carefully for correctness, past record, etc.

vet-er-an /'vetərən/ *n, adj* **1** (person) with long service or (former) experience, esp. as a soldier **2** (thing) that has grown old with long use: *a veteran car* (= one built before 1905)

vet-e-ri-na-ry /'vetərɪnəri‖-neri/ *adj* of the medical care of animals: *veterinary surgeon*

ve-to /'viːtəʊ/ *vt* **vetoed**; *pres. p.* **vetoing** officially refuse to allow ◆ *n* **vetoes** [C;U] (act of) vetoing

vex /veks/ *vt fml* displease; trouble **~ation** /vekˈseɪʃən/ *n* [C;U]

vexed ques-tion /,· '··/ *n* matter that causes fierce argument and is difficult to decide

vi-a /'vaɪə‖'vɪə/ *prep* travelling through

vi·a·ble /'vaɪəbəl/ *adj* able to succeed in actual use: *an economically viable plan* **–bility** /ˌvaɪə'bɪləti/ *n* [U]

vi·a·duct /'vaɪədʌkt/ *n* high bridge across a valley

vi·brant /'vaɪbrənt/ *adj* **1** powerful and exciting **2** (of colour or light) bright and strong **~ly** *adv* **vibrancy** *n* [U]

vi·brate /vaɪ'breɪt‖'vaɪbreɪt/ *vi/t* (cause to) move with a slight continuous shake **vibration** /vaɪ'breɪʃən/ *n* [C;U]

vic·ar /'vɪkər/ *n* priest in charge of an area (PARISH)

vic·ar·age /'vɪkərɪdʒ/ *n* vicar's house

vi·car·i·ous /vɪ'keəriəs‖vaɪ-/ *adj* experienced indirectly, by watching, reading, etc.: *vicarious pleasure* **~ly** *adv*

vice¹ /vaɪs/ *n* [C;U] **1** (kind of) evil behaviour or living: *She was arrested by the vice squad for prostitution.* **2 a** fault of character: *Laziness is his one vice.* **b** bad habit: *Smoking is my only vice.*

vice² *BrE n* tool with metal jaws for holding things firmly

vice-chan·cel·lor /ˌ· '···/ *n* (in Britain) head of a university

vice-roy /'vaɪsrɔɪ/ *n* person ruling as a representative of a king or queen

vice ver·sa /ˌvaɪs 'vɜːsə, ˌvaɪsi-‖-ɜːr-/ *adv* the opposite way around

vi·cin·i·ty /və'sɪnəti/ *n* [U] area nearby

vi·cious /'vɪʃəs/ *adj* **1** showing an unpleasant desire to hurt: *a vicious kick* **2** dangerous: *a vicious-looking knife* **~ly** *adv*

vicious cir·cle /ˌ·· '··/ *n* situation in which unpleasant causes and effects lead back to the original starting point

vi·cis·si·tudes /və'sɪsɪtjuːdz‖-tuːdz/ *n* [P] *fml* changes, esp. from good to bad, that have an effect on one

vic·tim /'vɪktəm/ *n* one who suffers as the result of something: *the murderer's victim* (= the person he killed) | *the victims of the plane crash* **~ize** *vt* cause to suffer unfairly **~ization** /ˌvɪktəmaɪ'zeɪʃən‖-mə-/ *n* [U]

vic·tor /'vɪktər/ *n fml or lit* winner

Vic·to·ri·an /vɪk'tɔːriən/ *adj* **1** of the time when Queen Victoria ruled Britain (1837-1901) **2** very respectable (esp. in matters of sex)

vic·to·ry /'vɪktəri/ *n* [C;U] winning: *her victory in the election/golf tournament* **–torious** /vɪk'tɔːriəs/ *adj* **1** that has won: *the victorious team* **2** showing victory: *a victorious shout*

vid·e·o /'vɪdiəʊ/ *adj* for (recording and) showing pictures on television **♦** *n* **-os** [C;U] videotape recording **2** [C] machine for making and showing

these **♦** *vt* **videoed**; *pres. p.* **videoing** videotape

video nas·ty /ˌ··· '··/ *n infml* video film including scenes of extremely unpleasant violence

vid·e·o·re·cord·er /'vɪdiəʊrɪˌkɔːdər‖-ɜːr-/ *n* VIDEO (2)

vid·e·o·tape /'vɪdiəʊteɪp/ *n* [C;U] band of MAGNETIC material on which moving pictures are recorded **♦** *vt* record on videotape

vie /vaɪ/ *vi* **vied**; *pres. p.* **vying** compete

view /vjuː/ *n* **1** [C;U] what one can see: *The train came into view round the corner.* | *You get a beautiful view of the sea from this window.* **2** [C] opinion: *In my view, he's a fool.* **3 in view of** taking into consideration: *In view of the unusual circumstances, we'll cancel it.* **4 on view** being shown to the public **5 with a view to** with the intention of **♦** *vt* **1** consider; regard: *I view the matter very seriously.* **2** examine by looking **3** watch television **~er** *n* person watching television

view·find·er /'vjuːˌfaɪndər/ *n* apparatus on a camera showing a small picture of what is to be photographed

view·point /'vjuːpɔɪnt/ *n* POINT OF VIEW

vig·il /'vɪdʒəl/ *n* act of staying (awake and) watchful for some purpose

vig·i·lance /'vɪdʒələns/ *n* [U] watchful care **-lant** *adj fml* always prepared for possible danger **-lantly** *adv*

vigilance com·mit·tee /ˈ··· ·ˌ·-/ *n AmE* group of vigilantes

vig·i·lan·te /ˌvɪdʒə'lænti/ *n* sometimes *derog* person who tries by unofficial means to punish crime: *vigilantes on the New York subway*

vi·gnette /vɪ'njet/ *n* short effective written description

vig·our *BrE* **-or** *AmE* /'vɪgər/ *n* [U] active strength or force **–orous** *adj* **-orously** *adv*

Vi·king /'vaɪkɪŋ/ *n* Scandinavian attacker (and settler) in northern and western Europe from the 8th to the 10th centuries

vile /vaɪl/ *adj* **1** *fml* low, shameful, and worthless: *a vile slander* **2** extremely unpleasant: *vile food* **~ly** /'vaɪl-li/ *adv*

vil·i·fy /'vɪləfaɪ/ *vt fml* say unfairly bad things about **–fication** /ˌvɪləfə'keɪʃən/ *n* [C;U]

vil·la /'vɪlə/ *n* **1** house in a holiday area, esp. which one can hire **2** large ancient Roman country house

vil·lage /'vɪlɪdʒ/ *n* collection of houses, shops, etc., in a country area, smaller than a town **villager** *n* person who lives in a village

vil·lain /'vɪlən/ *n* **1** (esp. in stories) bad person **2** *BrE infml* criminal **3** the

villain of the piece *infml* person or thing to be blamed **~ous** *adj* threatening great harm; evil

vin·ai·grette /ˌvɪnɪˈgret, ˌvɪneɪ-/ n [U] mixture of oil, VINEGAR, etc., put ON SALADS

vin·di·cate /ˈvɪndɪkeɪt/ vt 1 free from blame 2 prove (something that was in doubt) to be right **~cation** /ˌvɪndɪˈkeɪʃən/ n [S;U]

vin·dic·tive /vɪnˈdɪktɪv/ adj wishing to harm someone who has harmed you **~ly** adv **~ness** n [U]

vine /vaɪn/ n climbing plant, esp. one that produces GRAPEs

vin·e·gar /ˈvɪnɪgəʳ/ n [U] acid-tasting liquid used in preparing food **~y** adj

vine·yard /ˈvɪnjəd‖-jərd/ n piece of land with vines for making wine

vin·tage /ˈvɪntɪdʒ/ n particular year in which a wine is made ♦ adj 1 of the best quality 2 BrE (of a car) made between 1919 and 1930

vi·nyl /ˈvaɪnl̩/ n [U] firm bendable plastic

vi·o·la /viˈəʊlə/ n musical instrument like a large VIOLIN

vi·o·late /ˈvaɪəleɪt/ vt 1 act against (something solemnly promised or officially agreed): violate a treaty 2 fml come violently into (and spoil) 3 have sex (with a woman) by force **~lation** /ˌvaɪəˈleɪʃən/ n [C;U]

vi·o·lent /ˈvaɪələnt/ adj using, showing or produced by great damaging force: He became violent and began to hit her.|a violent storm|a violent death **~ly** adv **~lence** n [U] 1 extreme (and damaging) force 2 use of force to hurt people

vi·o·let /ˈvaɪəlɪt/ n small plant with sweet-smelling purple flowers — see also SHRINKING VIOLET

vi·o·lin /ˌvaɪəˈlɪn/ n small 4-stringed wooden musical instrument played by drawing a BOW² (2) across the strings **~ist** n

VIP /ˌviː aɪ ˈpiː/ n person of great influence or fame

vi·per /ˈvaɪpəʳ/ n small poisonous snake

vir·gin /ˈvɜːdʒɪn‖ˈvɜːr-/ n person who has not had sex ♦ adj unused; unspoiled **~ity** /vɜːˈdʒɪnɪti‖vɜːr-/ n [U] state of being a VIRGIN

vir·ile /ˈvɪraɪl‖ˈvɪrəl/ adj having the strong and forceful qualities expected of a man, esp. in matters of sex **~ility** /vɪˈrɪlɪti/ n [U]

vir·tu·al /ˈvɜːtʃuəl‖ˈvɜːr-/ adj almost or unofficially the stated thing: Though her husband was king, she was the virtual ruler of the country. **~ly** adv almost; very nearly

vir·tue /ˈvɜːtʃuː‖ˈvɜːr-/ n 1 [U] fml condition of being morally good 2 [C]

morally good quality, such as truthfulness or loyalty 3 [C;U] advantage: The plan's great virtue is its simplicity. 4 by virtue of as a result of; by means of **~tuous** adj morally good

vir·tu·o·so /ˌvɜːtʃuˈəʊzəʊ‖ˌvɜːrtʃuˈəʊsəʊ/ n -si extremely skilled (musical) performer **~osity** /-ˈɒsɪti‖-ˈɑːs-/ n [U] virtuoso's skill

vir·u·lent /ˈvɪrʊlənt/ adj 1 (of a poison, disease, etc.) very powerful and dangerous 2 fml full of bitter hatred: virulent abuse **~ly** adv **~lence** n [U]

vi·rus /ˈvaɪərəs/ n extremely small living thing that causes infectious disease: the flu virus viral adj

vi·sa /ˈviːzə/ n official mark put on a PASSPORT to allow someone to enter or leave a particular country

vis·age /ˈvɪzɪdʒ/ n lit face

vis-à-vis /ˌviːz ɑː ˈviː, ˌviːz ə ˈviː/ prep fml with regard to

vis·count /ˈvaɪkaʊnt/ n British nobleman between an EARL and a BARON in rank

vis·count·ess /ˈvaɪkaʊntɪs/ n the wife of a viscount, or a woman of the rank of viscount in her own right

vis·cous /ˈvɪskəs/ adj (of a liquid) thick and sticky **~cosity** /vɪsˈkɒsɪti‖-ˈkɑː-/ n [U]

vise /vaɪs/ n AmE for VICE²

vis·i·ble /ˈvɪzəbəl/ adj 1 that can be seen 2 noticeable **~bly** adv noticeably: He was visibly shaken by the unpleasant experience. **~bility** /ˌvɪzɪˈbɪlɪti/ n [U] 1 clearness with which things can be seen over a particular distance 2 ability to give a clear view

vi·sion /ˈvɪʒən/ n 1 [U] ability to see 2 [U] wise understanding of the future 3 [C] picture in the mind: I had visions of missing (= thought I might miss) my plane. 4 [C] something supposedly seen when in a sleeplike state or as a religious experience

vi·sion·a·ry /ˈvɪʒənəri‖-neri/ adj 1 having VISION (2) 2 grand but impractical ♦ n visionary person

vis·it /ˈvɪzɪt/ v 1 vi/t go to and spend time in (a place) or with (a person): We visited my sick uncle in hospital. 2 vt go to (a place) to make an official examination 3 vi AmE stay ♦ n act or time of visiting: We paid him a visit. (= visited him) **~or** n

visit on phr vt direct (anger, etc.) against

visit with phr vt AmE talk socially with

vi·sor /ˈvaɪzəʳ/ n face or eye protector on a hat or HELMET

vis·ta /ˈvɪstə/ n view stretching away into the distance

vi·su·al /ˈvɪʒuəl/ adj 1 of or done by seeing 2 having an effect on the sense

of sight: *the visual arts* ~**ly** *adv* ~**ize**
vt imagine, esp. as if by seeing

vi·tal /'vaɪtl/ *adj* **1** extremely necessary or important **2** necessary to stay alive **3** full of life and force ~**ly** *adv* in the highest possible degree

vi·tal·i·ty /vaɪ'tælɪti/ *n* [U] **1** cheerful forceful quality **2** ability to remain alive or effective

vital sta·tis·tics /,·· ·'··/ *n* [P] measurements round a woman's chest, waist, and HIPS

vi·ta·min /'vɪtəmɪn, 'vaɪ-‖'vaɪ-/ *n* chemical substance found in certain foods and important for growth and good health: *Oranges contain vitamin C.*

vi·ti·ate /'vɪʃieɪt/ *vt fml* weaken: *inaccuracies that vitiated his argument*

vit·ri·ol /'vɪtriəl/ *n* [U] **1** extremely powerful acid **2** cruel wounding quality of speech and writing ~**ic** /,vɪtri'ɒlɪk‖-'aːl-/ *adj fml* fiercely cruel in speech or judgment

vi·tro /'vɪtrəʊ/ *see* IN VITRO

vi·tu·pe·ra·tive /vɪ'tjuːpərətɪv‖vaɪ-'tuː-/ *adj fml* full of angry disapproval

vi·va·cious /vɪ'veɪʃəs/ *adj* (esp. of a woman) full of life and fun ~**ly** *adv* ~**city** /vɪ'væsɪti/ *n* [U]

viv·id /'vɪvɪd/ *adj* **1** (of light or colour) bright and strong **2** producing sharp clear pictures in the mind: *a vivid description* ~**ly** *adv*

viv·i·sec·tion /,vɪvɪ'sekʃən/ *n* [U] performing of operations on animals to test medical treatments, new products, etc.

vix·en /'vɪksən/ *n* female fox

V-neck /'viː nek/ *n* V-shaped neck opening of a dress, shirt, etc.

vo·cab·u·la·ry /və'kæbjʊlɒri, vəʊ-leri/ *n* [C;U] **1** words known, learnt, used, etc.: *a child's limited vocabulary* **2** [C] short list of words with their meanings

vo·cal /'vəʊkəl/ *adj* **1** of or produced by the voice: *vocal music* **2** expressing one's opinion loudly ~**ly** *adv* ~**ist** *n* singer

vocal cords /'·· ·, ,·· '·/ *n* [P] muscles in the throat that produce sounds when air passes through them

vo·ca·tion /vəʊ'keɪʃən/ *n* **1** [S] particular fitness or ability for a certain worthy kind of work, such as being a nurse **2** [C] job, esp. one which you do because you have a vocation ~**al** *adj* of or for a job: *vocational training*

vo·cif·er·ous /və'sɪfərəs, vəʊ-‖vəʊ-/ *adj fml* expressing oneself forcefully or noisily ~**ly** *adv*

vod·ka /'vɒdkə‖'vaːdkə/ *n* [U] strong colourless Russian alcoholic drink

vogue /vəʊg/ *n* [C;U] popular fashion: *Short skirts were in vogue then.* ♦ *adj* popular at present: *vogue words*

voice /vɔɪs/ *n* **1** [C;U] sound(s) produced in speaking or singing: *a loud/ kind voice* | *She shouted at the top of her voice.* (= very loudly) **2** [C] ability to produce such sounds: *She's lost her voice.* **3** [S;U] right to express oneself: *I have no voice in* (= influence over) *the decision.* ♦ *vt* express in words, esp. forcefully: *voicing their opinions*

voice-o·ver /'· ,··/ *n* voice of an unseen person on a film or television show

void /vɔɪd/ *n* empty space ♦ *adj law* having no value or effect ♦ *vt* make void

vol·a·tile /'vɒlətaɪl‖'vaːlətl/ *adj* **1** quickly changing, esp. easily becoming angry or dangerous **2** (of a liquid) easily changing into gas ~**tility** /,vɒlə'tɪlɪti‖,vaː-/ *n* [U]

vol-au-vent /,vɒl əʊ 'vɒn‖,vɔːl əʊ 'vɑːn/ *n* small pastry case filled with meat, vegetables, etc.

vol·ca·no /vɒl'keɪnəʊ‖vɑːl-/ *n* -**noes** or -**nos** mountain which sometimes throws out hot gases and melted rock ~**canic** /-'kænɪk/ *adj* **1** of a volcano **2** violently forceful

vo·li·tion /və'lɪʃən‖vəʊ-, və-/ *n* **of one's own volition** *fml* because one wishes to, not because one is told to by someone else

vol·ley /'vɒli‖'vaːli/ *n* **1** many shots fired together: (fig.) *a volley of blows/ curses* **2** kicking or hitting of a ball before it has hit the ground ♦ *v* **1** *vi* (of guns) be fired together **2** *vi/t* hit or kick (as) a VOLLEY (2)

vol·ley·ball /'vɒlibɔːl‖'vaː-/ *n* [U] team game played by hitting a large ball across a net with the hands

volt /vəʊlt/ *n* unit of electrical force ~**age** *n* [C;U] electrical force measured in volts

vol·u·ble /'vɒljʊbəl‖'vaː-/ *adj fml* talking a lot ~**bly** *adv* ~**bility** /,vɒljʊ'bɪlɪti‖,vaː-/ *n* [U]

vol·ume /'vɒljuːm‖'vaːljəm/ *n* **1** [U] (degree of) loudness of sound: *Turn down the volume on the TV.* **2** [U] size of something measured by multiplying its length by its height by its width **3** [C] any of a set of books: *volume 9 of the encyclopedia* **4** [C;U] amount: *the increasing volume of passenger traffic* **5 speak volumes (for something)** show or express (something) very clearly or fully

vo·lu·mi·nous /və'luːmɪnəs, və-'ljuː-‖və'luː-/ *adj fml* **1** filling or containing a lot of space: *a voluminous skirt/suitcase* **2** producing or containing (too) much writing

vol·un·ta·ry /'vɒləntəri‖'vaːlənteri/ *adj* acting or done willingly, without being forced ~**arily** *adv*

vol·un·teer /ˌvɒlənˈtɪəʳ‖ˌvɑː-/ n person who has volunteered ♦ v 1 vi/t offer to do something without payment or reward, or without being forced: *Jenny volunteered to clear up afterwards.* 2 vt tell without being asked: *He volunteered a statement to the police.*

vo·lup·tu·ous /vəˈlʌptʃuəs/ adj 1 suggesting or expressing sexual pleasure 2 giving a fine delight to the senses

vom·it /ˈvɒmət‖ˈvɑː-/ vi throw up (the contents of the stomach) through the mouth ♦ n [U] swallowed food thrown back up through the mouth

voo·doo /ˈvuːduː/ n [U] set of magical religious practices in esp. Haiti

vo·ra·cious /vəˈreɪʃəs, vɒ-‖vɔː-, və-/ adj eating or wanting a lot of food: (fig.) *a voracious reader* (= who reads a lot) ~**ly** adv ~**city** /vəˈræsəti/ n [U]

vor·tex /ˈvɔːteks‖ˈvɔːr-/ n -**texes** or -**tices** /-təsiːz/ 1 powerful circular moving mass of water or wind 2 lit situation that makes one powerless: *sucked into the vortex of war*

vo·ta·ry /ˈvəʊtəri/ n fml regular worshipper, admirer, etc.

vote /vəʊt/ v 1 vi express one's choice officially, esp. by marking a piece of paper or raising one's hand: *Which candidate will you vote for at the election?* | *As we can't reach an agreement, let's vote on it.* 2 vt agree, by a vote, to provide (something) 3 vt infml agree as the general opinion: *I vote we leave now.* ♦ n 1 [C;U] (choice or decision made by) voting: *I shall cast my vote for Tom Smith.* | *Let's put the matter to a vote.* 2 [U] number of such choices made by or for a particular person or group: *an increase in the Liberal vote* 3 [U] right to vote in political elections **voter** n

vouch /vaʊtʃ/ v **vouch for** phr vt state one's firm belief in the good qualities of, based on experience

vouch·er /ˈvaʊtʃəʳ/ n 1 BrE ticket usable instead of money 2 official paper given to prove that money has been paid

vouch·safe /vaʊtʃˈseɪf/ vt lit give, say, or do as a favour

vow /vaʊ/ vt, n (make) a solemn promise or declaration of intention: *He vowed he would never steal again.*

vow·el /ˈvaʊəl/ n speech sound made without closing the air passage in the mouth or throat: *In English, vowels are represented by the letters* a, e, i, o, *and* u.

voy·age /ˈvɔɪ-ɪdʒ/ n long journey by ship ♦ vi lit make a voyage ~**ager** n

voy·eur /vwɑːˈjɜːʳ/ n person who gets sexual excitement by (secretly) watching others have sex ~**ism** n [U]

vs AmE abbrev. for: VERSUS

vul·can·ize ‖ also -**ise** BrE /ˈvʌlkənaɪz/ vt strengthen (rubber) by chemical treatment

vul·gar /ˈvʌlgəʳ/ adj 1 very rude or bad-mannered 2 showing bad judgment in matters of beauty, style, etc. ~**ly** adv ~**ity** /vʌlˈgærəti/ n [U]

vul·ne·ra·ble /ˈvʌlnərəbəl/ adj 1 easy to attack 2 (of a person) easily harmed; sensitive -**bility** /ˌvʌlnərəˈbɪləti/ n [U]

vul·ture /ˈvʌltʃəʳ/ n 1 large tropical bird which feeds on dead animals 2 person who has no mercy and who uses people

vy·ing /ˈvaɪ-ɪŋ/ pres. p. of VIE

W

W, **w**/ˈdʌbəljuː/ the 23rd letter of the English alphabet

W written abbrev. for: 1 west(ern) 2 WATT

wack·y /ˈwæki/ adj esp. AmE silly -**iness** n [U]

wad /wɒd‖wɑːd/ n 1 many thin things pressed or folded thickly together: *a wad of bank notes* 2 small thick soft mass: *a wad of cotton wool*

wad·ding /ˈwɒdɪŋ‖ˈwɑː-/ n [U] soft material used esp. for packing or in medicine

wad·dle /ˈwɒdl‖ˈwɑːdl/ vi walk like a duck

wade /weɪd/ vi/t walk through (water) **wader** n 1 bird that wades to find its food 2 either of a pair of high rubber boots to protect the legs while wading

wade into phr vt begin (to attack) forcefully and with determination

wade through phr vt do or complete (something long or dull) with an effort

wadge /wɒdʒ‖wɑːdʒ/ n BrE infml for WAD (1)

wa·fer /ˈweɪfəʳ/ n 1 thin BISCUIT 2 thin round piece of special bread used in the Christian ceremony of COMMUNION

wafer-thin /ˌ·· ˈ·◂/ adj extremely thin

waf·fle[1] /ˈwɒfəl‖ˈwɑː-/ n light sweet cake marked with raised squares

waffle[2] vi BrE infml talk or write meaninglessly and at great length **waffle** n [U]

waft /wɑːft, woft‖wɑːft, wæft/ vi/t move lightly (as if) on wind or waves

wag¹ /wæg/ vi/t -gg- shake (esp. a body part) or be shaken from side to side: *The dog wagged its tail.* **wag** n

wag² n infml amusing man

wage /weɪdʒ/ vt carry on (a war)

wage freeze /'··/n attempt, esp. by government, to keep pay from rising

wa·ger /'weɪdʒəʳ/ n, vi fml for BET

wag·es /'weɪdʒɪz/ n [P] also **wage** [S] — payment for work done: *He gets his wages every Friday.* | *a wage rise*

wag·gle /'wægəl/ vi/t move quickly from side to side

wag·on ‖ also **waggon** BrE/'wægən/ n 1 strong usu. horse-drawn goods vehicle 2 BrE railway goods vehicle 3 esp. AmE TROLLEY: *a drinks wagon* 4 **on the wagon** no longer willing to drink alcohol

waif /weɪf/ n esp. lit uncared-for or homeless child or animal

wail /weɪl/ vi, n (make) a long cry (as if) in grief or pain

wain·scot /'weɪnskət, -skɒt‖-skət, -skɑːt/ n SKIRTING BOARD

waist /weɪst/ n 1 narrow part of the human body below the chest 2 narrow part of a garment or apparatus

waist·band /'weɪstbænd/ n strengthened part of trousers, a skirt, etc., that fastens round the waist

waist·coat /'weɪskəʊt, 'weskət‖ 'weskət/ n esp. BrE garment without arms worn under a JACKET

waist·line /'weɪstlaɪn/ n (length or height of) an imaginary line round the waist: (fig.) *No sugar for me — I'm watching my waistline.* (= trying not to become fatter)

wait /weɪt/ v 1 vi do nothing in the expectation of something happening: *I had to wait 2 hours for the bus!* | *Are you waiting to use the phone?* 2 vt not act until: *You'll have to wait your turn.* 3 vi remain unspoken, unheard, etc.: *My news can wait till later.* 4 **wait and see** delay an action or decision until the future becomes clearer 5 **wait at table** serve meals, esp. as a regular job ♦ n [S] act or period of waiting ~**er**, ~**ress** /-trəs/ fem. — n someone who serves food to people

wait on phr vt 1 serve food to, esp. in a restaurant 2 **wait on someone hand and foot** serve someone very humbly

waiting list /'··/n list of people who will be dealt with later

waiting room /'·· ·/ n room at a station, doctor's office, etc., where people wait

waive /weɪv/ vt fml state that (a rule, claim, etc.) is no longer in effect **waiver** n written statement waiving a right, etc.

wake¹ /weɪk/ vi/t woke /wəʊk/ or **waked, woken** /'wəʊkən/ or **waked** (cause to) stop sleeping: *I woke up late.* ~**ful** adj sleepless **waking** adj of the time when one is awake: *all my waking hours*

wake² n 1 track left by a ship: (fig.) *The car left clouds of dust in its wake.* 2 **in the wake of** as a result of: *war, with hunger and disease in its wake*

wake³ n gathering to grieve over a dead person

wak·en /'weɪkən/ vi/t fml wake

walk /wɔːk/ v 1 vi move slowly on foot so that at least one foot is always touching the ground 2 vt walk along: *He'd walked the streets looking for work.* 3 vt go with on foot: *I'll walk you to the bus stop.* 4 vt take (an animal) for a walk ♦ n 1 [C] (short) journey on foot: *Let's go for a walk.* | *The station's just a 5-minute walk from here.* 2 [S] way of walking 3 [C] place, path, or course for walking ~**er** n

walk into phr vt 1 get caught by (something) through carelessness 2 get (a job) very easily

walk off/away with phr vt 1 steal and take away 2 win easily

walk out phr vi 1 leave suddenly and disapprovingly 2 go on STRIKE²

walk out on phr vt leave suddenly

walk over phr vt treat badly

walk·ie·talk·ie /ˌwɔːki 'tɔːki/ n radio for talking as well as listening, that can be carried

walking stick /'·· ·/ n stick for support while walking

walk·man /'wɔːkmən/ n tdmk for PERSONAL STEREO

walk of life /ˌ· · '·/ n position in society, esp. one's job

walk-on /'· ·/ n small usu. non-speaking part in a play

walk·out /'wɔːk-aʊt/ n 1 action of disapprovingly leaving a meeting, organization, etc. 2 STRIKE² (1)

walk·o·ver /'wɔːkˌəʊvəʳ/ n easy victory

wall /wɔːl/ n 1 upright surface, esp. of brick or stone, for enclosing something: *the garden wall* | (fig.) *a wall of flames* 2 side of a room or building: *pictures hanging on the wall* 3 enclosing or inside surface: *the walls of a blood vessel* 4 **bang one's head against a (brick) wall** infml try to do the impossible 5 **go to the wall** (esp. in business) be ruined 6 **go up the wall** infml get very angry ~**ed** adj surrounded with a wall

wall off phr vt separate with a wall

wall up phr vt close or enclose with a wall

wal·let /'wɒlɪt‖'wɑː-/ n small flat case for papers and paper money

wall-flow-er /'wɔːl,flauə^r/ n 1 garden plant with sweet-smelling flowers 2 person who gets left out of social activity

wal-lop /'wɒləp‖'wɑː-/ vt, n infml (hit with) a powerful blow

wal-low /'wɒləʊ‖'wɑː-/ vi move, roll, or lie about happily in deep mud, water, etc.: wallowing in a hot bath |(fig.) in self-pity

wall-pa-per /'wɔːl,peɪpə^r/ n [U] decorative paper (for) covering the walls of a room ♦ vt cover the walls of (a room) with wallpaper

Wall Street /'· ·/ n centre of the American business and money world, in New York

wall-to-wall /,· · '·◄/ adj covering the whole floor: (fig.) wall-to-wall advertising

wal-ly /'wɒli‖'wɑː-/ n BrE infml fool

wal-nut /'wɔːlnʌt/ n 1 [C] eatable brain-shaped nut 2 [U] wood from its tree, used for furniture

wal-rus /'wɔːlrəs‖'wɒːl-, 'wɑːl-/ n -ruses or -rus large sea animal with 2 very long downward-pointing teeth

waltz /wɔːls‖wɔːlts/ vi, n (do) a rather slow dance for a man and a woman

wan /wɒn‖wɑːn/ adj esp. lit weak and tired

wand /wɒnd‖wɑːnd/ n stick used by someone doing magic tricks

wan-der /'wɒndə^r‖'wɑːn-/ v 1 vi/t move about without a fixed course or purpose: the wandering tribes of the Sahara. | (fig.) The discussion seems to have wandered from its main point. 2 vi be or become confused and unable to make or follow ordinary conversation ~er n ~ings n [P] long travels

wan-der-lust /'wɒndəlʌst‖'wɑːn-dər-/ n [S:U] strong desire to travel to faraway places

wane /weɪn/ vi get gradually smaller ♦ n on the wane becoming smaller or weaker

wan-gle /'wæŋgəl/ vt infml get by a trick

wank /wæŋk/ vi BrE taboo sl for MASTURBATE ~er n fool

want /wɒnt‖wɔːnt, wɑːnt/ vt 1 have a strong desire for: I don't want to go. 2 wish the presence of: Your mother wants you. 3 wish to find; hunt: He's wanted by the police for murder. 4 infml need: The house wants painting. 5 fml lack: to be found wanting (= not considered good, strong, etc., enough) ♦ n 1 [C;U] lack: The plants died for/ from want of water. 2 [U] severe lack of things necessary for life ~ing adj fml 1 lacking 2 not good enough

want for phr vt fml lack: The children want for nothing.

wan-ton /'wɒntən‖'wɑːn-, 'wɑːn-/ adj fml 1 (of something bad) having

no just cause: wanton disregard of the rules 2 (esp. of a woman) sexually improper

war /wɔː^r/ n [C;U] 1 (example or period of) armed fighting between nations: The 2 countries are at war.|the Second World War|(fig.) waging a war against poverty and ignorance 2 in the wars infml having been hurt or damaged ~ring adj fighting (each other)

war-ble /'wɔːbəl‖'wɔːr-/ vi (esp. of a bird) sing with a continuous varied note –bler n any of various songbirds

war clouds /'· ·/ n lit [P] signs that a war is getting likelier

war crime /'· ·/ n illegal act done while fighting a war

ward[1] /wɔːd‖wɔːrd/ n 1 large room in a hospital 2 political division of a city 3 person legally protected by another: The children were made wards of court.

ward[2] v ward off phr vt keep away (something bad)

war-den /'wɔːdn‖'wɔːrdn/ n person in charge of a place or people

ward-er /'wɔːdə^r‖'wɔːr-/ n BrE prison guard

war-drobe /'wɔːdrəʊb‖'wɔːr-/ n 1 large cupboard for storing clothes 2 person's collection of clothes

ward-room /'wɔːdrʊm, -ruːm‖ 'wɔːr-/ n officers' room in a warship

ware-house /'weəhaʊs‖'weər-/ n large building for storing things

wares /weəz‖weərz/ n [P] esp. lit things for sale

war-fare /'wɔːfeə^r‖'wɔːr-/ n [U] war

war game /'· ,·/ n pretended battle to test military plans

war-head /'wɔːhed‖'wɔːr-/ n explosive front end of a MISSILE

war-like /'wɔːlaɪk‖'wɔːr-/ adj fierce; liking to fight

war-lock /'wɔːlɒk‖'wɔːrlɑːk/ n male WITCH

warm[1] /wɔːm‖wɔːrm/ adj 1 having enough heat or pleasant heat: a warm bath 2 able to keep one warm: warm clothes 3 showing strong good feelings: a warm welcome 4 seeming cheerful or friendly: warm colours

warm[2] vi/t make or become warm ~ly adv

warm to phr vt 1 begin to like 2 become interested in

warm up phr vi/t prepare for action or performance by exercise or operation in advance

war-mon-ger /'wɔː,mʌŋgə^r‖'wɔːr-,mɑːŋ-, -,mʌŋ-/ n derog person who wants war

warmth /wɔːmθ‖wɔːrmθ/ n [U] being warm

warn /wɔːn‖wɔːrn/ v 1 vi/t tell of something bad that may happen, or of how to prevent it **2** vt give knowledge of some future need or action: *We warned we'd be away.* ~**ing** n [C;U] **1** telling in advance: *They attacked without warning.* **2** something that warns: *That's the second warning we've had.* — see also EARLY WARNING SYSTEM

warp /wɔːp‖wɔːrp/ vi/t turn or twist out of shape: *a warped plank*/(fig.) *mind* ♦ vt **1** warped place **2** threads running along the length of cloth

war-path /'wɔːpɑːθ‖'wɔːrpæθ/ n **on the warpath** angry and looking for someone to fight or punish

war-rant /'wɒrənt‖'wɔː-, 'wɑː-/ n [C] official paper allowing something: *The police have a warrant for her arrest.* **2** [U] fml proper reason for action ♦ vt **1** cause to seem right or reasonable **2** promise (that something is so)

warrant of-fic-er /'·· ,···/ n one just below an officer in rank

war-ran-ty /'wɒrənti‖'wɔː-, 'wɑː-/ n written GUARANTEE

war-ren /'wɒrən‖'wɔː-, 'wɑː-/ n **1** area where rabbits live **2** place where one can easily get lost

war-ri-or /'wɒriə‖'wɔː-, 'wɑː-/ n lit soldier

war-ship /'wɔː,ʃɪp‖'wɔːr-/ n naval ship used for war

wart /wɔːt‖wɔːrt/ n small hard swelling on the skin

war-time /'wɔːtaɪm‖'wɔːr-/ n [U] period during which a war is going on

war-y /'weəri/ adj careful; looking out for danger **-ily** adv

was /wəz; strong wɒz‖wəz; strong wɑːz/ v 1st and 3rd person sing. past t. of BE

wash /wɒʃ‖wɔːʃ, wɑːʃ/ v **1** vt clean with liquid **2** vi be able to be cleaned with liquid without damage: *This shirt doesn't wash well.* **3** vi wash oneself **4** vt carry by the force of moving water: *crops washed away by the floods* **5** vi/t esp. lit flow (against or over) continually **6** vi be (easily) believed: *His story won't wash.* **7 wash one's dirty linen (in public)** make public unpleasant subjects which ought to be kept private **8 wash one's hands of** refuse to have anything more to do with or to accept responsibility for ♦ n **1** [S] act of washing **2** [U] things to be washed **3** [S;U] movement of water caused by a passing boat **4 come out in the wash** infml **a** (of something shameful) become known **b** turn out all right in the end **5 in the wash** being washed ~**able** adj ~**ing** [U] clothes that are to be washed or have just been washed

wash down phr vt **1** clean with a lot of water **2** swallow with the help of liquid

wash out phr vt **1** cause to wash free of an unwanted substance **2** destroy or prevent by the action of water, esp. rain

wash up phr v **1** vi BrE wash dishes, knives, etc., after a meal **2** vt (of the sea) bring in to the shore **3** vi AmE for WASH (3)

wash-ba-sin /'wɒʃ,beɪsən‖'wɔːʃ-, 'wɑːʃ-/ BrE ‖ **washbowl** /-,bəʊl/ AmE — n fixed basin for washing the hands and face

washed-out /,· '·◄/ adj **1** faded **2** very tired **3** prevented because of rain: *The match was washed-out.*

washed-up /,· '·◄/ adj infml with no further possibilities of success

wash-er /'wɒʃə'‖'wɔː-, 'wɑː-/ n **1** ring of metal, plastic, etc., for making a joint tight under a screw, between 2 pipes, etc. **2** person or machine that washes

wash-er-wom-an /'wɒʃə,wʊmən‖'wɔːʃər-, 'wɑː-/ n **-women** /-,wɪmɪn/ (in former times) woman who washed other people's clothes

washing ma-chine /'·· ·,·/ n machine for washing clothes

washing-up /,·· '·/ n [U] BrE dishes, knives, etc., (to be) washed after a meal

wash-out /'wɒʃ-aʊt‖'wɔːʃ-, 'wɑːʃ-/ n failure

wash-room /'wɒʃrʊm, -ruːm‖'wɔːʃ-/ n AmE for TOILET (1)

wasn't /'wɒzənt‖'wɑː-/ short for: was not

wasp /wɒsp‖wɑːsp, wɔːsp/ n black and yellow beelike insect ~**ish** adj sharply bad-tempered and cruel ~**ishness** n [U]

WASP, Wasp n esp. AmE White Anglo-Saxon Protestant; an American whose family was originally from N. Europe, esp. considered as a member of the class which has power or influence in society

wast-age /'weɪstɪdʒ/ n [S;U] **1** wasteful loss **2** reduction in numbers

waste /weɪst/ n **1** [S;U] loss through wrong use or less than full use: *a waste of time*|*Don't let it go to waste.* (= be wasted) **2** [U] used or unwanted matter: *industrial/bodily waste* **3** [U] wide empty lonely stretch of water or land ♦ vt **1** use wrongly or not at all: *wasting his money on silly things* **2** fml make (the body) extremely thin ♦ adj **1** (of ground) empty and unused **2** got rid of as used or useless: *waste paper/products* ~**ful** adj tending to waste things ~**fully** adv

waste-pa-per bas-ket /,weɪst'peɪpə ,bɑːskət, 'weɪst,peɪpə-‖'weɪst,-peɪpər,bæ-/ ‖ also **wastebasket** /'weɪst,bɑːskət‖-,bæ-/ esp. AmE — n small container for throwing away unwanted paper, etc.

watch /wɒtʃ‖wɑːtʃ, wɔːtʃ/ v **1** vi/t look (at) attentively: *Watch me and you'll see how it's done.* **2** vt be careful about: *Watch what you're doing with that knife!* **3 watch it!** be careful **4 watch one's step** act with great care **5 watch the clock** be waiting for one's working day to end rather than thinking about one's work ♦ n **1** [C] small clock worn esp. on the wrist **2** [S;U] act of watching: *The police are keeping (a) watch on their activities.* **3** [C;U] period of duty on a ship ~**er** n ~**ful** adj careful to notice things

watch for phr vt look for; expect and wait for

watch out phr vi take care

watch out for phr vt **1** keep looking for **2** be careful of

watch over phr vt guard and protect; take care of

watch·dog /'wɒtʃdɒg‖'wɑːtʃdɔːg, 'wɔːtʃ-/ n **1** dog kept to guard property **2** person or group that tries to prevent loss, waste, or undesirable practices

watch·man /'wɒtʃmən‖'wɑːtʃ-, 'wɔːtʃ-/ n -men /-mən/ guard, esp. of a building

watch·word /'wɒtʃwɜːd‖'wɑːtʃ-wɜːrd, 'wɔːtʃ-/ n **1** PASSWORD **2** word or phrase expressing a guiding principle

wa·ter /'wɔːtəʳ‖'wɑː-, 'wɔː-/ n [U] **1** liquid found as rain, in the sea, etc., and commonly drunk **2** a mass of this: *She dived into the water.* | *After the flood the fields were under water.* | *The goods came by water.* (= by boat) **3 above water** out of difficulty: *keep one's head above water* (= keep oneself out of difficulty) **4 hold water** be true or reasonable: *Your story doesn't hold water.* **5 like water** in great quantity: *The wine flowed like water.* **6 make/pass water** URINATE **7 throw cold water on** point out difficulties in (a plan, idea, etc.) — see also HOT WATER ♦ v **1** vt pour water on (a plant or area) **2** vt supply (esp. animals) with water **3** vi (of the mouth or eyes) form or let out watery liquid **waters** n [P] **1** sea near or round a country: *in Icelandic waters* **2** water of the stated river, lake, etc. ~**y** adj **1** containing too much water **2** very pale

water down phr vt **1** weaken by adding water **2** reduce the force of: *a watered-down report*

water can·non /'·· ,··/ n apparatus for shooting out a powerful stream of water, esp. for controlling crowds

water clos·et /'·· ,··/ n WC

wa·ter·col·our /'wɔːtə,kʌləʳ‖'wɔː-tər-, 'wɑː-/ n **1** [C;U] paint mixed with water rather than oil **2** [C] picture painted with this

wa·ter·cress /'wɔːtəkres‖'wɔːtər-, 'wɑː-/ n [U] water plant with leaves used as food

wa·ter·fall /'wɔːtəfɔːl‖'wɔːtər-, 'wɑː-/ n very steep fall of water in a river, etc.

wa·ter·front /'wɔːtəfrʌnt‖'wɔːtər-, 'wɑː-/ n land along a stretch of water, esp. in a port

wa·ter·hole /'wɔːtəhəʊl‖'wɔːtər-, 'wɑː-/ n pool where animals come to drink

watering can /'··· ·/ n container for pouring water onto garden plants

water lev·el /'·· ,··/ n height to which a mass of water has risen or sunk

wa·ter·line /'wɔːtəlaɪn ‖ 'wɔːtər-, 'wɑː-/ n level reached by water up the side of a ship

wa·ter·logged /'wɔːtəlɒgd‖'wɔːtər-lɔːgd, 'wɑː-, -lɑːgd/ adj **1** (of ground) very wet **2** (of a boat) full of water

Wa·ter·loo /,wɔːtə'luː ‖ ,wɔːtər-, ,wɑː-/ n (deserved) defeat after a time of unusual success

wa·ter·mark /'wɔːtəmɑːk‖'wɔːtər-mɑːrk, 'wɑː-/ n **1** partly transparent mark in paper **2** mark that shows a level reached: *the high watermark of her success*

wa·ter·mel·on /'wɔːtə,melən‖'wɔː-tər-, 'wɑː-/ n large round green fruit with juicy red flesh

wa·ter·mill /'wɔːtəmɪl ‖ 'wɔːtər-, 'wɑː-/ n MILL (1) driven by moving water

water po·lo /'·· ,··/ n [U] game played by 2 teams of swimmers with a ball

wa·ter·pow·er /'wɔːtə,paʊəʳ‖'wɔː-tər-, 'wɑː-/ n [U] power from moving water to drive machines

wa·ter·proof /'wɔːtəpruːf‖'wɔːtər-, 'wɑː-/ adj, n (an outer garment) which does not allow water, esp. rain, through ♦ vt make waterproof

wa·ter·shed /'wɔːtəʃed ‖ 'wɔːtər-, 'wɑː-/ n point of very important change

wa·ter·side /'wɔːtəsaɪd ‖ 'wɔːtər-, 'wɑː-/ n [U] edge of a river, lake, etc.

water ski·ing /'·· ,··/ n [U] sport of being pulled across water on SKIs -er n

water sup·ply /'·· ·,··/ n flow of water provided for a building or area, and system of lakes, pipes, etc., that provides it

water ta·ble /'·· ,··/ n level below which water can be found in the ground

wa·ter·tight /'wɔːtətaɪt‖'wɔːtər-, 'wɑː-/ adj **1** which water cannot pass

weak

through **2** allowing or having no mistakes or possibility of doubt: *a watertight plan*

wa·ter·way /'wɔːtəweɪ ‖ 'wɔːtər-, 'wɑː-/ *n* stretch of water which ships travel along

wa·ter·wheel /'wɔːtəwiːl‖'wɔːtər-, 'wɑː-/ *n* wheel which is turned by moving water, esp. to give power to machines

wa·ter·works /'wɔːtəwɜːks‖'wɔːtərwɜːrks, 'wɑː-/ **1** place from which a public water supply is provided **2** *infml* body's system for removing water from the body **3 turn on the waterworks** start to cry, esp. to get attention, or what one wants

watt /wɒt‖wɑːt/ *n* measure of electrical power

wat·tle /'wɒtl‖'wɑːtl/ *n* [U] thin sticks woven over poles to form a fence or wall

wave /weɪv/ *v* **1** *vi/t* move (one's hand or something in it) as a signal: *We waved as the train pulled out.* **2** *vt* direct with a movement of the hand: *The policeman waved the traffic on.* **3** *vi* move gently from side to side in the air: *The flags waved.* **4** *vi/t* (cause to) curve regularly: *waved hair* ♦ *n* **1** raised moving area of water, esp. on the sea **2** movement of the hand in waving **3** feeling, way of behaving, etc., that suddenly starts and increases: *a wave of nausea* | *a crime wave* **4** form in which light, sound, etc., move: *radio waves* **5** evenly curved part of the hair **wavy** *adj* having regular curves

wave aside *phr vt* push aside without giving attention to (esp. ideas, etc.)

wave·length /'weɪvleŋθ/ *n* **1** distance between 2 WAVES (4) **2** radio signal sent out on radio WAVES that are a particular distance apart: (fig.) *We're on completely different wavelengths.* (= are completely different, cannot understand each other, etc.)

wa·ver /'weɪvəʳ/ *vi* be uncertain or unsteady in direction or decision: *Her loyalty never wavered.*

wax¹ /wæks/ *n* [U] solid meltable fatty or oily substance ♦ *vt* put wax on, esp. as a polish **~y** *adj*

wax² *vi* **1** (esp. of the moon) get gradually larger **2** *lit* (of a person) become: *He waxed eloquent as he described his plans.*

wax·works /'wækswɜːks‖-wɜːrks/ *n* -works (place with) models of people made in wax

way /weɪ/ *n* **1** [C] road, path, etc., to follow in order to reach a place: *She asked me the way to the station.* | *We lost our way.* **2** [C] direction: *He went that way.* **3** [S] distance: *We're a long*

way *from home.* **4** [C] method: *Do it this way.* **5** [C] manner: *the cruel way in which he treats his animals* **6** [C] single part of a whole; detail; point: *In many ways I agree with you, but I don't think you're completely right.* **7 by the way** (used to introduce a new subject in speech) **8 by way of: a** by going through **b** as a sort of: *a few sandwiches by way of lunch* **9 get one's own way** do or get what one wants in spite of others **10 go one's own way** do what one wants **11 go out of the/one's way** (to do) take the trouble (to do); make a special effort **12 have a way with one** have an attractive quality which persuades others **13 have it both ways** gain advantage from 2 opposing opinions or actions **14 out of/in the way** (of) (not) blocking space for forward movement: *You're in the way; move!* **15 make one's way** go **16 make way for** leave so as to allow so: develop freely **17 no way** *infml* no: *'Will you help me?' 'No way!'* **18 out of the way** unusual or not commonly known **19 see one's way (clear) to (doing)** feel able to do **20 under way** moving forwards — see also **give way** (GIVE¹), **RIGHT OF WAY** ♦ *adv* far: *That's way outside my area.* **ways** *n* [P] customs; habits: *mend one's ways* (= improve one's manners, etc.)

way·far·er /'weɪˌfeərəʳ/ *n* *lit* traveller

way·lay /weɪ'leɪ/ *vt* **-laid** /-'leɪd/, **-lain** /-'leɪn/ *or* **-laid 1** attack (a traveller) **2** find or stop (someone) to speak to them

way-out /ˌ· '·◄/ *adj* *infml* strange; unusual

way·side /'weɪsaɪd/ *n* side of the road or path

way·ward /'weɪwəd‖-ərd/ *adj* **1** difficult to guide or control **2** not well aimed

WC /ˌdʌbəljuː 'siː/ *n* TOILET (1)

we /wi; *strong* wiː/ *pron* (used as the subject of a sentence) **1** the people speaking; oneself and one or more others **2** *fml* (used by a king or queen) I

weak /wiːk/ *adj* **1** having little power: *weak muscles/eyes* **2** easily becoming broken, changed, destroyed, or ill: *a weak heart* **3** having little taste: *weak tea* **4** unable to control people: *a weak teacher* **5** not reaching a good standard: *His maths is rather weak.* **~ly** *adv* **~en** *vi/t* (cause to) become weaker **~ness** *n* **1** [U] fact or state of being weak **2** [C] part that spoils the rest: *The plan's only weakness is its cost.* **3** [C] fault in character **4** [C] strong liking: *a weakness for chocolate*

weak-kneed /ˌ·ˈ·◂/ adj cowardly

weak-ling /ˈwiːk-lɪŋ/ n derog weak person

weal /wiːl/ n mark on the skin where one has been hit

wealth /welθ/ n 1 [U] (large amount of) money and possessions 2 [S] fml large number: a wealth of examples ~y adj rich

wean /wiːn/ vt gradually give (a baby) solid food instead of milk

wean from phr vt gradually persuade to give up (something one disapproves of)

weap-on /ˈwepən/ n something to fight with, such as a gun or sword ~ry n [U] weapons

wear /weəʳ/ v wore /wɔːʳ/, worn /wɔːn‖wɔːrn/ 1 vt have (esp. clothes) on the body 2 vt have (a particular expression) on the face 3 vi/t (cause to) show the effects of continued use, rubbing, etc.: You've worn a hole in your sock.|(fig.) That excuse is wearing thin. (= becoming unbelievable) 4 vi last in the stated condition: an old person who has worn well 5 vt infml find acceptable ♦ n [U] 1 clothes: evening wear|men's wear 2 act of wearing esp. clothes 3 damage from use: signs of wear 4 quality of lasting in use: There's a lot of wear in these shoes.

wear down phr vt weaken

wear off phr vi (of a feeling, effect, etc.) become gradually less

wear on phr vi pass slowly in time

wear out phr v 1 vi/t (cause to) be reduced to nothing or a useless state by use 2 vt tire greatly

wear and tear /ˌ· · ˈ·/ n [U] damage from use; WEAR (3)

wear-i-some /ˈwɪərɪsəm/ adj tiring and boring (BORE²) or annoying

wea-ry /ˈwɪəri/ adj very tired ♦ vi/t (cause to) become weary **-ily** adv **-iness** n [U]

wea-sel¹ /ˈwiːzəl/ n small fierce furry animal

weasel² v **weasel out** phr vi AmE infml escape a duty by clever dishonest means

weath-er /ˈweðəʳ/ n [U] 1 particular condition of wind, sunshine, rain, snow, etc.: a day of fine weather 2 **make heavy weather of** make (something) seem difficult for oneself 3 **under the weather** slightly ill ♦ v 1 vt pass safely through (a storm or difficulty) 2 vi/t change from the effects of air, rain, etc.: weathered stone

weather-beat-en /ˈ·· ˌ··/ adj marked or damaged by the wind, sun, etc.

weather fore-cast /ˈ·· ˌ··/ n description of weather conditions as they are expected to be

weath-er-man /ˈweðəmæn‖-ər-/ n **-men** /-men/ person who describes likely future weather conditions, esp. on television or radio

weather sta-tion /ˈ·· ˌ··/ n place for noting weather conditions

weather vane /ˈ·· ·/ n small apparatus that is blown round to show the direction of the wind

weave /wiːv/ v wove /wəʊv/, woven /ˈwəʊvən/ 1 vi/t form threads into (material) by drawing them singly under and over a set of longer threads 2 vt twist; wind: a bird's nest woven from straws 3 vt produce (a story) esp. from a suggestion 4 (past t. and p. weaved) vi move twistingly: The cyclist weaved through the traffic. ♦ n style or pattern of woven material: a loose weave **weaver** n

web /web/ n 1 net of thin threads made by a SPIDER: (fig.) a web of lies 2 skin between the toes of certain swimming birds and animals ~**bed** /webd/ adj having a WEB (2) between the toes

web-bing /ˈwebɪŋ/ n [U] strong woven bands used for belts, supports, etc.

wed /wed/ vi/t wedded or wed esp. lit marry

we'd /wid; strong wiːd/ short for: 1 we had 2 we would

wed-ding /ˈwedɪŋ/ n marriage ceremony

wedding ring /ˈ·· ·/ n ring worn to show that one is married

wedge /wedʒ/ n 1 V-shaped piece of wood, etc., for keeping something in place or splitting something 2 V-shaped piece: a wedge of cake 3 something shaped like this: shoes with wedge heels — see also **thin end of the wedge** (THIN) ♦ vt fix firmly (as if) with a wedge: Wedge the door open.|I got wedged between 2 people on the bus.

Wedg-wood /ˈwedʒwʊd/ n [U] tdmk fine CHINA, esp. blue and white

wed-lock /ˈwedlɒk‖-lɑːk/ n [U] lit 1 being married 2 **out of wedlock** to unmarried parents

Wednes-day /ˈwenzdi/ n the 3rd day of the week

wee /wiː/ adj very small

weed¹ /wiːd/ n 1 unwanted wild plant 2 physically weak person ~**y** adj 1 thin and weak 2 full of weeds

weed² vi/t remove weeds from (a garden)

weed out phr vt get rid of (less good ones)

week /wiːk/ n 1 period of 7 days, usu. thought of as starting on Monday and ending on Sunday, but sometimes measured from Sunday to Saturday 2 period worked during a week: a 35-

hour **week 3 week after week** also **week in, week out** — continuously

week-day /'wi:kdeɪ/ *n* day other than Saturday or Sunday

week-end /ˌwiːk'end, 'wɪkend‖ 'wiːkend/ *n* Saturday and Sunday, esp. when considered a holiday

week-ly /'wiːkli/ *adj, adv* (happening) every week or once a week ♦ *n* magazine or newpaper which appears once a week

weep /wiːp/ *vi* wept /wept/ *fml or lit* cry ~**ing** *adj* (of a tree) with branches hanging down

wee-vil /'wiːvəl/ *n* small insect which eats (and spoils) grain, seeds, etc.

weft /weft/ *n* threads running across cloth

weigh /weɪ/ *v* **1** *vt* find the weight of: *weigh oneself* **2** *vi* have the stated weight: *It weighs 6 kilos.* **3** *vt* consider or compare carefully **4** *vt* raise (an ANCHOR)

weigh down *phr vt* make heavy with a load: (fig.) *weighed down with grief*

weigh in *phr vi* join in a fight or argument

weigh on *phr vt* worry: *His responsibilities weighed on him.*

weigh up *phr vt* form an opinion about, esp. by balancing opposing arguments

weigh-bridge /'weɪˌbrɪdʒ/ *n* a machine for weighing vehicles and their loads

weight /weɪt/ *n* **1** [C;U] (measured) heaviness of something: *The weight of the sack is 2 kilos.* **2** [C] something heavy: *lifting weights* **3** [C] piece of metal of known heaviness, used for weighing things **4** [U] system of standard measures of heaviness: *metric weight* **5** [U] value; importance: *I don't attach much weight to these rumours.* **6** [C] (something that causes) a feeling of anxiety: *a great weight off my mind* **7 pull one's weight** do one's full share of work **8 put on/lose weight** (of a person) become heavier/lighter **9 throw one's weight about** give orders to others ♦ *vt* **1** make heavy, esp. by fastening weights **2** include conditions in (something) that give a (dis)advantage: *The competition is weighted against younger children.* ~**less** *adj: a weightless flight in space* ~**y** *adj* **1** heavy **2** *fml* important and serious

weight lift-ing /'·ˌ··/ also **weight training** — *n* [U] sport of lifting heavy weights -**er** *n*

weir /wɪə/ *n* wall-like structure across a river controlling its flow

weird /wɪəd‖wɪərd/ *adj* **1** strange; unusual: *a weird shriek* **2** unusual and

not sensible or acceptable: *weird ideas* ~**ly** *adv* ~**ness** *n* [U]

weird-o /'wɪədəʊ‖'wɪər-/ *n* -**os** *sl* strange person

wel-come /'welkəm/ *interj* (a greeting to someone who has arrived) ♦ *vt* **1** greet (someone newly arrived), esp. with friendliness **2** wish to have; like: *I'd welcome some help.* ♦ *adj* **1** acceptable and wanted: *A cool drink is always welcome on a hot day.* **2** allowed freely (to have): *I've plenty of cigarettes; you're welcome to one.* **3 You're welcome** (a polite expression when thanked for something) ♦ *n* greeting

weld /weld/ *vt* join (metal) by melting ~**er** *n*

wel-fare /'welfeə/ *n* [U] **1** comfort, health, and happiness: *I was concerned for her welfare.* (= thought she might be in trouble) **2** help with living conditions, social problems, etc.

welfare state /ˌ·· '·‖'·· ·/ *n* (country with) a system of social help for poor, sick, etc., people

well¹ *adv* better /'betə/, best /best/ **1** in a good way: *She sings well.* | *a well-dressed man* **2** thoroughly: *They were well beaten.* **3** much; quite: *She finished well within the time allowed.* **4** suitably; properly: *I couldn't very well refuse.* **5 as well: a** also: *She came as well.* **b** with as good a result: *We might just as well have stayed at home.* **6 as well as** in addition to **7 come off well** be lucky in the end **8 do well** succeed or improve **9 do well out of** gain profit from **10 do well to** act wisely in **11 just as well** it is fortunate (that); there's no harm done **12 may well** could suitably **13 pretty well** almost **14 well and truly** completely **15 well away: a** getting ahead **b** *infml* starting to be drunk **16 Well done!** (said when someone has been successful) **17 well in with** having a good relationship with **18 well out of** lucky enough to be free from (an affair) ♦ *adj* better, best **1** in good health **2** in an acceptable state **3 It's all very well** (an expression of dissatisfaction when comparing what is practical to what is suggested): *It's all very well for you to laugh but what was I supposed to do?* ♦ *interj* **1** (expresses surprise) **2** (introduces an expression of surprise, doubt, etc.)

well² *n* **1** place where water can be taken from underground **2** OIL WELL **3** deep narrow space inside a building, for stairs or a LIFT² (2) ♦ *vi* flow

we'll /wɪl; *strong* wiːl/ *short for:* **1** we will **2** we shall

well-ad-jus-ted /ˌ· ·'··◂/ *adj* (of a person) fitting in well with society

well-ad-vised /ˌ· ·'··◂/ *adj* sensible

well-be·ing /ˌwel'biːɪŋ◂‖'welˌbiːɪŋ/ n [U] personal and physical comfort, esp. good health and happiness

well-bred /ˌ· '·◂/ adj having or showing high social rank, with good manners

well-con·nect·ed /ˌ· ·'·◂/ adj knowing or esp. related to people of high social rank or influence

well-done /ˌ· '·◂/ adj thoroughly cooked

well-groomed /ˌ· '·◂/ adj neat and clean

well-heeled /ˌ· '·◂/ adj infml rich

wel·lie /'weli/ n BrE infml wellington

well-in·formed /ˌ· ·'·◂/ adj knowing a lot about several subjects or parts of a particular subject

wel·ling·ton /'welɪŋtən/ n esp. BrE rubber boot for keeping the foot and lower leg dry

well-in·ten·tioned /ˌ· ·'··◂/ adj acting in the hope of good results, though often failing

well-known /ˌ· '·◂/ adj known by many people; famous

well-mean·ing /ˌ· '··◂/ adj well-intentioned

well-nigh /'· ·/ adv almost: well-nigh impossible

well-off /ˌ· '·◂/ adj 1 rich 2 lucky

well-pre·served /ˌ· ·'·◂/ adj (of someone or something old) still in good condition

well-read /ˌ· '·◂/ adj having read many books and got a lot of information

well-spok·en /ˌ· '·◂/ adj having a socially acceptable way of speaking

well-timed /ˌ· '·◂/ adj said or done at the most suitable time

well-to-do /ˌ· · '·◂/ adj rich

well-wish·er /'· ˌ··/ n person who wishes another to succeed, have good luck, etc.

well-worn /ˌ· '·◂/ adj (of a phrase) overused

welsh /welʃ/ vi derog avoid payment

Welsh adj of Wales

wel·ter /'weltəʳ/ n [S] confused mixture: a welter of statistics

wel·ter·weight /'weltəweɪt‖-ər-/ n boxer (BOX²) of middle weight

wench /wentʃ/ n lit young woman

wend /wend/ v **wend one's way: a** travel (slowly) **b** leave

went /went/ past t. of GO

wept /wept/ past t. and p. of WEEP

were /wəʳ; strong wɜːʳ/ v past t. of BE

we're /wɪəʳ; strong wɪəʳ/short for: we are

were-wolf /'weəwʊlf, 'wɪə-‖'weər-, 'wɪər-/ n (in stories) person who sometimes turns into a WOLF (1)

west /west/ n 1 (often cap.) direction towards which the sun sets 2 [the + S] (cap.) western Europe and the US ♦ adj 1 in the west 2 (of wind) from the west ♦ adv 1 towards the west 2 go **west: a** to die **b** be damaged or broken ~**ward** adj, adv

West End /ˌ· '·◂/ n [the], western part of central London, where shops, theatres, etc. are

west·er·ly /'westəli‖-ərli/ adj west

west·ern /'westən‖-ərn/ adj of the west part of the world or of a country ♦ n story about life in the middle of the US in the past, with COWBOYs and gunfights ~**er** n someone who lives in or comes from the WEST (2)

west·ern·ize ‖ also **-ise** BrE /'westənaɪz‖-ər-/ vt cause to have or copy the customs typical of America and Europe) **-ization** /ˌwestən-aɪ'zeɪʃən‖-ərnə-/ n [U]

wet /wet/ adj **-tt- 1** covered with or being liquid: wet grass/paint **2** rainy: a wet day **3** BrE weak in character and unable to get things done **4 wet through** completely covered in or with liquid ♦ n 1 [the + S] rainy weather **2** [C] BrE infml MODERATE¹ (2) person in the British Conservative Party ♦ vt **wet** or **wetted**; pres. p. **-tt-** make wet ~**ness** n [U]

wet blan·ket /ˌ· '··‖ˌ· ˌ··/ n person who discourages others or prevents them from enjoying themselves

wet dream /ˌ· '·/n sexually exciting dream resulting in a male ORGASM

wet-nurse /'· ·/vt treat with too much care

wet suit /'· ·/ n rubber garment for keeping the body warm in sea sports

we've /wiv; strong wiːv/ short for: we have

whack /wæk/ vt hit with a noisy blow ♦ n 1 (noise of) a hard blow **2** BrE infml (fair) share ~**ed** adj BrE infml very tired ~**ing** adj, adv infml (very) big

whale /weɪl/ n 1 extremely large fishlike animal **2 a whale of a time** a very enjoyable time **whaler** n a person who hunts whales **b** ship from which whales are hunted **whaling** n [U] hunting whales

wham /wæm/ n (sound of) a hard blow

wharf /wɔːf‖wɔːrf/ n **wharfs** or **wharves** /wɔːvz‖wɔːrvz/ place where ships are tied up to unload and load goods

what /wɒt‖wɑːt, wʌt/ predeterminer, determiner, pron 1 (used in questions about an unknown thing or person): What are you doing?| What colour is it? **2** the thing(s) that: He told me what to do. **3** (shows surprise): What a strange hat! **4 what for?** why? **5 what if?** what will happen if? **6 what's more** and this is more important **7**

what's what the true state of things: *to know what's what* ♦ *adv* 1 (used esp. in questions when no answer is expected) in what way: *What do you care?* (= I don't think you care at all) 2 **what with** (used for introducing the cause of something, esp. something bad)

what-ev-er /wɒt'evəʳ‖wɑː-, wʌ-/ *determiner, pron* 1 no matter what: *Whatever I said, he'd disagree.* 2 anything: *They eat whatever they can find.* 3 (shows surprise) what: *Whatever is that peculiar thing?* ♦ *adj* at all: *I have no money whatever.*

what-not /'wɒtnɒt‖'wɑːtnɑːt, 'wʌt-/ *n* [U] *infml* anything (else): *carrying his bags and whatnot*

wheat /wiːt/ *n* [U] (plant producing) grain from which flour is made

whee-dle /'wiːdl/ *vi/t* try to persuade (someone) by pleasant but insincere words

wheel /wiːl/ *n* 1 circular frame which turns to allow vehicles to move, to work machinery, etc. 2 movement by which a group of marching soldiers curve to the left or right 3 [*the* + S] the STEERING WHEEL of a car or ship 4 **at the wheel: a** driving or guiding a car or ship **b** in control 5 **wheels within wheels** hidden influences having effects on surface behaviour ♦ *v* 1 *vt* move (a wheeled object) with the hands 2 *vi* turn round suddenly 3 *vi* (of birds) fly round and round in circles 4 **wheel and deal** *vi infml* make deals, esp. in business or politics, in a skilful and perhaps dishonest way **~ed** *adj* having wheels

wheel-bar-row /'wiːl,bærəʊ/ *n* small 1-wheeled cart pushed by hand

wheel-chair /'wiːltʃeəʳ/ *n* wheeled chair for someone who cannot walk

wheeler-deal-er /,·· '··/ *n* someone skilled at doing clever (but perhaps not always honest) deals, esp. in business or politics

wheel-ie /'wiːli/ *n* act of riding a bicycle on its back wheel

wheeze /wiːz/ *vi* make a noisy whistling sound in breathing ♦ *n* 1 wheezing sound 2 *infml* joke or clever trick **wheezy** *adj*

whelk /welk/ *n* sea animal that lives in a shell

whelp /welp/ *n esp. lit derog* young animal, esp. a dog

when /wen/ *adv, conj* 1 at what time; at the time that: *When will they come?* | *He looked up when she came in.* 2 considering that; although: *Why did you do it when I told you not to?*

whence /wens/ *adv, conj lit* from where

when-ev-er /wen'evəʳ/ *adv, conj* 1 at whatever time 2 every time

where /weəʳ/ *adv, conj* at or to what place; at or to the place that: *Where do you live?* | *Sit where you like.*

where-a-bouts /,weərə'baʊts◂‖'weərəbaʊts/ *adv* where in general (not exactly): *Whereabouts did I leave my glasses?* ♦ *n* [U] place where a person or thing is

where-as /weər'æz/ *conj* (shows an opposite) but: *They live in a house, whereas we have a flat.*

where-by /weə'baɪ‖weər-/ *adj fml* by means of which

where-fore /'weəfɔːʳ‖'weər-/ *adv, conj lit* why

where-u-pon /,weərə'pɒn‖'weərəpɑːn,-pɔːn/ *conj* without delay after and because of which: *He stood up to speak, whereupon everyone cheered.*

wher-ev-er /weər'evəʳ/ *adv* 1 to or at whatever place 2 (shows surprise) where

where-with-al /'weəwɪðɔːl‖-'weər-/ *n* [U] enough money

whet /wet/ *vt* -tt- **whet someone's appetite** make someone wish for more

wheth-er /'weðəʳ/ *conj* if ... or not: *I'm trying to decide whether to go.*

whey /weɪ/ *n* [U] watery part of milk

which /wɪtʃ/ *determiner, pron* 1 (used in questions, when a choice is to be made): *Which shoes shall I wear, the red ones or the brown?* 2 (shows what thing is meant): *This is the book which I told you about.* 3 (used to add more information about something): *The train, which only takes an hour, is quicker than the bus.* — see also EVERY WHICH WAY

which-ev-er /wɪtʃ'evəʳ/ *determiner, pron* 1 only (one) of the set that: *Take whichever seat you like.* 2 no matter which: *It has the same result, whichever way you do it.*

whiff /wɪf/ *n* [S] 1 short-lasting smell of something 2 an act of breathing in: *A few whiffs of gas and she'll fall asleep.*

while¹ /waɪl/ *n* [S] 1 length of time: *He's been gone quite a while.* (= a fairly long time) 2 **once in a while** sometimes, but not often 3 **worth one's/someone's while** WORTH-WHILE to one/someone: *We'll make it worth your while.* ♦ *conj* 1 during the time that: *They arrived while we were having dinner.* 2 although: *While I agree with your reasons, I can't allow it.* 3 WHEREAS 4 and what is more

while² *v* **while away** *phr vt* pass (time) in a pleasantly lazy way

whilst /waɪlst/ *conj* while

whim /wɪm/ *n* sudden (often unreasonable) idea or wish

whim-per /'wɪmpəʳ/ *vi* make small weak trembling cries **whimper** *n*

whim·sy /ˈwɪmzi/ *n* [U] strange humour **–sical** *adj* fanciful; with strange ideas

whine /waɪn/ *vi* **1** make a high sad sound **2** complain (too much) in an unnecessarily sad way **whine** *n*: *the whine of the jet engines*

whinge /wɪndʒ/ *vi derog* complain, esp. of unfair treatment

whin·ny /ˈwɪni/ *vi* make a gentle sound which horses make

whip¹ /wɪp/ *n* **1** long piece of esp. rope or leather on a handle, used for striking sharp blows **2** esp. BrE (person who gives) an order to a member of Parliament to attend and vote

whip² *v* **-pp- 1** *vt* hit with a whip **2** *vi/t* move quickly: *He whipped out his gun.* **3** *vt* beat (esp. cream or eggs) until stiff **4** *vt infml* defeat **5** *vt BrE infml* steal **~ping** *n* beating as a punishment

whip up *phr vt* **1** cause (feelings) to become stronger, etc. **2** make quickly

whip hand /ˈ· ·/ *n* [U] control

whip·lash /ˈwɪp-læʃ/ *n* **1** blow from a whip **2** harm done by sudden violent movement of the head and neck, as in a car accident: *a whiplash injury*

whip·ping boy /ˈ·· ·/ *n* person who (unfairly) gets the blame and/or punishment

whip-round /ˈ· ·/ *n esp. BrE* collection of money within a group

whirl /wɜːl‖wɜːrl/ *vi/t* move round and round very fast ♦ *n* **1** [S] act or sensation of whirling: (fig.) *My head's in a whirl.* (= confused) **2** [C] very fast (confused) movement or activity **3 give something a whirl** *infml* try something

whirl·pool /ˈwɜːlpuːl‖ˈwɜːrl-/ *n* fast circular current of water

whirl·wind /ˈwɜːl.wɪnd‖ˈwɜːrl-/ *n* tall tube of air moving dangerously at high speed: (fig.) *a whirlwind romance* (= happening very quickly)

whirr /wɜːr/ *vi, n* (make) the regular sound of something whirring and beating against the air

whisk /wɪsk/ *vt* **1** remove, either by quick light brushing or by taking suddenly: *She whisked my cup away before I'd finished.* **2** beat (esp. eggs), esp. with a whisk ♦ *n* small hand-held apparatus for beating eggs, cream, etc.

whis·ker /ˈwɪskər/ *n* long stiff hair near an animal's mouth **whiskers** *n* [P] hair on the sides of a man's face

whis·key /ˈwɪski/ *n* [U] Irish or US whisky

whis·ky /ˈwɪski/ *n* [U] strong alcoholic drink made from grain, esp. in Scotland

whis·per /ˈwɪspər/ *v* **1** *vi/t* speak or say very quietly **2** *vt* suggest or pass (information) secretly: *It's whispered* he may resign. ♦ *n* **1** very quiet voice **2** RUMOUR

whist /wɪst/ *n* [U] card game for 4 players

whis·tle /ˈwɪsəl/ *n* **1** simple (musical) instrument played by blowing **2** high sound made by air blowing through a narrow opening ♦ *v* **1** *vi* make a WHISTLE (2), esp. by blowing through the lips: (fig.) *The wind whistled round us.* **2** *vt* produce (a tune) by doing this

whit /wɪt/ *n* [S] *fml* small amount: *not a whit less interesting*

white /waɪt/ *adj* **1** of the colour of snow and milk **2** pale **3** of a pale-skinned race **4** (of coffee) with milk or cream ♦ *n* **1** [U] white colour **2** [C] WHITE (3) person **3** [C] part of an egg surrounding the central yellow part **–whiten** *vi/t* (cause to) become white(r)

white-col·lar /ˌ· ˈ··◂/ *adj* of or being office workers, indoor workers, etc.

white el·e·phant /ˌ· ˈ···/ *n* useless article

white flag /ˌ· ˈ·/ *n* sign that one accepts defeat

White·hall /ˈwaɪthɔːl, ˌwaɪtˈhɔːl/ *n* [U] **1** (street in London containing many of the offices of) the British government **2** the British Government itself

white heat /ˌ· ˈ·/ *n* [U] temperature at which metal turns white

white hope /ˌ· ˈ·/*n* person who is expected to bring great success

White House /ˈ· ·/ *n* [the] official Washington home of the US president

white knight /ˌ· ˈ·/*n* person or organization that puts money into a business company to save it from being taken over by another company

white lie /ˌ· ˈ·/ *n* harmless lie

white pa·per /ˌ· ˈ··/ *n* official British government report explaining what the government intends to do

white-tie /ˌ· ˈ·◂/ *adj* (of parties and other social occasions) at which the men wear white BOW TIEs and TAILs

white·wash /ˈwaɪtwɒʃ‖-wɔːʃ, -wɑːʃ/ *n* **1** [U] white liquid for covering walls **2** [C;U] *derog* attempt to hide something wrong **3** [C] complete defeat ♦ *vt* **1** cover with WHITEWASH (1) **2** make (what is bad) seem good

whith·er /ˈwɪðər/ *adv lit* to which place

Whit·sun /ˈwɪtsən/ *n* (period around) the 7th Sunday after Easter

whit·tle /ˈwɪtl/ *vt* cut thin pieces off (wood): (fig.) *We've whittled the list of candidates down* (= reduced it) *to 5.*

whizz, whiz /wɪz/ *vi* **-zz-** move very fast (and noisily) ♦ *n* **1** [S] whizzing sound **2** [C] *infml* someone who is

whizz kid /'· ·/ n person who makes quick successes in life

who /huː/ pron (used esp. as the subject of a sentence) **1** what person?: Who said that? **2** (shows what person is meant): the people who live in that house **3** (adds more information about a person): This is my father, who lives in Glasgow.

whoa /wəʊ, həʊ/ interj (call to a horse to stop)

who-dun-it, **whodunnit** /ˌhuː'dʌnɪt/ n story, film, etc., about a crime mystery

who-ev-er /huː'evəʳ/ pron **1** anyone at all: I'll take whoever wants to go. **2** no matter who: Whoever it is, I don't want to see them. **3** (shows surprise) who: Whoever can that be at the door?

whole /həʊl/ adj **1** all; complete: I spent the whole day in bed.|She swallowed it whole. (= not divided up) **2** **swallow something whole** accept something without questioning it ♦ n **1** complete amount, thing, etc. **2** **on the whole** generally; mostly **wholly** /'həʊl-li/ adv: not wholly to blame

whole-food /'həʊlfuːd/ n [C;U] food in a simple natural form

whole-heart-ed /ˌ· '··◄/ adj with all one's ability, interest, etc.; full: wholehearted support

whole-meal /'həʊlmiːl/ adj (made from flour) without the grain-covering removed

whole num-ber /ˌ· '··/ n INTEGER

whole-sale /'həʊlseɪl/ adj, adv **1** sold in large quantities to shopkeepers (rather than directly to customers) **2** usu. derog very great or complete: wholesale slaughter **–saler** n seller of goods wholesale

whole-some /'həʊlsəm/ adj **1** good for the body: wholesome food **2** having a good moral effect **~ness** n [U]

whom /huːm/ pron fml (object form of **who**): To whom did you speak?

whoop /wuːp, huːp/ vi **1** make a loud cry, as of joy **2** **whoop it up** infml enjoy oneself a lot ♦ n a loud shout of joy

whoo-pee /wʊ'piː/ interj (cry of joy) ♦ n **make whoopee** enjoy oneself a lot

whoop-ing cough /'huːpɪŋ kɒf‖-kɔːf/ n [U] (children's) disease with attacks of severe coughing and difficult breathing

whoops /wʊps/ interj (said when one has made a mistake)

whoosh /wʊʃ‖wuːʃ/ vi, n (move quickly with) a rushing sound

whop-per /'wɒpəʳ‖'wɑː-/ n infml **1** big thing **2** big lie **–ping** adj, adv very (big): a whopping (great) bonus

whore /hɔːʳ/ n lit or derog for PROSTITUTE

whorl /wɜːl‖wɜːrl/ n shape of a line curving outwards from a centre

whose /huːz/ determiner, pron of whom: Whose car is that? (= who does it belong to?)|That's the man whose house burnt down.

why /waɪ/ adv, conj **1** for what reason: Why did you do it? **2** the reason why: Is that why you did it? **3** **why not** (used in suggestions): Why not sell it? (= I suggest you sell it) ♦ n **the whys and wherefores (of)** reasons and explanations (for)

wick /wɪk/ n **1** burning thread in a candle or lamp **2** **get on someone's wick** BrE infml annoy someone

wick-ed /'wɪkɪd/ adj **1** morally bad; evil **2** playfully bad: a wicked twinkle in his eye **~ly** adv **~ness** n [U]

wick-er-work /'wɪkəwɜːk‖'wɪkərwɜːrk/ n [U] (objects made from) woven CANES, sticks, etc. ♦ adj also **wicker** /'wɪkəʳ/ — made of wickerwork: wicker baskets

wick-et /'wɪkɪt/ n **1** set of 3 sticks (STUMPS¹ (3)) at which the ball is aimed in cricket **2** stretch of grass on which cricket is played

wide /waɪd/ adj **1** large from side to side: The car's too wide to go through the gate. **2** covering a large range: wide experience ♦ adv **1** completely (open or awake) **2** (in sport) away from the correct or central point **3** **wide of the mark** not suitable, correct, etc., at all **~ly** adv over a wide range: It's widely believed (= believed by many people) that the government will lose the election. **widen** vi/t make or become wider

wide boy /'· ·/ n BrE infml cleverly dishonest person, esp. a businessman

wide-eyed /ˌ· '··◄/ adj **1** with eyes very fully open **2** accepting or admiring things too easily

wide-spread /'waɪdspred/ adj common

wid-ow /'wɪdəʊ/ n woman whose husband has died

wid-ow-er /'wɪdəʊəʳ/ n man whose wife has died

width /wɪdθ/ n [C;U] size from side to side

wield /wiːld/ vt have and/or use (power, influence, etc.)

wife /waɪf/ n **wives** woman to whom a man is married

wig /wɪg/ n covering of false hair for the head

wig-gle /'wɪgəl/vi/t move with quick small movements: He wiggled his toes.

wig-wam /'wɪgwæm‖-wɑːm/ n North American Indian tent

wild /waɪld/ adj **1 a** living in natural conditions, not changed by human beings: *wild animals* **b** (of people) not civilized **2** uncontrollably violent **3** showing very strong feelings, esp. of anger **4** showing lack of thought or control: *a wild guess/throw* **5** *infml* having a very eager liking: *He's wild about football.* **6** *infml* good ♦ *n* [U] natural areas full of animals and plants, with few people ♦ *adv* **1 go wild** be filled with feeling, esp. anger or joy **2 run wild** behave as one likes, without control —**ly** *adv: wildly* (= too greatly) *optimistic*

wild-cat strike /'waɪldkæt ˌstraɪk/ *n* sudden unofficial stopping of work

wil-der-ness /'wɪldənɪs‖-dər-/ *n* **1** unchanging stretch of land, etc., with no sign of human presence **2 into the wilderness** (sent) out of political life, esp. for doing wrong

wild-fire /'waɪldfaɪər/ *n* **like wildfire** very quickly

wild-fowl /'waɪldfaʊl/ *n* [P] (water) birds shot for sport

wild-goose chase /ˌ· '· ·/ *n* useless search for something that cannot be found

wild-life /'waɪldlaɪf/ *n* [U] animals living in natural conditions

wild oats /ˌ· '·/ *n* **sow one's wild oats** behave wildly while young, esp. having many sexual partners

wiles /waɪlz/ *n* [P] tricks; deceitful persuading

wil-ful *BrE* ‖ **willful** *AmE* /'wɪlfəl/ *adj* **1** doing what one wants in spite of other people **2** (of something bad) done on purpose —**ly** *adv* —**ness** *n* [U]

will¹ /wɪl/ *v aux 3rd person sing.* **will**, *pres. t. negative short form* **won't** (expresses the future tense): *Will it rain tomorrow?* **2** be willing to: *I won't go!* **3** (used in requests): *Shut the door, will you?* **4** (shows what always happens): *Oil will float on water.* **5** (used like **can** to show what is possible): *This car will hold 5 people.* **6** (used like **must** to show what is likely): *That will be the postman at the door now.*

will² *n* **1** [C;U] power of the mind to make decisions and act in accordance with them: *You need a strong will to give up smoking.* — see also FREE WILL **2** [U] what someone wishes or intends: *She was forced to sign a confession against her will.* **3** [U] stated feelings towards someone: *I bear you no ill will.* **4** [S] force and interest: *They set to work with a will.* **5** [C] official statement of the way someone wants their property to be shared out after they die **6 at will** as one wishes **7 of one's own free will** according to one's own wish **8 -willed** having a certain kind of WILL² (1) ♦ *vt* **1** make or intend to

happen, esp. by the power of the mind **2** leave to someone in a WILL² (5)

will-ing /'wɪlɪŋ/ *adj* **1** ready: not refusing: *Are you willing to help?* **2** done or given gladly: *willing help* **3** eager: *a willing helper* —**ly** *adv* —**ness** *n* [U]

wil-low /'wɪləʊ/ *n* tree which grows near water, with long thin branches —**y** *adj* pleasantly thin and graceful

will-pow-er /'wɪlˌpaʊər/ *n* [U] strength of WILL² (1)

wil-ly-nil-ly /ˌwɪli 'nɪli/ *adv* regardless of whether it is wanted, or not

wilt /wɪlt/ *v* **1** *vi/t* become or cause (a plant) to become less fresh and start to die **2** *vi* (of a person) become tired and weaker

wil-y /'waɪli/ *adj* clever, esp. at getting what one wants **wiliness** *n* [U]

wimp /wɪmp/ *n* weak or useless person, esp. a man —**ish** *adj*

win /wɪn/ *v* **won** /wʌn/, *pres. p.* **-nn-1** *vi/t* be first or best (in) beating one's opponent(s): *Who won the race?* **2** *vt* be given as the result of success: *I won £100 in the competition.* **3** *vt* gain: *trying to win his friendship* **4** *vi* be right in a guess or argument **5 win hands down** win easily ♦ *n* (esp. in sport) victory; success —**ner** *n* —**ning** *adj* very pleasing or attractive: *a winning smile* —**nings** *n* [P] money won

win over *phr vt* gain the support of by persuading

wince /wɪns/ *vi* move back suddenly (as if) from something unpleasant, often twisting the face

winch /wɪntʃ/ *n* apparatus that turns to pull up heavy objects ♦ *vt* pull up with a winch

wind¹ /wɪnd/ *n* **1** [C;U] strongly moving air **2** [U] breath or breathing — see also SECOND WIND **3** [U] *esp. BrE* (condition of having) gas in the stomach **4 get wind of** hear about, esp. accidentally or unofficially **5 it's an ill wind (that blows no good/no one any good)** even bad things may have good results **6 put/get the wind up** *infml* make/become afraid or anxious **7 see/find out which way the wind blows** find out what the situation is before taking action **8 (something) in the wind** (something, esp. that is secret or not generally known) about to happen/being done **9 take the wind out of someone's sails** *infml* take away someone's confidence or advantage, esp. by saying or doing something unexpected ♦ *vt* make breathless —**y** *adj* with a lot of wind: *a windy day*

wind² /waɪnd/ *v* **wound** /waʊnd/ **1** *vt* turn round and round: *wind a handle* **2** *vt* make into a twisted round shape: *winding wool* **3** *vi* go twistingly: *The* *path winds through the woods.* **4** vt tighten the working parts of by turning: *I wound the clock (up).* **5** vt move by turning a handle: *Wind down the car window.* **6** vt place around several times: *She wound a bandage round his arm.* **7 wind someone round one's little finger** make someone do what one wants

wind down *phr vi* **1** (of a clock or watch) work more slowly before at last stopping **2** (of a person) to rest until calmer, after work or excitement **3** cause to be no longer in operation, esp. gradually: *They're winding down their business in Hong Kong.*

wind up *phr v* **1** vt bring to an end **2** vi get into the stated unwanted situation in the end: *I wound up having to pay for it myself.* **3** vt annoy or deceive (someone) playfully

wind-bag /'wɪndbæg/ n person who talks too much

wind-fall /'wɪndfɔːl/ n **1** fruit blown down off a tree **2** unexpected lucky gift

wind in·stru·ment /'wɪnd ˌɪnstrumənt/ n musical instrument played by blowing air through it

wind·mill /'wɪnd‚mɪl/ n building with a corn-crushing machine driven by large sails turned by the wind

win·dow /'wɪndəʊ/ n (glass-filled) opening in the wall of a building, in a car, etc., to let in light and air — see also FRENCH WINDOWS

window box /'·· ·/ n box of earth for growing plants outside a window

window dress·ing /'·· ˌ·/n [U] **1** art of arranging goods in shop windows **2** *usu. derog* something additional intended to attract people but hiding the true purpose

win·dow·pane /'wɪndəʊpeɪn/ n one whole piece of glass in a window

window-shop /'·· ·/ vi -pp- look at goods in shop windows without necessarily intending to buy

wind-pipe /'wɪndpaɪp/ n air passage from the throat to the lungs

wind-screen /'wɪndskriːn/ BrE | **windshield** /'wɪndfiːld/ AmE — n piece of transparent material across the front of a vehicle, for the driver to look through

windscreen wip·er /'·· ˌ·/ also **wiper** /-n one of 2 movable arms which clears rain from the WINDSCREEN of a car

wind·surf·ing /'wɪnd‚sɜːfɪŋ‖-ˌsɜːr-/ n [U] sport of riding on SAILBOARDS -er n

wind·swept /'wɪndswept/ adj **1** open to continual strong wind: *a windswept moor* **2** as if blown into an untidy state: *a windswept appearance*

wind tun·nel /'wɪnd ˌtʌnl/ n enclosed place through which air is forced at fixed speeds to test aircraft

wind·ward /'wɪndwəd‖-ərd/ n, adj, adv [U] (direction) against or facing the wind

wine[1] /waɪn/ n [C;U] alcoholic drink made from GRAPEs

wine[2] vt **wine and dine** (cause to) have a meal and wine

wing /wɪŋ/ n **1** limb used by a bird, insect, etc., for flying **2** part standing out from a plane that supports it in flight **3** part standing out from the side: *the west wing of the palace* **4** BrE side part of a car that covers the wheels **5** (in sport) far left or right of the field **6** group with different opinions or purposes from the main organization: *the left wing of the Labour Party* **7 on the wing** (of a bird) flying **8 take wing** fly (away) **9 under someone's wing** being protected, helped, etc., by someone ♦ v **1** vi fly (as if) on wings **2** vt wound slightly **wings** n [P] **1** sides of a stage, where an actor is hidden from view **2 in the wings** hidden and waiting for action ~ed adj having wings ~er n **1** player on the WINGs (5) **2** person on the stated WING (6)

winge /wɪndʒ/ vi WHINGE

wing·span /'wɪŋspæn/ also **wing-spread** /-spred/ — n distance from the end of one wing to the end of the other when both are stretched out

wink /wɪŋk/ vi/t **1** close and open (an eye) quickly **2** flash or cause (a light) to flash on and off ♦ n **1** [C] winking of the eye **2** [S] very short period of sleep: *I didn't get a wink all night.* (= didn't sleep at all) **3 tip someone the wink** give someone information or a sign about something — see also FORTY WINKS

wink at *phr vt* pretend not to notice (something bad)

win·kle[1] /'wɪŋkəl/ n small sea animal with a shell

winkle[2] v **winkle out** *phr vt esp. BrE* get or remove with difficulty

win·some /'wɪnsəm/ adj lit attractive

win·ter /'wɪntəʳ/ n cold season between autumn and spring ♦ vi spend the winter **–try** /'wɪntri/ adj

winter sports /ˌ·· '·/n [P] sports done on snow or ice

wipe /waɪp/ vt **1** rub (a surface or object) to remove (dirt, liquid, etc.): *Wipe your shoes on the mat.* | *She wiped the tears away.* **2 wipe the floor with someone** make someone feel deeply ashamed by severe scolding or by defeat in an argument ♦ n act of wiping

wipe off *phr vt* get rid of on purpose: *to wipe off a debt*

wipe out *phr vt* destroy or remove all of 2 *sl* make very tired

wipe up *phr v vt* remove with a cloth: *Wipe up that mess!*

wip·er /'waɪpəʳ/ n WINDSCREEN WIPER

wire /waɪəʳ/ n 1 [C;U] (piece of) thin threadlike metal: *a wire fence* | *electric wires* 2 [C] *AmE* for TELEGRAM ♦ *vt* 1 connect up wires in (esp. an electrical system) 2 fasten with wire(s) 3 *AmE* send a TELEGRAM to **wiring** *n* [U] system of (electric) wires **wiry** *adj* rather thin, with strong muscles

wire·less /'waɪəlɪs||'waɪər-/ *n old-fash.* radio

wire-tap·ping /'· ,··/ n [U] listening secretly to other people's telephone conversations with an electrical connection

wis·dom /'wɪzdəm/ *n* [U] quality of being wise

wisdom tooth /'·· ·/ n large late-growing back tooth

wise[1] /waɪz/ *adj* 1 sensible 2 having long experience and much knowledge 3 **none the wiser** knowing no more, after being told ~**ly** *adv*

wise[2] *v* **wise up** *phr vi/t AmE* (cause to) learn or become conscious of the true situation or true nature of someone or something

wise·crack /'waɪzkræk/ *vi, n* (make) a clever joke

wish /wɪʃ/ 1 *vt* want (something impossible): *I wish I hadn't agreed.* | *I wish I were a bird.* 2 *vt* want and try to cause something (as if) by magic: *If you wish hard enough you may get what you want.* 3 *vt* hope that (someone) will have (something), esp. expressed as a greeting: *We wished him a safe journey.* 4 *vt fml* want ♦ *n* 1 feeling of wanting something: *the wish for these peace talks to succeed* 2 thing wished for 3 attempt to make a wanted thing happen (as if) by magic

wish·bone /'wɪʃbəʊn/ *n* V-shaped chicken bone pulled apart before making a wish

wishful think·ing /,·· '··/ n false belief that something is true or will happen simply because one wishes it

wish·y-wash·y /'wɪʃi ,wɒʃi||-,wɔːʃi, -,wɑːʃi/ *adj* without determination or clear aims and principles

wisp /wɪsp/ *n* small twisted bunch, piece (of something): *a wisp of hair/ steam* ~**y** *adj*

wist·ful /'wɪstfəl/ *adj* sad because of unfulfilled hopes or thoughts of the past ~**ly** *adv* ~**ness** *n* [U]

wit[1] /wɪt/ *n* 1 [U] ability to say clever amusing things 2 [C] witty person 3 [U] also **wits** *pl.* — power of thought;

cleverness: *He hadn't the wit to say no.* | (fig.) *It scared me out of my wits.* (= very much) 4 **at one's wits end** too worried by difficulties to know what to do next 5 **have/keep one's wits about one** be ready to act quickly and sensibly ~**ty** *adj* having or showing WIT[1] (1) ~**tily** *adv*

wit[2] *v* **to wit** *lit or law* that is (to say)

witch /wɪtʃ/ *n* woman with magic powers

witch·craft /'wɪtʃkrɑːft||-kræft/ n [U] performing of magic

witch-doc·tor /'wɪtʃ ,dɒktəʳ||-,dɑːk-/ *n* man who cures people by magic

witch-hunt /'· ·/ n search for people with disliked political views, in order to remove them from power

with /wɪð, wɪθ/ *prep* 1 in the presence or company of: *I went to the cinema with Jim.* 2 having: *a book with a green cover* 3 by means of; using: *Cut it with scissors.* | *Fill it with sugar.* 4 in support of: *Are you with us or against us?* 5 against: *competing with foreign companies* 6 with regard to; in the case of: *Be careful with that glass.* | *He's in love with you.* 7 at the same time and rate as: *This wine improves with age.* 8 (used in comparisons): *The window is level with the street.* 9 in spite of: *With all his faults, I still like him.* 10 because of: *trembling with fear* 11 **in with** a friend of (a person or group) 12 **with it** giving proper attention to what is going on 13 **with me/you** following my/your argument: *I'm not with you, what do you mean?* 14 **with that** at once after that; then

with·draw /wɪð'drɔː, wɪθ-/ *v* -**drew** /-'druː/, -**drawn** /-'drɔːn/ 1 *vt* take away or back: *She withdrew £50 from her bank account.* | *I withdraw that remark.* 2 *vi/t* move away or back: *I withdrew from* (= left) *the room.* 3 *vi/t* (cause to) not take part: *She withdrew from the election.* ~**al** *n* [C;U] (act of) withdrawing -**drawn** *adj* quiet and not interested in other people

with·draw·al symp·toms /·'·· ,··/ n [P] painful or unpleasant effects which are the result of breaking or stopping a habit, esp. the taking of a drug

with·er /'wɪðəʳ/ *vi/t* (cause to) become dry, pale, and lifeless: *The heat had withered the plants.* ~**ing** *adj* sharply severe: *withering scorn*

with·hold /wɪð'həʊld, wɪθ-/ *vt* -**held** /-'held/ refuse to give: *withhold payment*

with·in /wɪð'ɪn||wɪð'ɪn, wɪθ'ɪn/ *adv, prep* 1 not more than: *He'll arrive within an hour.* 2 inside: *within the castle walls*

with·out /wɪð'aʊt||wɪð'aʊt, wɪθ'aʊt/ *prep, adv* 1 not having; lacking: *a pot* *without a lid*\ *He went out without telling me.* **2 do/go without** continue as usual in spite of the lack (of)

with-stand /wɪð'stænd, wɪθ-/ vt -**stood** /-'stʊd/ not be defeated or damaged by

wit-ness /'wɪtnɪs/ n **1** person who saw something happen **2** person who gives information to a court of law **3** person who watches another sign an official paper, and then signs it as proof of having seen them **4 bear witness to** show or prove (a quality) ◆ vt **1** be present at and see **2** watch or sign as a WITNESS (3) **3** be a sign or proof of

witness box /'·· ·/ BrE ‖ **witness stand** AmE — n enclosed area where witnesses stand in a court

wit-ti-cis-m /'wɪtɪsɪzəm/ n clever amusing remark

wives /waɪvz/ pl. of WIFE — see also OLD WIVES' TALE

wiz-ard /'wɪzəd‖-ərd/ n **1** (in stories) old man with magical powers **2** extremely skilful person: *a computer wizard* ~**ry** n [U]

wiz-ened /'wɪzənd/ adj (as if) dried up, with lines on the skin

wob-ble /'wɒbəl‖'wɑː-/ vi/t move unsteadily from side to side: *Don't wobble the table.* **wobble** n –**bly** adj wobbling: *wobbly jelly*

woe /wəʊ/ n fml or lit **1** [U] great sorrow **2** [C] trouble ~**ful** adj **1** esp. lit very sad **2** (of something bad) very great: *woeful ignorance* ~**fully** adv

wok /wɒk‖wɑːk/ n deep round Chinese cooking pan

woke /wəʊk/ past t. of WAKE

wok-en /'wəʊkən/ past p. of WAKE

wolf /wʊlf/ n **wolves** /wʊlvz/ **1** fierce wild animal of the dog family **2** man who seeks woman for sex only **3 cry wolf** call for help unnecessarily **4 keep the wolf from the door** earn enough to eat and live **5 a wolf in sheep's clothing** person who seems harmless but is hiding evil intentions ◆ vt eat quickly in large amounts

wolf whis-tle /'· ,··/ n whistle of admiration for an attractive woman

wom-an /'wʊmən/ n **women** /'wɪmɪn/ **1** adult female person **2** women in general **3** female nature or qualities **4 woman of the world** an experienced woman who knows how people behave ~**hood** n [U] quality or time of being a woman ~**ly** adj having good qualities suitable to a woman

wom-an-ize ‖ also -**ise** BrE /'wʊmənaɪz/ vi (of a man) habitually pay attention to many women for sexual purposes -**izer** n

womb /wuːm/ n round organ inside female MAMMALs in which young develop

women's move-ment /'··· ,··/ n [the + S] (all the women who join in making) a united effort to improve the social and political position of women

won /wʌn/ past t. and p. of WIN

won-der /'wʌndər/ n **1** [U] feeling of strangeness, surprise, and usu. admiration **2** [C] wonderful or surprising thing — see also NINE DAYS' WONDER **3 do/work wonders** bring unexpectedly good results **4 (it's) no/little/small wonder** it is not surprising; naturally ◆ vi/t **1** express a wish to know, in words or silently: *I wonder how you work this machine.* **2** be surprised: *It's not to be wondered at that she's angry.* ◆ adj unusually good or effective: *a wonder drug* ~**ful** adj unusually good; causing pleasure or admiration ~**fully** adv ~**ment** n [U] WONDER (1)

won-drous /'wʌndrəs/ adj lit wonderful

won-ky /'wɒŋki‖'wɑːŋki/ adj BrE infml **1** unsteady and likely to break or fail **2** not in a straight line

wont /wəʊnt‖wɔːnt/ adj fml likely (to) ◆ n [S] fml what the stated person usually does ~**ed** adj fml customary

won't /wəʊnt/ short for: will not

woo /wuː/ vt **1** lit try to make (a woman) love and marry one **2** try to gain the support of

wood /wʊd/ n **1** [U] substance of which trees are made **2** [C] also **woods** pl. — place where trees grow, smaller than a forest **3** [the + S] barrels **4 not see the wood for the trees** miss what is clear by looking too closely **5 out of the wood** BrE free from danger, difficulty, etc. ~**ed** adj covered with trees ~**en** adj **1** made of wood **2** stiff; unbending ~**y** adj of or like wood

wood-en spoon /,·· '·/ n BrE imaginary prize for finishing last in a competition

wood-land /'wʊdlənd, -lænd/ also **woodlands** pl. — n [U] wooded country

wood-peck-er /'wʊd,pekər/ n bird with a long beak that makes holes in trees

wood-wind /'wʊd,wɪnd/ n [U;P] (players of) WIND INSTRUMENTs made of wood

wood-work /'wʊdwɜːk‖-wɜːrk/ n [U] **1** esp. BrE skill of making wooden objects **2** parts of a house that are made of wood

wood-worm /'wʊdwɜːm‖-wɜːrm/ n [U] damaged condition of wood caused by the young of certain BEETLEs, which make holes

woof¹ /wʊf/ n, interj sound made by a dog

woof² /wuːf‖wʊf, wuːf/ n WEFT

woof-er /'wuːfə‖'wʊ-/ n LOUD-SPEAKER that gives out deep sounds

wool /wʊl/ n [U] 1 soft thick hair of sheep 2 thick thread made from this 3 **pull the wool over someone's eyes** trick someone by hiding the facts ~**len** BrE ‖ ~**en** AmE — adj made of wool ~**ly** adj 1 of or like wool 2 (of thoughts) not clear in the mind ♦ n woollen garment

wool-gath-er-ing /'wʊl,gæðərɪŋ/ n [U] thinking of other things instead of what one should be playing attention to

woo-zy /'wuːzi/ adj infml having an unsteady feeling in the head **-iness** n [U]

word /wɜːd‖wɜːrd/ n 1 [C] (written representation of) 1 or more sounds which can be spoken to represent an idea, object, etc. 2 [S] shortest (type of) statement: Don't say a word (= anything) about it to anyone. 3 [S] short conversation: I'd like a word with you. 4 [U] message or piece of news: He sent word that he wanted to see me. 5 [S] promise: I give you my word that I'll do it. 6 [C] suggestion or RECOMMENDATION: put in/say a good word for someone 7 **by word of mouth** by speaking and not by writing 8 **eat one's words** admit to having said something wrong 9 **get a word in edgeways** infml get a chance to speak 10 **have a word with someone/in someone's ear** (speak to someone) secretly, esp. giving advice or asking a question 11 **(have) the last word (on)** (make) the remark which finishes an argument, etc. 12 **have words (with)** argue angrily (with) 13 **in other words** expressing the same thing in different words 14 **(not) in so many words** (not) directly expressed in those words but only suggested 15 **put words in(to) someone's mouth: a** tell someone what to say **b** claim falsely that someone has said a particular thing 16 **take someone's word for it** accept what someone says as correct 17 **the last word in** the most recent development in 18 **word for word** in exactly the same words ♦ vt express in words ~**ing** n [U] words in which something is expressed ~**y** adj using or containing more words than necessary

word-per-fect /ˌ·'··/ adj repeating or remembering every word correctly

word pro-cess-or /'·ˌ···/ n small computer for esp. ordinary office work

wore /wɔːr/ past t. of WEAR

work[1] /wɜːk‖wɜːrk/ n 1 [U] activity done to produce something or gain a result rather than for amusement 2 [U] job; business: I go to work by train.

3 [U] something produced by work, esp. of the hands: This mat is my own work. (= I made it)|(fig.) The murder was the work of a madman. 4 [C] object produced by painting, writing, etc.: a work of art|the works of Shakespeare 5 **all in a day's work** not unusual 6 **at work (on)** doing something, esp. work 7 **go/set to work (on)** start doing 8 **have one's work cut out** have something difficult to do, esp. in the time allowed 9 **in/out of work** having a job/unemployed 10 **make short work of** finish quickly and easily — see also WORKS

work[2] v 1 vi do an activity which uses effort, esp. as one's job: She works at the factory. 2 vi (of a machine, plan, etc.) operate (properly): It works by electricity.|Your scheme will never work. 3 vt make (a person) do work: They work us too hard. 4 vt make (a machine) do work: How do you work this lift? 5 vt make (one's way) by work or effort 6 vi/t make or become by small movements: This little screw has worked loose. 7 vt produce (an effect): This medicine works wonders. 8 vt arrange, esp. unofficially: We'll work it so that we can all go together. 9 vi move or act for a certain result: This will work against you in the future. 10 **work to rule** obey the rules of one's work so exactly that one causes inconvenience to others, in order to support a claim for higher wages, etc. ~**able** adj which can be put into effect; usable: a workable plan ~**er** n 1 person who works: an office worker 2 member of the WORKING CLASS

work off phr vt get rid of by work or effort: He worked off his anger by chopping wood.

work out phr v 1 vt calculate (the answer to) 2 vi have a result; develop: The plan worked out very well in practice. 3 vt plan; decide: We're trying to work out how to get there. 4 vi reach the stated amount by being calculated: The cost works out at £10 each. 5 vi exercise 6 vt complete the use of (esp. a mine)

work up phr vt 1 excite the feelings of: He gets very worked up (= anxious and upset) about exams. 2 cause oneself to have: I couldn't work up much enthusiasm for it. 3 develop steadily: She worked the firm up from nothing.

work-a-day /'wɜːkədeɪ‖'wɜːrk-/ adj ordinary and/or dull

work-a-hol-ic /ˌwɜːkə'hɒlɪk‖ˌwɜːrk-ə'hɔː-/ n person who likes to work too hard

work-bench /'wɜːkbentʃ‖'wɜːrk-/ n (a table with) a hard surface for working on with tools

work·book /'wɜːkbuk‖'wɜːrk-/ n school book with questions and exercises

work coat /'· ·/ n AmE for OVERALL (1)

work·force /'·· ·/ n all the workers in a factory or in industry generally

work·horse /'wɜːkhɔːs‖'wɜːrkhɔːrs-/ n 1 person who does most of the (dull) work 2 useful machine, vehicle, etc., for performing continuous jobs

work·house /'wɜːkhaus‖'wɜːrk-/ n (in former times) place where unemployed people lived

work·ing /'wɜːkɪŋ‖'wɜːr-/ adj 1 used for work: working clothes 2 (of time) spent in work 3 useful as a base for further development: a working hypothesis

working class /,·· '·◄/ n social class of people who work with their hands **working-class** adj

working knowl·edge /,·· '·-/ n [S] enough practical knowledge to do something

working or·der /,·· '·-/ n [U] state of working well, with no trouble

working par·ty /'·· ,··/ n committee which examines and reports on a particular matter

work·ings /'wɜːkɪŋz‖'wɜːr-/ n [P] 1 way something works or acts: the workings of an engine/of his mind 2 parts of a mine which have been dug out

work·load /'wɜːkləud‖'wɜːrk-/ n amount of work that a person or machine is expected to do in a particular period of time

work·man /'wɜːkmən‖'wɜːrk-/ n -men /-mən/ man who works with his hands, esp. in a particular skill or trade ~**like** adj showing the qualities of a good workman ~**ship** n [U] (signs of) skill in making things

work·out /'wɜːkaut‖'wɜːr-/ n period of physical exercise

works /wɜːks‖wɜːrks/ n works 1 [P] moving parts of a machine 2 [C] factory: a dye works 3 **give someone the works** sl a give someone everything: They gave us supper, wine, chocolates, the works. b attack violently

work·shop /'wɜːkʃɒp‖'wɜːrkʃɑːp/ n 1 room where heavy repairs and jobs on machines are done 2 period of group activity and study: a drama workshop

work-shy /'· ·/ adj not liking work and trying to avoid it

work·top /'wɜːktɒp‖'wɜːrktɑːp/ n flat surface in a kitchen for preparing food

work-to-rule /,·· '·/ n act of working to rule (WORK[2] (10))

world /wɜːld‖wɜːrld/ n 1 [the + S] the Earth: the richest man in the world b particular part of it: the Old World 2 the + S] the universe 3 [the + S] group of living things: the animal world 4 [the + S] a particular area of human activity: the world of football 5 [the + S] people generally: We don't want the whole world (= everyone) to know about it. 6 [the + S] human life and its affairs: the ways of the world 7 [C] PLANET: life on other worlds 8 [the + S] large number or amount: This medicine did me the world of good. 9 the + S] fml material standards: to give up the world to serve God 10 **all the world to** very important to 11 **for all the world like/as if** exactly like/as if 12 **(have) the best of both worlds** (to have) the advantage which each choice offers, without having to choose between them 13 **in the world** (in a question expressing surprise): Where in the world have you been? 14 **not for the world** certainly not: I wouldn't hurt her for the world. 15 **on top of the world** very happy 16 **out of this world** unusually good; wonderful 17 **worlds apart** completely different ~**ly** adj 1 material: all my worldly goods (= everything I own) 2 too much concerned with human society, rather than religious things ~**liness** n [U]

world-beat·er /'· ,··/ n person or thing thought able to compete successfully with anyone/anything in the world

world-class /,· '·◄/ adj among the best in the world

world-fam·ous /,· '·-◄/ adj known all over the world

world pow·er /,· '·-/ n nation with very great power and influence

world-wear·y /,· '·-◄/ adj tired of life

world·wide /,wɜːld'waɪd‖,wɜːr-/ adj, adv in or over all the world

worm /wɜːm‖wɜːrm/ n 1 small thin creature with no bones or limbs, like a tube of flesh 2 worthless, cowardly, etc., person ♦ vt move by twisting or effort: We wormed our way through the crack in the wall. | (fig.) He wormed his way into her affections.

worm out phr vt obtain gradually by questioning

worn /wɔːn‖wɔːrn/ past p. of WEAR

worn-out /,· '·◄/ adj 1 no longer usable 2 very tired

wor·ry /'wʌri‖'wɜːri/ v 1 vi/t (cause to) be anxious or uncomfortable: worrying about the exams | Heights don't worry me. 2 vt (esp. of a dog) chase and bite (an animal) ♦ n [C;U] 1 feeling of anxiety 2 (person or thing that causes) anxiety -**ried** adj anxious ~**ing** adj

wor·ry·wart /'wʌriwɔːt‖'wɜːriwɔːrt/ *n AmE infml* person who worries a lot about unimportant things

worse /wɜːs‖wɜːrs/ *adj* **1** (*comparative of* BAD) of lower quality; more bad **2** more ill (than before) **3 none the worse (for)** not harmed (by) **4 the worse for wear** harmed by use over a period ♦ *adv* in a worse way or to a worse degree ♦ *n* [U] something worse

worsen *vi/t* (cause to) become worse

wor·ship /'wɜːʃɪp‖'wɜːr-/ *n* [U] (showing of) strong (religious) feelings of love, respect, and admiration ♦ *vi/t* -**pp**- *BrE* ‖ -**p**- *AmE* show worship (to): *to worship God│She worships her brother.* (= admires him (too) greatly) ~**per** *BrE* ‖ ~**er** *AmE n*

worst /wɜːst‖wɜːrst/ *adj* (*superlative of* BAD) of lowest quality; most bad ♦ *n* **1 worst** worst thing or part: *These ones are the worst.* **2 at (the) worst** if the worst happens **3 get the worst of** suffer most from **4 if the worst comes to the worst** if there is no better way ♦ *adv* (*superlative of* BADLY) most badly: *the worst-dressed man in the office*

wor·sted /'wʊstɪd/ *n* [U] wool cloth

worth /wɜːθ‖wɜːrθ/ *prep* **1** of the stated value: *a painting worth £5000* **2** deserving: *That film isn't worth seeing.* **3 for all one is worth** with all possible effort **4 for what it's worth** though I'm not sure it's of any value **5 worth** it useful; worthwhile **6 worth one's salt** worthy of respect or of being so called **7 worth one's/ someone's while** worthwhile to one/ someone ♦ *n* [U] value ~**less** *adj* **1** of no value **2** (of a person) of bad character

worth·while /ˌwɜːθ'waɪl‖ˌwɜːr-/ *adj* with a good enough result to deserve the trouble taken

wor·thy /'wɜːði‖'wɜːrði/ *adj* **1** deserving respect or serious attention **2** deserving: *worthy of admiration* **3** good but not very exciting or interesting -**thily** *adv* -**thiness** *n* [U]

would /wʊd/ *v aux* **1** (*past of* will): *They said they would meet us at 10.30.* **2** (shows what is likely or possible): *What would you do if you won a million pounds?* **3** (shows what always happened): *We would meet for a drink after work.* **4** (shows choice): *I'd rather have tea.* **5** (expressing a polite request): *Would you lend me your pencil?* **6 would better** *AmE* had better (HAVE[1])

would-be /'··/ *adj* which one wants or intends to be, but isn't: *a would-be musician*

wouldn't /'wʊdnt/ *short for*: would not

wound¹ /wuːnd/ *n* damaged place on the body, esp. caused by a weapon:

a bullet wound ♦ *vt* cause a wound to: *a wounded leg│*(fig.) *wounded pride*

wound² /waʊnd/ *past t. and p. of* WIND[2]

wound-up /ˌwaʊnd 'ʌp/ *adj* anxiously excited

wove /wəʊv/ *past t. of* WEAVE

wov·en /'wəʊvən/ *past p. of* WEAVE

wow /waʊ/ *interj infml* (expresses surprise and admiration) ♦ *n* [S] *sl* a great success ♦ *vt sl* cause surprise and admiration in someone

wraith /reɪθ/ *n lit for* GHOST

wran·gle /'ræŋgəl/ *vi, n* (take part in) an angry or noisy quarrel

wrap /ræp/ *vt* -**pp**- cover in material folded over: *I wrapped the box in brown paper.│She had a bandage wrapped round her finger.* ♦ *n* **1** *esp. AmE* garment for covering a woman's shoulders **2 under wraps** secret ~**per** *n* loose paper cover ~**ping** *n* [C;U] material for folding round and covering something

wrap up *phr vt* **1** wear warm clothes **2** complete (a business arrangement, meeting, etc.) **3 wrapped up in** giving complete attention to

wrath /rɒθ‖ræθ/ *n* [U] *fml or lit* strong fierce anger ~**ful** *adj*

wreak /riːk/ *vt esp. lit* perform or bring about (something violent or unpleasant)

wreath /riːθ/ *n usu.* circular arrangement of flowers or leaves **a** given at a funeral **b** placed on the head as a sign of honour

wreathe /riːð/ *vt esp. lit* circle round and cover completely: *Mist wreathed the hilltops.*

wreck /rek/ *n* **1** [C] sunken or destroyed ship **2** [C] something in a very bad condition: *Have you seen the old wreck he drives around in!* **3** *fml* ruin; destruction: *the wreck of our hopes* **4** [C] person whose health is destroyed ♦ *vt* destroy: *a ship wrecked on the rocks│The bad weather wrecked our plans.* ~**age** *n* [U] broken parts of a destroyed thing

wren /ren/ *n* very small brown European bird

wrench /rentʃ/ *vt* **1** pull hard with a twist **2** twist and damage (a joint of the body) ♦ *n* **1** act of or damage caused by wrenching **2** separation that causes suffering of the mind **3** SPANNER

wrest /rest/ *vt* **1** pull (away) violently **2** *esp. lit* obtain with difficulty

wres·tle /'resəl/ *vi/t* fight by trying to hold or throw one's opponent: (fig.) *wrestling with a difficult problem* -**tler** *n* person who wrestles as a sport

wretch /retʃ/ *n* **1** unfortunate person **2** annoying person

wretch-ed /'retʃɪd/ adj **1** very unhappy of a bad type which makes one unhappy: *a wretched headache* **3** annoying: *Why can't that wretched child behave himself!* ~**ly** adv ~**ness** n [U]

wrig-gle /'rɪgəl/ vi/t move from side to side: *He wriggled uncomfortably on the hard seat.* ♦ n wriggling movement

wriggle out of phr vt escape (a difficulty) by clever tricks

wring /rɪŋ/ vt **wrung** /rʌŋ/ **1** twist or press (wet clothes) to remove (water) **2** twist (the neck) hard, causing death **3** press hard on, esp. hands: *wringing her hands in sorrow* **4** obtain by severe or cruel methods: *Her torturers wrung a confession out of her.* **5 wringing wet** very wet ~**er** n machine for wringing clothes

wrin-kle /'rɪŋkəl/ n **1** small line or fold, esp. on the skin owing to age **2** infml useful suggestion or trick ♦ vi/t (cause to) form wrinkles –**kly** adj

wrist /rɪst/ n joint between the hand and the arm

wrist-watch /'rɪstwɒtʃ‖-wɑːtʃ, -wɔːtʃ/ n watch with a band for fastening round the wrist

writ /rɪt/ n official legal paper telling someone (not) to do a particular thing

write /raɪt/ v **wrote** /rəʊt/, **written** /'rɪtn/ **1** vi/t make (marks representing letters or words) with a tool, esp. a pen or pencil **2** vt think of and record, esp. on paper: *He wrote a report on the match.* **3** vt complete by writing words: *write a cheque* **4** vi/t produce and send (a letter): *He writes to me every week.* **5** vi be a writer (of books, plays, etc.): *She writes for television.* **6 be written on/all over** clearly showing because of the expression on: *Guilt was written all over his face.* **7 writ large** lit on a larger or grander scale **writer** n **writing** n [U] **1** handwriting **2** written work or form: *Put it down in writing.* **3** activity of writing books, etc. **writings** n [P] written works

write away phr vi write to a far-off place, esp. to buy something

write down phr vt record (esp. what has been said) in writing

write off phr vt **1** accept as lost or useless or as a failure **2** remove (esp. a debt) from the record **3** WRITE away

write-off /'· ·/ n something completely ruined and unrepairable

write out phr vt write in full

write up phr vt write (again) in a complete and useful form **write-up**

/'· ·/ n written report giving a judgment

writhe /raɪð/ vi twist the body (as if) in great pain

writ-ten /'rɪtn/ v past p. of WRITE

wrong /rɒŋ‖rɑːŋ/ adj **1** not correct: *the wrong answer* **2** morally bad **3** not in a proper or healthy state: *There's something wrong with the engine.* **4** not suitable: *the wrong time to visit* ♦ adv **1** wrongly **2 go wrong: a** stop working properly **b** make a mistake **c** end badly ♦ n **1** [U] morally bad behaviour **2** [C] fml unjust or bad action **3 in the wrong** mistaken or deserving blame ♦ vt be unfair to or cause to suffer ~**ful** adj unjust or illegal: *wrongful arrest* ~**fully** adv

wrong-do-ing /'rɒŋ,duːɪŋ‖,rɔːŋ'-duːɪŋ/ n [C;U] (example of) bad or illegal behaviour **wrongdoer** n [C]

wrote /rəʊt/ past t. of WRITE

wrought /rɔːt/ adj lit made: *wrought of steel*

wrought i-ron /,· '··◄/ n [U] iron shaped into a useful, pleasing form

wrung /rʌŋ/ past t. and p. of WRING

wry /raɪ/ adj showing a mixture of amusement and dislike, disappointment, etc.: *a wry smile* ~**ly** adv

X, x /eks/ the 24th letter of the English alphabet

xen-o-pho-bi-a /,zenə'fəʊbiə/ n [U] unreasonable fear and dislike of foreigners –**bic** adj

xe-rox /'zɪərɒks, 'ze-‖'zɪərɑːks, 'ziː-/ vt, n (make) a photographic copy on an electric copying machine

X-mas /'krɪsməs, 'eksməs/ n infml CHRISTMAS

X-ray /'eks reɪ/ n **1** powerful unseen beam which can pass through solid things, used esp. for photographing conditions inside the body **2** photograph taken with this **3** medical examination with this **x-ray** vt photograph, examine, or treat with X-rays

xy-lo-phone /'zaɪləfəʊn/ n musical instrument with many small wooden bars hit with a hammer

Y

Y, y /waɪ/ the 25th letter of the English alphabet

yacht /jɒt‖jɑːt/ *n* **1** light sailing boat used esp. for racing **2** large motor-driven pleasure boat ~**ing** *n* [U] sailing in a yacht

yachts·man /ˈjɒtsmən ‖ ˈjɑːts-/ **yachtswoman** /-ˌwʊmən/ *fem.* — *n* **-men** /-mən/ sailor in a yacht

yak[1] /jæk/ *n* long-haired cow of central Asia

yak[2] *vi* **-kk-** *derog* talk continuously about unimportant things

yam /jæm/ *n* tropical plant with a root eaten as a vegetable

yank /jæŋk/ *vi/t* pull suddenly and sharply **yank** *n*

Yank *n BrE derog* American person

yap /jæp/ *vi* **-pp-** *derog* **1** (of a dog) BARK continuously **2** talk noisily about unimportant things

yard[1] /jɑːd‖jɑːrd/ *n* a measure of length equal to 3 feet or 9.144 metres

yard[2] *n* **1** (partly) enclosed area next to a building **2** area enclosed for the stated activity or business: *a coalyard*

yard·arm /ˈjɑːd-ɑːm‖ˈjɑːrd-ɑːrm/ *n* either end of a long pole that supports a sail

yard·stick /ˈjɑːdˌstɪk ‖ ˈjɑːrd-/ *n* standard of measurement or comparison

yarn /jɑːn‖jɑːrn/ *n* **1** [U] long continuous thread used esp. in making cloth **2** [C] story

yash·mak /ˈjæʃmæk/ *n* cloth worn across the face by Muslim women

yaw /jɔː/ *vi* (of a ship, aircraft, etc.) turn to the side out of the proper course

yawn /jɔːn/ *vi* **1** open the mouth wide and breathe deeply, esp. from tiredness **2** be(come) wide open: *a yawning chasm* ♦ *n* **1** act of yawning **2** *infml* something dull

yd *written abbrev. for:* YARD(s)[1]

ye /jiː/ *pron lit* (used of more than 1 person) you

yea /jeɪ/ *adv lit* yes

yeah /jeə/ *adv infml* yes

year /jɪəʳ, jɜːʳ‖jɪər/ *n* **1** period of 365 (or 366) days, or 12 months, esp. as measured from January 1st to December 31st **2** period of about a year in the life of an organization: *the school year* **3** *all the year round* during the whole year **4** *year after year* continuously for many years **5** *year in, year out* regularly each year ~**ly** *adj, adv* (happening) every year or once a year

year dot /ˌ ·ˈ·/ *n* [*the* + S] *BrE infml* a very long time ago

year·ling /ˈjɪəlɪŋ, ˈjɜː-‖ˈjɪr-/ *n* animal between 1 and 2 years old

year·long /ˈjɪəlɒŋ, ˈjɜː-‖ˈjɪr lɔːŋ/ *adj* lasting a whole year

yearn /jɜːn‖jɜːrn/ *vi esp. lit* have a strong (sad) desire: *I yearn for your return.* ~**ing** *n* [C;U] *esp. lit* strong desire

yeast /jiːst/ *n* [U] form of very small plant with a chemical action used for producing alcohol in making wine and beer and for making bread light and soft ~**y** *adj*

yell /jel/ *vi/t, n* shout

yellow /ˈjeləʊ/ *adj* **1** of the colour of gold **2** *infml* cowardly ♦ *vi/t* (cause to) become yellow ~**ish** *adj*

yellow fe·ver /ˌ·· ˈ··/ *n* [U] serious tropical disease

Yellow Pag·es /ˌ·· ˈ··/ *n* [P] book with telephone numbers of businesses

yelp /jelp/ *vi, n* (make) a sharp high cry, esp. of pain

yen[1] /jen/ *n* yen unit of Japanese money

yen[2] *n* strong desire

yeo·man /ˈjəʊmən/ *n* **-men** /-mən/ *BrE, esp. lit* farmer who owns and works his own land

yes /jes/ *adv* **1** (used for accepting or agreeing) **2** (used for replying to a call)

yes-man /ˈjes mæn/ *n* **-men** /men/ *derog* someone who always agrees with their leader or employer

yes·ter·day /ˈjestədi‖ˈ-ər-/ *adv, n* (on) the day before today

yes·ter·year /ˈjestəjɪəʳ, -jɜːʳ‖ˈjestər-jɪər/ *n* [U] *esp. lit* the recent past

yet /jet/ *adv* **1** up until this time: *He hasn't arrived yet.* **2** in future, and in spite of how things seem now: *We may yet win.* **3** even: *a yet bigger problem* **4** still: *I have yet to be told.* (= I have still not been told) **5** *as yet* YET (1) ♦ *conj* but even so: *strange yet true*

yet·i /ˈjeti/ *n* large hairy manlike animal said to live in the Himalaya mountains

yew /juː/ *n* tree with small dark leaves and red berries

Y-fronts /ˈwaɪ frʌnts/ *n* [P] *BrE* type of men's UNDERPANTS

yield /jiːld/ *v* **1** *vt* produce: *a tree which yields a large crop* **2** *vt fml* give up control of: *yield a position of advantage* **3** *vi fml or lit* admit defeat ♦ *n* amount produced: *a high yield of fruit* ~**ing** *adj* **1** not stiff or fixed **2** (too) easily persuaded

yip·pee /jɪˈpiː‖ˈjɪpi/ *interj* (shout of delight or success)

yob /jɒb‖jɑːb/ *also* **yobbo** /ˈjɒbəʊ‖ˈjɑː-/ *-bos n BrE infml* rude or troublesome young man

yo·del /ˈjəʊdl/ *vi/t* **-ll-** *BrE* ‖ **-l-** *AmE* sing with many changes between the natural voice and a very high voice

yo-ga /'jəʊgə/ n [U] Hindu system of control of the mind and body, often including special exercises

yog-hurt /'jɒgət‖'jəʊgərt/ n [U] milk that has thickened and turned slightly acid through the action of certain bacteria

yo-gi /'jəʊgi/ n person who practises (and teaches) yoga

yoke /jəʊk/ n **1** bar joining 2 animals for pulling a vehicle or heavy load **2** frame across someone's shoulders for carrying 2 equal loads **3** lit controlling power: *the hated yoke of their conquerors* **4** part of garment from which the rest hangs ♦ vt join (as if) with a yoke

yo-kel /'jəʊkəl/ n simple or foolish country person

yolk /jəʊk‖jəʊk, jelk/n [C;U] yellow part of an egg

yon-der /'jɒndə'‖'jɑːn-/ adj, adv esp. lit that; over there

yonks /jɒŋks‖jɑːŋks/ n [U] BrE infml very long time

yore /jɔː'/ n [U] lit very long time ago

you /ja, jʊ; strong juː/ pron (used as subject or object) **1** person or people being spoken to: *I love you.* **2** anyone; one: *You can't trust such people.* **3** (used for addressing someone, esp. angrily): *You fool!*

you'd /jəd, jʊd; strong juːd/ short for: **1** you had **2** you would

you'll /jəl, jʊl; strong juːl/ short for: **1** you will **2** you shall

young /jʌŋ/ adj younger /'jʌŋgə'/, youngest /'jʌŋgɪst/ in an early stage of life or development ♦ n [P] **1** young people generally **2** young animals

young-ster /'jʌŋstə'/ n young person

your /jə'; strong jɔː' ‖ jər; strong jʊər, jɔːr/ determiner of you: *your house*

you're /jə'; strong jɔː'‖jər; strong jʊər, jɔːr/ short for: you are

yours /jɔːz‖jʊərz, jɔːrz/ pron **1** of you; your one(s) **2** (used at the end of a letter): *Yours sincerely, Janet Smith* **3 yours truly: a** (polite phrase written at the end of a letter) **b** infml I; me; myself

your-self /jə'self‖jər-/ pron -selves /-'selvz/ **1** (reflexive form of **you**): *Don't hurt yourself.* **2** (strong form of **you**): *Did you make it yourself?* **3 (all) by yourself: a** alone **b** without help **4 to yourself** not shared

youth /juːθ/ n youths /juːðz‖juːðz, juːθs/ **1** [U] period of being young **2** [C] often derog young person, esp. male **3** [U;P] young people as a group: *the youth of today* ~**ful** adj (seeming) young

you've /jəv; strong juːv/ short for: you have

yuck-y /'jʌki/ adj infml extremely unpleasant

yule /juːl/ n [U] lit for CHRISTMAS

yup-pie , yuppy /'jʌpi/ n young person in a professional job with a high income, esp. one who enjoys spending money and having a fashionable way of life

Z

Z , **z** /zed‖ziː/ the 26th and last letter of the English alphabet

za-ny /'zeɪni/ adj amusingly foolish

zap /zæp/ v -pp- infml **1** vt attack and/or destroy **2** vi/t move quickly and forcefully ~**py** adj full of life and force

zeal /ziːl/ n [U] fml eagerness ~**ous** /'zeləs/ adj eager; keen ~**ously** adv

zeal-ot /'zelət/ n someone who is (too) eager in their beliefs

ze-bra /'ziːbrə, 'ze-‖'ziːbrə/ n -bra or -bras horselike African animal with broad black and white lines

zebra cross-ing /ˌ·· '··/ n (in Britain) set of black and white lines across a road where people have a right to walk across

ze-nith /'zenɪθ‖'ziː-/ n highest or greatest point of development, success, etc.

ze-ro[1] /'zɪərəʊ‖'ziːrəʊ/ n -ros or -roes **1** (sign representing) the number 0 **2** point between + and - on a scale: *The temperature was below zero.* (= below the freezing point of water) **2** nothing: *zero growth*

zero[2] v **zero** in on phr vt **1** aim a weapon directly at **2** aim one's attention directly towards

zero hour /'·· ·/ n [U] time at which something important is to begin

zest /zest/ n **1** [S;U] pleasantly exciting quality: *The danger adds zest to the affair.* **2** [S;U] eagerness: *a zest for life* **3** [U] outer skin of an orange or LEMON ~**ful** adj

zig-zag /'zɪgzæg/ vi n -gg- (go in) a line shaped like a row of z's: *The path zigzags up the hill.*

zil-lion /'zɪljən/ determiner, n, pron infml extremely large number

zinc /zɪŋk/ n [U] bluish-white metal

Zi-on-is-m /'zaɪənɪzəm/ n [U] political movement to establish and develop an independent state of Israel for the Jews —**ist** adj, n

zip /zɪp/ n **1** [C] fastener with 2 sets of teeth and a sliding piece that joins the edges of an opening by drawing the

teeth together **2** [U] liveliness ♦ *v* **-pp-**
1 *vt* fasten with a ZIP (1) **2** *vi/t* move
very quickly and forcefully **~per** *n*
AmE for ZIP (1)

zip code /'· ·/ *n AmE* for POSTCODE

zith-er /'zɪðə'/ *n* flat musical instrument played by pulling sharply at its
strings

zits /zɪts/ *n* [P] *sl* spots on the skin

zo-di-ac /'zəʊdiæk/ *n* [*the* + S] imaginary belt in space along which the sun,
moon, and nearest PLANETs seem to
travel, divided into 12 equal parts
used in ASTROLOGY

zom-bie /'zɒmbi‖'zɑːm-/ *n* **1** *derog*
someone who moves or acts very
slowly or lifelessly **2** dead person
made to move by magic

zone /zəʊn/ *n* area marked off from
others by particular qualities or activities: *a war/danger zone* ♦ *vt* give a
particular purpose to (an area): *a part*
of town zoned for industrial develop-
ment **zonal** *adj*

zonked /zɒŋkt‖zɑːŋkt/ *adj infml*
extremely tired

zoo /zuː/ *n* **zoos** park where many
types of wild animal are kept for show

zo-ol-o-gy /zuː'ɒlədʒi, zəʊ'ɒ-‖-'ɑːl-/
n [U] scientific study of animals *adj*
-gist *n* **-gical** /ˌzuːə'lɒdʒɪkəl, ˌzəʊə-‖
-'lɑː-/ *adj*

zoom /zuːm/ *vi* **1** go quickly with a
loud noise **2** (of a cinema camera)
move quickly between a distant and a
close view **3** increase suddenly and
greatly

zoom lens /'· ˌ·/ *n* curved piece of
glass by which a camera can zoom in
and out while keeping the picture
clear

zuc-chi-ni /zʊ'kiːni/ *n* **-ni** *or* **-nis**
AmE for COURGETTE

Word beginnings

Afro- /ˈæfrəʊ/ **1** of Africa: *an Afro-American* **2** African and: *Afro-Asian peoples*

Anglo- /ˈæŋgləʊ/ **1** of England or Britain: *an Anglophile (someone who loves Britain)* **2** English or British and: *an Anglo-American treaty*

ante- /ˈænti/ before: *antenatal care* — compare POST-

anti- /ˈænti/ against; not in favour of; trying to prevent or destroy: *an anticancer drug* | *an antitank gun* | *He's very anti-war.* — compare PRO-

arch- /ɑːtʃ, ɑːk‖ɑːr-/ chief; main: *our archenemy*

astro- /ˈæstrəʊ/ of or about the stars and space: *astrophysics*

audio- /ˈɔːdiəʊ/ of, for, or using sound, esp. recorded sound: *audiovisual teaching aids* — compare VIDEO

Austro- /ˈɒstrəʊ‖ ɔː-, ɑː-/ **1** Australian and: *Austro-Malayan* **2** Austrian and: *the Austro-Italian border*

be- /bɪ/ (makes verbs and adjectives) cause to be or have: *a bewigged judge (= wearing a WIG)* | *She befriended me.*

bi- /baɪ/ two; twice: *a biannual publication (= coming out twice a year)*

bio- /ˈbaɪəʊ/ connected with (the study of) living things: *biochemistry*

centi- /ˈsenti/ hundredth part: *a centimetre (= a hundredth of a metre)*

co- /kəʊ/ with; together: *my co-author, who wrote the book with me*

counter- /ˈkaʊntəʳ/ done in return or so as to have an opposite effect or make ineffective: *a counterattack* | *counterespionage operations*

cross- /krɒs‖krɔːs/ going between the stated things: *cross-cultural influences*

de- /diː, dɪ/ **1** (showing an opposite): *a depopulated area (= which all or most of the population has left)* **2** to remove: *to dethrone a king* | *to debug a computer program* **3** to make less: *devalue the currency*

deca- /ˈdekə/ ten: *a decalitre (= ten litres)*

deci- /ˈdesi/ tenth part: *a decilitre (= a tenth of a litre)*

dis- /dɪs/ **1** not; the opposite of: *I disagree.* | *He is dishonest.* **2** removal: *nuclear disarmament*

em- /ɪm; em/ (before b, m, or p) EN-: *emboldened*

en- /ɪn, en/ (makes verbs) cause to be (more): *Enlarge the hole.*

equi- /ˈekwɪ, ˈiːkwɪ/ equally: *two points equidistant from a third*

Euro- /ˈjʊərəʊ/ of Europe, esp. the EEC: *the Europarliament*

ex- /eks/ former: *my ex-fiancé*

extra- /ˈekstrə/ not (usu.) included; beyond; outside: *extracurricular lessons* | *extravehicular activity by astronauts*

fore- /fɔːʳ/ **1** before; in advance: *I was forewarned of their visit.* **2** in or at the front: *a boat's foresail*

foster- /ˈfɒ stəʳ/ giving or receiving parental care although not of the same family: *my foster-parents*

Franco- /ˈfræŋkəʊ/ **1** of France: *a Francophile (= someone who loves France)* **2** French and: *the Franco-Prussian war*

geo- /ˈdʒiːəʊ/ connected with the study of the Earth or its surface: *geophysics*

hecto- /ˈhektəʊ/ hundred: *a hectolitre (= a hundred litres)* — compare CENTI-

hydro- /ˈhaɪdrəʊ/ concerning or using water: *hydroelectricity*

hyper- /ˈhaɪpəʳ/ very or too much: *hyperactive* | *hypercritical*

il- /ɪ/ (before l) not: *illiberal*

im- /ɪm/ (before b, m, or p) IN-: *impossible*

in- /ɪn/ **1** not: *indecisive* | *insane* **2** inwards: *a sudden inrush of water*

inter- /ˈɪntəʳ/ between or including both or all: *the intercity train service* | *an interdenominational marriage ceremony*

ir- /ɪ/ (before r) not: *irrational*

kilo- /ˈkɪlə/ thousand: *a kilogram (= a thousand grams)* — compare MILLI-

mal- /mæl/ bad(ly); wrong(ly): *a malformed body* | *maladministration*

maxi- /ˈmæksi/ unusually large or long — compare MINI-

mega- /ˈmegə/ **1** million: *a ten-megaton nuclear bomb* **2** *sl* very great: *a movie megastar*

micro- /ˈmaɪkrəʊ/ **1** (esp. with scientific words) extremely small: *a microcomputer* **2** using a microscope: *microsurgery* **3** millionth part: *a microsecond (= a millionth of a second)*

mid- /mɪd/ middle; in the middle of: *midwinter* | *in mid-Atlantic* | *She's in her mid-20s. (= is about 25 years old)*

milli- /ˈmɪlɪ/ thousandth part: *a millilitre (= a thousandth of a litre)* — compare KILO-

mini- /ˈmɪni/ unusually small or short: *a miniskirt* | *a TV miniseries*

mis- /mɪs/ **1** bad(ly); wrong(ly): *He mistreats his dog terribly.* | *I misheard what you said.* **2** lack of; opposite of: *mistrust* | *misfortune*

mono- /ˈmɒnəʊ‖ˈmɑː-/ one; single; UNI-: *monosyllabic* | *a monoplane* (with one wing on each side) — compare POLY-

multi- /mʌltɪ/ many: *a multipurpose tool* | *a multistorey carpark*

non- /nɒn‖nɑːn/ not: *nonaddictive* | *non-profitmaking*

over- /əʊvər/1 too much: *an overindulgent parent* | *an overcooked dish* — compare UNDER- 2 above; across: *We took the overland route.*

poly- /pɒlɪ‖pɑːli/ many: *polysyllabic* — compare MONO-

post- /pəʊst/ after; later than: *the postwar years* — compare PRE-

pre- /priː/ before; earlier than: *the prewar years* | *a prelunch drink* — compare POST-

pro- /prəʊ/ in favour of; supporting: *She's pro-Conservative.* — compare ANTI-

pseudo- /sjuːdəʊ‖suː-/ only pretending to be; false: *pseudo-intellectuals*

psycho- /saɪkəʊ/ connected with (illness of) the mind: *psychotherapy* | *psychosexual disorders*

quasi- /kwɑːzɪ, kweɪzaɪ/ seeming to be; almost like: *a quasijudicial function*

re- /riː/ again: *The body was dug up and then reburied.*

self- /self/of or by oneself or itself: *a self-charging battery* | *self-deception.* | *She's completely self-taught.*

semi- /semɪ/ half: *a semicircle* 2 partly; incomplete(ly): *semipermanent* | *in the semidarkness*

step- /step/ related through a parent who has remarried

sub- /sʌb/ 1 under; below: *subsoil* | *subzero temperatures* 2 smaller part of: *a subcategory* 3 less than; worse than: *subhuman intelligence* 4 next in rank below: *a sublieutenant* — compare SUPER-

super- /suːpər, sjuː-‖suː-/ greater or more than: *superhuman strength* | *supertankers* (= very large ships) *carrying oil* — compare SUB-

trans- /træns, trænz/ across; on or to the other side of: *a transatlantic flight*

tri- /traɪ/ three: *trilingual* (= speaking three languages)

ultra- /ʌltrə/ very, esp. too: *ultramodern* | *ultracautious*

un- /ʌn/ 1 (makes adjectives and adverbs) not: *uncomfortable* | *unfairly* | *unwashed* 2 (makes verbs) make or do the opposite of: *She tied a knot, and then untied it.*

under- /ʌndər/ 1 too little: *undercooked potatoes* | *underproduction* 2 below: *an undersea cable* — compare OVER-

uni- /juːnɪ/ one; single; MONO-: *unicellular*

vice- /vaɪs/ next in rank below: *the vice-chairman of the committee*

video- /vɪdɪəʊ/ of, for, or using recorded pictures, esp. as produced by a VIDEO (2): *a videocassette*

Word endings

-able /əbəl/ also **-ible** (*in adjectives*) that can have the stated thing done to it: *a washable fabric*

-age /ɪdʒ/ (*in nouns*) **1** the action or result of doing the stated thing: *to allow for shrinkage* (= getting smaller) | *several breakages* (= things broken) **2** the cost of doing the stated thing: *Postage is extra.* **3** the state or rank of: *given a peerage*

-al /əl, əl/ **1** (*in adjectives*) of; connected with: *autumnal mists* | *a musical performance* **2** (*in nouns*) (an) act of doing something: *the arrival of the bus* | *several rehearsals*

-an /ən, ən/-IAN: *the Elizabethan Age*

-ance /əns, əns/ (*in nouns*) (an example of) the action, state or quality of doing or being the stated thing: *his sudden appearance* (= he appeared suddenly) | *her brilliance* (= she is BRILLIANT)

-ant /ənt, ənt/ (*in adjectives and nouns*) (person or thing) that does the stated thing: *in the resultant confusion* | *a bottle of disinfectant*

-ar /ər, ɑːr/ **1** (*in adjectives*) of; connected with; being: *the Polar regions* **2** (*in nouns*) -ER²: *a liar*

-arian /eəriən/ (*in nouns*) person who supports and believes in: *a libertarian* (= person who supports freedom)

-ary /əri, æri | eri/ (*in adjectives*) being: *with his customary* (= usual) *caution* | *her legendary* (= very famous) *courage*

-ate /ət, eɪt/ **1** (*in verbs*) (cause to) become or have: *a hyphenated word* **2** (*in adjectives*) having: *a fortunate* (= lucky) *woman*

-ation /eɪʃən/ (*in nouns*) (an) act or result of doing the stated thing: *the continuation of the story*

-ative /ətɪv/ (*in adjectives*) **1** liking or tending to have or do: *argumentative* | *talkative* **2** for the purpose of the stated thing: *a consultative meeting*

-bound /baʊnd/ (*in adjectives*) limited, kept in, or controlled in the stated way: *a fog-bound aircraft*

-cy /si/ (*makes nouns from adjectives ending in* /t/ *or* /tɪk/) -ITY: *several inaccuracies in the report*

-d /d, t/ (*after* e) -ED: *a wide-eyed stare*

-dom /dəm/ (*in nouns*) **1** condition of being the stated thing: *freedom* | *boredom* **2** country or area ruled by: *a kingdom* **3** people of the stated sort: *despite the opposition of officialdom*

-ean /iən/ -IAN

-ed /d, ɪd, t/ **1** (*makes regular past t. and p. of verbs*): *We landed safely.* **2** (*in adjectives*) having or wearing the stated thing; with: *a long-tailed dog* | *a bowler-hatted man*

-ee /iː/ (*in nouns*) **1** person to whom the stated thing is done: *an employee* | *a trainee* **2** person who is or does the stated thing: *an absentee*

-eer /ɪər/ (*in nouns*) person who does or is connected with the stated thing: *a mountaineer* | *The auctioneer asked for bids.*

-en /ən, ən/ **1** (*in adjectives*) made of: *a wooden box* **2** (*in verbs*) make or become (more): *unsweetened tea* | *The sky darkened.*

-ence /əns, əns/ (*in nouns*) -ANCE: *its existence* | *reference* | *occurrence*

-ent /ənt, ənt/ -ANT: *nonexistent*

-er¹ /ər/ (*in comparative of short adjectives and adverbs*) more: *faster* | *colder*

-er ² /ər/ (*in nouns*) **1** person or thing that does the stated thing: *a singer* | *a footballer* (= person who plays football) | *an electric water heater* **2** person who comes from or lives in the stated place: *a Londoner*

-ery /əri, əri/ (*in nouns*) **1** the stated condition; -NESS: *bravery* **2** the stated art or practice; -ING (2): *cookery* **3** place where the stated thing is done: *a brewery*

-es /ɪz/ (*after* /s, z, ʃ, tʃ, dʒ/) -S: *bosses* | *matches*

-ese /iːz/ (*in nouns and adjectives*) (language) of the stated country: *Do you speak Japanese?* | *Portuguese food*

-esque /esk/ (*in adjectives*) in the manner or style of; like: *statuesque beauty* | *Kafkaesque*

-ess /ɪs, es/ (*in nouns*) female: *an actress* (= a female actor) | *a lioness*

-est /ɪst/ (*in superlative of short adjectives and adverbs*) most: *slowest* | *loveliest*

-eth /ɪθ/ -TH: *the twentieth time*

-ette /et/ (*in nouns*) small: *a kitchenette*

-ey /i/ (*esp. after* y) -Y: *clayey soil*

-fashion /fæʃən/ (*in adverbs*) in the way of: *They ate Indian-fashion, using their fingers.*

-fold /fəʊld/ (*in adjectives and adverbs*) multiplied by the stated number: *a fourfold increase*

-free /friː/ **1** (*in adjectives*) -LESS (1): *a troublefree journey*

-friendly /frendli/ (*in adjectives*) not difficult for the stated people to use: *a user-friendly computer*

-ful /fəl/ **1** (*in adjectives*) having or giving: *a sinful man* | *a restful day* **2** /fʊl/ (*in nouns*) amount contained by:

a handful of coins | *two spoonfuls of sugar*

-hood /hʊd/ (*in nouns*) condition or period of being the stated thing: *falsehood* | *during her childhood*

-ial /ɪəl, əl/-**AL** (1): *a commercial transaction* | *the presidential car*

-ian /ɪən, ən/ **1** (*in adjectives and nouns*) of or connected with the stated place or person: *Parisian restaurants* | *I speak Russian.* **2** (*in nouns*) person who studies the stated subject; EXPERT: *a historian* | *a theologian*

-ible /əbəl/-**ABLE**: *deductible*

-ic /ɪk/ also **-ical** /ɪkəl/ (*in adjectives*) connected with; having or showing: *The design is completely symmetric/symmetrical.* | *an historic occasion* | *a historical novel*

-icide /ɪsaɪd/ (*in nouns*) killing of: *infanticide*

-ics /ɪks/ (*in nouns*) science or skill: *linguistics* | *aeronautics* (2)

-ie /i/ -Y (2)

-ify /ɪfaɪ/ (*in verbs*) make or become: *purify* | *simplify*

-ine /aɪn/ **1** of or concerning: *equine* (= of horses) **2** made of; like: *crystalline*

-ing /ɪŋ/ **1** (*makes pres. p. of verbs*): *I'm coming.* **2** *a sleeping child* **2** (*makes nouns from verbs*): *Eating sweets makes you fat.* | *a fine painting*

-ise /aɪz/ *esp. BrE* for -IZE

-ish /ɪʃ/ **1** (*in nouns and adjectives*) (language) of the stated country: *I speak Swedish.* | *British customs* **2** (*in adjectives*) **a** typical of: *a foolish man* | *girlish giggles* **b** rather: *a reddish glow* **c** about the stated number: *He's fortyish.* | *Come at sixish.*

-ism /ɪzəm/ (*in nouns*) **1** set of beliefs: *Buddhism* | *socialism* **2** quality or way of behaving: *heroism* | *male chauvinism* **3** way of speaking: *Americanisms*

-ist /ɪst/ **1** (*in nouns*) person who works with or does the stated thing: *A violinist plays the violin.* | *A machinist works machines.* **2** (*in adjectives and nouns*) (follower) of a set of beliefs: *a Buddhist* **3** making unfair differences between people because of the stated thing: *racist* | *ageist*

-ite /aɪt/ -IST (2): *a Trotskyite*

-itude /ɪtjuːd‖ɪtuːd/ (*in nouns*) the state or degree of being: *exactitude* | *certitude* (= being certain)

-ity /ɪti/ (*in nouns*) the stated condition or quality; -NESS: *stupidity* | *sublimity*

-ive /ɪv/ (*in adjectives*) tending to do the stated thing: *a creative child* | *a supportive partner*

-ize /aɪz/ (*in verbs*) make or become: *popularizing a new brand of soap* | *to modernize our procedures*

-less /ləs/ (*in adjectives*) **1** without: *a windless day* | *We are powerless to act.* **2** that never does the stated thing: *a tireless worker*

-let /lət/ (*in nouns*) small: *lived in a flatlet*

-like /laɪk/ (*in adjectives*) typical of: *childlike innocence*

-ly /li/ **1** (*in adverbs*) in the stated way: *Drive carefully!* **2** (*in adjectives and adverbs*) every: *an hourly report* | *I see him daily.* **3** (*in adjectives*) typical of: *brotherly love* **4** (*in adverbs*) from the stated point of view: *Musically she's very gifted.*

-man /mən/ **1** man who comes from the stated place: *a Frenchman* **2** person with the stated job or skill: *a postman*

-manship /mənʃɪp/ (*in [U] nouns*) the art or skill of a person of the stated type: *seamanship* | *horsemanship*

-ment /mənt/ (*in nouns*) act or result of doing the stated thing; -ING (2): *enjoyment* | *encouragement*

-most /məʊst/ -EST: *the northernmost parts of the country*

-ness /nəs/ (*in nouns*) the stated condition or quality: *loudness* | *gentleness*

-nik /nɪk/ (*in nouns*) person who is connected with or keen on: *a peacenik*

-ology /ɒlədʒi‖ɑː-/ (*in nouns*) science or study of: *toxicology* (= the study of poisons) | *musicology*

-or /əʳ/ -ER²: *a sailor*

-ory¹ /əri‖ɔːri, əri/ (*in nouns*) place or thing used for doing the stated thing: *an observatory*

-ory² (*in adjectives*) that does the stated thing: *a congratulatory telegram*

-ous /əs/ (*in adjectives*) having; full of: *a dangerous place* | *a spacious room*

-phile /faɪl/ (*in nouns*) person who likes the stated thing or place very much: *an Anglophile* (= who likes England)

-phobe /fəʊb/ (*in nouns*) person who dislikes the stated thing or person very much: *an Anglophobe* (= who dislikes England)

-phobia /fəʊbiə/ (*in nouns*) great dislike: *Anglophobia*

-proof /pruːf/ **1** (*in adjectives*) treated or made so as not to be harmed by the stated thing: *a bulletproof car* | *an ovenproof dish* **2** (*in verbs*) to treat or make in this way: *to soundproof a room*

-r /əʳ/ (*after e*) -ER

-ridden /rɪdn/ (*in adjectives*) **1** suffering from the effects of: *guilt-ridden* **2** too full of: *mosquito-ridden*

-ry /ri/ (*in nouns*) -ERY: *sheer wizardry*

-s /z, s/ **1** (*makes the pl. of nouns*): *one cat and two dogs* **2** (*makes the 3rd* *person; pres. sing. of verbs*): *She laughs too much.*

-'s 1 (*forms the possessive case of sing. nouns and of plural nouns that do not end in -s*): *my sister's husband | yesterday's lesson | the sheep's heads* 2 *BrE* the shop or home of: *I met him at Mary's.*

-s' (*forms the possessive case of plural nouns*): *the girls' dresses*

-scape /skeɪp/ (*in nouns*) a wide view of the stated area: *some old Dutch seascapes*

-ship /ʃɪp/ (*in nouns*) 1 condition of having or being the stated thing: *a business in partnership with his brother | kingship* 2 the stated skill: *her masterly musicianship*

-some /səm/ 1 (*in adjectives*) causing; producing: *a troublesome problem* 2 (*in nouns*) group of the stated number of people or things: *a twosome*

-speak /spiːk/ *often derog* (*in nouns*) the special language, esp. slang words, used in the stated business or activity: *computerspeak*

-st /st/ (*after e*) -EST

-th /θ/ (*makes adjectives from numbers, except those ending in 1, 2, or 3*): *the seventh day*

-tion /ʃən/ (*in nouns*) -ION

-tude /tjuːd‖tuːd/ (*in nouns*) -ITUDE: *disquietude*

-ty /ti/-ITY: *cruelty*

-ure /jʊəʳ, jəʳ, əʳ/(*in nouns*) act or result of doing the stated thing; -ING (2): *the closure of the factory*

-ward /wəd‖wɔrd/ also **-wards** /wədz‖wɔrdz/ (*in adjectives and adverbs*) in the stated direction: *the homeward journey | travelling north-wards*

-ware /weəʳ/(*in nouns*) containers, tools, etc., made of the stated material or for the stated purpose: *pewterware | kitchenware (= for cooking)*

-ways /weɪz/ -WISE: *sideways*

-wise /waɪz/ (*in adverbs*) 1 in the stated way or direction: *walked crabwise* 2 with regard to: *very inexperienced businesswise*

-y /i/1 (*in adjectives*) of; like; having: *a lemony smell | a noisy room* 2 (*makes nouns more informal; used esp. when speaking to children*): *my granny | a nice little doggy* 3 (*in nouns*) -ITY: *jealousy*

Irregular verbs

verb	past tense	past participle
abide	abided, abode	abided
arise	arose	arisen
awake	awoke, awakened	awoken
baby-sit	baby-sat	baby-sat
be	*see dictionary entry*	
bear	bore	borne
beat	beat	beaten
become	became	become
befall	befell	befallen
beget	begot (*also* begat *bibl*)	begotten
begin	began	begun
behold	beheld	beheld
bend	bent	bent
beseech	besought, beseeched	besought, beseeched
beset	beset	beset
bet	bet, betted	bet, betted
bid	bade, bid	bid, bidden
bind	bound	bound
bite	bit	bitten
bleed	bled	bled
bless	blessed, blest	blessed, blest
blow	blew	blown
break	broke	broken
breed	bred	bred
bring	brought	brought
broadcast	broadcast	broadcast
build	built	built
burn	burned, burnt	burned, burnt
burst	burst	burst
buy	bought	bought
cast	cast	cast
catch	caught	caught
chide	chided, chid	chid, chidden
choose	chose	chosen
cleave	cleaved, cleft, clove	cleaved, cleft, cloven
cling	clung	clung
come	came	come
cost	cost	cost
creep	crept	crept
cut	cut	cut
deal	dealt /delt/	dealt
dig	dug	dug
dive	dived, (*AmE*) dove	dived
do	did	done
draw	drew	drawn
dream	dreamed, dreamt	dreamed, dreamt
drink	drank	drunk
drive	drove	driven
dwell	dwelt, dwelled	dwelt, dwelled
eat	ate	eaten
fall	fell	fallen
feed	fed	fed
feel	felt	felt

verb	past tense	past participle
fight	fought	fought
find	found	found
flee	fled	fled
fling	flung	flung
fly	flew	flown
forbear	forbore	forborne
forbid	forbade, forbad	forbidden
forecast	forecast, forecasted	forecast, forecasted
foresee	foresaw	foreseen
foretell	foretold	foretold
forget	forgot	forgotten
forgive	forgave	forgiven
forgo	forwent	forgone
forsake	forsook	forsaken
freeze	froze	frozen
gainsay	gainsaid	gainsaid
get	got	got (also gotten *AmE*)
gird	girded, girt	girded, girt
give	gave	given
go	went	gone
grind	ground	ground
grow	grew	grown
hamstring	hamstringed, hamstrung	hamstringed, hamstrung
hang	hung, hanged	hung, hanged
have	had	had
hear	heard	heard
heave	heaved, hove	heaved, hove
hew	hewed	hewn, hewed
hide	hid	hidden, hid
hit	hit	hit
hold	held	held
hurt	hurt	hurt
keep	kept	kept
kneel	knelt, (*esp. AmE*) kneeled	knelt, (*esp. AmE*) kneeled
knit	knitted, knit	knitted, knit
know	knew	known
lay	laid	laid
lead	led	led
lean	leaned, (*esp. BrE*) leant	leaned, (*esp. BrE*) leant
leap	leapt, (*esp. AmE*) leaped	leapt, (*esp. AmE*) leaped
learn	learned, (*esp. BrE*) learnt	learned, (*esp. BrE*) learnt
leave	left	left
lend	lent	lent
let	let	let
lie	lay	lain
light	lit, lighted	lit, lighted
lose	lost	lost
make	made	made
mean	meant	meant
meet	met	met

verb	past tense	past participle
miscast	miscast	miscast
mislay	mislaid	mislaid
mislead	misled	misled
misspell	misspelt, misspelled	misspelt, misspelled
misspend	misspent	misspent
mistake	mistook	mistaken
misunderstand	misunderstood	misunderstood
mow	mowed	mown, mowed
outdo	outdid	outdone
outgrow	outgrew	outgrown
outshine	outshone	outshone
overcome	overcame	overcome
overdo	overdid	overdone
overhang	overhung	overhung
overload	overloaded	overladen
overrun	overran	overrun
oversee	oversaw	overseen
oversleep	overslept	overslept
overtake	overtook	overtaken
overthrow	overthrew	overthrown
partake	partook	partaken
pay	paid	paid
prove	proved	proved (*also* proven *AmE*)
put	put	put
read	read /red/	read /red/
rend	rent	rent
repay	repaid	repaid
rethink	rethought	rethought
rid	rid, ridded	rid, ridded
ride	rode	ridden
ring	rang	rung
rise	rose	risen
run	ran	run
saw	sawed	sawn, sawed
say	said	said
see	saw	seen
seek	sought	sought
sell	sold	sold
send	sent	sent
set	set	set
sew	sewed	sewn, sewed
shake	shook	shaken
shear	sheared	shorn, sheared
shed	shed	shed
shine	shone, shined	shone, shined
shoe	shod	shod
shoot	shot	shot
show	showed	shown, showed
shrink	shrank, shrunk	shrunk
shut	shut	shut
sing	sang	sung
sink	sank, sunk	sunk
sit	sat	sat
slay	slew	slain
sleep	slept	slept

verb	past tense	past participle
slide	slid	slid
sling	slung	slung
slink	slunk	slunk
slit	slit	slit
smell	(*esp. BrE*) smelt, (*esp. AmE*) smelled	(*esp. BrE*) smelt, (*esp. AmE*) smelled
smite	smote	smitten
sow	sowed	sown, sowed
speak	spoke	spoken
speed	sped, speeded	sped, speeded
spell	(*esp. BrE*) spelt, (*esp. AmE*) spelled	(*esp. BrE*) spelt, (*esp. AmE*) spelled
spend	spent	spent
spill	(*esp. BrE*) spilt, (*esp. AmE*) spilled	(*esp. BrE*) spilt, (*esp. AmE*) spilled
spin	spun, span	spun
spit	spat (*also* spit *AmE*)	spat (*also* spit *AmE*)
split	split	split
spoil	spoiled, spoilt	spoiled. spoilt
spread	spread	spread
spring	sprang (*also* sprung *AmE*)	sprung
stand	stood	stood
steal	stole	stolen
stick	stuck	stuck
sting	stung	stung
stink	stank, stunk	stunk
strew	strewed	strewn, strewed
stride	strode	stridden
strike	struck	struck
string	strung	strung
strive	strove, strived	striven, strived
swear	swore	sworn
sweep	swept	swept
swell	swelled	swollen, swelled
swim	swam	swum
swing	swung	swung
take	took	taken
teach	taught	taught
tear	tore	torn
tell	told	told
think	thought	thought
thrive	thrived, throve	thrived
throw	threw	thrown
thrust	thrust	thrust
tread	trod	trodden, trod
unbend	unbent	unbent
undergo	underwent	undergone
understand	understood	understood
undertake	undertook	undertaken
undo	undid	undone
unwind	unwound	unwound
uphold	upheld	upheld
upset	upset	upset
wake	woke, waked	woken, waked

verb	past tense	past participle
wear	wore	worn
weave	wove	woven
wed	wedded, wed	wedded, wed
weep	wept	wept
wet	wetted, wet	wetted, wet
win	won	won
wind /waɪnd/	wound	wound
withdraw	withdrew	withdrawn
withhold	withheld	withheld
withstand	withstood	withstood
wring	wrung	wrung
write	wrote	written

Symbols used with words
in the same family

Words which are related to the headword are often given at the end of an entry. Sometimes they have a definition. Sometimes, if their meaning is clear, there is no definition. Sometimes a word is exactly the same as the headword, and so it is not written again. Sometimes a word has a different ending from the headword, and so the new ending is shown.

The following symbols are used to show exactly how these related words are formed:

♦ shows that a related word is exactly the same as the headword

an·ger /ˈæŋgə/ n [U] fierce displeasure and annoyance ♦ vt make angry

~ shows that a related word is formed by adding an ending directly to the headword

an·nounce /əˈnaʊns/ vt state loudly or publicly: *He announced the winner of the competition.* ~ **ment** n public statement

— shows that the form of the headword changes slightly before the new ending can be added

a·nom·a·ly /əˈnɒməli‖əˈnɑː-/ n fml something different from the usual type: *A cat with no tail is an anomaly.* —**lous** adj

ap·pro·ri·ate² /əˈprəʊprieɪt/ vt 1 set aside for a purpose 2 take for oneself —**ation** /ə,prəʊprɪˈeɪʃən/ n [C;U]